Financial Reporting and Statement Analysis

A STRATEGIC PERSPECTIVE

FIFTH EDITION

CLYDE P. STICKNEY

The Signal Companies Professor of Management
Tuck School of Business
Dartmouth College

PAUL R. BROWN

Professor of Accounting
Academic Director, TRIUM Executive MBA
Leonard N. Stern School of Business
New York University

JAMES M. WAHLEN

Associate Professor of Accounting and
Ford Motor Company Teaching Fellow
Kelley School of Business
Indiana University

THOMSON
™
SOUTH-WESTERN

Australia · Canada · Mexico · Singapore · Spain · United Kingdom · United States

THOMSON
SOUTH-WESTERN

Financial Reporting and Statement Analysis: A Strategic Perspective, 5e

Clyde P. Stickney, Paul R. Brown, James M. Wahlen

VP/Editorial Director:
Jack W. Calhoun

VP/Editor-in-Chief:
George Werthman

Acquisitions Editor:
Julie Lindsay

Senior Developmental Editor:
Craig Avery

Marketing Manager:
Keith Chassé

Production Editor:
Heather Mann

Manufacturing Coordinator:
Doug Wilke

Media Developmental Editor:
Josh Fendley

Media Production Editor:
Kelly Reid

Design Project Manager:
Stacy Jenkins Shirley

Production House:
Navta Associates, Inc.

Cover Designer:
Joseph Pagliaro Graphic Design

Internal Designer:
Joseph Pagliaro Graphic Design

Printer:
Phoenix Color
Hagerstown, MD

For permission to use material
from this text or product, contact
us by
Tel (800) 730-2214
Fax (800) 730-2215
http://www.thomsonrights.com

For more information
contact South-Western,
5191 Natorp Boulevard,
Mason, Ohio, 45040.
Or you can visit our Internet site
at: http://www.swlearning.com

For our students,
with thanks for permitting us to take the journey with you

For our families, with love,
Kathy, Joan, Emma, Debbie, Jessica, and Jaymie

The usual goal of financial statement analysis is to value a firm. The effective analysis of a set of financial statements begins with an understanding of (1) the industry economics characteristics and current conditions of a firm's businesses, and (2) the particular strategies the firm selects to compete in each of these businesses. It then moves to (3) assessing how well the firm's financial statements reflect the economic effects of the firm's decisions and actions. This assessment requires an understanding of the generally accepted accounting principles (GAAP), the procedures that underlie the financial statements, and the appropriate adjustments that the analyst should make to improve the quality of the information provided. Next, the analyst (4) assesses the profitability and risk of the firm in the recent past, using financial statements ratios and other analytical tools, and forecasts its expected future profitability and risk, incorporating information about expected changes in economics of the firm's industry and the firm's strategies. Finally, the analyst (5) values the firm using various valuation methods. This five-step process forms the conceptual and pedagogical flow for this book.

All textbooks in financial statement analysis include step (4), assessing the profitability and risk of a company. Textbooks differ, however, with respect to their emphases on the other four steps. Consider the following depiction of these steps.

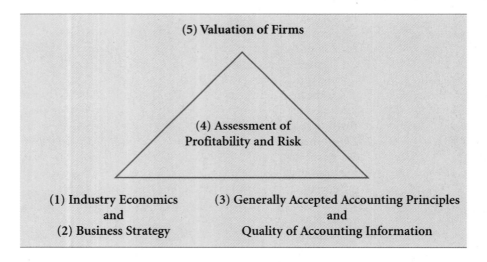

Our view is that these five steps must form an integrated whole for effective financial statement analysis. We have therefore positioned this book so that we provide balanced, integrated coverage of all five elements. We sequence our study by beginning with industry economics and strategy, then moving to consideration of GAAP and the quality of accounting information, and then concluding with valuation. We anchor each step in the sequence on the analysis of a firm's profitability and risk, the fundamental drivers of value. We continually relate each part to those preceding and succeeding it to maintain this balanced, integrated perspective.

The premise of this book is that students learn financial statement analysis most effectively by performing the analysis on actual companies. The book's narrative sets forth the important concepts and analytical tools and demonstrates their application using the financial statements of PepsiCo. Each chapter contains a set of problems and/or cases based primarily on financial statement data of actual companies. A financial statement analysis package (FSAP) is available to aid in the analytical tasks (discussed later).

OVERVIEW OF TEXT

This section describes briefly the content of each chapter, indicating the major changes made since the previous edition.

Chapter 1 Overview of Financial Reporting and Financial Statement Analysis. This chapter introduces the five key interrelated sequential steps in financial statement analysis that serve as an organization structure for this book. It presents several frameworks for understanding the industry economics and business strategy of a firm and applies them to PepsiCo. It also reviews the purpose, underlying concepts, and content of each of the three principal financial statements, including those of non-U.S. companies appearing in a different format. End-of-chapter materials include a new "ratio detective" problem involving U.S. and non-U.S. companies, an updated version of the Nike integrated review case, and updated information for most of the other problems from the previous edition.

Chapter 2 Asset and Liability Valuation and Income Measurement. This chapter is new to this edition. It covers three topics we believe our students need to review and reinforce from previous courses before delving into the more complex topics in this book. First, we discuss the link between the valuation of assets and liabilities on the balance sheet and the measurement of income. We believe that students understand topics such as revenue recognition and accounting for marketable securities, derivatives, pensions, and other topics more easily and in greater depth when they examine them from the perspective of both the balance sheet valuation and income measurement. We also examine whether firms should recognize value changes immediately in net income or delay their recognition, sending them temporarily through other comprehensive income. Second, and related to the first, we present a framework for analyzing the dual effects of transactions and other events on the financial statements. This framework relies on the balance sheet equation to trace through these dual effects. Even students that are well grounded in double-entry accounting find this framework helpful in visually identifying the effects of various complex business transactions, such as corporate acquisitions, derivatives, and leases. We use this framework in later chapters as we discuss various GAAP topics. Third, we discuss the measurement of income tax expense, particularly with regard to the treatment of temporary differences between book income and taxable income. Virtually every business transaction has income tax consequences. Delaying consideration of the income tax consequences until later in the text hinders effective coverage of such topics as restructuring charges, asset impairments, depreciation, and leases.

Chapter 3 Income Flows Versus Cash Flows: Key Relationships in the Dynamics of a Business. Chapter 3 reviews the statement of cash flows and presents a model for relating the cash flows from operating, investing, and financing activities to a firm's position in its product life cycle. The chapter demonstrates procedures for preparing the statement of cash flows when a firm provides no cash flow information. The chapter includes several new interpretative problems involving the Coca-Cola Company (Coke), The Gap, and Sunbeam.

Chapter 4 Profitability Analysis. The previous edition of this book introduced tools for analyzing profitability and risk in Chapter 3 and then explored them more fully in Chapters 8 and 9. This edition brings these materials into an integrated whole, examining profitability analysis in Chapter 4 and risk analysis in Chapter 5. Chapter 4 discusses and illustrates the calculation and interpretation of profitability ratios for PepsiCo, including the rate of return on assets and its disaggregated components and the rate of return on common shareholders' equity and its disaggregated components. We emphasize the importance of industry economics and firms' strategies when interpreting profitability ratios. This chapter also considers analytical tools unique to certain industries, such as airlines, service firms, and financial institutions. Chapter-end materials include new problems on Coke, Sun Microsystems, McDonalds, and Brinker, as well as updated problems or cases involving Hasbro, Wal-Mart, The Gap, and Limited Brands.

Chapter 5 Risk Analysis. This chapter describes and illustrates the calculation and interpretation of risk ratios for PepsiCo, focusing on both short-term liquidity risk and long-term solvency risk. We also explore credit risk and bankruptcy risk in greater depth. A new section for this edition examines the risk of financial reporting manipulation, illustrating Beneish's multivariate model for identifying potential manipulators. A unique feature of the problems in Chapters 4 and 5 is the linking of the analysis of several companies across the two chapters, including problems involving Coke, Hasbro, Lands' End, and Sun Microsystems. A new problem applies Beneish's model to Enron. Chapter-end cases involve credit analysis (Massachusetts Stove Company), bankruptcy prediction (Fly-By-Night International Group), and financial reporting manipulation (Millennial Technologies).

Chapter 6 Quality of Accounting Information and Adjustments to Reported Financial Statement Data. This chapter begins with an expanded discussion of the quality of accounting information, emphasizing substantive economic content and earnings persistence as the key characteristics. This discussion sets the stage for the discussion of various GAAP in Chapters 6 to 9. We then consider several financial reporting topics that primarily affect the persistence of earnings, including discontinued operations, extraordinary gains and losses, changes in accounting principles, restructuring charges, and asset impairment charges. The chapter concludes with a discussion of earnings management, contrasting it with earnings manipulation discussed in Chapter 5. Chapter-end materials include new problems involving H.J. Heinz, Parametric Technology, Ruby Tuesday, Wyeth, and Sapient. Chapter-end materials also include an integrative case involving the analysis of profitability and risk of International Paper Company in light of the inclusion of several potentially nonrecurring items in earnings. It also includes two related cases involving financial reporting in Japan.

Chapter 7 Revenue Recognition and Related Expenses. This chapter discusses various GAAP topics that affect the assessment of a firm's profitability. The chapter begins with an expanded discussion of revenue recognition, incorporating SEC *Staff*

Accounting Bulletin No. 101, and applying it to several recent purported reporting abusers, including Xerox, Global Crossing, Qwest Communications, and Microstrategy. We then consider GAAP for inventories, fixed assets, and intangible assets. The discussion of intangible assets incorporates FASB *Statement No. 141* and *Statement No. 142.* Several new chapter-end problems explore revenue recognition in greater depth. Cases involve revenue recognition (Arizona Land Development Company), intangibles (Chiron), changing pricing (Chilgener) and an updated case involving AOL's treatment of subscriber acquisition costs.

Chapter 8 Liability Recognition and Related Expenses. Chapter 8 discusses various GAAP topics that primarily affect the assessment of a firm's risk. The chapter begins with a conceptual discussion of an accounting liability, including an expanded discussion of off-balance sheet financing. We apply the principles for liability recognition to various potential off-balance sheet transactions, including the sale of receivables, product financing, R&D partnerships, and joint ventures. We then explore several GAAP topics in depth, including leases, derivatives, retirement benefits, income taxes, and reserves. The discussion of derivatives incorporates the provisions of FASB *Statement No. 133* and of retirement benefits incorporates the provisions of FASB *Statement No. 132.* Chapter-end materials include updated problems involving Wal-Mart, The Gap, Limited Brands, and Sun Microsystems and new problems involving Sears, Ford, Northwest Airlines, Coke, General Electric, Goodyear, and Boeing, as well as an updated case from the previous edition involving leases and retirement benefits for American Airlines and United Airlines.

Chapter 9 Intercorporate Entities. Chapter 9 examines various GAAP topics that affect many accounts on the financial statements, including corporate acquisitions, investments in securities and consolidated financial statements, and foreign currency translation. The discussion of corporate acquisitions incorporates the new provisions of FASB *Statements No. 141* and *142.* The discussion of consolidation policy includes consideration of the treatment of variable interest entities, including special purpose entities and the provisions of FASB *Interpretation No. 46.* A new section to this edition discusses the accounting for stock options and their impact on both financial statement amounts and firm value. The problem material at the end of the chapter has been revised to reflect elimination of the pooling of interests method and the required amortization of goodwill. New problems relating to stock options involve Nike, John Deere, and General Electric. The case involving Fisher Corporation illustrates the effects of accounting, tax, and financing decisions on the structure of a corporate acquisition and the related financial statements. The case involving Clark Equipment Company analyzes the effect on the financial statements of various ways of accounting for a joint venture. The case involving Loucks Corporation illustrates the choice of a functional currency and the financial statement impact of alternatives methods of foreign currency translation.

Chapter 10 Forecasting Pro Forma Financial Statements. This chapter describes and illustrates the procedures for preparing forecasted financial statements. This material plays a central role in the valuation of companies, a topic discussed in Chapters 11 to 13. The chapter begins with an overview of forecasting and the importance of creating integrated and articulated pro forma financial statements. It then illustrates the preparation of pro forma financial statements for PepsiCo. New to this edition is the addition of a Forecast spreadsheet within FSAP that aids in the preparation of pro forma financial statements. We illustrate the use of this spreadsheet with PepsiCo. The Forecast spreadsheet does not perform all of the programming for the preparation of pro forma financial statements but provides a template on which students can build their own forecasts. Short chapter-end problems illustrate techniques for determining the cost structure of a firm and dealing with irregular changes in accounts. Longer problems require the preparation of pro forma financial statements for cases discussed in earlier chapters involving Wal-Mart, The Gap and Limited Brands. The chapter-end case involves the preparation of pro forma financial statements to assist a firm in its decision to add gas stoves to its wood stove line. The problems and cases specify the assumptions students should make to illustrate the preparation procedure. Cases in later chapters and on the web site for this book require students to make their own pro forma assumptions.

Chapter 11 Valuation: Cash-Flow Based Approaches. Chapters 11 to 13 form a unit in which we explore various approaches to valuing a firm. Chapter 11 focuses on valuation using the present value of free cash flows. This chapter distinguishes free cash flows to all debt and equity stakeholders and free cash flows to common equity shareholders and the settings where one or the other measure of free cash flows is appropriate for valuation. We also consider and apply techniques for measuring the continuing value after the forecast horizon. The chapter also provides extensive discussion of the measurement of the cost of debt and equity capital and the weighted average cost of capital. We apply the discounted free cash flows valuation methods to PepsiCo, demonstrating how to measure the free cash flows to all debt and equity stakeholders, as well as the free cash flows to common equity. The valuations for PepsiCo use the forecasted amounts from PepsiCo's pro forma financial statements discussed in Chapter 10. The chapter also presents techniques for assessing the sensitivity of value estimates, varying key assumptions such as the costs of capital and long-term growth rates. New to this edition is the addition of a Valuation spreadsheet to FSAP. This spreadsheet takes the pro forma amounts from the Forecast spreadsheet and other relevant information and values the firm using the various valuation methods discussed in Chapters 11 to 13. New problem material includes the valuation of Wal-Mart, The Gap, Limited Brands, and Massachusetts Stove Company from pro forma financial statements developed in Chapter 10 problems and cases. Other problems give students the pro forma free cash flows, asking them to value firms using the present value of free cash flows valuation method. The Holmes Corporation case is an integrated case relevant for Chapter 10 to 13 in which students select pro forma assumptions, prepare pro forma financial statements, and value the firm using the various methods discussed in Chapters 10 to 13. This case can be assigned piecemeal with each chapter or as an integrated case after Chapter 13.

Chapter 12 Valuation: Earnings-Based Approaches. Chapter 12 emphasizes the role of accounting earnings in valuation, focusing on valuation methods using the residual income approach. The residual income approach uses the ability of a firm to generate comprehensive income in excess of the cost of capital as the principal driver of a firm's value in excess of its book value. We apply the residual income valuation method to the forecasted amounts for PepsiCo from Chapter 10. The chapter also demonstrates that the free cash flows valuation methods and the residual income valuation methods are consistent with a fundamental dividends-based valuation approach. The Valuation spreadsheet in FSAP includes valuation models that use the residual income valuation method as well as the dividends valuation method. Chapter-end materials apply the residual income approach to The Gap and Limited Brands considered in Chapters 10 and 11. Short problems also involve the valuation of other firms in which the needed pro forma financial statement information is given.

Chapter 13 Valuation: Market-Based Approaches. Chapter 13 demonstrates how to analyze and use the information in market value. In particular, the chapter describes and applies market-based valuation multiples, including the market-to-book ratio and the price-to-earnings ratio. The chapter describes and illustrates the theoretical and conceptual approaches to market multiples, and contrasts them with the practical approaches to market multiples. The chapter demonstrates how the market-to-book ratio is consistent with residual ROCE valuation and the residual income model discussed in Chapter 12. The chapter also describes the factors that drive market multiples, so analysts can adjust multiples appropriately to reflect differences in profitability, growth, and risk across comparable firms. The chapter also demonstrates how to reverse engineer a firm's stock price to infer the valuation assumptions that the stock market appears to be making. We apply all of these valuation methods to PepsiCo. The chapter ends with a brief discussion of market efficiency with respect to earnings, including evidence on post-earnings-announcement drift in stock returns. Chapter-end materials continue problems involving The Gap, Limited Brands, and Steak N Shake and a new comprehensive problem involving Coke.

Appendices. Appendix A includes the financial statements and notes for PepsiCo used in the illustrations throughout the book. Appendix B is PepsiCo's management discussion and analysis of operations, which we use when interpreting PepsiCo's financial ratios and developing our pro forma projections. Appendix C is the printout of the profitability and risk ratio analyses for PepsiCo from FSAP for Year 7 to Year 11. Appendix D is the printout of the Forecasts and Valuations spreadsheets from FSAP for PepsiCo discussed in Chapters 10 to 13.

CHAPTER SEQUENCE AND STRUCTURE

Our own experience and our discussions with other professors suggest that there are various approaches to teaching the financial statement analysis course, each of which works well in particular settings. We have therefore designed this book for flexibility with respect to the sequence of chapter assignments. The diagram on the following page sets forth the overall structure of the book.

The chapter sequence follows the five steps in financial statement analysis discussed in Chapter 1. Chapters listed in left-side boxes relate primarily to income statement and balance sheet information and profitability analysis. Chapters listed in right-side boxes relate primarily to cash flow information and risk analysis. Chapters in boxes extending to both sides relate to topics affecting all three financial statements and both profitability and risk analysis. Chapters 2 and 3 provide the concep-

Chapter 1: Overview of Financial Reporting and Financial Statement Analysis	
Chapter 2: Asset Valuation and Income Measurement	Chapter 3: Income Flow Versus Cash Flows
Chapter 4: Profitability Analysis	Chapter 5: Risk Analysis
Chapter 6: Quality of Accounting Information and Adjustments to Reported Financial Statement Data	
Chapter 7: Revenue Recognition and Related Expenses	Chapter 8: Liability Recognition and Related Expenses
Chapter 9: Intercorporate Entities	
Chapter 10: Forecasting Pro Forma Financial Statements	

Chapter 12: Valuation: Earnings-based Approaches	Chapter 13: Valuation: Market-based Approaches	Chapter 11: Valuation: Cash-Flow-based Approaches

tual foundation for the three financial statements. Chapters 4 and 5 present tools for analyzing the financial statements. Chapters 6 to 9 examine the quality of accounting information and various GAAP. Chapters 10 to 13 focus primarily on forecasting and valuation.

Some schools teach GAAP topics and financial statement analysis in separate courses. Chapters 6 to 9 are an integrated unit and sufficiently rich for the GAAP course. The remaining chapters will then work well in the financial statement analysis course. Some schools leave the topic of valuation to finance courses. Chapters 1 to 9 will then work well for the accounting prelude to the finance course. Some instructions may wish to begin with valuation (Chapters 11 to 13) and then examine data issues that might impact the numbers used in the valuations (Chapters 6 to 9). This textbook is adaptable to other sequences of the various topics.

SIGNIFICANT CHANGES IN THIS EDITION

The preceding sections discussed the major changes in this edition, summarized by the following:

1. Chapter 2 relates asset valuation and income measurement, both conceptually and procedurally through an analytical framework. It also introduces the accounting for income taxes to enrich discussions of various GAAP topics covered in subsequent chapters.
2. Chapter 4 consolidates materials related to profitability analysis into a single chapter and Chapter 5 consolidates materials related to risk analysis into a single chapter, instead of spread over three chapters as in the previous edition.
3. Chapter 5 includes new material related to earnings manipulation and Chapter 6 includes new material on quality of accounting information and earnings management.

4. Chapters 6 to 9 contain materials necessitated by new FASB pronouncements, including asset impairments (Chapter 6), revenue recognition and intangibles (Chapter 7), off-balance sheet financing, derivatives, and retirement benefits (Chapter 8), and corporate acquisitions and stock options (Chapter 9).

5. Chapters 11 to 13 present significantly revised materials on valuation, demonstrating the relation between cash-based and earnings-based valuation methods.

6. All chapters use the financial statements and notes of PepsiCo to illustrate the various topics covered.

7. The book contains substantial new or updated assignment material for all chapters. Additional case material will be available on the web site for this book on an ongoing basis.

8. The financial statement analysis package (FSAP) has been substantially enhanced to include spreadsheets for preparing pro forma financial statements and valuing a firm.

OVERVIEW OF THE ANCILLARY PACKAGE

An enhanced financial statement analysis package (FSAP) is available for download to students and instructors alike from the Web site for the book (http://stickney.swlearning.com). FSAP calculates profitability and risk ratios and presents common-size and percentage-change income statements and balance sheets for any company for which a file of financial statement data has been created. In addition, the enhanced FSAP also provides user-friendly templates to create pro forma financial statements and to calculate share value estimates using free-cash flow and residual income valuation models. The valuation models also permit extensive sensitivity analyses of the share value estimates, enabling the user to vary discount rates and growth rates to assess their impact on firm value. **FSAP data files,** also available for download by students and instructors, have been created for many of the problems and cases in the book (an **icon** in the margin denotes items with data sets). Moreover, an **example version** of FSAP, complete with financial data from Pepsico, is downloadable from the book's Web site. Finally, instructors and students can download an **FSAP User's Guide** for help. The website also includes data files for many of the problems and cases in the book (noted in the book adjacent to the problem or case). A user manual for FSAP also appears on the web site.

In addition to FSAP, which is designed to maximize the teaching and learning goals of the book, students are provided with **Thomson Analytics—Business School Edition** for the purpose of supplementary financial research beyond the problems and cases in the book. Thomson Analytics—Business School Edition is an educational version of the same financial data provided by Thomson Financial that experts use on a daily basis. For 500 companies, this online resource provides:

- Worldscope®, which includes company profiles, financials and accounting results, market per-share data, annual information, and monthly prices going back to 1980.

- I/B/E/S Consensus Estimates, which provides consensus estimates, analyst-by-analyst earnings coverage, and analysts' forecasts.
- Disclosure SEC Database, which includes company profiles, annual and quarterly company financials, pricing information and earnings.

An access card allowing entry to the Thomson Analytics—Business School Edition Web site is packaged with all new copies of the textbook. Detailed instructions for accessing the url and a serial number are printed on the card to allow purchasers of new books to get online immediately.

An **Instructor's Manual/Solutions Manual** is also available to faculty who adopt this book. It contains suggestions for using the textbook, solutions to all problems and cases, and teaching notes to cases.

ACKNOWLEDGMENTS

Many individuals provided invaluable assistance in the preparation of this book and we wish to acknowledge their help in a formal manner here.

The following professional colleagues have assisted in the development of this edition by reviewing or providing helpful comments:

Messod Daniel Beneish, *Indiana University*
Aaron Hipscher, *New York University*
Robert Howell, *Dartmouth College*
Amy Hutton, *Dartmouth College*
Prem Jain, *Georgetown University*
Ross Jennings, *University of Texas at Austin*

D. Craig Nichols, *Indiana University*
James Ohlson, *New York University*
Stephen Ryan, *New York University*
Virginia Soybel, *Babson College*
Christine Wiedman, *University of Western Ontario*
Michael Williamson, *Indiana University*

We wish to thank the following individuals at South-Western, who provided guidance, encouragement, or assistance in various phases of the revision: Melissa Acuña, Craig Avery, Julie Lindsay, and Heather Mann. Navta Associates, Inc. did an excellent job of copyediting. Deborah Gibbs and Marcia Diefendorf provided assistance with various technical aspects of manuscript preparation. Katherine Rybowiak did an outstanding job assisting with preparation of the solutions/instructor's manual. Bob Burnham provided much needed technical expertise in revising FSAP.

Finally, we wish to acknowledge the role played by former students in our financial statement analysis classes for being challenging partners in our learning endeavors and to our families for being encouraging and patient partners in this work. We dedicate this book to each of you.

Clyde P. Stickney
Paul R. Brown
James M. Wahlen

ABOUT THE AUTHORS

Clyde P. Stickney is The Signal Companies Professor of Management at the Amos Tuck School at Dartmouth College. He received his doctoral degree from Florida State University and served on the faculties of the University of Chicago and the University of North Carolina at Chapel Hill before joining the faculty of the Tuck School in 1977. He has also taught at the International University of Japan, Swinburne Institute of Technology, and Helsinki School of Economics and Business Administration.

Professor Stickney's teaching and research interests center around the analysis and interpretation of financial statements. Recent research has examined the impact of different accounting principles on U.S. versus Japanese price-earnings ratios, the use of financial statement ratios to infer the content, and to evaluate the success, of corporate-level strategies. He has authored and co-authored books on financial accounting, managerial accounting, and financial statement analysis. Professor Stickney is a member of the American Accounting Association.

Paul R. Brown, Ph.D., CPA is a Professor of Accounting and immediate past Chairman of the Department of Accounting, Taxation and Business Law of the Leonard N. Stern School of Business, New York University. Currently, Professor Brown is Academic Director of the TRIUM executive MBA program (http://www.triumemba.org). He received his doctoral degree from the University of Texas at Austin and has served on the faculties of the Yale School of Management and INSEAD.

Professor Brown publishes in a wide range of academic and professional publications. He appears on television and is quoted in the press often, providing commentary on such topics as financial statement analysis, earnings management, financial reporting regulation and reform, IASB reporting, and auditor independence. The professional activities of Professor Brown include lead researcher on a number of sponsored projects; executive education development and training at NYU Stern, investment banks and financial services firms; and corporate board membership and board consulting. Prior to entering academe, he worked as an auditor for Andersen & Co., and as a staff member of the Financial Accounting Standards Board. Professor Brown is a member of the New York State Society of CPAs, American Institute of CPAs, and the American Accounting Association.

James M. Wahlen is the Ford Motor Company Teaching Fellow in accounting at the Kelley School of Business at Indiana University. He received his doctoral degree from the University of Michigan in 1991, and has served on the faculties of the Kenan-Flagler Business School at the University of North Carolina, and at Pacific Lutheran University. He has also taught at INSEAD, at the University of Washington, and in executive education programs for KPMG, Arthur Andersen & Co., Bank of America, the Amsterdam Institute of Finance, and others.

Professor Wahlen's teaching and research interests focus on financial accounting, financial statement analysis, and the capital markets. He has published in leading research journals in accounting and finance. He has had public accounting experience in both Milwaukee and Seattle. Professor Wahlen is a member of the American Accounting Association.

BRIEF CONTENTS

CONTENTS

Chapter 1

OVERVIEW OF FINANCIAL REPORTING AND FINANCIAL STATEMENT ANALYSIS

Learning Objectives

1. Understand the links between the economic characteristics and strategies of a firm, its financial statements and notes, assessments of its current and forecasted profitability and risk, and its market value.

2. Review three tools for studying the economic characteristics of an industry in which a firm operates.

3. Introduce PepsiCo, the specimen firm that we analyze throughout the book, as well as provide an initial overview of its financial statements.

4. Review the purpose, underlying concepts, and format of the balance sheet, the income statement, and the statement of cash flows.

5. Provide an overview of the tools available to the analyst to conduct a financial analysis of profitability and risk.

6. Provide an overview of how the analyst might use financial statement information in the valuation of a firm.

7. Discuss the role of financial statement analysis in an efficient capital market.

8. Review sources of financial information available for publicly held firms.

The principal activity of security analysts is to value business firms. Security analysts use financial statements and other information to evaluate a firm's success in the past and to predict its likely future performance. They then use the predicted information to measure the value of the firm's shares. Comparisons of their estimates of the firm's share value with the market's price for the shares provide the basis for making buy, hold, or sell investment recommendations.

This book has two principal purposes:

1. **To enhance understanding of the accounting principles and methods that firms use to prepare their financial statements and the adjustments that the analyst might make to reported amounts to increase their relevance and reliability.**
2. **To illustrate the use of financial statement data in the valuation of firms.**

Financial analysis is an exciting and rewarding activity, particularly when the objective is assessing whether a firm's stock is fairly valued. Studying the intrinsic characteristics of a firm—its business model, product and service market share, financing and investing decisions, for example—and employing this information to make informed judgments can be a very satisfying endeavor. Financial statements play a central role in the study and analysis of a firm.

The tools of effective financial statement analysis adapt to many settings in addition to measuring firm value. Other settings include (1) extending credit, either for a short-term period (for example, a bank loan used to finance accounts receivable or inventories), or for a long-term period (for example, a bank loan or public bond issue used to finance the acquisition of property, plant, or equipment); (2) assessing the operating performance and financial health of a supplier, customer, competitor, or potential employer; (3) valuing a firm in the initial public offering of its stock; (4) forming a judgment about damages sustained in a lawsuit; and (5) assessing the extent of auditing needed to form an opinion on a client's financial statements.

OVERVIEW OF FINANCIAL STATEMENT ANALYSIS

The effective analysis of financial statements involves five interrelated, sequential steps, depicted in Exhibit 1.1:

1. **Identify the economic characteristics of the industry in which a particular firm participates.** For example, does the industry include a large number of firms selling similar products, such as grocery stores, or is the industry characterized by a small number of competitors selling unique products, such as pharmaceutical companies? Does technological change play an important role in maintaining a competitive advantage, as in computer software? Are industry sales growing rapidly or slowly?
2. **Identify the strategies that a particular firm pursues to gain a competitive advantage.** Are its products designed to meet the needs of specific market segments, such as ethnic or health foods, or are they intended for a broader

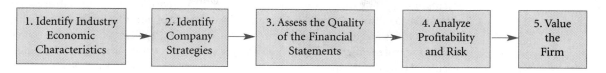

EXHIBIT 1.1

Interrelated Sequential Steps in Financial Statement Analysis

1. Identify Industry Economic Characteristics → 2. Identify Company Strategies → 3. Assess the Quality of the Financial Statements → 4. Analyze Profitability and Risk → 5. Value the Firm

consumer market, such as cafeterias and family restaurants? Has the firm integrated backwards into the growing or manufacture of raw materials for its products, such as a steel company that owns iron ore mines? Has the firm integrated forward into retailing to final consumers, such as an athletic footwear manufacturer that operates retail stores to sell its products? Is the firm diversified across several geographic markets or industries?

3. **Assess the quality of a firm's financial statements and, if necessary, adjust them for such characteristics as sustainability or comparability.** For example, do the firm's financial statements provide a clear and informative representation of the firm's economic performance and risk? Has the firm prepared its financial statements in accordance with generally accepted accounting principles of the United States, Japan, Mexico, or some other country, or are they prepared in accordance with principles established by the International Accounting Standards Board? Do earnings include nonrecurring gains and losses, such as a write-down of an equity investment or goodwill, that the analyst should evaluate differently than recurring components of earnings? Has the firm structured transactions or selected accounting principles that make it appear more profitable or less risky than economic conditions otherwise suggest? Do earnings include revenues that appear to be mismatched with the business model employed by the firm?

4. **Forecast the expected future profitability and risk of the firm using information in the financial statements.** Most financial analysts assess the profitability of a firm relative to the risks involved. Assessments of the recent profitability provide the basis for projecting the likely future profitability and, in turn, the likely future returns from investing in the company. Forecasts of a firm's ability to manage risks, particularly those elements of risk with measurable financial consequences, permit the analyst to estimate the likelihood that the firm will experience financial difficulties in the future.

5. **Value the firm.** Financial statement analysis is most frequently applied to value companies. Financial analysts make recommendations to buy, sell, or hold the equity securities of various firms whose price they think is too low, too high, or about right. Investment banking firms that underwrite the initial public offering of a firm's common stock must set the initial offering price. Translating information from the financial statements into intelligent estimates of firm value, and therefore into intelligent investment decisions, is the principal activity of financial analysts.

These five interrelated steps represent the subject matter of this book. This chapter briefly explores each step. Subsequent chapters develop the important concepts and tools in considerably more depth. Throughout this book, we use the financial statements, notes, and other information provided by PepsiCo, Inc. and Subsidiaries (PepsiCo) to illustrate the various topics discussed. Appendix A at the end of the book includes recent financial statements and notes for PepsiCo, as well as the opinion of the independent auditor and of management regarding these financial statements. Appendix B includes a financial review provided by management that discusses the business strategy of PepsiCo, as well as offers explanations for changes in its profitability and risk over time. Appendix C presents the output of a financial statement analysis software package, called FSAP, showing the profitability and risk ratios for PepsiCo for recent years. FSAP is available at the text's web site (http://stickney.swlearning.com). Many of the problems and cases in this book use FSAP to aid the analysis. Data files for the companies used in these problems and cases also appear on this web site.

STEP 1: IDENTIFY THE INDUSTRY ECONOMIC CHARACTERISTICS

The economic characteristics of an industry play a key role in dictating the types of financial statement relationships the analyst might expect to observe when analyzing a set of financial statements. Consider, for example, the financial statement data for firms in four different industries in Exhibit 1.2. This exhibit expresses all items on the balance sheet and income statement as a percentage of revenue. Consider how the economic characteristics of these industries affect their financial statement relationships.

Grocery Store Chain

The products of a particular grocery store chain are difficult to differentiate from similar products of other grocery store chains. In addition, low barriers to entry exist in the grocery store industry; an entrant simply needs retail space and access to food products distributors. Thus, extensive competition and nondifferentiated products result in a relatively low net income to sales, or profit margin, percentage (3.5 percent in this case). Grocery stores, however, need relatively few assets in order to generate sales (34.2 cents in assets for each dollar of sales in this case). The assets are described as turning over 2.9 times (= 100.0%/34.2%) per year. Each time the assets of this grocery store chain turn over, or generate one dollar of revenue, it generates a profit of 3.5 cents. Thus, during a one-year period, the grocery store earns 10.15 cents (= 3.5 percent × 2.9) for each dollar invested in assets.

Pharmaceutical Company

The barriers to entry in the pharmaceutical industry are much higher than for grocery stores. Pharmaceutical firms must invest considerable amounts in research

EXHIBIT 1.2

Common-size Financial Statement Data for Four Firms

	Grocery Store Chain	Pharmaceutical Company	Electric Utility	Commercial Bank
Balance Sheet at End of Year				
Cash and Marketable Securities	.7%	11.0%	1.5%	261.9%
Accounts and Notes Receivable.	.7	18.0	7.8	733.5
Inventories	8.7	17.0	4.5	—
Property, Plant, Equipment (net).	22.2	28.7	159.0	18.1
Other Assets	1.9	72.8	29.2	122.6
Total Assets	34.2%	147.5%	202.0%	1,136.1%
Current Liabilities.	7.7%	30.8%	14.9%	936.9%
Long-term Debt	7.6	12.7	130.8	71.5
Other Noncurrent Liabilities	2.6	24.6	1.8	27.2
Shareholders' Equity.	16.3	79.4	54.5	100.5
Total Equities	34.2%	147.5%	202.0%	1,136.1%
Income Statement for Year				
Revenue.	100.0%	100.0%	100.0%	100.0%
Cost of Goods Sold.	(74.1)	(31.6)	(79.7)	—
Operating Expenses	(19.7)	(37.1)	—	(41.8)
Research and Development	—	(10.1)	—	—
Interest	(.5)	(3.1)	(4.6)	(36.6)
Income Taxes	(2.2)	(6.0)	(5.2)	(8.6)
Net Income.	3.5%	12.1%	10.5%	13.0%

and development to create new drugs. After a lengthy government approval process, firms receive a patent for new drugs. The patent gives firms exclusive rights to manufacture and sell the drug for an extended period. These high entry barriers permit pharmaceutical firms to realize much higher profit margins than grocery stores. Exhibit 1.2 indicates that the pharmaceutical firm generated a profit margin of 12.1 percent, more than three times that reported by the grocery store chain. Pharmaceutical firms, however, face product liability risks as well as the risk that competitors will develop superior drugs that make a particular firm's drug offerings obsolete. Because of these business risks, pharmaceutical firms tend to take on relatively small amounts of debt financing.

Electric Utility

The principal assets of an electric utility are its capital-intensive generating plants. Thus, property, plant, and equipment dominate the balance sheet. Because of the large investments required in such assets, electric utility firms in the past have generally demanded a monopoly position in a particular locale. Government regulators permitted this monopoly position but set the rates that utilities charged customers for electric services. Thus, electric utilities have traditionally realized relatively high profit margins (10.5 percent in this case) to offset their relatively low total assets turnovers (.495 = 100.0%/202.0% in this case). The monopoly position and regulatory protection reduced the risk of financial failure and permitted electric utilities to take on relatively high proportions of debt in their capital structures. The economic characteristics of electric utilities have changed dramatically in recent years. The elimination of monopoly positions and the setting of rates as market conditions dictate have considerably reduced profit margins.

Commercial Bank

The principal assets of commercial banks are investments in financial securities and loans to businesses and consumers. The principal financing for commercial banks comes from customers' deposits and short-term borrowing. Because customers can generally withdraw deposits at any time, commercial banks invest in securities that they can quickly sell for cash, if necessary. The lending of money is a commodity business: money borrowed from one bank is similar to money borrowed from another bank. Thus, one would expect a commercial bank to realize a small excess margin on the price it earns from lending (interest revenue) over the price it pays for funds (interest expense). The profit margins on lending are indeed relatively small. The 13.0 percent margin for the commercial bank shown in Exhibit 1.2 reflects the much higher profit margins it generates from offering fee-based financial services, such as arranging mergers and acquisitions, structuring financing packages for businesses, and guaranteeing financial commitments of business customers. Note that the assets of this commercial bank turn over just .09 (=100.0%/1,136.1%) times per year, reflecting the net effect of interest revenues from investments and loans of six to eight percent per year and fee-based revenues which require relatively few assets.

TOOLS FOR STUDYING INDUSTRY ECONOMICS

Three tools for studying the economic characteristics of an industry are (1) value chain analysis, (2) Porter's five forces classification, and (3) an economic attributes framework we have found helpful. The microeconomics literature suggests other analytical frameworks as well.

VALUE CHAIN ANALYSIS

The value chain for an industry sets forth the sequence or chain of activities involved in the creation, manufacture, and distribution of its products and services.

Exhibit 1.3 describes a value chain for the pharmaceutical industry. Pharmaceutical companies invest in research and development to discover and develop new drugs. When promising drugs emerge, a lengthy drug approval process begins. Estimates suggest that it takes 8–12 years and more than $300 million to discover, and then obtain approval, of new drugs. To expedite the approval process, reduce costs, and permit their scientists to devote energies to the more creative drug discovery phase, pharmaceutical companies have contracted with clinical research firms to conduct the testing and shepherding of new drugs through the approval process.

The manufacture of drugs involves the combining of various chemicals and other elements. For quality control and product purity reasons, the manufacturing process is heavily automated.

Pharmaceutical companies employ sales forces to market drugs to doctors and hospitals. In an effort to create demand, these companies have increasingly advertised new products through multiple advertising media, suggesting that consumers ask their doctors about the drug. Drug distribution typically channels through pharmacies, although bulk mail order purchases are increasingly common (and encouraged by health insurers).

To the extent that prices are available for products or services at any of the stages in the value chain, the analyst can study where value gets added within an industry. For example, the analyst can look at the prices paid to acquire firms with promising or newly discovered drugs to ascertain the value of the drug discovery phase. The prices charged by clinical research firms to test and obtain approval of new drugs provide a signal of the value added by this activity. The higher the value added from any activity, the higher should be the profitability from engaging in that phase (see Problem 1.4).

The analyst can also use the value chain to identify the strategic positioning of a particular firm within the industry. Pharmaceutical firms have traditionally maintained a presence in the discovery through demand creation phases, leaving distribution to pharmacies and, increasingly, contracting out the drug testing and approval phase.

Exhibit 1.4 sets forth a value chain for the soft drink/beverage industry. Almost 40 percent of PepsiCo's recent sales were generated in the beverage industry. PepsiCo operates in three business segments, with worldwide snacks (Frito-Lay) and cereal and related products (Quaker Foods) as the other two segments. Appendix B

EXHIBIT 1.3

Value Chain for the Pharmaceutical Industry

| Research to Discover Drugs | Approval of Drugs by Government Regulators | Manufacture of Drugs | Creation of Demand for Drugs | Distribution to Consumers |

EXHIBIT 1.4

Value Chain for the Soft Drink/Beverage Industry

New Beverage Product Development → Manufacture of Concentrate → Mixing of Concentrate, Water, and Sweetener to Produce Beverage or Syrup → Containerizing Beverage or Syrup in Bottles, Cans, or Other Container → Distribution to Retail Outlets

---

includes PepsiCo's description of its worldwide soft drink/beverage business, which consists of three segments, Pepsi-Cola North America, Gatorade/Tropicana North America, and PepsiCo Beverage International, as well as its involvement along the value chain.

Although the classic PepsiCo soft drinks (Pepsi, Mountain Dew, Slice, among others) have not changed for many years, the company continually engages in new product development. Once a product appears to have commercial feasibility, PepsiCo combines raw materials into a concentrate or syrup base. The ingredients and their mixes are highly secret. PepsiCo then ships the concentrate to its franchise bottlers (or, in the case of syrup, to its national fountain accounts), who combine it with water and sweeteners to produce the finished soft drink beverage.

PepsiCo relies on non-controlled affiliates to bottle and distribute its beverages. That is, PepsiCo primarily contracts outs the bottling operation (we discuss the rationale for this arrangement in the strategy section later in this chapter), a decision it made in Year 9 and discussed in Appendix B. The bottlers transport the bottled beverages and syrups to retail establishments.

Because the analyst can obtain separate financial statements for PepsiCo and for its bottlers, one can observe where value gets added along the value chain. We examine the profitability and risk of PepsiCo and its bottlers in Chapters 4, 5, and 9.

PORTER'S FIVE FORCES CLASSIFICATION

Porter suggests that five forces influence the average profitability of an industry.[1]

1. **Buyer Power.** Are consumers sensitive to product prices? If products are similar to those offered by competitors, consumers may switch to the lowest priced offering. If consumers view a particular firm's products as unique, however, they will likely be less sensitive to price differences. Another dimension of price sensitivity is the relative cost of a product. We are less sensitive to prices of products that represent a small portion of our income, such as beverages, than we are to higher-priced products, such as automobiles.

---

[1]Michael E. Porter, *Competitive Strategy: Techniques for Analyzing Industries and Competitors* (New York: The Free Press), 1998.

Buyer power relates to relative bargaining power. If there are many sellers of a product and a small number of buyers, such as military equipment and weapons systems bought by governments, the buyer can exert significant downward pressure on prices and therefore the profitability of suppliers. If there are few sellers and many buyers, as with beverages, it is the sellers who have more bargaining power. Brand loyalty, control of distribution channels, low price, and the small number of suppliers result in low buyer power in the beverage industry.

2. **Supplier Power.** A similar set of factors applies on the input side as well. Beverage companies purchase the raw materials that make up their concentrate or syrup. Although PepsiCo does not disclose every ingredient, it is unlikely that PepsiCo is dependent on one or even a few suppliers for any of its raw materials. It is also unlikely that any of these ingredients are sufficiently unique that the suppliers could exert much power over PepsiCo. Given PepsiCo's size, the power more likely resides with PepsiCo than with its suppliers. By contrast, certain suppliers of microchips, operating systems, and software are very powerful suppliers to PC manufacturers.

3. **Rivalry Among Existing Firms.** Pepsi and Coke dominate the soft drink/ beverage industry in the United States. Because some consumers view their products as similar, intense competition based on price could develop. Also, the soft drink market in the United States is mature (that is, not growing rapidly), so price could become a weapon to gain market share.

   While intense rivalries have a tendency to reduce profitability, in this case Pepsi and Coke, the only two major players, can tacitly minimize competition based on price and compete instead on image, access to key distribution channels (for example, fast-food chains), or other attributes. Growth opportunities do exist in other countries, which these companies pursue aggressively. Thus, we might characterize industry rivalry as moderate.

4. **Threat of New Entrants.** How easily can new firms enter a market? Are there entry barriers, such as large capital investment, technological expertise, patents, or regulation that inhibit new entrants? If so, firms in the industry will likely generate higher earnings than if new entrants can easily enter the market and compete away the excess profitability.

   Entry barriers in the soft drink industry are high. Brand recognition by Pepsi and Coke serves as one entry barrier. Another barrier is domination of the distribution channels by these two firms. Most restaurant chains sign exclusive contracts to serve the beverages of one or the other of these two firms. Also, Pepsi and Coke often dominate shelf space in grocery stores.

5. **Threat of Substitutes.** How easily can customers switch to substitute products? How likely are they to switch? When there are close substitutes in a market, profitability is dampened, as between restaurants and grocery stores for certain types of prepared foods; and between airlines, driving an automobile, and other means of leisure travel for shorter distances. Unique products with few substitutes, such as certain prescription medications, enhance profitability. Fruit juices, tonic waters and sports drinks serve a similar thirst-

quenching function as soft drinks, which is the reason PepsiCo purchased Tropicana and Gatorade. Consumer buying habits, brand loyalty, and channel availability, however, minimize the threat of substitutes in the soft drink industry.

Thus, the soft drink/beverage industry rates low on buyer power, supplier power, threat of new entrants, and threat of substitutes, and moderate on rivalry within the industry. Unless either Pepsi or Coke decides to compete on the basis of low price, the analyst might expect these firms to report relatively high profitability.

ECONOMIC ATTRIBUTES FRAMEWORK

We have found the following framework useful in studying the economic attributes of a business, in part because it ties in with items reported in the financial statements.

1. **Demand**
   - Are customers highly price sensitive, as in the case of automobiles, or are they relatively insensitive, as in the case of soft drinks?
   - Is demand growing rapidly, as in the case with long-term health care, or is the industry relatively mature, as in the case of grocery stores?
   - Does demand move with the economic cycle, as in the case of construction of new homes and offices, or is it insensitive to business cycles, as in the case of the demand for food products or medical care?
   - Does demand vary with the seasons of a year, as with summer clothing or ski equipment, or is it relatively stable throughout the year, as in the case with gasoline for automobiles?

2. **Supply**
   - Are there many suppliers offering similar products, or few suppliers offering unique products?
   - Are there high barriers to entry or can new entrants gain easy access?
   - Are there high barriers to exit?

3. **Manufacturing**
   - Is the manufacturing process capital intensive, as in the case of electric power generation; labor intensive, as in the case of advertising and auditing services; or a combination of the two, as in the case of automobile manufacturing or airline transportation?
   - Is the manufacturing process complex with low tolerance for error, as for heart pacemakers or microchips, or relatively simple with ranges of acceptable-quality products, such as clothing and nonmechanized toys?

4. **Marketing**
   - Is the product promoted to other businesses, where a sales staff plays a key role, or is it marketed to consumers, where advertising, location, and coupons serve as the principal promotion mechanisms?
   - Does steady demand pull products through distribution channels, or must firms continually create demand?

5. **Investing and Financing**
   - Are the assets of firms in the industry relatively short term, as in the case of commercial banks, which require assets to match their short-term sources of funds? Or, are assets relatively long term, as in the case of electric utilities, requiring primarily long-term financing?
   - Is there relatively little risk in the assets of firms in the industry so firms can carry high proportions of debt financing? Alternatively, are there high risks resulting from short product life cycles or product liability concerns that dictate low debt and high shareholders' equity financing?
   - Is the industry relatively profitable and mature, generating more cash flow from operations than is needed for acquisitions of property, plant, and equipment? Alternatively, is the industry growing rapidly and in need of external financing?

Exhibit 1.5 summarizes the economic characteristics of the soft drink/beverage industry.

STEP 2: IDENTIFY THE COMPANY STRATEGY

Firms establish business strategies in an attempt to differentiate themselves from competitors, but an industry's economic characteristics affect the flexibility that firms have in designing these strategies. In some cases, firms can create sustainable competitive advantages. Pepsi's size and brand name give it a sustainable competitive advantage, although Coke can boast similar advantages. The reputation for quality family entertainment provides Disney with a sustainable advantage.

In many industries, however, products and ideas quickly get copied. Consider, for example, computer hardware; chicken, pizza, and hamburger restaurant chains; and financial services. In these cases, firms may achieve competitive advantage by being the first with new concepts or ideas (referred to as *first mover advantage*) or by continually investing in product development to remain on the leading edge of change within an industry.

FRAMEWORK FOR STRATEGY ANALYSIS

The set of strategic choices confronting a particular firm varies across industries. A framework dealing with product and firm characteristics helps in structuring the choice set.

1. **Nature of Product or Service.** Is a firm attempting to create unique products or services for particular market niches and thereby achieving relatively high profit margins (referred to as a *product differentiation strategy*) or it is offering nondifferentiated products at low prices, accepting a lower profit margin in return for a higher total assets turnover (referred to as a *low-cost leadership strategy*)? Is it possible to achieve both objectives by creating brand loyalty and maintaining control over costs?

EXHIBIT 1.5

Economic Characteristics of Soft Drink/Beverage Industry

Demand
- Relatively insensitive to price.
- Low growth in the United States but more rapid growth opportunities in other countries.
- Demand is not cyclical.
- Demand is higher during warmer weather.

Supply
- Two principal suppliers (PepsiCo and Coke) selling branded products.
- Branded products and domination of distribution channels by two principal suppliers create high barriers to entry.

Manufacturing
- Manufacturing process for concentrate and syrup is not capital intensive.
- Bottling and distribution of final product is capital intensive.
- Manufacturing process is simple (essentially a mixing operation) with some tolerance for quality variation.

Marketing
- Brand recognition and established demand pull products through distribution channels but advertising can stimulate demand to some extent.

Investing and Financing
- Bottling operations and transportation of products to retailers require long-term financing.
- Profitability is relatively high and growth is slow in the United States, leading to excess cash flow generation. Growth markets in other countries require financing from internal domestic cash flow or from external sources.

---

2. **Degree of Integration within Value Chain.** Is the firm pursuing a vertical integration strategy, participating in all phases of the value chain, or selecting just certain phases within the chain? With respect to manufacturing, is the firm conducting all manufacturing operations itself (as usually occurs in steel manufacturing), outsourcing all manufacturing (common in athletic shoes), or outsourcing the manufacturing of components but conducting the assembly operation in-house (common in automobile and computer hardware manufacturing)?

   With respect to distribution, is the firm maintaining control over the distribution function or outsourcing it? Some restaurant chains, for example, own all of their restaurants while other chains operate through independently owned franchises. Computer hardware firms have recently shifted from selling through their own sales staffs to using various indirect sellers, such as value-added resellers and systems integrators, in effect shifting from in-house sourcing to outsourcing of the distribution function.

3. **Degree of Geographical Diversification.** Is the firm targeting its products to its domestic market or integrating horizontally across many countries? Operating in other countries creates opportunities for growth but exposes firms to risks from exchange rate changes, political uncertainties, and additional competitors.

4. **Degree of Industry Diversification.** Is the firm operating in a single industry or diversifying across multiple industries? Operating in multiple industries permits firms to diversify product, cyclical, regulatory, and other risks encountered when operating in a single industry but raises questions about management's ability to understand and manage multiple and different businesses effectively.

APPLICATION OF STRATEGY FRAMEWORK TO PEPSICO'S BEVERAGE SEGMENT

To apply this strategy framework to PepsiCo's beverage segment of its operations, we rely on the description by PepsiCo's management found in Appendix B. Most U.S. firms include this information in their Form 10-K filing with the Securities and Exchange Commission.

1. **Nature of Product or Service.** PepsiCo competes broadly within the beverage industry, with offerings in soft drinks, fruit juices, tonic waters, and sports drinks. However, its principal product is soft drinks. Although one might debate whether its products differ from similar products offered by Coke and other competitors, brand recognition and domination of distribution channels permit it to sell a somewhat differentiated product.

2. **Degree of Integration within Value Chain.** PepsiCo engages in new product development, manufactures concentrates and syrups, and promotes its products, while it allows its bottlers to manufacture and distribute soft drink products. This arrangement exists because PepsiCo realizes that the principal value added is the secret formulas that make up the concentrates and syrups, and in product and brand promotion to maintain its brand name and brand loyalty. Maintaining product quality and efficient and effective distribution channels are critical to PepsiCo's success, so PepsiCo emphasizes the important role played by the bottlers and the oversight role played by PepsiCo to insure their financial strength and efficient operation. Thus, there is a close operational relationship between PepsiCo and its bottlers. However, bottling operations are relatively simple, yet capital intensive; require long-term financing, typically debt; and are not particularly value enhancing. By not owning the bottling and distribution operations, PepsiCo reports less debt on its balance sheet and appears less risky.

   Because of its heavy influence (seller power) over its bottlers, PepsiCo is able to price its concentrate sales to these bottlers to garner a significant portion of the profit margin for itself. The bottlers are willing to accept a lower margin because of the monopoly power given them by PepsiCo in a particular locale, and the strong demand for the products of PepsiCo that they produce. (In subsequent chapters, we consider PepsiCo's strategy with respect to its bottlers when we assess its profitability, quality of financial information, and risk.)

It's interesting to note that PepsiCo's main competitor in the soft drink industry, Coke, structures its operations similarly. Just as with PepsiCo, Coke's principal product is concentrates that it sells to bottlers, who are responsible for bottling and distributing the final Coke soft drinks.

3. **Degree of Geographical Diversification.** Note 21 to PepsiCo's financial statements discloses the geographical distribution of its operations. During Year 11, PepsiCo derived 10 percent of its beverage revenues and 5 percent of its beverage operating income from outside of North America. PepsiCo indicates that the largest international growth came from sales in Russia, China, and Brazil. International and North American beverage sales grew at a compound annual growth rate of 4 percent during the last three years ending December 31, Year 11. As opposed to Coke, which is geographically diverse, Pepsi's soft drink/beverage segment generates most of its sales in North America. PepsiCo reports in Appendix A that it generates 32 percent of its combined sales for Year 11 internationally.

4. **Degree of Industry Diversification.** As discussed earlier, PepsiCo segments its business into three industries: soft drinks/beverages; snack foods (Frito-Lay); and cereals and related products (Quaker Foods). For Year 11, PepsiCo generated 39 percent of its revenues and 35 percent of its operating profits from the soft drink/beverage segment; 54 percent of its revenues and 56 percent of its operating profits from the snack food segment; and 7 percent of its revenues and 9 percent of its operating profits from cereals and related products. Although PepsiCo is more industry diverse than Coke, many economic characteristics of the beverage, snack food, and cereal industries are similar in nature (importance of brand recognition and distribution channels, for example).

STEP 3: ASSESS THE QUALITY OF THE FINANCIAL STATEMENTS

Business firms prepare three principal financial statements to report the results of their activities: (1) balance sheet, (2) income statement, and (3) statement of cash flows. Many firms prepare a fourth statement, the statement of shareholders' equity, which provides further detail of the shareholders' equity section of the balance sheet. Firms also include a set of notes that elaborate on items included in these statements. This section presents a brief overview of the purpose and content of each of these three financial statements, using the financial statements and notes for PepsiCo in Appendix A as examples.

Generally accepted accounting principles, or GAAP, determine the valuation and measurement methods used in preparing the financial statements. Official rule-making bodies set these principles. The Securities and Exchange Commission (SEC), an agency of the federal government, has the legal authority to specify acceptable accounting principles in the United States. The SEC has, for the most part, delegated the responsibility for setting GAAP to the Financial Accounting Standards Board (FASB), a private-sector body within the accounting profession. The FASB specifies acceptable accounting principles only after receiving extensive comments on proposed accounting standards from various preparers, auditors, and users of financial statements.

The process followed in other countries varies widely. In some countries, the amounts reported for financial and tax reporting closely conform. In these cases, legislative arms of the government play a major role in setting acceptable accounting principles. Japan and Germany are examples of such countries. Other countries employ a model similar to that in the United States, where financial and tax-reporting methods differ and the accounting profession plays a major role in establishing GAAP. The United Kingdom and Canada are examples of such countries.

The International Accounting Standards Board, or IASB, is an independent entity comprised of fourteen members and a full-time professional staff. The IASB strives to reduce diversity in accounting principles across countries and to encourage greater standardization. Its pronouncements, however, have no enforceability of their own. Rather, the representatives to the IASB pledge their best efforts in establishing the pronouncements of the IASB as GAAP within their countries.

The IASB has increased its activity in recent years, and the FASB has pledged to work with the IASB in an attempt to harmonize reporting worldwide. Many still believe, however, that it will be some time before accounting standards conform worldwide.

BALANCE SHEET—MEASURING FINANCIAL POSITION

The balance sheet, or statement of financial position, presents a snapshot of the resources of a firm (assets) and the claims on those resources (liabilities and shareholders' equity) as of a specific date.

The assets portion of the balance sheet reports the effects of a firm's investing decisions. Refer to the balance sheet for PepsiCo on December 31, Year 10 and Year 11, in Exhibit 1.6. PepsiCo's principal assets are accounts and notes receivable (PepsiCo allows customers to delay their cash payments which results in an implicit investment of cash in these customers by PepsiCo); investments in property, plant and equipment; investments in the equity securities of bottlers (unconsolidated affiliates); and intangible assets.

The liabilities and shareholders' equity portion of the balance sheet reports the effects of a firm's financing decisions. PepsiCo obtains financing from suppliers of goods and services (reported as accounts payable and other current liabilities), bank loans (reported as short-term borrowings), long-term debt and other long-term liabilities, and shareholders' equity.

The balance sheet derives its name from the fact that it shows the following balance or equality:

$$\text{Assets} = \text{Liabilities} + \text{Shareholders' Equity}$$

That is, a firm's assets or resources are in balance with, or equal to, the claims on

EXHIBIT 1.6		
PepsiCo, Inc. and Subsidiaries		
Consolidated Balance Sheets		

Consolidated Balance Sheets *December 29, Year 11, and December 30, Year 10* (in millions except per share amounts)	Year 11	Year 10
ASSETS		
Current Assets		
Cash and cash equivalents	$ 683	$ 1,038
Short-term investments, at cost	966	467
	1,649	1,505
Accounts and notes receivable, net	2,142	2,129
Inventories	1,310	1,192
Prepaid expenses and other assets	752	791
Total Current Assets	5,853	5,617
Property, Plant, and Equipment, net	6,876	6,558
Intangible Assets, net	4,841	4,714
Investments in Unconsolidated Affiliates	2,871	2,979
Other Assets	1,254	889
Total Assets	$21,695	$20,757

those assets by creditors (liabilities) and owners (shareholders' equity). The balance sheet views resources from two perspectives: a list of the specific forms in which a firm holds the resources (cash, inventory, equipment) and a list of the persons or entities that provided the funds to obtain the assets and therefore have claims on them (suppliers, employees, governments, shareholders). Thus, the balance sheet portrays the equality of investing and financing.

Formats of balance sheets in some countries differ from that in the United States. In Germany and France, for example, property, plant, and equipment and other non-current assets appear first, followed by current assets. On the financing side, share-holders' equity appears first, followed by noncurrent liabilities and then current liabilities. This format maintains the balance between investing and financing but presents accounts in the opposite sequence to that common in the United States.

In the United Kingdom, the balance sheet equation takes the following form:

Noncurrent Assets + [Current Assets – Current Liabilities]

– Noncurrent Liabilities = Shareholders' Equity

This format takes the perspective of shareholders by reporting the assets available for shareholders after subtracting claims by creditors. Financial analysts can rearrange

EXHIBIT 1.6		
continued		

Consolidated Balance Sheets *December 29, Year 11, and December 30, Year 10* **(in millions except per share amounts)**	**Year 11**	**Year 10**
LIABILITIES AND SHAREHOLDERS' EQUITY		
Current Liabilities		
Short-term borrowings.....................................	$ 354	$ 202
Accounts payable and other current liabilities....................	4,461	4,529
Income taxes payable	183	64
Total Current Liabilities	4,998	4,795
Long-term Debt	2,651	3,009
Other Liabilities.......................................	3,876	3,960
Deferred Income Taxes	1,496	1,367
Preferred Stock, no par value	26	49
Deferred Compensation – preferred	—	(27)
Common Shareholders' Equity		
Common stock, par value 1²/₃¢ per share (issued 1,782 and 2,029 shares, respectively).....................................	30	34
Capital in excess of par value	13	375
Deferred compensation.....................................	—	(21)
Retained earnings	11,519	16,510
Accumulated other comprehensive loss	(1,646)	(1,374)
	9,916	15,524
Less: repurchased common stock, at cost (26 and 280 shares, respectively)	(1,268)	(7,920)
Total Common Shareholders' Equity	8,648	7,604
Total Liabilities and Shareholders' Equity	$21,695	$20,757

See accompanying notes to Consolidated Financial Statements.

the components of published balance sheets to whichever format they consider most informative, although ambiguity may exist for some balance sheet categories.

Assets—Recognition, Valuation, and Classification

Which of its resources does a firm recognize as assets? At what amount does the firm report these assets? How does it classify them within the assets portion of the balance sheet? GAAP determines responses to these questions.

Assets are resources that have the potential for providing a firm with future economic benefits: the ability to generate future cash inflows (as with accounts receivable and inventories) or to reduce future cash outflows (as with prepayments). A firm recognizes as assets those resources (1) for which its has acquired rights to their future use as a result of a past transaction or event, and (2) for which the firm can measure, or quantify, the future benefits with a reasonable degree of precision.[2] Resources that firms do not normally recognize as assets because they fail to meet one or both of the criteria include purchase orders received from customers, employment contracts with corporate officers, and a quality reputation with employees, customers, or citizens of the community.

Perhaps the most valuable resources of PepsiCo are its brand names (Pepsi, Frito-Lay, Quaker Oats). PepsiCo has created these brand names through past expenditures on advertising, event sponsorships, product development, and quality control. Yet, ascertaining the portion of these expenditures that creates sustainable future benefits and the portion that simply stimulates sales during the current period is too uncertain to justify recognition of an asset. On the contrary, the amounts that PepsiCo does report for goodwill and other intangible assets result from PepsiCo's purchase (that is, transaction-based event) of other companies.

Most assets on the balance sheet are either *monetary* or *nonmonetary*. Using the definition for these categories as discussed in Chapter 9 (foreign currency translation), monetary assets include cash and claims to a fixed amount of cash receivable in the future. PepsiCo's monetary assets include cash, accounts and notes receivable, and investments in the debt securities of other firms. The balance sheet reports monetary assets at the amount of cash the firm expects to receive in the future. If the date or dates of receipt extend beyond one year, the firm reports the monetary asset at the present value of the future cash flows (using a discount rate that reflects the underlying uncertainty of collecting the cash as assessed at the time the claim initially arose).

Nonmonetary assets include assets that are *tangible*, such as inventories, buildings, and equipment, and assets that are *intangible*, including goodwill, patents, trademarks, and licenses. Nonmonetary assets do not represent claims to fixed amounts of cash. Firms might report nonmonetary assets at the amounts initially paid to acquire them (acquisition, or historical, cost); the amounts required currently to acquire them (current replacement cost); the amounts for which firms could currently sell the asset (current net realizable value); or the present values of the amounts firms expect to receive in the future from selling or using the assets (present value of future cash flows). GAAP generally requires the reporting of nonmonetary assets on the balance sheet at their acquisition cost amounts because this valuation is usually more objective and verifiable than other possible valuation bases. GAAP in some countries, such as the United Kingdom and the Netherlands, permits periodic revaluation of property, plant, and equipment to current values. Chapter 2 discusses alternative valuation methods and their implications for measuring earnings.

The classification of assets within the balance sheet varies widely in published annual reports. The principal asset categories are as follows:

Current Assets. Current assets include cash and other assets that a firm expects to sell or consume during the normal operating cycle of a business, usually one year.

---

[2]Financial Accounting Standards Board, *Statement of Financial Accounting Concepts No. 6,* "Elements of Financial Statements," 1985, par. 25.

Cash, short-term investments, accounts and notes receivable, inventories, and pre-payments appear as current assets for PepsiCo.

Investments. This category includes long-term investments in the debt and equity securities of other entities. If a firm makes such investments for short-term purposes, it classifies them under current assets. A principal asset for PepsiCo is the investments in its bottlers (Pepsi Bottling Group (PBG), PepsiAmericas, and other bottlers). Note 10 to PepsiCo's financial statements indicates that it owns less than 50 percent of the common stock of these bottlers. PepsiCo therefore does not prepare consolidated financial statements with these bottlers but, instead, reports the investments on the balance sheet using the equity method (discussed in Chapter 9).

Property, Plant, and Equipment. This category includes the tangible, long-lived assets that a firm uses in operations over a period of years. Note 8 to PepsiCo's financial statements indicates that land and improvements, buildings and improvements, machinery and equipment, and construction in progress are included in this category. It reports property, plant, and equipment at acquisition cost and then subtracts the accumulated depreciation recognized on these assets since acquisition.

Intangibles. Intangibles include the rights established by law or contract to the future use of property. Patents, trademarks, and franchises are intangible assets. The most troublesome asset recognition questions revolve around which rights satisfy the criteria for an asset. As the discussion in Chapter 7 makes more clear, firms generally recognize as assets intangibles acquired in external market transactions with other entities (as is the case for goodwill included in PepsiCo's balance sheet under the category of intangible assets, net, that it details in Note 9) but do not recognize as assets intangibles developed internally by the firm (PepsiCo's brand names, for example).

Liabilities—Recognition, Valuation, and Classification

A liability represents a firm's obligation to make payments of cash, goods, or services in a reasonably predictable amount at a reasonably predictable future time for benefits or services received in the past.[3] Liabilities for PepsiCo include obligations to suppliers of goods and services (accounts payable and other current liabilities), banks (short-term borrowings), governments (income taxes payable), and lenders (long-term debt).

Most troublesome questions regarding liability recognition relate to executory contracts. GAAP does not recognize labor contracts, purchase order commitments, and some lease agreements as liabilities because firms will receive the benefits from these items in the future instead of having received them in the past. Notes to the financial statements disclose material, executory contracts, and other contingent claims. Chapter 8 discusses these claims more fully.

Most liabilities are monetary, requiring payments of fixed amounts of cash. GAAP reports those due within one year at the amount of cash the firm expects to pay to discharge the obligation. If the payment dates extend beyond one year, then GAAP

---

[3]Financial Accounting Standards Board, ibid., par. 35.

states the liability at the present value of the required future cash flows (discounted at an interest rate that reflects the underlying uncertainty of paying the cash as assessed at the time the obligation initially arose). Some liabilities, such as warranties, require the delivery of goods or services instead of the payment of cash. The balance sheet states those liabilities at the expected future cost of providing these goods and services.

Published balance sheets classify liabilities in various ways. Virtually all firms (except banks) use a current liabilities category, which includes obligations that a firm expects to settle within one year. Balance sheets report the remaining liabilities in a section labeled noncurrent liabilities or long-term debt. PepsiCo uses three noncurrent liability categories: long-term debt, other liabilities, and deferred income taxes. Chapters 2 and 8 discuss deferred income taxes.

Shareholders' Equity Valuation and Disclosure

The shareholders' equity in a firm is a residual interest or claim. That is, the owners have a claim on all assets not required to meet the claims of creditors. The valuation of assets and liabilities in the balance sheet therefore determines the valuation of total shareholders' equity.[4]

Balance sheets separate total shareholders' equity into (1) amounts initially contributed by shareholders for an interest in a firm (PepsiCo uses the accounts, common stock, and capital in excess of par value), (2) cumulative net income in excess of dividends declared (PepsiCo's account is retained earnings), (3) equity effects of the recognition or valuation of certain assets or liabilities (PepsiCo includes items related to deferred compensation and accumulated other comprehensive income), and (4) treasury stock (PepsiCo shares repurchased by PepsiCo).

Assessing the Quality of the Balance Sheet as a Complete Representation of Economic Position

Analysts frequently examine the relation between items in the balance sheet when assessing a firm's financial position and credit risk. For example, an excess of current assets over current liabilities suggests that a firm has sufficient liquid resources to pay short-term creditors. A relatively low percentage of long-term debt to shareholders' equity suggests that a firm has sufficient permanent shareholders' capital in place to reduce the risk of being unable to repay the long-term debt at maturity.

When using the balance sheet for these purposes, however, the analyst must recognize that:

1. Certain valuable resources of a firm that generate future cash flows, such as a patent for a pharmaceutical firm or a brand name for a consumer products

---

[4]The issuance of bonds with equity characteristics, such as convertible bonds, and the issuance of preferred stock with debt characteristics, such as redeemable preferred stock, cloud the distinction between liabilities and shareholders' equity. In fact, Note 15 of PepsiCo's financial statements details the small amount of convertible preferred stock that the firm has outstanding at the end of Year 11.

firm such as PepsiCo, will only appear as assets if they were acquired from another firm and therefore have a measurable historical cost.

2. Nonmonetary assets appear at acquisition cost, even though their current market values might exceed their recorded amounts. An example is the market value versus recorded value of land on the balance sheets of railroads and many urban department stores.

3. Certain commitments to make future payments may not appear as liabilities. We generally do not see on the balance sheet, for example, the commitments by airlines to make future lease payments on their aircraft or the commitments to make future payments for labor by steel, tire, and automobile companies under labor union contracts.

4. Noncurrent liabilities appear at the present value of expected cash flows discounted at an interest rate determined at the time the liability initially arose, instead of at a current market interest rate.

These factors result in the balance sheet reporting incomplete measures of the economic position of a firm. When using the balance sheet, the analyst should consider making adjustments for items that impact balance sheet quality. Chapters 7 through 9 discuss these issues more fully.

INCOME STATEMENT—MEASURING OPERATING PERFORMANCE

The total assets of a firm change over time because of investing and financing activities. For example, a firm may issue common stock for cash, acquire a building by assuming a mortgage for part of the purchase price, or issue common stock in exchange for convertible bonds. These investing and financing activities affect the amount and structure of a firm's assets, liabilities, and shareholders' equity.

The total assets of a firm also change over time because of operating activities. A firm sells goods or services to customers for a larger amount than the cost to the firm to acquire or produce the goods and services. Creditors and owners provide capital to a firm with the expectation that the firm will use it to generate a profit and provide an adequate return to the suppliers of capital for the level of risk involved.

The second principal financial statement, the income statement, provides information about the operating profitability of a firm for a period of time. We use the terms net income, earnings, and profit interchangeably in referring to the bottom line amount in the income statement. Exhibit 1.7 presents an income statement for PepsiCo for Year 9, Year 10, and Year 11.

Net income equals revenues and gains minus expenses and losses. Revenues measure the inflows of assets from selling goods and providing services. Expenses measure the outflows of assets that a firm uses, or consumes, in the process of generating revenues. As a measure of operating performance, revenues reflect resources generated by a firm, and expenses indicate the resources consumed. Gains and losses result from selling assets or settling liabilities peripherally related to a firm's central operations for more or less than their book values. For example, the sale of a building by PepsiCo for more than its book value would appear as a gain on the income statement.

PepsiCo generates revenues from selling goods in three principal product lines: various soft drink concentrates to its bottlers and other beverages directly to consumers; Frito-Lay snack foods; and Quaker Foods cereals and related items. Revenues

---

EXHIBIT 1.7			
PepsiCo, Inc. and Subsidiaries **Consolidated Statements of Income**			
Fiscal years ended December 29, Year 11, December 30, Year 10, and December 25, Year 9.			
(in millions except per share amounts)	**Year 11**	**Year 10**	**Year 9**
Net Sales			
New PepsiCo	$26,935	$25,479	$22,970
Bottling Operations.	—	—	2,123
Total Net Sales	26,935	25,479	25,093
Costs and Expenses			
Costs of sales	10,754	10,226	10,326
Selling, general, and administrative expenses.	11,608	11,104	11,018
Amortization of intangible assets	165	147	193
Merger-related costs	356	—	—
Other impairment and restructuring charges	31	184	73
Total Costs and Expenses	22,914	21,661	21,610
Operating Profit			
New PepsiCo	4,021	3,818	3,430
Bottling operations and equity investments.	—	—	53
Total Operating Profit.	4,021	3,818	3,483
Bottling equity income and transaction gains/(losses), net	160	130	1,083
Interest expense.	(219)	(272)	(421)
Interest income	67	85	130
Income Before Income Taxes	4,029	3,761	4,275
Provision for Income Taxes	1,367	1,218	1,770
Net Income	$ 2,662	$ 2,543	$ 2,505
Net Income per Common Share			
Basic.	$ 1.51	$ 1.45	$ 1.41
Diluted.	$ 1.47	$ 1.42	$ 1.38

See accompanying notes to consolidated financial statements.

also include interest income from investments in debt instruments and equity method income from investments in affiliated but noncontrolled bottlers.

Costs of sales include the cost of producing concentrates sold to bottlers, and the cost of snack foods, cereals, and other products. Expenses include selling, general, and administrative expenses (including advertising and other promotion costs), and interest expense on short- and long-term borrowing.

PepsiCo also reported two unusual charges in its Year 11 income statement: merger-related costs for the acquisition of Quaker Oats, and impairment and restructuring charges for the supply chain reconfiguration project began in Year 9. In addition, PepsiCo reported an expense for amortization of its intangible assets, an amount that will be reduced in future years because a new FASB ruling (FASB *Statement No. 142*) no longer requires the amortization of goodwill (see the subsection in Note 1 to PepsiCo's financial statements titled "Accounting Changes").

Accrual Basis of Accounting

Exhibit 1.8 depicts the operating, or earnings, cycle for a manufacturing firm. Net income from this series of activities equals the amount of cash received from customers minus the amount of cash paid for raw materials, labor, and the services of production facilities. If the entire operating cycle occurred within one accounting period, few difficulties would arise in measuring operating performance. Net income would equal cash inflows minus cash outflows related to these operating activities. However, firms acquire raw materials in one accounting period and use them in several future accounting periods. They acquire buildings and equipment in one accounting period and use them during many future accounting periods. A firm often sells goods or services in an earlier period than the one in which it receives cash from customers.

Under a cash basis of accounting, a firm recognizes revenue when it receives cash from customers and recognizes expenses when it pays cash to suppliers, employees, and other providers of goods and services. Because a firm's operating cycle usually extends over several accounting periods, the cash basis of accounting provides a poor measure of operating performance for specific periods of time. To overcome this deficiency of the cash basis, GAAP generally requires that firms use the accrual basis of accounting in measuring operating performance.

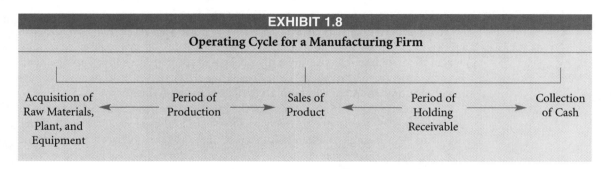

EXHIBIT 1.8
Operating Cycle for a Manufacturing Firm

Acquisition of Raw Materials, Plant, and Equipment ← Period of Production → Sales of Product ← Period of Holding Receivable → Collection of Cash

Under the accrual basis of accounting, a firm recognizes revenue when it performs all, or a substantial portion, of the services it expects to perform and receives either cash or a receivable whose cash-equivalent amount the firm can measure objectively. Most firms recognize revenue at the time they sell goods or render services. They match expenses with the associated revenues. Consider the accrual basis of accounting applied to a manufacturing firm. The cost of manufacturing a product remains on the balance sheet as an asset (inventory) until the time of sale. At the time of sale, the firm recognizes revenue in the amount of cash it expects to collect. It recognizes the cost of manufacturing the product as a matching expense. When a firm cannot easily link costs to a particular revenue (for example, the salary of the chief executive officer), it recognizes an expense in the period when it consumes services in operations.

Note that a firm need not delay revenue recognition until it receives cash from customers as long as the firm can estimate with reasonable precision the amount of cash it will ultimately receive. The amount will appear in accounts receivable prior to the receipt of cash. The accrual basis provides a better measure of operating performance than the cash basis because it matches inputs with outputs more accurately.

Classification and Format within the Income Statement

Investors commonly assess a firm's value based on the firm's expected future earnings stream. As detailed in Chapter 10 of this book, analysts form predictions of the future earnings, or net income, of a firm by studying the past trend of earnings. Inaccurate projections from past data can occur if net income includes unusual or nonrecurring amounts. To provide more useful information for prediction, GAAP requires that the income statement include some or all of the following sections or categories, depending on the nature of the firm's income for a period:

1. Income from continuing operations.
2. Income, gains, and losses from discontinued operations.
3. Extraordinary gains and losses.
4. Adjustments for changes in accounting principles.

The first section, Income from Continuing Operations, reports the revenues and expenses of activities in which a firm anticipates an ongoing involvement. If a firm does not have any of the other three categories of income in a particular year, it will probably not use the continuing operations label as such.

Firms report their expenses in various ways. Most firms in the United States report expenses by their function: cost of goods sold for manufacturing, selling expenses for marketing, administrative expenses for administrative management, interest expense for financing. Other firms report expenses by their nature: raw materials, compensation, advertising, research and development.

The continuing operations section of the income statement frequently appears in two formats. The single-step format lists all revenues, all expenses, and then derives net income in a single mathematical step as the difference between the two. The multiple-step format generally lists revenues from selling a firm's goods and services and then shows subtractions for the cost of goods and services sold and the costs of selling and administrative services. The multiple-step format then reports a subtotal for operating income. The income statement will then report nonoperating revenues (interest income, equity income), nonoperating expenses (interest expense), and nonoperating gains and losses. The multiple-step format derives its name from the various subtotals that generally appear before the disclosure of net income. PepsiCo uses this multiple step format, but many variations in income statement format appear in corporate annual reports.

A firm that intends to remain in a line of business but decides to sell or close down some portion of that line would report any income, gain, or loss from such an action under continuing operations. On the other hand, if a firm decides to terminate its involvement in a line of business, it would report the income, gain, or loss in the second section of the income statement labeled Income, Gains, and Losses from Discontinued Operations.

Extraordinary gains and losses arise from events that are (1) unusual, given the nature of a firm's activities, (2) nonrecurring, and (3) material in amount. Corporate annual reports rarely disclose such items.

Many firms in recent years have reported restructuring charges and impairment losses in their income statements. Such items often reflect the write-down of assets or the recognition of liabilities arising from changes in economic conditions and corporate strategies. Because restructuring charges and impairment losses do not usually satisfy the criteria for discontinued operations or extraordinary items, firms report them in the continuing operations section of the income statement. If the amounts are material, they will appear on a separate line to distinguish them from recurring income items.

Note 3 of PepsiCo's financial statements details the asset impairment charges taken by the firm in Years 9, 10, and 11. The income statement separately discloses these charges as part of continuing operations, even though the amounts are relatively small.

When firms change their methods of accounting, GAAP generally requires them to report the cumulative difference between the income reported under the old and the new methods in a separate section of the income statement labeled Adjustments for Changes in Accounting Principles.

All four categories of income items appear in the income statement, net of any income tax effects. The majority of published income statements include only the first section because discontinued operations, extraordinary gains and losses, and changes in accounting principles occur infrequently.

Comprehensive Income

The recognition and valuation of assets and liabilities usually give rise to an adjustment to some other account. This other account is often a revenue or expense account. For example, a firm might sell inventory for cash. Cash increases by the amount of the selling price, and revenues, a component of retained earnings, increase. Inventory decreases by the amount of the acquisition cost of the inventory item sold, and expenses, a negative component of retained earnings, increase.

Some changes in the recognition and valuation of assets and liabilities do not immediately affect net income and retained earnings but will likely affect them in future periods. Chapter 9 discusses, for example, the effect of exchange rate changes on the valuation of assets and liabilities of a foreign subsidiary of a U.S. company. Any gain or loss from exchange rate changes is unrealized until the foreign unit makes a currency conversion from its currency into U.S. dollars or vice versa. These unrealized "gains" and "losses" appear in a separate shareholders' equity account.

Review the Consolidated Statement of Common Shareholders' Equity for PepsiCo in Appendix A. It details three items in accumulated other comprehensive loss that relate to the valuation of assets and liabilities: (1) currency translation adjustment, (2) cash flow hedges, net of tax, and (3) minimum pension liability adjustment, net of tax. (Later chapters discuss the accounting for each of these items.)

FASB is aware that users of financial statements might overlook items of this nature that affect the market value of firms but which do not yet appear in net income. It therefore requires firms to report an amount in one of its financial statements that the FASB refers to as comprehensive income.[5]

Comprehensive income equals net income for a period plus or minus the changes in shareholders' equity accounts other than from net income and transactions with owners. Comprehensive income for PepsiCo for Year 11 is as follows (in millions):

Net Income	$2,662
Currency translation adjustment	(218)
Cash flow hedges, net of tax	(18)
Minimum pension liability adjustment (and other), net of tax	(36)
Comprehensive Income	$2,390

Firms have considerable flexibility as to where they report comprehensive income in the financial statements. It may appear in the income statement, in a separate statement of comprehensive income, or as part of the analysis of changes in shareholders' equity accounts.

Firms also have flexibility as to how they label disclosures related to comprehensive income. That is, firms need not use the term "comprehensive income" but instead may label the amount, for example, as net income plus or minus changes in other non-owner equity accounts. The balance sheet disclosure might use the term "accumulated other comprehensive income/loss" for the portions of comprehensive income not related to reported earnings, or use a term such as "accumulated non-owner equity account changes."

Appendix A indicates that PepsiCo uses the term "Accumulated Other Comprehensive Loss" in its Consolidated Balance Sheet. In addition, PepsiCo reports the accumulated balances for each component of its comprehensive income in Note 16 to the financial statements.

---

[5]Financial Accounting Standards Board, *Statement of Financial Accounting Standards Statement No. 130,* "Reporting Comprehensive Income," 1997.

Assessing the Quality of Earnings as a Complete Representation of Economic Performance

The capital markets frequently use earnings figures in the valuation of firms (witness, for example, the frequent references to the price-earnings ratio in the financial press), so the analyst needs to be alert to the possibility that reported earnings for a particular period represent an incomplete measure of current period profitability, or are a poor predictor of ongoing profitability. For example, reported net income may exclude certain gains or losses that have not yet been realized in cash, and may exclude certain items that are not yet required to be expensed under U.S. GAAP (executive stock options grants). Reported net income may also include amounts that are not likely to recur in the future, such as restructuring or impairment charges, income, gains, and losses from discontinued operations, extraordinary gains or losses, or adjustments for changes in accounting principles. As discussed above, for example, PepsiCo reports in Note 3 that it recognized impairment and restructuring charges in Years 9, 10, and 11 for a supply chain reconfiguration project to optimize Quaker Foods' manufacturing and distribution system. (The Year 9 charge also included closure and write-down costs for three Frito-Lay plants.) The analyst may wish to eliminate the effects of nonrecurring items when assessing operating performance for purposes of forecasting future earnings.

Management can also use subtle means to manage earnings. The firm might cut back on advertising or research and development expenditures or delay maintenance expenditures as a means of increasing earnings in a particular period. Chapter 6 discusses the concept of the quality of accounting information and illustrates the adjustments that the analyst might make to improve the quality of earnings.

STATEMENT OF CASH FLOWS

The third principal financial statement is the statement of cash flows. Exhibit 1.9 presents the statement of cash flows for PepsiCo for Year 9, Year 10, and Year 11. This statement reports for a period of time the net cash flows (inflows minus outflows) from three principal business activities: operating, investing, and financing.

Rationale for the Statement of Cash Flows

The statement of cash flows provides information on the sources and uses of cash. Even profitable firms, and especially those growing rapidly, sometimes find themselves strapped for cash and unable to pay suppliers, employees, and other creditors. This can occur for two principal reasons:

1. The timing of cash receipts from customers does not necessarily coincide with the recognition of revenue, and the timing of cash expenditures does not necessarily coincide with the recognition of expenses under the accrual basis of accounting. In the usual case, cash expenditures precede the recognition of expenses and cash receipts occur after the recognition of revenue. Thus, a firm might have positive net income for a period but the cash outflow for operations exceeds the cash inflow.

EXHIBIT 1.9			
PepsiCo, Inc. and Subsidiaries **Consolidated Statements of Cash Flows**			
Fiscal years ended December 29, Year 11, December 30, Year 10, and December 25, Year 9.			
(in millions)	Year 11	Year 10	Year 9
Operating Activities			
Net income	$2,662	$2,543	$2,505
Adjustments to reconcile net income to net cash provided by operating activities			
Bottling equity income and transaction (gains)/losses, net . .	(160)	(130)	(1,083)
Depreciation and amortization.	1,082	1,093	1,156
Merger-related costs	356	—	—
Other impairment and restructuring charges.	31	184	73
Cash payments for merger-related costs and other restructuring charges.	(273)	(38)	(98)
Deferred income taxes.	162	33	573
Deferred compensation—ESOP	48	36	32
Other noncash charges and credits, net	209	303	368
Changes in operating working capital, excluding effects of acquisitions and dispositions			
Accounts and notes receivable.	7	(52)	(141)
Inventories	(75)	(51)	(202)
Prepaid expenses and other current assets	(6)	(35)	(209)
Accounts payable and other current liabilities	(236)	219	357
Income taxes payable.	394	335	274
Net change in operating working capital	84	416	79
Net Cash Provided by Operating Activities	4,201	4,440	3,605
Investing Activities			
Capital spending	(1,324)	(1,352)	(1,341)
Acquisitions and investments in unconsolidated affiliates.	(432)	(98)	(430)
Sales of businesses	—	33	513
Sales of property, plant, and equipment.	—	57	130
Short-term investments, by original maturity			
More than three months—purchases	(2,537)	(4,950)	(2,209)
More than three months—maturities.	2,078	4,585	2,220
Three months or less, net	(41)	(9)	12
Other, net.	(381)	(262)	(67)
Net Cash Used for Investing Activities	(2,637)	(1,996)	(1,172)

EXHIBIT 1.9			

continued

Consolidated Statements of Cash Flows
December 29, Year 11, December 30, Year 10, and December 25, Year 9.

(in millions)	Year 11	Year 10	Year 9
Financing Activities			
Proceeds from issuances of long-term debt	324	130	3,480
Payments of long-term debt	(573)	(879)	(1,216)
Short-term borrowings, by original maturity			
More than three months—proceeds.	788	198	3,699
More than three months—payments	(483)	(155)	(2,758)
Three months or less, net	(397)	1	(2,814)
Cash dividends paid	(994)	(949)	(935)
Share repurchases—common	(1,716)	(1,430)	(1,285)
Share repurchases—preferred.	(10)	—	—
Quaker share repurchases	(5)	(254)	(382)
Proceeds from reissuance of shares.	524	—	—
Proceeds from exercises of stock options	623	690	383
Net Cash Used for Financing Activities	(1,919)	(2,648)	(1,828)
Effect of exchange rate changes on cash and cash equivalents. .	—	(4)	3
Net (decrease)/Increase in Cash and Cash Equivalents	(355)	(208)	608
Cash and Cash Equivalents, Beginning of Year	1,038	1,246	638
Cash and Cash Equivalents, End of Year.	$ 683	$1,038	$1,246
Supplemental Cash Flow Information			
Interest paid.	$ 159	$ 226	$ 384
Income taxes paid	$ 857	$ 876	$ 689
Acquisitions:			
Fair value of assets acquired	$ 604	$ 80	$ 717
Cash paid and debt issued.	(432)	(98)	(438)
Liabilities assumed.	$ 172	$ (18)	$ 279

See accompanying notes to Consolidated Financial Statements.

2. The firm may need to acquire new property, plant, and equipment; retire outstanding debt; or reacquire shares of its common stock when there is insufficient cash available.

In many cases, a profitable firm finding itself short of cash can obtain the needed funds from either short- or long-term creditors or owners. The firm must repay with interest the funds borrowed from creditors. Owners may require that the firm pay periodic dividends as an inducement to invest in the firm. Eventually, the firm must generate sufficient cash from operations if it is to survive.

Cash flows are the connecting link between operating, investing, and financing activities. They permit each of these three principal business activities to continue functioning smoothly and effectively. The statement of cash flows also can be helpful in assessing a firm's past ability to generate *free cash flows* and for predicting future free cash flows. The concept of free cash flows is first introduced in Chapter 3. As discussed in Chapter 11, free cash flows are central to cash-flow-based valuation models.

An examination of the statement of cash flows for PepsiCo reveals that cash flow from operations exceeded the net cash outflow for investing activities in each of the three years. PepsiCo used the excess cash flow to reduce debt, to pay dividends to shareholders, and to repurchase shares of its common stock.

Classification of Cash Flows

The statement of cash flows classifies cash flows as relating to either operating, investing, or financing activities.

Operating. Selling goods and providing services are among the most important ways that a financially healthy company generates cash. Assessing cash flow from operations over several years indicates the extent to which operating activities have provided the necessary cash to maintain operating capabilities, and the extent to which firms have had to rely on other sources of cash.

Investing. The acquisition of noncurrent assets, particularly property, plant, and equipment, usually represents a major ongoing use of cash. Firms must replace such assets as they wear out and acquire additional noncurrent assets if they are to grow. Firms obtain a portion of the cash needed to acquire noncurrent assets from sales of existing noncurrent assets. However, such cash inflows are seldom sufficient to cover the cost of new acquisitions.

Financing. A firm obtains cash from short- and long-term borrowing and from issuing preferred and common stock. It uses cash to repay short- and long-term borrowing, to pay dividends, and to reacquire shares of outstanding preferred and common stock.

Firms sometimes engage in investing and financing transactions that do not directly involve cash. For example, a firm might acquire a building by assuming a mortgage obligation. It might issue common stock upon conversion of long-term debt. Firms disclose these transactions in a supplementary schedule or note to the statement of cash flows in a way that clearly indicates that they are investing and financing transactions that do not affect cash. PepsiCo's statement of cash flows in Appendix A reports the portion of its acquisitions in recent years that did not directly involve the use of cash.

The statement of cash flows is required under U.S. GAAP but it is not a required financial statement in some countries. Increasingly, however, large international firms are providing the statement on a voluntary basis. Chapter 3 describes and illustrates analytical procedures for preparing a statement of cash flows in situations where firms provide only a balance sheet and income statement.

SUMMARY OF FINANCIAL STATEMENTS AND NOTES

Exhibit 1.10 summarizes the principal activities of a business and the three principal financial statements. The environmental assessment includes consideration of the economic characteristics of an industry and the strategies of competitors. The setting of corporate goals and strategies addresses how a particular firm intends to compete within the industry to gain competitive advantage. The balance sheet reflects the results of a firm's investing and financing activities. The income statement reports the results of a firm's operating activities. Firms prepare their balance sheets and income statements using the accrual basis of accounting. The statement of cash flows reports the cash effects of operating, investing, and financing activities.

EXHIBIT 1.10

Summary of Principal Business Activities and Financial Statements

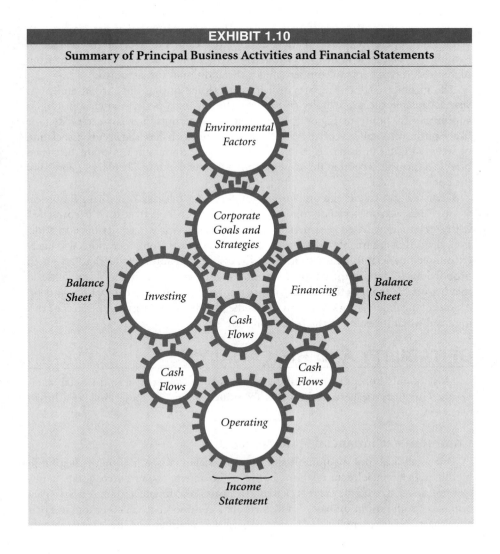

STEP 4: ANALYZE PROFITABILITY AND RISK

Armed with three key building blocks: (1) an understanding of the economics of the industry in which a firm competes, (2) an understanding of the particular strategies that the firm has chosen to compete in its industry, and (3) an assessment of the quality of the financial statements and notes that report the results of a firm's operating, investing, and financing activities, the analyst is ready to conduct a financial statement analysis.

Most financial statement analyses aim to assess a firm's *profitability* and its *risk*. This two-fold focus stems from the emphasis of investment decisions on returns and risk. Investors acquire shares of common stock in a company because of the return they expect from such investments. This return includes any dividends received plus the change in the market price of the shares of stock while the investor holds them. An investor will not be indifferent between two investments that are expected to yield, say, 20 percent return, if there are differences in the uncertainty, or risk, of earning 20 percent. The investor will likely demand a higher expected return from higher risk investments to compensate for the additional risk assumed.

The income statement reports a firm's net income during the current and prior years. Assessing the profitability of the firm during these periods, after adjusting as appropriate for nonrecurring or unsustainable items, permits the analyst to predict the likely future profitability of the firm. Empirical research has shown an association between earnings and market rates of return on common stock, a point discussed briefly in the next section in this chapter and in greater depth in Chapters 12 and 13 of the book.

Financial statements are also useful for assessing the risk of a firm. Empirical research has also shown that volatility in reported earnings over time is correlated with stock market-based measures of firm risk, such as market equity beta. In addition, firms that are unable to generate sufficient cash flow from operations will likely encounter financial difficulties and perhaps even bankruptcy. Firms that have high proportions of debt in their capital structures will experience financial difficulties if they are unable to repay the debt at maturity or replace maturing debt with new debt. Assessing the financial risk of a firm assists the investor in identifying the level of risk incurred when investing in the firm's common stock.

TOOLS OF PROFITABILITY AND RISK ANALYSIS

Most of this book describes and illustrates tools for analyzing financial statements. Our purpose here is simply to introduce several of these tools as a broad overview.

Common-size Financial Statements

One analytical tool is common-size financial statements, a tool that is helpful in highlighting financial data relations both within statements and across statements. Common-size statements express all items in a particular financial statement as a percentage of some common base. Total assets are a common base in common-size balance sheets. Sales revenue is a common base in the common-size income statement.

The first two columns of Exhibit 1.11 present common-size balance sheets for PepsiCo for Year 10 and Year 11. Note the stability of various common-size percentages for PepsiCo over this two-year period. PepsiCo experienced a significant decrease in the proportion of retained earnings and treasury stock during Year 11. Note 2 to PepsiCo's financial statements reports on the purchase of the Quaker Oats Company during Year 11, indicating that the merger was accounted for as a pooling-

EXHIBIT 1.11
Common-size and Percentage Change Balance Sheets for PepsiCo

	Common-size		Percentage Change	
	Year 10	Year 11	Year 11	Five-Year Compound Annual Growth Rate
Assets				
Cash and Marketable Securities.	7.3%	7.6%	9.6%	13.0%
Accounts/Notes Receivable	10.3	9.9	(0.6%)	(5.3%)
Inventories	5.7	6.0	9.9%	0.0%
Other Current Assets	3.8	3.5	(4.9%)	(5.7%)
Total Current Assets.	27.1%	27.0%	4.2%	(0.6%)
Investments	14.3	13.2	(3.6%)	15.9%
Property, Plant, and Equipment	31.6	31.7	4.8%	(9.6%)
Intangible and Other Assets.	27.0	28.1	8.8%	(9.6%)
Total Assets.	100.0%	100.0%	4.5%	(5.6%)
Liabilities and Shareholders' Equity				
Accounts Payable	5.8%	5.7%	2.1%	(7.0%)
Short-term Borrowing.	1.0	1.6	75.2%	(9.8%)
Other Current Liabilities	16.3	15.7	0.7%	(3.8%)
Total Current Liabilities.	23.1%	23.0%	4.2%	(5.1%)
Long-term Debt.	14.5	12.2	(11.9%)	(22.4%)
Deferred Tax	6.6	6.9	9.4%	(5.8%)
Other Noncurrent Liabilities.	19.1	17.9	(2.1%)	4.6%
Total Liabilities.	63.3%	60.0%	(0.8%)	(9.1%)
Preferred Stock.	0.1%	0.1%	18.2%	6.5%
Common Stock	2.0%	0.2%	(89.5%)	(53.9%)
Retained Earnings	79.5	53.1%	(30.2%)	1.5%
Accumulated Other Comprehensive Loss.	(6.7)	(7.6)	18.0%	11.9%
Treasury Stock	(38.2)	(5.8)	(84.0%)	(20.5%)
Total Shareholders' Equity.	36.7%	40.0%	13.7%	2.0%
Total Liabilities and Shareholders' Equity	100.0%	100.0%	4.5%	(5.6%)

of-interests. With this technique, discussed in more depth in Chapter 9 and no longer permitted by GAAP, PepsiCo issued approximately 306 million shares of its stock to holders of Quaker common stock. The accounting for the transaction resulted in both a significant reissuance of PepsiCo's treasury stock and a reduction in retained earnings, as the Consolidated Statement of Common Shareholders' Equity in Appendix A indicates.

The first two columns of Exhibit 1.12 present common-size income statements for PepsiCo for Year 10 and Year 11. Note that net income as a percentage of sales (also known as net profit margin) remained flat between the two years. Also note the stability of the various revenue and expense percentages for this period. There is a slight reduction in the selling, general, and administrative expenses and interest expense as a percentage of sales, but they are offset by higher percentages for nonrecurring items and income tax expense. Management's discussion and analysis of operations presented in Appendix B provide explanations for some of these changes. The task of the financial analyst is to delve into the reasons for such changes, taking into consideration industry economics, company strategies, management's explanations, and the operating results for competitors.

The analyst must interpret common-size financial statements carefully. The amount for any one item in these statements is not independent of all other items. The dollar amount for an item might increase between two periods but its relative percentage in the common-size statement would decrease (or remain the same) if it increased at a smaller rate than other items. This is the case with the amortization of

EXHIBIT 1.12				
Common-size and Percentage Change Income Statements for PepsiCo				
		Common-size		Percentage Change
		Year 10	Year 11	Year 11	Five-Year Compound Annual Growth Rate
Sales		100.0%	100.0%	5.7%	1.0%
Other Revenues		0.8	0.8	5.6%	16.1%
Cost of Sales................................		(40.1)	(39.9)	5.2%	(0.8%)
Selling, General, and Administrative Expenses.....		(43.6)	(43.1)	4.5%	0.9%
Amortization of Intangibles		(0.6)	(0.6)	12.2%	(4.6%)
Merger-related Costs and Other					
Nonrecurring Items.......................		(0.7)	(1.4)	110.3%	(31.7%)
Interest Expense............................		(1.1)	(0.8)	(19.5%)	(21.1%)
Income Before Income Taxes..................		14.7%	15.0%	7.1%	26.5%
Income Tax Expense		(4.7)	(5.1)	12.2%	18.9%
Net Income		10.0%	9.9%	4.7%	21.7%

intangibles for PepsiCo between Year 10 and Year 11. Common-size percentages provide a general overview of financial position and operating performance but the analyst must supplement them with other analytical tools.

Percentage Change Statements

Another analytical tool is percentage change statements, a tool that is helpful in highlighting the magnitude of changes in financial statement data over time. These statements present the percentage change in the amount of an item relative to its amount in the previous period, or the average change over several prior periods. The third and fourth columns of Exhibit 1.11 present changes in balance sheet items between Year 10 and Year 11 and the compound annual growth rates between Year 6 and Year 11. PepsiCo has increased its investments in bottlers at a faster rate than it has increased property, plant, and equipment during the previous five years. Thus, it appears that PepsiCo has shifted more operating responsibility to its nonconsolidated bottlers. Also note that PepsiCo decreased its long-term debt during this five-year period, in line with its decision to rely more heavily on bottlers.

The analyst must exert particular caution when interpreting percentage change balance sheets for any particular year. If the amount for the preceding year that serves as the base is relatively small, then even a small change in dollar amount can result in a large percentage change. Note, for example, that the percentage change in short-term borrowing for Year 11 was 75.2 percent. This change reflects an increase from $202 million in Year 10, to $354 million in Year 11. However, note that short-term borrowing comprises only 1.0 percent of total liabilities plus shareholders' equity at the end of Year 10. A large percentage change in an account that comprises only a small portion of total financing is not as meaningful as a smaller percentage change in an account that makes up a larger portion of total assets or total financing.

The third and fourth columns of Exhibit 1.12 present percentage change income statement amounts for PepsiCo. Note that for the four-year period, net income for PepsiCo increased significantly faster than sales. Cost of goods sold decreased during the period, suggesting improved manufacturing efficiencies or a higher proportion of sales from higher margin activities. Selling, general, and administrative expenses increased, but not quite as fast as sales, and interest expense significantly decreased during the five-year period.

Financial Statement Ratios

Perhaps the most useful analytical tools for assessing profitability and risk are financial statement ratios. Financial ratios express relationships between various items from the three financial statements. Researchers and practitioners have found that financial ratios serve as effective indicators of dimensions of profitability and risk. Chapters 4 and 5 discuss these financial ratios in depth. This discussion here merely introduces several of them.

Profitability Ratios. Perhaps the most commonly encountered financial ratio is earnings per common share (EPS). EPS equals net income allocable to the common shareholders' divided by the weighted average number of common shares outstanding.

For Year 11, EPS for PepsiCo (see Exhibit 1.7 and Note 5 to the financial statements) is $1.51 (= $2,657/1,763). Firms typically report earnings per share in their income statements. As Chapter 13 makes clear, financial analysts often use a multiple of EPS to derive what they consider an appropriate price for a firm's common stock.

Another profitability ratio is the rate of return on common shareholders' equity (ROCE). ROCE equals net income allocable to the common shareholders divided by average common shareholders' equity for the year. ROCE for PepsiCo for Year 11 is 32.7 percent [= $2,657/(0.5($7,604 + $8,648))]. This ROCE is large relative to many firms, but is difficult to interpret without a frame of reference. Analysts compare ratios to corresponding ratios of earlier periods (time-series analysis), to corresponding ratios of other firms in similar industries (cross-sectional analysis), and to average industry ratios in order to interpret the ratios. Chapter 4 provides an in-depth analysis of PepsiCo's ROCE and other profitability ratios.

Risk Ratios. To assess the volatility in a firm's earnings over time, and to gauge the uncertainty inherent in the firm's future earnings, analysts can calculate the standard deviation in ROCE over time. To assess the ability of firms to repay short-term obligations, analysts frequently calculate the current ratio, which equals current assets divided by current liabilities. The ratio for PepsiCo at the end of Year 11 is 1.17 (= $5,853/$4,998). As with profitability ratios, this ratio is only meaningful when the analyst performs a time-series and cross-sectional analysis. Most firms have current ratios that exceed 1.0, so PepsiCo would appear to have minimal short-term risk.

To assess the ability of firms to continue operating for a longer term (that is, avoid bankruptcy), the analyst looks at the amount of long-term debt in the capital structure. The ratio of long-term debt to shareholders' equity for PepsiCo at the end of Year 11 is 30.6 percent (=$2,651/$8,648). This percentage has steadily declined for PepsiCo in recent years, from a peak of 81.2 percent in Year 7. Thus, PepsiCo would appear to have low debt levels. Given PepsiCo's level of profitability and low debt levels, bankruptcy risk is very low. Chapter 5 provides an in-depth analysis of PepsiCo's debt to equity ratio and other risk ratios.

STEP 5: VALUE THE FIRM

Capital market participants most commonly use financial statement analysis to value firms. Financial statements and, specifically, key metrics from the statements such as earnings and operating cash flows, play a central role in firm valuation. Thus, the emphasis of this book is to arm the analyst with the knowledge necessary to prepare sophisticated and comprehensive valuation models. Chapters 10 through 13 discuss various approaches to valuation.

As discussed earlier in this chapter, performing financial analysis that relies on the analysis, forecasting, and valuation of key accounting measures from a firm's financial statements can be very rewarding. To illustrate the striking linkage between accounting earnings and stock returns, and to foreshadow the potential to generate positive excess returns through analysis and forecasting, consider the results from seminal empirical research by Ray Ball and Philip Brown.[6] They studied the average market-adjusted returns generated by firms during the 12 months leading up to and including the month in which each firm announced annual earnings numbers. For a sample of several hundred firms per year over a period of nine years, they found that the average firm that announced an increase in earnings (over the prior year's earnings) experienced stock returns that exceeded market average returns by roughly 7 percent. On the other hand, the average firm that announced a decrease in earnings experienced stock returns that were roughly 9 percent lower than the market average. Their results suggest that merely the *sign* of the change in earnings is associated with a 16 percent stock return differential in one year, on average.

To an analyst, the results of the Ball and Brown study indicate the magnitude of potential returns to be earned by forecasting the changes in earnings one year ahead. To be sure, analysts will not be able to beat the market consistently by 16 percent per year—Ball and Brown had the advantage of perfect foresight, which analysts do not have. Using historical data, Ball and Brown knew with certainty which firms would announce earnings increases or decreases. Analysts must forecast earnings changes, and take positions in stocks on the basis of their earnings expectations.

Analysts should view the Ball and Brown results as very encouraging because they imply that if analysts can forecast earnings changes correctly more often than not, then they should be able to earn some portion of the excess returns documented in Ball and Brown. Empirical research in accounting subsequent to Ball and Brown has continued to observe the same strong relations between earnings and market-adjusted returns. It has also deepened our understanding of these relations by documenting that share prices react strongly to the magnitude of the change in earnings and the persistence of the change in earnings for future periods, and that financial statement ratios are useful for predicting future earnings changes. We will refer to important research results like these throughout this book.

ROLE OF FINANCIAL STATEMENT ANALYSIS IN AN EFFICIENT CAPITAL MARKET

There are differing views as to the benefits of analyzing a set of financial statements. One view is that stock market prices react efficiently to published information about a firm. That is, market participants react intelligently and quickly to information they receive, so that market prices continually reflect underlying economic values. One implication of an efficient capital market is that financial statement users cannot routinely analyze financial statements to find "undervalued" or "overvalued" securities. The market quickly impounds new information into security prices.

Opposing views include the following:

1. Even if markets are perfectly efficient, someone must do the analysis to bring about the appropriate prices. Financial analysts, with their expertise and

---
[6]Ray Ball and Philip Brown, "An Evaluation of Accounting Income Numbers," *Journal of Accounting Research*, Autumn 1968, pp. 159–178.

access to information about firms, do the analysis quickly and engage in the trading necessary to achieve efficient pricing.

2. Research on capital market efficiency aggregates financial data for individual firms and studies the average reaction of the market to earnings and other financial statement information. A finding that the market is efficient on average does not preclude temporary mispricing of individual firms' shares.[7] A principal task of the financial analyst is to identify mispriced securities of particular firms and to take actions to bring about appropriate pricing.

3. Research has shown that equity markets are not perfectly efficient. Anomalies include the tendency for market prices to adjust with a lag to new information, systematic underreaction to the information contained in earnings announcements, and the ability to use a combination of financial ratios to detect under- and overpriced securities.[8]

4. Management has incentives related to job security and compensation to report as favorable a picture as possible in the financial statements within the constraints of GAAP. These reports may therefore represent biased indicators of the economic performance and financial position of firms. Financial analysts should adjust these financial statements of such biases if market prices are to reflect underlying economic values.

5. There are numerous settings outside of equity capital markets where financial statement analysis is valuable (for example, credit analysis by a bank to support corporate lending; competitor analysis to identify competitive advantages; merger and acquisition analysis to identify buyout candidates).

SOURCES OF FINANCIAL STATEMENT INFORMATION

Firms in the United States whose bonds or capital stock trade in public markets typically make available the following information:

1. **Annual Report to Shareholders.** The "glossy" annual report includes balance sheets for the most recent two years and income statements and statements of cash flows for the most recent three years, along with various notes and supporting schedules. The annual report also includes a letter from the chairperson of the board of directors and chief executive officer summarizing the activities of the most recent year. It also includes a discussion and analysis by management of the firm's operating performance, financial position, and liquidity. Firms vary with respect to the information provided in this Management Discussion and Analysis of operations. Some firms, such as

---

[7]For an elaboration on the role of financial statement analysis in an efficient capital market and the insights provided by academic research to this process, see Clyde P. Stickney, "The Academic's Approach to Securities Research: Is It Relevant to the Analyst?" *The Journal of Financial Statement Analysis*, Summer 1997, pp. 52–60.

[8]For a summary of the issues and related research, see Ray Ball, "The Theory of Stock Market Efficiency: Accomplishments and Limitations," *Journal of Applied Corporate Finance* (Spring 1995), pp. 4–17.

PepsiCo as shown in Appendix B, give helpful information about the firm's strategy and reasons for the changes in profitability, financial position, and risk. Other firms merely repeat amounts presented in the financial statements without providing helpful explanations for operating results.

2. **Form 10-K Annual Report.** The Form 10-K annual report filed with the Securities and Exchange Commission (SEC) includes the same financial statements and notes as the corporate annual report plus additional supporting schedules required by the SEC. For example, the 10-K often includes more detailed information than the corporate annual report on changes in the allowance for uncollectible accounts and other valuation accounts.

3. **Form 10-Q Quarterly Report.** The Form 10-Q quarterly report filed with the SEC includes condensed balance sheet and income statement information for the most recent three months, as well as comparative data for earlier quarters.

4. **Prospectus or Registration Statement.** Firms intending to issue new bonds or capital stock file a prospectus with the SEC that describes the offering (amount, intended uses of proceeds). The prospectus includes much of the financial information found in the 10-K annual report.

5. **Form 20-F Annual Report.** Non-U.S. firms whose bonds or capital stock trade in capital markets in the United States must file annual reports with the SEC. The Form 20-F annual report is similar to the 10-K except that it includes schedules to reconcile net income and shareholders' equity from GAAP of the domicile of the non-U.S. firm to GAAP in the United States.

A large number of firms include all or a portion of their annual reports and Form 10-K on a web site home page. For example, PepsiCo provides all of the financial data and analysis provided in Appendices A and B on the firm's web site: http://www.pepsico.com. In addition, many firms provide additional financial data at these sites that is not published in the annual reports. For example, Gap, Inc., consisting of The Gap, Banana Republic, and Old Navy clothing chains, provides monthly sales data for each of these chains. It also provides information on the opening and closing of stores.

Firms are required to file reports electronically with the SEC, with these filings for recent years available at the web site for the SEC: http://www.sec.gov by searching the Edgar database. There are also numerous commercial on-line and CD-ROM services that provide financial statement information (Thomson Analytics, Bloomberg, Standard & Poor, Moody's, and others).

SUMMARY

The purpose of this chapter is to provide a broad overview of five interconnected activities related to financial statement analysis:

1. Identify the economic characteristics of the industry in which a firm participates.
2. Identify the corporate strategy that a firm pursues to compete within its industry.

3. Assess the quality of a firm's financial statements and adjust them for items lacking sustainability or comparability.
4. Analyze and interpret the profitability and risk of a firm, assessing how well the firm performed and the strength of its financial position.
5. Value the particular firm.

You should not expect to fully understand any of these five steps at this stage of your studies. Future chapters discuss each in greater depth. Chapter 2 discusses the important links between the valuation of assets and liabilities on the balance sheet, and revenues and expenses on the income statement. Chapter 3 details the preparation and interpretation of the statement of cash flows for firms in various industries at various stages in their growth. Chapter 4 describes common financial statement ratios for assessing profitability and illustrates their calculation and interpretation for PepsiCo. Chapter 5 parallels the previous chapter by describing common financial statement ratios for assessing risk. Chapters 6 through 9 examine GAAP for various financial statement items, and address concerns that affect the quality of earnings and financial position.

Chapters 10 to 13 shift our focus to valuation. Chapter 10 demonstrates the preparation of pro forma financial statements. Chapters 11 through 13 examine various valuation models based on cash flows, earnings, and amounts for comparable firms. With firm valuation the most frequent objective of financial statement analysis, these chapters represent a fitting culmination to the book.

PROBLEMS AND CASES

1.1 EFFECT OF INDUSTRY CHARACTERISTICS ON FINANCIAL STATEMENT RELATIONSHIPS. Effective financial statement analysis requires an understanding of a firm's economic characteristics. The relations between various financial statement items provide evidence of many of these economic characteristics. Exhibit 1.13 presents common-size condensed balance sheets and income statements for 12 firms in different industries. These common-size balance sheets and income statements express various items as a percentage of operating revenues (that is, the statement divides all amounts by operating revenues for the year). Exhibit 1.13 also shows the ratio of cash flow from operations to capital expenditures. A dash for a particular financial statement item does not necessarily mean that the amount is zero. It merely indicates that the amount is not sufficiently large for the firm to disclose it. The 12 companies and a brief description of their activities appear below.

1. Abercrombie & Fitch: Sells retail apparel primarily through stores to the fashion-conscious adult and has established itself as a trendy, popular player in the specialty apparel industry.
2. AK Steel: Manufactures and sells a broad line of steel products.
3. Allstate Insurance: Sells property and casualty insurance, primarily on buildings and automobiles. Operating revenues include insurance premiums collected or due from customers and revenues earned from investments made

with cash received from customers prior to the time that Allstate pays customers' claims. Operating expenses include amounts actually paid or expected to be paid in the future on insurance coverage outstanding during the year.

4. Gillette: Manufactures and sells a variety of consumer personal care and household products. Gillette has acquired several branded consumer products companies in recent years. Gillette includes the costs incurred on new product development in selling and administrative expenses.

5. Hewlett-Packard: Develops, manufactures, and sells computer hardware. The firm outsources many of its computer components.

6. Household International: Lends money to consumers for periods ranging from several months to several years. Operating expenses represent estimated uncollectible loans.

7. Kelly Services: Provides temporary office services to businesses and other firms. Operating revenues represent amounts billed to customers for temporary help services and operating expenses include amounts paid to the temporary help employees of Kelly.

8. Lands' End: Sells apparel through catalogs, primarily through third-party credit cards.

9. McDonald's: Operates fast food restaurants worldwide. A large percentage of McDonald's' restaurants are owned and operated by franchisees. McDonald's frequently owns the restaurant buildings of franchisees and leases them to franchisees under long-term leases.

10. Merck: A leading research-driven pharmaceutical products and services company. Merck discovers, develops, manufactures, and markets a broad range of products (primarily ethical drugs) to improve human and animal health, directly and through its joint ventures.

11. Newmont Mining: Mines for gold and other minerals. Research and development expense includes exploration costs for Newmont.

12. Omnicom Group: Creates advertising copy for clients and is the largest marketing services firm in the world. Purchases advertising time and space from various media and sells it to clients. Operating revenues represent the commission or fee earned by Omnicom for advertising copy created and media time and space sold. Operating expenses include compensation paid to employees. Omnicom acquired a large number of marketing services firms in recent years.

Required

Use whatever clues that you can to match the companies in Exhibit 1.13 with the firms listed above.

1.2 EFFECT OF INDUSTRY CHARACTERISTICS ON FINANCIAL STATEMENT RELATIONSHIPS—GLOBAL PERSPECTIVE. Effective financial statement analysis requires an understanding of a firm's economic characteristics. The relations between various financial statement items provide evidence of many of these economic characteristics. Exhibit 1.14 presents common-size condensed balance sheets

EXHIBIT 1.13

Common-size Financial Statement Data for Firms in 12 Industries
(Problem 1.1)

	(1)	(2)	(3)	(4)
Balance Sheet at End of Year				
Cash and Marketable Securities	2.0%	7.8%	9.6%	6.9%
Receivables	12.7	.8	14.7	10.9
Inventories.	—	14.5	11.5	9.3
Property, Plant, and Equipment Cost.	6.5	21.9	25.5	39.7
Accumulated Depreciation	(2.8)	(9.6)	(15.4)	(12.2)
Net.	3.7	12.3	10.1	27.5
Other Assets	3.7	2.7	26.1	37.6
Total Assets	22.1%	38.1%	72.0%	92.2%
Current Liabilities.	8.7%	11.8%	30.9%	24.2%
Long-term Debt	—	—	8.2	10.1
Other Noncurrent Liabilities	—	.8	2.1	24.3
Shareholders' Equity.	13.4	25.5	30.9	33.6
Total Equities.	22.1%	38.1%	72.1%	92.2%
Income Statement for Year				
Operating Revenues	100.0%	100.0%	100.0%	100.0%
Cost of Goods Sold (excluding depreciation)				
or Operating Expenses[a].	(81.6)	(54.9)	(67.1)	(57.6)
Depreciation	(.8)	(1.2)	(3.9)	(3.1)
Selling and Administrative	(14.6)	(36.7)	(14.5)	(13.0)
Interest.	—	—	(.8)	(.7)
Research and Development	—	—	(5.4)	(5.1)
Income Taxes.	(1.2)	(2.6)	(2.2)	(6.5)
All Other Items (net)	—	.3	1.1	1.4
Total Expenses.	98.2%	95.1%	92.8%	84.6%
Net Income	1.8%	4.9%	7.2%	15.4%
Cash Flow from Operations/				
Capital Expenditures.	2.4	6.1	1.6	3.3

[a]See the problem narrative for items included in operating expenses.

and income statements for 12 firms in different industries. These common-size balance sheets and income statements express various items as a percentage of operating revenues (that is, the statement divides all amounts by operating revenues for the year). A dash for a particular financial statement item does not necessarily mean that the amount is zero. It merely indicates that the amount is not sufficiently large for the

EXHIBIT 1.13

continued

(5)	(6)	(7)	(8)	(9)	(10)	(11)	(12)
31.1%	2.2%	10.6%	2.8%	7.6%	13.5%	276.7%	41.1%
2.7	8.9	19.9	5.9	68.5	1.1	13.8	791.0
14.1	20.5	11.3	.7	—	28.7	—	—
59.4	103.0	58.1	162.1	16.9	266.8	4.6	17.5
(12.1)	(43.7)	(18.5)	(45.8)	(8.9)	(101.2)	(1.6)	(12.2)
47.3	59.3	39.6	116.3	8.0	165.6	3.0	5.3
—	19.2	31.9	23.0	70.2	33.2	84.7	54.9
95.2%	110.1%	113.3%	148.7%	154.3%	242.1%	378.2%	892.3%
21.2%	17.5%	54.0%	15.1%	96.4%	29.2%	232.2%	185.5%
—	28.7	21.5	57.5	7.1	65.5	39.3	567.1
1.5	41.5	9.0	11.7	18.9	58.5	47.1	57.8
72.5	22.4	28.8	64.4	31.9	88.9	59.6	81.9
95.2%	110.1%	113.3%	148.7%	154.3%	242.1%	378.2%	892.3%
100.0%	100.0%	100.0%	100.0%	100.0%	100.0%	100.0%	100.0%
(56.1)	(81.1)	(38.1)	(56.4)	(54.1)	(62.0)	(67.2)	(20.2)
(3.0)	(5.8)	(3.3)	(6.8)	(3.2)	(16.2)	—	(5.1)
(20.9)	(6.4)	(42.2)	(18.0)	(28.6)	(6.3)	(20.2)	(24.6)
—	(2.3)	(1.6)	(3.0)	(1.1)	(5.7)	—	(30.0)
—	—	—	—	—	(7.6)	—	—
(7.9)	(1.7)	(4.6)	(4.7)	(5.1)	(2.5)	(3.3)	(7.2)
.3	—	—	—	(.6)	11.4	—	—
87.6%	97.3%	89.8%	88.9%	92.7%	88.9%	90.7%	87.1%
12.4%	2.7%	10.2%	11.1%	7.3%	11.1%	9.3%	12.9%
2.5	.6	1.2	1.2	2.7	.6	25.1	18.7

firm to disclose it. The 12 companies, the country of their headquarters, and a brief description of their activities appear below.

1. Accor (France): World's largest hotel group, operating hotels under the names of Sofitel, Novotel, Motel 6, and others. Accor has grown in recent years by acquiring established hotel chains.

EXHIBIT 1.14

**Common-size Financial Statement Data for Firms in 12 Industries
(Problem 1.2)**

	(1)	(2)	(3)	(4)
Balance Sheet at End of Year				
Cash and Marketable Securities	4.7%	16.4%	8.9%	8.4%
Receivables	8.5	15.9	16.5	27.6
Inventories.	9.9	2.8	9.9	5.8
Property, Plant, and Equipment Cost.	40.8	20.9	59.0	69.6
Accumulated Depreciation	(15.0)	(9.1)	(33.2)	(17.8)
Net.	25.8	11.8	25.8	51.8
Intercorporate Investments.	4.0	14.3	3.0	.6
Other Assets	15.0	10.9	11.7	3.6
Total Assets	67.9%	72.1%	75.8%	97.8%
Current Liabilities.	37.3	25.5%	29.7%	26.4%
Long-term Debt	12.0	6.1	6.6	9.1
Other Noncurrent Liabilities	2.1	1.8	5.9	2.3
Shareholders' Equity	16.5	38.7	33.6	60.0
Total Equities.	67.9%	72.1%	75.8%	97.8%
Income Statement for Year				
Operating Revenues	100.0%	100.0%	100.0%	100.0%
Other Revenues.	1.1	2.7	1.0	.2
Cost of Goods Sold (excluding depreciation)				
or Operating Expenses[a].	(87.8)	(45.2)	(44.5)	(64.6)
Depreciation and Amortization	(3.0)	(4.9)	(4.1)	(3.2)
Selling and Administrative	(6.3)	(24.8)	(38.9)	(24.3)
Interest.	(1.4)	(.4)	(2.0)	(1.3)
Research and Development	—	(9.8)	(1.3)	—
Income Taxes.	(1.3)	(5.8)	(3.1)	(2.4)
All Other Items (net)	.8	—	(.8)	(.3)
Total Expenses.	99.0%	90.9%	94.7%	96.1%
Net Income	2.1%	11.8%	6.3%	4.1%

[a]See the problem narrative for items included in operating expenses.

2. Arbed-Acier (Luxembourg): Offers flat-rolled steel products, primarily to the European automobile industry.
3. Carrefour (France): Operates grocery supermarket and hypermarkets in Europe, Latin America, and Asia.
4. Deutsche Telekom (Germany): Europe's largest provider of wired and wireless

EXHIBIT 1.14

continued

(5)	(6)	(7)	(8)	(9)	(10)	(11)	(12)
16.7%	7.4%	16.1%	21.3%	72.0%	8.3%	1.4%	338.8%
35.9	17.7	81.1	29.6	24.0	10.5	5.9	533.4
6.4	25.7	—	1.3	20.0	2.9	—	—
88.3	130.9	23.0	110.3	83.3	278.9	535.4	15.3
(50.5)	(67.7)	(11.8)	(35.5)	(35.2)	(112.5)	(284.9)	(12.9)
37.8	63.2	11.2	74.8	48.1	166.4	250.5	2.4
18.8	10.3	1.3	10.7	7.7	22.4	16.9	41.9
7.1	1.9	63.5	42.1	69.1	56.3	5.4	61.9
122.7%	126.2%	173.2%	179.8%	240.9%	266.8%	280.1%	978.4%
42.7%	34.5%	106.0%	65.1%	48.3%	42.6%	51.3%	820.8%
22.2	23.3	22.7	49.6	56.4	95.8	167.7	76.9
4.2	17.2	10.6	10.9	24.5	27.8	24.7	42.2
53.6	51.2	33.9	54.2	111.7	100.6	36.4	38.5
122.7%	126.2%	173.2%	179.8%	240.9%	266.8%	280.1%	978.4%
100.0%	100.0%	100.0%	100.0%	100.0%	100.0%	100.0%	100.0%
.7	2.3	1.9	.3	13.8	.7	—	—
(68.0)	(81.0)	(55.3)	(74.5)	(27.2)	(45.0)	(57.3)	(32.6)
(5.9)	(5.3)	(2.0)	(7.1)	(9.9)	(23.9)	(19.9)	—
(16.4)	(13.6)	(27.8)	(8.1)	(40.0)	(15.2)	(7.3)	(22.5)
(.4)	(3.5)	(1.9)	(3.0)	(5.2)	(8.6)	(8.6)	(35.4)
(3.7)	—	—	—	(13.8)	—	—	—
(2.5)	(.3)	(5.9)	(3.7)	(4.4)	(3.9)	(2.8)	(2.2)
(.6)	2.1	(.8)	.6	—	(.6)	—	(1.7)
97.5%	101.6%	93.7%	95.8%	100.5%	97.2%	95.9%	94.4%
3.2%	.7%	8.2%	4.5%	13.3%	3.5%	4.1%	5.6%

telecommunication services. The telecommunications industry has experienced increased deregulation in recent years.

5. Fortis (Netherlands): Offers both insurance and banking services. Operating revenues include insurance premiums received, investment income, and interest revenue on loans. Operating expenses include amounts actually paid or

amounts it expects to pay in the future on insurance coverage outstanding during the year.

6. Interpublic Group (U.S.): Creates advertising copy for clients. Purchases advertising time and space from various media and sells it to clients. Operating revenues represent the commission or fee earned by Interpublic for advertising copy created and media time and space sold. Operating expenses include compensation paid to employees. Interpublic acquired other marketing services firms in recent years.

7. Marks & Spencer (U.K.): Operates department stores in England and other retail stores in Europe and the United States. Offers its own credit card for customers' purchases.

8. Nestle (Switzerland): World's largest food processor, offering prepared foods, coffees, milk-based products, and mineral waters.

9. Roche Holding (Switzerland): Creates, manufactures, and distributes a wide variety of prescription drugs.

10. Sun Microsystems (U.S.): Designs, manufactures, and sells engineering workstations and servers used to maintain integrated computer networks. Sun outsources the manufacture of many of its computer components.

11. Tokyo Electric Power (Japan): Provides electric power services, primarily to the Tokyo community. It maintains almost a monopoly in its service area.

12. Toyota Motor (Japan): Manufactures automobiles and offers financing services to its customers.

Required

Use whatever clues you can to match the companies in Exhibit 1.14 with the companies and industries listed above.

1.3 EFFECT OF INDUSTRY CHARACTERISTICS ON FINANCIAL STATEMENT RELATIONSHIPS. Effective financial statement analysis requires an understanding of a firm's economic characteristics. The relations between various financial statement items provide evidence of many of these economic characteristics. Exhibit 1.15 presents common-size condensed financial statement information for firms in 12 industries. These common-size balance sheets and income statements express various items as a percentage of operating revenues (that is, the statements divide all amounts by operating revenues for the year). Exhibit 1.15 also shows the cash flow from operations to capital expenditures ratio for the year. A dash does not necessarily indicate that the amount is zero for a particular firm. It merely indicates that the amount is not sufficiently large for the firm to disclose it. The 12 companies and a brief description of their activities appear below.

1. AT&T: Provides telecommunication services. AT&T has made major acquisitions of other companies in recent years.

2. Brown Forman: Distills hard liquors, which require aging, and manufactures tonic waters.

3. Champion: Harvests timber and processes pulp into various paper products.

4. Citibank: Lends money to businesses and consumers, and conducts financial consulting services. Operating expenses for Citibank include compensation expense and estimated losses from uncollectible loans.
5. Commonwealth Edison: Generates and sells electricity to businesses and households. Currently operates under regulatory authority that sets electric rates but will transition into more competitive, less regulatory environment in the years ahead.
6. Delta: Provides airline transportation services.
7. Eli Lilly: Develops, manufactures, and markets prescription drugs.
8. Kellogg: Manufactures and markets breakfast cereals.
9. Marriott: Manages hotels owned by others.
10. Microsoft: Designs, manufactures, and markets computer software.
11. Nike: Designs and markets athletic footwear and apparel. Nike outsources the manufacturing to firms in East Asia and outsources the retailing to retail and specialty stores.
12. USLife: Provides life insurance services. During the lag between collecting insurance premiums from policyholders and paying out benefits, USLife invests the cash in various financial securities. Operating expenses include the current year's portion of the amount USLife expects ultimately to pay to policyholders.

Required

Use whatever clues that you can to match the companies in Exhibit 1.15 with the firms listed above.

1.4 VALUE CHAIN ANALYSIS AND FINANCIAL STATEMENT RELATIONSHIPS. Exhibit 1.16 presents common-size income statements and balance sheets for seven firms that operate at various stages in the value chain for the pharmaceutical industry. These common-size statements express all amounts as a percentage of sales revenue. Exhibit 1.16 also shows the cash flow from operations to capital expenditures ratios for each firm. A dash for a particular financial statement item does not necessarily mean that the amount is zero. It merely indicates that the amount is not sufficiently large for the firm to disclose it. The seven companies and a brief description of their activities appear below.

1. Wyeth: Engages in the development, manufacture, and sale of ethical drugs (that is, drugs requiring a prescription). The drugs of Wyeth primarily represent mixtures of chemical compounds. Ethical drug companies must obtain approval of new drugs from the Food and Drug Administration (FDA). Patents protect such drugs from competition until either other drug companies develop more effective substitutes or the patent expires.
2. Amgen: Engages in the development, manufacture, and sale of drugs based on biotechnology research. Biotechnology drugs must obtain approval from the FDA and enjoy patent protection similar to those for chemical-based drugs. The biotechnology segment is less mature than the ethical drug industry, with relatively few products having received FDA approval.

EXHIBIT 1.15				
Common-size Financial Statement Data for Firms in 12 Industries **(Problem 1.3)**				
	(1)	**(2)**	**(3)**	**(4)**
Balance Sheet at End of Year				
Cash and Marketable Securities	2.6%	4.0%	3.7%	3.5%
Current Receivables.	7.4	20.8	8.9	16.6
Inventories.	1.7	14.4	6.4	28.0
Property, Plant, and Equipment Cost.	22.7	17.1	73.2	38.5
Accumulated Depreciation	(4.1)	(7.2)	(29.3)	(20.3)
Net.	18.6	9.9	43.9	18.2
Other Assets	19.6	11.9	12.7	23.1
Total Assets	49.9%	61.0%	75.6%	89.4%
Current Liabilities.	17.3%	22.7%	32.9%	19.6%
Long-term Debt	9.9	.2	10.9	13.7
Other Noncurrent Liabilities	10.3	.6	12.6	15.0
Owners' Equity	12.4	37.5	19.2	41.1
Total Equities.	49.9%	61.0%	75.6%	89.4%
Income Statement for Year				
Operating Revenues	100.0%	100.0%	100.0%	100.0%
Cost of Goods Sold (excluding depreciation) or Operating Expenses[a].	(92.3)	(60.4)	(43.0)	(40.6)
Depreciation	(1.5)	(1.5)	(3.8)	(2.4)
Selling and Administrative	(.8)	(23.1)	(36.8)	(39.2)
Interest.	(.8)	(.6)	(1.0)	(1.3)
Research and Development	—	—	—	—
Income Taxes.	(1.9)	(5.3)	(5.6)	(6.3)
All Other Items (net)	.3	(.6)	(.5)	.2
Total Expenses.	97.0%	91.5%	90.7%	89.6%
Net Income	3.0%	8.5%	9.3%	10.4%
Cash Flow from Operations/ Capital Expenditures.	1.8	1.5	2.3	2.9

[a]See the problem narrative for items included in operating expenses.

EXHIBIT 1.15

continued

(5)	(6)	(7)	(8)	(9)	(10)	(11)	(12)
.3%	80.0%	13.3%	3.0%	13.0%	.4%	364.8%	271.9%
17.2	7.4	7.8	9.9	20.1	9.5	22.2	518.7
—	—	.6	7.8	12.0	6.7	—	—
75.7	27.1	213.8	198.3	96.6	414.0	2.5	26.0
(37.8)	(11.8)	(96.2)	(62.0)	(38.0)	(165.5)	(1.9)	(11.7)
37.9	15.3	117.6	136.3	58.6	248.5	.6	14.3
51.1	13.7	21.9	10.0	91.0	69.7	48.7	57.0
106.5%	116.4%	161.2%	167.0%	194.7%	334.8%	436.3%	861.9%
31.3%	28.0%	29.2%	16.1%	57.5%	28.1%	348.4%	740.5%
15.1	—	80.5	52.5	34.2	92.8	16.6	57.8
21.2	—	31.1	34.4	20.0	113.4	3.6	—
38.9	88.4	20.4	64.0	83.0	100.5	67.7	63.6
106.5%	116.4%	161.2%	167.0%	194.7%	334.8%	436.3%	861.9%
100.0%	100.0%	100.0%	100.0%	100.0%	100.0%	100.0%	100.0%
(49.5)	(11.7)	(60.6)	(80.4)	(25.9)	(61.3)	(70.7)	(19.2)
(5.3)	(5.5)	(5.1)	(6.9)	(7.4)	(13.7)	(.6)	(2.2)
(28.3)	(30.8)	(17.9)	(6.2)	(24.3)	—	(19.9)	(21.9)
(.6)	—	(8.0)	(3.8)	(3.9)	(7.3)	(2.4)	(38.1)
—	(16.5)	—	—	(14.5)	—	—	—
(6.2)	(13.7)	(3.3)	(1.1)	(6.9)	(6.7)	(2.2)	(7.0)
.6	3.5	.5	.8	3.6	—	—	—
89.3%	74.7%	94.4%	97.6%	79.3%	89.0%	95.8%	88.4%
10.7%	25.3%	5.6%	2.4%	20.7%	11.0%	4.2%	11.6%
1.4	5.7	1.5	.8	4.5	1.7	53.0	6.4

EXHIBIT 1.16

Common-size Financial Statement Data for Seven Firms in the Pharmaceutical Industry (Problem 1.4)

	1	2	3	4	5	6	7
Income Statement							
Sales	100.0%	100.0%	100.0%	100.0%	100.0%	100.0%	100.0%
Cost of Goods Sold	(47.0)	(11.0)	(24.0)	(58.4)	(28.9)	(73.3)	(92.5)
Selling and Administrative.	(18.8)	(24.2)	(36.7)	(31.0)	(36.3)	(21.0)	(4.2)
Research and Development	(8.0)	(21.5)	(13.2)	—	(10.9)	—	—
Interest	—	(.3)	(1.0)	(2.6)	(1.6)	—	(.3)
Income Taxes	(10.6)	(14.1)	(7.0)	(3.2)	(6.8)	(2.2)	(1.0)
Other	3.5	5.2	(1.5)	1.0	1.4	.1	(.2)
Net Income	19.1%	34.1%	16.6%	5.8%	16.9%	3.6%	1.8%
Balance Sheet							
Cash	33.7%	66.3%	21.4%	34.9%	24.2%	.1%	1.9%
Receivables	27.5	12.3	19.4	26.4	14.0	3.2	5.0
Inventories	19.1	8.9	12.4	—	9.1	14.1	13.1
Other Current	7.6	8.6	15.9	5.4	8.7	.4	2.3
Intercorporate Investments	—	—	—	—	—	—	—
Property, Plant, and							
Equipment (net)	19.9	48.5	44.6	22.4	23.4	17.7	3.8
Other Noncurrent Assets	49.9	15.9	48.9	31.2	37.2	.4	4.4
Total Assets	157.7%	160.5%	162.6%	120.3%	116.6%	35.9%	30.5%
Current Liabilities	34.4%	25.0%	51.4%	28.5%	24.4%	12.2%	13.7%
Long-term Debt	2.8	5.6	11.4	2.0	6.5		3.9
Other Noncurrent Liabilities	2.2	—	23.8	—	12.3	2.6	1.6
Shareholders' Equity	118.3	129.9	76.0	89.8	73.4	21.1	11.3
Total Equities	157.7%	160.5%	162.6%	120.3%	116.6%	35.9%	30.5%
Cash Flow from Operations/							
Capital Expenditures	2.2	3.4	2.3	1.3	2.8	.6	1.3

3. Mylan Laboratories: Engages in the development, manufacture, and sale of generic drugs. Generic drugs have the same chemical compositions as drugs that had previously benefited from patent protection but for which the patent has now expired. Generic drug companies have benefited in recent years from the patent expiration of several major ethical drugs. The major ethical drug companies, however, have increasingly offered generic versions of their ethical drugs to compete against the generic drug companies.

4. Johnson & Johnson: Engages in the development, manufacture, and sale of over-the-counter health care products. Such products do not require a prescription and often benefit from brand recognition.

5. Quintiles: Offers laboratory testing services and expedition of the drug approval process through the FDA for ethical drug companies that have discovered new drugs. Cost of goods sold for this company represents the salaries of personnel conducting the laboratory testing and drug approval services.

6. Cardinal Health: Distributes drugs as a wholesaler to drugstores, hospitals, and mass merchandisers. Also offers pharmaceutical benefit management services in which it provides customized databases designed to help customers order more efficiently, contain costs, and monitor their purchases. Cost of goods sold for Cardinal Health includes the cost of drugs sold plus the salaries of personnel providing pharmaceutical benefit management services.

7. Walgreen: Operates a chain of drug stores nationwide. The data in Exhibit 1.16 for Walgreen include the recognition of operating lease commitments for retail space.

Required

Use whatever clues that you can to match the seven companies above with the seven companies in Exhibit 1.16.

1.5 RECASTING THE FINANCIAL STATEMENTS OF A U.K. COMPANY INTO U.S. FORMATS, TERMINOLOGY, AND ACCOUNTING PRINCIPLES. WPP Group, headquartered in the United Kingdom, is one of the largest marketing and communication services firms in the world. It offers advertising, market research, public relations, and other marketing services through a worldwide network of offices. The firm employs over 65,000 individuals and is located in approximately 100 countries. WPP Group, as the parent company, operates through activities of its individual operating companies.

The financial statements of WPP Group for Year 10 and Year 11 appear in Exhibit 1.17 (balance sheet), Exhibit 1.18 (profit and loss account), and Exhibit 1.19 (cash flow statement). These financial statements reflect reporting formats, terminology, and accounting principles employed in the United Kingdom.

Required

Recast the consolidated balance sheet, consolidated profit and loss account, and the consolidated cash flow statement of WPP Group using reporting formats, terminology, and accounting principles customarily used in the United States.

EXHIBIT 1.17

WPP Group
Consolidated Balance Sheet
(amounts in millions of pounds)
(Problem 1.5)

	December 31	
	Year 11	Year 10
Fixed Assets		
Intangible Assets (Corporate Brands and Goodwill – see Note 1).......	£ 5,389	£ 4,447
Tangible Assets.....................................	432	390
Investments	553	552
Total Fixed Assets.............................	£ 6,374	£ 5,389
Current Assets		
Stocks and Work In Progress................................	£ 237	£ 241
Debtors (Note 2)	2,640	2,414
Investments	77	
Cash at Bank and In Hand	586	1,068
	£ 3,540	£ 3,723
Creditors: Amounts Falling Due Within One Year (Note 3)............	(4,322)	(4,252)
Net Current Liabilities..	£ (782)	£ (529)
Total Assets Less Current Liabilities	£ 5,592	£ 4,860
Creditors: Amounts Falling Due After One Year....................	(1,712)	(1,280)
Provisions for Liabilities and Charges (Note 4)	(105)	(98)
Net Assets Excluding Pension Provision	3,775	3,482
Pension Provision	(135)	(88)
Net Assets	£ 3,640	£ 3,394
Capital and Reserves		
Called Up Share Capital.......................................	£ 115	£ 111
Share Premium Account	1,044	1,096
Reserves (Note 5)..	2,488	2,374
Profit & Loss Account	(48)	(211)
Share Owners' Funds...	£ 3,599	£ 3,370
Minority Interests	41	24
Total Capital Employed	£ 3,640	£ 3,394

NOTES TO EXHIBIT 1.17

Note 1: Intangible Assets represent the portion of the purchase price of marketing services agencies acquired that WPP allocated to the brand names of these agencies. WPP breaks out the £ 5,389 for Year 11 as Corporate Brands, £ 950 and Goodwill, £ 4,439. For Year 10, the breakdown is Corporate Brands, £ 950 and Goodwill, £ 3,497.

Note 2: Debtors include the following:

	December 31	
	Year 11	Year 10
Trade Debtors....................................	£ 2,392	£ 2,181
Other Debtors....................................	248	233
Total..	£ 2,640	£ 2,414

Note 3: Creditors falling due within one year include the following:

	December 31	
	Year 11	Year 10
Bank Loans.....................................	£ 319	£ 298
Trade Creditors.................................	2,506	2,575
Taxation	166	164
Other Creditors and Accruals.....................	1,331	1,215
Total	£ 4,322	£ 4,252

Note 4: Provisions include the following:

	December 31	
	Year 11	Year 10
Deferred Taxation................................	£ 41	£ 30
Pensions	18	11
Other...	46	57
Total	£ 105	£ 98

Note 5: Reserves include the following amounts:

	December 31	
	Year 11	Year 10
Cumulative Translation Adjustment	£ 80	£ 133
Retirement Benefit Reserves	45	27
Merger Reserve (a)	2,363	2,214
Total	£ 2,488	£ 2,374

(a) WPP Group issued common shares in Year 10 and Year 11 for the acquisition of additional agencies. The increase in the reserve represents the "share premium" (using WPP's terminology) above the "called up share capital" (again, using WPP's terminology). The equivalent terminology in U.S. GAAP is additional paid-in capital for share premium; and common stock, par value for called up share capital.

EXHIBIT 1.18

WPP Group
Consolidated Profit and Loss Account
(amounts in millions of pounds)
(Problem 1.5)

	Year 11	Year 10
Turnover	£ 20,887	£ 13,949
Gross Profit	£ 20,655	£ 13,704
Other Operating Expenses	20,149	13,325
Operating Profit	£ 506	£ 379
Other income (expense) items, net	(24)	38
Interest Payable	(71)	(52)
Profit on Ordinary Activities Before Taxation	£ 411	£ 365
Tax on Profit on Ordinary Activities..............	(126)	(110)
Profit/(Loss) on Ordinary Activities After Taxation...	£ 285	£ 255
Minority Interest	(14)	(11)
Profit/(Loss) for the Financial Year...............	£ 271	£ 244
Ordinary Dividends............................	(52)	(38)
Retained Profit/(Loss) for the Year	£ 219	£ 206

EXHIBIT 1.19

WPP Group
Consolidated Cash Flow Statement
(amounts in millions of pounds)
(Problem 1.5)

	December 31	
	Year 11	Year 10
Operating Activities		
Operating Profit	£ 506	£ 379
Depreciation Charge	125	79
(Increase) Decrease in Stocks	(18)	(15)
(Increase) Decrease in Debtors	(5)	(434)
Increase (Decrease) in Trade Creditors	(473)	539
Increase in Provisions	27	74
Other Adjustments	12	2
Net Cash Flow from Operating Activities	£ 174	£ 624
Returns on Investments and Servicing of Finance		
Interest and Dividends Received	£ 53	£ 25
Interest Paid	(84)	(78)
Dividend Paid	(44)	(26)
Net Cash Flow from Investments and Servicing of Finance	£ (75)	£ (79)
Taxation	£ (78)	£ (81)
Investing Activities		
Purchase of Tangible Fixed Assets	£ (218)	£ (112)
Acquisitions.	(696)	(230)
Other Investing Activities	(125)	(51)
Net Cash Outflow from Investing Activities	£(1,039)	£ (393)
Financing Activities		
Proceeds from Issue of Share Capital	69	£ 78
Increase (Decrease) in Bank Loans	£ 439	£ 128
Net Cash Flow from Financing Activities	£ 508	£ 206
Effect of Exchange Rate Changes on Cash and Cash Equivalents.	£ 10	£ 35
Cash and Cash Equivalents—Beginning of Year	£ 1,086	£ 774
Cash and Cash Equivalents—End of Year	£ 586	£ 1,086

1.6 COMPREHENSIVE INCOME.   Refer to the financial statements of the WPP Group reported in Problem 1.5 as Exhibits 1.17, 1.18, and 1.19. You will note that the U.S. requirement of reporting comprehensive income does not exist in the United Kingdom as the WPP Group does not report comprehensive income anywhere in these statements. However, WPP Group does report several changes in the recognition and valuation of assets and liabilities that are not reported currently in the consolidated profit and loss account, but likely will be in the future. Examples of these types of changes are detailed in the chapter for PepsiCo, which are reported as part of the firm's comprehensive income.

Required

   a. Prepare a Statement of Comprehensive Income for the WPP Group for Year 11. Use whatever disclosures from WPP Group's financial statements and notes you believe are appropriate to prepare the statement. Clearly label the components reported in the statement.
   b. Calculate WPP Group's net income as a percent of turnover (equivalent to revenues in the United States) for Year 11. Recalculate this ratio using comprehensive income instead of net income and assess the effect of the difference between the two calculations.

1.7 RECASTING THE FINANCIAL STATEMENTS OF A GERMAN COMPANY INTO U.S. FORMATS AND TERMINOLOGY.   Volkswagen Group AG manufactures passenger cars and commercial vehicles, and provides financing for its customers' purchases. The firm also provides financing to dealers that sell its products. Brand names include Volkswagen, Audi, SEAT, Rolls-Royce, and Bentley. Exhibit 1.20 presents a balance sheet at the end of Year 9 and Year 10, and Exhibit 1.21 presents an income statement for Year 9 and Year 10 for Volkswagen.

Required

   a. Prepare a balance sheet for Volkswagen on December 31, Year 9 and Year 10, using reporting formats and terminology commonly encountered in the United States.
   b. Prepare an income statement for Volkswagen for Year 9 and Year 10, using terminology commonly encountered in the United States. Separate operating revenues and expenses from nonoperating revenues and expenses.

EXHIBIT 1.20

Balance Sheet for Volkswagen Group AG
(in millions of €)
(Problem 1.7)

	December 31	
	Year 10	**Year 9**
Assets		
Fixed Assets		
Intangible Assets (Note 1)	€ 6,596	€ 5,355
Tangible Assets (net)	21,735	19,726
Financial Assets	3,999	4,216
Total Fixed Assets...	€ 32,330	€ 29,297
Leasing and Rental Assets (Note 2).............................	€ 7,284	€ 4,783
Current Assets		
Inventories	€ 9,945	€ 9,335
Receivables	45,166	41,432
Securities..	3,610	3,886
Cash on Hand...	4,285	2,156
Total Current Assets	€ 63,006	€ 56,809
Prepaid and Deferred Charges (Note 3).........................	€ 378	€ 299
Deferred Tax Assets...	€ 1,426	€ 1,377
Balance Sheet Total	€104,424	€ 92,565
Shareholders' Equity and Liabilities		
Shareholders' Equity		
Subscribed Capital: Ordinary Shares	€ 815	€ 803
Preferred Shares	272	268
Capital Reserve...	4,415	4,296
Revenue Reserves (Note 4).....................................	14,546	13,690
Accumulated Profits...	3,947	2,314
Minority Interests (Note 5)	53	49
Total Shareholders' Equity..................................	€ 24,048	€ 21,420
Deferred Tax Liabilities.......................................	2,299	2,095
Provisions (Note 6)...	21,782	21,128
Current Borrowings	30,044	26,201
Non-current Borrowings	12,750	8,383
Trade Payables...	7,055	7,435
Other Payables (Note 7)	6,161	5,699
Deferred Income (Note 8)	285	204
Balance Sheet Total	€104,424	€ 92,565

EXHIBIT 1.21

Income Statement for Volkswagen Group AG
(in millions of €)
(Problem 1.7)

	Year Ended December 31	
	Year 10	Year 9
Sales	€ 88,540	€ 83,127
Cost of Sales	(75,586)	(71,130)
Gross Profit—Automotive Division	€ 12,954	€ 11,997
Gross Profit—Financial Services Division (Note 9)	1,328	1,213
Selling and Distribution Expenses........................	(7,554)	(7,080)
General and Administrative Expenses......................	(2,154)	(2,001)
Other Operating Income (Note 10)........................	4,118	3,656
Other Operating Expenses (Note 11)	(3,268)	(3,761)
Operating Profit.....................................	5,424	4,024
Share of Profit and Losses of Group Companies (Note 12)	289	335
Other Income (Expenses)	(419)	99
Other Financial Results (Note 13)..........................	(885)	(739)
Profit before Tax....................................	€ 4,409	€ 3,719
Taxes on Income.....................................	(1,483)	(1,105)
Minority Interest	(11)	(7)
Net Earnings..	€ 2,915	€ 2,607

NOTES TO EXHIBITS 1.20 AND 1.21

Note 1: Intangible Assets consist of license rights, goodwill, and miscellaneous other intangible assets.

Note 2: Leasing and Rental Assets represents vehicles leased to customers. The leases are treated as operating leases, which means that the vehicle remains on the balance sheet of Volkswagen Group AG as vehicle property.

Note 3: Prepaid and Deferred Charges consist of the following:

	December 31	
	Year 10	Year 9
Prepaid Operating Costs...........................	€ 78	€ 63
Other..	300	236
Total	€ 378	€ 299

Note 4: Revenue Reserves represent earnings not officially designated by the board of directors as available for dividends.

Note 5: Minority Interests represent the ownership interests of shareholders outside of the Volkswagen Group AG in a consolidated entity within the Group. The minority interests at the end of Year 10 consisted primarily of Audi AG shareholders.

Note 6: Provisions include the following:

	December 31	
	Year 10	Year 9
Pensions	€ 9,984	€ 9,558
Warranties	3,884	3,704
Restructuring	1,920	2,063
Taxable Payable.	1,418	1,424
Other Provisions.	4,576	4,379
Total.	€ 21,782	€ 21,128

Note 7: Other liabilities that are primarily due within one year related to various aspects of the firm's operations (such items as accrued wages and salaries, social security taxes, and other payroll taxes).

Note 8: Consists of up-front payments from operating lease customers and other operating lease-related items.

Note 9: Gross Profit—Financial Services Division consists of the following:

	Year Ended December 31	
	Year 10	Year 9
Interest Income—Dealer Financing.	€ 499	€ 463
Interest Income—Customer Financing	1,587	1,412
Interest Income—Finance Leases.	1,122	1,150
Interest Expense	(1,880)	(1,812)
Gross Profit	€ 1,328	€ 1,213

Note 10: Other Operating Income consists primarily of reversing provisions made in prior years and other unspecified operating income.

Note 11: Other Operating Expenses consist of the effects of exchange rate changes and other unspecified operating expenses.

Note 12: Results from participation represent Volkswagen Group AG's share in the earnings of less than majority owned entities.

Note 13: Other Financial Results consist of pension expenses and related provisions.

CASE 1.1

NIKE: SOMEWHERE BETWEEN A SWOOSH AND A SLAM DUNK

Nike's principal business activity involves the design, development, and worldwide marketing of high quality footwear, apparel, equipment, and accessory products. Almost 23,000 employees work for the firm. Nike boasts the largest worldwide market share in the athletic footwear industry and a leading market share in sports and athletic apparel. Nike, Reebok, and Adidas combine for over two-thirds of the market share in the athletic footwear industry in the United States.

This case uses the financial statements for Nike and excerpts from its notes to review important concepts underlying the three principal financial statements (balance sheet, income statement, and statement of cash flows) and relationships among them. The case also introduces tools for analyzing financial statements, comparing amounts for Nike (Year 11 sales of $9.5 billion) to those of Reebok (Year 11 sales of $3.0 billion) and Adidas (Year 11 sales of $6.1 billion, assuming parity between the dollar and euro). Nike and Reebok are U.S.-based companies and Adidas is headquartered in Germany.

INDUSTRY ECONOMICS

Product Lines

Industry analysts debate whether the athletic footwear industry is a performance-driven athletic footwear industry or a fashion-driven sneaker industry. Proponents of the performance view point to Nike's dominant market position, which results in part from continual innovation in product development. Proponents of the fashion view point to the difficulty of protecting technological improvements from competitor imitation, the large portion of total expenses comprising advertising, the role of sports and other personalities in promoting athletic shoes, and the fact that only a small percentage of athletic footwear consumers use the footwear for its intended purpose (that is, basketball, running).

Growth

There are only modest growth opportunities for footwear in the United States. Concern exists with respect to both volume increases (how many pairs of athletic shoes will consumers tolerate in their closets) and price increases (will consumers continue to pay prices for innovative athletic footwear that is often twice as costly as other footwear).

Athletic footwear companies have diversified their revenue sources in two directions in recent years. One direction involves increased emphasis on international sales. With dress codes becoming more casual in Europe and East Asia and interest in American sports such as basketball and football becoming more widespread, industry analysts view international markets as the major growth markets during the next several years. Increased emphasis on soccer in the United States aids companies such as Adidas with reputations for quality soccer footwear.

The second direction for diversification is sports and athletic apparel. The three leading athletic footwear companies capitalize on their brand name recognition and distribution channels to create a line of sportswear that coordinates with their footwear. Team uniforms and matching apparel for coaching staffs have become a major growth avenue recently. For example, Bauer/Nike Hockey manufactures and distributes ice skates, skate blades, in-line roller skates, protective gear, hockey sticks, and hockey jerseys and accessories under both the Bauer and Nike brand names.

Production

Essentially all athletic footwear and most apparel come from factories in Asia, primarily China (40 percent), Indonesia (31 percent), Vietnam, South Korea, Taiwan, and Thailand. The footwear companies do not own any of these manufacturing facilities. They typically hire manufacturing representatives to source and oversee the manufacturing process, helping to insure quality control and serving as a link between the design and the manufacture of products. The manufacturing process is labor intensive, with sewing machines used as the primary equipment. Footwear companies typically price their purchases from these factories in U.S. dollars.

Marketing

Athletic footwear and sportswear companies sell their products through various independent department, specialty, and discount stores. Their sales forces educate retailers on new product innovations, store display design, and similar activities. The dominant market shares of Nike, Reebok, and Adidas, limits on retailers' shelf space, and slower growth in sales make it increasingly difficult for the remaining athletic footwear companies to gain market share.

Nike, Reebok, and Adidas have typically used independent distributors to market their products in other countries. With increasing brand recognition and anticipated growth in international sales, these companies have recently acquired an increasing number of their distributors to capture more of the profits generated in other countries and maintain better control of international marketing.

Finance

Compared to other apparel firms, the athletic footwear firms generate higher profit margins and rates of return. These firms use cash flow generated from this superior profitability to finance needed working capital investments (receivables and inventories). Long-term debt tends to be minimal, reflecting the absence of significant investments in manufacturing facilities.

NIKE

Nike targets the serious athlete with performance-driven footwear. In recent years, the firm has particularly emphasized growth outside of the United States. Philip Knight, Chairman, CEO, and major shareholder, sums up the company's philosophy and driving force behind Nike's success by saying: "We are midway on our journey to becoming a truly global company. We are creating a product that is meaningful beyond the stick-and-ball shores of the United States. Consumers around the world are seeing and embracing Nike."

To maintain its technological edge, Nike engages in extensive research at its research facilities in Beaverton, Oregon. It continually alters its product line to introduce new footwear and evolutionary improvements in existing products.

Nike maintains a reputation for timely delivery of footwear products to its customers, primarily as a result of its "Futures" ordering program. Under this program, retailers book orders five to six months in advance. Nike guarantees 90 percent delivery of the order within a set time period at the agreed price at the time of ordering. Approximately 86 percent of footwear orders received by Nike during Year 11 came though its Futures program. This program allows the company to improve production scheduling, thereby reducing inventory risk. However, the program locks in prices and increases Nike's risk of change in raw materials and labor costs.

Independent contractors manufacture virtually all of Nike's products. Nike sources all of its footwear from other countries and approximately 95 percent of its apparel.

The following exhibits present information for Nike, Reebok, and Adidas:

Exhibit 1.22: Consolidated balance sheets for Nike for Year 10 and Year 11.

Exhibit 1.23: Consolidated income statements for Nike for Year 9, Year 10, and Year 11.

Exhibit 1.24: Consolidated statements of cash flows for Nike for Year 9, Year 10, and Year 11.

Exhibit 1.25: Excerpts from the Notes to the Nike's financial statements.

Exhibit 1.26: Common-size and percentage change income statements for Nike, Reebok, and Adidas.

Exhibit 1.27: Common-size and percentage change balance sheets for Nike, Reebok, and Adidas.

Required

Study the financial statements and notes for Nike and then respond to each of the following questions.

INCOME STATEMENT

a. Identify the time at which Nike recognizes revenues. Does this timing of revenue recognition seem appropriate? Explain.
b. Identify the cost-flow assumption(s) that Nike uses to measure cost of goods sold. Does Nike's choice of cost-flow assumption(s) seem appropriate? Explain.

EXHIBIT 1.22

Consolidated Balance Sheet for Nike
(amounts in millions)
(Case 1.1)

May 31:	Year 11	Year 10
Assets		
Cash and Cash Equivalents	$ 304	$ 254
Accounts Receivable, less Allowance for Doubtful		
Accounts of $72 and $65	1,621	1,569
Inventories	1,424	1,446
Deferred Income Taxes	113	112
Prepayments.	163	215
Total Current Assets.	$3,625	$3,596
Property, Plant, and Equipment, net of		
Accumulated Depreciation of $934 and $810	1,619	1,583
Identifiable Intangible Assets and Goodwill	397	411
Deferred Income Taxes and Other Assets	178	266
Total Assets.	$5,819	$5,856
Liabilities and Shareholders' Equity		
Accounts Payable	$ 432	$ 544
Notes Payable.	855	924
Current Portion of Long-term Debt	5	50
Other Current Liabilities	494	622
Total Current Liabilities.	$1,786	$2,140
Long-term Debt.	436	470
Deferred Income Taxes	103	110
Other Liabilities	—	—
Total Liabilities.	$2,325	$2,720
Common Stock	$ 452	$ 360
Accumulated Other Comprehensive Income		
(foreign currency)	(152)	(111)
Retained Earnings	3,194	2,887
Total Shareholders' Equity.	$3,494	$3,136
Total Liabilities and Shareholders' Equity	$5,819	$5,856

EXHIBIT 1.23

Consolidated Income Statement for Nike
(amounts in millions)
(Case 1.1)

Year Ended May 31:	Year 11	Year 10	Year 9
Sales Revenue....................	$9,489	$8,995	$8,777
Cost of Goods Sold	(5,785)	(5,404)	(5,493)
Selling and Administrative..........	(2,690)	(2,606)	(2,427)
Restructuring Charge, net	—	3	(45)
Interest	(59)	(45)	(44)
Other Income (Expense), net	(34)	(23)	(22)
Income Before Income Taxes........	$ 921	$ 920	$ 746
Income Taxes	(332)	(340)	(295)
Net Income.....................	$ 589	$ 580	$ 451

c. Nike reports property, plant, and equipment on its balance sheet and discloses the amount of depreciation for each year in its statement of cash flows. Why doesn't depreciation expense appear among its expenses on the income statement?

d. Identify the portions of Nike's income tax expense of $332 million for Year 11 that is currently payable to governmental entities and the portion that is deferred to future years. Why do governmental entities permit firms to defer payment of their income taxes to future years?

BALANCE SHEET

a. Why do accounts receivable appear net of allowance for doubtful accounts? Identify the events or transactions that cause the allowance account to increase or decrease.

b. Identify the depreciation method(s) that Nike uses for its buildings and equipment. Does Nike's choice of depreciation method(s) seem appropriate?

c. Nike includes identifiable intangible assets and goodwill on its balance sheet as an asset. Does this account include the value of the Nike name and "swoosh" trademark? Explain.

d. Nike includes deferred income taxes among current assets, noncurrent assets, and noncurrent liabilities. Under what circumstances will deferred income taxes give rise to an asset? To a liability?

e. Nike reports accumulated other comprehensive income related to foreign currency translation of ($152) million at the end of Year 11 and ($111) million at the end of Year 10. Why are these "losses" reported as part of shareholders' equity and not as part of net income in the income statement?

EXHIBIT 1.24

Consolidated Statement of Cash Flows for Nike
(amounts in millions)
(Case 1.1)

Year Ended May 31:	Year 11	Year 10	Year 9
Operations			
Net Income...	$ 589	$ 580	$ 451
Depreciation.......................................	197	188	198
Non-cash Portion of Restructuring Charge................	—	—	28
Deferred Income Taxes................................	66	46	—
Other...	50	50	64
(Increase) Decrease in Accounts Receivable	(141)	(83)	114
(Increase) Decrease in Inventories......................	(17)	(312)	214
(Increase) Decrease in Other Current Assets..............	78	61	24
Increase (Decrease) in Accounts Payable and			
Other Current Liabilities............................	(165)	169	(153)
Cash Flow from Operations.........................	$ 657	$ 699	$ 940
Investing			
Additions to Property, Plant, and Equipment.............	$(318)	$(420)	$(384)
Disposals of Property, Plant, and Equipment	13	25	27
Additions to Other Assets.............................	(43)	(51)	(61)
Increases in Other Liabilities	5	6	(1)
Cash Flow from Investing..........................	$(343)	$(440)	$(419)
Financing			
Additions to Long-term Debt	$ —	$ —	$ —
Reductions in Long-term Debt	(50)	(2)	(2)
Increase (Decrease) in Notes Payable....................	(69)	505	(61)
Proceeds from Exercise of Stock Options	56	24	54
Repurchase of Common Stock..........................	(157)	(646)	(300)
Dividends	(130)	(133)	(136)
Other...	86	49	13
Cash Flow from Financing.........................	$(264)	$(203)	$(432)
Change in Cash.....................................	$50	$56	$89
Cash—Beginning of Year..............................	254	198	109
Cash—End of Year...................................	$ 304	$ 254	$ 198

EXHIBIT 1.25

Excerpts from Notes to Consolidated Financial Statements for Nike
(amounts in millions)
(Case 1.1)

Summary of Significant Accounting Policies

Recognition of Revenues: Nike recognizes revenue at time of sale to its customers and as it earns fees on sales by licensees. Provisions for sales discounts and returns are made at the time of sale.

Inventory Valuation: Inventories appear at lower of cost or market. Nike determines cost using the first-in, first-out (FIFO) method. The firm changed to this method in Year 9.

Property, Plant, and Equipment and Depreciation: Property, plant, and equipment appear at acquisition cost. Nike computes depreciation using the straight-line method for buildings and leasehold improvements and a declining balance method for machinery and equipment, based on estimated useful lives ranging from three to thirty-two years.

Identifiable Intangible Assets and Goodwill: This account represents the excess of the purchase price of acquired businesses over the market values of identifiable net assets, net of amortization to date.

Foreign currency translation: Adjustments resulting from translating foreign functional currency financial statements into U.S. dollars are included in the foreign currency translation adjustment, a component of accumulated other comprehensive income.

Income Taxes: Nike provides deferred income taxes for temporary differences between income before taxes for financial reporting and tax reporting. Income tax expense includes the following:

	Year 11	Year 10	Year 9
Currently Payable	$266	$294	$295
Deferred	66	46	—
Income Tax Expense.	$332	$340	$295

Stock Repurchases: Nike repurchases outstanding shares of its common stock each year and retires them. Any difference between the price paid and the book value of the shares appears as an adjustment of retained earnings.

Restructuring Charges: Nike recorded a restructuring charge in Year 9 (and a minor reversal of that charge in Year 10) related primarily to the cost of severing employees and the write-down of assets no longer in use.

EXHIBIT 1.26

Common-size and Percentage Change Income Statements
for Nike, Reebok, and Adidas
(Case 1.1)

Nike	Common-size Income Statements Fiscal Year Ended May 31:			Percentage Change Income Statements Fiscal Year Ended May 31:		
	Year 11	Year 10	Year 9	Year 11	Year 10	Year 9
Sales Revenues.............	100.0%	100.0%	100.0%	5.5%	2.5%	(8.1%)
Cost of Goods Sold.........	(61.0)	(60.1)	(62.6)	7.1%	(1.6%)	(9.4%)
Selling and Administrative Expenses	(28.3)	(29.0)	(27.7)	3.2%	7.3%	(7.5%)
Restructuring Charge	—	—	(.5)	—	—	(65.1%)
Other Income (Expense)......	(.4)	(.2)	(.2)	47.8%	4.5%	16.1%
Interest Expense	(.6)	(.5)	(.5)	31.1%	2.3%	(26.7%)
Income Before Taxes........	9.7%	10.2%	8.5%	.1%	23.3%	14.2%
Income Taxes..............	(3.5)	(3.8)	(3.4)	(2.4%)	15.2%	16.2%
Net Income	6.2%	6.4%	5.1%	1.6%	28.6%	13.0%

	Common-size Income Statements Calendar Year Ended December 31:				Percentage Change Income Statements Calendar Year Ended December 31:	
	Year 11	Year 10	Year 11	Year 10	Year 11	Year 11
	Reebok		Adidas		Reebok	Adidas
Sales Revenues.............	100.0%	100.0%	100.0%	100.0%	4.5%	4.8%
Other Revenues.............	—	—	.6	.7		
Cost of Goods Sold.........	(63.2)	(62.1)	(59.6)	(58.7)	6.5%	6.2%
Selling and Administrative Expenses	(30.5)	(31.9)	(33.3)	(34.5)	(.2%)	1.2%
Interest Expense	(.5)	(.7)	(1.7)	(1.6)	(20.3%)	(2.3%)
Special Charge.............	(.4)	(.4)	(.1)	—	—	583.1%
Minority Interest............	(.1)	(.2)	(.1)	(.4)	(19.4%)	(17.5%)
Income Before Taxes........	5.3%	4.7%	5.8%	5.5%	14.7%	8.6%
Income Taxes..............	(1.6)	(1.7)	(2.4)	(2.4)	(1.4%)	5.3%
Net Income	3.7%	3.0%	3.4%	3.1%	27.1%	14.8%

EXHIBIT 1.27

Common-size and Percentage Change Balance Sheets for Nike, Reebok, and Adidas (Case 1.1)

| | Percentage Change Balance Sheets | | Common-size Balance Sheets | | | | |
| | Nike | | Nike | | | Reebok | Adidas |
	Year 11	Year 10	Year 11	Year 10	Year 9	Year 11	Year 11
Assets							
Cash	19.7%	28.2%	5.2%	4.3%	6.2%	26.7%	2.2%
Accounts Receivable	3.3%	1.7%	27.9	26.8	31.7	24.8	24.9
Inventories	(1.5%)	23.6%	24.5	24.7	22.0	23.5	45.3
Prepayments	(24.7%)	1.8%	4.7	5.6	4.4	8.6	5.4
Total Current Assets	.8%	10.2%	62.3%	61.4%	64.3%	83.6%	77.8%
Property, Plant, and Equipment	2.3%	23.6%	27.8	27.0	22.0	9.0	15.1
Other Noncurrent Assets	2.2%	(5.9%)	9.9	11.6	13.7	7.4	7.1
Total Assets	(.6%)	11.6%	100.0%	100.0%	100.0%	100.0%	100.0%
Liabilities and Shareholders' Equity							
Accounts Payable	(20.4%)	14.8%	7.4%	8.7%	10.7%	8.2%	19.3%
Notes Payable	(7.5%)	120.5%	14.7	11.7	10.5	.7	23.0
Current Portion of Long-term Debt	(90.0%)	490.0%	—	.9	.2	—	—
Other Current Liabilities	(24.0%)	12.3	8.5	11.3	13.2	20.2	17.0
Total Current Liabilities	(16.5%)	48.0%	30.6%	32.6%	34.6%	29.1%	59.3%
Long-term Debt	(7.4%)	21.8%	7.5	7.9	7.1	22.8	5.5
Deferred Income Taxes	(7.3%)	(39.2%)	1.8	.5	—	—	.1
Other Noncurrent Liabilities	—	—	—	1.3	1.0	—	2.9
Total Liabilities	(14.5%)	42.2%	39.9%	42.3%	42.7%	51.9%	67.8%
Minority Interest	—	—	—	—	—	1.5	1.2
Common Stock	25.6%	10.5%	7.8%	.1%	.1%	.1%	12.2%
Additional Paid-in Capital	—	—	—	3.6	3.7	—	.8
Retained Earnings	10.6%	(5.8%)	54.9	54.0	54.0	94.2	18.0
Foreign Currency Translation	36.9%	63.2%	(2.6)	—	(.5)	(4.9)	—
Treasury Stock	—	—	—	—	—	(42.8)	—
Total Shareholders' Equity	11.4%	(5.9%)	60.1%	57.7%	57.3%	48.1%	32.2%
Total Liabilities and Shareholders' Equity	(.6%)	11.6%	100.0%	100.0%	100.0%	100.0%	100.0%

STATEMENT OF CASH FLOWS

a. Why does the amount of net income differ from the amount of cash flow from operations?

b. Why does Nike report depreciation as an addition to net income in calculating cash flow from operations?

c. Why does Nike report deferred income taxes as an addition to net income in calculating cash flow from operations for Year 11 (as well as each of the previous years)?

d. Why does Nike subtract increases in accounts receivable from net income when calculating cash flow from operations for Year 11?

e. Why does Nike subtract increases in inventory from net income when calculating cash flow from operations for Year 11?

f. Why does Nike add increases in accounts payable and other current liabilities to net income when calculating cash flow from operations for Year 10?

g. Given that firms often sell property, plant, and equipment at a gain or loss, why does Nike include the proceeds of disposal of these assets as an investing activity instead of as an operating activity?

h. Given that notes payable appear on the balance sheet as a current liability, why does Nike include changes in this liability as a financing activity instead of as an operating activity?

RELATIONS BETWEEN FINANCIAL STATEMENT ITEMS

a. Compute the amount of cash collected from customers during Year 11.

b. Compute the amount of cash payments made to suppliers of merchandise during Year 11.

c. Prepare an analysis that accounts for the change in the property, plant, and equipment account and the accumulated depreciation account during Year 11. Calculate the gain or loss that Nike recognized on the disposal of property, plant, and equipment during Year 11.

d. Identify the reasons for the change in retained earnings during Year 11.

INTERPRETING FINANCIAL STATEMENT RELATIONSHIPS

a. Exhibit 1.26 presents common-size and percentage change income statements for Nike for Year 9, Year 10, and Year 11. Exhibit 1.26 also presents similar information for Reebok and Adidas, Nike's two principal competitors. What are the likely reasons for the higher net income/sales revenue percentages for Nike for Years 11 and 10 versus Year 9?

b. What is the likely reason for the increase in Selling and Administrative Expenses between year Year 9 and Year 10?

c. What does the relation between the percentage change in sales and the percentage change in cost of goods sold for Nike for Year 9 and Year 11 suggest about the behavior of this expense item? What could be the reason for the different relation between these percentage change items in Year 10?

d. The three companies report cost of goods sold/sales percentages between 59 percent and 63 percent during Year 11. Why might these percentages be so similar (Hint: consider how these firms likely set purchase and selling prices for their products)?

e. Nike experienced the highest net income/sales percentage of the three companies for all three years. What is the apparent source of its competitive advantage?

f. Exhibit 1.27 presents common-size and percentage change balance sheets for Nike at the end Year 9, Year 10, and Year 11. Exhibit 1.27 also presents common-size balance sheets for Reebok and Adidas at the end of Year 10 and Year 11, and percentage change balance sheets for Year 11. What is the likely explanation for the relatively small percentages for property, plant, and equipment for these three companies?

g. What is the likely explanation for the relatively small percentages for long-term debt for these three companies?

h. What is the likely explanation for the small increase in the percentage change for property, plant, and equipment for Nike for Year 11?

i. The proportion of total financing comprised of notes payable increased steadily during the three years for Nike, while the portion comprised of accounts payable decreased steadily during this same period. What might this suggest about financing options available to Nike? Explain.

j. Which of the three firms appears to be the most risky from a financial structure perspective? Explain your reasoning.

k. Refer to the statement of cash flows for Nike in Exhibit 1.24. Net income increased between Year 9 and Year 10, but cash flow from operations decreased. What is the likely reason for the different direction of these changes?

l. Continuing with part k above, net income increased between Year 10 and Year 11, but cash flow from operations decreased at a rate much slower than in the previous year. Why does this decrease in cash flow pattern differ from that between Year 9 and Year 10?

m. Cash flow from operations exceeded net income during all three years. Why is this the case?

n. How has Nike primarily financed its acquisitions of property, plant, and equipment during the three years?

o. What are the likely reasons for the repurchases of common stock during the three years?

p. The dividends paid by Nike decreased slightly each year ($136 million in Year 9, $133 million in Year 10, and $130 million in Year 11). Do you speculate that Nike reduced its dividend rate each year, or is there some other possible explanation for the reduction?

Chapter 2

ASSET AND LIABILITY VALUATION AND INCOME MEASUREMENT

Learning Objectives
1. **Understand the difference between measuring assets and liabilities using historical values versus current values.**
2. **Understand the relation between the valuation of assets and liabilities on the balance sheet and the measurement of net income on the income statement.**
3. **Measure the income tax effects of various income transactions.**
4. **Use an analytical framework to identify the effects of various business transactions on the balance sheet and the income statement.**

Chapter 1 provided a broad overview of financial statement analysis, introducing the five-step framework for financial statement analysis that we use throughout this text. Chapter 1 described tools to analyze industry economics and firm strategies and the effects of economic and strategic factors on profitability and risk. Chapter 1 also described the purpose and content of the three principal financial statements, tools for analyzing them, and links between financial statement information and valuation. The remainder of the text develops all of these ideas more completely and provides tools for each step of the framework. To lay the groundwork for these tools for effective analysis of financial statements, we must first understand three fundamental elements that are part of the foundation of financial statements: (1) the principles that underlie the measurement and reporting of financial position and profitability; (2) the pervasive role of taxes; and (3) the impact of business transactions on financial statements. This chapter explores these three fundamental elements by demonstrating their effects on the balance sheet and income statement. Specifically, we:

- Examine the critical link between the valuation of assets and liabilities and the measurement of net income and comprehensive income.
- Examine the income tax effects of recognizing changes in the value of assets and liabilities on net income and comprehensive income.
- Provide an analytical framework for identifying the effects of value changes on individual balance sheet and income statement accounts.

Chapter 3 discusses the important concepts and analytical tools for the statement of cash flows in greater depth.

ASSET AND LIABILITY VALUATION

The balance sheet reports the assets of a firm and the claims on those assets by creditors (liabilities) and owners (shareholders' equity) at a moment in time. Assets are economic resources that provide a firm with future services, or benefits. Liabilities are obligations to sacrifice economic resources in the future for services, or benefits, already received. Shareholders' equity is the residual claim on assets not required to satisfy the claims of creditors. Chapter 7 discusses the economic resources that firms recognize as assets (for example, inventories, buildings, and equipment) and those that GAAP does not recognize as assets (for example, internally developed brand names and technologies). Chapter 8 discusses the obligations that firms recognize as liabilities (for example, advances from customers, accounts payable to suppliers) and those not normally recognized (for example, obligations related to unsettled lawsuits or mutually unexecuted contracts). Our concern in this section is the valuation of *recognized* assets and liabilities.

Assets provide benefits to a firm in the future, and liabilities require firms to sacrifice resources in the future. Although assets and liabilities clearly have a future orientation, their valuation on the balance sheet might reflect historical information, current information, or future information. Historical values use information about the value of an asset when a firm acquired it, and the value of a liability when a firm initially incurred it. Current values use information about the value of an asset and a liability at the date of the balance sheet. Valuation methods that reflect historical values include:

1. acquisition cost,
2. adjusted acquisition cost, and
3. present value of cash flows using historical interest rates.

Valuation methods that reflect current values include:

1. current replacement cost,
2. net realizable value, and
3. present value of cash flows using current interest rates.

Both present value methods use projected cash flows but discount those cash flows to a present value using either historical interest rates or current interest rates. Thus, we view these two present value methods as reflecting either historical values or current values.

HISTORICAL VALUE: ACQUISITION COST

The acquisition cost of an asset is the amount paid initially to acquire the asset. Acquisition cost includes all costs required to prepare the asset for its intended use.

Example 1

Red Lobster Restaurants acquired a tract of land for a restaurant site at a cost of $120,000. It paid attorneys $4,500 to conduct a title search and prepare the required legal documents for the purchase. It paid a state real estate transfer tax of $1,200. The acquisition cost of the land is $125,700 (= $120,000 + $4,500 + $1,200).

Example 2

Gallo Wines paid employees $1,040,000 to oversee the growing of grapes in its orchards, to harvest the grapes, and to process the grapes into wine. Depreciation on buildings and equipment related to wine production totaled $220,000. Gallo incurred insurance, taxes, and other operating costs of $146,000. The acquisition cost of the wine in inventory prior to commencement of aging totals $1,406,000 (= $1,040,000 + $220,000 + $146,000). Gallo Wines will increase the inventory account in later periods for costs incurred during the aging process.

Acquisition cost valuations are relatively objective in that invoices, cancelled checks, and other documents evidence the amount. One valuation question that often arises concerns the costs to include in the asset amount. Should the acquisition cost of the land in Example 1 include the salaries of Red Lobster personnel engaged in selecting the site? Should the acquisition cost of the wine in Example 2 include interest on funds borrowed to finance the production of the wine? A second valuation question concerns the relevancy of acquisition cost valuations to users of the financial statements. At the time that a firm acquires an asset, acquisition cost valuations are reliably, or objectively, measured, and are the relevant valuation method to users of financial statements desiring to value a firm's assets. As time passes, the acquisition cost valuation is still reliably measured but loses relevance for current users desiring to value the firm. Thus, acquisition cost valuations often require trade-offs between *reliability* and *relevance*.

HISTORICAL VALUE: ADJUSTED ACQUISITION COST

The service potential of some assets, such as land, typically do not decline with usage over time and therefore remain at acquisition cost on the balance sheet. Firms consume the service potential of assets such as inventory all at once at the time of sale. The acquisition cost of the asset becomes an expense (cost of goods sold) at that time. Firms consume the service potential of assets such as buildings, equipment, license fees, and contractual rights gradually over time. Firms initially record these assets on the balance sheet at acquisition cost and then amortize or depreciate them over time in some systematic manner.

Example 3

Citicorp, a financial services firm, acquires a computer from IBM for $5 million. Citicorp expects to use the computer for five years and then to sell it for $1 million. Citicorp depreciates $4 million over the five-year useful life to the bank. It matches the remaining $1 million of book value at the end of five years against the selling price and recognizes a gain or loss for any difference.

Example 4

American Airlines acquires a regional airline in the Midwestern United States for $450 million. American Airlines allocates $150 million of the purchase price to landing rights at various airports. The landing rights expire in five years. American Airlines amortizes the $150 million over the five years of usage.

Adjusted acquisition cost valuations share the advantages and disadvantages of acquisition cost valuations discussed above. In addition, the difficulty of physically observing the consumption of service potential that results from usage makes measuring the amount of depreciation or amortization inevitably subjective. Firms must estimate the expected useful life and salvage value of the assets. Furthermore, GAAP permits firms to select from among several time-series patterns (straight line, accelerated) for measuring depreciation and amortization expenses.

Firms use acquisition cost valuations and adjusted acquisition cost valuations for assets that do not have fixed amounts of future cash flows. For example, nonmonetary assets have no fixed amount of cash the firm will receive when it uses or sells these assets. Inventories; land; buildings; equipment; legal rights to use another entities' facilities, name, or distribution channels; and goodwill are examples of nonmonetary assets. When the future economic benefits (future cash flows) of an asset are uncertain, firms use acquisition cost and adjusted acquisition cost as a reliable measure of the asset's value.

Monetary assets and liabilities, on the other hand, represent amounts of cash the firm can expect to receive or pay in the future. Cash, accounts and notes receivable, and accounts, notes, and bonds payable are examples of monetary items that represent claims on pre-set amounts of cash flows. Firms typically value monetary assets and liabilities using present values, although GAAP permits firms to ignore the discounting process for monetary assets and liabilities due within one year. Firms might also value nonmonetary assets at the present value of expected future cash flows, as a later section discusses.

HISTORICAL VALUE: PRESENT VALUE OF CASH FLOWS USING HISTORICAL INTEREST RATES

Selling goods or services on account to customers or lending funds to others creates either an accounts receivable or notes receivable for the selling or lending firm. Purchasing goods or services on account from a supplier or borrowing funds from others creates a liability (for example, accounts payable, notes payable, bonds payable). Discounting the expected future cash flows under such arrangements to a present value expresses those cash flows in terms of a current cash-equivalent value. The discounting procedure might use (1) the interest rate appropriate to the particular financing arrangement at the time the firm initially enters it, referred to as the *historical interest rate*, or (2) the interest rate appropriate to the particular financing arrangement at the date of the balance sheet, referred to the *current interest rate*. This section discusses present values based on historical interest rates. A later section on valuation methods reflecting current values discusses present values based on current interest rates.

Example 5

Sun Microsystems sells computer equipment to Sun Trust Banks. Sun Trust Banks agrees to pay Sun Microsystems $250,000 at the end of each of the next five years, pledging the equipment as collateral for the loan. An assessment of the credit standing of Sun Trust Banks and of the value of the collateral suggests that 8 percent is an appropriate interest rate for this loan. The present value of $250,000 per year for five years when discounted at 8 percent is $998,178. Sun Microsystems records a note receivable and Sun Trust Banks records a note payable in the amount of $998,178. During the first year, interest on the note of $79,854 (= .08 × $998,178) increases the book value of the note and the cash payment of $250,000 reduces the book value of the note to $828,032 (= $998,178 + $79,854 − $250,000). The book value of the note of $828,032 equals the present value of the four remaining annual cash flows of $250,000 when discounted at the historical interest rate of 8 percent.

Example 6

Sears, a department store chain, sells a refrigerator to a customer on July 1, permitting the customer to delay payment of the $500 selling price until December 31. An assessment of the credit standing of the customer suggests that 6 percent per year is an appropriate interest rate for this extension of credit. The present value of $500 when discounted back for one-half year at 6 percent is $485.44. A strict application of the present value of cash flows valuation method results in reporting sales revenue of $485.44 on July 1 and interest revenue of $14.56 (= .06 × ½ × $485.44) for the six-month period from July 1 to December 31. As indicated earlier, GAAP permits firms to ignore the discounting process for monetary assets and liabilities due within one year on the grounds that the financial statement effects of discounting or not discounting are not materially different.

Valuing monetary assets and liabilities at the present value of cash flows using historical interest rates is relatively objective. The arrangement between the two entities usually specifies the required future cash flows. Some subjectivity might exist in establishing an appropriate interest rate at the time of the transaction. The borrower, for example, might choose to use the interest rate at which it could borrow on similar terms from a bank, whereas the seller might use the interest rate that would discount the pre-set cash flows to a present value equal to the cash selling price of good or service sold. These small differences in interest rates usually do not result in material differences in valuation between the entities involved in the transaction.

CURRENT VALUES: CURRENT REPLACEMENT COST

Current replacement cost is the amount a firm would have to pay currently to acquire an asset it now holds. Current replacement cost should reflect normal purchases and sales between unrelated parties, and not distressed purchases and sales where one party or the other holds a major advantage in setting prices.

Example 7

Refer to Example 1. Red Lobster Restaurants initially recorded the land on its books for $125,700. The land would remain on the books for this amount under the acquisition cost valuation method. Assume that real estate values in the vicinity of this tract of land increased during the next two years. A study of recent real estate transactions suggests that the current cost of purchasing this land or replacing it with similar land is now $145,700.

Example 8

Refer to Example 4. American Airlines amortizes the landing rights for one year in the amount of $30 million (= $150 million/5 years), resulting in a book value of $120 million. Assume now that a curtailment of air travel results in a decline in the replacement cost of these landing rights. A study of recent sales of landing rights suggests that the current replacement cost of landing rights with a four-year remaining life is $55 million.

Current replacement cost valuations generally reflect somewhat greater subjectivity than acquisition cost valuations. When active markets exist, recent transactions provide evidence of current replacement costs. When active markets do not exist, as is often the case for equipment specifically designed for a particular firm's needs, then the degree of subjectivity increases. Yet, users of financial statements may find current replacement cost valuations more relevant to their needs than out-of-date acquisition cost valuations. Thus, tradeoffs exist between the greater reliability of acquisition cost valuations and the greater relevance of replacement cost valuations.

CURRENT VALUES: NET REALIZABLE VALUE

Net realizable value is the net amount a firm would receive if it sold an asset or the net amount it would pay to settle a liability. As with current replacement cost valuation, net realizable value should reflect normal, instead of distressed, sales.

Example 9

Microsoft, a computer software firm, holds investments in various marketable securities of other firms. It could use the closing price of each security on the nearest trading day to the date of its balance sheet to value these securities at their net realizable value.

Example 10

Refer to Example 3. Citicorp uses the computer equipment for two years and records depreciation of $.8 million [= ($5 million − $1 million)/5 years] each year. The book value of the computer based on adjusted acquisition cost valuation is $3.4 million [= $5 million − (2 × $.8)]. Assume now that new technologies render the computer equipment partially obsolete. A study of used computer equipment offered for sale in business computer magazines indicates an average offering price for similar equipment of $2.5 million. IBM offers Citicorp $2.7 million for the equipment as a trade-in on a new, technologically superior computer. The net realizable value of the used computer likely falls in the range of $2.5 million to $2.7 million.

Using net realizable values to value assets encounters the same advantages and disadvantages as using current replacement costs. Net realizable values may provide more relevant information to users of the financial statements but result in greater subjectivity when active markets for the assets do not exist.

CURRENT VALUES: PRESENT VALUE OF CASH FLOWS USING CURRENT INTEREST RATES

The present value of a series of cash flows changes with the passage of time, as Example 5 illustrates. Even though the pre-set cash flows do not change, the present value of those cash flows will change if the interest, or discount, rate changes. The discount rate might change either because of changes in interest rates in the economy or because of a change in the credit risk of the particular borrower.

Example 11

Refer to Example 5. At the end of the first year, the note receivable on the books of Sun Microsystems and the note payable on the books of Sun Trust Banks has a book value of $828,032, which equals the present value of the remaining four payments of $250,000 when discounted at the historical interest rate of 8 percent. Assume now the market interest rate appropriate to this note declines to 6 percent. The present value of these payments at 6 percent is $866,276. These firms could revalue the receivables and payables to $866,276 to reflect the change in value caused by the change in the discount rate.

Example 12

Hilton Hotels owns a chain of hotels throughout the world. It reports these hotels at adjusted acquisition cost. Hilton Hotels could forecast the net cash flows it anticipates from each hotel in the future and discount them to a present value using current interest rates to value these hotels on its balance sheet at a current value.

Using the present value of cash flows to value a monetary asset or liability with pre-set cash flows is relatively objective. Selecting the appropriate current interest rate to revalue the monetary item each period entails a degree of subjectivity. Valuing nonmonetary assets, such as the hotels of Hilton Hotels in Example 12, entails considerable subjectivity. Unlike the case for a monetary asset, the cash flows for a nonmonetary asset are not pre-set. The accountant must forecast the timing and amount of the expected cash flows for some number of years into the future. The accountant must also revalue the asset each period for either changes in expected cash flows or for changes in the discount (interest) rate.

GAAP VALUATIONS

GAAP does not utilize a single valuation method for all assets and liabilities. Instead, GAAP stipulates that firms use historical values for some assets and liabilities, and fair values for other assets and liabilities. GAAP uses the term *fair value* instead of current value. When GAAP requires firms to use fair value for an asset or liability, firms can measure fair value using either current market prices (that is, current replacement cost or net realizable value) or present value of cash flows using current interest rates as the discount rate. GAAP has increasingly required use of fair values in the valuation of certain assets and liabilities in recent years. Exhibit 2.1 summarizes the use of these valuations methods for various assets and liabilities, which later chapters discuss more fully.

EXHIBIT 2.1
Summary of Valuation Methods for Various Assets and Liabilities

Historical Values
- Acquisition Cost: Prepayments, Land, Intangibles with Indefinite Lives, Goodwill
- Adjusted Acquisition Cost: Buildings, Equipment and Other Depreciable Assets, Intangibles with Limited Lives
- Present Value of Cash Flows Using Historical Interest Rates: Investments in Bonds Held to Maturity, Long-term Receivables and Payables. This valuation method in theory applies to current receivables and payables but GAAP ignores the discounting process on the grounds that discounted and undiscounted cash flows do not result in materially different valuations.

Fair Values (current market price or present value of cash flows using current interest rates)
- Investments in Marketable Equity Securities
- Investments in Debt Securities Classified as either Trading Securities or as Securities Available for Sale
- Financial Instruments and Derivative Instruments Subject to Hedging Activities
- Assets and Liabilities of a Business to be Discontinued

Combination of Values
- Lower of Cost or Market for Inventories
- Lower of Cost or Fair Value for Assets Experiencing an Asset Impairment

INCOME RECOGNITION

The income statement reports the results of a firm's operating activities for a period of time. Net income equals revenues and gains minus expenses and losses. In an ideal world, net income would equal all changes in economic value for a period. Users of the financial statements would then forecast future value changes, using the current period's value changes as a base to value the shareholders' equity of a firm.

GAAP recognizes, however, that the measurement of value changes often requires tradeoffs between the relevance of value changes to the user and the reliability of those measurements. The preceding section discussed the types of judgments often required to value assets and liabilities using current values. GAAP treats value changes in one of three ways:

Treatment 1: Value changes recognized on the balance sheet and the income statement when realized in a market transaction (that is, when a firm sells an asset or pays a liability).

Treatment 2: Value changes recognized on the balance sheet when the value changes occur over time but not recognized in net income until realized in a market transaction.

Treatment 3: Value changes recognized on the balance sheet and the income statement when they occur over time, even though not yet realized in a market transaction.

Exhibit 2.2 summarizes these three treatments, which the following sections discuss. An important guiding principle in asset valuation and income measurement is:

Over sufficiently long time periods, net income equals cash inflows minus cash outflows, other than cash flows with owners (for example, issuing or repurchasing common stock, paying dividends). Asset valuation and income measurement merely affect when and how the financial statements report these value changes. All value changes eventually affect net income and retained earnings.

TREATMENT 1: VALUE CHANGES RECOGNIZED ON THE BALANCE SHEET AND INCOME STATEMENT WHEN REALIZED

The traditional accounting model rests on the *realization convention* for the recognition of revenues and gains, and the *matching convention* for the recognition of expenses and losses. Firms typically recognize revenues when they receive cash, a receivable, or some other asset subject to reasonably reliable measurement from a customer for goods sold or services performed. The receipt of this asset validates the amount of the value change. Accountants characterize the firm as having *realized* the value change. Accountants match all costs incurred to create and sell the good or service as expenses against this revenue. The objective is to match inputs with outputs and thereby measure the net value change, or incremental value added.

	EXHIBIT 2.2	
	Treatment of Fair Value Changes	
	Recognized in the Indicated Financial Statement When Fair Value Change Realized	*Recognized in the Indicated Financial Statement When Fair Value Change Occurs*
Balance Sheet	Treatment 1	Treatment 2 Treatment 3
Income Statement	Treatment 1 Treatment 2	Treatment 3

Delaying the recognition of value changes for assets and liabilities until realized means that the balance sheet reports assets and liabilities at historical values. Note that realization of the value change is the driver for recognition on both the balance sheet and the income statement. The receipt or disbursement of cash is not a requirement for either realization or matching. Because the cash flows may precede, coincide with, or follow the value change, the balance sheet reports various accruals (for example, accounts receivable, accounts payable, prepayments).

Example 13

Refer to Example 2 for Gallo Wines. The firm accumulates various costs of producing the wine in its inventory account while the aging occurs. When the aging is complete and the firm sells the wine, it recognizes the value increase in both its assets and its net income. Assume that Gallo Wines incurs total costs of processing and aging the wine of $1,600,000 (= $1,406,000 for the initial processing and $194,000 for aging) and sells the wine at the completion of the aging for $2,000,000 on account. Gallo Wines reports inventories on its balance sheet each year during aging at the accumulated acquisition cost, even though the current value of the wine likely exceeds the accumulated acquisition cost. At the time of sale to a customer, Gallo Wines receives an account receivable of $2,000,000 and gives inventory with a book value of $1,600,000 in exchange. The firm realizes and recognizes revenues of $2,000,000 and matches the accumulated cost of goods sold of $1,600,000 against the revenue to report the net value increase of $400,000 in net income. Assets on the balance sheet increase by a corresponding $400,000 (= $2,000,000 increase in accounts receivable offset by a $1,600,000 decrease in inventories).

Example 14

Refer to Example 7. Red Lobster reports the land on the balance sheet at $125,700, its acquisition cost, as long as the firm continues to hold it. Suppose that Red Lobster decides to sell the land two years after acquiring it for $145,700 in cash. The firm recognizes the $20,000 value increase in its assets (= $145,700 increase in cash minus the $125,700 decrease in land) and simultaneously reports a gain on sale of the land of $20,000 in net income. Firms typically report the income from sales of assets peripheral to their main business as a net amount, $20,000, instead of showing the selling price of $145,700 as revenue and the cost of the asset sold of $125,700 as an expense. In contrast, income from a firm's principal business activities appears as gross amounts. Gallo Wines in Example 13 reports revenue of $2,000,000 and expense for the cost of goods sold of $1,600,000 because selling wines is its primary business.

TREATMENT 2: VALUE CHANGES RECOGNIZED ON THE BALANCE SHEET WHEN THEY OCCUR BUT RECOGNIZED IN NET INCOME WHEN REALIZED

The traditional accounting model delays the recognition of value changes of assets and liabilities until a market transaction validates their amounts (that is, realization occurs). The value changes of some assets and liabilities are of particular interest to users and are measurable with a sufficiently high degree of objectivity that GAAP requires firms to revalue them to fair value each period. GAAP recognizes, however, that the value change is *unrealized* until the firm sells the asset or settles the liability. The ultimate *realized* gain or loss will likely differ from the unrealized gain or loss each period. GAAP therefore requires firms to delay including the gain or loss in net income until the gain or loss is realized. In the meantime, the firm must include the unrealized gain or loss arising in each period in Other Comprehensive Income and the cumulative unrealized gain or loss in Accumulated Other Comprehensive Income. Recall from Chapter 1 that Accumulated Other Comprehensive Income is a balance sheet account appearing in shareholders' equity. Accumulated Other Comprehensive Income changes each period by the amount of Other Comprehensive Income for the period. Only at the time of realization of the value change will the firm include the realized gain or loss in net income. The firm must simultaneously remove any amounts in Accumulated Other Comprehensive Income related to the asset or liability. Accumulated Other Comprehensive Income serves as a "holding tank" for value changes recognized for assets and liabilities but not yet for net income.

Example 15

Refer to Example 9. Assume that Microsoft has cash in excess of its near-term needs. Rather than allow the cash to remain in its bank account, Microsoft purchases marketable equity securities costing $4,500,000. The fair value of these securities on December 31 is $4,900,000. Microsoft intends to sell these securities when it needs cash. The current fair value of these securities is likely of more interest to users of the firm's financial statements than acquisition cost. The ready market for these securities provides reliable evidence of their fair value.

GAAP requires Microsoft to revalue the securities to fair value and recognize an unrealized holding gain of $400,000 in Other Comprehensive Income. Thus, assets increase by $400,000 and shareholders' equity increases by $400,000.

Next, suppose that Microsoft sells the securities in early June of the following year for $5,000,000. The firm recognizes a realized gain on sale in net income of $500,000 (= $5,000,000 – $4,500,000). It must also eliminate the $400,000 unrealized gain from Accumulated Other Comprehensive Income. Thus, assets increase $100,000 (cash increases by $5,000,000 and Marketable Securities decreases by $4,900,000) and shareholders' equity increases by $100,000 (net income causes retained earnings to increase by $500,000, and Accumulated Other Comprehensive Income decreases by $400,000). Chapter 9 discusses the accounting for marketable securities more fully.

Example 16

Ford Motor Company operates in Europe through its subsidiary, Ford Europe. Ford Europe keeps its accounts in euros each period. Ford Motor Company must translate these euro amounts into their U.S. dollar equivalent amounts each period in order to prepare consolidated financial statements for the two entities. As the exchange rate between the U.S. dollar and the euro changes each period, the U.S. dollar equivalent of the euro-measured assets and liabilities of Ford Europe changes.

GAAP requires firms in most circumstances to use the current exchange rate on the date of the balance sheet to translate the assets and liabilities of foreign entities into U.S. dollars. The U.S. parent will not realize the economic effect of the value change, however, until the foreign unit remits cash to the parent and the parent converts the euro cash into U.S. dollars. GAAP therefore does not permit firms to flow through the unrealized foreign exchange gain or loss to net income immediately. Instead, firms must include the unrealized gain or loss in Other Comprehensive Income for the period. Later, when Ford Motor Company makes a currency conversion with the cash received, it realizes an exchange gain or loss and includes it in net income. It simultaneously reduces Accumulated Other Comprehensive Income for a portion of the unrealized gain or loss recognized in earlier periods. Chapter 9 discusses the accounting for foreign entities more fully.

TREATMENT 3: VALUE CHANGES RECOGNIZED ON THE BALANCE SHEET AND THE INCOME STATEMENT WHEN THEY OCCUR

The third possibility is that firms revalue assets and liabilities to fair value each period and recognize the unrealized gains and losses in net income in that same period. GAAP generally does not permit firms to revalue assets upward for value increases and recognize the unrealized gain in net income. Firms must await the validation of the value increase through a market transaction (that is, realization) to justify recognizing the gain.

GAAP, however, is not consistent with value decreases. Firms must generally write down assets whose fair values decrease below their book values and flow through the value decrease to net income immediately. This inconsistent treatment of gains and losses rests on the *conservatism convention*. Given the judgments often required in measuring net income, GAAP is more concerned that firms not overstate net income than that they understate it.

Example 17

Refer to Example 8. At the end of the first year after their acquisition, the landing rights of American Airlines have a book value of $120 million and a fair value of $55 million. The decrease in air travel results in an impairment in the value of the landing rights of $65 million (= $120 million − $55 million). American Airlines must write down the value of the landing rights and recognize an asset impairment loss of $65 million on its income statement. Thus, assets and shareholders' equity decrease by $65 million. It must recognize this loss even though the firm has not realized the loss in a market transaction. Chapter 6 discusses asset impairment losses more fully.

Example 18

Refer to Example 10. The book value of the computer equipment on Citicorp's books is $3,400,000. Assume that the fair value of the equipment is $2,600,000 as a result of technological obsolescence. GAAP requires Citicorp to write down the computer to $2,600,000 and recognize an asset impairment loss of $800,000 (= $3,400,000 − $2,600,000). Thus, assets and shareholders' equity decrease by $800,000.

Example 19

Refer to Example 11. Recall that the present value of the note payable on the books of Sun Trust Banks is $828,032 based on the historical interest rate of 8 percent. The decrease in interest rates to 6 percent results in an increase in the fair value of the note to $866,276. GAAP generally does not permit firms to revalue financial instruments to market value to reflect changes in interest rates. However, Sun Trust Banks may wish to repay the note prior to maturity. Sun Microsystems, the holder of the note, will likely set a price for earlier repayment that reflects current market interest rates at the time of repayment. For example, Sun Microsystems would probably require Sun Trust Banks to pay $866,276 to repay the note at this time if interest rates have declined to 6 percent.

Sun Trust Banks may obtain a hedging contract, referred to as a *derivative*, from another entity that protects the net amount Sun Trust Banks must pay to retire the debt prior to maturity. When firms acquire derivatives to hedge changes in value of a financial instrument, GAAP requires the firms to revalue both the financial instrument and the derivative to fair value each period and recognize unrealized gains and losses in net income immediately. In this example, Sun Trust Banks writes up the note payable from $828,032 to $866,272 and recognizes a loss in net income for the difference, $38,240. It would also revalue the derivative, which in this case is an asset. If the derivative perfectly hedges the change in interest rates, it will increase in value by $38,240 as well. Sun Trust Banks increases the derivative asset and recognizes a gain of $38,240. If the hedge is not perfectly effective, the gain and loss will not precisely offset and net income will increase or decrease for the difference (net of any tax effect). Chapter 8 discusses the accounting for financial instruments and derivatives. The discussion there indicates that not all unrealized gains and losses immediately flow through to net income, but instead may first flow through Other Comprehensive Income.

SUMMARY OF ASSET AND LIABILITY VALUATION AND INCOME RECOGNITION

The traditional accounting model relies mostly on historical values for assets and liabilities, and the realization and matching conventions for income recognition (Treatment 1 above). In this model, asset and liability valuation directly link to income measurement. Standard-setting bodies have increasingly required the use of fair values in the valuation of certain assets and liabilities in recent years. Some of these value changes (generally, declines in asset values) affect net income immediately (Treatment 3 above). GAAP invokes the conservatism convention to justify recognition of value declines but not value increases. Other value changes affect asset and liability amounts before they affect net income (Treatment 2 above). In the intervening time, firms park the unrealized gains and losses in Accumulated Other Comprehensive Income. When the firm realizes the value change, it reclassifies the unrealized gains and losses from Accumulated Other Comprehensive Income to net income. GAAP has not yet evolved to the point of providing a sufficient conceptual rationale for these three different approaches to asset and liability valuation and income measurement to permit the user of financial statements to anticipate, apart from prescribed GAAP, how firms account for any particular transaction. Given the tradeoffs between reliability and objectivity often encountered in setting GAAP for particular assets and liabilities and the different preferences and concerns of the various constituencies involved in the standard-setting process, obtaining agreement on a single valuation approach in the near future seems unlikely.

ACCOUNTING FOR INCOME TAXES

The discussion thus far in this chapter has considered the measurement of revenues, gains, expenses, and losses before considering any income tax effects. Income taxes affect virtually every transaction in which a firm engages. Consider the following examples:

- American Airlines in Example 17 and Citicorp in Example 18 must recognize impairment losses for financial reporting as the fair values of its assets decline. These firms cannot deduct such losses immediately for tax purposes, but instead must continue to depreciate or amortize them over time. Thus, GAAP and the income tax law treat these decreases in value differently.
- Microsoft in Example 15 includes the $400,000 increase in fair value of marketable equity securities in Other Comprehensive Income. The firm will report the effect of any value changes in taxable income only when it sells the securities. Should Microsoft recognize any income tax expense now on the $400,000 of Other Comprehensive Income?
- Ford Motor Company in Example 16 must include unrealized foreign exchange gains and losses in Other Comprehensive Income. The firm will not include such gains and losses in taxable income until the foreign unit remits cash to the parent company. If the foreign unit intends to reinvest its earnings permanently,

then it may never pay a dividend to its parent. When and how much income tax expense should Ford Motor Company recognize on the unrealized foreign exchange gain or loss?

Thus, in order to fully understand business transactions, we need to understand their income tax effects. Before discussing various financial reporting topics in Chapters 6 to 9, we need an overview of the required accounting for income taxes under GAAP. Chapter 8 discusses the accounting for income taxes more fully.

OVERVIEW OF INCOME TAX ACCOUNTING

Income taxes affect the analysis of a firm's profitability (income tax expense is a subtraction in computing net income) and its cash flows (income taxes paid are an operating use of cash). Income tax expense for a period does not necessarily equal income taxes payable for that period. The balance sheet recognizes the difference between the two amounts as a deferred tax asset or a deferred tax liability.

A simple example illustrates the issues in accounting for income taxes. Exhibit 2.3 sets forth information for a firm for its first two years of operations. The first column for each year shows the amounts reported to shareholders (referred to as "book amounts" or "financial reporting"). The second column shows the amounts reported to income tax authorities (referred to as "tax amounts" or "tax reporting"). The third

EXHIBIT 2.3						
Illustration of the Effects of Income Taxes on Net Income, Taxable Income, and Cash Flows						
	First Year			**Second Year**		
	Book Amounts	Tax Amounts	Cash Flow Amounts	Book Amounts	Tax Amounts	Cash Flow Amounts
Sales Revenue	$500	$500	$500	$500	$500	$500
Interest on Municipal Bonds . .	25	—	25	25	—	25
Depreciation Expense	(60)	(80)	—	(60)	(40)	—
Warranty Expense	(10)	(4)	(4)	(10)	(12)	(12)
Other Expenses	(300)	(300)	(300)	(300)	(300)	(300)
Net Income before Taxes or Taxable Income	$155	$116		$155	$148	
Income Tax Expense or Payable	(52)	(46.4)	(46.4)	(52)	(59.2)	(59.2)
Net Income	$103			$103		
Depreciation Addback	60			60		
Change in Warranty Liability . .	6			(2)		
Change in Deferred Taxes	5.6			(7.2)		
Cash Flow from Operations . . .	$174.6		174.6	$153.8		$153.8

column indicates the effect of each item on cash flows. Assume for this example and those throughout this chapter that the income tax rate is 40 percent. Additional information on each item is as follows:

- Sales Revenue: The firm reports sales of $500 each year for both book and tax reporting. We assume that it collects the full amount each year in cash (that is, the firm has no accounts receivable).
- Interest Revenue on Municipal Bonds: The firm earns $25 of interest on municipal bonds. The firm includes this amount in its book income. The federal government does not subject interest on state and municipal bonds to taxation, so we exclude this amount from the computation of taxable income. We assume that the firm receives the full amount of interest revenue in cash each year.
- Depreciation Expense: The firm has equipment costing $120 with a two-year life. It depreciates the equipment using the straight-line method for financial reporting, recognizing $60 of depreciation expense on its books each year. Income taxing authorities permit the firm to write off a larger portion of the asset's cost in the first year, $80, than the straight-line method. Because total depreciation over the life of an asset cannot exceed acquisition cost, the firm recognizes only $40 of depreciation for tax reporting in the second year.
- Warranty Expense: The firm estimates that the cost of providing warranty services on products sold equals 2 percent of sales. It recognizes warranty expense of $10 (=.02 × $500) each year for financial reporting, which matches the estimated cost of warranties against the revenue from the sale of products subject to warranty. Income tax laws do not permit firms to claim a deduction for warranties in computing taxable income until they make cash expenditures to provide warranty services. We assume that the firm incurs cash costs of $4 in the first year and $12 in the second year.
- Other Expenses: The firm incurs and pays in cash other expenses of $300 each year.
- Income Before Taxes and Taxable Income: Income before taxes for financial reporting is $155 each year. Taxable income is $116 in the first year and $148 in the second year.

Income before taxes for financial reporting differs from taxable income for two principal reasons:

1. **Permanent Differences:** Revenues and expenses that firms include in net income to shareholders but which never appear in the income tax return. Interest revenue on the municipal bond is a permanent difference.
2. **Temporary Differences:** Revenues and expenses that firms include in both net income to shareholders and in taxable income but in different periods. Depreciation expense is a temporary difference. The firm recognizes total depreciation of $120 over the life of the equipment for both financial and tax reporting but in a different pattern over time. Warranty expense is likewise a temporary difference. The firm recognizes $20 of warranty expense over the two-year period for financial reporting. It recognizes only $16 over the two-year period for tax reporting. If the firm's estimate of total warranty costs turn

out to be correct, then the firm will recognize the remaining $4 of warranty expense for tax reporting in future years as it provides warranty services.

A central conceptual question in accounting for income taxes concerns the measurement of income tax expense on the income statement for financial reporting:

1. Should the firm compute income tax expense based on book income before taxes ($155 for each year in Exhibit 2.3)?
2. Should the firm compute income tax expense based on book income before taxes but excluding permanent differences, ([$130 (= $155 − $25)] for each year in Exhibit 2.3)?
3. Should the firm compute income tax expense based on taxable income ($116 in the first year and $148 in the second year in Exhibit 2.3)?

Standard-setting bodies require firms to follow the second approach. Income tax expense is not simply the amount of income taxes currently payable (the third approach). Firms must also recognize the benefit of future tax deductions and the obligations related to future taxable income that arise because of temporary differences. The underlying concept is matching: matching income tax expense with the income reported for financial reporting, even though the associated cash flows for income taxes will not occur until future periods.

Permanent differences do not affect taxable income or income taxes paid in any year. Because total expenses over sufficiently long time periods must equal the related cash outflows, firms never recognize income tax expense or income tax savings on permanent differences (the first approach). Thus, income tax expense is $52 (=.40 × $130) in each year.

The firm makes the following entry to recognize income tax expense in the first year:

Income Tax Expense (.40 × $130)	52.0	
Deferred Tax Asset—Warranty (.40 × $6)	2.4	
Deferred Tax Liability—Depreciation (.40 × $20)		8.0
Income Taxes Payable (.40 × $116)		46.4

The deferred tax asset measures the future tax saving that the firm will realize when it provides warranty services in future years and claims a tax deduction on products sold in the first year. The firm expects to incur $6 (=$10 − $4) of warranty costs in the second and later years. When it incurs these costs, it will reduce its taxable income and reduce income taxes payable for the year. For financial reporting, the firm follows the matching principle and recognizes all of the $10 expected costs of providing warranty services on products sold during the first year.

The deferred tax liability measures the income taxes saved in the first year as a result of recognizing $20 more depreciation for tax purposes than for financial reporting purposes, taxes that the firm must pay in the second year when its recognizes $20 less depreciation for tax reporting than for financial reporting.

Now consider the effect on cash flows. The third column for each year in Exhibit 2.3 shows that the increases and decreases in cash net to $174.6 for the first year. This reporting format follows the *direct method* of computing cash flow from operations. As Chapter 3 discusses more fully, most firms report cash flow from operations using the *indirect method.* The indirect method begins with net income and then adjusts that amount to compute cash flow from operations.

The lower portion of the book income amounts in the first column demonstrates the calculation for the indirect method. Depreciation is an expense that does not use cash, so we add back the $60 of depreciation recognized for book purposes to offset its subtraction in measuring net income. The firm recognized warranty expense of $10 in measuring net income but used only $4 of cash in satisfying warranty claims. The firm adds back the $6 difference, which is the credit change in the warranty liability account during the period. The warranty liability account begins with a zero balance and ends the year with a balance of $6 (= $10 – $4). Likewise, the firm recognized $52 of income tax expense in measuring net income but used only $46.4 cash for income taxes. The firm adds back the $5.6 difference, which is the net credit change in the Deferred Tax Asset ($2.4 debit change) and Deferred Tax Liability ($8 credit change) accounts (see the preceding journal entry).

The firm makes the following entry in the second year to recognize income tax expense:

Income Tax Expense (.40 × $130)	52	
Deferred Tax Liability—Depreciation (.40 × $20)	8	
Deferred Tax Asset—Warranty (.40 × $2)		.8
Income Tax Payable (.40 × $148)		59.2

The temporary difference related to depreciation completely reversed in the second year, so the firm reduces the deferred tax liability to zero, which increases income taxes currently payable by $8. The temporary difference related to the warranty partially reversed during the second year, but the firm created additional temporary differences in that year. For the two years as a whole, warranty expense for financial reporting of $20 (= $10 + $10) exceeds the amount recognized for tax reporting of $16 (= $4 + $12). Thus, the firm will recognize tax savings of $1.6 (= .4 × $4) in future years. The deferred tax asset had a balance of $2.4 at the end of the first year. The entry for the second year reduces the balance in the deferred tax assets by $.8 (= $2.4 – $1.6) for the net tax benefit realized during that year.

Now consider the cash flow effects for the second year. Cash flow from operations is $153.8. The firm again adds back to net income depreciation expense of $60. The firm recognized warranty expense of $10 for financial reporting but used $12 of cash to satisfy warranty claims. It subtracts the additional $2 of cash used in excess of the expense. The $2 subtraction also equals the debit change in the warranty liability accounting during the second year, as the following analysis shows:

Warranty Liability, beginning of second year	$ 6
Warranty Expense, second year	10
Warranty Claims, second year	(12)
Warranty Liability, end of second year	$ 4

The firm recognized $52 of income tax expense but used $59.2 of cash for income taxes. It subtracts the additional $7.2 of cash used in excess of the expense. The $7.2 subtraction also equals the net debit change in the Deferred Tax Asset ($.8 credit change) and Deferred Tax Liability ($8 debit change) during the second year, as the following analysis shows:

Net Deferred Tax Liability, beginning of second year ($8 – $2.4)	$ 5.6
Income Tax Expense, second year	52.0
Income Taxes Payable, second year	(59.2)
Net Deferred Tax Asset, end of second year	$(1.6)

MEASURING INCOME TAX EXPENSE: A BIT MORE TO THE STORY

The illustration above followed what we might term an *income statement approach* to measuring income tax expense. We compared revenues and expenses recognized for book and tax purposes, eliminated permanent differences, and then computed income tax expense based on book income before taxes excluding permanent differences. Financial Accounting Standards Board *Statement 109*[1], however, requires firms to follow a *balance sheet approach* when computing income taxes expense. We describe the approach next.

1. Identify at each balance sheet date all differences between the book basis of assets, liabilities, and tax loss carryforwards (that is, the book values for financial reporting) and the tax basis of assets, liabilities, and tax loss carryforwards. Tax loss carryforwards represent net losses incurred in one year that the income tax law allows a firm to carry forward to offset positive taxable income in future years and thereby reduce taxes otherwise payable in those future years. In the illustration above, the book basis of the equipment at the end of the first year is $60 (= $120 – $60) and the tax basis is $40 (= $120 – $80). The book and tax basis are zero at the end of the second year. The book basis of the warranty liability at the end of the first year is $6 (= $10 – $4) and the tax basis is zero (that is, the firm recognizes a deduction for tax purposes when it

---

[1]Financial Accounting Standards Board, *Statement of Financial Accounting Standards No. 109,* "Accounting for Income Taxes," 1992.

pays warranty claims and therefore has no liability on its tax books). The book basis of the warranty liability at the end of the second year is $4 (= $6 + $10 − $12) and the tax basis is zero.

2. Eliminate differences from step 1 that will not have a future tax consequence (that is, permanent differences). Assume, for example, that the firm in the illustration above had not received the $25 of interest on the municipal bond investment by the end of the first year. It would show an Interest Receivable on its financial reporting books of $25, but no receivable would appear on its tax books. Because the tax law does not tax such interest, the difference between the book and tax basis is a permanent difference. The firm would eliminate this book/tax difference before moving to the next step.

3. Separate the remaining differences into those that give rise to future tax deductions and those that give rise to future taxable income. Exhibit 2.4 summarizes the possibilities and gives several examples of these temporary differences, as later chapters discuss. The difference between the book basis ($6) and the tax basis ($0) of the warranty liability at the end of the first year gives rise to future tax deductions. The difference between the book basis ($60) and the tax basis ($40) of the equipment at the end of the first year gives rise to future taxable income. Multiply differences that give rise to future tax deductions by the enacted marginal tax rate expected to apply in those future periods. The result is a deferred tax asset. The deferred tax asset related to warranties at the end of the first year is $2.4 [= .4 × ($6 − $0)]. Multiply differences that give rise to future taxable income by the enacted marginal tax rate expected to apply in those future periods. The result is a deferred tax liability. The deferred tax liability related to the equipment at the end of the first year is $8 [= .4 × ($60 − $40)]. A firm may have recognized net losses in its income statement for financial reporting but which the firm cannot then recognize for tax reporting. It can carry forward this net loss and offset taxable income of future years, thereby saving taxes. The firm includes the tax effect of tax loss carryforwards (reduce future taxable income) and tax credit carryforwards (reduce future taxes payable) in deferred tax assets at each balance sheet date.

4. Assess the likelihood that the firm will realize the benefits of deferred tax *assets* in the future. This assessment should consider the nature (whether cyclical or noncyclical, for example) and characteristics (growing, mature, or declining, for example) of a firm's business and its tax planning strategies for the future. If realization of the benefits of deferred tax assets is "more likely than not" (that is, exceeds 50 percent), then deferred tax assets equal the amounts computed in step 3. If it is more likely than not that the firm will *not* realize some or all of the deferred tax assets, then the firm must reduce the deferred tax asset for a *valuation allowance* (similar in concept to the allowance for uncollectible accounts receivable). The valuation allowance reduces the deferred tax assets to the amounts the firm expects to realize by way of reduced taxes in the future. Assume that the firm in the illustration above considers it more likely than not that it will realize the tax benefits of the deferred tax assets related to warranties and therefore recognizes no valuation allowance.

EXHIBIT 2.4
Examples of Temporary Differences

	Assets	*Liabilities*
Future Tax Deduction (results in deferred tax assets)	Tax Basis of Assets Exceeds Book (Financial Reporting) Basis[a]	Tax Basis of Liabilities is Less than Book (Financial Reporting) Basis[b]
Future Taxable Income (results in deferred tax liabilities)	Tax Basis of Assets is Less than Book (Financial Reporting) Basis[c]	Tax Basis of Liabilities Exceeds Book (Financial Reporting) Basis[d]

Examples

[a]Accounts receivable using the direct charge-off method for uncollectible accounts for tax purposes exceeds accounts receivable (net) using the allowance method for financial reporting.

[b]Tax reporting does not recognize an estimated liability for warranty claims (firms can deduct only actual expenditures on warranty claims), whereas firms must recognize such a liability for financial reporting to match warranty expense with sales revenue in the period of sale.

[c]Depreciation computed using accelerated depreciation for tax purposes and the straight-line method for financial reporting.

[d]Leases recognized by a *lessee*, the user of the leased assets, as a capital lease for tax reporting and an operating lease for financial reporting.

The result of this four-step procedure is a deferred tax asset and a deferred tax liability at each balance sheet date. The amounts in the illustration above are as follows:

	January 1, First Year	December 31, First Year	December 31, Second Year
Deferred Tax Asset— Warranties.	$0	$ 2.4	$1.6
Deferred Tax Liability— Equipment	0	8.0	0
Net Deferred Tax Asset (Liability)	$0	$(5.6)	$1.6

Income tax expense for each period equals:

1. Income taxes currently payable on taxable income;
2. Plus a credit change in the net deferred tax asset and liability, or minus a debit change in the net deferred tax asset and liability.

Income tax expense in the illustration above is:

	First Year	Second Year
Income Taxes Currently Payable on Taxable Income	$46.4	$59.2
Plus Credit Change in Net Deferred Tax Asset and Liability	5.6	—
Minus Debit Change in Net Deferred Tax Asset and Liability	—	(7.2)
Income Tax Expense................	$52.0	$52.0

The income statement approach illustrated in the first section and the balance sheet approach illustrated in this section yield identical results whenever (1) enacted tax rates applicable to future periods do not change, and (2) the firm recognizes no valuation allowance on deferred tax assets. Legislated changes in tax rates applicable to future periods will cause the tax effects of previously recognized temporary differences to differ from the amounts in the deferred tax asset and deferred tax liability accounts. The firm revalues the deferred tax assets and liabilities for the change in tax rates and flows through the effect of the change to income tax expense in the year of the legislated change. A change in the valuation allowance for deferred tax assets likewise flows through immediately to income tax expense.

REPORTING INCOME TAXES IN THE FINANCIAL STATEMENTS

Firms may not include all income taxes for a period on the line for income tax expense in the income statement. Some amounts may appear elsewhere:

1. Discontinued Operations, Extraordinary Items, Adjustments for Changes in Accounting Principles: Firms with any of the above categories of income for a particular period report them in separate sections of the income statement, each net of their income tax effects. Thus, income tax expense reflects income taxes on income from continuing operations only.
2. Other Comprehensive Income: Unrealized changes in the market value of marketable equity securities classified as "available for sale," unrealized changes in the market value of hedged financial instruments and derivatives classified as cash flow hedges, unrealized foreign translation adjustments, and changes in the minimum pension liability appear in Other Comprehensive Income, net of

their tax effects. These items almost always give rise to deferred tax assets or deferred tax liabilities because the income tax law does include such gains and losses in taxable income until realized in a market transaction. Thus, a portion of the change in deferred tax assets and liabilities on the balance sheet does not flow through income tax expense on the income statement.

We will return to our study of income taxes in Chapter 8 to explore in greater depth the concepts and procedures of accounting for income taxes.

FRAMEWORK FOR ANALYZING THE EFFECTS OF TRANSACTIONS ON THE FINANCIAL STATEMENTS

Each period, firms prepare financial statements that aggregate and summarize the results of numerous transactions. This section presents and illustrates an analytical framework for understanding the effects of various transactions on the financial statements.

One might legitimately ask the question: Why do I need to understand individual transactions when my concern is the analysis of financial statements as a whole? After all, firms engage in millions of transactions during the year, with no single transaction likely having a material effect on the financial statements. The response to this question is two-fold.

First, one must understand the effects of the numerous similar, repetitive transactions that dominate balance sheet and income statement amounts in order to make appropriate interpretations about a firm's profitability and risk. Consider the following examples from recent annual reports of several publicly traded corporations.

Example 20

PepsiCo combines various ingredients to produce syrup for its soft drinks. It sells the syrup to its bottlers, who add water and other ingredients to manufacture the finished soft drink and then bottle it. PepsiCo owns 30 to 40 percent of the common stock of its bottlers, with individuals and other entities owning the remainder. What is the effect on PepsiCo's net income when it sells syrup to its bottlers? Should it recognize revenue immediately in an amount equal to the selling price of the syrup, the same as it would if it sold the syrup to nonaffiliated bottlers? Or, should PepsiCo delay the recognition of revenue until the bottlers manufacture and sell soft drinks to customers? Should PepsiCo include all of the assets and liabilities of the bottlers in its balance sheet, a proportion of the assets and liabilities equal to its ownership percentage, or none of these assets and liabilities? How would the analysis of PepsiCo's profitability and risk differ depending on PepsiCo's accounting method for transactions with its bottlers?

Example 21

Xerox Corporation sells photocopying machines, photographic paper, and after-sale maintenance services in a bundled package to customers on a multi-year installment payment plan. Xerox generates four types of income from this activity: (1) manufacturing income from selling the machines for more than their manufacturing cost, (2) income from selling photographic paper for more than the cost of that paper to Xerox, (3) maintenance income from providing services over the life of the maintenance contract, and (4) interest income from providing financing services over the life of the installment sales contract. What is the impact on total assets and net income each year if Xerox attributes too much of the cash it will receive to the manufacturing activity and too little to the maintenance services? What is the impact on total assets and net income each year if Xerox uses a discount rate of 7 percent instead of 8 percent to discount the cash flows to their present value? What amount, if any, will appear among liabilities related to Xerox's obligation under the maintenance agreement?

Example 22

Enron entered into multi-year contracts to purchase and sell energy products at pre-set prices. To neutralize the risk of price changes during the term of the contracts, Enron also sold and purchased financial instruments, called *derivatives*. Enron created special purpose entities (SPEs), to which it transferred some of these energy contracts and derivatives in return for an equity interest. The SPEs also obtained equity capital from other investors. GAAP does not require firms to consolidate the financial statements of the SPEs with their own as long as the investor is not the primary beneficiary of the SPE, as discussed in Chapter 9. What is the effect on Enron's balance sheet if it retains the energy contracts and derivatives versus transferring them to the SPE? What is the effect on the income statement? Will it make a difference if Enron sells the energy contracts and derivatives versus transferring them for an equity interest?

A second response to the question about the need to understand the effects of individual transactions on the financial statements relates to the increased complexity of many nonrecurring transactions in recent years. Consider the following examples.

Example 23

Tyco International engaged in extensive restructuring of its operations, closing down or selling manufacturing facilities and severing employees. GAAP requires firms to recognize restructuring expenses when they commit to a restructuring plan, even though several years may elapse before completing the plan. Will the recognition of restructuring expense result in an immediate decrease in assets, an increase in liabilities, or both? What is the effect on the income statement when the firm actually closes or sells a manufacturing facility or severs employees? What is the effect on subsequent balance sheet and income statement amounts if the firm discovers later that its initial restructuring expense was too small or too large?

Example 24

Nortel Networks made numerous corporate acquisitions totaling $33.5 billion in recent years. It allocated $14.5 billion of the purchase price to identifiable assets, such as accounts receivable, inventories, plant, and equipment, and to identifiable liabilities, such as accounts payable and long-term debt. Nortel allocated the remaining $19 billion to goodwill. What is the effect on net income of subsequent years if Nortel had allocated more of the purchase price to identifiable assets and liabilities and less to goodwill? Nortel subsequently recognized a $12.3 billion goodwill impairment loss because the fair value of the acquired firms had declined since the acquisitions. What is the impact of the goodwill impairment loss on total assets, total liabilities, and shareholders' equity?

It is likely at this point that you experienced some difficulty in understanding the effects of each of these transactions on the financial statements. This is expected. Later chapters discuss these transactions in greater depth. The purpose of these examples is to illustrate the need for an analytical framework to structure your thinking about business transactions and their effect on the financial statements.

OVERVIEW OF ANALYTICAL FRAMEWORK

The analytical framework relies on the balance sheet equation:

$$\textbf{Assets} \quad = \textbf{Liabilities} \quad + \quad \textbf{Shareholders' Equity}$$

We can expand the equation as follows:

| | | | | | | **Contributed** | | **Accumulated Other** | | **Retained** |
| **Cash** | + | **Non-cash Assets** | = | **Liabilities** | + | **Capital** | + | **Comprehensive Income** | + | **Earnings** |

Using symbols:

| C | + | N$A | = | L | + | CC | + | AOCI | + | RE |

Firms prepare balance sheets at the beginning and end of a period. Thus:

C	+	N$A	=	L	+	CC	+	AOCI	+	RE
								Other Comprehensive Income		Net Income − Dividends
C	+	N$A	=	L	+	CC	+	AOCI	+	RE

Transactions during a period link balance sheets at the beginning and end of the period. Many value changes affect net income for the period and thereby affect changes in retained earnings for the period. Other value changes affect Other Comprehensive Income for the period and thereby affect changes in Accumulated Other Comprehensive Income for the period.

We illustrate this analytical framework using several of the transactions discussed earlier in this chapter.

Example 25

Refer to Example 13. Gallo Wines (1) sold for $2,000,000 on account (2) wine costing $1,600,000 to produce. (3) Gallo Wines recognizes revenues and expenses in the same period for financial and tax reporting and pays income taxes at a rate of 40 percent immediately. We use the following abbreviations throughout the examples:

BS-BOP: Balance Sheet at the Beginning of the Period
IBT: Income Before Taxes
OCE: Other Comprehensive Income
NI: Net Income
BS-EOP: Balance Sheet at the End of the Period

	C	+	N$A	=	L	+	CC	+	AOCI	+	RE
BS-BOP											
(1)			+2,000,000								+2,000,000
(2)			−1,600,000								−1,600,000
IBT											+ 400,000
(3)	−160,000										− 160,000
NI											+ 240,000
BS-EOP	−160,000		+ 400,000								+ 240,000

Net assets increase by $240,000 (= $400,000 - $160,000) and net income and retained earnings increase by $240,000.

Example 26

Refer to Example 14. (1) Red Lobster Restaurants sells for $145,700 land with a book value of $125,700. (2) Red Lobster recognizes the gain at the time of sale for both financial and tax reporting and pays taxes at a rate of 40 percent.

	C	+	N$A	=	L	+	CC	+	AOCI	+	RE
BS-BOP											
(1)	+145,700		−125,700								+20,000
IBT											+20,000
(2)	− 8,000										− 8,000
NI											+12,000
BS-EOP	+137,700		−125,700								+12,000

Net assets increase by $12,000 (= $137,700 − $125,700) and net income and retained earnings increase by $12,000.

Example 27

Refer to Example 15. Microsoft (1) purchases marketable securities costing $4,500,000 for cash, (2) revalues them to their $4,900,000 market value at the end of the period, (3) recognizes income taxes for the period, and (4) sells them for $5,000,000 during the next period. (5) The income tax law taxes gains and losses when realized at an income tax rate of 40 percent.

	C	+	N$A	=	L	+	CC	+	AOCI	+	RE
BS-BOP											
(1)	−4,500,000		+4,500,000								
(2)			+ 400,000						+400,000		
IBT									+400,000		
(3)					+160,000				−160,000		
OCI									+240,000		
BS-EOP	−4,500,000		+4,900,000		+160,000				+240,000		
(4)	+5,000,000		−4,900,000						−400,000		+500,000
IBT											+500,000
(5)	− 200,000				−160,000				+160,000		−200,000
NI											+300,000
BS-EOP	+ 300,000		0		0				0		+300,000

During the first year, Microsoft revalues the securities to market value and includes the $400,000 increase in Other Comprehensive Income. It recognizes a liability for future income taxes on the increase in value of $160,000 (= .4 × $400,000). Because Microsoft includes the pre-tax increase in value in Other Comprehensive Income, it reports the tax effect there as well (matching convention). The income tax law does not tax the unrealized gain immediately, so Microsoft increases its Deferred Tax Liability for $160,000. During the second year, Microsoft includes the realized gain of $500,000 in net income. It must reduce Accumulated Other Comprehensive Income for the $400,000 unrealized gain recognized in the first year. Thus, net income before taxes for the second year increases by $500,000 but shareholders' equity increases by only $100,000 (= $500,000 − $400,000), the value increase during the second year. The firm recognizes and pays $200,000 of income taxes on the realized gain. It must also eliminate the deferred tax liability of $160,000 recognized during the first year and eliminate income taxes of the same amount included in Accumulated Other Comprehensive Income.

Example 28

Refer to Examples 4, 8, and 17. American Airlines (1) purchases landing rights for $150 million, (2) amortizes the landing rights $30 million during the first year for both financial and tax reporting, (3) recognizes an asset impairment loss for the decline in fair value to $65 million at the end of the first year, and (4) recognizes the immediate tax savings from the amortization and the delayed tax savings from the asset impairment loss. The income tax law does not permit the firm to claim a tax deduction for the asset impairment immediately. Instead, it must continue to amortize the landing rights over their original expected life of five years.

	C	+	N$A	=	L	+	CC	+	AOCI	+	RE
BS-BOP											
(1)	−150		+150								
(2)			− 30								−30
(3)			− 65								−65
IBT											−95
(4)	+ 12		+ 26								+38
NI											−57
BS-EOP	−138		+ 81								+57

The income tax effects deserve elaboration. The income tax law requires firms to specify at the outset an expected useful life for the landing rights and to amortize them over this period. American Airlines selects five years as the useful life and amortizes $30 million a year. The firm realizes an immediate tax savings of $12 million for the $30 million of amortization expense recognized for financial and tax reporting. GAAP requires the firm to recognize the $65 million asset impairment loss, but the tax law does not permit American Airlines to claim an immediate tax deduction. Instead, it implicitly includes this amount as part of its amortization deduction over the remaining four years of useful life. Thus, the $65 million asset impairment loss gives rise to a $26 million (= .4 × $65 million) deferred tax asset for the future tax benefits of writing off the landing rights for tax purposes.

Example 29

Refer to Example 5. Sun Trust Bank (1) purchases a computer by giving a note with a present value of $998,178 (= present value of $250,000 a year for five years at 8 percent), (2) recognizes depreciation of $199,636 (= $998,178/5) on the computer for the first year based on a five-year useful life, (3) recognizes interest expense for the first year of $79,854 (= .08 × $998,178), the cash payment of $250,000, and the reduction in principal of $170,146 (= $250,000 − $79,854), and (4) recognizes the tax savings from depreciation and interest deductions.

	C	+	N$A	=	L	+	CC	+	AOCI	+	RE
BS-BOP											
(1)			+998,178		+998,178						
(2)			−199,636								−199,636
(3)	250,000				−170,146						− 79,854
IBT											−279,490
(4)	+111,796										+111,796
NI											−167,694
BS-EOP	−138,204		+798,542		+828,032						−167,694

SUMMARY OF ANALYTICAL FRAMEWORK

This analytical framework may seem a bit unfamiliar at this stage in your study. Repeated use in later chapters will not only increase your comfort but demonstrate its richness in understanding the financial statement effects of a variety of complex business transactions. You may find it useful to practice using the framework with several familiar transactions. Several problems at the end of the chapter require the use of this analytical framework.

SUMMARY

This chapter provides the conceptual foundation for understanding the balance sheet and the income statement. Assets and liabilities on the balance sheet may reflect either historical values or current values. The conventional accounting model uses historical, or acquisition, costs to value assets and liabilities, and delays the recognition of value changes until external market transactions validate their amounts. Use of acquisition costs generally results in more objective financial statements than current values, but such statements might provide less relevant information to users desiring to value the firm. Recognizing value changes for assets and liabilities still leaves open the question of when the value change should affect net income. Such value changes might affect net income immediately or affect it later, initially lodging in Accumulated Other Comprehensive Income until validated by an external market transaction. Over sufficiently long time periods, net income equals cash inflows minus cash outflows, other than cash transactions with owners. Different approaches to asset and liability valuation and to income measurement affect the pattern of net income over time but not its ultimate amount.

Virtually every transaction affecting net income has an income tax effect. The accounting issue is whether firms should recognize the income tax effect when the related revenue or expense affects net income for financial reporting, or when it affects taxable income. That is, should the income tax match against the book amounts or the tax amounts? GAAP requires firms to measure income tax expense each period based on the pre-tax income for financial reporting. When income tax expense differs from income taxes currently payable on taxable income, firms recognize deferred tax assets and deferred tax liabilities. Deferred tax assets arise when taxable income exceeds book income. Firms prepay taxes now but reduce taxes paid later when the temporary difference reverses and book income exceeds taxable income. Deferred tax liabilities arise when book income exceeds taxable income. Firms delay paying taxes now but will pay the taxes later when the temporary differences reverse and taxable income exceeds book income.

Later chapters discuss the accounting for various assets, liabilities, revenues, and expenses. The analytical framework discussed in this chapter provides a tool for analyzing business transactions and understanding their effects on the financial statements. The analytical framework uses the balance sheet equation and changes in balance sheet amounts between the beginning and end of a period as its structuring device. You may not yet feel comfortable using this analytical framework, but repeated use in later chapters will demonstrate its richness as a tool of analysis.

PROBLEMS AND CASES

2.1 EFFECT OF VALUATION METHOD FOR NONMONETARY ASSET ON BALANCE SHEET AND INCOME STATEMENT.   Wal-Mart acquires a tract of land on January 1, Year 11, for $100,000 cash. On December 31, Year 11, the current market value of the land is $150,000. On December 31, Year 12, the current market value of the land is $120,000. The firm sells the land on December 31, Year 13, for $180,000 cash.

Required

Ignore income taxes. Using the analytical framework discussed in the chapter, indicate the effect of the information above for Year 11, Year 12, and Year 13 under each of the following valuation methods:
  a. Valuation of the land at acquisition until sale of the land.
  b. Valuation of the land at current market value but include unrealized gains and losses in Accumulated Other Comprehensive Income until sale of the land.
  c. Valuation of the land at current market value and include market value changes each year in net income.
  d. Why is retained earnings on December 31, Year 13, equal to $80,000 in all three cases despite the reporting of different amounts of net income each year?

2.2 EFFECT OF VALUATION METHOD FOR MONETARY ASSET ON BALANCE SHEET AND INCOME STATEMENT.   Refer to Problem 2.1. Assume that Wal-Mart sells the land on December 31, Year 13, for a note receivable with a present value of $180,000 instead of for cash. The note bears interest at 8 percent and requires cash payments of $100,939 on December 31, Year 14 and Year 15. Interest rates for notes of this risk level increase to 10 percent on December 31, Year 14, resulting in a market value for the note on this date of $91,762.

Required

Ignore income taxes. Using the analytical framework discussed in the chapter, indicate the effect of the information above for Year 14 and Year 15 under each of the following valuation methods:

a. Valuation of the note at the present value of future cash flows using the historical market interest rate of 8 percent.

b. Valuation of the note at the present value of future cash flows using the current market interest rate of 8 percent for Year 14, and 10 percent for Year 15. Include unrealized holding gains and losses in net income.

c. Why is retained earnings on December 31, Year 15, equal to $101,878 in both cases despite the reporting of different amounts of net income each year?

2.3 EFFECT OF VALUATION METHOD FOR NONMONETARY ASSET ON BALANCE SHEET AND INCOME STATEMENT. General Motors (GM) acquired equipment used in its administrative activities for $100,000 on January 1, Year 11. The equipment had an expected useful life of four years and zero salvage value. GM calculates depreciation using the straight-line method over the remaining expected useful life in all cases. On December 31, Year 11, after recognizing depreciation for the year, GM learns that new equipment now offered on the market makes the equipment that GM purchased partially obsolete. The market value of the equipment on December 31, Year 11, reflecting this obsolescence, is $60,000. The expected useful life does not change. On December 31, Year 12, the market value of the equipment is $48,000. GM sells the equipment on January 1, Year 14, for $26,000.

Required

Ignore income taxes.

a. Assume for this part that GM accounts for the equipment using acquisition cost adjusted for depreciation and impairment losses. Using the analytical framework discussed in the chapter, indicate the effect of the following events on the balance sheet and income statement:

   (1) Acquisition of the equipment for cash on January 1, Year 11.
   (2) Depreciation for Year 11.
   (3) Impairment loss for Year 11.
   (4) Depreciation for Year 12.
   (5) Depreciation for Year 13.
   (6) Sale of the equipment on January 1, Year 14.

b. Assume for this part that GM accounts for the equipment using current market values adjusted for depreciation and impairment losses. Using the analytical framework discussed in the chapter, indicate the effect of the following events on the balance sheet and income statement.

   (1) Acquisition of the equipment for cash on January 1, Year 11.
   (2) Depreciation for Year 11.
   (3) Impairment loss for Year 11.
   (4) Depreciation for Year 12.

(5) Recognition of unrealized holding gain or loss for Year 12.

(6) Depreciation for Year 13.

(7) Recognition of unrealized holding gain or loss for Year 13.

(8) Sale of the equipment on January 1, Year 14.

c. After selling the equipment, why is retained earnings on January 1, Year 14, equal to a negative $74,000 in both cases, despite showing a different pattern of expenses, gains, and losses over time?

2.4 EFFECT OF VALUATION METHOD FOR MONETARY ASSET ON BALANCE SHEET AND INCOME STATEMENT. Mercedes Benz (MB) incurs costs of $30,000 in manufacturing an automobile during Year 11. Assume that it incurs all of these costs in cash. MB sells this automobile to you on January 1, Year 12, for $45,000. You pay $5,000 immediately and agree to pay $14,414 on December 31 of Year 12, Year 13, and Year 14. Based on the interest rate appropriate for this note of 4 percent on January 1, Year 12, the present value of the note is $40,000. The interest rate appropriate to this note is 5 percent on December 31, Year 13, resulting in a present value of the remaining cash flows of $26,802. The interest rate appropriate to this note is 8 percent on December 31, Year 14, resulting in a present value of the remaining cash flows of $13,346.

Required

Ignore income taxes.

a. Assume for this part that MB accounts for this note throughout the three years using the historical market interest rate of 4 percent. Using the analytical framework discussed in the chapter, indicate the effect of the following events on the balance sheet and income statement.

(1) Manufacture of the automobile during Year 10.

(2) Sale of the automobile on January 1, Year 11.

(3) Cash received and interest revenue recognized on December 31, Year 12.

(4) Cash received and interest revenue recognized on December 31, Year 13.

(5) Cash received and interest revenue recognized on December 31, Year 14.

b. Assume for this part that MB accounts for this note using the current market interest rate each year. Changes in market interest rates affect the valuation of the note on the balance sheet immediately and the computation of interest revenue for the next year.

(1) Manufacture of the automobile during Year 10.

(2) Sale of the automobile on January 1, Year 11.

(3) Cash received and interest revenue recognized on December 31, Year 12.

(4) Note receivable revalued and an unrealized holding gain or loss recognized on December 31, Year 12.

(5) Cash received and interest revenue recognized on December 31, Year 13.

(6) Note receivable revalued and an unrealized holding gain or loss recognized on December 31, Year 13.

(7) Cash received and interest revenue recognized on December 31, Year 14.

c. Why is retained earnings on December 31, Year 14, equal to $18,241 in both cases, despite showing a different pattern of income over time?

2.5 INTERPRETING INCOME TAX DISCLOSURES. The financial statements of Target Corporation, a retail chain, reveal the following information (amounts in millions).

For the Year Ended December 31:	Year 11	Year 10
Income Before Income Taxes		
United States	$2,216	$2,063
Income Tax Expense		
Current:		
Federal	$ 686	$ 675
State and Local.............................	107	113
Total Current.............................	$ 793	$ 788
Deferred:		
Federal	$ 43	$ (1)
State and Local.............................	6	2
Total Deferred	$ 49	$ 1
Total.....................................	$ 842	$ 789

December 31:	Year 11	Year 10	Year 9
Components of Deferred Tax Assets			
and Liabilities			
Deferred Tax Assets:			
Self-insured Benefits....................	$ 172	$ 167	$ 146
Deferred Compensation................	160	143	130
Inventory	138	100	84
Post Retirement Health Care Obligation...	41	40	41
Uncollectible Accounts................	99	64	63
Other................................	97	99	106
Total Deferred Tax Assets	$ 707	$ 613	$ 570
Deferred Tax Liabilities:			
Depreciation..........................	(519)	(460)	(408)
Pensions	(109)	(53)	(45)
Other................................	(71)	(43)	(59)
Total Deferred Tax Liabilities	$(699)	$(556)	$(512)
Net Deferred Tax Asset	$ 8	$ 57	$ 58

Required

a. Assuming that Target had no significant permanent differences between book income and taxable income, did income before taxes for financial reporting exceed or fall short of taxable income for Year 10? Explain.

b. Did income before taxes for financial reporting exceed or fall short of taxable income for Year 11? Explain.

c. Will the adjustment to net income for deferred taxes to compute cash flow from operations in the statement of cash flows result in an addition or subtraction for Year 10? For Year 11?

d. Target does not contract with an insurance agency for property and liability insurance, but instead self-insures. Target recognizes an expense and a liability each year for financial reporting to reflect its average expected long-term property and liability losses. When it experiences an actual loss, it charges it against the liability. The income tax law permits a deduction for such losses only in the year sustained when firms self-insure. Why are deferred taxes related to self-insurance disclosed as a deferred tax asset instead of a deferred tax liability? Suggest reasons for the direction of the change in amounts for this deferred tax asset between Year 9 and Year 11.

e. Target treats certain storage and other inventory costs as expenses in the year incurred for financial reporting but must include these in inventory for tax reporting. Why are deferred taxes related to inventory disclosed as a deferred tax asset? Suggest reasons for the direction of the change in amounts for this deferred tax asset between Year 9 and Year 11.

f. Firms must recognize expenses related to postretirement health care and pension obligations as employees provide services but claim an income tax deduction only when they make cash payments under the benefit plan. Why are deferred taxes related to health care obligation disclosed as a deferred tax asset? Why are deferred taxes related to pensions disclosed as a deferred tax liability? Suggest reasons for the direction of the change in amounts for these deferred tax items between Year 9 to Year 11.

g. Firms must recognize expenses related to uncollectible accounts when they recognize sales revenues but claim an income tax deduction when they deem a particular customer's accounts uncollectible. Why are deferred taxes related to this item disclosed as a deferred tax asset? Suggest reasons for the direction of the change in amounts for this deferred tax asset between Year 9 and Year 11.

h. Target uses the straight-line depreciation method for financial reporting and accelerated depreciation methods for income tax purposes. Why are deferred taxes related to depreciation disclosed as a deferred tax liability? Suggest reasons for the direction of the change in amounts for this deferred tax liability between Year 9 and Year 11.

2.6 INTERPRETING INCOME TAX DISCLOSURES.

The financial statements of Starbucks Corporation, a retail coffeehouse chain, reveal the following information (amounts in millions).

For the Year Ended December 31:	Year 11	Year 10
Income Before Income Taxes		
United States	$289	$161
Income Tax Expense		
Current:		
Federal	$ 95	$ 72
State and Local	18	12
Total Current	$113	$ 84
Deferred	(5)	(18)
Total	$108	$ 66

December 31:	Year 11	Year 10	Year 9
Components of Deferred Tax Assets and Liabilities			
Deferred Tax Assets:			
Loss on Investments	$ 24	$ 23	$ —
Deferred Compensation	10	9	6
Accrued Rent	12	10	8
Other	21	17	12
Gross Deferred Tax Assets	$ 67	$ 59	$ 26
Valuation Allowance	(9)	(6)	—
Net Deferred Tax Assets	$ 58	$ 53	$ 26
Deferred Tax Liabilities:			
Depreciation	(39)	(36)	(30)
Investments in Joint Ventures	(5)	(5)	(4)
Other	(1)	(4)	(2)
Total Deferred Tax Liabilities	$(45)	$(45)	$(36)
Net Deferred Tax Asset (Liability)	$ 13	$ 8	$(10)

Required

a. Assuming that Starbucks had no significant permanent differences between book income and taxable income, did income before taxes for financial reporting exceed or fall short of taxable income for Year 10? Explain.

b. Did book income before taxes for financial reporting exceed or fall short of taxable income for Year 11? Explain.

c. Will the adjustment to net income for deferred taxes to compute cash flow from operations in the statement of cash flows result in an addition or subtraction for Year 10? For Year 11?

d. Starbucks holds investments in the equity securities of several Internet companies for which it recognized impairment losses for financial reporting. Starbucks cannot claim an income tax deduction for these losses until it realizes the loss at the time of sale. Why do the deferred taxes for losses on these investments appear as deferred tax assets instead of deferred tax liabilities?

e. Starbucks recognizes an expense related to retirement benefits as employees rendered services but cannot claim an income tax deduction until it pays cash to a retirement fund. Why do the deferred taxes for deferred compensation appear as a deferred tax asset? Suggest possible reasons why the deferred tax asset increased between the end of Year 9 and the end of Year 11.

f. Starbucks rents retail space for its coffeehouses. It must recognize rent expense as it uses rental facilities but cannot claim an income tax deduction until it pays cash to the landlord. Suggest the scenario that would give rise to a deferred tax asset instead of a deferred tax liability related to rent.

g. Starbucks recognizes a valuation allowance on its deferred tax assets related to losses on investments because the benefits of some of these losses will expire before the firm will realize the benefits. Why might the valuation allowance have increased between Year 10 and Year 11?

h. Starbucks uses the straight-line depreciation method for financial reporting and accelerated depreciation for income tax reporting. Why do the deferred taxes related to depreciation appear as deferred tax liabilities? Suggest possible reasons why the amount of the deferred tax liability related to depreciation increased between Year 9 and Year 11.

i. Starbucks recognizes its share of the earnings from investments in joint ventures each year for financial reporting but recognizes income from these investments for income tax reporting only when it receives a dividend. Why do the deferred taxes related to joint ventures appear as a deferred tax liability?

2.7 INTERPRETING INCOME TAX DISCLOSURES.   The financial statements of
Ford Motor Company reveal the following information (amounts in millions).

For the Year Ended December 31:	Year 11	Year 10
Income Before Income Taxes		
United States	$(6,015)	$9,559
Non-United States	(1,085)	(1,241)
Total	$(7,100)	$8,318
Income Tax Expense		
Current:		
Federal	$ 22	$ 154
Non-United States	103	760
State and Local	—	116
Total Current	$ 125	$1,030
Deferred:		
Federal	$(2,126)	$2,617
Non-United States	(248)	(1,153)
State and Local	98	211
Total Deferred	$(2,276)	$1,675
Total	$(2,151)	$2,705

December 31:	Year 11	Year 10	Year 9
Components of Deferred Tax Assets and Liabilities			
Deferred Tax Assets:			
Employee Benefit Plans	$ 5,895	$ 5,138	$ 4,195
Dealer and Customer Allowances			
and Claims	1,919	2,365	2,709
Credit Losses	1,518	1,067	1,006
Other	8,297	4,026	2,068
Total Deferred Tax Assets	$ 17,629	$ 12,596	$ 9,978
Deferred Tax Liabilities:			
Depreciation	(11,784)	(11,753)	(9,902)
Finance Receivables	(2,388)	(2,593)	(1,328)
Other	(5,084)	(2,153)	(976)
Total Deferred Tax Liabilities	$(19,256)	$(16,499)	$(12,206)
Net Deferred Tax Asset (Liability)	$ (1,627)	$ (3,903)	$ (2,228)

Required

a. Assuming that Ford had no significant permanent differences between book income and taxable income, did income before taxes for financial reporting exceed or fall short of taxable income for Year 10? Explain.

b. Did net loss before taxes for financial reporting exceed or fall short of taxable loss for Year 11? Explain.

c. Will the adjustment to net income for deferred taxes to compute cash flow from operations in the statement of cash flows result in an addition or subtraction for Year 10? For Year 11?

d. Firms must recognize expenses related to employee benefit plans as employees provide services but claim an income tax deduction only when they make cash payments to the benefit plan. Why are deferred taxes related to employee benefit plans disclosed as a deferred tax asset instead of a deferred tax liability? Suggest reasons for the direction of the change in amounts for this deferred tax asset between Year 9 to Year 11.

e. Firm must recognize expenses related to dealer and customer allowances and claims when they recognize sales revenues but claim an income tax deduction when they make cash payments or provide warranty services. Why are deferred taxes related to this item disclosed as a deferred tax asset? Suggest reasons for the direction of the change in amounts for this deferred tax asset between Year 9 and Year 11.

f. Firms must recognize expenses for credit losses as they recognize sales revenues but claim an income tax deduction when they establish the uncollectibility of a particular customer's account. Why are deferred taxes related to credit losses disclosed as a deferred tax asset? Suggest reasons for the direction of the change in amounts for this deferred tax asset between Year 9 and Year 11.

g. Ford uses the straight-line depreciation method for financial reporting and accelerated depreciation methods for income tax purposes. Why are deferred taxes related to depreciation disclosed as a deferred tax liability? Suggest reasons for the direction of the change in amounts for this deferred tax liability between Year 9 and Year 11.

h. Ford leases automobiles and trucks to customers under multi-year leases. For financial reporting, Ford treats these leases as capital, or financing, leases, with income from the manufacturing activity recognized at the time of delivery of the vehicle to the customer and interest revenue on the finance receivable recognized over time. For tax reporting, Ford treats these arrangements as operating leases, with rent revenue recognized over time as customers make periodic lease payments. Why are deferred taxes related to finance receivables disclosed as a deferred tax liability? Suggest reasons for the direction of the change in amounts for this deferred tax liability between Year 9 and Year 11.

2.8 ANALYZING TRANSACTIONS. Using the analytical framework illustrated in the chapter, indicate the effect of the following related transactions of a firm:

a. January 1: Issued 10,000 shares of common stock for $50,000.

b. January 1: Acquired a building costing $35,000, paying $5,000 in cash and borrowing the remainder from a bank.

c. During the year: Acquired inventory costing $40,000 on account from various suppliers.

d. During the year: Sold inventory costing $30,000 for $65,000 on account.

e. During the year: Paid employees $15,000 as compensation for services rendered during the year.

f. During the year: Collected $45,000 from customers related to sales on account.

g. During the year: Paid merchandise suppliers $28,000 related to purchases on account.

h. December 31: Recognized depreciation on the building of $7,000 for financial reporting. Depreciation expense for income tax purposes was $10,000.

i. December 31: Recognized compensation for services rendered during the last week in December but not paid by year end of $4,000.

j. December 31: Recognized and paid interest on the bank loan in b of $2,400 for the year.

k. Recognized income taxes on the net effect of the transactions above at an income tax rate of 40 percent. Assume that the firm pays cash immediately for any taxes currently due to the government.

2.9 ANALYZING TRANSACTIONS. Using the analytical framework illustrated in the chapter, indicate the effect of each of the three independent sets of transactions described next.

a. (1) January 15, Year 10: Purchased marketable equity securities for $100,000.

  (2) December 31, Year 10: Revalued the marketable securities to their market value of $90,000. Unrealized changes in the market value of marketable equity securities appear in Accumulated Other Comprehensive Income.

  (3) December 31, Year 10: Recognized income tax effects of the revaluation in item (2) at an income tax rate of 40 percent. The income tax law includes changes in the market value of equity securities in taxable income only when the investor sells the securities.

  (4) January 5, Year 11: Sold the marketable equity securities for $94,000.

  (5) January 5, Year 11: Recognized the tax effect of the sale of the securities in transaction (4). Assume that the tax effect affects cash immediately.

b. (1) During Year 11: Sells inventory on account for $500,000.

  (2) During Year 11: The cost of the goods sold in (1) is $400,000.

  (3) During Year 11: Estimated that uncollectible accounts on the goods sold in (1) will equal 2 percent of the selling price.

  (4) During Year 11: Estimated that warranty claims on the goods sold in (1) will equal 4 percent of the selling price.

  (5) During Year 11: Actual accounts written off as uncollectible totaled $3,000.

  (6) During Year 11: Actual cash expenditures on warranty claims totaled $8,000.

  (7) December 31, Year 11: Recognized income tax effects of the six transactions

above. The income tax rate is 40 percent. The income tax law permits a deduction for uncollectible accounts when a firm writes off accounts as uncollectible and for warranty claims when a firm makes warranty expenditures. Assume that any tax effect on taxable income affects cash immediately.

c. (1) January 1, Year 11: Purchased $100,000 face value of zero-coupon bonds for $68,058. These bonds mature on December 31, Year 15, and are priced on the market at the time of issuance to yield 8 percent compounded annually. Zero-coupon bonds earn interest as time passes for financial and tax reporting but the issuer does not pay interest until maturity. Assume that any tax effect on taxable income affects cash immediately.

(2) December 31, Year 11: Recognized interest revenue on the bonds for Year 11.

(3) December 31, Year 11: Recognized income tax effect of the interest revenue for Year 11. The income tax law taxes interest on zero-coupon bonds as it accrues each year.

(4) December 31, Year 12: Recognized interest revenue on the bonds for Year 12.

(5) December 31, Year 12: Recognized income tax effect of the interest revenue for Year 12.

(6) January 2, Year 13: Sold the zero-coupon bonds for $83,683.

(7) January 2, Year 13: Recognized the income tax effect of the gain or loss on the sale. The applicable income tax rate is 40 percent and affects cash immediately.

Chapter 3

INCOME FLOWS VERSUS CASH FLOWS: KEY RELATIONSHIPS IN THE DYNAMICS OF A BUSINESS

Learning Objectives
1. Understand the relation between net income and cash flow from operations for firms in various industries.
2. Understand the relation between cash flows from operating, investing, and financing activities for firms in various stages of their life cycles.
3. Prepare a statement of cash flows from balance sheet and income statement data.

The income statement reports the revenues and expenses of a firm during a period of time following the principles of the accrual basis of accounting. The objective in preparing an income statement is to obtain a measure of operating performance that matches a firm's outputs (revenues) with associated inputs (expenses). Accrual accounting aims to provide a measure of operating performance that accomplishes this desired matching. The accrual basis of accounting ignores the timing of cash receipts when recognizing revenues and the timing of cash expenditures when recognizing expenses. The desire to match revenues and expenses in measuring operating performance overrides the desirability of reporting information on an important ingredient for remaining in business: cash flows. Thus, the need arises for another financial statement that reports the flows of cash in and out of a firm: the statement of cash flows.

Chapter 1 points out that a firm's cash flows will not precisely track, or mirror, its income flows[1] each period because (1) cash receipts from customers do not necessarily occur in the same period that a firm recognizes revenues, (2) cash expenditures to employees, suppliers, and governments do not necessarily occur in the same period that a firm recognizes expenses, and (3) cash inflows and outflows occur relating to investing and financing activities that do not immediately flow through the income statement. Thus, to augment information on operating performance in accrual-based net income, firms prepare a statement of cash flows that reports the relation between income flows and cash flows from operations. It also reports the cash flow effects of investing and financing activities.

---

[1]This chapter uses income flows to mean net income and not revenues.

An understanding of cash flows is helpful in each of the five steps in financial statement analysis discussed in Chapter 1:

- Identifying the Economic Characteristics of a Business: The pattern of cash flows from operating, investing, and financing activities differs for various types of businesses and for firms in various stages of their life cycle. High growth, capital-intensive firms likely experience insufficient cash flow from operations to finance capital expenditures and require external financing to maintain their growth. Mature consumer products companies usually generate more than sufficient cash flow from operations to finance their modest needs for capital expenditures and can use the excess cash flow to repay debt, pay dividends, or repurchase common stock.
- Identify the Strategy of the Firm: The analyst should expect a rapidly growing capital-intensive firm to invest heavily in fixed assets. A firm pursuing a strategy of growth by acquiring other firms should report significant cash outflows for corporate acquisitions. A firm divesting of non-core businesses should report cash inflows from disposing of these businesses.
- Adjust the Financial Statements for Nonrecurring, Unusual Items: An analyst who chooses to eliminate nonrecurring or unusual items from net income to assess ongoing operating performance should also adjust cash flow from operations for these items.
- Analyze Profitability and Risk: Chapter 2 makes clear that, over sufficiently long periods, net income equals the net cash flow from operating, investing, and non-owner financing activities. Thus, a reality check on net income is that it should converge on this net cash flow amount. Also, the ability of a firm to generate sufficient cash flow from operations to finance capital expenditures and repay borrowing is a key signal of the financial health of the firm.
- Value the Firm: Chapter 11 discusses the use of free cash flow in the valuation of a firm. Free cash flow to all debt and common equity stakeholders approximately equals cash flow from operations in excess of cash flow from investing. Free cash flow to common equity shareholders equals cash flows from operations in excess of cash flow from investing and cash flow from non-owner (debt) financing. Discounting these cash flows at the appropriate discount rate yields the value of total debt plus equity and total equity, respectively.

This chapter explores the statement of cash flows in greater depth than the overview presented in Chapter 1. We look at the relation between income flows and cash flow from operations for various types of businesses and at the relation between the cash flows from operating, investing, and financing activities for firms in various stages of their life cycles. We also describe and illustrate procedures for preparing the statement of cash flows using information from the balance sheet and income statement.[2]

---

[2]*Statement No. 95* defines cash flows in terms of their effect on cash and cash equivalents. Cash equivalents include highly liquid investments that are both readily convertible into cash and so near to maturity that changes in interest rates present an insignificant risk to their market value. Cash equivalents usually include Treasury bills, commercial paper, and money market funds. Throughout this book, we use the term *cash* to mean cash and cash equivalents. See Financial Accounting Standards Board, *Statement of Financial Accounting Standards No. 95,* "Statement of Cash Flows," 1987.

INCOME FLOWS, CASH FLOWS, AND LIFE CYCLE RELATIONS

Interpreting the statement of cash flows requires an understanding of two relations:

1. The relation between net income and cash flow from operations.
2. The relation among the net cash flows from operating, investing, and financing activities.

NET INCOME AND CASH FLOW FROM OPERATIONS

The first section of the statement of cash flows reports the amount of cash flow from operations: the cash received from selling goods and services to customers net of the cash paid to suppliers, employees, governments, and other providers of goods and services. Firms present cash flow from operations in one of two formats: the direct method or the indirect method. Under the *direct method*, firms list the cash inflows from selling goods and services and then subtract the cash outflows to providers of goods and services. The top panel of Exhibit 3.1 shows the direct method of calculating cash flow from operations for Forest City Enterprises, a real estate development company.

Under the *indirect method*, firms begin with net income to calculate cash flow from operations for the period. The provisional assumption is that cash increased by the amount of revenues and decreased by the amount of expenses. However, not all revenues result in simultaneous cash receipts and not all expenses result in simultaneous cash expenditures. Firms must then adjust net income for noncash revenues and expenses to obtain cash flow from operations. The lower panel of Exhibit 3.1 illustrates the indirect method of presentation. The vast majority of firms use the indirect method because it reconciles net income for a period with the net amount of cash received or paid from operations. Critics of the indirect method suggest that the rationale for some of the reconciling items is difficult for less sophisticated users to understand. We use the indirect method throughout this text because of its widespread use by business firms.

The calculation of cash flow from operations under the indirect method involves two types of adjustments: (1) adjusting revenues and expenses for changes in non-working capital accounts (for example, depreciation, deferred income taxes), and (2) adjusting revenues and expenses for changes in operating working capital accounts (for example, accounts receivable, inventories, accounts payable).

Changes in Non-working Capital Accounts

Certain revenues and expenses relate to changes in noncurrent asset or noncurrent liability accounts and have cash flow effects that differ from their income effects. For example, depreciation expense reduces net property, plant, and equipment and net income. However, depreciation expense does not require an *operating* cash outflow in the period of the expense (on the contrary, firms classify the cash outflow to

EXHIBIT 3.1

Cash Flow from Operations Presented in Direct and Indirect Methods for Forest City Enterprises (amounts in millions)

	Year Ended January 31		
	Year 11	Year 10	Year 9
Direct Method			
Rents and Other Revenues Received..........................	$531	$508	$480
Proceeds from Land Sales.......................	44	45	42
Land Development Expenditures	(26)	(24)	(33)
Operating Expenditures	(352)	(324)	(238)
Interest Paid........................	(135)	(132)	(119)
Cash Flow from Operations....................	$ 62	$ 73	$132
Indirect Method			
Net Income (Loss)........................	$7	$ 6	$(49)
Depreciation and Amortization	66	66	66
Deferred Income Taxes	10	11	24
Write-down of Real Estate to Market Value	12	10	10
(Gain) Loss on Disposition of Properties........................	(18)	1	31
Working Capital from Operations	$ 77	$ 94	$ 82
(Increase) Decrease in Accounts and Notes Receivable	(41)	29	1
(Increase) Decrease in Land Held for Development	(12)	—	19
Increase (Decrease) in Accounts Payable	40	(29)	37
Increase (Decrease) in Other Current Liabilities	(2)	(21)	(7)
Cash Flow from Operations....................	$ 62	$ 73	$132

acquire depreciable assets as an *investing* activity in the year of acquisition). The addback of depreciation expense to net income (see Exhibit 3.1) offsets the effect of the subtraction of depreciation expense (that is, nets its effect to zero) when computing cash flow for operations.

Firms that sell an item of property, plant, or equipment report the full cash proceeds as an investing activity.[3] Because net income includes any gain or loss on the sale (that is, sale proceeds minus the book value of the item sold), the operating section of the statement of cash flows shows an addback for a loss and a subtraction for a gain to offset their inclusion in net income. Forest City Enterprises reports adjustments for gains and losses on dispositions of properties in computing cash flow from

---

[3]The sale of land by a land development company, such as Forest City Enterprises in Exhibit 3.1, represents an operating activity because land is "inventory" to such a business.

operations (see Exhibit 3.1). These properties are buildings that Forest City Enterprises had previously rented to others and has now sold.

Chapter 9 points out that a firm holding an investment of 20 percent to 50 percent in another entity uses the equity method to account for the investment (a noncurrent asset). The investor recognizes its share of the investee's earnings each period, increasing the investment account and net income. It reduces the investment account for dividends received. Thus, net income reflects the investor's share of earnings, not the cash received. The statement of cash flows usually shows a subtraction from net income for the excess of the investor's share of the investee's earnings over dividends received (see PepsiCo's statement of cash flows in Appendix A, where it shows a subtraction from net income for "bottling equity income").

Other examples of revenues and expenses that relate to changes in noncurrent asset or noncurrent liability accounts include amortization of intangible assets, the deferred portion of income tax expense, minority interest in the earnings of consolidated subsidiaries, and some restructuring charges and adjustments for changes in accounting principles. Later chapters discuss each of these items more fully.

Published statements of cash flows sometimes report a subtotal after adjusting net income for the above items and may label the subtotal "working capital from operations." Firms with high proportions of noncurrent assets on the balance sheet, such as capital-intensive manufacturing and transportation companies, will find that net income and working capital from operations will likely differ by a substantial amount. Firms with high proportions of current assets, such as retailers that rent their retail space, will find that net income and working capital from operations are similar in amount. Reporting a subtotal for working capital from operations is not a requirement of *Statement No. 95*, however.

Changes in Operating Working Capital Accounts

The second type of adjustment to reconcile net income to cash flow from operations involves changes in operating current asset and current liability accounts. Firms must adjust the amounts for revenues and expenses included in net income to the corresponding amounts of cash receipts and disbursements. For example, an increase in accounts receivable for a period indicates that a firm did not collect as much cash as the amount of revenues included in net income. The operating section of the statement of cash flows shows a subtraction from net income for the increase in accounts receivable, thereby converting sales revenue on an accrual basis to cash received from customers. An increase in current operating liabilities means that a firm did not use as much cash for operating expenses as the amounts appearing on the income statement. An addition to net income for the increase in current operating liabilities converts operating expenses on an accrual basis to cash paid to suppliers of various goods and services. Similar adjustments for changes in inventories, prepayments, and accounts payable convert accrual basis income amounts to their associated cash flow amounts.

Firms that are mature and not growing rapidly will report relatively small amounts for changes in operating current asset and current liability accounts. Cash flow from operations for such firms will not differ substantially from working capital from operations. Firms that grow rapidly will report more substantial adjustments for changes in accounts receivable, inventories, and operating current liabilities. If a firm uses current operating liabilities to finance the increases in accounts receivable and inventories, then the adjustments for changes in working capital will net to a relatively small amount and working capital from operations will approximately equal cash flow from operations. Most growing firms, however, expand their accounts receivable and inventories more rapidly than their current operating liabilities and find that cash flow from operations will be less than both net income and working capital from operations.

Another factor that may cause cash flow from operations to differ from working capital from operations is the length of the operating cycle (see Exhibit 1.8 for a graphic depiction). The operating cycle encompasses the period of time from when a firm commences the manufacture of its products until it receives cash from customers from the sale of the products. Firms such as construction companies and aerospace manufacturers with relatively long operating cycles will often experience a lag between the time they expend cash for raw materials and labor costs and the time when they receive cash from customers. Unless such firms receive cash advances from their customers prior to completion and delivery of the products or delay payments to their suppliers, cash flow from operations will be less than working capital from operations. The longer the operating cycle and the more rapid the growth of a firm, the larger will be the difference between these two amounts. Firms with short operating cycles, such as restaurants and service firms, will experience less of a lag between the creation and delivery of their products and the collection of cash from customers. Thus, cash flow from operations will not differ substantially from working capital from operations.

A study of the relation between net income, working capital from operations, and cash flow from operations revealed (1) a high correlation between net income and working capital from operations, and (2) low correlations between net income and cash flow from operations, and between working capital from operations and cash flow from operations.[4] The primary difference between net income and working capital from operations for most firms is the addback for depreciation expense. If a firm's income growth tracks its additions to property, plant, and equipment, one would expect a high correlation between net income and working capital flow from operations. The low correlation between these two measures and cash flow from operations suggests that changes in operating working capital accounts do not track changes in net income.

Other studies have looked at the information content of net income versus cash flow from operations in predicting future cash flow from operations. As Chapter 11 discusses more fully, future cash flow from operations plays an important role in the valuation of firms. Knowing whether net income or cash flow from operations correlates more highly with future operating cash flows should enhance the analysts' valuation task. These studies have had mixed results, some showing the superiority of net income and some the superiority of cash flow from operations.[5]

---

[4]Robert M. Bowen, David Burgstahler, and Lane A. Daley, "Evidence on the Relationship Between Earnings and Various Measures of Cash Flow," *Accounting Review* (October, 1986), pp. 713–725.

[5]Patricia M. Dechow, S.P. Kothari, and Ross L. Watts, "The Relation Between Earnings and Cash Flows," *Journal of Accounting and Economics 25* (1998), pp. 133–168; David Burgstahler, Jim Jiambalvo, and Y. Pyo, "The Informativeness of Cash Flows for Future Cash Flows," *Working paper*, Univerity of Washington, 1998.

An extension of these studies examined the information content of various adjustments to net income to compute cash flow from operations (for example, changes in accounts receivable, inventories, accounts payable, depreciation, and amortization), referred to in the literature as *accruals.*[6] This study examined the predictive ability of aggregate earnings versus aggregate cash flow from operations plus individual accrual items. The study found that individual accrual items had information content. Individual accrual items, coupled with past cash flow from operations, outperformed aggregate earnings alone as a predictor of future cash flow from operations. Increases in accounts receivable, for example, correlated with increases in future cash flow from operations, thus signaling a growing firm. Increases in depreciation likewise signaled increased future cash flow from operations, thus signaling the building of capacity to support growth.

The next section uses the product life cycle concept to enhance understanding of the behavior of working capital accounts as firms grow, mature, and decline.

RELATION BETWEEN CASH FLOWS FROM OPERATING, INVESTING, AND FINANCING ACTIVITIES

A helpful framework for understanding more fully the relation between income flows and cash flows is the product life cycle concept from marketing and microeconomics. Individual products (goods or services) move through four more or less identifiable phases: introduction, growth, maturity and decline, as the top panel of Exhibit 3.2 depicts. The length of these phases and the steepness of the revenue curve vary by the type of product. Products subject to rapid technological change, such as semiconductors and computer software, move through these four phases in two to three years. Other products, such as PepsiCo's soft drinks, can remain in the maturity phase for many years. Although the analyst will experience difficulty pinpointing the precise location of a product on its life cycle curve at any particular time, it is usually possible to identify the phase and whether the product is in the early or later portion of that phase.

The middle panel of Exhibit 3.2 shows the trend of net income over the product life cycle. Net losses usually occur in the introduction and early growth phases as revenues do not cover the cost of designing and launching new products. Net income peaks during the maturity phase and then begins to decline.

The lower panel of Exhibit 3.2 shows the cash flows from operating, investing, and financing activities during the four life-cycle phases. During the introduction and early growth phases, negative cash flow from operations results from the cash outflows needed to launch the product. Negative cash flow from investing activities also occurs during these early phases to build productive capacity. The relative size of this negative cash flow for investing activities depends on the degree of capital intensity of the business. Firms must obtain the cash needed for operating and investing

---

[6]Mary E. Barth, Donald P. Cram, and Karen K. Nelson, "Accruals and the Prediction of Future Cash Flows," *The Accounting Review* (January 2001), pp. 27–58.

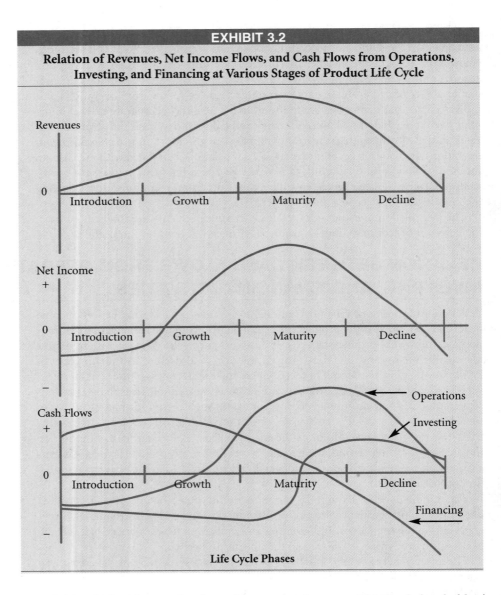

EXHIBIT 3.2

Relation of Revenues, Net Income Flows, and Cash Flows from Operations, Investing, and Financing at Various Stages of Product Life Cycle

activities during these early phases from external sources (debt and shareholders' equity).

As the growth phase accelerates, operations become profitable and begin to generate cash. However, firms must use the cash generated to finance accounts receivable and build inventories for expected higher sales levels in the future. Thus, net income usually turns positive earlier than cash flow from operations. The extent of the negative cash flow from investing activities depends on the rate of growth and the degree of capital intensity. As in the introduction phase, firms obtain most of the cash needed during the growth phase from external sources (a multi-product firm can use cash generated from products in the maturity phase of their life cycle to finance products in the introduction and growth phases and therefore not need as much external financing).

As products move through the maturity phase, the cash flow pattern changes dramatically. Operations become a net provider of cash, both because of market acceptance of the product and a leveling off of working capital needs. Also, with revenues leveling off, firms invest to maintain rather than increase productive capacity. During the later stages of the maturity phase, net cash flows from sales of unneeded plant assets may sometimes result in a net positive cash flow from investing activities. Firms can use the excess cash flow from operations and, to a lesser extent, from the sale of investments to repay debt incurred during the introduction and growth phases, to pay dividends, and to repurchase their common stock.

During the decline phase, cash flow from operations and investing activities tail off as sales decrease. Firms repay their remaining debt, pay dividends, and repurchase common stock.

The product life cycle model discussed above provides helpful insights about the relation between sales, net income, and cash flows from operating, investing, and financing activities for a single product. Few business firms, however, rely on a single product; most have a range of products at different stages of their life cycles. Furthermore, the statement of cash flows reports amounts for a firm as a whole and not for each product. If the life cycle concept is to assist in interpreting published statements of cash flows, the analyst needs a multi-product view.

The analyst obtains such a multi-product view by aggregating the position of each product in its respective life cycle into a reading on the average life cycle position of the firm. For example, the average position of a firm in technology-driven industries, such as biotechnology, is probably in the growth phase. Although such firms will have some products fresh off the drawing board and other products in their decline phase because of the emergence of new technologies, most of these firms' products are in their high growth phase. Most consumer food companies have an average life cycle position in the maturity phase. Branded consumer food products can remain in their maturity phase for many years with proper product quality control and promotion (consider, for example, PepsiCo's and Coca-Cola's soft drinks). Such companies continually bring new products to the market and eliminate products that do not meet consumer acceptance, but their average position is probably in the maturity phase. Certain industries in the United States, such as textiles and steel, are probably in the early decline phase because of foreign competition and outdated technology. Some companies in these industries have built technologically advanced production facilities to compete more effectively on a worldwide basis and have, therefore, essentially reentered the maturity phase. Other firms have diversified into more growth-oriented industries.

ILLUSTRATIONS OF CASH FLOW RELATIONS

Refer to the statement of cash flows for PepsiCo in Appendix A. Cash flow from operations exceeds net income each year, primarily as a result of the addback for depreciation and amortization. Pepsi also reports an addition for deferred income taxes, indicating that Pepsi did not use as much cash for income taxes as the amount of income tax expense subtracted in measuring net income would indicate. We discuss the other adjustments to net income related to changes in noncurrent assets and liability accounts (for example, bottling equity income, impairment and restructuring charges) as we discuss these topics in later chapters. Changes in operating working capital accounts net to relatively small amounts each year ($79 million in Year 9, $416 million in Year 10, and $84 million in Year 11). Pepsi's revenues grew only 1.5 percent between Year 9 and Year 10, and 5.7 percent between Year 10 and Year 11, so we would not expect changes in working capital to play a significant role in converting net income to cash flow from operations.

PepsiCo experienced an excess of cash inflows from operations over cash outflows for investing, typical of a mature firm. Thus, PepsiCo did not need external financing for purchases of property, plant, equipment, and corporate acquisitions. Note that changes in short-term investments appear as investing activities. The amounts might seem relatively large, compared to other amounts in the statement of cash flows. However, firms must report cash flows related to each purchase and sale during the year. Turning over such securities several times during the year will increase the amounts reported. The analyst might gain better insight about changes in marketable securities by looking at the net increase or decrease during the year. PepsiCo, for example, used $500 million (= $2,078 − $2,537 − $41) net in cash during Year 11 to increase its short-term investments.

Some analysts label the excess of cash flow from operations over cash flows for investing activities as *free cash flows to all debt and common equity shareholders*. Firms can then use the excess cash flow to repay borrowing, pay dividends, and repurchase common stock, or allow the excess to accumulate in the cash account on the balance sheet. PepsiCo primarily used the excess cash flow to pay dividends and repurchase shares of its common stock, activities typical of a mature firm.

Exhibits 3.3 to 3.7 present statements of cash flows for firms in five different industries to illustrate the point that a firm's phase in its aggregate product life cycle affects the interpretation of its statement of cash flows. These statements of cash flows also reveal information about the economic characteristics and strategy of the firms.

Amazon.com

Exhibit 3.3 shows a statement of cash flows for Amazon.com (Amazon), an Internet-based retailer. Amazon was in the rapid growth phase of its life cycle, particularly during Year 9 and Year 10. The firm operated at a net loss and generated a negative cash flow from operations in all three years. Cash flow from operations is not as negative as net income, in part because of the addback for depreciation and amortization. In addition, Amazon recognized a substantial restructuring charge in Year 10, increasing the net loss. The restructuring charge did not require cash in the amount of the charge, so the firm added it back to net income when computing cash flow from operations (see Other Addbacks for Year 10). Amazon also increased its accounts payable and other current liabilities in Year 9 and Year 10 to somewhat reduce the negative cash flow from operations.

EXHIBIT 3.3
Amazon.com
Statement of Cash Flows
(amounts in thousands)

	Year 11	Year 10	Year 9
Operations			
Net Loss	$(567,277)	$(1,411,273)	$ (719,968)
Depreciation and Amortization.....................	265,742	406,232	251,500
Other Addbacks	147,550	697,109	153,318
Other Subtractions................................	(1,335)	(280)	0
Working Capital Provided by Operations	$(155,320)	$ (308,212)	$ (315,150)
(Increase) Decrease in Inventories....................	30,628	46,083	(172,069)
(Increase) Decrease in Other Current Assets...........	20,732	(8,585)	(54,927)
Increase (Decrease) in Accounts Payable..............	(44,438)	22,357	330,166
Increase (Decrease) in Other Current Liabilities........	28,616	117,915	121,105
Cash Flow from Operations	$(119,782)	$ (130,442)	$ (90,875)
Investing			
Fixed Assets Acquired.............................	$ (50,321)	$ (134,758)	$ (287,055)
Change in Marketable Securities	(196,775)	361,269	(295,297)
Other Investing Transactions.......................	(6,198)	(62,533)	(369,607)
Cash Flow from Investing	$(253,294)	$ 163,978	$ (951,959)
Financing			
Increase in Long-term Borrowing	$ 10,000	$ 665,377	$1,228,488
Issue of Common Stock............................	116,456	44,697	64,469
Decrease in Long-term Borrowing	(19,575)	(16,927)	(188,886)
Other Financing Transactions	(15,958)	(37,557)	489
Cash Flow from Financing	$ 90,923	$ 655,590	$1,104,560
Change in Cash...................................	$(282,153)	$ 689,126	$ 61,726
Cash—Beginning of Year..........................	822,435	133,309	71,583
Cash—End of Year...............................	$ 540,282	$ 822,435	$ 133,309
Growth in Revenues from Previous Year..............	3.5%	68.4%	68.9%

The negative cash flow from operations coupled with negative cash flows from investing in Year 9 and Year 11 required Amazon to obtain cash from financing sources. The firm primarily relied on long-term borrowing in Year 9 and Year 10, and on issuing common stock in all three years. It did not use all of the cash obtained for operations, capital expenditures, and acquisition immediately, so Amazon invested the temporarily excess cash in marketable securities in Year 9 and Year 11. It sold some of these marketable securities in Year 10 when it needed cash. Note that the firm did not pay dividends, a typical characteristic of a start-up or high-growth firm.

EXHIBIT 3.4			
Wal-Mart Stores			
Statement of Cash Flows			
(amounts in millions)			
	Year 11	Year 10	Year 9
Operations			
Net Income.................................	$ 6,671	$ 6,295	$ 5,575
Depreciation and Amortization.....................	3,290	2,868	2,375
Working Capital Provided by Operations.............	$ 9,961	$ 9,163	$ 7,950
(Increase) Decrease in Accounts Receivable	(210)	(422)	(255)
(Increase) Decrease in Inventories....................	(1,235)	(1,795)	(2,088)
(Increase) Decrease in Other Current Assets...........	(180)	75	(307)
Increase (Decrease) in Accounts Payable.............	368	2,061	1,849
Increase (Decrease) in Other Current Liabilities........	1,556	522	1,045
Cash Flow from Operations	$10,260	$ 9,604	$ 8,194
Investing			
Fixed Assets Acquired.............................	$(8,383)	$(8,042)	$ (6,183)
Corporate Acquisitions	—	(627)	(10,419)
Other Investing Transactions.......................	1,237	(45)	(244)
Cash Flow from Investing	$(7,146)	$(8,714)	$(16,846)
Financing			
Increase in Short-term Borrowing....................	$ —	$ —	$ 4,316
Increase in Long-term Borrowing....................	4,591	3,778	6,000
Issue of Common Stock............................	—	581	—
Decrease in Short-term Borrowing	(1,533)	(2,022)	—
Decrease in Long-term Borrowing	(3,686)	(1,692)	(996)
Acquisition of Common Stock	(1,214)	(193)	(101)
Dividends	(1,249)	(1,070)	(890)
Other Financing Transactions	84	(74)	300
Cash Flow from Financing	$(3,007)	$ (692)	$ 8,629
Change in Cash..................................	$ 107	$ 198	$ (23)
Cash—Beginning of Year	2,054	1,856	1,879
Cash—End of Year................................	$ 2,161	$ 2,054	$ 1,856
Growth in Revenues from Previous Year..............	13.8%	15.9%	19.9%

EXHIBIT 3.5			
Merck & Co.			
Statement of Cash Flows			
(amounts in millions)			
	Year 11	**Year 10**	**Year 9**
Operations			
Net Income.................................	$ 7,281.8	$ 6,821.7	$ 5,890.5
Depreciation and Amortization.....................	1,463.8	1,277.3	1,144.8
Other Additions (Subtractions).....................	(359.5)	777.2	(496.6)
Working Capital Provided by Operations.............	$ 8,386.1	$ 8,876.2	$ 6,538.7
(Increase) Decrease in Accounts Receivable	(9.2)	(885.8)	(1,021.4)
(Increase) Decrease in Inventories....................	(557.5)	(210.1)	(223.0)
Increase (Decrease) in Accounts Payable.............	458.3	(37.7)	673.0
Increase (Decrease) in Other Current Liabilities........	802.2	(55.3)	163.4
Cash Flow from Operations	$ 9,079.9	$ 7,687.3	$ 6,130.7
Investing			
Fixed Assets Acquired.............................	$(2,724.7)	$(2,727.8)	$(2,560.5)
Change in Marketable Securities	(1,397.4)	(969.6)	(1,902.5)
Other Investing Transactions.......................	(190.2)	56.1	1,646.0
Cash Flow from Investing	$(4,312.3)	$(3,641.3)	$(2,817.0)
Financing			
Increase in Short-term Borrowing (net)	$ 259.8	$ 905.6	$ 2,137.9
Increase in Long-term Borrowing	1,694.4	442.1	11.6
Issue of Common Stock............................	300.6	2,140.7	322.9
Decrease in Long-term Borrowing	(11.0)	(443.2)	(17.5)
Acquisition of Common Stock	(3,890.8)	(3,545.4)	(3,582.1)
Dividends..	(3,145.0)	(2,798.0)	(2,589.7)
Other Financing Transactions	(368.4)	(232.9)	(181.1)
Cash Flow from Financing	$(5,160.4)	$(3,531.1)	$(3,898.0)
Change in Cash....................................	$ (392.8)	$ 514.9	$ (584.3)
Cash—Beginning of Year..........................	2,536.8	2,021.9	2,606.2
Cash—End of Year	$ 2,144.0	$ 2,536.8	$ 2,021.9
Growth in Revenues from Previous Year.............	18.2%	23.4%	21.6%

EXHIBIT 3.6			
American Airlines Statement of Cash Flows (amounts in millions)			
	Year 11	Year 10	Year 9
Operations			
Net Income....................................	$(1,762)	$ 770	$ 656
Depreciation and Amortization....................	1,404	1,202	1,092
Other Additions	1,214	475	183
Other Subtractions..............................	(755)	(57)	(110)
Working Capital Provided by Operations	$ 101	$ 2,390	$ 1,821
(Increase) Decrease in Accounts Receivable	120	(169)	261
(Increase) Decrease in Inventories...................	(39)	(111)	(140)
Increase (Decrease) in Accounts Payable..............	379	579	42
Increase (Decrease) in Other Current Liabilities........	(50)	453	280
Cash Flow from Operations	$ 511	$ 3,142	$ 2,264
Investing			
Fixed Assets Acquired............................	$(3,640)	$ (3,678)	$(3,539)
Change in Marketable Securities	(728)	(438)	(253)
Other Investing Transactions.......................	(323)	841	342
Cash Flow from Investing	$(4,691)	$ (3,275)	$(3,450)
Financing			
Increase in Short-term Borrowing (net)	$ —	$ —	$ 300
Increase in Long-term Borrowing	5,096	836	2,010
Issue of Common Stock............................	37	67	25
Decrease in Long-term Borrowing	(922)	(766)	(280)
Acquisition of Common Stock	—	—	(871)
Cash Flow from Financing	$ 4,211	$ 137	$ 1,184
Change in Cash.................................	$ 31	$ 4	$ (2)
Cash—Beginning of Year...........................	89	85	87
Cash—End of Year................................	$ 120	$ 89	$ 85
Growth in Revenues from Previous Year.............	−3.8%	11.1%	1.2%

Wal-Mart Stores

Exhibit 3.4 presents a statement of cash flows for Wal-Mart Stores (Wal-Mart), a rapidly growing discount store, warehouse club, and grocery store chain. Working capital from operations exceeded net income each year because of the addback for depreciation and amortization expense. Cash flow from operations exceeded working capital from operations in all three years, primarily because accounts payable and other current liabilities increased more than inventories. Thus, Wal-Mart used its suppliers to finance some of its working

	EXHIBIT 3.7		
	Interpublic Group		
	Statement of Cash Flows		
	(amounts in millions)		
	Year 11	**Year 10**	**Year 9**
Operations			
Net Income......................................	$ (505.3)	$ 420.3	$ 359.4
Depreciation and Amortization.....................	451.2	397.4	339.3
Other Additions	620.0	130.5	120.8
Other Subtractions...............................	(196.8)	(52.2)	(58.1)
Working Capital Provided by Operations	$ 369.1	$ 896.0	$ 761.4
(Increase) Decrease in Accounts Receivable	780.6	(230.6)	(928.5)
(Increase) Decrease in Inventories...................	84.6	(30.0)	(24.4)
Prepayments.....................................	(106.4)	(56.6)	(8.3)
Increase (Decrease) in Accounts Payable.............	(896.0)	13.1	1,004.6
Increase (Decrease) in Other Current Liabilities........	(83.4)	15.3	(35.4)
Cash Flow from Operations	$ 148.5	$ 607.2	$ 769.4
Investing			
Fixed Assets Acquired.............................	$ (268.0)	$ (259.5)	$ (249.7)
Change in Marketable Securities	5.6	(3.1)	(25.9)
Change in Long-term Investments	7.4	(64.0)	134.3
Corporate Acquisitions	(310.6)	(670.1)	(318.6)
Other Investing Transactions.......................	(130.9)	(95.4)	(65.3)
Cash Flow from Investing	$ (696.5)	$(1,092.1)	$ (525.2)
Financing			
Increase in Short-term Borrowing (net)	$ (670.6)	$ 105.8	$ 50.0
Increase in Long-term Borrowing	1,804.7	1,013.9	433.9
Issue of Common Stock............................	85.6	60.0	133.5
Decrease in Long-term Borrowing	(281.8)	(521.8)	(111.1)
Acquisition of Common Stock	(118.0)	(248.1)	(313.4)
Dividends.......................................	(144.4)	(153.4)	(133.7)
Other Financing Transactions	(36.9)	(74.2)	(46.0)
Cash Flow from Financing	$ 638.6	$ 182.2	$ 13.2
Change in Cash...................................	$ 90.6	$ (302.7)	$ 257.4
Cash—Beginning of Year...........................	844.6	1,147.3	889.9
Cash—End of Year................................	$ 935.2	$ 844.6	$1,147.3
Growth in Revenues from Previous Year..............	−6.3%	11.9%	13.8%

capital needs. Wal-Mart permits customers to use cash or bank credit cards, so it does not need to carry heavy investments in receivables.

Wal-Mart's cash flow from operations was $8 billion to $10 billion a year, more than sufficient in all three years to finance the spending on new stores. Note that the acquisition of fixed assets exceeded depreciation expense each year, an indicator of growth in property, plant, and equipment. Wal-Mart made a significant corporate acquisition in Year 9 (ASDA Corporation in the United Kingdom) for which it needed external financing. The firm used short- and long-term financing for the acquisition. There are a variety of reasons Wal-Mart used debt as opposed to equity financing, including the predictable cash flows of a large retailer, the collateral value of its stores and store equipment, and the lower cost of debt financing. It repaid most of the short-term financing in Year 10 and Year 11, in part by using cash from new long-term borrowing.

Merck

Exhibit 3.5 shows the statement of cash flows for Merck, a pharmaceutical company. Net income, working capital from operations, and cash flow from operations experienced similar growth each year. Merck is not heavily capital intensive, as indicated by the relatively small percentage of depreciation and amortization expense to net income. Changes in its current operating liabilities approximately matched changes in its current operating assets for the three years as a whole, although the amounts for individual years show some variation.

Merck's cash flow from operations exceeded its capital expenditures in all three years. Merck used the excess cash flow to purchase marketable securities, pay dividends, and repurchase its common stock. The repurchase of common stock reduced the proportion of equity and increased the proportion of debt in the capital structure, thereby increasing the degree of financial leverage. Chapter 4 discusses the benefits of financial leverage. Merck's cash flow pattern is typical of a mature company, although the growth rates in revenues for Merck are more characteristic of a firm in its rapid growth phase.

American Airlines

Exhibit 3.6 presents a statement of cash flows for American Airlines (American). Cash flow from operations significantly exceeds net income or net loss in each year because of the large addback of depreciation expense. The high percentage of depreciation to net income indicates the capital-intensive nature of airline operations. Reporting cash flow from operations significantly in excess of net income is typical of capital-intensive firms. American operated at a net loss in Year 11 in part because of a downturn in the economy and because of recognizing an asset impairment loss on fixed assets. This loss did not use cash, so American added it back to net income when computing cash flow from operations (included in Other Additions).

Although American experienced a positive cash flow from operations each year, this cash flow was not sufficient to finance capital expenditures. It used long-term debt to finance these acquisitions. Debt is a less costly source of capital than equity.

The assets acquired serve as collateral for the borrowing. The heavy use of debt financing adds considerable risk, however, to the capital structure of airlines.

Interpublic Group

Finally, Exhibit 3.7 presents a statement of cash flows for Interpublic Group (Interpublic), an advertising agency. Depreciation represents a less significant addback for Interpublic, a service firm, than for American. The primary source of variation between net income and cash flow from operations is management of working capital, particularly accounts receivable and accounts payable. An advertising agency serves as a conduit between clients wishing to place advertisements (giving rise to an accounts receivable for the agency), and the various media in which the agency places advertisements for clients (giving rise to an accounts payable). Interpublic manages its position so that the receivables and payables closely offset (except for Year 10), resulting in a close relationship between working capital from operations and cash flow from operations.

Cash flow from operations was sufficient to finance acquisitions of fixed assets and of other companies in Year 9. However, cash flow from operations declined in Year 10 and Year 11, and was not sufficient to finance these investing activities. Interpublic engaged in long-term borrowing to make up the shortfall. Interpublic also used some of the cash flow from long-term borrowing to pay dividends and acquire its common stock.

These five statements of cash flows present typical patterns for firms in different types of industries and in different stages of their product life cycles. They also illustrate some of the interpretations that an analyst can make about the economic characteristics, strategy, and performance of an entity by studying its statement of cash flows.

PREPARING THE STATEMENT OF CASH FLOWS

Publicly held firms in the United States must include a statement of cash flows in their published financial statements each period.[7] Smaller, privately held firms often prepare just a balance sheet and an income statement. Firms outside of the United States also usually include a statement of cash flows in their published statements. However, some provide only a balance sheet and an income statement. This section illustrates a procedure for preparing a statement of cash flows using information from the balance sheet and income statement. The resulting statement merely approximates the amounts that the statement of cash flows would report if the analyst had full access to a firm's accounting records. However, the estimated amounts should approximate the actual amounts closely enough for the analyst to make meaningful interpretations.

---

[7]Financial Accounting Standards Board, *Statement of Financial Accounting Standards No. 95*, "Statement of Cash Flows," 1987.

ALGEBRAIC FORMULATION

We know from the accounting equation that:

$$\text{Assets} = \text{Liabilities} + \text{Shareholders' Equity}$$

This equality holds for balance sheets at the beginning and end of each period. If we subtract the amounts on the balance sheet at the beginning of the period from the corresponding amounts on the balance sheet at the end of the period, we obtain the following equality for changes (Δ) in balance sheet amounts:

$$\Delta \text{ Assets} = \Delta \text{ Liabilities} + \Delta \text{ Shareholders' Equity}$$

We can now expand the change in assets as follows:

$$\Delta \text{ Cash} + \Delta \text{ Non-cash Assets} = \Delta \text{ Liabilities} + \Delta \text{ Shareholders' Equity}$$

Rearranging terms:

$$\Delta \text{ Cash} = \Delta \text{ Liabilities} + \Delta \text{ Shareholders' Equity} - \Delta \text{ Non-cash Assets}$$

The statement of cash flows explains the reasons for the change in cash during a period. We can see that the change in cash equals the change in all other (non-cash) balance sheet amounts.

Refer to Exhibit 3.8, which shows the comparative balance sheet of Logue Shoe Store for the years ending December 31, Year 11, Year 10, and Year 9. The balance sheets at the end of Year 9 and Year 10 report the following equalities:

	Cash	+	Non-cash Assets	=	Liabilities	+	Shareholders' Equity
Year 9	$13,698	+	$132,136	=	$105,394	+	$40,440
Year 10	$12,595	+	$129,511	=	$ 85,032	+	$57,074

Subtracting the amounts at the end of Year 9 from the amounts at the end of Year 10, we obtain:

$$\Delta \text{ Cash} + \Delta \text{ Non-cash Assets} = \Delta \text{ Liabilities} + \Delta \text{ Shareholders' Equity}$$
$$-\$1,103 + \qquad -\$2,625 \qquad = \quad -\$20,362 \quad + \qquad \$16,634$$

Rearranging terms:

$$\Delta \text{ Cash} = \Delta \text{ Liabilities} + \Delta \text{ Shareholders' Equity} - \Delta \text{ Non-cash Assets}$$
$$-\$1,103 = \quad -\$20,362 \quad + \qquad \$16,634 \qquad - \qquad -\$2,625$$

The decrease in cash of $1,103 equals the decrease in liabilities plus the increase in shareholders' equity minus the decrease in non-cash assets.

CLASSIFYING CHANGES IN BALANCE SHEET ACCOUNTS

The statement of cash flows classifies the reasons for the change in cash as being either an operating, investing, or financing activity. The remaining task then is to

EXHIBIT 3.8			
Logue Shoe Store **Balance Sheet**			
	December 31, Year 11	December 31, Year 10	December 31 Year 9
Assets			
Cash	$ 5,815	$ 12,595	$ 13,698
Accounts Receivable..................	1,816	1,978	1,876
Inventories	123,636	106,022	98,824
Other Current Assets	1,560	—	3,591
Total Current Assets	$132,827	$120,595	$117,989
Property, Plant, and Equipment (cost)	$ 64,455	$ 65,285	$ 63,634
Less Accumulated Depreciation.............	(54,617)	(45,958)	(37,973)
Net Property, Plant, and Equipment	$ 9,838	$ 19,327	$ 25,661
Other Assets	2,184	2,184	2,184
Total Assets	$144,849	$142,106	$145,834
Liabilities and Shareholders' Equity			
Accounts Payable	$ 13,954	$ 15,642	$ 21,768
Notes Payable	10,814	—	—
Current Portion of Long-term Debt	7,288	10,997	18,256
Other Current Liabilities	5,489	6,912	4,353
Total Current Liabilities	$ 37,545	$ 33,551	$ 44,377
Long-term Debt.....................	43,788	51,481	61,017
Total Liabilities	$ 81,333	$ 85,032	$105,394
Common Stock	$ 1,000	$ 1,000	$ 1,000
Additional Paid-in Capital...............	124,000	124,000	124,000
Retained Earnings	(61,484)	(67,926)	(84,560)
Total Shareholders' Equity..............	$ 63,516	$ 57,074	$ 40,440
Total Liabilities and Shareholders' Equity.....	$144,849	$142,106	$145,834

classify the change in each non-cash balance sheet account (right-hand side of the equation above) into one of these three categories. The analyst injects approximations into the preparation of the statement of cash flows at this step. Some of the changes in balance sheet accounts unambiguously fit into one of the three categories (for example, the change in common stock is a financing transaction). However, some balance sheet changes (for example, retained earnings) result from the netting of several changes, some of which relate to operations (net income) and some of which relate to investing or financing (dividends) activities. The analyst should use whatever information that the financial statements and notes provide about changes in balance sheet accounts to classify the net change each period.

The change in balance sheet accounts of publicly traded companies will not always equal the amounts reported on their statement of cash flows related to these accounts. For example, the balance sheet for PepsiCo in Appendix A indicates that inventories increased during Year 11 from $1,192 million to $1,310 million, an increase of $118 million. The statement of cash flows shows a subtraction from net income to compute cash flow from operations of $75 million for the increase in inventories. The usual explanation for a difference is that the firm made acquisitions or dispositions of businesses during the period and classified the change in the balance sheet accounts partially as an operating activity (excess of purchases over sales of inventory, $75 million for Pepsi) and partially as an investing activity (inventories of the acquired or disposed businesses, $118 million – $75 million, or $43 million for PepsiCo). PepsiCo's statement of cash flows uses the label "Changes in operating working capital, excluding effects of acquisitions and dispositions" to alert the reader that changes in operating working capital accounts on the balance sheet and statement of cash flows differ. Unless we have information that indicates otherwise, we assume that each change in a balance sheet account affects only one of the three categories in the statement of cash flows.

Exhibit 3.9 classifies the changes in the non-cash balance sheet accounts. The next section discusses the classification of each account.

1. Accounts Receivable

Cash collections from customers during a period equal sales for the period plus accounts receivable at the beginning of the period minus accounts receivable at the end of the period. Thus, the change in accounts receivable clearly relates to operations. Line (18) of Exhibit 3.9 shows net income as a source of cash from operations. Net income includes sales revenue. The amount for sales revenue included in the amount on line (18) plus or minus the change in accounts receivable on line (1) results in the amount of cash received from customers.

2. Marketable Securities

Firms typically acquire marketable securities when they temporarily have excess cash and sell these securities when they need cash. The holding of marketable securities for a relatively short period might make their purchases and sales appear as operating activities. However, the temporarily excess cash could result from selling fixed assets, issuing bonds or common stock, or from operating activities. Likewise, firms might use the cash inflow from the sale of marketable securities to purchase fixed assets, retire debt, repurchase common or preferred stock, or finance operating activities. GAAP in the United States ignores the reason for the excess cash (with which firms purchase marketable securities) and the use of the cash proceeds (from the sale of marketable securities), and classifies the cash flows associated with purchases and sales of marketable securities as investing activities. (The analyst, however, can feel free to reclassify purchases and sales of marketable securities as operating or financing activities if deemed appropriate for purposes of analysis.) Because net income includes gains or losses on sales of marketable securities, the analyst must subtract gains and add back losses to net income in deriving cash flow from operations if

	EXHIBIT 3.9			
	Worksheet for Preparation of Statement of Cash Flows			
	Balance Sheet Changes	Operations	Investing	Financing
(Increase) Decrease in Assets				
(1) Accounts Receivable		x		
(2) Marketable Securities			x	
(3) Inventories.		x		
(4) Other Current Assets.		x		
(5) Investments in Securities.			x	
(6) Property, Plant, and Equipment Cost.			x	
(7) Accumulated Depreciation		x		
(8) Other Assets.		x	x	
Increase (Decrease) in Liabilities and Shareholders' Equities				
(9) Accounts Payable.		x		
(10) Notes Payable.				x
(11) Current Portion of Long-term Debt.				x
(12) Other Current Liabilities.		x		
(13) Long-term Debt.				x
(14) Deferred Income Taxes		x		
(15) Other Noncurrent Liabilities . . .				x
(16) Common Stock				x
(17) Additional Paid-in Capital				x
(18) Retained Earnings		x (net income)		x (dividends)
(19) Treasury Stock				x
(20) Cash				

purchases and sales are viewed as investing activities. Failure to offset the gain or loss included in earnings results in reporting too much (sales of marketable securities at a gain) or too little (sales of marketable securities at a loss) cash flow from operations. Cash flow from operations should include none of the cash flows associated with sales of marketable securities if such transactions are viewed as investing activities.

3. Inventories

Purchases of inventory during a period equal cost of goods sold for the period plus inventories at the end of the period minus inventories at the beginning of the period. Line (18) includes cost of goods sold as an expense in measuring net income. The change in inventories on line (3) coupled with cost of goods sold included in the amount on line (18) results in the amount of purchases for the period. The presumption at this point is that the firm made a cash outflow equal to the amount of purchases. If the firm does not pay cash for all of these purchases, then accounts payable changes. We adjust for the change in accounts payable on line (9), discussed later.

4. Other Current Assets

This balance sheet account typically includes prepayments for various operating costs such as insurance or rent. Unless the financial statements and notes present information to the contrary, the presumption is that the change in Other Current Assets relates to operations.

5. Investments in Securities

The Investments in Securities account can change for the following possible reasons:

Source of Change	Classification in Statement of Cash Flows
Acquisition of New Investments	Investing (outflow)
Recognition of Income or Loss Using Equity Method	Operations (subtraction or addition)
Receipt of Dividend from Investee	Operations (inflow)
Sale of Investments	Investing (inflow)

If the balance sheet, income statement, or notes provide information that permits the disaggregation of the net change in Investments in Securities into these components, then the analyst can make appropriate classifications of the components. Absent such information, we classify the change in the account as an investing activity.

6. Property, Plant, and Equipment

GAAP classifies the cash flows related to purchases and sales of fixed assets as investing activities. Because net income includes any gains or losses from sales of fixed assets, we offset their effect on earnings by adding back losses and subtracting gains from net income when computing cash flow from operations.

7. Accumulated Depreciation

The amount of depreciation expense recognized each period reduces net income but does not use cash. Thus, we classify depreciation expense as an operating item with a positive sign on line (7). When we add the amount for depreciation expense included under operations on line (7) to depreciation expense included as a negative element in net income on line (18), we eliminate the effect of depreciation expense from the Operations column. This treatment is appropriate since depreciation expense is not a cash flow (ignoring income tax consequences). If a firm sells depreciable assets during a period, the net change in accumulated depreciation includes both the accumulated depreciation removed from the account for assets sold as well depreciation expense for the period. Thus, the analyst cannot assume that the change in the accumulated depreciation account relates to depreciation expense only, unless disclosures indicate that the firm did not sell depreciable assets during the year.

8. Other Assets

Other Assets on the balance sheet include patents, copyrights, goodwill, and similar assets. A portion of the change in these accounts represents amortization, which requires an addback to net income when computing cash flow from operations. Unless the financial statements and notes provide contrary information, the presumption is that the remaining change in these accounts is an investing activity.

9. Accounts Payable

The cash outflow for purchases equals purchases during the period plus accounts payable at the beginning of the period minus accounts payable at the end of the period. We derived the amount for purchases of the period as part of the calculations in line (3) for inventories. The adjustment on line (9) for the change in accounts payable converts purchases to cash payments on purchases and, like inventories, is an operating transaction.

10. Notes Payable

Notes Payable is the account generally used when a firm engages in short-term borrowing from a bank or other financial institution. GAAP in the United States classifies such borrowing as a financing activity on the statement of cash flows, even though the firm might use the proceeds to finance accounts receivable, inventories, or other working capital needs. The presumption underlying the classification of bank borrowing as a financing activity is that firms derive operating cash inflows from their customers, not by borrowing from banks.

11. Current Portion of Long-term Debt

The change in the current portion of long-term debt during a period equals (a) the reclassification of long-term debt from a noncurrent liability to a current liability (that is, debt that the firm expects to repay within one year as of the end-of-the-period balance sheet) minus (b) long-term debt actually repaid during the period. The latter amount represents the cash outflow from this financing transaction. We consider the amount arising from the reclassification in connection with line (13) below.

12. Other Current Liabilities

Firms generally use this account for obligations related to goods and services used in operations other than purchases of inventories. Thus, changes in Other Current Liabilities appear as operating activities.

13. Long-term Debt

This account changes for the following reasons:

Issuance of New Long-term Debt

Reclassification of Long-term Debt from a Noncurrent to a Current Liability

Retirement of Long-term Debt

Conversion of Long-term Debt to Preferred or Common Stock

These items are clearly financing transactions but they do not all affect cash. The issuance of new debt and the retirement of old debt do affect cash flows. The reclassification of long-term debt included in the amount on line (13) offsets the corresponding amount included in the change on line (11) and they effectively cancel each other. This is appropriate because the reclassification does not affect cash flow. Likewise, any portion of the change in long-term debt on line (13) due to a conversion of debt into common stock offsets a similar change on line (16). The analyst enters reclassifications and conversions of debt, such as those described above, on the worksheet for the preparation of a statement of cash flows since such transactions help explain changes in balance sheet accounts. However, these transactions do not appear on the formal statement of cash flows because they do not involve actual cash flows.

14. Deferred Income Taxes

Income taxes currently payable equal income tax expense (included on line (18) as a negative element of net income) plus or minus the change in deferred taxes during the period. Thus, changes in Deferred Income Taxes appear as an operating activity. Chapter 2 discussed deferred income taxes.

15. Other Noncurrent Liabilities

This account includes unfunded pension or retirement benefit obligations, long-term deposits received, and other miscellaneous long-term liabilities. Changes in pension and retirement benefit obligations are operating activities. Absent information to the contrary, however, we classify the change in other noncurrent liability accounts as financing activities.

16. and 17. Common Stock and Additional Paid-in Capital

These accounts change when a firm issues new common stock or repurchases and retires outstanding common stock, and they appear as financing activities.

18. Retained Earnings

Retained earnings increase by the amount of net income and decrease with the declaration of dividends each period. Net income is an operating activity and dividends are a financing activity.

19. Treasury Stock

Repurchases of a firm's outstanding capital stock are a financing activity.

ILLUSTRATION OF THE PREPARATION PROCEDURE

We illustrate the procedure for preparing the statement of cash flows using the data for Logue Shoe Store in Exhibit 3.8. Net income was $16,634 for Year 10 and $6,442 for Year 11.

Exhibit 3.10 presents the worksheet for Year 10. The first column shows the change in each non-cash balance sheet account that nets to the $1,103 decrease in cash for the period. One should observe particular caution with the direction of the change. Recall from the earlier equation:

Δ Cash	=	Δ Liabilities	+	Δ Shareholders' Equity	−	Δ Non-cash Assets
Increase	=	Increase				
Decrease	=	Decrease				
Increase	=			Increase		
Decrease	=			Decrease		
Decrease	=					Increase
Increase	=					Decrease

EXHIBIT 3.10

Worksheet for Statement of Cash Flows for Logue Shoe Store
Year 10

	Balance Sheet Changes	Operations	Investing	Financing
(Increase) Decrease in Assets				
Accounts Receivable	$ (102)	$ (102)		
Inventories.	(7,198)	(7,198)		
Other Current Assets.	3,591	3,591		
Property, Plant, & Equipment.	(1,651)		$(1,651)	
Accumulated Depreciation	7,985	7,985		
Other Assets.	—			
Increase (Decrease) in Liabilities and				
Shareholders' Equities				
Accounts Payable.	$(6,126)	$(6,126)		
Notes Payable.	—			—
Current Portion of Long-term Debt.	(7,259)			$ (7,259)
Other Current Liabilities.	2,559	2,559		
Long-term Debt.	(9,536)			(9,536)
Common Stock	—			—
Additional Paid-in Capital	—		—	—
Retained Earnings	16,634	16,634		
Cash.	$(1,103)	$17,343	$(1,651)	$(16,795)

Thus, changes in liabilities and shareholders' equity have the same directional effect on cash, whereas changes in non-cash assets have just the opposite directional effect. Bank borrowings increase liabilities and cash; debt repayments decrease liabilities and cash. Issuing common stock increases shareholders' equity and cash; paying dividends or repurchasing outstanding common stock reduces shareholders' equity and cash. Purchasing equipment increases non-cash assets and reduces cash; selling equipment reduces non-cash assets and increases cash.

We classify the change in each account as an operating, investing, or financing activity, because we have no information that more than one activity caused the change in the account. Observe the following for Year 10:

1. Operating activities were a net source of cash for the period. Cash flow from operations approximately equaled net income. Logue Shoe Store increased its inventories but reduced accounts payable. Most firms attempt to increase accounts payable to finance increases in inventories. The reduced accounts payable suggests either a desire to pay more quickly, perhaps to take advantage of cash discounts, or pressure from suppliers to pay more quickly.
2. Cash flow from operations was more than sufficient to finance the increase in property, plant, and equipment. Note that capital expenditures were small relative to the amount of depreciation for the year.
3. Logue Shoe Store used the cash derived from operations in excess of capital expenditures to repay long-term debt.

Exhibit 3.11 presents a worksheet for Year 11. The preparation procedure is identical to that in Exhibit 3.10. Note in this case that operations were a net user of cash. The increase in accounts payable did not match the substantial increase in inventories. Long-term debt was again redeemed in Year 11, but it appears that the firm used short-term bank borrowing to finance the redemption. The negative cash flow from operations coupled with the use of short-term debt to redeem long-term debt suggests an increase in short-term liquidity risk.

Exhibit 3.12 presents the statement of cash flows for Logue Shoe Store for Year 10 and Year 11 using the amounts taken from the worksheets in Exhibits 3.10 and 3.11.

SUMMARY

Compared to the balance sheet and income statement, the statement of cash flows is a relatively new statement. The Financial Accounting Standards Board issued its most recent comprehensive standard on the statement of cash flows in 1987, although GAAP in the United States has required some form of "funds flow" statement since the late 1960s.

The statement of cash flows will continue its usefulness in the future for the following reasons:

1. Analysts will understand better the types of information that this statement presents and the kinds of interpretations that are appropriate.

EXHIBIT 3.11

Worksheet for Statement of Cash Flows for Logue Shoe Store
Year 11

	Balance Sheet Changes	Operations	Investing	Financing
(Increase) Decrease in Assets				
Accounts Receivable	$ 162	$ 162		
Inventories............................	(17,614)	(17,614)		
Other Current Assets....................	(1,560)	(1,560)		
Property, Plant, and Equipment...........	830		$830	
Accumulated Depreciation	8,659	8,659		
Other Assets..........................	—			
Incease (Decrease) in Liabilities and				
and Shareholders' Equities				
Accounts Payable......................	$(1,688)	$(1,688)		
Notes Payable.........................	10,814			$10,814
Current Portion of Long-term Debt........	(3,709)			(3,709)
Other Current Liabilities................	(1,423)	(1,423)		
Long-term Debt.......................	(7,693)			(7,693)
Common Stock........................	—			—
Additional Paid-in Capital	—		—	—
Retained Earnings.....................	6,442	6,442	—	—
Cash.................................	$(6,780)	$(7,022)	$830	$ (588)

2. Analysts increasingly recognize that cash flows do not necessarily track income flows. A firm with a healthy income statement is not necessarily financially healthy. Cash requirements to service debt, for example, may outstrip the ability of operations to generate cash.

3. Differences in accounting principles have less of an impact on the statement of cash flows than on the balance sheet and income statement. Such differences in accounting principles between countries are a major issue as capital markets become more integrated across countries.

4. The statement of cash flows reveals information about the economic characteristics of a firm's industry, its strategy, and the stage in its life cycle.

5. The statement of cash flows provides information to assess the financial health of a firm.

6. The statement of cash flows permits the calculation of free cash flows, an important factor in the valuation of firms.

EXHIBIT 3.12		
Statement of Cash Flows for Logue Shoe Store		
	Year 11	Year 10
Operations		
Net Income	$ 6,442	$ 16,634
Depreciation.......................	8,659	7,985
(Inc.) Dec. in Accounts Receivable	162	(102)
(Inc.) Dec. in Inventories......................	(17,614)	(7,198)
(Inc.) Dec. in Other Current Assets..............	(1,560)	3,591
Inc. (Dec.) in Accounts Payable.................	(1,688)	(6,126)
Inc. (Dec.) in Other Current Liabilities...........	(1,423)	2,559
Cash Flow from Operations	$ (7,022)	$ 17,343
Investing		
Sale (Acquisition) of Property, Plant, and		
Equipment.....................	$ 830	$ (1,651)
Financing		
Increase in Notes Payable.....................	$ 10,814	—
Repayment of Long-term Debt.................	$(11,402)	$(16,795)
Cash Flow from Financing	$ (588)	$(16,795)
Net Change in Cash........................	$ (6,780)	$ (1,103)

PROBLEMS AND CASES

3.1 INTERPRETING THE STATEMENT OF CASH FLOWS. The Coca-Cola Company (Coke), like PepsiCo, manufactures and markets a variety of beverages. Exhibit 3.13 presents a statement of cash flows for Coke for Year 7 to Year 11.

Required

Discuss the relationship between net income, working capital from operations, and cash flow from operations, and between cash flows from operating, investing, and financing activities for the firm over the five-year period. Identify characteristics of Coke's cash flows that one would expect for a mature company.

3.2 INTERPRETING THE STATEMENT OF CASH FLOWS. Texas Instruments primarily develops and manufactures semiconductors for use in technology-based products for various industries. The manufacturing process is capital intensive and subject to cyclical swings in the economy. Because of overcapacity and a cutback in spending on technology products, semiconductor prices collapsed during Year 8 and Year 11. Exhibit 3.14 presents a statement of cash flows for Texas Instruments for Year 7 to Year 11.

EXHIBIT 3.13

The Coca-Cola Company
Statement of Cash Flows
(amounts in millions)
(Problem 3.1)

	Year 11	Year 10	Year 9	Year 8	Year 7
Operations					
Net Income	$ 3,979	$ 2,177	$ 2,431	$ 3,533	$ 4,129
Depreciation and Amortization	803	773	792	645	626
Gains on Sales of Bottlers	(176)	(127)	(49)	(333)	(1,002)
Asset Impairment Charges	—	916	799	—	—
Other Addbacks..........................	90	698	508	176	435
Other Subtractions	(124)	—	(41)	(38)	(108)
Working Capital from Operations	$ 4,572	$ 4,437	$ 4,440	$ 3,983	$ 4,080
(Increase) Decrease in Accounts Receivable	(73)	(39)	(96)	(237)	(164)
(Increase) Decrease in Inventories	(17)	(2)	(163)	(12)	(43)
(Increase) Decrease in Prepayments	(349)	(618)	(547)	(318)	(145)
Increase (Decrease) in Accounts Payable	(179)	(84)	281	(70)	299
Increase (Decrease) in Other					
Current Liabilities......................	156	(109)	(32)	87	6
Cash Flow from Operations	$ 4,110	$ 3,585	$ 3,883	$ 3,433	$ 4,033
Investing					
Fixed Assets Sold	$ 91	$ 45	$ 45	$ 54	$ 71
Fixed Assets Acquired	(769)	(733)	(1,069)	(863)	(1,093)
Acquisition of Bottlers.....................	(651)	(397)	(1,876)	(1,428)	(1,100)
Change in Marketable Securities.............	(1)	(218)	(342)	426	1,540
Other Investing Transactions................	142	138	(179)	(350)	82
Cash Flow from Investing................	$(1,188)	$(1,165)	$(3,421)	$(2,161)	$ (500)
Financing					
Increase in Long-term Borrowing.............	$ 3,011	$ 3,671	$ 3,411	$ 1,818	$ 155
Issue of Common Stock	164	331	168	302	150
Decrease in Long-term Borrowing	(3,937)	(4,256)	(2,455)	(410)	(751)
Acquisition of Common Stock	(277)	(133)	(15)	(1,563)	(1,262)
Dividends................................	(1,791)	(1,685)	(1,580)	(1,480)	(1,387)
Other	(45)	(140)	(28)	(28)	(134)
Cash Flow from Financing	$(2,875)	$(2,212)	$ (499)	$(1,361)	$(3,229)
Change in Cash	$ 47	$ 208	$ (37)	$ (89)	$ 304
Cash—Beginning of Year...................	1,819	1,611	1,648	1,737	1,433
Cash—End of Year........................	$ 1,866	$ 1,819	$ 1,611	$ 1,648	$ 1,737
Change in Sales from Previous Year	− 1.8%	+ 3.3%	+ 5.3%	− .3%	+ 4.6%

Required

Discuss the relationship between net income, working capital from operations, and cash flows from operations, and between cash flows from operating, investing, and financing activities for the firm over the five-year period.

3.3 INTERPRETING THE STATEMENT OF CASH FLOWS.   The Gap operates chains of retail clothing stores under the names of The Gap, Banana Republic, and Old Navy Stores. Exhibit 3.15 presents the statement of cash flows for The Gap for Year 7 to Year 11.

Required

Discuss the relationship between net income, working capital from operations, and cash flow from operations, and between cash flows from operating, investing, and financing activities for the firm over the five-year period.

3.4 INTERPRETING THE STATEMENT OF CASH FLOWS. Sunbeam Corporation manufactures and sells a variety of small household appliances, including toasters, food processors, and waffle grills. Exhibit 3.16 presents a statement of cash flows for Sunbeam for Year 5, Year 6, and Year 7. After experiencing decreased sales in Year 5, Sunbeam hired Albert Dunlap in Year 6 try to turn the company around. Albert Dunlap, known in the industry as "Chainsaw Al," had directed restructuring efforts at Scott Paper Company previously. The restructuring effort generally involved firing employees and cutting costs aggressively. Most of these restructuring efforts took place during Year 6. The market expected significantly improved results in Year 7. Reported sales increased 18.7 percent between Year 6 and Year 7 and net income improved. However, subsequent revelations showed that almost one-half of the sales increase resulted from recognizing revenues in the fourth quarter of Year 7 that the firm should have recognized in the first quarter of Year 8.

Required

a. Using information in the statement of cash flows for Year 5, identify any signals that Sunbeam was experiencing operating difficulties and in need of restructuring.
b. Using information in the statement of cash flows for Year 6, identify indicators of the turnaround efforts and any relations between cash flows that trouble you.
c. Using information in the statement of cash flows for Year 7, indicate any signals that the firm might have overstated its revenues and had not yet fixed its operating problems.

EXHIBIT 3.14

Texas Instruments
Statement of Cash Flows
(amounts in millions)
(Problem 3.2)

	Year 11	Year 10	Year 9	Year 8	Year 7
Operations					
Net Income (Loss)	$ (201)	$ 3,087	$ 1,451	$ 407	$ 302
Depreciation	1,599	1,216	1,005	1,144	1,109
Other Addbacks	252	284	157	25	476
Other Subtractions	—	(1,636)	(11)	(54)	—
Working Capital from Operations	$ 1,650	$ 2,951	$ 2,602	$ 1,522	$ 1,887
(Increase) Decrease in Accounts Receivable	977	(348)	(444)	288	39
(Increase) Decrease in Inventories	482	(372)	(207)	74	(34)
(Increase) Decrease in Prepayments	(254)	27	(20)	(17)	(19)
Increase (Decrease) in Accounts Payable	(687)	246	96	(427)	(36)
Increase (Decrease) in Other					
Current Liabilities	(349)	(319)	330	(189)	6
Cash Flow from Operations	$ 1,819	$ 2,185	$ 2,357	$ 1,251	$ 1,843
Investing					
Fixed Assets Acquired	$(1,790)	$(2,762)	$(1,398)	$(1,031)	$(1,238)
Change in Marketable Securities	793	(1,231)	(292)	293	(1,978)
Sale of Discontinued Businesses	—	2,198	—	—	2,195
Other Investing Transactions	(629)	(29)	(284)	(732)	(127)
Cash Flow from Investing	$(1,626)	$(1,824)	$(1,974)	$(1,470)	$(1,148)
Financing					
Increase in Short-term Borrowing	$ —	$ 23	$ 11	$ —	$ —
Increase in Long-term Borrowing	3	250	400	—	28
Issue of Common Stock	183	242	225	196	140
Decrease in Short-term Borrowing	(3)	(19)	(13)	(4)	(314)
Decrease in Long-term Borrowing	(132)	(307)	(262)	(68)	(256)
Acquisition of Common Stock	(395)	(155)	(473)	(253)	(86)
Dividends	(147)	(141)	(134)	(133)	(131)
Other Financing Transactions	(16)	(290)	(61)	6	(25)
Cash Flow from Financing	$ (507)	$ (397)	$ (307)	$ (256)	$ (644)
Change in Cash	$ (314)	$ (36)	$ 76	$ (475)	$ 51
Cash—Beginning of Year	745	781	705	1,180	1,129
Cash—End of Year	$ 431	$ 745	$ 781	$ 705	$ 1,180
Change in Sales from Previous Year	− 30.9%	+ 21.7%	+ 10.0 %	− 13.2%	− 1.9%

EXHIBIT 3.15					
The Gap					
Statement of Cash Flows					
(amounts in millions)					
(Problem 3.3)					
	Year 11	**Year 10**	**Year 9**	**Year 8**	**Year 7**
Operations					
Net Income (Loss)	$ (8)	$ 877	$ 1,127	$ 825	$ 534
Depreciation	811	590	436	326	270
Other Addbacks.	30	92	214	45	10
Working Capital from Operations	$ 833	$ 1,559	$ 1,777	$ 1,196	$ 814
(Increase) Decrease in Inventories	213	(455)	(404)	(322)	(156)
(Increase) Decrease in Prepayments	(13)	(61)	(56)	(77)	(45)
Increase (Decrease) in Accounts Payable	42	250	118	265	64
Increase (Decrease) in Other					
Current Liabilities.	243	(3)	42	332	168
Cash Flow from Operations	$1,318	$ 1,290	$ 1,477	$ 1,394	$ 845
Investing					
Fixed Assets Acquired	$ (940)	$(1,859)	(1,239)	(797)	(466)
Other Investing Transactions.	(11)	(16)	(40)	(29)	152
Cash Flow from Investing	$ (951)	$(1,875)	$(1,279)	$ (826)	$ (314)
Financing					
Increase in Short-term Borrowing	$ —	$ 621	$ 85	$ 1	$ 44
Increase in Long-term Borrowing.	1,194	250	312	—	496
Issue of Capital Stock	139	152	76	49	31
Decrease in Short-term Borrowing.	(735)	0	0	0	0
Decrease in Long-term Borrowing	(250)	—	—	—	—
Acquisition of Capital Stock	(1)	(393)	(707)	(892)	(593)
Dividends.	(76)	(75)	(76)	(77)	(80)
Other	(11)	(11)	(3)	3	(1)
Cash Flow from Financing	$ 260	$ 544	$ (313)	$ (916)	$ (103)
Change in Cash	$ 627	$ (41)	$ (115)	$ (348)	$ 428
Cash—Beginning of Year.	409	450	565	913	485
Cash—End of Year.	$1,036	$ 409	$ 450	$ 565	$ 913
Change in Sales from Previous Year	+ 1.3%	+17.5%	+ 28.5%	+39.1%	+23.2%

EXHIBIT 3.16

Sunbeam Corporation
Statement of Cash Flows
(amounts in millions)
(Problem 3.4)

	Year 7	Year 6	Year 5
Operations			
Net Income (Loss)...................................	$109.4	$(228.3)	$ 50.5
Depreciation and Amortization	38.6	47.4	44.2
Restructuring and Asset Impairment Charges	—	283.7	—
Deferred Income Taxes	57.8	(77.8)	25.1
Other Additions..................................	13.7	46.2	10.8
Other Subtractions	(84.6)	(27.1)	(21.7)
Working Capital Provided by Operations....................	$134.9	$ 44.1	$ 108.9
(Increase) Decrease in Accounts Receivable	(84.6)	(13.8)	(4.5)
(Increase) Decrease in Inventories	(100.8)	(11.6)	(4.9)
(Increase) Decrease in Prepayments	(9.0)	2.7	(8.8)
Increase (Decrease) in Accounts Payable......................	(1.6)	14.7	9.2
Increase (Decrease) in Other Current Liabilities	52.8	(21.9)	(18.4)
Cash Flow from Operations	$ (8.3)	$ 14.2	$ 81.5
Investing			
Fixed Assets Acquired	$(58.3)	$ (75.3)	$(140.1)
Sale of Businesses.....................................	91.0	—	65.3
Acquisitions of Businesses..............................	—	(.9)	(33.0)
Cash Flow from Investing...............................	$ 32.7	$ (76.2)	$(107.4)
Financing			
Increase (Decrease) in Short-term Borrowing	$ 5.0	$ 30.0	$ 40.0
Increase in Long-term Debt	—	11.5	—
Issue of Common Stock..............................	26.6	9.2	9.8
Decrease in Long-term Debt............................	(12.2)	(1.8)	(5.4)
Acquisition of Common Stock	—	—	(13.0)
Dividends..	(3.4)	(3.3)	(3.3)
Other Financing Transactions...........................	.5	(.4)	(.2)
Cash Flow from Financing	$ 16.5	$ 45.2	$ 27.9
Change in Cash	$ 40.9	$ (16.8)	$ 2.0
Cash—Beginning of Year...............................	11.5	28.3	26.3
Cash—End of Year....................................	$ 52.4	$ 11.5	$ 28.3
Growth in Revenues from Previous Year.....................	18.7%	−3.2%	−2.6%

3.5 INTERPRETING THE STATEMENT OF CASH FLOWS.   Kemet designs and manufactures capacitors for electronic circuit boards used in the telecommunications, computer, and automotive industries. Capacitors store electric charges within the board, in contrast to processors, which control the use of the board. Demand for electronic equipment drives the demand for capacitors. The demand for electronic equipment is cyclical with conditions in the economy. The manufacturing process is highly capital intensive. Changes in revenues can impact net income significantly. Exhibit 3.17 presents a statement of cash flows for Kemet for Year 10, Year 11, and Year 12.

Required

a. Discuss the cash flow relations for Year 10 and Year 11 that are consistent with the rapid growth in revenues experienced by Kemet in those years.
b. Discuss the cash flow relations for Year 12 that are consistent with the rapid decline in revenues experienced by Kemet in that year.

3.6 INTERPRETING THE STATEMENT OF CASH FLOWS.   Montgomery Ward operates a retail department store chain. It filed for bankruptcy during the first quarter of Year 12. Exhibit 3.18 presents a statement of cash flows for Montgomery Ward for Year 7 to Year 11. The firm acquired Lechmere, a discount retailer of sporting goods and electronic products, during Year 9. It acquired Amoco Enterprises, an automobile club, during Year 11. During Year 10, it issued a new series of preferred stock and used the cash proceeds in part to repurchase a series of outstanding preferred stock. The "other subtractions" in the operating section for Year 10 and Year 11 represent reversals of deferred tax liabilities.

Required

Discuss the relationship between net income, working capital from operations, and cash flow from operations, and between cash flows from operating, investing, and financing activities for the firm over the five-year period. Identify signals of Montgomery Ward's difficulties that might have led to its filing for bankruptcy.

3.7 IDENTIFYING INDUSTRY DIFFERENCES IN STATEMENT OF CASH FLOWS.   Exhibit 3.19 presents common-size statements of cash flows for eight firms in various industries. All amounts in the common-size statements of cash flows are expressed as a percentage of cash flow from operations. To construct the common-size percentages for each firm, reported amounts for each firm for three consecutive years were summed and the common-size percentages are based on the summed amounts. This procedure reduces the effects of a nonrecurring item in a particular year, such as a major debt or common stock issue. Exhibit 3.19 also shows the compound annual rate of growth in revenues over the three-year period. The eight companies are as follows:

(continued on page 147)

	EXHIBIT 3.17		

Kemet Corporation
Statement of Cash Flows
(amounts in thousands)
(Problem 3.5)

	Year 12	Year 11	Year 10
Operations			
Net Income..........................	$ (27,289)	$ 352,346	$ 70,119
Depreciation and Amortization....................	43,060	63,601	55,699
Other Additions	11,162	5,266	14,510
Other Subtractions.............................	(12,887)	(12,046)	(17,536)
Working Capital Provided by Operations	$ 14,046	$ 409,167	$ 122,792
(Increase) Decrease in Accounts Receivable	74,482	(2,456)	(38,025)
(Increase) Decrease in Inventories...................	(57,115)	(71,318)	(5,140)
(Increase) Decrease in Prepayments	34,465	(45,805)	(55)
Increase (Decrease) in Accounts Payable..............	(128,710)	78,059	58,958
Increase (Decrease) in Other Current Liabilities........	(43,979)	17,874	39,187
Cash Flow from Operations	$(106,811)	$ 385,521	$ 177,717
Investing			
Fixed Assets Sold	$ 62,917	$ —	$ —
Fixed Assets Acquired...........................	(78,500)	(210,559)	(82,009)
Change in Marketable Securities	—	123,687	(123,687)
Other Investing Transactions......................	100	2,339	81
Cash Flow from Investing	$ (15,483)	$ (84,533)	$(205,615)
Financing			
Issue of Common Stock..........................	$ 2	$ 8,629	$ 163,719
Decrease in Long-term Borrowing	—	—	(64,000)
Acquisition of Common Stock	(5,296)	(29,315)	—
Other Financing Transactions	1,452	4,721	—
Cash Flow from Financing	$ (3,842)	$ (15,965)	$ 99,719
Change in Cash...............................	$(126,136)	$ 285,023	$ 71,821
Cash—Beginning of Year........................	360,758	75,735	3,914
Cash—End of Year............................	$ 234,622	$ 360,758	$ 75,735
Growth in Revenues from Previous Year..............	−63.8%	71.0%	45.4%

EXHIBIT 3.18					
Montgomery Ward					
Statement of Cash Flows					
(amounts in millions)					
(Problem 3.6)					
	Year 7	Year 8	Year 9	Year 10	Year 11
Operating					
Net Income..............................	$ 100	$ 101	$ 109	$ (9)	$(237)
Depreciation.............................	97	98	109	115	122
Other Addbacks	32	25	24	8	13
Other Subtractions.......................	—	—	(29)	(119)	(197)
Working Capital from Operations	$ 229	$ 224	$ 213	$ (5)	$(299)
(Increase) Decrease in Accounts Receivable	9	(9)	(38)	(54)	(32)
(Increase) Decrease in Inventories................	(38)	(204)	(229)	(112)	225
(Increase) Decrease in Prepayments	36	(58)	(39)	(32)	27
Increase (Decrease) in Accounts Payable...........	(17)	148	291	85	(222)
Increase (Decrease) in Other					
Current Liabilities	(64)	28	(45)	(64)	(55)
Cash Flow from Operations	$ 155	$ 129	$ 153	$(182)	$(356)
Investing					
Fixed Assets Acquired.........................	$(146)	$(142)	$(184)	$(122)	$ (75)
Change in Marketable Securities	137	(27)	(4)	(14)	20
Other Investing Transactions.....................	9	6	(113)	27	(93)
Cash Flow from Investing	$ —	$(163)	$(301)	$(109)	$(148)
Financing					
Increase in Short-term Borrowing.................	$ —	$ —	$ 144	$ 16	$ 588
Increase in Long-term Borrowing	—	100	168	205	—
Issue of Capital Stock...........................	1	1	78	193	3
Decrease in Short-term Borrowing	—	—	—	—	—
Decrease in Long-term Borrowing	(403)	(18)	(275)	(17)	(63)
Acquisition of Capital Stock	(97)	(11)	(9)	(98)	(20)
Dividends	(19)	(23)	(24)	(4)	(9)
Other...	2	2	1	—	—
Cash Flow from Financing	$(516)	$ 51	$ 83	$ 295	$ 499
Change in Cash	$(361)	$ 17	$ (65)	$ 4	$ (5)
Cash—Beginning of Year.......................	442	81	98	33	37
Cash—End of Year	$ 81	$ 98	$ 33	$ 37	$ 32
Change in Sales from Previous Year..............	+2.0%	+3.7%	+17.2%	−.5%	−10.0%

1. Biogen: creates and manufactures biotechnology drugs. Many drugs are still in the development phase in this high-growth, relatively young industry. Research and manufacturing facilities are capital intensive, although the research process requires skilled scientists.

2. Chevron: explores, extracts, refines, and markets petroleum products. Extraction and refining activities are capital intensive. Petroleum products are in the mature phase of their product life cycles.

3. H.J. Heinz: manufactures and markets branded consumer food products. Heinz has acquired several other branded food products companies in recent years.

4. Home Depot: retails home improvement products. Home Depot competes in a new retail category known as "category killer" stores. Such stores offer a wide selection of products in a particular product category (for example, books, pet products, office products). These stores have taken significant market share away from the more diversified department and discount stores in recent years.

5. Inland Steel: manufactures steel products. Although steel plants are capital intensive, they also utilize unionized workers to process iron into steel products. Demand for steel products follows cyclical trends in the economy. Steel manufacturing in the United States is in the mature phase of its life cycle.

6. Pacific Gas & Electric: provides electric and gas utility services. The electric utility industry in the United States has excess capacity. Increased competition from less regulated, more open markets has forced down prices and led some utilities to reduce their capacity.

7. Servicemaster: provides home cleaning and restoration services. Servicemaster has recently acquired firms offering cleaning services for health care facilities and broadened its home services to include termite protection, garden care, and other services. Servicemaster operates as a partnership. Partnerships do not pay income taxes on their earnings each year. Instead, partners (owners) include their share of the earnings of Servicemaster in their taxable income.

8. Sun Microsystems: creates, manufactures, and markets computers, primarily to the scientific and engineering markets and to network applications. Sun follows an assembly strategy in manufacturing computers, outsourcing the components from various other firms worldwide. Sun has been rumored to be a takeover target by larger technology companies in recent years.

Required

Use whatever clues you can to match the companies in Exhibit 3.19 with the companies listed above. Discuss the reasoning for your selection in each case.

3.8 PREPARING A STATEMENT OF CASH FLOWS FROM BALANCE SHEETS AND INCOME STATEMENTS. Fuso Pharmaceutical Industries develops, manufactures, and markets pharmaceutical products in Japan. Its main product is a solution used by individuals with artificial kidneys. Most individuals in Japan are covered by a national health insurance system. The Japanese government sets the policies for the proportion of health care costs covered by the government versus the proportion that is the responsibility of the individual. The government also establishes the prices

EXHIBIT 3.19

Common-size Statements of Cash Flows for Selected Companies (Problem 3.7)

	1	2	3	4	5	6	7	8
Operations								
Net Income	34.9%	38.6%	40.9%	45.4%	61.2%	62.4%	76.5%	97.6%
Depreciation	47.9	55.2	62.9	37.7	46.0	22.3	38.0	23.3
Other	3.1	24.3	5.1	(5.0)	9.4	11.6	2.3	3.9
Working Capital from Operations	85.9%	118.1%	108.9%	78.1%	116.6%	96.3%	116.8%	124.8%
(Increase) Decrease in Accounts Receivable	6.5	(4.8)	(.6)	(12.4)	(34.2)	(7.8)	(6.8)	(8.5)
(Increase) Decrease in Inventories	1.5	(15.1)	(1.2)	(14.4)	(11.9)	(3.1)	(7.4)	(58.4)
Increase (Decrease) in Accounts Payable	1.5	3.1	(5.6)	12.4	3.0	2.9	12.6	39.9
Increase (Decrease) in Other Current Liabilities	4.6	(1.3)	(1.5)	36.3	26.5	11.7	(15.2)	2.2
Cash Flow from Operations	100.0%	100.0%	100.0%	100.0%	100.0%	100.0%	100.0%	100.0%
Investing								
Fixed Assets Acquired	(37.1)%	(64.0)%	(81.1)%	(165.7)%	(44.7)%	(13.4)%	(39.3)%	(153.4)%
Change in Marketable Securities	—	—	(2.8)	(75.1)	(14.8)	(3.5)	5.9	(17.5)
Other Investing Transactions	(7.7)	8.5	16.4	(28.4)	(15.9)	(17.3)	(40.6)	23.2
Cash Flow from Investing	(44.8)%	(55.5)%	(67.5)%	(269.2)%	(75.4)%	(34.2)%	(74.0)%	(147.7)%
Financing								
Change in Short-term Debt	(.6)%	—	(7.4)%	—	(2.4)%	—	7.9%	—
Increase in Long-term Debt	19.5	41.4%	8.4	75.7%	—	33.1%	24.0	46.9%
Issue of Capital Stock	11.2	9.9	—	82.5	17.7	1.7	6.7	13.5
Decrease in Long-term Debt	(36.0)	(85.0)	(9.1)	(2.7)	(7.0)	(27.6)	(3.1)	(1.2)
Repurchase of Capital Stock	(18.9)	(1.5)	(.1)	—	(50.7)	(21.4)	(26.9)	—
Dividends	(29.5)	(10.9)	(29.9)	—	—	(46.1)	(43.5)	(11.5)
Other Financing Transactions	—	—	(.2)	—	—	.6	9.8	1.9
Cash Flow from Financing	(54.3)%	(46.1)%	(38.3)%	155.5%	(42.4)%	(59.7)%	(25.1)%	49.6%
Net Change in Cash	.9%	(1.6)%	(5.8)%	13.7%	(17.8)%	6.1%	.9%	1.9%
Growth in Revenues	(3.6)%	5.7%	5.7%	23.0%	18.2%	7.7%	8.6%	28.3%

for prescription drugs. The Japanese economy experienced recessionary conditions during recent years. In response to these conditions, the Japanese government increased the proportion of medical costs that is the patient's responsibility and lowered the prices for prescription drugs. Exhibit 3.20 presents the firm's balance sheets for the years ending March 31, Year 8 to Year 11, and Exhibit 3.21 presents the firm's income statements for the years ending March 31, Year 9 to Year 11.

Required

a. Prepare a worksheet for the preparation of a statement of cash flows for Fuso Pharmaceutical Industries for each of the years ending March 31, Year 9 to Year 11. Follow the format of Exhibit 3.9 in the text. Notes to the financial statements indicate the following:

   (1) The changes in Marketable Securities and Investments in Securities represent purchases and sales. Assume that Fuso sold these securities and investments at no gain or loss.

   (2) There were no sales of property, plant, and equipment during the three-year period.

   (3) The changes in the Other Noncurrent Assets account represent investing activities.

   (4) The changes in the Employee Retirement Benefits account relate to provisions made for retirement benefits net of payments made to retired employees, both of which the statement of cash flows classifies as operating activities.

b. Discuss the relation between net income and cash flow from operations, and the pattern of cash flows from operating, investing, and financing transactions for Year 9, Year 10, and Year 11.

3.9 PREPARING A STATEMENT OF CASH FLOWS FROM BALANCE SHEETS AND INCOME STATEMENTS.

Flight Training Corporation is a privately held firm that provides fighter pilot training under contracts with the U.S. Air Force and U.S. Navy. The firm owns approximately 100 Lear jets that it equips with radar jammers and other sophisticated electronic devices to mimic enemy aircraft. The company recently experienced cash shortages to pay its bills. The owner and manager of Flight Training Corporation stated: "I was just dumbfounded. I never had an inkling that there was a problem with cash."

Exhibit 3.22 presents comparative balance sheets for Flight Training Corporation on December 31, Year 1 through Year 4, and Exhibit 3.23 presents income statements for Year 2 through Year 4.

Required

a. Prepare a worksheet for the preparation of a statement of cash flows for Flight Training Corporation for each of the years ending December 31, Year 2 through Year 4. Follow the format in Exhibit 3.9 in the text. Notes to the financial statements indicate the following: (continued on page 152)

EXHIBIT 3.20

Fuso Pharmaceutical Industries
Balance Sheets
(amounts in millions of yen)
(Problem 3.8)

March 31:	Year 11	Year 10	Year 9	Year 8
Assets				
Cash	¥ 5,265	¥ 3,872	¥ 6,038	¥ 6,792
Marketable Securities...........................	2,481	3,121	2,402	2,367
Accounts and Notes Receivable—Trade	19,560	19,154	18,940	18,121
Inventories	8,893	9,308	9,191	8,110
Prepayments................................	222	203	182	524
Total Current Assets	¥36,421	¥35,658	¥36,753	¥35,914
Investments................................	3,847	3,820	4,364	4,738
Property, Plant, and Equipment..................	66,685	64,937	63,601	61,659
Less Accumulated Depreciation..................	(31,964)	(29,576)	(27,214)	(24,964)
Other Assets	3,140	3,220	3,277	1,926
Total Assets	¥78,129	¥78,059	¥80,781	¥79,273
Liabilities and Shareholders' Equity				
Accounts and Notes Payable—Trade..............	¥11,344	¥10,260	¥11,329	¥10,206
Notes Payable to Banks	5,833	6,284	8,022	8,067
Current Portion of Long-term Debt	2,635	2,239	1,670	1,119
Other Current Liabilities	7,461	7,840	7,940	8,310
Total Current Liabilities	¥27,273	¥26,623	¥28,961	¥27,702
Long-term Debt	8,629	9,024	9,346	8,530
Employee Retirement Benefits..................	1,592	1,593	1,564	2,305
Total Liabilities	¥37,494	¥37,240	¥39,871	¥38,537
Common Stock..............................	¥10,758	¥10,758	¥10,758	¥10,758
Additional Paid-in Capital.....................	15,012	15,012	15,012	15,012
Retained Earnings	14,865	15,049	15,140	14,966
Total Shareholders' Equity	¥40,635	¥40,819	¥40,910	¥40,736
Total Liabilities and Shareholders' Equity	¥78,129	¥78,059	¥80,781	¥79,273

EXHIBIT 3.21

Fuso Pharmaceutical Industries
Income Statements
(amounts in millions of yen)
(Problem 3.8)

Year Ended March 31:	Year 11	Year 10	Year 9
Sales	¥ 44,544	¥ 43,770	¥ 43,373
Cost of Goods Sold	(28,117)	(27,012)	(26,443)
Selling and Administrative Expenses.............	(14,130)	(14,423)	(14,003)
Interest Expense............................	(475)	(505)	(576)
Income Tax Expense	(1,045)	(954)	(1,218)
Net Income................................	¥ 777	¥ 876	¥ 1,133

EXHIBIT 3.22

Flight Training Corporation
Balance Sheets
(amounts in thousands)
(Problem 3.9)

December 31:	Year 4	Year 3	Year 2	Year 1
Current Assets				
Cash	$ 159	$ 583	$ 313	$ 142
Accounts Receivable.	6,545	4,874	2,675	2,490
Inventories	5,106	2,514	1,552	602
Prepayments.	665	829	469	57
Total Current Assets	$ 12,475	$ 8,800	$ 5,009	$ 3,291
Property, Plant, and Equipment	$106,529	$76,975	$24,039	$17,809
Less Accumulated Depreciation.	(17,231)	(8,843)	(5,713)	(4,288)
Net	$ 89,298	$68,132	$18,326	$13,521
Other Assets	$ 470	$ 665	$ 641	$ 1,112
Total Assets	$102,243	$77,597	$23,976	$17,924
Current Liabilities				
Accounts Payable	$ 12,428	$ 6,279	$ 993	$ 939
Notes Payable	—	945	140	1,021
Current Portion of Long-term Debt	60,590	7,018	1,789	1,104
Other Current Liabilities	12,903	12,124	2,423	1,310
Total Current Liabilities	$ 85,921	$26,366	$ 5,345	$ 4,374
Noncurrent Liabilities				
Long-term Debt.	$ —	$41,021	$ 9,804	$ 6,738
Deferred Income Taxes	—	900	803	—
Other Noncurrent Liabilities	—	—	226	—
Total Liabilities.	$ 85,921	$68,287	$16,178	$11,112
Shareholders' Equity				
Common Stock	$ 34	$ 22	$ 21	$ 20
Additional Paid-in Capital.	16,516	5,685	4,569	4,323
Retained Earnings	(29)	3,802	3,208	2,469
Treasury Stock	(199)	(199)	—	—
Total Shareholders' Equity.	$ 16,322	$ 9,310	$ 7,798	$ 6,812
Total Liabilities and Shareholders' Equity	$102,243	$77,597	$23,976	$17,924

EXHIBIT 3.23

Flight Training Corporation
Comparative Income Statement for the Year Ended December 31
(amounts in thousands)
(Problem 3.9)

Year Ended December 31:	Year 4	Year 3	Year 2
Continuing Operations			
Sales..............................	$54,988	$36,597	$20,758
Expenses			
Cost of Services......................	47,997	29,594	14,247
Selling and Administrative	5,881	2,972	3,868
Interest.............................	5,841	3,058	1,101
Income Taxes........................	(900)	379	803
Total Expenses......................	$58,819	$36,003	$20,019
Net Income	$(3,831)	$ 594	$ 739

(1) The firm did not sell any aircraft during the three-year period.
(2) Changes in Other Noncurrent Assets are investing transactions.
(3) Changes in Deferred Income Taxes are operating transactions.
(4) Changes in Treasury Stock are financing transactions.
(5) The firm violated covenants in its borrowing agreements during Year 4. The lenders can therefore require Flight Training Corporation to repay its long-term debt immediately. Although the banks have not yet demanded payment, the firm reclassified its long-term debt as a current liability.

b. Prepare a comparative statement of cash flows for Flight Training Corporation for each of the years ending December 31, Year 2 through Year 4.
c. Comment on the relation between net income and cash flow from operations and the pattern of cash flows from operating, investing, and financing activities for each of the three years.
d. Describe the likely reasons for the cash flow difficulties of Flight Training Corporation.

3.10 PREPARING A STATEMENT OF CASH FLOWS FROM BALANCE SHEETS AND INCOME STATEMENTS. GTI, Inc. manufactures parts, components, and processing equipment for electronics and semiconductor applications in the communication, computer, automotive, and appliance industries. Its sales tend to vary with changes in the business cycle since the sales of most of its customers are cyclical. Exhibit 3.24 presents balance sheets for GTI as of December 31, Year 7 through Year 9, and Exhibit 3.25 presents income statements for Year 8 and Year 9.

EXHIBIT 3.24

GTI, Inc.
Balance Sheets
(amounts in thousands)
(Problem 3.10)

December 31:	Year 9	Year 8	Year 7
Assets			
Cash	$ 367	$ 475	$ 430
Accounts Receivable.	2,545	3,936	3,768
Inventories	2,094	2,966	2,334
Prepayments.	122	270	116
Total Current Assets	$5,128	$ 7,647	$ 6,648
Property, Plant, and Equipment (net).	4,027	4,598	3,806
Other Assets	456	559	193
Total Assets	$9,611	$12,804	$10,647
Liabilities and Shareholders' Equity			
Accounts Payable	$ 796	$ 809	$ 1,578
Notes Payable to Banks	2,413	231	11
Other Current Liabilities	695	777	1,076
Total Current Liabilities	$3,904	$ 1,817	$ 2,665
Long-term Debt.	2,084	4,692	2,353
Deferred Income Taxes	113	89	126
Total Liabilities	$6,101	$ 6,598	$ 5,144
Preferred Stock.	$ 289	$ 289	$ —
Common Stock	85	85	83
Additional Paid-in Capital.	4,395	4,392	4,385
Retained Earnings	(1,259)	1,440	1,035
Total Shareholders' Equity	$3,510	$ 6,206	$ 5,503
Total Liabilities and Shareholders' Equity	$9,611	$12,804	$10,647

EXHIBIT 3.25

GTI, Inc.
Income Statements
(amounts in thousands)
(Problem 3.10)

	Year 9	Year 8
Sales	$11,960	$22,833
Cost of Goods Sold	(11,031)	(16,518)
Selling and Administrative Expenses.	(3,496)	(4,849)
Interest Expense.	(452)	(459)
Income Tax Expense.	328	(590)
Net Income.	$ (2,691)	$ 417
Dividends on Preferred Stock	(8)	(12)
Net Income Available to Common	$ (2,699)	$ 405

Required

   a. Prepare a worksheet for the preparation of a statement of cash flows for GTI, Inc. for Year 8 and Year 9. Follow the format in Exhibit 3.9 in the text. Notes to the firm's financial statements reveal the following (amounts in thousands):

     (1) Depreciation expense was $641 in Year 8 and $625 in Year 9.

     (2) Other Assets represent patents. Patent amortization was $25 in Year 8 and $40 in Year 9.

     (3) Changes in Deferred Income Taxes are operating transactions.

   b. Discuss the relation between net income and cash flow from operations, and the pattern of cash flows from operating, investing, and financing activities.

CASE 3.1

W.T. GRANT CO.[8]

At the time that it filed for bankruptcy in October 1975, W.T. Grant (Grant) was the 17th largest retailer in the United States, with almost 1,200 stores, over 82,000 employees, and sales of $1.7 billion. It had paid dividends consistently since 1906. The collapse of Grant came largely as a surprise to the capital markets, particularly to the banks that provided short-term working capital loans. Grant had altered its business strategy in the mid-1960s to transform itself from an urban discount store chain to a suburban housegoods store chain. Its failure serves as a classic study of poor implementation of what seemed like a sound business strategy. What happened to Grant, and why, are questions that, with some analysis, can be answered. On the other hand, why the symptoms of Grant's prolonged illness were not diagnosed and treated earlier is difficult to understand.

THE STRATEGIC SHIFT

Prior to the mid-1960s, Grant built its reputation on sales of low-priced soft goods (clothing, linens, sewing fabrics). It placed its stores in large, urban locations and appealed primarily to lower income consumers.

The mid-1960s marked the beginning, however, of urban unrest and a movement to the suburbs. To service the needs of these new homeowners, suburban shopping centers experienced rapid growth. Sears led the way in this movement, establishing itself as the anchor store in many of the more upscale locations. Montgomery Ward and JC Penney followed suit. At this time, Sears held a dominant market share in the middle-income consumer market. It saw an opportunity, however, to move its product line more upscale to compete with the established department stores (Macy's, Marshall Field), which had not yet begun their move to the suburbs. To implement this new strategy, Sears introduced its Sears Best line of products.

---

[8]Source: This case was coauthored with Professor James A. Largay.

The outward population move to the suburbs and increased competition from growing discount chains such as KMart caused Grant to alter its strategy as well. One aspect of this strategic shift was rapid expansion of new stores into suburban shopping centers. Between 1963 and 1973, Grant opened 612 new stores and expanded 91 others. It concentrated most of that expansion in the 1969–1973 period when it opened 369 new stores, 15 on one particularly busy day. Because Grant's reputation had been built on sales to lower income consumers, it was often unable to locate its new stores in the choicest shopping centers. Louis C. Lustenberger, president of Grant from 1959 to 1968, started the expansion program, although later, as a director, he became concerned over dimensions of the growth and the problems it generated. After Lustenberger stepped down, the pace of expansion accelerated under the leadership of Chairman Edward Staley and President Richard W. Mayer.

A second aspect of Grant's strategy involved a change in its product line. Grant perceived a vacuum in the middle-income consumer market when Sears moved more upscale. Grant introduced a higher quality, medium-priced line of products into its new shopping center stores to fill this vacuum. In addition, it added furniture and private-brand appliances to its product line and implemented a credit card system. With much of the move to the suburbs representing middle-income consumers, Grant attempted to position itself as a primary supplier to outfit the new homes being constructed.

To implement this new strategy, Grant chose a decentralized organizational structure. Each store manager controlled credit extension and credit terms. At most stores, Grant permitted customers 36 months to pay for their purchases; the minimum monthly payment was $1, regardless of their total purchases. Bad debt expenses averaged 1.2 percent of sales each year until fiscal 1975, when a provision of $155.7 million was made. Local store managers also made inventory and pricing decisions. Merchandise was acquired either from regional Grant warehouses or ordered directly from the manufacturer. At this time, Grant did not have an information system in place that permitted one store to check the availability of a needed product from another store. Compensation of employees was considered among the most generous in the industry, with most employees owning shares of Grant's common stock acquired under employee stock option plans. Compensation of store managers included salary plus stated percentages of the store's sales and profits.

To finance the expansion of receivables and inventory, Grant used commercial paper, bank loans, and trade credit. To finance the expansion of store space, Grant entered into leasing arrangements. Because Grant was liquidated before the Financial Accounting Standards Board issued *Statement of Financial Accounting Standards No. 13,* requiring the capitalization of capital leases on the balance sheet and the disclosure of information on operating leases in the notes to the financial statements, it did not disclose its long-term leasing arrangements. Property, plant, and equipment reported on its balance sheet consisted mostly of store fixtures. Grant's long-term debt included debentures totaling $200 million issued in 1971 and 1973. Based on per square foot rental rates at the time, Grant's disclosures of total square footage of space, and an 8 percent discount rate, the estimated present values of Grant's leases are as follows (in thousands):

January 31	Present Value of Lease Commitments	January 31	Present Value of Lease Commitments
1966	$394,291	1971	$496,041
1967	$400,090	1972	$626,052
1968	$393,566	1973	$708,666
1969	$457,111	1974	$805,785
1970	$486,837	1975	$821,565

ADVANCE AND RETREAT—THE ATTEMPT TO SAVE GRANT

By 1974, it became clear that Grant's problems were not of a short-term operating nature. In the spring of 1974, both Moody's and Standard & Poor's eliminated their credit rating for Grant's commercial paper. Banks entered the picture in a big way in the summer of 1974. To provide financing, a group of 143 banks agreed to offer lines of credit totaling $525 million. Grant obtained a short-term loan of $600 million in September 1974, with three New York money center banks absorbing approximately $230 million of the total. These three banks also loaned $50 million out of a total of $100 million provided to Grant's finance subsidiary.

Support of the banks during the summer of 1974 was accompanied by a top management change. Messrs. Staley and Mayer stepped down in the spring and were replaced in August 1974, by James G. Kendrick, brought in from Zeller's Ltd., Grant's Canadian subsidiary. As Chief Executive Officer, Kendrick moved to cut Grant's losses. He slashed payroll significantly, closed 126 unprofitable stores and phased out the big-ticket furniture and appliance lines. New store space brought on line in 1975 was 75 percent less than in 1974.

The positive effects of these moves could not overcome the disastrous events of early 1975. In January, Grant defaulted on about $75 million in interest payments and in February, results of operations for the year ended January 31, 1975, were released. Grant reported a loss of $177 million, with substantial losses from credit operations accounting for 60 percent of the total.

The banks now assumed a more active role in what was becoming a struggle to save Grant. Robert H. Anderson, a vice president of Sears, was offered a lucrative $2.5 million contract. He decided to accept the challenge to turn the company around, and joined Grant as its new president in April 1975. Kendrick remained as chairman of the board. The banks holding 90 percent of Grant's debt extended their loans from June 2, 1975, to March 31, 1976. The balance of about $56 million was repaid on June 2. A major problem confronting Anderson was how to maintain the continued flow of merchandise into Grant stores. Suppliers became skeptical of Grant's ability to pay for merchandise and, in August 1975, the banks agreed to subordinate $300 million of debt to the suppliers' claims for merchandise shipped. With the approach of the Christmas shopping season, the need for merchandise became critical. Despite the banks' subordination of their claims to those of suppliers and the intensive cultivation of suppliers by Anderson, Grant did not receive sufficient quantities of merchandise in the stores.

During this period, Grant reported a $111.3 million net loss for the six months ended on July 31, 1975. Sales had declined 15 percent from the comparable period in 1974. Kendrick observed that a return to profitability before the fourth quarter was unlikely.

On October 2, 1975, Grant filed a Chapter 11 bankruptcy petition. The rehabilitation effort was formally underway and the protection provided by Chapter 11 permitted a continuation of the reorganization and rehabilitation activities for the next four months. On February 6, 1976, after store closings and liquidations of inventories had generated $320 million in cash, the creditors committee overseeing the bankruptcy voted for liquidation, and W.T. Grant ceased to exist.

FINANCIAL STATEMENTS FOR GRANT

Two changes in accounting principles affect Grant's financial statements. Prior to fiscal 1970, Grant accounted for the investment in its wholly owned finance subsidiary using the equity method. Beginning with the year ending January 31, 1970, Grant consolidated the finance subsidiary. Prior to fiscal 1975, Grant recorded the total finance charge on credit sales as income in the year of the sale. Accounts receivable therefore included the full amount to be received from customers, not the present value of such amount. Beginning with the fiscal year ending January 31, 1975, Grant recognized finance changes on credit sales over the life of the installment contract.

Exhibit 3.26 presents comparative balance sheets and Exhibit 3.27 presents statements of income and retained earnings for Grant, based on the amounts as originally reported for each year. Exhibits 3.28, 3.29, and 3.30 present balance sheets, income statements, and statements of cash flow, respectively, based on revised amounts reflecting retroactive restatement for the two changes in accounting principles discussed above. These latter statements consolidate the finance subsidiary for all years. Grant provided the necessary data to restate for the change in income recognition of finance charges for the 1971 to 1975 fiscal years only. Exhibit 3.31 presents selected other data for Grant, the variety chain store industry, and the aggregate economy.

Required

Using the narrative information and the financial data provided in Exhibits 3.26 through 3.31, your mission is to apply tools of financial analysis to determine the major causes of Grant's financial problems. If you had been performing this analysis contemporaneously with the release of publicly reported information, when would you have become skeptical of the ability of Grant to continue as a viable going concern? To assist in this analysis, Exhibits 3.32 through 3.34 present selected ratio and growth rate information based on the following assumptions:

Exhibit 3.32: Based on the amounts as originally reported for each year (Exhibits 3.26 and 3.27).

Exhibit 3.33: Based on the amounts as retroactively restated for changes in accounting principles (Exhibits 3.28, 3.29 and 3.30).

Exhibit 3.34: Same as Exhibit 3.32, except assets and liabilities reflect the capitalization of leases using the amounts presented in the case.

EXHIBIT 3.26

W.T. GRANT COMPANY
Comparative Balance Sheets
(as originally reported)
(Case 3.1)

January 31:	1966	1967	1968	1969
Assets				
Cash and Marketable Securities	$ 22,559	$ 37,507	$ 25,047	$ 28,460
Accounts Receivable[c].	110,943	110,305	133,406	154,829
Inventories.	151,365	174,631	183,722	208,623
Other Current Assets	—	—	—	—
Total Current Assets.	$284,867	$322,443	$342,175	$391,912
Investments.	38,419	40,800	56,609	62,854
Property, Plant, and Equipment (net).	40,367	48,071	47,572	49,213
Other Assets	1,222	1,664	1,980	2,157
Total Assets.	$364,875	$412,978	$448,336	$506,136
Equities				
Short-term Debt	$ —	$ —	$ 300	$ 180
Accounts Payable—Trade	58,252	75,885	79,673	102,080
Current Deferred Taxes.	37,590	47,248	57,518	64,113
Total Current Liabilities.	$ 95,842	$123,133	$137,491	$166,373
Long-term Debt	70,000	70,000	62,622	43,251
Noncurrent Deferred Taxes	6,269	7,034	7,551	7,941
Other Long-term Liabilities	4,784	4,949	4,858	5,519
Total Liabilities.	$176,895	$205,116	$212,522	$223,084
Preferred Stock	$ 15,000	$ 15,000	$ 14,750	$ 13,250
Common Stock.	15,375	15,636	16,191	17,318
Additional Paid-in Capital	25,543	27,977	37,428	59,945
Retained Earnings.	132,062	149,249	167,445	192,539
Total	$187,980	$207,862	$235,814	$283,052
Less Cost of Treasury Stock	—	—	—	—
Total Stockholders' Equity.	$187,980	$207,862	$235,814	$283,052
Total Equities	$364,875	$412,978	$448,336	$506,136

[a]In the year ending January 31, 1970, W.T. Grant changed its consolidation policy and commenced consolidating its wholly owned finance subsidiary.
[b]In the year ending January 31, 1975, W.T. Grant changed its method of recognizing finance income on installment sales. In prior years, Grant recognized all finance income in the year of the sale. Beginning in the 1975 fiscal period, it recognized finance income over the time the installment receivable was outstanding.
[c]Accounts receivable comprises the following:

	1966	1967	1968	1969
Customer Installment Receivables.	$114,470	$114,928	$140,507	$162,219
Less Allowances for Uncollectible Accounts.	(7,065)	(9,383)	(11,307)	(13,074)
Unearned Credit Insurance.	—	—	—	—
Unearned Finance Income	—	—	—	—
Net	$107,405	$105,545	$129,200	$149,145
Other Receivables.	3,538	4,760	4,206	5,684
Total Receivables.	$110,943	$110,305	$133,406	$154,829

EXHIBIT 3.26

continued

1970[a]	1971	1972	1973	1974	1975[b]
$ 32,977	$ 34,009	$ 49,851	$ 30,943	$ 45,951	$ 79,642
368,267	419,731	477,324	542,751	598,799	431,201
222,128	260,492	298,676	399,533	450,637	407,357
5,037	5,246	5,378	6,649	7,299	6,581
$628,409	$719,478	$831,229	$ 979,876	$1,102,686	$ 924,781
20,694	23,936	32,367	35,581	44,251	49,764
55,311	61,832	77,173	91,420	100,984	101,932
2,381	2,678	3,901	3,821	5,063	5,790
$706,795	$807,924	$944,670	$1,110,698	$1,252,984	$1,082,267
$182,132	$246,420	$237,741	$ 390,034	$ 453,097	$ 600,695
104,144	118,091	124,990	112,896	104,883	147,211
80,443	94,785	112,846	130,137	132,085	2,000
$366,719	$459,296	$475,577	$ 633,067	$ 690,065	$ 749,906
35,402	32,301	128,432	126,672	220,336	216,341
8,286	8,518	9,664	11,926	14,649	—
5,700	5,773	5,252	4,694	4,196	2,183
$416,107	$505,888	$618,925	$ 776,359	$ 929,246	$ 968,430
$11,450	$ 9,600	$ 9,053	$ 8,600	$ 7,465	$ 7,465
17,883	18,180	18,529	18,588	18,599	18,599
71,555	78,116	85,195	86,146	85,909	83,914
211,679	230,435	244,508	261,154	248,461	37,674
$312,567	$336,331	$357,285	$ 374,488	$ 360,434	$ 147,652
(21,879)	(34,295)	(31,540)	(40,149)	(36,696)	(33,815)
$290,688	$302,036	$325,745	$ 334,339	$ 323,738	$ 113,837
$706,795	$807,924	$944,670	$1,110,698	$1,252,984	$1,082,267

1970	1971	1972	1973	1974	1975
$381,757	$433,730	$493,859	$ 556,091	$ 602,305	$ 518,387
(15,270)	(15,527)	(15,750)	(15,770)	(18,067)	(79,510)
(5,774)	(9,553)	(12,413)	(8,768)	(4,923)	(1,386)
—	—	—	—	—	(37,523)
$360,713	$408,650	$465,696	$ 531,553	$ 579,315	$ 399,968
7,554	11,081	11,628	11,198	19,484	31,233
$368,267	$419,731	$477,324	$ 542,751	$ 598,799	$ 431,201

EXHIBIT 3.27

W.T. GRANT COMPANY
Statements of Income and Retained Earnings
(as originally reported)
(Case 3.1)

Year Ended January 31	1967	1968	1969
Sales.....................................	$920,797	$979,458	$1,096,152
Concessions.............................	2,249	2,786	3,425
Equity in Earnings	2,072	2,987	3,537
Finance Charges	—	—	—
Other Income	1,049	2,010	2,205
Total Revenues	$926,167	$987,241	$1,105,319
Cost of Goods Sold.......................	$631,585	$669,560	$ 741,181
Selling, General & Administration	233,134	253,561	287,883
Interest..................................	4,970	4,907	4,360
Taxes: Current	13,541	17,530	25,600
Deferred	11,659	9,120	8,400
Total Expenses	$894,889	$954,678	$1,067,424
Net Income	$ 31,278	$ 32,563	$ 37,895
Dividends	(14,091)	(14,367)	(17,686)
Change in Accounting Principles:			
Consolidation of Finance Subsidiary........	—	—	4,885
Recognition of Financing Charges..........	—	—	—
Change in Retained Earnings	$ 17,187	$ 18,196	$ 25,094
Retained Earnings—Beginning of Period	132,062	149,249	167,445
Retained Earnings—End of Period	$149,249	$167,445	$ 192,539

EXHIBIT 3.27

continued

1970	1971	1972	1973	1974	1975
$1,210,918	$1,254,131	$1,374,811	$1,644,747	$1,849,802	$1,761,952
3,748	4,986	3,439	3,753	3,971	4,238
2,084	2,777	2,383	5,116	4,651	3,086
—	—	—	—	—	91,141
2,864	2,874	3,102	1,188	3,063	3,376
$1,219,614	$1,264,768	$1,383,735	$1,654,804	$1,861,487	$1,863,793
$ 817,671	$ 843,192	$ 931,237	$1,125,261	$1,282,945	$1,303,267
307,215	330,325	374,334	444,879	491,287	769,253
14,919	18,874	16,452	21,127	78,040	86,079
24,900	21,140	13,487	9,588	(6,021)	(19,439)
13,100	11,660	13,013	16,162	6,807	(98,027)
$1,177,805	$1,225,191	$1,348,523	$1,617,017	$1,853,058	$2,041,133
$ 41,809	$ 39,577	$ 35,212	$ 37,787	$ 8,429	$ (177,340)
(19,737)	(20,821)	(21,139)	(21,141)	(21,122)	(4,457)
(2,932)	—	—	—	—	—
$ —	$ —	$ —	$ —	$ —	$ (28,990)
$ 19,140	$ 18,756	$ 14,073	$ 16,646	$ (12,693)	$ (210,787)
192,539	211,679	230,435	244,508	261,154	248,461
$ 211,679	$ 230,435	$ 244,508	$ 261,154	$ 248,461	$ 37,674

EXHIBIT 3.28

W.T. GRANT COMPANY
Comparative Balance Sheets
(as retroactively reported for changes in accounting principles)
(Case 3.1)

January 31:	1966	1967	1968	1969
Assets				
Cash and Marketable Securities..........	$ 22,638	$ 39,040	$ 25,141	$ 25,639
Accounts Receivable[c]	172,706	230,427	272,450	312,776
Inventories	151,365	174,631	183,722	208,623
Other Current Assets	3,630	4,079	3,982	4,402
Total Current Assets	$350,339	$448,177	$485,295	$551,440
Investments.........................	13,405	14,791	16,754	18,581
Property, Plant, and Equipment (net).	40,372	48,076	47,578	49,931
Other Assets	1,222	1,664	1,980	2,157
Total Assets	$405,338	$512,708	$551,607	$622,109
Equities				
Short-term Debt.....................	$ 37,314	$ 97,647	$ 99,230	$118,125
Accounts Payable	58,252	75,885	79,673	102,080
Current Deferred Taxes	36,574	44,667	56,545	65,073
Total Current Liabilities	$132,140	$218,199	$235,448	$285,278
Long-term Debt	70,000	70,000	62,622	43,251
Noncurrent Deferred Taxes	6,269	7,034	7,551	7,941
Other Long-term Liabilities	4,785	5,159	5,288	5,519
Total Liabilities	$213,194	$300,392	$310,909	$341,989
Preferred Stock......................	$ 15,000	$ 15,000	$ 14,750	$ 13,250
Common Stock.......................	15,375	15,636	16,191	17,318
Additional Paid-in Capital..............	25,543	27,977	37,428	59,945
Retained Earnings....................	136,226	153,703	172,329	189,607
Total..............................	$192,144	$212,316	$240,698	$280,120
Less Cost of Treasury Stock	—	—	—	—
Total Stockholders' Equity...........	$192,144	$212,316	$240,698	$280,120
Total Equities.....................	$405,338	$512,708	$551,607	$622,109

[a]See Note a to Exhibit 3.26.
[b]See Note b to Exhibit 3.26.
[c]Accounts receivable comprises the following:

	1966	1967	1968	1969
Customer Installment Receivables				
Less Allowances for Uncollectible	NOT DISCLOSED ON A FULLY			
Accounts				
Unearned Credit Insurance	CONSOLIDATED BASIS			
Unearned Finance Income.........				
Net	WITH FINANCE SUBSIDIARY			
Other Receivables....................				
Total Receivables	$172,706	$230,427	$272,450	$312,776

EXHIBIT 3.28

continued

1970[a]	1971	1972	1973	1974	1975[b]
$ 32,977	$ 34,009	$ 49,851	$ 30,943	$ 45,951	$ 79,642
368,267	358,428	408,301	468,582	540,802	431,201
222,128	260,492	298,676	399,533	450,637	407,357
5,037	5,246	5,378	6,649	7,299	6,581
$628,409	$658,175	$762,206	$ 905,707	$1,044,689	$ 924,781
20,694	23,936	32,367	35,581	44,251	49,764
55,311	61,832	77,173	91,420	100,984	101,932
2,381	2,678	3,901	3,821	5,063	5,790
$706,795	$746,621	$875,647	$1,036,529	$1,194,987	$1,082,267
$182,132	$246,420	$237,741	$ 390,034	$ 453,097	$ 600,695
104,144	118,091	124,990	112,896	104,883	147,211
80,443	58,536	72,464	87,431	103,078	2,000
$366,719	$423,047	$435,195	$ 590,361	$ 661,058	$ 749,906
35,402	32,301	128,432	126,672	220,336	216,341
8,286	8,518	9,664	11,926	14,649	—
5,700	5,773	5,252	4,694	4,196	2,183
$416,107	$469,639	$578,543	$ 733,653	$ 900,239	$ 968,430
$ 11,450	$ 9,600	$ 9,053	$ 8,600	$ 7,465	$ 7,465
17,883	18,180	18,529	18,588	18,599	18,599
71,555	78,116	85,195	86,146	85,909	83,914
211,679	205,381	215,867	229,691	219,471	37,674
$312,567	$311,277	$328,644	$ 343,025	$ 331,444	$ 147,652
(21,879)	(34,295)	(31,540)	(40,149)	(36,696)	(33,815)
$290,688	$276,982	$297,104	$ 302,876	$ 294,748	$ 113,837
$706,795	$746,621	$875,647	$1,036,529	$1,194,987	$1,082,267

1970	1971	1972	1973	1974	1975
$381,757	$433,730	$493,859	$ 556,091	$ 602,305	$ 518,387
(15,270)	(15,527)	(15,750)	(15,770)	(18,067)	(79,510)
(5,774)	(9,553)	(12,413)	(8,768)	(4,923)	(1,386)
—	(61,303)	(69,023)	(74,169)	(57,997)	(37,523)
$360,713	$347,347	$396,073	$ 457,384	$ 521,318	$ 399,968
7,554	11,081	11,628	11,198	19,484	31,233
$368,267	$358,428	$408,301	$ 468,582	$ 540,802	$ 431,201

EXHIBIT 3.29

W.T. GRANT COMPANY
Statements of Income and Retained Earnings
(as retroactively revised for changes in accounting principles)
(Case 3.1)

Year Ended January 31	1967	1968	1969
Sales..................................	$920,797	$979,458	$1,096,152
Concessions...........................	2,249	2,786	3,425
Equity in Earnings	1,073	1,503	1,761
Finance Charges	—	—	—
Other Income	1,315	2,038	2,525
Total Revenues	$925,434	$985,785	$1,103,311
Cost of Goods Sold......................	$631,585	$669,560	$ 741,181
Selling, General & Administration	229,130	247,093	278,031
Interest................................	7,319	8,549	9,636
Taxes: Current	14,463	18,470	27,880
Deferred	11,369	9,120	8,400
Total Expenses	$893,866	$952,792	$1,065,128
Net Income	$ 31,568	$ 32,993	$ 38,183
Dividends	(14,091)	(14,367)	(17,686)
Change in Accounting Principles:			
Consolidation of Finance Subsidiary........	—	—	(3,219)
Recognition of Financing Charges..........	—	—	—
Change in Retained Earnings	$ 17,477	$ 18,626	$ 17,278
Retained Earnings—Beginning of Period	136,226	153,703	172,329
Retained Earnings—End of Period	$153,703	$172,329	$ 189,607

EXHIBIT 3.29

continued

1970	1971	1972	1973	1974	1975
$1,210,918	$1,254,131	$1,374,812	$1,644,747	$1,849,802	$1,761,952
3,748	4,986	3,439	3,753	3,971	4,238
2,084	2,777	2,383	5,116	4,651	3,086
—	63,194	66,567	84,817	114,920	91,141
2,864	2,874	3,102	1,188	3,063	3,376
$1,219,614	$1,327,962	$1,450,303	$1,739,621	$1,976,407	$1,863,793
$ 817,671	$ 843,192	$ 931,237	$1,125,261	$1,282,945	$1,303,267
307,215	396,877	445,244	532,604	601,231	769,253
14,919	18,874	16,452	21,127	78,040	86,079
24,900	22,866	13,579	11,256	(6,021)	(19,439)
13,100	9,738	12,166	14,408	9,310	(98,027)
$1,177,805	$1,291,547	$1,418,678	$1,704,656	$1,965,505	$2,041,133
$ 41,809	$ 36,415	$ 31,625	$ 34,965	$ 10,902	$ (177,340)
(19,737)	(20,821)	(21,139)	(21,141)	(21,122)	(4,457)
—	—	—	—	—	—
—	(21,892)	—	—	—	—
$ 22,072	$ (6,298)	$ 10,486	$ 13,824	$ (10,220)	$ (181,797)
189,607	211,679	205,381	215,867	229,691	219,471
$ 211,679	$ 205,381	$ 215,867	$ 229,691	$ 219,471	$ 37,674

EXHIBIT 3.30

W.T. GRANT COMPANY
Statement of Cash Flows
(as retroactively revised for changes in accounting principles)
(Case 3.1)

	1967	1968	1969
Operations			
Net Income	$ 31,568	$ 32,993	$ 38,183
Depreciation	7,524	8,203	8,388
Other	66	(856)	(1,140)
(Inc.) Dec. in Receivables	(57,721)	(42,023)	(40,326)
(Inc.) Dec. in Inventories	(23,266)	(9,091)	(24,901)
(Inc.) Dec. in Prepayments.	(449)	97	(420)
Inc. (Dec.) in Accounts Payable	17,633	3,788	22,407
Inc. (Dec.) in Other Cur. Liab.	8,093	11,878	8,528
Cash Flow from Operations	$(16,552)	$ 4,989	$ 10,719
Investing			
Acquisition of Property, Plant, and Equipment.	$(15,257)	$ (7,763)	$(10,626)
Acquisition of Investments.	(269)	(418)	(35)
Cash Flow from Investing.	$(15,526)	$ (8,181)	$(10,661)
Financing			
Inc. (Dec.) in Short-term Borrowing	$ 60,333	$ 1,583	$ 18,895
Inc. (Dec.) in Long-term Borrowing	—	(1,500)	(1,500)
Inc. (Dec.) in Capital Stock	2,695	3,958	844
Dividends	(14,091)	(14,367)	(17,686)
Cash Flow from Financing	$ 48,937	$(10,326)	$ 553
Other	$ (457)	$ (381)	$ (113)
Change in Cash.	$ 16,402	$(13,899)	$ 498

EXHIBIT 3.30

continued

1970	1971	1972	1973	1974	1975
$ 41,809	$ 36,415	$ 31,625	$ 34,965	$ 10,902	$(177,340)
8,972	9,619	10,577	12,004	13,579	14,587
(1,559)	(2,470)	(1,758)	(1,699)	(1,345)	(16,993)
(55,491)	(11,981)	(49,873)	(60,281)	(72,220)	109,601
(13,505)	(38,364)	(38,184)	(100,857)	(51,104)	43,280
(635)	(209)	(132)	(1,271)	(650)	718
2,064	13,947	6,899	(12,094)	(8,013)	42,328
15,370	(21,907)	13,928	14,967	15,647	(101,078)
$ (2,975)	$(14,950)	$(26,918)	$(114,266)	$(93,204)	$ (84,897)
$(14,352)	$(16,141)	$(25,918)	$ (26,251)	$(23,143)	$ (15,535)
—	(436)	(5,951)	(2,216)	(5,700)	(5,282)
$(14,352)	$(16,577)	$(31,869)	$ (28,467)	$(28,843)	$ (20,817)
$ 64,007	$ 64,288	$ (8,679)	$ 152,293	$ 63,063	$ 147,598
(1,687)	(1,538)	98,385	(1,584)	93,926	(3,995)
(17,860)	(8,954)	7,407	(8,227)	1,833	886
(19,737)	(20,821)	(21,139)	(21,141)	(21,122)	(4,457)
$ 24,723	$ 32,975	$ 75,974	$ 121,341	$137,700	$ 140,032
$ (58)	$ (416)	$ (1,345)	$ 2,484	$ (645)	$ (627)
$ 7,338	$ 1,032	$ 15,842	$ (18,908)	$ 15,008	$ 33,691

EXHIBIT 3.31				

W.T. GRANT COMPANY
Other Data
(Case 3.1)

December 31:	1965	1966	1967	1968
W.T. Grant Co.				
Sales (millions of dollars)[a]	$ 839.7	$ 920.8	$ 975.5	$1,096.1
Number of Stores	1,088	1,104	1,086	1,092
Store Area (thousands of square feet)[a]		——DATA NOT AVAILABLE——		
Dividends per Share[a]	$ .80	$ 1.10	$ 1.10	$ 1.30
Stock Price—High	$ 31⅛	$ 35⅛	$ 37⅜	$ 45⅛
—Low	$ 18	$ 20½	$ 20¾	$ 30
—Close (12/31)	$ 31⅛	$ 20¾	$ 34⅜	$ 42⅝
Variety Chain Store Industry				
Sales (millions of dollars)	$5,320.0	$5,727.0	$6,078.0	$6,152.0
Standard & Poor's Variety				
Chain Stock Price Index—High	31.0	31.2	38.4	53.6
—Low	24.3	22.4	22.3	34.7
—Close (12/31)	31.0	22.4	37.8	50.5
Aggregate Economy				
Gross National Product				
(billions of dollars)	$ 684.9	$ 747.6	$ 789.7	$ 865.7
Average Bank Short-term Lending Rate	4.99%	5.69%	5.99%	6.68%
Standard & Poor's 500				
Stock Price Index—High	92.6	94.1	97.6	108.4
—Low	81.6	73.2	80.4	87.7
—Close (12/31)	92.4	80.3	96.5	103.9

[a]These amounts are for the fiscal year ending January 31 of year after the year indicated in the column. For example, sales for W.T. Grant of $839.7 in the 1965 column are for the fiscal year ending January 31, 1966.

EXHIBIT 3.31

continued

1969	1970	1971	1972	1973	1974
$1,210.9	$ 1,254.1	$ 1,374.8	$ 1,644.7	$ 1,849.8	$ 1,762.0
1,095	1,116	1,168	1,208	1,189	1,152
——	38,157	44,718	50,619	53,719	54,770
1.40	$ 1.40	$ 1.50	$ 1.50	$ 1.50	$ .30
$ 59	$ 52	$ 70^5⁄$_8$	$ 48^3⁄$_4$	$ 44^3⁄$_8$	$ 12
$ 39^1⁄$_4$	$ 26^7⁄$_8$	$ 41^7⁄$_8$	$ 38^3⁄$_4$	$ 9^7⁄$_8$	$ 1^1⁄$_2$
$ 47	$ 47^1⁄$_8$	$ 47^3⁄$_4$	$ 43^7⁄$_8$	$ 10^7⁄$_8$	$ 1^7⁄$_8$
$6,426.0	$ 6,959.0	$ 6,972.0	$ 7,498.0	$ 8,212.0	$ 8,714.0
66.1	61.4	92.2	107.4	107.3	73.7
48.8	40.9	60.2	82.1	60.0	39.0
59.6	60.4	88.0	106.8	66.2	41.9
$ 932.1	$ 1,075.3	$ 1,107.5	$ 1,171.1	$ 1,233.4	$ 1,210.0
8.21%	8.48%	6.32%	5.82%	8.30%	11.28%
106.2	93.5	104.8	119.1	120.2	99.8
89.2	69.3	90.2	101.7	92.2	62.3
92.1	92.2	102.1	118.1	97.6	68.6

ᵃThese amounts are for the fiscal year ending January 31 of year after the year indicated in the column. For example, sales for W.T. Grant of $839.7 in the 1965 column are for the fiscal year ending January 31, 1966.

EXHIBIT 3.32			

W.T. GRANT COMPANY
Financial Ratios and Growth Rates for W.T. Grant Based on Amounts as Originally Reported
(Case 3.1)

Financial Ratios	1967	1968	1969
Profitability Analysis			
Profit Margin.	3.7%	3.6%	3.7%
Assets Turnover.	2.4	2.3	2.3
Return on Assets	8.7%	8.2%	8.4%
Return on Common Shareholders' Equity.	16.8%	15.5%	15.2%
Operating Performance			
Cost of Goods Sold/Sales	68.6%	68.4%	67.6%
Sell. & Admin. Exp./Sales	25.3%	25.9%	26.3%
Asset Turnovers			
Accounts Receivable	8.3	8.0	7.6
Inventory.	3.9	3.7	3.8
Fixed Asset.	20.8	20.5	22.7
Short-term Liquidity Risk			
Current Ratio	2.62	2.49	2.36
Quick Ratio.	1.20	1.15	1.10
Days Receivables	44	45	48
Days Inventory	94	98	97
Days Payables	37	42	43
Operating Cash Flow/Current Liabilities	(15.1%)	3.8%	7.1%
Long-term Solvency Risk			
Liabilities/Assets	49.7%	47.4%	44.1%
LT Debt/Assets.	17.0%	14.0%	8.5%
Operating Cash Flow/Liabilities	(8.7%)	2.4%	4.9%
Interest Coverage.	12.4	13.1	17.5

Growth Rates		1968	1969
Accounts Receivable.		20.9%	16.1%
Inventories		5.2%	13.6%
Fixed Assets		(1.0%)	3.4%
Total Assets.		8.6%	12.9%
Accounts Payable		5.0%	28.1%
Bank Loans.		—	(40.0%)
Long-term Debt.		(10.5%)	(30.9%)
Shareholders' Equity		13.4%	20.0%
Sales		6.4%	11.9%
Cost of Goods Sold		6.0%	10.7%
Sell. & Admin. Expense		8.8%	13.5%
Net Income.		4.1%	16.4%

EXHIBIT 3.32

continued

1970	1971	1972	1973	1974	1975
4.1%	3.9%	3.2%	3.0%	2.6%	(7.5%)
2.0	1.7	1.6	1.6	1.6	1.5
8.2%	6.5%	5.0%	4.7%	4.1%	(11.4%)
15.1%	13.7%	11.4%	11.7%	2.5%	(84.1%)
67.5%	67.2%	67.7%	68.4%	69.4%	74.0%
25.4%	26.3%	27.2%	27.0%	26.6%	43.7%
4.6	3.2	3.1	3.2	3.2	3.4
3.8	3.5	3.3	3.2	3.0	3.0
23.2	21.4	19.8	19.5	19.2	17.4
1.71	1.57	1.75	1.55	1.60	1.23
1.09	.99	1.11	.91	.93	.68
79	115	119	113	113	107
96	104	110	113	121	120
45	46	46	35	30	37
(1.1%)	(3.6%)	(5.8%)	(20.6%)	(14.1%)	(11.8%)
58.9%	62.6%	65.5%	69.9%	74.2%	85.9%
5.0%	4.0%	13.6%	11.4%	17.6%	20.0%
(.9%)	(3.2%)	(4.8%)	(16.4%)	(10.9%)	(9.0%)
6.4	4.8	4.8	4.0	1.1	(2.4)

1970	1971	1972	1973	1974	1975
137.9%	14.0%	13.7%	13.7%	10.3%	(28.0%)
6.5%	17.3%	14.7%	33.8%	12.8%	(9.6%)
12.4%	11.8%	24.8%	18.5%	10.5%	.9%
39.6%	14.3%	17.0%	17.6%	12.8%	(13.6%)
2.0%	13.4%	5.8%	(9.7%)	(7.1%)	40.4%
N/A	35.3%	(3.5%)	64.1%	16.2%	32.6%
(18.1%)	(8.8%)	297.6%	(1.4%)	73.9%	(1.8%)
2.7%	3.9%	7.8%	2.6%	(3.2%)	(64.8%)
10.5%	3.6%	9.6%	19.6%	12.5%	(4.7%)
10.3%	3.1%	10.4%	20.8%	14.0%	1.6%
6.7%	7.5%	13.3%	18.8%	10.4%	56.6%
10.3%	(5.3%)	(11.0%)	7.3%	(77.7%)	(2,203.9%)

EXHIBIT 3.33

W.T. GRANT COMPANY
Financial Ratios and Growth Rates for W.T. Grant Based on Amounts Retroactively Restated
for Changes in Accounting Principles (Leases Not Capitalized)
(Case 3.1)

Financial Ratios	1967	1968	1969
Profitability Analysis			
Profit Margin...........................	3.8%	3.8%	3.9%
Assets Turnover.........................	2.0	1.8	1.9
Return on Assets........................	7.7%	7.0%	7.4%
Return on Common Shareholders' Equity.........	16.6%	15.3%	15.3%
Operating Performance			
Cost of Goods Sold/Sales	68.6%	68.4%	67.6%
Sell. & Admin. Exp./Sales	24.9%	25.2%	25.4%
Asset Turnovers			
Accounts Receivable	4.6	3.9	3.7
Inventory...................................	3.9	3.7	3.8
Fixed Asset.................................	20.8	20.5	22.5
Short-term Liquidity Risk			
Current Ratio	2.05	2.06	1.93
Quick Ratio...............................	1.23	1.26	1.19
Days Receivables	80	94	97
Days Inventory	94	98	97
Days Payables	37	42	43
Operating Cash Flow/Current Liabilities	(9.4%)	2.2%	4.1%
Long-term Solvency Risk			
Liabilities/Assets	58.6%	56.4%	55.0%
LT Debt/Assets..............................	13.7%	11.4%	7.0%
Operating Cash Flow/Liabilities	(6.4%)	1.6%	3.3%
Interest Coverage............................	8.8	8.1	8.7

Growth Rates		1968	1969
Accounts Receivable............................		18.2%	14.8%
Inventories		5.2%	13.6%
Fixed Assets		(1.0%)	4.9%
Total Assets..................................		7.6%	12.8%
Accounts Payable		5.0%	28.1%
Bank Loans...................................		1.6%	19.0%
Long-term Debt...............................		(10.5%)	(30.9%)
Shareholders' Equity		13.4%	16.4%
Sales		6.4%	11.9%
Cost of Goods Sold		6.0%	10.7%
Sell. & Admin. Expense		7.8%	12.5%
Net Income...................................		4.5%	15.7%

EXHIBIT 3.33

continued

1970	1971	1972	1973	1974	1975
4.1%	3.7%	2.9%	2.8%	2.8%	(7.5%)
1.8	1.7	1.7	1.7	1.7	1.5
7.5%	6.4%	5.0%	4.8%	4.6%	(11.6%)
15.1%	13.2%	11.3%	11.9%	3.6%	(90.2%)
67.5%	67.2%	67.7%	68.4%	69.4%	74.0%
25.4%	31.6%	32.4%	32.4%	32.5%	43.7%
3.6	3.5	3.6	3.8	3.7	3.6
3.8	3.5	3.3	3.2	3.0	3.0
23.0	21.4	19.8	19.5	19.2	17.4
1.71	1.56	1.75	1.53	1.58	1.23
1.09	.93	1.05	.85	.89	.68
103	106	102	97	100	101
96	104	110	113	121	120
45	46	46	35	30	37
(.9%)	(3.8%)	(6.3%)	(22.3%)	(14.9%)	(12.0%)
58.9%	62.9%	66.1%	70.8%	75.3%	89.5%
5.0%	4.3%	14.7%	12.2%	18.4%	20.0%
(.8%)	(3.4%)	(5.1%)	(17.4%)	(11.4%)	(9.1%)
6.4	4.7	4.5	3.9	1.2	(2.4)

1970	1971	1972	1973	1974	1975
17.7%	(2.7%)	13.9%	14.8%	15.4%	(20.3%)
6.5%	17.3%	14.7%	33.8%	12.8%	(9.6%)
10.8%	11.8%	24.8%	18.5%	10.5%	.9%
13.6%	5.6%	17.3%	18.4%	15.3%	(9.4%)
2.0%	13.4%	5.8%	(9.7%)	(7.1%)	40.4%
54.2%	35.3%	(3.5%)	64.1%	16.2%	32.6%
(18.1%)	(8.8%)	297.6%	(1.4%)	73.9%	(1.8%)
3.8%	(4.7%)	7.3%	1.9%	(2.7%)	(61.4%)
10.5%	3.6%	9.6%	19.6%	12.5%	(4.7%)
10.3%	3.1%	10.4%	20.8%	14.0%	1.6%
10.5%	29.2%	12.2%	19.6%	12.9%	27.9%
9.5%	(12.9%)	(13.2%)	10.6%	(68.8%)	(1,726.7%)

EXHIBIT 3.34

W.T. GRANT COMPANY

Financial Ratios and Growth Rates for W.T. Grant Based on Amounts Retroactively Restated for Changes in Accounting Principles (Leases Capitalized)

(Case 3.1)

Financial Ratios	1967	1968	1969
Profitability Analysis			
Profit Margin.	3.8%	3.8%	3.9%
Assets Turnover.	1.1	1.1	1.1
Return on Assets	4.1%	4.0%	4.3%
Return on Common Shareholders' Equity.	16.6%	15.3%	15.3%
Operating Performance			
Cost of Goods Sold/Sales	68.6%	68.4%	67.6%
Sell. & Admin. Exp./Sales	24.9%	25.2%	25.4%
Asset Turnovers			
Accounts Receivable	4.6	3.9	3.7
Inventory.	3.9	3.7	3.8
Fixed Asset.	2.1	2.2	2.3
Short-term Liquidity Risk			
Current Ratio	2.05	2.06	1.93
Quick Ratio.	1.23	1.26	1.19
Days Receivables	80	94	97
Days Inventory	94	98	97
Days Payables	37	42	43
Operating Cash Flow/Current Liabilities	(9.4%)	2.2%	4.1%
Long-term Solvency Risk			
Liabilities/Assets	76.7%	74.5%	74.0%
LT Debt/Assets.	51.5%	48.3%	46.4%
Operating Cash Flow/Liabilities	(2.5%)	.7%	1.4%
Interest Coverage.	8.8	8.1	8.7

Growth Rates		1968	1969
Accounts Receivable.		18.2%	14.8%
Inventories		5.2%	13.6%
Fixed Assets		1.6%	14.9%
Total Assets.		3.5%	14.2%
Accounts Payable		5.0%	28.1%
Bank Loans.		1.6%	19.0%
Long-term Debt		(3.0%)	9.7%
Shareholders' Equity		13.4%	16.4%
Sales		6.4%	11.9%
Cost of Goods Sold		6.0%	10.7%
Sell. & Admin. Expense		7.8%	12.5%
Net Income.		4.5%	15.7%

EXHIBIT 3.34

continued

1970	1971	1972	1973	1974	1975
4.1%	3.7%	2.9%	2.8%	2.8%	(7.5%)
1.1	1.0	1.0	1.0	1.0	.9
4.4%	3.8%	2.9%	2.8%	2.7%	(6.8%)
15.1%	13.2%	11.3%	11.9%	3.6%	(90.2%)
67.5%	67.2%	67.7%	68.4%	69.4%	74.0%
25.4%	31.6%	32.4%	32.4%	32.5%	43.7%
3.6	3.5	3.6	3.8	3.7	3.6
3.8	3.5	3.3	3.2	3.0	3.0
2.3	2.3	2.2	2.2	2.2	1.9
1.71	1.56	1.75	1.53	1.58	1.23
1.09	.93	1.05	.85	.89	.68
103	106	102	97	100	101
96	104	110	113	121	120
45	46	46	35	30	37
(.9%)	(3.8%)	(6.3%)	(22.3%)	(14.9%)	(12.0%)
75.6%	77.7%	80.2%	82.6%	85.3%	94.0%
43.8%	42.5%	50.2%	47.9%	51.3%	54.5%
(.3%)	(1.6%)	(2.5%)	(8.6%)	(5.9%)	(4.9%)
6.4	4.7	4.5	3.9	1.2	(2.4)

1970	1971	1972	1973	1974	1975
17.7%	(2.7%)	13.9%	14.8%	15.4%	(20.3%)
6.5%	17.3%	14.7%	33.8%	12.8%	(9.6%)
6.9%	2.9%	26.1%	13.8%	13.3%	1.8%
10.6%	4.1%	20.8%	16.2%	14.6%	(4.8%)
2.0%	13.4%	5.8%	(9.7%)	(7.1%)	40.4%
54.2%	35.3%	(3.5%)	64.1%	16.2%	32.6%
4.4%	1.2%	42.8%	10.7%	22.8%	1.1%
3.8%	(4.7%)	7.3%	1.9%	(2.7%)	(61.4%)
10.5%	3.6%	9.6%	19.6%	12.5%	(4.7%)
10.3%	3.1%	10.4%	20.8%	14.0%	1.6%
10.5%	29.2%	12.2%	19.6%	12.9%	27.9%
9.5%	(12.9%)	(13.2%)	10.6	(68.8%)	(1,726.7%)

Chapter 4

PROFITABILITY ANALYSIS

Learning Objectives
1. Analyze and interpret levels of, and changes in, the operating profitability of a firm using the rate of return on assets and its components, profit margin and total assets turnover.
2. Understand the effect of economic and strategic factors on the interpretation of the rate of return on assets and its components.
3. Examine financial ratios in addition to the rate of return on assets for analyzing the operating profitability of a firm.
4. Analyze and interpret levels of, and changes in, the rate of return on common shareholders' equity, including the conditions when a firm uses financial leverage successfully to increase the return to the common shareholders.
5. Calculate earnings per common share and understand the strengths and weaknesses of this financial ratio as a measure of return to common shareholders.

The primary objective in most financial statement analysis is to value a firm's equity securities. As Chapters 11 to 13 make clear, the value of an equity security relates to the *return* an investor anticipates relative to the *risk* involved. Most financial statement analysis examines aspects of a firm's *profitability* and its *risk*. Examining the profitability of a firm in the recent past provides information to help the analyst project its likely future profitability and the expected return from investing in the firm's equity securities. Evaluations of risk involve judgments about a firm's success in managing various dimensions of risk in the past and its ability to manage risks in the future.

This chapter describes several commonly used financial statement ratios for analyzing profitability. Chapter 5 explores the use of financial statements in assessing risk. We illustrate the application of these tools of analysis to the financial statements of PepsiCo in Appendix A. The analytical tools discussed in Chapters 4 and 5 provide the framework for the discussion of alternative accounting principles and other data issues in Chapters 6 through 9 and the valuation of firms in Chapters 10 to 13. Although we will make some preliminary interpretations of the analytical results for PepsiCo in Chapters 4 and 5, a deeper understanding requires consideration of data issues relating to PepsiCo's financial statements discussed in later chapters.

Our analysis examines changes in the financial ratios for PepsiCo over time, a process referred to as *time-series analysis*. Is Pepsi becoming more or less profitable over time? Is it becoming more or less risky? Are changes in PepsiCo's strategy, economic conditions, competition, or other factors causing its profitability and risk to change? Time-series analysis attempts to answer these questions.

It is also useful to compare the financial ratios for PepsiCo to those of its competitors, a process referred to as *cross-section analysis*. PepsiCo's principal competitor is The Coca-Cola Company (Coke). We might compare our analysis of PepsiCo to the corresponding financial ratios for Coke to gain a cross-section perspective (see problem 4.11). We might also compare the results for PepsiCo with average industry ratios, such as those published by Moody's, Robert Morris Associates, Dun and Bradstreet, and others (discussed later in this chapter).

We view effective financial statement analysis as a three-legged stool, as Exhibit 4.1 depicts. Three building blocks for effective analysis are:

1. Understanding the financial statements and the accounting concepts and methods that underlie them.
2. Understanding the economic characteristics of the industries in which a firm participates and the relation of those economic characteristics to the various financial statement ratios.
3. Understanding the strategies that a firm pursues to differentiate itself from competitors in order to evaluate the sustainability of a firm's earnings and its risks.

EXHIBIT 4.1

Building Blocks for Financial Statement Analysis

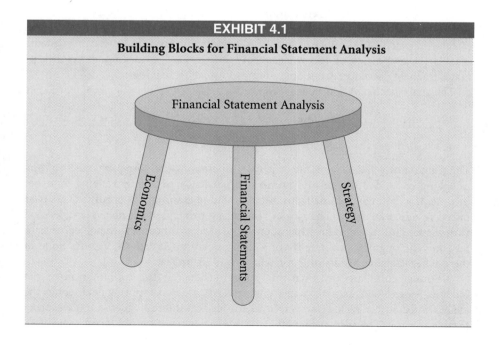

Chapter 1 introduced the economic characteristics of the beverage industry and the strategy of PepsiCo to compete in this industry. We incorporate this information and other information provided by the management of PepsiCo in its discussion and analysis of operations in Appendix B into our interpretations of PepsiCo's financial ratios. Appendix C provides a printout for PepsiCo of the financial statement analysis package, called FSAP, available with this book.

PROFITABILITY ANALYSIS

The analysis of profitability addresses two broad questions:

1. How profitable are the operations of a firm independent of how the firm finances its assets? We use the rate of return on assets (ROA) to answer this question.
2. How profitable is the firm in generating a return for the common shareholders? That is, how much of ROA is left for the common shareholders after subtracting amounts owed to lenders and others senior to the common shareholders in the capital structure? We use the rate of return on common shareholders' equity (ROCE) and earnings per share (EPS) to answer this question.

RATE OF RETURN ON ASSETS

The rate of return on assets measures a firm's success in using assets to generate earnings independent of the financing of those assets. Refer to Exhibit 4.2. ROA takes as given the particular set of environmental factors and strategic choices that a firm makes and focuses on the profitability of its operations relative to the investments (assets) in place. ROA ignores, however, the means of financing these investments (that is, the proportion of debt versus equity financing). This measure therefore separates financing activities from operating and investing activities.

The analyst calculates ROA as follows:

$$\text{ROA} = \frac{\text{Net Income} + (1 - \text{Tax Rate})(\text{Interest Expense}) + \text{Minority Interest in Earnings}}{\text{Average Total Assets}}$$

The numerator of ROA is net income from operations excluding the effects of any financing costs. Calculating the numerator is usually easiest by starting with net income. If a firm has income from discontinued operations, extraordinary gains or losses, or adjustments for changes in accounting principles, the analyst might start with income from continuing operations instead of net income if the objective is to measure the ongoing profitability of a firm's operations. PepsiCo reports none of these other categories of income for Year 9, Year 10, or Year 11.

We must eliminate any financing costs included in the computation of net income. Because accountants subtract interest expense in computing net income, the analyst must add it back. However, firms can deduct interest expense in measuring taxable income. The *incremental* effect of interest expense on net income therefore

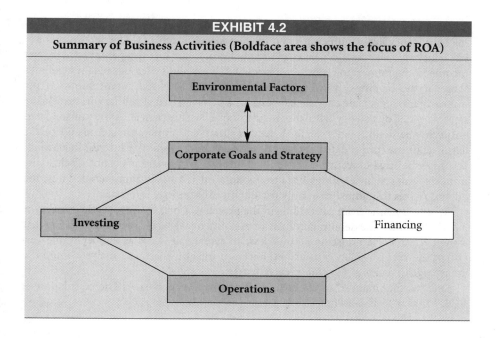

EXHIBIT 4.2

Summary of Business Activities (Boldface area shows the focus of ROA)

equals one minus the marginal tax rate times interest expense. That is, the analyst adds back the full amount of interest expense to net income and then subtracts, or eliminates, the tax savings from that interest expense. The tax savings from interest expense depend on the marginal tax rates in the tax jurisdiction where the firm raises its debt. The federal tax savings from interest expense depends on the statutory tax rate, which is currently 35 percent in the United States. Firms must disclose in a note to the financial statements why the average tax rate (defined as income tax expense divided by net income before income taxes) differs from the federal statutory tax rate of 35 percent. The statutory federal rate will differ from a firm's average tax rate because of (1) state and foreign tax rates that differ from 35 percent, and (2) revenues and expenses that firms include in book income but which do not impact taxable income (that is, permanent differences as described in Chapter 2). The analyst can attempt to approximate the combined marginal federal, state, and foreign tax rate applicable to income tax deductions from these disclosures. We will use the statutory federal tax rate of 35 percent in our computations of the tax savings from interest in the numerator of ROA throughout this book. Because accountants do not subtract dividends on preferred and common stocks in measuring net income, calculating the numerator of ROA requires no adjustment for dividends.[1]

---

[1]One could argue that the analyst should exclude returns from short-term investments of excess cash (that is, interest revenue) from the numerator of ROA and the short-term investments from the denominator of ROA under the view that such investments are really negative financings (that is, savings rather than borrowings). We do not make this adjustment when computing ROA, although we consider the effect of such short-term investments in the discussion of valuation in Chapters 11 to 13.

The rationale for adding back the minority interest in earnings relates to attaining consistency in the numerator and the denominator of ROA. The denominator of ROA includes all assets of the consolidated entity, not just the parent's share. Net income in the numerator, however, represents the parent's earnings plus the parent's share of the earnings of consolidated subsidiaries. The accountant subtracts the minority interest's claim on the earnings of a consolidated subsidiary in measuring net income. Consistency with the inclusion of all of the assets of the consolidated entity in the denominator of ROA requires that the numerator include all of the earnings of the consolidated entity. The addback of the minority interest in earnings accomplishes this objective. Most publicly traded corporations do not disclose the minority interest in earnings because its amount is usually immaterial. Thus, the analyst makes this adjustment only for significant minority interests.

Because income from operations in the numerator of ROA reports the results for a period of time, the denominator uses a measure of average assets in use during that same period. For a nonseasonal business, an average of assets at the beginning and end of the year is usually satisfactory. For a seasonal business, the analyst should use an average of assets at the end of each quarter.

Refer to the financial statements for PepsiCo in Appendix A. The calculation of ROA for Year 11 is as follows:

$$\text{ROA} = \frac{\text{Net Income} + (1 - \text{Tax Rate})(\text{Interest Expense}) + \text{Minority Interest in Earnings}}{\text{Average Total Assets}}$$

$$13.2\% = \frac{\$2,662 + (1 - .35)(\$219) + \$0}{.5(\$20,757 + \$21,695)} = \frac{\$2,804}{\$21,226}$$

An examination of PepsiCo's financial statements and notes in Appendix A indicates that net income includes some unusual or nonrecurring items in Year 11. If the objective is to measure the ongoing operating profitability of PepsiCo, it is desirable to adjust the reported amounts for such items. Chapter 6 discusses and illustrates these adjustments more fully. We adjust Pepsi's net income for two items for Year 11.

1. PepsiCo reports $356 million of pre-tax charges related to the merger with Quaker Oats.
2. Pepsi reports impairment and restructuring charges of $31 million pre-tax.

We add back these two items to net income, net of their income tax effects. If firms disclose the income tax effect, we use the reported amounts. Otherwise, we assume that the marginal federal tax rate of 35 percent applies. Note 2 to PepsiCo's financial statements indicates that the after-tax charge for the merger was $322 million. Note 3 indicates that the after-tax charge for impairment and restructuring charges was $19 million. Thus, we add $341 million (= $322 + $19) to the numerator. The adjusted ROA for PepsiCo for Year 11 is:

$$14.8\% = \frac{\$2,662 + \$341 + (1 - .35)(\$219) + \$0}{.5(\$20,757 + \$21,695)} = \frac{\$3,145}{\$21,226}$$

We make similar adjustments for asset impairment and restructuring charges in Year 9 and Year 10, and a nonrecurring gain from investments in bottlers in Year 9 (see Note 10 to PepsiCo's financial statements). The adjusted ROA for PepsiCo is 11.3 percent for Year 9 and 13.9 percent for Year 10. Thus, PepsiCo's ROA increased continually during the three-year period.

DISAGGREGATING ROA

The analyst obtains further insight into the behavior of ROA by disaggregating it into profit margin and total assets turnover (hereafter referred to as *assets turnover*) components as follows:

ROA	=	**Profit Margin for ROA**	×	**Assets Turnover**
Net Income + Interest Expense (net of taxes) + Minority Interest in Earnings		Net Income + Interest Expense (net of taxes) + Minority Interest in earnings		
———————————	=	———————————	×	———————
Average Total Assets		Sales		Average Total Assets
				Sales

The profit margin indicates the ability of a firm to generate income from operations for a particular level of sales.[2] The assets turnover indicates the ability to manage the level of investment in assets for a particular level of sales or, to put it another way, the ability to generate sales from a particular investment in assets.

The disaggregation of ROA for PepsiCo for Year 11, after adjusting for nonrecurring items, is as follows:

ROA	=	**Profit Margin for ROA**	×	**Assets Turnover**
$\dfrac{\$3,145}{\$21,226}$	=	$\dfrac{\$3,145}{\$26,935}$	×	$\dfrac{\$26,935}{\$21,226}$
14.8%	=	11.7%	×	1.3

Exhibit 4.3 summarizes ROA, profit margin, and assets turnover for PepsiCo for Year 9, Year 10, and Year 11. PepsiCo's profit margin steadily increased, while its assets turnover increased between Year 9 and Year 10, and remained stable between Year 10 and Year 11. After exploring economic and strategic factors underlying ROA and its components in the next section, we return to analyzing the profit margin and assets turnover of PepsiCo in greater depth.

---

[2]One might argue that the analyst should use total revenues, not just sales, in the denominator because assets generate returns in forms other than sales (for example, interest revenue, equity in earnings of affiliates). However, interpretations of various expense ratios (discussed later in this chapter) are usually easier when we use sales in the denominator.

EXHIBIT 4.3			
ROAs, Profit Margins for ROA, and Assets Turnovers for PepsiCo—Year 9 to Year 11			
	Year 9	Year 10	Year 11
ROA.	11.3%	13.9%	14.8%
Profit Margin for ROA	10.2%	11.1%	11.7%
Assets Turnover.	1.1	1.3	1.3

ECONOMIC AND STRATEGIC FACTORS IN THE INTERPRETATION OF ROA[3]

ROA and its components will differ across industries depending on their economic characteristics, and across firms within an industry depending on the design and implementation of their strategies. This section explores economic and strategic factors that impact the interpretation of ROA and its components.

Exhibit 4.4 depicts graphically the 12-year average of the median annual ROAs, profit margins, and assets turnovers of 23 industries for the years 1990 to 2001. The two isoquants reflect ROAs of 3 percent and 6 percent. The isoquants show the various combinations of profit margin and assets turnover that yield an ROA of 3 percent and 6 percent. For instance, an ROA of 6 percent results from any of the following profit margin/assets turnover combinations: 6%/1.0, 3%/2.0, 2%/3.0, 1%/6.0.

The data for ROA, profit margin, and assets turnover underlying the plots in Exhibit 4.4 reflect aggregated amounts across firms and across years. The focus of financial statement analysis is on the ROAs of specific firms, or even segments of specific firms, for particular years (or even quarters). We can obtain useful insights about the behavior of ROA at the segment or firm level, however, by examining the average industry-level data. In particular,

1. What factors explain the consistently high or consistently low ROAs of some industries relative to the average of all industries (that is, reasons for differences in the distribution of industries in the bottom left versus the top right in Exhibit 4.4)?

2. What factors explain the fact that certain industries have high profit margins and low assets turnovers, while other industries experience low profit margins and high assets turnovers (that is, reasons for differences in the distribution of industries in the upper left versus the lower right in Exhibit 4.4)?

---

[3]The material in this section draws heavily from Thomas I. Selling and Clyde P. Stickney, "The Effects of Business Environments and Strategy on a Firm's Rate of Return on Assets," *Financial Analysts Journal* (January/February 1989), pp. 43–52.

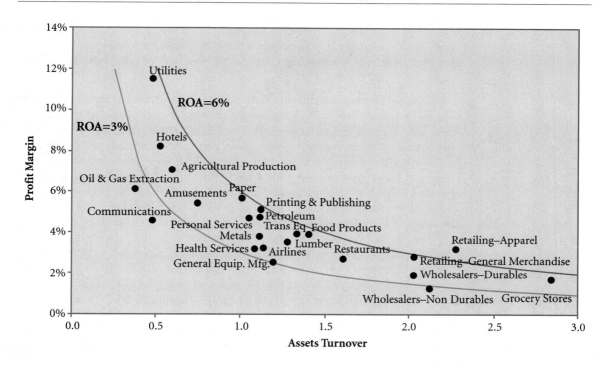

EXHIBIT 4.4

**Average Median ROAs, Profit Margins, and Assets Turnovers
for 23 Industries 1990 to 2001**

The microeconomics and business strategy literatures provide useful background for interpreting the behavior of ROA, profit margin, and assets turnover.

Differences or Changes in ROA

Economic theory suggests that higher levels of perceived risk in any activity should lead to higher levels of expected return if that activity is to attract capital. The extra return compensates for the extra risk assumed. Realized rates of return (ROAs) derived from financial statement data for any particular period will not necessarily correlate perfectly with expected returns or with the level of risk involved in an activity as economic theory suggests if:

1. Faulty assumptions were used in deriving expected ROAs.
2. Changes in the environment after forming expectations cause realized ROAs to deviate from expectations (for example, an unexpected recession).
3. ROA is an incomplete measure of economic rates of return (that is, rates of return that include all changes in economic value) because generally accepted

accounting principles rely on acquisition costs for reliable measurement of assets and conservatism in measuring income.

Despite these potential weaknesses, ROAs based on reported financial statement data do provide useful information for tracking the past, periodic performance of a firm and its segments, and for developing expectations about future earnings potential. Three elements of risk help in understanding differences across firms and changes over time in ROAs: (1) operating leverage, (2) cyclicality of sales, and (3) stage and length of product life cycles.

Operating Leverage. Firms operate with different mixtures of fixed and variable costs in their cost structures. Firms in the utilities, communications, hotel, petroleum, and chemical industries are capital-intensive. Depreciation and many operating costs are more or less fixed for any given period. Most retailers and wholesalers, on the other hand, have high proportions of variable costs in their cost structures. Firms with high proportions of fixed costs will experience significant increases in operating income as sales increase. The increased income occurs because the firms spread fixed costs over a larger number of units sold, resulting in a decrease in average unit cost. Likewise, when sales decrease, these firms experience sharp decreases in operating income. Economists refer to this process of operating with high proportions of fixed costs as *operating leverage*. Firms with high levels of operating leverage experience greater variability in their ROAs than firms with low levels of operating leverage. All else being equal (see the discussion of cyclicality of sales in the next section), firms with high levels of operating leverage incur more risk in their operations and should earn higher rates of return.

Measuring the degree of operating leverage of a firm or its segments requires information about the fixed and variable cost structure. The top panel of Exhibit 4.5 shows the total revenue and total cost functions of two firms, A and B. The graphs assume that the two firms are the same size, have the same total revenue functions, and the same break-even points. These assumptions simplify the discussion of operating leverage but are not necessary when comparing actual companies.

Firm B has a higher level of fixed costs than Firm A, as measured by the intersection of the vertical axis at zero sales in the top panel of Exhibit 4.5. Firm A has a higher level of variable costs than Firm B, as measured by the slope of its total cost functions as revenues increase above zero. The lower panel nets the total revenue and total cost functions to derive the operating income function. Operating income is negative in an amount equal to fixed costs when revenues are zero and operating income is zero at break-even revenues. We use the slope of the operating income line as a measure of the extent of operating leverage. Firm B, with its higher fixed cost and lower variable cost mix, has more operating leverage. As revenues increase, its operating income increases more than that for Firm A. On the downside, however, income decreases more sharply for Firm B as revenues decrease.

Unfortunately, firms do not publicly disclose information about their fixed and variable cost structures. To examine the influence of operating leverage on the behavior of ROA for a particular firm or its segments, the analyst must estimate the

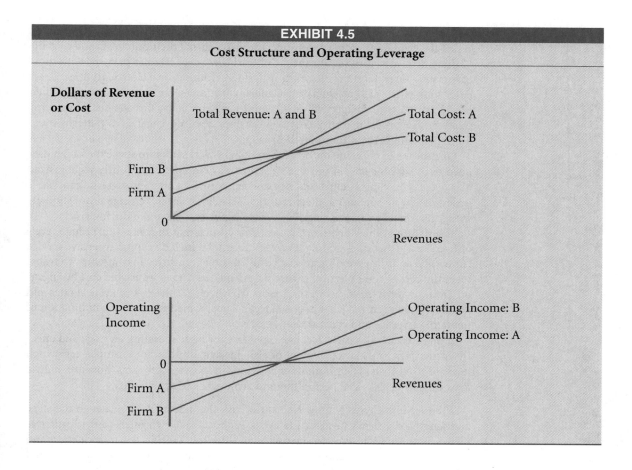

EXHIBIT 4.5

Cost Structure and Operating Leverage

fixed/variable cost structure. One approach to such estimation is to study the various cost items of a firm and attempt to identify those items that are likely to behave as fixed costs. Firms incur some costs in particular amounts, referred to as *committed fixed costs*, regardless of the actual level of activity during the period. Examples include depreciation, amortization, and rent. Firms can alter the amount of other costs, referred to as *discretionary fixed costs*, in the short run in response to operating conditions but, in general, these costs do not vary directly with the level of activity. Examples include research and development, maintenance, advertising, and central corporate staff expenses. Whether the analyst should classify these latter costs as fixed costs or as variable costs in measuring operating leverage depends on their behavior in a particular firm.

Cyclicality of Sales. The sales of certain goods and services are sensitive to conditions in the economy. Examples include construction services, industrial equipment, computers, automobiles, and other durable goods. When the economy is in an upswing (healthy GNP growth, low unemployment, low interest rates), customers purchase these relatively high-priced items and sales of these firms grow accordingly. When the economy enters a recession, customers curtail their purchases and the sales of these firms decrease significantly. Contrast these cyclical sales patterns with those of grocery stores, food processors, non-fashion clothing, and electric utilities. These latter industries sell products that most consumers consider necessities. Their products also tend to carry lower per unit costs, reducing the benefits of delaying purchases in order to realize cost savings. Firms with cyclical sales patterns incur more risk than firms with noncyclical sales.

One means of reducing the risk inherent in cyclical sales is to strive for a high proportion of variable cost in the cost structure. Pay employees an hourly wage instead of a fixed salary, and rent buildings and equipment under short-term cancelable leases instead of purchasing these facilities. Cost levels should change proportionally with sales, thereby maintaining profit margin percentages and reducing risk.

The nature of the activities of some firms is such that they must carry high levels of fixed costs (that is, operating leverage). Examples include capital-intensive service firms such as airlines and railroads. Firms in these industries may attempt to transform the cost of their physical capacity from a fixed cost to a variable cost by engaging in short-term leases. However, lessors will then bear the risk of cyclical sales and demand higher returns (that is, rental fees). Thus, some firms bear a combination of operating leverage and cyclical sales risks.

A noncyclical sales pattern can compensate for high operating leverage and effectively neutralize this latter element of risk. Electric utilities, for example, carry high levels of fixed costs. Their dominant positions in most service areas, however, reduce their operating risks and permit them to achieve stable profitability.

Product Life Cycle. A third element of risk that affects ROA relates to the stage and length of a firm's product life cycle. Products move through four identifiable phases: introduction, growth, maturity, and decline. During the introduction and growth phases, a firm focuses on product development (product R&D spending) and capacity enlargement (capital spending). The objective is to gain market acceptance and market share. Considerable uncertainty may exist during these phases regarding the market viability of a firm's products. Products that have survived into the maturity phase have gained market acceptance. Also, firms have probably been able to cut back capital expenditures on new operating capacity. During the maturity phase, however, competition becomes more intense, and the emphasis shifts to reducing costs through improved capacity utilization (economies of scale) and more efficient production (process R&D spending aimed at reducing manufacturing costs through better utilization of labor and materials). During the decline phase, firms exit the industry as sales decline and profit opportunities diminish.

Exhibit 4.6 depicts the behavior of revenues, operating income, investment, and ROA that corresponds to the four phases of the product life cycle. During the introduction and early growth phases, expenditures on product development and marketing, coupled with relatively low sales levels, lead to operating losses and negative ROAs. As sales accelerate during the high growth phase, operating income and ROAs turn positive. Extensive product development, marketing, and depreciation expenses

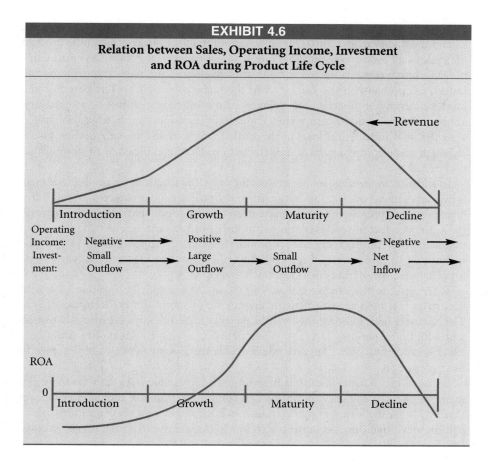

EXHIBIT 4.6

Relation between Sales, Operating Income, Investment and ROA during Product Life Cycle

during this phase moderate operating income, while heavy capital expenditures to build capacity for expected higher future sales increase the denominator of ROA. Thus, ROA does not grow as rapidly as sales. ROA increases significantly during the maturity phase due to benefits of economies of scale and learning curve phenomena, and to curtailments of capital expenditures. ROA deteriorates during the decline phase as operating income decreases, but may remain positive or even increase for some time into this phase. Thus, as products move through their life cycles, their ROAs should move to the upper right area in Exhibit 4.4, peak during the maturity stage, and then move to the lower left area as the decline phase sets in. This movement in ROA appears negatively correlated with the level of risk. Risks are probably highest in the introduction and growth stages, when ROA is low or negative, and least in the maturity phase, when ROA is high. Taking a weighted average of ROAs over several years will reflect more accurately the economic returns generated by high growth firms.

Note that the product life cycle theory focuses on individual products. We can extend the theory to an industry level by examining the average stage in the product life cycle of all products within that industry. For instance, the products in the computer industry range from the introduction to the decline phases, but the overall industry is probably in the latter part of the high growth phase. The beverage and food processing industries, the primary involvements of PepsiCo, are mature, although PepsiCo and its competitors continually introduce new products. We might view the steel industry, at least in the United States, as in the early decline phase, although some companies have modernized production sufficiently to stave off the decline.[4]

In addition to the stage in the product life cycle, the length of the product life cycle is also an element of risk. Products with short product life cycles require more frequent expenditures to develop replacement or new products and thereby increase risks. The product life cycles of most computer products run one to two years. Most pharmaceutical products experience product life cycles of approximately seven years. In contrast, the life cycles of PepsiCo's soft drinks, branded food products, and some toys (for example, Barbie dolls) are much longer.

Refer again to the average industry ROAs in Exhibit 4.4. The location of several industries is consistent with their incurring one or more of these elements of risk. The relatively high ROAs of the utilities, paper, and petroleum industries are consistent with high operating leverage. Paper, petroleum, and transportation equipment experience cyclical sales. Apparel retailers face the risk of fashion obsolescence of their products.

Some of the industry locations in Exhibit 4.4 appear inconsistent with these elements of risk. Oil and gas exploration and communications are capital intensive, yet their ROAs are the lowest of the 23 industries. One might view these positions as disequilibrium situations. Generating such low ROAs will not likely attract capital over the longer term.

The ROA locations of several industries appear to be affected by generally accepted accounting principles (GAAP). A principal resource of food products firms, such as General Mills or Kellogg's, is the value of their brand names. Yet, GAAP requires these firms to expense immediately advertising and other costs incurred to develop these brand names. Thus, their asset bases are understated and their ROAs are overstated.[5] Likewise, the publishing industry does not recognize the value of copyrights or authors' contracts as assets, resulting in an overstatement of ROAs. A similar overstatement problem occurs for service firms, where the value of their employees does not appear as an asset.

---

[4]Empirical support for a link between life cycle stage, sales growth, capital expenditure growth, and stock market reaction appears in Joseph H. Anthony and K. Ramesh, "Association Between Accounting Performance Measures and Stock Prices: A Test of the Life Cycle Hypothesis," *Journal of Accounting and Economics*, 15 (1992), pp. 203–227.

[5]The immediate expensing of advertising costs understates net income as well, but the difference between the amount expensed and amortization of amounts from the current and prior periods that perhaps should have been capitalized will result in less distortion of net income than of total assets.

Differences in the Profit Margin/Assets Turnover Mix

In addition to differences in ROA depicted in Exhibit 4.4, we must also examine reasons for differences in the relative mix of profit margin and assets turnover. Explanations come from both the microeconomics and business strategy literatures.

Microeconomic Theory. Exhibit 4.7 sets out some important economic factors that constrain certain firms and industries to operate with particular combinations of profit margins and assets turnovers. Firms and industries characterized by heavy fixed capacity costs and lengthy periods required to add new capacity operate under a capacity constraint. There is an upper limit on the size of assets turnover achievable. In order to attract sufficient capital, these firms must generate a relatively high profit margin. Such firms will therefore operate in the area of Exhibit 4.7 marked **Ⓐ**. The firms usually achieve the high profit margin through some form of entry barrier. The entry barrier may take the form of large required capital outlays, high risks, or regulation. Such factors help explain the profit margin/assets turnover mix of utilities, oil and gas exploration, communications, hotels, and amusements in Exhibit 4.4.

EXHIBIT 4.7
Economic Factors Affecting the Profit Margin/Assets Turnover Mix

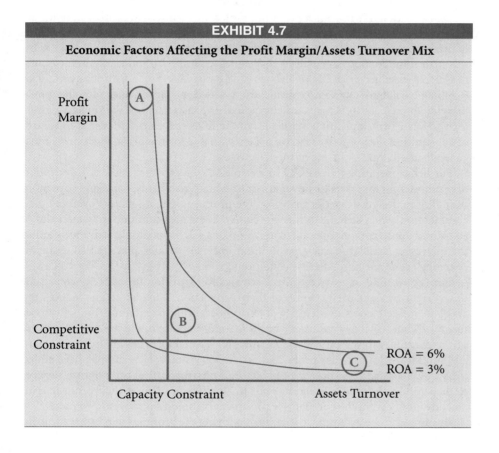

Firms whose products are commodity-like in nature, where there are few entry barriers, and where competition is intense, operate under a competitive constraint. There is an upper limit on the level of profit margin achievable. In order to attract sufficient capital, these firms must strive for high assets turnovers. Such firms will therefore operate in the area of Exhibit 4.7 marked **Ⓒ**. Firms achieve the high assets turnovers by keeping costs as low as possible (for example, minimizing fixed overhead costs, purchasing in sufficient quantities to realize discounts, and integrating vertically or horizontally to obtain cost savings). These firms match such actions to control costs with aggressively low prices to gain market share and drive out marginal firms. Most retailers and wholesalers operate in the low profit margin/high assets turnover area of Exhibit 4.4.

Firms that operate in the area of Exhibit 4.7 marked as **Ⓑ** are not as subject to either capacity or competitive constraints as severe as those that operate in the tails of the ROA curves. Therefore, they have more flexibility to take actions that will increase profit margin, assets turnover, or both, to achieve a higher ROA.

The notion of flexibility in trading off profit margin for assets turnover (or vice versa) is important when a firm considers strategic alternatives. The underlying economic concept is the marginal rate of substitution.

Consider first a firm with a profit margin/assets turnover combination that puts it in the **Ⓐ** area of Exhibit 4.7. Such a firm will have to give up a significant amount of profit margin to obtain a meaningful increase in assets turnover. To increase ROA, this firm should emphasize actions that increase profit margin; it might, for example, increase selling prices or reduce variable costs. Likewise, a firm in area **Ⓒ** of Exhibit 4.7 will have to give up considerable assets turnover to achieve a higher profit margin. To increase ROA, such a firm should emphasize actions that increase assets turnover. For firms operating in the tails of the ROA curves, the poor marginal rates of substitution do not favor trading off one variable for the other. Such firms must generally emphasize only one of these factors.

For firms operating in area **Ⓑ** in Exhibit 4.7, the marginal rates of substitution of profit margin for assets turnover are more equal. Such firms, therefore, have more flexibility to design strategies that promote profit margin, assets turnover, or some combination, when striving to increase ROA. Unless the economic characteristics of a business constrain it to operate in area **Ⓐ** or **Ⓒ**, firms should strive to position themselves in area **Ⓑ**. Such positioning provides greater potential to adapt to changing economic and business conditions.

Firms operating in area **Ⓐ** might attempt to reposition the capacity constraint to the right by outsourcing some of their production. Such an action reduces the amount of fixed assets needed per dollar of sales (that is, increases the fixed asset turnover), but will likely reduce the profit margin (because of the need to share some of the margin with the outsourcing company). Firms operating in area **Ⓒ** might add products with a higher profit margin. Grocery stores, for example, have added fresh flowers, salad bars, bakery products, and pharmaceutical prescription services to their product offerings in recent years in an effort to increase their profit margin and advance beyond the competitive constraint common for grocery products.

In summary, the economic concepts underlying the profit margin/assets turnover mix are the following:

Area in Exhibit 4.7	Capital Intensity	Competition	Likely Strategic Focus
(A)	High	Monopoly	Profit Margin
(B)	Medium	Oligopolistic or Monopolistic Competition	Profit Margin, Assets Turnover, or Some Combination
(C)	Low	Pure Competition	Assets Turnover

Business Strategy. Both Hall[6] and Porter[7] suggest that firms have two generic, alternative strategies for any particular product: product differentiation and low-cost leadership. The thrust of the product-differentiation strategy is to differentiate a product in such a way as to obtain market power over revenues and, therefore, profit margins. The differentiation could relate to product capabilities, product quality, service, channels of distribution, or some other factor. The thrust of the low-cost leadership strategy is to become the lowest cost producer, thereby enabling the firm to charge the lowest prices and to achieve higher volumes. Such firms can achieve the low-cost position through economies of scale, production efficiencies, outsourcing, or similar factors, or by asset parsimony (maintaining strict controls on investments in receivables, inventories, and capital expenditures).[8]

In terms of Exhibit 4.4, movements in the direction of area **(A)** from any point along the ROA curves focus on product differentiation. Likewise, movements in the direction of area **(C)** from any point along the ROA curves focus on low-cost leadership. To illustrate, let us look at the average profit margins and assets turnovers for three types of retailers during the period 1990 to 2001:

	Profit Margin	Assets Turnover
Specialty Retailers....................	3.27%	2.27
General Merchandise Stores.............	2.87%	2.02
Grocery Stores	1.78%	2.83

Within the retailing industry, specialty retailers have differentiated themselves by following a niche strategy and achieved a higher profit margin than the other two segments. Competition severely constrains the profit margin of grocery stores and they must pursue more low-cost leadership strategies. Thus, a firm does not have to be in the tails of the ROA curves to be described as a product differentiator or low-cost

---

[6]W.K. Hall, "Survival Strategies in a Hostile Environment," *Harvard Business Review* (September–October 1980), pp. 78–85.

[7]M.E. Porter, *Competitive Strategy: Techniques for Analyzing Industries and Competitors*, (New York: Free Press, 1998). Porter suggests that firms might also pursue a niche strategy. Because a niche strategy essentially represents differentiation within a market segment, we include it here under product differentiation strategy.

[8]Research in business strategy suggests that firms can simultaneously pursue product differentiation and low-cost leadership since product differentiation is revenue (output) oriented and low-cost leadership is more expense (input) oriented.

leader. The appropriate basis of comparison is not other industries but other firms in the same industry. Remember, however, that the relative location along the ROA curve affects a firm's flexibility to trade off profit margin (product differentiation) for assets turnover (low-cost leadership).

Summarizing, differences in the profit margin/assets turnover mix relate to economic factors external to a firm, such as degree of competition, extent of regulation, entry barriers and similar factors, and to internal strategic choices, such as product differentiation and low-cost leadership. The external and internal factors are, of course, interdependent and in a continual state of change.

PepsiCo's Positioning Relative to Consumer Foods Industry

PepsiCo is part of the food products industry. The average of the median ROA, profit margin, and assets turnover for the food products industry for Year 9, Year 10, and Year 11, and the amounts for PepsiCo for each year, are as follows:

	Food Products Industry	PepsiCo
ROA........................	5.3%	13.3%
Profit Margin for ROA	4.1%	11.0%
Total Assets Turnover	1.3	1.2

Note that the average ROA of PepsiCo significantly exceeds that for the food products industry, primarily as a result of the higher profit margins earned by PepsiCo. Possible economic or strategic explanations for the higher profit margin include (1) more value to its brand names than other food products companies, (2) greater pricing power because of domination of the beverage industry by PepsiCo and Coke, (3) greater pricing power because of PepsiCo's influence over its bottlers, and (4) greater efficiencies due it its size or quality of management. The next section explores this higher profit margin more fully.

ANALYZING THE PROFIT MARGIN FOR ROA

We disaggregated ROA into its profit margin and assets turnover components. One might liken this disaggregation to peeling an onion. ROA is the outer layer (Level 1). Peeling away that layer reveals the profit margin for ROA and assets turnover (Level 2). We can peel the onion an additional layer by examining the components of the profit margin for ROA and the components of total assets turnover (Level 3).

A study of the relation between individual expenses and sales can identify reasons for differences in the profit margin percentage. Exhibit 4.8 presents these expense percentages for PepsiCo, which expresses each expense as a percentage of sales. We should note that these percentages can change because of (a) changes in expenses in the numerator independent of changes in sales (for example, an increase in employee compensation levels), (b) changes in sales independent of changes in expenses (for example, because the expense is fixed for the period), (c) interaction effects between

EXHIBIT 4.8			
Analysis of the Profit Margin for PepsiCo—Year 9 to Year 11			
	Year 9	**Year 10**	**Year 11**
Sales	100.0%	100.0%	100.0%
Other Revenues	.8	.8	.8
Cost of Goods Sold	(41.1)	(40.1)	(39.9)
Selling and Administrative............	(43.9)	(43.6)	(43.1)
Goodwill Amortization	(.8)	(.6)	(.6)
Income Taxes	(4.8)	(5.4)	(5.5)
Profit Margin	10.2%	11.1%	11.7%

numerator and denominator (an increase in advertising expenses leads to an increase in sales), or (d) coincident but independent changes in the numerator and denominator (that is, combinations of the other three possibilities).

Note from Exhibit 4.8 that decreases in the cost of goods sold to sales percentage, and in the selling and administrative expenses to sales percentage offset by an increase in the income tax expense to sales percentage, account for the increase in the profit margin for ROA during this period.

The task for the financial analyst is to identify likely reasons for the changes in these expense percentages. As Chapter 1 indicates, the annual report to shareholders and the Form 10-K report to the SEC include a narrative discussion by management of reasons for changes in a firm's profitability and risk. Appendix B includes management's discussion for PepsiCo. Firms vary with respect to the informativeness of these discussions. Some firms give specific reasons for changes in various financial ratios. Other firms simply indicate the rate of increase or decrease without providing explanations for the changes. Even when firms provide explanations, the analyst should assess their reasonableness in light of conditions in the economy and in the industry, as well as the firm's stated strategy, and the results for the firms' competitors.

Cost of Goods Sold

Interpreting changes in the cost of goods sold to sales percentage are often difficult because explanations might relate to sales revenue only, to cost of goods sold only, or to common factors affecting both the numerator and the denominator. Consider, for example, the following possible explanations for a decrease in the cost of goods sold to sales percentage for a firm:

1. An increase in demand for products in excess of available capacity in an industry will likely result in an increase in selling prices. Even though the cost of manufacturing the product does not change, the cost of goods sold percentage will decrease.
2. As a result of product improvements or effective advertising, a firm's market

share for its product increases. The firm allocates the fixed cost of manufacturing the product over a larger volume of production, thereby lowering its per unit cost. Even though selling prices do not change, the cost of goods sold to sales percentage will decrease.

3. A firm lowers the price for its product in order to gain a larger market share. It lowers its manufacturing cost per unit by purchasing raw materials in larger quantities to take advantage of quantity discounts. Cost of goods sold per unit declines more than selling price per unit, causing the cost of goods sold to sales percentage to decline.

4. A firm sells multiple products with different cost of goods sold to sales percentages. The product mix shifts toward higher profit margin products, thereby lowering the overall cost of goods sold to sales percentage.

Thus, the analyst must consider changes in selling prices, manufacturing costs, and product mix when interpreting changes in the cost of goods sold percentage.

Exhibit 4.8 indicates that PepsiCo's cost of goods sold to sales percentage continually decreased during the three-year period. Management's discussion of the results of operations in Appendix B does not provide a separate discussion of the reasons for the changes in the cost of goods sold percentage. We can gain additional insight into the likely reasons for the decreasing cost of goods sold percentage by examining data for each of PepsiCo's operating segments. We do so after considering changes in the selling and administrative expenses to sales percentage.

Selling and Administrative Expenses

Most firms combine selling and administrative expenses on the income statement. Combining these expense items is unfortunate from an analysis perspective because different factors tend to drive these two expenses. Selling expenses include sales commissions, advertising, and promotion materials, and usually vary with the level of sales. Administrative expenses include top management's salaries and the cost of operating staff departments such as information systems, legal services, and research and development costs that tend not to vary with the level of sales.

PepsiCo's selling and administrative expenses to sales percentage decreased continually over the three-year period. Management's discussion of operations in Appendix B also does not provide a separate discussion of the reasons for the changes in selling and administrative expenses. Note 1 under Marketing Costs discloses the amount of advertising expenses each year. These expenses were $1.6 billion in Year 9 and $1.7 billion in Year 10 and Year 11. Advertising expense as a percentage of sales was 7.0 percent in Year 9, 6.7 percent in Year 10, and 6.3 percent in Year 11. Thus, virtually all of the decrease in the selling and administrative expense to sales percentage results from spreading a relatively fixed advertising expense over a larger sales base. PepsiCo may have strategically maintained its advertising levels, expecting consumer loyalty to its brand names to provide continuing sales increases. Alternatively, either excess supply of media time and space or decreased demand for such media time and space in a recessionary period may have lowered advertising rates, permitting PepsiCo to advertise more but at a similar total cost as in the past.

Segment Data

Most firms in the United States provide profitability data for product and geographical segments. Note 21 to PepsiCo's financial statements presents segment data for each of its product segments. It separates operations in its snack foods (Frito-Lay) and Pepsi-Cola segments into the portions attributable to North American and to international operations. Firms report segment sales, operating income, assets, capital expenditures, and depreciation and amortization for each segment.

The segment disclosures permit the analyst to examine ROA, profit margin, and assets turnover at an additional level (Level 4) of depth, in effect peeling the onion one more layer. Unfortunately, firms do not report cost of goods sold and selling and administrative expenses for each segment, so we cannot reconcile changes in segment profit margins to changes in the overall levels of these two expense percentages. Firms also report segment data pre-tax, so the segment ROAs and profit margins exceed those for the overall company to a considerable extent.

Exhibit 4.9 presents sales mix data for PepsiCo. Exhibit 4.10 presents ROAs, profit margins, and assets turnovers for each of PepsiCo's segments. Observe that the profit margin increased over the three-year period for each of PepsiCo's segments except Pepsi North America beverages. One likely explanation for the increasing segment profit margins is the spreading of the relatively fixed amount of advertising expense over a larger sales level. This explanation ties in with the decrease in the selling and administrative expense to sales percentage for PepsiCo as a whole.

Another explanation might relate to a change in the sales mix. The proportion of sales from Pepsi North America beverages increased during the three-year period. This is PepsiCo's segment with the largest profit margin. A shift in the sales mix toward a segment with a higher profit margin percentage can result in a decrease in the expense percentages (either cost of goods sold, selling and administrative, or both).

EXHIBIT 4.9			
Sales Mix Data for PepsiCo			
	Year 9	Year 10	Year 11
Snacks:			
North America	35.9%	35.2%	34.8%
International	18.6	19.1	19.0
Beverages:			
Pepsi North America..............	11.3	12.9	14.3
Pepsi International	10.5	10.0	9.6
Other Beverages	15.0	15.1	14.9
Quaker Oats......................	8.7	7.7	7.4
Total........................	100.0%	100.0%	100.0%

EXHIBIT 4.10
Product Segment Profitability Analysis for PepsiCo

	ROA		
	Year 9	**Year 10**	**Year 11**
Snacks:			
North America.	40.5%	44.7%	44.5%
International	10.3%	12.6%	14.3%
Total Snacks.	26.0%	29.8%	31.2%
Beverages:			
Pepsi North America	103.0%	99.6%	70.0%
Pepsi International	5.4%	8.8%	12.7%
Other Beverages.	11.0%	12.1%	12.2%
Total Beverages	19.4%	21.8%	22.7%
Quaker Oats	35.0%	41.2%	45.3%

	Profit Margin				Assets Turnover		
	Year 9	**Year 10**	**Year 11**		**Year 9**	**Year 10**	**Year 11**
Snacks:							
North America	20.4%	21.3%	21.9%		2.0	2.1	2.0
International.	10.6%	11.2%	12.2%		1.0	1.1	1.2
Total Snacks	17.2%	18.0%	18.8%		1.5	1.6	1.7
Beverages:							
Pepsi North America . . .	28.8%	25.3%	24.1%		3.6	3.9	2.9
Pepsi International.	4.5%	6.7%	8.6%		1.2	1.3	1.5
Other Beverages	12.5%	13.0%	13.2%		.9	.9	.9
Total Beverages.	15.3%	15.5%	16.1%		1.3	1.4	1.4
Quaker Oats	18.2%	19.9%	20.8%		1.9	2.1	2.2

Although the profit margin of Pepsi North America is larger than those for PepsiCo's other segments, the profit margin for Pepsi North America decreased during the three years. PepsiCo indicates in Appendix B that only one percentage point of the 8.3 percent increase in sales in Year 10 and only four percentage points of the 18.1 percent increase in sales in Year 11 were due to volume increases. Thus, most of the increasing sales of Pepsi North America each year resulted from price increases. Substantial price increases should have led to decreased expense percentages and increased profit margins for this segment. The decreasing profit margin for this segment might result from the need to share more of the gross profit with bottlers that PepsiCo previously owned entirely but now owns less than 50 percent.

Income Taxes

Exhibit 4.8 indicates that income taxes as a percentage of sales increased each year. These changes in the income tax percentage do not necessarily mean that PepsiCo's income tax burden is changing. Governmental entities impose income taxes on income (that is, revenues minus expenses), not on sales. A more appropriate measure of the income tax burden, referred to as the *effective tax rate*, relates income tax expense to net income before income taxes. Refer to Exhibit 4.11. Instead of using the dollar amounts from PepsiCo's income statement, Exhibit 4.11 uses the percentages from Exhibit 4.8 to compute the effective tax rate. Exhibit 4.11 indicates that PepsiCo had a stable effective tax rate during the three-year period. Thus, income taxes do not account for the overall increase in the profit margin for ROA.

Firms must disclose in notes to the financial statements their effective tax rate and the reasons why this rate differs from the statutory federal tax rate. Note 14 to PepsiCo's financial statements in Appendix A presents this information. Note that PepsiCo reports an effective tax rate of 41.4 percent in Year 9, 32.4 percent in Year 10, and 33.9 percent in Year 11. PepsiCo reports reconciling items, however, for the gain on sale of bottlers and merger, impairment, and restructuring costs. Earlier, we eliminated these items and their income tax effects before calculating ROA for PepsiCo. Eliminating the tax effects of these items results in a stable effective tax rate of approximately 32 percent. Chapter 8 discusses the analysis of the effective tax rate more fully.

EXHIBIT 4.11			
Calculation of Effective Tax Rate on Operating Income **(Amounts Taken from Exhibit 4.8)**			
	Year 9	Year 10	Year 11
Numerator			
(1) Income Taxes	4.8%	5.4%	5.5%
Denominator			
(2) Profit Margin for ROA.	10.2%	11.1%	11.7%
(3) Income Taxes	4.8	5.4	5.5
(4) Profit Margin Before Income Taxes.	15.0%	16.5%	17.2%
(5) Effective Tax Rate on Operations (1) ÷ (4)	32.0%	32.7%	32.0%

Summary of Profit Margin Analysis

We noted at the beginning of this section that PepsiCo's profit margin increased steadily between Year 9 and Year 11. The increased profit margin results from a decreasing cost of goods sold to sales percentage, and a decreasing selling and administrative expense to sales percentage. The decline in the cost of goods sold to sales percentage may result from a shift in the sales mix toward Pepsi North America, its most profitable segment. The decline in the selling and administrative expense to sales percentage likely results from a relatively constant advertising expense compared to increases in sales revenues.

ANALYZING TOTAL ASSETS TURNOVER

We noted earlier that PepsiCo's total assets turnover increased from 1.1 in Year 9 to 1.3 in Year 10 and Year 11. The assets turnover for Year 9 is not comparable to those for Year 10 and 11. During Year 8, PepsiCo owned a controlling interest in most of its bottlers. The assets of these bottlers appeared on PepsiCo's consolidated balance sheet. PepsiCo reduced its ownership interest in these bottlers in Year 9 to below 50 percent and therefore discontinued consolidating the bottlers (Chapter 9 discusses the criteria for preparing consolidated financial statements). PepsiCo's balance sheet for the end of Year 8 consolidates these bottlers but the balance sheet for Year 9 excludes the individual assets of these bottlers. The amount for average assets for Year 9 used in the denominator of the total assets turnover is therefore overstated and the total assets turnover is understated. Thus, the increase in the total assets turnover between Year 9 and Year 10 may not represent a real increase but may simply be a result of the change in accounting for investments in bottlers.

We can gain greater insight into changes in the total assets turnover by examining turnover ratios for particular assets. Analysts frequently calculate three turnover ratios: accounts receivable turnover, inventory turnover, and fixed asset turnover. The management discussion and analysis of operations usually does not include explanations for changes in asset turnovers, so the analyst will need to search for possible clues. Note in this case that, like the total assets turnover, the individual asset turnovers for Year 9 are not comparable to those for Year 10 and Year 11 because of the change in the accounting for bottlers.

Accounts Receivable Turnover

The rate at which accounts receivable turn over gives an indication of how soon they will convert into cash. The analyst calculates the accounts receivable turnover by dividing net sales on account by average accounts receivable. Most sales transactions between businesses are on account instead of for cash. Except for retailers and restaurants that deal directly with consumers, the assumption that all sales are on account is usually reasonable. The calculation of the accounts receivable turnover for Year 11 for PepsiCo, assuming that it makes all sales on account, is as follows:

$$\frac{\text{Accounts Receivable}}{\text{Turnover}} = \frac{\text{Net Sales on Account}}{\text{Average Accounts Receivable}}$$

$$12.6 = \frac{\$26,935}{.5(\$2,129 + \$2,142)}$$

PepsiCo's accounts receivable turnover was 10.7 in Year 9 and 12.5 in Year 10. The lower accounts receivable turnover in Year 9 results from PepsiCo's consolidation of its bottlers at the end of Year 8 but not the end of Year 9. PepsiCo's accounts receivable turnover changed very little between Year 10 and Year 11.

The analyst often expresses the accounts receivable turnover in terms of the average number of days receivables are outstanding before their conversion into cash. The calculation divides 365 days by the accounts receivable turnover. The average number of days that accounts receivable were outstanding is 34.1 days (= 365/10.7) for Year 9, 29.2 days (= 365/12.5) for Year 10, and 29.0 days (=365/12.6) for Year 11.

The interpretation of the average collection period depends on the terms of sale. If customers must pay within 30 days, then it appears that most of PepsiCo's customers pay within the required period. If the terms of sales are, say, 15 days, then PepsiCo does not collect on average within the required period. Many firms transact business with terms of 30 days. Thus, PepsiCo does not appear to have a major problem with collecting its accounts receivable.

The interpretation of changes in the accounts receivable turnover and average collection period also relates to a firm's credit extension policies. Firms will often use credit terms as a means of stimulating sales. For example, firms might permit customers to delay making payments on purchases of lawn mowers until after the summer and on snowmobiles until after the winter in an effort to stimulate sales. Such actions would lead to a decrease in the accounts receivable turnover and an increase in the days receivables are outstanding. The changes in these accounts receivable ratios would not necessarily signal negative news if the increase in net income from the additional sales exceeded the cost of carrying accounts receivable for the extra time.

Retailing firms, particularly department store chains such as Sears and JC Penney, offer their own credit cards to customers. They use credit cards both to stimulate sales and to earn interest revenue from delayed payments by customers. Interpreting an increase in the number of days accounts receivable are outstanding involves two conflicting signals. The increase might suggest greater risk of uncollectibility but it also provides additional interest revenues. Some firms price their products to obtain a relatively low gross margin from the sale and depend on interest revenues as their principal source of earnings. Thus, the analyst must consider a firm's credit strategy and policies when interpreting the accounts receivable turnover and days receivable outstanding ratios.

Inventory Turnover

The rate at which inventories turn over gives an indication of how soon they will be sold. The analyst calculates the inventory turnover by dividing cost of goods sold by the average inventory during the period. The calculation of inventory turnover for PepsiCo for Year 11 is as follows:

$$\frac{\text{Inventory}}{\text{Turnover}} = \frac{\text{Cost of Goods Sold}}{\text{Average Inventories}}$$

$$8.6 = \frac{\$10,754}{.5(\$1,192 + \$1,310)}$$

Thus, PepsiCo's inventory was on hand for 42.4 days (=365/8.6) on average during Year 11. Pepsi's inventory turnover was 8.5 (42.9 days) in Year 9 and 8.7 (42.0 days) in Year 10. The increase in the inventory turnover between Year 9 and Year 10 results in large part from the deconsolidation of its bottlers. However, the changes in inventory turnover and days inventory for all three years were minor.

The interpretation of the inventory turnover figure involves two opposing considerations. A firm would like to sell as many goods as possible with a minimum of capital tied up in inventories. An increase in the rate of inventory turnover between periods would seem to indicate more profitable use of the investment in inventory. On the other hand, a firm does not want to have so little inventory on hand that shortages result and the firm must turn away customers. An increase in the rate of inventory turnover in this case may mean a loss of customers and thereby offset any advantage gained by a decreased investment in inventory. Firms must make trade-offs in deciding the optimum level of inventory and thus the desirable rate of inventory turnover.

The analyst often gains insights into changes in the inventory turnover by examining changes in both the inventory turnover and the cost of goods sold to sales percentage simultaneously. Consider the following scenarios and possible interpretations:

1. **Increasing cost of goods sold to sales percentage, coupled with an increasing inventory turnover.** Firm lowers prices to sell inventory more quickly. Firm shifts its product mix toward lower margin, faster moving products. Firm outsources the production of a higher proportion of its products, requiring the firm to share profit margin with the outsourcer but reducing the amount of raw materials and work-in-process inventories.

2. **Decreasing cost of goods sold to sales percentage, coupled with a decreasing inventory turnover.** Firm raises prices to increase its gross margin but inventory sells more slowly. Firm shifts its product mix toward higher margin, slower moving products. Firm produces a higher proportion of its products instead of outsourcing, thereby capturing more of the gross margin but requiring the firm to carry raw materials and work-in-process inventories.

3. **Increasing cost of goods sold to sales percentage, coupled with a decreasing inventory turnover.** Weak economic conditions lead to reduced demand for a firm's products, necessitating price reductions to move goods. Despite price reductions, inventory builds up.

4. **Decreasing cost of goods sold to sales percentage, coupled with an increasing inventory turnover.** Strong economic conditions lead to increased demand for a firm's products, allowing price increases. An inability to replace

inventory as fast as the firm sells it leads to an increased inventory turnover. Firm implements a just-in-time inventory system, reducing storage costs, product obsolescence, and the amount of inventory held.

Some analysts calculate the inventory turnover ratio by dividing sales, rather than cost of goods sold, by the average inventory. As long as there is a reasonably constant relation between selling prices and cost of goods sold, the analyst can identify changes in the trend of the inventory turnover with either measure. It is inappropriate to use sales in the numerator if the analyst desires to use the inventory turnover ratio to calculate the average number of days inventory is on hand until sale.

The cost-flow assumption (FIFO, LIFO, weighted average) for inventories and cost of goods sold can significantly affect both the inventory turnover ratio and the cost of goods sold to sales percentage. Chapter 7 discusses the impact of the cost-flow assumption and illustrates adjustments the analyst might make to deal with these effects.

Fixed Asset Turnover

The fixed asset turnover ratio measures the relation between sales and the investment in property, plant, and equipment. The analyst calculates the fixed asset turnover by dividing sales by average fixed assets (net of accumulated depreciation) during the year. The fixed assets turnover ratio for PepsiCo for Year 11 is as follows:

$$\frac{\text{Fixed Asset}}{\text{Turnover}} = \frac{\text{Sales}}{\text{Average Fixed Assets}}$$

$$4.0 = \frac{\$26,935}{.5(\$6,558 + \$6,876)}$$

The fixed asset turnover for PepsiCo was 3.4 in Year 9 and 3.9 in Year 10. The increase in the fixed asset turnover between Year 9 and Year 10 results from the deconsolidation of the fixed-asset intensive bottlers. The fixed asset turnover changed very little between Year 10 and Year 11.

The analyst must carefully interpret changes in the fixed asset turnover ratio. Firms make investments in fixed assets in anticipation of higher sales in future periods. Thus, a low or decreasing rate of fixed asset turnover may indicate an expanding firm preparing for future growth. On the other hand, a firm may cut back its capital expenditures if the near-term outlook for its products is poor. Such an action could lead to an increase in the fixed asset turnover ratio.

In recent years, many firms have increased the proportion of production outsourced to other manufacturers. This action allows firms to achieve the same (or increasing) sales levels with less fixed assets, thereby increasing the fixed asset turnover. A reduction in the number of consolidated bottlers by PepsiCo essentially represents increased outsourcing.

Summary of Assets Turnover Analysis

To summarize, the deconsolidation of PepsiCo's bottlers led to increases in the total assets turnover ratios for accounts receivable, inventories, and fixed assets between Year 9 and Year 10. Each of these assets turnover ratios was stable between Year 10 and Year 11.

Summary of ROA Analysis

Our analysis of operating profitability involves four levels of depth:

Level 1: ROA for the firm as a whole.

Level 2: Disaggregation of ROA into profit margin and assets turnover for the firm as a whole.

Level 3a: Disaggregation of profit margin into expense ratios for various cost items.

Level 3b: Disaggregation of assets turnover into turnovers for individual assets.

Level 4: Analysis of profit margins and asset turnovers for the segments of a firm.

Exhibit 4.12 summarizes this analysis in a format we use throughout the remainder of this book.

SUPPLEMENTING ROAS IN PROFITABILITY ANALYSIS

ROA uses average total assets as a base for assessing a firm's effectiveness in using resources to generate earnings from operations. For some firms and industries, total assets may not serve an informative role for this purpose because GAAP (1) excludes certain valuable resources from assets (brand names, technological knowledge, human capital), and (2) reports assets at their acquisition costs instead of current market values (forests for forest products companies, land and buildings for department stores). Analysts often supplement ROA by relating sales, expenses, and earnings to nonfinancial bases when evaluating profitability. This section discusses techniques for assessing profitability unique to certain industries. The discussion is not intended to be exhaustive of all industries but to provide a flavor for the types of supplemental measures used.

Analyzing Retailers

A key resource of retailers is their retail space. Some retailers own their stores while others lease their space. The analyst can capitalize the present value of operating lease commitments to insure that total assets include store buildings under operating leases (Chapter 8 discusses this adjustment). An alternative approach when analyzing retailers is to express sales, operating expenses, and operating income on a per square foot basis. This supplemental base for evaluating profitability circumvents the issue of whether firms own or lease their space. It also eliminates the effects of using different depreciation methods and depreciable lives, and having fixed assets with different ages.

Exhibit 4.13 presents per square foot data for The Gap and Limited Brands for a recent year, as well as profit margin, assets turnover, and ROA. The superior ROA of The Gap results from a much higher sales per square foot. Although its expenses per

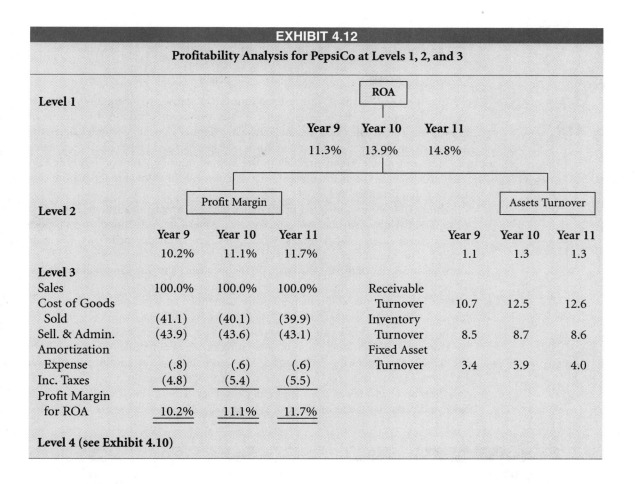

EXHIBIT 4.12

Profitability Analysis for PepsiCo at Levels 1, 2, and 3

Level 1

ROA

	Year 9	Year 10	Year 11
	11.3%	13.9%	14.8%

Level 2

Profit Margin

	Year 9	Year 10	Year 11
	10.2%	11.1%	11.7%

Assets Turnover

	Year 9	Year 10	Year 11
	1.1	1.3	1.3

Level 3

	Year 9	Year 10	Year 11		Year 9	Year 10	Year 11
Sales	100.0%	100.0%	100.0%	Receivable			
Cost of Goods				Turnover	10.7	12.5	12.6
Sold	(41.1)	(40.1)	(39.9)	Inventory			
Sell. & Admin.	(43.9)	(43.6)	(43.1)	Turnover	8.5	8.7	8.6
Amortization				Fixed Asset			
Expense	(.8)	(.6)	(.6)	Turnover	3.4	3.9	4.0
Inc. Taxes	(4.8)	(5.4)	(5.5)				
Profit Margin							
for ROA	10.2%	11.1%	11.7%				

Level 4 (see Exhibit 4.10)

EXHIBIT 4.13

Profitability Ratios for The Gap and Limited Brands

Per Square Foot:	The Gap	Limited Brands
Sales	$ 418	$ 304
Cost of Goods Sold	(243)	(202)
Selling and Administrative.	(100)	(65)
Operating Income	$ 75	$ 37
Profit Margin for ROA.	11.2%	8.0%
Assets Turnover	1.1	1.0
ROA	12.6%	7.9%

square foot are higher than those of Limited Brands, its ability to obtain higher sales from its space largely accounts for its superior profitability in the year analyzed.

Analyzing Airlines

Aircraft provide airlines with a fixed amount of capacity during any particular period. The total number of seats available to carry passengers times the number of miles flown equals the available capacity. The number of seats occupied times the number of miles flown equals the amount of capacity used (referred to as revenue passenger miles). Common practice in the airline industry is to compute the revenues and expenses per available seat mile and per seat mile flown to judge both cost structure and profitability.

Exhibit 4.14 presents selected profitability data for American Airlines, Southwest Airlines, and United Airlines for a recent year. American and United operate both domestic and international routes, while Southwest provides primarily domestic services. The employees of American and United are unionized while those of Southwest are not. All three airlines are publicly owned. The first three columns present revenues, expenses, and operating income before income taxes per available seat mile, and the last three columns present the same income items per actual seat mile flown.

The costs of an airline (for example, depreciation, fuel, compensation) are largely fixed for any particular year. Thus, the operating expenses per available seat mile indicate the costs of operating each airline. The operating costs of Southwest are lower than those of American and United. The advantage of Southwest relates to lower compensation costs and lower other operating expenses. The income data per seat mile flown indicates the usage of the available capacity. American generates the highest

EXHIBIT 4.14						
Profitability Ratios for American Airlines, Southwest Airlines, and United Airlines						
	Per Available Seat Mile			Per Seat Mile Flown		
	American	Southwest	United	American	Southwest	United
Operating						
Revenues	10.60¢	8.36¢	10.05¢	15.48¢	12.58¢	14.02¢
Compensation.	(3.56)	(2.45)	(3.31)	(5.20)	(3.69)	(4.63)
Fuel	(1.16)	(1.19)	(1.28)	(1.69)	(1.79)	(1.78)
Other Operating						
Expenses	(4.94)	(3.86)	(4.77)	(7.21)	(5.80)	(6.65)
Operating Income.	.94¢	.86¢	.69¢	1.38¢	1.30¢	.96¢
Profit Margin for ROA				6.2%	6.8%	4.5%
Assets Turnover.				.61	.65	.65
ROA.				3.8%	4.4%	2.9%

revenues per seat mile flown but also has the highest costs. Its compensation costs and other operating expenses are the highest of the three airlines. Southwest realizes less revenues per seat mile flown than American but its lower cost structure permits it to generate almost the same operating income before income taxes. United falls between American and Southwest on both revenues and operating expenses per seat mile flown but has the lowest operating income before income taxes. The ROA data are consistent with the per seat mile data, except that the profit margin of Southwest reflects higher interest revenues from investments of excess cash relative to American and United.

The analyst can apply similar metrics to other firms with fixed capacity. The analysis of hospitals focuses on income data per available bed or per patient day. The analysis of hotels uses income data per room. The analysis of cable or telecommunications companies examines income data per subscriber or customer.

Analyzing Advertising Firms

Using ROA to analyze the profitability of firms that provide services can result in misleading conclusions because their most important resource, their employees, do not appear on the balance sheet as assets under GAAP. One approach to deal with this omission is to express income data on a per-employee basis. The analyst must use this data cautiously because of differences among firms in their use of full- versus part-time employees, and their mix of direct service providers versus support personnel.

Exhibit 4.15 presents profitability data for three advertising agencies. Grey Advertising has the highest revenue per employee but also the highest compensation per employee. Its administrative expenses are similar to those of Interpublic but its higher compensation leads to the lowest operating income before income taxes per employee and the lowest profit margin and ROA. Interpublic and Omnicom have similar operating revenues per employee but Omnicom's higher compensation,

	EXHIBIT 4.15		
	Profitability Data for Grey Advertising, Interpublic Group, and Omnicom Group		
Per Employee:	**Grey Advertising**	**Interpublic Group**	**Omnicom Group**
Operating Revenues	$121,508	$116,936	$116,373
Compensation.	(75,347)	(61,946)	(68,527)
Administration Expenses	(36,870)	(36,653)	(33,460)
Operating Income Before Income Taxes	$ 9,291	$ 18,337	$ 14,386
Profit Margin for ROA	4.6%	9.7%	9.2%
Assets Turnover.	.75	.56	.70
ROA.	3.4%	5.4%	6.4%

offset by its lower administrative expenses, yields it lower operating income per employee and a lower profit margin. Omnicom has a faster assets turnover than Interpublic, so it has the highest ROA.

Other service industries for which per-employee data might usefully supplement traditional financial ratios include management consulting, temporary help services, and engineering services. The use of per-employee data might also supplement the analysis of firms that use fixed assets in the provision of services, such as airlines, health care providers, and hotels.

Analyzing Technology-Based Firms

ROA can be an even more misleading ratio for analyzing technology-based firms than for service firms because the two most important resources of technology firms do not appear in their assets: (1) their people, and (2) their technologies. Employees contribute to the creation of technologies but the most important resource not recognized is the value of the technologies. GAAP requires firms to expense research and development (R&D) costs in the year incurred. Thus, both assets and net income are understated.

Chapter 7 discusses research by Lev and Sougiannis[9] to document the value of technologies that might provide a basis for recognizing a technology asset on the balance sheet and recomputing net income each year. The methodology involves studying the relationship between R&D expenditures in a particular year and revenues of subsequent years. The technology "asset" equals the present value of the future revenue stream net of the R&D expenditure during the year. The analyst would then amortize this "asset" over the future periods of benefit based on the projected stream of revenues.

The research described above is in an early development stage and not yet used widely by analysts of technology companies. Traditional financial ratio analysis works reasonably well for established technology firms that have products in all stages of their life cycles. Traditional financial ratio analysis does not work as well for start-up firms and firms with most of their products in the early, high-growth stages of their life cycles.

RATE OF RETURN ON COMMON SHAREHOLDERS' EQUITY

The rate of return on assets measures the profitability of operations before considering the effects of financing. That is, ROA ignores the proportion of debt versus equity financing that a firm uses to finance the assets. The rate of return on common shareholders' equity (ROCE) measures the return to common shareholders after subtracting from revenues not only operating expenses (for example, cost of goods

---

[9]Baruch Lev and Theodore Sougiannis, "The Capitalization, Amortization and Value-Relevance of R&D," *Journal of Accounting and Economics*, 1996, pp. 107–138.

sold, selling and administration expenses, income taxes) but also the costs of financing debt and preferred stock that are senior to the common stock. The latter includes interest expense on debt and dividends on preferred stock (if any). Thus, ROCE incorporates the results of a firm's operating, investing, and financing decisions.

The analyst calculates ROCE as follows:

$$\text{ROCE} = \frac{\text{Net Income} - \text{Preferred Stock Dividends}}{\text{Average Common Shareholders' Equity}}$$

The numerator measures the amount of income for the period allocable to the common shareholders after subtracting all amounts allocable to senior claimants. The accountant subtracts interest expense on debt in measuring net income, so the calculation of the numerator of ROCE requires no adjustment for creditors' claims on earnings. The analyst must subtract dividends paid or payable on preferred stock from net income to obtain income attributable to the common shareholders.[10]

The denominator of ROCE measures the average amount of common shareholders' equity in use during the period. An average of the total common shareholders' equity at the beginning and end of the year is appropriate unless a firm made a significant new common stock issue or buyback during the year. If the latter occurred, the analyst should use an average of the common shareholders' equity at the end of each quarter.

Common shareholders' equity equals total shareholders' equity minus the minority interest in the net assets of consolidated subsidiaries and minus the par value of preferred stock. Because net income to common shareholders in the numerator reflects a subtraction for the minority interest in earnings of consolidated subsidiaries, the denominator should exclude the minority interest in net assets (if any). Chapter 9 discusses consolidated financial statements more fully. Firms seldom issue preferred stock significantly above par value, so the analyst can assume that the amount in the Additional Paid-in Capital account relates to common stock.

PepsiCo reports no minority interest in either its income statement or balance sheet. It does have preferred stock outstanding. The calculation of the ROCE of PepsiCo for Year 11 is as follows:

$$\text{ROCE} = \frac{\text{Net Income} - \text{Preferred Stock Dividends}}{\text{Average Common Shareholders' Equity}}$$

$$36.9\% = \frac{\$3,003 - \$4}{.5(\$7,604 + \$8,648)}$$

---

[10]Chapter 12 indicates that for purposes of valuation, the analyst might compute ROCE using comprehensive income available to common shareholders, not net income available to the common shareholders. Recall from Chapter 2 that comprehensive income equals net income plus or minus changes in the value of certain assets and liabilities that GAAP requires firms to include in Other Comprehensive Income until realized.

The amount for net income reflects adjustments for nonrecurring merger expenses and impairment and restructuring charges, the same adjustments made earlier to compute ROA. The amount for the preferred stock dividend appears in the statement of common shareholders' equity in Appendix A. The amount for common shareholders' equity in the denominator equals total shareholders' equity minus the par value of preferred stock. The ROCE of PepsiCo was 33.4 percent in Year 9 and 36.1 percent in Year 10, reflecting an increase over the three-year period.

Relating ROA to ROCE

ROA measures operating performance independent of financing while ROCE explicitly considers the cost of debt and preferred stock financing. The relation between ROA and ROCE is as follows[11]:

Return on Assets	→	Return to Creditors	Return to Preferred Shareholders	Return to Common Shareholders
$\dfrac{\text{Net Income + Interest Expense Net of Taxes}}{\text{Average Total Assets}}$	→	$\dfrac{\text{Interest Expense Net of Taxes}}{\text{Average Total Liabilities}}$	$\dfrac{\text{Preferred Dividends}}{\text{Average Preferred Shareholders' Equity}}$	$\dfrac{\text{Net Income to Common}}{\text{Average Common Shareholders' Equity}}$

The analyst allocates each dollar of return generated from using assets to the various providers of capital. Creditors receive their return in the form of interest. The cost of this capital is interest expense net of the income tax benefit derived from deducting interest in calculating taxable income. Many liabilities, such as accounts payable and salaries payable, carry no explicit cost.

The preferred stock carries a cost equal to the preferred dividend amount. Firms historically could not deduct preferred dividends in calculating taxable income. Firms in recent years have been successful in structuring preferred stock issues so that they qualify for tax deductibility of dividends paid. In those cases, the analyst should adjust preferred dividends for the related tax savings.

The income from operations (that is, the numerator of ROA) that is not allocated to creditors or preferred shareholders belongs to the common shareholders as the residual claimants. Likewise, the portion of a firm's assets not financed with capital provided by creditors or preferred shareholders represents the capital provided by the common shareholders.[12]

---

[11]Note that the relation does not appear as an equation. We use an arrow instead of an equal sign to indicate that the return on assets gets allocated to the various suppliers of capital. To express the relation as an equality requires that we weight each rate by the proportion of each type of capital in the capital structure.

[12]If a firm does not own 100 percent of the common stock of a consolidated subsidiary, the accountant must allocate a portion of the ROA to the minority shareholders. Thus, a fourth term would appear on the righthand side of the arrow: minority interest in earnings/average minority interest in net assets.

Consider now the relation between ROA and ROCE. Under what circumstances will ROCE exceed ROA? Under what circumstances will ROCE be less than ROA?

ROCE will exceed ROA whenever ROA exceeds the cost of capital provided by creditors and preferred shareholders. If a firm can generate a higher return on capital provided by creditors and preferred shareholders than the cost of that capital, the excess return belongs to the common shareholders.

To illustrate, recall that PepsiCo generated an ROA of 14.8 percent during Year 11. The after-tax cost of capital provided by creditors during Year 11 was 1.1 percent [= $(1 - .35)(\$219)/.5(\$13,131 + \$13,021)$].[13] The difference between the 1.1 percent cost of creditor capital and the 14.8 percent ROA generated on assets financed with debt capital belongs to the common shareholders. The preferred shareholders received a dividend of $4 million, which as a percentage of average preferred stockholders' equity represented a cost of 16.7 percent [= $\$4/.5(\$22 + \$26)$]. The cost of preferred shareholders' capital appears to exceed ROA slightly and reduced the return to the common shareholders. The common shareholders also have a full claim on the 14.8 percent ROA generated on the assets financed with the equity capital that they provided. Thus, the ROCE of PepsiCo for Year 11 comprises the following (calculations use rates taken to more decimal points than the three decimal points shown):

Excess Return on Capital Provided by Creditors:	
$[.148 - .011][.5(\$13,131 + \$13,021)]$	$1,795.3
Excess Return on Capital Provided by Preferred Shareholders:	
$[.148 - .167][.5(\$22 + \$26)]$	(.4)
Return on Capital Provided by Common Shareholders:	
$[.148][.5(\$7,604 + \$8,848)]$	1,204.1
Total Return to Common Shareholders	$2,999.0
ROCE: $\$2,999/[.5(\$7,604 + \$8,648)]$	36.9%

Common business terminology refers to the practice of using lower-cost creditor and preferred stock capital to increase the return to common shareholders as *financial leverage*. Financial leverage worked to the advantage of PepsiCo's shareholders in Year 9, Year 10, and Year 11 because its ROCE exceeds its ROA.

We can measure the incremental effect of financial leverage beyond ROA by computing the ratio of ROCE divided by ROA. The ratios for PepsiCo are as follows:

Year 9: 33.4%/11.3% = 2.96
Year 10: 36.1%/13.9% = 2.60
Year 11: 36.9%/14.8% = 2.49

Thus, financial leverage worked less effectively each succeeding year for PepsiCo. We explore next the possible reasons for this decreased effectiveness.

---

[13]The amounts in the denominator for PepsiCo equal total assets minus total shareholders' equity, or total liabilities. The after-tax cost of creditor capital seems low, but recall that many liabilities do not carry an explicit interest cost.

Disaggregating ROCE

We can disaggregate ROCE into several components to aid in its interpretation, much as we did earlier with ROA. The disaggregated components of ROCE are profit margin for ROCE, total assets turnover, and capital structure leverage.

ROCE	=	Profit Margin for ROCE	×	Assets Turnover	×	Capital Structure Leverage
$\dfrac{\text{Net Income to Common}}{\text{Average Common Shareholders' Equity}}$	=	$\dfrac{\text{Net Income to Common}}{\text{Sales}}$	×	$\dfrac{\text{Sales}}{\text{Average Total Assets}}$	×	$\dfrac{\text{Average Total Assets}}{\text{Average Common Shareholders' Equity}}$

The profit margin for ROCE indicates the earnings allocable to the common shareholders after subtracting from revenues all operating expenses and all financing costs of capital senior to the common shareholders. Note that the profit margin for ROA, used in the disaggregation of ROA, is before financing costs. The profit margin for ROCE is after financing costs. The total assets turnover is identical to that used in the disaggregation of ROA. The capital structure leverage (CSL) ratio measures the degree to which a firm uses common shareholders' funds to finance assets. The difference between the numerator and denominator of CSL is the amount of liabilities and preferred shareholders' equity in the capital structure. The larger is the amount of capital obtained from these senior sources, the smaller will be the amount of capital obtained from common shareholders and the larger will be the CSL ratio.

The disaggregation of ROCE for PepsiCo for Year 11 appears as follows:

ROCE	=	Profit Margin for ROCE	×	Assets Turnover	×	Capital Structure Leverage
$\dfrac{\$3,003 - \$4}{.5(\$7,604 + \$8,648)}$		$\dfrac{\$3,003 - \$4}{\$26,935}$	×	$\dfrac{\$26,935}{.5(\$20,757 + \$21,695)}$		$\dfrac{.5(\$20,757 + \$21,695)}{.5(\$7,604 + \$8,648)}$
36.9%	=	11.1%	×	1.3	×	2.6

Exhibit 4.16 presents the disaggregation of ROCE of PepsiCo for Year 9 to Year 11. The increasing ROCEs of PepsiCo result from an increasing profit margin for ROCE each year and an increased total assets turnover between Year 9 and Year 10. Offsetting these positive effects on ROCE is a steady decline in the CSL ratio during the three-year period. PepsiCo had net repayments of debt during Year 10 and Year 11 (see PepsiCo's statement of cash flows in Appendix A). Also, the retention of earnings and new stock issuances exceeded dividends and stock repurchases, resulting in an increase in common shareholders' equity. Although financial leverage worked to

EXHIBIT 4.16						
Disaggregation of ROCE of PepsiCo for Year 9 to Year 11						
	ROCE	=	Profit Margin for ROCE	×	Total Assets Turnover	×	Capital Structure Leverage
Year 9	33.4%	=	9.1%	×	1.1	×	3.3
Year 10	36.1%	=	10.4%	×	1.3	×	2.8
Year 11	36.9%	=	11.1%	×	1.3	×	2.6

the benefit of the common shareholders in all three years, the decreasing CSL ratio moderated the positive effects of the increasing profit margin for ROCE and assets turnover.

EARNINGS PER COMMON SHARE

A second financial statement ratio besides ROCE that common equity investors frequently use to assess profitability is earnings per common share (EPS). As Chapter 12 discusses more fully, analysts and investors frequently use EPS to value firms. EPS is the only financial ratio covered explicitly by the opinion of the independent auditor. This section briefly describes the calculation of EPS[14] and discusses some of its uses and limitations.

CALCULATING EPS

Simple Capital Structure

Firms that do not have (1) outstanding convertible bonds or convertible preferred stock that holders can exchange for shares of common stock, or (2) options or warrants that holders can use to acquire common stock, have simple capital structures. For such firms, the accountant calculates basic EPS as follows:

$$\text{Basic EPS (Simple Capital Structure)} = \frac{\text{Net Income} - \text{Preferred Stock Dividends}}{\text{Weighted Average Number of Common Shares Outstanding}}$$

The numerator of basic EPS for a simple capital structure is identical to the numerator of ROCE. The denominator is a daily weighted average of common shares outstanding during the period, reflecting new stock issues, treasury stock acquisitions, and similar transactions.

---

[14]Financial Accounting Standards Board, *Statement of Financial Accounting Standards No. 128*, "Earnings per Share," 1997.

Example 1. Brown Corporation had the following capital structure during its most recent year.

	January 1	December 31
Preferred Stock, $20 par Value, 500 Shares Issued and Outstanding.........	$ 10,000	$ 10,000
Common Stock, $10 par Value, 4,000 Shares Issued	40,000	40,000
Additional Paid-in Capital	50,000	50,000
Retained Earnings........................	80,000	85,600
Treasury Shares—Common (1,000 shares)	—	(30,000)
Total Shareholders' Equity................	$180,000	$155,600

Retained earnings changed during the year as follows:

Retained Earnings, January 1	$80,000
Plus Net Income	7,500
Less Dividends:	
Preferred Stock.........................	(500)
Common Stock	(1,400)
Retained Earnings, December 31	$85,600

The preferred stock is not convertible into common stock. The firm acquired the treasury stock on July 1. There are no stock options or warrants outstanding. The calculation of basic earnings per share for Brown Corporation appears below:

$$\text{Basic EPS} = \frac{\$7,500 - \$500}{(.5 \times 4,000) + (.5 \times 3,000)} = \frac{\$7,000}{3,500} = \$2.00 \text{ per share}$$

Complex Capital Structure

Firms that have either convertible securities or stock options or warrants outstanding have complex capital structures. Such firms must present two EPS amounts: basic EPS and diluted EPS. Diluted EPS reflects the dilution potential of convertible securities, options, and warrants. Dilution refers to the reduction in basic EPS that would result if holders of convertible securities exchanged them for shares of common stock, or holders of stock options or warrants exercised them. This section describes the calculation of diluted EPS in general terms.

$$\text{Diluted EPS} \atop \text{(Complex Capital Structure)} \quad = \quad \frac{\text{Net Income-Preferred Stock Dividends} \; + \; \text{Adjustments for Dilutive Securities}}{\text{Weighted Average Number of Common Shares Outstanding} \; + \; \text{Weighted Average Number of Shares Issuable from Dilutive Securities}}$$

To calculate diluted EPS, the accountant assumes the conversion of convertible bonds and convertible preferred stock, and the exercise of stock options and warrants. The accountant adds back any interest expense (net of taxes) on convertible bonds and dividends on convertible preferred stock that the firm subtracted in computing net income to common. The accountant also adds back any amount recognized as compensation expense on stock options to the numerator.

The additional common shares issuable upon conversion of bonds and preferred stock, and exercise of stock options and warrants, are added to the denominator. The computation of the additional shares to be issued upon the exercise of stock options assumes that the firm would use any cash proceeds from such exercise to repurchase common shares on the open market. Only the net incremental shares issued (shares issued under options minus assumed shares repurchased) enter the computation of diluted EPS.

Example 2. Assume the preferred stock of Brown Corporation is convertible into 1,000 shares of common stock. Also assume that Brown Corporation has stock options outstanding that holders can currently exchange for 300 incremental shares of common stock. Brown Corporation recognized $600 of compensation expense (net of taxes) related to these stock options during the current year. The calculation of diluted EPS is as follows:

$$\text{Diluted EPS} = \frac{\$7{,}500 - \$500 + \$500 + \$600}{(.5 \times 4{,}000) + (.5 \times 3{,}000) + (1.0 \times 1{,}000) + (1.0 \times 300)} = \frac{\$8{,}100}{4{,}800}$$

$$= \$1.69 \text{ per share}$$

The calculation assumes the conversion of the convertible preferred stock into common stock as of January 1. If conversion had taken place, the firm would not have paid preferred dividends during the year. Thus, the analyst adds back to the numerator of fully diluted earnings per share the $500 of preferred dividends, which the accountant subtracted in computing net income available to common stock when calculating basic earnings per share. The weighted average number of shares in the denominator increases for the 1,000 common shares that the firm would issue upon conversion of the preferred stock. The accountant likewise adds back to net income the after-tax cost of stock options initially recognized as expense in computing net income. The weighted average number of shares in the denominator increases for the incremental shares issuable.

The accountant makes these adjustments to EPS for complex capital structures only if their effect is dilutive (that is, the adjustments reduce basic EPS). Both EPS amounts appear on the income statement.

Refer to the income statements of PepsiCo in Appendix A. PepsiCo reports both basic and diluted EPS. PepsiCo's Note 5 shows the calculation of its EPS amounts. Basic EPS shows a subtraction from net income for preferred dividends. Diluted EPS shows an addition for the portion of the preferred dividend that relates to convertible preferred stock. PepsiCo also reports the additional common shares issuable under stock option plans, from convertible preferred stock, and for stock awards.

CRITICISMS OF EPS

Critics of EPS as a measure of profitability point out that it does not consider the amount of assets or capital required to generate a particular level of earnings. Two firms with the same earnings and EPS are not equally profitable if one firm requires twice the amount of assets or capital to generate those earnings as does the other firm. Also, the number of shares of common stock outstanding serves as a poor measure of the amount of capital in use. The number of shares outstanding usually relates to a firm's attempts to achieve a desirable trading range for its common stock. For example, suppose a firm has an aggregate market value for its common shares of $10 million. If the firm has 500,000 shares outstanding, the shares will sell for $20 per share. If the firm has 1,000,000 shares outstanding, the shares will sell for $10 per share. The amount of capital in place is the same in both instances but the number of shares outstanding, and therefore EPS, are different.

For similar reasons, analysts cannot compare EPS amounts across firms. Two firms can have identical earnings, common shareholders' equities, and ROCEs but their EPSs will differ if they have different numbers of shares outstanding.

EPS is also an ambiguous measure of profitability because it reflects (1) operating performance in the numerator, and (2) capital structure decisions in the denominator. For example, a firm can experience reduced earnings during the year but report a higher EPS than the previous year if it has repurchased sufficient shares during the period. When assessing earnings performance, the analyst must separate the impact of these two factors on EPS.

Despite these criticisms of EPS as a measure of profitability, analysts frequently use it in valuing firms. Chapter 13 discusses the use of EPS in valuation.

INTERPRETING FINANCIAL STATEMENT RATIOS

The analyst can compare financial ratios for a particular firm with similar ratios for the same firm for earlier periods (time-series analysis), as we have done in this chapter for PepsiCo, or with those of other firms for the same period (cross-section analysis). This section discusses some of the issues involved in making such comparisons.

COMPARISONS WITH CORRESPONDING RATIOS OF EARLIER PERIODS

A time-series analysis of a particular firm's financial statement ratios permits a historical tracking of the trends and variability in the ratios over time. A firm's financial ratios in the past serve as a benchmark for interpreting its financial ratios during the current period. The analyst can study the impact of economic conditions (recession, inflation), industry conditions (shift in regulatory status, new technology), and firm-specific conditions (shift in corporate strategy, new management) on the time-series pattern of these ratios. For example, our study of PepsiCo on a time-series basis permits us to assess the effect of its strategic shift to deconsolidate its bottlers.

Some of the questions that the analyst should raise before using ratios of past financial statement data as a basis for interpreting ratios for the current period include:

1. Has the firm made a significant change in its product, geographical, or customer mix that affects the comparability of financial statement ratios over time?
2. Has the firm made a major acquisition or divestiture?
3. Has the firm changed its methods of accounting over time? For example, does the firm now consolidate a previously unconsolidated entity?

One concern with using past performance as a basis for comparison is that the earlier performance might have been at an unsatisfactory level. Any improvement during the current year may still leave the firm at an undesirable level. An improved profitability ratio may mean little if a firm ranks last in its industry in terms of profitability in all years.

Another concern involves interpreting the rate of change in a ratio over time. The analyst's interpretation of a 10 percent increase in profit margin differs depending on whether other firms in the industry experienced a 15 percent versus a 5 percent increase. Comparing a particular firm's ratios with those of similar firms lessens the concerns discussed above.

COMPARISONS WITH CORRESPONDING RATIOS OF OTHER FIRMS

The major task confronting the analyst in performing a cross-section analysis is identifying the other firms to use for comparison. The objective is to select firms with similar products and strategies and similar size and age. Few firms may meet these criteria. Coke, for example, is a logical comparison firm for PepsiCo. Coke, however, derives virtually all of its revenues from beverages, whereas PepsiCo derives only about 39 percent from beverages.

An alternative approach uses average industry ratios, such as those published by Moody's, Dun & Bradstreet, and Robert Morris Associates, or as derived from computerized databases. These average industry ratios provide an overview of the performance of an industry.

The analyst should consider the following issues when using industry ratios:

1. Definition of the industry: Publishers of average industry ratios generally classify diversified firms into the industry of their major product. PepsiCo, for example, appears as a "beverage" company, even though it generates a large percentage of its revenues from packaged consumer foods. The "industry" also excludes privately held and foreign firms. If these types of firms are significant

for a particular industry, the analyst should recognize the possible impact of their absence from the published data.

2. Calculation of industry average: Is the published ratio a simple (unweighted) average of the ratios of the included firms or is it weighted by size of firm? Is the weighting based on sales, assets, market value, or some other factor? Is the median of the distribution used instead of the mean?

3. Distribution of ratios around the mean: To interpret a deviation of a particular firm's ratio from the industry average requires information on the distribution around the mean. The analyst interprets a ratio that is 10 percent larger than the industry mean differently depending on whether the standard deviation is 5 percent versus 15 percent greater or less than the mean. The published sources of industry ratios give either the quartiles or the range of the distribution.

4. Definition of financial statement ratios: The analyst should examine the definition of each published ratio to insure that it is consistent with that calculated by the analyst. For instance, is the rate of return on common shareholders' equity based on average or beginning-of-the-period common shareholders' equity?

Average industry ratios serve as a useful basis of comparison as long as the analyst recognizes their possible limitations.

SUMMARY

This chapter presents various financial statement ratios for assessing profitability. The large number of financial ratios discussed is probably overwhelming at this point. Enhanced understanding of these financial ratios results from using and interpreting the ratios, not from memorizing them. The FSAP software package available with this book facilitates calculation of the ratios and permits the analyst to devote more time to interpretations.

Exhibit 4.17 summarizes the financial ratios discussed in this chapter. Profitability analysis proceeds through four levels of depth. Level 1 involves measures of profitability for a firm as a whole: the rate of return on assets and the rate of return on common shareholders' equity. Level 2 disaggregates ROA and ROCE into important components. ROA disaggregates into profit margin for ROA and assets turnover. ROCE disaggregates into profit margin for ROCE, assets turnover, and capital structure leverage components. Level 3 disaggregates the profit margin into various expense-to-sales percentages and disaggregates the total assets turnover into individual asset turnovers. Level 4 uses product and geographical segment data to study ROA, profit margin, and assets turnover more fully.

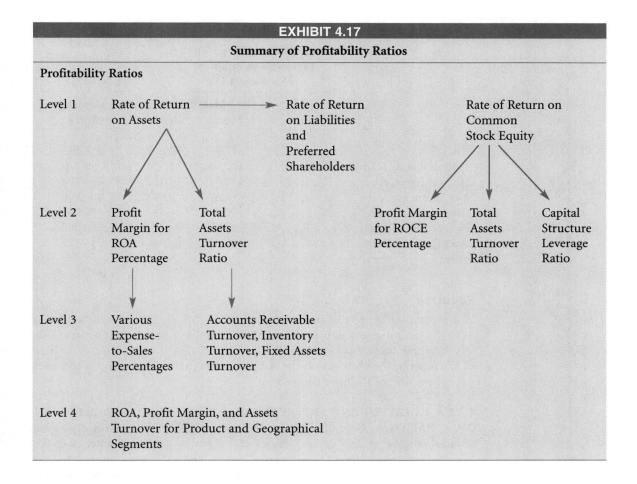

EXHIBIT 4.17
Summary of Profitability Ratios

Profitability Ratios

Level 1 — Rate of Return on Assets → Rate of Return on Liabilities and Preferred Shareholders — Rate of Return on Common Stock Equity

Level 2 — Profit Margin for ROA Percentage — Total Assets Turnover Ratio — Profit Margin for ROCE Percentage — Total Assets Turnover Ratio — Capital Structure Leverage Ratio

Level 3 — Various Expense-to-Sales Percentages — Accounts Receivable Turnover, Inventory Turnover, Fixed Assets Turnover

Level 4 — ROA, Profit Margin, and Assets Turnover for Product and Geographical Segments

PROBLEMS AND CASES

4.1 ANALYZING OPERATING PROFITABILITY. Exhibit 4.18 presents selected operating data for three retailers for a recent year. Wal-Mart sells a wide variety of household, personal, and grocery products following an everyday low-price strategy. It locates its stores in both urban and rural areas. Home Depot sells products for the home improvement industry, which includes products ranging from riding lawn-mowers to lighting fixtures to kitchen countertops. It locates its stores in suburban locations. May Department Stores operates several department store chains selling products ranging from clothing to china, cosmetics and bedding. It locates its stores in urban and suburban areas.

EXHIBIT 4.18		
Selected Data for Three Retailers **(amounts in millions)** **(Problem 4.1)**		
	Wal-Mart Stores	**Home Depot**	**May Department Stores**
Sales.	$217,799	$53,553	$14,175
Cost of Goods Sold.	171,562	37,406	9,770
Interest Expense	1,326	112	378
Net Income	6,671	3,044	706
Average Inventory.	22,028	6,641	2,907
Average Fixed Assets	47,973	14,222	5,082
Average Total Assets	85,422	23,890	11,477

Required

a. Compute the rate of return on assets for each firm. Disaggregate the rate of return on assets into profit margin and assets turnover components. The income tax rate is 35 percent.
b. Describe the likely reasons for the differences in the profit margins and assets turnovers of the three companies.

4.2 CALCULATING AND INTERPRETING ACCOUNTS RECEIVABLE TURN-OVER RATIOS. Microsoft Corporation (Microsoft) and Oracle Corporation (Oracle) engage in the design, manufacture, and sale of computer software. Microsoft sells and licenses a wide range of systems and application software to businesses, computer hardware manufacturers, and consumer retailers. Oracle sells software for information management almost exclusively to businesses. Exhibit 4.19 presents selected data for the two firms for Year 9, Year 10, and Year 11.

Required

a. Calculate the accounts receivable turnover ratio for Microsoft and Oracle for Year 9, Year 10, and Year 11.
b. Suggest possible reasons for the differences in the accounts receivable turnovers of Microsoft versus Oracle during the three-year period.
c. Suggest possible reasons for the changes in the accounts receivable turnover for the two firms over the three-year period.

4.3 CALCULATING AND INTERPRETING INVENTORY TURNOVER RATIOS. Eli Lilly and Merck develop, manufacture, and market prescription drugs worldwide. Merck also provides managed prescription drug programs for various businesses, purchasing drugs in bulk quantities for distribution to health care providers and

EXHIBIT 4.19			
Selected Data for Microsoft and Oracle			
(amounts in millions)			
(Problem 4.2)			
	Year 11	Year 10	Year 9
Microsoft			
Sales.................................	$25,296	$22,956	$19,747
Average Accounts Receivable.............	3,461	2,748	1,853
Change in Sales from Previous Year......	+10.2%	+16.3%	+36.3%
Oracle			
Sales.................................	$ 9,673	$10,860	$10,130
Average Accounts Receivable.............	2,375	2,752	2,635
Change in Sales from Previous Year......	−10.9%	+ 7.2%	+14.8%

monitoring usage patterns, costs, effectiveness, and other factors. Both firms use the same cost-flow assumptions for measuring inventories and cost of goods sold. Selected data for each firm for Year 9, Year 10, and Year 11 appear in Exhibit 4.20.

Required

a. Calculate the inventory turnover ratio for each firm for Year 9, Year 10, and Year 11.

b. Suggest reasons for the differences in the inventory turnover ratios of these two firms.

c. Suggest reasons for the changes in the inventory turnover ratios of Merck during the three-year period.

4.4 CALCULATING AND INTERPRETING ACCOUNTS RECEIVABLE AND INVENTORY TURNOVER RATIOS. AK Steel and Nucor are steel manufacturers. AK Steel is an integrated steel producer, transforming ferrous metals into rolled steel and then into various steel products for the automobile, appliance, construction, and other industries. Its steel falls on the higher end in terms of quality (that is, strength, durability). Nucor produces steel in mini-mills. Mini-mills transform scrap ferrous metals into standard sizes of rolled steel, which Nucor then sells to steel service centers and distributors. Its steel falls on the lower end in terms of quality. Exhibit 4.21 sets forth various data for these two companies for Year 10 and Year 11.

Required

a. Calculate the accounts receivable turnovers for AK Steel and Nucor for Year 10 and Year 11.

b. Describe the likely reasons for the differences in the accounts receivable turnovers for these two firms.

EXHIBIT 4.20

Selected Data for Eli Lilly and Merck
(amounts in millions)
(Problem 4.3)

	Year 11	Year 10	Year 9
Eli Lilly			
Cost of Goods Sold......................	$ 2,160	$ 2,056	$ 2,098
Average Inventories......................	972	892	950
Change in Sales from Previous Year.........	+ 6.3%	+ 9.6%	+ 7.3%
Merck			
Cost of Goods Sold......................	$28,977	$22,401	$17,534
Average Inventories......................	3,301	2,935	2,736
Change in Sales from Previous Year.........	+18.2%	+23.4%	+21.6%
Percentage of Sales from Prescription			
Drug Management Programs	58.6%	54.1%	51.4%

EXHIBIT 4.21

Selected Data for AK Steel and Nucor
(amounts in millions)
(Problem 4.4)

	Year 11	Year 10
AK Steel		
Sales...	$ 3,994	$ 4,612
Cost of Goods Sold..............................	3,599	4,000
Average Accounts Receivable	464	513
Average Inventories.............................	896	823
Change in Sales from Previous Year	−35.5%	− 7.4%
Nucor		
Sales...	$ 4,139	$ 4,586
Cost of Goods Sold..............................	3,820	3,925
Average Accounts Receivable	341	372
Average Inventories.............................	464	463
Change in Sales from Previous Year	− 9.7%	+14.4%

c. Describe the likely reasons for the trend of the accounts receivable turnovers of these two firms during the two-year period.

d. Calculate the inventory turnovers for AK Steel and Nucor for Year 10 and Year 11.

e. Describe the likely reasons for the differences in the inventory turnovers of these two firms.

f. Describe the likely reasons for the trend in the inventory turnovers of these two firms during the two-year period.

4.5 CALCULATING AND INTERPRETING FIXED ASSET TURNOVER RATIOS.

Texas Instruments (TI) designs and manufactures semiconductor products for use in computers, telecommunications equipment, automobiles, and other electronics-based products. The manufacturing of semiconductors is highly capital intensive. Hewlett-Packard Corporation (HP) manufactures computer hardware and various imaging products, such as printers and fax machines. HP outsources the manufacture of a portion of the components for its products. Exhibit 4.22 presents selected data for TI and HP for Year 9, Year 10, and Year 11.

Required

a. Compute the fixed asset turnover for each firm for Year 9, Year 10, and Year 11.

b. Suggest reasons for the differences in the fixed asset turnovers of TI and HP.

c. Suggest reasons for the changes in the fixed asset turnovers of TI and HP during the three-year period.

EXHIBIT 4.22

Selected Data for Texas Instruments and Hewlett-Packard
(amounts in millions)
(Problem 4.5)

	Year 11	Year 10	Year 9
Texas Instruments			
Sales.....................................	$ 8,201	$11,860	$ 9,468
Cost of Goods Sold......................	5,577	6,065	4,900
Capital Expenditures....................	1,790	2,762	1,373
Average Fixed Assets	5,518	4,641	3,604
Percentage Fixed Assets Depreciated	42.3%	40.0%	46.1%
Percentage Change in Sales...............	−30.9%	+25.3%	+11.9%
Hewlett-Packard			
Sales.....................................	$45,226	$48,782	$42,370
Cost of Goods Sold......................	33,474	34,864	29,720
Capital Expenditures....................	1,527	1,737	1,134
Average Fixed Assets	4,449	4,417	5,346
Percentage Fixed Assets Depreciated	55.0%	52.7%	51.4%
Percentage Change in Sales...............	− 7.3%	+15.1%	−10.0%

4.6 CALCULATING AND INTERPRETING THE RATE OF RETURN ON COMMON SHAREHOLDERS' EQUITY AND ITS COMPONENTS.   Delta Air Lines (Delta) provides airline transportation services. Exhibit 4.23 presents selected data for Delta for Year 9, Year 10, and Year 11.

Required

a. Calculate the rate of return on assets for Year 9, Year 10, and Year 11. Disaggregate ROA into the profit margin for ROA and total assets turnover components.
b. Calculate the rate of return on common shareholders' equity for Year 9, Year 10, and Year 11. Disaggregate ROCE into the profit margin for ROCE, total assets turnover, and capital structure leverage components.
c. Suggest reasons for the changes in ROCE over the three years.
d. Did financial leverage work to the advantage of the common shareholders in each of the three years? Explain.

4.7 INTERPRETING THE RATE OF RETURN ON COMMON SHAREHOLDERS' EQUITY AND ITS COMPONENTS.   Selected financial data for Georgia-Pacific Company, a forest products firm, appear in Exhibit 4.24.

Required

a. In which years did financial leverage work to the advantage of the common shareholders and in which years did it work to their disadvantage? Explain.

EXHIBIT 4.23

Selected Data for Delta Air Lines
(amounts in millions)
(Problem 4.6)

	Year Ended June 30:		
	Year 11	Year 10	Year 9
Sales.....................................	$13,879	$16,741	$14,711
Net Income (Loss)...........................	(1,216)	928	1,101
Interest Expense	442	426	199
Preferred Stock Dividend	14	13	11
Income Tax Rate	35%	35%	35%

	June 30			
	Year 11	Year 10	Year 9	Year 8
Total Assets	$23,605	$21,931	$16,544	$14,603
Preferred Stock	452	460	471	475
Total Common Shareholders' Equity	3,572	5,117	4,172	3,723

	EXHIBIT 4.24				

**Selected Data for Georgia Pacific Corporation
(Problem 4.7)**

	Year 11	Year 10	Year 9	Year 8	Year 7
Rate of Return on Common					
Shareholders' Equity	(9.1%)	7.4%	20.6%	3.3%	(2.4%)
Rate of Return on Assets	.8%	3.3%	7.4%	3.1%	1.4%
Profit Margin for ROA.....................	.9%	3.3%	5.6%	2.7%	.9%
Profit Margin for ROCE	(1.9%)	1.6%	4.0%	.8%	(.7%)
Total Assets Turnover......................	.9	1.0	1.3	1.1	1.1
Capital Structure Leverage	5.3	4.8	3.9	3.5	3.5
Growth Rate in Sales	13.4%	24.1%	34.6%	2.0%	−.4%

b. Identify possible reasons for the changes in the capital structure leverage ratio during the five-year period.

4.8 CALCULATING AND INTERPRETING THE RATE OF RETURN ON COMMON SHAREHOLDERS' EQUITY AND EARNINGS PER COMMON SHARE.
Selected data for General Mills for Year 2, Year 3, and Year 4 appear below (amounts in millions):

	Year 4	Year 3	Year 2
Net Income	$ 506.1	$ 505.6	$472.7
Weighted Average Number of			
Common Shares Outstanding..........	163.1	165.7	164.5
Average Common Shareholders' Equity.....	$1,294.7	$1,242.2	$961.6

a. Compute the rate of return on common shareholders' equity (ROCE) for Year 2, Year 3, and Year 4.
b. Compute basic earnings per common share (EPS) for Year 2, Year 3, and Year 4.
c. Interpret the changes in ROCE versus EPS over the three-year period.

4.9 CALCULATING AND INTERPRETING PROFITABILITY RATIOS.
Hasbro is a leading firm in the toy, game, and amusement industry. Its promoted brands group includes products from Playskool, Tonka, Milton Bradley, Parker Brothers, Tiger, and Wizards of the Coast.

Exhibit 4.25 presents the balance sheets for Hasbro for the years ended December 31, Year 8 through Year 11. Exhibit 4.26 presents the income statement and Exhibit 4.27 presents the statement of cash flows for Year 9 through Year 11.

Required

a. Exhibit 4.28 presents profitability ratios for Hasbro for Year 9 and Year 10. Calculate each of these financial ratios for Year 11. The income tax rate is 35 percent.

b. Analyze the changes in ROA and its components of Hasbro over the three-year period, suggesting reasons for the changes observed.

c. Analyze the changes in ROCE and its components of Hasbro over the three-year period, suggesting reasons for the changes observed.

EXHIBIT 4.25

Hasbro
Balance Sheets
(amounts in millions)
(Problem 4.9)

	December 31			
	Year 11	Year 10	Year 9	Year 8
Assets				
Cash	$ 233	$ 127	$ 280	$ 178
Accounts Receivable......................	572	686	1,084	959
Inventories	217	335	409	335
Prepayments................................	346	432	359	319
Total Current Assets......................	$1,368	$1,580	$2,132	$1,791
Property, Plant, and Equipment (net)...............	236	296	319	330
Other Assets	1,765	1,952	2,013	1,674
Total Assets...............................	$3,369	$3,828	$4,464	$3,795
Liabilities and Shareholders' Equity				
Accounts Payable	$ 123	$ 192	$285	$ 209
Short-term Borrowing.....................	36	228	715	372
Other Current Liabilities	599	820	1,072	785
Total Current Liabilities.................	$ 758	$1,240	$2,072	$1,366
Long-term Debt	1,166	1,168	421	407
Other Noncurrent Liabilities	92	93	92	76
Total Liabilities...........................	$2,016	$2,501	$2,585	$1,849
Common Stock............................	$ 105	$ 105	$ 105	$ 70
Additional Paid-in Capital...............	455	457	468	556
Retained Earnings (Note A)...............	1,622	1,583	1,764	1,624
Accumulated Other Comprehensive Income..............	(68)	(45)	(33)	(10)
Treasury Stock	(761)	(773)	(425)	(294)
Total Shareholders' Equity.	$1,353	$1,327	$1,879	$1,946
Total Liabilities and Shareholders' Equity..............	$3,369	$3,828	$4,464	$3,795

Note A: The change in retained earnings does not equal the net income amount in Exhibit 4.26 minus the dividends amounts in Exhibit 4.27 because of adjustments to net income for nonrecurring items discussed in later chapters.

EXHIBIT 4.26

Hasbro
Income Statements
(amounts in millions)
(Problem 4.9)

	For the Year Ended December 31		
	Year 11	Year 10	Year 9
Sales	$ 2,856	$ 3,787	$ 4,232
Cost of Goods Sold	(1,223)	(1,642)	(1,651)
Selling and Administrative Expenses:			
Advertising.	(291)	(453)	(457)
Research and Development and Royalties	(126)	(209)	(255)
Other Selling and Administrative	(1,016)	(1,486)	(1,462)
Interest Expense	(104)	(114)	(69)
Income Tax Expense.	(34)	43	(107)
Net Income.	$ 62	$ (74)	$ 231

EXHIBIT 4.27

Hasbro
Statements of Cash Flows
(amounts in millions)
(Problem 4.9)

	For the Year Ended December 31		
	Year 11	Year 10	Year 9
Operations			
Net Income.	$ 62	$ (74)	$ 231
Depreciation and Amortization.	226	264	277
Addbacks and Subtractions—Net	(160)	(99)	(83)
(Inc.) Dec. in Accounts Receivable	99	396	(11)
(Inc.) Dec. in Inventories.	109	70	(44)
Inc. (Dec.) in Accounts Payable and Other Current Liabilities.	31	(401)	17
Cash Flow from Operations	$367	$ 156	$ 387
Investing			
Property, Plant, and Equipment Acquired.	$ (50)	$ (125)	$ (107)
Other Investing Transactions.	(8)	(56)	(322)
Cash Flow from Investing	$ (58)	$ (181)	$ (429)

	For the Year Ended December 31		
Exhibit 4.27—continued	Year 11	Year 10	Year 9
Financing			
Inc. in Short-term Borrowing	$ 0	$ 0	$226
Inc. in Long-term Borrowing...........................	250	913	$460
Inc. in Common Stock.....................................	8	3	50
Dec. in Short-term Borrowing........................	(190)	(342)	0
Dec. in Long-term Borrowing	(250)	(292)	(308)
Acquisition of Common Stock	0	(368)	(238)
Dividends..	(21)	(42)	(46)
Cash Flow from Financing	$(203)	$(128)	$144
Change in Cash	$ 106	$(153)	$102
Cash—Beginning of Year...............................	127	280	178
Cash—End of Year......................................	$ 233	$ 127	$280

EXHIBIT 4.28

Hasbro
Financial Statement Ratio Analysis
(Problem 4.9)

	Year 11	Year 10	Year 9
Profit Margin for ROA.....................................		0.0%	6.5%
Assets Turnover		.9	1.0
Rate of Return on Assets		0.0%	6.7%
Profit Margin for ROCE.....................................		(2.0%)	5.5%
Capital Structure Leverage....................................		2.6	2.2
Rate of Return on Common Shareholders' Equity..............		(4.6%)	12.1%
Cost of Goods Sold ÷ Sales		43.4%	39.0%
Advertising Expense ÷ Sales..................................		12.0%	10.8%
Research and Development and Royalties ÷ Sales		5.5%	6.0%
Other Selling and Administrative Expense ÷ Sales..............		39.2%	34.5%
Income Tax Expense (excluding tax effects of interest expense) ÷ Sales...............................		(.1%)	2.5%
Accounts Receivable Turnover..............................		4.3	4.1
Inventory Turnover		4.4	4.4
Fixed Asset Turnover		12.3	13.0

4.10 CALCULATING AND INTERPRETING PROFITABILITY RATIOS. Lands' End Corporation sells men's, women's, and children's clothing through catalogs. Financial statements for Lands' End for fiscal years ending January 31, Year 5, Year 6, and Year 7 appear in Exhibit 4.29 (balance sheet), Exhibit 4.30 (income statement), and Exhibit 4.31 (statement of cash flows). Exhibit 4.32 presents financial statement ratios for Lands' End for Year 5 and Year 6. Sales increased 14 percent between Year 4 and Year 5, 4 percent between Year 5 and Year 6, and 8.5 percent between Year 6 and Year 7.

EXHIBIT 4.29			

Lands' End—Balance Sheets
(amounts in thousands)
(Problem 4.10)

	January 31			
	Year 7	Year 6	Year 5	Year 4
Assets				
Cash	$ 92,827	$ 17,176	$ 5,426	$ 21,569
Accounts Receivable.	8,739	8,064	4,459	3,644
Inventories	142,445	164,816	168,652	149,688
Prepayments.	28,028	32,033	19,631	17,375
Total Current Assets	$272,039	$222,089	$198,168	$192,276
Property, Plant, and Equipment (net).	103,684	98,985	96,991	79,691
Other Assets	2,322	2,423	2,453	1,863
Total Assets	$378,045	$323,497	$297,612	$273,830
Liabilities and Shareholders' Equity				
Accounts Payable	$ 76,585	$ 62,380	$ 52,762	$ 54,855
Short-term Borrowing.	11,195	9,319	7,579	0
Current Portion of Long-term Debt	0	0	0	40
Other Current Liabilities	57,786	43,045	42,369	36,154
Total Current Liabilities	$145,566	$114,744	$102,710	$ 91,049
Long-term Debt.	0	0	0	40
Other Noncurrent Liabilities.	9,474	7,561	5,774	5,456
Total Liabilities	$155,040	$122,305	$108,484	$ 96,545
Common Stock	$ 402	$ 402	$ 402	$ 201
Additional Paid-in Capital.	34,630	34,565	34,217	33,288
Retained Earnings	310,069	259,276	228,417	191,705
Treasury Stock	(122,096)	(93,051)	(73,908)	(47,909)
Total Shareholders' Equity.	$223,005	$201,192	$189,128	$177,285
Total Liabilities and Shareholders' Equity	$378,045	$323,497	$297,612	$273,830

Because of capacity shortages, paper prices rose significantly during Lands' End's year ending January 31, Year 6, but declined in its fiscal Year 7. Lands' End shipped 88 percent of orders at the time customers placed their orders during fiscal Year 5, 90 percent during fiscal Year 6, and 86 percent during fiscal Year 7.

Required

a. Calculate the ratios in Exhibit 4.32 for Year 7. The income tax rate is 35 percent.
b. Analyze the changes in ROA of Lands' End during the three-year period, suggesting possible reasons for the changes observed.
c. Analyze the changes in ROCE of Lands' End during the three-year period, suggesting possible reasons for the changes observed.

4.11 INTERPRETING PROFITABILITY RATIOS IN A CROSS-SECTIONAL SETTING. The Coca-Cola Company (Coke) is the principal competitor of PepsiCo in the soft drink beverage business. Coke engages almost exclusively in beverages, where PepsiCo also engages in the manufacture and distribution of packaged foods, such as chips, salsas, and cereals.

The value chain for beverages involves:

1. Manufacturing of syrup to be used in the beverages.
2. Mixing of syrup, water, and other ingredients and then placing the finished beverage in a container (can, bottle). This process is relatively capital intensive.
3. Distribution of packaged beverages to food distributors and retail establishments. This activity is also capital intensive.

Coke and PepsiCo are primarily engaged in the manufacture of syrup (step 1). Coke uses other entities to perform steps 2 and 3. Prior to Year 9, PepsiCo engaged in all

---

EXHIBIT 4.30

Lands' End—Income Statements
(amounts in thousands)
(Problem 4.10)

	For the Year Ended January 31		
	Year 7	Year 6	Year 5
Sales	$1,118,743	$1,031,548	$992,106
Cost of Goods Sold	(609,168)	(588,017)	(571,265)
Selling and Administrative Expenses	(424,390)	(392,484)	(357,516)
Interest Expense..........................	(510)	(2,771)	(1,769)
Other Income (Expense)...................	244	2,649	(1,893)
Income Tax Expense	(33,967)	(20,370)	(23,567)
Net Income	$ 50,952	$ 30,555	$ 36,096

EXHIBIT 4.31

Lands' End
Statements of Cash Flows
(amounts in thousands)
(Problem 4.10)

	For the Year Ended January 31		
	Year 7	**Year 6**	**Year 5**
Operations			
Net Income	$ 50,952	$ 30,555	$ 36,096
Depreciation and Amortization	13,558	12,456	10,311
Addbacks and Subtractions—Net.	2,030	1,140	(987)
(Inc.) Dec. in Accounts Receivable	(675)	(4,888)	(264)
(Inc.) Dec. in Inventories.	22,371	1,423	(16,544)
(Inc.) Dec. in Prepayments	4,613	(9,929)	597
Inc. (Dec.) in Accounts Payable.	14,205	9,618	(2,093)
Inc. (Dec.) in Other Current Liabilities	14,741	1,017	7,345
Cash Flow from Operations	$121,795	$ 41,392	$ 34,461
Investing			
Property, Plant, and Equipment Acquired	$(18,481)	$(13,904)	$(32,102)
Other Investing Transactions.	0	1,665	0
Cash Flow from Investing.	$(18,481)	$(12,239)	$(32,102)
Financing			
Inc. in Short-term Borrowing.	$ 1,876	$ 1,780	$ 7,539
Inc. in Common Stock	604	858	1,978
Dec. in Short-term Borrowing	0	0	0
Dec. in Long-term Borrowing.	0	(40)	(40)
Dec. in Common Stock	(30,143)	(20,001)	(27,979)
Dividends.	0	0	0
Other Financing Transactions.	0	0	0
Cash Flow from Financing	$(27,663)	$(17,403)	$(18,502)
Change in Cash	$ 75,651	$ 11,750	$(16,143)
Cash—Beginning of Year.	17,176	5,426	21,569
Cash—End of Year.	$ 92,827	$ 17,176	$ 5,426

EXHIBIT 4.32			
Lands' End			
Financial Statement Ratio Analysis			
(Problem 4.10)			
	Year 7	Year 6	Year 5
Profit Margin for ROA.....................................		3.1%	3.8%
Assets Turnover		3.3	3.5
Rate of Return on Assets		10.4%	13.0%
Profit Margin for ROCE....................................		3.0%	3.6%
Capital Structure Leverage.................................		1.6	1.6
Rate of Return on Common Shareholders' Equity		15.7%	19.7%
Cost of Goods Sold ÷ Sales		57.0%	57.6%
Selling and Administrative Expense ÷ Sales		38.0%	36.0%
Income Tax Expense (excluding tax effects			
of interest expense) ÷ Sales.............................		2.1%	2.4%
Accounts Receivable Turnover..............................		164.7	244.9
Inventory Turnover		3.5	3.6
Fixed Asset Turnover		10.5	11.2

three steps in the value chain. Beginning in Year 9, PepsiCo began selling its ownership interest in the entities performing steps 2 and 3.

The value chain for packaged foods involves:

1. Combining ingredients, cooking as appropriate, and then packaging the finished food products.
2. Distribution of packaged food products to food distributors and retail establishments.

Exhibit 4.33 presents ROA and its disaggregated components for Coke and PepsiCo for Year 9 to Year 11. Exhibit 4.34 presents ROCE and its disaggregated components, and Exhibit 4.35 presents segment data for these two companies. The ratio amounts for PepsiCo correspond to those discussed in the chapter but appear next to those for Coke to ease interpretation. The segment profitability data are based on operating income before interest and income taxes. Thus, the profit margins and ROAs for the segments exceed those for the companies as a whole. The two firms experienced similar rates of sales growth between Year 9 and Year 11.

Required

a. What are the likely reasons that the cost of goods sold to sales percentage for Coke is lower than that for PepsiCo?

b. What are the likely reasons that PepsiCo's inventory turnover ratio exceeds that for Coke?
c. What are the likely reasons that Coke's fixed asset turnover exceeds that for PepsiCo?
d. For which firm is financial leverage helping the common shareholders more? Explain in such a way as to demonstrate your understanding of financial leverage.
e. What are the likely reasons that PepsiCo reduced its capital structure leverage ratio between Year 9 and Year 11?

EXHIBIT 4.33

ROA and its Disaggregated Components for Coke and PepsiCo
(Problem 4.11)

ROA	Year 9	Year 10	Year 11
Coke	15.6%	16.0%	19.0%
PepsiCo	11.3%	13.9%	14.8%

Profit Margin for ROA	Year 9	Year 10	Year 11		Assets Turnover	Year 9	Year 10	Year 11
Coke	16.5%	17.1%	20.5%		Coke	.9	.9	.9
PepsiCo	10.2%	11.1%	11.7%		PepsiCo	1.1	1.3	1.3

	Coke			PepsiCo				Year 9	Year 10	Year 11
	Year 9	Year 10	Year 11	Year 9	Year 10	Year 11	Receivables Turnover			
Sales	100.0%	100.0%	100.0%	100.0%	100.0%	100.0%	Coke	11.1	11.2	11.0
Other Rev.	.9	.8	2.6	.8	.8	.8	PepsiCo	10.7	12.5	12.6
CGS	(31.2)	(31.2)	(30.1)	(41.1)	(40.1)	(39.9)	Inventory Turnover			
S&A	(44.0)	(43.0)	(43.3)	(44.7)	(44.2)	(43.7)	Coke	6.1	5.8	5.7
Inc. Taxes	(9.3)	(9.5)	(8.7)	(4.8)	(5.4)	(5.5)	PepsiCo	8.5	8.7	8.6
							Fixed Asset Turnover			
Profit Margin for ROA	16.5%	17.1%	20.5%	10.2%	11.1%	11.7%	Coke	4.9	4.7	4.7
							PepsiCo	3.4	3.9	4.0

EXHIBIT 4.34

ROCE and its Disaggregated Components for Coke and PepsiCo
(Problem 4.11)

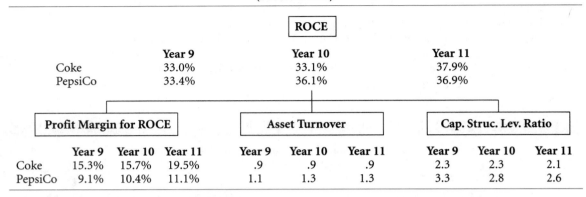

	ROCE		
	Year 9	Year 10	Year 11
Coke	33.0%	33.1%	37.9%
PepsiCo	33.4%	36.1%	36.9%

	Profit Margin for ROCE			Asset Turnover			Cap. Struc. Lev. Ratio		
	Year 9	Year 10	Year 11	Year 9	Year 10	Year 11	Year 9	Year 10	Year 11
Coke	15.3%	15.7%	19.5%	.9	.9	.9	2.3	2.3	2.1
PepsiCo	9.1%	10.4%	11.1%	1.1	1.3	1.3	3.3	2.8	2.6

EXHIBIT 4.35

Segment Data for Coke and PepsiCo
(Problem 4.11)

	Coke			PepsiCo		
	Year 9	Year 10	Year 11	Year 9	Year 10	Year 11
Geographical Segment Data						
Sales Mix						
North America	37.1%	37.3%	37.8%	70.9%	70.9%	71.6%
Other Countries	62.9%	62.7%	62.2%	29.1%	29.1%	28.5%
Profitability						
North America						
Profit Margin	20.4%	19.1%	19.7%	19.8%	20.1%	20.4%
Asset Turnover	1.97	1.72	1.59	1.66	1.77	1.72
ROA	40.4%	33.0%	31.2%	32.8%	35.6%	35.1%
Other Countries						
Profit Margin	26.2%	27.0%	37.1%	8.4%	9.7%	11.0%
Asset Turnover	1.88	2.24	1.87	1.04	1.18	1.26
ROA	49.3%	60.4%	69.5%	8.8%	11.4%	13.8%
Product Segment Data						
Sales Mix						
Beverage	100.0%	100.0%	100.0%	36.8%	38.0%	38.8%
Snack Foods	—	—	—	63.2%	62.0%	61.2%
Profitability						
Beverages						
Profit Margin	24.0%	24.0%	30.5%	15.3%	15.5%	16.1%
Asset Turnover	1.92	2.01	1.75	1.27	1.40	1.41
ROA	46.0%	48.4%	53.5%	19.4%	21.8%	22.7%
Snack Foods						
Profit Margin	—	—	—	17.2%	18.0%	18.8%
Asset Turnover	—	—	—	1.51	1.65	1.66
ROA	—	—	—	26.0%	29.8%	31.2%

4.12 INTERPRETING PROFITABILITY RATIOS. Sun Microsystems (Sun) has historically operated primarily in the engineering workstation segment of the computer hardware market. The workstation market was initially developed to meet the computation, design, and graphics needs of technical users such as scientists, architects, and engineers. High-quality graphics, design flexibility, and the need to integrate the work of several individuals on a design team were the primary product objectives. Sun has built on the networking technologies of its workstations to branch out into the design and manufacture of computer servers for use on intranet and Internet applications. It emphasizes networking capabilities and open system architecture as its principal strategic weapons. Sun is currently attempting to differentiate itself by emphasizing its experience and long-term commitment to these two needed qualities of integrated systems. Sun has also developed the Java computer language for use in writing software for network systems and applications. It has obtained agreements from IBM, Microsoft, Oracle Systems, Netscape Communications and others to use Java in their network software. Sun now characterizes itself as a "global supplier of network computing products, including workstations, servers, software, microprocessors, and a full range of services and support." Sun has also increasingly invested in emerging technology companies in recent years. Sun outsources virtually all of the components of its computers, employing an assembly manufacturing strategy for the final product. It has increasingly relied on indirect sellers for more than 60 percent of its sales in recent years, with Sun's own sales force accounting for the remainder. Sun operates in two principal business segments: (1) Computer Systems and Network Storage, which includes workstations and servers, and (2) Enterprise Services, which includes information systems consulting, education, and after-sale customer support. Exhibit 4.36 presents profitability ratios for Sun for Year 10, Year 11, and Year 12.

Required

a. What are the likely reasons for the decreasing profit margin for ROA between Year 10 and Year 12?

b. What are the likely reasons for the decreasing total assets turnover between Year 10 and Year 12?

c. Did financial leverage work to the advantage or disadvantage of the common shareholders in Year 10, Year 11, and Year 12? Explain.

4.13 ANALYZING THE PROFITABILITY OF A SERVICE FIRM. Kelly Services (Kelly) places employees at clients' businesses on a temporary basis. It segments its services into (1) commercial, (2) professional and technical, and (3) international. Kelly recognizes revenues for the amount billed to clients. Kelly includes the amount it pays to temporary employees in cost of services sold. It includes the compensation paid to permanent employees that administer its offices in selling and administrative expenses. The latter expense also includes data processing costs relating to payroll records for all employees, and rent, taxes, and insurance on office space. Amounts receivable from clients appear in accounts receivable, and amounts payable to permanent and temporary employees appear in current liabilities.

	EXHIBIT 4.36		
	Sun Microsystems		
	Profitability Ratios		
	(Problem 4.12)		
	Year 12	Year 11	Year 10
Profit Margin for ROA..................................	(1.7)%	5.7%	12.1%
Assets Turnover	.7	1.1	1.3
Rate of Return on Assets	(1.2)%	6.1%	16.1%
Profit Margin for ROCE	(2.0)%	5.4%	11.8%
Capital Structure Leverage	1.8	1.9	2.0
Rate of Return on Common Shareholders' Equity.............	(2.5)%	11.0%	30.6%
Other Revenues (primarily interest) ÷ Sales.................	2.1%	2.0%	2.9%
Cost of Goods Sold ÷ Sales..............................	60.7%	55.0%	48.0%
Selling and Administrative Expense ÷ Sales	30.5%	26.3%	26.3%
Research and Development Expense ÷ Sales	14.7%	11.5%	10.4%
Income Tax Expense (credit) (excluding tax effects			
of interest expense) ÷ Sales...........................	(2.1)%	3.5%	6.0%
Accounts Receivable Turnover............................	4.4	6.5	6.3
Inventory Turnover	9.2	12.5	17.5
Fixed Asset Turnover	3.4	5.6	6.5
Growth Rate in Sales	(31.5)%	+16.1%	+33.2%
Sales Mix:			
Computer Systems.......................................	72.8%	82.3%	85.4%
Enterprise Services......................................	27.2	17.7	14.6
	100.0%	100.0%	100.0%
Gross Margin Percentage			
Computer Systems.......................................	39.4%	47.0%	54.6%
Enterprise Services......................................	39.1%	35.7%	36.8%
Sales Mix:			
United States	46.5%	47.4%	51.7%
Europe	31.8	30.2	28.6
Asia Pacific...	17.4	17.2	15.3
Other International	5.3	5 2	4.4
	100.0%	100.0%	100.0%

The temporary supply business offers clients flexibility in adjusting their number of workers to meet changing capacity needs. Temporary employees are typically less costly than permanent workers because they have fewer fringe benefits. Temporary workers, however, generally are not as well-trained as permanent workers and have less loyalty to clients.

Barriers to entry in the personnel supply business are low. This business does not require capital for physical facilities (most space is rented), does not need specialized assets (most temporary employees do not possess unique skills; needed data processing technology is readily available), and operates with little government regulation. Thus, competition is intense and margins tend to be thin.

Exhibit 4.37 presents selected profitability ratios and other data for Kelly Services, the largest temporary personnel supply firm in the United States. The data in Exhibit 4.37 reflect the capitalization of operating leases, a topic discussed in Chapter 8.

Required

Analyze the changes in the profitability of Kelly Services during the three-year period in as much depth as permitted by the data provided.

EXHIBIT 4.37
Profitability Ratios and Other Data for Kelly Services
(Problem 4.13)

	Year 11	Year 10	Year 9
Profit Margin for ROA..........................	.4%	1.8%	2.0%
Assets Turnover	3.6	3.8	3.8
Rate of Return on Assets	1.6%	7.1%	7.8%
Profit Margin for ROCE........................	.4%	1.8%	2.0%
Capital Structure Leverage Ratio.................	1.9	1.9	2.0
Rate of Return on Common Shareholders' Equity ...	2.8%	13.4%	15.2%
Revenues.....................................	100.0%	100.0%	100.0%
Compensation of Temporary Employees/Revenues ..	83.6%	82.3%	82.0%
Selling and Administrative Expense/Revenues	15.7%	14.6%	14.6%
Income Tax Expense/Revenues	.3%	1.3%	1.4%
Accounts Receivable Turnover....................	7.3	7.3	7.2
Fixed Asset Turnover	13.6	14.8	15.4
Number of Offices	2,300	1,800	1,500
Number of Permanent Employees................	8,600	7,400	7,200
Number of Temporary Employees................	690,000	750,000	740,000
Growth Rate in Revenues.......................	−5.1%	5.1%	4.3%
Per Office Data:			
Revenues.....................................	$1,850,823	$2,492,939	$2,846,075
Net Income...................................	7,195	45,337	56,740
Permanent Employees	3.7	4.1	4.8
Temporary Employees	300	417	493
Per Permanent Employee Data:			
Revenues.....................................	$ 494,987	$ 606,391	$ 592,932
Net Income...................................	$ 1,924	$ 11,028	$ 11,821
Temporary Employees	80.2	101.4	102.8
Per Temporary Employee Data:			
Revenues.....................................	$ 6,169	$ 5,983	$ 5,769
Net Income...................................	24	108	115

4.14 ANALYZING THE PROFITABILITY OF TWO HOTELS. La Quinta Inns (La Quinta) operates a chain of mid-priced hotels aimed at the cost-conscious business traveler. Its targeted guests desire quality rooms in convenient locations at attractive prices but do not require banquet and convention facilities, in-house restaurants, cocktail lounges, or room service. Exhibit 4.38 presents selected profitability ratios and other data for La Quinta.

Prime Hospitality Corporation (Prime) operates several hotel chains with different targeted customers. Its AmeriSuites and Wellesley Inns offer hotel suites in primarily suburban commercial centers and corporate office parks. These hotels are located with easy access to shopping, food, and entertainment amenities. Prime also operates full-service hotels under national brand names (Marriott, Sheraton, Crown Plaza) which offer banquet and convention facilities. Exhibit 4.39 presents selected profitability and other data for Prime.

Required

Analyze the changes and the differences in the profitability of these two hotel chains to the maximum depth permitted by the given data.

EXHIBIT 4.38

Profitability Ratios and Other Data for La Quinta Inns
(Problem 4.14)

	Year 9	Year 8	Year 7
Profit Margin for ROA	19.9%	18.8%	17.4%
Assets Turnover	.43	.46	.45
Rate of Return on Assets	8.6%	8.6%	7.9%
Profit Margin for ROCE	13.5%	12.2%	10.6%
Capital Structure Leverage Ratio	3.0	3.5	4.7
Rate of Return on Common Shareholders' Equity	17.4%	19.7%	22.4%
Number of Hotels	248	237	228
Number of Rooms	32,728	31,363	29,712
Rooms/Hotel	132	132	130
Occupancy Rate	68.9%	70.8%	70.1%
Revenue/Available Room Night	$ 37.09	$ 36.16	$ 33.40
Operating Income/Available Room Night	$ 7.39	$ 6.78	$ 5.82
Revenue/Occupied Room Night	$ 53.83	$ 51.07	$ 47.65
Operating Income/Occupied Room Night	$ 10.73	$ 9.58	$ 8.30
Revenue/Hotel	$1,786,528	$1,746,494	$1,588,781
Operating Income/Hotel	$ 356,141	$ 327,629	$ 276,640

EXHIBIT 4.39

Profitability Ratios and Other Data for Prime Hospitality Corporation
(Problem 4.14)

	Year 9	Year 8	Year 7
Profit Margin for ROA	13.8%	15.3%	20.4%
Assets Turnover	.38	.41	.32
Rate of Return on Assets	5.2%	6.3%	6.5%
Profit Margin for ROCE	8.5%	8.5%	13.2%
Capital Structure Leverage Ratio	2.1	2.3	2.3
Rate of Return on Common Shareholders' Equity	6.8%	8.0%	9.7%
Number of Hotels	108	95	86
Number of Rooms..........................	16,232	11,110	8,965
Rooms/Hotel	150	117	104
Occupancy Rate...........................	69.0%	69.2%	68.0%
Revenue/Available Room Night	$ 43.09	$ 50.71	$ 41.04
Operating Income/Available Room Night	$ 5.96	$ 7.77	$ 8.36
Revenue/Occupied Room Night	$ 62.45	$ 73.28	$ 60.36
Operating Income/Occupied Room Night.......	$ 8.64	$ 11.23	$ 12.30
Revenue/Hotel............................	$2,363,944	$2,164,505	$1,561,663
Operating Income/Hotel....................	$ 208,620	$ 331,653	$ 318,058

4.15 ANALYZING THE PROFITABILITY OF TWO RESTAURANT CHAINS.
Analyzing the profitability of restaurants requires consideration of their strategies
with respect to ownership of restaurants versus franchising. Firms that own and
operate their restaurants will report the assets and financing of those restaurants on
their balance sheets, and the revenues and operating expenses of the restaurants on
their income statements. Firms that franchise their restaurants to others (that is,
franchisees) will often own the land and buildings of franchised restaurants and lease
them to the franchisees. The income statement includes fees received from franchisees in the form of license fees for using the franchiser's name, rent for facilities
and equipment, and various fees for advertising, menu planning, and food and paper
products used by the franchisee. The revenues and operating expenses of the franchised restaurants appear on the financial statements of the franchisees.

Exhibit 4.40 presents profitability ratios and other data for Brinker, and Exhibit
4.41 presents similar data for McDonald's. Brinker operates chains of specialty, sit-
down restaurants in the United States under the names of Chili's, Macaroni Grill, and
On The Border. Its restaurants average approximately 7,000 square feet. Brinker owns
and operates approximately 79 percent of its restaurants. McDonald's operates
chains of fast food restaurants in the United States and other countries under the
names of McDonald's, Boston Market, Chipotle, and Donato's Pizzeria. Its restaurants average approximately 2,800 square feet. McDonald's owns and operates

approximately 28 percent of its restaurants. It also owns approximately 25 percent of the restaurant land and buildings of franchisees. The financial ratios and other data in Exhibits 4.40 and 4.41 reflect the capitalization of operating leases in property, plant, and equipment and long-term debt, a topic discussed in Chapter 8.

Required

a. Suggest reasons for the changes in the profitability of Brinker during the three-year period.

b. Suggest reasons for the changes in the profitability of McDonald's during the three-year period.

c. Suggest reasons for differences in the profitability of Brinker and McDonald's during the three-year period.

EXHIBIT 4.40

Profitability Ratios and Other Data for Brinker International
(Problem 4.15)

	Year 11	Year 10	Year 9
Profit Margin for ROA	6.1%	5.9%	5.6%
Assets Turnover	1.4	1.4	1.3
Rate of Return on Assets	8.5%	8.1%	7.3%
Profit Margin for ROCE	5.9%	5.5%	5.1%
Capital Structure Leverage	2.2	2.2	2.3
Rate of Return on Common Shareholders' Equity	17.4%	16.6%	15.3%
Cost of Goods Sold ÷ Revenues	86.3%	86.3%	86.6%
Selling and Administrative Expenses ÷ Revenues	4.4%	4.6%	4.8%
Income Tax Expense (excluding tax effects of interest expense) ÷ Revenues	3.3%	3.2%	3.0%
Accounts Receivable Turnover	97.0	105.4	93.6
Inventory Turnover	99.3	120.3	111.8
Fixed Asset Turnover	1.7	1.7	1.6
Revenues per Restaurant (000's)	$2,164	$2,081	$2,005
Operating Income per Restaurant (000's)	$ 127	$ 114	$ 103
Fixed Assets per Restaurant (000's)	$1,290	$1,246	$1,244
Percentage of Restaurants Owned and Operated	79.0%	75.8%	77.2%
Growth in Revenues	14.5%	15.4%	18.9%
Growth in Number of Restaurants	10.1%	11.3%	17.5%

	EXHIBIT 4.41		

Profitability Ratios and Other Data for McDonald's
(Problem 4.15)

	Year 11	Year 10	Year 9
Profit Margin for ROA...............................	13.7%	15.9%	16.7%
Assets Turnover	.5	.5	.5
Rate of Return on Assets	7.3%	8.5%	9.0%
Profit Margin for ROCE	11.7%	13.9%	14.7%
Capital Structure Leverage	2.8	2.6	2.5
Rate of Return on Common Shareholders' Equity	17.5%	19.5%	19.6%
Cost of Goods Sold ÷ Revenues	69.0%	66.9%	64.6%
Selling and Administrative Expenses ÷ Revenues............	11.2%	11.1%	11.1%
Income Tax Expense (excluding tax effects			
of interest expense) ÷ Revenues	6.1%	7.4%	8.1%
Accounts Receivable Turnover..........................	17.7	18.9	20.1
Inventory Turnover	100.0	104.6	107.1
Fixed Asset Turnover	.6	.6	.6
Revenues per Restaurant (000's)	$494	$496	$504
Operating Income per Restaurant (000's)..................	$ 58	$ 69	$ 74
Fixed Assets per Restaurant (000's)	$770	$765	$780
Percentage of Restaurants Owned and Operated	27.8%	26.7%	23.0%
Growth in Revenues....................................	4.4%	7.4%	6.7%
Growth in Number of Restaurants	4.8%	9.1%	7.3%

4.16 ANALYZING TWO COMMERCIAL BANKS. Commercial banks generate their revenues from two principal sources: (1) lending and investing, and (2) fee-based services. Commercial banks obtain the majority of their funds from deposits by customers and short-term borrowing. They invest a portion of the funds in relatively liquid government and high-grade corporate debt securities and lend most of the remainder to businesses and consumers. Some banks conduct trading activities in various securities both to help establish an active market and to trade on their own account for profit.

Competition among banks and other financial institutions has reduced the net interest margin banks generate from the spread between the rate paid for funds and the return generated from lending. As a consequence, commercial banks have increasingly turned to fee-based revenues to increase their profitability. Service charges for bank services (checking accounts, trust services, investment advisory and management services) are one avenue pursued. Another avenue involves structuring new financing, mergers and acquisitions, and other advisory services for businesses. The principal expenses of commercial banks, besides interest, are compensation of employees, occupancy costs, information systems cost, and uncollectible accounts.

The commercial banking industry has experienced major consolidation during the last decade, the result of (1) reduced restrictions on interstate banking, (2) the desirability of building a national, and even international, presence to serve customers more effectively, and (3) perceived benefits of economies of scale in information processing and one-stop customer shopping for financial services. Mergers between commercial banks and investment banks are currently occurring at a rapid pace with the relaxation of restrictions previously imposed by the Glass-Steagall Act of 1933.

Analyzing the profitability of a commercial bank uses rate of return on assets and on common shareholders' equity and their disaggregated components, profit margin, assets turnover, and capital structure leverage ratio. One difference in the calculation of these ratios is that the analyst makes no adjustment to ROA and profit margin for interest expense, since interest expense for a commercial bank is similar to cost of goods sold for a manufacturing or retailing firm. Commercial banks provide sufficient information to compute the return from loans, bank deposits, investments in securities, and trading securities, and the cost of deposits and other borrowing. Because most balance sheet accounts experience significant increases and decreases each day, commercial banks provide the average daily balances in various accounts to serve as the basis for computing various rates of return.

The sources of risk for commercial banks include (1) credit risk from lending, (2) interest rate risk from borrowing and lending activities, and (3) liquidity risk. Analysis of credit risk utilizes the following ratios:

(1) Loan Loss Reserve Ratio = Loan Loss Reserve/Loans Receivable.
(2) Net Charge-Offs Ratio = Net Charge-Offs/Average Loans Receivable during the Year. Net charge-offs equal loans charged off minus recoveries of loans charged off in a previous year.
(3) Nonperforming Loan Percentage = Nonperforming Loans/Total Loans Receivable. Nonperforming loans are loans that the bank does not expect to collect in full in accordance with the original lending agreement. Some of these loans no longer accrue interest and some have been restructured.

Commercial banks have become quite sophisticated in managing their interest rate risk. They utilize computer software to insure that the level and term structure of their interest-sensitive assets match their interest-sensitive liabilities on a daily basis. Commercial banks disclose their interest-sensitive position by maturity date.

The analyst assesses liquidity risk by examining the proportion of long-term debt and shareholders' equity in the capital structure. The higher is this proportion, the more cushion the banks have to cover deposits by customers and repay short-term borrowing. The Federal Reserve Board establishes minimum capital requirements that are a stated percentage of risk-adjusted assets. Tier 1 capital primarily includes common and preferred stock. Tier 2 capital includes certain long-term debt. Risk-adjusted assets include most assets reported on the balance sheet plus various off-balance sheet commitments. Commercial banks apply various risk-adjustment factors to these assets to form the denominator of the capital ratios. Tier 1 capital as a percentage of risk-adjusted assets must reach a minimum of 4 percent. Tier 1 plus Tier 2 capital must reach a minimum of 8 percent of risk-adjusted assets.

Exhibit 4.42 presents various profitability and risk ratios and Exhibit 4.43 presents a common-size balance sheet for Wells Fargo for Year 6 through Year 8. Exhibits 4.44 and 4.45 present similar information for J.P. Morgan. Wells Fargo maintains its principal presence in the West and Southwest portion of the United States. It maintains a

---

EXHIBIT 4.42

**Profitability and Risk Ratios for Wells Fargo
(Problem 4.16)**

	Year 8	Year 7	Year 6
Company-Level Profitability Analysis			
Profit Margin for Rate of Return on Assets	12.28%	21.92%	16.94%
Assets Turnover	.09	.11	.10
Rate of Return on Assets	1.15%	2.44%	1.62%
Capital Structure Leverage Ratio..........................	8.21	14.93	14.57
Rate of Return on Shareholders' Equity	8.78%	35.21%	22.68%
Operating Performance Analysis			
Gross Yield on Earning Assets.............................	8.80%	9.14%	8.01%
Rate Paid on Funds	2.70%	3.20%	2.46%
Net Interest Margin	6.10%	5.94%	5.55%
Non-Interest Revenue Percentage	25.22%	26.36%	24.17%
Non-Interest Expense Percentage	69.84%	60.60%	65.12%
Loan Loss Provision Percentage	1.61%	0.00%	5.31%
Segment Profitability Analysis			
Return on Bank Deposits	3.04%	3.05%	2.88%
Return on Domestic Loans	9.40%	9.86%	8.86%
Return on Foreign Loans.................................	6.90%	8.70%	6.45%
Return on Investment Securities...........................	6.40%	6.75%	5.85%
Cost of Domestic Deposits	3.23%	3.19%	2.62%
Cost of Foreign Deposits.................................	5.06%	5.93%	4.76%
Cost of Other Borrowing.................................	6.09%	6.18%	5.11%
Risk Analysis			
Loan Loss Reserve Ratio	2.99%	5.04%	5.73%
Net Charge-off Ratio....................................	1.06%	.83%	.71%
Non-Performing Loan Percentage..........................	1.06%	1.51%	1.56%
Risk-Adjusted Capital Ratio—Tier 1.......................	7.68%	8.81%	9.09%
Risk-Adjusted Capital Ratio—Tier 1 and 2	11.70%	12.46%	13.16%

network of branch banks to obtain deposits from customers and to lend to businesses and consumers. It emphasizes the traditional borrowing and lending activities of commercial banks. Wells Fargo acquired First Interstate Bancorp during the second quarter of Year 8 through an exchange of common stock in a transaction accounted for using the purchase method. J.P. Morgan maintains a minor presence in traditional borrowing and lending. Instead, it emphasizes investing and trading activities, and the offering of fee-based financial advisory services.

Required

a. Analyze the changes in the profitability and risk of Well Fargo during the three-year period.
b. Analyze the changes in the profitability and risk of J.P. Morgan during the three-year period.
c. Analyze the differences in the profitability and risk of Wells Fargo and J.P. Morgan, indicating how differences in their strategies affect their operating performance and risk.

EXHIBIT 4.43

Common-size Balance Sheets for Wells Fargo
(Problem 4.16)

	Year 8	Year 7	Year 6
Interest Bearing Deposits.	1.1%	.3%	.5%
Investment Securities.	13.5	20.2	24.5
Domestic Loans	64.7	69.3	65.6
Foreign Loans.	.2	.1	.1
Total Earning Assets	79.5%	89.9%	90.7%
Other Assets	20.5	10.1	9.3
Total Assets	100.0%	100.0%	100.0%
Domestic Interest Bearing Deposits	52.0%	55.0%	59.6%
Foreign Interest Bearing Deposits	.4	3.5	1.8
Non-Interest Bearing Deposits	24.3	17.9	17.4
Short-term Borrowing.	2.3	7.8	4.7
Long-term Borrowing	5.0	6.1	6.6
Other Non-Interest Bearing Liabilities	3.0	2.2	2.0
Total Liabilities	87.0%	92.5%	92.1%
Preferred Stock Equity.	.8%	1.0%	1.0%
Common Stock Equity.	12.2	6.5	6.9
Total Shareholders' Equity	13.0%	7.5%	7.9%
Total Liabilities and Shareholders' Equity.	100.0%	100.0%	100.0%

EXHIBIT 4.44

Profitability and Risk Ratios for J. P. Morgan
(Problem 4.16)

	Year 8	Year 7	Year 6
Company-Level Profitability Analysis			
Profit Margin for Rate of Return on Assets	9.92%	9.37%	10.20%
Assets Turnover	.73	.08	.07
Rate of Return on Assets	.35%	.73%	.70%
Capital Structure Leverage Ratio.	20.68	19.06	18.63
Rate of Return on Shareholders' Equity	15.14%	13.58%	12.90%
Operating Performance Analysis			
Gross Yield on Earning Assets	6.24%	7.30%	6.24%
Rate Paid on Funds	5.25%	5.83%	4.76%
Net Interest Margin	.99%	1.47%	1.47%
Non-Interest Revenue Percentage	32.48%	28.19%	29.68%
Non-Interest Expense Percentage	33.42%	33.51%	36.59%
Loan Loss Provision Percentage	0.00%	0.00%	0.00%
Segment Profitability Analysis			
Return on Bank Deposits	2.76%	3.64%	5.17%
Return on Resale Agreements	5.17%	6.00%	4.63%
Return on Domestic Loans	6.66%	7.21%	5.58%
Return on Foreign Loans.	6.24%	6.97%	6.02%
Return on Trading Account Securities	12.44%	11.50%	9.84%
Return on Investment Securities.	17.95%	16.33%	13.90%
Cost of Domestic Deposits	5.15%	4.79%	4.64%
Cost of Foreign Deposits.	5.18%	5.80%	4.89%
Cost of Other Borrowing.	5.67%	6.27%	5.06%
Risk Analysis			
Loan Loss Reserve Ratio	4.06%	5.06%	6.06%
Net Charge-off Ratio	.05%	.00%	.11%
Non-Performing Loan Percentage.	.44%	.52%	1.01%
Risk-Adjusted Capital Ratio—Tier 1.	8.8%	8.8%	9.6%
Risk-Adjusted Capital Ratio—Tier 1 and 2	12.2%	13.0%	14.2%

EXHIBIT 4.45

Common-size Balance Sheets for J. P. Morgan
(Problem 4.16)

	Year 6	Year 7	Year 8
Interest Bearing Deposits.........................	1.9%	2.6%	2.2%
Resale Agreements	31.8	26.3	27.7
Investment Securities........................	11.6	12.3	11.6
Trading Account Securities	21.6	21.5	22.4
Domestic Loans	2.9	3.7	4.5
Foreign Loans..........................	10.1	9.8	9.4
Total Earning Assets	79.8%	76.2%	77.8%
Other Assets	20.2	23.8	22.2
Total Assets	100.0%	100.0%	100.0%
Domestic Interest Bearing Deposits	1.8%	1.2%	1.3%
Foreign Interest Bearing Deposits	21.0	23.4	21.9
Non-Interest Bearing Deposits	1.4	2.6	3.0
Short-term Borrowing.......................	48.1	43.5	47.6
Long-term Borrowing	5.0	4.9	3.4
Other Non-Interest Bearing Liabilities	17.6	18.9	17.1
Total Liabilities	94.9%	94.5%	94.3%
Preferred Stock Equity.......................	.3%	.3%	.3%
Common Stock Equity........................	4.8	5.2	5.4
Total Shareholders' Equity	5.1%	5.5%	5.7%
Total Liabilities and Shareholders' Equity....................	100.0%	100.0%	100.0%

CASE 4.1

PROFITABILITY AND RISK ANALYSIS OF WAL-MART STORES

Wal-Mart Stores (Wal-Mart) is the world's largest retailer. It employs an "everyday low-price" strategy and operates through four principal store concepts:

1. Wal-Mart Stores: Discount department stores that offer clothing, housewares, electronic equipment, pharmaceuticals, health and beauty products, sporting goods, and similar items. The number of Wal-Mart Stores decreased at a compound annual rate of 4.1 percent and square footage decreased at a compound annual rate of 3.8 percent between fiscal Year 10 and fiscal Year 12. The average size of a Wal-Mart Store was 95,750 square feet at the end of fiscal Year 12.
2. Wal-Mart Supercenters: A full-line supermarket combined with a discount department store. Supercenters represent for Wal-Mart a move to grocery

products. Combining grocery products with Wal-Mart's traditional discount department store offerings attempts to capitalize on one-stop shopping by consumers and to gain efficiencies in product distribution, stocking, and advertising. Compound annual growth rates between fiscal Year 10 and fiscal Year 12 for Wal-Mart Supercenters are 23.6 percent in the number of stores and 24.5 percent in square footage. A portion of the growth in Wal-Mart Supercenters represents conversions of previous Wal-Mart Stores. The average size of a Wal-Mart Supercenter was 185,180 square feet at the end of fiscal Year 12.

3. Sam's Clubs: Members-only warehouse stores that offer large quantities of food and household products as well as automotive, electronic, sporting goods, and similar products at wholesale prices. Compound annual growth rates between fiscal Year 10 and fiscal Year 12 for Sam's Clubs are 3.5 percent in the number of stores and 4.2 percent in square footage. The average size of a Sam's Club store was 123,600 square feet at the end of fiscal Year 12.

4. International: Wal-Mart expanded its international operations significantly in recent years and now conducts operations (number of stores in parentheses) in Canada (196), Mexico (551), Puerto Rico (17), Brazil (22), Argentina (11), United Kingdom (250), China (19), Korea (9), and Germany (95). Wal-Mart operates internationally through discount stores, supercenters, and some specialty stores and restaurants. It grew its international operations 17.9 percent in number of stores and 22.8 percent in square footage between Year 10 and Year 12. Wal-Mart's principal acquisitions included CIFRA in Mexico on September 1, Year 7; Interspar in Germany on December 29, Year 8; and ASDA in the United Kingdom on September 1, Year 9. Wal-Mart allocated the purchase price to the identifiable assets and liabilities acquired based on their market values. It allocated any remaining purchase price to goodwill. Income and cash flows from these acquisitions are included in consolidated net income and cash flows from the date of acquisition. The effects of these and several smaller acquisitions on the balance sheet at the date of acquisition were as follows:

Acquisitions During Fiscal:	Year 8	Year 9	Year 10	Year 11
Cash	$ 500	$137	$ 195	—
Accounts Receivable	97	—	16	—
Inventories	266	200	655	—
Prepayments	—	—	403	—
Property, Plant, and Equipment (net)	2,105	219	5,902	—
Goodwill	1,213	576	7,020	452
Accounts Payable	(431)	(112)	(1,159)	—
Other Current Liabilities	(132)	(60)	(847)	—
Long-term Debt	—	—	(1,272)	—
Deferred Income Taxes	(353)	32	(58)	—
Other	(900)	—	(7)	165
Purchase Price	$2,365	$992	$10,848	$617

The average size of a store in the International segment was 83,330 square feet at the end of fiscal Year 12.

Wal-Mart has recently added a small number of "Neighborhood Markets" to its retail line. These stores, totaling 31 and averaging 45,742 square feet in size at the end of fiscal Year 12, are located in residential neighborhoods, and primarily offer grocery products.

Wal-Mart uses centralized purchasing through its home office for substantially all of its merchandise. It distributes products to its stores through regional distribution centers. During fiscal Year 12, the proportion of merchandise channeled through its regional distribution centers was as follows:

Wal-Mart Stores and Supercenters	84%
Sam's Club	62%
International	71%

Wal-Mart increased its use of consignment arrangements during the last three years. The manufacturers of consigned products keep the inventory on their books and bear the risks of inventory obsolescence and theft. Unsold products physically revert back to the manufacturer. Wal-Mart records the sales of such products as Sales Revenue and the amount it must pay the manufacturer as Cost of Goods Sold.

Exhibit 4.46 sets out various operating data for Wal-Mart for its most recent three years. Exhibit 4.47 presents segment data. The "Other" segment represents Wal-Mart's distribution centers. These distribution centers not only distribute products to Wal-Mart stores but to other retailers as well. Exhibit 4.48 presents comparative balance sheets, Exhibit 4.49 presents comparative income statements, and Exhibit 4.50 presents comparative statements of cash flows for Wal-Mart for fiscal Year 10, Year 11, and Year 12. Exhibit 4.51 presents selected financial statement ratios for Wal-Mart for fiscal Year 10, Year 11, and Year 12. The income tax rate is 35 percent.

Required

a. What are the likely reasons for the changes in Wal-Mart's rate of return on assets during the three-year period? Analyze the financial ratios to the maximum depth possible.

b. What are the likely reasons for the changes in Wal-Mart's rate of return on common shareholders' equity during the three-year period?

NOTE: Parts c and d require coverage of material from Chapter 5.

c. How has the short-term liquidity risk of Wal-Mart changed during the three-year period?

d. How has the long-term liquidity risk of Wal-Mart changed during the three-year period?

EXHIBIT 4.46

Operating Data for Wal-Mart Stores, Inc.
(Case 4.1)

	Fiscal Year Ended January 31:		
	Year 12	Year 11	Year 10
Wal-Mart Stores (Domestic)			
Number	1,647	1,736	1,801
Square Footage (millions)	157.7	165.4	170.8
Wal-Mart Supercenters (Domestic)			
Number	1,066	888	721
Square Footage (millions)	197.4	162.6	130.7
Wal-Mart Stores and Supercenters (combined)			
Sales per Square Foot	$391.81	$371.61	$360.60
Operating Income per Square Foot	$ 29.02	$ 29.68	$ 27.92
Sam's Club (Domestic)			
Number	500	475	463
Square Footage (millions)	61.8	58.0	56.4
Sales per Square Foot	$475.65	$462.03	$439.73
Operating Income per Square Foot	$ 16.63	$ 16.76	$ 13.45
International			
Number	1,170	1,071	1,004
Square Footage (millions)	97.5	80.4	74.9
Sales per Square Foot	$363.95	$399.25	$303.44
Operating Income per Square Foot	$ 14.95	$ 13.83	$ 10.90
Domestic Comparable Store Sales Increase	6%	5%	8%
Employees (full and part time)	1,383,000	1,244,000	1,140,000

EXHIBIT 4.47

Segment Profitability Analysis for Wal-Mart Stores, Inc.
(Case 4.1)

	Year 12	Year 11	Year 10
Sales Mix			
Wal-Mart Discount Stores and Supercenters....................	63.9%	63.7%	65.9%
Sam's Club	13.5	14.0	15.0
International...	16.3	16.8	13.8
Other...	6.3	5.5	5.3
	100.0%	100.0%	100.0%
Wal-Mart Discount Stores and Supercenters			
Profit Margin	7.4%	8.0%	8.0%
Total Assets Turnover	6.4	6.0	6.0
Rate of Return on Assets	47.1%	48.0%	47.8%
Sam's Club			
Profit Margin	3.5%	3.5%	3.4%
Total Assets Turnover	7.4	7.0	6.9
Rate of Return on Assets	26.0%	24.5%	23.7%
International			
Profit Margin	4.1%	3.5%	3.6%
Total Assets Turnover	1.3	1.2	.9
Rate of Return on Assets	5.5%	4.3%	3.2%
Other			
Profit Margin	(5.2%)	(2.8%)	(3.0%)
Total Assets Turnover	.4	.4	.4
Rate of Return on Assets	(2.3%)	(1.1%)	(1.1%)

Wal-Mart Stores, Inc.
Comparative Balance Sheets
(amounts in millions)
(Case 4.1)

	January 31:			
	Year 12	Year 11	Year 10	Year 9
Assets				
Cash	$ 2,161	$ 2,054	$ 1,856	$ 1,879
Accounts Receivable...............................	2,000	1,768	1,341	1,118
Inventories	22,614	21,442	19,793	17,076
Prepayments......................................	1,471	1,291	1,366	1,059
Total Current Assets.............................	$28,246	$26,555	$24,356	$21,132
Property, Plant, and Equipment (net)	50,529	45,417	39,001	28,756
Other Assets	9,455	10,641	10,024	2,891
Total Assets....................................	$88,230	$82,613	$73,381	$52,779
Liabilities and Shareholders' Equity				
Accounts Payable	$15,617	$15,092	$13,105	$10,257
Notes Payable	743	2,286	3,323	—
Current Portion of Long-term Debt	2,405	4,375	2,085	1,006
Other Current Liabilities	8,517	7,196	7,290	5,499
Total Current Liabilities...........................	$27,282	$28,949	$25,803	$16,762
Long-term Debt	23,511	20,138	19,706	12,390
Other Noncurrent Liabilities	2,335	2,183	2,038	2,515
Total Liabilities.................................	$53,128	$51,270	$47,547	$31,667
Common Stock....................................	$ 445	$ 447	$ 446	$ 445
Additional Paid-in Capital	1,484	1,411	714	435
Retained Earnings.................................	33,173	29,485	24,674	20,232
Total Shareholders' Equity.........................	$35,102	$31,343	$25,834	$21,112
Total Liabilities and Shareholders' Equity.............	$88,230	$82,613	$73,381	$52,779

EXHIBIT 4.49

Wal-Mart Stores, Inc.
Comparative Income Statements
(amounts in millions)
(Case 4.1)

	Year Ended January 31:		
	Year 12	Year 11	Year 10
Sales Revenue	$217,799	$191,329	$165,013
Other Revenues	2,013	1,966	1,796
Total Revenues.	$219,812	$193,295	$166,809
Expenses:			
Cost of Goods Sold	$171,562	$150,255	$129,664
Marketing and Administrative	36,356	31,679	27,210
Interest.	1,326	1,374	1,022
Income Taxes	3,897	3,692	3,338
Total Expenses	$213,141	$187,000	$161,234
Net Income.	$ 6,671	$ 6,295	$ 5,575

EXHIBIT 4.50

Wal-Mart Stores, Inc.
Comparative Statements of Cash Flows
(amounts in millions)
(Case 4.1)

	Year Ended January 31:		
	Year 12	Year 11	Year 10
Operations			
Net Income.	$ 6,671	$ 6,295	$ 5,575
Depreciation.	3,290	2,868	2,375
(Increase) in Accounts Receivable	(210)	(422)	(255)
(Increase) in Inventories	(1,235)	(1,795)	(2,088)
(Increase) in Prepayments	(180)	75	(307)
Increase in Accounts Payable	368	2,061	1,849
Increase in Other Current Liabilities.	1,556	522	1,045
Cash Flow from Operations	$10,260	$ 9,604	$ 8,194
Investing			
Acquisition of Property, Plant, and Equipment	$(8,383)	$(8,042)	$ (6,183)
Other	1,237	(672)	(10,663)
Cash Flow from Investing	$(7,146)	$(8,714)	$(16,846)
Financing			
Increase (Decrease) in Short-term Borrowing	$(1,533)	$(2,022)	$ 4,316
Increase in Long-term Borrowing	4,591	3,778	6,000

Exhibit 4.50—continued	Year Ended January 31:		
	Year 12	Year 11	Year 10
Increase in Common Stock	0	581	0
Decrease in Long-term Borrowing	(3,686)	(1,692)	(996)
Acquisition of Common Stock	(1,214)	(193)	(101)
Dividends	(1,249)	(1,070)	(890)
Other	84	(74)	300
Cash Flow from Financing	$(3,007)	$ (692)	$8,629
Change in Cash	$ 107	$ 198	$ (23)
Cash, Beginning of Year	2,054	1,856	1,879
Cash, End of Year	$ 2,161	$ 2,054	$1,856

EXHIBIT 4.51

Wal-Mart Stores, Inc.
Financial Ratio Analysis
(Case 4.1)

	Year 12	Year 11	Year 10
Profitability Ratios			
Rate of Return on Assets	8.8%	9.2%	9.9%
Profit Margin for ROA	3.5%	3.8%	3.8%
Total Assets Turnover	2.55	2.45	2.62
Cost of Goods Sold/Sales	78.8%	78.5%	78.6%
Marketing and Administrative Expense/Sales	16.7%	16.6%	16.5%
Interest Expense (net of taxes)/Sales	.4%	.4%	.4%
Income Tax Expense (excluding tax effects of interest expense)/Sales	2.0%	2.2%	2.2%
Accounts Receivable Turnover Ratio	115.6	123.1	134.2
Inventory Turnover Ratio	7.8	7.3	7.0
Fixed Assets Turnover Ratio	4.5	4.5	4.9
Rate of Return on Common Shareholders' Equity	20.1%	22.0%	23.8%
Profit Margin for ROCE	3.1%	3.3%	3.4%
Capital Structure Leverage Ratio	2.57	2.73	2.68
Risk Ratios			
Current Ratio	1.04	.92	.94
Quick Ratio	.15	.13	.12
Accounts Payable Turnover	11.2	10.8	11.3
Cash Flow from Operations to Current Liabilities Ratio	36.5%	35.1%	38.5%
Long-term Debt Ratio	40.1%	39.1%	43.3%
Total Liabilities/Total Assets Ratio	60.2%	62.1%	64.8%
Cash Flow from Operations to Total Liabilities Ratio	19.7%	19.4%	20.7%
Interest Coverage Ratio	9.0	8.3	9.7

SPECIALTY APPAREL RETAILING: THE GAP AND LIMITED BRANDS

The Gap and Limited Brands compete in the specialty apparel segment of the retailing industry. This segment experienced its most significant growth during the 1980s. During the decades before that, traditional department stores held the leadership position in retailing. Department stores offered the advantage of one-stop shopping by carrying broad lines of clothing, household, furniture, and other products. The size and product line diversity of department stores provided them with economies of scale in purchasing, storage, and transportation. The two main disadvantages of department stores became the competitive weapons of specialty retailers: breadth and depth of a specialty product line, and expertise in services offered in support of that product line. The specialty retailers tended to locate in shopping centers anchored by established department stores, benefiting from shopping center traffic without incurring much of the promotion cost to attract customers.

The 1990s witnessed several changes in the economics of specialty apparel retailing. Competition increased significantly as the number of specialty apparel retailers reached the saturation point in many locales. In addition, department stores adopted a "mini-boutique" strategy, whereby their stores became a collection of specialty retail shops under one roof. Firms in the industry responded to this heightened competition and market saturation by adding new store concepts and expanding into other countries.

A second factor affecting specialty apparel retailing is a change from a "shop 'til you drop" mentality to a "value" emphasis. Firms in the industry are responding to this change by placing more emphasis on periodic sales, 2-for-1 offers, and other discounting mechanisms. They are also creating new store concepts that emphasize lower prices.

A third factor affecting specialty apparel retailing is the increased sensitivity to time constraints, related in part to a demographic shift whereby increasing proportions of women are entering the work force. Consumers are more focused on what they want to purchase when they go shopping (referred to as "precision shopping"). Convenience of store location and layout, and ease of conducting the purchase are becoming increasingly important to consumers. At-home shopping (catalogs, Internet) is capturing an increasing proportion of consumer spending on apparel in response to both time pressures and sensitivity to prices.

The Gap and Limited Brands initially entered the specialty retail market with clothing designed for teenage and young working female customers. The Gap subsequently expanded its product line to include men's and children's apparel. The product line of The Gap includes basic clothes (jeans, shirts, etc.), which it sells in a variety of sizes and colors to customers of all ages. It tends to rely heavily on print advertising both to stimulate demand and promote its brands. It operates stores under the names of The Gap, Gap Kids, Banana Republic, and Old Navy. The Gap recently expanded significantly the number of its Banana Republic stores, retailers of a more upscale, stylish line of clothes than traditional Gap retail stores. It also recently expanded the number of Old Navy stores, retailers of casual basic clothing at a lower price point than the other Gap retail chains. Between Year 10 and Year 12, The Gap expanded the number of Gap stores at a compound annual rate of 14.0 percent, the number of Banana Republic Stores at a compound annual rate of 12.7 percent, and the number of Old Navy Stores at a compound annual rate of 22.7 percent. Catalog and web site sales are an increasing, but still small, proportion of its sales. The Gap has increasingly placed new stores in non-mall locations. It is also expanding abroad.

From its initial entry into apparel for teenage and young working female customers, Limited Brands subsequently expanded its product line to include men's, women's and children's apparel as well as personal care products. It operated stores during the Year 12 fiscal year in three segments:

Apparel: Limited Stores, Express, Lerner New York, and Structure
Intimate: Victoria's Secret, Bath and Body Works
Other: Henri Bendel

Limited Brands gives the managers of each of its chains considerable freedom to make strategic and operating decisions. The apparel of Limited Brands tends to be more stylish than that of The Gap. The strategy of Limited Brands has been to locate several stores from its chains in the same shopping mall. This strategy provides the firm with bargaining power on lease terms and with possible economies of scale in transportation, information processing, and other support services. The stores compete with each other, with the consumer often not even aware that the competing stores are owned by Limited Brands. Limited Brands relies on in-store promotions (2-for-1 discounts and special daily price reductions) as well as advertising to stimulate sales. The Limited divested of several of its chains in recent years. Limited Brands spun off Limited Too in fiscal Year 10 and sold Lane Bryant in fiscal Year 12.

Both firms lease the space in their stores, primarily under operating lease arrangements. Both firms also source the majority of their apparel from suppliers in East Asia and price their purchases in U.S. dollars.

Exhibit 4.52 presents selected data for The Gap and Limited Brands. Exhibits 4.53 to 4.55 present the financial statements of The Gap for fiscal Year 10 through fiscal Year 12, and Exhibits 4.56 to 4.58 present the financial statements for Limited Brands for these same years. These financial statements reflect the capitalization of lease commitments for store space, a topic discussed in Chapter 8. Cost of goods sold for both companies includes the cost of merchandise sold as well as occupancy expense (rent, depreciation). Exhibits 4.59 and 4.60 present segment data for each company. Exhibits 4.61 and 4.62 present financial ratios for The Gap and Limited Brands, respectively, for fiscal Year 10 through fiscal Year 12. The economy entered into a recession at the beginning of fiscal Year 11 and the recession continued through fiscal Year 12.

Required

a. Analyze the changes in the profitability of The Gap during the three-year period, offering possible reasons for the changes observed.

b. Repeat part a for Limited Brands.
c. Compare the profitability of The Gap versus Limited Brands during the three-year period, suggesting possible reasons for the differences observed.

NOTE: Parts d through f require coverage of material from Chapter 5.

d. Analyze the changes in the risk of The Gap during the three-year period.
e. Repeat part d for Limited Brands.
f. Compare the risk of The Gap versus Limited Brands during the three-year period.

EXHIBIT 4.52

Selected Data for The Gap and Limited Brands
(Case 4.2)

For the Year Ended January 31:	The Gap			Limited Brands		
	Year 12	Year 11	Year 10	Year 12	Year 11	Year 10
Number of Stores	4,071	3,740	3,058	4,614	5,129	5,023
Total Square Feet (000's)	36,333	31,373	23,978	23,470	23,372	23,592
Average Square Feet per Store	8,925	8,389	7,838	5,087	4,557	4,697
Sales per Store (000's)	$ 3,402	$ 3,656	$ 3,805	$ 2,029	$ 1,970	$ 1,936
Sales per Average Square Foot...............	$ 394	$ 482	$ 548	$ 398	$ 432	$ 412
Inventory per Square Foot...............	$ 49	$ 54	$ 53	$ 45	$ 47	$ 46
Fixed Assets per Square Foot...............	$ 215	$ 218	$ 221	$ 168	$ 173	$ 183
Sales per Employee (000's)..............	$ 84	$ 82	$ 83	$ 93	$ 82	$ 85
Total Sales Growth.......	1.3%	17.5%	28.5%	(7.3%)	3.9%	4.0%
Comparable Store Sales Growth[a]	(13%)	(5%)	7%	(4%)	5%	9%
Advertising Expense/ Sales	3.1%	3.6%	4.3%	4.8%	4.8%	4.4%

[a]Increase in sales of stores open at least two full years.

EXHIBIT 4.53

Balance Sheets for The Gap
(amounts in millions)
(Case 4.2)

	January 31			
	Year 12	Year 11	Year 10	Year 9
Assets				
Cash	$ 1,036	$ 409	$ 450	$ 565
Inventories	1,677	1,904	1,462	1,056
Prepayments	332	335	286	251
Total Current Assets	$ 3,045	$ 2,648	$2,198	$1,872
Property, Plant, and Equipment (net)	8,004	7,596	6,051	4,525
Other Assets	382	358	276	216
Total Assets	$11,431	$10,602	$8,525	$6,613
Liabilities and Shareholders' Equity				
Accounts Payable	$ 1,105	$ 1,067	$ 806	$ 684
Short-term Borrowing	42	1,030	169	91
Current Portion of Long-term Debt	0	0	0	0
Other Current Liabilities	909	702	778	778
Total Current Liabilities	$ 2,056	$ 2,799	$1,753	$1,553
Long-term Debt	5,803	4,369	4,121	3,145
Other Noncurrent Liabilities	564	505	418	341
Total Liabilities	$ 8,423	$ 7,673	$6,292	$5,039
Common Stock	$ 47	$ 47	$ 50	$ 33
Additional Paid-in Capital	454	283	670	366
Retained Earnings	4,890	4,975	4,150	3,090
Accumulated Other Comprehensive Income	(62)	(20)	(7)	(13)
Treasury Stock	(2,321)	(2,356)	(2,630)	(1,902)
Total Shareholders' Equity	$ 3,008	$ 2,929	$2,233	$1,574
Total Liabilities and Shareholders' Equity	$11,431	$10,602	$8,525	$6,613

EXHIBIT 4.54

Income Statements for The Gap
(amounts in millions)
(Case 4.2)

	For the Year Ended January 31		
	Year 12	Year 11	Year 10
Sales	$13,848	$13,673	$11,635
Other Revenues	—	53	22
Cost of Goods Sold	(9,418)	(8,333)	(6,575)
Selling and Administrative Expenses.	(3,718)	(3,629)	(3,043)
Interest Expense.	(421)	(383)	(254)
Income Tax Expense	(267)	(504)	(658)
Net Income.	$ 24	$ 877	$ 1,127

EXHIBIT 4.55

Statements of Cash Flows for The Gap
(amounts in millions)
(Case 4.2)

	For the Year Ended January 31		
	Year 12	Year 11	Year 10
Operations			
Net Income.	$ 24	$ 877	$ 1,127
Depreciation.	810	590	436
Addbacks and Subtractions—Net	261	294	421
(Inc.) Dec. in Inventories	213	(455)	(404)
Inc. (Dec.) in Current Liabilities	9	(16)	(103)
Cash Flow from Operations	$1,317	$ 1,290	$ 1,477
Investing			
Property, Plant, and Equipment Acquired.	$ (940)	$(1,859)	$(1,239)
Other Investing Transactions	(11)	(16)	(40)
Cash Flow from Investing	$ (951)	$(1,875)	$(1,279)
Financing			
Inc. in Short-term Borrowing	$ —	$ 621	$ 85
Inc. in Long-term Borrowing.	1,194	250	312
Inc. in Common Stock.	139	152	76
Dec. in Short-term Borrowing.	(735)	0	0
Dec. in Long-term Borrowing	(250)	0	0
Dec. in Common Stock	(1)	(393)	(707)
Dividends	(76)	(75)	(76)
Other Financing Transactions	(10)	(11)	(3)
Cash Flow from Financing	$ 261	$ 544	$ (313)
Change in Cash.	$ 627	$ (41)	$ (115)
Cash—Beginning of Year	409	450	565
Cash—End of Year	$1,036	$ 409	$ 450

EXHIBIT 4.56

Balance Sheets for Limited Brands
(amounts in millions)
(Case 4.2)

	January 31			
	Year 12	Year 11	Year 10	Year 9
Assets				
Cash	$1,375	$ 564	$ 817	$ 870
Accounts Receivable...........................	79	94	109	78
Inventories	966	1,157	1,051	1,120
Prepayments...................................	262	253	269	250
Total Current Assets	$2,682	$2,068	$2,246	$2,318
Property, Plant, and Equipment (net).............	3,839	4,046	4,052	4,577
Other Assets...................................	678	626	612	870
Total Assets	$7,199	$6,740	$6,910	$7,765
Liabilities and Shareholders' Equity				
Accounts Payable	$ 245	$ 273	$ 256	$ 290
Short-term Borrowing..........................	150	0	250	100
Other Current Liabilities	924	727	732	858
Total Current Liabilities......................	$1,319	$1,000	$1,238	$1,248
Long-term Debt................................	2,730	3,051	3,222	4,117
Other Noncurrent Liabilities....................	229	228	184	56
Total Liabilities	$4,278	$4,279	$4,644	$5,421
Minority Interest in Subsidiaries.................	$ 177	$ 143	$ 119	$ 111
Common Stock	216	216	190	180
Additional Paid-in Capital......................	53	84	178	157
Retained Earnings	2,729	2,312	6,228	5,648
Accumulated Other Comprehensive Income	(177)	(143)	(119)	(111)
Treasury Stock	(77)	(151)	(4,330)	(3,641)
Total Shareholders' Equity	$2,921	$2,461	$2,266	$2,344
Total Liabilities and Shareholders' Equity	$7,199	$6,740	$6,910	$7,765

EXHIBIT 4.57

Income Statements for Limited Brands
(amounts in millions)
(Case 4.2)

	For the Year Ended January 31		
	Year 12	Year 11	Year 10
Sales.....	$9,363	$10,105	$9,723
Other Revenues.....	22	20	51
Cost of Goods Sold.....	(5,898)	(6,442)	(6,109)
Selling and Administrative Expenses	(2,505)	(2,561)	(2,460)
Interest Expense.....	(246)	(284)	(335)
Income Tax Expense	(304)	(334)	(358)
Minority Interest in Subsidiary.....	(64)	(69)	(73)
Net Income	$ 368	$ 435	$ 439

EXHIBIT 4.58

Statements of Cash Flows for Limited Brands
(amounts in millions)
(Case 4.2)

	For the Year Ended January 31		
	Year 12	Year 11	Year 10
Operations			
Net Income.....	$ 368	$ 435	$ 439
Depreciation.....	277	271	272
Addbacks and Subtractions—Net	(113)	106	89
(Inc.) Dec. in Accounts Receivable.....	15	15	(37)
(Inc.) Dec. in Inventories.....	82	(106)	(54)
Inc. (Dec.) in Current Liabilities	189	55	(123)
Cash Flow from Operations	$ 818	$ 776	$ 586
Investing			
Property, Plant, and Equipment Acquired.....	$ (337)	$(446)	$(375)
Investments Acquired.....	0	0	0
Other Investing Transactions.....	420	(29)	544
Cash Flow from Investing.....	$ 83	$(475)	$ 169
Financing			
Inc. in Short-term Borrowing	0	0	$ 300
Dec. in Long-term Borrowing	0	(250)	(300)
Dec. in Common Stock	0	(200)	(815)
Dividends	(129)	(128)	(130)
Other Financing Transactions	39	24	137
Cash Flow from Financing	$ (90)	$(554)	$(808)
Change in Cash.....	$ 811	$(253)	$ (53)
Cash—Beginning of Year.....	564	817	870
Cash—End of Year.....	$1,375	$ 564	$ 817

EXHIBIT 4.59

Segment Data for The Gap
(Case 4.2)

	Year 12	Year 11	Year 10
Number of Stores			
Gap	2,832	2,643	2,181
Banana Republic	441	408	347
Old Navy	798	689	530
Total	4,071	3,740	3,058

	Year 12	Year 11	Year 10
Sales Mix			
Gap	49.3%	52.2%	52.1%
Banana Republic	13.7	13.2	15.1
Old Navy	37.0	34.6	32.8
Total	100.0	100.0	100.0

EXHIBIT 4.60

Segment Data for Limited Brands
(Case 4.2)

	Year 12	Year 11	Year 10
Number of Stores			
Apparel	1,996	2,085	2,258
Intimate	2,617	2,390	2,110
Other.......	1	654	655
	4,614	5,129	5,023
Sales Mix			
Apparel	40.7%	39.8%	38.8%
Intimate	53.6	50.6	47.4
Other.......	5.7	9.6	13.8
	100.0%	100.0%	100.0%
Sales per Square Foot			
Apparel	$ 288	$ 291	$ 256
Intimate	$ 547	$ 601	$ 596
Comparable Store Sales Increase			
Apparel	(3%)	8%	7%
Intimate	(5%)	4%	12%
Profit Margin			
Apparel	1.7%	2.9%	2.8%
Intimate	13.3%	14.7%	17.6%

EXHIBIT 4.61

Ratio Analysis for The Gap
(Case 4.2)

	Year 12	Year 11	Year 10
Profit Margin for ROA....................................	2.1%	8.2%	11.1%
Assets Turnover	1.3	1.4	1.5
Rate of Return on Assets	2.7%	11.8%	17.1%
Profit Margin for ROCE..................................	.2%	6.4%	9.7%
Capital Structure Leverage Ratio	3.7	3.7	4.0
Rate of Return on Common Shareholders' Equity	.8%	34.0%	59.2%
Cost of Goods Sold ÷ Sales	68.0%	60.9%	56.5%
Selling and Administrative Expense ÷ Sales	26.8%	26.5%	26.2%
Income Tax Expense ÷ Sales[a].............................	3.0%	4.7%	6.4%
Inventory Turnover	5.3	5.0	5.2
Fixed Asset Turnover	1.8	2.0	2.2
Current Ratio	1.5	1.0	1.3
Quick Ratio	.5	.2	.3
Cash Flow from Operations ÷ Current Liabilities.................	54.3%	56.7%	89.4%
Days Inventory..	69	74	70
Days Accounts Payable....................................	43	39	39
Net Days Working Capital	26	35	31
Long-term Debt Ratio	65.9%	59.9%	64.9%
Debt-Equity Ratio	73.7%	72.4%	73.8%
Cash Flow from Operations ÷ Total Liabilities..................	16.4%	18.5%	26.1%
Interest Coverage Ratio	1.7	4.6	8.0

[a]Excluding tax effects of interest expense.

EXHIBIT 4.62			
Ratio Analysis for Limited Brands **(Case 4.2)**			
	Year 12	Year 11	Year 10
Profit Margin for ROA....................................	6.3%	6.8%	7.5%
Assets Turnover	1.3	1.5	1.3
Rate of Return on Assets	8.5%	10.1%	9.9%
Profit Margin for ROCE...................................	3.9%	4.3%	4.5%
Capital Structure Leverage Ratio..........................	2.6	2.9	3.2
Rate of Return on Common Shareholders' Equity	13.7%	18.4%	19.0%
Cost of Goods Sold ÷ Sales	63.0%	63.8%	62.8%
Selling and Administrative Expense ÷ Sales	26.8%	25.3%	25.3%
Income Tax Expense ÷ Sales[a].............................	4.2%	4.3%	4.9%
Accounts Receivable Turnover.............................	108.2	99.6	104.0
Inventory Turnover	5.6	5.8	5.6
Fixed Asset Turnover	2.4	2.5	2.3
Current Ratio	2.0	2.1	1.8
Quick Ratio	1.1	.7	.8
Cash Flow from Operations ÷ Current Liabilities.............	70.5%	69.3%	47.1%
Days Accounts Receivable	3	4	4
Days Inventory..	66	63	65
Days Accounts Payable....................................	17	15	16
Net Day Working Capital..................................	52	52	53
Long-term Debt Ratio	48.3%	55.4%	58.7%
Debt-Equity Ratio	59.4%	63.5%	67.2%
Cash Flow from Operations ÷ Total Liabilities	19.1%	17.4%	11.6%
Interest Coverage Ratio	4.0	4.0	3.6

[a]Excluding tax effects of interest expense.

Chapter 5

RISK ANALYSIS

Learning Objectives
1. **Understand the importance of effective working capital management, and apply analytical tools for assessing short-term liquidity risk.**
2. **Understand the benefits and risks of financial leverage, and apply analytical tools for assessing long-term solvency risk.**
3. **Use risk analysis tools in assessing credit risk.**
4. **Use risk analysis tools in assessing bankruptcy risk.**
5. **Understand the distinction between firm-specific risks, as measured by various financial statement ratios, and systematic risk, as measured by market equity beta, and relationships between these types of risks.**
6. **Examine factors that might lead firms to manipulate reported financial statement amounts and apply tools for analyzing the risk of fraudulent reporting.**

Individuals make investment decisions based on the return expected from investments relative to the risks of realizing those returns. Lenders make lending decisions based on the return expected in the form of interest revenue relative to the risks of repayment. The analysis of risk is central to any decision to commit economic resources. This chapter explores the analysis of risk using various financial statement ratios and other analytical tools.

FRAMEWORK FOR RISK ANALYSIS

The sources and types of risk that a firm faces are numerous and often interrelated. They include:

Source	Type or Nature
International	Host government regulations and attitudes
	Political unrest
	Exchange rate changes
Domestic	Recession
	Inflation or deflation
	Interest rate changes
	Demographic changes
	Political changes
Industry	Technology
	Competition
	Regulation
	Availability of raw materials
	Labor and other input price changes
	Unionization
Firm-Specific	Management competence
	Strategic direction
	Lawsuits

Although a firm should continually monitor each of these types of risk, we focus our attention on the financial consequences of these elements of risk using data from the financial statements. Each of these types of risk ultimately affects net income and cash flows. A firm usually enters bankruptcy because it is unable either to generate sufficient cash internally or to obtain needed cash from external sources to sustain operating, investing, and financing activities. The statement of cash flows (discussed in Chapter 3), which reports the net amount of cash generated or used by operating, investing, and financing activities, is an important source of information for studying risk.

Exhibit 5.1 relates the factors affecting a firm's ability to generate cash with its need to use cash. Most financial statement-based risk analysis focuses on a comparison of the supply of cash and demand for cash. Risk analysis using financial statement data typically examines (1) *short-term liquidity risk*, the near-term ability to generate cash to service working capital needs and debt service requirements, and (2) *long-term solvency risk*, the longer-term ability to generate cash internally or from external sources to satisfy plant capacity and debt repayment needs. We structure our discussion of the analytical tools for assessing risk around short-term liquidity risk and long-term solvency risk.

The field of finance identifies two types of firm-specific risk: *credit risk* and *bankruptcy risk*. Credit risk concerns a firm's ability to make interest and principal payments on borrowings as they come due. Bankruptcy risk relates to the likelihood that

	EXHIBIT 5.1		
	Framework for Financial Statement Analysis of Risk		
Activity	**Ability to Generate Cash**	**Need to Use Cash**	**Financial Statement Analysis Performed**
Operations	Profitability of goods and services sold	Working capital requirements	Short-term liquidity risk
Investing	Sales of existing plant assets or investments	Plant capacity requirements	Long-term solvency risk
Financing	Borrowing capacity	Debt service requirements	

a firm will file for bankruptcy and perhaps subsequently liquidate. The analyst might view these two types of risk as states of financial distress that fall along a continuum of increasing gravity from (1) failing to make a required interest payment on time, to (2) defaulting on a principal payment on debt, to (3) filing for bankruptcy, to (4) liquidating a firm. Analysts concerned with the economic loss of a portion or the entire amount lent to or invested in a firm would examine a firm's position on this financial distress continuum. We demonstrate how the analysts can use tools of short-term liquidity and long-term solvency risk in assessing credit risk and bankruptcy risk.

Less than 5 percent of publicly traded firms experience financial distress as defined by one of the four states above. Yet, to value firms, we need a broader definition that encompasses elements of risk common to all firms. A research stream that strives for a broader definition of risk is one that attempts to explain differences in market rates of return on common stocks. Economic theory teaches that differences in market returns must relate to differences in perceived risk. Studies of this risk/return relation use market equity beta as the measure of *market equity risk*. Market equity beta measures the covariability of a firm's returns with the returns of all securities in the market. Because only a small percentage of publicly traded firms experience significant risk from financial distress, additional factors besides short-term liquidity risk, long-term solvency risk, credit risk, and bankruptcy risk must explain market beta. We discuss the research relating financial statement data and market equity beta later in this chapter, and then elaborate on it more fully in Chapters 11 to 13.

This chapter examines various tools of financial statement analysis for identifying and measuring the five types of risk described above. The presumption is that a firm follows generally accepted accounting principles (GAAP) in preparing its financial statements so that the analyst can use the reported amounts to assess each of these types of risk. In some cases, however, firms intentionally report amounts outside, or beyond the limits of, GAAP in an effort to portray a more profitable or less risky profile than is appropriate. In these cases, the analyst cannot rely on reported amounts as meaningful indicators of risk. Assessing *financial reporting manipulation risk* is an important element of risk analysis.

Thus, the discussion of risk analysis in this chapter considers analysis of the following types of risk:

1. Short-term liquidity risk
2. Long-term solvency risk
3. Credit risk
4. Bankruptcy risk
5. Market equity beta risk
6. Financial reporting manipulation risk

As will become clear, these elements of risk are interrelated. Analysts use short-term liquidity and long-term solvency risk ratios in assessing both credit risk and bankruptcy risk. Some of the factors affecting long-term solvency risk affect market equity betas. Firms with particularly high levels of financial risk are more prone to manipulate reported amounts.

We illustrate the analyses of various dimensions of risk using the financial statements of PepsiCo in Appendix A. As we did in Chapter 4, we compare financial ratios for PepsiCo for Year 11 with the corresponding ratios for Year 9 and Year 10 in a time-series setting. We might also compare the ratios for PepsiCo with average industry ratios or with those of PepsiCo's competitors. Problem 5.3 at the end of the chapter compares PepsiCo's risk ratios with those of Coke.

ANALYZING SHORT-TERM LIQUIDITY RISK

The analysis of short-term liquidity risk requires an understanding of the operating cycle of a firm, introduced in Chapter 1. Consider a typical manufacturing firm. It acquires raw materials on account, promising to pay suppliers within 30 to 60 days. The firm then combines the raw materials, labor services, and other factor inputs to produce a product. It pays for some of these costs at the time of incurrence and delays payment of other costs. At some point, the firm sells the product to a customer, probably on account. It then collects the customer's account and pays suppliers and others for purchases on account.

If a firm (1) can delay all cash outflows to suppliers, employees, and others until it receives cash from customers, and (2) receives more cash than it must disburse, then the firm will not likely encounter short-term liquidity problems. Most firms, however, cannot time their cash inflows and outflows precisely. Employees may require weekly or semi-monthly payments, whereas customers may delay payments for 30 days or more. Firms may experience rapid growth and need to produce more units of product than they sell during a period. Even if perfectly timed, the cash outflows to support the higher level of production this period can exceed the cash inflows from customers this period from the lower level of sales of prior periods. Firms that operate at a net loss for a period often find that the completion of the operating cycle results in a net cash outflow instead of a net cash inflow.

Short-term liquidity problems also arise from longer-term solvency difficulties. For example, a firm may assume a relatively high percentage of debt in its capital structure, as many firms did in the leveraged buyout movement in the late 1980s. This level of debt usually requires periodic interest payments and may require repayments of principal as well. For some firms, interest expense is their largest single cost. The operating cycle must not only generate sufficient cash to supply operating working capital needs, it must generate sufficient cash to service debt as well.

Financially healthy firms frequently close any cash flow gap in their operating cycles with short-term borrowing. Such firms may issue commercial paper on the market or obtain three- to six-month bank loans. Most firms maintain a line of credit with their banks so they can obtain cash quickly for working capital needs. The notes to the financial statements usually disclose the amount of the line of credit and the level of borrowing utilized on that line during the year.

We discuss six financial statement ratios for assessing short-term liquidity risk: (1) current ratio, (2) quick ratio, (3) operating cash flow to current liabilities ratio, (4) accounts receivable turnover, (5) inventory turnover, and (6) accounts payable turnover.

Current Ratio

The current ratio equals current assets divided by current liabilities. It indicates the amount of cash available at the balance sheet date plus the amount of other current assets that the firm expects to turn into cash within one year of the balance sheet date (from collection of receivables and sale of inventory) relative to obligations coming due during that period. The current ratio for PepsiCo on December 31, Year 11, is:

$$\text{Current Ratio} = \frac{\text{Current Assets}}{\text{Current Liabilities}}$$

$$1.17 = \$5,853 / \$4,998$$

The current ratio for PepsiCo was 1.09 at the end of Year 9 and 1.17 at the end of Year 10. Thus, PepsiCo has experienced a relatively stable current ratio at a level slightly above 1.0.

Banks, suppliers, and others that extend short-term credit to a firm generally prefer a current ratio substantially in excess of 1.0. Large current ratios indicate abundant cash and near-cash assets to repay obligations coming due within the next year. Prior to the 1980s, the average current ratios for most industries exceeded 2.0. As interest rates increased in the early 1980s, firms attempted to stretch their accounts payable and use suppliers to finance a greater portion of their working capital needs (that is, receivables, inventories). Also, firms increasingly instituted just-in-time inventory systems that reduced the amount of raw materials and finished goods inventories. As a consequence of these two factors, current ratios began moving in the direction of 1.0. Current ratios hovering around this level, or even just below 1.0, are now common. Although this directional movement suggests an increase in short-term liquidity risk, the level of risk is not necessarily intolerable. Recall that accountants report inventories, a major component of current assets for many firms, at acquisition cost. The cash that firms expect to generate from inventories is larger than the amount used in calculating the current ratio. PepsiCo, for example, has a cost of goods sold to sales percentage of approximately 40 percent. Thus, inventories have selling prices of 2.5 (= 1.00/.40) times the amount appearing on the balance sheet. Also, PepsiCo reports in Note 12 that it has a $750 million unused line of credit on its revolving credit facility at the end of Year 11. Thus, a current ratio just slightly greater than 1.0 is not a major concern for PepsiCo.

Several additional interpretive problems arise with the current ratio:

1. An increase of equal amounts in both current assets and current liabilities (for example, purchasing inventory on account) results in a decrease in the current ratio when the ratio is greater than 1.0 before the transaction but an increase in the current ratio if it is less than 1.0 before the transaction. Similar interpretive difficulties arise when current assets and current liabilities decrease by an equal amount. With current ratios for many firms now in the neighborhood of 1.0, this concern with the current ratio gains greater significance.

2. A very high current ratio may accompany unsatisfactory business conditions, whereas a falling ratio may accompany profitable operations. During a recession, businesses contract, firms pay current liabilities, and, even though current assets reach a low point, the current ratio can increase to very high levels. In a boom period, just the reverse can occur.

3. The current ratio is susceptible to "window dressing;" that is, management can take deliberate steps at the balance sheet date to produce a better current ratio than is the normal or average ratio for the period. For instance, towards the end of the period a firm may accelerate normal purchases on account (current ratio is less than 1.0) or delay such purchases (current ratio is greater than 1.0) in an effort to improve the current ratio. Alternatively, a firm may collect loans previously made to officers, classified as noncurrent assets, and use the proceeds to reduce current liabilities.

Given these interpretive problems with the current ratio, the analyst may find its widespread use as a measure of short-term liquidity risk surprising. The explanation lies partially in its ease of calculation. In addition, empirical studies of bond default, bankruptcy, and other conditions of financial distress have found that the current ratio has strong predictive power. A later section of this chapter discusses this empirical research more fully.

Quick Ratio

A variation of the current ratio is the quick, or acid test, ratio. The analyst computes the quick ratio by including in the numerator only those current assets that the firm could convert quickly into cash. The numerator customarily includes cash, marketable securities, and receivables. However, the analyst should study the facts in each case before deciding whether to include receivables and to exclude inventories. Some businesses can convert their inventory of merchandise into cash more quickly (for example, a retail chain like Wal-Mart) than other businesses can collect their receivables (for example, an automobile manufacturer like Ford that provides financing for its customers' purchases).

Assuming that we include accounts receivable but exclude inventories, the quick ratio of PepsiCo at the end of Year 11 is:

$$\text{Quick Ratio} = \frac{\text{Cash} + \text{Marketable Securities} + \text{Receivables}}{\text{Current Liabilities}}$$

$$.76 = \frac{\$683 + \$966 + \$2,142}{\$4,998}$$

The quick ratio for PepsiCo was .70 at the end of Year 9 and .76 at the end of Year 10. Unless inventory turnovers have changed dramatically, the trends in the quick ratio and the current ratio correlate highly. That is, the analyst obtains the same information about improving or deteriorating short-term liquidity by examining either ratio. Note that the current and quick ratios for PepsiCo follow similar trends. With current ratios recently trending toward 1.0, quick ratios have trended toward .5.

The quick ratio is subject to some of the same concerns as the current ratio. With quick ratios typically less than 1.0, equal increases in the numerator and denominator increase the ratio and equal decreases decrease the ratio. The quick ratio is also susceptible to year-end window dressing.

Operating Cash Flow to Current Liabilities Ratio

The analyst can overcome the deficiencies discussed above in using current assets measured at a point in time as an indicator of a firm's ability to generate cash in the near term by using cash flow from operations instead. Cash flow from operations, reported on the statement of cash flows, indicates the excess amount of cash that the firm derived from operations after funding working capital needs. Because the numerator of this ratio uses amounts for a period of time, the denominator uses an average of current liabilities for the period. This ratio for PepsiCo for Year 11 is:

$$\text{Operating Cash Flow to Current Liabilities Ratio} = \frac{\text{Cash Flow from Operations}}{\text{Average Current Liabilities}}$$

$$85.8\% = \frac{\$4,201}{.5(\$4,795 + \$4,998)}$$

The ratio was 52.8 percent for Year 9 and 93.3 percent for Year 10. An empirical study utilizing the operating cash flow to current liabilities ratio found that a ratio of 40 percent or more was common for a healthy manufacturing or retailing firm.[1] PepsiCo consistently has an operating cash flow to current liabilities ratio in excess of 40 percent. Thus, even though the current and quick ratios appear somewhat low, PepsiCo does not display much short-term liquidity risk.

---

[1]Cornelius Casey and Norman Bartzcak, "Cash Flow—It's Not the Bottom Line," *Harvard Business Review* (July-August 1984), pp. 61–66.

Working Capital Activity Ratios

The analyst uses three measures of the rate of activity in working capital accounts to study the cash-generating ability of operations and the short-term liquidity risk of a firm:

$$\text{Accounts Receivable Turnover} = \frac{\text{Sales}}{\text{Average Accounts Receivable}}$$

$$\text{Inventory Turnover} = \frac{\text{Cost of Goods Sold}}{\text{Average Inventories}}$$

$$\text{Accounts Payable Turnover} = \frac{\text{Purchases}}{\text{Average Accounts Payable}}$$

Chapter 4 discussed the accounts receivable and inventory turnovers, components of the total assets turnover, as measures of profitability. We use these ratios here as measures of the speed with which firms turn accounts receivable into cash and sell inventories. The accounts payable turnover indicates the speed at which a manufacturing or retailing firm pays for purchases of inventories on account. Purchases is not an amount that the financial statements typically disclose. The analyst can approximate purchases as follows:[2]

Purchases = Cost of Goods Sold + Ending Inventory − Beginning Inventory

The analyst often expresses these three ratios in terms of the number of days each balance sheet item (that is, receivables, inventories, accounts payable) is outstanding. To do so, divide 365 days by the three turnover amounts.

Exhibit 5.2 presents the calculation of these three turnover ratios and the related number of days for PepsiCo for Year 11. PepsiCo combines accounts payable and other current liabilities on its balance sheet. Note 11 disaggregates this combined amount into its various elements and reports the amounts for accounts payable separately. We use the amounts for accounts payable from Note 11 to compute the accounts payable turnover.

The number of days that firms hold inventory until sale plus the number of days that firms hold accounts receivable until collection indicates the total number of days between purchase of inventory on account until collection of cash from the sale of inventory to customers. This combined number of days indicates the period of time that the firm must obtain financing for its primary working capital assets. The number of days that accounts payable is outstanding indicates the portion of the days of needed working capital financing that the firm obtained financing from suppliers. The difference between the total number of days that the firm requires financing for

---

[2]The accounts payable turnover ratio will be skewed upward if cost of goods sold includes a high proportion of costs (for example, depreciation, labor) that do not flow through accounts payable. This skewness is more of a concern for manufacturing firms than for retailing firms. The skewness is more of an issue in cross-sectional comparisons than in time-series analyses.

EXHIBIT 5.2
Working Capital Activity Ratios for PepsiCo for Year 11

Accounts Receivable Turnover

$$\frac{\$26{,}935}{.5(\$2{,}129 + \$2{,}142)} = 12.6 \text{ times per year}$$

Days Receivables Outstanding

$$\frac{365}{12.6} = 29 \text{ days}$$

Inventory Turnover

$$\frac{\$10{,}754}{.5(\$1{,}192 = \$1{,}310)} = 8.6 \text{ times per year}$$

Days Inventory Held

$$\frac{365}{8.6} = 42 \text{ days}$$

Accounts Payable Turnover

$$\frac{(\$10{,}754 + \$1{,}310 - \$1{,}192)}{.5(\$1{,}212 + \$1{,}238)} = 8.9 \text{ times per year}$$

Days Accounts Payable Outstanding

$$\frac{365}{8.9} = 41 \text{ days}$$

its working capital and the portion of those days it obtained financing from suppliers of inventory indicates the additional days for which it must obtain financing. We depict these relations below:

Days of Working Capital Financing Required:

Days Inventory Held	Days Accounts Receivable Outstanding

Days of Working Capital Financing Provided:

Days Account Payable Outstanding	Days of Working Capital Financing Needed from Other Sources

Exhibit 5.3 shows the net number of days of financing needed from other sources for PepsiCo for Year 9, Year 10, and Year 11. PepsiCo's days accounts payable approximately equals its days inventory, indicating that suppliers provided the financing for PepsiCo's inventory. The net days financed from other sources approximately equal the days accounts receivable were outstanding. PepsiCo used short-term borrowing to finance part of the net days of needed financing. The analysis of changes in operating working capital in the statement of cash flows also indicates that PepsiCo might have stretched out payments to suppliers of other goods and services to finance the net days of needed financing.

In general, the shorter the number of days of needed financing, the larger is the cash flow from operations to average current liabilities ratio. A small number of net days indicates either relatively little need to finance accounts receivable and inventories (that is, the firm sells inventory quickly and receives cash from customers soon

EXHIBIT 5.3				
Net Days of Working Capital Financing Needed from Other Sources for PepsiCo				
Year	Days Accounts Receivable Outstanding	Days Inventory Held	Days Accounts Payable Outstanding	Days Other Financing Required
Year 9	34	43	(48)	29
Year 10	29	42	(45)	26
Year 11	29	42	(41)	30

after sale) or aggressive use of suppliers to finance these current assets (that is, the firm delays paying cash to suppliers). Both scenarios enhance cash flow from operations in the numerator of this ratio. Furthermore, firms with a shorter number of days of financing required from other sources need not engage in short-term borrowing from banks and other financing institutions. Such borrowing increases current liabilities in the denominator of the cash flow from operations to average current liabilities ratio and, therefore, lowers this ratio.

Summary of Short-term Liquidity Risk

The short-term liquidity risk ratios suggest that PepsiCo has relatively little short-term liquidity risk. Although the current and quick ratios are on the low side, the operating cash flow to current liabilities ratio exceeds 40 percent in all years. PepsiCo has an established brand name and dominates (along with Coke) the soft drink industry. Chapter 4 discussed PepsiCo's healthy profitability picture, suggesting that it could obtain short-term financing if needed. Its established line of credit provides a cushion if short-term liquidity becomes a problem.

ANALYZING LONG-TERM SOLVENCY RISK

Chapter 4 discussed the concept of financial leverage. When firms obtain funds from borrowing and invest those funds in assets that generate a higher return than the after-tax cost of the borrowing, the common shareholders benefit. Common shareholders continue to benefit with increasing proportions of debt in the capital structure as long as the firm maintains the excess of ROA over the after-tax cost of the debt. Financial leverage therefore enhances the return to the common shareholders. Increasing the proportion of debt in the capital structure, however, increases the risk that the firm cannot pay interest and repay the principal on the amount borrowed. That is, credit and bankruptcy risk increases and the incremental cost of borrowing likely also increases. When the excess of ROA over the after-tax cost of borrowing declines, additional financial leverage begins to reduce the return to the common shareholders. Analysts use measures of long-term solvency risk to examine a firm's ability to make interest and principal payments on long-term debt and similar obligations as they come due.

Perhaps the best indicator for assessing long-term solvency risk is a firm's ability to generate earnings over a period of years. Profitable firms either generate sufficient cash from operations or obtain needed cash from creditors or owners. The measures of profitability discussed in Chapter 4 therefore apply for this purpose as well. Also, firms must survive in the short term if they are to survive in the long term. Thus, analysis of long-term solvency risk must begin with an analysis of short-term liquidity risk. Three measures used in examining long-term solvency risk are (1) debt ratios, (2) interest coverage ratio, and (3) operating cash flow to total liabilities ratio.

Debt Ratios

Analysts use debt ratios to measure the amount of liabilities, particularly long-term debt, in a firm's capital structure. The higher this proportion, the greater the long-term solvency risk. Several variations in debt ratios exist. Three commonly encountered measures are:

$$\text{Long-term Debt Ratio} = \frac{\text{Long-term Debt}}{\text{Long-term Debt} + \text{Shareholders' Equity}}$$

$$\text{Debt / Equity Ratio} = \frac{\text{Long-term Debt}}{\text{Shareholders' Equity}}$$

$$\text{Liabilities to Assets Ratio} = \frac{\text{Total Liabilities}}{\text{Total Assets}}$$

The debt ratios for PepsiCo at the end of Year 11 are as follows:

$$\text{Long-term Debt Ratio} = \frac{\$2,651}{\$2,651 + \$8,648} = 23.4\%$$

$$\text{Debt / Equity Ratio} = \frac{\$2,651}{\$8,648} = 30.6\%$$

$$\text{Liabilities to Assets Ratio} = \frac{\$21,695 - \$8,648 - \$26}{\$21,695} = 60.0\%$$

Exhibit 5.4 shows the debt ratios for PepsiCo at the end of Year 9, Year 10, and Year 11. The debt ratios declined during the three-year period. Although PepsiCo issued additional long-term debt during the period, its shareholders' equity increased even more due to the retention of earnings in excess of dividends and common stock repurchases.

Note the high correlation between changes in the two long-term debt ratios over time. This result is not surprising since they use the same financial statement data. The analyst can generally select one of these ratios and use it consistently over time. Because different debt ratios exist, the analyst should use caution when reading financial periodicals and discussing debt ratios with others to be sure of the

EXHIBIT 5.4			
Debt Ratios for PepsiCo at the End of Year 9 to Year 11			
	Year 9	Year 10	Year 11
Long-term Debt Ratio	33.2%	28.3%	23.4%
Debt/Equity Ratio	49.7%	39.5%	30.6%
Liabilities to Assets Ratio	64.4%	63.3%	60.0%

particular version of the debt ratio used. A debt/equity ratio greater than 1.0 (that is, more long-term debt than shareholders' equity) is not unusual, but a long-term debt ratio or liabilities to assets ratio greater than 1.0 is highly unusual (requires a negative shareholders' equity in the case of the latter ratio).

In addition to computing debt ratios, the analyst should study the note to the financial statements on long-term debt. The note includes information on the types of debt that a firm has issued and the interest rates and maturity dates of the debt. The analyst should also examine the debt contract for each debt issue to assess if the firm is nearing violation of any debt covenants.

In an effort to appear less risky and lower their cost of financing or perhaps to avoid violating debt covenants in existing borrowing arrangements, firms often attempt to structure financing in a manner that keeps debt off of the balance sheet. Chapter 8 discusses some of the avenues available under GAAP (for example, accounting for leases as operating leases instead of capital leases) to minimize reported long-term debt. The analyst should recognize the possibility of such actions when interpreting debt ratios.

Interest Coverage Ratio

The interest coverage ratio indicates the number of times that net income before interest expense and income taxes exceeds interest expense. The interest coverage ratio for PepsiCo for Year 11 is:[3]

$$\text{Interest Coverage Ratio} = \frac{\begin{array}{c}\text{Net Income} + \text{Interest Expense} \\ + \text{Income Tax Expense} + \text{Minority Interest in Earnings}\end{array}}{\text{Interest Expense}}$$

$$19.4 = \frac{\$2,662 + \$219 + \$1,367 + \$0}{\$219}$$

---

[3]Increased precision suggests that the denominator include total interest cost for the year, not just the amount recognized as interest expense. If a firm self-constructs fixed assets, it must capitalize a portion of its interest cost each year and add it to the cost of the self-constructed assets. The analyst should probably apply this refinement of the interest coverage ratio only to electric utilities, which engage in heavy borrowing to construct their capital-intensive plants.

The interest coverage ratio for PepsiCo was 11.2 in Year 9 and 14.8 in Year 10. PepsiCo's profitability increased during the three-year period (see the discussion in Chapter 4) while its debt levels decreased, resulting in an increasing interest coverage ratio. Analysts typically view coverage ratios of less than approximately 2.0 as risky situations. Thus, PepsiCo exhibits low long-term solvency risk by this measure.

If a firm must make other required periodic payments (for example, pensions, leases), then the analyst could include these amounts in the calculation as well. If so, the analyst refers to the ratio as the *fixed charges coverage ratio.*

One criticism of the interest and the fixed charges coverage ratios as measures of long-term solvency risk is that they use earnings rather than cash flows in the numerator. Firms pay interest and other fixed charges with cash, not with earnings. When the value of the ratio is relatively low (that is, less than approximately 2.0), the analyst should use cash flow from operations before interest and income taxes in the numerator to calculate coverage ratios.

To illustrate, cash flow from operations for PepsiCo for Year 11 was $4,201 million. The supplemental cash flow information at the bottom of the statement of cash flows indicates that the cash payment for interest is $159 million and for income taxes totaled $857 million. The calculation of the interest coverage ratio using cash flows is as follows:

$$\text{Interest Coverage Ratio Based on Cash Flows} = \frac{\text{Cash Flow from Operations} + \text{Payments for Interest and Income Taxes}}{\text{Cash Payments for Interest}}$$

$$32.8 = \frac{\$4,201 + \$159 + \$857}{\$159}$$

Operating Cash Flow to Total Liabilities Ratio

The debt ratios give no recognition to the ability of a firm to generate cash flow from operations to service debt. The ratio of cash flow from operations to average total liabilities overcomes this deficiency. This cash flow ratio is similar to the one used in assessing short-term liquidity, but here the denominator includes all liabilities (current and noncurrent).

The operating cash flow to total liabilities ratio for Year 11 for PepsiCo is as follows:

$$\text{Operating Cash Flow to Total Liabilities Ratio} = \frac{\text{Cash Flow from Operations}}{\text{Average Total Liabilities}}$$

$$32.1\% = \frac{\$4,201}{.5(\$20,757 - \$7,604 - \$26 + \$21,695 - \$8,648 - \$49 + \$27)}$$

The ratio for PepsiCo was 22.9 percent in Year 9 and 34.2 percent in Year 10. A ratio of 20 percent or more[4] is common for a financially healthy company. Thus, PepsiCo appears to have low long-term solvency risk by this measure.

Summary of Long-term Solvency Risk

The debt, interest coverage, and cash flow ratios indicate that PepsiCo has low long-term solvency risk. PepsiCo is profitable and generates the needed cash flow to service its debt.

ANALYZING CREDIT RISK

Lenders to a firm, whether short- or long-term, want to be sure that the firm can pay periodic interest and repay the principal amount lent. Lenders use the short-term liquidity and long-term solvency ratios discussed thus far in this chapter to assess credit risk. Lenders also consider other factors when extending credit. Common practice uses a set of terms that begin with the letter "C" to characterize factors to consider in lending decisions. This section discusses a number of such "C" terms. The list is not an exhaustive catalogue of the factors that lenders consider in assessing credit risk.

1. Circumstances Leading to Need for the Loan

The reason that a firm needs to borrow affects the riskiness of the loan and the likelihood of repayment. Consider the following examples.

Example 1. W.T. Grant Company, a discount retail chain, filed for bankruptcy in 1975. Its bankruptcy has become a classic example of how poorly designed and implemented controls can lead a firm into financial distress (see Case 3.1). Between 1968 and 1975, Grant experienced increasing difficulty collecting its accounts receivable from credit card customers. To finance the buildup of its accounts receivable, Grant borrowed short-term funds from commercial banks. Grant, however, failed to fix the credit extension and cash collection problems with its receivables. The bank loans simply kept Grant in business in an ever-worsening credit situation. Lending to satisfy cash-flow needs related to an unsolved problem or difficulty can be highly risky.

Example 2. Toys"R"Us purchases toys, games, and other entertainment products in September and October in anticipation of heavy demand during the end-of-the-year holiday season. It typically pays its suppliers within 30 days for these purchases but doesn't collect cash from customers until December, January, or later. To finance its inventory, Toys"R"Us borrows short term from its banks. It repays these loans with cash collected from customers. Lending to satisfy cash-flow needs related to ongoing seasonal business operations is generally relatively low risk. Toys"R"Us has an established brand name and predictable demand. Although some risk exists that the products offered will not meet customer preferences in a particular year,

---

[4]Casey and Bartzak, *op.cit.*

Toys"R"Us offers a sufficiently diverse product line so failure to collect sufficient cash to repay the bank loan is low.

Example 3. Wal-Mart Stores has grown the number of its stores at a rate of approximately 12 percent per year during the last five years (see Case 4.1). The fastest growth is in its superstores, which represent a combination of its traditional discount store and a grocery store. Wal-Mart borrows a large portion of the funds needed to construct new stores using 20- to 25-year loans. (Wal-Mart also enters into leases for a portion of the space needed for its new stores.) Such loans are relatively low risk, given the operating success of Wal-Mart in the past and the existence of land and buildings that serve as collateral for the loans.

Example 4. National Semiconductor designs and manufactures semiconductors for use in computers and other electronic products. Its principal competitor, Intel, maintains the dominant market share for semiconductors. National Semiconductor has increasingly lost market share to Intel in recent years. Assume now that National Semiconductor desires to develop new semiconductors and needs to borrow funds to finance the design and development effort. Such a loan would likely be relatively high risk. Technological change occurs rapidly in semiconductors, which could make obsolete any semiconductors developed by National Semiconductor. In addition, expenditures on semiconductors would not likely result in assets that can serve as collateral for the loan.

Thus, lending to established firms for ongoing operating needs presents the lowest credit risk. Lending to firms experiencing operating problems, lending to emerging businesses, and lending to support investments in intangible assets typically carry higher risks. Lenders should be wary of borrowers that are unclear as to how they intend to use the proceeds of a loan.

2. Cash Flows

A second "C" term is cash flows. Lenders prefer that firms generate sufficient cash flows to pay interest and repay principal on a loan rather than having to rely on selling the collateral. Tools for studying the cash-generating ability of a firm include examining the statement of cash flows for recent years, computing various cash flow financial ratios, and studying cash flows in projected financial statements.

Statement of Cash Flows. An examination of a firm's statement of cash flows for the most recent three or four years will indicate whether certain relations expected for a particular business occurred. Some of the indicators of potential cash flow problems, if observed for several years in a row, include:

1. Growth in accounts receivable or inventories that exceeds the growth rate in sales.
2. Increases in accounts payable that exceed the increase in inventories.
3. Other operating current liabilities that grow at a faster rate than sales.
4. Persistent negative cash flow from operations, either because of net losses or substantial increases in net working capital (current assets minus current liabilities).

5. Capital expenditures that substantially exceed cash flow from operations. Although the analyst should expect such an excess for a rapidly growing, capital-intensive firm, the negative excess cash flow (cash flow from operations minus capital expenditures) indicates a firm's continuing need for external financing to sustain that growth.

6. Reductions in capital expenditures over time. Although such reductions conserve cash in the near term, they might signal that the firm expects declines in future sales, earnings, and operating cash flows.

7. Sales of marketable securities in excess of purchases of marketable securities. Such sales provide cash immediately but might signal the inability of a firm's operations to provide adequate cash flow to finance working capital and long-term investments. Firms sell the marketable securities to obtain the cash needed for these purposes. Such sales, however, may not be an indicator of cash flow problems if the firm invested temporarily excess cash that it now plans to use to make a corporate acquisition or to acquire fixed assets.

8. A substantial shift from long-term borrowing to short-term borrowing. The increase in short-term borrowing may signal a firm's inability to obtain long-term loans because lenders are uncertain about a firm's future.

9. A reduction or elimination of dividend payments. Although such actions conserve cash in the near term, dividend changes can provide a negative signal about a firm's future prospects.

Although none of these indicators by themselves represent conclusive evidence of cash flow problems, they signal the need to obtain explanations from management to see if an emerging cash flow problem may exist.

Cash Flow Financial Ratios. Previous sections of this chapter discussed two cash flow ratios that might signal a cash flow problem: (1) cash flow from operations to average current liabilities, and (2) cash flow from operations to average total liabilities.

Cash Flows in Projected Financial Statements. Projected financial statements, sometimes referred to as *pro forma* financial statements, represent forecasted income statements, balance sheets, and statements of cash flows for some number of years in the future. Lenders may require potential borrowers to prepare such statements to demonstrate the borrower's ability to repay the loan with interest as it comes due. The credit analyst should question each of the important assumptions (for example, sales growth, cost structure, capital expenditures plans) underlying these projected financial statements. The credit analyst should also assess the sensitivity of the projected cash flows to changes in key assumptions. Suppose, for example, that sales grow by 4 percent instead of the 6 percent projected. Suppose that raw materials costs increase 5 percent instead of the 3 percent projected. Suppose that additional plant expenditures are necessary because a firm reaches capacity limits with a higher than expected sales increase. What impact will each of these changed assumptions have on cash flow from operations? Chapter 10 illustrates the preparation of projected, or pro forma, financial statements. Case 5.1 illustrates the use of projected financial statements in a lending decision.

3. Collateral

A third consideration when assessing credit risk is the availability and value of collateral for a loan. If cash flows are insufficient to pay interest and repay the principal on a loan, the lender has the right to take possession of any collateral pledged in support of the loan. Depending on the nature of the collateral pledged, the analyst might examine the following:

1. **Marketable Securities:** Chapter 9 discusses the accounting for marketable securities. Marketable equity securities representing less than a 20 percent ownership appear on the balance sheet at market value. The analyst can assess whether the market value of securities pledged as collateral exceeds the unpaid balance of a loan. Marketable securities representing 20 percent or more of another entity appear on the balance sheet using the equity method. Determining whether the market value of such securities adequately covers the unpaid balance of a loan is more difficult. The analyst might examine the amount reported as equity in earnings of affiliates in recent years to assess the level and changes in profitability of the investee.

2. **Accounts Receivable:** A lender should assess whether the current value of accounts receivable is sufficient to cover the unpaid portion of a loan collateralized by accounts receivable. Determining whether the book value of accounts receivable accurately reflects their market value involves an examination of changes in the provision for uncollectible accounts relative to sales, the balance in allowance for uncollectible accounts relative to gross accounts receivable, the amount of accounts written off as uncollectible relative to gross accounts receivable, and the number of days receivables are outstanding.

3. **Inventories:** The analyst should examine changes in the inventory turnover ratio, in the cost of goods sold to sales percentage, and in the mix of raw materials, work-in-process, and finished goods inventories to identify possible inventory obsolescence problems. The analyst should remember that the market value of inventories would likely differ more from their book value for a firm using LIFO than for a firm using FIFO. Firms using LIFO must report the excess of market or FIFO value over LIFO cost, permitting the analyst to assess the adequacy of LIFO inventories to cover the unpaid balance on a loan collateralized by inventories. (See the discussion of inventories in Chapter 7.)

4. **Property, Plant, and Equipment:** Firms often pledge fixed assets as collateral for long-term borrowing. Determining the market values of such assets is difficult using reported financial statement information because of the use of acquisition cost valuations. Market values of unique, firm-specific assets are particularly difficult to ascertain. Clues indicating market value declines include restructuring charges or asset impairment charges or recent sales of such assets at a loss. (See the discussion of property, plant, and equipment in Chapter 7.)

Some lending occurs on a non-secured basis (that is, the borrower pledges no specific collateral in support of the loan). In these cases, the lender should study the notes to the financial statements to ascertain how much, if any, of the borrower's assets are not already pledged or otherwise restricted. The liquidation value of such assets represents the available resources of a firm to repay unsecured creditors. For smaller, family-owned businesses, an additional source of collateral may be the personal assets of management or major shareholders. Has management or the shareholders pledged their personal residence, debt or equity securities owned, or other assets to serve as additional collateral for a business loan?

4. Capacity for Debt

Closely related to a firm's cash-generating ability and available collateral is a firm's capacity to assume additional debt. The cash flows and the collateral represent the means to repay the debt. Most firms do not borrow up to the limit of their debt capacity. Lenders want to be sure that a margin of safety exists. Although no precise methodology exists to measure debt capacity, the analyst can study various financial statement ratios when assessing debt capacity.

1. Debt Ratios: An earlier section described several ratios that relate the amount of long-term debt or total liabilities to shareholders' equity or total assets as measures of the proportion of liabilities in the capital structure. In general, the higher are the debt ratios, the higher is the credit risk and the lower is the unused debt capacity of the firm. When measuring debt ratios, the analyst must be careful to consider possible off-balance-sheet obligations (for example, operating lease commitments, underfunded pension or health care benefit obligations). The analyst can compare a particular firm's debt ratios with those of similar firms in the same industry.

2. Interest Coverage Ratio: The number of times that interest payments are covered by operating income before interest and income taxes serves as a gauge of the margin of safety provided by operations to service debt. When firms make heavy use of operating leases for their fixed assets, as is common for airlines and retail stores, the analyst might convert the operating leases to capital leases for the purpose of computing the interest coverage ratio (see the discussion of leases in Chapter 8). The analyst adds back the lease payments (that is, rent expense) to net income when computing cash flows from operations in the numerator of this ratio and includes the lease payments in the denominator. When the interest coverage ratio falls below approximately 2, the credit risk is generally considered high. Interest coverage ratios that exceed 4 or 5 usually suggest a capacity to carry additional debt.

5. Contingencies

The credit standing of a firm could change abruptly in the future if current uncertainties turn out negatively for the firm. Questions that the analyst might ask include the following:

1. Is the firm a defendant in a major lawsuit involving its principal products, its technological advantages, its income tax returns, or other core endeavors that

could change its profitability and cash flows in the future? Consider, for example, the uncertainty confronting the tobacco and asbestos industries at the present time with the unsettled status of lawsuits in the United States. Most large firms are continually engaged in lawsuits as a normal part of their business. Most of their losses are insured. Negative legal judgments will likely have a more pronounced effect on smaller firms, however, because they have less of a resource base to defend themselves and sustain such losses and may not carry adequate insurance.

2. Has the firm sold receivables with recourse or served as guarantor on a loan by a subsidiary, joint venture, special purpose entity, or corporate officer that, if payment is required, will consume cash flows otherwise available to service other debt obligations?

3. Has the firm committed itself to make payments related to derivative financial instruments that could adversely affect future cash flows if interest rates, exchange rates, or other prices change significantly in an unexpected direction (see the discussion of derivatives in Chapter 8)?

4. Is the firm dependent on one or a few key employees, contracts or license agreements, or technologies, the loss of which could substantially affect the viability of the business?

Obtaining answers to such questions will require the analyst to read the notes to the financial statement carefully and to ask astute questions of management, attorneys, and others.

6. Character of Management

An intangible that can offset to some extent otherwise weak signals about the credit worthiness of a firm is the character of its management. Has the management team successively weathered previous operating problems and challenges that could have bankrupted most firms? Has the management team delivered in the past on projections made with regard to sales levels, cost reductions, new product development, and similar operating targets? Does the firm have a reputation for honest and fair dealings with suppliers, customers, bankers, and others? Lenders are also more comfortable lending to firms where management has a substantial portion of its personal wealth invested in the firm's common equity. Managers desiring to increase the value of their equity holdings have incentives to operate the firm profitably and avoid defaulting on debt.

7. Conditions

Lenders often place restrictions, or constraints, on a firm to protect their interests. Such restrictions might include minimum or maximum levels of certain financial ratios (for example, the current ratio cannot decline below 1.2; the debt-equity ratio cannot exceed 75 percent). Firms may also be precluded from paying dividends or taking on new financing with rights senior to existing lenders in the event of bankruptcy. Violation of these debt constraints, or covenants, could result in the need to repay borrowing immediately. Although these covenants can protect the interest of senior, collateralized lenders, they can place less senior lenders in jeopardy if the firm must quickly liquidate assets to repay debt. Thus, debt covenants are a double-edged sword from the viewpoint of credit risk. They provide protection against undue deterioration in the financial condition of a firm but increase the likelihood of default or bankruptcy if the constraints are too tight.

Summary of Credit Risk Analysis

The analysis of credit risk is a multi-faceted endeavor. The financial statements and notes provide evidence on a firm's cash-generating ability, extent of collateralized assets, amount of unused debt capacity, and constraints imposed by existing borrowing agreements. Although the financial statements might provide some clues, the credit analyst must search beyond the financial statements for information on the market value of collateral, contingencies confronting the firm, and the character of management. Existing lenders should monitor a firm's credit risk on an ongoing basis. New lenders should assess how their loan will incrementally affect the firm's credit risk.

ANALYZING BANKRUPTCY RISK

This section discusses the analysis of bankruptcy risk using information in the financial statements.

THE BANKRUPTCY PROCESS

Firms may file a petition for bankruptcy in the local federal bankruptcy court of their jurisdiction. Most firms file under Chapter 11 of the National Bankruptcy Code. Under Chapter 11, firms have six months in which to present a plan of reorganization to the court. After that period elapses, creditors, employees, and others can file their plans of reorganization. One such plan might include immediately selling the assets of the business and paying creditors the amounts due. The court decides which plan provides the fairest treatment for all parties concerned. While in bankruptcy, creditors cannot demand payment of their claims. The court oversees the execution of the reorganization. When the court determines that the firm has executed the plan of reorganization successfully and appears to be a viable entity, the firm is released from bankruptcy.

A Chapter 7 filing entails an immediate sale, or liquidation, of the firm's assets and a distribution of the proceeds to the various claimants in the order of their priority.

Firms typically file for bankruptcy when they have insufficient cash to pay creditors' claims coming due. If such firms did not file for bankruptcy, creditors could exercise their right to take possession of any collateral pledged to secure their lending and effectively begin liquidation of the firm. In an effort to keep assets intact and allow time for the firm to reorganize, the firm files for bankruptcy. In recent years, some firms have filed for bankruptcy for reasons other than insufficient liquid resources to pay creditors. Some firms have filed for bankruptcy to avoid labor contracts that they consider too costly. Other firms facing potentially costly litigation have filed for bankruptcy as a means of forcing the contending party to negotiate a settlement.

MODELS OF BANKRUPTCY PREDICTION

Empirical studies of bankruptcy attempt to distinguish the financial characteristics of firms that file for bankruptcy from those that do not, a dichotomous outcome state. The objective is to develop a model that predicts which firms will likely file for bankruptcy one or more years before the filing. These models use financial statement ratios and other data.

Univariate Bankruptcy Prediction Models

Early research on bankruptcy prediction in the mid-1960s used univariate analysis. Univariate models examine the relation between a particular financial statement ratio and bankruptcy. Multivariate models, discussed next, combine several financial statement ratios to determine if the set of ratios together can improve bankruptcy prediction. Beaver[5] studied 29 financial statement ratios for the five years preceding bankruptcy for a sample of bankrupt and nonbankrupt firms. The objective was to identify the ratios that distinguished best between these two groups of firms and to determine how many years prior to bankruptcy the differences in the ratios emerged. The six ratios with the best discriminating power (and the nature of the risk each ratio measures) were:

1. Net Income plus Depreciation, Depletion, and Amortization/Total Liabilities (long-term solvency risk).[6]
2. Net Income/Total Assets (profitability).
3. Total Debt/Total Assets (long-term solvency risk).
4. Net Working Capital/Total Assets (short-term liquidity risk).
5. Current Assets/Current Liabilities (short-term liquidity risk).
6. Cash, Marketable Securities, Accounts Receivable/Operating Expenses excluding Depreciation, Depletion, and Amortization (short-term liquidity risk).[7]

Note that this list includes profitability, short-term liquidity risk, and long-term solvency risk ratios. Beaver's best predictor was net income before depreciation, depletion, and amortization divided by total liabilities. Exhibit 5.5 summarizes the success

---

[5]William Beaver, "Financial Ratios as Predictors of Failure," *Empirical Research in Accounting: Selected Studies, 1966*, supplement to *Journal of Accounting Research* (1966), pp. 71–102.
[6]This ratio is similar to the cash flow from operations to total liabilities ratio discussed earlier in this chapter except that the numerator of Beaver's ratio does not include changes in working capital accounts. Published "funds flow" statements at the time of Beaver's study defined funds as working capital (instead of cash).
[7]This ratio, referred to as the *defensive interval*, indicates the proportion of a year that a firm could continue to operate by paying cash operating expenses with cash and near-cash assets.

		EXHIBIT 5.5		

Classification Accuracy and Error Rates for Net Income before Depreciation, Depletion and Amortization/Total Liabilities

Years Prior to Bankruptcy	Proportion Correctly Classified	Error Rate	
		Type I	Type II
5	78%	42%	4%
4	76%	47%	3%
3	77%	37%	8%
2	79%	34%	8%
1	87%	22%	5%

Source: Beaver, "Financial Ratios as Predictors of Failure," *Empirical Research in Accounting: Selected Studies, 1966,* supplement to *Journal of Accounting Research* (1966), p. 90.

of this ratio in correctly classifying sample firms as bankrupt or not for each of the five years preceding bankruptcy. The classification accuracy increased as bankruptcy approached, but was close to 80 percent for as early as five years preceding bankruptcy.

The error rates deserve particular attention however. A Type I error is classifying a firm as nonbankrupt when it ultimately goes bankrupt. A Type II error occurs when a firm is classified as bankrupt and ultimately survives. A Type I error is more costly to an investor because of the likelihood of losing the full amount invested. A Type II error costs the investor the opportunity cost of funds invested. Note in Exhibit 5.5 that the Type I error rates are much higher than the Type II error rates in Beaver's study. Four years prior to bankruptcy, the net income before depreciation, depletion, and amortization to total liabilities ratio does only slightly better in predicting which firms will enter bankruptcy than flipping a coin.

Univariate analysis helps to identify factors related to bankruptcy and is therefore a necessary step in the initial development of a theory of bankruptcy risk. However, univariate analysis does not provide a means of measuring the relative importance of individual financial statement ratios or of combining them when assessing risk. For example, does a firm with a high current ratio and a high debt to assets ratio have more bankruptcy risk than a firm with a low current ratio and a low debt to assets ratio? The analyst must also judge subjectively the level of each financial ratio that signals a high probability of bankruptcy.

Multivariate Bankruptcy Prediction Models Using Multiple Discriminant Analysis

Deficiencies of univariate analysis led researchers during the late 1960s and throughout the 1970s to use multiple discriminant analysis (MDA), a multivariate statistical technique, to develop bankruptcy prediction models. Researchers typically selected a sample of bankrupt firms and matched these firms with healthy firms of approximately the same size and in the same industry. This matching attempts to control for size and industry factors so the researcher can examine the impact of other factors that might explain bankruptcy. The researcher then calculates a large number of financial statement ratios expected *a priori* to explain bankruptcy. Using these financial ratios as inputs, the MDA model selects the subset (usually four to six ratios) that best discriminates between bankrupt and nonbankrupt firms. The resulting MDA model includes a set of coefficients that, when multiplied times the particular financial statement ratios and then summed, yields a multivariate score. Scores below a critical cutoff point suggest a high probability of bankruptcy, and scores above that point suggest a low probability. Researchers usually develop the MDA model on an estimation sample and then apply the resulting model to a separate holdout, or prediction, sample to check on the general applicability and predictability of the model.

Perhaps the best-known MDA bankruptcy prediction model is Altman's Z-score.[8] Altman used data for manufacturing firms to develop the model. The calculation of the Z-score appears below:

$$Z\text{-score} = 1.2 \left[\frac{\text{Net Working Capital}}{\text{Total Assets}} \right] + 1.4 \left[\frac{\text{Retained Earnings}}{\text{Total Assets}} \right]$$

$$+ 3.3 \left[\frac{\text{Earnings Before Interest and Taxes}}{\text{Total Assets}} \right] + .6 \left[\frac{\text{Market Value of Equity}}{\text{Book Value of Liabilities}} \right]$$

$$+ 1.0 \left[\frac{\text{Sales}}{\text{Total Assets}} \right]$$

Each of the ratios captures a different dimension of profitability or risk:

1. **Net Working Capital/Total Assets:** The proportion of total assets comprising relatively liquid net current assets (current assets minus current liabilities). This ratio serves as a measure of short-term liquidity risk.
2. **Retained Earnings/Total Assets:** Accumulated profitability and relative age of a firm.
3. **Earnings before Interest and Taxes/Total Assets:** A version of ROA. This ratio measures current profitability.
4. **Market Value of Equity/Book Value of Liabilities:** This is a form of the debt/equity ratio, but it incorporates the market's assessment of the value of the firm's shareholders' equity. This ratio therefore measures long-term solvency risk and the market's overall assessment of the profitability and risk of the firm.
5. **Sales/Total Assets:** This ratio is similar to the total assets turnover ratio discussed in Chapter 4 and indicates the ability of a firm to use assets to generate sales.

---

[8]Edward Altman, "Financial Ratios, Discriminant Analysis, and the Prediction of Corporate Bankruptcy," *Journal of Finance* (September 1968), pp. 589–609.

In applying this model, Altman found that Z-scores of less than 1.81 indicated a high probability of bankruptcy, while Z-scores higher than 3.00 indicated a low probability of bankruptcy. Scores between 1.81 and 3.00 were in the gray area.

Altman obtained 95 percent correct classification accuracy rate one year prior to bankruptcy, with a Type I error rate of 6 percent and a Type II error rate of 3 percent. The correct classification rate two years before bankruptcy was 83 percent, with a Type I error rate of 28 percent and a Type II error rate of 6 percent. As with Beaver's study, the more costly Type I error rate is larger than the Type II error rate.

Exhibit 5.6 shows the calculation of Altman's Z-score for PepsiCo for Year 11, the most recent year reported in Appendix A. PepsiCo's Z-score of 6.6472 clearly indicates a low probability of bankruptcy.

The principal strengths of MDA are:

1. It incorporates multiple financial ratios simultaneously.
2. It provides the appropriate coefficients for combining the independent variables.
3. It is easy to apply once the initial model has been developed.

The principal criticisms of MDA are:

1. As in univariate applications, the researcher cannot be sure that the MDA model includes all relevant discriminating financial ratios. Most early studies, for example, used accrual-basis income statement and balance sheet data instead of cash-flow data. MDA selects the best ratios from those provided to it, but that set does not necessarily provide the best explanatory power.

EXHIBIT 5.6	
Altman's Z-Score for PepsiCo	
Net Working Capital/Total Assets	
1.2[($5,853 − $4,998)/$21,695]	.0473
Retained Earnings/Total Assets	
1.4[$11,519/$21,695]	.7433
Earnings before Interest and Taxes/Total Assets	
3.3[($2,662 + $1,367 + $219)/$21,695]	.6462
Market Value of Equity/Book Value of Liabilities	
.6[($49.05 × 1,756)/$13,021]	3.9689
Sales/Total Assets	
1.0[$26,935/$21,695]	1.2415
Z-Score...	6.6472

2. As in univariate applications, the researcher must judge subjectively the value of the cutoff score that best distinguishes bankrupt from nonbankrupt firms, taking into consideration the level of Type I and Type II errors.
3. The development and application of the MDA model requires firms to disclose the necessary information to compute each financial ratio. Firms excluded because they do not provide the necessary data may bias the MDA model.
4. MDA assumes that each of the financial ratios for bankrupt and nonbankrupt firms is normally distributed. Firms experiencing financial distress often display unusually large or small ratios that can skew the distribution away from normal. In addition, the researcher cannot include dummy variables (for example, 0 if financial statements are audited, 1 if they are not audited). Dummy variables are not normally distributed.
5. MDA requires that the variance-covariance matrix of the explanatory variables be the same for bankrupt and nonbankrupt firms.[9]

Multivariate Bankruptcy Prediction Models Using Logit Analysis

A third stage in the methodological development of bankruptcy prediction research was the move during the 1980s and early 1990s to using logit analysis instead of MDA. Logit does not require that the data display the underlying statistical properties described above for MDA. In addition, logit provides a probability of bankruptcy, which is more easily interpretable than the numerical score obtained from MDA. Interpreting the MDA score requires the researcher to choose subjectively the range of scores that indicate high, low, and uncertain likelihoods of bankruptcy.

The development of the logit model follows a similar procedure to MDA: (1) initial calculation of a large set of financial ratios, (2) reduction of the set of financial ratios to a subset that best discriminates bankrupt and nonbankrupt firms, and (3) estimation of coefficients for each included variable.

The logit model defines the probability of bankruptcy as follows:

$$\text{Probability of Bankruptcy for a Firm} = \frac{1}{1+e^{-y}}$$

where e equals approximately 2.718282. The exponent y is a multivariate function that includes a constant and coefficients for a set of explanatory variables (that is, financial statement ratios).

Ohlson[10] used logit to discriminate bankrupt from nonbankrupt firms. Ohlson's model for one year prior to bankruptcy defined y as follows:

---

[9]For an elaboration of these criticisms, see James A. Ohlson, "Financial Ratios and the Probabilistic Prediction of Bankruptcy," *Journal of Accounting Research* (Spring 1980), pp. 109–131 and Mark E. Zmijewski, "Methodological Issues Related to the Estimation of Financial Distress Prediction Models," *Journal of Accounting Research—Supplement,* 1984, pp. 59–82.
[10]Ohlson, *op.cit.*

$$y = -1.32 - .407(\text{SIZE}) + 6.03(\text{TLTA}) - 1.43(\text{WCTA}) + .0757(\text{CLCA})$$
$$-2.37(\text{NITA}) - 1.83(\text{FUTL}) + .285(\text{INTWO}) - 1.72(\text{OENEG})$$
$$-.521(\text{CHIN})$$

The definition of the independent variables is as follows:

SIZE = Natural log of (Total Assets/GNP implicit price deflator index). The price index is as of the end of the year prior to the year end of the balance sheet to allow for real-time implementation of the model. Ohlson's model was developed using a GNP index of 100 in 1978.[11] Total assets equal the full dollar value of assets, not the amount reported on the balance sheet with zeroes omitted (for example, when the balance sheet reports amounts in thousands or millions).[12]

TLTA = Total Liabilities/Total Assets

WCTA = (Current Assets – Current Liabilities)/Total Assets

CLCA = Current Liabilities/Current Assets

NITA = Net Income/Total Assets

FUTL = Funds (Working Capital) from Operations/Total Liabilities
Ohlson developed his model when firms presented a statement of sources and uses of funds, with funds defined as working capital, instead of a statement of cash flows. As Chapter 3 discusses, working capital from operations equals net income plus addbacks for expenses (for example, depreciation) and subtractions for revenues (for example, equity in earnings of affiliates in excess of dividends received) that do not provide cash. Thus, working capital from operations is an intermediate subtotal between net income and cash flow from operations before adjusting for changes in working capital accounts.

INTWO = One if net income was negative for the last two years and zero otherwise.

OENEG = One if total liabilities exceed total assets and zero otherwise.

CHIN = $(\text{Net Income}_t - \text{Net Income}_{t-1})/(|\text{Net Income}_t| + |\text{Net Income}_{t-1}|)$.

Explanatory variables with a positive coefficient increase the probability of bankruptcy because they decrease e^{-y} towards zero, with the result that the bankruptcy probability function approaches 1/1 or 100 percent. Likewise, independent variables with a negative coefficient decrease the probability of bankruptcy. The analyst must interpret the sign of the coefficient for a particular financial statement ratio cautiously because the coefficients of the various ratios in a multivariate model are not independent of each other. With this caveat in mind, consider each of the nine explanatory variables in Ohlson's logit model.

---

[11]The GNP index for the fourth quarter of 1978 was 49.59 and for the fourth quarter of 2001 was 109.78 when 1996 = 100. With 1978 = 100, the equivalent index for the fourth quarter of 2001 is 221.4 (109.78/49.59). *The Survey of Current Business* regularly publishes values for the GNP implicit price deflator index.

[12]Most calculators have a button labeled "ln" for calculating natural logs.

1. **SIZE:** Larger firms have greater flexibility to curtail capacity, sell assets, and attract debt or equity capital than smaller firms. Thus, the coefficient on SIZE carries a negative coefficient.

2. **TLTA:** Higher debt ratios increase the probability of bankruptcy. TLTA is a measure of long-term solvency risk. Thus, the coefficient on TLTA is appropriately positive.

3. **WCTA:** The higher the proportion of net working capital to total assets, the more liquid are the assets and the lower the probability (negative coefficient) of bankruptcy. WCTA is a measure of short-term liquidity risk.

4. **CLCA:** An excess of current liabilities over current assets is also an indicator of short-term liquidity risk, consistent with the positive sign for this coefficient.

5. **NITA:** The higher is the rate of profitability, the less likely a firm will experience difficulty servicing debt and therefore the lower the probability (negative coefficient) of bankruptcy.

6. **FUTL:** The greater is the ability of working capital from operations to cover total liabilities, the lower is the probability (negative coefficient) of bankruptcy. This reasoning is similar to that for the cash flow from operations to total liabilities ratio discussed earlier in this chapter in connection with assessing credit risk. Thus, FUTL is a measure of short- and long-term solvency risk.

7. **INTWO:** A recent history of net losses increases the probability of bankruptcy and results in the positive coefficient for this explanatory variable.

8. **OENEG:** This variable would appear to be redundant with TLTA. One would also expect that this variable would carry a positive, instead of a negative, coefficient. The appearance and sign of this variable in the logit model illustrates the difficulty in interpreting individual coefficients in a multivariate statistical model.

9. **CHIN:** The change in net income indicates the direction and magnitude of earnings growth or decline. Increased earnings coupled with the negative coefficient suggest a lower probability of bankruptcy. Decreased earnings coupled with the negative coefficient (net positive effect on y) suggest a higher probability of bankruptcy.

Ohlson developed this logit model on 105 bankrupt and 2,058 nonbankrupt firms. Ohlson found that using a probability cut-off of 3.8 percent for classifying firms as bankrupt (that is, firms are likely to go bankrupt if the probability derived from applying the logit model exceeds 3.8 percent) minimizes Type I and Type II errors. At this probability cut-off point, the model correctly classified 87.6 percent of the bankrupt firms and 82.6 percent of the nonbankrupt firms.

Exhibit 5.7 shows the calculation of the value of y in Ohlson's logit model for PepsiCo for Year 11. The calculation of the probability of bankruptcy is as follows:[13]

$$1/(1 + e^{-(-9.4122)}) = 1/(1 + 12,236.77) = .008\%$$

---

[13]Most calculators have a function for computing e.

EXHIBIT 5.7	
Applying Ohlson's Bankruptcy Prediction Model to PepsiCo	
Constant.	−1.3200
SIZE: −.407($18.40038)*	−7.4890
TLTA: 6.03($13,047/$21,695)	3.6263
WCTA: −1.43[($5,853 − $4,998)/$21,695]	.0564
CLCA: .0757($4,998/$5,853)	.0646
NITA: −2.37($2,662/21,695)	−3.7221
FUTL: −1.83[($4,201 − $84)/$13,021].	−.5786
INTWO: .285(0)	.0000
OENEG: −1.72(0)	.0000
CHIN: −.521[($2,662 − $2,543)/($2,662 + $2,543)].	−.0498
Value of *y*.	−9.4122

*Natural log of ($21,695,000,000/221.4) = $18.40038.

As one would expect, the probability of bankruptcy for PepsiCo is very small. The value of the SIZE variable for PepsiCo dominates the value of *y*. Its healthy profitability increased the values for NITA, FUTL, and CHIN and lowered the value of *y* (that is, made it more negative).

Application of Bankruptcy Prediction Models to W.T. Grant Company

W. T. Grant Company (Grant), one of the largest retailers in the United States at the time, filed for bankruptcy in October 1975. Case 3.1 at the end of Chapter 3 includes financial statement data for Grant for its fiscal years ended January 31, 1968 through 1975. Exhibit 5.8 shows the calculation of Altman's Z-score and Ohlson's probability of bankruptcy for each of these fiscal years using amounts from Exhibits 3.28 and 3.30 of Case 3.1.[14]

Altman's model shows a low probability of bankruptcy prior to the 1973 fiscal year, a move into the gray area in 1973 and 1974, and a high probability of bankruptcy in 1975. The absolute levels of these Z-scores are inflated because Grant is a retailer, whereas Altman developed the model using manufacturing firms. Retailing

---

[14]The web site for this book contains an Excel spreadsheet, called Bankruptcy Prediction Models, for use in calculating Altman's Z-score and Ohlson's probability of bankruptcy.

EXHIBIT 5.8		
Application of Altman's and Ohlson's Bankruptcy Prediction Models to W.T. Grant		
Fiscal Year	1968	1969
Altman's Z-Score Model		
Net Working Capital/Assets..................	.54353	.51341
Retained Earnings/Assets	.43738	.42669
EBIT/Assets................................	.41358	.44611
Market Value Equity/Book Value Liabilities.....	.86643	1.01740
Sales/Assets	1.77564	1.76199
Score.....................................	4.03656	4.16560
Probability of Bankruptcy Range.............	Low	Low
Ohlson's Logit Model		
Constant	−1.320	−1.320
SIZE......................................	−6.504	−6.536
TLTA	3.399	3.315
WCTA	−.648	−.612
CLCA......................................	.037	.039
NITA	−.142	−.148
FVTL......................................	−.237	−.243
INTWO....................................	.000	.000
OENEG....................................	.000	.000
CHIN......................................	−.011	−.042
Total......................................	−5.426	−5.547
Probability of Bankruptcy	.4%	.4%

firms typically have a faster assets turnover than manufacturing firms. In this case, the trend of the Z-score is more meaningful than its absolute level. Note that the Z-score declined steadily beginning in the 1970 fiscal year. With a few exceptions in individual years, each of the five components also declined steadily.[15]

The lower panel of Exhibit 5.8 shows the probability of bankruptcy using Ohlson's model. The model indicates a steady increase in the probability of bankruptcy beginning with the 1970 fiscal year, primarily as a result of increased borrowing. However, it is not until the 1975 fiscal year that the probability of bankruptcy would show

---

[15]The solution to the Grant case indicates that, prior to its 1975 fiscal year, Grant failed to provide adequately for uncollectible accounts. The effect of this action was to overstate the net working capital/assets, retained earnings/assets, and EBIT/assets components of the Z-score, understate the sales/assets component, and probably overstate the overall Z-score.

EXHIBIT 5.8					

continued

1970	1971	1972	1973	1974	1975
.44430	.37791	.44814	.36508	.38524	.19390
.41929	.38511	.34513	.31023	.25712	.04873
.44228	.38848	.27820	.26029	.25470	−.63644
.95543	.89539	.69788	.50578	.10211	.01730
1.71325	1.67974	1.57005	1.58678	1.54797	1.62802
3.97455	3.72663	3.33940	3.02816	2.54714	1.25151
Low	Low	Low	Gray	Gray	High
−1.320	−1.320	−1.320	−1.320	−1.320	−1.320
−6.652	−6.686	−6.730	−6.779	−6.801	−6.700
3.550	3.793	3.984	4.268	4.543	5.396
−.529	−.450	−.534	−.435	−.459	−.231
.044	.049	.043	.049	.048	.061
−.139	−.116	−.086	−.080	−.022	.398
−.216	−.170	−.128	−.113	−.047	.340
.000	.000	.000	.000	.000	.000
.000	.000	.000	.000	.000	.000
−.018	.034	.037	−.026	.273	.521
−5.280	−4.866	−4.734	−4.436	−3.785	−1.535
.5%	.8%	.9%	1.2%	2.2%	17.7%

cause for alarm (the Ohlson model, using a 3.8 percent cut-off, would not classify Grant as a likely bankruptcy candidate prior to this time). The seemingly late classification of Grant as a bankruptcy candidate relates again to the influence of the SIZE variable in Ohlson's model. An alternative logit model by Zavgren[16] that does not use size as an explanatory variable shows an increase in the probability of bankruptcy for Grant from 35.0 percent in 1967 to 93.5 percent in 1975.

Other Methodological Issues in Bankruptcy Prediction Research

Bankruptcy prediction research has addressed several other methodological issues.

[16]Christine V. Zavgren, "Assessing the Vulnerability to Failure of American Industrial Firms: A Logistic Analysis," *Journal of Business Finance and Accounting* (Spring 1985), pp. 19–45.

1. **Equal Sample Sizes of Bankrupt and Nonbankrupt Firms.** The proportion of bankrupt firms in the economy is substantially smaller than the proportion of nonbankrupt firms. The matched pairs research design common in most studies results in overfitting the MDA and logit models toward the characteristics of bankrupt firms. This overfitting is not necessarily a problem if the objective is to identify characteristics of bankrupt firms. However, it will likely result in classifying too many nonbankrupt firms as bankrupt (a Type II error) when the model is applied to the broader population of firms. Researchers (such as Ohlson in the study discussed above) have addressed this criticism by using a larger proportion of nonbankrupt firms.

2. **Matching Bankrupt and Nonbankrupt Firms on Size and Industry Characteristics.** This matching precludes consideration of either of these factors as possible explanatory variables for bankruptcy. Yet, small firms may experience greater difficulty obtaining funds when needed than larger firms (consistent with the results for Ohlson's SIZE variable). Industry membership, particularly for cyclical industries, may be an important factor explaining bankruptcy. Some researchers select a random sample of nonbankrupt firms. Another approach is to develop the MDA or logit models for each industry. Platt,[17] for example, developed models for sixteen two-digit SIC industries. The explanatory variables and their coefficients varied across the various industries. Platt and Platt[18] normalized the financial ratios of each firm by relating them to the corresponding average industry ratio of the firm's industry. They found that normalized financial ratios increased the classification accuracy of their sample to 90 percent, versus 78 percent based on a model of non-normalized ratios.

3. **Use of Accrual versus Cash Flow Variables.** Until the mid-1980s, most bankruptcy research used accrual basis balance sheet and income statement ratios or ratios from the "funds flow" statement, which defined funds as working capital. The transition to a cash definition of funds in the statement of cash flows led researchers to add cash flow variables to bankruptcy prediction models. Casey and Bartczak,[19] among others, found that adding cash flow from operations/current liabilities and cash flow from operations/total liabilities did not significantly add explanatory power to models based on accrual basis amounts. Other researchers have found contrary results.[20]

4. **Stability in Bankruptcy Prediction Models over Time.** A final methodological issue in bankruptcy prediction research concerns the stability of the bankruptcy prediction models over time, both with regard to the explanatory

---

[17]Harlan D. Platt, "The Determinants of Interindustry Failure," *Journal of Economics and Business* (1989), pp. 107–126.

[18]Harlan D. Platt and Marjorie B. Platt, "Development of a Class of Stable Predictive Variables: The Case of Bankruptcy Prediction," *Journal of Business, Finance, and Accounting* (Spring 1990), pp. 31–51.

[19]Cornelius J. Casey and Norman J. Bartczak, "Cash Flow—It's Not the Bottom Line," *Harvard Business Review* (June 1984), pp. 61–67.

[20]For a summary of this research, see M. F. Gombola, M.E. Haskins, J. E. Ketz, and D. D. Williams, "Cash Flow in Bankruptcy Prediction," *Financial Management* (Winter 1987), pp. 55–65.

variables included and their coefficients. Bankruptcy laws and their judicial interpretation change over time. The frequency of bankruptcy filings changes as economic conditions change. New financing vehicles emerge (for example, redeemable preferred stock, debt and equity securities with various option rights) that previous MDA or logit models did not consider in their formulation. To apply these models in practical settings, the analyst should periodically update them.

Begley, Ming, and Watts[21] applied Altman's MDA model and Ohlson's logit model to a sample of bankrupt and nonbankrupt firms in the 1980s, a later period than those used by Altman and Ohlson. They found that the Type I and Type II errors rates increased substantially relative to those in the original studies. They then re-estimated the coefficients for each model using data for a portion of their 1980s sample. The coefficients on the liquidity ratios increased and the coefficients on the debt ratio decreased relative to those in the original studies. When they applied the original and re-estimated coefficients to the 1980s sample, they observed a reduction in Type II errors but no improvement in Type I errors for the Altman model. For the Ohlson model, they found that a reduction in Type II errors was offset by an increase in Type I error of equal amount. Thus, the revised coefficients result in fewer errors in classifying nonbankrupt firms as bankrupt, but similar or worse errors occur in classifying bankrupt firms as nonbankrupt.

SYNTHESIS OF BANKRUPTCY PREDICTION RESEARCH

The preceding sections of this chapter discussed bankruptcy prediction models. Similar streams of research relate to commercial bank lending,[22] bond ratings,[23] corporate restructurings,[24] corporate liquidations,[25] and earnings management.[26] Although the statistical models used and the relevant financial statement ratios vary across the numerous studies, certain commonalities appear as well. This section attempts to summarize the factors that seem to explain bankruptcy most consistently across various studies.

Investment Factors

Two factors relate to the asset side of the balance sheet.

[21]Joy Begley, Jin Ming, and Susan Watts, "Bankruptcy Classification Errors in the 1980s: An Empirical Analysis of Altman's and Ohlson's Models," *Review of Accounting Studies, Vol. 1 (4)*, (1996), pp. 267–284.

[22]Edward Altman, *Corporate Financial Distress and Bankruptcy*, 2nd edition, New York: John Wiley & Sons (1993), pp. 245–266.

[23]G. E. Pinches and K.A. Mingo, "A Multivariate Analysis of Industrial Bond Ratings," *Journal of Finance* (March 1973), pp. 1–18.

[24]James E. Seward, "Corporate Restructuring and Reorganization," in *Handbook of Modern Finance*, edited by Dennis Logue, New York: Warren, Gorham & Lamont (1993), pp. E8–1 to E8–36.

[25]Cornelius J. Casey, Victor McGee, and Clyde P. Stickney, "Discriminating Between Reorganized and Liquidated Firms in Bankruptcy," *Accounting Review* (April 1986), pp. 249–262.

[26]Messod D. Beneish, "Detecting GAAP Violation: Implications for Assessing Earnings Management among Firms with Extreme Financial Performance," *Journal of Accounting and Public Policy* (1997), pp. 271–309.

1. Relative Liquidity of a Firm's Assets. The probability of financial distress decreases as the relative liquidity of a firm's assets increases. Firms with relatively large proportions of current assets tend to experience less financial distress than firms with fixed assets or intangible assets as the dominant assets. Greater asset liquidity means that the firm will either have or will soon generate the necessary cash to meet creditors' claims. It is of interest to note that the expected return from more liquid assets, such as cash, marketable securities, and accounts receivable, is usually less (reflecting lower risk) than the expected return from fixed and intangible assets. Thus, firms must balance their mix of assets to obtain the desired return/risk profile. Researchers typically use the following ratios to measure relative liquidity: cash/total assets, current assets/total assets, and net working capital/total assets; or relative illiquidity: fixed assets/total assets.

2. Rate of Asset Turnover. The investment of funds in any asset eventually ends up in cash. Firms acquire fixed assets or create intangibles to produce a salable product (inventory) or create a desired service. Goods or services are often sold on account (accounts receivable) and later collected in cash. The faster assets turn over, the more quickly funds work their way toward cash on the balance sheet. Thus, a retailer may have the same proportion of fixed assets to total assets as a manufacturing firm. The other assets of the retailer (that is, accounts receivable, inventories) likely turn over more quickly and are thus more liquid. Commonly used financial ratios for this factor are total assets turnover, accounts receivable turnover, and inventory turnover. The working capital turnover ratio [= sales/(current assets minus current liabilities)] and fixed asset turnover ratios have not generally showed statistical significance in studies of financial distress.

Financing Factors

Two factors relate to the liability side of the balance sheet.

1. Relative Proportion of Debt in the Capital Structure. Firms experience bankruptcy because they are unable to pay liabilities as they come due. The higher is the proportion of liabilities in the capital structure, the higher is the probability that firms will experience bankruptcy. Firms with lower proportions of debt tend to have unused borrowing capacity that they can use in times of difficulty. Some measure of the proportion of debt in the capital structure appears in virtually all bankruptcy prediction models. Commonly used ratios include total liabilities/total assets and total liabilities/shareholders' equity.

2. Relative Proportion of Short-term Debt in the Capital Structure. This factor has a similar rationale to that above except that the nearer due date of short-term debt increases the risk of bankruptcy. Thus, considering only the financing side of the balance sheet, a retailer using extensive bank and creditor financing will likely have greater risk of bankruptcy than a manufacturer with a similar proportion of total liabilities but whose liabilities are primarily long-term debt. A commonly used ratio for this factor is current liabilities/total assets.

Operating Factors

Two factors relate to the operating activities of a firm.

1. Relative Level of Profitability. Profitable firms ultimately turn their earnings into cash. Profitable firms are also usually able to borrow funds more easily than unprofitable firms. Firms with low or negative profitability must often rely on available cash or additional borrowing to meet financial commitments as they come due. Research has demonstrated that most bankruptcies initiate with one or more years of poor operating performance. Firms with unused debt capacity can often borrow for a year or two until the operating difficulties reverse. A combination of weak profitability and high debt ratios usually spells "financial distress." Commonly used financial ratios for profitability are net income/assets, income before interest and taxes/assets, net income/sales, and cash flow from operations/assets. The second profitability measure above identifies profitability problems in the core input/output markets of a firm before considering debt service costs and income taxes. The third measure appears in bankruptcy distress prediction models because profit margin, rather than assets turnover, is usually the driving force behind return on assets. The fourth measure substitutes cash flow from operations for net income in measuring profitability on the premise that cash pays the bills, not earnings.

2. Variability of Operations. Firms that experience variability in their operations, such as from cyclical sales patterns, exhibit a greater likelihood of bankruptcy than do firms with low variability. During the down times in the cycle, such firms must obtain financing to meet financial commitments and maintain operating levels. The risk of bankruptcy in these cases relates to the unknown length of the down portion of the cycle. For how many years can a firm hold on until the cycle reverses? Researchers typically use the change in sales or the change in net income from the previous year to measure variability, although a longer period would seem more reasonable.

Other Possible Explanatory Variables

Three other factors examined in bankruptcy research warrant discussion.

1. Size. Studies of bankruptcy, particularly since the early 1980s, have increasingly identified size as an important explanatory variable. Larger firms generally have access to a wider range of financing sources and more flexibility to redeploy assets than smaller firms. Larger firms therefore experience a lower probability of bankruptcy than smaller firms. Most studies use total assets as the measure of size.

2. Growth. Studies of bankruptcy often include some measure of growth (for example, growth in sales, assets, or net income) as a possible explanatory variable. The statistical significance of growth as an independent variable has varied considerably across studies. It is therefore difficult to conclude much about its relative importance. The mixed results may relate in part to ambiguity as to how growth relates to bankruptcy. Rapidly growing firms often need external financing to cover cash shortfalls from operations and permit acquisitions of fixed assets. These firms often display financial ratios typical of a firm in financial difficulty (that is, high debt ratios, weak profitability). Yet, their growth potential provides access to capital that permits them to survive. Firms in the late maturity or early decline phase of their life cycles may display healthy financial ratios but prospects are sufficiently poor that the probability of future financial difficulty is high.

3. Qualified Audit Opinion. Several studies have examined the information value of a qualified audit opinion in predicting bankruptcy. Hopwood, McKeown, and Mutchler compared the predictive accuracy of a qualified audit opinion versus models that include only financial ratios in predicting bankruptcy.[27] They found that the qualified audit opinion had similar predictive accuracy as the models based on financial ratios. This result is not surprising if auditors use bankruptcy prediction models in deciding whether or not to issue a qualified opinion. Chen and Church found that the negative stock price reaction at the time of a bankruptcy filing was less for firms that had previously had a qualified audit opinion than firms that had only clean audit opinions, suggesting that the audit opinion had information content.[28]

Some Final Thoughts

Bankruptcy prediction research represents an effort to integrate traditional financial statement analysis with statistical modeling. This area of research evolved between the mid-1960s and mid-1980s from relatively simple univariate models to multivariate models. Despite the importance of predicting bankruptcy, this area of research has provided few new insights since the mid-1980s. The models developed by Altman and by Ohlson rely on data that are decades old and based on business activities and bankruptcy laws that differ from those currently encountered. Yet, the models continue to be used by security analysts and academic researchers.[29]

MARKET EQUITY BETA RISK

Firms face additional risks besides credit and bankruptcy risk. Recessions, inflation, changes in interest rates, rising unemployment, and similar economic factors affect all firms but in varying degrees, depending on the nature of their operations. The investor in a firm's common stock must consider these dimensions of risk when making investment decisions. Economic theory teaches that differences in expected rates of return between investment alternatives should relate to differences in risk.

---

[27]William Hopwood, James C. McKeown, and Jane F. Mutchler, "A Reexamination of Auditor versus Model Accuracy within the Context of the Going-Concern Opinion Decision," *Contemporary Accounting Research* (Spring 1994), pp. 409–431.

[28]Kevin C.W. Chen and Bryan K. Church, "Going Concern Opinions and the Market's Reaction to Bankruptcy Filings," *Accounting Review* (January 1996), pp. 117–128.

[29]A recent study models bankruptcy prediction as an option pricing valuation using market values. The authors compare the prediction accuracy of this market-based model with the Altman and Ohlson models and find that their model has better prediction accuracy. However, using either the Altman or Ohlson model in addition to the option pricing model adds to the prediction accuracy. See Stephen A. Hillegeist, Donald P. Cram, Elizabeth K. Keating, and Kyle G. Lundstedt, "Assessing the Probability of Bankruptcy," *Working Paper*, Northwestern University, 2002.

Thus, we can turn to equity markets to obtain a broader measure of risk. We will then relate this market measure of risk to financial statement information.

Studies of market rates of return have traditionally used the capital asset pricing model (CAPM). The research typically regresses the returns on a particular firm's common shares (dividends plus (minus) capital gains (losses)) over some period of time on the excess of the returns of all common stocks over the risk-free rate. The regression takes the following form:

$$\begin{array}{l}\text{Returns on Common Stock} \\ \text{of a Particular Firm}\end{array} = \begin{array}{l}\text{Risk-Free} \\ \text{Interest Rate}\end{array} + \begin{array}{l}\text{Market} \\ \text{Beta}\end{array} \left[\begin{array}{l}\text{Market} \\ \text{Return}\end{array} - \begin{array}{l}\text{Risk-Free} \\ \text{Interest Rate}\end{array}\right]$$

The beta coefficient measures the covariability of a firm's returns with those of all shares traded on the market (in excess of the risk-free interest rate). Firms with a market beta of 1.0 experience variability equal to the average. Firms with a beta greater than 1.0 experience greater variability than the average. Firms with a beta less than 1.0 experience less variability than the average firm. A beta of 1.20 suggests 20 percent greater variability. A beta of .80 suggests 20 percent less variability.

Beta captures the *systematic risk* of the firm. The market, through the pricing of a firm's shares, rewards shareholders for the systematic risk assumed. Elements of risk that do not contribute to systematic risk are referred to as *nonsystematic risk*. By constructing a diversified portfolio of securities, the investor can eliminate nonsystematic risk. Thus, market pricing should provide no returns for the assumption of nonsystematic risk.

Studies of the determinants of market beta have identified three principal explanatory variables:[30]

1. Degree of operating leverage
2. Degree of financial leverage
3. Variability of sales

Each of these factors causes the earnings of a particular firm to vary over time.

Operating leverage refers to the extent of fixed operating costs in the cost structure. Costs such as depreciation and amortization do not vary with the level of sales. Other costs, such as research and development and advertising, may vary somewhat with the level of sales but remain relatively fixed for any particular period. The presence of fixed operating costs leads to variations in operating earnings as sales increase and decrease. Likewise, the presence of debt in the capital structure adds a fixed cost for interest and creates the potential for causing earnings to increase or decrease as sales vary.

---

[30]Robert S. Hamada, "The Effect of a Firm's Capital Structure on the Systematic Risk of Common Stocks," *Journal of Finance* (May 1972), pp. 435–452; Barr Rosenberg and Walt McKibben, "The Prediction of Systematic and Specific Risk in Common Stocks," *Journal of Financial and Quantitative Analysis* (March 1973), pp. 317–333; James M. Gahlon and James A. Gentry, "On the Relationship Between Systematic Risk and Degrees of Operating and Financial Leverage," *Financial Management* (Summer 1982), pp. 15–23.

The presence of these fixed costs does not necessarily lead to earnings fluctuations over time. A firm with stable or growing sales may be able to adjust the level of fixed assets and related financing (for example, through leasing) to the level of sales, in effect converting fixed costs into variable costs. Firms such as electric utilities with high fixed costs from operating and financial leverage have historically had monopoly power to price their services to cover costs regardless of demand. Such firms likewise have not experienced wide variations in earnings. Operating and financial leverage create variations in earnings when sales vary and firms cannot alter their level of fixed costs. Thus, we would expect capital-intensive firms in cyclical industries to experience wide variations in earnings over the business cycle.

Research has shown a link between changes in earnings and changes in stock prices.[31] Thus, operating leverage, financial leverage, and variability of sales should result in fluctuations in the market returns for a particular firm's common shares. The average returns for all firms in the market should reflect the average level of operating leverage, financial leverage, and sales variability of these firms. Therefore, the market beta for a particular firm reflects its degree of variability relative to the average firm. Chapters 11 to 13 discuss the relation between financial statement information and market beta more fully and the use of market beta in the valuation of firms.

FINANCIAL REPORTING MANIPULATION RISK

Enron, WorldCom, Global Crossing, Qwest Communications, Sunbeam, Cendant, and others have been the subject of SEC investigations and negative media coverage in recent years for allegedly preparing financial statements outside the limits of GAAP in an effort to portray the firm in a more favorable light than is appropriate. Analysts cannot rely on intentionally misleading financial statements when assessing profitability and risk. This section explores the characteristics of firms accused of falsifying their financial statements and describes tools for assessing this type of risk.

At the outset, we need to recognize the distinction between earnings manipulation and earnings management. *Earnings manipulation* refers to reporting amounts outside the limits of GAAP and is the subject of this section. *Earnings management* refers to choices made within the limits of GAAP and is a principal topic of Chapter 6. Regulations of the SEC and rules of various stock exchanges require the preparation of financial reports according to, or within the bounds of, GAAP. Thus, firms that intentionally report outside the limits of GAAP in an effort to mislead financial statement users are potentially subject to legal and regulatory actions for fraudulent reporting.

---

[31]Ray Ball and Philip Brown, "An Empirical Evaluation of Accounting Income Numbers," *Journal of Accounting Research* (Autumn 1968), pp. 159–178.

MOTIVATIONS FOR EARNINGS MANIPULATION

Reasons that firm might manipulate earnings include:

1. Obtain debt financing at a lower cost because of appearing more profitable or less risky.
2. Positively influence stock prices, or delay inevitable stock price declines.
3. Increase management bonuses that are based on earnings or stock prices.
4. Avoid violation of debt covenants.

EMPIRICAL RESEARCH ON EARNINGS MANIPULATION

Dechow, Sloan, and Sweeney[32] examined the governance characteristics of firms subject to enforcement actions by the SEC. They found that such firms have weak corporate governance structures, including the absence of an audit committee within their board of directors, the appointment of the founder of the company as the chief executive officer (CEO), the appointment of the CEO as the chairperson of the board, and the domination of the board by insiders (employees, consultants, or individuals otherwise closely associated with the firm). The SEC enforcement action led to a 9 percent reduction in stock price on average, an increase in the bid-ask spread, less analyst consensus on earnings forecasts, and increased short interest, each of which likely increases the firm's cost of capital.

Beneish developed a probit model, similar to the logit model of Ohlson for bankruptcy prediction discussed earlier, to identify the financial characteristics of firms likely to engage in earnings manipulation. Beneish developed both a 12-factor model[33] and an 8-factor model.[34] The 12-factor model relies on a combination of financial statement items and changes in stock prices for a firm's shares. The 8-factor model uses only financial statement items. Beneish developed the models using data for firms subject to SEC enforcement actions.

Developing these models involves identifying characteristics of firms likely to manipulate earnings, selecting financial statement ratios or other measures of these characteristics, and then using a probit statistical program to select the significant factors and the appropriate coefficient for each factor. Applying the coefficient to the value of each factor for a particular firm yields a score that becomes the value of y.

Unlike logit models, which convert the value of y into a probability using $\dfrac{1}{1 + e^{-y}}$,

---

[32]Patricia M. Dechow, Richard G. Sloan, and Amy P. Sweeney, "Causes and Consequences of Earnings Manipulation: An Analysis of Firms Subject to Enforcement Actions by the SEC," *Contemporary Accounting Research* (Spring 1996), pp. 1–36.

[33]Messod D. Beneish, "Detecting GAAP Violation: Implications for Assessing Earnings Management among Firms with Extreme Financial Performance," *Journal of Accounting and Public Policy* (1997), pp. 271–309. For an instructional case applying this model to an actual company, see Christine I. Wiedman, "Instructional Case: Detecting Earnings Manipulation," *Issues in Accounting Education* (February 1999), pp. 145–176. Also see Messod D. Beneish, "A Note on Wiedman's (1999) Instructional Case: Detecting Earnings Manipulation," *Issues in Accounting Education* (May 1999), pp. 369–370.

[34]Messod D. Beneish, "The Detection of Earnings Manipulation," *Financial Analyst Journal* (September/October 1999), pp. 24–36.

probit converts y into a probability using a standardized normal distribution and a specified prior probability of earnings manipulation. The command NORMSDIST within Excel, when applied to a particular value of y, converts it to the appropriate probability value. As with Ohlson's bankruptcy model, positive coefficients increase the probability of earnings manipulation.

Beneish's eight factors and the rationale for their inclusion are as follows:

1. **Days in Receivables Index (DSRI).** The index relates the ratio of accounts receivable at the end of the current year as a percentage of sales for the current year to the corresponding amounts for the preceding year. A large increase in accounts receivable as a percentage of sales might indicate an overstatement of accounts receivable and sales during the current year to boost earnings. Such an increase might also result from a change in the firm's credit policy (for example, liberalizing credit terms).

2. **Gross Margin Index (GMI).** This index relates gross margin (that is, sales minus cost of goods sold) as a percentage of sales last year to the gross margin as a percentage of sales for the current year. A decline in the gross margin percentage will result in an index greater than 1.0. Firms with weaker profitability this year are more likely to engage in earnings manipulation.

3. **Asset Quality Index (AQI).** Asset quality refers to the proportion of total assets comprising assets other than current assets and property, plant, and equipment. The remaining assets include intangibles for which future benefits are less certain than for current assets and property, plant, and equipment. The asset quality index equals the proportion of these lower quality assets during the current year relative to the preceding year. An increase in the proportion suggests an increased effort to capitalize and defer costs that the firm should have expensed.

4. **Sales Growth Index (SGI).** This index equals sales of the current year relative to sales of the preceding year. Growth does not necessarily imply manipulation. Growing companies, however, usually rely on external financing more than mature companies. The need for low-cost external financing might motivate managers to manipulate sales and earnings. Young, growing companies also often have less developed governance practices to monitor manager's manipulation efforts.

5. **Depreciation Index (DEPI).** This index equals depreciation expense as a percentage of net property, plant, and equipment before depreciation for the preceding year relative to the corresponding percentage for the current year. A ratio greater than 1.0 indicates that the firm has slowed down the rate of depreciation, perhaps by lengthening depreciable lives, and thereby increased earnings.

6. **Selling and Administrative Expense Index (SAI).** This index equals selling and administrative expenses as a percentage of sales for the current year to the corresponding percentage for the preceding year. An index greater than 1.0 might suggest increased marketing expenditures that would lead to increased sales in future periods. Firms not able to sustain the sales growth would then

more likely engage in earnings manipulation. An alternative interpretation is that an index greater than 1.0 suggests that the firm has not taken advantage of capitalizing various costs but instead has expensed them. Firms attempting to manipulate earnings would defer costs and the index value would be less than 1.0. If this latter explanation is descriptive, then the coefficient on this variable will be negative.

7. **Leverage Index (LVGI).** This index equals the proportion of total financing comprised of current liabilities and long-term debt for the current year relative to the proportion for the preceding year. An increase in the proportion of debt likely subjects a firm to a greater risk of violating debt covenants and the need to manipulate earnings to avoid the violation.

8. **Total Accruals to Total Assets (TATA).** Total accruals equals the difference between income from continuing operations and cash flow from operations. Dividing total accruals by total assets at the end of the year scales total accruals across firms and across time. Beneish used this variable as an indicator of the extent that earnings result from accruals instead of from cash flows. A large excess of income from continuing operations over cash flow from operations indicates that accruals play a large part in measuring income. Accruals can serve as a means of manipulating earnings.

Beneish developed both a weighted probit model that takes the proportion of earnings manipulations into account and an unweighted probit model. We illustrate the unweighted model in this section. The unweighted model tends to classify more non-manipulating firms as manipulators (higher Type II error), but lowers the most costly Type I error rate. The value of y is as follows:

$$y = -4.840 + .920 \text{ (DRRI)} + .528 \text{ (GMI)} + .404 \text{ (AQI)} + .892 \text{ (SGI)} + .115 \text{ (DEPI)} - .172 \text{ (SAI)} - .327 \text{ (LVGI)} + 4.670 \text{ (TATA)}$$

The coefficient on SAI is negative, suggesting that a lower selling and administrative expense to sales percentage in the current year relative to the preceding year increases the likelihood that the firm engaged in earnings manipulation to boost earnings. The coefficient on the leverage variable is also negative. A decrease in the proportion of debt in the capital structure may suggest decreased ability to obtain funds from borrowing and the need to engage in earnings manipulation to portray a healthier firm. The coefficients on the SAI or the LVGI variables were not statistically significant. As indicated earlier in the discussion of the coefficients in Ohlson's bankruptcy prediction model, one cannot interpret the sign or statistical significance of a coefficient in a multivariate model independent of the other variables in the model.

APPLICATION OF BENEISH'S MODEL TO SUNBEAM CORPORATION

We illustrate the application of Beneish's probit model to the financial statements of Sunbeam Corporation (Sunbeam). Sunbeam manufactures countertop kitchen appliances and barbeque grills. Its sales growth and profitability slowed considerably in the mid-1990s and the firm experienced market price declines for its common stock. The firm hired Al Dunlap in mid-1996 as CEO. Known as "Chainsaw Al," he had developed a reputation for dispassionately cutting costs and strategically redirecting troubled companies. Mr. Dunlap laid off one-half of the work force, closed or consolidated more than one-half of Sunbeam's factories, and divested several businesses in 1996 and 1997. He also announced major growth initiatives centering on new products and corporate acquisitions.

The reported results for 1997 showed significant improvement over 1996. Sales increased 18.7 percent while gross margin increased to 28.3 percent from 8.5 percent. The stock price more than doubled between the announcement of Dunlap's hiring in mid-1996 and the end of 1997.

The turnaround appeared to proceed according to plan until the firm announced earnings for the first quarter of 1998, seven quarters into the turnaround effort. To the surprise of analysts and the stock market, Sunbeam reported a net loss for the quarter. Close scrutiny by analysts and the media suggested that Sunbeam might have manipulated earnings in 1997. The SEC instituted a formal investigation into this possibility in mid-1997. Sunbeam responded in October 1997 by restating its financial statements from the fourth quarter of 1996 to the first quarter of 1998. The restatements revealed that Sunbeam had engaged in various actions that boosted earnings for 1997. The actions included:

1. Sunbeam instituted "early buy" and "bill and hold" programs in 1997 to encourage retailers to make purchases during the last few months of 1997. Sunbeam did not adequately provide for returns and cancelled transactions, resulting in an overstatement of sales and net income for 1997.
2. Overstated a restructuring charge in the fourth quarter of 1996 for expenses that should have appeared in the income statement for 1997.
3. Understated bad debt expense for 1997.

Exhibit 5.9 shows the application of Beneish's earnings manipulation model to the originally reported and the restated financial statement amounts for 1996 and 1997.[35]

Selecting the cut-off probability that signals earnings manipulation involves tradeoffs between Type I and Type II errors, in a similar manner as with Ohlson's bankruptcy discussed earlier. A Type I error involves failing to identify a firm as an income manipulator when it turns out to be one. A Type II error involves identifying a firm as an income manipulator when it turns out not to be one. The Type I error is more costly to the investor than a Type II error. The cut-off probability depends on the analyst's view of the relative cost of the Type I error compared to a Type II error. That is, how much more costly is failing to classify an actual earnings manipulator as a nonmanipulator than classifying an actual nonmanipulator as a manipulator. A Type I error can result in an investor losing all of the investment in a firm when the

---

[35]The web site for this book contains an Excel spreadsheet, called Beneish's Manipulation Index, for use in calculating the probability of earnings manipulation using Beneish's probit model. This spreadsheet is adapted from one prepared by Professor Christine I. Wiedman (see footnote 33).

EXHIBIT 5.9				
Application of Beneish's Earnings Manipulation Model to Sunbeam Corporation				
	Originally Reported		**Restated**	
Value of Variable before Applying Coefficient	**1996**	**1997**	**1996**	**1997**
Days in Receivables Index...............	1.020	1.167	1.020	.982
Gross Margin Index	2.403	.300	2.303	.393
Asset Quality Index...................	.912	.928	.912	.919
Sales Growth Index...................	.968	1.187	.968	1.090
Depreciation Index...................	.752	1.284	.752	1.290
Selling and Administrative Expense Index...........	1.608	.516	1.665	.632
Leverage Index	1.457	.795	1.457	.917
Total Accruals/Total Assets	−.196	.117	−.208	.055
Beneish's Manipulation y Value	−2.983	−1.827	−3.101	−2.388
Probability of Manipulation...................	.143%	3.386%	.096%	.848%

Note: The amounts in this table are rounded to three decimal places.

manipulation comes to light. Misclassifying an actual nonmanipulator results in the investor losing the return that might have been earned on that investment. The investor, however, presumably invested the funds in another firm. Thus, as with bankruptcy prediction, the Type I error is more costly. If a particular investment makes up a small proportion of an investor's diversified portfolio of investments, then a Type I error is less costly than if the investment comprises a more significant proportion of a less diversified portfolio of investments. The cut-off probabilities for various relative mixtures of Type I and Type II error costs are:

Cost of Type I Error Relative to Type II Error	Cut-off Probability
10:1	6.85%
20:1	3.76%
30:1	3.76%
40:1 or higher	2.94%

Exhibit 5.9 indicates that the probability of manipulation for Sunbeam for 1996 is .143% based on its originally reported amounts. This probability level falls below the cut-off probabilities listed above for all mixtures of Type I and Type II errors and therefore does not suggest earnings manipulation. On the other hand, the probability for 1997 of 3.386% (see Exhibit 5.9) suggests manipulation for Type I error costs 40 times or more higher than Type II error costs. An examination of changes in the

individual variables between 1996 and 1997 signals the nature of the manipulation that might have occurred. Total accruals to total assets increased significantly. Sunbeam reported a significant increase in income from continuing operations from a net loss of $196.7 million in 1996 to a net profit of $123.1 million 1997, but cash flow from operations turned from $13.3 million in 1996 to a negative $8.2 million in 1997. Buildups of accounts receivable and inventories are the major reasons for the negative cash flow from operations in 1997. The days receivable index increased between these two years, consistent with the buildup of receivables related to the early buy and bill and hold programs. The sales growth index also increased, consistent with the aggressive recognition of revenues. The depreciation index variable increased between the two years, but there is no obvious explanation from the firm's financial statements and notes to suggest manipulation. The gross margin improved significantly between the two years, moderating the increased probability of earnings manipulation. This improvement is misleading, however, because of failure to provide adequately for returns and cancelled transactions.

Exhibit 5.9 indicates that the probabilities of manipulation based on the restated data are below the cut-off points for both 1996 and 1997. The most important difference between the reported and restated probabilities arises for 1997. The downward restatement of income from continuing operations results in fewer accruals, moderating the influence of this variable on the manipulation index. It is interesting to note that the model would not indicate that Sunbeam was an income manipulator if it had reported accurately to begin with (that is, reported the restated data). Initially reporting the restated data, however, would likely have decreased Sunbeam's stock price, which Dunlap tried to avoid.

SUMMARY OF INCOME MANIPULATION RISK

The recent revelations of corporate reporting abuses add to the importance of assessing if firms have intentionally manipulated earnings. Academic research on earnings manipulation is at a relatively early stage of development. The data in the studies discussed above deal with reporting violations prior to the mid-1990s. The business environment since that time has changed dramatically, particularly for technology-based companies. One might expect additional research in this area in coming years.

SUMMARY

An effective analysis of risk requires the analyst to consider a wide range of factors (government regulatory status, technological change, management's health, competitors' actions). This chapter examines those dimensions of risk that have financial consequences and impact the financial statements.

This chapter examined the analysis of financial risk along three dimensions.

1. With Respect to Time Frame: First, we examined the analysis of a firm's ability to pay liabilities coming due within the next year (short-term liquidity risk analysis) and its ability to pay liabilities coming due over a longer term

(long-term solvency risk analysis). The financial ratios examined a firm's need for cash and other liquid resources relative to amounts coming due within various time frames.

2. **With Respect to the Degree of Financial Distress:** We emphasized the need to consider risk as falling along a continuum from low risk to high risk of financial distress. Most credit analysis occurs on the low- to medium-risk side of this continuum. Most bankruptcy risk analysis occurs on the medium- to high-risk side of this continuum.

3. **With Respect to Covariability of Returns with Other Securities in the Market.** We introduced the use of market equity beta as an indicator of systematic risk with the market, a topic discussed more fully in Chapters 11 to 13.

Analysts and academic researchers refer to the first two dimensions of risk as non-systematic, or firm-specific, risk. They refer to the third dimension of risk as systematic risk. Common factors come into play in all three settings for risk analysis. Fixed costs related either to operations or to financing constrain the flexibility of a firm to adapt to changing economic, business, and firm-specific conditions. The profitability and cash-generating ability of a firm permit it to operate within its constraints or to change the constraints in some desirable direction. If the constraints are too high or the capabilities to adapt are too low, then a firm faces the risk of financial distress.

This chapter also explored recent efforts to model earnings manipulation risk and to identify firms most likely to have measured earnings outside the bounds of GAAP. Chapter 6 explores a related element of risk, the risk of managing earnings within the bounds of GAAP.

PROBLEMS AND CASES

5.1 CALCULATING AND INTERPRETING RISK RATIOS.   Refer to the financial statement data for Hasbro in problem 4.9 in Chapter 4. Exhibit 5.10 presents risk ratios for Hasbro for Year 9 and Year 10.

Required

a. Calculate the amounts of these ratios for Year 11.
b. Assess the changes in the short-term liquidity risk of Hasbro between Year 9 and Year 11 and the level of that risk at the end of Year 11.
c. Assess the changes in the long-term solvency risk of Hasbro between Year 9 and Year 11 and the level of that risk at the end of Year 11.

5.2 CALCULATING AND INTERPRETING RISK RATIOS.   Refer to the financial statement data for Lands' End in problem 4.10 in Chapter 4. Exhibit 5.11 presents risk ratios for Lands' End for Year 5 and Year 6.

Required

a. Compute the amounts of these ratios for Year 7.

EXHIBIT 5.10

Risk Ratios for Hasbro
(Problem 5.1)

	Year 11	Year 10	Year 9
Current Ratio		1.3	1.0
Quick Ratio.		.7	.7
Operating Cash Flow ÷ Average			
Current Liabilities		9.4%	22.5%
Days Accounts Receivable.		85	88
Days Inventory		83	82
Days Accounts Payable		56	52
Net Days Working Capital		112	118
Long-term Debt Ratio		46.8%	18.3%
Debt-Equity Ratio.		88.0%	22.4%
Liabilities ÷ Total Assets		65.3%	57.9%
Operating Cash Flow ÷ Average			
Total Liabilities.		6.1%	17.5%
Interest Coverage Ratio.		(.03)	5.9

EXHIBIT 5.11

Risk Ratios for Lands' End
(Problem 5.2)

	Year 7	Year 6	Year 5
Current Ratio		1.9	1.9
Quick Ratio.		.2	.1
Operating Cash Flow ÷ Average			
Current Liabilities		38.1%	35.6%
Days Accounts Receivable.		2	1
Days Inventory		103	102
Days Accounts Payable		36	33
Net Days Working Capital		69	70
Long-term Debt Ratio		—	—
Debt-Equity Ratio.		—	—
Liabilities ÷ Total Assets		37.8%	36.5%
Operating Cash Flow ÷ Average			
Total Liabilities.		35.9%	33.6%
Interest Coverage Ratio.		19.4	34.7

b. Assess the changes in the short-term liquidity risk of Lands' End between Year 5 and Year 7 and the level of that risk at the end of Year 7.

c. Assess the changes in the long-term solvency risk of Lands' End between Year 5 and Year 7 and the level of that risk at the end of Year 7.

5.3 INTERPRETING RISK RATIOS.   Refer to the profitability ratios of Coke in problem 4.11 in Chapter 4. Exhibit 5.12 presents risk ratios for Coke for Year 9, Year 10, and Year 11.

Required

a. Assess the changes in the short-term liquidity risk of Coke between Year 9 and Year 11.

b. Assess the changes in the long-term solvency risk of Coke between Year 9 and Year 11.

c. Compare the short-term liquidity ratios of Coke with those of PepsiCo discussed in the chapter. Which firm appears to have more short-term liquidity risk? Explain.

d. Compare the long-term solvency ratios of Coke with those of PepsiCo discussed in the chapter. Which firm appears to have more long-term solvency risk? Explain.

EXHIBIT 5.12			
Risk Ratios for Coke **(Problem 5.3)**			
	Year 11	Year 10	Year 9
Current Ratio	.9	.7	.7
Quick Ratio............................	.5	.4	.4
Operating Cash Flow ÷ Average			
Current Liabilities	46.3%	37.4%	42.0%
Days Accounts Receivable.................	33	33	33
Days Inventory	64	63	60
Days Accounts Payable	126	126	117
Net Days Working Capital	(29)	(30)	(24)
Long-term Debt Ratio	9.7%	8.2%	8.2%
Debt-Equity Ratio......................	10.7%	9.0%	9.0%
Liabilities ÷ Total Assets	49.3%	55.3%	56.0%
Operating Cash Flow ÷ Average			
Total Liabilities......................	36.4%	30.3%	34.0%
Interest Coverage Ratio..................	20.3	11.8	14.7

5.4 INTERPRETING RISK RATIOS.   Refer to the profitability ratios of Sun Microsystems (Sun) in problem 4.12 in Chapter 4. Exhibit 5.13 presents risk ratios for Sun for Year 10, Year 11, and Year 12.

Required

a. Assess the changes in the short-term liquidity risk of Sun during the three-year period and the level of that risk at the end of Year 12.
b. Assess the changes in the long-term solvency risk of Sun during the three-year period and the level of that risk at the end of Year 12.

5.5 COMPUTING AND INTERPRETING BANKRUPTCY PREDICTION RATIOS.   Payless Cashways operates a chain of retail stores that offers home improvement products for professional craftsmen (carpenters, plumbers, painters) as well as do-it-yourself homeowners. The firm filed for Chapter 11 bankruptcy protection on July 21, Year 7. Exhibit 5.14 presents selected financial data for Payless Cashways for each of the four fiscal years ending November 30, Year 3, Year 4, Year 5, and Year 6 that preceded its bankruptcy filing.

Required

a. Compute the value of each the following risk ratios for Year 4, Year 5, and Year 6.
   (1) Current Ratio (at year end).

EXHIBIT 5.13			
Risk Ratios for Sun Microsystems **(Problem 5.4)**			
	Year 12	Year 11	Year 10
Current Ratio	1.5	1.5	1.5
Quick Ratio.	1.1	.9	1.1
Operating Cash Flow ÷ Average			
Current Liabilities	17.2%	43.1%	96.6%
Days Accounts Receivable.	83	56	58
Days Inventory	39	29	21
Days Accounts Payable	54	34	39
Net Days Working Capital	68	51	40
Long-term Debt Ratio	21.0%	21.2%	24.3%
Debt-Equity Ratio.	26.6%	27.0%	32.0%
Liabilities ÷ Total Assets	44.6%	45.2%	50.5%
Operating Cash Flow ÷ Average			
Total Liabilities.	10.6%	25.8%	64.8%
Interest Coverage Ratio.	(8.2)	16.8	34.0

EXHIBIT 5.14

Financial Data for Payless Cashways
(amounts in thousands)
(Problem 5.5)

Year Ended November:	Year 6	Year 5	Year 4	Year 3
Sales	$2,642,829	$2,680,186	$2,722,539	$2,601,003
Net Income (Loss) Before				
Interest and Taxes	$ 10,458	$ (60,562)	$ 161,792	$ 151,086
Interest Expense	$ 60,488	$ 61,067	$ 65,571	$ 125,247
Net Income (Loss)	$ (19,078)	$ (128,549)	$ 44,889	$ (36,159)
Current Assets	$ 450,497	$ 442,679	$ 449,870	$ 427,702
Total Assets..................	$1,293,118	$1,344,436	$1,495,882	$1,458,481
Current Liabilities	$ 319,593	$ 344,279	$ 310,742	$ 345,560
Long-term Debt	$ 618,667	$ 608,627	$ 654,131	$ 640,127
Total Liabilities................	$1,003,387	$1,036,273	$1,060,017	$1,071,170
Retained Earnings (Deficit)	$ (238,997)	$ (219,919)	$ (91,370)	$ (136,259)
Working Capital Provided by				
Operations.................	$ 95,400	$ 78,257	$ 127,335	$ 96,411
Cash Flow Provided by				
Operations.................	$ 32,447	$ 108,428	$ 117,330	$ 109,027
Capital Expenditures	$ 40,117	$ 67,281	$ 81,906	$ 49,982
Common Shares Outstanding	39,959	39,914	39,874	39,537
Market Price per Share...........	$ 1.125	$ 3.625	$ 8.25	$ 11.00
Applicable GNP Implicit Price				
Deflation for Ohlson Model	207.5	202.7	197.7	192.7

(2) Cash Flow from Operations to Average Current Liabilities.
(3) Debt-Equity Ratio (at year end).
(4) Total Liabilities to Total Assets Ratio (at year end).
(5) Cash Flow from Operations to Average Total Liabilities.
(6) Interest Coverage Ratio.

b. Compute the value of Altman's Z-score for Payless Cashways for Year 3, Year 4, Year 5, and Year 6.

c. Compute the value of Ohlson's probability of bankruptcy for Payless Cashways for Year 3, Year 4, Year 5, and Year 6. The firm generated a net loss of $15,902,000 in Year 2.

d. Using the analyses in parts a, b, and c above, discuss the most important factors that signal the bankruptcy of Payless Cashways in Year 7.

5.6 APPLYING AND INTERPRETING BANKRUPTCY PREDICTION MODELS.

Exhibit 5.15 presents selected financial data for Harvard Industries and Marvel Entertainment for fiscal Year 5 and Year 6. Harvard Industries manufactures automobile components that it sells to automobile manufacturers. Competitive conditions in the automobile industry in recent years have led automobile manufacturers to put pressure on suppliers like Harvard Industries to reduce costs and selling prices. Marvel Entertainment creates and sells comic books, trading cards, and other youth entertainment products, and licenses others to use fictional characters created by Marvel Entertainment in their products. Youth readership of comic books and interest in trading cards have been in steady decline in recent years. Marvel Entertainment recognized a significant asset impairment charge in fiscal Year 6.

Required

a. Compute Altman's Z-score for Harvard Industries and Marvel Entertainment for fiscal Year 5 and Year 6.
b. Compute Ohlson's probability of bankruptcy for Harvard Industries and Marvel Entertainment for fiscal Year 5 and Year 6.
c. How did the bankruptcy risk of Harvard Industries change between fiscal Year 5 and Year 6? Explain.
d. How did the bankruptcy risk of Marvel Entertainment change between Year 5 and Year 6? Explain.

EXHIBIT 5.15

Financial Data for Harvard Industries and Marvel Entertainment
(amounts in thousands)
(Problem 5.6)

	Harvard Industries		Marvel Entertainment	
	Year 6	Year 5	Year 6	Year 5
Sales..........................	$ 824,835	$ 631,832	$ 745,400	$ 828,900
Net Income (Loss) Before Interest and Taxes	$ (11,012)	$ 40,258	$(370,200)	$ 25,100
Net Income (Loss) Current Year......	$ (68,712)	$ 6,921	$(464,400)	$ (48,400)
Net Income (Loss) Previous Year	$ 6,921	$ 7,630	$ (48,400)	$ 61,800
Current Assets....................	$ 156,226	$ 195,417	$ 399,500	$ 490,600
Total Assets	$ 617,705	$ 662,262	$ 844,000	$1,226,310
Current Liabilities.................	$ 163,384	$ 176,000	$ 345,800	$ 318,100
Total Liabilities	$ 648,934	$ 624,817	$ 999,700	$ 948,100
Retained Earnings (Deficit)	$(184,308)	$(115,596)	$(350,300)	$ 114,100
Working Capital Provided (Used) by Operations..................	$ 12,321	$ 55,054	$(116,200)	$ (7,200)
Common Shares Outstanding	7,014	6,995	101,810	101,703
Market Price per Share	$ 85.00	$ 100.50	$ 1.625	$ 10.625
Applicable GNP Implicit Price Deflator Index for Ohlson Model ..	206.3	201.3	207.5	202.7

e. Which firm do you think is more likely to file for bankruptcy during fiscal Year 7? Explain, using the analyses from parts a and b.

5.7 APPLYING AND INTERPRETING BANKRUPTCY PREDICTION MODELS.
Exhibit 5.16 presents selected financial data for Old America Stores and Levitz Furniture for fiscal Year 6 and Year 7. Old America Stores operates a chain of retail stores that sells craft supplies, framing services, artificial flowers and flower arranging services, baskets, and knick-knacks. Levitz Furniture operates a chain of retail stores offering furniture in a warehouse-showroom format. The firm switched to a value pricing strategy beginning in fiscal Year 6.

Required
a. Compute Altman's Z-score for Old America Stores and Levitz Furniture for fiscal Year 6 and Year 7.
b. Compute Ohlson's probability of bankruptcy for Old America Stores and Levitz Furniture for fiscal Year 6 and Year 7.
c. How did the bankruptcy risk of Old America Stores change between fiscal Year 6 and Year 7? Explain.

EXHIBIT 5.16
Financial Data for Old America Stores and Levitz Furniture
(amounts in thousands)
(Problem 5.7)

	Old America Stores Year Ended January		Levitz Furniture Year Ended March	
	Year 7	Year 6	Year 7	Year 6
Sales..............................	$134,605	$117,943	$ 965,855	$ 986,622
Net Income (Loss) Before Interest and Taxes	$ 7,560	$ 7,986	$ 43,859	$ 42,208
Net Income (Loss)—Current Year	$ 3,911	$ 4,154	$ (27,586)	$ (23,753)
Net Income (Loss)—Previous Year......	$ 4,154	$ 2,937	$ (23,753)	$ 2,386
Current Assets.....................	$ 56,753	$ 48,944	$ 222,859	$ 198,046
Total Assets	$ 87,991	$ 76,059	$ 934,368	$ 606,867
Current Liabilities..................	$ 19,002	$ 19,779	$ 271,276	$ 217,915
Total Liabilities	$ 36,150	$ 28,323	$1,028,440	$ 674,539
Retained Earnings (Deficit)	$ 9,537	$ 5,627	$ (305,951)	$(278,365)
Working Capital Provided (Used) by Operations....................	$ 6,603	$ 6,071	$ (3,653)	$ (800)
Common Shares Outstanding	4,515	4,483	30,321	30,321
Market Price Per Share	$ 7.50	$ 8.137	$ 2.125	$ 2.50
Applicable GNP Implicit Price Deflator Index for Ohlson Model	207.5	202.7	209.0	204.3

d. How did the bankruptcy risk of Levitz Furniture change between fiscal Year 6 and Year 7? Explain.

e. Which firm do you think is more likely to file for bankruptcy during fiscal Year 8? Explain, using the analyses from parts a and b.

5.8 APPLYING AND INTERPRETING EARNINGS MANIPULATION MODEL.
Exhibit 5.17 presents selected financial statement data for Enron Corporation for Year 7, Year 8, Year 9, and Year 10. These data reflect amounts from the financial statements as originally reported for each year. In Year 11, Enron restated its financial statements for earlier years because it reported several items beyond the limits of generally accepted accounting principles.

a. Compute the probability that Enron engaged in earnings manipulation for Year 8, Year 9, and Year 10 using Beneish's probit model.

b. Identify the major reasons for the changes in the probability of earnings manipulation during the three-year period.

EXHIBIT 5.17
Financial Statement Data for Enron Corporation
(amounts in millions)
(Problem 5.8)

	Year 10	Year 9	Year 8	Year 7
Accounts Receivable	$ 10,396	$ 3,030	$ 2,060	$ 1,697
Current Assets	30,381	7,255	5,933	4,669
Property, Plant, and Equipment—Net	11,743	10,681	10,657	9,170
Total Assets	65,503	33,381	29,350	23,422
Current Liabilities	28,406	6,759	6,107	4,412
Long-term Debt	8,550	7,151	7,357	6,254
Sales	100,789	40,112	31,260	20,273
Cost of Goods Sold	94,517	34,761	26,381	17,311
Selling and Administrative Expenses	3,184	3,045	2,473	1,406
Income from Continuing Operations	979	1,024	703	105
Cash Flow from Operations	4,779	1,228	1,640	501
Depreciation Expense	485	565	563	480

MASSACHUSETTS STOVE COMPANY—BANK LENDING DECISION

Massachusetts Stove Company manufactures wood-burning stoves for the heating of homes and businesses. The company has approached you as chief lending officer for the Massachusetts Regional Bank seeking to increase its loan from the current level of $93,091 as of January 15, Year 12, to $143,091. Jane O'Neil, Chief Executive Officer and majority stockholder of the company, indicates that the company needs the loan to finance the working capital required for an expected 25 percent annual increase in sales during the next two years, to repay suppliers, and to provide funds for expected nonrecurring legal and retooling costs.

The company's wood stoves have two distinguishing characteristics: (1) the metal frame of the stoves includes inlaid soapstone, which increases the intensity and duration of the heat provided by the stoves and enhances their appearance as an attractive piece of furniture, and (2) a catalytic combuster, which adds heating potential to the stoves and reduces air pollution.

The company manufactures wood-burning stoves in a single plant located in Greenfield, Massachusetts. It purchases metal castings for the stoves from foundries located in Germany and Belgium. The soapstone comes from a supplier in Canada. These purchases are denominated in U.S. dollars. The catalytic combuster is purchased from a supplier in the United States. The manufacturing process is essentially an assembly operation. The plant employs an average of eight workers. The two keys to quality control are structural air tightness and effective operation of the catalytic combuster.

The company rents approximately 60 percent of the 25,000-square-foot building that it uses for manufacturing and administrative activities. This building also houses the company's factory showroom. The remaining 40 percent of the building is not currently rented.

The company's marketing of wood stoves follows three channels:

1. Wholesaling of stoves to retail hardware stores. This channel represents approximately 20 percent of the company's sales in units.
2. Retail direct marketing to individuals in all 50 states. This channel utilizes (a) national advertising in construction and design magazines, and (b) the sending of brochures to potential customers identified from personal inquiries. This channel represents approximately 70 percent of the company's sales in units. The company is the only firm in the industry with a strategic emphasis on retail direct marketing.
3. Retailing from the company's showroom. This channel represents approximately 10 percent of the company's sales in units.

The company offers three payment options to retail purchasers of its stoves:

1. Full Payment: Check, money order, or charge to a third-party credit card.

2. Layaway Plan: Monthly payments over a period not exceeding one year. The company ships the stove after receiving the final payment.
3. Installment Financing Plan: The company has a financing arrangement with a local bank to finance the purchase of stoves by credit-approved customers. The company is liable if customers fail to repay their installment bank loans.

The imposition of strict air emission standards by the Environmental Protection Agency (EPA) has resulted in a major change in the wood stove industry. By December 31, Year 9, firms were required by EPA regulations to demonstrate that their wood stoves met or surpassed specified air emission standards. These standards were not only stricter than industry practices at the time, but firms had to engage in numerous company-sponsored and independent testing of their stoves to satisfy EPA regulators. As a consequence, the number of firms in the wood stove industry decreased from over 200 in the years prior to Year 10 to approximately 35 by December 31, Year 11.

The company received approval for its Soapstone Stove I in Year 11, after incurring retooling and testing costs of $63,001. It capitalized these costs in the Property, Plant, and Equipment account. It depreciates these costs over the five-year EPA approval period. A second stove, Soapstone Stove II, is currently undergoing retooling and testing. The company incurred costs of $19,311 in Year 10 and $8,548 in Year 11 on this stove and has received preliminary EPA approval. It anticipates additional design, tooling, and testing costs of approximately $55,000 in Year 12 and $33,000 in Year 13 in order to obtain final EPA approval.

The company holds an option to purchase the building in which it is located for $608,400. The option also permits the company to assume the unpaid balance on a low interest rate loan on the building from the New England Regional Industrial Development Authority. The interest rate on this loan is adjusted annually and equals 80 percent of the bank prime interest rate. The unpaid balance on the loan exceeds the option price and will result in a cash transfer to the company from the owner of the building at the time of transfer. The company exercised its option in Year 9, but the owner of the building refused to comply with the option provisions. The company sued the owner. The case has gone through the lower court system in Massachusetts and is currently under review at the Massachusetts Supreme Court. The company incurred legal costs totaling $68,465 through Year 11 and anticipates additional costs of approximately $45,000 in Year 12. The lower courts have ruled in favor of the company's position on all of the major issues in the case. The company expects the Massachusetts Supreme Court to concur with the decisions of the lower courts when it renders its final decision in the spring of Year 12. The company has held discussions with two prospective tenants for the 10,000 square feet of the building that it does not use in its operations.

Jane O'Neil owns 51 percent of the company's common stock. The remaining stockholders include John O'Neil (Chief Financial Officer and father of Jane O'Neil), Mark Forest (Vice President for Manufacturing), and four independent local investors.

To assist in the loan decision, the company provides you with financial statements (see the first three columns of Exhibits 5.18 to 5.20) and notes for the three years ending December 31, Year 9, Year 10, and Year 11. These financial statements were prepared by John O'Neil, Chief Financial Officer, and are not audited. The company also provides you with pro forma financial statements for Year 12 and Year 13 (see the last two columns of Exhibits 5.18 to 5.20) to demonstrate both its need for the loan and its ability to repay. The loan requested involves an increase in the current loan amount from $93,091 to $143,091. The company will pay interest monthly and repay the $50,000 additional amount borrowed by December 31, Year 13. Exhibit 5.21 presents financial statement ratios for the company.

The assumptions underlying the pro forma financial statements are as follows:

Sales: Projected to increase 25 percent annually during the next two years, after increasing 17.7 percent in Year 10 and 21.9 percent Year 11. The increase reflects continuing market opportunities related to the company's strategic emphasis on retail direct marketing and to the expected continuing contraction in the number of competitors in the industry.

Cost of Goods Sold: Most manufacturing costs vary with sales. The company projects cost of goods sold to equal 51 percent of sales in Year 12 and 49 percent of sales in Year 13, having declined from 69.2 percent of sales in Year 9 to 53.9 percent of sales in Year 11. The reductions resulted from a higher proportion of retail sales in the sales mix (which have a higher gross margin than wholesale sales), a more favorable pricing environment in the industry (fewer competitors), switching to lower-cost suppliers, and more efficient production.

Selling and Administrative Expenses: The company projects these costs to equal 41 percent of sales, having increased from 26.7 percent of sales in Year 9 to 40.9 percent of sales in Year 11. The increases resulted from a heavier emphasis on retail sales, which require more aggressive marketing than wholesale sales.

Legal Expenses: The additional $45,000 of legal costs represents the best estimate by the company's attorneys.

EXHIBIT 5.18

Massachusetts Stove Company
Income Statements
(Case 5.1)

	Actual			Pro Forma	
	Year 9	Year 10	Year 11	Year 12	Year 13
Sales	$665,771	$783,754	$955,629	$1,194,535	$1,493,170
Cost of Goods Sold	(460,797)	(474,156)	(514,907)	(609,213)	(731,653)
Selling and Administrative............	(177,631)	(290,719)	(390,503)	(489,760)	(612,200)
Legal (Note 1)	(28,577)	(30,092)	(9,796)	(45,000)	—
Interest...........................	(25,948)	(24,122)	(23,974)	(26,510)	(26,510)
Income Tax (Note 2)	—	—	—	—	—
Net Income (Loss)...................	$(27,182)	$(35,335)	$ 16,449	$ 24,052	$ 122,807

		EXHIBIT 5.19				

Massachusetts Stove Company
Balance Sheets
(Case 5.1)

	Actual				Pro Forma	
December 31:	Year 8	Year 9	Year 10	Year 11	Year 12	Year 13
Assets						
Cash........................	$ 3,925	$ 11,707	$ 8,344	$ 37,726	$ 11,289	$ 6,512
Accounts Receivable............	94,606	54,772	44,397	31,964	40,035	49,964
Inventories...................	239,458	208,260	209,004	225,490	291,924	329,480
Total Current Assets.........	$ 337,989	$ 274,739	$ 261,745	$ 295,180	$ 343,248	$385,956
Property, Plant, and Equipment (at Cost).................	$ 258,870	$ 316,854	$ 362,399	$ 377,784	$ 440,284	$487,784
Accumulated Depreciation	(205,338)	(228,985)	(250,189)	(274,347)	(302,502)	(333,694)
Property, Plant, and Equipment (Net)....................	$ 53,532	$ 87,869	$ 112,210	$ 103,437	$ 137,782	$154,090
Other Assets..................	$ 17,888	$ 17,888	$ 17,594	$ 17,006	$ 17,006	$ 17,006
Total Assets..............	$ 409,409	$ 380,496	$ 391,549	$ 415,623	$ 498,036	$557,052
Liabilities and Shareholders' Equity						
Accounts Payable..............	$ 148,579	$ 139,879	$ 189,889	$ 160,905	$ 198,206	$176,915
Notes Payable—Banks (Note 3) ..	152,985	140,854	125,256	93,091	143,091	93,091
Other Current Liabilities (Note 4)	13,340	11,440	23,466	62,440	33,500	41,000
Total Current Liabilities......	$ 314,904	$ 292,173	$ 338,611	$ 316,436	$ 374,797	$311,006
Long-term Debt (Note 3)	248,000	269,000	268,950	298,750	298,750	298,750
Total Liabilities............	$ 562,904	$ 561,173	$ 607,561	$ 615,186	$ 673,547	$609,756
Common Stock	$ 2,000	$ 2,000	$ 2,000	$ 2,000	$ 2,000	$ 2,000
Additional Paid-in Capital	435,630	435,630	435,630	435,630	435,630	435,630
Accumulated Deficit	(591,125)	(618,307)	(653,642)	(637,193)	(613,141)	(490,334)
Total Shareholders' Equity	$(153,495)	$(180,677)	$(216,012)	$(199,563)	$(175,511)	$ (52,704)
Total Liabilities and Shareholders' Equity.......	$ 409,409	$ 380,496	$ 391,549	$ 415,623	$ 498,036	$557,052

Interest Expense: Interest expense has averaged approximately 6 percent of short- and long-term borrowing during the last three years. The pro forma income statement assumes a continuation of the 6 percent average rate.

Income Tax Expense: The company has elected to be taxed as a Subchapter S corporation, which means that the net income of the firm is taxed at the level of the individual shareholders and not at the corporate level. Thus, the pro forma financial statements include no income tax expense. The firm has operated at a net loss for tax purposes for several years prior to Year 11, primarily because of losses of a lawn

EXHIBIT 5.20

Massachusetts Stove Company
Statements of Cash Flows
(Case 5.1)

	Actual			Pro Forma	
	Year 9	Year 10	Year 11	Year 12	Year 13
Operations					
Net Income (Loss).........................	$(27,182)	$(35,335)	$ 16,449	$ 24,052	$122,807
Depreciation and Amortization	23,647	21,204	24,158	28,155	31,192
(Increase) Decrease in Accounts Receivable.....	39,834	10,375	12,433	(8,071)	(9,929)
(Increase) Decrease in Inventories	31,198	(744)	(16,486)	(66,434)	(37,556)
Increase (Decrease) in Accounts Payable	(8,700)	50,010	(28,984)	37,301	(21,291)
Increase (Decrease) in Other Current Liabilities	(1,900)	12,026	38,974	(28,940)	7,500
Cash Flow from Operations	$ 56,897	$ 57,536	$ 46,544	$(13,937)	$ 92,723
Investing					
Fixed Assets Acquired	$(57,984)	$(45,545)	$(15,385)	$(62,500)	$(47,500)
Other Investing	—	294	588	—	—
Cash Flow from Investing..................	$(57,984)	$(45,251)	$(14,797)	$(62,500)	$(47,500)
Financing					
Increase (Decrease) in Short-term Borrowing.............................	$(12,131)	$(15,598)	$(32,165)	$ 50,000	$(50,000)
Increase (Decrease) in Long-term Borrowing.............................	21,000	(50)	29,800	—	—
Cash Flow from Financing	$ 8,869	$(15,648)	$ (2,365)	$ 50,000	$(50,000)
Change in Cash	$ 7,782	$ (3,363)	$ 29,382	$(26,437)	$ (4,777)
Cash—Beginning of Year	3,925	11,707	8,344	37,726	11,289
Cash—End of Year	$ 11,707	$ 8,344	$ 37,726	$ 11,289	$ 6,512

products business that it acquired ten years ago. The company discontinued the lawn products business in Year 10.

Cash: The pro forma amounts for cash represent a plug to equate projected assets with projected liabilities and shareholders' equity. Projected liabilities include the requested loan during Year 12 and its repayment at the end of Year 13.

Accounts Receivable: Days accounts receivable outstanding, calculated on the average accounts receivable balances, will be 11 days in Year 12 and Year 13.

Inventories: Days inventory held, calculated on the average inventory balances, will be 155 days in Year 12 and Year 13.

Property, Plant, and Equipment: Capital expenditures for Year 12 include a $55,000 cost for retooling the Soapstone Stove II and $7,500 for other equipment, and for

EXHIBIT 5.21

Massachusetts Stove Company
Profitability and Risk Ratios
(Case 5.1)

	Actual			Pro Forma	
	Year 9	Year 10	Year 11	Year 12	Year 13
Profit Margin for ROA	(.2)%	(1.4)%	4.2%	4.2%	10.0%
Assets Turnover	1.7	2.0	2.4	2.6	2.8
Return on Assets	(.3)%	(2.9)%	10.0%	11.1%	28.3%
Cost of Goods Sold ÷ Sales.	69.2%	60.5%	53.9%	51.0%	49.0%
Selling and Administrative ÷ Sales	26.7%	37.1%	40.9%	41.0%	41.0%
Legal Expense ÷ Sales	4.3%	3.8%	1.0%	3.8%	—
Interest Expense ÷ Sales	3.9%	3.1%	2.5%	2.2%	1.8%
Days Accounts Receivable	41	23	15	11	11
Days Inventory	177	161	154	155	155
Days Accounts Payable	122	127	122	96	89
Fixed Asset Turnover.	9.4	7.8	8.9	9.9	10.2
Current Ratio.	.9	.8	.9	.9	1.2
Quick Ratio	.2	.2	.2	.1	.2
Cash Flow from Operations ÷					
Average Current Liabilities.	18.7%	18.2%	14.2%	(4.0%)	27.0%
Total Liabilities ÷ Total Assets.	147.5%	155.2%	148.0%	135.2%	109.5%
Long-term Debt ÷ Total Assets.	70.7%	68.7%	71.9%	60.0%	53.6%
Cash Flow from Operations ÷					
Average Total Liabilities	10.1%	9.8%	7.6%	(2.2%)	14.5%
Interest Coverage Ratio.	.0	(.5)	1.7	1.9	5.6

Year 13 include $33,000 for retooling the Soapstone Stove II and $14,500 for other equipment. The pro formas exclude the cost of acquiring the building, its related debt, the cash to be received at the time of transfer, and rental revenues from leasing the unused 40 percent of the building to other businesses.

Accumulated Depreciation: Continuation of the historical relation between depreciation expense and the cost of property, plant, and equipment.

Other Assets: A new financial reporting standard no longer requires amortization of intangibles after Year 11.

Accounts Payable: Days accounts payable outstanding, based on the average accounts payable balances, will be 97 days in Year 12 and 89 days in Year 13. The decrease in days payable reflects the ability to pay suppliers more quickly with the proceeds of the increased bank loan.

Notes Payable: Projected to increase in the amount of the bank loan in Year 12 and to decrease by the loan repayment at the end of Year 13.

Other Current Liabilities: The large increase at the end of Year 11 resulted from a major promotional offer in the fall of Year 11, which increased the amount of deposits by customers. The projected amounts for Year 12 and Year 13 represent more normal expected levels of deposits.

Long-term Debt: Long-term borrowing represents loans from shareholders to the company. The company does not plan to repay any of these loans in the near future.

Retained Earnings: The change each year represents net income or net loss from operations. The company does not pay dividends.

Statement of Cash Flows: Amounts are taken from the changes in various accounts on the actual and pro forma balance sheets.

NOTES TO FINANCIAL STATEMENTS

Note 1: The company has incurred legal costs to enforce its option to purchase the building used in its manufacturing and administrative activities. The case is under review at the Massachusetts Supreme Court, with a decision expected in the spring of Year 12.

Note 2: The company is not subject to income tax because it has elected Subchapter S tax status.

Note 3: The notes payable to banks are secured by machinery and equipment, shares of common stock of companies traded on the New York Stock Exchange owned by two shareholders, and by personal guarantees of three of the shareholders. The long-term debt consists of unsecured loans from three shareholders.

Note 4: Other current liabilities include the following:

	Year 8	Year 9	Year 10	Year 11
Customer Deposits	$11,278	$ 9,132	$20,236	$59,072
Employee Taxes Withheld	2,062	2,308	3,230	3,368
	$13,340	$11,440	$23,466	$62,440

Required (Excel spreadsheet available on-line for this case.)

Would you make the loan to the company in accordance with the stated terms? In responding, consider the reasonableness of the company's projections, positive and negative factors affecting the industry and the company, and the likely ability of the company to repay the loan.

FLY-BY-NIGHT INTERNATIONAL GROUP: CAN THIS COMPANY BE SAVED?

Douglas C. Mather, Founder, Chairman, and Chief Executive of Fly-By-Night International Group (FBN), lived the fast-paced, risk-seeking life that he tried to inject into his company. Flying the company's Learjets, he logged 28 world speed records. Once he throttled a company plane to the top of Mount Everest in $3\frac{1}{2}$ minutes.

These activities seemed perfectly appropriate at the time. Mather was a Navy fighter pilot in Vietnam and then flew commercial airlines. In the mid-1970s, he started FBN as a pilot training school. With the defense buildup beginning in the early 1980s, Mather branched out into government contracting. He equipped the company's Learjets with radar jammers and other sophisticated electronic devices to mimic enemy aircraft. He then contracted his "rent-an-enemy" fleet to the Navy and Air Force for use in fighter pilot training. The Pentagon liked the idea and FBN's revenues grew to $55 million in the fiscal year ending April 30, Year 14. Its common stock, issued to the public in Year 9 at $8.50 a share, reached a high of $16.50 in mid-Year 13. Mather and FBN received glowing write-ups in *Business Week* and *Fortune*.

In mid-Year 14, however, FBN began a rapid descent. Although still growing rapidly, its cash flow was inadequate to service its debt. According to Mather, he was "just dumbfounded. There was never an inkling of a problem with cash."

In the fall of Year 14, the Board of Directors withdrew the company's financial statements for the year ending April 30, Year 14, stating that there appeared to be material misstatements that needed investigation. In December of Year 14, Mather was asked to step aside as manager and director of the company pending completion of an investigation of certain transactions between Mather and the company. On December 29, Year 14, NASDAQ (over-the-counter stock market) discontinued quoting the company's common shares. In February, Year 15, the Board of Directors, following its investigation, terminated Mather's employment and membership on the Board.

Exhibits 5.22 to 5.24 present the financial statements and related notes of FBN for the five years ending April, Year 10, through April, Year 14. The financial statements for Year 10 to Year 12 use the amounts as originally reported for each year. The amounts reported on the statement of cash flows for Year 10 (for example, the change in accounts receivable) do not precisely reconcile to the amounts on the balance sheet at the beginning and end of the year because certain items classified as relating to continuing operations on the balance sheet at the end of Year 9 were reclassified as relating to discontinued operations on the balance sheet at the end of Year 10. The financial statements for Year 13 and Year 14 represent the restated financial statements for those years after the Board of Directors completed its investigation of suspected material misstatements that caused it to withdraw the originally issued financial statements for fiscal Year 14. Exhibit 5.25 lists the members of the Board of Directors. Exhibit 5.26 presents profitability and risk ratios for FBN.

EXHIBIT 5.22

Fly-By-Night International Group
Comparative Balance Sheets
(amounts in thousands)
(Case 5.2)

April 30:	Year 14	Year 13	Year 12	Year 11	Year 10	Year 9
Assets						
Cash	$ 159	$ 583	$ 313	$ 142	$ 753	$ 192
Notes Receivable.	—	—	—	1,000	—	—
Accounts Receivable.	6,545	4,874	2,675	1,490	1,083	2,036
Inventories	5,106	2,514	1,552	602	642	686
Prepayments.	665	829	469	57	303	387
Net Assets of Discontinued						
Businesses	—	—	—	—	1,926	—
Total Current Assets.	$ 12,475	$ 8,800	$ 5,009	$ 3,291	$ 4,707	$ 3,301
Property, Plant, and Equipment	$106,529	$76,975	$24,039	$17,809	$37,250	$17,471
Less Accumulated Depreciation.	(17,231)	(8,843)	(5,713)	(4,288)	(4,462)	(2,593)
Net	$ 89,298	$68,132	$18,326	$13,521	$32,788	$14,878
Other Assets	$ 470	$ 665	$ 641	$ 1,112	$ 1,566	$ 1,278
Total Assets.	$102,243	$77,597	$23,976	$17,924	$39,061	$19,457
Liabilities and Shareholders' Equity						
Accounts Payable	$ 12,428	$ 6,279	$ 993	$ 939	$ 2,285	$ 1,436
Notes Payable	—	945	140	1,021	4,766	—
Current Portion of Long-term Debt . . .	60,590	7,018	1,789	1,104	2,774	1,239
Other Current Liabilities..	12,903	12,124	2,423	1,310	1,845	435
Total Current Liabilities.	$ 85,921	$26,366	$ 5,345	$ 4,374	$11,670	$ 3,110
Long-term Debt	—	41,021	9,804	6,738	20,041	9,060
Deferred Income Taxes	—	900	803	—	1,322	1,412
Other Noncurrent Liabilities	—	—	226	—	248	—
Total Liabilities.	$ 85,921	$68,287	$16,178	$11,112	$33,281	$13,582
Common Stock	$ 34	$ 22	$ 21	$ 20	$ 20	$ 20
Additional Paid-in Capital.	16,516	5,685	4,569	4,323	3,611	3,611
Retained Earnings	(29)	3,802	3,208	2,469	2,149	2,244
Treasury Stock	(199)	(199)	—	—	—	—
Total Shareholders' Equity	$ 16,322	$ 9,310	$ 7,798	$ 6,812	$ 5,780	$ 5,875
Total Liabilities and Shareholders'						
Equity	$102,243	$77,597	$23,976	$17,924	$39,061	$19,457

		EXHIBIT 5.23			

Fly-By-Night International Group
Comparative Income Statements
For the Year Ended April 30
(amounts in thousands)
(Case 5.2)

	Year 14	Year 13	Year 12	Year 11	Year 10
Continuing Operations					
Sales................................	$54,988	$36,597	$20,758	$19,266	$31,992
Expenses					
Cost of Services........................	$38,187	$26,444	$12,544	$ 9,087	$22,003
Selling and Administrative	5,880	3,020	3,467	2,989	4,236
Depreciation	9,810	3,150	1,703	2,798	3,003
Interest...............................	5,841	3,058	1,101	2,743	2,600
Income Taxes..........................	(900)	379	803	671	74
Total Expenses........................	$58,818	$36,051	$19,618	$18,288	$31,916
Income—Continuing Operations	$(3,830)	$ 546	$ 1,140	$ 978	$ 76
Income—Discontinued Operations........	—	47	(400)	(659)	(171)
Net Income	$(3,830)	$ 593	$ 740	$ 319	$ (95)

Required

You are asked to study these financial statements and notes and respond to the following questions:

a. What evidence can you observe from analyzing the financial statements that might signal the cash flow problems experienced in mid-Year 14?

b. Can FBN avoid bankruptcy during Year 15? What changes in either the design or implementation of FBN's strategy would you recommend? To compute Altman's Z-score, use the low bid market price for the year to determine the market value of common shareholders' equity. To compute Ohlson's probability of bankruptcy, use the following values for the GNP Implicit Price Deflator: Year 11: 148.29; Year 12: 152.45; Year 13, 156.81; Year 14, 161.74. Note that the case does not provide sufficient information to compute the probability of bankruptcy for Year 10.

NOTES TO FINANCIAL STATEMENTS

1. Summary of Significant Accounting Policies

Consolidation The consolidated financial statements include the accounts of the company and its wholly owned subsidiaries. The company uses the equity method for subsidiaries not majority owned (50 percent or less) and eliminates significant intercompany transactions and balances.

EXHIBIT 5.24

Fly-By-Night International Group
Comparative Statements of Cash Flows
For the Year Ended April 30
(amounts in thousands)
(Case 5.2)

	Year 14	Year 13	Year 12	Year 11	Year 10
Operations					
Income—Continuing Operations	$ (3,830)	$ 546	$ 1,140	$ 978	$ 76
Depreciation	9,810	3,150	1,703	2,798	3,003
Other Adjustments	1,074	1,817	1,119	671	74
Working Capital from Operations	$ 7,054	$ 5,513	$ 3,962	$ 4,447	$ 3,153
Changes in Working Capital:					
(Inc.) Dec. in Receivables	(1,671)	(2,199)	(1,185)	(407)	403
(Inc.) Dec. in Inventories	(2,592)	(962)	(950)	40	19
(Inc.) Dec. in Prepayments.............	164	(360)	(412)	246	36
Inc. (Dec.) in Accounts Payable	6,149	5,286	54	(1,346)	359
Inc. (Dec.) in Other Current Liabilities	779	9,701	1,113	(535)	596
Cash Flow from Continuing Operations	$ 9,883	$ 16,979	$ 2,582	$ 2,445	$ 4,566
Cash Flow from Discontinued Operations ..	—	(77)	(472)	(752)	(335)
Net Cash Flow from Operations..........	$ 9,883	$ 16,902	$ 2,110	$ 1,693	$ 4,231
Investing					
Sale of Property, Plant, and Equipment.....	$ 259	$ 3	$ 119	$ 18,387	$ 12
Acquisition of Property,					
Plant, and Equipment	(33,035)	(52,960)	(6,573)	(2,424)	(20,953)
Other.............................	(1,484)	78	1,017	(679)	30
Net Cash Flow from Investing	$(34,260)	$(52,879)	$(5,437)	$ 15,284	$(20,911)
Financing					
Increase in Short-term Borrowing	$ —	$ 805	$ —	$ —	$ 4,766
Increase in Long-term Borrowing	43,279	42,152	5,397	5,869	14,739
Issue of Common Stock	12,266	191	428	—	—
Decrease in Short-term Borrowing	(945)	—	(881)	(3,745)	—
Decrease in Long-term Borrowing........	(30,522)	(7,024)	(1,647)	(19,712)	(2,264)
Acquisition of Common Stock...........	—	(198)	—	—	—
Other.............................	(125)	321	201	—	—
Net Cash Flow from Financing...........	$ 23,953	$ 36,247	$ 3,498	$(17,588)	$ 17,241
Change in Cash......................	$ (424)	$ 270	$ 171	$ (611)	$ 561
Cash, Beginning of Year	583	313	142	753	192
Cash, End of Year	$ (159)	$ 583	$ 313	$ 142	$ 753

EXHIBIT 5.25

Fly-By-Night International Group
Members of the Board of Directors
(Case 5.2)

Charles A. Barry, USAF (Ret.), Executive Vice President of Wicks and Associates, Inc., a management consulting firm

Thomas P. Gilkey, Vice President, Marketing

Lawrence G. Hicks, Secretary and General Counsel

Michael S. Holt, Vice President, Finance, and Chief Financial Officer

Gordon K. John, Executive Vice President and Chief Operating Officer

Douglas C. Mather, Chairman of the Board, President and Chief Executive Officer

Edward F. O'Hara, President of the O'Hara Companies, which manufactures aircraft products

E. William Shapiro, Professor of Law, Emory University

Inventories Inventories, which consist of aircraft fuel, spare parts, and supplies, appear at lower of FIFO cost or market.

Property and Equipment Property and equipment appear at acquisition cost. The company capitalizes major inspections, renewals, and improvements, while it expenses replacements, maintenance, and repairs that do not improve or extend the life of the respective assets. The company computes depreciation of property and equipment using the straight-line method.

Contract Income Recognition Contractual specifications (that is, revenue rates, reimbursement terms, functional considerations) vary among contracts; accordingly, the company recognizes guaranteed contract income (guaranteed revenue less related direct costs) either as it logs flight hours or on a straight-line monthly basis over the contract year, whichever method better reflects the economics of the contract. The company recognizes income from discretionary hours flown in excess of the minimum guaranteed amount each month as it logs such discretionary hours.

Income Taxes The company recognizes deferred income taxes for temporary differences between financial and tax reporting amounts.

2. Transactions with Major Customers

The company provides contract flight services to three major customers: the U.S. Air Force, the U.S. Navy, and the Federal Reserve Bank System. These contracts have termination dates in Year 16 or Year 17. Revenues from all government contracts as a percentage of total revenues were as follows: Year 14, 62 percent; Year 13, 72 percent; Year 12, 73 percent; Year 11, 68 percent; Year 10, 31 percent.

EXHIBIT 5.26

Profitability and Risk Ratios for FBN
(Case 5.2)

	Year 14	Year 13	Year 12	Year 11	Year 10
Profit Margin for ROA.................	(.1)%	6.9%	9.0%	14.5	5.6%
Assets Turnover	.6	.7	1.0	.7	1.1
Return on Assets	0.0%	5.0%	8.9%	9.8%	6.1%
Cost of Goods and Services ÷ Sales	69.4%	72.3%	60.4%	47.2%	68.8%
Selling and Administrative ÷ Sales	10.7%	8.3%	16.7%	15.5%	13.2%
Depreciation Expense ÷ Sales	17.8%	8.6%	8.2%	14.5%	9.4%
Income Tax Expense (excluding					
tax effects of interest) ÷ Sales	2.1%	4.0%	5.7%	8.3%	3.0%
Interest Expense ÷ Sales	10.6%	8.4%	5.3%	14.2%	8.1%
Days Accounts Receivable	38	38	37	24	18
Days Accounts Payable	84	48	26	65	31
Fixed Asset Turnover	.7	.8	1.3	.8	1.3
Profit Margin for ROCE	(7.0)%	1.5%	5.5%	5.1%	.2%
Capital Structure Leverage Ratio..........	7.0	5.9	2.9	4.5	5.0
Rate of Return on Common Equity	(29.9)%	6.4%	15.6%	15.5%	1.3%
Current Ratio........................	.2	.3	.9	.8	.4
Quick Ratio	.1	.2	.6	.6	.2
Cash Flow from Operations ÷ Average					
Current Liabilities...................	17.6%	107.1%	53.1%	30.5%	61.8%
Total Liabilities ÷ Total Assets...........	84.0%	88.0%	67.5%	62.0%	85.2%
Long-term Debt Ratio.................	0.0%	81.5%	55.7%	49.7%	77.6%
Cash Flow from Operations ÷ Average					
Total Liabilities	12.8%	40.2%	18.9%	11.2%	19.5%
Interest Coverage Ratio	.2	1.3	2.8	1.6	1.1

3. Segment Data

During Year 10, the company operated in five business segments as follows:

Flight Operations—Business Provides combat readiness training to the military and nightly transfer of negotiable instruments for the Federal Reserve Bank System, both under multi-year contracts.

Flight Operations—Transport Provides charter transport services to a variety of customers.

Fixed Base Operations Provides ground support operations (fuel, maintenance) to commercial airlines at several major airports.

Education and Training Provides training for non-military pilots.

Aircraft Sales and Leasing Acquires aircraft that the company then either resells or leases to various firms.

The company discontinued the Flight Operations—Transport and Education and Training segments in Year 11. It sold most of the assets of the Aircraft Sales and Leasing segment in Year 11.

Segment revenue, operating profit, and asset data for the various segments appear below (amounts in thousands).

April 30:	Year 14	Year 13	Year 12	Year 11	Year 10
Revenues					
Flight Operations—Business	$ 44,062	$31,297	$16,026	$11,236	$10,803
Flight Operations—Transport	—	—	—	—	13,805
Fixed Base Operations	9,597	4,832	4,651	3,911	3,647
Education and Training	—	—	—	—	542
Aircraft Sales and Leasing.	1,329	468	81	4,119	3,195
Total	$ 54,988	$36,597	$20,758	$19,266	$31,992
Operating Profit					
Flight Operations—Business	$ 5,707	$ 4,863	$ 3,455	$ 2,463	$ 849
Flight Operations—Transport	—	—	—	—	(994)
Fixed Base Operations	(2,041)	1,362	1,038	174	332
Education and Training	—	—	—	—	12
Aircraft Sales and Leasing.	1,175	378	(15)	1,217[b]	2,726[a]
Total	$ 4,841	$ 6,603	$ 4,478	$ 3,854	$ 2,925
Assets					
Flight Operations—Business	$ 85,263	$64,162	$17,738	$11,130	$13,684
Flight Operations—Transport	—	—	—	—	1,771
Fixed Base Operations	16,544	13,209	5,754	5,011	4,784
Education and Training	—	—	—	—	1,789
Aircraft Sales and Leasing.	436	226	438	1,262	18,524
Total	$102,243	$77,597	$23,930	$17,403	$40,552

[a]Includes a gain of $2.6 million on the sale of aircraft.
[b]Includes a gain of $1.2 million on the sale of aircraft.

4. Discontinued Operations

Income from discontinued operations consists of the following (amounts in thousands):

Year 13
Income from Operations of Flight Operations—Transport
($78), net of income taxes of $31. . . . . $ 47

Year 12

Loss from write-off of Airline Operations Certificates in
Flight Operations—Transport Business. . . . . $(400)

Year 11

Loss from Operations of Flight Operations—Transport
($1,261) and Education and Training ($172) Segments,
net of income tax benefits of $685. . . . . $(748)

Gain on Disposal of Education and Training Business, net
of income taxes of $85   89

Total . . . . $(659)

Year 10

Loss from Operations of Charter Tour Business, net of
income tax benefits of $164 . . . . $(171)

5. Relation Party Transactions

On April 30, Year 11, the company sold most of the net assets of the Aircraft Sales and Leasing segment to Interlease, Inc., a Georgia corporation wholly owned by the company's majority stockholder, whose personal holdings represented at that time approximately 75 percent of the company.

Under the terms of the sale, the sales price was $1,368,000, of which the buyer paid $368,000 in cash and gave a promissory note for the remaining $1,000,000. The company treated the proceeds received in excess of the book value of the net assets sold of $712,367 as a capital contribution due to the related party nature of the transaction. FBN originally acquired the assets of the Aircraft Sales and Leasing segment during Year 10.

On September 29, Year 14, the company's Board of Directors established a Transaction Committee to examine certain transactions between the company and Douglas Mather, its Chairman, President, and majority stockholder. These transactions appear below:

Certain Loans to Mather In early September, Year 13, the Board of Directors authorized a $1,000,000 loan to Mather at the company's cost of borrowing plus 1/8 percent. On September 19, Year 13, Mather tendered a $1,000,000 check to the company in repayment of the loan. On September 22, Year 13, at Mather's direction, the company made an additional $1,000,000 loan to him, the proceeds of which Mather apparently used to cover his check in repayment of the first $1,000,000 loan. The Transaction Committee concluded that the Board of Directors neither authorized the September 22, Year 13 loan to Mather nor was any director aware of the loan at the time other than Mather. The company's Year 13 Proxy Statement, dated September 27, Year 13, incorrectly stated that "as of September 19, Year 13, Mather had repaid the principal amount of his indebtedness to the company." Mather's $1,000,000 loan remained outstanding until it was cancelled in connection with the ESOP Transaction discussed below.

ESOP Transaction On February 28, Year 14, the company's Employee Stock Ownership Plan (ESOP) acquired 100,000 shares of the company's common stock from Mather at $14.25 per share. FBN financed the purchase. The ESOP gave the company a $1,425,000 unsecured demand note. To complete the transaction, the company cancelled a $1,000,000 promissory note from Mather and paid the remaining $425,000 in cash. The Transaction Committee determined that the Board of Directors did not authorize the $1,425,000 loan to the ESOP, the cancellation of Mather's $1,000,000 note, or the payment of $425,000 in cash.

Eastwind Transaction On April 27, Year 14, the company acquired four Eastwind aircraft from a German company. FBN subsequently sold these aircraft to Transreco, a corporation owned by Douglas Mather, for a profit of $1,600,000. In late September and early October, Transreco sold these four aircraft at a profit of $780,000 to unaffiliated third parties. The Transactions Committee determined that none of the officers or directors of the company were aware of the Eastwind transaction until late September, Year 14.

On December 12, Year 14, the company announced that Mather had agreed to step aside as Chairman and a Director and take no part in the management of the company pending resolution of the matters presented to the Board by the Transactions Committee. On February 13, Year 15, the company announced that it had entered into a settlement agreement with Mather and Transreco resolving certain of the issues addressed by the Transactions Committee. Pursuant to the agreement, the company will receive $211,000, the bonus paid to Mather for fiscal Year 14, and $780,000, the gain recognized by Transreco on the sale of the Eastwind aircraft. Also pursuant to the settlement, Mather will resign all positions with the company and waive his rights under his employment agreement to any future compensation or benefits to which he might otherwise have a claim.

6. Long-term Debt

Long-term debt consists of the following (amounts in thousands):

April 30	Year 14	Year 13	Year 12	Year 11	Year 10
Notes Payable to Banks:					
Variable Rate	$44,702	$30,495	$ 2,086	$2,504	$ 3,497
Fixed Rate	13,555	14,679	6,292	3,562	1,228
Notes Payable to Finance Companies:					
Variable Rate	—	—	1,320	1,667	10,808
Fixed Rate	—	—	—	—	325
Capitalized Lease Obligations	2,333	2,865	1,295	70	5,297
Other	—	—	600	39	1,660
Total	$60,590	$48,039	$11,593	$7,842	$22,815
Less Current Portion	(60,590)	(7,018)	(1,789)	(1,104)	(2,774)
Net	$ —	$41,021	$ 9,804	$6,738	$20,041

Substantially all of the company's property, plant, and equipment serve as collateral for this debt. The borrowings from bank and finance companies contain restrictive covenants, the most restrictive of which appear below:

	Year 14	Year 13	Year 12	Year 11	Year 10
Liabilities/Tangible Net Worth	<2.5	<3.0	<4.2	<5.5	<6.7
Tangible Net Worth	>20,000	>5,800	>5,400	>5,300	>5,100
Working Capital	>5,000	—	—	—	—
Interest Coverage Ratio	>1.15	—	—	—	—

As of April 30, Year 14, the company is in default of its debt covenants. It is also in default with respect to covenants underlying its capitalized lease obligations. As a result, lenders have the right to accelerate repayment of their loans. Accordingly, the company has classified all of its long-term debt as a current liability.

The company has entered into operating leases for aircraft and other equipment. The estimated present value of the minimum lease payments under these operating leases as of April 30 of each year is

Year 10:	$4,083
Year 11:	3,971
Year 12:	3,594
Year 13:	3,142
Year 14:	2,706

7. Income Taxes

Income tax expense consists of the following:

	Year Ended April 30:				
	Year 14	Year 13	Year 12	Year 11	Year 10
Current					
Federal	$ —	$ —	$ —	$—	$ —
State	—	—	—	—	—
Deferred					
Federal	$(845)	$380	$685	$67	$(85)
State	(55)	30	118	4	(5)
Total	$(900)	$410	$803	$71	$(90)

The cumulative tax loss and tax credit carryovers as of April 30 of each year are as follows:

April 30:	Tax Loss	Tax Credit
Year 14	$10,300	$250
Year 13	5,200	280
Year 12	1,400	300
Year 11	2,100	450
Year 10	4,500	750

The deferred tax provision results from temporary differences in the recognition of revenues and expenses for income tax and financial reporting. The sources and amounts of these differences for each year are as follows:

	Year 14	Year 13	Year 12	Year 11	Year 10
Depreciation...............................	$ —	$ 503	$336	$(770)	$ 778
Aircraft Modification Costs	—	1,218	382	982	703
Net Operating Losses	(900)	(1,384)	290	—	(1,729)
Other.......................................	—	73	(205)	(141)	158
	$(900)	$ 410	$803	$ 71	$ (90)

A reconciliation of the effective tax rate with the statutory tax rate is as follows:

	Year 14	Year 13	Year 12	Year 11	Year 10
Federal Taxes at Statutory Rate..............	(35.0)%	35.0%	34.0%	34.0%	(34.0)%
State Income Taxes	(2.5)	3.0	3.0	3.0	(3.0)
Effect of Net Operating Loss and					
Investment Credits.....................	16.5	—	(7.2)	(29.9)	—
Other.......................................	2.0	2.9	22.2	11.1	(12.0)
	(19.0)%	40.9%	52.0%	18.2%	(49.0)%

8. Market Price Information

The company's common stock trades on the NASDAQ National Market System under the symbol FBN. Trading in the company common stock commenced on January 10, Year 10. High and low bid prices during each fiscal year are as follows:

Fiscal Year	High Bid	Low Bid
Year 14	$16.50	$9.50
Year 13	$14.63	$6.25
Year 12	$11.25	$3.25
Year 11	$ 4.63	$3.00
Year 10	$ 5.25	$3.25

On December 29, Year 14, the company announced that the NASDAQ decided to discontinue quoting the company's common stock because of the company's failure to comply with NASDAQ's filing requirements.

Ownership of the company's stock at various dates appears below:

April 30:	Year 14	Year 13	Year 12	Year 11	Year 10
Douglas Mather	42%	68%	72%	75%	75%
Public	48	23	24	25	25
Company ESOP	10	9	4	—	—
	100%	100%	100%	100%	100%
Common Shares Outstanding (000's)	3,357.5	2,222.8	2,095.0	2,000.0	2,000.0

CASE 5.3

MILLENNIAL TECHNOLOGIES: APOCALYPSE NOW

Millennial Technologies, a designer, manufacturer, and marketer of PC cards for portable computers, printers, telecommunications equipment, and equipment diagnostic systems, was the darling of Wall Street during Year 6. Its common stock price was the leading gainer for the year on the New York Stock Exchange. Its bubble burst during the third quarter of Year 7 when revelations about seriously misstated financial statements for prior years became known. This case seeks to identify signals of the financial shenanigans and to assess the likelihood of the firm's future survival.

INDUSTRY AND PRODUCTS

Digital computing and processing have expanded beyond desktop computing systems in recent years to include a broad array of more mobile applications, including portable computers, cellular telephones, digital cameras, and medical and automobile diagnostic equipment. A PC card is a rugged, lightweight, credit card-sized device inserted into a dedicated slot in these products that provides programming, processing, and storage capabilities normally provided on hard drives and floppy disks in conventional desktop computers. The PC card has high shock and vibration tolerance, low power consumption, small size, and high access speed. The market for PC cards is one of the fastest growing segments of the electronics industry.

Millennial Technologies designs PC cards for four principal industries: (1) communications (routers, cellular telephones, and local area networks), (2) transportation (vehicle diagnostics, navigation), (3) mobile computing (hand-held data collection terminals, notebook computers), and (4) medical (blood gas analysis systems, defibrillators). The firm targets its engineering and product development, all of which it conducts in-house, to these four industry groups. It works closely with original equipment manufacturers (OEMs) to design PC cards that meet specific needs of products aimed at these four industries. Its customers include, among others,

Lucent Technologies, Philips Electronics, 3Com Corporation, and Bay Networks. Millennial Technologies also conducts its manufacturing in-house, which allows it to respond quickly to changing requirements and schedules of these OEMs. The firm markets its products using its own sales force.

Millennial Technologies was incorporated in Year 4 in Delaware as the successor of M. Millennial, a Massachusetts corporation. The firm made its initial public offering of common stock (1,000,000 shares) on April 19, Year 4, at a price of $5.625 per share. Each common share issued included a redeemable common stock purchase warrant that permitted the holder to purchase one share of the firm's common stock for $7.20. Prior to its initial public offering, Millennial Technologies obtained a $550,000 bridge loan during Year 4, which it repaid with proceeds from the initial public offering. Holders of the stock purchase warrants exercised their options during Year 5 and Year 6. The firm obtained equity capital during Year 5 as a result of a private placement of its common stock at $5.83 a share. It issued additional shares to the public during Year 6 at $18 a share. Its stock price was $5.25 on June 30, Year 4; $22.625 on June 30, Year 5; $29.875 on June 30, Year 6; and $52 on December 31, Year 6.

Millennial Technologies maintained a line of credit throughout Year 4 to Year 6 with a major Boston bank to finance its accounts receivables and inventories. The borrowing is at the bank's prime lending rate. Substantially all of the assets of the firm collateralize this borrowing.

The firm's chief executive officer, Manuel Pinoza, is also its major shareholder. The firm maintains an employment agreement with Pinoza under which it pays his compensation to a Swiss executive search firm, which then pays Pinoza.

Beginning in Year 6, Millennial Technologies made minority investments in five corporations engaged in technology development, four of which the firm accounts for using the cost method and one of which it accounts for using the equity method. Products developed by these companies could conceivably use PC cards. Millennial Technologies also advanced amounts to some of these companies using interest-bearing notes.

Exhibits 5.27 to 5.29 present the financial statements for the fiscal years ended June 30, Year 4, Year 5, and Year 6 for Millennial Technologies based on the amounts originally reported for each year. Exhibit 5.30 presents selected financial statement ratios based on these reported amounts.

FINANCIAL STATEMENT IRREGULARITIES

On February 10, Year 7, after receiving information regarding various accounting and reporting irregularities, the Board of Directors fired Pinoza and relieved the Chief Financial Officer of his duties. The Board formed a special committee of outside directors to investigate the purported irregularities, obtaining the assistance of legal counsel and the firm's independent accountants. On February 21, Year 7, the New York Stock Exchange announced the suspension of trading in the firm's common stock. The stock was delisted on April 25, Year 7. On February 14, Year 7, the major Boston bank providing working capital financing notified the firm that the

EXHIBIT 5.27

Balance Sheets for Millennial Technologies
As Originally Reported
(amounts in thousands)
(Case 5.3)

	June 30			
	Year 6	Year 5	Year 4	Year 3
Assets				
Cash	$ 6,182	$ 970	$ 981	$ —
Marketable Securities	4,932	—	—	—
Accounts Receivable	12,592	3,932	1,662	730
Inventories	18,229	8,609	3,371	2,257
Other Current Assets	6,256	1,932	306	234
Total Current Assets	$48,191	$15,443	$6,320	$3,221
Investments in Securities	2,472	—	—	—
Property, Plant, and Equipment (net)	4,698	1,323	669	208
Other Assets	421	1,433	601	666
Total Assets	$55,782	$18,199	$7,590	$4,095
Liabilities and Shareholders' Equity				
Accounts Payable	$ 3,494	$ 3,571	$ 616	$1,590
Notes Payable	4,684	1,153	—	980
Current Portion of Long-term Debt	336	103	—	—
Other Current Liabilities	614	765	516	457
Total Current Liabilities	$ 9,128	$ 5,592	$1,132	$3,027
Long-term Debt	367	162	—	—
Deferred Tax Liability	242	—	39	24
Total Liabilities	$ 9,737	$ 5,754	$1,171	$3,051
Common Stock	$ 165	$ 110	$ 90	$ 60
Additional Paid-in Capital	38,802	10,159	5,027	146
Retained Earnings	7,078	2,176	1,302	838
Total Shareholders' Equity	$46,045	$12,445	$6,419	$1,044
Total Liabilities and Shareholders' Equity	$55,782	$18,199	$7,590	$4,095

EXHIBIT 5.28

**Income Statements for Millennial Technologies
as Originally Reported
(amounts in thousands)
(Case 5.3)**

	For the Year Ended June 30		
	Year 6	Year 5	Year 4
Sales	$37,848	$12,445	$8,213
Other Revenues	353	10	9
Cost of Goods Sold	(23,636)	(6,833)	(4,523)
Selling and Administrative..............	(4,591)	(3,366)	(1,889)
Research and Development.............	(1,434)	(752)	(567)
Interest	(370)	(74)	(495)[a]
Income Taxes	(3,268)	(556)	(284)
Net Income...........................	$ 4,902	$ 874	$ 464

[a]Includes the cost of selling receivables to a factor and interest on bridge financing obtained and repaid during the year.

firm had defaulted on its line of credit agreement. Although this bank subsequently extended the line of credit through July 31, Year 7, it increased the interest rate significantly above prime. Millennial Technologies decided to seek a new lender.

The investigation by the Board's special committee revealed the following accounting and reporting irregularities:

1. Recording of invalid sales transactions: The firm created fictitious purchase orders from regular customers using their purchase order forms from legitimate purchase transactions. The firm then shipped empty PC card housings purportedly to these customers at bogus addresses. Pinoza then apparently paid the accounts receivable underlying these sales with his personal funds.
2. Recording of revenues from bill and hold transactions: The firm kept its books open beyond June 30 each year and recorded as sales of each year products that were shipped in July and should have been recorded as revenues of the next fiscal year.
3. Manipulation of physical counts of inventory balances and inclusion of empty PC card housings in finished goods inventories.
4. Failure to write down inventories adequately for product obsolescence.
5. Inclusion of certain costs in property, plant, and equipment that the firm should have expensed in the period incurred.
6. Inclusion in advances to other technology companies of amounts that represent prepaid license fees. The firm should have amortized these fees over the license period.

7. Failure to provide adequately for uncollectible amounts related to advances to other technology companies.
8. Failure to write down or write off investments in other technology companies when their market value was less than the cost of the investment.

EXHIBIT 5.29

Statements of Cash Flows for Millennial Technologies as Originally Reported
(amounts in thousands)
(Case 5.3)

	For the Year Ended June 30		
	Year 6	Year 5	Year 4
Operations			
Net Income..........................	$ 4,902	$ 874	$ 464
Depreciation........................	645	337	193
Other Addbacks and Subtractions (net)	1,159	(5)	219
Working Capital Provided by Operations...	$ 6,706	$ 1,206	$ 876
(Increase) Decrease in Accounts			
Receivables........................	(8,940)	(2,433)	(981)
(Increase) Decrease in Inventories.........	(9,620)	(5,238)	(1,115)
(Increase) Decrease in Other Current			
Assets.............................	(836)	(2,406)	(71)
Increase (Decrease) in Accounts Payable....	(76)	2,955	(974)
Increase (Decrease) in Other Current			
Liabilities.........................	(152)	251	87
Cash Flow from Operations	$(12,918)	$(5,665)	$(2,178)
Investing			
Sale of Investments	$ 3,981	$ —	$ —
Acquisition of Fixed Assets	(3,899)	(862)	(525)
Acquisitions of Investments.............	(11,186)	—	—
Other Investing Transactions.............	(2,800)	—	—
Cash Flow from Investing.............	$(13,904)	$ (862)	$ (525)
Financing			
Increase in Short-term Borrowing	$ 3,531	$ 1,153	$ 550
Increase in Long-term Borrowing.........	691	320	—
Increase in Common Stock	28,064	5,099	4,663
Decrease in Short-term Borrowing........	—	—	(1,529)
Decrease in Long-term Borrowing	(252)	(56)	—
Cash Flow from Financing	$ 32,034	$ 6,516	$ 3,684
Net Change in Cash....................	$ 5,212	$ (11)	$ 981
Cash—Beginning of Year................	970	981	—
Cash—End of Year....................	$ 6,182	$ 970	$ 981

EXHIBIT 5.30

Financial Ratios for Millennial Technologies
Based on Originally Reported Amounts
(Case 5.3)

	Year 6	Year 5	Year 4
Profit Margin for ROA................	13.6%	7.4%	9.6%
Assets Turnover	1.0	1.0	1.4
Rate of Return on Assets	13.9%	7.2%	13.5%
Profit Margin for ROCE...............	13.0%	7.0%	5.6%
Capital Structure Leverage.............	1.3	1.4	1.6
Rate of Return on Common			
Shareholders' Equity	16.8%	9.3%	12.4%
Cost of Goods Sold/Sales..............	62.4%	54.9%	55.1%
Selling and Administrative/Sales	12.1%	27.0%	23.0%
Research and Development/Sales.........	3.8%	6.0%	6.9%
Income Tax Expense (excluding tax			
effects of interest expense)/Sales.......	9.0%	4.7%	5.5%
Accounts Receivable Turnover...........	4.6	4.4	6.9
Inventory Turnover	1.8	1.1	1.6
Fixed Asset Turnover	12.6	12.5	18.7
Current Ratio	5.3	2.8	5.6
Quick Ratio..........................	2.6	.9	2.3
Days Accounts Payable.................	39	63	71
Cash Flow from Operations/Current			
Liabilities	(175.5%)	(168.5%)	(104.7%)
Long-term Debt Ratio	.8%	1.3%	—
Liabilities/Assets.....................	17.5%	31.6%	15.4%
Cash Flow from Operations/			
Total Liabilities.....................	(166.8%)	(163.6%)	(103.2%)
Interest Coverage Ratio	23.1	20.3	2.5

Exhibits 5.31 to 5.33 present the restated financial statements for Millennial Technologies for the fiscal years ending June 30, Year 4, Year 5, and Year 6 after correcting for the irregularities described above. These exhibits also present the financial statements for the nine months ended March 30, Year 7. The firm decided during February of Year 7 to change its fiscal year to a March year end. Exhibit 5.34 presents selected financial ratios based on the restated financial statements.

Required

   a. Using information in the financial statements as originally reported in Exhibits 5.27 to 5.29, compute the value of Beneish's manipulation index for fiscal Year 5 and Year 6.

EXHIBIT 5.31

Balance Sheets for Millennial Technologies
Using Restated Data
(amounts in thousands)
(Case 5.3)

	March 31	June 30			
	Year 7	Year 6	Year 5	Year 4	Year 3
Assets					
Cash	$ 57	$ 6,182	$ 970	$ 981	$ —
Marketable Securities....................	—	4,932	—	—	—
Accounts Receivable.....................	5,571	11,260	2,802	1,280	730
Inventories	7,356	8,248	2,181	1,581	2,257
Other Current Assets	14,229	6,395	2,284	839	669
Total Current Assets	$27,213	$37,017	$ 8,237	$4,681	$3,656
Investments in Securities	20,332	1,783	—	—	—
Property, Plant, and Equipment (net)	3,087	2,033	923	399	243
Other Assets	566	299	390	123	172
Total Assets	$51,198	$41,132	$ 9,550	$5,203	$4,071
Liabilities and Shareholders' Equity					
Accounts Payable	$ 4,766	$ 3,025	$ 3,303	$ 772	$1,590
Notes Payable	10,090	4,684	1,153	—	980
Current Portion of Long-term Debt	671	336	103	—	—
Other Current Liabilities	7,117	811	562	116	457
Total Current Liabilities.................	$22,644	$ 8,856	$ 5,121	$ 888	$3,027
Long-term Debt	—	367	162	—	—
Total Liabilities	$22,644	$ 9,223	$ 5,283	$ 888	$3,027
Common Stock.........................	$ 177	$ 165	$ 110	$ 90	$ 60
Additional Paid-in Capital.................	82,240	42,712	10,843	5,059	146
Retained Earnings........................	(53,630)	(10,968)	(6,686)	(834)	838
Foreign Currency Adjustment	(233)	—	—	—	—
Total Shareholders' Equity..............	$28,554	$31,909	$ 4,267	$4,315	$1,044
Total Liabilities and Shareholders' Equity...	$51,198	$41,132	$ 9,550	$5,203	$4,071

EXHIBIT 5.32

Income Statements for Millennial Technologies
Using Restated Data
(amounts in thousands)
(Case 5.3)

	Nine Months March 31	Year Ended June 30		
	Year 7	Year 6	Year 5	Year 4
Sales	$ 28,263	$33,412	$ 8,982	$ 7,801
Other Revenues	67	353	10	9
Cost of Goods Sold	(24,453)	(29,778)	(11,575)	(6,508)
Selling and Administrative.................	(7,318)	(3,803)	(2,442)	(2,083)
Research and Development	(1,061)	(1,434)	(753)	(567)
Loss on Investments.......................	(14,096)[a]	(2,662)[a]	—	—
Investigation Costs........................	(3,673)[b]	—	—	—
Provision for Settlement of Shareholder Litigation....................	(20,000)[c]	—	—	—
Interest	(391)	(370)	(74)	(495)
Income Taxes	—[d]	—[d]	—[d]	171
Net Income (Loss)	$(42,662)	$(4,282)	$(5,852)	$(1,672)

[a]Write-offs of advances, and write-downs or write-offs of investments, in technology companies.
[b]Legal, accounting, and related costs of investigating misstatements of financial statements.
[c]Estimated cost of class action lawsuits arising from misstatements of financial statements. Millennial Technologies reached an agreement on June 18, Year 7 to pay the plaintiffs $1,475,000 in cash (included in Accounts Payable on March 31, Year 7 balance sheet) and common stock of $18,525,000 (included in Additional Paid-in Capital on March 31, Year 7 balance sheet). The common stock portion of the settlement represents 37 percent of the common stock of Millennial Technologies.
[d]Millennial Technologies incurred net losses for income tax purposes and maintains a valuation allowance equal to the balance in deferred tax assets.

b. Using information from part a and the financial ratios in Exhibit 5.30, indicate possible signals that Millennial Technologies might have been manipulating its financial statements.

c. Describe the effect of each of the eight accounting irregularities on the balance sheet, income statement, and statement of cash flows.

d. Using information in the restated financial statements in Exhibits 5.31 to 5.33, the financial ratios in Exhibit 5.34, and the information provided in this case, would you as a commercial banker be willing to offer Millennial Technologies a line of credit as of July 31, Year 7? State the conditions that would induce you to offer such a line of credit.

e. Exhibit 5.35 presents the values of Altman's Z-score for fiscal Year 4, Year 5, and Year 6 based on both the originally reported amounts and the restated amounts. Compute the value of Altman's Z-score for the fiscal year ended

EXHIBIT 5.33

Statements of Cash Flows for Millennial Technologies
Using Restated Data
(amounts in thousands)
(Case 5.3)

	Nine Months Ended March 31	Year Ended June 30		
	Year 7	Year 6	Year 5	Year 4
Operations				
Net Loss..................................	$(42,662)	$ (4,282)	$(5,852)	$(1,672)
Depreciation and Amortization	831	471	281	176
Other Addbacks and Subtractions (net).........	28,812	2,005	224	352
Working Capital Provided by Operations	$(13,019)	$ (1,806)	$(5,347)	$(1,144)
(Increase) Decrease in Accounts Receivable......	5,289	(8,883)	(1,693)	(599)
Increase (Decrease) in Inventories	454	(6,067)	(600)	676
(Increase) Decrease in Other Current Assets	(8,092)	(5,213)	(1,932)	(176)
Increase (Decrease) in Accounts Payable	6,572	(9)	3,072	(818)
Increase (Decrease) in Other Current Liabilities	—	(20)	(96)	(340)
Cash Flow from Operations...............	$ (8,796)	$(21,998)	$(6,596)	$(2,401)
Investing				
Sale of Investments	$ 32,182	$ 3,981	$ —	$ —
Acquisition of Fixed Assets..................	(2,074)	(1,459)	(583)	(332)
Acquisition of Investments..................	(38,892)	(11,186)	—	—
Cash Flow from Investing...................	$ (8,784)	$ (8,664)	$ (583)	$ (332)
Financing				
Increase in Short-term Borrowing	$ 5,406	$ 3,531	$ 1,153	$ 550
Increase in Long-term Borrowing	250	691	320	—
Increase in Capital Stock....................	4,060	28,813	5,099	4,663
Decrease in Short-term Borrowing	—	—	—	(1,529)
Decrease in Long-term Borrowing............	(282)	(252)	(56)	—
Proceeds from Related Party Transaction........	2,021	3,091	652	30
Cash Flow from Financing.................	$ 11,455	$ 35,874	$ 7,168	$ 3,714
Change in Cash............................	$ (6,125)	$ 5,212	$ (11)	$ 981
Cash—Beginning of Year	6,182	970	981	—
Cash—End of Year	$ 57	$ 6,182	$ 970	$ 981

EXHIBIT 5.34

Financial Ratios for Millennial Technologies
Based on Restated Data
(Case 5.3)

	Year 7[a]	Year 6	Year 5	Year 4
Profit Margin for ROA	(150.0%)	(12.1%)	(64.6%)	(17.2%)
Assets Turnover	.6	1.3	1.2	1.7
Rate of Return on Assets	(91.9%)	(15.9%)	(78.7%)	(29.0%)
Profit Margin for ROCE	(150.9%)	(12.8%)	(65.2%)	(21.4%)
Capital Structure Leverage	1.5	1.4	1.7	1.7
Rate of Return on Common Shareholders' Equity	(141.1%)	(23.7%)	(136.4%)	(62.4%)
Cost of Goods Sold/Sales	86.5%	89.1%	128.9%	83.4%
Selling and Administrative/Sales	25.9%	11.4%	27.2%	26.7%
Research and Development/Sales	3.8%	4.3%	8.4%	7.3%
Special Provisions/Sales	133.6%	8.0%	—	—
Accounts Receivable Turnover	3.4	4.8	4.4	7.8
Inventory Turnover	3.1	5.7	6.2	3.4
Fixed Asset Turnover	11.0	22.6	13.6	24.3
Current Ratio	1.2	4.2	1.6	5.3
Quick Ratio	.3	2.5	.7	2.6
Days Accounts Payable	60	32	61	74
Cash Flow from Operations/Current Liabilities	(55.8%)	(314.8%)	(219.5%)	(122.7%)
Long-term Debt Ratio	—	1.1%	3.7%	—
Liabilities/Assets	44.2%	22.4%	55.3%	17.1%
Cash Flow from Operations/Total Liabilities	(55.2%)	(303.3%)	(213.8%)	(122.7%)
Interest Coverage Ratio	(108.1)	(10.6)	(78.1)	(2.7)

[a]Amounts based on a nine-month fiscal year.

March 31, Year 7. Although not technically correct, use the income amounts for the nine-month period ending March 31, Year 7. Based on the amounts in the proposed settlement of the class action lawsuits, the value of the common equity on March 31, Year 7, is $50,068,568.

f. Exhibit 5.36 presents the values of y and the probability of bankruptcy for Millennial Technologies according to Ohlson's model for fiscal Year 4, Year 5, and Year 6. Compute the value of y and the probability of bankruptcy for the fiscal year ended March 31, Year 7. The gross national product implicit price index on March 31, Year 7, was 209.0. Use the income amounts for the nine-month period ending March 31, Year 7.

g. Can Millennial Technologies avoid bankruptcy as of mid-Year 7? Why don't the Altman and Ohlson models signal the financial difficulties earlier than they do?

EXHIBIT 5.35

Altman's Z-Score for Millennial Technologies
(Case 5.3)

	Originally Reported Data			Restated Data		
	Year 6	Year 5	Year 4	Year 6	Year 5	Year 4
Net Working Capital/Total Assets	.8403	.6496	.8203	.8216	.3915	.8748
Retained Earnings/Total Assets	.1776	.1674	.2402	−.3733	−.9801	−.2244
Income Before Interest and Taxes/ Total Assets	.5052	.2727	.5404	−.3139	−1.9966	−.8550
Market Value of Equity/Book Value of Liabilities	15.3089	13.1911	8.0700	16.1620	14.3672	10.6419
Sales/Total Assets	.6785	.6838	1.0821	.8123	.9405	1.4993
Z-Score	17.5106	14.9646	10.7530	17.1088	12.7225	11.9366

EXHIBIT 5.36

Ohlson's Probability of Bankruptcy for Millennial Technologies
(Case 5.3)

	Originally Reported Data			Restated Data		
	Year 6	Year 5	Year 4	Year 6	Year 5	Year 4
Size	−5.0926	−4.6474	−4.30007	−4.9866	−4.3849	−4.1470
TLTA	1.0526	1.9065	.9303	1.3521	3.3357	1.0291
WCTA	−1.0014	−.7740	−1.0014	−.9790	−.4666	−1.0425
CLCA	.0143	.0274	.0143	.0181	.0471	.0144
NITA	−.2083	−.1138	−.2083	.2467	1.4523	.7616
FUTL	−1.2603	−.3836	−1.2603	.3583	1.8522	2.3576
INTWD	—	—	—	.2850	.2850	—
OENEG	—	—	—	—	—	—
CHIN	−.3633	−.1596	−.3633	−.0807	.2894	.5210
CONSTANT	−1.3200	−1.3200	−1.3200	−1.3200	−1.3200	−1.3200
Value of Y	−8.1790	−5.4645	−8.1790	−5.0881	1.0902	−1.8258
Probability of Bankruptcy	.03%	4.2%	.08%	.6%	74.8%	13.9%

Chapter 6

QUALITY OF ACCOUNTING INFORMATION AND ADJUSTMENTS TO REPORTED FINANCIAL STATEMENT DATA

Learning Objectives
1. **Understand the concept of quality of accounting information, including the attributes of economic content and earnings sustainability.**
2. **Understand GAAP reporting for various items that typically occur infrequently and yet can have a large economic impact on the reported financial data, including gains and losses from discontinued operations, extraordinary gains and losses, changes in accounting principles, other comprehensive income, impairment losses, restructuring charges, changes in estimates, and gains and losses from peripheral activities.**
3. **Develop the skills to know when and how to adjust the current period's earnings for income items not expected to persist.**
4. **Understand the issues the analyst faces in dealing with retroactively restated financial statements, account classification differences, and differences in accounting principles across countries.**
5. **Review the distinction between earnings management and earnings fraud, and understand the conditions under which managers might more likely engage in earnings management.**

The third step of the five-step financial analysis process introduced in Chapter 1 stresses assessing the quality of a firm's financial statements prior to performing profitability and risk analysis and prior to valuing the firm. This step in the process is the emphasis of both this chapter, and Chapters 7 through 9 that discuss various generally accepted accounting principles (GAAP) in greater depth.

Chapters 4 and 5 provided a framework and tools for analyzing the profitability and risk of a firm using financial statement data. The presumption in using reported financial statement data is that they portray accurately the economic effects of a firm's decisions and actions during the current period, and are informative about the firm's likely future profitability and risk. However, to make insightful decisions about profitability and risk based on relations among data (that is, ratios, time-series trends, etc.), we must first assess whether the unadjusted, reported data are the appropriate inputs in the profitability and risk measures used. In this chapter, we develop the concept of accounting quality as the basis for assessing the information content of reported financial statement data, and discuss whether the analyst needs to adjust that data before analyzing a firm's profitability and risk and valuing the firm.

This chapter illustrates financial reporting for a wide array of items, primarily income statement-related, that typically occur infrequently and yet can have a large economic impact on the financial statements. Specifically, the chapter discusses reporting for discontinued operations, extraordinary gains and losses, changes in accounting principles, other comprehensive income items, impairment losses, restructuring charges, changes in estimates, and gains and losses from peripheral activities. The important objectives in analyzing each of these items are to assess (1) their economic effect on the current period's performance, and (2) their likely persistence in the future. This distinction, as you will see, is important for identifying when to consider making adjustments to the reported financial data.

This chapter also discusses additional accounting and reporting items that may require adjustment. These include retroactively restated financial statements, account classification differences, and different accounting principles across countries.

The chapter concludes with a discussion of the distinction between earnings management and earnings fraud, and the conditions that might trigger earnings management. Chapter 5 discusses earnings manipulation and fraud as reporting accounting data outside the limits of GAAP. This chapter discusses earnings management, defined as reporting accounting data based on rules within the limits of GAAP but probably not the best economic characterization of the firm. The chapter concludes with a discussion of earnings management because the concepts of accounting quality and earnings management often are linked when discussing the need to adjust financial data to better reflect the economic information content of financial data.

ACCOUNTING QUALITY

Recent financial reporting abuses by companies such as Enron, WorldCom, Global Crossing, and others have raised questions about the quality of accounting information. Terms such as *earnings quality* and, less frequently, *balance sheet quality* appear in the financial press, but often are poorly defined and used loosely to capture a myriad of reporting and accountability concerns.

We prefer to use the broader concept of quality of accounting information. Accounting quality encompasses the *economic information content* of reported earnings, the balance sheet, the statement of cash flows, notes to the financial statements, and management's discussion and analysis. We define accounting quality broadly because each of these elements integrate and articulate, and thus, a firm's accounting quality depends on the quality of all of them. Our analysis of the firm's accounting quality is intended to be broad so that it can fully inform our assessment of the firm's reported financial position, performance, and risk.

Our view of accounting quality is also broader than, and should not be confused with, conservatism, sometimes construed as a measure of reporting quality. Conservative accounting numbers in their own right are not high quality for purposes of financial statement analysis and valuation, but conservatism is a prudent response by accountants when faced with uncertainty.

Although accounting quality has many dimensions, we focus on two elements that are central to analysis and valuation:

1. Accounting information should be a fair and complete representation of the firm's economic performance, position, and risk.
2. Accounting information should provide relevant information to forecast the firm's expected future earnings and cash flows.

Next, we explore each of these two elements more fully.

HIGH QUALITY REFLECTS ECONOMIC INFORMATION CONTENT

Quality accounting information portrays fairly and completely the economic effects of a firm's decisions and actions. Quality accounting information paints an accurate economic portrait of the firm's financial position, performance, and risk.

A high quality balance sheet should portray the economic resources under a firm's control that can be reasonably expected to generate future economic benefits, and the claims on those resources at a point in time. The assets on the balance sheet should reflect resources the firm can control—collectible receivables, sellable inventory, leased or owned plant and equipment, intangible rights—that the firm expects to use to generate future economic benefits. If measurement of the expected future economic benefits is highly uncertain (as in the case of the benefits from certain R&D, advertising, or brand management expenditures), or outside of the firm's control (for example, human capital), or if the expected future economic benefits have expired, then a high quality balance sheet should exclude these items. A high quality balance sheet should provide a complete and fair portrayal of all of the obligations of the firm at a point in time, including the present value of long-term liabilities for future payments such as pension obligations. Shareholders' equity on a high quality balance sheet represents the net asset position of the firm at that point in time—the residual value of the assets of the firm at that time, after deducting the obligations of the firm.

Net income should reflect the operating performance of a firm during a period. High quality measure of performance would include all of the revenues that the firm earned during the period and can reasonably expect to collect. A high quality measure of operating performance would include the costs of all of the resources consumed, including resources consumed in the production process to generate revenues (that is, costs that can be matched to revenues such as costs of sales), as well as resources consumed during the period as a function of time that might not match directly with revenues (for example, fixed administrative costs, interest expenses, and the like). High quality measures of performance should also include the effects of any gains or losses from other transactions and events of that period. Accounting quality is low if net income includes revenues that the firm did not earn during the period or may not be able to collect; if it fails to include expenses or losses of the period; or if it includes expenses or losses that are attributable to other periods.

Notes to the financial statements should disclose additional information that enhances understanding of the judgments made in measuring economic values and changes in those values. Often the disclosures provided in the notes to the financial statements are further enhanced by the qualitative discussions of operations and risks in the Management's Discussion and Analysis section of the annual report and 10-K (see Appendix B for PepsiCo's MDA discussions of key assumptions, policies, and estimates made by the firm).

Measuring the economic effects of firms' activities guides standard setters when establishing GAAP. Standard setters recognize, however, that measuring these economic effects often requires subjectivity. Managers must estimate the rate, for example, at which a long-lived asset such as a building or machine loses service potential; the point when a particular customer's account becomes uncollectible; and the point when a firm has earned revenues. As the degree of subjectivity in measuring economic effects increases, it also increases the potential for firms to report accounting information that includes unintentional measurement error, or intentional bias to portray the firm in a light most favorable to the firm or its managers. Standard setters often react to this potential for intentional bias or unintentional estimation error when establishing GAAP by making tradeoffs between accurately reflecting economic reality and obtaining reliable accounting information. Thus, quality accounting information seeks to maximize relevance and economic faithfulness, subject to the constraints of the reliability of the measurements.

Standard setters recognize that a single accounting method may not always portray the economic effects of a particular transaction for all firms. Firms' choices and estimates within GAAP should be determined by the firm's underlying economic circumstances, including conditions in their industry, competitive strategy, and technology. For example, firms use up the services of buildings and equipment at different rates over time, so GAAP allows firms to select from among several depreciation methods. Firms structure leasing arrangements so that the lessor bears most of the economic risk in some cases, whereas the lessee bears most of the economic risk in other cases. GAAP allows two methods of accounting for leases, the operating lease method and the capital lease method, to reflect differences in the economics of these leasing arrangements. Thus, to obtain quality accounting information, firms should select the accounting principles that best portray the economics of their activities from the set permitted by GAAP.

Even when firms select the accounting principles, or methods, that best portray the economics of their activities, firms must still make estimates in applying those accounting principles. Firms must estimate the period of time during which buildings and equipment will provide benefits. Firms must estimate the amount of cash they will ultimately receive from customers from credit sales. Firms must estimate the expected future cost of warranty plans on products sold during the period. Thus, obtaining quality accounting information requires firms' judgments and estimates in applying GAAP.

Given that firms have discretion in choosing their accounting principles in some cases and must make estimates in applying those accounting principles in most cases, firms should disclose sufficient information in the financial statements and notes to permit users to assess the economic appropriateness of those choices. Thus, informative disclosures are an essential element of quality accounting information.

Summarizing, the user of financial statements should consider the following when evaluating the quality of accounting information:

1. Economic faithfulness of the measurements made.
2. Reliability of the measurements made.
3. Fit of GAAP selections to the activities of a firm.
4. Reasonableness of the estimates made in applying GAAP.
5. Adequacy of disclosures.

The analyst may conclude that the reported financial statements for a particular firm fall short of the desired level of accounting quality. In these cases, the analyst might adjust reported amounts to enhance the accounting quality before using them to assess operating performance, financial position, or risk. For example, the analyst might judge that an accelerated depreciation method reflects more accurately than the straight-line method the economic decline in service potential of a building or machine. Converting the reported amounts from straight-line to accelerated depreciation enhances accounting quality. Or, the analyst might judge that a bad debt provision of 3 percent of sales, instead of the 2 percent rate used by the firm, reflects more accurately the likely uncollectible accounts. Adjusting the reported amounts enhances accounting quality. Chapters 7 to 9 discuss various GAAP and the choices firms must make in applying them. These chapters discuss the types of adjustments that the analyst might make to reported amounts to enhance the quality of accounting information.

The analyst can use the adjusted financial statement amounts for the current period to evaluate the firm's managers, to assess risk, and to test for earnings management or fraud. The analyst will also likely use the adjusted financial statement amounts to value the firm. This use requires consideration of a second element of quality accounting information: persistence over time.

HIGH QUALITY SIGNALS EARNINGS PERSISTENCE OVER TIME

When using financial statements to value firms, the analyst should ask: what do the reported or restated amounts for the current period suggest about the long-run persistence of income, and therefore the economic value of a firm? This question points out the importance of judging the economic content of current period earnings in the context of whether it should be relied on to assess earnings persistence over time.

Recall that we use a two-prong definition of accounting quality. Quality accounting information should be informative as to *both* the economic value implications of the current period's earnings and the long-run sustainability of profits. For accounting to be deemed of high quality, both components—a fair and complete representation of current economic performance, and informative about expected future earnings and cash flows—are necessary. Consider the following four possibilities.

1. Earnings could be very informative about current performance, and tell you that current performance is sustainable. This constitutes high quality on both counts (for example, a big jump in sales and earnings this period because of new products that will continue to be successful for a long time).

2. Earnings could be very informative about current performance and tell you that current performance is non-sustainable. Again, this constitutes high quality on both counts (for example, a firm realizes an unexpected gain (or loss) this year, but it is clearly non-recurring; there is no ambiguity, it is informative in that it will not likely affect future earnings).

3. Earnings could be informative about current performance but not informative (that is, do not reduce uncertainty) about the future. In this case, we have high current period information quality, but low information quality for the future. For example, a firm recognizes a fair value gain on a financial asset as a result of a favorable move in interest rates and the asset is marked to observable market value. The measure is relevant and reliable, but this year's gain does not help you forecast whether interest rates will move up or down next year, so it is not informative about sustainable earnings.

4. Earnings are not informative about current period performance but are informative about sustainability of future earnings. Here, we have low current period information quality, but high information quality for the long run (for example, earnings this period include expenses for pre-opening costs for new stores; the new stores are operational and are expected to be profitable in the future).

Chapters 1 and 4 point out that the value of an equity security is a function of the returns expected from investing in the equity security relative to the level of risk. Chapters 10 to 13 discuss and illustrate how the analyst uses financial statement amounts to derive appropriate equity values. Our concern in this section is with understanding the different signals that quality accounting information might provide about economic values. To link our discussion so far about current period earnings and expected future earnings to the value implications of earnings, consider the following four scenarios. In each case, we assume that the analyst has adjusted or restated reported earnings amounts to achieve the desired level of economic information content as discussed in the previous section.

Scenario 1: Earnings for the current period are considered high quality, are in line with previous expectations, and do not suggest any changes in expected future earnings. There should not be a change in the market price of the equity securities.

Market prices already reflect the expected earnings levels. Earnings are informative in the sense that they signal no change in expectations.

Scenario 2: Earnings for the current period differ from expectations and the new earnings level is expected to persist. A firm may have introduced a new product not previously anticipated in pricing the equity security. The new product should enhance earnings for some number of years in the future. The market price of the security should increase for the realized additional earnings of the current period and for the present value of the expected additional earnings in the future. Earnings are informative if they signal the portion of the current period's earnings due to the new product and the additional earnings in the future as a result of the persistence of this new earnings stream. Consider a second example. A firm unexpectedly loses a patent infringement lawsuit enjoining it from selling a key line of products and requiring it to pay immediate damages. The value of the firm's equity securities should decline in the amount of the damages paid. In addition, the level of expected earnings for the future will decline relative to those previously anticipated. The market price of the firm's equity securities should decline for the present value of the lower expected future earnings. Earnings are informative if they signal the amount of the immediate economic loss and the persistent negative effect on future earnings.

Scenario 3: Earnings for the current period differ from expectations but expected future earnings do not change. A firm receives an unexpected rebate on property taxes previously paid because of a processing error made by the local government. The market value of the firm's equity securities should increase in the amount of the rebate. Because expected future earnings do not change, there should be no further market price reaction for the equity securities. Earnings are informative if they disclose the amount of the rebate and signal its one-time nature.

Scenario 4: Earnings for the current period do not differ from expectations but expected future earnings do change. A firm acquires a new factory at the end of the current period, which it records as an asset on the balance sheet. The new factory adds to the firm's manufacturing capacity, increasing expected earnings for future periods. The acquisition of the factory results in a shift between cash and buildings on the balance sheet and should not materially affect the market value of the firm's equity securities. The market price of the equity securities should increase, however, for the present value of the higher expected future earnings. Earnings are informative if they disclose sufficient information for the analyst to forecast the increase in expected future earnings.

The next section discusses the accounting and disclosure of various income items that typically occur infrequently, but can have an economically large impact. These income items may or may not signal (1) an unexpected change in earnings for the current period, or (2) a change in expected earnings for future periods. Understanding GAAP reporting for each item should assist the analyst in making judgments about the effect of each item on market equity values. When using earnings of the current period to forecast expected future earnings, the analyst might choose to ignore or eliminate income items that the analyst does not expect to persist and therefore should not affect equity values.

The topics discussed are:

1. Discontinued operations.
2. Extraordinary gains and losses.
3. Changes in accounting principles.
4. Items in other comprehensive income.
5. Impairment losses on long-lived assets.
6. Restructuring and other charges.
7. Changes in estimates.
8. Gains and losses from peripheral activities.

Of these eight categories, financial disclosures related to the first five are the most comprehensive and consistent across firms because the FASB has issued specific pronouncements on the topics. Exhibit 6.1 presents an income statement that separates the income effects of the first four items from income from continuing operations.

DISCONTINUED OPERATIONS

When a firm decides to exit a particular component of its business, it classifies that business as a *discontinued business*. GAAP stipulates that a discontinued business is either a separable business or a component of the firm with clearly distinguishable

EXHIBIT 6.1
Statement of Comprehensive Income for a Hypothetical Company for Year 12

Income from Continuing Operations:	
Sales Revenue.	X
Cost of Goods Sold	(X)
Selling and Administrative Expenses	(X)
Operating Income	X
Gain on Sale of Equipment.	X
Interest Income	X
Interest Expense.	(X)
Income before Income Taxes	X
Income Tax Expense	(X)
Income from Continuing Operations	X
Income from Discontinued Operations (net of taxes)	X
Extraordinary Gains and Losses (net of taxes)	X
Adjustments for Changes in Accounting Principles (net of taxes) . . .	X
Net Income.	X
Items of Other Comprehensive Income (net of taxes)	X
Comprehensive Income	X

operations and cash flows.[1] The most recent ruling on discontinued operations, *Statement No. 144*, maintained the basic provisions of *Opinion No. 30* for presenting discontinued operations, but broadened the presentation to include more disposal transactions.

The degree to which a particular divested component operationally integrates with ongoing businesses will likely vary across firms depending on their organizational structures and operating policies. Thus, the gain or loss from the sale of a business might appear in income from continuing operations for one firm (that is, the divested business is operationally integrated) and in discontinued operations for another firm (that is, the divested business is not operationally integrated).

Two dates are important in measuring the income effects of discontinued operations. The *measurement date* is the date on which a firm commits itself to a formal plan to dispose of a segment. The *disposal date* is the date of closing the sale, if the firm intends to sell the segment, or the date operations cease, if the firm intends to abandon the segment.

A firm reports the net income or loss from operating the discontinued business prior to the disposal date as a separate item in the discontinued operations section of the income statement. Firms also report the gain or loss on disposal (net of tax effects) in this same section of the income statement, often labeled "Income, Gains, and Loss from Discontinued Operations." Most U.S. firms include three years of income statement information in their income statements. A firm that decides during the current year to divest a business will include the net income or loss of this business in discontinued operations not only for the current year but in comparative income statements for the preceding two years as well, even though the firm had previously reported the latter income in continuing operations in the income statements originally prepared for those two years.

At the measurement date, the firm estimates (1) the net income or loss it expects the discontinued business to generate between the measurement date and the disposal date, and (2) the gain or loss it expects from the sale or abandonment of the segment. The firm then nets these two amounts. If the net amount is an estimated *loss*, the firm recognizes the loss in the year that includes the measurement date. It simultaneously increases an account, Estimated Losses from Discontinued Operations, which appears among liabilities on the balance sheet. Realized losses (or gains) subsequent to the measurement date from either (1) or (2) above reduce (increase) this account instead of appearing in the income statements of those years. Only when cumulative losses exceed the amount initially established in the Estimated Losses from Discontinued Operations account will additional losses appear in the income statement.

If the net amount from netting (1) and (2) above is a *gain*, the firm recognizes the income and gains only when realized in subsequent years. These provisions rest on the conservatism convention of recognizing losses as soon as they become evident but postponing the recognition of gains until realization occurs.

---

[1]Accounting Principles Board, *Opinion No. 30*, "Reporting the Results of Operations," 1973 and Financial Accounting Standards Board, *Statement of Financial Accounting Standards No. 144*, "Accounting for the Impairment or Disposal of Long-Lived Assets," 2001.

Example 1

During Year 10, Halliburton, an energy and construction services firm, decided to sell portions of the Dresser Equipment Group that it acquired in Year 9 when it merged with Dresser Industries. Disposals occurred in Year 10 and Year 11. Halliburton also disposed of other businesses in Year 9, Year 10, and Year 11. Exhibit 6.2 presents selected data from the financial statements related to discontinued operations.

Note that Halliburton sets forth the net income or net loss from operating discontinued businesses separately from the gain or loss on disposal, each net of their tax effects. Halliburton reports gains on disposals each year that exceed the net

EXHIBIT 6.2			
Halliburton, Inc.			
Selected Information Related to Discontinued Operations			
(in millions of dollars)			
Years ended December 31	**Year 11**	**Year 10**	**Year 9**
Income Statement			
Income from Continuing Operations	$ 551	$ 188	$ 174
Income from Discontinued Operations:			
Net Income (Loss) of Discontinued Businesses	$ (41)	$ 98	$ 124
Gain on Disposal of Discontinued Businesses	299	215	159
Income from Discontinued Operations	$ 258	$ 313	$ 283
Net Income	$ 809	$ 501	$ 457
December 31	**Year 11**	**Year 10**	**Year 9**
Balance Sheet			
Net Assets of Discontinued Businesses	$ 0	$ 689	$1,103
Years ended December 31	**Year 11**	**Year 10**	**Year 9**
Statement of Cash Flows			
Operations			
Net Income	$ 809	$ 501	$ 457
Adjustment for Discontinued Operations	(258)	(313)	(283)
Other Adjustments	478	(245)	(232)
Cash Flow from Operations	$1,029	$ (57)	$ (58)
Cash Flow from Investing (details omitted)	(858)	(411)	(107)
Cash Flow from Financing (details omitted)	(1,375)	(593)	194
Cash Flow from Discontinued Operations	1,263	826	234
Net Change in Cash	$ 59	$(235)	$ 263

income or loss from operating these units. Thus, it is likely that Halliburton estimated the net effect on earnings from both operating and selling these units and concluded that a net gain would ultimately result. The firm therefore recognized the income, gains, and losses as they were realized each year.

Given that Halliburton reports income and gains from discontinued operations in each of the three years, the analyst might conclude that they are a recurring source of income for the firm. In this case, the analyst would add the amounts for discontinued operations to income from continuing operations when forecasting future earnings. Note, however, that Halliburton reports no assets on its balance sheet related to discontinued operations as of the end of Year 11, suggesting that the firm has completed disposal activities. If the analyst concludes that such income and gains will not represent a recurring source of earnings in future years, then leaving the amounts in discontinued operations and basing forecasts of future profitability on income from continuing operations is appropriate.

Halliburton reports the amount of assets net of liabilities related to discontinued operations on its balance sheet each year (except Year 11). Consistency with ignoring income from discontinued operations suggests that the analyst exclude these amounts from assets on the balance sheet. The analyst would reduce assets by $1,103 million at the end of Year 9 and $689 million at the end of Year 10. To keep the balance sheet in balance, the analyst must either increase some other asset or decrease shareholders' equity. The firm will ultimately sell these assets for cash. However, increasing cash at this point is inappropriate because the firm does not yet have the cash, nor does it know how much cash it will ultimately realize. Decreasing shareholders' equity implies that the firm will realize no cash on the disposal of these assets and therefore report a loss equal to the book value of the net assets. Neither adjustment seems appropriate. The best approach is to leave the assets of the discontinued operations on the balance sheet but to exclude them from the calculation of any financial ratios that relate an income statement item to a balance sheet item. For example, excluding income from discontinued operations from the numerator of the rate of return on assets suggests excluding the related assets from the denominator of this ratio as well. Excluding sales of discontinued operations from the numerator of the total assets turnover suggests excluding the net assets of discontinued operations from the denominator of this ratio.

Exhibit 6.2 indicates that Halliburton eliminated the effect of discontinued operations from the calculation of cash flow from operations and classified all of the cash flows related to discontinued operations in a separate section of the statement of cash flows after financing activities. Because cash flow from operations contains no amounts related to discontinued operations, the analyst can use it when computing cash flow ratios (for example, cash flow from operations to average current liabilities) without making additional adjustments. If the firm had not excluded the cash flow effects of discontinued operations from cash flow from operations, the analyst would want to do so.

In general, the overriding task for the analyst is to judge firms' strategies regarding the purchase and sale of businesses. For some firms, income from discontinued operations is an ongoing source of profitability and the analyst might decide to include this income in forecasts of future earnings. For most firms, however, income from discontinued operations represents a source of earnings that cannot persist. Recall that the definition of a discontinued operation envisions a firm's exit from a major area of business as opposed to divestment of a portion of an ongoing business, such as a plant or a geographical division. Most firms do not change the major areas of business in which they are involved on a sufficiently regular basis to justify considering income from discontinued operations as a recurring source of profitability.

A second argument for excluding income from discontinued operations from forecasts of future earnings relates to its measurement. Recall that at the measurement date, the firm estimates (1) the net income or loss it expects the discontinued business to generate between the measurement date and the disposal date, and (2) the gain or loss it expects from the sale or abandonment of the segment. The amount reported as income from discontinued operations for a particular year may represent (a) an estimated amount applicable to the current and future years, if the netting of (1) and (2) above at the measurement date is an estimated loss; or (b) an actual, or realized, amount applicable to the current year only if the netting of (1) and (2) above at the measurement date is an estimated gain. These measurement and reporting procedures cloud the interpretation of the time-series behavior of income from discontinued operations.

Thus, in most cases, the analyst should exclude income from discontinued operations from forecasts of future earnings and focus instead on income from continuing operations.

EXTRAORDINARY ITEMS

The income statement can include extraordinary gains and losses. An income item classified as extraordinary must meet all three of the following criteria:[2]

1. Unusual in nature.
2. Infrequent in occurrence.
3. Material in amount.

A firm applies these criteria as they relate to its own operations and to similar firms in the same industry, taking into consideration the environment in which the entities operate. Thus, an item might be extraordinary for some firms but not for others. Income items that meet all three of these criteria are rarely found in corporate annual reports in the United States.

Example 2

Fountain Powerboats manufactures high-performance sport boats, sport cruisers, express cruisers, and sport fishing boats. According to the firm, "Fountain is the most widely recognized brand name denoting quality in the North American boating industry." The firm is located on the coast of North Carolina, and uses the Pamlico River and Atlantic Ocean to test the boats it builds in nearby facilities.

---

[2]*Ibid.*

In April, Year 10, Fountain Powerboats recognized an extraordinary gain of $1.3 million from the settlement of a class action lawsuit alleging antitrust violations against a supplier of the firm. The supplier manufactures sterndrive and inboard engines for boats of the type manufactured by Fountain Powerboats and other boat manufacturers. Fountain Powerboats and other boat manufacturers claimed that the supplier used its dominant market share in sterndrive and inboard engines to gain excessive competitive advantage.

The income statement for the company reveals the following (in thousands):

	Year 10
Earnings from continuing operations before extraordinary items . . .	$ 468.3
Gain on settlement of lawsuit	
(net of $523.1 in income taxes).	790.0
Net earnings	$1,258.3
Basic and diluted earnings per share	
Continuing operations	$ 0.10
Gain from lawsuit	0.17
	$ 0.27

Using the analytical framework described and illustrated in Chapter 2, the effect of (1) the lawsuit and (2) related taxes are as follows:

	C	+	N$A	=	L	+	CC	+	AOCI	+	RE
BS-BOP											
(1)	+1,313.1										+1,313.1
IBT											+1,313.1
(2)	− 523.1										− 523.1
NI	_____										+ 790.0
BS-EOP	+ 790.0										+ 790.0

This analysis assumes that the firm received cash at the time of settlement of the law-suit and paid income taxes immediately.

The question for the analyst is whether to include or exclude extraordinary gains and losses in current period earnings when using current earnings to forecast expected future earnings.[3] The response depends on the persistence of these gains and losses for

---

[3]Note that regardless of the decision to adjust for the extraordinary gain for assessing persistent earnings, the gain has real economic content for the current period. That is, the gain positively affects current period performance, regardless of whether it recurs.

a particular firm. By definition, the analyst can assume that they are infrequent in occurrence and in most cases will exclude them from forecasts of future profitability, focusing instead on income from continuing operations. As with discontinued operations, the income statement reports the amounts net of any tax effects.

In the case of Fountain Powerboats, the analyst probably should not consider the extraordinary gain on the lawsuit settlement as an ongoing source of earnings because Year 10 is the only year in the last three that it reported such a gain or loss.

Fountain Powerboats includes the cash provided by the settlement of the lawsuit in cash flow from operations in the statement of cash flows (not reported here). Consistent with excluding this extraordinary gain from earnings when using it to assess future profitability, the analyst should exclude the cash provided by the settlement when forecasting future cash flow from ongoing operations. Eliminating the amount entirely from the statement of cash flows, however, results in the change in cash on the cash flow statement not reconciling to the change in cash on the balance sheet. This would be inappropriate. If the company has not done so, as is the case with Fountain Powerboats, the analyst might create a separate section of operating cash flows for unusual or extraordinary items and reclassify the cash provided by the settlement there. This was the approach followed by Halliburton in Example 1. When calculating financial ratios that use cash flow from operations, the analyst should use cash flow from ongoing operations only.

CHANGES IN ACCOUNTING PRINCIPLES

Firms highlight the effect of a change in an accounting principle on a separate line item on the income statement. Firms may voluntarily change their accounting principles, such as shift from a first-in, first-out (FIFO) to a last-in, first-out (LIFO) cost flow assumption for inventories or from an accelerated to the straight-line depreciation method. New FASB pronouncements often mandate a change in accounting principles, with these highlighted as a separate line item on the income statement. For example, a spate of pronouncements by the FASB in the 1990s required the reporting of changes in accounting principles for health care benefits for retired employees,[4] income taxes,[5] postemployment benefits,[6] and derivative instruments.[7]

Firms that change their accounting principles must calculate, as of the *beginning* of the year of the change, the cumulative difference between net income under the accounting principle used previously and under the new accounting principle. The firm reports this cumulative difference (net of taxes) in a separate section of the income statement.[8]

---

[4]Financial Accounting Standards Board, *Statement of Financial Accounting Standards No. 106*, "Employers' Accounting for Postretirement Benefits Other Than Pensions," 1990.

[5]Financial Accounting Standards Board, *Statement of Financial Accounting Standards No. 109*, "Accounting for Income Taxes," 1992.

[6]Financial Accounting Standards Board, *Statement of Financial Accounting Standards No. 112*, "Employers' Accounting for Postemployment Benefits," 1992.

[7]Financial Accounting Standards Board, *Statement of Financial Accounting Standards No. 133*, "Accounting for Derivative Instruments and Hedging Activities," 1998.

[8]Accounting Principles Board, *Opinion No. 20*, "Accounting Changes," 1971.

Example 3

Tenneco Automotive is one of the world's largest designers, manufacturers, and distributors of automotive ride control and emission control products and systems. Its primary customers are automotive original equipment manufacturers. They sell products under such well-recognized brand names as Monroe, Walker, and Gillet.

In Year 9, Tenneco Automotive reports the cumulative effects of changes in accounting principles of $134 million, comprised of *two* changes as described in Exhibit 6.3. The firm reports the effects as if both changes took place as of the beginning of the year, January 1, Year 9, which is a requirement of *Opinion No. 20.* Tenneco Automotive reports the cumulative effect of the changes in its income statement as follows:

EXHIBIT 6.3

Tenneco Automotive
Note 1: Summary of Accounting Policies

In April, Year 8, the AICPA issued SOP 98-5, "Reporting on the Costs of Start-up Activities," which requires costs of start-up activities to be expensed as incurred. This statement was effective for fiscal years beginning after December 31, Year 8. The statement requires previously capitalized costs related to start-up activities to be expensed as a cumulative effect of a change in accounting principle when the statement is adopted. Prior to January 1, Year 9, we capitalized certain costs related to start-up activities, primarily pre-production design and development costs for new automobile original equipment platforms. We adopted SOP 98-5 on January 1, Year 9, and recorded an after-tax charge for the cumulative effect of this change in accounting principle of $102 million (net of a $50 million tax benefit), or $3.04 per diluted common share.

The change in accounting principle decreased income from continuing operations by $19 million (net of an $11 million tax benefit), or $.56 per diluted common share, for the year ended December 31, Year 9. If the new accounting method had been applied retroactively, income from continuing operations for the years ended December 31, Year 8 and Year 7, would have been lower by $19 million (net of a $12 million tax benefit), or $.57 per diluted common share, and $18 million (net of a $12 million tax benefit), or $.54 per diluted common share, respectively.

Effective January 1, Year 9, we changed our method of accounting for customer acquisition costs from a deferral method to an expense-as-incurred method. In connection with the decision to separate the automotive and specialty packaging businesses into independent public companies, we determined that a change to an expense-as-incurred method of accounting for automotive after-market customer acquisition costs was preferable in order to permit improved comparability of stand-alone financial results with our after-market industry competitors. We recorded an after-tax charge for the cumulative effect of this change in accounting principle of $32 million (net of a $22 million tax benefit), or $.95 per diluted common share.

The change in accounting principle increased income from continuing operations by $10 million (net of $6 million in income tax expense), or $.30 per diluted common share for the year ended December 31, Year 9. If the new accounting principle had been applied retroactively, income from continuing operations for the years ended December 31, Year 8 and Year 7, would have been lower by $4 million (net of a $3 million income tax benefit), or $.11 per diluted common share, and $12 million (net of a $8 million income tax benefit), or $.35 per diluted common share, respectively.

in millions	Year 9
Income (loss) before Cumulative Effect of Change in Accounting Principles.................................	$ (289)
Cumulative Effect of Change in Accounting Principles, net of income tax....................................	(134)
Net Income..	$ (423)
Basic and Diluted Earnings per Share—after Cumulative Effect of Change in Accounting Principles.......................	$(3.99)

First, note the magnitude of the accounting changes relative to income before the cumulative effect of the changes. Several additional disclosures in Exhibit 6.3 are worth noting as well. Tenneco Automotive argues for changing to the expense-as-incurred method for customer acquisition cost because it improves comparability with its competitors in the after-market industry. This same argument probably would have led the analyst to adjust Tenneco Automotive's financial statements reported prior to this accounting change, and is the reason why the analyst benefits from the retroactive disclosures provided by the firm for Year 8 and Year 7. Also, note that Tenneco Automotive reports the cumulative amounts of both changes net of the tax benefits. The firm also discloses the tax effects of applying the new accounting methods retroactively, allowing the analyst to restate income tax expense for the previous periods together with the two expenses using the new accounting method.

Example 4

Brunswick Corporation operates in three segments: marine engines, boat, and recreation. It is a manufacturer and marketer of leading consumer brands, including such well-known products as Mercury outboard engines, Baja high-performance boats, Hammer fitness equipment, Brunswick bowling equipment, and Brunswick billiard tables. The firm also owns and operates Brunswick family bowling centers across the United States and internationally.

Effective January 1, Year 11, Brunswick adopted *Statement No. 133* that addresses accounting for derivative instruments. In the first note to a recent Brunswick Corporation annual report, the firm states: "As a result of the adoption of this standard, on January 1, Year 11, the Company recorded a $2.9 million after-tax loss ($4.7 million pre-tax) as a cumulative effect of a change in accounting principle, primarily resulting from interest rate swaps."

Brunswick Corporation's income statement reports the cumulative effect of the change as follows:

in millions	Year 11
Earnings from Continuing Operations	$ 84.7
Cumulative Effect of Change in Accounting Principles, net of income tax.	(2.9)
Net Income.	$(81.8)
Basic and Diluted Earnings per Share—after Cumulative Effect of Change in Accounting Principles	$ (.03)

Example 5

The final example of accounting for a change in accounting principles provides an interesting historical perspective. For many companies, the "catch-up" effect of implementing the mandated accounting change for health care benefits for retired employees *(Statement No. 106)* resulted in especially large charges on the income statement. Exhibit 6.4 illustrates the case for Ford Motor Company, taken from an annual report of the firm issued in the previous decade.

The $7.5 billion charge related to *Statement No. 106* represented the obligation (net of taxes) as of the beginning of Year 3 to provide health care benefits to employees during retirement. Prior to *Statement No. 106*, firms recognized an expense each year as it paid health insurance premiums on behalf of retired employees, a so-called "pay as you go" system. The current reporting standard requires firms to recognize an expense each year during the employees' working years for a portion of the present value of the health insurance premiums expected to be paid during the employees' retirement years. The adoption of *Statement No. 106* resulted in an immediate obligation for health care benefits already earned by employees but not previously recognized as either an expense or a liability by the employer.

EXHIBIT 6.4			
Ford Motor Company **Consolidated Statement of Earnings** **(in millions)**			
	Year 1	Year 2	Year 3
Income from Continuing Operations	$860.1	$(2,258.0)	$ (501.8)
Cumulative Effect of Changes in Accounting Principles:			
Adoption of FASB Statement No. 106 . . .	—	—	(7,540.2)
Adoption of FASB Statement No. 109 . . .	—	—	657.0
Net Income (Loss)	$860.1	$(2,258.0)	$(7,385.0)

This reporting standard gave firms the option of either recognizing the full amount of the health care obligation immediately, as Ford did, or recognizing it piecemeal over the remaining working lives of employees.[9]

When analysts evaluated Ford during this period, the case for excluding the effect of adopting *Statement No. 106*—and similar mandated accounting changes—when assessing operating profitability was: (1) the charge occurred because the firm did not recognize health care benefit expenses in prior years; one might view the charge as a correction of cumulative misstatements of previously reported expenses; (2) a charge of this magnitude was nonrecurring; and (3) the amount of the obligation and timing of its recognition varied across firms depending on the reporting option selected.

In Ford's case, excluding the charge from assessments of operating profitability for the year of adoption but allowing it to flow through to retained earnings resulted in a reduction in retained earnings and a recognition of a health care obligation (long-term liability) and a deferred tax asset on the balance sheet at the beginning of the year of adoption. The amounts reported in Ford's financial statements are as follows (in millions):

Health Care Benefits Liability	$12,040
Deferred Tax Asset Related to Above	(4,500)
Cumulative Effect of Change in Accounting Principle	$ 7,540

The analyst obtains a consistent comparative balance sheet at the beginning and end of the year of adoption of *Statement No. 106* by reflecting this obligation on the balance sheet as of the end of the year preceding the year of adoption (that is, Year 2 for Ford). The analytical entry to reflect this health care obligation on Ford's balance sheet at the end of Year 2 is:

December 31, Year 2

Deferred Tax Asset	$4,500	
Retained Earnings	7,540	
Health Care Liabilities		12,040

The debit of $7,540 million to retained earnings reflects the cumulative reduction in retained earnings that would have occurred if Ford had applied *Statement No. 106* in all years prior to Year 3.

---

[9]A examination of the motivation for firms' decisions to recognize the full amount of the obligation immediately or to recognize it piecemeal over the remaining working lives of employees can be found in Eli Amir and Joshua Livnat, "Adoption Choices of SFAS No. 106: Implications for Financial Analysis," *The Journal of Financial Statement Analysis*, Winter 1997, pp. 51–60. The authors also examine the effect of the different implementation methods on the financial statements.

Income from continuing operations for Year 3 includes an expense for the increase in the present value of the health care benefits obligation as a result of employees working an additional year and perhaps generating increased health care benefits. The amount reported in the notes to Ford's financial statements for Year 3 was $723 million pre-tax and $455 million after taxes. Charges of this nature continued in future years as employees render services, so including the $455 million after-tax amount in income related to continuing operations is appropriate.

The inclusion of this $455 million expense in net income for Year 3 resulted in an inconsistency with prior years, however. To adjust net income of prior years, the analyst needs to know the expense actually recognized on a pay-as-you-go basis in each prior year analyzed relative to the amount that the firm would have recognized if the firm had applied *Statement No. 106* each year. Ford did not disclose this information.

Thus, to assess profitability from continuing operations, the adjustment for adoption of *Statement No. 106* involves: (1) ignoring the cumulative effect of the change in accounting principles in the year of adoption, in effect focusing on income from continuing operations when assessing profitability, and (2) reflecting the health care benefits obligation on the balance sheet at the end of the year preceding the year of adoption. The analyst should consider the effects of omitting the health care obligation from financial statements of earlier years when making interpretations of profitability and risk ratios.

Exhibit 6.4 also shows a mandated accounting change for Ford related to income taxes *(Statement No. 109)*. The rationale for excluding the effect of the change from income and the adjustments to the financial statements are the same as for recognition of health care benefits.

Summary of Adjustments for Changes in Accounting Principles

The FASB continues to issue new reporting standards that require recognition of the effects of a change in an accounting principle on the income statement. Firms periodically change reporting principles on a voluntary basis as well. The analysts should examine carefully any voluntary changes in accounting principles made by firms. Such changes may have some bearing on assessing management's attempts to manage earnings upward or downward. We discuss earnings management at the conclusion of the chapter.

ITEMS OF OTHER COMPREHENSIVE INCOME

Chapter 2 indicates that GAAP often requires firms to restate certain assets and liabilities to market value each period and to include the unrealized gains and losses from changes in market value in Other Comprehensive Income, even though firms have not yet realized the value change in a market transaction. Examples include marketable equity securities, derivatives held as cash flow hedges, minimum pension obligations, and investments in certain foreign operations. Later chapters discuss the accounting for each of these items more fully.

Example 6

Refer to Note 16 in Appendix A in which PepsiCo details three items that comprise "other comprehensive loss" for Year 11: (1) currency translation adjustment; (2) derivatives held as cash flow hedges; and (3) minimum pension liability adjustment. (Chapters 8 and 9 discuss the accounting for these three items.) PepsiCo's Statement of Common Shareholders' Equity, also reported in Appendix A, details the changes in these items for Year 11.

Example 7

Cisco Systems Inc., an information technology company, in recent years invested a large amount of its excess cash in publicly traded equity securities. In a footnote to the financial statements reported in a recent annual report, Cisco states: "At July 28, Year 10 and July 29, Year 9, substantially all of the Company's investments were classified as available for sale. Unrealized gains and losses on these investments are included as a separate component of accumulated other comprehensive income (loss), net of any related tax effect."

Chapter 9 provides a discussion of accounting for investments in marketable equity securities. Among other requirements, the rules require Cisco to report at the balance sheet date its equity investments at their fair values as reported in actively traded markets. The change in their values between balance sheet dates is reported as part of comprehensive income. For fiscal year ending July 29, Year 9, Cisco reports a net *positive* change in unrealized gain on investments of $3.2 billion in the subsection of the Consolidated Statement of Shareholders' Equity labeled, "Accumulated Other Comprehensive Income (Loss)." Comprehensive income for the year was $5.9 billion, which is comprised of net income for the year ($2.7 billion) and the unrealized gain on holding marketable equity securities ($3.2 billion).

Dramatic changes occurred in both the information technology industry and the economy in general between Year 9 and Year 10. For the fiscal year ending July 29, Year 10, Cisco reports a net *negative* change in unrealized gains on investments of $3.8 billion in the same section of the statement shareholders' equity referred to above. Comprehensive *loss* for the year was $4.8 billion, consisting of a net loss for the year ($1.0 billion) and the unrealized losses on holding marketable equity securities ($3.8 billion).

The analyst must decide whether to include the unrealized gains and losses when assessing earnings persistence and predicting future profitability. The case for considering these gains and losses as part of sustainable earnings is: (1) such gains and losses closely relate to ongoing operating activities and will likely recur, and (2) measuring the amount of the gain or loss on certain assets is relatively objective in that active markets exist to indicate the amount of the value changes. The case against including the value changes in assessments of profitability is: (1) the amount of gain or loss that firms ultimately realize when they sell the assets or settle the liabilities will differ from the amount reported each period, (2) the gains and losses could easily reverse in future years prior to disposal or settlement, (3) the gain or loss does not have an immediate effect on cash flows, and (4) measuring the amount of the gain or loss on certain types of assets can be subjective if they are not traded in active markets.

IMPAIRMENT LOSSES ON LONG-LIVED ASSETS

When a firm acquires assets such as property, plant, equipment and intangible assets, it assumes that it will generate future benefits through their use. This is not always the case, however. The development of new technologies by competitors, changes in government regulations, changes in demographic trends, and other factors external to a firm may reduce the future benefits originally anticipated from the assets. Financial reporting requires firms to assess whether the carrying amounts of long-lived assets are recoverable and, if they are not, to write down the assets to their fair values and recognize an impairment loss in income from continuing operations.[10]

It is impractical to expect firms to evaluate every asset each reporting period, so financial reporting generally requires testing for asset impairment only when events or circumstances indicate that their carrying amounts may be not recovered. Nurnberg and Dittmar suggest the following events or circumstances as examples that may signal recoverability problems:

1. A significant decrease in the market value of an asset.
2. A significant change in the extent or manner in which an asset is used, or a significant physical change in an asset.
3. A significant adverse change in legal factors or in the business climate that affects the value of an asset, or an adverse action or assessment by a regulator.
4. An accumulation of costs significantly in excess of the amount originally anticipated to acquire or construct an asset.
5. A current-period operating or cash flow loss combined with a history of operating or cash flow losses, or a projection or forecast that demonstrates continuing losses associated with an asset used for the purpose of producing revenue.
6. Insufficient rental demand for a rental project currently under construction.
7. Write-downs by competitors and other industry leaders.[11]

What is particularly noteworthy about this list is that a firm, in effect, must disclose when it anticipates that assets previously acquired will no longer provide the future benefits initially anticipated. This is a valuable disclosure for the analyst attempting to assess a past strategic decision by a firm. GAAP does require the testing of goodwill and other intangibles not requiring amortization for asset impairment annually, independent of the triggering events listed above. Chapter 7 discusses the nature of the impairment test for various types of long-lived assets.

---

[10]Financial Accounting Standards Board, *Statement of Financial Accounting Standards No. 144,* "Accounting for the Impairment or Disposal of Long-Lived Assets," 2001. *Statement No. 144* superseded *Statement No. 121,* "Accounting for the Impairment of Long-lived Assets and for Long-lived Assets to be Disposed of," 1995. *Statement No. 144* retains the fundamental provisions of *Statement No. 121* for recognizing and measuring impairment losses on long-lived assets held for use and long-lived assets to be disposed of by sale, while also resolving significant implementation issues associated with *Statement No. 121.*

[11]Hugo Nurnberg and Nelson Dittmar, "Reporting Impairments of Long-Lived Assets: New Rules and Disclosures," *The Journal of Financial Statement Analysis,* Winter 1997, pp. 37–50. The article includes examples of how these impairment indicators are applied by firms in the oil and gas, restaurant, retail food, and service-related industries.

Example 8

Refer to Appendix A in which PepsiCo provides several disclosures related to its impaired assets. In Note 1, "Summary of Significant Accounting Policies," PepsiCo indicates that, while *Statement No. 144* is first effective for the firm in Year 12, it anticipates no impact on the financial statements in that year. In that same note, PepsiCo also points out that "an impaired asset is written down to its estimated fair market value based on the best information available. Estimated fair value is generally measured by discounting estimated future cash flows. Considerable management judgment is necessary to estimate discounted future cash flows."

PepsiCo reports a small impairment charge in Year 11 (and previous years) as required under *Statement No. 121*. In Note 3, PepsiCo reports an asset impairment charge of $19 million for Year 11, $125 million for Year 10, and $8 million for Year 9. The note details the reason for the charges, and indicates that the asset impairment charges "primarily reflect the reduction in the carrying value of the land, buildings, and production machinery and equipment to their estimated fair market value based on analyses of the liquidation values of similar assets."

Note 3 also details restructuring charges taken by the firm in recent years, a topic that the next section discusses. Note that PepsiCo reports the after-tax effect of the asset impairment and restructuring charges *combined*, rather than disclosing the amounts related to each item.

Statement No. 144 requires that firms include impairment losses in income before taxes from continuing operations. Although asset impairments do not warrant disclosure in a separate section of the income statement, such as that given discontinued operations or extraordinary gains or losses discussed earlier, alternative methods for disclosing the losses include a separate line item on the income statement, or a detailed note that describes what line item on the income statement includes the impairment losses.

Example 9

Exhibit 6.5 details asset impairment charges and restructuring charges taken by JDS Uniphase Corporation in Year 11. JDS Uniphase is a technology company that designs, develops, manufactures, and distributes fiber optic components, modules, and subsystems for the fiber optic communication industry. The company was founded in Year 3 and is the product of several large mergers and acquisitions, including, among others, JDS FITEL, OCLI, E-TEK Dynamics, and SDL, Inc.

The magnitude of the asset impairment charge by JDS Uniphase—over $50 billion as detailed in Exhibit 6.5—is record-breaking and the result of a dramatic downturn in the telecommunications industry beginning in Year 10. JDS Uniphase attributed the downturn to a precipitous decrease in network deployment and capital spending by telecommunications carriers. The firm also states in its notes to the financial statements that it anticipates additional reductions and charges in future years.

The majority of the $50 billion asset impairment charge relates to goodwill associated with the acquisitions of E-TEK Dynamics, SDL, Inc., and OCLI. Note (a) in Exhibit 6.5 explains how JDS Uniphase determined the fair value of the asset impairment, with management acknowledging that the process entails a large amount of estimation. The firm also points out, both in its statement of cash flows and in its notes to the financial statements, that all of the $50 billion asset impairment is a non-cash charge.

The analyst must assess whether to exclude impairment losses from reported earnings when using the current period's earnings to forecast future earnings. JDS

EXHIBIT 6.5
JDS Uniphase Corporation
Note 12—Special Charges
(in millions)

	Year Ended June 30, Year 11
Reduction of Goodwill and	
Other Long-lived Assets[a]	$50,085.0
Restructuring Activities:	
Worldwide Workforce Reduction[b]	79.1
Facilities and Equipment[c]	122.2
Lease Commitments[d]	63.0
Restructuring Charges[e]	264.3
Special Charges	$50,349.3

[a]Fair value was determined based on discounted cash flows for the operating entities that had separately identifiable cash flows. The cash flow periods used were five years using annual growth rates of 15 percent to 60 percent, the discount rate used was 13.0 percent in the third quarter of Year 11 and 14.5 percent in the fourth quarter of Year 11, and the terminal values were estimated based upon terminal growth rates of 7 percent. The assumptions supporting the estimated future cash flows, including the discount rate and estimated terminal values, reflect management's best estimates. The discount rate was based upon the Company's weighted average cost of capital as adjusted for the risks associated with its operations.
[b]Primarily relates to severance and fringe benefits associated with the reduction of 9,000 employees.
[c]Property and equipment that was disposed of or removed from operations during Year 11.
[d]Primarily relates to exiting and terminating leases for excess or closed facilities with planned exit dates.
[e]Write-downs of facilities and equipment totaled $122.2 million in Year 11 and $2.7 million in Year 12. Cash payments to severed employees and lessors totaled $25.8 million in Year 11 and $50.7 million in Year 12. The firm adjusted its restructuring liability by $4.7 million pre-tax in Year 12 because it appeared that actual costs would be less than originally expected.

Uniphase indicates that it anticipates additional impairment charges in the future, suggesting a recurring pattern. However, it is unlikely that a charge as large as that in Year 11 will recur. Because firms report asset impairment losses pre-tax, a decision to eliminate a particular asset impairment loss requires the analyst to adjust for the income tax effect as well. In some cases, firms disclose the tax effect in notes to the financial statements. In other cases, firms do not disclose tax effects directly. In such cases, the analyst should study the note on income taxes to see whether the firm discloses any information related to the impairment charge. If the firm can claim a deduction later, then a deferred tax asset will appear. If the firm cannot take a tax deduction at any time, as is often the case for goodwill, then the analysis of the firm's effective tax rate will show an increase because of the nondeductibility of the impairment charge.

JDS Uniphase reports an increase in its effective tax rate reconciliation for Year 11 of $17.5 billion because of asset impairments. This amount equals the 35 percent statutory tax rate times the $50.1 billion asset impairment change. Thus, the charge does not give rise to a tax deduction. If no information appears in the notes, then one must assume that the asset impairment charge gives rise to an immediate tax deduction in an amount equal to the statutory tax rate times the asset impairment change.

RESTRUCTURING AND OTHER CHARGES

Assessing the quality of earnings as related to the five topics discussed to this point—discontinued operations, extraordinary gains and losses, changes in accounting principles, items of other comprehensive income, and impairment losses on long-lived assets—benefit from the fact that the FASB has issued specific pronouncements on each of the topics. Disclosures for restructuring and other charges and the remaining topics presented in this section—changes in estimates, and gains and losses from peripheral activities—are not as comprehensive and consistent across firms because rulings on the topic either do not exist or are general in nature.

Firms will frequently remain in a segment of its business, but decide to make major changes in the strategic direction or level of operations of that business.[12] In many of these cases, firms record a restructuring charge against earnings for the estimated cost of implementing the decision. The treatment of restructuring charges in assessing earnings persistence and assessing profitability is important for the following reasons:

1. Recessionary conditions often induce firms to include restructuring charges in their reported earnings for the current period. Furthermore, the conditions might have a bearing on forecasting earnings in the future as well.
2. The Financial Accounting Standards Board has not issued a specific pronouncement regarding how firms should measure restructuring charges and

---

[12]If the firm decides to abandon a business segment or component altogether, the reporting policies discussed earlier for discontinued operations apply. In many cases, however, firms are not abandoning current areas of business, but "restructuring" them to improve profitability.

when firms should include such charges in measuring income. Because of this, the analyst must judge whether to include the charges in forecasts of future earnings, or whether they relate only to the current and past periods.

Interpreting a particular firm's restructuring charge is difficult because firms vary in their treatment of these items:

1. Some firms apply their accounting principles conservatively (for example, use relatively short lives for depreciable assets, expense immediately expenditures for repairs of equipment, use relatively short amortization lives for intangible assets). Such firms have smaller amounts to write off as restructuring charges than if they had applied their accounting principles less conservatively.

2. Some firms attempt to minimize the amount of the restructuring charge each year so as not to penalize reported earnings too much. Such firms often must take restructuring charges for several years in order to provide adequately for restructuring costs.

3. Some firms attempt to maximize the amount of the restructuring charge in a particular year. This approach communicates the "bad news" all at once (referred to as the "big bath" approach) and reduces or eliminates the need for additional restructuring charges in the future. If the restructuring charge later turns out to have been too large, income from continuing operations in a later period includes a restructuring credit which increases reported earnings (such as Hershey Foods in Example 14 below).

Firms also report "other charges" on the income statement using a variety of different account titles. These other charges have characteristics similar to restructuring charges, but often are not directly related to any strategic decision by the firm related to the level or direction of its operations. Two illustrations of restructuring and other similar charges are provided in the examples below.

Example 10

As described in Example 9, JDS Uniphase recorded both restructuring and asset impairment charges in Year 11. Exhibit 6.5 reports a restructuring charge totaling $264.3 million, comprised of laying off employees, closing facilities, disposing of equipment, and terminating leases. These items typify the activities captured in restructuring charges, and exemplify the consequences of the recessionary conditions in the telecommunications industry during the Year 9 through Year 11 period.

JDS Uniphase makes no mention of taxing savings related to the restructuring charge. However, its income tax note shows an increase in deferred tax assets related to net operating losses. Firms generally cannot claim income tax deductions for restructuring charges until the firm makes severance payments to employees, terminates leases, and closes down or disposes of facilities and equipment. The restructuring charge likely created a net operating loss, which will give rise to future tax deductions. Thus, the recognition of the $264.3 million restructuring charge in Year 11 likely increased deferred tax assets by $92.5 million (= .35 × $264.3).

The following analysis summarizes the effects on the balance sheets and income statements of JDS Uniphase from the:

(1) restructuring charge during Year 11
(2) tax effect of the restructuring charge
(3) disposal or removal of facilities and equipment during Year 11
(4) tax effect of the disposals in (3)
(5) cash payments to severed employees and to lessors for termination of leases during Year 11
(6) tax effect of (5)
(7) disposal or removal of facilities and equipment during Year 12
(8) tax effect of the disposals in (7)
(9) cash payments to severed employees and to lessors for termination of leases during Year 12
(10) tax effect of (9)
(11) adjustment to the restructuring liability account because of a change in the estimated amount needed
(12) tax effect of (11)

	C	+	N$A	=	L	+	CC	+	AOCI	+	RE
BS-BOP											
(1)					+264.3						−264.3
IBT											−264.3
(2)			+ 92.5								+ 92.5
NI											−171.8
(3)			−133.1		−133.1						
(4)	+46.7		− 46.7								
(5)	−25.8				− 25.8						
(6)	+ 9.0		− 9.0								
BS-EOP	**+29.9**		**− 96.3**		**+105.4**						**−171.8**
(7)			− 2.7		− 2.7						
(8)	+ .9		− .9								
(9)	−50.7				− 50.7						
(10)	+17.7		− 17.7								
(11)					− 4.7						+ 4.7
IBT											+ 4.7
(12)			− 1.7								− 1.7
NI											+ 3.0
BS-EOP	**− 2.2**		**−119.3**		**+ 47.3**						**−168.8**

Note several aspects of the accounting for the restructuring charge. JDS Uniphase establishes the restructuring charge and the related liability in Year 11 and then charges actual costs against the liability in Year 11, Year 12, and later years. Except for the adjustment for the change in estimate in Year 12, net income of subsequent years remains unchanged. The remaining liability at the end of Year 12 is $47.3 million. The remaining deferred tax asset is $16.6 million (= .35 × $47.3).

After illustrating additional examples of restructuring and unusual charges, we discuss how the analyst might treat the restructuring charge of JDS Uniphase.

Example 11

Brunswick Corporation, discussed in Example 4, reported "Unusual Charges" on its income statement for both Year 9 and Year 10. Exhibit 6.6 provides a portion of the income statement taken from the firm's annual report. Note that Brunswick includes the charges as part of operating earnings for each year. (Although not reported in Exhibit 6.6, the firm reported no "unusual charges" in Year 11.)

Exhibit 6.7 illustrates additional disclosures provided by Brunswick for the charges reported on the income statement. Note 4 to the annual report details the composition of the charge. In addition, Management's Discussion and Analysis (MDA) section of Brunswick's 10-K provides a discussion of the charges. Particularly note in Exhibit 6.7 that the firm reports the after-tax amount for the charges. Thus, as opposed to the previous example, the analyst does not have to estimate the tax savings related to the unusual charges.

Example 12

Refer to Appendix A and Note 2 of PepsiCo's annual report. During Year 11, PepsiCo reported a $356 million charge associated with its merger with Quaker Foods. The firm also discloses the charge as a separate line on the Consolidated Statement of Income ("Merger-related Costs" as detailed in Appendix A), reducing

---

EXHIBIT 6.6

Brunswick Corporation
Partial Consolidated Statements of Income
For the Years Ended December 31
(in millions)

	Year 10	Year 9
Net Sales	$3,811.9	$3,541.3
Cost of Sales	(2,723.3)	(2,527.3)
Selling, General and Administrative Expense.	(534.2)	(533.7)
Research and Development Expense	(102.2)	(89.7)
Unusual Charges.	(55.1)	(116.0)
Operating Earnings	$ 397.1	$ 274.6

EXHIBIT 6.7

Brunswick Corporation
Selected Annual Report and Form 10-K Disclosures
(in millions)

Note 4. Unusual Charges

Unusual charges consist of the following:

	Year 10	Year 9
Environmental Provisions	$41.0	$ —
Investment Write-downs	14.1	—
Antitrust Litigation Settlements		116.0
Total.	$55.1	$116.0

Management's Discussion and Analysis (MDA)

Results for Year 10 include a $55.1 million pre-tax unusual charge to operating earnings ($40.0 million after tax or $0.45 per diluted share) to increase environmental reserves related to the cleanup of contamination from a former manufacturing facility and to account for the write-down of investments in certain Internet-related businesses.

Results for Year 9 included a $116.0 million pre-tax charge to operating earnings ($71.4 million after tax or $0.77 per diluted share) related to litigation settlements.

operating profit for the year. PepsiCo breaks the charge into (1) transactions costs ($117 million), and (2) integration and restructuring costs ($239 million), and provides a discussion of each category in Note 2. (Chapter 4 also includes a discussion of this charge when assessing PepsiCo's profitability for Year 11.)

Similar to the example above, PepsiCo discloses the tax savings resulting from the charge. It appears that the vast majority of the merger-related costs did not qualify as tax deductions. Note 2 reports an after-tax amount for the charge of $322 million, representing a tax savings of only $34 million ($356 − $322). The analyst would use this actual tax savings reported by PepsiCo, rather than multiplying the statutory rate times the charge, if a decision is made to adjust for the charge. Using actual amounts reported by firms is preferable to hypothetical calculations.

The analyst must assess in each of these three examples whether (1) similar restructuring and unusual charges are likely to recur and therefore represent an ongoing drain on earnings, and (2) whether the restructuring and other charges adequately provide for the costs encompassed by the charges. If not, estimates of future earnings must take this into account.

With respect to restructuring charges, the assessment is more difficult because firms follow different reporting strategies with respect to the charges. As stated earlier, some firms make restructuring charges for several years in a row, attempting perhaps to minimize the negative news by making smaller charges than are appropriate. Also as stated earlier, other firms make a single, presumably larger, restructuring charge as an opportunity to get the bad news behind them.

It is also possible that firms use the restructuring charge as an opportunity to write down assets that do not even relate directly to the restructuring action. This is possible given the lack of specific reporting guidance in the area by policymakers. For example, firms might have previously selected long depreciable lives for property and equipment and long amortization periods for intangibles to increase reported earnings. The same firms may hope that the stock market will view a restructuring charge as nonrecurring and exclude it from estimates of future earnings. Writing down assets now relieves future periods of depreciation and similar charges and increases reported earnings of those periods. Thus, restructuring charges may signal the practice of earnings management, a topic discussed later in this chapter. The analyst must examine carefully the rationale for, the amount of, and the time pattern of restructuring charges when judging the economic value-added of current earnings.

Let's now consider the analyst's treatment of the three restructuring charges described above.

JDS Uniphase

JDS Uniphase reported no restructuring charges in the year ended June 30, Year 10. It reported restructuring charges of $264.3 million in fiscal Year 11, as discussed above, and $260.0 million in fiscal Year 12. It also reported an additional $8,285.0 million asset impairment charge related to goodwill and other long-lived assets in fiscal Year 12. Thus, it would not appear that the charge in Year 11 was a one-time event. Conditions in the telecommunications industry have not yet improved to the point where additional charges would be a surprise. Thus, the analyst could easily justify not eliminating the restructuring charges in Year 11 and Year 12 when forecasting future earnings.

Brunswick Corporation

The three unusual charges for Brunswick (detailed in Exhibit 6.7) do in fact appear unusual. There is only one charge for each of the three items over the two-year period. Each relates to a specific event that is unlikely to be a normal part of the firm's ongoing operations. Thus, the analyst appears justified in excluding them and their related tax effects from income from continuing operations when forecasting future profitability.

PepsiCo

The merger-related costs incurred by PepsiCo are material and occur in Year 11 only. Although PepsiCo acquires other companies each year, a charge of this magnitude is unusual. Thus, eliminating the charge and its related tax effect from income from continuing operations when forecasting future earnings seems appropriate.

CHANGES IN ESTIMATES

As discussed earlier in this chapter, application of GAAP often requires firms to make estimates. Examples include the amount of uncollectible accounts receivable, the depreciable lives for fixed assets, the percentage of completion rate for a long-term project, the return rate for warranties, and interest, compensation, and inflation rates for pensions, health care, and other retirement benefits.

Firms periodically make changes in these estimates. The amounts reported in prior years for various revenues and expenses will differ from the amount suggested by the new estimates. Firms might conceivably (1) retroactively restate prior years' revenues and expenses to reflect the new estimates, (2) include the cumulative effect of the change in estimate in income in the year of the change (similar to a change in accounting principle), or (3) spread the effect of the prior years' misstatement over the current and future years.

GAAP requires firms to follow the third procedure described above.[13] Policymakers view the making of estimates and the revising of those estimates as an integral and ongoing part of applying accounting principles. They are concerned about the credibility of financial statements if firms revise their financial statements each time they change an accounting estimate. Policymakers are also concerned that users of the financial statements will overlook a change in an estimate if its effect does not appear in the income statement of the current and future years.

Example 13

DriveTime is the largest chain of car dealerships in the United States that both sells used cars and provides financing for the purchase of the cars. Prior to Year 11, the firm operated under the not-so-flattering name of Ugly Duckling, Inc. In a recent SEC filing, the firm indicated that the name change was made "in an attempt to attract a high volume of our better customers, reduce loan losses, and improve profitability."

DriveTime sells and finances used vehicles to customers within what is referred to as the "sub-prime" segment of the used car market. The sub-prime market is comprised of customers who typically have limited credit histories, low income, or past credit problems.

Exhibit 6.8 provides an excerpt from a recent quarterly filing by DriveTime. In the excerpt taken from the notes to the quarterly financial statements, DriveTime describes its accounting policy for credit losses on loans. The judgments necessary to assess credit losses are heavily dependent on estimates and uncertainties. In the exhibit, DriveTime identifies five factors that it considers in evaluating whether the allowance and the provision for credit losses are adequate. Moreover, it makes clear that this list is not an exhaustive one.

Given the demographics of DriveTime's typical customers, the judgments necessary by management for calculating the effect of these items on reported earnings are extremely subjective and subject to change fairly quickly. Exhibit 6.9 illustrates a

---

[13]Accounting Principles Board, *Opinion No. 20.*

EXHIBIT 6.8

DriveTime (formerly Ugly Duckling, Inc.)
Excerpt from Notes to Consolidated Quarterly Financial Statements

---

Revenue Recognition

Direct loan origination costs related to loans originated at Company dealerships are deferred and charged against finance income over the life of the related installment sales loan using the interest method. The accrual of interest for accounting purposes is suspended if collection becomes doubtful, generally 90 days past due, and is resumed when the loan becomes current. Interest income also includes income on the Company's residual interests from its securitization program.

Allowance for Credit Losses

An allowance for credit losses (allowance) is established by charging the provision for credit losses. To the extent that the allowance is considered insufficient to absorb anticipated credit losses over the next 12 months, additions to the allowance are established through a charge to the provision for credit losses. The evaluation of the allowance considers such factors as (1) the performance of each dealership's loan portfolio, (2) the Company's historical credit losses, (3) the overall portfolio quality and delinquency status, (4) the value of underlying collateral, and (5) the current economic conditions that may affect the borrower's ability to pay.

---

change made by DriveTime in Year 11 for estimating the provision for credit losses. The magnitude of the change is dramatic. The firm attributes the need to adjust the provision upward because of a decrease in new loans originated and the effects of the recession experienced in Year 10 and Year 11.

Example 14

The earlier discussion on restructuring charges points out that if the firm subsequently deems the charge too high, income from continuing operations in a later period includes a restructuring credit—in effect, increasing reported earnings in the later period. In a report several years ago, Hershey Foods reports a reversal of a previous year's restructuring charge and attributes it to a change in estimates. The company states:

> As of December 31, Year 5, $81.1 million of restructuring reserves had been utilized and $16.7 million had been reversed to reflect revisions and changes in estimates to the original restructuring program.

Given the difficulty in estimating the cost of restructuring programs prior to their implementation, this disclosure is not surprising. Unless the magnitude of the reversal is large relative to the original estimate (Hershey Food's restructuring charge

	EXHIBIT 6.9		
	DriveTime (formerly Ugly Duckling, Inc.)		
	Excerpt from Form 10-K Notes—Provision for Credit Losses		
	Year 11	**Year 10**	**Percent Change**
Provision for Credit Losses (000s)	$151,071	$141,971	6.4%
Provision per Loan Originated	$3,183	$2,513	26.7%
Provision as a Percentage of Principal Balances Originated	35.4%	30.1%	

Provision for Credit Losses ("Provision") is the amount we charge to current operations on each car sold to establish an Allowance for Credit Losses ("Allowance"). The Provision in total, per loan originated, and as a percent of principal balances originated, increased in both Year 11 and Year 10.

The Provision for Year 11 increased to 35.4% of the amount financed versus 30.1% in Year 10. The Company's policy is to maintain an Allowance for all loans in its portfolio to cover estimated net charge-offs for the next twelve months. Our loans have experienced lifetime net losses in the 31% to 34% range for the past few years. With origination growth rate over this time, we have been able to maintain an adequate Allowance in accordance with GAAP and Company policy by providing between 27% and 31% of the amount financed. However, in Year 11 the volume of portfolio originations decreased from Year 10 due to the implementation of higher credit standards and the effects of the recession. Due to the decreased volume of originations, an increase in the Provision as a percentage of loan originations was needed in order to maintain an adequate Allowance.

The Company has begun to improve the underlying credit quality mix of its originations due to improved credit standards and the introduction of loan grading. As a result, Year 11 originations are performing better to date than prior year originations. Offsetting these improvements are the effects of the recession and the performance of loans originated prior to Year 11 that do not have the benefit of the new higher credit standards and are emerging at loss levels higher than previously estimated. As a result, the Provision for Credit Losses increased to $151 million in Year 11 compared to $142 million in Year 10. The Allowance as a percentage of loan principal is 19.8% at December 31, Year 11, up from 19.4% at December 31, Year 10.

originally was estimated at $106.1 million), most analysts are not wary of this type of disclosure.

The analyst needs to address a set of issues when evaluating changes in estimates. How reasonable are management's stated explanations for the change? For example,

DriveTime changed estimates because of a strategic business decision (reduce loan originations to generate higher quality loans) and a deterioration in economic conditions. Is this reasonable? Often an extensive set of factors needs to be considered. Has technology changed necessitating shorter useful lives for depreciable assets to incorporate obsolescence? Has a firm improved quality control on products manufactured necessitating lower warranty liability levels? Are the firm's new estimates in line with those of its competitors?

GAINS AND LOSSES FROM PERIPHERAL ACTIVITIES

Firms often enter into transactions that are peripheral to their core operations but generate gains and losses that must be reported on the income statement. For example, to create, manufacture, and market products, firms generally need to invest in assets such as buildings and equipment that provide the capacity to carry out business activities. The sale of such peripheral assets usually results in a gain or loss. Similar to restructuring charges, gains and losses from activities peripheral to the primary activities of a firm are included in income from continuing operations. The analyst should search for such items and decide whether to exclude them when assessing current profitability and forecasting future earnings.

Example 15

In the annual report of Delta Air Lines, income from continuing operations for three years includes gains from the disposition of flight equipment of $18 million, $17 million, and $35 million. Such gains relate, although indirectly, to providing transportation services. Clearly, Delta Air Lines needs to replenish its aircraft inventory periodically to carry out its business activities.

Example 16

Refer to PepsiCo's financial statements in Appendix A. Income Before Income Taxes includes the following category (in millions):

	Year 11	Year 10	Year 9
Bottling equity income and transaction gains/(losses), net......................	$160	$130	$1,083

Note 1 in Appendix A describes PepsiCo's policy of accounting for gains on issuance of stock by subsidiaries. The firm also provides a discussion of the policy in the section in Appendix B titled, "Bottling Equity Income and Transaction Gains and Losses." In this section, PepsiCo indicates that a gain of $59 million from the sale of approximately 2 million shares of PBG stock is included in the $160 million.

Example 17

Refer to the previous example involving PepsiCo's bottling equity income and transaction gains and losses. For Year 9, the firm included a $1.0 billion transaction gain in this income statement category, significantly larger than any amount reported in this category in the subsequent two years. (Chapter 4 also includes a discussion of this gain when assessing PepsiCo's profitability for Year 9.)

Appendix B discusses the transaction that dominated the amount reported in this category. PepsiCo states in the section titled, "Bottling Equity Income and Transaction Gains and Losses":

> In Year 9, reported bottling equity income and transaction gains and losses include a gain on bottling transactions of $1.0 billion ($270 million after-tax or $0.15 per share) relating to the second quarter PBG and Whitman bottling transactions.

This large transaction is the result of a strategic decision by PepsiCo in Year 9 to exit the business of converting the PepsiCo concentrate into the final product, bottling it, and then distributing it to customers. It is interesting to note that Coke, PepsiCo's main competitor in the soft drink/beverage industry, has implemented this same strategy for many years.

The analyst in each of these examples must assess whether to remove peripheral gains and losses from income from continuing operations. In many cases, even though the gains and losses do not relate to the sale of the firm's principal products and services, such gains and losses recur and should enter into estimates of future earnings. Of course, firms that rely heavily on such gains and losses for their earnings will not likely survive for long. Thus, a large percentage of reported earnings comprising gains and losses from peripheral activities might signal the need to revise downward the estimates of sustainable earnings.

Similar to impairment and restructuring charges, firms report peripheral gains and losses on a *pre-tax* basis. Income tax expense includes the tax effects of the gain or loss. If the analyst decides to eliminate the gain or loss from income from continuing operations, the analyst must also eliminate the related tax effect from income tax expense using the statutory rate as described for restructuring charges above.

Summary of Raw Data Adjustments

This section discussed the reporting of various types of disclosures related to earnings. A large set of factors are identified that may affect the quality of the accounting information as a predictor of future sustainable earnings. The nature and extent of adjustments made to current earnings in order to use it as a predictor requires knowledge of the industry, the firm and its strategy, and the required financial reporting. The process is more art than science and requires considerable judgment on the part of the analyst.

RESTATED FINANCIAL STATEMENT DATA

A notion embedded in the concept of high quality financial statement data is the ability to compare financial statement data across years for any particular firm. Comparability of data is crucial for effective time-series analysis, a technique used by analysts to judge trends over time. Policymakers also recognize the importance of comparability and in some cases require firms to provide restated, comparable data. Firms retroactively restate the financial statements of prior years when the current year's annual report includes prior years' financial statements in the following situations:

1. A firm that decides during the current year to discontinue its involvement in a particular line of business reclassifies the income of that business for prior years as a discontinued operation, even though the firm had included this income in continuing operations in income statements originally prepared for these years. The firm may also reclassify the net assets of the discontinued business as of the end of the preceding year to a single line, Net Assets of Discontinued Business, even though these net assets appeared among individual assets and liabilities in the balance sheet originally prepared for the preceding year.

2. Certain changes in accounting principles (for example, a change from a LIFO cost-flow assumption for inventories to any other cost-flow assumption, or a change in the method of income recognition on long-term contracts, both discussed in Chapter 7) require the restatement of prior years' financial statements to reflect the new method.[14]

The analyst must decide whether to use the financial statement data as originally reported for each year or as restated to reflect the new conditions. Because the objective of most financial statement analysis is to evaluate the past as a guide for projecting the future, the logical response is to use the restated data.

The analyst encounters difficulties, however, in using restated data. Most companies include balance sheets for two years and income statements and statements of cash flows for three years in their annual reports. Analysts can calculate ratios and perform other analyses based on balance sheet data only (for example, current assets/current liabilities, long-term debt/shareholders' equity) for two years at most on a consistent basis. Analysts can calculate ratios based on data from the income statement (for example, cost of goods sold/sales) or from the statement of cash flows (for example, cash flow from operations/capital expenditures) for three years at most on a consistent basis. However, many important ratios and other analyses rely on

---

[14]Prior to 2002, if a firm merged with another firm in a transaction that qualified for pooling of interests accounting, it restated prior years' financial statements to reflect the results for the two entities combined. Chapter 9 briefly discusses pooling of interests accounting, which was eliminated as a reporting option with the adoption of Financial Accounting Standards Board, *Statement of Financial Accounting Standards No. 141*, "Business Combinations." As discussed in Appendix A, note that PepsiCo accounted for its merger with Quaker Oats Company using the pooling of interests method because that merger was initiated in December 2000.

data from both the balance sheet and either the income statement or the statement of cash flows. For example, the rate of return on common shareholders' equity equals net income to common stock divided by average common shareholders' equity. The denominator of this ratio requires two years of balance sheet data. Thus, it is possible to calculate ratios based on average data from the balance sheet and one of the other two financial statements for only one year under the new conditions. The analysts could obtain balance sheet amounts for prior years from earlier annual reports, but this results in comparing restated income statement or statement of cash flow data with non-restated balance sheet data for those earlier years.

Example 18

Refer to the financial statements of General Mills (Mills) in Exhibits 6.10 (income statement) and 6.11 (balance sheet). The notes to Mills' financial statements indicate that Mills decided in Year 5 to dispose of its toy and fashion segments and the non-apparel retailing businesses within its specialty retailing segment. It reported a loss of $188.3 million from these discontinued operations in its income statement for Year 5 (see first column of Exhibit 6.10). In its comparative income statements for Year 4 and Year 3 (second and third columns), the income from these discontinued operations appears on the line, Discontinued Operations After Tax. Exhibit 6.10 also shows the amounts as originally reported for Year 4 and Year 3 (columns four and five) in which Mills included the revenues and expenses from these operations in continuing operations. Exhibit 6.11 shows the comparative balance sheets for Year 5 and Year 4. Note that the net assets of these discontinued businesses appear on a separate line in the Year 5 balance sheet. However, individual asset and liability accounts include the amounts for these discontinued activities in the Year 4 balance sheet. Thus, Mills provides three years of income statements with the operations of these discontinued businesses set out separately, but only one balance sheet. The analyst cannot even calculate ratios using income statement and average balance sheet data for one year on a consistent basis in this case.

When a firm provides sufficient information to restate prior years' financial statements without injecting an intolerable number of assumptions, the analyst should use retroactively restated financial statement data. When the firm does not provide sufficient information to do the restatements, the analysts should use the amounts as originally reported for each year. Then to interpret the resulting ratios, the analyst attempts to assess how much of the change in the ratios results from the new reporting condition and how much relates to other factors.

ACCOUNT CLASSIFICATION DIFFERENCES

Accounting classification differences also affect comparability and time-series analysis. Firms frequently classify items in their financial statements in different ways. The goal when comparing two or more companies is to obtain comparable data sets. A scan of the financial statements should permit the analyst to identify significant differences that might affect the analysis and interpretations.

EXHIBIT 6.10

General Mills, Inc., and Subsidiaries
Consolidated Statement of Earnings
(amounts in millions, except per share data)

	Fiscal Year Ended			As Originally Reported	
	May 26, Year 5 (52 weeks)	May 27, Year 4 (52 Weeks)	May 29, Year 3 (52 Weeks)	May 27, Year 4 (52 Weeks)	May 29, Year 3 (52 Weeks)
Continuing Operations:					
Sales	$4,285.2	$4,118.4	$4,082.3	$5,600.8	$5,550.8
Costs and Expenses: Cost of sales,					
exclusive of items below ...	2,474.8	2,432.8	2,394.8	3,165.9	3,123.3
Selling, general and					
administrative expenses ...	1,368.1	1,251.5	1,288.3	1,849.4	1,831.6
Depreciation and					
amortization expenses	110.4	99.0	94.2	133.1	127.5
Interest expense	60.2	31.5	39.5	61.4	58.7
Total Costs and Expenses	4,013.5	3,814.8	3,816.8	5,209.8	5,141.1
Earnings from Continuing					
Operations—Pre-tax	271.7	303.6	265.5	391.0	409.7
Gain (Loss) from Redeployments	(75.8)	53.0	2.7	7.7	—
Earnings from Continuing Operations					
after Redeployments—Pre-tax	195.9	356.6	268.2	398.7	409.7
Income Taxes	80.5	153.9	106.1	165.3	164.6
Earnings from Continuing Operations					
after Redeployments	115.4	202.7	162.1	233.4	245.1
Earnings per Share—Continuing					
Operations after Redeployments	$2.58	$4.32	$3.24	$4.98	$4.89
Discontinued Operations after Tax	(188.3)	30.7	83.0	—	—
Net Earnings (Loss)	$(72.9)	$233.4	$245.1	$233.4	$245.1
Net Earnings (Loss) per Share	$(1.63)	$4.98	$4.89	$4.98	$4.89
Average Number of Common Shares	44.7	46.9	50.1	46.9	50.1

EXHIBIT 6.11

General Mills, Inc., and Subsidiaries
Consolidated Balance Sheets
(in millions)

		Fiscal Year Ended	
Assets		May 26, Year 5	May 27, Year 4
Current Assets:	Cash and short-term investments	$ 66.8	$ 66.0
	Receivables, less allowance for doubtful accounts of $4.0 in Yr. 5 and $18.8 in Yr. 4	284.5	550.6
	Inventories	377.7	661.7
	Investments in tax leases	—	49.6
	Prepaid expenses	40.1	43.6
	Net assets of discontinued operations and redeployments	517.5	18.4
	Total Current Assets	1,286.6	1,389.9
Land, Buildings, and Equipment at Cost:	Land	93.3	125.9
	Buildings	524.4	668.6
	Equipment	788.1	904.7
	Construction in progress	80.2	130.0
	Total Land, Buildings, and Equipment	1,486.0	1,829.2
	Less accumulated depreciation	(530.0)	(599.8)
Net Land, Buildings, and Equipment	....	956.0	1,229.4
Other Assets:	Net noncurrent assets of businesses to be spun off ...$	206.5	$ —
	Intangible assets, principally goodwill	50.8	146.0
	Investments and miscellaneous assets	162.7	92.8
	Total Other Assets	420.0	238.8
Total Assets	....	**$2,662.6**	**$2,858.1**
Liabilities and Stockholders' Equity			
Current Liabilities:	Accounts payable	$ 360.8	$ 477.8
	Current portion of long-term debt	59.4	60.3
	Notes payable	379.8	251.0
	Accrued taxes	1.4	74.3
	Accrued payroll	91.8	119.1
	Other current liabilities	164.0	162.9
	Total Current Liabilities	1,057.2	1,145.4
Long-term Debt	....	449.5	362.6
Deferred Income Taxes	....	29.8	76.5
Deferred Income Taxes—Tax Leases	....	60.8	—
Other Liabilities and Deferred Credits	....	42.0	49.0
	Total Liabilities	1,639.3	1,633.5

(continued)

Exhibit 6.11—continued		Fiscal Year Ended	
		May 26, Year 5	May 27, Year 4
Stockholders' Equity:	Common stock	$ 213.7	$ 215.4
	Retained earnings	1,201.7	1,375.0
	Less common stock in treasury, at cost	(333.9)	(291.8)
	Cumulative foreign currency adjustment	(58.2)	(74.0)
	Total Stockholders' Equity	1,023.3	1,224.6
Total Liabilities and Stockholders' Equity		**$2,662.6**	**$2,858.1**

Example 19

Exhibit 6.12 shows the disclosure of operating expenses for three leading manufacturers of cellular phones: Ericsson (Swedish), Motorola (U.S.), and Nokia (Finnish). Ericsson and Motorola report depreciation separately, whereas Nokia includes it in cost of goods sold and selling and administrative expenses. Nokia reports research and development (R&D) expense separately, whereas Ericsson and Motorola include it in selling and administrative expenses. The analyst must be aware of these classification differences when comparing financial statement ratios directly across these three firms.

To deal with the depreciation differences, the analyst must either allocate the depreciation amount for Ericsson and Motorola to cost of goods sold and selling and administrative expenses, or extract from cost of goods sold and selling and administrative expenses the depreciation amount of Nokia (Nokia reports total depreciation expense as an addback to net income in computing cash flow from operations). Both of these approaches require the analyst to make assumptions about the proportion of depreciation applicable to cost of goods sold versus selling and administrative expenses.

EXHIBIT 6.12

Disclosure of Operating Expenses by Cellular Phone Companies
(in millions)

	Ericsson	Motorola	Nokia
Sales	SEK 124,266	$27,973	FIM 39,321
Cost of Goods Sold	(70,106)	(18,990)	(28,029)
Selling and Administrative	(40,803)	(4,715)	(3,512)
Depreciation	(4,216)	(2,308)	—
Research and Development	—	—	(3,514)
Operating Income	SEK 9,141	$ 1,960	FIM 4,266

The classification differences for R&D expense are easier to fix. Ericsson and Motorola report the amount of R&D expense in their notes. Thus, the analyst can subtract the amounts from selling and administrative expenses.

When the analyst can easily and unambiguously reclassify accounts, the reclassified data should serve as the basis for analysis. If the reclassifications require numerous assumptions, then it is necessary to make them as precisely as possible. If the assumptions cannot be reasonably precise, then it may be best to avoid making them. The analyst should make note of the differences in account classification for further reference when interpreting the financial statement analysis.

FINANCIAL REPORTING WORLDWIDE

Thus far, we have identified many reasons why accounting quality and comparability may be lacking. The concerns discussed in the chapter to this point equally apply to firms that follow reporting systems employed outside the United States. However, important additional concerns also exist when comparing financial data for firms that operate in different countries.

Cross-national analysis of firms entails a two-step approach:

1. Achieve comparability of the reporting methods and accounting principles employed by the firms under scrutiny.
2. Understand corporate strategies, institutional structures, and cultural practices unique to the countries in which the firms operate.

Ideally, financial reporting would be the same worldwide. That has not happened to date, however, and differences in accounting principles worldwide may severely affect both time-series and cross-sectional comparisons of data reported by multinational firms.[15] The analyst needs to thoroughly understand the reporting system employed by the firms under scrutiny in order to decide what data adjustments are necessary.[16]

Firms headquartered outside of the United States which have debt or equity securities traded in U.S. capital markets must file a Form 20-F report with the SEC each year. The Form 20-F report must include a reconciliation of shareholders' equity and net income as reported under GAAP of the firm's local country with GAAP in the

---

[15]As discussed in Chapter 1, one objective of the International Accounting Standards Board (IASB) is to improve and harmonize standards of financial reporting worldwide. In addition, recently the IASB and FASB pledged to use their best efforts to make existing U.S. and IASB standards fully compatible as soon as is practicable and to coordinate their future work programs to insure that once achieved, compatibility is maintained. The IASB's overarching objective is to reduce diversity in accounting principles across countries and to encourage greater standardization. Its pronouncements, however, have no enforceability of their own.

[16]A study of international accounting standards is beyond the scope of this book. However, an extensive summary of accounting principle differences around the world is available in Frederick D. S. Choi, *International Accounting and Finance Handbook*, Second Edition, New York: John Wiley & Sons, Inc., 1997. The largest public accounting firms also prepare comprehensive guides of financial reporting practices worldwide.

United States. With this information, the analyst can convert the financial statements of a non-U.S. firm to achieve comparable accounting principles with U.S. firms.

Example 20

Exhibit 6.13 presents the Form 20-F reconciliation for three recent years for Ericsson, a Swedish manufacturer of cellular phones. (We study the particular accounting principles requiring adjustment in later chapters and will therefore not discuss them at this time.) Note, however, that net income under U.S. GAAP significantly exceeds that under Swedish GAAP, primarily because of differences in the treatment of software development costs.

Achieving comparability in reporting is important to the analysis of multinational firms, but the data needs to be carefully interpreted. Analysis of multinational firms is complicated by the fact that the environments in which the firms operate may vary extensively across countries. Operational strategies may exist in one firm's base country that are not common in another. Institutional arrangements, such as significant alliances with banks and extensive intercorporate holdings, may be common in one country and not in another. Cultural characteristics may exist in one country that affect how firms do business in that country—with those same characteristics foreign to other business settings.

EXHIBIT 6.13

Form 20-F Reconciliations for Ericsson
(in millions)

	Year 6	Year 5	Year 4
Adjustments to Shareholders' Equity			
Reported Shareholders' Equity	SEK 40,456	SEK 34,263	SEK 23,302
Capitalization of Software.	6,100	5,158	3,916
Capitalization of Interest Expense	349	325	310
Pensions.	746	588	406
Revaluation of Fixed Assets.	(500)	(608)	(729)
Deferred Taxes	(2,230)	(1,848)	(1,510)
Approximate Equity According to U.S. GAAP	SEK 44,921	SEK 37,878	SEK 25,695
Adjustments to Net Income			
Reported Net Income	SEK 7,110	SEK 5,439	SEK 3,949
Depreciation of Revalued Fixed Assets	108	121	—
Capitalization of Software Development Costs	942	1,242	1,004
Capitalization of Interest Expenses.	24	15	16
Pensions.	158	182	112
Deferred Income Taxes	(382)	(338)	(190)
Approximate Net Income According to U.S. GAAP . . .	SEK 7,960	SEK 6,661	SEK 4,891

For example, in a study addressing comparability of Japanese and U.S. financial reporting, Herrmann, Inoue, and Thomas identify the following environmental characteristics that may influence interpretation of the data:

1. Profitability ratios often are more conservative in Japan, attributable in part to the close link between tax and financial reporting systems.
2. Japanese companies often have higher debt ratios. High debt ratios are sometimes considered a sign of financial strength because debt is the primary source of capital.
3. The corporate group is different in Japan in that Japanese grouping is often based on bank dependence, intercompany loans, mutual shareholding, preferred business transactions, and multiple personal ties.[17]

Herrmann, Inoue, and Thomas stress that environmental factors unique to Japan may influence the financial data reported by Japanese firms in such a way that the data, although comparable to data reported by U.S. firms once the necessary adjustments are made, can only be effectively interpreted when taking these unique factors into consideration.

Other countries have their own unique environmental and business practices. When analyzing multinational firms, the analyst needs to incorporate these factors into the interpretation of the data and understand that, although the data may be comparable from a measurement perspective, they may not be comparable on other dimensions.

EARNINGS MANAGEMENT

We conclude the chapter with a discussion of earnings management because the concepts of accounting quality and earnings management often are linked when discussing the need to adjust financial data to better reflect the economic information content of financial data.

As with other concepts discussed in this chapter, earnings management connotes different things to different users of the term.[18] Healy and Wahlen provide the following definition of earnings management:

> Earnings management occurs when managers use judgment in financial reporting and in structuring transactions to alter financial reports to either mislead some stakeholders about the underlying economic performance of the company or to influence contractual outcomes that depend on reporting accounting numbers.[19]

---

[17]Don Herrmann, Tatsuo Inoue, and Wayne Thomas, "Are There Benefits to Restating Japanese Financial Statements According to U.S. GAAP?" *Journal of Financial Statement Analysis*, Fall 1996, pp. 61–73.

[18]As Chapter 5 notes, earnings management also is linked at times with earnings manipulation, a topic discussed in that chapter and defined as preparing financial reports based on reporting techniques outside the limits of generally accepted accounting principles.

[19]Paul M. Healy and James M. Wahlen, "A Review of the Earnings Management Literature and its Implications for Standard Setting," *Accounting Horizons*, December 1999, pp. 365–383.

In the chapter we established that choices, judgments, and estimates are an inevitable consequence of the reporting process. Healy and Wahlen recognize this and define earnings management as the use of these inherent aspects of the reporting model to mask the underlying economic performance of a firm. Any judgments employed by management that result in lower economic information content of the financial reports, and provide a skewed basis for making decisions, are probably the result of a firm practicing earnings management.

Ferreting out earnings management is difficult because there are so many ways that managers can exercise judgment in financial reporting. One of our objectives in Chapters 7 through 9 is to illustrate the judgments that firms must make to apply the accounting principles under investigation in those chapters so that the analyst can discern whether a firm practices earnings management.

Motives to Practice Earnings Management[20]

Suggested reasons *for* earnings management by a firm and its managers include:

1. Firms manage earnings to create optimal manager compensation payments under compensation contracts.
2. Firms manage earnings to create optimal job security for senior management.
3. Firms manage earnings to create optimal lending environments and to mitigate potential violation of debt covenants.
4. Firms use earnings management in an attempt to influence short-term stock price performance and wealth resource allocation over time.
5. Firms have incentives to minimize/manage reported earnings to thwart industry-specific actions and anti-trust actions against the firm.

Disincentives to Practice Earnings Management

Suggested reasons *against* earnings management by a firm and its managers include:

1. Earnings and cash flows ultimately coincide, so firms cannot manage earnings forever. Eventually, earnings aggressively reported in early years must be offset by lower earnings or even losses in later years to compensate.
2. Capital markets and regulators such as the Securities and Exchange Commission penalize firms identified as flagrant earnings managers.
3. Legal consequences can result from aggressive earnings management, as well as from earnings management that reverts to earnings manipulations and fraud.[21]

---

[20]Often the motivations for practicing earnings management and earnings manipulation (discussed in Chapter 5) are similar; however, the legal consequences of earnings manipulation are generally more severe.
[21]Messod D. Beneish, "Detecting GAAP Violation: Implications for Assessing Earnings Management among Firms with Extreme Financial Performance," *Journal of Accounting and Public Policy* (1997), pp. 271–309; and "The Detection of Earnings Management," *Financial Analyst Journal* (September/October, 1999), pp. 24–36.

The questions as to whether analysts of financial reports can detect earnings management and make appropriate adjustments to reported amounts in making investment decisions has been the subject of extensive but inconclusive research in recent years.[22]

Boundaries of Earnings Management

It is important to note that earnings management has some boundaries. Securities regulations and stock exchanges require annual audits by independent accountants. Auditors can monitor particularly aggressive actions taken by management to influence earnings, although their power to thwart actions taken within the bounds of generally accepted accounting principles is limited. In addition, the ongoing scrutiny of financial analysts and investors serves as a check on earnings management. Security analysts typically follow several firms within an industry and have a sense of the corporate reporting "personalities" of various firms. The frequency, timeliness, and quality of management's communications with shareholders and analysts serve as a signal of the forthrightness of management and of the likelihood of earnings being highly managed.[23]

The task for the analyst is to identify those situations where earnings management is possible and the avenues management might pursue in those situations to carry out earnings management. Understanding when GAAP provides flexibility to manage earnings should permit the analyst to distinguish high economic information content from what some call "cosmetic" (that is, earnings managed) content of the reported data. As stated earlier, a close study of the selected accounting principles presented in Chapters 7 to 9 will aid in this task.

SUMMARY

The financial analysis framework discussed in Chapters 1 to 5, and the discussion of valuation presented in Chapters 10 to 13 assume that a firm's reported financial statement data reflect accurately the economic effects of a firm's decisions. The assumption also is that the financial data are informative about the firm's likely future profitability and risk. This chapter develops the concept of accounting quality as the basis for assessing the information content of reported financial statement data, and for adjusting that data before assessing a firm's profitability and risk or before valuing the firm.

The illustrations in this chapter identify items that are part of the current period's performance but may not recur in future years. The chapter indicates the adjustments the analyst might make to eliminate the effect of such items from forecasts of future earnings. The chapter also identifies adjustments that the analyst might make to enhance comparability of a particular firm's reported amounts over time.

---

[22]See, *op. cit.*, for an extensive list of research related to earnings management provided in the reference list at the end of the article.

[23]See, Mark H. Lang and Russell J. Lundholm, "Corporate Disclosure Policy and Analyst Behavior," *Accounting Review*, October 1996, pp. 467–492.

Analyzing accounting quality and adjusting financial data are themes that continue in Chapters 7 through 9. In this regard, Chapters 6 through 9 represent a unit that together addresses the relevant financial data for analysis. Chapter 7 focuses on revenue recognition and related expenses. Chapter 8 examines the recognition and valuation of liabilities, together with related expenses. Chapter 9 explores topics that have pervasive effects on all three principal financial statements, including corporate acquisitions, intercorporate investments, and foreign currency translation.

The chapter concludes with examining the distinction between earnings management and earnings fraud, and the conditions that might trigger earnings management. The concepts of accounting quality and earnings management often are linked when discussing the need to adjust financial data to better reflect the economic information content of financial data.

PROBLEMS AND CASES

6.1 ADJUSTING FOR UNUSUAL INCOME STATEMENT AND CLASSIFICATION ITEMS.   H.J. Heinz Company is one of the world's leading marketers of branded foods to retail and food service channels. According to the firm, Heinz holds the number one or two branded products in more than 50 world product markets. Among the company's well-known brands are Heinz, Starkist, Kibbles 'n Bits, and 9-Lives. Exhibit 6.14 presents an income statement for Heinz for Year 10, Year 11, and Year 12. Notes to the financial statements reveal the following information:

1. *Gain on Sale of Weight Watchers.* In Year 10, Heinz completed the sale of the Weight Watchers classroom business for $735 million. The transaction resulted in a pre-tax gain of $464.5 million. The sale did not include Weight Watcher frozen meals, desserts, and breakfast items. Heinz did not disclose the tax effect of the gain reported in Exhibit 6.14.

2. *Accounting Change for Revenue Recognition.* In Year 11, Heinz changed its method of accounting for revenue recognition to recognizing revenue upon the passage of title, ownership, and risk of loss to the customer. The change was driven by a new ruling of the Securities and Exchange Commission on revenue recognition. The cumulative effect of the change on prior years resulted in a charge to income of $17 million, net of income taxes of $10 million. Heinz indicated that the effect on Year 11 and prior years was not material.

3. *Sale and Promotion Costs.* In Year 11, Heinz changed the classification of certain sale and promotion incentives provided to customers and consumers. In the past, Heinz classified these incentives as selling and administrative expenses (see Exhibit 6.14), with the gross amount of the revenue associated with the incentives reported in sales. Beginning in Year 11, Heinz changed to reporting the incentives as a reduction of revenues. As a result of this change, the firm reported lower revenues of $693 million in Year 12, $610 million in Year 11, and $469 million in Year 10. The firm stated that selling and administrative expenses were "correspondingly reduced such that net earnings were not affected." Exhibit 6.14 already reflects the adjustments to sales revenues

EXHIBIT 6.14

Income Statement
H.J. Heinz Company
(amounts in millions)
(Problem 6.1)

	Year 12	Year 11	Year 10
Sales	$9,431	$8,821	$8,939
Gain on Sale of Weight Watchers	—	—	465
Cost of Goods Sold	(6,094)	(5,884)	(5,789)
Selling and Administrative Expenses	(1,746)	(1,955)	(1,882)
Interest Income	27	23	25
Interest Expense.	(294)	(333)	(270)
Other (Income) Expense.	(45)	1	(25)
Income Before Income Taxes and Cumulative			
Effect of Accounting Changes	$1,279	$ 673	$1,463
Income Tax Expense	(445)	(178)	(573)
Income before Cumulative Effect of Accounting Change	$ 834	$ 495	$ 890
Cumulative Effect of Accounting Change.	—	(17)	—
Net Income	$ 834	$ 478	$ 890

and selling and administrative expenses for Years 10 through 12. (Note that Management's Discussion and Analysis by PepsiCo in Appendix B (section titled, "New Accounting Standards") discusses a similar reclassification adjustment the firm will make to its Year 12 income statement.)

4. **Tax Rate.** The U.S. federal statutory income tax rate was 35 percent for each of the years presented in Exhibit 6.14.

Required

a. Discuss whether or not you would adjust for each of the following items when using earnings to forecast the future profitability of Heinz:
   (1) Gain on Sale of Weight Watchers Classroom Business
   (2) Accounting Change for Revenue Recognition
b. Indicate the adjustment you would make to Heinz's net income for each of the items in part a.
c. Discuss whether you believe that the reclassification adjustments made by Heinz for the sale and promotion incentive costs (item 3) are appropriate.
d. Prepare a common size income statement for Year 10, Year 11, and Year 12 using the amounts in Exhibit 6.14. Set sales equal to 100 percent.
e. Repeat part d after making the income statement adjustments in part b.
f. Assess the changes in the profitability of Heinz during the three-year period.

6.2 ADJUSTING FOR UNUSUAL INCOME STATEMENT ITEMS. Parametric Technology Corporation (PTC) was founded almost twenty years ago. It develops, markets, and supports software that helps manufacturers improve the competitiveness of their products. PTC offers a suite of mechanical computer-aided design tools and a range of Internet-based software technologies. The firm employed over 4,500 people at the end of Year 11. Exhibit 6.15 shows the income statement for PTC for Years 9 through Year 11.

1. *Goodwill and Other Intangible Asset Amortization.* PTC amortizes goodwill over five to seven years and trademarks over seven years. It amortizes other intangible assets, such as customer lists and developed technology (software), over seven years. Beginning in Year 12, GAAP no longer requires firms to amortize goodwill and other intangibles with indefinite lives, such as trademarks. Firms must, however, test such intangibles annually for impairment and write down those assets when an impairment occurs.

2. *Acquisition and Nonrecurring Charges.* In Years 9 through Year 11, PTC reorganized its sales force, wrote down some impaired assets, provided severance and termination packages to employees, and implemented several cost reduction programs—all related to acquisitions undertaken by PTC during the three-year period. Year 9 also included a write-off of purchased in-process research and development costs related to acquisitions made in that year. PTC did not disclose the tax effects of the charges reported in Exhibit 6.15.

EXHIBIT 6.15

Parametric Technology Corporation
Income Statement
(amounts in thousands)
(Problem 6.2)

	Year 11	Year 10	Year 9
License and Service Revenues	$934,606	$928,414	$1,057,601
Cost of License and Service Revenues	(252,571)	(244,984)	(207,655)
Research and Development	(148,942)	(143,763)	(124,131)
Sales and Marketing	(380,902)	(416,665)	(407,936)
General and Administration	(74,683)	(71,263)	(62,852)
Amortization of Goodwill and Other Intangible Assets	(37,942)	(38,432)	(22,888)
Acquisition and Nonrecurring Charges	(42,568)	(21,534)	(53,347)
Interest Income and Expense, net	2,495	3,160	2,450
Write-down of Investments	(10,354)	—	—
Income (Loss) before Income Taxes	$(10,861)	$ (5,067)	$ 181,242
(Provision) Benefit for Income Taxes	2,647	1,087	(61,949)
Net Income (Loss)	$ (8,214)	$ (3,980)	$ 119,293

3. **Write-down of Investments.** In Year 11, PTC recorded a $10.4 million non-cash write-down on several equity investments. PTC did not disclose the tax effects of the write-down reported in Exhibit 6.15.

4. **Tax Rate.** The U.S. federal statutory income tax rate was 35 percent for each of the years presented in Exhibit 6.15.

Required

a. Discuss the appropriate treatment of the (1) goodwill and other intangible asset amortization, (2) acquisition and nonrecurring charges, and (3) write-down of investments items when using earnings to forecast the future profitability of PTC.

b. Assume for this part that you have decided to eliminate items 2 and 3 in part a. Indicate the adjustments to net income of PTC to eliminate each of the items.

6.3 ADJUSTING FOR NONRECURRING ITEMS.   Ruby Tuesday, Inc. owns and operates Ruby Tuesday casual dining restaurants. The firm also franchises the Ruby Tuesday concept in selected domestic and international markets. As of the end of Year 12, it owned and operated almost 400 restaurants, and had over 200 franchised restaurants. Exhibit 6.16 presents an income statement for Ruby Tuesday, Inc. for Year 12, Year 11, and Year 10. The notes to the financial statements reveal the following additional information:

1. **Peripheral Losses.** In Years 12 and 10, Ruby Tuesday recorded pre-tax losses on restaurants it sold. For Year 10, the firm recognized the sale of a set of restaurants—American Café, L&N Seafood, and Tia's Tex-Mex restaurants—to Specialty Restaurant Group and recorded a pre-tax and after-tax loss of $10.0 million. Ruby Tuesday received a note payable of $28.9 million from the Specialty Restaurant Group as partial payment for the restaurants. In Year 12, Ruby Tuesday recorded an additional loss on the sale by writing off the note due to the firm from the Specialty Restaurant Group. Ruby Tuesday indicated that the write-off generated a $11.4 million tax benefit.

2. **Accounting Change.** Ruby Tuesday adopted *Statement No. 133* in Year 12. *Statement No. 133* addresses accounting for derivative instruments. The firm reports the cumulative effect of the accounting change net of tax affects.

Required

a. Discuss the appropriate treatment of items and 1 and 2 when using earnings to forecast the future profitability of Ruby Tuesday.

b. Indicate the adjustments to the income statement to eliminate the items in part a.

c. Ruby Tuesday's statement of cash flows shows an addback to net income for the losses on the restaurant sales for both Year 12 ($28.9 million) and Year 10 ($10.0 million). What is the interpretation of this addback?

EXHIBIT 6.16

Ruby Tuesday, Inc.
Income Statement
(amounts in milllion)
(Problem 6.3)

	Year 12	Year 11	Year 10
Restaurant Sales and Operating Revenue	$ 819	$ 770	$ 785
Franchise Revenues	14	12	8
Total Revenues	$ 833	$ 782	$ 793
Payroll and Related Costs	(268)	(248)	(251)
Cost of Merchandise	(221)	(213)	(214)
Other Restaurant Operating Costs	(155)	(148)	(159)
Depreciation and Amortization	(34)	(34)	(42)
Loss on Specialty Restaurant Group, LLC	(29)	—	—
Loss on Sale of Various Restaurants	—	—	(10)
Selling and Administrative Expenses	(45)	(50)	(53)
(Interest) Income Expense	6	4	(1)
Income Before Income Taxes and Cumulative Effect of Accounting Change	$ 87	$ 93	$ 63
Provision for Income Taxes	(30)	(33)	(26)
Income Before Cumulative Effect of Change in Accounting Principle	$ 57	$ 60	$ 37
Cumulative Effect of Change in Accounting Principle	$ (1)	—	—
Net Income	$ 56	$ 60	$ 37

6.4 ADJUSTMENTS FOR PERIPHERAL GAINS, IMPAIRMENT OF LONG-LIVED ASSETS, AND OTHER UNUSUAL ITEMS. Wyeth (formerly American Home Products) is a global leader in prescription pharmaceuticals, non-prescription medicines, and animal health care products. Wyeth's products are sold in more than 140 countries, with a product portfolio that includes treatments across a wide range of therapeutic areas. It employs more than 52,000 individuals.

Exhibit 6.17 presents a recent income statement for Wyeth. A set of transactions and activities during Years 9 through 11 led to a number of nonrecurring items on the income statement.

1. *Special Charges.* In Year 10, Wyeth took two special charges: (1) $80 million ($52 million after-tax) to provide for product returns and the write-off of

EXHIBIT 6.17

Wyeth and Subsidiaries
Partial Income Statement
(amounts in millions)
(Problem 6.4)

	Year 11	Year 10	Year 9
Net Revenue	$14,129	$13,214	$11,815
Cost of Goods Sold	(3,389)	(3,269)	(3,022)
Selling, General, and Administration.	(5,179)	(4,983)	(4,322)
Research and Development Expenses	(1,870)	(1,689)	(1,588)
Interest Expense, net	(146)	(58)	(214)
Other Income, net	274	161	256
Gain on Sale of Immunex Common Stock	—	2,061	—
Termination	—	1,709	—
Litigation	(950)	(7,500)	(4,750)
Goodwill Impairment	—	(401)	—
Special Charges.	—	(347)	(82)
Income before Income Taxes	$ 2,869	$(1,102)	$(1,907)
Income Tax (Provision) Benefit.	(583)	200	700
Income from Continuing Operations.	$ 2,286	$ (902)	$(1,207)

inventory that included phenylpropanolamine (PPA) (The U.S. Food and Drug Administration requested that all firms cease production and shipment of any product containing PPA.); and (2) $267 million ($173 million after-tax) for the discontinuation of certain products manufactured in Wyeth's facilities in Pennsylvania and New York. In Year 9, the firm recorded a special charge of $82 million ($53 million after-tax) for estimated costs associated with the suspension of shipments and the voluntary market withdrawal of RotaShield, a rotavirus vaccine.

2. *Goodwill Impairment.* In Year 10, Wyeth determined that the goodwill associated with the Solgar consumer health care product line was impaired. The firm recorded a charge of $401 million ($341 million after-tax) to write down the carrying value of the goodwill to its fair value, based upon discounted future cash flows.

3. *Litigation Charges.* Wyeth was named as a defendant in numerous legal actions related to the diet drugs Redux and Pondimin. The drugs were used in the United States by approximately 5.8 million people until their voluntary market withdrawal in Year 7. The legal actions alleged that the use of the diet drugs caused certain serious conditions, including valvular heart disease. Extensive class action lawsuits and court-administered settlements took place since Year 7. Wyeth recorded litigation charges related to these drugs in Year 9

of $4,750 million, ($3,288 million after-tax), Year 10 $7,500 million ($5,375 million after-tax), and Year 11 $950 million ($615 million after-tax).

4. ***Gain on Sale of Immunex Common Stock.*** In Year 10, Wyeth sold 60.5 million shares of Immunex common stock. The firm recorded a gain on the sale of $2,061 million ($1,415 million after-tax).

5. ***Termination Fee.*** In Year 9, Wyeth and Warner-Lambert Company entered into an agreement to combine the two companies in a "merger-of-equals" transaction. Early in Year 10, the two firms terminated the merger agreement. Wyeth recorded termination "income" of $1,709 million ($1,111 million after-tax) resulting from the receipt of a $1,800 million termination fee provided for under the merger agreement, offset in part by certain related expenses.

Required

a. Discuss whether or not you would adjust for each of the five items when using earnings to forecast the future profitability of Wyeth. Discuss each item separately.

b. Indicate the adjustments to the income statement of Wyeth to eliminate each of the items in part a. The statutory income tax rate was 35 percent in each of the years.

c. The statement of cash flows shows an addback to net income for items 1 through 3, a subtraction for item 4, and nothing for item 5. Why is this the case?

6.5 ADJUSTING FOR UNUSUAL ITEMS.   Prior to Year 14, Borden, Inc. derived approximately 75 percent of its revenues from branded food products and 25 percent from packaging and industrial products. The geographical sales mix was comprised of approximately 67 percent in the United States and 33 percent from other countries, although, interestingly, the firm's manufacturing and processing facilities were equally split between the United States and other countries. In Year 14 and Year 15, Borden was acquired by a firm that specialized in takeovers and buyouts of established firms. As a result, the firm experienced substantial business realignments and financial restructuring during this period. Exhibit 6.18 presents an income statement and Exhibit 6.19 presents a statement of cash flow for Borden for Year 14, Year 15, and Year 16. The notes to the financial statements reveal the following additional information.

1. ***Restructuring Charges and Discontinued Operations.*** For years, Borden reported continually increasing sales while maintaining a profit margin of approximately 4 percent. Borden regularly purchased branded food products companies and other businesses with the cash flows generated by its mature food products business. Sales and earnings started declining in Year 10, however, brought on by deteriorating market positions in certain branded food products segments and difficulties in managing the diverse set of businesses in which Borden competed. As a result, Borden embarked on a major restructuring program in Year 10. The restructuring program involved both organizational changes and divestiture of its North American snacks, seafood, jams

EXHIBIT 6.18

Borden, Inc.
Income Statement
(amounts in millions)
(Problem 6.5)

	Year 16	Year 15	Year 14
Continuing Operations			
Sales	$5,944	$6,261	$6,226
Other Income (Expense)—Net.	(18)	(138)	35
Cost of Goods Sold	(4,136)	(4,240)	(4,083)
Selling and Administrative	(1,811)	(1,963)	(2,045)
Restructuring Expense.	11	(15)	(115)
(Loss) Gain on Divestitures.	(245)	59	15
Impairment Losses	(8)	(293)	0
Interest.	(140)	(143)	(140)
Minority Interest	(15)	(41)	(41)
Income Taxes	(24)	(53)	51
Income (Loss) from Continuing Operations	$ (442)	$ (566)	$ (97)
Discontinued Operations (net of tax effects)			
Income (Loss) from Operations	$ 9	$ 27	$ (26)
Gain (Loss) on Disposal	67	(59)	(490)
Income (Loss) from Discontinued Operations.	$ 76	$ (32)	$ (516)
Accounting Changes (net of tax effect)			
Postretirement Benefits Other than Pensions.	—	—	(18)
Net Income (Loss).	$ (366)	$ (598)	$ (631)

and jellies, and other businesses. Four years later, Borden embarked on another restructuring brought on by factors similar to those identified in Year 10. (The firm reported no restructuring charges in Year 11, Year 12, or Year 13.) The restructuring charges/credits in Year 14, Year 15, and Year 16 related to streamlining operations and the charges involved employee severances and relocations and plant closings, part of which Borden included in continuing operations and part of which it included in income from discontinued operations. The loss on disposal recognized in Year 14 represented a pre-tax charge of $637 million ($490 million after taxes) to provide for the expected future disposal of the North American businesses described above. The charges and credits in Year 15 and Year 16 related to these businesses as well.

2. **Loss/Gain on Divestitures.** In Year 16, the firm redesigned its operating structure and made the decision to divest additional businesses. The firm recorded

EXHIBIT 6.19

Borden, Inc.
Statement of Cash Flows
(amounts in millions)
(Problem 6.5)

	Year 16	Year 15	Year 14
Operations			
Net Income (Loss).....................................	$(366)	$(598)	$(631)
Depreciation and Amortization	157	193	224
Loss on Disposal—Discontinued Operations........	245	95	637
Restructuring..	(53)	(57)	53
Impairment Losses	8	293	—
(Increase) Decrease in Accounts Receivable	7	(41)	61
(Increase) Decrease in Inventories	10	(44)	30
Increase (Decrease) in Accounts Payable	(27)	50	3
Increase (Decrease) in Current and Deferred Taxes..	9	24	(242)
Other Changes in Working Capital Accounts........	92	(7)	17
Cash Flow from Operations........................	$ 82	$ (92)	$ 152
Investing			
Capital Expenditures.................................	$(203)	$(150)	$(177)
Divestiture of Businesses and Sale of Securities....	289	409	53
Purchase of Businesses	(6)	—	(9)
Cash Flow from Investing..........................	$ 80	$ 259	$(133)
Financing			
Increase (Decrease) in Short-term Debt...........	$(192)	$ (85)	$(536)
Increase in Long-term Debt	3	616	275
Issuance of Capital Stock...........................	998	6	12
Reduction in Long-term Debt.......................	(436)	(493)	(129)
Dividends...	(43)	(36)	(127)
Other	(472)	(150)	400
Cash Flow from Financing.........................	$(142)	$(142)	$(105)
Change in Cash	20	25	(86)
Cash—Beginning of Year	125	100	186
Cash—End of Year	$ 145	$ 125	$ 100

a $245 million charge related to the estimated losses on the disposal or consolidation of these businesses. The firm indicated that a large portion of the charge related to the excess of net book values over expected proceeds.

3. ***Impairment Losses.*** In Year 15, Borden wrote down goodwill, plant, and equipment totaling $293 million. The firm concluded that ongoing and projected operating losses reported by the businesses represented by these assets indicated that the carrying values of the assets were not expected to be recovered by their future cash flows. The firm stated that the future cash flow projections were measured at the business level, which is the level at which the business is managed. A similar write-down of $8 million was recorded in Year 16.

Required

a. Why do the amounts for restructuring charges in the income statement in Exhibit 6.18 differ from the amounts for restructuring charges reported in the operations section of the statement of cash flows in Exhibit 6.19?

b. Why does the amount for loss on disposal of discontinued operations in the income statement in Exhibit 6.18 in Year 14 differ from the amount reported in the operations section of the statement of cash flows in Exhibit 6.19?

c. Discuss whether or not you would eliminate each of the following items when using earnings to forecast the future profitability of Borden: (1) restructuring charges, (2) discontinued operations, (3) loss or gain on divestitures, and (4) impairment losses.

d. Assume for this part that you have decided to eliminate each of the four items in part c plus the adjustment for the accounting change. Indicate the change in net income as a result of such eliminations. The income tax rate is 35 percent for Year 14, Year 15, and Year 16.

e. Prepare a common-size income statement for Borden after eliminating the items in part d. Set sales equal to 100 percent.

f. Assess the changes in the profitability of Borden during the three-year period.

6.6 RESTRUCTURING CHARGES. Sapient Corporation, a leading technology consultancy firm, was founded in Year 3. It focuses on helping clients achieve business outcomes through the rapid application and support of advanced information technology. Most of its contracts are negotiated on a fixed-price basis. After a decade of success, the firm recently experienced a significant decline in the demand for its services. Exhibit 6.20 presents a recent income statement for Sapient Corporation. A note to the firm's financial statements stated that "the Company announced restructurings of its work force and operations in March, Year 11, and July, Year 11." The March, Year 11, charge was $60.5 million, and the July, Year 11, charge was $40.1 million. Under both plans, the charges consisted of work force reduction costs, consolidation of facilities, and termination of leases. Exhibit 6.20 reports the total of these two charges, $100.6 million, as "Restructuring and Other Related Charges."

EXHIBIT 6.20		
Sapient Corporation		
Partial Income Statement		
(amounts in thousands)		
(Problem 6.6)		
	Year 11	**Year 10**
Revenues	$ 329,698	$503,339
Project Personnel Costs	$ 235,766	$249,279
Selling and Marketing Costs.	27,949	33,903
General and Administrative Expenses	131,729	135,424
Restructuring and Other Related Charges	100,640	—
Amortization of Intangible Assets	28,126	11,328
Stock-based Compensation	4,449	2,165
Total Operating Expenses	$ 528,659	$432,099
Income (Loss) from Operations.	$(198,961)	$ 71,240
Gain on Equity Investment Change in Interest	1,407	—
Other Expense	(4,677)	(1,250)
Interest Income.	9,407	11,678
Income Tax (Provision) Benefit	3,091	(33,925)
Income (Loss) before Net Equity Loss		
from Investees and Minority Interest	(189,733)	47,743
Net Equity Loss from Investees	(499)	(878)
Minority Interest in Net Loss of Consolidated		
Subsidiary.	464	95
Net Income	$(189,768)	$ 46,960

Required

a. Discuss whether or not you would eliminate the restructuring charge from the income statement of Sapient Corporation when using earnings to forecast future profitability.

b. The statement of cash flows for Sapient Corporation (not included here) includes an addback for "restructuring costs" in Year 11 of $19.7 million. Speculate why this amount differs from the $100.6 million reported on the income statement for Year 11 for the restructuring charges.

c. Restructuring charges often cover a wide range of different cost categories. Identify the categories of costs often included in restructuring charges, including identifying those that usually entail the use of cash and those that do not use cash.

6.7 USING ORIGINALLY REPORTED VERSUS RESTATED DATA. Prior to Year 8, General Dynamics Corporation engaged in a wide variety of industries, including weapons manufacturing under government contracts, information technologies, commercial aircraft manufacturing, missile systems, coal mining, material service, ship management, and ship financing. During Year 8, General Dynamics sold its information technologies business. During Year 9, General Dynamics sold its commercial aircraft manufacturing business. During Year 9, it also announced its intention to sell its missile systems, coal mining, material service, ship management, and ship financing businesses. These strategic moves left General Dynamics with only its weapons manufacturing business. Financial statements for General Dynamics for Year 9 as reported, Year 8 as restated in the Year 9 annual report for discontinued operations, and Year 8 as originally reported appear in Exhibit 6.21 (balance sheet), Exhibit 6.22 (income statement), and Exhibit 6.23 (statement of cash flows).

EXHIBIT 6.21
General Dynamics Corporation
Balance Sheet
(amounts in millions)
(Problem 6.7)

	Year 9 as Reported	Year 8 as Restated in Year 9 Annual Report	Year 8 as Originally Reported
Assets			
Cash and Cash Equivalents....................	$ 513	$ 507	$ 513
Marketable Securities..........................	432	307	307
Accounts Receivable...........................	64	99	444
Contracts in Process...........................	1,550	1,474	2,606
Net Assets of Discontinued Businesses.............	767	1,468	—
Other Current Assets..........................	329	145	449
Total Current Assets.......................	$3,655	$4,000	$4,319
Property, Plant, and Equipment (net).............	322	372	1,029
Other Assets..................................	245	300	859
Total Assets..............................	$4,222	$4,672	$6,207
Liabilities and Shareholders' Equity			
Accounts Payable and Accruals...................	$ 553	$ 642	$2,593
Current Portion of Long-term Debt..............	145	450	516
Other Current Liabilities.......................	1,250	1,174	—
Total Current Liabilities.....................	$1,948	$2,266	$3,109
Long-term Debt...............................	38	163	365
Other Noncurrent Liabilities....................	362	263	753
Total Liabilities..........................	$2,348	$2,692	$4,227
Common Stock................................	$ 42	$ 55	$ 55
Additional Paid-in Capital......................	—	25	25
Retained Earnings.............................	2,474	2,651	2,651
Treasury Stock................................	(642)	(751)	(751)
Total Shareholders' Equity....................	$1,874	$1,980	$1,980
Total Liabilities and Shareholders' Equity.........	$4,222	$4,672	$6,207

EXHIBIT 6.22

General Dynamics Corporation
Income Statement
(amounts in millions)
(Problem 6.7)

	Year 9 as Reported	Year 8 as Restated in Year 9 Annual Report	Year 8 as Originally Reported
Continuing Operations			
Sales....................................	$3,472	$3,322	$8,751
Operating Costs and Expenses....................	(3,297)	(3,207)	(8,359)
Interest Income (Expense), net....................	25	4	(34)
Other Expense, net	27	(27)	(27)
Earnings Before Income Taxes	$ 227	$ 92	$ 331
Income Tax Credit	21	114	43
Income from Continuing Operations	$ 248	$ 206	$ 374
Discontinued Operations			
Earnings from Operations	$ 193	$ 299	$ 131
Gain on Disposal	374	—	—
Net Income..................................	$ 815	$ 505	$ 505

Required

a. Refer to the balance sheets of General Dynamics in Exhibit 6.21. Why does the restated amount for total assets for Year 8 of $4,672 million differ from the originally reported amount of $6,207 million?

b. Refer to the income statement for General Dynamics in Exhibit 6.22. Why are the originally reported and restated net income amounts for Year 8 the same (that is, $505 million) when each of the individual revenues and expenses decreased upon restatement?

c. Refer to the statement of cash flows for General Dynamics in Exhibit 6.23. Why is the restated amount of cash flow from operations for Year 9 of $609 million less than the originally reported amount of $673 million?

d. If the analyst wished to analyze changes in the structure of assets and equities between Year 8 and Year 9, which columns and amounts in Exhibit 6.21 would the analyst use? Explain.

e. If the analyst wished to analyze changes in the operating profitability between Year 8 and Year 9, which columns and amounts in Exhibit 6.22 would the analyst use? Explain.

f. If the analyst wished to use cash flow ratios to assess short-term liquidity and long-term solvency risk, which columns and amounts in Exhibit 6.23 would the analyst use? Explain.

EXHIBIT 6.23

General Dynamics Corporation
Statement of Cash Flows
(amounts in millions)
(Problem 6.7)

	Year 9 as Reported	Year 8 as Restated in Year 9 Annual Report	Year 8 as Originally Reported
Operations			
Income from Continuing Operations	$ 248	$ 206	$ 374
Depreciation and Amortization	56	140	303
(Inc.) Dec. in Accounts Receivable.	35	4	(91)
(Inc.) Dec. in Contracts in Process.	(76)	(83)	237
(Inc.) Dec. in Other Current Assets	(6)	8	13
Inc. (Dec.) in Accounts Payable and Accruals	(66)	51	262
Inc. (Dec.) in Other Current Liabilities.	11	(41)	(469)
Cash Flow from Continuing Operations	$ 202	$ 285	$ 629
Cash Flow from Discontinued Operations	288	324	44
Cash Flow from Operations	$ 490	$ 609	$ 673
Investing			
Proceeds from Sale of Discontinued Operations.	$ 1,039	$ 184	$ 184
Capital Expenditures	(18)	(29)	(82)
Purchase of Marketable Securities	(125)	(307)	(307)
Other.	32	3	56
Cash Flow from Investing	$ 928	$(149)	$(149)
Financing			
Issue of Common Stock	$ 57	$ —	$ —
Repayment of Debt.	(454)	(11)	(61)
Purchase of Common Stock.	(960)	—	—
Dividends	(55)	(42)	(42)
Other.	—	—	(17)
Cash Flow from Financing	$(1,412)	$ (53)	$(120)
Change in Cash.	$ 6	$ 407	$ 404
Cash—Beginning of Year	507	100	109
Cash—End of Year	$ 513	$ 507	$ 513

6.8 USING ORIGINALLY REPORTED VERSUS RESTATED DATA. INTERCO is a manufacturer and retailer of a broad line of consumer products, including London Fog, Florsheim Shoes, Converse, Ethan Allen Furniture, and Lane Furniture. During Year 9, INTERCO became the target of an unfriendly takeover attempt. In an effort to defend itself against the takeover, INTERCO declared a special dividend of $1.4 billion. It financed the dividend by issuing long-term debt and preferred stock. INTERCO planned to dispose of certain businesses to repay a portion of this debt. Exhibits 6.24, 6.25, and 6.26 present balance sheets, income statements, and statements of cash flows, respectively, for INTERCO. The first column of each exhibit shows the amounts as reported for Year 9. The second column shows the restated amounts for Year 8 to reflect the decision to dispose of certain businesses that the company had previously included in continuing operations. The third column shows the amounts originally reported for Year 8. The income tax rate is 35 percent.

EXHIBIT 6.24
INTERCO
Balance Sheet
(amounts in thousands)
(Problem 6.8)

	Year 9 as Reported	Year 8 as Restated in Year 9 Annual Report	Year 8 as Originally Reported
Cash and Marketable Securities.	$ 77,625	$ 23,299	$ 31,882
Receivables.	329,299	310,053	486,657
Inventories	490,967	514,193	805,095
Prepayments.	41,625	24,984	35,665
Net Assets of Discontinued Businesses	346,372	521,644	—
Total Current Assets	$ 1,285,888	$1,394,173	$1,359,299
Property, Plant, and Equipment (net).	327,070	317,238	479,499
Other Assets.	162,344	118,989	146,788
Total Assets	$ 1,775,302	$1,830,400	$1,985,586
Current Liabilities	$ 736,268	$ 269,315	$ 373,343
Long-term Debt.	1,986,837	266,191	299,140
Other Noncurrent Liabilities.	57,947	43,557	61,766
Total Liabilities	$ 2,781,052	$ 579,063	$ 734,249
Contributed Capital.	$ 339,656	$ 256,740	$ 256,740
Retained Earnings	(1,208,250)	1,179,964	1,179,964
Treasury Stock	(137,156)	(185,367)	(185,367)
Total Shareholders' Equity	$(1,005,750)	$1,251,337	$1,251,337
Total Liabilities and Shareholders' Equity	$ 1,775,302	$1,830,400	$1,985,586

EXHIBIT 6.25
INTERCO
Income Statement
(amounts in thousands)
(Problem 6.8)

	Year 9 as Reported	Year 8 as Restated in Year 9 Annual Report	Year 8 as Originally Reported
Sales	$2,011,962	$1,995,974	$3,341,423
Other Income.	18,943	13,714	29,237
Total Revenues.	$2,030,905	$2,009,688	$3,370,660
Cost of Goods Sold	$1,335,678	$1,288,748	$2,284,640
Selling and Administrative.	537,797	493,015	799,025
Interest	141,735	29,188	33,535
Income Taxes	19,977	85,303	108,457
Total Expenses.	$2,035,187	$1,896,254	$3,225,657
Income from Continuing Operations	$ (4,282)	$ 113,434	$ 145,003
Income from Discontinued Operations	74,432	31,569	—
Net Income	$ 70,150	$ 145,003	$ 145,003

Required

a. Refer to the balance sheets of INTERCO in Exhibit 6.24. Why is the restated amount for total assets for Year 8 of $1,830,400 different from the originally reported amount for total assets of $1,985,566?

b. Refer to the income statement of INTERCO in Exhibit 6.25. Why is the originally reported and restated net income the same ($145,003) when each of the company's individual revenues and expenses decreased upon restatement?

c. Refer to the statement of cash flows for INTERCO in Exhibit 6.26. Why is the restated amount of cash flow from operations for Year 8 of $94,447 less than the originally reported amount of $117,774?

d. If the analyst wished to analyze changes in the structure of assets and equities between Year 8 and Year 9, which columns and which amounts in Exhibit 6.24 would the analyst use? Explain.

e. If the analyst wished to compare the change in operating performance between Year 8 and Year 9, which columns and which amounts in Exhibit 6.25 would the analyst use? Explain.

f. Describe briefly how INTERCO's actions during Year 9 might thwart an unfriendly takeover attempt.

EXHIBIT 6.26

INTERCO

Statement of Cash Flows

(amounts in thousands)

(Problem 6.8)

	Year 9 as Reported	Year 8 as Restated in Year 9 Annual Report	Year 8 as Originally Reported
Operations			
Income (Loss) from Continuing Operations	$ (4,282)	$113,434	$ 145,003
Depreciation.	40,037	40,570	62,772
Other Addbacks (Subtractions).	(24,230)	8,750	13,957
Change in Operating Working Capital Accounts . . .	29,015	(96,271)	(103,958)
Cash Flow from Continuing Operations.	$ 40,540	$ 66,483	$ 117,774
Cash Flow from Discontinued Operations	249,704	27,964	—
Cash Flow from Operations	$ 290,244	$ 94,447	$ 117,774
Investing			
Sale of Fixed Assets	$ 4,134	$ 1,145	$ 8,102
Acquisition of Fixed Assets	(50,966)	(45,925)	(65,880)
Cash Flow from Investing.	$ (46,832)	$ (44,780)	$ (57,778)
Financing			
Increase in Short-term Borrowing	$ —	$ 1,677	$ 1,677
Increase in Long-term Borrowing.	1,967,500	205,533	205,673
Decrease in Long-term Borrowing	(617,401)	(85,570)	(95,841)
Increase in Capital Stock	19,994	4,606	4,606
Decrease in Capital Stock	(102,341)	(160,442)	(160,442)
Dividends.	(1,456,162)	(64,219)	(64,219)
Other	(676)	252	54
Cash Flow from Financing	$ (189,086)	$ (98,163)	$ (108,492)
Net Change in Cash	$ 54,326	$ (48,496)	$ (48,496)

6.9 ADJUSTING FINANCIAL STATEMENTS FOR DIFFERENT ACCOUNTING PRINCIPLES. In Year 6, Glaxo Holdings acquired Wellcome, maintaining its position as one of the largest pharmaceutical companies in the United Kingdom. Glaxo prepares financial statements in accordance with generally accepted accounting principles (GAAP) in the United Kingdom. The statements prepared by Glaxo prior to the acquisition of Wellcome appear in Exhibit 6.27 (balance sheet), Exhibit 6.28 (income statement), and Exhibit 6.29 (statement of cash flows). Exhibit 6.30 presents a reconciliation of shareholders' equity and net income from U.K. accounting principles to U.S. accounting principles. A description of the reconciling items appears below.

EXHIBIT 6.27
Glaxo
Balance Sheet
(amounts in millions)
(Problem 6.9)

	June 30		
	Year 4	Year 3	Year 2
Assets			
Cash.....	£ 119	£ 390	£ 225
Marketable Securities	2,644	2,107	1,524
Accounts Receivable	908	916	720
Inventories	575	595	475
Other Current Assets	234	234	211
Total Current Assets.....	£4,480	£4,242	£3,155
Investments in Securities	55	61	32
Property, Plant, and Equipment (net)	3,184	2,959	2,341
Other Assets	168	196	154
Total Assets.....	£7,887	£7,458	£5,682
Liabilities and Shareholders' Equity			
Accounts Payable	£ 188	£ 178	£ 162
Short-term Debt.....	400	597	366
Other Current Liabilities	1,542	1,425	1,040
Total Current Liabilities.....	£2,130	£2,200	£1,568
Long-term Debt	298	243	137
Deferred Income Taxes.....	139	193	179
Other Noncurrent Liabilities	154	165	159
Total Liabilities.....	£2,721	£2,801	£2,043
Minority Interests in Subsidiaries	£ 123	£ 111	£ 67
Common Stock.....	£ 762	£ 758	£ 753
Additional Paid-in Capital	229	151	77
Retained Earnings.....	4,052	3,637	2,742
Total Shareholders' Equity.....	£5,043	£4,546	£3,572
Total Liabilities and Shareholders' Equity.....	£7,887	£7,458	£5,682

Deferred Taxation. U.K. GAAP requires the recognition of deferred taxes only when it is probable that deferred tax benefits or liabilities will crystallize. U.S. GAAP requires the recognition of deferred taxes for all temporary differences between financial and tax reporting.

Post-retirement Benefits Other than Pensions. U.K. GAAP allows recognition of post-retirement benefits other than pensions on a cash basis. U.S. GAAP requires

EXHIBIT 6.28

Glaxo
Income Statement
(amounts in millions)
(Problem 6.9)

	Year Ended June 30	
	Year 4	Year 3
Sales	£5,656	£4,930
Other Revenues	65	206
Cost of Goods Sold	(1,007)	(871)
Selling and Administrative	(1,972)	(1,795)
Research and Development.	(858)	(739)
Interest.	(44)	(56)
Income Taxes	(525)	(461)
Minority Interest in Net Income.	(12)	(7)
Net Income	£1,303	£1,207

recognition of this benefit obligation on an accrual basis. The post-retirement benefit obligation was £26 million on July 1, Year 3.

Goodwill. U.K. GAAP allows firms to write off goodwill against retained earnings. Up until Year 5, U.S GAAP required firms to capitalize and amortize goodwill over a maximum period of 40 years.

Dividends. U.K. GAAP provides for the recognition of a liability when the Board of Directors recommends a dividend to shareholders for their approval. U.S. GAAP does not recognize a dividend until declared by the Board of Directors, which occurs in the U.K. after shareholders' approval.

Required

a. Indicate the adjustments to the balance sheet, income statement, and statement of cash flows of Glaxo to convert its financial statements from U.K. GAAP to U.S. GAAP. Glaxo includes the dividend recommended to shareholders in other current liabilities.

b. Compute the rate of return on assets (ROA), the rate of return on common shareholders' equity (ROCE), and the capital structure leverage ratio using the reported amounts (U.K. GAAP) and the adjusted amounts (U.S. GAAP). The income tax rate is 33 percent.

c. Why are ROCE and ROA larger and the capital structure leverage ratio smaller using the reported amounts (U.K. GAAP) than using the adjusted amounts (U.S. GAAP)?

EXHIBIT 6.29

Glaxo
Statement of Cash Flows
(amounts in millions)
(Problem 6.9)

	Year Ended June 30	
	Year 4	Year 3
Operations		
Net Income....................................	£ 1,303	£1,207
Depreciation and Amortization...................	282	225
Other Addbacks	120	86
Other Subtractions............................	(11)	(29)
	£ 1,694	£1,489
(Inc.) Dec. in Accounts Receivable................	8	(196)
(Inc.) Dec. in Inventories	5	29
(Inc.) Dec. in Other Current Assets................	0	102
Inc. (Dec.) in Accounts Payable	10	16
Inc. (Dec.) in Other Current Liabilities	41	30
Cash Flow from Operations	£ 1,758	£1,470
Investing		
Property, Plant, and Equipment Sold...............	£ 22	£ 84
Property, Plant, and Equipment Acquired...........	(575)	(608)
Investments Acquired..........................	(814)	(337)
Other Investing Transactions....................	4	3
Cash Flow from Investing	£(1,363)	£ (858)
Financing		
Inc. (Dec.) in Short-term Borrowing...............	£ (12)	£ 27
Issue of Common Stock........................	51	69
Dividends	(705)	(543)
Cash Flow from Financing	£ (666)	£ (447)
Change in Cash................................	£ (271)	£ 165
Cash—Beginning of Year	390	225
Cash—End of Year	£ 119	£ 390

EXHIBIT 6.30
Glaxo
Reconciliation of U.K. and U.S. GAAP
(amounts in millions)
(Problem 6.9)

	June 30		
	Year 4	Year 3	Year 2
Shareholders' Equity, U.K. GAAP	£5,043	£4,546	£3,572
Deferred Taxation.	(307)	(279)	(218)
Post-retirement Benefits Other Than Pensions.................	(26)	—	—
Goodwill...	35	27	23
Dividends	549	455	330
Shareholders' Equity, U.S. GAAP...........................	£5,294	£4,749	£3,707

	Year Ended June 30	
	Year 4	Year 3
Net Income, U.K. GAAP	£1,303	£1,207
Deferred Taxation.	(28)	(61)
Post-retirement Benefits Other than Pensions	(26)	—
Goodwill Amortization	(1)	(1)
Net Income, U.S. GAAP....................................	£1,248	£1,145

CASE 6.1

INTERNATIONAL PAPER: A RECURRING DILEMMA

International Paper Company is the largest forest products company in the world. It operates in five segments of the forest products industry:

1. **Printing Paper.** Uncoated and coated papers used for reprographic and printing, envelopes, writing tablets, file folders, and magazines.
2. **Packaging.** Liner board used for corrugated boxes and bleached packaging board used for food, pharmaceutical, cosmetic, and other consumer products.
3. **Distribution.** Sale of printing, graphic, packaging, and similar products through wholesale and retail outlets. Sales of these outlets comprise approximately 20 percent of International Paper's products and 80 percent of other manufacturers' products.
4. **Specialty Products.** Film, door facings, wood siding, fabrics, and chemicals used for adhesives and paints.

5. **Forest Products.** Logs, lumber, plywood, and wood panels. International Paper has the largest timber holdings of any private-sector entity in the United States.

Exhibit 6.31 presents product segment data for International Paper for Year 7 thought Year 10. The proportion of sales generated from within the United States decreased from 79 percent in Year 7 to 71 percent in Year 10. The proportion generated from within Europe fluctuated between 17 and 19 percent during the four-year period. The proportion from the rest of the world, primarily East Asia, increased from 3 percent in Year 7 to 12 percent in Year 10.

EXHIBIT 6.31

International Paper
Product Line Segment Profitability Analysis
(Case 6.1)

	Year 10	Year 9	Year 8	Year 7
Sales Mix				
Printing Papers	26%	29%	28%	27%
Packaging	23	21	22	22
Distribution	22	24	22	22
Specialty Products	16	16	17	17
Forest Products	13	10	11	12
	100%	100%	100%	100%
Rate of Return on Assets				
Printing Papers	2.1%	15.3%	.3%	(1.9%)
Packaging	6.9%	17.9%	9.5%	6.2%
Distribution	8.1%	7.3%	6.1%	5.3%
Specialty Products	(1.4%)	5.7%	9.6%	10.1
Forest Products	17.2%	8.7%	27.3%	30.4%
Profit Margin				
Printing Papers	3.3%	17.7%	.5%	(3.1%)
Packaging	8.5%	16.8%	8.7%	6.1%
Distribution	2.3%	2.1%	2.1%	1.8%
Specialty Products	(1.5%)	6.3%	10.3%	10.7%
Forest Products	34.7%	18.5%	24.4%	28.7%
Assets Turnover				
Printing Papers	.65	.87	.66	.60
Packaging	.81	1.07	1.09	1.03
Distribution	3.47	3.46	2.86	2.89
Specialty Products	.96	.91	.93	.94
Forest Products	.50	.47	1.12	1.06

The financial statements for International Paper for Year 7 through Year 10 appear in Exhibit 6.32 (income statement), Exhibit 6.33 (balance sheet), and Exhibit 6.34 (statement of cash flows). Exhibit 6.35 presents financial ratios for International Paper based on the reported amounts.

The notes to the financial statements reveal the following information:

1. **Change in Accounting Principle.** Effective January 1, Year 8, International Paper changed its method of accounting for start-up costs on major projects to expensing these costs as incurred. Prior to Year 8, the firm capitalized these costs as part of property, plant, and equipment and amortized them over a five-year period. The firm made the change to increase the focus on controlling costs associated with facility start-ups. International Paper recorded a pre-tax charge of $125 million ($75 million after taxes) as the cumulative effect of an accounting change in Year 8.

2. **Gain on Sale of Partnership Interest.** On March 29, Year 10, International Paper sold its general partnership interest in a partnership that owned 300,000 acres of forestlands located in Oregon and Washington. Included in the partnership were forestlands, roads, and $750 million of long-term debt. As a result of this transaction, International Paper recognized a pre-tax gain of $592 million ($336 million after taxes). International Paper maintains general partnership interests in several partnerships created by the firm as a means of raising capital from outside investors. International Paper consolidates the

---

EXHIBIT 6.32

International Paper
Income Statement
(amounts in millions)
(Case 6.1)

| | Year Ended December 31 | | | |
	Year 10	Year 9	Year 8	Year 7
Sales	$20,143	$19,797	$14,966	$13,685
Gain on Sale of Partnership Interest	592	—	—	—
Cost of Goods Sold	(16,095)	(14,927)	(11,977)	(11,051)
Selling and Administrative Expenses.	(2,628)	(2,349)	(1,925)	(1,786)
Restructuring and Asset Impairment Charges	(680)	—	—	—
Interest Expense.	(530)	(493)	(349)	(310)
Income Taxes	(330)	(719)	(236)	(213)
Minority Interest in Earnings	(169)	(156)	(47)	(36)
Income from Continuing Operations	$ 303	$ 1,153	$ 432	$ 289
Changes in Accounting Principles.	—	—	(75)	—
Net Income.	$ 303	$ 1,153	$ 357	$ 289

EXHIBIT 6.33

International Paper
Balance Sheet
(amounts in millions)
(Case 6.1)

	December 31				
	Year 10	Year 9	Year 8	Year 7	Year 6
Assets					
Cash.............................	$ 352	$ 312	$ 270	$ 242	$ 225
Accounts Receivable..................	2,553	2,571	2,241	1,856	1,861
Inventories	2,840	2,784	2,075	2,024	1,938
Prepayments	253	206	244	279	342
Total Current Assets..............	$ 5,998	$ 5,873	$ 4,830	$ 4,401	$ 4,366
Investments in Securities	1,178	1,420	1,032	631	599
Property, Plant, and Equipment (net) ...	16,559	13,800	9,941	9,658	9,643
Other Assets	4,517	2,884	2,033	1,941	1,851
Total Assets....................	$28,252	$23,977	$17,836	$16,631	$16,459
Liabilities and Shareholders' Equity					
Accounts Payable	$ 1,426	$ 1,464	$ 1,204	$ 1,089	$ 1,259
Notes Payable	3,296	2,283	2,083	2,089	2,356
Other Current Liabilities	1,172	1,116	747	831	916
Total Current Liabilities...........	$ 5,894	$ 4,863	$ 4,034	$ 4,009	$ 4,531
Long-term Debt	7,141	6,396	4,464	3,601	3,096
Deferred Income Taxes..............	2,768	1,974	1,612	1,614	1,417
Other Noncurrent Liabilities	1,240	980	870	1,182	1,226
Total Liabilities..................	$17,043	$14,213	$10,980	$10,406	$10,270
Minority Interest in Subsidiaries	$ 1,865	$ 1,967	$ 342	$ —	$ —
Common Stock....................	301	263	256	127	127
Additional Paid-in Capital	3,426	1,963	1,658	1,704	1,792
Retained Earnings..................	5,639	5,627	4,711	4,553	4,472
Treasury Stock....................	(22)	(56)	(111)	(159)	(202)
Total Shareholders' Equity	$11,209	$ 9,764	$ 6,856	$ 6,225	$ 6,189
Total Liabilities and Shareholders' Equity	$28,252	$23,977	$17,836	$16,631	$16,459

EXHIBIT 6.34

International Paper
Statement of Cash Flows
(amounts in millions)
(Case 6.1)

| | Year Ended December 31 | | | |
	Year 10	Year 9	Year 8	Year 7
Operations				
Net Income..	$ 303	$ 1,153	$ 357	$ 289
Depreciation......................................	1,194	1,031	885	898
Restructuring and Asset Impairment Charges	680	—	—	—
Changes in Accounting Principles...................	—	—	75	—
Gain on Sale of Partnership Interest	(592)	—	—	—
Other Addbacks and Subtractions..................	240	54	8	32
	$ 1,825	$ 2,238	$ 1,325	$ 1,219
(Inc.) Dec. in Accounts Rec.	192	45	(339)	78
(Inc.) Dec. in Inventories.........................	174	(320)	8	(93)
(Inc.) Dec. in Prepayments	(47)	38	(35)	63
Inc. (Dec.) in Accounts Payable....................	(38)	260	115	(170)
Inc. (Dec.) in Other Current Liabilities..............	(367)	(13)	169	(168)
Cash Flow from Operations	$ 1,739	$ 2,248	$ 1,243	$ 929
Investing				
Capital Expenditures	$(1,394)	$(1,518)	$(1,114)	$ (971)
Investments Acquired (net)	(1,586)	(1,038)	(396)	(151)
Cash Flow from Investing......................	$(2,980)	$(2,556)	$(1,510)	$(1,122)
Financing				
Increase in Short-term Borrowing	$ —	$ 57	$ —	$ —
Decrease in Short-term Borrowing	(23)	—	(115)	—
Increase in Long-term Borrowing...................	1,909	1,505	1,059	1,276
Decrease in Long-term Borrowing	(375)	(950)	(275)	(1,016)
Issue of Common Stock...........................	100	66	67	225
Dividends..	(291)	(237)	(210)	(208)
Other Financing Transactions	(39)	(91)	(231)	(67)
Cash Flow from Financing	$ 1,281	$ 350	$ 295	$ 210
Change in Cash	$ 40	$ 42	$ 28	$ 17
Cash—Beginning of Year..........................	312	270	242	225
Cash—End of Year...............................	$ 352	$ 312	$ 270	$ 242

EXHIBIT 6.35

International Paper
Financial Statement Ratios
(Case 6.1)

	Year 10	Year 9	Year 8	Year 7
Profit Margin for ROA..................................	4.1%	8.2%	4.2%	3.8%
Assets Turnover	.8	.9	.9	.8
Rate of Return on Assets	3.1%	7.8%	3.7%	3.2%
Profit Margin for ROCE	1.5%	5.8%	2.4%	2.1%
Capital Structure Leverage.............................	3.0	2.9	2.9	2.7
Rate of Return on Common Shareholders' Equity...........	3.5%	16.1%	5.6%	4.7%
Cost of Goods Sold ÷ Sales	79.9%	75.4%	80.0%	80.8%
Selling and Administrative Expense ÷ Sales	13.0%	11.9%	12.9%	13.1%
Interest Expense ÷ Sales...............................	2.6%	2.5%	2.3%	2.3%
Income Tax Expense ÷ Sales	1.7%	3.6%	1.6%	1.5%
Accounts Receivable Turnover...........................	7.9	8.2	7.3	7.4
Inventory Turnover	5.7	6.1	5.8	5.6
Fixed Asset Turnover	1.3	1.7	1.5	1.4
Current Ratio..	1.0	1.7	1.5	1.4
Quick Ratio	.5	.6	.6	.5
Cash Flow from Operations ÷ Average Current Liabilities.....	32.3%	50.5%	30.9%	21.8%
Days Accounts Receivable	46	44	50	50
Days Inventory...	64	59	62	65
Days Accounts Payable..................................	33	31	35	38
Liabilities ÷ Assets	60.3%	59.3%	61.6%	62.6%
Long-term Debt Ratio	43.3%	45.1%	40.7%	36.6%
Long-term Debt ÷ Shareholders' Equity...................	76.4%	82.0%	68.5%	57.8%
Cash Flow from Operations ÷ Average Total Liabilities	9.9%	16.3%	11.4%	9.0%
Interest Coverage Ratio	2.5	5.1	3.1	2.7
Cash Flow from Operations ÷ Capital Expenditures	1.3	1.5	1.1	1.0

financial statements of these partnerships with its own financial statements and shows the interest of the remaining partners (limited partners) as a minority interest.

3. **Restructuring and Asset Impairment Charges.** During the first quarter of Year 10, the firm's Board of Directors authorized a series of management actions to restructure and strengthen existing businesses that resulted in a pre-tax charge of $515 million ($362 million after taxes). The charge included $305 million for the write-off of certain assets, $100 million for asset impairments, $80 million in associated severance costs, and $30 million in other expenses, including the cancellation of leases.

During the fourth quarter of Year 10, International Paper recorded a $165 million pre-tax charge ($105 million after taxes) for the write-down of its investments in a company that markets digital communications products and to record its share of a restructuring charge announced by that investee.

These restructuring charges were the first recognized by International Paper since Year 6. In November, Year 6, the firm recorded a pre-tax charge of $398 million ($263 million after taxes) to establish a productivity improvement reserve. Over 80 percent of this charge represented asset write-downs for facility closings or realignments and related severance and relocation costs. The balance covers one-time costs of environmental clean-up, remediation, and legal costs. In December, Year 5, the firm recorded a $60 million ($37 million after taxes) reduction in work force charge to cover severance costs associated with the elimination of more than 1,000 positions from its worldwide work force. In December, Year 4, International Paper completed a review of operations in the context of its ongoing programs to emphasize value-added products in growing markets and improve the efficiency of its facilities. As a result, the firm recorded a pre-tax charge of $212 million ($137 million after taxes), principally related to the planned sale or closure of certain wood products and converting facilities, the estimated costs of environmental remediation, and severance and other personnel expenses associated with the business improvement program.

On July 9, Year 11, International Paper announced a plan to restructure or eliminate certain production operations and cut 9,000 jobs, more than 10 percent of its work force. It recognized a restructuring charge of $385 million pre-tax. It also recognized a $93 million charge related to pending litigation.

Required

a. For each of the three categories of income items described above for Year 7 through Year 10, discuss (1) whether you would eliminate it when using earnings to forecast the future profitability of International Paper and, if so, (2) the adjustments you would make to the income statement, balance sheet, and statement of cash flows.

b. Taking into consideration the adjustments from part a, analyze and interpret the changes in the profitability and risk of International Paper during this four-year period. The statutory tax rate is 35 percent in each year.

CASE 6.2

TANAGUCHI CORPORATION—PART A*

Dave Ando and Yoshi Yashima, recent business school graduates, work as research security analysts for a mutual fund specializing in international equity investments. Based on several strategy meetings, senior managers of the fund decided to invest in the machine tool industry. One international company under consideration is Tanaguchi Corporation, a Japanese manufacturer of machine tools. As staff analysts

---

*This case, co-authored by Paul R. Brown and Clyde P. Stickney, appeared in *Issues in Accounting Education* (Spring, 1992), pp. 57–59 and is reproduced with permission of the American Accounting Association.

assigned to perform fundamental analysis on all new investment options, Ando and Yashima obtain a copy of Tanaguchi Corporation's unconsolidated financial statements and notes (Appendix 6.1) and set out to calculate their usual spreadsheet of financial statement ratios. Exhibit 6.36 presents the results of their efforts. As a basis for comparison, Exhibit 6.36 also presents the median ratios for U.S. machine tool companies for a comparable year. The following conversation ensues.

APPENDIX 6.1 (CASE 6.2)

UNCONSOLIDATED FINANCIAL STATEMENTS FOR TANAGUCHI CORPORATION

Tanaguchi Corporation
Balance Sheet
(in billions of yen)
(Case 6.2)

	March 31:	
	Year 5	Year 4
ASSETS		
Current Assets		
Cash..	¥ 27	¥ 30
Marketable Securities (Note 1)........................	25	20
Notes and Accounts Receivable (Note 2):		
Trade Notes and Accounts........................	210	200
Affiliated Company	45	30
Less: Allowance for Doubtful Accounts...............	(7)	(5)
Inventories (Note 3)	150	130
Other Current Assets.............................	30	25
Total Current Assets.............................	¥480	¥430
Investments		
Investment in and Loans to Affiliated		
Companies (Note 4)..............................	¥140	¥110
Investments in Other Companies (Note 5)	60	60
Total Investments................................	¥200	¥170
Property, Plant, and Equipment (Note 6)		
Land..	¥ 25	¥ 25
Buildings......................................	130	110
Machinery and Equipment..........................	180	155
Less: Depreciation to Date........................	(165)	(140)
Total Property, Plant, and Equipment	¥170	¥150
Total Assets....................................	¥850	¥750

Balance Sheet—continued	March 31:	
	Year 5	Year 4
LIABILITIES AND STOCKHOLDERS' EQUITY		
Current Liabilities		
Short-term Bank Loans..............................	¥200	¥185
Notes and Accounts Payable:		
Trade Notes and Accounts	164	140
Affiliated Company	20	25
Other Current Liabilities............................	50	40
Total Current Liabilities	¥434	¥390
Long-Term Liabilities		
Bonds Payable (Note 7).............................	¥ 20	¥ 20
Convertible Debt..................................	20	20
Retirement and Severance Allowance (Note 8)	153	122
Total Long-term Liabilities........................	¥193	¥162
Stockholders' Equity		
Common Stock, 10 par value	¥ 15	¥ 15
Capital Surplus	40	40
Legal Reserve (Note 9)	17	16
Retained Earnings (Note 9)	151	127
Total Stockholders' Equity	¥223	¥198
Total Liabilities and Stockholders' Equity	¥850	¥750

Dave: Tanaguchi Corporation does not appear to be as profitable as comparable U.S. firms. Its operating margin and rate of return on assets are significantly less than the median ratios for U.S. machine tool operators. Its rate of return on common equity is only slightly less than its U.S. counterparts, but this is at the expense of assuming much more financial leverage and therefore risk. Most of this leverage is in the form of short-term borrowing. You can see this in its higher total liabilities to total assets ratio combined with its lower long-term debt ratio. This short-term borrowing and higher risk are also evidenced by the lower current and quick ratios. Finally, the market price of Tanaguchi Corporation's shares reflects a higher multiple of net income and stockholders' equity than U.S. machine tool companies. I can't see how we can justify paying more for a company that is less profitable and more risky than comparable U.S. companies. It doesn't seem to me that it is worth exploring this investment possibility any further.

**Tanaguchi Corporation
Statement of Income and
Retained Earnings For Fiscal Year 5
(in billions of yen)
(Case 6.2)**

Revenues

Sales (Note 10)...	¥1,200
Interest and Dividends (Note 11)	5
Total Revenues..	¥1,205

Expenses

Cost of Goods Sold	¥ 878
Selling and Administrative.................................	252
Interest	13
Total Expenses......................................	¥1,143
Income before Income Taxes	¥ 62
Income Taxes (Note 12)....................................	(34)
Net Income...	¥ 28

Retained Earnings

Balance, Beginning of Fiscal Year 5	¥ 127
Net Income...	28
Deductions:	
Cash Dividends	(3)
Transfer to Legal Reserve (Note 9)	(1)
Balance, End of Fiscal Year 5	¥ 151

Yoshi: You may be right, Dave. However, I wonder if we are not comparing apples and oranges. As a Japanese company, Tanaguchi Corporation operates in an entirely different institutional and cultural environment than U.S. machine tool companies. Furthermore, it prepares its financial statements in accordance with Japanese generally accepted accounting principles (GAAP), which differ from those in the United States.

Dave: Well, I think we need to explore this further. I recall seeing a report on an associate's desk comparing U.S. and Japanese accounting principles. I will get a copy for us (Appendix 6.2).

EXHIBIT 6.36

Comparative Financial Ratio Analysis for Tanaguchi Corporation and U.S. Machine Tool Companies
(Case 6.2)

	Tanaguchi Corporation	Median Ratio for U.S. Machine Tool Companies[a]
Profitability Ratios		
Operating Margin After Taxes		
(before interest expense and related tax effects)	2.8%	3.3%
Assets Turnover..................................	1.5	1.8
Return on Assets..................................	4.2%	5.9%
Capital Structure Leverage	3.8	2.6
Return on Common Equity.....................	13.3%	13.9%
Operating Margin Analysis		
Sales...	100.0%	100.0%
Other Revenue/Sales	.4	—
Cost of Goods Sold/Sales..........................	(73.2)	(69.3)
Selling and Administrative/Sales.....................	(21.0)	(25.8)
Income Taxes/Sales	(3.4)	(1.6)
Operating Margin (excluding interest		
and related tax effects)	2.8%	3.3%
Asset Turnover Analysis		
Receivable Turnover	5.1	6.9
Inventory Turnover	6.3	5.2
Fixed Asset Turnover..............................	7.5	7.0
Risk Analysis		
Current Ratio....................................	1.1	1.6
Quick Ratio	.7	.9
Total Liabilities/Total Assets	73.8%	61.1%
Long-term Debt/Total Assets.......................	4.7%	16.1%
Long-term Debt/Stockholders' Equity	17.9%	43.2%
Times Interest Covered	5.8	3.1
Market Price Ratios (per common share)		
Market Price/Net Income	45.0	9.0
Market Price/Stockholders' Equity	5.7	1.2

[a]Source: Robert Morris Associates, *Annual Statement Studies* (except price-earnings ratio).

Required

Using the report comparing U.S. and Japanese accounting principles (Appendix 6.2) and Tanaguchi Corporation's financial statements and notes (Appendix 6.1), identify the most important differences between U.S. and Japanese GAAP. Consider both the differences in acceptable methods and in the methods commonly used. For each major difference, indicate the likely effect (increase, decrease, or no effect) of converting Tanaguchi's financial statements to U.S. GAAP (1) on net income, (2) on total assets, and (3) on the ratio of liabilities divided by stockholders' equity .

TANAGUCHI CORPORATION NOTES TO FINANCIAL STATEMENTS

Note 1: *Marketable Securities*

Marketable securities appear on the balance sheet at acquisition cost.

Note 2: *Accounts Receivable*

Accounts and notes receivable are noninterest bearing. Within 15 days of sales on open account, customers typically sign noninterest-bearing, single-payment notes. Customers usually pay these notes within 60 to 180 days after signing. When Tanaguchi Corporation needs cash, it discounts these notes with Menji Bank. Tanaguchi Corporation remains contingently liable in the event customers do not pay these notes at maturity. Receivables from (and payables to) the affiliated company are with Takahashi Corporation (see Note 4) and are noninterest bearing.

Note 3: *Inventories*

Inventories appear on the balance sheet at lower of cost or market. The measurement of acquisition cost uses a weighted average cost-flow assumption.

Note 4: *Investments and Loans to Affiliated Companies*

Intercorporate investments appear on the balance sheet at acquisition cost. The balances in this account at the end of Year 4 and Year 5 comprise the following:

	Year 5	Year 4
Investments in Tanaka Corporation (25%)	¥ 15	¥ 15
Investment in Takahashi Corporation (80%)	70	70
Loans to Takahashi Corporation	55	25
	¥140	¥110

Note 5: *Investments in Other Companies*

Other investments represent ownership shares of less than 20 percent and appear at acquisition cost.

Note 6: *Property, Plant, and Equipment*

Fixed assets appear on the balance sheet at acquisition cost. The firm capitalizes expenditures that increase the service lives of fixed assets, whereas it expenses immediately expenditures that maintain the originally expected useful lives. It computes depreciation using the declining balance method. Depreciable lives for buildings are 30 to 40 years and for machinery and equipment are 6 to 10 years.

Note 7: *Bonds Payable*

Bonds payable comprises two bond issues as follows:

	Year 5	Year 4
12% semi-annual, ¥10 billion face value bonds, with interest payable on March 31 and September 30 and the principal payable at maturity on March 31, Year 20; the bonds were initially priced on the market to yield 10%, compounded semi-annually	¥11.45	¥11.50
8% semi-annual, ¥10 billion face value bonds, with interest payable on March 31 and September 30 and the principal payable at maturity on March 31, Year 22; the bonds were initially priced on the market to yield 10%, compounded semi-annually.	¥ 8.55	¥ 8.50
	¥20.00	¥20.00

Note 8: *Retirement and Severance Allowance*

The firm provides amounts as a charge against income each year for estimated retirement and severance benefits but does not fund these amounts until it makes actual payments to former employees.

Note 9: *Legal Reserve and Retained Earnings*

The firm reduces retained earnings and increases the Legal Reserve account for a specified percentage of dividends paid during the year. The following plan for appropriation of retained earnings was approved by shareholders at the annual meeting held on June 29, Year 5:

Transfer to Legal Reserve	¥(1)
Cash Dividend	(3)
Directors' and Statutory Auditors' Bonuses.	(1)
Elimination of Special Tax Reserve Relating to Sale of Equipment	1

Note 10: *Sales Revenue*

The firm recognizes revenues from sales of machine tools at the time of delivery. Reported sales for Year 5 are net of a provision for doubtful accounts of ¥50 billion.

Note 11: *Interest and Dividend Revenue*

Interest and Dividend Revenue includes ¥1.5 billion from loans to Takahashi Corporation, an unconsolidated subsidiary.

Note 12: *Income Tax Expense*

The firm computes income taxes based on a statutory tax rate of 55 percent for Year 5. Deferred tax accounting is not a common practice in Japan.

APPENDIX 6.2 (CASE 6.2)

COMPARISON OF U.S. AND JAPANESE GAAP

1. STANDARD-SETTING PROCESS

U.S.   The U.S. Congress has the legal authority to prescribe acceptable accounting principles, but it has delegated that authority to the Securities and Exchange Commission (SEC). The SEC has stated that it will recognize pronouncements of the Financial Accounting Standard Board (FASB), a private-sector entity, as the primary vehicle for specifying generally accepted accounting standards.

Japan   The Japanese Diet has the legal authority to prescribe acceptable accounting principles. All Japanese corporations (both publicly and privately held) must periodically issue financial statements to their stockholders following provisions of the Japanese Commercial Code. This Code is promulgated by the Diet. The financial statements follow strict legal-entity concepts.

Publicly-listed corporations in Japan must also file financial statements with the Securities Division of the Ministry of Finance following accounting principles promulgated by the Diet in the Securities and Exchange Law. The Diet, through the Ministry of Finance, obtains advice on accounting principles from the Business Advisory Deliberations Council (BADC), a body composed of representatives from business, the accounting profession, and personnel from the Ministry of Finance. The BADC has no authority on its own to set acceptable accounting principles. The financial statements filed with the Securities Division of the Ministry of Finance tend to follow economic entity concepts, with intercorporate investments either accounted for using the equity method or consolidated.

All Japanese corporations file income tax returns with the Taxation Division of the Ministry of Finance. The accounting principles followed in preparing tax returns mirror closely those used in preparing financial statements for stockholders under the Japanese Commercial Code. The Minister of Finance will sometimes need to reconcile conflicting preferences of the Securities Division (desiring financial information better reflecting economic reality) and the Taxation Division (desiring to raise adequate tax revenues to run the government).

2. PRINCIPAL FINANCIAL STATEMENTS

U.S.   Balance sheet, income statement, statement of cash flows.

Japan   Balance sheet, income statement, proposal for appropriation of profit or disposition of loss. The financial statements filed with the Ministry of Finance contain some supplemental information on cash flows.

3. INCOME STATEMENT

U.S.   Accrual basis.

Japan   Accrual basis.

4. REVENUE RECOGNITION

U.S.   Generally at time of sale; percentage-of-completion method usually required on long-term contracts; installment and cost-recovery-first methods permitted when there is high uncertainty regarding cash collectibility.

Japan   Generally at time of sale; percentage-of-completion method permitted on long-term contracts; installment method common when collection period exceeds two years regardless of degree of uncertainty of cash collectibility.

5. UNCOLLECTIBLE ACCOUNTS

U.S.   Allowance method.

Japan   Allowance method.

6. INVENTORIES AND COST OF GOODS SOLD

U.S.   Inventories valued at lower of cost or market. Cost determined by FIFO, LIFO, weighted average, or standard cost. Most firms use LIFO for domestic inventories and FIFO for non-domestic inventories.

Japan   Inventories valued at lower of cost or market. Cost determined by specific identification, FIFO, LIFO, weighted average, or standard cost. Most firms use weighted average or specific identification.

7. FIXED ASSETS AND DEPRECIATION EXPENSE

U.S.   Fixed assets valued at acquisition cost. Depreciation computed using straight-line, declining balance, and sum-of-the-years'-digits methods. Permanent declines in value are recognized. Most firms use straight line for financial reporting and an accelerated method for tax reporting.

Japan   Fixed assets valued at acquisition cost. Depreciation computed using straight-line, declining balance, and sum-of-the-years'-digits methods. Permanent declines in value are recognized. Most firms use a declining balance method for financial and tax reporting.

8. INTANGIBLE ASSETS AND AMORTIZATION EXPENSE

U.S.   Internally developed intangibles expensed when expenditures are made. Externally purchased intangibles capitalized as assets and tested annually for impairment.

Japan   The cost of intangibles (both internally developed and externally purchased) can be expensed when incurred or capitalized and amortized over the period allowed for tax purposes (generally 5 to 20 years). Goodwill is amortized over 5 years. Some intangibles (for example, property rights) are not amortized.

9. LIABILITIES RELATED TO ESTIMATED EXPENSES (WARRANTIES, VACATION PAY, EMPLOYEE BONUSES)

U.S.   Estimated amount recognized as an expense and as a liability. Actual expenditures are charged against the liability.

Japan   Estimated amount recognized as an expense and as a liability. Actual expenditures are charged against the liability. Annual bonuses paid to members of the Board of Directors and to the Commercial Code auditors are not considered expenses, but a distribution of profits. Consequently, such bonuses are charged against retained earnings.

10. LIABILITIES RELATED TO EMPLOYEE RETIREMENT AND SEVERANCE BENEFITS

U.S.   Liability recognized for unfunded accumulated benefits.

Japan   Severance benefits more common than pension benefits. An estimated amount is recognized each period as an expense and as a liability for financial reporting. The maximum liability recognized equals 40 percent of the amount payable if all eligible employees were terminated currently. There is wide variability in the amount recognized. Benefits are deducted for tax purposes only when actual payments are made to severed employees. Such benefits are seldom funded beforehand.

11. LIABILITIES RELATED TO INCOME TAXES

U.S.   Income tax expense based on book income amounts. Deferred tax expense and deferred tax asset or liability recognized for temporary (timing) differences between book and taxable income.

Japan   Income tax expense based on taxable income amounts. Deferred tax accounting not practiced. In consolidated statements submitted to the Ministry of Finance by listed companies (see No. 18), deferred tax accounting is permitted.

12. NONINTEREST-BEARING NOTES

U.S.   Notes stated at present value of future cash flows and interest recognized over term of the note.

Japan   Notes stated at face amount and no interest recognized over term of the note. Commonly used as a substitute for Accounts Payable.

13. BOND DISCOUNT OR PREMIUM

U.S.   Subtracted from or added to the face value of the bond and reported among liabilities on the balance sheet. Amortized over the life of the bond as an adjustment to interest expense.

Japan   Bond discount usually included among intangible assets and amortized over the life of the bonds. Bond discount and premium may also be subtracted from or added to face value of bonds on the balance sheet and amortized as an adjustment of interest expense over the life of the bonds.

14. LEASES

U.S.   Distinction made between operating leases (not capitalized) and capital leases (capitalized).

Japan   All leases treated as operating leases.

15. LEGAL RESERVE (PART OF SHAREHOLDERS' EQUITY)

U.S. Not applicable.

Japan When dividends are declared and paid, unappropriated retained earnings and cash are reduced by the amount of the dividend. In addition, unappropriated retained earnings are reduced and the legal reserve account is increased by a percentage of this dividend, usually 10 percent, until such time as the legal reserve equals 25 percent of stated capital. The effect of the latter entry is to capitalize a portion of retained earnings to make it part of permanent capital.

16. APPROPRIATIONS OF RETAINED EARNINGS

U.S. Not a common practice in the United States. Appropriations have no legal status when they do appear.

Japan Stockholders must approve each year the "proposal for appropriation of profit or disposition of loss." Four items commonly appear: dividend declarations, annual bonuses for directors and Commercial Code auditors, transfers to legal reserves, and changes in reserves.

The income tax law permits certain costs to be deducted earlier for tax than for financial reporting and permits certain gains to be recognized later for tax than for financial reporting. To obtain these tax benefits, the tax law requires that these items "be reflected on the company's books." The *pretax effect* of these timing differences *do not appear* on the income statement. Instead, an entry is made decreasing unappropriated retained earnings and increasing special retained earnings reserves (a form of appropriated retained earnings). When the timing difference reverses, the above entry is reversed. The *tax effects* on these timing differences *do appear* on the income statement, however. In the year that the timing difference originates, income tax expense and income tax payable are reduced by the tax effect of the timing difference. When the timing difference reverses, income tax expense and income tax payable are increased by a corresponding amount.

17. TREASURY STOCK

U.S. Shown at acquisition cost as a subtraction from total shareholders' equity. No income recognized from treasury stock transactions.

Japan Reacquired shares are either cancelled immediately or shown as a current asset on the balance sheet.

18. INVESTMENTS IN SECURITIES

A. Marketable Securities (Current Asset)

U.S.   Fair value method.

Japan   Reported at acquisition cost, unless price declines are considered permanent, in which case lower of cost or market.

B. Investments (Noncurrent Asset)

U.S.   Accounting depends on ownership: Less than 20 percent, market value method; 20 percent to 50 percent, equity method; greater than 50 percent, consolidated.

Japan   The principal financial statements are those of the parent company only (that is, unconsolidated statements). Intercorporate investments are carried at acquisition cost. Listed companies must provide consolidated financial statements as supplements to the principal statements in filings to the Ministry of Finance. The accounting for investments in securities in these supplementary statements is essentially the same as in the United States.

19. CORPORATE ACQUISITIONS

U.S.   Purchase method.

Japan   Purchase method.

20. FOREIGN CURRENCY TRANSLATION

U.S.   The translation method depends on whether the foreign unit operates as a self-contained entity (all-current method) or as an extension of the U.S. parent (monetary/nonmonetary method).

Japan   For branches, the monetary/nonmonetary translation method is used, with any translation adjustment flowing through income. For subsidiaries, current monetary items are translated using the current rate, other balance sheet items use the historical rate, and the translation adjustment is part of shareholders' equity.

21. SEGMENT REPORTING

U.S.   Segment information (sales, operating income, assets) disclosed by industry segment, geographical location, and type of customer.

Japan   Sales data by segment (industry, geographical location).

Sources: The Japanese Institute of Certified Public Accountants, *Corporate Disclosure in Japan* (July 1987); KPMG Peat Marwick, *Comparison of Japanese and U.S. Reporting and Financial Practices* (1989); PricewaterhouseCoopers, *Doing Business in Japan* (1993); and recent FASB rulings.

CASE 6.3

TANAGUCHI CORPORATION—PART B*

Dave Ando and Yoshi Yashima spent the next several days converting the financial statements of Tanaguchi Corporation from Japanese to U.S. GAAP. Although their conversions required them to make several estimates, Dave and Yoshi felt comfortable that they had largely filtered out the effects of different accounting principles. Exhibit 6.37 of this case presents the profitability and risk ratios for Tanaguchi Corporation based on Japanese GAAP (column 1) and as restated to U.S. GAAP (column 2). Column 3 shows the median ratios for U.S. machine tool companies (the same data as those reported in Exhibit 6.36). After studying the financial statement ratios in Exhibit 6.37, the following conversation ensues.

> **Dave:** The operating profitability of Tanaguchi Corporation, as evidenced by the rate of return on assets, is still lower than comparable U.S. firms, even after adjusting for differences in accounting principles. Although Tanaguchi's rate of return on common equity is now higher than its U.S. counterparts, the higher return occurs at the expense of taking on substantially more debt and therefore more risk. A significant portion of the differences in price-earnings ratios between Tanaguchi Corporation and U.S. companies results from differences in accounting principles. However, large differences still remain. I'm still not convinced that investing in Tanaguchi Corporation makes sense. Yoshi, am I on track with my interpretations or am I missing something?

> **Yoshi:** I'm not sure we are yet to the point where we can make a recommendation regarding an investment in the shares of Tanaguchi Corporation. We need to develop a better understanding of why the restated financial ratios for Tanaguchi Corporation still differ so much from those for U.S. machine tool companies.

One possible explanation might relate to the practice of many Japanese companies to operate in corporate groups, which the Japanese call *keiretsu.* Tanaguchi Corporation is a member of the Menji keiretsu. Each keiretsu typically comprises firms in eight or ten different industries (for example, one keiretsu might include firms in the steel, chemicals, forest products, retailing, insurance, and banking industries). The companies usually hold stock in each other; investments in the 25 percent to 30 percent range are common. These investments are not made for the purpose of controlling or even significantly influencing other members of the corporate group. Rather, they serve as a mechanism for

---

*Refer to Case 6.2, Tanaguchi Corporation—Part A, for background for this case. The case, co-authored by Paul R. Brown and Clyde P. Stickney, appeared in *Issues in Accounting Education* (Spring 1992), pp. 57–59 and is reproduced with permission of the American Accounting Association.

EXHIBIT 6.37

Comparative Financial Ratio Analysis For Tanaguchi Corporation and U.S. Machine Tool Companies
(Case 6.3)

	Tanaguchi Corp. (Japanese GAAP) (1)	Tanaguchi Corp. (U.S. GAAP) (2)	Median Ratio for U.S. Machine Tool Cos.[a] (3)
Profitability Ratios			
Operating Margin After Taxes (before interest expense and related tax effects)	2.8%	2.9%	3.3%
Assets Turnover	1.5	1.5	1.8
Return on Assets	4.2%	4.5%	5.9%
Capital Structure Leverage	3.8	4.0	2.6
Return on Common Equity	13.3%	14.8%	13.9%
Operating Margin Analysis			
Sales	100.0%	100.0%	100.0%
Other Revenue/Sales	.4	.4	—
Cost of Goods Sold/Sales	(73.2)	(73.4)	(69.3)
Selling and Administrative/Sales	(21.0)	(20.6)	(25.8)
Income Taxes/Sales	(3.4)	(3.5)	(1.6)
Operating Margin (excluding interest and related tax effects)	2.8%	2.9%	3.3%
Asset Turnover Analysis			
Receivable Turnover	5.1	5.0	6.9
Inventory Turnover	6.3	6.5	5.2
Fixed Asset Turnover	7.5	7.2	7.0
Risk Analysis			
Current Ratio	1.1	1.0	1.6
Quick Ratio	.7	.7	.9
Total Liabilities/Total Assets	73.8%	74.5%	61.1%
Long-term Debt/Total Assets	4.7%	5.1%	16.1%
Long-term Debt/Stockholders' Equity	17.9%	18.3%	43.2%
Times Interest Covered	5.8	5.7	3.1
Market Price Ratios (per common share)			
Market Price/Net Income	45.0	30.9	9.0
Market Price/Stockholders' Equity	5.7	4.6	1.2

[a]Source: Robert Morris Associates, *Annual Statement Studies* (except price-earnings ratio).

providing operating links between the entities. It is common for one corporation in the keiretsu to source many of its raw materials from another group member and to sell a substantial portion of its products to entities within the group. Each keiretsu includes a bank that provides needed funds to group members. It is rare that the bank would allow a member of the group to experience significant operating problems or to go bankrupt due to lack of funds.

A second, but related, institutional difference between the United States and Japan concerns stock ownership patterns. Roughly one-third of Japanese companies' shares is held by members of its keiretsu and another one-third is held by financial institutions, typically banks and insurance companies not affiliated with the keiretsu. This leaves only one-third of the shares held by individuals. The large percentage of intercorporate stock holdings has historically lessened the concern about keeping investors happy by paying large dividends or reporting ever-increasing earnings per share, as seems to be the case in the United States.

Instead, the emphasis of Japanese companies has been on serving new or growing markets, increasing market share, and strengthening the members of the keiretsu. The Japanese economy has grown more rapidly than the U.S. economy during the last several decades. In addition, Japanese companies have built their export markets and added operations abroad. The strategic emphasis has been on gaining market dominance in this growth environment and not on attaining particular levels of profit margin, rates of return, or earnings per share.

Finally, stock price changes in Japan appear related more to changes in real estate values than to the operating performance of individual companies. Real estate values and stock prices moved dramatically upward during the 1980s, although significant decreases have occurred recently. The increasing stock prices appeared to keep investors happy, leading them to deemphasize the kinds of profitability performance evaluation common in the United States.

Required

After studying the financial statements and notes for Tanaguchi Corporation, develop explanations for the differences in the profitability and risk ratios for Tanaguchi Corporation reported in column 2 of Exhibit 6.37 as compared to those reported in column 3 for U.S. machine tool companies.

Chapter 7

REVENUE RECOGNITION AND RELATED EXPENSES

Learning Objectives

1. Review the criteria for recognizing revenue and expenses under the accrual basis of accounting and apply these criteria to various types of businesses.

2. Calculate the income statement, balance sheet, and statement of cash flow effects of recognizing income prior to the point of sale, at the time of sale, and subsequent to sale.

3. Analyze and interpret the effects of FIFO versus LIFO on financial statements and convert the statements of a firm from a LIFO to a FIFO basis.

4. Use financial statement disclosures for depreciable assets to calculate average depreciable lives and age of such assets, and convert the financial statements of a firm from a straight-line to an accelerated depreciation basis.

5. Understand the alternative ways that firms account for intangible assets (highlighting research and development expenditures, software development expenditures, and goodwill) and the difficulties that these alternatives present when analyzing high-technology firms.

6. Review the rules for evaluating the impairment of long-lived assets, including goodwill, and analyze how to apply the rules to different categories of long-lived assets.

7. Understand the distinction between changes in the general purchasing power of the monetary unit and changes in the prices of specific assets and liabilities, and the accounting methods designed to adjust financial statements for these two types of changing prices.

This chapter and the next two describe the selection and application of alternative methods of accounting for assets, liabilities, revenues, and expenses commonly encountered in corporate annual reports. These chapters emphasize those methods that have the greatest effect on the income statement and balance sheet. We continue our focus on how a firm's selection of accounting methods and the way it implements them affect its *accounting quality*, its *earnings quality* and its *balance sheet quality*, topics introduced in Chapter 6.

The assessment of accounting quality begins with understanding GAAP. In this chapter, we examine accounting for revenue recognition, inventory cost-flow assumptions, depreciable and intangible assets, and impairment of long-lived assets. The focus is on acceptable reporting methods in the United States, although the chapter notes differences between the United States and other countries. For firms operating in countries that experience high inflation, Appendix 7.1 is especially relevant as it illustrates how significant changes in the general purchasing power of the reporting unit affect performance and risk analysis, and firm valuation.

As Chapter 6 discusses, quality accounting information should portray fairly and completely the economic effects of a firm's decisions and actions. That is, quality accounting information must paint the most accurate economic portrait of the firm's financial position, performance, and risk that is possible given the complexity of today's business environment. In this chapter (and Chapters 8 and 9), we explain the various reporting principles under investigation, describe the choices firms make in applying them, and discuss whether adjustments are needed to the reported amounts to enhance the quality of accounting information. In this regard, Chapters 6 through 9 represent a unit that addresses understanding both the *reported* corporate financial data and determining the relevant *adjusted* financial data for analyzing the profitability and risk of a firm.

INCOME RECOGNITION

Earnings from any operating activity undertaken by a firm are ultimately the difference between the economic resources received from customers and the economic resources paid to suppliers, employees, and other providers of goods and services. Economic value-added is the difference between the present value of these inflows and outflows.

Although the incremental flows measure the *amount* of added value, a timing problem often arises because the cash received from a particular operating activity may occur in a different period than the period when a firm expends cash for that operating activity. The accrual basis of accounting addresses this problem by developing criteria for recognizing revenues and expenses that are not driven by the immediate period's cash flows, but rather, by the economic value-added generated by the firm during the period. The economic value-added affects both income for the period and changes in the valuation of assets and liabilities on the balance sheet, an important relation discussed in Chapter 2. The difficulty at times is developing criteria that accurately and reliably capture economic value-added.

Under the accrual basis of accounting, firms apply a set of criteria for revenue recognition that attempts to capture the point when a firm has substantially completed its value-adding activities. And after calculating revenue based on the criteria, firms attempt to match against this revenue all costs incurred to generate that revenue. Following this process, earnings match inputs with outputs, aiming to provide an accurate measure of the economic value-added during the period. We discuss the criteria for revenue and expense recognition shortly.

Accepting the accrual basis of accounting, however, does not settle the question of *when* firms recognize revenues and matching expenses. Options for recognizing revenues include, for example, (1) during the period of production, (2) at the completion of production, (3) at the time of sale, (4) during the period while receivables are outstanding, or (5) at the time of cash collection. Subsequent sections of this chapter provide examples of applying the accrual basis of accounting at various revenue recognition points.

CRITERIA FOR REVENUE RECOGNITION

One of the most important reporting decisions firms must make is when to recognize revenue. The reason for its importance is straightforward: a firm needs to generate and report persistent revenues to survive long term. For the analyst, then, no other reporting decision deserves more scrutiny than this one. The analyst needs to be confident that the revenues (net of related expenses) reported by the firm represent economic value-added.

Policymakers recognize the importance of revenue recognition to the reporting model and spend considerable time attempting to refine the criteria for recognizing revenues. In fact, financial reporting policymakers at the SEC have given the topic high priority and have issued numerous rulings on revenue recognition in recent years.[1] In addition, both the FASB and IASB have identified revenue recognition as a key topic in their future agendas.

GAAP requires firms to identify the significant accounting policies employed for recognizing revenues in notes to the financial statements. Exhibit 7.1 illustrates a recent disclosure by Halliburton describing how it recognizes revenues on long-term construction contracts, a technique discussed later in the chapter. Halliburton reported over $13 billion in revenues in a recent year, representing one of the largest energy-related firms in the world. PepsiCo discloses its revenue recognition policy in both Note 1 to the financial statements (Appendix A) and the first section of Management's Discussion and Analysis (Appendix B).

The complexity of today's business environment has heightened the importance of understanding a firm's business model and its relation to the revenue recognition principles chosen for reporting. Although there are many cases where it is relatively

---

[1]The SEC issued Staff Accounting Bulletin No. 101, "Revenue Recognition in Financial Statements," in December 1999. SAB 101, as it is commonly referred to, is one of the more important documents issued by the SEC in recent years and summarizes in one location all existing guidance on revenue recognition. SAB 101 and related documents issued subsequently by the SEC significantly impact the choices made by many publicly held companies for recognizing revenue.

EXHIBIT 7.1

Halliburton, Inc.
Excerpt from Note 1 to the Consolidated Financial Statements

Note 1: Significant Accounting Policies

Revenue and income recognition. Revenues from engineering and construction contracts are reported on the percentage of completion method of accounting using measurements of progress toward completion appropriate for the work performed. Progress is generally based upon physical progress, man-hours, or costs incurred based upon the appropriate method for the type of job. All known or anticipated losses on contracts are provided for currently. Claims and change orders that are in the process of being negotiated with customers for extra work, or changes in the scope of work, are included in revenues when collection is deemed probable.

---

easy to determine when to recognize revenue, there are more than a few cases where it is not. Businesses with sales that include future performance obligations, sales that involve a barter exchange of services between firms, and sales that bundle several services are just a few examples where the selection and application of revenue recognition principles can have a dramatic effect on the amount and timing of reported revenue.

Financial reporting requires the recognition of revenue under the accrual basis of accounting when a firm *both*:

1. Has provided all, or a substantial portion, of the services to be performed.
2. Has received either cash, a receivable, or some other asset whose cash-equivalent amount the firm can measure with reasonable precision.

Revenue Recognition Principles

Most firms recognize revenue at the time of sale (delivery) of goods or services. At this point, a firm has completed production of the goods or creation of the services, so that the first criterion is satisfied. The firm has either already incurred or can estimate the amount of total cash outflow related to the production and sale of the goods or services. Such measurement of total costs permits an appropriate matching of expenses with revenues, as discussed in the next section.

The benefit that a firm obtains from providing goods or services is the cash or other consideration that the firm expects to receive. If the customer promises to pay cash in the future, the firm examines the credit standing of the customer and assesses the likelihood of receiving the cash. The second criterion is satisfied so long as the firm can reasonably predict the amount of cash it will collect.

Revenue Recognition and Economic Value-Added

The recognition of revenue at the time of sale (delivery) is so common that analysts may neglect to assess whether this timing is appropriate for a particular firm.

Firms may attempt to report as favorable a picture of themselves as possible by accelerating the timing of revenues or estimating the collectible amounts too aggressively. If so, the quality of accounting information suffers because it does not represent high economic content, is probably managed, and is probably not sustainable.

Consider the following three conditions, each of which is a signal that revenue recognition at the time of sale may be too early: (1) large and volatile amounts of uncollectible accounts receivable; (2) unusually large amount of returned goods, and (3) excessive warranty expenditures. Each of these sales-related expenses should bear a reasonably stable relationship to revenues over time. Either large percentages of these expenses as a percentage of sales, or widely varying percentages from year to year, should raise questions about the appropriateness of revenue recognition at the time of sale.

Another possible signal related to accounts receivable is an increase in their days' outstanding. (Chapter 4 provides a discussion of how to calculate receivable days' outstanding.) Customers taking longer to pay for their purchases may suggest an overstatement of revenues and earnings. Note that the analyst should assess the receivable days' outstanding and the stability of bad debt expense to revenue in tandem because either ratio by itself may provide a misleading signal. A firm that adequately recognizes bad debt expense for an increasing proportion of uncollectible sales will likely show a stable accounts receivable turnover, because providing for estimated uncollectible accounts has the same effect on accounts receivable (that is, reduction) as collecting the accounts in cash. Thus, examining just the accounts receivable turnover does not signal the collection problem. The analyst must examine the ratio of bad debt expense to sales to observe the increasing proportion of uncollectible sales. A firm that does not adequately recognize bad debt expense for an increasing proportion of uncollectible sales will experience a buildup of accounts receivable relative to sales and therefore higher accounts receivable days' outstanding. Examining just the ratio of bad debt expense to sales will not signal the slow rate at which customers pay.

Recognizing revenues at the *time of sale* suffers from an even more fundamental problem at times: What is the definition of *sale*? Does the receipt of firm customer orders for goods held in inventory constitute a sale or is physical delivery of the product to the customer necessary? Is completion of the production of custom-ordered goods sufficient to recognize revenue or is physical delivery necessary? In an effort to achieve sales targets for a period, firms sometimes record sales earlier than physical delivery.

Some firms, hungry for sales revenue, even record sales based on merely an indication of possible interest in a product by a customer. Inevitably in these situations the pressure placed on sales personnel, either by themselves or senior management, leads to this violation of the revenue recognition criteria. A related ploy is to accelerate the recognition of revenues and then hide sales returns by customers. Firms store the returned goods in a remote or independently owned warehouse, hoping that the independent auditor will not detect them.

Chapter 5 points out that the distinction between earnings management and management fraud is often a thin line. In these ploys, however, it is clear that management crosses the line. The actions are fraudulent in nature because they are outside the bounds of generally accepted accounting principles, and management takes the actions to intentionally mislead statement users.[2]

As stated earlier, the analyst cannot be too vigilant in assessing whether firms have managed their revenues. Revenues are at the core of a firm's ability to grow and prosper. A firm experiencing declining sales growth, particularly relative to other firms in its industry, is the type most likely to be tempted to manage earnings by "stretching" the revenue recognition rules. Although this type of earnings management eventually catches up with the firm, it is precisely in these situations when a firm's sustainable earnings are likely to be declining. The analyst needs to take this into account when forecasting future earnings.

CRITERIA FOR EXPENSE RECOGNITION

Financial reporting requires the recognition of expenses under the accrual basis of accounting as follows:

1. Costs directly associated with revenues become expenses in the period when a firm recognizes the revenues.
2. Costs not directly associated with revenues become expenses in the period when a firm consumes the services or benefits of the costs in operations.

Most of the costs of manufacturing a product closely relate to particular revenues. The firm matches expense recognition with revenue recognition for such costs, referred to as *product* costs. Other costs, such as insurance and property taxes on administrative facilities, salaries of corporate officers, and depreciation on computer equipment, for example, bear only an indirect relation to revenues generated during the period. Such costs become expenses in the period in which the firm consumes the benefits of insurance, governmental, administrative, and computer services. Accountants refer to such costs as *period* expenses.

Since a large proportion of the expenses that firms report in the income statement associate directly with revenue recognized, assessing the economic value-added and manageability of expenses and revenues are closely related. However, there are certain period expenses that are more susceptible to management than others. The analyst should carefully monitor advertising, research and development, and maintenance expenditures, as examples, in order to discern whether substantive reasons exist for changes in the levels of these expenditures, or whether the changes are the result of managed earnings. Expenditures that are somewhat discretionary in nature and reported on the income statement as period costs are prime candidates for managing earnings.

Similar to revenue recognition, GAAP requires firms to identify in notes to the financial statements the significant policies employed for recognizing expenses.

---

[2]A summary of celebrated cases in which management abused the reporting system for recognizing revenue appears in Chapter 6 of Martin S. Fridson and Fernando Alvarez, *Financial Statement Analysis: A Practitioner's Guide,* Third Edition, New York: John Wiley & Sons, Inc., 2002; and Chapters 3 through 10 of Kathryn F. Staley, *The Art of Short Selling.* New York: John Wiley & Sons, Inc., 1997.

Exhibit 7.2 illustrates a recent quarterly disclosure by DriveTime for recognition of expenses for credit losses on loans (DriveTime is also discussed in Chapter 6.). DriveTime's primary line of business is to sell and finance used vehicles to customers in the "sub-prime" segment of the used car market. The sub-prime market is comprised of customers who typically have limited credit histories, low income, or past credit problems. The judgment necessary for calculating the effect of credit losses is particularly strewn with estimates and uncertainties. DriveTime identifies five factors in Exhibit 7.2 that it considers in evaluating whether the allowance and the provision for credit losses is adequate. Moreover, it makes clear that this list is not an exhaustive one.

APPLICATION OF REVENUE AND EXPENSE RECOGNITION CRITERIA

Applying the revenue recognition and matching principles to actual business settings is not always as straightforward as the criteria might appear. The common expression, "the devil is in the detail," aptly describes the problem of assessing whether the principles are correctly applied in the particular circumstances. The reporting system currently employed in the United States often entails making subjective measurement judgments. Coupling this problem with the complexities of businesses today, it is not surprising that appropriate application of revenue recognition criteria is not always obvious.

To obtain a flavor for the complexities often involved in applying the principles, consider the six examples that follow.

Example 1

Xerox Corporation typically manufactures and leases copiers to customers under multi-year leases. The length of the leases often approximates the useful life of the

---

EXHIBIT 7.2
DriveTime (formerly Ugly Duckling, Inc.)
Excerpt from Notes to Consolidated Quarterly Financial Statements

Allowance for Credit Losses

An allowance for credit losses (allowance) is established by charging the provision for credit losses. To the extent that the allowance is considered insufficient to absorb anticipated credit losses over the next 12 months, additions to the allowance are established through a charge to the provision for credit losses. The evaluation of the allowance considers such factors as (1) the performance of each dealership's loan portfolio, (2) the Company's historical credit losses, (3) the overall portfolio quality and delinquency status, (4) the value of underlying collateral, and (5) the current economic conditions that may affect the borrower's ability to pay.

copiers. Thus, the arrangement is equivalent to a sale of the copier, with Xerox providing financing to the customer signing the lease. (Chapter 8 describes and illustrates the accounting for leases by both the lessor and lessee.) The accounting is complex, however, because the lease contract usually entails a bundled monthly payment that covers not just use of the copier by the customer over the life of the lease, but also maintenance services, photocopying paper up to certain minimum usage, and financing costs. The revenue recognition question is when Xerox should recognize revenue from the four services covered in the lease: (1) copier use, (2) maintenance services, (3) photocopying paper, and (4) financing.

The question is most easily answered by first considering how Xerox accounts for outright sales of copiers. If Xerox sells a copier to a credit-worthy customer, it recognizes revenue from the sale of the copier at the time of delivery. For the items (2) through (4), Xerox meets the substantial performance criterion for revenue recognition over time as it provides these goods and services.

However, in the typical situation, the copier is *not* an outright sale but, rather, a lease arrangement that involves a bundled periodic lease payment. Xerox must unbundle the monthly payment to ascertain the proportion related to each revenue component. If the leasing arrangement is equivalent in economic substance to a sale, then Xerox must determine (1) how much revenue it should recognize up front for manufacturing the copier and providing its use to the customer over its entire life, and (2) how much it should allocate to the remaining three categories of the arrangement and recognize later. In fact, Xerox does make these allocations, but in the recent past the SEC accused Xerox of allocating too much of the monthly payment to the sale of the copiers and too little to maintenance, paper, and financing. The result was an acceleration of revenues and earnings that authorities contended was too aggressive. Xerox accordingly restated its earnings.

Example 2

Metropolitan Life Insurance Company sells life insurance policies to customers. The firm receives premium payments each year and invests the cash in stocks, bonds, real estate, and other income-producing assets. The premiums received from customers plus the income from investments over the life of insured individuals provide the funds to pay the required death benefits.

Life insurance companies receive cash from premiums and from investments each period. They invest in readily marketable securities for the most part, so that they can measure objectively the changes in the market value of their investments. Measuring the amount of revenue each period while the life insurance policy is outstanding presents few difficulties. The only issue on the revenue side is whether these firms should recognize as revenue the unrealized gains and losses from changes in the market value of investments. Common practice in the insurance industry is to recognize such gains and losses each year in computing net income.[3]

---

[3]Chapter 9 provides a discussion of how firms other than life insurance companies account for investments in readily marketable debt and equity securities.

There is usually little question about the total expense on a life insurance policy. Other than selling commissions and administrative costs, the only expense is the face value of the policy. The income recognition issue is how much of this total cost life insurance companies should recognize as an expense each year to match against premium and investment revenues. The objective is to spread these costs over the life of the insured. Determining the length of this period and the pattern of expense recognition requires actuarial calculations of expected life, investment returns, and similar factors. Note that allocating an equal portion of the total cost to each year of expected life will not necessarily provide an appropriate matching of revenues and expenses. Although insurance premiums typically remain level over the contract period, investment revenues increase over time as premiums and investment returns accumulate. Life insurance companies increase a liability each period, often called Policyholder Reserves, for the amount of expense recognized. They reduce this account when they pay insurance claims. An analyst examining the financial statements of a life insurance company should study carefully the amount shown for Policyholder Reserves and the change in this account each year. Such an assessment provides information about both the adequacy of assets to cover potential claims and the amount of net income each period.

Example 3

Microstrategy, Inc. is a software and consulting firm in the information technology sector. The firm specializes in tailoring proprietary software to analyze large databases of clients. Clients often sign two- or three-year contracts with the firm that cover tailoring the software to the specific needs of the client and then licensing (as opposed to selling) the use of software for the length of the contract. The contracts often require Microstrategy to train the client's personnel to use the software in mining large databases and to assist the client in designing reports and analyses based on this data mining. The contracts establish key deliverables, together with a schedule for the payment of fees over the life of the contract.

Assuming reasonable assurance of the collectibility of fees from the client, the revenue recognition issue is when Microstrategy meets the substantial performance criterion for revenue recognition. The situation is complicated because Microstrategy is providing both (1) use of a product, that is, its proprietary software tailored to the client's needs, and (2) a service in the form of consulting to insure that client personnel can produce value-added reports and analyses. What proportion of the contract relates to the software and what proportion to the consulting services? How precise are the deliverables, and what happens if Microstrategy misses a contract deadline?

In the past, Microstrategy recognized approximately fifty percent of the amount of the total contract as revenue at the time of signing the contract. The firm, in other words, concluded that substantial performance was met for about half of what it promised to the customer at the contract signing date. The SEC disagreed with this assessment, however, and concluded that fifty percent was far too aggressive and represented an inappropriate acceleration of revenue. Microstrategy scaled back the amount of revenue recognized at the contract signing date to approximately ten percent and restated past financial statements. The news of the need to restate previously reported earnings led to a substantial drop in Microstrategy's stock price.

Example 4

AOL, the Internet services division of AOL Time Warner, generates advertising revenues for advertisements it places on various web sites.

In the past, AOL entered into one such arrangement with eBay. Under the arrangement, AOL located firms that wished to advertise on the eBay web site. AOL sold the advertising space to various companies and then remitted a portion of this amount to eBay. AOL bore no credit risk if the firms failed to pay for the advertising space. AOL guaranteed the sale of a certain minimum amount of advertising space each month. Failure to sell the minimum space required AOL to make payments to eBay. AOL booked the amount to be received from the various companies as revenues and the amount paid to eBay as an expense. eBay booked the net amount received from AOL as revenue.

The issue is whether AOL is a principal or an agent in purchasing and selling advertising space. The accounting described above considers AOL a principal, since it entails booking the full revenue and expense. GAAP requires a firm to assume substantial product risk if it is to be considered a principal, which does not appear to be the case here because AOL probably can sell sufficient advertising space each month to cover the minimum obligation to eBay. With this the case, AOL bears little risk of unsold advertising space and should have accounted for its services as an agent and recognized only the net amount as revenue. The distinction is an important one because, although there is no effect on net income, the magnitude of revenues reported as a principal are substantially higher than those reported as an agent.

Example 5

Global Crossing, Qwest Communications, and other telecommunication companies have created worldwide fiber optic networks in recent years. Companies in the industry typically enter into long-term leases for the use of the networks developed by other companies in the industry. For example, Global Crossing might create a fiber optic network in India, Qwest Communications might create a similar network in China, and each in turn might lease part of the capacity of the networks to each other. The leases often give the lessee an indefeasible right of use to the capacity, essentially a legal transfer of title to the capacity. Each company books the "sale" of the legal rights to the capacity as revenue in the year they sign the leases. They treat the "purchase" of the legal rights to the capacity as a capital expenditure, much like the purchase of a long-lived asset.

The issue is whether these firms satisfy the revenue recognition criterion that requires receipt of an asset with a measurable cash-equivalent value when they swap legal rights to capacity. Recognize that, as opposed to the manufacture and sale of physical equipment, these situations simply involve the sale of legal rights to use capacity. If the capacity is already in place, then the "manufacturing" activity is complete. As long as there are not significant restrictions on the ability of the buyer to use the capacity purchased, then the purchaser of the capacity receives an asset, the right to use capacity of the other firm in the future.

The analyst must consider at least two other issues, however. First, is it likely that the seller of the capacity will exist for the full period of the contract and be in a position to provide the services? The free-fall of the telecommunications industry in recent years makes this an important consideration. Second, how should the firms establish the value of the contract? Given that the contracts often entail the swapping of promises to provide capacity in the future with no cash changing hands, it is difficult to determine the true value of the contracts. What is the appropriate value to attach to the revenue for the seller at the signing of the contract? What is the appropriate value to attach to the expense recorded by the buyer during the course of the contract? GAAP has not definitively answered how to account for these types of transactions.

Example 6

Walgreen Company operates over 3,500 drugstores in the United States and is one of the most recognized names in its field. Walgreen often receives rebates from its suppliers when its purchases during any given year reach established minimum levels. In some cases, formal agreements exist that state the minimum purchases required for the rebate. In other cases, the arrangement is less formal. Although the supplier decides the amount of rebates to pay as the reporting year progresses, it is fairly predictable from year to year. The issue is how Walgreen should recognize supplier rebates in its quarterly reports issued during the course of any reporting year.

The key issue is whether realization of the rebate is necessary to justify recognition of the benefit, or whether estimates of its amounts are sufficient to justify recognition. If the probability of realizing the rebate is high and its amount is predictable, the matching principle supports recognition in each quarter. In this way, Walgreen matches cost of goods sold net of the rebates against the revenues earned in the quarter. In fact, reporting the entire rebate credit in one quarter (the quarter when it is received, for example) would be inappropriate because it provides a poor matching of revenues and expenses. However, if the probability of receiving the rebate is low or its amount difficult to predict, then delaying recognition until it is received seems appropriate. Having a contract in place enhances the predictability, but it is not necessary if customary practice is for the suppliers to make rebates. The key is being able to make reasonably solid estimates of the rebate's amount.

Firms in the drugstore and retail discount industry handle rebates differently. The firm's first note to the financial statements often provides an explanation of its policy on accounting for rebates.

These six examples illustrate the difficulty at times of applying the general principles for recognizing revenues and expenses to business practices specific to particular industries. The analyst needs to ratchet up the usual degree of healthy skepticism practiced in analyzing reported financial data when the activities of the firms or industries under scrutiny involve the level of uncertainty and subjectivity represented by these six illustrations.

The next section explores more fully the impact on the financial statements of recognizing income either earlier than the time of sale (a common practice among long-term contractors) or later than the time of sale (a common practice when firms sell goods on an installment payment basis and experience high uncertainty regarding the collectibility of cash).

INCOME RECOGNITION FOR LONG-TERM CONTRACTORS

The operating cycle for a long-term contractor (for example, building contractor, aerospace manufacturer, ship builder) differs from that of a manufacturing firm in three important respects:

1. The period of construction (production) may span many accounting periods.
2. Contractors identify customers and agree upon a contract price in advance (or at least in the early stages of construction).
3. Customers often make periodic payments of the contract price as work progresses.

The operating activities of long-term contractors often satisfy the criteria for the recognition of revenue during the period of construction. Exhibit 7.1 describes this form of revenue recognition for Halliburton, a long-term contractor in the energy-related industry. The existence of a contract indicates that the contractor has identified a buyer and agreed upon a price. The contractor either collects cash in advance or concludes, based on an assessment of the customer's credit standing, that it will receive cash equal to the contract price after completion of construction. Although the contract may obligate the contractor to perform substantial future services, the contractor should be able to estimate the cost of these services with reasonable precision. In agreeing to a contract price, the firm must have some confidence in the estimates of the total costs it will incur on the contract.

Percentage-of-Completion Method

When contractors meet the criteria for revenue recognition as construction progresses, they usually recognize revenue during the period of construction using the percentage-of-completion method. Under the percentage-of-completion method, contractors recognize a portion of the total contract price, based on the degree of completion of the work during the period, as revenue for the period. They base this proportion either on engineers' or architects' estimates of the degree of completion or on the ratio of costs incurred to date to the total expected costs for the contract. The actual schedule of cash collections is *not* a determining factor in measuring the amount of revenue recognized each period under the percentage-of-completion method. Even if a contractor expects to collect the entire contract price at the completion of construction, it would still use the percentage-of-completion method as long as it can make reasonable estimates as construction progresses of the amount of cash it will collect and of the costs it will incur.

As contractors recognize portions of the contract price as revenues, they recognize corresponding proportions of the total estimated costs of the contract as expenses.

The percentage-of-completion method, following the principles of the accrual basis of accounting, matches expenses with related revenues.

Example 7

To illustrate the percentage-of-completion method, assume that a firm agrees to construct a bridge for $5,000,000. Estimated costs are as follows: Year 1, $1,500,000; Year 2, $2,000,000; and Year 3, $500,000. Thus, the expected gross margin from the contract is $1,000,000 (= $5,000,000 − $1,500,000 − $2,000,000 − $500,000).

Assuming that the contractor bases the degree of completion on the percentage of total costs incurred to date and that it incurs actual costs as anticipated, revenue and expense from the contract are as follows:

Year	Degree of Completion	Revenue	Expense	Gross Margin
1	$1,500,000/$4,000,000 = 37.5%	$1,875,000	$1,500,000	$ 375,000
2	$2,000,000/$4,000,000 = 50.0%	2,500,000	2,000,000	500,000
3	$500,000/$4,000,000 = 12.5%	625,000	500,000	125,000
		$5,000,000	$4,000,000	$1,000,000

Actual costs on contracts seldom coincide precisely with expectations. As new information on expected total costs becomes available, contractors must adjust reported income on the contract. They make the adjustment to reported income for this change in estimated total costs during the current and future periods rather than retroactively restating income of prior periods.

Example 8

Look at Example 7 again. Assume now that actual costs incurred in Year 2 for the contract were $2,200,000 instead of $2,000,000 and that total expected costs on the contract are now $4,200,000. Revenue, expense, and gross margin from the contract are as follows:

Year	Cumulative Degree of Completion	Revenue	Expense	Margin
1	$1,500,000/$4,000,000 = 37.5%	$1,875,000	$1,500,000	$375,000
2	$3,700,000/$4,200,000 = 88.1%	2,530,000[a]	2,200,000	330,000
3	$4,200,000/$4,200,000 = 100%	595,000[b]	500,000	95,000
		$5,000,000	$4,200,000	$800,000

[a] (.881 × $5,000,000) − $1,875,000 = $2,530,000

[b] $5,000,000 − $1,875,000 − $2,530,000 = $595,000

Example 9

If it appears that the contractor will ultimately realize a loss upon completion of a contract, the contractor must recognize the loss in full as soon as it becomes evident. For example, if at the end of Year 2 the contractor expects to realize a loss of $200,000 on the contract, it must recognize a loss of $575,000 in Year 2. The $575,000 amount offsets the income of $375,000 recognized in Year 1 plus a loss of $200,000 anticipated on the overall contract.

Contractors report actual contract costs on the balance sheet in a Contracts in Process account. This account includes not only accumulated costs to date but any income or loss recognized on the contract. Assume that the firm in Example 7 pays cash for all costs incurred each year and receives cash from the customer upon completion of the contract. Using the analytical framework from Chapter 2, the effect on the financial statements of incurring costs on the contract each year (transactions (1), (3), and (5)), recognizing revenue and expense each year (transactions (2), (4), and (6)), and completing the contract (transaction (7)) are as follows (ignoring income taxes).

	C	+	N$A	=	L	+	CC	+	AOCI	+	RE
BS-BOP											
(1)	− 1,500,000		+1,500,000								
(2)			+1,875,000								+1,875,000
			−1,500,000								−1,500,000
IBT											+ 375,000
BS-EOP	**−1,500,000**		**+1,875,000**								**+ 375,000**
(3)	− 2,000,000		+2,000,000								
(4)			+2,500,000								+2,500,000
			−2,000,000								−2,000,000
IBT											+ 500,000
BS-EOP	**− 3,500,000**		**+4,375,000**								**+ 875,000**
(5)	− 500,000		+ 500,000								
(6)			+ 625,000								+ 625,000
			− 500,000								− 500,000
IBT											+ 125,000
(7)	+5,000,000		−5,000,000								
BS-EOP	**+1,000,000**		**—**								**+1,000,000**

Exhibit 7.3 shows the Contracts in Process account for Examples 7 through 9. If the contractor periodically billed the customer for portions of the contract price, it would report the amount billed in Accounts Receivable and as a subtraction from the amount in the Contracts in Process account.

	EXHIBIT 7.3

**Calculation of Balance in Contracts in Process Account
Using the Percentage-of-Completion Method**

	Accumulated Costs	Accumulated Income	Amount in Contracts in Process Account
Example 7 (Profit = $1,000,000)			
During Year 1....................	$1,500,000	$ 375,000	$1,875,000
Balance, December 31, Year 1	$1,500,000	$ 375,000	$1,875,000
During Year 2.....................	2,000,000	500,000	2,500,000
Balance, December 31, Year 2	$3,500,000	$ 875,000	$4,375,000
During Year 3.....................	500,000	125,000	625,000
Completion of Contract during Year 3.........	(4,000,000)	(1,000,000)	(5,000,000)
Balance, December 31, Year 3	$ -0-	$ -0-	$ -0-
Example 8 (Profit = $800,000)			
During Year 1....................	$1,500,000	$ 375,000	$1,875,000
Balance, December 31, Year 1	$1,500,000	$ 375,000	$1,875,000
During Year 2.....................	2,200,000	330,000	2,530,000
Balance, December 31, Year 2	$3,700,000	$ 705,000	$4,405,000
During Year 3.....................	500,000	95,000	595,000
Completion of Contract during Year 3.........	(4,200,000)	(800,000)	(5,000,000)
Balance, December 31, Year 3	$ -0-	$ -0-	$ -0-
Example 9 (Loss = $200,000)			
During Year 1....................	$1,500,000	$ 375,000	$1,875,000
Balance, December 31, Year 1	$1,500,000	$ 375,000	$1,875,000
During Year 2.....................	2,200,000	(575,000)	1,625,000
Balance, December 31, Year 2	$3,700,000	$(200,000)	$3,500,000
During Year 3.....................	1,500,000	—	1,500,000
Completion of Contract during Year 3.........	(5,200,000)	200,000	(5,000,000)
Balance, December 31, Year 3	$ -0-	$ -0-	$ -0-

Completed-Contract Method

Some long-term contractors postpone the recognition of revenue until they complete the construction project. Such firms use the completed-contract method of recognizing revenue, which, in effect, is the "time of sale" method of recognizing revenue. If the firm in Example 8 had used the completed-contract method, it would have recognized no revenue or expense from the contract during Year 1 or Year 2. It would recognize contract revenue of $5,000,000 and contract expenses of $4,200,000 in Year 3. Note that total gross margin is $800,000 under both the percentage-of-completion and completed-contract methods, equal to cash inflows of $5,000,000 less cash outflows of $4,200,000. If the contractor anticipates a loss on a contract, it recognizes the loss as soon as the loss becomes evident, even if the contract is incomplete.

The Contracts in Process account under the completed-contract method shows a balance of $1,500,000 on December 31, Year 1, the accumulated costs to date. This account shows a balance on December 31, Year 2 of $3,500,000 under Example 7, $3,700,000 under Example 8, and $3,500,000 under Example 9. These amounts reflect accumulated costs to date minus, in Example 9, the estimated loss on the contract.

These amounts are less than the amounts shown in the Contracts in Process account for Examples 7 and 8 under the percentage-of-completion method (see Exhibit 7.3) by the amount of accumulated income recognized under the latter method. Accelerating the recognition of income under the percentage-of-completion method increases both assets and net income (part of retained earnings). Thus, as Chapter 2 discussed, income recognition and asset valuation closely interrelate.

Choice of Reporting Method by Long-term Contractors

The primary reason that a contractor would not use the percentage-of-completion method when a contract exists is that there is substantial uncertainty regarding the total costs it will incur in completing the project. If the contractor cannot estimate the total costs, it will be unable to estimate the percentage of total costs incurred as of a given date and thereby the percentage of services already rendered. It will also be unable to estimate the total income from the contract.

In some cases, contractors use the completed-contract method because the contracts are of such short duration (such as a few months) that earnings reported with the percentage-of-completion method and the completed-contract method are not significantly different. In these cases, the lower costs of implementing the completed-contract method explain its use. Contractors also use the completed-contract method in situations when they have not obtained a specific buyer during the construction phase, as is sometimes the case in the construction of residential housing. These cases require future selling efforts. Substantial uncertainty may exist regarding the ultimate contract price and the amount of cash that the contractor will receive.

Contractors must use the percentage-of-completion method for income tax purposes. Although most firms would prefer to use the completed-contract method for tax purposes, thereby delaying the recognition of income and payment of income taxes, the Internal Revenue Code does not permit it.

Examples 7 through 9 dramatically illustrate the level of estimation and uncertainty involved with income recognition for long-term contractors. Sometimes a project can take up to five years to complete. In some cases, contractors are working with hundreds of subcontractors. Renegotiating contracts several times during the course of a large contract is commonplace. Estimating persistent earnings using historical data for firms that construct (and sell) long-term products must take into consideration these factors, and other firm factors, including the volume of projects underway currently, the success in completing projects on time and within budget, the length of typical projects, and the types of projects undertaken. Long-term construction firms usually address many of these factors in the analysis of operations found in the annual report and Form 10-K filing. (Again, see Exhibit 7.1 for an excerpt from Halliburton's annual report.). Because both (1) the time period between cash inflows and outflows for these firms is so long, and (2) a large degree of estimation is needed to measure revenues and expenses, the potential for earnings management is high. The analyst evaluating firms in the residential construction, aircraft, and defense-related industries, for example, must be particularly sensitive to this fact.

REVENUE RECOGNITION WHEN CASH COLLECTIBILITY IS UNCERTAIN

Occasionally, estimating the amount of cash or cash equivalent value of other assets that a firm will receive from customers is difficult. This may occur because the future financial condition of the customer is highly uncertain or because the customer may have the right to return the items purchased, thereby avoiding the obligation to make cash payments. This uncertainty regarding future cash inflows may prevent the selling firm from measuring—at the time of sale—the present value of the cash it expects to receive. The firm will therefore recognize revenue at the time it collects cash using either the installment method or the cost-recovery-first method.

Unlike the cash method of accounting, these revenue recognition methods follow accrual principles by matching expenses with associated revenues. The installment and cost-recovery-first methods exist because, without these options, applying the time of sale method to situations with high uncertainty as to cash inflows could result in widespread earnings management. Given the difficulty in estimating the cash inflows in these situations, the opportunity to manage earnings may cloud even management's best intentions to measure earnings accurately. The uncertainty of future cash flows also affects assessments of earnings persistence. The task for the analyst is to judge whether a firm recognizing revenue using the time of sale method should be using one of these two, more conservative, methods because the level of uncertainty introduced in the reporting system is intolerable.

Installment Method

Under the installment method, a firm recognizes revenue as it collects portions of the selling price in cash. At the same time, it recognizes corresponding portions of the cost of the good or service sold as an expense. For example, assume that a firm sells for $100 merchandise costing $60. The buyer agrees to pay (ignoring interest) $20 each month for 5 months. The firm recognizes revenue of $20 each month as it receives cash. Likewise, it recognizes cost of goods sold of $12 (=$20/$100 × $60) each month. By the end of 5 months, the firm recognizes total income of $40 [= 5 × ($20 – $12)].

Land development companies, which typically sell undeveloped land and promise to develop it over several future years, sometimes use the installment method. The buyer makes a nominal down payment and agrees to pay the remainder of the purchase price in installments over 10, 20, or more years. In these cases, future development of the land is a significant aspect of the earnings process. Also, substantial uncertainty often exists as to the ultimate collectibility of the installment notes, particularly those not due until many years in the future. The customer can always elect to stop making payments, losing the right to own the land.

Cost-Recovery-First Method

When firms experience substantial uncertainty about cash collection, they can also use the cost-recovery-first method of income recognition. The cost-recovery-first method matches the costs of generating revenues dollar for dollar with cash receipts until the firm recovers all such costs. Revenues equal expenses in each period until full cost recovery occurs. Only when cumulative cash receipts exceed total costs will a firm show profit (that is, revenue without any matching expenses) in the income statement.

To illustrate the cost-recovery-first method, refer to the previous example relating to the sale of merchandise for $100. During the first 3 months, the firm would recognize revenue of $20 and expense of $20. By the end of the third month, cumulative cash receipts of $60 exactly equal the cost of the merchandise sold. During the fourth and fifth months, the firm would recognize revenue of $20 each month but without an offsetting expense. For the five months as a whole, total income is again $40 (equal to cash inflow of $100 less cash outflow of $60) but the income recognition pattern differs from that of the installment method.

Comprehensive Illustration of Income Recognition Methods for Installment Sales

Technor Computer Corporation (TCC) sold a computer costing $16,000,000 to the City of Boston for $20,000,000 on January 1, Year 10. The City of Boston agreed to make annual payments of $5,548,195 on December 31, Year 10 to December 31, Year 14 (five payments in total). The top panel of Exhibit 7.4 shows an amortization table for the note receivable underlying this transaction. The five payments of $5,548,195 each when discounted at 12 percent have a present value equal to the $20,000,000 selling price. Thus, 12 percent is the interest rate implicit in the note. Column (2) shows the interest revenue that TCC recognizes each year from providing financing services to the City of Boston (that is, permitting the city to delay payment of the $20,000,000 selling price).

The middle panel shows the revenue and expense that TCC recognizes under three income recognition methods. Columns (6) and (7) assume TCC recognizes income from the sale of the computer at the time of sale. Such immediate recognition rests on the premise that the City of Boston will pay the amounts due under the note with a high probability.

If substantial uncertainty exists regarding cash collectibility of the notes, then TCC should use either the installment or cost-recovery-first methods. Columns (8) and (9) show the amounts for the installment method. Revenues in column (8) represent collections of the $20,000,000 principal amount of the note (that is, the portion of each

EXHIBIT 7.4

Illustration of Income Recognition Methods from Installment Sales

Amortization Schedule for Note Receivable

Year	Note Receivable, January 1: (1)	Interest Revenue at 12 Percent (2)	Cash Payment Received (3)	Repayment of Principal (4)	Note Receivable, December 31: (5)
1	$20,000,000	$2,400,000	$ 5,548,195	$ 3,148,195	$16,851,805
2	16,851,805	2,022,217	5,548,195	3,525,978	13,325,827
3	13,325,827	1,599,099	5,548,195	3,949,096	9,376,731
4	9,376,731	1,125,208	5,548,195	4,422,987	4,953,744
5	4,953,744	594,449	5,548,193	4,953,744	-0-
		$7,740,973	$27,740,973	$20,000,000	

Column (2) = .12 × Column (1)
Column (3) = Given
Column (4) = Column (3) − Column (2)
Column (5) = Column (1) − Column (4)

Income Recognition from Sale of Computer

Year	Time of Sale Revenue (6)	Expense (7)	Installment Method Revenue (8)	Expense (9)	Cost-Recovery-First Method Revenue (10)	Expense (11)	All Three Methods Interest Revenue (12)
1	$20,000,000	$16,000,000	$ 3,148,195	$ 2,518,556	$ 3,148,195	$ 3,148,195	$2,400,000
2	—	—	3,525,978	2,820,782	3,525,978	3,525,978	2,022,217
3	—	—	3,949,096	3,159,277	3,949,096	3,949,096	1,599,099
4	—	—	4,422,987	3,538,390	4,422,987	4,422,987	1,125,208
5	—	—	4,953,744	3,962,995	4,953,744	953,744	594,449
	$20,000,000	$16,000,000	$20,000,000	$16,000,000	$20,000,000	$16,000,000	$7,740,973

Column (8) = Column (4)
Column (9) = .80 × Column (8)
Column (10) = Column (4)
Column (11) = Column (10) until Cumulative Revenues = $16,000,000
Column (12) = Column (2)

Exhibit 7.4—(continued)

Notes Receivable-Net Reported on Balance Sheet

| | Time of Sale | Installment Method | | | | Cost-Recovery-First Method | | |
| | | | | | | | | |
	Notes Receivable (13)	Notes Receivable (14)	Less Deferred Gross Margin (15)	Notes Receivable Net (16)	Notes Receivable (17)	Less Deferred Gross Margin (18)	Notes Receivable Net (19)
January 1, Year 1	$20,000,000	$20,000,000	$4,000,000	$16,000,000	$20,000,000	$4,000,000	$16,000,000
December 31, Year 1	16,851,805	16,851,805	3,370,361	13,481,444	16,851,805	4,000,000	12,851,805
December 31, Year 2	13,325,827	13,325,827	2,665,165	10,660,662	13,325,827	4,000,000	9,325,827
December 31, Year 3	9,376,731	9,376,731	1,875,346	7,501,385	9,376,731	4,000,000	5,376,731
December 31, Year 4	4,953,744	4,953,744	990,749	3,962,995	4,953,744	4,000,000	953,744
December 31, Year 5	—	—	—	—	—	—	—

Column (13), Column (14), Column (17) = Column (1)
Column (15) = $4,000,000 minus cumulative income recognized = Column (8) – Column (9) for the current and prior years. For example, $3,370,361 = $4,000,000 – ($3,148,195 – $2,518,556).
Column (16) = Column (14) – Column (15)
Column (18) = $4,000,000 minus cumulative income recognized = Column (10) – Column (11) for the current and prior years.
Column (19) = Column (17) – Column (18).

cash payment made by the city that does not represent interest). Column (9) shows the expense each year, which represents 80 percent (= $16,000,000 ÷ $20,000,000) of the revenue recognized. Columns (10) and (11) show the amounts for the cost-recovery-first method. Note that TCC recognizes no income until Year 5, when cumulative cash receipts exceed the $16,000,000 cost of manufacturing the computer.

Note that total cash inflows of $27,740,973 (column 3) equal total revenue, sales revenue (columns 6, 8, and 10) plus interest revenue (column 12), and total cash outflows of $16,000,000 equal total expense (columns 7, 9, and 11).

The last panel of Exhibit 7.4 shows the amounts that TCC reports on its balance sheet for each of the three income recognition methods. Recognizing income at the time of sale results in the largest cumulative income through the first four years and the largest assets. Recognizing income using the installment method results in the next largest cumulative income and the next largest assets. The cost-recovery-first method results in the smallest cumulative income and the smallest assets. The differences in assets equal the differences in cumulative income recognized. Thus, we see again that asset valuation closely relates to income recognition. Note also that at the end of five years, cumulative income and assets are identical for all three income recognition methods.

Choice of Installment and Cost-Recovery-First Methods

Financial reporting permits firms to use the installment method and the cost-recovery-first method only when substantial uncertainty exists about cash collection. For most sales of goods and services, past experience and an assessment of the credit standing of customers provide a sufficient basis for estimating the amount of cash firms will receive. In these cases, firms do not use the installment method and the cost-recovery-first method. These firms must generally recognize revenue at the time of sale.

Income tax laws allow the installment method for income tax reporting under some circumstances, even when no uncertainty exists regarding cash collections. Manufacturing firms selling on extended payment plans often use the installment method for income tax reporting (while recognizing revenue at the time of sale for financial reporting). Firms seldom use the cost-recovery-first method for tax reporting.

INVENTORY COST-FLOW ASSUMPTION

Firms selling relatively high dollar-valued items, such as automobiles, trailers, and real estate, can ascertain from the accounting records the specific cost of each item sold. They recognize this amount as an expense, cost of goods sold, and match it against sales revenue in measuring net income.

In most cases, firms cannot identify the cost of the specific items sold. Inventory items are sufficiently similar and their unit costs sufficiently small that firms cannot justify economically the cost of designing an accounting system to keep track of specific unit costs. To measure cost of goods sold in these cases, firms must make some assumption about the *flow of costs* (not the flow of units, since firms usually sell the oldest goods first). With the introduction of cost-flow assumptions into the reporting system, however, comes the possibility of earnings management and varying degrees of earnings quality. Analyzing earnings quality in the context of inventory accounting first requires understanding the reporting options available to management.

Financial reporting permits three cost-flow assumptions:

1. First-in, first-out (FIFO).
2. Last-in, first-out (LIFO).
3. Weighted average.

FIFO assigns the cost of the earliest purchases to the units sold and the cost of the most recent purchases to ending inventory. LIFO assigns the cost of the most recent purchases to the cost of goods sold and the earliest purchases to inventory. Weighted average assigns the average cost of all units available for sale during the period (units in beginning inventory plus units purchased) to both units sold and units in ending inventory. Exhibit 7.5 depicts these relationships graphically assuming that a firm purchases units evenly over the year.

FIFO

FIFO results in balance sheet amounts for ending inventory that are closest to current replacement cost. The cost of goods sold tends to be somewhat out of date, however, because FIFO charges to expense the earlier prices of beginning inventory and the earliest purchases during the year. When inventory costs are rising, FIFO leads to the highest reported net income (lowest cost of goods sold) of the three methods, and when inventory costs fall it leads to the smallest net income.

LIFO

LIFO results in amounts for cost of goods sold that closely approximate current replacement costs. Balance sheet amounts, however, can contain the cost of inventory acquisitions made many years previously. Consider the diagram in Exhibit 7.6 that shows purchases, LIFO ending inventory, and LIFO cost of goods sold over several periods for a firm.

During each of the first four periods, the firm purchases more units than it sells. Thus, the physical units in ending inventory grow each year. The firm assigns costs to the units in inventory at the end of Year 1 based on the earliest purchases in Year 1. We refer to the costs assigned to these units as the base LIFO layer (denoted with the letter *a* in Exhibit 7.6).

LIFO prices the units in inventory at the end of Year 2 in two layers. Units equal to those on hand at the end of Year 1 carry unit costs based on purchase prices paid at the beginning of Year 1. Units added to ending inventory during Year 2 carry unit costs

---

EXHIBIT 7.5

Cost-flow Assumptions

Purchases
January 1   January 1

| FIFO Cost of Goods Sold | FIFO Ending Inventory |

| Weighted Average Cost for Goods Sold and in Ending Inventory |

| LIFO Ending Inventory | LIFO Cost of Goods Sold |

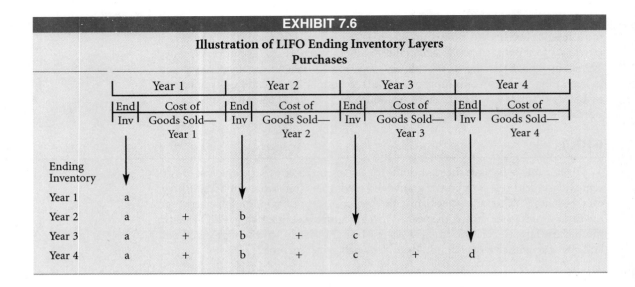

EXHIBIT 7.6

Illustration of LIFO Ending Inventory Layers

	Year 1		Year 2		Year 3		Year 4
	End Inv	Cost of Goods Sold— Year 1	End Inv	Cost of Goods Sold— Year 2	End Inv	Cost of Goods Sold— Year 3	End Inv	Cost of Goods Sold— Year 4
Ending Inventory							
Year 1	a						
Year 2	a	+	b				
Year 3	a	+	b	+	c		
Year 4	a	+	b	+	c	+	d

based on purchase prices paid at the beginning of Year 2 (denoted with the letter *b* in Exhibit 7.6). The balance sheet at the end of Year 2 states the inventory at the sum of the costs assigned to these two layers. Note that LIFO does not assume that the actual physical flow of units sold will track a LIFO assumption. LIFO is a *cost flow*, or cost assignment, method and not a means of tracking the physical movement of goods.

As the quantity of units in ending inventory continues to increase in Year 3 and Year 4, the firm adds new LIFO layers. At the end of Year 4, LIFO assigns costs to ending inventory based on purchases made at the beginning of Year 1, Year 2, Year 3, and Year 4. Thus, the longer a firm remains on LIFO, the more its ending inventory valuation will differ from current replacement costs.

During periods of rising inventory costs, LIFO generally results in the highest cost of goods sold and the lowest net income of the three cost-flow assumptions. It is for this reason that firms usually prefer LIFO for income tax purposes. If a firm chooses a LIFO cost-flow assumption for tax purposes, the income tax law requires the firm to use LIFO for financial reporting to shareholders.

LIFO Liquidation

One exception to the generalization that LIFO produces the lowest net income during periods of rising prices occurs when a firm sells more units during a period than it purchases (referred to as a LIFO layer liquidation). In this case, LIFO assigns the cost of all of the current period's purchases plus the costs assigned to the most recent LIFO layers to the cost of goods sold. For example, assume that sales exceeded purchases in Year 5 in the example above. The firm assigns the cost of all of Year 5's purchases to the units sold. LIFO then assigns the cost of Year 4's LIFO layer (reflecting purchase prices at the beginning of Year 4) to the excess units sold, then assigns Year 3's LIFO layer (reflecting purchase prices at the beginning of Year 3) to any remaining excess units, and so on until it has assigned a cost to all units sold. Because LIFO assigns older, lower costs to a portion of the units sold, LIFO cost of goods sold may not exceed FIFO cost of goods sold, despite experiencing rising inventory costs during the current period.

When firms experience LIFO liquidations, two cash flow effects likely occur. First, firms delay purchasing inventory items, thereby delaying a cash outflow. Second, firms increase taxable income and the required cash outflow for taxes. Researchers have examined the effect of LIFO liquidations on abnormal stock price behavior at the time firms disclose such liquidations. No abnormal stock price reaction was observed on average in these studies when those firms' tax positions (for example, availability of net operating loss carryforwards) were ignored. However, when this tax position was considered, low tax-paying firms had a higher abnormal price reaction to a LIFO liquidation than other firms.[4]

Characteristics of LIFO Adopters

Researchers have examined the characteristics of firms that do and do not adopt LIFO. Although these research studies do not always show consistent results, the following factors appear related to the decision to adopt LIFO[5]:

Direction and rate of factor price changes for inventory items. Firms experiencing rapidly increasing factor prices for raw materials, labor, or other product costs obtain greater tax benefits from LIFO than firms who experience smaller factor price increases or who experience price decreases.

Variability in the rate of inventory growth. LIFO adopters show more variable rates of inventory growth before adopting LIFO than firms that remain on FIFO. The variability of inventory growth declines after adopting LIFO. Because LIFO tends to match more recent inventory costs with sales than does FIFO or weighted average (these methods use costs that are six to fifteen months old relative to current replacement costs), LIFO tends to result in less variability in the gross margin percentage over the business cycle. Firms with variable rates of inventory growth (perhaps because of cyclicality in their industry) can more easily accomplish an income smoothing reporting objective using LIFO than if they use FIFO or average cost.

Tax savings opportunities. LIFO adopters tend not to have tax loss carryforwards available to offset future taxable income. These firms instead adopt LIFO to provide future tax savings. LIFO adopters also realize larger tax savings in the year of adoption than in the surrounding years, suggesting that the decision is in part motivated by tax rather than financial reporting considerations.

---

[4]Thomas L. Stober, "The Incremental Information Content of Financial Statement Disclosures: The Case of LIFO Inventory Liquidations," *Journal of Accounting Research*, Supplement 1986, pp. 138–160, and Senyo Tse, "LIFO Liquidations," *Journal of Accounting Research*, Spring 1990, pp. 229–238.

[5]For a review of these studies, see Frederick W. Lindahl, "Dynamic Analysis of Inventory Accounting Choice," *Journal of Accounting Research*, Autumn 1989, pp. 201–226, and Nicholas Dopuch and Morton Pincus, "Evidence on the Choice of Inventory Accounting Methods: LIFO versus FIFO," *Journal of Accounting Research*, Spring 1988, pp. 28–59.

Industry membership. Firms in certain industries are more likely to adopt LIFO than firms in other industries. Since firms in an industry face similar factor price changes and variability in their inventory growth rates, one would expect similar choices of cost-flow assumptions.

Asset size. Larger firms are more likely to adopt LIFO than smaller firms. LIFO increases record-keeping costs, relative to FIFO, both in the year of adoption and in subsequent years. Larger firms realize larger amounts of tax savings than smaller firms to absorb the adoption and ongoing record-keeping costs of LIFO.

One hypothesis examined in this research is the relation between LIFO adoption and managerial compensation. Because LIFO usually results in lower earnings, one would expect that managerial compensation of LIFO adopters would either be less than compensation of non-LIFO adopters or else include a lower component of compensation based on earnings. Studies have found no difference in managerial compensation of LIFO and non-LIFO adopters, although adopters had a smaller earnings component to their compensation.

WEIGHTED AVERAGE

The weighted average cost-flow assumption falls between the other two in its effect on the balance sheet and the income statement. It is, however, much more like FIFO than like LIFO in its effects on the balance sheet. When inventory turns over rapidly, purchases during the current period receive a heavy weight in the weighted average unit cost. The weighted average assumption therefore reflects current prices almost as much as FIFO.

CONVERSION FROM LIFO TO FIFO

No cost-flow assumption based on historical cost can simultaneously report current cost data in both the income statement and the balance sheet. If a firm reports current costs in the income statement under LIFO, its balance sheet amount for ending inventory contains some very old costs. The out-of-date LIFO inventory valuation results in low accounting information quality and provides potentially misleading information to users of financial statements. Consequently, the Securities and Exchange Commission requires firms using LIFO to disclose in notes to the financial statements the amounts by which LIFO inventories are less than if the firm had reported inventories at FIFO or current cost. Analysts sometimes refer to the difference in ending inventory valuation between LIFO and FIFO or current cost as the *LIFO reserve*. From this disclosure, it is possible to restate a LIFO firm's income to a FIFO basis. In this way, the analyst can place firms using LIFO on a basis more comparable to firms using FIFO.

Example 10

Note 1 to PepsiCo's financial statements (Appendix A) indicates that it uses a combination of FIFO, LIFO, and average cost-flow assumptions for inventories and cost of goods sold. A subsequent note indicates that the differences between the LIFO and FIFO methods for valuing inventories are immaterial for both Year 11 and Year 10.

In previous reporting periods, however, the differences were material enough that PepsiCo provided a reconciliation between the LIFO and FIFO valuation methods. In Year 8's annual report, for example, PepsiCo indicates that the current cost of inventories exceeds their LIFO amounts by $11 million at the end of Year 7 and $8 million at the end of Year 8. Exhibit 7.7 shows the conversion of PepsiCo's inventories and cost of goods sold from a combination of three cost-flow assumptions to a combination of FIFO and average costs.

Because reporting standards do not require the disclosure of the excess of current cost over average cost of inventories, it is not possible to restate inventories and cost of goods sold fully to a FIFO basis. It appears that PepsiCo's use of a combination of FIFO, LIFO, and average costs has no effect on measures of its operating profitability.

Example 11

In Year 11, Bethlehem Steel Company changed the method of valuing inventories from the LIFO method to the FIFO method.[6] An annual report of Bethlehem Steel issued prior to the change provides substantial information on its inventories, as illustrated in Exhibit 7.8. Exhibit 7.9 shows the conversion from LIFO to FIFO for Bethlehem Steel Company.

EXHIBIT 7.7			
Year 8 Restatement of PepsiCo's Inventories and Cost of Goods Sold for Differences in Cost-flow Assumptions (in millions)			
	FIFO/LIFO/ Average Cost	**Excess of Current Cost Over LIFO Cost**	**FIFO/ Average Cost**
Beginning Inventory.......	$ 1,051[a]	$11[c]	$ 1,062[d]
Purchases...............	15,370		15,370
Available	$16,421		$16,432
Less Ending Inventory	1,038[a]	8[c]	1,046[e]
Cost of Goods Sold........	$15,383[b]	$ 3	$15,386[b]

[a]As reported in Pepsi's Year 8 balance sheet.
[b]As reported in Pepsi's Year 8 income statement.
[c]As reported in Pepsi's Year 8 note on inventories.
[d]$1,062 = $1,051 + $11.
[e]$1,046 = $1,038 + $8.

---

[6]The change is reported as a "change in accounting principle" as discussed in Chapter 6. However, a firm *restates* prior years' financial statements to reflect the change, a financial reporting requirement specific to a change from the LIFO to FIFO inventory cost-flow assumption.

The gross margin percentage under LIFO is 16.2 percent [=($5,250.9 − $4,399.1) ÷ $5,250.9] and under FIFO is 16.8 percent [= ($5,250.9 − $4,366.7) ÷ $5,250.9]. The lower gross margin value under LIFO suggests that the manufacturing costs of steel increased during Year 9.

The calculation of the inventory turnover ratio, a measure that indicates the efficiency with which a firm manages its inventory, is:

LIFO: $4,399.1 ÷ .5($369.0 + $410.3) = 11.3
FIFO: $4,366.7 ÷ .5($899.1 + $972.8) = 4.7

The dramatic difference in the inventory turnover ratio under LIFO and FIFO reflects the many years that have elapsed since Bethlehem Steel Company adopted

EXHIBIT 7.8

Bethlehem Steel Company
Annual Report Excerpts
(in millions)

December 31:	Year 8	Year 9
Inventories at FIFO Cost.	$ 899.1	$ 972.8
Excess of FIFO Cost Over LIFO Cost.	(530.1)	(562.5)
Inventories at LIFO Cost	$ 369.0	$ 410.3
Current Assets (LIFO).	$1,439.8	$1,435.2
Current Liabilities.	870.1	838.0

	For Year 9
Sales.	$5,250.9
Cost of Goods Sold (LIFO).	4,399.1
Net Income	245.7
Income Tax Rate	35%

EXHIBIT 7.9

Conversion of Bethlehem Steel Company from
LIFO to FIFO
(in millions)

	LIFO	Excess of FIFO Cost Over LIFO Cost	FIFO
Beginning Inventory	$ 369.0	$530.1	$ 899.1
Purchases.	4,440.4		4,440.4
Available.	$4,809.4	$530.1	$5,339.5
Less Ending Inventory	(410.3)	(562.5)	(972.8)
Cost of Goods Sold	$4,399.1	$(32.4)	$4,366.7

LIFO. The current (FIFO) cost of its inventory is more than twice as large as its book (LIFO) value. The inventory turnover ratio based on LIFO amounts gives a poor indication of the actual physical turnover of inventory items because it divides a cost of goods sold amount reflecting current costs by an average inventory amount reflecting very old costs. The inventory turnover ratio under FIFO provides a better indication of the physical turnover of inventory items because it divides a cost of goods sold reflecting only slightly out-of-date costs by an average inventory reflecting relatively recent costs. Although the trend in the inventory turnover ratio for a particular firm is likely to be similar under LIFO and FIFO, cross-sectional comparisons are inappropriate if one firm uses LIFO and another uses FIFO. Also, the LIFO measure of the inventory turnover ratio does not accurately portray the number of days inventories are held.

The inventory cost-flow assumption also affects the current ratio, a measure commonly used to assess short-term liquidity risk that is introduced in Chapter 5. The conversion from LIFO to FIFO increases inventories at the end of Year 9 by $562.5 million, increasing the current ratio. However, *cumulative* pre-tax income and taxable income would have been $562.5 million higher under FIFO. Income tax laws do not permit a firm to use LIFO for taxes if it uses FIFO for financial reporting. Thus, Bethlehem Steel Company would have paid $196.9 million (= .35 × $562.5) more in income taxes under FIFO than under LIFO. (We assume that the income taxes saved by adopting LIFO are now partly in cash and partly in other assets.) If the $196.9 million reduces cash on the December 31, Year 9 balance sheet, the current ratio under LIFO and FIFO appears below:

LIFO: $1,435.2 ÷ $838.0 . . . .   1.71

FIFO: [$1,435.2 + (1 − .35)($562.5)] ÷ $838.0 . . . .   2.15

Thus, the current ratios differ significantly. The assumption that the extra income taxes paid under FIFO reduce cash only and not other assets moderates the differences in the current ratios. The current ratio on December 31, Year 9 under FIFO would likely exceed 2.15.

Conversion of the financial statements of Bethlehem Steel Company from LIFO to FIFO requires the following adjustments:

	December 31	
Balance Sheet	Year 8	Year 9
Cash: .35 × $530.1; .35 × $562.5	$−185.5	$−196.9
Inventories	$+530.1	$+562.5
Retained Earnings: .65 × $530.1; .65 × $562.5.	$+344.6	$+365.6

Income Statement	For Year 9
Reduction in Cost of Goods Sold	$−32.4
Increase in Income Tax Expense: .35 × $32.4	$+11.3
Net Income: .65 × $32.4.	$+21.1

Statement of Cash Flows	For Year 9
Net Income.	$+21.1
Increase in Inventories:	
($410.3 − $369.0) − ($972.8 − $899.1)	$(+32.4)
Cash Flow from Operations.	$−11.3

Cash flow from operations decreases for the extra income taxes paid under FIFO.

Users of financial statements find the conversion procedure illustrated in Exhibits 7.7 and 7.9 especially useful when comparing U.S. and non-U.S. firms. Most industrialized countries do not permit the use of LIFO for financial reporting. One important exception is Japan, but even in Japan most firms use specific identification or average costs rather than LIFO. Thus, the analyst should restate inventories and cost of goods sold for U.S. firms using LIFO to make them more comparable to cost-flow assumptions used outside of the United States.

STOCK PRICE REACTION TO CHANGES IN INVENTORY COST-FLOW ASSUMPTION

The required conformity of tax and financial reporting for firms choosing a LIFO cost-flow assumption provides fertile ground for researchers studying the efficiency of capital markets. LIFO saves taxes when inventory costs are rising. A switch to LIFO could result in a positive stock price reaction if the capital markets react to the expected future tax savings to arise from the switch. The switch also signals that the firm expects future inventory costs to rise, which could trigger a negative stock price reaction. The switch to LIFO also results in lower reported earnings to shareholders, and could trigger a negative stock price reaction if capital markets fixate on reported earnings rather than the underlying economic effects driving the firm's accounting method choices.

Numerous research studies[7] have examined this question, some observing positive price reactions and others observing negative price reactions at the time of the switch. Refinements to the research methodology to provide for different earnings expectation models, tax positions, and other factors have not yet resulted in a definitive answer to the question about the efficiency of the market's reaction. Research studies have examined the characteristics of firms that remain on FIFO versus firms that switch to LIFO (see the discussion earlier in this section) in an attempt to sort out these conflicting results.

---

[7]For a summary of this research, see Dopuch and Pincus, "Evidence on the Choice of Inventory Accounting Methods: LIFO versus FIFO," *op. cit.*

PERSISTENT EARNINGS AND THE COST-FLOW ASSUMPTION

For most firms, cost of goods sold represents the largest expense on the income statement. Inventory represents one of the most active accounts on the balance sheet because the creation and selling of goods and services is the central activity of most firms. Thus, monitoring cost of goods sold and inventory for their effect on the quality of accounting information is critical. To do this, the analyst considers:

1. The inventory cost-flow assumption chosen by management.
2. Price variation and the speed at which inventory turns over.
3. Any liquidation of LIFO inventory layers.
4. Any physical deterioration or obsolescence of inventory.
5. The financing of inventory acquisitions.

Choice of Cost-Flow Assumption

Because LIFO generally matches the most recent acquisition costs again revenues in measuring earnings, LIFO-based earnings generally provide the best measure of economic value-added and of sustainable earnings. A firm must replace goods sold if it is to continue operating and the most recent cost of the items purchased serves as the best predictor of their replacement costs. A FIFO cost-flow assumption matches older acquisition costs with current revenues and a weighted-average cost-flow assumption provides results between LIFO and FIFO. Researchers examining the relation between market returns for a firm's equity securities and earnings based on LIFO versus FIFO cost of goods sold found that those based on LIFO explain more of the cross-sectional returns across firms than FIFO.[8]

Although LIFO generally provides higher quality earnings measures, FIFO generally provides higher *quality financial position* measures. This is because the inventory values under LIFO can be considerably less than current market values, which FIFO values often approximate. (Exceptions are discussed below.) A firm cannot use LIFO for measuring cost of goods sold on the income statement, and FIFO for measuring inventory on the balance sheet, however. All is not lost because, as Examples 10 and 11 reveal, firms using LIFO must disclose the difference between the FIFO cost and LIFO cost of inventories. With this information, the analyst can convert inventory on the balance sheet to an amount more closely approximating current economic value.

Rapid Inventory Turnover and Price Stability

The preference for LIFO as the best indicator of economic value-added is tempered significantly when (1) inventory turns over quickly or (2) acquisition costs of inventory items do not vary much. LIFO, FIFO, and weighted-average cost-flow assumptions all yield approximately the same amounts for cost of goods sold if inventory turns over roughly four or more times each year.

---

[8]Ross Jennings, Paul J. Simko, and Robert B. Thompson II, "Does LIFO Inventory Accounting Improve the Income Statement at the Expense of the Balance Sheet?" *Journal of Accounting Research*, Spring 1996, pp. 85–109.

For some firms, inventory does not turn over quickly but prices are so stable that the choice of the cost-flow assumption is of little consequence. This is an unusual situation, however, and probably should lead to questions by the analyst regarding demand for the firm's products.

Liquidation of LIFO Inventory Layers

When firms dip into LIFO layers, they must report the amount by which cost of goods sold was reduced (the usual case) and earnings were increased. This is a classic example of lower quality of earnings despite higher reported profits. When using earnings of the current period to estimate sustainable earnings, the analyst should eliminate the effect of the dip into old LIFO layers from the current period's earnings. The analyst should also ascertain from management the reason why inventory levels were depleted.

Obsolete or Damaged Inventory

When the current value of inventories decline below acquisition cost because of obsolescence or physical deterioration, firms must write down their inventories to reflect the decline. The analyst needs to rely on management and the auditors to determine when inventory is overvalued, but a good gauge is whether competitors are taking write-downs. Another signal comes from industry-wide publications addressing the demand for the firm's products. In certain cases, it is reasonable for the analyst to estimate independently the economic value of inventory and adjust the reported values accordingly.

Inventory Financing Arrangements

Firms often need substantial amounts of cash early in their operating cycle to finance the purchase of raw materials. Firms may finance these purchases through short-term borrowing agreements with suppliers that appear on the balance sheet as accounts payable. However, firms sometimes obtain financing for their inventories in a manner that avoids reporting a liability on the balance sheet. For example, a firm might create a legal trust with the sole purpose of purchasing raw materials that the firm needs in its operations. The trust purchases the raw materials on account from various suppliers. The firm later purchases the needed raw materials from the trust at agreed-upon prices and reimburses the trust for the cost of carrying the raw materials until needed by the firm. The supplier is willing to sell to the trust on account because of the firm's purchase commitment.

The economic substance of this arrangement is that the firm has purchased raw material on account, and yet no accounts payable appears in the financial statements of the firm. Current financial reporting rules sometimes allow the firm to leave both the inventory and the accounts payable off the balance sheet, thereby lowering its debt levels and increasing inventory and accounts payable turnover ratios. The analyst should examine the notes to the financial statements for significant purchase commitments and consider adding them to inventories and accounts payable. Chapter 8 discusses these arrangements more fully.

ACCOUNTING FOR FIXED ASSETS

Virtually all firms report some amount of property, plant, and equipment (sometimes collectively referred to as long-lived fixed assets) on their balance sheets. The higher the degree of capital intensity of a firm, the higher will be the proportion of total assets represented by property, plant, and equipment. Among the questions analysts should raise about property, plant, and equipment are the following:

1. At what amount does the balance sheet report gross property, plant, and equipment?
2. Over what useful lives does the firm depreciate its plant and equipment?
3. What depreciation method does the firm use to write off the cost of plant and equipment?
4. Are the carrying amounts of the fixed assets recoverable through productive use of the assets?

The following sections consider each of these questions.

FIXED ASSET VALUATION

GAAP in the United States and virtually all other countries requires the valuation of fixed assets at acquisition costs. An exception is the Netherlands, where financial reporting permits periodic revaluations to current replacement cost. (Appendix 7.1 discusses the accounting for such revaluations.) Accounting's use of acquisition cost valuations rests on the presumption that such amounts are more objectively measurable than the current market values of fixed assets.

Difficulties encountered in determining current market values include (1) the absence of active markets for many used fixed assets, particularly those specific to a particular firm's needs, (2) the need to identify comparable assets currently available in the market to value assets in place, and (3) the need to make assumptions about the effect of technological and other improvements when using the prices of new assets currently available on the market in the valuation process.

The disclosures of property, plant, and equipment on the balance sheet or in the notes permit the analyst to estimate the relative age of depreciable assets and get some sense of the extent to which acquisition costs reflect outdated valuations. Appendix A (Note 8 to the financial statements) discloses the following information for PepsiCo at the end of Year 11 (in millions):

	PepsiCo
Depreciable Assets (excluding land and construction in progress)	$10,981
Accumulated Depreciation	(5,304)
Net Depreciable Assets	$ 5,677
Depreciation Expense	$ 843

PepsiCo also discloses in Appendix A that it primarily uses the straight-line depreciation method (discussed later in this section). At the end of Year 11, PepsiCo's depreciable assets were approximately 6.3 years old on average (= $5,304 ÷ $843). Given relatively low inflation rates in the United States in recent years, the historical cost values shown on PepsiCo's balance sheet are probably not significantly out of date.

A second issue related to the gross amount of long-lived assets is the treatment of expenditures to add to or improve existing plant and equipment. GAAP stipulates that firms should capitalize (that is, add to the asset's cost) expenditures that increase the service potential (either in quantity or quality) of an asset beyond that originally anticipated. Firms should expense immediately those expenditures that merely maintain the originally expected service potential. A firm's capitalization versus expense policy with respect to such expenditures affects its reported earnings and provides management with some flexibility to manage earnings. Unfortunately, firms do not provide sufficient information to permit the analyst to assess the quality of earnings with respect to such expenditures.

Example 12

American Airlines, one of the largest airlines in the world, follows a rigorous maintenance program for all of its aircraft. In a recent annual report, the firm provides the following information about its maintenance and repair costs:

> *Maintenance and Repair Costs.* Maintenance and repair costs for owned and leased flight equipment are charged to operating expense as incurred, except engine overhaul costs incurred by AMR Eagle Holding Corporation and costs incurred for maintenance and repair under power-by-the-hour maintenance contract agreements, which are accrued on the basis of hours flown.

DEPRECIABLE LIFE

Depreciation is a process of allocating the historical cost of depreciable assets to the periods of their use in a reasonably systematic manner. One factor in this depreciation process is the expected useful life. Both physical wear and tear and technological obsolescence affect this life. Firms make estimates of this expected total life, a process that again offers management an opportunity to manage reported earnings.

The disclosures firms make about depreciable lives are usually not very helpful to the analyst in assessing a firm's aggressiveness in lengthening depreciable lives to manage earnings. The problem often is the aggregated nature of the disclosures.

Example 13

American, Delta, and United Airlines are dominant players in the airline industry worldwide, and account for a large percentage of domestic travel in the United States. These firms depreciate leased and owned aircraft, along with other fixed assets integral to operating airlines, following the policies detailed in Exhibit 7.10. The range of depreciable lives chosen by the three airlines is large. In addition, note that

---

EXHIBIT 7.10
American, Delta, and United Airlines
Note Disclosure Policies—Depreciable Lives

American Airlines

Equipment and Property. The provision for depreciation of operating equipment and property is computed on the straight-line method applied to each unit of property, except that rotable parts, avionics, and assemblies are depreciated on a group basis. The depreciable lives and residual values used for the principal depreciable asset classifications are:

	Depreciable Life	Residual Value
Fokker 100 aircraft	9 years	None
ATR 42 and Saab 340 aircraft	4 years	None
Other American jet aircraft	20–30 years	5–10%
Other regional aircraft and engines	16–20 years	5–10%
Major rotable parts, avionics, and assemblies	Life of equipment to which applicable	5–10%
Improvements to leased flight equipment	Term of lease	None
Buildings and improvements (principally on leased land)	10–30 years or term of lease	None
Furniture, fixtures, and equipment	3–20 years	
Capitalized software	3–10 years	None

Delta Air Lines

Depreciation and Amortization.   Flight equipment is depreciated on a straight-line basis to residual values (5% of cost) over a 20-year period from the dates placed in service (unless earlier retirement of the aircraft is planned). Flight equipment under capital leases is amortized on a straight-line basis over the term of the respective leases, which range from 6 to 12 years. Ground property and equipment are depreciated on a straight-line basis over their estimated service lives, which range from 3 to 30 years.

United Airlines

Depreciation and amortization of owned depreciable assets is based on the straight-line method over their estimated service lives. Leasehold improvements are amortized over the remaining period of the lease or the estimated service life of the related asset, whichever is less. Aircraft are depreciated to estimated salvage values, generally over lives of 10 to 30 years; buildings are depreciated over lives of 25 to 45 years; and other property and equipment are depreciated over lives of 3 to 15 years.

Properties under capital leases are amortized on the straight-line method over the life of the lease, or in the case of certain aircraft, over their estimated service lives. Lease terms are 10 to 30 years for aircraft and flight simulators, and 25 years for buildings. Amortization of capital leases is included in depreciation and amortization expense.

depreciable lives for *leased* aircraft equipment are often determined by the length of the leases, which are not necessarily the same as the useful lives of the aircraft. (Chapter 8 discusses accounting for capital leases by the lessee.)

Because most firms in the United States use the straight-line depreciation method, the analyst can measure the average total life of depreciable assets by dividing average depreciable assets (gross, assuming zero salvage value) by depreciation expense for the year.[9] The calculations for PepsiCo follow (in millions):

	PepsiCo
Depreciable Assets (Gross):	
December 31, Year 10.....................................	$10,244.0
December 31, Year 11.....................................	10,981.0
Average Depreciable Assets (Gross) for Year 11.............	$10,612.5
Depreciation Expense, Year 11	$ 843.0
Average Total Depreciable Life...........................	12.6 years

DEPRECIATION METHOD

The third factor in the calculation of depreciation (in addition to the acquisition cost and expected useful life of depreciable assets) is the depreciation method. Financial reporting permits firms to write off assets evenly over their useful lives (straight-line method) or to write off larger amounts during the early years and smaller amounts in later years (accelerated depreciation methods). Note that total depreciation over an asset's life cannot exceed acquisition costs unless firms revalue such assets to current market values. Thus, straight-line and accelerated depreciation methods differ only in the timing of depreciation expense, not in its total amount over time.

Virtually all firms in the United States use the straight-line method for financial reporting. They use accelerated depreciation methods for tax reporting based on depreciable lives specified in the income tax law. These lives are usually shorter than the depreciable lives firms use for financial reporting purposes.

Financial reporting in most countries other than the United States also permits both accelerated and straight-line depreciation methods. In countries where tax laws heavily influence financial reporting (Germany, France, and Japan are examples), most firms use accelerated deprecation methods for both financial and tax reporting. Thus, comparisons of U.S. firms with those of some other countries require the analyst to assess the effect of different depreciation methods. The analyst must either

---

[9]Note that all three of the airlines in Example 13 used the straight-line method for calculating depreciation expense.

restate reported U.S. amounts to an accelerated basis or convert reported amounts for other countries to a straight-line basis.

The analyst can place U.S. firms on an accelerated depreciation basis using information in the income tax note. *Statement No. 109*[10] requires firms to report in notes to the financial statements the deferred tax liability related to depreciation timing differences at the beginning and end of the year. PepsiCo, for example, reports in Note 14 (see Appendix A) that its deferred tax liability related to property, plant, and equipment was $742.0 million on December 31, Year 10, and $804.0 million on December 31, Year 11. These deferred taxes relate to differences in both depreciable lives and depreciation methods. Converting PepsiCo's financial statements to amounts reported for tax purposes requires the following adjustments (assuming a 35 percent income tax rate, a rate PepsiCo discloses in the same note):

	December 31	
Balance Sheet	**Year 10**	**Year 11**
Property, Plant, and Equipment (Net):		
$742.0 ÷ .35; $804.0 ÷ .35	$–2,120.0	$–2,297.1
Deferred Tax Liability.	– 742.0	– 804.0
Retained Earnings.	$–1,378.0	$–1,493.1

Income Statement	**For Year 11**
Increase in Depreciation Expense: ($742.0 – $804.0) ÷ .35. . .	$+177.1
Decrease in Income Tax Expense: .35 × $177.1	– 62.0
Net Income: .65 × $177.1	$–115.1

Statement of Cash Flows	**For Year 11**
Net Income.	$–115.1
Depreciation Expense.	+177.1
Change in the Increase in Deferred Tax Liability for Depreciation Timing Difference ($804.0 – $742.0).	– 62.0
Cash Flow from Operations.	$ 0

Note that PepsiCo's Deferred Tax Liability related to property, plant, and equipment increased during the year by approximately 8.4 percent [= ($804.0/$742.0) – 1]. This increase accounts for the increase in Year 11's depreciation expense reported for tax purposes.

---

[10]Financial Accounting Standards Board, *Statement No. 109*, "Accounting for Income Taxes," 1992. Chapter 2 provides an initial discussion of this statement, with the discussion continuing in Chapter 8.

IMPAIRMENT OF FIXED ASSETS

Chapter 6 addresses how income statement charges for the impairment of fixed assets affect forecasts of future earnings. The development of new technologies by competitors, changes in government regulations, changes in demographic trends, and other factors external to a firm may reduce the future benefits originally anticipated from the assets. Financial reporting requires firms to assess whether the carrying amounts of fixed assets are recoverable and, if they are not, to write down the assets to their market values and recognize impairment losses in income from continuing operations.[11]

Chapter 6 provides several examples involving impairment charges, including a description of PepsiCo's disclosures in this area. Firms recognize an impairment loss when the carrying amount (net book value) of a fixed asset or asset group exceeds its fair value and is deemed not recoverable. *Statement No. 144* defines a carrying amount as "not recoverable" if it is greater than the sum of the *undiscounted* cash flows expected from the asset's use and disposal. The actual impairment charge recorded is the difference between the amount by which the carrying value exceeds an asset's fair value. Fair value means market value or present (*discounted*) value of expected cash flows from the fixed asset.

Firms do not have to judge impairment for every asset every reporting period. However, tests for impairment are required when circumstances change indicating the possibility of a significant change in carrying amounts. Chapter 6 provides examples of changing circumstances that might warrant the need for impairment testing.

Financial reporting does not require separate disclosure of impaired assets, although firms often voluntarily provide this information. Also, *Statement No. 144* requires that firms include impairment losses in income before taxes from continuing operations.

PERSISTENT EARNINGS AND FIXED ASSET REPORTING

For many firms, but particularly for those operating in such capital-intensive industries as freight transportation (trucking and rail), defense, or utilities, expenditures for fixed assets are a large and recurring outflow of cash. The beverage and snack food industry in which PepsiCo operates is moderately capital intensive. PepsiCo reports capital expenditures by business segments in Note 21 of Appendix A totaling $1,324.0 million in Year 11 ($1,352.0 million in Year 10 and $1,341.0 million in Year 9). As PepsiCo also reports in the Appendix, purchases of fixed assets for Year 9 through 11, on average, represent approximately 33 percent of cash generated by operations (see the Consolidated Statement of Cash Flows).

---

[11]Financial Accounting Standards Board, *Statement of Financial Accounting Standards No. 144,* "Accounting for the Impairment or Disposal of Long-lived Assets," 2001. *Statement No. 144* superseded *Statement No. 121,* "Accounting for the Impairment of Long-lived Assets and for Long-lived Assets to be Disposed of," 1995. *Statement No. 144* retains the fundamental provisions of *Statement No. 121* for recognizing and measuring impairment losses on long-lived assets held for use and long-lived assets to be disposed of by sale, while also resolving significant implementation issues associated with *Statement No. 121.*

Analyzing valuation and depreciation of fixed assets for their effects on the quality of accounting information is an important task of the analyst. The analyst needs to consider the:

1. Disparity between amounts reported for fixed assets and current economic values.
2. Depreciable lives established by management.
3. Depreciation method employed to match fixed asset costs to reported revenues.

Fixed Assets and Current Economic Values

The valuation most consistent with economic value-added and high quality accounting information is the current cost of replacing fixed assets. Difficulties arise in measuring objectively current replacement cost, however. For example, the absence of active, secondhand markets for many used fixed assets means that the analyst must estimate replacement cost by referring to the cost of a similar new asset and then adjusting that replacement cost for the used condition, and perhaps lower productivity, of the asset owned. Adjusting to replacement costs is even more difficult because firms do not provide sufficient detailed information about the nature, location, condition, and age of their fixed assets. The most disaggregated information usually provided in dollar form is the book value of land, buildings, machinery, and equipment. (Note that PepsiCo reports in Appendix A an additional category in Note 8, labeled "Construction in Progress." PepsiCo will transfer the expenditures represented by this category to either buildings and improvements, or machinery and equipment once it completes the construction.)

As demonstrated earlier for PepsiCo, analysts can estimate the average age of depreciable assets by dividing the balance in the accumulated depreciation account at the end of the most recent year by the amount of depreciation expense for the current year. The analyst can use the average age in concert with data on subsequent price increases to estimate current value, but probably the amount of subjectivity introduced is intolerable. Unless firms operate in an industry where fixed assets are at the core of their activities (for example, real estate firms), probably the analyst should work with the unadjusted numbers and take this into consideration when interpreting the financial analysis.[12]

Choice of Depreciable Lives

Choosing the number of years during which firms receive benefits from fixed assets can be difficult. Furthermore, firms report any change in depreciable lives as a "change in estimates" (discussed in Chapter 6) and account for its effect prospectively. These two facts make choosing depreciable lives a fruitful avenue for practicing earnings management. The analyst should compare the depreciable lives (or the

---

[12]The underlying assumption in this discussion is that fixed assets are *undervalued* on the balance sheet when compared to current economic values. If firms experience fixed asset value impairments, the analyst benefits from the reporting rules of *Statement No. 144* discussed earlier, which requires firms to write down fixed assets to their fair values.

average of the depreciable lives, a calculation illustrated earlier for PepsiCo) across firms in the same industry to assess whether the firm under scrutiny is an outlier.

Choice of Depreciation Method

The vast majority of the publicly traded firms in the United States use the straight-line method of depreciation. Although the straight-line method may not accurately reflect the actual deterioration in the usefulness of the fixed assets to help generate revenues, it does not appear that firms use their choice of depreciation method to manage reported earnings. However, there is still an accounting quality issue because many analysts consider earnings based on accelerated depreciation methods to be of higher quality than that based on straight-line depreciation. This is because both (1) the biases caused by using acquisition costs instead of replacement cost to calculate depreciation, and (2) the opportunities to manage earnings through the choice of depreciable lives are tempered by the fact that more conservative measures of earnings result from the use of accelerated depreciation methods. In many cases, accelerated depreciation of acquisition costs also produces depreciation amounts closer to replacement cost than straight-line depreciation during the early years of assets' lives, thereby providing an enhanced measure of value-added. (Just the opposite effect occurs during the later years of assets' lives, however.)

The preference for accelerated depreciation methods by analysts is not universal. Some analysts judge earnings quality by its comparability to competitor firms. Analysts favoring the straight-line method from an earnings quality perspective observe that at least firms are using the method favored by the vast majority of publicly traded firms.

ACCOUNTING FOR INTANGIBLE ASSETS

Intangible assets include trade and brand names, trademarks, patents, copyrights, franchise rights, customer lists, goodwill and similar items. Two characteristics distinguish intangible assets: their intangibility (that is, lacking physical attributes) and their multiple-period useful life. Financial reporting in the United States accounts for intangible assets as follows:

1. Firms expense the cost of developing intangibles in the period incurred.[13] The rationale for immediate expensing of such costs is the difficulty in ascertaining whether a particular expenditure results in a future benefit (that is, an asset) or not (an expense). Accountants provide more conservative measures of earnings by expensing such costs immediately. Thus, although PepsiCo spends millions of dollars each year promoting its products, and the names *Pepsi* and *Frito-Lay* represent some of the most valuable "assets" of the firm, financial reporting does not permit the firm to recognize an asset for the

---

[13]An exception to this policy is made for certain software development costs discussed later in this section.

expenditures made to develop and maintain its trade name. PepsiCo's balance sheet reported in Appendix A does not include an asset labeled, "Trade Name—Pepsi," or "Brand Name—Frito-Lay," although these assets are undoubtedly worth hundreds of millions of dollars to the firm.

2. Firms recognize as an asset expenditures made to acquire intangible assets from others.[14] In this case, the firm makes an expenditure on a specifically identifiable intangible asset. The existence of an external market transaction provides evidence of the value of the intangible asset. The acquiring firm must consider the future benefits of the intangible to at least equal the price paid.[15]

3. Specifically identifiable intangible assets acquired from others may have a finite useful life, such as a patent, or an indefinite useful life, such as a brand name. Firms amortize intangibles with a finite useful life over their expected useful lives, taking into consideration the legal, regulatory, economic, competitive or contractual provisions that may limit the useful life. Common practice uses straight-line amortization if the actual pattern in which the economic benefits are consumed or used up cannot be reliably determined.

4. The intangible asset, goodwill, may be recorded by a firm when acquiring another firm in a business combination. Goodwill is assumed to have an indefinite useful life and is not amortized unless its useful life is determined to no longer be indefinite.

5. Firms periodically test intangible assets requiring amortization for asset impairment following a similar procedure to that described earlier for fixed assets. For intangibles not requiring amortization (for example, brand names, goodwill) firms must test annually for asset impairment, or more frequently if events and circumstances indicate that the asset may be impaired. The test compares the carrying value to the fair value of the intangibles and requires recognition of an impairment loss whenever the carrying value exceeds the fair value. The test for asset impairment for an intangible not requiring amortization differs from that for fixed and intangible assets requiring amortization. Recall that the test for asset impairment for an asset requiring amortization (for example, fixed assets) compares the undiscounted cash flows from the asset to the asset's carrying value. Intangibles not requiring

---

[14]An exception to this policy is made for "purchased in-process research and development costs." Firms immediately expense any in-process, but unproven, technology purchased in a corporate acquisition, a requirement stipulated by Financial Accounting Standards Board, *Interpretation No. 4*, "Applicability of FASB Statement No. 2 to Business Combinations Accounted for by the Purchase Method," 1975. In a *Barron's* article addressing this controversial requirement, ("Big Blue Haze," December 23, 1996), Abraham Briloff points out that more than half the $3.2 billion IBM paid for the Lotus Development Corporation was expensed at the date of acquisition because it represented what is often labeled "in-process technology."

[15]Some financial statement preparers and users have criticized the differing treatment of internally developed versus externally purchased intangibles. They point out that internally developed intangibles also result from external market exchanges (payments to advertising agencies for promotion services, payments to employees for research and development services). Supporters of the current rules point out that the market exchange in the case of externally acquired intangibles validates the existence of a "completed asset," whereas the market exchange in the case of internally developed intangibles validates only that the firm has made an expenditure. It does not validate the existence and value of future benefits.

amortization have an indefinite life, and thus, no defined period over which to estimate undiscounted cash flows. Chapter 6 provides several impairment charge examples, including PepsiCo's disclosures in this area.

ACCOUNTING FOR RESEARCH AND DEVELOPMENT COSTS

Controversy surrounds application of the general principles of intangible asset accounting to research and development (R&D) costs. Financial reporting requires firms to expense immediately all R&D costs incurred internally.[16] For industries with high R&D expenditures, this requirement is especially troublesome because financial reporting requires firms to assume that the economic value of all R&D expenditures is zero. Thus, a major asset never appears on the balance sheet.

Consider the three examples that follow from financial reports of biotechnology firms. Firms in the research-intensive biotechnology industry cannot survive without making significant R&D expenditures responsible for generating future revenues, and yet GAAP requires firms to expense these expenditures when incurred.

Example 14

Biogen, Inc. develops biotechnology and other drug-related products internally in its research laboratories. Founded in 1978, it is principally engaged in discovering and developing drugs for human health care through genetic engineering. As required by *Statement No. 2*, Biogen, Inc. states in a recent annual report that "research and development costs, including fees and milestones paid to collaborative partners, are expensed as incurred." Its R&D expense/sales percentage averaged 34 percent in three recent years, and the firm showed no asset on its balance sheet related to this research activity.

Example 15

Genzyme Corporation is a biotechnology and health care products firm engaged in the development of medical products and services. It follows a strategy of both internal development of technology and acquisition of other companies involved in biotechnology research. Genzyme expenses the portion of the acquisition price of companies related to *in-process technology*, but it capitalizes and subsequently amortizes any portion of the price related to *completed* technologies.

Genzyme's R&D expense/sales percentage for internal R&D costs and amortization of previously capitalized costs was approximately 22.6 percent for the third quarter ending September 30, Year 10. However, because it made an acquisition of a company during the same year, it also expensed the portion of the purchase price related to in-process technology. Thus, the total R&D expense/sales percentage for the year was 48.8 percent. In the same quarter a year later, ending September 30, Year 11, the total R&D expense/sales percentage was only 22.0 percent because only a small portion of in-process technology (.5 percent) was purchased (and expensed).

---

[16]Financial Accounting Standards Board, *Statement of Financial Accounting Standards No. 2*, "Accounting for Research and Development Costs," 1974.

Example 16

Amgen's top-selling product, Epogen, accounted for almost 60 percent of the firm's sales in Year 11. Epogen (Epoetin Alfa) is a recombinant version of a human protein that stimulates the production of red blood cells. It is used in the treatment of anemia associated with chronic renal failure for patients on dialysis. Amgen is continually striving to develop new products and enhance existing ones. The firm follows a strategy of both internal development of biotechnology and external development through a series of joint ventures and partnerships. Amgen contributes preliminary research findings for its interest in these joint ventures and partnerships. The other participants provide funding to continue development of this preliminary research.

In some cases, Amgen contracts with the joint venture or partnership to perform the continued development in its own laboratories. In this case, Amgen receives a fee each period in an amount approximately equal to the R&D costs incurred in conducting the research. In other cases, the joint venture or partnership entity conducts the research, in which case Amgen may show no R&D expense on its books. Amgen generally maintains a right of first refusal to any products developed, in which case it must pay the owners of the joint venture a periodic royalty. (Chapters 8 and 9 discuss the accounting for investments in these joint ventures and partnerships.)

Amgen's R&D expense/sales percentage for Year 11 was 21.4 percent, the lowest of the three firms for the most recent year. It shows only minor amounts on its balance sheet for investments in joint ventures and partnerships, relating to cash advances. Because Amgen must expense initial development costs when incurred, its contribution of preliminary research findings for an interest in these joint ventures and partnerships does not result in increasing an asset.

Examples 14 through 16 illustrate three different strategies firms pursue in developing biotechnologies, and highlight the problem with current R&D reporting rules. The different strategies firms follow, especially when combined with the required accounting for R&D costs, complicate any cross-sectional analysis of firms' financial data. To the extent that the economic substance of these arrangements differ, then different accounting treatments may be appropriate. If, on the other hand, the economic substance is similar and the principal aim is to keep R&D costs out of the income statement, then the differing accounting treatments seem unwarranted.

The economic characteristics of R&D arrangements suggest a two-fold approach to dealing with these different reporting standards:

1. Capitalize and subsequently amortize all expenditures on R&D that have future service potential, whether a firm incurs the R&D cost internally or whether it purchases in-process or completed technology externally. Expense immediately all R&D costs that have no future service potential.
2. Consolidate the firm's share of the assets, liabilities, revenues, and expenses of R&D joint ventures or partnerships with its own financial statements.

Unfortunately, current financial statement disclosures do not permit the analyst to implement the two-fold approach. Without these disclosures, the analyst must proceed with caution when analyzing R&D-intensive firms. The analyst especially benefits from scientific and other disclosures provided by these firms that are outside the financial reporting model.

ACCOUNTING FOR SOFTWARE DEVELOPMENT COSTS

Financial reporting treats the cost of developing computer software somewhat differently than R&D costs. Firms must expense when incurred all costs incurred internally in developing computer software until such development proceeds to the point when the firm establishes the technological feasibility of a product. Thereafter, the firm must capitalize and subsequently amortize additional development costs.[17] The FASB defines *technological feasibility* as completion of a detailed program design or, in its absence, completion of a working model. A key issue in applying this reporting standard is the treatment of costs to improve an existing product.

Example 17

In the previous decade, IBM purchased Lotus Development Corporation as part of its strategic plan to remain on the cutting edge in the highly competitive information technology industry. Lotus 1-2-3, the firm's best-known product, was first developed in the early 1980s. The IBM subsidiary continually revises this software to increase its capabilities and adapt to changes in hardware capabilities and design.

In a recent annual report, IBM includes the following introductory note on its accounting for software development costs, including those costs incurred to maintain and enhance Lotus 1-2-3:

> **Software.** Costs that are related to the conceptual formulation and design of licensed programs are expensed as research and development. Also, for licensed programs, the company capitalizes costs that are incurred to produce the finished product after technological feasibility is established. The annual amortization of the capitalized amounts is the greater of the amount computed based on the estimated revenue distribution over the products' revenue-producing lives, or the straight-line method, and is applied over periods ranging up to three years. The company performs periodic assessments to insure that unamortized program costs remain recoverable from future revenue. The company charges costs to support or service license programs against net income as the costs are incurred.

---

[17]Financial Accounting Standards Board, *Statement of Financial Accounting Standards No. 86*, "Accounting for the Costs of Computer Software to Be Sold, Leased, or Otherwise Marketed," 1985. *Statement No. 86* applies to software developed for sale, and not software developed or obtained for internal use. Georgia-Pacific describes its implementation of current reporting practice for internal use software in a recent annual report by stating:

> The firm capitalizes incremental costs that are directly associated with the development of software for internal use and implementation of the related systems. Amounts are amortized over five years beginning when the assets are placed in service. Capitalized costs were $121 million at December 31, Year 6, and $65 million at December 31, Year 5. Amounts are included as property, plant, and equipment in the firm's balance sheet.

Example 18

Microsoft Corporation introduced its first version of Word in 1983. Microsoft also continually revises this software to enhance its capabilities. Microsoft expenses all software development costs as incurred. It reports software development expense of $4,307.0 million (15.2 percent of sales) for the year ended June 30, Year 12, and shows no asset on its balance sheet for capitalized software development costs.

Example 19

Adobe Systems is a leading developer of graphics software. It develops new software internally and through aggressive external acquisitions of other software companies. Adobe expenses initial software development costs incurred internally as research and development, which represents 18.2 percent of revenue in Year 11.

Adobe capitalizes software development costs once a program attains technological feasibility. It also capitalizes the cost of software acquired in corporate acquisitions to the extent that the software has achieved technological feasibility. However, in both cases, Adobe indicates that the amount of software costs capitalized in recent years has been immaterial to the financial statements.

Examples 17 through 19 illustrate the diversity in practice currently. Software development firms interpret *Statement No. 86* so differently that it is debatable whether the standard serves a purpose any longer. Furthermore, the Software Publishers Association, a trade association for firms in the software development industry, advocates expensing all software development costs when incurred. In a position paper submitted to the FASB, the Association requests rescission of *Statement No. 86*, suggesting that expensing these costs eliminates the concerns of extremely shortened software product cycles and uncertainty over realization of software assets.

Why would the Software Publishers Association advocate immediate expensing of all software development costs when current reporting offers the best of all worlds to software producers: capitalize *or* immediately expense the costs depending on their desires? A study[18] addressing this intriguing position of the Association shows that, in recent years, enhancing reported earnings through software capitalization schemes has diminished. The researchers conclude that since software capitalization no longer provides an opportunity for earnings management, nothing is lost by restricting software producers to only one allowable reporting technique. In addition, the study addresses the more substantive issue of whether software capitalization is "value-relevant" to investors. For those firms that capitalize software development costs (that is, report a cumulative software intangible asset on the balance sheet), the researchers find a significant association between these costs and future earnings, concluding that this finding supports continuation of *Statement No. 86*.

---

[18]David Aboody and Baruch Lev, "The Value-Relevance of Intangibles: The Case of Software Capitalization," *Journal of Accounting Research*, Supplement, 1998, pp. 161–191.

The flexibility firms enjoy in applying *Statement No. 86* currently should cause the analyst to proceed cautiously when analyzing computer software development companies. An added concern in this regard is the small size of many such companies and the rapid pace of technological change in this industry. The information technology industry, and particularly the software subsegment of the industry, experienced even a greater rate of change recently due to the surge of interest in the Internet and Internet-related services. The crash of the information technology industry in recent years is further reason to practice a high degree of skepticism when analyzing firms in the industry.

ACCOUNTING FOR GOODWILL

The most common setting in which intangibles arise is in corporate acquisitions. As Chapter 9 discusses more fully, acquiring firms must allocate the purchase price to the assets acquired and liabilities assumed when purchasing another entity. Acquiring firms usually allocate the purchase price to identifiable, tangible assets (inventories, land, equipment) and liabilities first. They then allocate any excess purchase price to specifically identifiable intangible assets such as patents, customer lists, or trade names, with the remainder allocated to goodwill. Goodwill is a residual and effectively represents all intangibles that are not specifically identifiable. Finally, as discussed at the beginning of this section, specifically identifiable, intangible assets may or may not be amortized, depending on whether they have a finite or indefinite useful life. Goodwill, on the other hand, has an indefinite useful life and is therefore not amortized but tested for impairment.[19]

The disclosures for intangible assets, including goodwill, vary significantly across firms. For example, as illustrated in Appendix A, PepsiCo reports a total of $4,841.0 million under "Intangible Assets, net" on its balance sheet. PepsiCo's Note 9 reports that the majority of this amount (over two-thirds) is goodwill. The remainder consists of trademarks and brands, which are amortized on a straight-line basis over their estimated useful lives, generally ranging from five to twenty years.[20]

How should an analyst treat goodwill that appears on a firm's balance sheet? One approach is to follow financial reporting rules, leaving goodwill among total assets. The justification for this approach is that the initial valuation of goodwill arose from an exchange between an independent buyer and seller of another corporate entity and simply represents valuable resources that accountants cannot separately identify. These valuable resources enable the firm to generate profits. The analyst should include these resources in the asset base on which management should be expected to generate a reasonable return. If these valuable resources are not likely to last forever, amortization of their cost over some period of years is appropriate.

---

[19]Financial Accounting Standards Board, *Statement of Financial Accounting Standards No. 142*, "Goodwill and Other Intangible Assets," 2001. Recall from the earlier discussion that testing for impairment of long-lived assets other than goodwill is also required and is addressed in *Statement No. 144*.

[20]PepsiCo reports the amortization policies for these specifically identifiable intangibles in Note 1 of Appendix A. PepsiCo also reports in Note 1 that it amortizes goodwill in Year 11. PepsiCo will cease amortizing goodwill in Year 12 and onward. *Statement No. 142* does not require firms to amortize after 2001.

Another approach eliminates goodwill from assets and subtracts its amount from retained earnings or other common shareholders' equity accounts. The justification for this approach is two-fold.

1. The amount allocated to goodwill from a corporate acquisition may simply occur because the firm paid too much and may not necessarily indicate the presence of resources with future service potential. Subtracting the amount allocated to goodwill from retained earnings suggests that the excess purchase price is a loss for the firm.
2. Immediate subtraction of goodwill from retained earnings treats goodwill arising from an acquisition similar to goodwill developed internally. In the latter case, firms expense advertising, training, and other costs when incurred, so no asset appears on the balance sheet.

PERSISTENT EARNINGS AND INTANGIBLE ASSET REPORTING

The quality of accounting information for *tangible assets* is often low because substantial adjustments for changes in economic values are often necessary. The analyst at least knows the acquisition cost of tangible assets to use as a starting point for such revaluations. For intangible assets such as the three highlighted above, the difficulty is more acute because firms seldom report such resources on the balance sheet. If such resources do appear on the balance sheet, usually because they arose from a corporate acquisition, they appear at some mixture of historical and amortized cost. Estimating the economic value of intangibles usually entails a high level of subjectivity.

The arguments for immediately expensing intangibles, from the perspective of quality of accounting information, include the following:

1. The expense occurs in the same period as the cash outflow, the latter being the economic resource sacrificed.
2. Firms must replace intangibles consumed if they are to continue operating profitably. The best measure of the replacement cost of intangibles consumed in generating revenue in a reporting period is the cost of expenditures made in the same period on such intangibles. Depreciating fixed assets using an accelerated depreciation method argued for earlier in this chapter is similar to this line of reasoning for intangibles consumed.
3. Immediate expensing eliminates the opportunities for earnings management that arise when firms must decide on the amortization period and pattern for capitalized intangibles.[21]

---

[21]Note, however, that opportunities for earnings management still exist under the immediate expensing option. Firms with a poor earnings year can eliminate or delay expenditures, thereby increasing reporting earnings. Accelerating expenditures reduces current earnings.

Chapter 6 addresses whether it is good business practice to manage earnings in this way. For example, firms that cut back on research and development costs to manage earnings may suffer a poor quality of accounting assessment by analysts. Similarly, firms that cut back on advertising expenditures or delay maintenance expenditures as a means of increasing earnings in a reporting period may suffer from the same fate.

4. For a stable or moderate growth firm, the expense each year from immediate expensing is approximately the same as the expense from capitalizing expenditures and subsequently amortizing them.

Most analysts tend to prefer immediate expending of *all* intangible assets.[22] Analysts often remove from the balance sheet any R&D costs, software development costs, and goodwill reported as assets before performing a financial analysis. By doing so, they argue that (1) quality of earnings information improves because the ability to manage earnings is reduced, and (2) quality of balance sheet information improves because the balance sheet is cleansed of "soft" assets lacking physical substance. Analysts eliminate the assets by subtracting them from retained earnings. The financial analysis must be interpreted carefully, however, because a firm's asset base undoubtedly is understated when these assets are eliminated—just as is the case with PepsiCo's asset base because the trade names *Pepsi* and *Frito-Lay* (among other important intangibles owned by the firm) are not reported on the balance sheet.

VALUING INTANGIBLES—IS IT POSSIBLE?

Robert Swieringa served as a member of the Financial Accounting Standards Board for ten years. He observes that:

> The current financial accounting model has been shaped by the existing corporate arrangements for large, complex, and more or less permanent business enterprises that invest heavily in tangible assets. Such a model will be challenged by more flexible and fluid organizations, increased investments in intangible or "soft" assets, more extensive use of financial instruments to manage various risks, and changes in information technology.[23]

Swieringa's point regarding "soft" assets increasingly is being made by others as well, and policymakers such as the SEC and FASB continue to explore ways for developing more relevant disclosures and measurement metrics for intangibles. Nobody doubts that the quality of accounting information improves if the balance sheet reports the economic value of a firm's intangible resources. If these resources cannot be measured with any degree of accuracy, however, the trade-off between relevance and reliability is simply too great. The challenge for the analyst (and accountants and policymakers) involves developing robust models for valuing intangibles because, as Examples 14 through 16 above point out, intangibles often are the essential drivers for a firm's success.

Recent research with respect to one intangible—future benefits accruing from R&D expenditures—is promising because it demonstrates a possible methodology

---

[22]Although advocating immediate expending of these costs, few analysts suggest that they are of no value. However, analysts are most concerned with how to value the economic assets represented by these costs, and the potential for earnings management, given the subjectivity involved in any valuation model employed.

[23]Robert J. Swieringa, "Should Accounting be 'Green and Smooth and Inviting?'" *The Journal of Financial Statement Analysis*, Winter 1997, pp. 75–87.

for valuing intangibles.[24] The research involves studying the relation between R&D expenditures in a particular year and revenues of subsequent years. The study shows that benefits accrue for five to nine years, depending on the industry, and that the pattern of benefits is not uniform over time.

Using this analysis, the researchers then calculate the present value of this revenue stream net of the current R&D expenditures to estimate the value of R&D expenditures in a particular year. By summing similar values over the past five to nine years (again, depending on the industry), the researchers obtained a value for the R&D expenditure. They then studied the relation between this value and market prices and found a statistically significant relationship, suggesting that investors implicitly incorporate the market values of firms' R&D efforts into the valuation of firms.

The researchers stress the industry-specific nature of their work. Because of this, extensive replication of the study is necessary across many industries before a general model can be developed. This limitation, coupled with the researchers' exclusive emphasis on R&D expenditures, makes valuing all intangibles an unsolved problem currently. Additional research emphasizing other categories of intangibles and across a wide range of industries is appropriate and necessary.[25]

SUMMARY

The unifying concept for the various financial reporting rules discussed in this chapter (revenue recognition, inventory cost-flow assumptions, depreciable asset accounting, and intangible asset accounting) are the links among revenue and expense recognition, and asset and liability valuation. The recognition of revenue usually coincides with an increase in assets (usually cash or a receivable). The recognition of expense usually coincides with a decrease in assets (cash, inventories, depreciable or intangible assets) or an increase in liabilities (which will require a decrease in assets in a later period). Thus, the income statement and balance sheet closely interrelate.

The next chapter discusses the financial reporting rules linking expenses to liability recognition and valuation. As with asset valuation issues, liability recognition and valuation issues demonstrate the link between expenses reported on the income statement and liabilities reported on balance sheet—and the fact that any discussion of income and economic value-added leads inevitably to a consideration of liabilities and their economic value-added as well. Similar to this chapter, Chapter 8 explains the various reporting principles under investigation, describes the choices firms make in applying them, and debates whether adjustments are needed to the reported amounts to enhance the quality of accounting information.

---

[24]Baruch Lev and Theodore Sougiannis, "The Capitalization, Amortization and Value-Relevance of R&D," *Journal of Accounting and Economics*, 1996, pp. 107–138.

[25]Baruch Lev, a co-author of the research cited in the previous footnote, spearheads *The Intangibles Research Project* that has as its goal the sharing of information, ideas, and research about the valuation and disclosure of corporate intangibles. Lev is a member of the faculty at New York University's Leonard N. Stern School of Business, and a description of this long-term project, including information on how practitioners and academics can become involved with the project, can be obtained by contacting him directly.

APPENDIX 7.1

ACCOUNTING FOR THE EFFECTS OF CHANGING PRICES

Changing prices affect financial reports in two principal ways:

Measuring Unit Problem

Changes in the *general* level of prices in an economy (as measured by the prices of a broad basket of goods and services) affect the purchasing power of the monetary unit (for example, the U.S. dollar). During periods of inflation (deflation), the measuring unit loses (gains) purchasing power. Because the measuring unit does not reflect a constant amount of purchasing power over time, accounting measurements of assets, liabilities, revenues, and expenses made with this measuring unit are not comparable. Adding the acquisition cost of land acquired ten years ago for $10 million to the acquisition cost of land acquired this year for $10 million is as inappropriate as adding the cost of land acquired in the United States for $10 million to the cost of land acquired by a subsidiary in the United Kingdom for £10 million. We refer to the accounting issues created by changes in the general level of prices as a *measuring unit problem.*

Valuation Problem

Changes in the *specific* prices of individual assets and liabilities (for example, inventories, fixed assets) affect the measurement of revenues and expenses on the income statement, and the valuation of assets and liabilities on the balance sheet. Land acquired last year for $10 million may now have a market value of $14 million. Should the accountant report this land on the balance sheet at its acquisition cost of $10 million or at its current market value of $14 million? Should net income include an unrealized holding gain of $4 million? We refer to the accounting issues created by changes in the prices of specific assets and liabilities as a *valuation problem.*

Summarizing,

1. Financial reporting can use either a *nominal* measuring unit (that is, one that gives no recognition to the changing value of the measuring unit), or a *constant* measuring unit (that is, one that restates measurements made over time to reflect a constant measuring unit).
2. Financial reporting can use either *acquisition cost* valuations or *current (replacement) cost* valuations for assets and liabilities; changes in current cost valuations over time affect the measurement of net income and shareholders' equity.

The combination of alternative measuring units and valuation methods presents four possible treatments of the effects of changing prices:

1. Acquisition Cost/Nominal Dollar Accounting
2. Acquisition Cost/Constant Dollar Accounting
3. Current Cost/Nominal Dollar Accounting
4. Current Cost/Constant Dollar Accounting

We illustrate each of these four combinations using a simple example. Exhibit 7.11 summarizes the data used in the illustration. A firm begins its first year of operations, Year 1, with $400 in cash and contributed capital. On January 1, Year 1, the Consumer Price Index (CPI) is 200. The firm immediately acquires two widgets for $100 each and a piece of equipment for $100. During the first six months of Year 1, general price inflation is 5 percent. Thus, the CPI increases from 200 to 210. On June 30, Year 1, the firm sells one widget for $240 and replaces it at the new higher replacement cost of $115. The firm also pays other expenses totaling $100 on June 30, Year 1. During the second six months of the year, general price inflation is 10 percent (the CPI increases from 210 to 231). On December 31, Year 1, the replacement cost of the widget is $140 and the replacement cost of the equipment in new condition is $120.

Financial statements prepared under each of the four combinations of measuring units and valuation methods appear in Exhibit 7.12. The sections below discuss each of these approaches to accounting for changing prices.

EXHIBIT 7.11
Data for Inflation Accounting Illustration

Balance Sheet as of Jan. 1, Year 1

Cash: $400		Contributed Capital: $400	

Date:	January 1, Year 1	June 30, Year 1	December 31, Year 1
CPI	200	210 (5% increase)	231 (10% increase)
Cost of One Widget	$100	$115	$140
Cost of Equipment	$100	$110	$120
Transactions	1. Buy 2 widgets at $100 each, $200	1. Sell 1 widget for $240; replace widget at $115	Close books and prepare statements
	2. Purchase equipment (5 yr. life) for $100	2. Pay other expenses of $100	

EXHIBIT 7.12

Illustration of Financial Statements Reflecting Inflation Accounting

	(1) Acquisition Cost/ Nominal Dollars		(2) Acquisition Cost/ Constant Dollars		(3) Current Cost/ Nominal Dollars		(4) Current Cost/ Constant Dollars	
Income Statement								
Sales		$240		$264.0[a]		$240		$264.0
Cost of Goods Sold	$100		$115.5[b]		$115		$126.5[n]	
Depreciation	20		23.1[c]		22[i]		24.2[o]	
Other Expenses	100	220	110.0[d]	248.6	100	237	110.0[d]	260.7
Operating Income		$ 20		$ 15.4		$ 3		$ 3.3
Realized Holding Gains:								
Goods Sold		—		—		15[j]		11.0[p]
Depreciation Assets Used		—		—		2[k]		1.1[q]
Unrealized Holding Gains:								
Inventory		—		—		65[l]		38.0[r]
Depreciation Assets		—		—		16[m]		3.6[s]
Purchasing Power Loss		—		(18.0)[e]		—		(18.0)[e]
Net Income (Loss)		$ 20		$ (2.6)		$101		$ 39.0
Balance Sheet								
Cash		$125		$125.0		$125		$125
Inventory		215		242.0[f]		280		280
Equipment	$100		$115.5[g]		$120		$120	
Accumulated Depreciation	(20)	80	(23.1)	92.4	(24)	96	(24)	96
Total Assets		$420		$459.4		$501		$501
Contributed Capital		$400		$462.0[h]		$400		$462[h]
Retained Earnings		20		(2.6)		101		39
Total Equity		$420		$459.4		$501		$501

[a]$240 × (231/210) = $264.0
[b]$100 × (231/200) = $115.5
[c]$100 × (231/200) = $115.5; $115.5/5 = $23.1
[d]$100 × (231/210) = $110
[e][$100 × (10/200) x (231/210)] +
    $125 × (21/210) = $5.50 + $12.50 = $18
[f]$100 × (231/200) + $115 × (231/210) = $242

[g]$100 × (231/200) = $115.5
[h]$400 × (231/200) = $462
[i]$110/5 = $22
[j]$115 − $100 = $15
[k]$22 − $20 = $2
[l]$280 − $215 = $65

[m]$96 − $80 = $16
[n]$115 × (231/210) = $126.5
[o]$22 × (231/210) = $24.2
[p]$126.5 − $115.5 = $11
[q]$24.2 − $23.1 = $1.1
[r]$280 − $242 = $38
[s]$96−$92.4=$3.6

ACQUISITION COST/NOMINAL DOLLAR ACCOUNTING

Column 1 of Exhibit 7.12 shows the results for Year 1 as they would appear in the conventional financial statements prepared in the United States. These financial statements give no explicit consideration to the effects of changing prices, either in general or for specific assets and liabilities.

Sales appear at the nominal dollars received when the firm sold the widget on June 30. Other expenses appear at the nominal dollars expended on June 30. Cost of goods sold, depreciation, and equipment reflect the nominal dollars expended on January 1. Inventories on the balance sheet reflect the nominal dollars expended on January 1 and June 30. Thus, the financial statements use a measuring unit of unequal size (purchasing power).

Likewise, the financial statements do not reflect the increase in the replacement cost of the inventory and the equipment during Year 1. Is the firm better off by the $20 of net income if it must replace the widget for a higher current cost? Is $20 of depreciation a sufficient measure of the cost of the equipment used during Year 1? Might the firm be better off by more than the $20 of net income because it held inventories and equipment while their replacement cost increased?

Nominal dollars as the measuring unit can be justified when the rate of general price inflation is relatively low (for example, less than 5 percent per year). The rapid turnover of assets for most businesses will not result in serious distortions in financial statement measurements. Likewise, the use of a last-in, first-out (LIFO) cost-flow assumption for cost of goods sold and accelerated depreciation for fixed assets provides at least a partial solution to the problems created by changes in specific prices (these accounting principles provide measures of expenses that approximate current replacement costs but result in balance sheet valuations for assets that can deviate widely from current costs).

ACQUISITION COST/CONSTANT DOLLAR ACCOUNTING

Column 2 of Exhibit 7.12 shows financial statements restated to dollars of constant general purchasing power. Acquisition cost valuations still underlie the measurement of revenues, expenses, assets, and liabilities. However, the nominal dollars underlying these measurements are restated to dollars of constant purchasing power at the end of Year 1. Other constant-dollar measuring units are also possible (for example, January 1, Year 1, constant dollars or June 30, Year 1, constant dollars).

Sales revenue was originally measured in dollars of June 30, Year 1, purchasing power. The restatement expresses the $240 of sales revenue in terms of dollars of December 31, Year 1, purchasing power. Likewise, inventories and equipment reflect restatements of nominal-dollar, acquisition-cost valuations to dollars of constant December 31, Year 1, purchasing power. Thus, an equivalent measuring unit underlies the amounts in column 2. Note that these restated amounts do not represent the current replacement costs of the specific assets and liabilities. The specific prices of assets and liabilities could have changed in an entirely different direction and pattern than prices in general.

One new element in column 2 of Exhibit 7.12 is the *purchasing power gain or loss on monetary items*. A firm that holds cash and claims to a fixed amount of cash (for example, accounts receivable, marketable debt securities) during a period of inflation loses general purchasing power. The dollars held or received later have less general purchasing power after the period of inflation than they had before. A firm that borrows from others, promising to pay a fixed amount in cash at a later time (for example, accounts payable, income taxes payable, bonds payable) gains general purchasing power during a period of inflation. The dollars paid later have less general purchasing power after the period of inflation than they had before. The purchasing power gain or loss is a measure of the increase or decrease in general purchasing power during a period due to being in a net lending position (purchasing power loss) or net borrowing position (purchasing power gain). The accountant calculates the purchasing power gain or loss on *monetary items*. Monetary items include cash and claims receivable or payable in a fixed amount of cash regardless of changes in the general price level.

In the illustration, the firm held $100 of cash during the first six months of the year while the general purchasing power of the dollar decreased 5 percent. It therefore lost $5 of general purchasing power. This $5 loss is measured in terms of dollars of June 30, Year 1, purchasing power. Measured in dollars of December 31, Year 1, constant dollars, the purchasing power loss for the first six months of Year 1 is $5.50. The firm held $125 of cash during the second six months of the year. With 10 percent inflation during this six-month period, an additional loss in purchasing power of $12.50 occurs. Note *e* of Exhibit 7.12 shows the calculations. This illustration is simplified in that the firm has no receivables or payables. In more typical settings, firms that engage in long-term borrowing will often be in a net monetary liability position (that is, monetary liabilities exceed monetary assets). During periods of inflation, these firms experience purchasing power gains.

Constant dollar accounting, in contrast to current cost accounting discussed next, carries a higher level of objectivity. Independent accountants can examine canceled checks, invoices, and other documents to verify acquisition cost valuations. The restatements to constant dollars use general price indexes published by governmental bodies.

Users of constant-dollar financial statements must remember, however, that the amounts reported for individual assets and liabilities do not reflect the current costs of these items. Also, the firm is not necessarily better or worse off in an amount equal to the purchasing power gain or loss on monetary items. Lenders and borrowers incorporate the *expected* rate of inflation into the interest rate charged for delayed payments. Conceptually, purchasing power gains should offset interest expense and purchasing power losses should offset interest revenue. Whether a firm is better or worse off depends on the actual rate of inflation relative to the expected rate incorporated into the interest rate.

CURRENT COST/NOMINAL DOLLAR ACCOUNTING

Column 3 of Exhibit 7.12 reports amounts in terms of the current replacement cost of specific assets and liabilities. Matched against sales are the current costs of replacing the widget sold and the services of the equipment used. Operating income (sales minus expenses measured at current replacement cost) reports the firm's ability to maintain its operating capacity. If sales revenue is not large enough to cover the cost of replacing goods and services used up, the firm will have to cut back its level of operations (unless it secures outside financing).

Current cost income also includes *realized and unrealized holding gains and losses.* A holding gain or loss arises from holding an asset (or liability) while its replacement cost changes. The widget purchased on January 1, Year 1, for $100 was held during the first six months of the year while its replacement cost increased to $115. When the firm sold the widget on June 30, it realized a holding gain of $15 (= $115 – $100). Likewise, the two widgets in ending inventory give rise to unrealized holding gains of $65: $40 (= $140 – $100) on the other widget acquired on January 1 and $25 (= $140 – $115) on the widget acquired on June 30.

Controversy surrounds whether holding gains constitute an increase in the value of a firm. Proponents argue that firms that purchase assets early in anticipation of increases in replacement costs are better off than firms that delay purchases and must pay the higher replacement costs. Opponents argue that firms cannot use such holding gains as the basis for dividend payments without impairing the ability to replace those assets used or sold.

Current cost/nominal dollar accounting is subject to two other criticisms. First, current replacement cost valuations are not as easy to verify or audit as acquisition cost valuations. Different appraisers will likely provide different replacement cost valuations for various assets. The variation in appraisal values will be particularly wide in the case of assets specific to a firm for which active secondhand markets do not exist. Second, the use of nominal dollars means that the measuring unit underlying current replacement cost valuations is not constant across time. Revenues and expenses reflect the purchasing power of the monetary unit during the year, whereas assets and liabilities reflect year-end purchasing power. Distortions caused by changes in the general purchasing power of the measuring unit are less severe in current cost/nominal dollar accounting than in acquisition cost/nominal dollar accounting because current replacement costs reflect more recent measurements.

CURRENT COST/CONSTANT DOLLAR ACCOUNTING

Column 4 of Exhibit 7.12 shows the results of accounting for changes in both general and specific prices. Sales, cost of goods sold, and other expenses measured in terms of replacement costs on June 30, Year 1 (column 3 amounts), are restated from dollars of June 30 purchasing power to dollars of December 31 purchasing power in column 4. Balance sheet amounts for assets reflect current replacement cost valuations and constant dollars on December 31, Year 1.

Perhaps the most interesting disclosures in column 4 are the holding gains. The reported amounts indicate the extent to which changes in prices of the firm's specific assets exceed (or fall short of) the change in the general price level. Economists refer to such holding gains (or losses) as *real holding gains and losses.* Column 4 also includes the purchasing power gain on monetary items.

Current cost/constant dollar accounting deals with both accounting problems caused by changing prices—the measuring unit problem and the valuation problem. Although current cost/constant dollar accounting provides a comprehensive solution to these problems, the user of financial statements based on this approach should keep in mind the concerns discussed previously: (1) current cost valuations are less objective than acquisition cost valuations, (2) the firm is not necessarily better or worse off in an amount equal to the purchasing power gain or loss on monetary items, and (3) the firm cannot distribute to shareholders an amount equal to the holding gains on nonmonetary items (for example inventories, equipment) if it is to maintain its operating capacity.

PROBLEMS AND CASES

7.1 INCOME RECOGNITION FOR VARIOUS TYPES OF BUSINESSES. Discuss when each of the following types of businesses is likely to recognize revenues and expenses.

a. A savings and loan association lending money for home mortgages.
b. A travel agency that books hotels, transportation, and similar services for customers and earns a commission from the providers of these services.
c. A major league baseball team that sells season tickets before the season begins and signs multi-year contracts with players. These contracts typically defer the payment of a significant portion of the compensation provided by the contract until the player retires.
d. A firm that manufactures and sells limited edition figurines. The firm agrees to repurchase the figurines at any time during the 20 years after sale if the market value of the figurine does not increase by at least 10 percent annually.
e. A producer of fine whiskey that ages 12 years before sale.
f. A timber-growing firm that contracts to sell all timber in a particular tract when it reaches 20 years of age. Each year, it harvests another tract. The price per board foot of timber equals the market price when the customer signs the purchase contract plus 10 percent for each year until harvest.
g. An airline that provides transportation services to customers. Each flight grants frequent-flier miles to customers. Customers earn a free flight when they accumulate sufficient frequent-flier miles.

7.2 MEASURING INCOME FOR A SOFTWARE MANUFACTURER. Dassault Systemes (DS), a French information technology firm, develops software that manufacturing firms, its customers, use to manage the life cycle of their products. The cycle begins with product concept and design, and continues through manufacturing simulation, production, and maintenance. Although DS also provides consulting services to customers, its proprietary software is the centerpiece of the services it offers. The firm's largest customers are most of the world's automobile and aircraft manufacturers. In some cases, DS tailors the software to the specific needs of the manufacturer, but typically this task is the responsibility of the customer.

DS generates software revenue from licensing (as opposed to selling) the firm's proprietary software to its customers. DS retains the ownership of the software and sells a "right of use" of the software to its customers. The following excerpt, taken from a recent annual report of DS, describes the two types of revenue streams it generates from licensing its software to customers:

> "The Company's revenue is derived from non-refundable, initial, software license charges, known as the primary license charge, and periodic license or maintenance fees. Primary license charges are recognized upon installation. After such installation, the Company has no further obligations with respect to the primary license charge.
>
> Periodic license and maintenance fee revenues are recognized over the license or maintenance period. An end-user customer with an active license, or an active maintenance contract, is provided with corrective software maintenance services and product updates at no additional charge, the costs of which are recorded in the period incurred.
>
> Revenues of all types of activities are not recognized unless collection is probable."

As the excerpt indicates, the primary license charge is non-refundable regardless of the duration of the license and maintenance charge. Typically, DS signs separate contracts for the primary license charge and the license and maintenance charge, but often the duration of each contract is similar. Contract lengths vary significantly.

Required

  a. Describe the key aspects to the two different charges, "primary license" charges and "periodic license and maintenance" charges, that allow revenues to be recognized differently for each one.
  b. What could be an alternative method for DS to recognize revenue on the "primary license" charges?
  c. Discuss the appropriateness of the revenue recognition techniques employed by DS for both its primary and periodic license and maintenance fees.

7.3 MEASURING INCOME FOR A LONG-HAUL TRANSPORT FIRM. Canadian National Railway Company (CN) spans Canada and mid-America, and provides freight transport services from the Atlantic Ocean to the Pacific Ocean and to the Gulf of Mexico. It is currently the largest private rail system in Canada and was privatized by the Canadian government at a time when it was considered one of the worst rail transport companies in North America. CN has been a success story since its privatization, and is now considered one of the strongest and most efficient rail freight transport companies. Its success is partly due to a fundamental change in the way it offers freight services to customers. CN runs what the firm refers to as a "scheduled railroad." Similar to rail passenger service, CN as much as possible maintains a fixed operating schedule and a fixed freight-car fleet movement across the continent. In this way, the customers know exactly what shipment options are available to them and know with a high degree of accuracy when shipments will arrive at designated locations.

Typically, a customer contracts a fixed fee with CN to provide the shipment of its freight from the point of origination (for example, the Port of Halifax) to the point of destination (for example, the Port of Vancouver). CN provides the entire transport (that is, CN does not contract out a portion of the shipment to other rail transport companies), and the length of time taken to deliver the freight depends on the distance and the type of service (fast delivery versus normal amount of time for delivery, for example) purchased by the customer. In a recent annual report, CN succinctly states its policy on recognizing revenue: "Freight revenues are recognized on services performed by the Company, based on the percentage of complete service method. Costs associated with movements are recognized as the service is performed."

Required

Discuss the appropriateness of the revenue recognition techniques employed by CN for recognizing freight revenues.

7.4 MEASURING INCOME FROM LONG-TERM CONTRACTS. Turner Construction Company agreed on January 1, Year 1, to construct an observatory for Dartmouth College for $120 million. Dartmouth College must pay $30 million upon signing and $30 million at the end of Year 1, Year 2, and Year 3. Expected constructed costs are $10 million for Year 1, $60 million for Year 2, and $30 million for Year 3. Assume that these cash flows occur at the end of each year. Also assume that an appropriate interest rate for this contract is 10 percent. Amortization schedules for the deferred cash flows appear below.

	Amortization Schedule for Cash Received				
Year	Balance Jan. 1	Interest Revenue	Payment	Reduction in Principal	Balance Dec. 31
1	$74,606	$7,460	$30,000	$22,540	$52,066
2	52,066	5,207	30,000	24,793	27,273
3	27,273	2,727	30,000	27,273	—

	Amortization Schedule for Cash Disbursed				
Year	Balance Jan. 1	Interest Expense	Payment	Reduction in Principal	Balance Dec. 31
1	$81,217	$8,122	$10,000	$ 1,878	$79,339
2	79,339	7,934	60,000	52,066	27,273
3	27,273	2,727	30,000	27,273	—

Required

a. Indicate the amount and nature of income (revenue and expense) that Turner would recognize during Year 1, Year 2, and Year 3 if it uses the completed-contract method. Ignore income taxes.

b. Repeat part a using the percentage-of-completion method.
c. Repeat part a using the installment method.
d. Indicate the balance in the Construction-in-Process account on December 31, Year 1, Year 2, and Year 3 (just prior to completion of the contract) under the completed-contract and the percentage-of-completion methods.

7.5 MEASURING INCOME FROM LONG-TERM CONTRACTS. Halliburton, Inc. is a multinational long-term construction firm in the energy-related field. It employs the percentage-of-completion method for recognizing revenue, as discussed in Exhibit 7.1. The exhibit also describes how Halliburton accounts for claims and change orders, which often represent changes resulting from disputes between the firm and its customers. These items are important to contractors because they have the potential for eroding forecasted profit margins. Halliburton states:

> "Claims and change orders which are in the process of being negotiated with customers, for extra work or changes in the scope of work, are included in revenues when collection is deemed probable."

Bracknell Corporation is a large construction firm that operates primarily in North America. It emphasizes construction of complex and critical components of a plant's infrastructure, such as plumbing, electrical power, ventilation, and automated controls. It often performs the function of general contractor as well. Similar to Halliburton, Bracknell uses the percentage-of-completion method for recognition of revenue. The firm's policy for accounting for claims and change orders is as follows:

> "The Company does not recognize any gross profit amounts related to change order work performed until it is known that the change orders have been approved by the customer. At that point, an amount equal to contract costs attributable to claims is included in revenues when realization is probable and the amount can be reliably estimated."

Required

a. Describe the differences and similarities between the policies of the two firms for accounting for claims and change orders.
b. What arguments can be made by Halliburton to justify its policy of recognizing revenues before the customer and the firm have agreed to the claims and change orders?
c. Which technique do you believe is preferable for recognizing revenue on claims and change orders? Why?

7.6 ANALYZING FINANCIAL STATEMENT DISCLOSURES REGARDING INVENTORIES AND FIXED ASSETS. USX derives revenues from the manufacture of steel and the refining and marketing of petroleum products. USX uses a LIFO cost-flow assumption for inventories, straight-line depreciation for financial reporting, and accelerated depreciation for tax reporting. Exhibit 7.13 presents selected data for USX for Year 7 and Year 8. The income tax rate is 35 percent.

<table>
<tr><td colspan="4" align="center">**EXHIBIT 7.13**</td></tr>
<tr><td colspan="4" align="center">USX
Financial Statement Data
(amounts in millions)
(Problem 7.6)</td></tr>
</table>

	December 31		
	Year 8	**Year 7**	**Year 6**
Inventories (LIFO)	$ 2,021	$ 1,973	$ 1,626
Property, Plant, and Equipment (net)	10,535	11,482	11,603
Total Assets	16,743	17,517	17,374
Deferred Tax Liability Relating to			
Temporary Depreciation Differences	2,530	2,733	2,680
Common Shareholders' Equity	4,328	4,302	3,864

	Year Ended December 31	
	Year 8	**Year 7**
Sales	$20,922	$19,330
Cost of Goods Sold	15,103	14,186
Depreciation Expense	1,160	1,065
Interest Expense.	501	461
Net Income (Loss).	214	501

Required

a. The excess of FIFO over LIFO inventories was $340 million on December 31, Year 6, $260 million on December 31, Year 7, and $320 on December 31, Year 8. Compute the cost of goods sold for USX for Year 7 and Year 8 assuming that it had used a FIFO cost-flow assumption.

b. Compute the inventory turnover ratio for USX for Year 7 and Year 8 using (1) a LIFO cost-flow assumption and (2) a FIFO cost-flow assumption.

c. Compute the amount of depreciation expense that USX recognized for income tax purposes for Year 7 and Year 8. Note that the amount reported as the deferred tax liability relating to temporary depreciation differences represents the cumulative income taxes delayed as of each balance sheet date because USX uses accelerated depreciation for tax purposes and straight-line depreciation for financial reporting.

d. Compute the fixed asset turnover ratio for Year 7 and Year 8 assuming use of (1) straight-line depreciation and (2) accelerated (tax) depreciation.

e. Compute the rate of return on assets for Year 7 and Year 8 based on the reported amounts (that is, LIFO for inventories and straight-line depreciation). Disaggregate ROA into profit margin and assets turnover components.

f. Repeat part e using FIFO for inventories and accelerated (tax) depreciation.

Assume USX uses FIFO for both financial and tax reporting. Any tax effects reduce or increase cash. Disaggregate ROA into profit margin and assets turnover components.

g. Compute the rate of return on common shareholders' equity for Year 7 and Year 8 based on the reported amounts. Disaggregate ROCE into ROA and capital structure leverage components.

h. Repeat part g using FIFO for inventories and accelerated (tax) depreciation.

i. Interpret the changes in the profitability and risk of USX between Year 7 and Year 8 in light of the preceding analyses.

7.7 ANALYZING DISCLOSURES REGARDING FIXED ASSETS. Exhibit 7.14 presents selected financial statement data for three chemical companies: Ethyl Corporation, Monsanto, and Olin Corporation.

Required

a. Compute the average total depreciable life of assets in use for each firm during Year 12.

b. Compute the average age to date of depreciable assets in use for each firm at the end of Year 12.

EXHIBIT 7.14
Three Chemical Companies
Selected Financial Statement Data on Depreciable Assets
(amounts in millions)
(Problem 7.7)

	Ethyl Corporation	Monsanto	Olin Corporation
Depreciable Assets at Cost:			
December 31, Year 11........	$769	$3,858	$1,661
December 31, Year 12........	768	4,459	1,718
Accumulated Depreciation:			
December 31, Year 11........	436	1,639	1,178
December 31, Year 12........	477	1,800	1,241
Net Income, Year 12	61	334	81
Depreciation Expense, Year 12 ...	66	546	85
Deferred Tax Liability			
Relating to Depreciable Assets			
December 31, Year 11........	34	203	64
December 31, Year 12........	44	234	66
Income Tax Rate..............	35%	35%	35%
Depreciation Method for			
Financial Reporting.........	Straight-line	Straight-line	Straight-line
Depreciation Method for			
Tax Reporting..............	Accelerated	Accelerated	Accelerated

c. Compute the amount of depreciation expense recognized for tax purposes for each firm for Year 12 using the amount of the deferred taxes liability related to depreciation timing differences.

d. Compute the amount of net income for Year 8 for each firm assuming depreciation expense for financial reporting equals the amount computed in part c for tax reporting.

e. Compute the amount each company would report for property, plant, and equipment (net) on December 31, Year 12, if it had used accelerated (tax reporting) depreciation instead of straight-line depreciation.

f. What factors might explain the difference in average total life of Ethyl Corporation and Olin Corporation relative to Monsanto?

g. What factors might explain the older average age for depreciable assets of Ethyl Corporation and Olin Corporation relative to Monsanto?

7.8 INTERPRETING FINANCIAL STATEMENT DISCLOSURES RELATING TO INCOME RECOGNITION. Deere & Company manufactures agricultural and industrial equipment and provides financing services for its independent dealers and their retail customers. Exhibit 7.15 presents an income statement and Exhibit 7.16 presents a balance sheet for Deere for Year 19 and Year 20. The notes to these financial statements appear below.

EXHIBIT 7.15

Deere & Company
Income Statement
(amounts in millions)
(Problem 7.8)

	Year Ended October 31	
	Year 20	Year 19
Revenues		
Equipment Sales Revenue (Note 1)	$11,077	$11,169
Finance Revenue (Note 2).	1,445	1,321
Investment Revenue	11	19
Other Income	759	627
Total Revenues	$13,292	$13,136
Expenses		
Cost of Goods Sold.	$ 9,376	$ 8,936
Research and Development Expenses.	590	542
Selling, Administrative, and Other Expenses	2,607	2,203
Interest Expense	766	677
Income Tax Expense	17	294
Total Expenses	$13,356	$12,652
Net Income (Loss).	$ (64)	$ 484

EXHIBIT 7.16

Deere & Company
Balance Sheet
(amounts in millions)
(Problem 7.8)

	October 31	
	Year 20	Year 19
Assets		
Cash....................................	$ 1,030	$ 292
Marketable Securities	176	127
Accounts and Notes Receivable (Note 2)..........	14,754	13,025
Inventories (Note 3)	1,506	1,553
Property, Plant, and Equipment (Note 4)	2,052	1,912
Intangible Assets, net	874	652
Other Assets	2,271	2,908
Total Assets..............................	$22,663	$20,469
Liabilities and Shareholders' Equity		
Short-term Borrowing	$ 6,199	$ 5,759
Accounts Payable and Accrued Expenses..........	3,257	3,130
Long-term Borrowing.........................	6,561	4,764
Deferred Income Taxes	13	75
Pension Liability	2,641	2,440
Total Liabilities...........................	$18,671	$16,168
Common Stock..............................	$ 527	$ 414
Accumulated Other Comprehensive Loss	(370)	(229)
Retained Earnings............................	3,835	4,116
Total Shareholders' Equity...................	$ 3,992	$ 4,301
Total Liabilities and Shareholders' Equity.......	$22,663	$20,469

Note 1: Deere recognizes income from equipment sales for financial reporting at the time of shipment to dealers. Provisions for sales incentives to dealers, returns and allowances, and uncollectible accounts are made at the time of sale. There is a time lag, which varies based on the timing and level of retail demand, between when Deere records sales to dealers and when dealers sell equipment to retail customers. Deere recognizes income from equipment sales using the installment method for tax reporting.

Note 2: Deere provides financing to independent dealers and retail customers for Deere products. Accounts and notes receivable appear net of unearned finance income. Deere recognizes the unearned finance income as finance revenue over the period that dealer and customer notes are outstanding.

Note 3: Deere uses a LIFO cost-flow assumption for inventories and cost of goods sold. The excess of FIFO over LIFO cost of inventories was $978 million on October 31, Year 19, and $1,004 on October 31, Year 20.

Note 4: Property, plant, and equipment includes the following:

	October 31	
	Year 20	**Year 19**
Land	$ 59	$ 58
Buildings.................................	1,238	1,166
Machinery and Equipment...................	2,458	2,315
Dies, Patterns, Tools	765	678
Other....................................	868	838
Total	$5,388	$5,055
Less Accumulated Depreciation	(3,336)	(3,143)
	$2,052	$1,912

Deere depreciates fixed assets using the straight-line method for financial reporting. Depreciation expense was $292 million in Year 19 and $308 in Year 20. Deere uses accelerated depreciation for tax reporting.

Required

a. Using the criteria for revenue recognition, justify the timing of revenue recognition by Deere for its equipment sales. Give consideration as to why recognition of revenue either earlier or later than the time of shipment to dealers would not be more appropriate.

b. Describe briefly how the balance sheet accounts of Deere & Company listed below would change if it recognized revenues during the period of production using the percentage-of-completion method. You need not give amounts but indicate the likely direction of the change and describe the computation of its amount.

   Accounts and Notes Receivable

   Inventories

   Retained Earnings

c. Respond to question b assuming that Deere & Company recognized revenue using the installment method.

   Accounts and Notes Receivable

   Inventories

   Retained Earnings

d. Compute the amount of cost of goods sold for Year 20 assuming that Deere & Company had used a FIFO instead of a LIFO cost-flow assumption.

e.　Did the quantities and costs of inventory items likely increase or decrease during Year 20? Explain.

f.　Compute the average age of Deere's depreciable assets at the end of Year 20.

7.9 INTERPRETING DISCLOSURES REGARDING CHANGING PRICES. Chilgener S.V. is one of the largest providers of electric transmission services in Chile. The firm also provides electricity to sections of Argentina. Exhibit 7.17 presents the balance sheet for Chilgener on December 31, Year 12 and Year 13. Exhibit 7.18 presents the income statement for Chilgener for Year 12 and Year 13. Excerpts from the notes to its financial statements appear below.

EXHIBIT 7.17

Chilgener S.A
Balance Sheet
(amounts in millions of constant December 31, Year 13 Chilean Pesos)
(Problem 7.9)

	December 31	
	Year 13	**Year 12**
Assets		
Cash....................................	P 30,140	P 4,031
Accounts Receivable	10,923	7,121
Inventories...............................	8,622	8,664
Other Current Assets......................	50,746	15,053
Total Current Assets	P100,431	P 34,869
Fixed Assets—at Cost	P438,067	P436,595
Technical Revaluation of Fixed Assets	29,075	29,075
Accumulated Depreciation	(171,353)	(165,394)
Net Fixed Assets	P295,789	P300,276
Other Assets.............................	P 93,840	P 37,606
Total Assets	P490,060	P372,751
Liabilities and Shareholders' Equity		
Short-term Borrowing......................	P 50,800	P 11,068
Accounts Payable..........................	15,860	10,127
Other Current Liabilities....................	6,233	5,839
Total Current Liabilities	P 72,893	P 27,034
Long-term Debt...........................	96,482	87,360
Other Noncurrent Liabilities.	9,245	5,347
Total Liabilities	P178,620	P119,741
Paid-in Capital...........................	P238,818	P190,233
Technical Revaluation of Fixed Assets	29,075	29,075
Retained Earnings	43,547	33,702
Total Shareholders' Equity	P311,440	P253,010
Total Liabilities and Shareholders' Equity	P490,060	P372,751

EXHIBIT 7.18

Chilgener, S.A.
Income Statement
(amounts in millions of constant December 31, Year 13 Chilean Pesos)
(Problem 7.9)

	December 31	
	Year 13	Year 12
Operating Revenues	P90,030	P70,514
Operating Costs	(53,556)	(38,871)
Operating Margin	P36,474	P31,643
Selling and Administrative Expense	(11,809)	(10,114)
Operating Income	P24,665	P21,529
Financial Income	P10,415	P 3,258
Share of Profits of Investees	4,278	1,123
Financing Expenses	(7,263)	(7,136)
Other Non-operating Expenses	(1,584)	(1,544)
Price Level Restatement	(1,250)	3,471
Non-operating Income	P 4,596	P (828)
Income Before Tax	P29,261	P20,701
Income Tax	(4,030)	(3,264)
Net Income	P25,231	P17,437

SUMMARY OF SIGNIFICANT ACCOUNTING PRINCIPLES

General

The consolidated financial statements have been prepared in conformity with generally accepted accounting principles in Chile and with the regulations issued by the Superintendency of Corporations and Insurance Companies.

Price Level Restatement

These consolidated financial statements have been restated through the application of an adjustment based on the change in the consumer price index in order to reflect the effect of fluctuations in the purchasing power of the Chilean peso. Restatements have been based on the official index published by the Chilean Institute of Statistics which amounts to a 12.1 percent increase for the year ended December 31, Year 13 (in Year 12, 14 percent). Moreover, income and expenses were also restated so as to express them at year-end purchasing power. The Year 12 financial statements and their relevant notes have been adjusted (without being reflected in the accounting records) by 12.1 percent, with the only purpose of allowing their comparison with the Year 12 financial statements in constant pesos of December, Year 13.

Inventories

Inventories consist of raw materials and spares which are valued at their replacement cost. The values thus determined do not exceed their net realizable value in accordance with generally accepted accounting principles.

Fixed Assets

Fixed assets are presented according to contribution values or at cost, as the case may be, plus price-level restatement. The value of fixed assets was adjusted on June 30, Year 6, in accordance with the Technical Appraisal Circulars of the Superintendency of Corporations and Insurance Companies. Depreciation has been calculated on a straight-line basis on the adjusted value of assets, in accordance with their remaining useful life. Depreciation for Year 13 amounted to P10,206, and to P9,941 for Year 12. It is included in operating costs and includes additional depreciation for technical reappraisal of fixed assets amounting to P1,166 in Year 13, and P1,195 in Year 12.

Bonds

Bonds are shown at nominal year-end value plus accrued interest.

Required

a. Does Chilgener's reporting most closely resemble (1) acquisition cost/constant peso reporting, (2) current cost/nominal peso reporting, or (3) current cost/constant peso reporting? Explain.

b. Interpret the last sentence in the note on price-level restatement.

c. What is the likely reason that Chilgener reported a price-level restatement gain on its income statement for Year 12, but a price-level restatement loss for Year 13?

d. Assume that sales and price-level changes occurred evenly during Year 12 and Year 13. Compute the *nominal* peso change in sales between Year 12 and Year 13.

e. Have the current replacement costs of Chilgener's fixed assets increased at a faster or slower rate than the general price level? Explain your reasoning. If you do not think that the disclosures permit an answer to this question, then explain your reasoning.

f. Why does the amount in the account, Technical Revaluation of Fixed Assets, remain at P29,075 during Year 13 if the note on fixed assets indicates that Chilgener recognized depreciation on the revalued fixed asset amount?

CASE 7.1

ARIZONA LAND DEVELOPMENT COMPANY

Joan Locker and Bill Dasher organized the Arizona Land Development Company (ALDC) on January 2, Year 1. They contributed land with a market value of $300,000 and cash of $100,000 for all of the common stock of the corporation. The land served as the initial inventory of property sold to customers.

ALDC sells undeveloped land, primarily to individuals approaching retirement. Within a period of nine years from the date of sale, ALDC promises to develop the land so that it is suitable for the construction of residential housing. ALDC makes all sales on an installment basis. Customers pay 10 percent of the selling price at the time of sale, and remit the remainder in equal installments over the next nine years.

ALDC estimates that development costs will equal 50 percent of the selling price of the land and that development work will take nine years to complete from the date of sale. Actual development costs have coincided with expectations. The firm incurs 10 percent of the development costs at the time of sale, and incurs the remainder evenly over the next nine years.

ALDC remained a privately held firm for its first six years. Exhibits 7.19 through 7.21 present the firm's income statement, balance sheet, and statement of cash flows, respectively, for Year 1 to Year 6. ALDC recognizes income from sales of undeveloped land at the time of sale. The amount shown for sales each year in Exhibit 7.19 represents the gross amount ALDC ultimately expects to collect from customers for

EXHIBIT 7.19

Arizona Land Development Company
Income Statements
Income Recognition at Time of Sale—No Discounting of Cash Flows
(Case 7.1)

	Year 1	Year 2	Year 3	Year 4	Year 5	Year 6
Sales.....................	$650,000	$900,000	$1,500,000	$2,500,000	$1,200,000	$400,000
Less:						
Cost of Land						
Inventory Sold.........	(65,000)	(90,000)	(150,000)	(250,000)	(120,000)	(40,000)
Estimated Development						
Costs...............	(325,000)	(450,000)	(750,000)	(1,250,000)	(600,000)	(200,000)
Gross Profit..............	$260,000	$360,000	$ 600,000	$1,000,000	$ 480,000	$160,000
Selling Expenses	(65,000)	(90,000)	(150,000)	(250,000)	(120,000)	(40,000)
Net Income Before						
Taxes.................	$195,000	$270,000	$ 450,000	$ 750,000	$ 360,000	$120,000
Income Taxes:						
Current	—	—	(9,778)	(26,091)	(73,009)	(94,902)
Deferred..............	(66,300)	(91,800)	(143,222)	(228,909)	(49,391)	54,102
Net Income..............	$128,700	$178,200	$ 297,000	$ 495,000	$ 237,600	$ 79,200

EXHIBIT 7.20

Arizona Land Development Company
Balance Sheets
Income Recognition at Time of Sale—No Discounting of Cash Flows
(Case 7.1)

	Year 1	Year 2	Year 3	Year 4	Year 5	Year 6
Assets						
Cash	$100,000	$ 132,500	$ 100,222	$ 126,631	$ 131,122	$ 273,720
Notes Receivable..........	520,000	1,175,000	2,220,000	3,915,000	4,320,000	3,965,000
Land Inventory............	235,000	145,000	95,000	45,000	125,000	185,000
Total Assets	$855,000	$1,452,500	$2,415,222	$4,086,631	$4,576,122	$4,423,720
Liabilities and Shareholders' Equity						
Estimated Development						
Cost Liability	$260,000	$ 587,500	$1,110,000	$1,957,500	$2,160,000	$1,982,500
Deferred Income Taxes......	66,300	158,100	301,322	530,231	579,622	525,520
Common Stock............	400,000	400,000	400,000	500,000	500,000	500,000
Retained Earnings.........	128,700	306,900	603,900	1,098,900	1,336,500	1,415,700
Total Liabilities and Shareholders' Equity ...	$855,000	$1,452,500	$2,415,222	$4,086,631	$4,576,122	$4,423,720

EXHIBIT 7.21

Arizona Land Development Company
Statements of Cash Flows
Income Recognition at Time of Sale—No Discounting of Cash Flows
(Case 7.1)

	Year 1	Year 2	Year 3	Year 4	Year 5	Year 6
Operations						
Net Income	$128,700	$178,200	$297,000	$495,000	$237,600	$ 79,200
(Inc.) Dec. in Notes Receivable..............	(520,000)	(655,000)	(1,045,000)	(1,695,000)	(405,000)	355,000
(Inc.) Dec. in Land Inventory	65,000	90,000	50,000	50,000	(80,000)	(60,000)
Inc. (Dec.) in Estimated Development Cost Liability................	260,000	327,500	522,500	847,500	202,500	(177,500)
Inc. (Dec.) in Deferred Income Taxes	66,300	91,800	143,222	228,909	49,391	(54,102)
Cash Flow from Operations	$ 0	$ 32,500	$(32,278)	$(73,591)	$ 4,491	$142,598
Financing						
Common Stock Issued	—	—	—	100,000	—	—
Change in Cash	$ 0	$ 32,500	$(32,278)	$ 26,409	$ 4,491	$142,598

land sold in that year. The amount shown for estimated development costs each year is the gross amount ALDC expects ultimately to disburse to develop land sold in that year. The firm treats selling expenses as a period expense. It is subject to a 34 percent income tax rate. ALDC uses the installment method of income recognition for income tax purposes.

ALDC contemplates making its initial public offering of common stock early in Year 7. The firm asks you to assess whether its income recognition method, as reflected in Exhibits 7.19 to 7.21, accurately reflects its operating performance and financial position. To assist you, the firm has prepared financial statements following three other income recognition methods as described next.

INCOME RECOGNITION AT TIME OF SALE BUT WITH DISCOUNTING OF FUTURE CASH FLOWS TO PRESENT VALUE

Exhibits 7.22 to 7.24 present the financial statements following this income recognition method. This method discounts future cash inflows from customers and future cash outflows for development work to their present values. The gross profit recognized at the time of sale equals the present value of cash inflows net of the present value of cash outflows. One might view this gross profit as the current cash equivalent value of the gross profit that the firm will ultimately realize over the nine-year period. This method reports the increase in the present value of cash inflows as time passes as interest revenue each year and the increase in the present value of cash outflows as interest expense. Thus, this income recognition method results in reporting two types of income: a gross profit from the selling of land and interest from delayed cash flows. The computations of present values underlying the financial statements in Exhibits 7.22 to 7.24 rest on the following assumptions.

1. ALDC makes all sales on January 1 of each year. It receives 10 percent of the gross selling price at the time of sale and also pays 10 percent of the gross development costs immediately.
2. The firm receives 10 percent of the gross selling price from customers and pays 10 percent of the gross development costs on December 31 of each year, beginning with the year of sale.
3. The interest rates used in discounting are as follows:

Sales In:	Interest Rate
Year 1	12%
Year 2	12%
Year 3	15%
Year 4	15%
Year 5	12%
Year 6	12%

EXHIBIT 7.22

Arizona Land Development Company
Income Statements
Income Recognition at Time of Sale—With Discounting of Cash Flows
(Case 7.1)

	Year 1	Year 2	Year 3	Year 4	Year 5	Year 6
Sales......................	$411,336[a]	$569,543	$865,737	$1,442,895	$759,390	$253,130
Less:						
Cost of Land Inventory						
Sold...................	(65,000)	(90,000)	(150,000)	(250,000)	(120,000)	(40,000)
Estimated Development						
Costs	(205,668)[b]	(284,771)	(432,869)	(721,448)	(379,695)	(126,565)
Gross Profit...............	$140,668	$194,772	$282,868	$ 471,447	$259,695	$ 86,565
Selling Expenses	(65,000)	(90,000)	(150,000)	(250,000)	(120,000)	(40,000)
Interest Revenue	41,560[c]	96,293	196,609	361,257	411,130	400,899
Interest Expense	(20,780)[d]	(48,147)	(98,304)	(180,628)	(205,566)	(200,449)
Net Income Before Taxes	$ 96,448	$152,918	$231,173	$ 402,076	$345,259	$247,015
Income Taxes:						
Current	—	—	(9,778)	(26,091)	(73,009)	(94,902)
Deferred	(32,792)	(51,992)	(68,821)	(110,615)	(44,379)	10,917
Net Income	$ 63,656	$100,926	$152,574	$ 265,370	$227,871	$163,030

[a]Represents the present value of $65,000 received on January 1, Year 1, plus the present value of a series of $65,000 cash inflows on December 31, Year 1 to Year 9, discounted at 12 percent.
[b]Represents the present value of $32,500 paid on January 1, Year 1, plus the present value of a series of $32,500 cash outflows on December 31, Year 1 to Year 9, discounted at 12 percent.
[c].12($411,336 − $65,000) = $41,560.
[d].12($205,668 − $32,500) = $20,780.

EXHIBIT 7.23

Arizona Land Development Company
Balance Sheets
Income Recognition at Time of Sale—With Discounting of Cash Flows
(Case 7.1)

	Year 1	Year 2	Year 3	Year 4	Year 5	Year 6
Assets						
Cash	$100,000	$ 132,500	$ 100,222	$ 126,631	$ 131,122	$ 273,720
Notes Receivable...........	322,896[a]	743,732	1,351,078	2,350,230	2,725,750	2,624,779
Land Inventory............	235,000	145,000	95,000	45,000	125,000	185,000
Total Assets	$657,896	$1,021,232	$1,546,300	$2,521,861	$2,981,872	$3,083,499

Exhibit 7.23—continued	Year 1	Year 2	Year 3	Year 4	Year 5	Year 6
Liabilities and Shareholders' Equity						
Estimated Development						
Cost Liability	$161,448[b]	$ 371,866	$ 675,539	$1,175,115	$1,362,876	$1,312,390
Deferred Income Taxes.	32,792	84,784	153,605	264,220	308,599	297,682
Common Stock.	400,000	400,000	400,000	500,000	500,000	500,000
Retained Earnings.	63,656	164,582	317,156	582,526	810,397	973,427
Total Liabilities and						
Shareholders' Equity . . .	$657,896	$1,021,232	$1,546,300	$2,521,861	$2,981,872	$3,083,499

[a]$411,336 – $65,000 + $41,560 – $65,000 = $322,896 (see Notes a and c to Exhibit 7.22).
[b]$205,668 – $32,500 + $20,780 – $32,500 = $161,448 (see Notes b and d to Exhibit 7.22).

EXHIBIT 7.24

Arizona Land Development Company
Statements of Cash Flows
Income Recognition at Time of Sale—With Discounting of Cash Flows
(Case 7.1)

	Year 1	Year 2	Year 3	Year 4	Year 5	Year 6
Operations						
Net Income	$ 63,656	$100,926	$152,574	$265,370	$227,871	$163,030
(Inc.) Dec. in Notes Receivable . .	(322,896)	(420,836)	(607,346)	(999,152)	(375,520)	100,971
(Inc.) Dec. in Land Inventory. . . .	65,000	90,000	50,000	50,000	(80,000)	(60,000)
Inc. (Dec.) in Estimated						
Development Cost Liability. . .	161,448	210,418	303,673	499,576	187,761	(50,486)
Inc. (Dec.) in Deferred						
Income Taxes	32,792	51,992	68,821	110,615	44,379	(10,917)
Cash Flow from Operations	$ 0	$ 32,500	$ (32,278)	$(73,591)	$ 4,491	$142,598
Financing						
Common Stock Issued	—	—	—	100,000	—	—
Change in Cash.	$ 0	$ 32,500	$ (32,278)	$ 26,409	$ 4,491	$142,598

INCOME RECOGNITION USING THE INSTALLMENT METHOD— WITH DISCOUNTING OF CASH FLOWS

Exhibits 7.25 to 7.27 present the financial statements following this income recognition method. ALDC uses this income recognition method for tax reporting.

EXHIBIT 7.25

Arizona Land Development Company
Income Statements
Income Recognition Using Installment Method—With Discounting of Cash Flows
(Case 7.1)

	Year 1	Year 2	Year 3	Year 4	Year 5	Year 6
Sales Revenue..................	$ 88,440[a]	$148,707	$258,391	$443,744	$383,868	$ 354,101
Cost of Goods Sold	(58,195)[a]	(97,852)	(172,963)	(297,634)	(254,699)	(235,427)
Gross Profit	$ 30,245[a]	$ 50,855	$ 85,428	$146,110	$129,169	$ 118,674
Selling Expenses...............	(65,000)	(90,000)	(150,000)	(250,000)	(120,000)	(40,000)
Interest Revenue	41,560[b]	96,293	196,609	361,257	411,130	400,899
Interest Expense...............	(20,780)[c]	(48,147)	(98,304)	(180,628)	(205,566)	(200,449)
Net Income Before Taxes.........	$(13,975)	$ 9,001	$ 33,733	$ 76,739	$214,733	$ 279,124
Income Taxes:						
Current	—[d]	—[d]	(9,778)[d]	(26,091)	(73,009)	(94,902)
Deferred....................	4.751	(3.060)	(1.691)	—	—	—
Net Income	$ (9,224)	$ 5,941	$ 22,264	$ 50,648	$141,724	$ 184,222

[a]Exhibit 7.22 indicates that the total gross profit from land sold in Year 1 is $140,668. The present value of the amounts that ALDC will receive from customers is $411,336 (see Exhibit 7.22). Thus, for each dollar of the $411,336 collected, the firm recognizes 34.2 cents (= $140,668 ÷ $411,336) of gross profit. During Year 1, ALDC collects $130,000 from sales of land made in Year 1 ($65,000 on January 1 and $65,000 on December 31). However, only $23,440 (= $65,000 − $41,560) of the December 31 payment represents payment of a portion of the $411,336 selling price. The remainder ($41,560) represents interest. Thus, the gross profit recognized in Year 1 is $30,245 [.342($65,000 + $23,440)].
[b]See Note c to Exhibit 7.22.
[c]See Note d to Exhibit 7.22.
[d]ALDC carries forward the $13,975 loss in Year 1 to offset taxable income in future years ($9,001 in Year 2 and $4,974 in Year 3).

EXHIBIT 7.26

Arizona Land Development Company
Balance Sheets
Income Recognition Using Installment Method—With Discounting of Cash Flows
(Case 7.1)

	Year 1	Year 2	Year 3	Year 4	Year 5	Year 6
Assets						
Cash	$100,000	$132,500	$ 100,222	$ 126,631	$ 131,122	$ 273,720
Notes Receivable	212,473[a]	489,392	899,298	1,573,113	1,818,107	1,749,245
Land Inventory	235,000	145,000	95,000	45,000	125,000	185,000
Deferred Tax Asset............	4,751	1,691	—	—	—	—
Total Assets	$552,224	$768,583	$1,094,520	$1,744,744	$2,074,229	$2,207,965

Exhibit 7.26—continued	Year 1	Year 2	Year 3	Year 4	Year 5	Year 6
Liabilities and Shareholders' Equity						
Estimated Development						
Cost Liability	$161,448[b]	$371,866	$ 675,539	$1,175,115	$1,362,876	$1,312,390
Deferred Income Taxes	—	—	—	—	—	—
Common Stock	400,000	400,000	400,000	500,000	500,000	500,000
Retained Earnings	(9,224)	(3,283)	18,981	69,629	211,353	395,575
Total Liabilities and						
Shareholders' Equity	$552,224	$768,583	$1,094,520	$1,744,744	$2,074,229	$2,207,965

[a]The derivation of this amount is as follows:

	Notes Receivable Gross	Deferred Gross Profit	Notes Receivable Net
January 1, Year 1	$411,336	$140,668	$270,668
Less Cash Received, January 1, Year 1	(65,000)	—	(65,000)
Plus Interest Revenue, Year 1	41,560	—	41,560
Less Cash Received, December 31, Year 1	(65,000)	—	(65,000)
Gross Profit Recognized,			
Year 1	—	(30,245)	30,245
Totals	$322,896	$110,423	$212,473

[b]See Note b to Exhibit 7.23.

EXHIBIT 7.27

Arizona Land Development Company
Statements of Cash Flows
Income Recognition Using Installment Method—With Discounting of Cash Flows
(Case 7.1)

	Year 1	Year 2	Year 3	Year 4	Year 5	Year 6
Operations						
Net Income (Loss)	$ (9,224)	$ 5,941	$ 22,264	$ 50,648	$141,724	$184,222
(Inc.) Dec. in Notes Receivable	(212,473)	(276,919)	(409,906)	(673,815)	(244,994)	68,862
(Inc.) Dec. in Land Inventory	65,000	90,000	50,000	50,000	(80,000)	(60,000)
(Inc.) Dec. in Deferred						
Tax Asset	(4,751)	3,060	1,691	—	—	—
(Inc.) Dec. in Estimated						
Development Cost Liability	161,448	210,418	303,673	499,576	187,761	(50,486)
Cash Flow from Operations	$ 0	$ 32,500	$(32,278)	$(73,591)	$ 4,491	$142,598
Financing						
Common Stock Issued	—	—	—	100,000	—	—
Change in Cash	$ 0	$ 32,500	$(32,278)	$ 26,409	$ 4,491	$142,598

INCOME RECOGNITION USING THE PERCENTAGE-OF-COMPLETION METHODS

Exhibits 7.28 to 7.30 present the financial statements following this income recognition method. The presumption underlying this method is that ALDC is primarily a developer of real estate and that its income should reflect its development activity, not its sales activity. The difference between the contract price and the total estimated costs of the land and development work represents the total income from development of the land. The percentage-of-completion method uses actual costs incurred to date as a percentage of estimated total costs to determine the degree of completion each period. Multiplying this percentage times the contract price yields sales revenue each year. Multiplying this percentage times the total expected costs yields cost of goods sold.

Required

a. For each of the four income recognition methods illustrated in Exhibits 7.19 through 7.30, show the supporting calculations for each of the following items for Year 2:

(1) Sales Revenue for Year 2

(2) Cost of Goods Sold for Year 2

(3) Gross Profit for Year 2

(4) Notes Receivable on December 31, Year 2, under the first three income recognition methods and the Contracts in Process account on December 31, Year 2, under the fourth income recognition method.

(5) Estimated Development Costs Liability on December 31, Year 2, under the first three income recognition methods and the Progress Billings account on December 31, Year 2, under the fourth income recognition method.

b. Evaluate each of the four income recognition methods described in the case relative to the criteria for revenue and expense recognition. Which method do you think best portrays the operating performance and financial position of ALDC? Discuss your reasoning.

c. Which income recognition method is ALDC likely to prefer in reporting to shareholders?

d. Why did ALDC choose the installment method for tax reporting?

e. With respect to maximizing cumulative reported earnings, the four income recognition methods rank order as follows:

1. Income Recognition at Time of Sale—No Discounting of Cash Flows

2. Income Recognition at Time of Sale—With Discounting of Cash Flows

3. Income Recognition Using the Percentage-of-Completion Method

4. Income Recognition Using the Installment Method—With Discounting of Cash Flows

What is the reason behind this rank ordering?

f. The difference in cumulative reported earnings between any two income recognition methods equals (1) the difference in Notes Receivable or

EXHIBIT 7.28

Arizona Land Development Company
Income Statements
Income Recognition Using Percentage-of-Completion Method
(Case 7.1)

	Year 1	Year 2	Year 3	Year 4	Year 5	Year 6
Sales	$216,667[a]	$354,167	$629,167	$1,087,500	$862,500	$695,833
Cost of Goods Sold	(130,000)[a]	(212,500)	(377,500)	(652,500)	(517,500)	(417,500)
Gross Profit.	$ 86,667[a]	$141,667	$251,667	$ 435,000	$345,000	$278,333
Selling Expenses	(65,000)	(90,000)	(150,000)	(250,000)	(120,000)	(40,000)
Net Income Before Taxes	$ 21,667	$ 51,667	$101,667	$ 185,000	$225,000	$238,333
Income Taxes:						
Current.	—	—	(9,778)	(26,091)	(73,009)	(94,902)
Deferred	(7,367)	(17,567)	(24,789)	(36,809)	(3,491)	13,869
Net Income.	$ 14,300	$ 34,100	$ 67,100	$ 122,100	$148,500	$157,300

[a]Land sold under contract in Year 1 had a contract price of $650,000 and estimated contract cost of $390,000 (= $65,000 + $325,000) (see Exhibit 7.19). ALDC incurred development costs of $130,000 (= $65,000 for land + $32,500 on January 1, Year 1 + $32,500 on December 31, Year 1) during Year 1. Thus, the percentage of completion as of the end of Year 1 is 33.3 percent (= $130,000 ÷ $390,000). Sales are 33.3 percent of $650,000 and cost of goods sold is 33.3 percent of $390,000.

EXHIBIT 7.29

Arizona Land Development Company
Balance Sheets
Income Recognition Using Percentage-of-Completion Method
(Case 7.1)

	Year 1	Year 2	Year 3	Year 4	Year 5	Year 6
Assets						
Cash	$100,000	$132,500	$ 100,222	$ 126,631	$ 131,122	$ 273,720
Contracts in Process.	216,667[a]	570,834	1,200,001	2,287,501	3,150,001	3,845,834
Less Progress Billings	(130,000)[b]	(375,000)	(830,000)	(1,635,000)	(2,430,000)	(3,185,000)
Contracts in Process (net)	$ 86,667	$195,834	$ 370,001	$ 652,501	$ 720,001	$ 660,834
Land Inventory.	235,000	145,000	95,000	45,000	125,000	185,000
Total Assets.	$421,667	$473,334	$ 565,223	$ 824,132	$ 976,123	$1,119,554
Liabilities and Shareholders' Equity						
Deferred Income Taxes	$ 7,367	$ 24,934	$ 49,723	$ 86,532	$ 90,023	$ 76,154
Common Stock	400,000	400,000	400,000	500,000	500,000	500,000
Retained Earnings	14,300	48,400	115,500	237,600	386,100	543,400
Total Liabilities and						
Shareholders' Equity	$421,667	$473,334	$ 565,223	$ 824,132	$ 976,123	$1,119,554

[a]Accumulated costs of $130,000 + gross profit recognized in Year 1 of $86,667 (see Note a to Exhibit 7.28).
[b]Down payment of $65,000 received on January 1, Year 1, plus $65,000 installment payment received on December 31, Year 1.

	EXHIBIT 7.30					

Arizona Land Development Company
Statements of Cash Flows
Income Recognition Using Percentage-of-Completion Method
(Case 7.1)

	Year 1	Year 2	Year 3	Year 4	Year 5	Year 6
Operations						
Net Income.....................	$ 14,300	$ 34,100	$ 67,100	$122,100	$148,500	$157,300
(Inc.) Dec. in Contracts in Process....................	(216,667)	(354,167)	(629,167)	(1,087,500)	(862,500)	(695,833)
Inc. (Dec.) in Progress Billings.....................	130,000	245,000	455,000	805,000	795,000	755,000
(Inc.) Dec. in Land Inventory	65,000	90,000	50,000	50,000	(80,000)	(60,000)
Inc. (Dec.) in Deferred Income Taxes................	7,367	17,567	24,789	36,809	3,491	(13,869)
Cash Flow from Operations........	$ 0	$ 32,500	$(32,278)	$ (73,591)	$ 4,491	$142,598
Financing						
Common Stock Issued............	—	—	—	100,000	—	—
Change in Cash.................	$ 0	$ 32,500	$(32,278)	$ 26,409	$ 4,491	$142,598

Contracts in Process (net) minus (2) the difference in the Estimated Development Cost Liability minus (3) the difference in the Deferred Income Taxes Liability. What is the rationale behind this relation?

g. Why is the amount shown on the income statement for "current" income taxes the same in each year for all four income recognition methods but the amount of total income tax expenses (current plus deferred) in each year different across income recognition methods?

h. Given that net income each year differs across the four income recognition methods, why is the amount of cash provided by operations the same? Under what conditions would a firm report different amounts of cash flow from operations for different income recognition methods?

CASE 7.2

CHIRON CORPORATION—AN R&D PUZZLE

Chiron Corporation is in the human health care industry, applying genetic engineering and other tools of biotechnology to develop products that diagnose, prevent, and treat human diseases. Exhibit 7.31 presents an income statement for Chiron for Year 5, Year 6, and Year 7. Total revenues increased from $141 million in Year 5 to $318 million in Year 7, a 49.8 percent compound annual growth rate. Net income increased from a $445 million loss in Year 5 to a $18 million profit in Year 7. The ana-

EXHIBIT 7.31

Income Statement
Chiron Corporation
(amounts in thousands)
(Case 7.2)

	Year 7	Year 6	Year 5
Revenues			
Product Sales:			
Related Parties	$ 23,156	$ 11,801	$ 10,576
Unrelated Parties	124,737	99,779	40,696
	$147,893	$111,580	$ 51,272
Research Revenues:			
Related Parties	$ 54,552	$ 24,486	$ 18,331
Unrelated Parties	14,391	16,017	12,144
	$ 68,943	$ 40,503	$ 30,475
License Fees—Unrelated Parties	22,960	19,939	9,906
Equity in Earnings of Joint Ventures	77,739	74,238	49,845
Total Revenues	$317,535	$246,260	$ 141,498
Expenses			
Research and Development	$140,030	$142,265	$ 80,001
Cost of Goods Sold	68,484	54,692	28,423
Selling and Administrative Expenses	95,790	99,707	44,068
Write-off of In-process Technologies	—	—	442,484
Other Operating Expenses	(1,907)	7,499	2,287
Total Expenses	$302,397	$304,163	$ 597,263
Income (Loss) from Operations	$ 15,138	$(57,903)	$(455,765)
Interest Income	7,949	6,973	12,997
Income (Loss) Before Income Taxes	$ 23,087	$(50,930)	$(442,768)
Income Tax Expense	(4,703)	(4,024)	(1,882)
Net Income	$ 18,384	$(54,954)	$(444,650)

lyst encounters difficulties understanding the reasons for the increased profitability because of the following:

1. The company has grown both internally and through corporate acquisitions.
2. The company uses joint ventures and collaborative research agreements to develop and market new products.
3. Sales to related parties comprise 41 percent of total revenues in Year 5, 38 percent in Year 6, and 43 percent in Year 7.

The sectors below elaborate on these complicating factors.

Chiron operates in four major product markets:

1. Therapeutics—The product emphasis in this segment is oncology.
2. Ophthalmic Surgical—The two principal products in this segment are equipment for removing cataracts using ultrasound technology and intraocular lenses for cataract surgeries.
3. Diagnostics—The primary product for this market is a blood screening device for the Hepatitis C virus. The company is conducting research on applying DNA probe testing technologies to develop new diagnostic products.
4. Vaccines—This segment offers immunizations for adult and pediatric diseases.

THERAPEUTICS

The company's involvement in Therapeutics is through its wholly owned, consolidated subsidiary, Cetus Corporation (Cetus). Chiron acquired Cetus on December 28, Year 5, by exchanging shares of its common stock with a market value of $887.8 million. The acquisition was accounted for using the purchase method. Chiron restated the assets and liabilities of Cetus to their market values on December 28, Year 5. The difference between the $887.8 million purchase price and the market value of identifiable assets and liabilities was allocated as $442 million to in-process technologies and $44.8 million to base technologies. Amortization expense on the capitalized amount was $3.9 million in Year 6 and Year 7 and is included in other operating expenses in Exhibit 7.31. The amounts allocated to in-process and base technologies are not deductible for tax purposes. Under the purchase method used in this acquisition, Chiron recognizes the earnings of Cetus subsequent to the date of acquisition.

OPHTHALMIC SURGICAL

The company's involvement in Ophthalmic Surgical is through its wholly owned, consolidated subsidiary, Intra Optics. Chiron acquired Intra Optics on January 5, Year 6, by exchanging shares of its common stock. Chiron accounted for the acquisition using the pooling of interests method. Under a pooling of interests, the book values of Intra Optic's assets and liabilities carry over after the acquisition. The earnings of Chiron are retroactively restated to include the earnings of Intra Optics for all years presented.

DIAGNOSTICS

The company's involvement in Diagnostics is through a joint venture with Ortho Diagnostic Systems, a subsidiary of Johnson & Johnson. Chiron conducts research, development, and manufacturing for the Chiron/Ortho joint venture. The joint venture reimburses Chiron at cost for these services, which were as follows:

	Research and Development	Manufacturing
Year 5............................	$8.0	$ 9.3
Year 6............................	$9.2	$10.6
Year 7............................	$9.8	$11.3

Chiron's 50 percent share of the earnings of this joint venture totaled $49.8 million in Year 5, $73.6 million in Year 6, and $77.1 million in Year 7.

VACCINES

The company's involvement in Vaccines is through a joint venture with CIBA-GEIGY. Chiron conducts research, development, and manufacturing services for the Chiron/CIBA-GEIGY joint venture. The joint venture reimburses Chiron at cost for these services, which were as follows:

	Research and Development	Manufacturing
Year 5............................	$10.3	$ 1.3
Year 6............................	$15.3	$ 1.2
Year 7............................	$44.8	$11.9

Chiron's equity in the earnings of the Chiron/CIBA-GEIGY joint venture were zero in Year 5, $.638 million in Year 6, and $.639 million in Year 7.

Required

a. Recast the income statement of Chiron Corporation for Year 5, Year 6, and Year 7 into a format that enhances understanding of the changes in its profitability during the three-year period. Describe the rationale for your treatment of each of the following items:
   1. The appropriate measure of total revenues and the classification of its components.
   2. The measurement of research and development expense, particularly with respect to the treatment of cost-reimbursed research and development services, and the cost of in-process purchased technologies.

b. Identify the principal reasons for the changes in the profitability of Chiron during the three-year period.

CASE 7.3

CORPORÃCION INDUSTRIAL SANLUIS: COPING WITH CHANGING PRICES

Corporãcion Industrial Sanluis (Sanluis) is a leading conglomerate firm in Mexico. It derives revenues from the manufacture of auto parts (springs and drums), the mining of precious metals (gold and silver), and the provision of hotel services (owner of several Hyatt resort hotels). The manufacture of coils, springs, and metal drums accounts for approximately 75 percent of Sanluis' revenues. Sanluis is the first Mexican company to have its shares traded in the United States through American Depository Receipts.

Sanluis follows generally accepted accounting principles in Mexico to prepare its financial statements. Its Year 8 financial statements and notes are attached as Exhibit 7.32 (balance sheet), Exhibit 7.33 (statement of income), and Exhibit 7.34 (statement of changes in financial position). Excerpts from the notes to its financial statements appear below. This case examines financial disclosures in Mexico with respect to changing prices and assesses Sanluis' success in coping with inflation.

EXCERPTS FROM NOTES TO THE FINANCIAL STATEMENTS

Note 1: Accounting Policies
  a. The consolidated financial statements have been prepared in conformity with generally accepted accounting principles in Mexico and are stated in pesos of December 31, Year 8, purchasing power.
  b. Marketable Securities and other investments in shares are stated at market value.
  c. Inventories are stated at estimated replacement cost. Cost of goods sold is determined by the last-in, first-out (LIFO) method.
  d. Property, plant, and equipment are recorded at net replacement cost determined on the basis of appraisals made by independent experts registered at the National Securities Commission. Depreciation, amortization, and depletion are calculated by the straight-line method based on the estimated useful lives of the assets determined by the appraisers.
  e. The restatement of capital stock represents the amount necessary to maintain the shareholders' investment in terms of purchasing power at the balance sheet date, and is determined by applying to the historical amounts factors derived from the National Consumer Price Index (NCPI).
  f. Retained Earnings is expressed in pesos of purchasing power as of the latest balance sheet date and is determined by applying to the historical amounts factors derived from the NCPI.
  g. The gain on net monetary position represents the effect of inflation, as measured by NCPI, on the company's monthly net monetary assets and liabilities during the year, restated in pesos of purchasing power as of the end of the most recent period.

EXHIBIT 7.32

Corporãcion Industrial Sanluis, S.A. DE C.V. and Subsidiaries
Consolidated Balance Sheet
(in thousands of constant December 31, Year 8 Mexican Pesos)
(Case 7.3)

	December 31	
	Year 8	Year 7
Assets		
Cash and Short-term Investment	P 219,490	P 177,670
Accounts Receivable	79,866	82,017
Inventories.	64,075	68,027
Prepayments	9,856	2,282
Total Current Assets	P 373,287	P 329,996
Property, Plant, and Equipment	P 810,026	P 854,628
Accumulated Depreciation	(240,632)	(294,622)
Total Property, Plant, and Equipment	P 569,394	P 560,006
Other Assets	P 28,395	P 27,193
Total Assets	P 971,076	P 917,195
Liabilities and Shareholders' Equity		
Bank Loans	P 308,323	P 195,090
Accounts Payable.	56,639	37,115
Accrued Liabilities.	38,960	27,275
Total Current Liabilities	P 403,922	P 259,480
Long-term Debt	125,957	184,993
Total Liabilities.	P 529,879	P 444,473
Preferred Stock—Nominal Value	P 59,796	P 59,796
Restatement Increase.	7,134	7,134
	P 66,930	P 66,930
Common Stock—Nominal Value.	P 15,000	P 15,000
Restatement Increase.	188,902	188,902
	P 203,902	P 203,902
Other Equity Accounts—Nominal Value	P 17,301	P 27,702
Restatement Increase.	62,725	58,729
	P 80,026	P 86,431
Retained Earnings—Nominal Value.	P 317,505	P 278,492
Restatement Increase.	830,050	851,497
	P 1,147,555	P 1,129,989
Deficit in the Restatement of Capital	P(1,057,216)	P(1,014,530)
Total Shareholders' Equity	P 441,197	P 472,722
Total Liabilities and Shareholders' Equity	P 971,076	P 917,195

EXHIBIT 7.33

Corporācion Industrial Sanluis, S.A. DE C.V. and Subsidiaries
Consolidated Statement of Income
(in thousands of constant December 31, Year 8 Mexican Pesos)
(Case 7.3)

	Year 8	Year 7
Sales	P429,471	P411,213
Cost of Goods Sold	(334,198)	(327,489)
Depreciation and Depletion	(21,032)	(17,924)
Gross Profit	P 74,241	P 65,800
Distribution and Selling Expenses.	(11,806)	(13,470)
General and Administrative Expenses.	(29,100)	(36,355)
Exploration and Development Expenses	(1,320)	(2,364)
Operating Profit.	P 32,015	P 13,611
Interest Expense—Net.	(19,536)	(18,733)
Exchange Loss—Net	(7,514)	(16,540)
Gain on Net Monetary Position	19,481	29,263
Other Income—Net.	3,463	8,390
Income from Continuing Operations Before Tax		
and Statutory Employee Profit Sharing	P 27,909	P 15,991
Taxes and Statutory Employee Profit Sharing.	(10,343)	(8,656)
Income from Continuing Operations.	P 17,566	P 7,335

EXHIBIT 7.34

Corporācion Industrial Sanluis, S.A. DE C.V. and Subsidiaries
Consolidated Statement of Changes in Financial Position
(in thousands of constant December 31, Year 8 Mexican Pesos)
(Case 7.3)

	Year 8	Year 7
Operations		
Income from Continuing Operations.	P17,566	P 7,335
Depreciation and Depletion	21,032	17,925
Variation in Current Assets	17,631	3,642
Resources Provided by Operations.	P56,229	P 28,902
Financing		
Increase in Capital Stock	P —	P 66,930
Bank Loans—Net.	53,104	(15,643)
Resources Provided by Financing.	P53,104	P 51,287

Exhibit 7.34—continued	Year 8	Year 7
Investing		
(Acquisition) Sale of Subsidiaries	P (9,963)	P 16,590
Acquisition of Property, Plant, and Equipment		
(net).	(57,550)	(63,965)
Resources Used for Investing	P (67,513)	P (47,375)
Increase in Cash and Short-term Investments	P 41,820	P 32,814
Cash and Short-term Investments at Beginning		
of Year	177,670	144,856
Cash and Short-term Investments at End of Year. . .	P219,490	P177,670

h. The gain or loss from holding nonmonetary assets represents the amount by which the increases in the values of nonmonetary assets exceeds or falls short of the inflation rate measured in terms of the NCPI, and is included in the deficit in the restatement of capital.

Required

a. Which of the methods of accounting for changing prices discussed in Appendix 7.1 does Sanluis apparently use? Indicate the clues supporting your conclusion.

b. Prepare a balance sheet for Sanluis as of December 31, Year 8, under each of the three methodologies indicated in the columns below. Aggregate individual assets in preparing this analysis. You should begin with liabilities and shareholders' equity and work backwards toward total assets.

	Historical Cost/ Nominal Pesos	Historical Cost/ Constant Pesos	Current Cost/ Constant Pesos
Assets			
Liabilities			
Preferred Stock.			
Common Stock			
Other Equity Accounts . . .			
Retained Earnings			
Deficit in Restatement of			
Capital.			
Total Equities			

c. What is the likely explanation for Sanluis' recognition of a purchasing power gain on its monetary items during Year 8?

d. Did Sanluis experience a holding gain or a holding loss on its nonmonetary items (that is, inventories, fixed assets) during Year 8? What is the interpretation of this gain or loss?

e. How well has Sanluis coped with changing prices during Year 7 and Year 8? Note: Mexico's consumer price index increased 18.8 percent in Year 7 and 11.9 percent in Year 8.

CASE 7.4

AMERICA ONLINE: PAST REPORTING VINDICATED?

America Online, Inc. (AOL) is currently the world's largest Internet service provider. At the time of the merger of AOL and Time Warner in Year 11, AOL had one of the largest subscriber bases in the world. Over 40 million individuals subscribed to AOL in a recent year, and the firm continually adjusts its strategic plan in an attempt to reach even a larger set of Internet users. Synergies with Time Warner, such as exclusive access to the film and television content of the Time Warner libraries, and bandwidth benefits provided by the extensive cable system of Time Warner for Internet access and content delivery, garner tremendous advantages to AOL over its competitors. The industry is a competitive one, however, and it is unclear whether AOL can continue to dominate in the future.

AOL subscriptions grew at a tremendous pace in its early years of existence. After only five fully operational years, AOL subscribers reached 8 million, making the firm substantially larger than any of its direct competitors. By end of Year 7, AOL reached its goal of 10 million subscribers worldwide.

PRICING POLICY

AOL's main source of revenue is on-line Internet service fees generated through customer subscriptions. In its early years of existence, AOL generated revenues from subscribers paying both (1) a monthly membership fee and (2) hourly charges based on usage in excess of the number of hours of usage provided as part of the monthly fee. In the last quarter of Year 6, however, AOL launched its unlimited-use pricing policy. During the quarter ended December 31, Year 6, both AOL membership and system usage showed record growth. Membership climbed 1.2 million to a total 7.8 million with a record 546,000 new members added in December alone. This included 7.4 million members in North America and approximately 400,000 in Europe.

Industry analysts praised AOL's move to flat-rate pricing, but the move also caused the company major problems. The network became so crowded that users were blocked from dialing in because there weren't enough open lines. State regulatory officials who had complained to AOL on behalf of their customers reached a settlement whereby AOL agreed to give customer refunds.

As part of the settlement, AOL also said it would sharply reduce marketing and advertising efforts, temporarily scale back its efforts to attract new members, and, for the time being, stop airing its television advertising as well as sharply reduce the distribution of free trial disks.

On January 16, Year 7, AOL announced that membership in its on-line Internet network has surpassed 8 million and also said it would increase investment in system expansion to address the extraordinary demand for its service. The increased investment in system expansion included increasing its previously announced investment to expand system capacity from $250 million to $350 million, increasing the current total of 200,000-plus modems by 75 percent to improve connectivity, and promoting and supporting alternative ways to get AOL through work or school connections.

But only months after a national controversy about its jammed networks, AOL started to recruit members again. Word of AOL's plans came from Chief Executive Steve Case in his April, Year 7, monthly letter to subscribers. On September 2, Year 7, AOL announced the company had more than 9 million subscribers worldwide, including more than 400,000 net new members since the quarter ending June 30.

KEY FINANCIAL REPORTING POLICIES

The financial statements of AOL are presented in Exhibits 7.35, 7.36, and 7.37. The statements presented are prior to the merger of AOL and Time Warner, which took place in Year 11.

As Exhibit 7.38 illustrates, total revenues grew along with AOL's membership. AOL's total revenues increased from $115.7 million in Year 4 to $394.3 million in Year 5, or a 241 percent growth. The increase was primarily attributable to a 233 percent increase in the number of AOL subscribers, which contributed 250 percent growth of on-line service revenues. For fiscal Year 6, total revenues increased to $1.1 billion, or 177 percent over fiscal Year 5. On-line service revenues increased 188 percent to $991.7 million, which was primarily attributable to 93 percent growth in the number of AOL subscribers. For Year 7, on-line service revenues increased to $1.4 billion, or 44 percent over Year 6. This increase was primarily attributable to a 53 percent increase in the quarterly average number of AOL North American subscribers for Year 7. Total revenues in Year 7 were $1.7 billion, or 54 percent over Year 6.

As Exhibit 7.39 illustrates, AOL's total assets increased from $155.2 million in Year 4 to $405.4 million in Year 5, a 161 percent growth. In Year 6, the company's total assets increased to $958.8 million, or 136 percent over Year 5. Due to the $385.2 million write-off of Deferred Subscriber Acquisition Costs in Year 7, AOL's total assets decreased to $846.7 million, a 12 percent decrease compared to Year 6.

Two categories of AOL costs are central to analyzing the quality of the accounting information provided by AOL during this period: product development costs and deferred subscriber acquisition costs.

EXHIBIT 7.35

AOL, Inc.
Comparative Balance Sheets
(amounts in thousands)
(Case 7.4)
June 30

	Year 3	Year 4	Year 5	Year 6	Year 7
Assets					
Cash	$ 9,224	$ 43,891	$ 45,877	$118,421	$124,340
Short-term Investments	5,105	24,052	18,672	10,712	268
Accounts Receivable	2,861	10,583	43,557	72,613	91,399
Other Current Assets	1,723	5,753	25,527	68,832	107,466
Total Current Assets..............	$18,913	$ 84,279	$133,633	$270,578	$323,473
Property, Plant, and Equipment (net)	2,402	20,306	70,919	101,277	233,129
Product Development Costs (net)	3,915	7,912	18,949	44,330	72,498
Deferred Subscriber Acquisition (net)....	6,890	26,392	77,229	314,181	
Goodwill			54,356	51,691	41,783
Other Assets	282	15,695	50,327	176,697	175,805
Total Assets......................	$32,402	$154,584	$405,413	$958,754	$846,688
Liabilities and Shareholders' Equity					
Accounts Payable	$ 3,766	$ 15,642	$ 84,640	$105,904	$ 69,703
Short-term Debt....................		2,287	2,329	2,435	1,454
Other Current Liabilities	4,851	18,460	46,393	181,567	483,313
Total Current Liabilities............	$ 8,617	$ 36,389	$133,362	$289,906	$554,470
Long-term Debt		7,015	17,369	19,306	50,000
Other Noncurrent Liabilities		12,883	37,870	137,040	114,184
Total Liabilities..................	$ 8,617	$ 56,287	$188,601	$446,252	$718,654
Common Stock.....................	$ 59	$ 308	$ 767	$ 926	$ 1,002
Preferred Stock				1	1
Unrealized Gain on Available-for-Sale Securities					16,924
Additional Paid-in Capital	22,652	98,836	252,668	519,342	617,221
Accumulated Deficit.................	1,074	(847)	(36,623)	(7,767)	(507,114)
Total Shareholders' Equity..........	$23,785	$ 98,297	$216,812	$512,502	$128,034
Total Liabilities and Shareholders' Equity......................	$32,402	$154,584	$405,413	$958,754	$846,688

		EXHIBIT 7.36			

AOL, Inc.
Comparative Income Statements
(amounts in thousands)
(Case 7.4)

			Year Ended June 30		
	Year 3	Year 4	Year 5	Year 6	Year 7
On-line Service Revenues	$37,648	$ 98,497	$344,309	$991,656	$1,429,445
Other Revenues	14,336	17,225	49,981	102,198	255,783
Total Revenues	$51,984	$115,722	$394,290	$1,093,854	$1,685,228
Cost of Revenues	28,820	69,043	229,724	627,372	1,040,762
Marketing Expenses	9,745	23,548	77,064	212,710	409,260
Write-off Deferred Subscriber					
Acquisition Costs					385,221
Product Development Expenses	2,913	5,288	14,263	53,817	58,208
Administrative Expenses	8,581	13,667	42,700	110,653	193,537
Acquired Research & Development . . .			50,335	16,981	
Amortization of Goodwill			1,653	7,078	6,549
Restructuring Charge					48,627
Contract Termination Charge					24,506
Settlement Charge					24,204
Total Costs and Expenses	$50,059	$111,546	$415,739	$1,028,611	$2,190,874
Income (loss) from Operations	$ 1,925	$ 4,176	$(21,449)	$ 65,243	$ (505,646)
Other Income (Expense), net	371	1,810	3,074	(2,056)	6,299
Merger Expenses			(2,207)	(848)	
Income (loss) Before Income Taxes . . .	$ 2,296	$ 5,986	$(20,582)	$ 62,339	$ (499,347)
Income Tax Expense	(764)	(3,832)	(15,169)	(32,523)	
Net Income (loss)	$ 1,532	$ 2,154	$(35,751)	$ 29,816	$ (499,347)

PRODUCT DEVELOPMENT COST

AOL capitalizes costs incurred for the production of computer software used in the sale of its services as Product Development Costs. Costs capitalized include direct labor and related overhead for software produced by the company, and the costs of software purchased from third parties. All costs in the software development process that are classified as research and development are expensed as incurred until technological feasibility has been established. Once technological feasibility has been established, such costs are capitalized until the software is commercially available.

Amortization is provided on a product-by-product basis, using the greater of the straight-line method or current year revenue as a percent of total revenue estimates

EXHIBIT 7.37

AOL, Inc.
Comparative Statements of Cash flows
(amounts in thousands)
(Case 7.4)

	Year Ended June 30				
	Year 3	Year 4	Year 5	Year 6	Year 7
Cash Flows from Operating Activities					
Net Income (loss)............................	$ 1,532	$ 2,154	$(35,751)	$ 29,816	$(499,347)
Write-off of Deferred Subscriber Acquisition Costs					$ 385,221
Non-cash Restructuring Charges...............					$ 22,478
Depreciation and Amortization................	1,957	2,822	12,266	33,366	64,572
Amortization of Subscriber Acquisition Costs	7,038	17,922	60,924	126,072	59,189
Loss (gain) on Sale of Property and Equipment...	(39)	5	37	44	
Charge of Acquired Research and Development...			50,335	16,981	
Changes in Assets and Liabilities:					
Accounts Receivable	(1,902)	(4,892)	(23,459)	(28,728)	(14,335)
Other Current Assets	(1,494)	(2,873)	(19,635)	(43,305)	(44,394)
Deferred Subscriber Acquisition Costs........	(10,685)	(37,424)	(111,761)	(363,024)	(130,229)
Accounts Payable	2,119	10,224	60,805	21,150	(36,944)
Other Current Liabilities	3,209	12,193	14,787	135,316	356,210
Other Assets and Liabilities	470	1,290	8,712	5,585	(39,372)
Net Cash (used in) Provided by Operating Activities	$ 2,205	$ 1,421	$ 17,260	$(66,727)	$ 123,049
Cash Flows from Investing Activities:					
Short-term Investments......................	$(5,105)	$(18,947)	$ 5,380	$ 7,960	$ 10,444
Purchase of Property and Equipment...........	(2,041)	(18,010)	(59,255)	(50,262)	(149,768)
Product Development Costs	(1,831)	(5,131)	(13,054)	(32,631)	(56,795)
Sale of Property and Equipment...............	62	95	180		
Purchase of Acquired Businesses..............			(20,523)	(4,133)	(475)
Net Cash Used in Investing Activities	$(8,915)	$(41,993)	$(87,272)	$(79,066)	$(196,594)
Cash Flows from Financing Activities:					
Proceeds from Issuance of Common Stock, net ...	$ 609	$ 68,120	$ 61,721	$189,359	$ 84,506
Proceeds from Issuance of Preferred Stock, net ...				28,315	
Proceeds from Issuance of Preferred Stock of Subsidiary.............................					15,000
Increases in Borrowings.....................	7,187	14,260	13,488	3,000	50,000
Restricted Cash					(50,000)
Decrease in Borrowings.....................	(7,036)	(7,878)	(3,413)	(2,337)	(20,042)
Net Cash Provided by Financing Activities.......	$ 760	$ 74,502	$ 71,796	$218,337	$ 79,464
Net Increase in Cash and Cash Equivalents	$(5,950)	$ 33,930	$ 1,784	$ 72,544	$ 5,919
Cash and Cash Equivalents at the Beginning of Year.................................	16,113	10,163	44,093	45,877	118,421
Cash and Cash Equivalents at the End of Year	$10,163	$ 44,093	$ 45,877	$118,421	$ 124,340

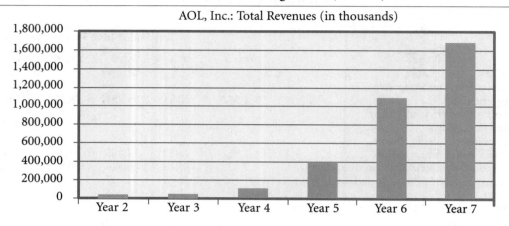

EXHIBIT 7.38

AOL, Inc.
Total Revenues, Year 2 through Year 7 (Case 7.4)

AOL, Inc.: Total Revenues (in thousands)

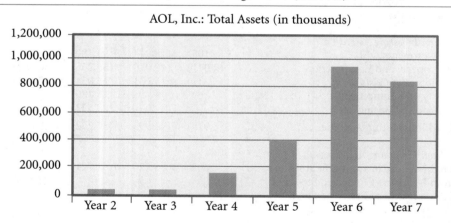

EXHIBIT 7.39

AOL, Inc.
Total Assets, Year 2 through Year 7 (Case 7.4)

AOL, Inc.: Total Assets (in thousands)

for the related software product, not to exceed five years, commencing the month after the date of product release.

DEFERRED SUBSCRIBER ACQUISITION COSTS

AOL expenses the costs of advertising as incurred, except direct response advertising, which is classified as Deferred Subscriber Acquisition Costs. Direct response advertising consists solely of the costs of marketing programs that result in subscriber registrations without further effort required by the company. These costs, which relate directly to subscriber solicitations, principally include the printing, production, and shipping of starter kits, and the costs of obtaining qualified prospects by various targeted direct marketing programs and from third parties.

The deferred costs are amortized, beginning the month after such costs are incurred, over a period determined by calculating the ratio of current revenues related to direct response advertising versus the total expected revenues related to this advertising, or twenty-four months, whichever is shorter. All other costs related to the acquisition of subscribers, as well as general marketing costs, are expensed as incurred.

In the first quarter of Year 7, AOL's practice of capitalizing and writing off the Subscriber Acquisition Costs over two years was abandoned. The effect of the decision was to eliminate Deferred Subscriber Acquisition Costs on the balance sheet, and charge the full amount to the income statement. Deferred Subscriber Acquisition Costs was $314,181,000 at the end of AOL's fiscal Year 6 (see Exhibit 7.35). As the result of capitalizing and amortizing subscriber acquisition costs during the first quarter of Year 7, before the company abandoned the practice, Deferred Subscriber Acquisition Costs increased to $385,221,000. That is the write-off amount shown on AOL's income statement for Year 7 (see Exhibit 7.36).

AOL presents the following logic in its Year 7 financial statements for changing the practice:

> As a result of a change in accounting estimate, the Company recorded a charge of $385,221,000 ($4.03 per share), as of September 30, Year 6 (that is, in the first quarter of Year 7), representing the balance of deferred subscriber acquisition costs of that date. The company previously had deferred the cost of certain marketing activities, to comply with the criteria of Statement of Position 93-7, "Reporting on Advertising Costs," and then amortized those costs over a period determined by calculating the ratio of current revenues related to direct response advertising versus the total expected revenues related to this advertising, or twenty-four months, whichever was shorter. The company's changing business model, which includes flat-rate pricing for its on-line service, increasingly is expected to reduce its reliance on on-line service subscriber revenues for the generation of revenues and profits. This changing business model, coupled with a lack of historical experience with flat-rate pricing, created uncertainties regarding the level of expected future economic benefits from on-line service subscriber revenues. As a result, the

company believed it no longer had an adequate accounting basis to support recognizing deferred subscriber acquisition costs as an asset.

Required

a. Prepare an analysis that accounts for the change in the Deferred Subscriber Acquisition Costs account on the balance sheet for each of the fiscal years from Year 4 through Year 7 by using Amortization of Subscriber Acquisition Costs and Deferred Subscriber Acquisition Costs accounts from the Statements of Cash Flows.

b. Compare the Subscriber Acquisition Costs amortized from part a with total Marketing Expenses on the Income Statement. Calculate the percentage that this amortization bears to total Marketing Expenses for each of the fiscal years from Year 3 to Year 7.

c. Prepare an analysis of the change in the Product Development Costs on the Balance Sheet account for each of the fiscal years from Year 4 to Year 7, given that the costs capitalized were $5,131,000, $13,054,000, $32,735,000, and $55,363,000, respectively, and cost amortized were $1,134,000, $2,017,000, $7,354,000, and $27,195,000, respectively.

d. Compare Amortization of Product Development Costs with Total Product Development Expenses in the Income Statement. Calculate the percentage that amortization bears to Total Product Development Expenses for each of the fiscal years from Year 3 to Year 7.

e. Recompute the Income (Loss) from Operations in the Income Statements for AOL for each of the fiscal years Year 4 to Year 7 assuming that (a) the company expensed Subscriber Acquisition Costs and Product Development Costs in the year incurred instead of capitalizing, then amortizing the costs, or (b) excludes Acquired Research & Development Costs and the Write-off of Subscriber Acquisition Costs from the Income from Operations because of its materiality and nonrecurring nature.

f. In May, Year 10, eight months prior to the merger of AOL and Time Warner, AOL was fined $3.5 million by the Securities and Exchange Commission to settle charges that it mislead investors by following the policy of capitalizing and amortizing subscriber acquisition costs. Comment on both the (1) timing of the settlement and (2) SEC requirement that AOL restate earnings during the periods that the firm capitalized subscriber acquisition costs.

Chapter 8

LIABILITY RECOGNITION AND RELATED EXPENSES

Learning Objectives

1. Review the criteria for the recognition of an accounting liability and apply these criteria to various obligations of a firm, including financing arrangements structured to keep debt off of the balance sheet.

2. Understand the effects of the operating and capital lease methods on the financial statements and the adjustments required to convert operating leases to capital leases.

3. Understand the use of derivative financial instruments for hedging risks and the effects of fair value hedges and cash flow hedges on the financial statements.

4. Understand the relation between the accounting records of the sponsoring employer of a pension or other retirement plan and the accounting records of the plan itself, and the reasons for differences between the two sets of records. Adjust the financial statements of the sponsoring employer to incorporate information from the accounting records of the retirement plan with respect to any unrecognized obligation.

5. Review the reasons for differences between the book values of assets and liabilities for financial reporting and their tax basis, and the effect of such differences on the measurement of income tax expense.

6. Use information in the financial statement note on income taxes to identify reasons for changes in the income tax burden of a firm.

7. Understand the various uses of reserve accounts and their potential for managing earnings over time.

This chapter discusses the accounting for liabilities and related expenses commonly encountered in corporate annual reports. The recognition and valuation of liabilities affect the analysis of financial statements in two important ways:

1. Profitability Analysis

Firms use, or consume, various goods (for example, inventories) and services (for example, employees' labor services) during a period in generating revenues for which they may not make cash payments until future periods. Also, firms promise to provide goods or perform services in the future related to revenues recognized during the current period (for example, under warranty plans). The cost of these goods and services that the firm has already consumed or will consume in the future is an expense of the current period. Effective analysis of profitability requires that the analyst assess whether the firm has measured these expenses properly.

2. Risk Analysis

The amount shown on the balance sheet for liabilities indicates the present value of the cash or other assets that the firm will need to discharge obligations coming due within the next year (current liabilities) and after one year (noncurrent liabilities). A firm with inadequate resources to satisfy these obligations runs the risk of insolvency or even bankruptcy. Effective analysis of risk requires the analyst to assess whether the firm has recognized and measured its liabilities properly. Recognition issues are particularly important because many firms engage in transactions that create financial risk but do not recognize a liability on the balance sheet for such risks. In fact, GAAP stipulates that the firm not recognize a liability in some cases.

This chapter discusses the concept of an accounting liability and the application of GAAP to various obligations commonly encountered in corporate financial statements, including (1) leases, (2) derivatives, (3) pension and other retirement benefits, and (4) income taxes. We continue our focus on how a firm's choice of accounting methods and the way it implements them affect its *accounting quality*, its *earnings quality* and its *balance sheet quality*, topics introduced in Chapter 6. A starting point for assessing accounting quality is to understand GAAP's required accounting for a particular transaction. This chapter describes and illustrates GAAP for each of the topics listed above. When the reported amounts for liabilities do not adequately include the economic risks assumed by a firm, the analyst should adjust the reported amounts to enhance the economic information content of the financial statements.

PRINCIPLES OF LIABILITY RECOGNITION

Financial reporting recognizes an obligation as a liability if it satisfies three criteria:[1]

1. The obligation involves a probable future sacrifice of resources—a future transfer of cash, goods, or services, or the foregoing of a future cash receipt—

---

[1]Financial Accounting Standards Board, *Statement of Financial Accounting Standards No. 6*, "Element of Financial Statement," 1985.

at a specified or determinable date. The firm can measure with reasonable precision the cash equivalent value of the resources needed to satisfy the obligation.

2. The firm has little or no discretion to avoid the transfer.
3. The transaction or event that gave rise to the obligation has already occurred.

PRINCIPLES OF LIABILITY VALUATION

The general principles underlying the valuation of liabilities are as follows:

1. Liabilities requiring future cash payments (for example, bonds payable) appear at the present value of the required future cash flows discounted at an interest rate that reflects the uncertainty that the firm will be able to make these cash payments. The firm establishes the discount rate at the time it initially records a liability in the accounts (often referred to as the *historical interest rate*) and uses this interest rate in accounting for the liability in all future periods.

   An exception to using the historical interest rate involves liabilities for which firms have hedged interest or foreign exchange risk. A later section of this chapter indicates that firms in these cases report the liability and the related hedge instrument at the present value of the cash flows using the current market interest rate. For some liabilities due within the next year (for example, accounts payable, income taxes payable, salaries payable), the difference between the amount of the future cash flows and their present value is sufficiently small that accounting ignores the discounting process and reports the liabilities at the amounts ultimately payable.

2. Liabilities requiring the future delivery of goods or services (for example, warranties payable) appear at the estimated cost of those goods and services.

3. Liabilities representing advances from customers (for example, Rental Fees Received in Advance, Subscription Fees Received in Advance) appear at the amount of the cash advance.

The current market value of a liability may differ from the amount appearing on the balance sheet, particularly for long-term debt. The current market value will reflect current interest rates and assessments of the firm's ability to make the required payments. GAAP requires firms to disclose the fair value of financial instruments, whether or not these financial instruments appear as liabilities (or assets) on the balance sheet.[2]

---

[2]Financial Accounting Standards Board, *Statement of Financial Accounting Standards No. 107,* "Disclosures about Fair Value of Financial Instruments," 1991.

APPLICATION OF CRITERIA FOR LIABILITY RECOGNITION

The criteria for liability recognition may appear straightforward and subject to unambiguous interpretation. Unfortunately, this is not so. Various obligations of an enterprise fall along a continuum with respect to how well they satisfy these criteria. Exhibit 8.1 classifies obligations into six groups. The following sections discuss each of these groups.

Obligations with Fixed Payment Dates and Amounts

The obligations that most clearly satisfy the liability recognition criteria are those with fixed payment dates and amounts (usually set by contract). Most obligations arising from borrowing arrangements fall into this category. A firm receives the benefit of having funds available for its use. The borrowing agreement specifies the timing and amount of interest and principal payments.

EXHIBIT 8.1
Classification of Accounting Liabilities by Degree of Certainty

Obligations with Fixed Payment Dates and Amounts	Obligations with Fixed Payment Amounts but Estimated Payment Dates	Obligations for Which the Firm Must Estimate Both Timing and Amount of Payment	Obligations Arising from Advances from Customers on Unexecuted Contracts and Agreements	Obligations Under Mutually Unexecuted Contracts	Contingent Obligations
Notes Payable Interest Payable Bonds Payable	Accounts Payable Salaries Payable Taxes Payable	Warranties Payable	Rental Fees Received in Advance Subscription Fees Received in Advance	Purchase Commitments Employment Commitments	Unsettled Lawsuits[a] Financial Instruments with Off-Balance Sheet Risk[a]

Most Certain ⟵――――――――――――――――――――――――――⟶ Least Certain

⟵―――― Recognized as Accounting Liabilities ――――⟶   ⟵―― Not Generally Recognized as ――⟶ Accounting Liabilities

[a]If an obligation meets certain criteria for a loss contingency, firms must recognize this obligation as a liability. See the discussion later in this chapter.

Obligations with Fixed Payment Amounts but Estimated Payment Dates

Most current liabilities fall into this category. Either oral agreements, written agreements, or legal statutes fix the amounts payable to suppliers, employees, and governmental agencies. Firms normally settle these obligations within a few months after incurring them. The firm can estimate the settlement date with sufficient accuracy to warrant recognizing a liability.

Obligations with Estimated Payment Dates and Amounts

Obligations in this group require estimation because the firm cannot identify the specific future recipients of cash, goods, or services at the time the obligation becomes a liability. In addition, the firm cannot compute precisely the amount of resources it will transfer in the future. For example, when a firm sells products under a warranty agreement, it promises to replace defective parts or perform certain repair services for a specified period of time. At the time of sale, the firm can neither identify the specific customers who will receive warranty benefits nor ascertain the amounts of their claims. Past experience, however, often provides the necessary information for estimating the likely proportion of customers who will make claims and the probable average amount of their claims. As long as the firm can estimate the probable amount of the obligation, it satisfies the first criterion for a liability. The selling price of goods sold under warranty includes an explicit or implicit charge for the warranty services. Thus, the receipt of cash or the right to receive cash in the sales transaction benefits the firm and creates the warranty liability.

Obligations Arising from Advances from Customers on Unexecuted Contracts and Agreements

A firm sometimes receives cash from customers in advance for goods or services it will provide in a future period. For example, a rental firm may receive cash in advance of the rental period on rental property. A magazine publisher may receive subscription fees in advance of the subscription period. Organizations and associations may receive membership dues prior to the membership period. These firms could recognize revenue upon the receipt of cash, as with the sale of products under warranty plans. In the case of advances from customers, however, all of the required transfer of resources (goods or services) will occur in the future. Revenue recognition generally requires that the firm deliver the goods or provide the services. Thus, the receipt of cash in advance creates a liability equal to the cash received. The firm might conceivably recognize a liability equal to the expected cost of delivering the promised goods or services, but doing so would result in recognizing the profit from the transaction before substantial performance had occurred.

Obligations Under Mutually Unexecuted Contracts

Mutually unexecuted contracts arise when two entities agree to make a transfer of resources but *neither* entity has yet made a transfer. For example, a firm may agree to purchase from its suppliers specified amounts of merchandise over the next two years. A baseball organization may agree to pay its "franchise" player a certain sum as compensation for services the player will render over the next five years. A bank may agree to provide lines of credit to its business customers in the event that these firms need funds in the future. Both parties have exchanged promises but neither party has transferred resources. Thus, no accounting liability arises at the time of the exchange of promises. A liability arises only when one party or the other transfers resources in the future. This category of obligation, called executory contracts, differs from the preceding two, where the contracts or agreements are partially executed. With warranty agreements, a firm received cash but has not fulfilled its warranty obligation. With rental, subscription, and membership fees, a firm receives cash but has not provided the required goods or services.

GAAP generally does not require firms to recognize obligations under mutually unexecuted contracts as accounting liabilities (exceptions occur for some leasing arrangements and for derivatives, discussed later in this chapter). If the amounts involved are material, the firm must disclose the nature of the obligation and its amount in notes to the financial statements. The analyst might conclude, however, that these obligations create sufficient risk for the firm to justify adjusting the reported financial statements to include such obligations.

Contingent Obligations

An event whose outcome today is unknown may create an obligation for the future transfer of resources. For example, a firm may be a defendant in a lawsuit, the outcome of which depends on the results of legal proceedings. The obligation is *contingent* on future events.

Contingent obligations may or may not give rise to accounting liabilities. Financial reporting requires firms to recognize an estimated loss from a contingency (called a *loss contingency*) and a related liability only if both of the following conditions are met:

1. Information available prior to the issuance of the financial statements indicates that it is probable that an asset has been impaired or that a liability has been incurred.
2. The firm can estimate the amount of the loss with reasonable precision.[3]

The first criterion for recognition of a loss contingency rests on the probability, or likelihood, that an asset has been impaired or a liability has been incurred. Financial reporting does not provide clear guidance as to what probability cutoff defines *likely* or *probable*. The FASB has stated that "probable is used with its usual general meaning, rather than in a specific accounting or technical sense, and refers to that which can be expected or believed on the basis of available evidence or logic but is neither certain or proved."[4]

---

[3]Financial Accounting Standards Board, *Statement of Financial Accounting Standards No. 5*, "Accounting for Contingencies," 1975.
[4]Financial Accounting Standards Board, *Statement of Financial Accounting Concepts No. 6*, "Elements of Financial Statements," 1985. Although the FASB has not defined *probable*, practice demands that firms and auditors define it. Currently, most firms and auditors appear to use *probable* to mean 80 to 85 percent or larger.

The second criterion requires reasonable estimation of the amount of the loss. Again, financial reporting does not define *reasonably estimated* in precise terms. Instead, if the firm can narrow the amount of the loss to a reasonable range, however large, financial reporting presumes that the firm has achieved sufficient precision to justify recognition of a liability. The amount of the loss is the most likely estimate within the range. If no amount within the range is more likely than any other, then the firm should use the amount at the lower end of the range.

Financial reporting refers to obligations meeting both of these two criteria as *loss contingencies*. One example suggested by the FASB relates to a toy manufacturer that sold toys later found to present a safety hazard. The toy manufacturer concludes that the likelihood of having to pay damages is high. The firm meets the second criterion if experience or other information enables the manufacturer to make a reasonable estimate of the loss. The toy manufacturer recognizes a loss and a liability in this case. As another example, firms in the tobacco and environmentally sensitive industries grapple with measuring loss contingencies related to litigation, and draw on lawyers and others to facilitate quantifying the loss.

Closely related to the concept of a loss contingency is a *guarantee*. For example, one firm may guarantee the repayment of another entity's borrowing in the event the other entity cannot repay the loan at maturity. As another example, a firm may sell a portion of its accounts receivable to another entity, promising to reimburse the other entity if uncollectible accounts exceed a specified amount. The need to make a future cash payment is contingent on future events. GAAP requires firms to recognize the market value of the guarantee as a liability.[5] Measuring this market value involves estimating the likelihood, timing, and amount that might become payable. However, a guarantee can have a market value even when the likelihood of making a future payment is low. A guarantee by a financially strong firm of a financially weaker firm's debt will reduce the weaker firm's cost of borrowing. The guarantor recognizes a receivable and a liability for the market value of the benefit granted to the borrower by the grantor. The obligation to reimburse a purchaser of accounts receivable for excess uncollectibles likely increases the amount the buyer pays the seller for the receivables. Recognizing the market value of this guarantee as a liability affects the amount of gain or loss the seller recognizes on the sale of the receivables. In addition to recognizing the market value of guarantees as liabilities, firms must disclose the maximum amount that could become payable and any available collateral that the guarantor could recover in the event it must execute the guarantee.

PepsiCo discloses the following in Note 13:

> We have unconditionally guaranteed $2.3 billion of Bottling Group, LLC's long-term debt. The guarantee had a fair value of $59 million at December 29, Year 11, and $66 million at December 30, Year 10, based on market rates.

---

[5]Financial Accounting Standards Board, *Interpretation No. 45*, "Guarantor's Accounting and Disclosure Requirements for Guarantees, Including Indirect Indebtedness of Others," 2002.

In Note 20, PepsiCo states:

> Contingent liabilities primarily reflect guarantees to support financial arrangements of certain unconsolidated affiliates, including the unconditional guarantee for $2.3 billion of Bottling Group, LLC's long-term debt. We believe that the ultimate liability, if any, in excess of amounts already recognized arising from such claims or contingencies is not likely to have a material adverse effect on our results of operations, financial condition, or liquidity.

The amount "already recognized" is $59 million on December 29, Year 11, and $66 million on December 30, Year 10. PepsiCo does not disclose the account on the balance sheet that includes these guarantees.

The financial statements and notes have high accounting quality if they disclose sufficient information for the analyst to judge whether a particular firm's contingencies and guarantees warrant recognition as a liability on the balance sheet and, if so, the appropriate amount. However, firms seldom disclose sufficient information for the analyst to make these judgments.

CONTROVERSIAL ISSUES IN LIABILITY RECOGNITION

Most obligations discussed in preceding sections clearly either were liabilities or were not liabilities. Recently, firms have structured innovative financing arrangements in ways that may not satisfy the criteria for the recognition of a liability. That is, firms attempted to structure financing in such a way that GAAP treats any obligation as either an executory contract or as a contingency. The principal aim of such arrangements is to reduce the amount shown as liabilities on the balance sheet. Investors and lenders often use the proportion of debt in a firm's capital structure as a measure of risk and therefore as a factor in establishing the cost of funds. (Chapter 5 discusses various ratios for measuring risk.) Other things being equal, firms prefer to obtain funds without showing a liability on the balance sheet in the hope that future lenders will ignore such financing in setting interest rates. Although there is little empirical evidence to support the notion that lenders ignore such financing in assessing a firm's risk, some firms *act* as if lenders do overlook such borrowing.

ISSUANCE OF HYBRID SECURITIES

One means of reducing the amount shown as liabilities is to issue securities that have both debt and equity characteristics (referred to as *hybrid securities*) but classify them as equity on the balance sheet. Some firms have issued preferred stock that is subject to mandatory redemption after some period of time by the issuing firm. For example, until recently Sears, Roebuck and Co. borrowed funds through the issuance of "Series A Mandatory Exchangeable Preferred Shares." The preferred stock paid an annual, cumulative dividend of $3.75 per share before it was retired. Stock of this nature often has more debt than equity characteristics. Firms have also issued preferred stock that is subject to a call option by the issuing firm. The firm sets out provisions in the preferred stock agreement that make exercise of the call option highly probable. This preferred stock also has more debt than equity characteristics.

On the other hand, some firms issue debt securities that have more equity than debt characteristics. For example, firms might issue bonds that are convertible into common stock. The firm sets out provisions in the debt instrument that make conversion into common stock highly probable. Or, the firm might issue debt with interest payments tied to the firm's operating performance or dividend yield. (Firms treat these equity-like securities as debt in an effort to obtain a tax deduction for "interest expense.")

As this book goes to press, the FASB is studying the accounting for hybrid securities. It has tentatively decided that firms should classify preferred stock subject to mandatory redemption as a liability. It is leaning toward valuing the separate components of securities that have both debt and equity characteristics and classifying each part as either a liability or a shareholders' equity account.

Although financial reporting attempts to classify all financial instruments as either a liability or a shareholders' equity account, the securities of most firms fall along a continuum from pure debt to pure equity. The dividing line is not always clear. Until the FASB provides more definitive guidance, the analyst should study the notes to the financial statements to assess whether the firm's classification of hybrid securities as debt versus equity seems reasonable.

OFF-BALANCE-SHEET FINANCING ARRANGEMENTS

Another means of reducing the amount shown as liabilities on the balance sheet is to structure a borrowing arrangement so that the firm does not recognize a liability (referred to as *off-balance-sheet financing*). Firms usually accomplish off-balance-sheet financing using one or a combination of two approaches: (1) sale of an existing asset, or (2) use of another entity to obtain the financing.

Sale of an Existing Asset

Firms may have accounts receivable, inventories, property, plant, and equipment, or other assets that it could use as collateral for a loan. If the firm borrowed funds, using the assets as collateral, it would increase cash and increase a liability. The notes to its financial statements would disclose that certain assets were serving as collateral for the loan. Structuring the transaction in this way places debt on the balance sheet.

If, on the other hand, the firm sold the same asset to the provider of the funds, it would increase cash, reduce the asset transferred, and recognize a gain or loss for the difference. It would have the cash but would not show a liability on the balance sheet. This is appropriate as long as the sale did not expose the selling firm to the risk of having to make payments to the purchaser in the future (as, for example, if the selling firm had to guarantee that the purchaser could resell the asset for a certain minimum amount).

Lenders, however, often do not want to assume all of the risks of such assets. They will often require the seller to make cash payments in the future if certain events occur. To qualify as a "sale" and not a collateralized loan, the contingency must be relatively unlikely. That is, the firm must attempt to structure the sale of the asset so that only a contingent obligation, not an accounting liability, arises. Recall from the earlier discussion in this chapter and Exhibit 8.1 that GAAP does not require recognition of contingent obligations as liabilities unless they qualify as loss contingencies or as guarantees.

Use of Another Entity to Obtain Financing

The general theme of this approach is that the firm obtains access to the asset that the funds finance, but neither the asset nor its financing appear on the firm's balance sheet. Instead, they appear on the balance sheet of another entity.

Suppose, for example, that a firm needs additional manufacturing capacity but does not want to borrow funds to build the extra plant assets. Instead, it gives a purchase commitment to an unaffiliated company to purchase a certain amount of output from a factory at a pre-specified cost that covers operating and debt service costs. The unaffiliated company takes the purchase commitment to a financial institution and obtains a loan. The unaffiliated company uses the loan proceeds to construct the needed capacity. The new plant assets and the loan appear on the balance sheet of the unaffiliated company. The purchase commitment is a mutually unexecuted contract of the firm initially needing the additional manufacturing capacity. Recall from the earlier discussion and Exhibit 8.1 that firms do not recognize mutually unexecuted contracts as liabilities.

Alternatively, the firm can accomplish the same result using an affiliated company, one over which it has a greater degree of influence than an unaffiliated one. The key to keeping debt off of the balance sheet in this case is that the firm not be required by GAAP to prepare consolidated financial statements with the affiliated company. Consolidated statements aggregate the separate financial statements of two or more entities under the control of one of the entities. The debt will appear on the consolidated balance sheet as long as it appears on the balance sheet of any one entity in the consolidated group. (Chapter 9 discusses consolidated financial statements more fully.) To avoid consolidation, the firm needing the financing must not effectively *control* the entity obtaining the financing.

One means of avoiding consolidation is to set up a joint venture with another entity, with each entity owning 50 percent of the common stock. In this case, neither firm controls the joint venture. GAAP currently does not require either firm to prepare consolidated financial statements with the joint venture.

Another means of avoiding consolidation is to set up a *special purpose entity (SPE)*. The SPE obtains financing and either (1) constructs or acquires the asset desired by the firm attempting to keep debt off of its balance sheet, or (2) purchases the particular asset from this firm. In both cases, the asset held by the SPE serves as collateral for the loan. The lender to the SPE will likely require some commitment from the firm that sets up the SPE to insure repayment of the loan. The commitment may take the form of a noncancelable purchase commitment or a loan guarantee. The key to avoiding consolidation is that effective control of the SPE must not reside primarily with the firm setting it up. The SPE must have economic substance of its own and other parties, either the lender or other equity owners, must be the primary beneficiary of the SPE.

Central to the bankruptcy of Enron was the misuse of SPEs to hold derivative instruments and securities initially acquired by Enron. Enron did not consolidate these SPEs, maintaining that it did not control them. Later revelations showed that effective control was in fact present, requiring Enron to restate its previously issued financial statements. The restatements increased assets and liabilities on the balance sheet and eliminated gains that Enron recognized on the "sale" of the assets to the SPEs. Chapter 9 discusses the accounting for SPEs.

The following sections describe several off-balance-sheet financing arrangements. In several cases, the FASB has issued a reporting standard setting out how firms should treat such transactions for financial reporting purposes. In other cases, the FASB has not issued a specific financial reporting standard and the accountant must apply the general criteria for liability recognition when deciding whether or not to recognize a liability.

Sale of Receivables

Firms sometimes sell their accounts receivable as a means of obtaining financing. If collections from customers are not sufficient to repay the amount borrowed plus interest, then the firm may have to pay the difference (that is, the lender has recourse against the borrowing firm).

The question arises as to whether the recourse provision creates an accounting liability. Some argue that the arrangement is similar to a collateralized loan. The firm should leave the receivables on its books and recognize a liability in the amount of the cash received. Others argue that the firm has sold an asset; it should recognize a liability only if it is *probable* that collections from customers will be insufficient and the firm will be required to repay some portion of the amount received.

The FASB requires that firms recognize transfers of receivables as sales only if the transferor surrenders control of the receivables. Firms surrender control only if all of the following conditions are met:

(1) the assets transferred (that is, receivables) have been isolated from the selling ("transferor") firm (that is, neither the transferor nor a creditor of the selling firm could access the receivables in the event of the seller's bankruptcy);
(2) the buying ("transferee") firm obtains the right to pledge or exchange the transferred assets, and no condition both constrains the transferee from taking advantage of its right and provides more than a trivial benefit to the transferor; and
(3) the selling firm does not maintain effective control over the assets transferred through either (a) an agreement that both entitles and obligates it to repurchase the assets, or (b) the ability to unilaterally cause the transferee to return specific assets.[6]

---

[6]Financial Accounting Standards Board, *Statement of Financial Accounting Standards No. 140,* "Accounting for Transfers and Servicing of Financial Assets and Extinguishments of Liabilities," 2000.

The principal refinement to the concept of an accounting liability brought out by *Statement No. 140* relates to identifying the party involved in the transaction that controls the determination of which party enjoys the economic benefits and sustains the economic risk of the *assets* (receivables in this case). If the selling (borrowing) firm controls the economic benefits/risks, then the transaction is a collateralized loan. If the arrangement transfers these benefits/risks to the buying (lending) firm, then the transaction is a sale.

Example 1

Sears, Roebuck, and Co., a retail department store chain, reported credit card receivables on its balance sheet of $28.2 billion on December 31, Year 11. Sears also states that it sold credit card receivables to SPEs. The SPEs securitize these receivables by selling debt and equity interests in the SPE to various lenders and investors, with Sears retaining a residual, subordinated interest. The subordinated status of Sears serves as a credit enhancement to the SPE. Lenders and investors in the SPE receive cash as Sears' customers repay the receivables. Credit card receivables sold to SPEs totaled $15.0 billion on December 31, Year 11. Sears does not guarantee the debt of the SPEs. Lenders to the SPE have no claim on Sears' assets. However, Sears must contribute additional credit card receivables to the SPEs if uncollectible accounts held in the SPEs exceed certain amounts. In this case, Sears has a continuing involvement with the receivables by bearing the risk of uncollectible accounts. The SPEs apparently cannot maintain their credit ratings over time unless Sears assumes the ongoing risk of changes in the amount of uncollectible accounts. This continuing involvement raises questions as to whether the transferred receivables have been isolated from Sears or whether creditors could lay claim to them in bankruptcy proceedings. Sears treats the transfer of receivables as a collateralized loan, concluding that the ongoing obligation to maintain the credit rating of the SPEs constitutes a continuing involvement with the receivables that violates the first condition to qualify as a sale.

Example 2

In a recent annual report, General Motors Corporation (GM) reports finance receivables on its balance sheet of $99.8 billion on December 31, Year 11. GM states that it sold automobile loans and other receivables totaling $132.9 billion to SPEs. The SPEs securitize these receivables by selling debt and equity interests to various investors, with GM retaining a residual equity interest as a credit enhancement to the SPE. GM's residual equity interest is at risk if cash flows from customers are insufficient to repay amounts borrowed. However, GM does not guarantee the debt of the SPEs, guarantee a return to other equity investors, or remain liable for excess uncollectibles. The SPEs in this case appear able to maintain their credit ratings on an ongoing basis and do not need a continuing involvement from GM to deal with excess uncollectibles. GM accounts for these receivables as a sale, not a collateralized loan. The lenders and investors bear the risk of any losses from uncollectible accounts beyond GM's residual equity interest.

Product Financing Arrangements

Product financing arrangements occur when a firm (sponsor):

1. Sells inventory to another entity and, in a related transaction, agrees to repurchase the inventory at specified prices over specified times.
2. Arranges for another entity to purchase inventory items on the firm's behalf and, in a related transaction, agrees to purchase the inventory items from the other entity.

The first arrangement is similar to the sale of receivables with recourse except that greater certainty exists that the inventory transaction will require a future cash outflow. The second arrangement is structured to appear as a purchase commitment. In this case, however, the sponsoring firm usually creates an SPE for the sole purpose of acquiring the inventory. The sponsoring firm usually guarantees the debt incurred by the SPE in acquiring the inventory.

Financial reporting requires that firms recognize product financing arrangements as liabilities if they meet two conditions:

1. The arrangement requires the sponsoring firm to purchase the inventory, substantially identical inventory, or processed goods of which the inventory is a component, at specified prices.
2. The payments made to the other entity cover all acquisition, holding, and financing costs.[7]

The second criterion suggests that the sponsoring firm recognize a liability whenever it incurs the economic risks (changing costs, interest rates) of purchasing and holding inventory, even though it may not physically control the inventory or have a legal obligation to the supplier of the inventory. Thus, as with sales of receivables with recourse, a firm recognizes a liability when it controls the determination of which party enjoys the economic benefits and incurs the economic risks of the asset involved. It also recognizes an asset of equal amount, usually inventory.

Research and Development Financing Arrangements

When a firm borrows funds to conduct research and development work, it recognizes a liability at the time of borrowing and recognizes expenses as it incurs research and development costs.

Firms have engaged in innovative means of financing aimed at both keeping liabilities off the balance sheet and effectively excluding research and development expenses from the income statement.

---

[7]Financial Accounting Standards Board, *Statement of Financial Accounting Standards No. 49*, "Accounting for Product Financing Arrangements," 1981.

Example 3

Merck, a pharmaceutical company, forms joint ventures with other pharmaceutical companies to develop, manufacture, and market new products. The joint venture between Merck and Schering-Plough focuses on cholesterol management and respiratory therapeutic products. The joint venture of Merck and Johnson & Johnson involves nonprescription medicines. Merck's joint venture with Aventis works in animal care products. Merck's joint venture with Aventis Pasteur focuses on vaccines. Thus, Merck conducts a significant amount of pharmaceutical research through joint ventures. Because the joint ventures are owned equally by the two entities in each case, Merck does not consolidate the financial statements of the joint ventures with its own financial statements. Any liabilities of the joint ventures appear on the financial statements of the joint ventures, not on Merck's balance sheet. Likewise, the research and development expense of the joint ventures appears on the income statement issued by the joint ventures, not on Merck's income statement.

Firms use other arrangements besides joint ventures. Although the structures vary somewhat across firms, they generally operate as follows:

1. The sponsoring firm contributes either preliminary development work or rights to future products to a partnership for a general interest in the partnership. It obtains limited partners (often corporate directors or officers) who contribute cash for their partnership interests.
2. The sponsoring firm conducts research and development work for the partnership for a fee. The sponsoring firm usually performs the research and development work on a best-efforts basis, with no guarantee of success. The sponsoring firm recognizes amounts received from the partnership for research and development services as revenues. The amount of revenue generally equals or exceeds the research and development costs it incurs.
3. The rights to any resulting products usually reside in the partnership. However, the partnership agreement usually constrains the returns and risks of the limited partners. The sponsoring firm can often acquire the limited partners' interests in the partnership if valuable products emerge. On the other hand, the sponsoring firm may have to guarantee certain minimum royalty payments to the partnership or agree to purchase the partnership's rights to the product.

In arrangements like these, a primary objective of the sponsoring firm involves obtaining financing for its research and development work without having to recognize a liability.

Criteria exist for when firms must recognize such financing arrangements as liabilities.[8] The sponsoring firm recognizes a liability:

---

[8]Financial Accounting Standards Board, *Statement of Financial Accounting Standards No. 68*, "Research and Development Arrangements," 1982.

1. If the contractual agreement requires the sponsoring firm to repay any of the funds provided by the other parties regardless of the outcome of the research and development work; or

2. If surrounding conditions indicate that the sponsoring firm bears the risk of failure of the research and development work, even though the contractual agreement does not obligate it to repay the other parties. For example, if a sponsoring firm guarantees the debt of the partnership, must make minimum royalty payments to the partnership, or must acquire the partnership's interest in any product, then the sponsoring firm bears the risk of the research and development work.

The joint ventures formed by Merck and the other pharmaceutical companies operate as independent entities, with broad oversight by the two joint owners. The joint ventures retain the rights to products developed. Neither joint owner guarantees any debt of the joint ventures. Neither joint owner must pay the other joint owner any amounts if the research effort is nonproductive. Although the two joint owners ultimately bear the risk of failure of the joint venture, GAAP accounting for joint ventures requires only that the joint owners recognize their equity investment in the joint venture on the balance sheet.

As with the off-balance-sheet financing arrangements involving receivables and inventories discussed above, firms recognize liabilities when they bear the risk associated with the asset or product involved in the financing.[9]

Take-or-Pay or Throughput Contracts

A take-or-pay contract is an agreement in which a purchaser agrees to pay specified amounts periodically to a seller for products or services. A throughput contract is similar to a take-or-pay contract except that the "product" purchased is transportation or processing services.

To understand the rationale for such arrangements, consider the following case. Suppose that two petroleum companies are in need of additional refining capacity. If either company builds a refinery, it will record an asset and any related financing on its balance sheet. Suppose instead that the two companies form a joint venture to construct a refinery. The joint venture, an entity separate from the two petroleum companies, obtains financing and constructs the refinery. In order to secure financing for the joint venture, the two petroleum companies sign take-or-pay contracts agreeing to make certain payments to the joint venture each period for refining services. The payments are sufficient to cover all operating and financing costs of the refinery. The joint owners must make the payments even if they acquire no refining services.

---

[9]A study of firms that conduct their research and development through limited partnerships found that the stock market appears to consider the call option that firms have on research findings in the valuation of the firm. The author calls for improved disclosure of these arrangements instead of recognition of a liability in the balance sheet. See Terry Shevlin, "The Valuation of R&D Firms with R&D Limited Partnerships," *Accounting Review*, January, 1991, pp. 1–21.

The economic substance of this arrangement is that each petroleum company owns half of the refinery and is obligated to the extent of half of the financing. The legal status of the arrangement is that the two firms have simply signed noncancelable purchase commitments (that is, executory contracts). Accounting likewise treats these arrangements as executory contracts. At the time of signing the contract, the firms are not viewed as yet having received any benefits that obligate them to pay. As they receive benefits over time, a liability arises. If one or the other entity guarantees the debt of the partnership, the guarantee is a contingent obligation, which GAAP does not recognize as a liability until future events indicate a high probability of payment.

Financial reporting requires firms to disclose take-or-pay and throughput commitments in the notes.[10] The analyst should examine disclosures of these commitments in notes to the financial statements to assess whether the firm incurs the risks and rewards of the arrangement and should therefore recognize a liability.

Summary of Off-Balance-Sheet Financing

The conventional accounting model based on historical cost is exchange- or transaction-oriented. Accounting recognizes events when an exchange takes place. The criteria for liability recognition discussed earlier in this chapter and in Exhibit 8.1 illustrate this exchange orientation. Accounting recognizes liabilities when a firm incurs an obligation to sacrifice resources in the future for benefits already received. Financial reporting has typically not recognized mutually unexecuted contracts as liabilities because the parties have merely exchanged promises to perform in the future. Financial reporting also does not generally require the recognition of contingent obligations as liabilities because some future event must occur to establish the existence of a liability.

The evolving concept of an accounting liability recognizes that exchanges of promises can have economic substance even though a legal obligation to pay does not immediately arise. When a firm controls the determination of which party enjoys the economic benefits and/or incurs the economic risks from an asset, then the firm should recognize the asset and its related financing.

The FASB closely monitors reporting issues related to off-balance-sheet commitments of firms, but it continues to be challenged because of the ever-changing nature of business financing arrangements and the flexible and fluid organizational arrangements that firms create.

LEASES

Many firms acquire rights to use assets through long-term leases. A company might, for example, agree to lease an office suite for five years or an entire building for forty years, promising to pay a fixed periodic fee for the duration of the lease. Leasing provides benefits to lessees, or the user, such as the following:

---

[10]Financial Accounting Standards Board, *Statement of Financial Accounting Standards No. 47*, "Disclosure of Long-term Obligations," 1981.

1. Ability to shift the tax benefits of depreciation and other deductions from a lessee that has little or no taxable income (such as an airline) to a lessor, or owner of the asset, that has substantial taxable income. The lessee expects the lessor to share some of the benefits of these tax deductions by allowing lower lease payments.
2. Flexibility to change capacity as needed without having to purchase or sell assets.
3. Ability to reduce the risk of technological obsolescence, relative to outright ownership, by maintaining the flexibility to shift to technologically more advanced assets.
4. Ability to finance the "acquisition" of an asset using lessor financing when alternative sources of financing are unavailable or more costly.

These potential benefits of leasing to lessees do not come without a cost. When the lessor assumes the risks of ownership, it will require the lessee to make larger lease payments than if the lessee incurs these risks. The party bearing the risks is a matter of negotiation between lessor and lessee.

Promising to make an irrevocable series of lease payments commits the firm just as surely as a bond indenture or mortgage, and the accounting is similar in many cases. This section examines two methods of accounting for long-term leases: the operating lease method and the capital lease method. The illustrations show the accounting by the lessee, the user of the leased asset. A later section illustrates the accounting for the lessor, the owner of the asset.

To illustrate these two methods, suppose that Myers Company wants to acquire a computer that has a three-year life and could be purchased for $45,000. Assume also that Myers Company must pay 10 percent per year to borrow money for three years. The computer manufacturer is willing to sell the equipment for $45,000 or to lease it for three years. Myers Company is responsible for property taxes, maintenance, and repairs of the computer whether it leases or purchases the computer.

Assume that Myers Company signs a lease on January 1, Year 1, and must make payments on the lease on December 31, Year 1, Year 2, and Year 3. (In practice, lessees usually make lease payments in advance, but the assumption of end-of-the-year payments simplifies the computations.) Compound interest computations show that each lease payment must be $18,095. (The present value of an annuity of $1 paid at the end of this year and each of the next 2 years is $2.48685 when the interest rate is 10 percent per year. Because the lease payments must have a present value equal to the current cash purchase price of $45,000 if the computer manufacturer is to be indifferent between selling and leasing the computer, each payment must be $45,000/2.48685 = $18,095.)

OPERATING LEASE METHOD

In an *operating lease*, the owner, or lessor, transfers only the rights to use the property to the lessee for specified periods of time. At the end of the lease period, the lessee returns the property to the lessor. For example, car rental companies lease cars by the day or week on an operating basis. In leasing arrangements where the lessee neither assumes the risks nor enjoys the rewards of ownership, GAAP requires the lessee to treat the lease as an operating lease. Accounting gives no recognition to the signing of an operating lease (that is, the lessee reports neither the leased asset nor a lease liability on its balance sheet; the lease is simply a mutually unexecuted contract). The lessee recognizes rent expense in measuring net income each year. The effect on the financial statements of Myers Company each year (ignoring income taxes) if its treats the lease as an operating lease, is:

	C	+	N$A	=	L	+	CC	+	AOCI	+	RE
BS-BOP											
(1)	−18,095										−18,095
IBT	_____										−18,095
BS-EOP	**−18,095**										**−18,095**

Myers Company makes the following journal entry on its books on December 31, Year 1, Year 2, and Year 3, under the operating lease method:

```
Rent Expense ..........................    18,095
    Cash...............................              18,095
To recognize annual expense of leasing computer.
```

CAPITAL LEASE METHOD

In leasing arrangements where the lessee assumes the risks and enjoys rewards of ownership, the arrangement is a form of borrowing and GAAP treats such leases as *capital leases*. This treatment recognizes the signing of the lease as the simultaneous acquisition of a long-term asset and the incurring of a long-term liability for lease payments. The effect on the financial statements of Myers Company at the time it signs the lease and the related journal entry that it makes in its accounting records are:

	C	+	N$A	=	L	+	CC	+	AOCI	+	RE
BS-BOP											
(1)			+ 45,000		+45,000						

```
Leased Asset ..........................    45,000
    Lease Liability ...................              45,000
To recognize acquisition of leased asset and the
related liability.
```

Lessees recognize two expense items each year on capital leases. First, the lessee must depreciate the leased asset over its useful life (that is, the term of the lease). Assuming that Myers Company uses straight-line depreciation (see Chapter 7 for a discussion of depreciation methods), it recognizes depreciation expense of $15,000 (= $45,000 ÷ 3) each year. Second, the lease payment made each year is part interest expense on the lease liability and part reduction in the liability itself. For Year 1, interest expense is $4,500 (= .10 × $45,000) and the repayment of the lease liability is $13,595 (= $18,095 − $4,500). The effects of (1) the signing of the capital lease on January 1, Year 1, and the recognition of (2) depreciation and (3) interest during Year 1 are as follows:

	C	+	N$A	=	L	+	CC	+	AOCI	+	RE
BS-BOP											
(1)			+ 45,000		+45,000						
(2)			− 15,000							−	15,000
(3)	−18,095				−13,595					−	4,500
IBT										−	19,500
BS-EOP	**−18,095**	**+**	**30,000**	**=**	**−31,405**					**−**	**19,500**

The journal entries on the books of Myers Company for depreciation and interest are as follows:

December 31, Year 1:

Depreciation Expense	15,000	
Accumulated Depreciation		15,000

To record depreciation of leased asset.

December 31, Year 1:

Interest Expense	4,500	
Lease Liability	13,595	
Cash		18,095

To recognize lease payment, interest on liability for Year 1 (.10 × $45,000 = $4,500), and the plug for reduction in the liability. The present value of the liability after this entry is $31,405 = $45,000 − $13,595.

Exhibit 8.2 shows the amortization schedule for this liability. Column (3) shows the amount of interest expense. The entries made for interest expense and the payment of $18,095 at the end of Year 2 and Year 3 are as follows:

December 31, Year 2:

Interest Expense	3,141	
Lease Liability	14,954	
Cash		18,095

To recognize lease payment, interest on liability for Year 2 (.10 × $31,405 = $3,141), and the plug for reduction in the liability. The present value of the liability after this entry is $16,451 = $31,405 − $14,954.

	EXHIBIT 8.2				
Amortization Schedule for $45,000 Lease Liability, Repaid in Three Annual Installments of $18,095 Each, Interest Rate 10 Percent, Compounded Annually					
Year (1)	Lease Liability, Start of Year (2)	Interest Expense for Year (3)	Payment (4)	Portion of Payment Reducing Lease Liability (5)	Lease Liability, End of Year (6)
1	$45,000	$4,500	$18,095	$13,595	$31,405
2	31,405	3,141	18,095	14,954	16,451
3	16,451	1,644[a]	18,095	16,451	0

Column (2) = column (6), previous period.
Column (3) = .10 × column (2).
Column (4) is given.

Column (5) = column (4) – column (3).
Column (6) = column (2) – column (5).
[a]Does not equal .10 × $16,451 due to rounding.

December 31, Year 3:
    Interest Expense   1,644
    Lease Liability   16,451
        Cash   18,095
To recognize lease payment, interest on liability for Year 3 (.10 × $16,451 = $1,644), and the plug for reduction in the liability. The present value of the liability after this entry is zero (= $16,451 – $16,451).

Notice that, in the capital lease method, the total expense over the three years is $54,285, comprising $45,000 (= $15,000 + $15,000 + $15,000) for depreciation expense and $9,285 (= $4,500 + $3,141 + $1,644) for interest expense. This total expense is exactly the same as that recognized under the operating lease method described previously ($18,095 × 3 = $54,285). The capital lease method recognizes expenses sooner than does the operating lease method, as Exhibit 8.3 summarizes. But, over sufficiently long time periods, total expense equals the cash expenditure. One difference between the operating lease method and the capital lease method is the *timing* of the expense recognition. The other difference is that the capital lease method recognizes both the asset and the liability on the balance sheet.

CHOOSING THE ACCOUNTING METHOD

When a lessee treats a lease as a capital lease, it increases both an asset account and a liability account, thereby increasing total liabilities and making the company appear more risky. Given a choice, most managers prefer not to show the asset and a related liability on the balance sheet. These managers prefer an operating lease to

	EXHIBIT 8.3	
	Comparison of Expense Recognized under Operating and Capital Lease Methods	

	Expense Recognized Each Year under:	
Year	**Operating Lease Method**	**Capital Lease Method**
1	$18,095	$19,500 (= $15,000 + $4,500)
2	18,095	18,141 (= 15,000 + 3,141)
3	18,095	16,644 (= 15,000 + 1,644)
Total	$54,285[a]	$54,285 (= $45,000[b] + $9,285[c])

[a]Rent expense.
[b]Depreciation expense.
[c]Interest expense.

either an installment purchase or a capital lease, where both the asset and liability appear on the balance sheet. Many managers also prefer to recognize expenses later rather than sooner for financial reporting. These preferences have led managers to structure asset acquisitions so that the financing takes the form of an operating lease, thereby achieving off-balance-sheet financing.

Conditions Requiring Capital Lease Accounting

GAAP provides detailed rules of accounting for long-term leases. The lessor and lessee must account for a lease as a capital lease if the lease meets any one of four conditions.[11] These conditions attempt to identify which party, the lessor or the lessee, bears most of the risk related to the asset under lease. When the lessor bears most of the risk, the lease is an operating lease. If the lessee bears most of the risk, the lease is a capital lease.

A lease is a capital lease if it meets any one of the following conditions:

(1) if it extends for at least 75 percent of the asset's total expected useful life (the lessee uses the asset for most of its life), or

(2) if it transfers ownership to the lessee at the end of the lease term (the lessee bears the risk of changes in the residual value of the asset at the end of the lease term), or

(3) if it seems likely that the lessor will transfer ownership to the lessee because of a "bargain purchase" option (the lessee again bears the residual value risk; a bargain purchase option gives the lessee the right to purchase the asset for a

[11]Financial Accounting Standards Board, *Statement of Financial Accounting Standards No. 13*, "Accounting for Leases," 1976.

price less than the expected fair market value of the asset when the lessee exercises its option), or

(4) the present value of the contractual minimum lease payments equals or exceeds 90 percent of the fair market value of the asset at the time of signing.

The first three conditions are relatively easy to avoid in lease contracts if lessors and lessees prefer to treat a lease as an operating lease instead of a capital lease. The most difficult of the four conditions to avoid is the fourth one. When the contractual minimum lease payments equal or exceed 90 percent of the fair market value of the asset at the time of signing, the lessor has less than or equal to 10 percent of the asset's value at risk to an uncertain residual value at the end of the lease term. The lease therefore transfers the major risks and rewards of ownership from the lessor (landlord) to the lessee. In economic substance, the lessee has acquired an asset, and has agreed to pay for it under a long-term contract, which the lessee recognizes as a liability. When the present value of the minimum lease payments is less than 90 percent of the fair market value of the asset at the time of signing, the lessor bears the major risks and rewards of ownership and the lease is an operating lease.

Firms often report both operating and capital leases because certain lease agreements meet one or more of these conditions, while others meet none of the conditions.

Example 4

Delta Air Lines leases many of its aircraft and ground facilities. In the notes to its financial statements, Delta provides a schedule of capital and operating lease commitments for Year 12 and beyond, as reported in Exhibit 8.4. The firm also reports the present value of its capital lease commitments ($99 million on December 31, Year 11, as reported in Exhibit 8.4). The capital leases reported by Delta on the balance sheet as long-term debt represent less than 1 percent of Delta's total long-term debt at the end of Year 11. Delta's commitments under operating leases are much more substantial, representing an important off-balance-sheet cash-flow commitment of the firm that we will analyze further later in this section.

Most countries outside of the United States also set out criteria for distinguishing operating and capital leases. The particular criteria differ somewhat from those described above but attempt to identify the party enjoying the rewards and bearing the risks of ownership.

EFFECTS ON LESSOR

The lessor (landlord) generally uses the same criteria for classifying a lease as an operating lease or a capital lease as does the lessee (tenant). Under the operating lease method, the lessor recognizes rent revenue in the same amounts as the lessee recognizes rent expense. At the time of the signing of a capital lease, the lessor recognizes an asset, Lease Receivable, and revenue in an amount equal to the present value of all future cash flows ($45,000 in the Myers Company lease) and recognizes expense (analogous to cost of goods sold) in an amount equal to the book value of the leased

---

EXHIBIT 8.4

Delta Air Lines
Lease Commitments

Minimum lease obligations, excluding taxes, insurance and other expenses payable directly by the Company, for leases in effect as of December 31, Year 11, were:

amounts in millions	Capital leases	Operating leases
Year 12	$ 39	$ 1,271
Year 13	30	1,238
Year 14	21	1,197
Year 15	14	1,177
Year 16	6	1,144
After Year 16..............................	10	8,068
Minimum payments	$120	$14,095
Imputed interest..........................	(21)	
Present value of minimum leases payments, principally long-term	$ 99	

---

asset. Assume that Myers Company manufactured the computer at a cost of $39,000. The difference between the revenue and expense is the lessor's gross margin from the "sale" of the asset. The effects on the financial statements of Myers Company of (1) manufacturing the leased asset, and then (2) signing a capital lease are as follows:

BS-BOP	C	+	N$A	=	L	+	CC	+	AOCI	+	RE
(1)	−39,000	+	39,000								
(2)		+	45,000							+	45,000
		−	39,000							−	39,000
IBT										+	6,000

The lessor records the lease receivable like any other long-term receivable at the present value of the future cash flows. It recognizes interest revenue over the term of the lease in amounts that closely mirror interest expense by the lessee. The effects on the financial statements of accounting for the lease as a capital lease by the lessor for Year 1 (we repeat the effects of manufacturing the asset and signing the lease) are as follows:

BS-BOP	C	+	N$A	=	L	+	CC	+	AOCI	+	RE
(1)	−39,000	+	39,000								
(2)		+	45,000							+	45,000
		−	39,000							−	39,000
(3)	+18,095	−	13,595							+	4,500
IBT										+	10,500
BS-EOP	**−20,905**	**+**	**31,405**							**+**	**10,500**

The lessor's entries under the operating and capital lease methods, assuming that it manufactured the computer for $39,000, are as follows:

Operating Lease Method
December 31 of each year:

Cash..............................	18,095	
Rent Revenue....................		18,095

To recognize annual revenue from renting computer.

Depreciation Expense.................	13,000	
Accumulated Depreciation		13,000

To recognize depreciation on rented computer ($13,000 = $39,000/3).

Capital Lease Method
January 1, Year 1:

Lease Receivable	45,000	
Sales Revenue.....................		45,000

To recognize the "sale" of a computer for a series of future cash flows with a present value of $45,000.

Cost of Goods Sold...................	39,000	
Inventory		39,000

To record the cost of the computer "sold" as an expense.

December 31, Year 1:

Cash..............................	18,095	
Interest Revenue..................		4,500
Lease Receivable.................		13,595

To recognize lease receipt, interest on receivable, and reduction in receivable for Year 1. See supporting calculations in the lessee's journal entries.

December 31, Year 2:

Cash..............................	18,095	
Interest Revenue..................		3,141
Lease Receivable..................		14,954

To recognize lease amounts for Year 2.

December 31, Year 3:

Cash..............................	18,095	
Interest Revenue..................		1,644
Lease Receivable..................		16,451

To recognize lease amounts for Year 3.

LEASE ACCOUNTING FOR TAX PURPOSES

An earlier section indicates that one of the benefits of leasing is that it permits the user of the property (the lessee) to shift the tax benefits of depreciation, interest, and other deductions to the lessor in the expectation of lowering the required lease payments. To achieve this benefit, the lease must satisfy the criteria for an operating lease for tax purposes. These criteria differ somewhat from those GAAP uses to classify leases for financial reporting. The five criteria for operating leases for tax reporting are:

1. Use of the property at the end of the lease term by someone other than the lessee is commercially feasible; and
2. The lease does not have a bargain purchase option; and
3. The lessor has a minimum 20 percent of its capital at risk; and
4. The lessor has a positive cash flow and profit from the lease independent of tax benefits; and
5. The lessee does not have an investment in the lease and has not lent any of the purchase price to the lessor.

These criteria attempt to identify the party to the lease that enjoys the rewards and bears the risks of ownership. Because the financial and tax reporting criteria for leases differ, lessors and lessees may treat particular leases one way for financial reporting and another way for tax reporting.

CONVERTING OPERATING LEASES TO CAPITAL LEASES

The analyst must address accounting quality issues for lessor and lessee firms that enter into substantial lease agreements, given the preference particularly by lessees to structure leases as operating leases. A slight change in the amount or pattern of cash flows can result in the present value of the minimum lease payments falling just above or just below the 90 percent threshold. Lease commitments by lessees accounted for as operating leases do not appear as liabilities on the balance sheet and can result in the analyst understating the capital structure risk of the firm. For these reasons, the analyst may wish to restate the financial statements of lessees to convert all operating leases into capital leases. Such a restatement provides a more conservative measure of total liabilities.

To illustrate the procedure followed, refer to PepsiCo's operating lease disclosures in Note 20 in Appendix A, and as summarized in Exhibit 8.5. Column (2) shows PepsiCo's commitments on noncancelable operating leases net of sublease revenues at the end of Year 11. The analyst must express the lease commitments in present value terms. The discount rate that the analyst uses is the lessee's incremental borrowing rate for secured debt with similar risk as the leasing arrangement. We assume a 6 percent rate in this case. To select a present value factor for payments after Year 16, we need to know the years and amounts in which PepsiCo will pay the $162 million. If we presume that payments after Year 16 will continue at the same amount as the $42 million payment in Year 16, then PepsiCo will pay $42 million a year for 3.86 periods (= $162/$42). The present value of an annuity of $42 million for 3.86 periods is $141.0. This amount represents the present value at the beginning of Year 17. The present value at the end of Year 11 requires that we discount $141.0 million five periods at 6 percent to obtain a present value of $105.4 million. Lease commitments usually decline over time as existing leases terminate, so assuming a level $42 million provides a more conservative measure of the obligation from the viewpoint of the analyst.

The analyst adds the $490.8 million lease to property, plant, and equipment and to long-term debt on the December 31, Year 11, balance sheet. For time-series analysis of PepsiCo, similar calculations would be necessary for at least two previous years. The long-term debt ratio of PepsiCo on December 31, Year 11, based on reported amounts is 23.4 percent (= $2,651/($2,651 + $26 + $8,648). Capitalizing the

---

EXHIBIT 8.5

PepsiCo., Inc.
Operating Lease Disclosures
(amounts in millions)

Operating Leases Commitments at the end of Year 11

Year (1)	Reported Lease Commitments (2)	Present Value Factor at 6%	Present Value
12	$138	.94340	$130.2
13	$111	.89000	98.8
14	$ 95	.83962	79.8
15	$ 57	.79209	45.2
16	$ 42	.74726	31.4
After Year 16	$162	*	105.4
			$490.8

*Present Value of an annuity of $42 million for 3.86 periods (= $162/$42) at 6 percent, then that present value discounted back five periods at 6 percent.

operating lease commitments increases the long-term debt ratio to 26.6 percent (= ($2,651 + $490.8)/($2,651 + $490.8 + $26 + $8,648).

Assuming that the analyst views the economic substance of this lease more as a means of financing the acquisition of long-term assets (that as, as a capital lease) than as a right to use such assets for a short period of time, the analyst could also convert the income statement for Year 11 from the operating to the capital lease method. Assume that the January 1, Year 11, capitalized value of operating leases was $602.4, that these leased assets had a remaining lease term of 8.5 years on that date, and that all new leases signed during Year 11 were signed on December 31, Year 11. Expenses under the operating and capital lease methods are as follows:

Operating Lease Method (as reported)

Lease Expense (see Note 20 in Appendix A)............	$165.0

Capital Lease Method (as restated)

Depreciation Expense ($602.4 ÷ 8.5)	$ 70.9
Interest Expense (.06 × $602.4).....................	36.1
Total	$107.0
Decrease in Expenses	$ 58.0

One possible reason for the significant difference in total expenses is that lease expense of $165 million under the operating lease method may contain some contingent rental amounts based on sales or other measures of performance. PepsiCo would pay this contingent rental amount even if it used the capital lease method. Thus, the difference in expenses may be smaller than $58.0 million. PepsiCo does not disclose the amount of any contingent rentals.

If the average lease is in the first half of its life, total expenses under the capital lease method tend to exceed total expenses under the operating lease method. If the average lease is in the last half of its life, total expenses under the capital lease method tend to be less than under the operating lease method. The two expense amounts are approximately equal at the mid-life point (see Exhibit 8.3). In general, balance sheet restatements are more significant than income statement restatements. Consequently, the analyst can usually ignore restatements of the income statement.[12]

The analyst could restate the statement of cash flows for the capitalization of operating leases. Under the operating lease method, the lease payment for the year is an operating use of cash. Its inclusion as a subtraction in computing net income results in reporting its negative effect on the operating section of the statement of

---

[12]For an alternative procedure for converting operating into capital leases, see Eugene A. Imhoff, Jr., Robert C. Lipe, and David W. Wright, "Operating Leases: Impact of Constructive Capitalization," *Accounting Horizons*, March, 1991, pp. 51–63. In this study, the authors found that capitalizing operating leases decreased the rate of return on assets 34 percent for high lease firms and 10 percent for low lease firms, and increased the debt-to-equity ratio 191 percent for high lease firms and 47 percent for low lease firms.

cash flows. Under the capital lease method, a portion of the cash payment represents a repayment of the lease liability, a financing instead of an operating use of cash. The analyst should reclassify this portion of the cash payment from the operating section to the financing section of the statement of cash flows. The analyst could also reduce net income for depreciation expense on the capitalized lease assets, but this same amount appears as an addback to net income for a non-cash expense. Thus, the net effect of depreciation expense on operating cash flows is zero.

IMPACT OF ACCOUNTING FOR OPERATING LEASES AS CAPITAL LEASES

Virtually all firms have some amount of commitments under operating leases. The change in debt ratios for some firms is relatively minor, as is the case for PepsiCo. For other firms, particularly airlines and retail stores, the effect can be significant. Refer again to the lease commitments for Delta Air Lines in Exhibit 8.4. The present value of Delta's lease commitments on December 31, Year 11, at a six-percent discount rate, based on the same procedure as Exhibit 8.5 illustrates for PepsiCo, is $8,908. Delta's long-term debt ratio without recognizing its commitments under operating leases is 67.5 percent. Including the present value of operating lease commitments in long-term debt increases long-term debt ratio to 90.2 percent. Even for firms for which the effect is relatively small, adding the effect of capitalizing operating leases to the effect of other off-balance-sheet obligations can result in a combined material effect. Thus, the analyst should examine the effect of leases when assessing the risk and accounting quality of a firm's financial statements.

DERIVATIVE INSTRUMENTS

Firms incur various risks when carrying out their business operations. A fire may destroy a warehouse of a retail chain and disrupt the flow of merchandise to stores. An automobile accident involving a member of the sales staff may injure the employee or others and damage the firm's automobile. A firm's products may injure customers and subject the firm to lawsuits. Most firms purchase property, medical, or liability insurance against such risks. The insurance shifts the risk of the loss, at least up to the limits in the insurance policy, to the insurance company. The firm pays insurance premiums for the right to shift the risk of these losses.

Firms engage in numerous other transactions that subject them to risks. Consider the following scenarios.

Example 5

Firm A, a U.S. firm, orders a machine on June 30, Year 1, for delivery on June 30, Year 2, from a British supplier for 10,000 Great Britain pounds (referred to as GBP throughout this section). The exchange rate between the U.S. dollar and the British pound is currently $1.60 per GBP, indicating a purchase price of $16,000. Firm A worries that the value of the U.S. dollar will decline between June 30, Year 1, and June

30, Year 2, when it must convert U.S. dollars into British pounds, requiring it to pay more than $16,000 to purchase the machine.

Example 6

Firm B gives a note payable to a supplier on January 1, Year 1, to acquire manufacturing equipment. The note has a face value of $100,000 and bears interest at the rate of 8 percent each year. Interest is payable annually on December 31 and the note matures on December 31, Year 3. Firm B has the option of repaying the note prior to maturity. It knows, though, that the equipment supplier will value the note at any time prior to maturity based on existing market interest rates at the time. Firm B worries that the value of the note will increase if interest rates decrease and require it to pay more than $100,000 if it decides to repay the note early.

Example 7

Firm C gives a note payable to a supplier on January 1, Year 1, to acquire manufacturing equipment. The note has a face value of $100,000 and bears interest at the prime lending rate. The prime lending rate is 8 percent on January 1, Year 1. The supplier resets the interest rate each December 31 to establish the interest charge for the next calendar year. Interest is payable on December 31 of each year and the note matures on December 31, Year 3. Firm C worries that interest rates will increase above 8 percent during the term of the note and negatively affect its cash flows.

Example 8

Firm D holds 10,000 gallons of whiskey in inventory on October 31, Year 1. Firm D expects to finish aging this whiskey by March 31, Year 2, at which time it intends to sell the whiskey. Uncertainties about the quality of the aged whiskey and economic conditions at the time, however, make predicting the selling price of whiskey on March 31, Year 2 difficult.

Many firms face risks of economic losses from changes in interest rate, foreign exchange rates, or commodity prices. Firm can purchase financial instruments to mitigate these business risks. The general term used for the financial instrument is a *derivative*. This section discusses the nature, use, accounting, and reporting of derivative instruments. Financial Accounting Standards Board *Statement of Financial Accounting Standards No. 133*[13] and *Statement of Financial Accounting Standards No. 138*[14] set forth the required accounting for derivative instruments.

---

[13]Financial Accounting Standards Board, *Statement of Financial Accounting Standards No. 133*, "Accounting for Derivative Instruments and Hedging Activities," 1998.
[14]Financial Accounting Standards Board, *Statement of Financial Accounting Standards No. 138*, "Accounting for Certain Derivative Instruments and Certain Hedging Activities, an Amendment to FASB Statement No. 133," 2000.

NATURE AND USE OF DERIVATIVE INSTRUMENTS

A derivative is a financial instrument that obtains its value from some other financial instrument. An option to purchase a share of stock derives its value from the market price of the stock. A commitment to purchase a certain amount of foreign currency in the future derives its value from changes in the exchange rate for that currency. Firms typically use derivative instruments to hedge the risk of losses from changes in interest rates, foreign exchange rates, and commodity prices. The general idea is that changes in the value of the derivative instrument offset changes in the value of an asset or liability or changes in future cash flows, thereby neutralizing the economic loss. Reconsider the four examples discussed previously.

Example 9

Refer to Example 5. Firm A desires to minimize the effect of changes in the exchange rate between the U.S. dollar and the Great Britain pound (GBP) while it awaits delivery of the equipment. It purchases a *forward foreign exchange contract* from a bank on June 30, Year 1, in which it promises to pay a fixed U.S. dollar amount on June 30, Year 2, in exchange for 10,000 GBP. The forward foreign exchange rate between U.S. dollars and British pounds on June 30, Year 1, for settlement on June 30, Year 2, establishes the number of U.S. dollars it must deliver. Assume that the forward rate on June 30, Year 1, for settlement of the forward contract on June 30, Year 2, is $1.64 per GBP. By purchasing the forward contract, Firm A locks in the cost of the equipment at $16,400 (= 10,000 pounds × $1.64 per GBP).

Example 10

Refer to Example 6. Firm B wants to neutralize the effect of changes in the market value of the note payable caused by changes in market interest rates. It engages in a *swap contract* with its bank. The swap in effect allows Firm A to swap its fixed interest rate obligation for a variable interest rate obligation. The market value of the note remains at $100,000 as long as the variable interest rate in the swap is the same as the variable rate used by the supplier to revalue the note while it is outstanding.

Example 11

Refer to Example 7. Firm C wants to protect itself against increases in the variable interest rate above the initial 8 percent rate. It also engages in a swap contract with its bank. The swap in effect allows Firm C to swap its variable interest rate obligation for a fixed interest rate obligation. The swap fixes its annual interest expense and cash expenditure to 8 percent of the $100,000 note. By engaging in the swap, Firm C cannot take advantage of decreases in interest rates below 8 percent, which it could have done with its variable rate note.

Example 12

Refer to Example 8. Firm D would like to fix the price at which it can sell the whiskey in its inventory on March 31, Year 2. It acquires a *forward commodity contract* in which it promises to sell 10,000 gallons of whiskey on March 31, Year 2, at a fixed price. The forward price of whiskey on October 31 Year 1, for delivery on March 31, Year 2, is $320 per gallon. Thus, it locks in a total cash inflow from selling the whiskey of $3,200,000.

Forward contracts and swap contracts are only two of many types of derivative instruments. Banks and other financial intermediaries structure derivatives for a fee to suit the particular needs of their customers. Thus, the nature and complexity of derivatives vary widely. We confine our discussion to forward and swap contracts to illustrate the accounting and reporting of derivatives.

With these examples of derivatives, consider the following elements of a derivative:

1. A derivative has one or more *underlyings.* An underlying is a specified interest rate, commodity price, foreign exchange rate, or other variable. The underlying in Example 9 is the foreign exchange rate; in Examples 10 and 11, is an interest rate; and in Example 12, is the price of whiskey.
2. A derivative has one or more *notional amounts.* A notional amount is a number of currency units, bushels, shares, or other units specified in the contract. The notional amount in Example 9 is 10,000 GBP; in Examples 10 and 11, is the $100,000 face value of the note; and in Example 12, is 10,000 gallons of whiskey.
3. A derivative often requires no initial investment, although it might. The firm usually acquires a derivative by exchanging promises with a counterparty, such as a commercial or investment bank. The acquisition of a derivative is usually an exchange of promises, a mutually unexecuted contract.
4. Derivatives typically require, or permit, *net settlement.* Firm A in Example 9 will not deliver $16,400 to the counterparty and receive in exchange 10,000 GBP. Firm A will actually purchase 10,000 GBP on the market on June 20, Year 2, at the exchange rate on that date, when it needs the British pounds to purchase the equipment. Firm A will receive cash from the counterparty to the extent that the exchange rate on June 30, Year 2, exceeds $1.64 per GBP and must pay the counterparty on this date to the extent that the exchange rate is less than $1.64 per GBP. Firm B in Example 10 will pay the supplier the 8 percent interest established in the fixed rate note. If the variable interest rate used in the swap contract decreases to 6 percent, the counterparty will pay Firm B an amount equal to 2 percent (= .08 − .06) of the notional amount of the note, $100,000. Paying interest of 8 percent to the supplier and receiving cash of 2 percent from the counterparty results in net interest cost of 6 percent. If the variable interest rate increases to 10 percent, Firm B still pays the supplier interest of 8 percent as specified in the original note. It would then pay the counterparty an additional 2 percent (= .10 − .08), resulting in total interest expense equal to the variable rate of 10 percent.

ACCOUNTING FOR DERIVATIVES

Firms must recognize derivatives in the balance sheet as assets or liabilities, depending on the rights and obligations under the contract. The forward contract in Example 9 is either an asset or a liability, depending on the exchange rate. The swap contracts in

Examples 10 and 11 may be assets or liabilities, depending on the level of interest rates. The forward contract in Example 12 may be an asset or liability, depending on the price of whiskey. A later section discusses the initial valuation of these assets and liabilities.

Firms must revalue the derivatives to market value each period. Common terminology refers to this as *marking to market*. The revaluation amount, in addition to increasing or decreasing the derivative asset or liability, also affects either (1) net income immediately, or (2) other comprehensive income immediately and net income later. Recall that Other Comprehensive Income is a temporary shareholders' equity account that reports changes during an accounting period in the recorded amounts of certain assets and liabilities, such as derivatives. Firms transfer the amount of other comprehensive income at the end of the period to the Accumulated Other Comprehensive Income account, a permanent shareholders' equity account. The income effect (that is, (1) or (2) above) depends on the nature of the hedge for which a firm acquires a derivative.

Generally accepted accounting principles (GAAP) classify derivatives as (1) speculative investments, (2) fair value hedges, or (3) cash flow hedges. Firms usually acquire derivatives to hedge particular risks. Thus, firms typically classify derivatives as either fair value hedges or cash flow hedges. Firms must choose to designate each derivative as one or the other, depending on their general hedging strategy and purpose in acquiring the particular derivative instrument. If a firm chooses not to designate a particular derivative as either a fair value hedge or a cash flow hedge, GAAP requires that the firm account for the derivative as a speculative investment.

Speculative Investment

Firms that acquire derivatives for reasons other than hedging a specific risk classify the derivative as a speculative investment. Firms must revalue derivatives held as speculative investments to market value each period and recognize the resulting gain or loss in net income.

Fair Value Hedges

Derivative instruments acquired to hedge exposure to changes in the fair value of an asset or liability are *fair value hedges*. Fair value hedges are of two general types (1) hedges of a *recognized* asset or liability, and (2) hedges of an *unrecognized* firm commitment. Firm B in Examples 6 and 10 entered into the interest swap agreement to neutralize the effect of changes in interest rates on the market value of its notes payable. Firm A in Examples 5 and 9 acquired the forward foreign exchange contract to neutralize the effect of changes in exchange rates on its commitment to purchase the equipment. These derivative instruments are therefore fair value hedges.

Cash Flow Hedges

Derivative instruments acquired to hedge exposure to variability in expected future cash flows are *cash flow hedges*. Cash flow hedges are of two general types: (1) hedges of cash flows of an *existing* asset or liability, and (2) hedges of cash flows of *forecasted* transactions. Firm C in Examples 7 and 11 entered into the interest swap agreement to neutralize changes in cash flows for interest payments on its variable rate notes payable. Firm D in Examples 8 and 12 acquired the forward contract on whiskey to protect itself from changes in the selling price of whiskey between October 31, Year 1, and March 31, Year 2. These derivative instruments are therefore cash flow hedges.

A particular derivative could be either a fair value hedge or a cash flow hedge, depending on the firm's reason for engaging in the hedge. Both the forward foreign exchange contract in Example 9 and the forward whiskey contract in Example 12 protect the firms' cash flows. The firms could conceivably classify both derivative instruments as cash flow hedges. Firm B in Example 9 acquires the derivative to protect the value of equipment acquired and therefore classifies it as a fair value hedge. Firm D in Example 12 acquires the derivative to protect its cash flows from changes in the price of whiskey and therefore classifies it as a cash flow hedge. One suspects that the FASB views the firm commitment to purchase the equipment by Firm A as having the economic substance of an asset and a liability, even though accounting treats it as a mutually unexecuted contract, whereas it views the anticipated transaction by Firm D to sell whiskey in the future as too uncertain to have the economic attributes of an asset at this point.

The four examples described thus far in this section illustrate the accounting for four possible scenarios:

Examples	Type of Hedge	Derivative Instrument Used
5 and 9	Fair Value—Firm Commitment	Forward Foreign Exchange Contract
6 and 10	Fair Value—Of Asset	Swap Contract—Variable for Fixed Rate
7 and 11	Cash Flow—Interest Payments	Swap Contract—Fixed for Variable Rate
8 and 12	Cash Flow—Forecasted Transaction	Forward Commodity Contract

Treatment of Hedging Gains and Losses

GAAP requires firms to recognize gains and losses from changes in the market value of financial instruments classified as fair value hedges in net income each period while the firm holds the financial instrument. GAAP also requires firms to revalue the asset or liability that is hedged and recognize a corresponding loss or gain. If the hedge is fully effective, the gain (loss) on the financial instrument will precisely offset the loss (gain) on the asset or liability hedged. The net effect on earnings is zero. If the hedge is not fully in effect, the net gain or loss increases or decreases net income.

GAAP require firms to include gains and losses from changes in the market values of financial instruments classified as cash flow hedges in other comprehensive income each period to the extent the financial instrument is "highly effective" in neutralizing the risk. Firms must include the ineffective portion in net income currently. FASB *Statement No. 133* gives general guidelines but leaves to professional judgment the meaning of "highly effective." The firm removes the accumulated amount in other comprehensive income related to a particular derivative instrument and transfers it to net income either periodically during the life of the derivative instrument or at the time of settlement, depending on the type of derivative instrument used.

The logic for the FASB's different treatment of gains and losses from changes in fair value of financial instruments results from applying the matching principle. In a fair value hedge of a recognized asset or liability, both the hedged asset (or liability) and its related derivative generally appear on the balance sheet. The firm revalues both the hedged asset (or liability) and its derivative to fair value each period and reports the gain or loss on the hedged asset (or liability) and the loss or gain on the derivative in net income. The net gain or loss indicates the effectiveness of the hedge in neutralizing the risk. In a cash flow hedge of an anticipated transaction, the hedged cash flow commitment does not appear on the balance sheet but the derivative instrument does appear. Recognizing a gain or loss on the derivative instrument in net income each period but recognizing the loss or gain on the anticipated transaction at the time an actual transaction occurs results in poor matching. Thus, the firm classifies the gain or loss on the derivative instrument in other comprehensive income and then, later, reclassifies it to net income when it records the actual transaction.

The logic for the FASB's different treatment would seem to break down for fair value hedges related to a firm commitment. GAAP usually does not recognize the firm commitment as an asset or a liability. Firms must recognize changes in the market value of the firm commitment as an asset and a liability, even though the initial commitment does not give rise to a recognized asset or liability.

ILLUSTRATIONS OF ACCOUNTING FOR DERIVATIVES

This section illustrates the accounting for the derivatives using the two examples involving interest rate swaps. (Problems 8.8 and 8.9 examine the accounting for the forward foreign exchange contract in Example 9 and the forward commodity contract in Example 12, respectively.) We use journal entries to illustrate the accounting for derivatives instead of the analytical framework described in Chapter 2. Exhibits 8.6 and 8.7 summarize the accounting in a format similar to the analytical framework.

Fair Value Hedge: Interest Rate Swap to Convert Fixed Rate Debt to Variable Rate Debt

Refer to Examples 6 and 10. Firm B desires to maintain the market value of its note payable in the event that it wishes to repay it prior to maturity. Changes in interest rates will change the market value of its fixed rate note. It enters into a swap contract to convert the fixed rate debt to variable rate debt. The market value of the debt will remain at $100,000 as long as the interest rate incorporated into the swap contract is the same as the rate used by the equipment supplier to value the note payable. Firm B designates the swap contract as a fair value hedge.

Firm B issues the note to the supplier on January 1, Year 1, and makes the following entry:

January 1, Year 1

Equipment	100,000	
Note Payable		100,000

The swap contract is a mutually unexecuted contract on January 1, Year 1. The variable interest rate on this date is 8 percent, the same as the fixed rate for the note to the equipment supplier. The swap contract has a market value of zero on this date. Thus, Firm B makes no entry to record the swap contract.

On December 31, Year 1, Firm B makes the required interest payment on the note for Year 1:

December 31, Year 1

Interest Expense (.08 × $100,000)	8,000	
Cash................................		8,000

Interest rates declined during Year 1. On December 31, the counterparty with whom Firm B entered into the swap contract resets the interest rate for Year 2 to 6 percent. Firm B must restate the note payable to market value and record the change in the market value of the swap contract caused by the decline in the interest rate.

The present value of the remaining cash flows on the note payable when discounted at 6 percent is:

Present Value of Interest Payments: $8,000 × 1.83339	$ 14,667
Present Value of Principal: $100,000 × .89000....................	89,000
Total Present Value	$103,667

Firm B makes the following entry to record the change in market value:

December 31, Year 1

Loss on Revaluation of Note Payable (Inc. State.)	3,667	
Note Payable (= $103,667 – $100,000)....		3,667

Firms typically do not revalue financial instruments, such as this note payable, to market value when interest rates change. They continue to account for the financial instruments using the interest rate at the time of the initial recording of the financial instrument in the accounts. When a firm hedges a financial instrument, however, it must recognize changes in market values. It must likewise recognize changes in the market value of the swap contract.

The decline in interest rates to 6 percent means that Firm B will save $2,000 each year in interest payments. The present value of a $2,000 annuity for two periods at 6 percent is $3,667 (= $2,000 × 1.83339). Thus, the value of the swap contract increased from zero at the beginning of Year 1 to $3,667 at the end of the year. Firm B makes the following entry:

December 31, Year 1

Swap Contract (Asset)	3,667	
Gain on Revaluation of Swap Contract (Inc. State.)		3,667

The loss from the revaluation of the note payable exactly offsets the gain from the revaluation of the swap contract, indicating that the swap contract was fully effective (that is, the Loss on Revaluation of Note Payable is 100 percent offset by the Gain on Revaluation of Swap Contract) in hedging the interest rate risk.

Firm B follows a similar process at the end of Year 2. First, it records interest expense on the note payable:

December 31, Year 2

Interest Expense (.06 × $103,667)	6,220	
Note Payable (plug)	1,780	
Cash (.08 × $100,000)		8,000

Firm B uses the effective interest method to compute interest expense for the year. The effective interest rate for Year 2 is 6 percent and the book value of the note payable at the beginning of the year is $103,667. The cash payment of $8,000 is the amount set forth in the original borrowing arrangement with the equipment supplier.

Second, the firm records interest revenue for the change in the present value of the swap contract for the year.

December 31, Year 2

Swap Contract (Asset)	220	
Interest Revenue (.06 × $3,667)		220

Interest expense (net) as a result of the two entries is $6,000 (= $6,220 − $220), which is the variable rate for Year 2 of 6 percent times the face value of the note.

Third, Firm B receives $2,000 under the swap contract with its counterparty because interest rate decreased from 8 percent to 6 percent.

December 31, Year 2

Cash [$100,000 × (.08 − .06)]	2,000	
Swap Contract (Asset)		2,000

The $2,000 cash received from the counterparty in a sense reimburses Firm B for paying interest at 8 percent on the note whereas the swap contract provides that the firm benefits when interest rates decline, in this case to 6 percent.

Fourth, Firm B must revalue the note payable and the swap contract for changes in market value. Interest rates increased during Year 2, so the bank resets the interest rate in the swap agreement to 10 percent for Year 3. The present value of the remaining payments on the note at 10 percent is:

Present Value of Interest Payment: $8,000 × .90909	$ 7,273
Present Value of Principal: $100,000 × .90909	90,909
Total Present Value	$98,182

The book value of the note payable before revaluation is $101,887 (= $103,667 − $1,780). The entry to revalue the note payable is:

Note Payable ($101,887 − $98,182)	3,705	
Gain on Revaluation of Note Payable		
(Inc. State.)		3,705

The market value of the swap contract decreases. Firm A must now *pay* an additional $2,000 in interest in Year 3 because of the swap contract. Thus, the swap contract becomes a liability instead of an asset. The present value of $2,000 when discounted at 10 percent is $1,818 (= $2,000 × .90909). The book value of the swap contract before revaluation is an asset of $1,887 (= $3,667 + $220 − $2,000). The entry to revalue the swap contract is:

Loss on Revaluation of Swap Contract (Inc. State.)	3,705	
Swap Contract (Asset).		1,887
Swap Contract (Liability)		1,818

The gain on revaluation of the note exactly offsets the loss on revaluation of the swap contract, so the swap contract hedges the change in interest rates.

The entries for Year 3 are as follows:

December 31, Year 3

Interest Expense (.10 × $98,182)	9,818	
Note Payable (plug).		1,818
Cash (.08 × $100,000)		8,000

December 31, Year 3

Interest Expense (.10 × $1,818)	182	
Swap Contract (Liability)		182

Interest expense (net) after these two entries is $10,000 (= $9,818 + $182), which equals the variable interest rate of 10 percent times the face value of the note.

Firm B must pay the counterparty an extra 2 percent because the variable interest rate of 10 percent exceeds the fixed interest rate of 8 percent.

December 31, Year 3

Swap Contract (Liability) [$100,000 × (.10 − .08)] . .	2,000	
Cash		2,000

Firm B must repay the note and close out the Swap Contract.

December 31, Year 3

Note Payable ($98,182 + $1,181)	100,000	
Cash.		100,000

The Swap Contract account has a zero balance on December 31, Year 3, after making the entries above (= $1,818 + $182 − $2,000), so it need make no additional entries to close out this account.

		Equipment	Notes	Swap	Income
	Cash	(at cost)	Payable	Contract	Statement
Year 1					
Issue Note for Equipment.............	$ —	$100,000	$(100,000)	$ —	$ —
Enter Swap Contract.................	—	—	—	—	—
Record Interest on Note	(8,000)	—	—	—	8,000
Revalue Note Payable	—	—	(3,667)	—	3,667
Revalue Swap Contract..............	—	—	—	3,667	(3,667)
December 31, Year 1	$ (8,000)	$100,000	$(103,667)	$ 3,667	$ 8,000
Year 2					
Record Interest on Note	(8,000)	—	1,780	—	$ 6,220
Record Interest on Swap Contract	—	—	—	220	(220)
Record Swap Interest Received	2,000	—	—	(2,000)	—
Revalue Note Payable	—	—	3,705	—	(3,705)
Revalue Swap Contract..............	—	—	—	(3,705)	3,705
December 31, Year 2	$ (14,000)	$100,000	$ (98,182)	$(1,818)	$ 6,000
Year 3					
Record Interest on Note	(8,000)	—	(1,818)	—	$ 9,818
Record Interest on Swap Contract	—	—	—	(182)	182
Record Swap Interest Paid............	(2,000)	—	—	2,000	—
Repay Note Payable.................	(100,000)	—	100,000	—	—
December 31, Year 3	$(124,000)	$100,000	$ —	$ —	$10,000

EXHIBIT 8.6
Effects on Various Accounts of $100,000 Fixed Rate Note and Related Interest Rate Swap Accounted for as a Fair Value Hedge

Note: Amounts in parentheses are credits to the various accounts.

Exhibit 8.6 summarizes the effects of these entries on various accounts (credit entries in parentheses). Note that net income reflects the variable interest rate each year, 8 percent for Year 1, 6 percent for Year 2, and 10 percent for Year 3. The note payable and the swap contract net to $100,000 at the end of each year.

Summary of the Accounting for a Fair Value Hedge of an Existing Asset or Liability

The following summarizes the accounting for a fair value hedge of an existing asset or liability.

1. The hedged asset or liability already appears on the books. Its valuation depends on GAAP's required accounting for the particular asset or liability

(for example, lower of cost or market for inventories, present value of future cash flows for long-term receivables and payables).

2. The firm recognizes the derivative as an asset on the date of acquisition to the extent it makes an initial investment. Otherwise, no amount appears on the balance sheet for the derivative.

3. At the end of each period, revalue the hedged asset or liability to fair value and include the resulting gain or loss in net income.

4. At the end of each period, revalue the derivative instrument to fair value and include the resulting loss or gain in net income.

5. Show the hedged asset and liability and its related derivative separately on the balance sheet.

6. Remove the hedged asset or liability and its related derivative from the accounts at the time of settlement (for example, at the time of interest payments).

Cash Flow Hedge: Interest Rate Swap to Convert Variable Rate Debt to Fixed Rate Debt

Refer to Examples 7 and 11. Firm C desires to hedge the risk of changes in interest rates on its cash payments for interest. It enters into a swap contract with a counterparty to convert its variable rate note payable to a fixed rate note. Firm C designates the swap contract as a cash flow hedge. The facts for the case are similar to those for Firm B. The note has a $100,000 face value, an initial variable interest rate of 8 percent, which the counterparty resets to 6 percent for Year 2, and 10 percent for Year 3. The note matures on December 31, Year 3.

The entry to record the note payable is:

January 1, Year 1

Equipment	100,000	
Note Payable		100,000

Firm C records interest on the note for Year 1.

December 31, Year 1

Interest Expense (.08 × $100,000)	8,000	
Cash.		8,000

The market value of the note in this case, unlike that for Firm B, will not change as interest rates change because the note carries a variable interest rate. The market value of the swap contract does change. The market value on December 31, Year 1, after the counterparty resets the interest rate to 6 percent, is $3,667. This amount is the present value of the $2,000 that Firm C will pay the counterparty on December 31 of Year 2 and Year 3 if the interest rate remains at 6 percent. The entry is:

December 31, Year 1

Other Comprehensive Income (Swap Contract)	3,667	
Swap Contract (Liability)		3,667

The loss from the revaluation of the swap contract does not affect net income immediately on a cash flow hedge. Instead, it reduces other comprehensive income. Other comprehensive income is an element of accumulated other comprehensive income, a shareholders' equity account.

Note that the book value of the note payable of $100,000 plus the book value of the swap contract of $3,667 is $103,667. This amount is the present value of the expected cash flows under the fixed rate note and swap contract combined, discounted at 6 percent.

The entry on December 31, Year 2, to recognize and pay interest on the variable rate note is:

December 31, Year 2
Interest Expense (.06 × $100,000)   6,000
    Cash.   6,000

Firm C must also increase the book value of the swap contract for the passage of time.

December 31, Year 2
Other Comprehensive Income (Swap Contract)
    (.06 × $3,667)   220
        Swap Contract (liability).   220

Note that the interest charge does not affect net income immediately but instead decreases other comprehensive income.

Firm C pays the counterparty the $2,000 [= $100,000 × (.08 − .06)] required by the swap contract. The entry is:

December 31, Year 2
Swap Contract (Liability).   2,000
    Cash.   2,000

Because the swap contract hedged cash flows related to interest rate risk during Year 2, Firm C reclassifies a portion of other comprehensive income to net income. The entry is:

December 31, Year 2
Interest Expense [= $100,000 × (.08 − .06)} . . .   2,000
    Other Comprehensive Income
        (Swap Contract)   2,000

At this point the swap contract account has a credit balance of $1,887 (= $3,667 + $220 − $2,000). Other comprehensive income related to this transaction likewise has a debit balance of $1,887. Interest expense on the income statement is $8,000 (= $6,000 + $2,000).

Restating the interest rate on December 31, Year 2, to 10 percent changes the value of the swap contract from a liability to an asset. The present value of the $2,000 that Firm C will receive from the counterparty at the end of Year 3 when discounted at 10 percent is $1,818. The entry to revalue to swap contract is:

December 31, Year 2

Swap Contract (Liability).................	1,887	
Swap Contract (Asset)	1,818	
Other Comprehensive Income (Swap Contract)		3,705

Other comprehensive income has a credit balance of $1,818, which equals the debit balance in the Swap Contract account.

The entry during Year 3 to recognize and pay interest on the variable rate note is:

December 31, Year 3

Interest Expense (.10 × $100,000)	10,000	
Cash................................		10,000

Firm C also increases the book value of the swap contract for the passage of time.

December 31, Year 3

Swap Contract (Asset) (.10 × $1,818)	182	
Other Comprehensive Income		
(Swap Contract)		182

The swap contract requires the counterparty to pay the firm $2,000 under the swap contract.

December 31, Year 3

Cash [$100,000 × (.10 − .08)]..............	2,000	
Swap Contract (Asset)................		2,000

Because the swap contract hedged cash flows related to interest rate risk during Year 3, Firm C reclassifies a portion of other comprehensive income to net income. The entry is:

December 31, Year 3

Other Comprehensive Income		
(Swap Contract)......................	2,000	
Interest Expense		2,000

Thus, interest expense (net) for Year 3 is $8,000 (= $10,000 − $2,000).

Firm C repays the note on December 31, Year 3:

December 31, Year 3

Notes Payable	100,000	
Cash................................		100,000

It must also close out the swap contract account. This account has a balance of zero on December 31, Year 3 (= $1,818 + $182 − $2,000). Thus, Firm C need make no entry. If the swap contract had been highly, but not perfectly, effective in neutralizing the interest rate risk, then accumulated other comprehensive income would have a balance related to the swap contract, which Firm C would reclassify to net income at this point.

	EXHIBIT 8.7					
	Effects on Various Accounts of $100,000 Variable Rate Note and Related Interest Rate Swap Accounted for as a Cash Flow Hedge					
	Cash	Equipment (at cost)	Notes Payable	Swap Contract	Income Statement	Other Comp. Income
Year 1						
Issue Note for Equipment.........	$ —	$100,000	$(100,000)	$ —	$ —	$ —
Enter Swap Contract.............	—	—	—	—	—	—
Record Interest on Note	(8,000)	—	—	—	8,000	—
Revalue Swap Contract...........	—	—	—	(3,667)		3,667
December 31, Year 1	$ (8,000)	$100,000	$(100,000)	$(3,667)	$ 8,000	$ 3,667
Record Interest on Note	(6,000)	—	—	—	6,000	
Record Interest on Swap Contract ..	—	—	—	(220)	—	220
Record Swap Interest Paid	(2,000)	—	—	2,000	—	—
Reclassify Portion of Other Comprehensive Income........	—	—	—	—	2,000	(2,000)
Revalue Swap Contract...........	—	—	—	3,705	—	(3,705)
December 31, Year 2	$ (16,000)	$100,000	$(100,000)	$ 1,818	$ 8,000	$(1,818)
Record Interest on Note	(10,000)	—	—	—	10,000	
Record Interest on Swap Contract ..	—	—	—	182		(182)
Record Swap Interest Received.....	2,000	—	—	(2,000)	—	—
Reclassify Portion of Other Comprehensive Income........	—	—	—	—	(2,000)	2,000
Repay Note Payable.............	(100,000)	—	100,000	—	—	
Close Out Swap Contract.........	—	—	—	—	—	—
December 31, Year 3	$(124,000)	$100,000	$ —	$ —	$ 8,000	$ —

Note: Amounts in parentheses are credits to the various accounts.

Exhibit 8.7 summaries the effect of these entries on various accounts (credit entries in parentheses). Note that interest expense is $8,000 each year, the fixed rate of 8 percent that Firm C accomplished by entering into the swap contract. The amounts in other comprehensive income reflect changes in the market value of the swap contract. The swap contract begins and ends with a zero value.

Summary of Accounting for a Cash Flow Hedge of an Existing Asset or Liability

The following summarizes the accounting for a cash flow hedge of an existing asset or liability:

1. The hedged asset or liability already appears on the books. Its valuation depends on GAAP's required accounting for the particular asset or liability (for example, lower of cost or market for inventories, present value of future cash flows for long-term receivables and payables).

2. The firm recognizes the derivative as an asset on the date of acquisition to the extent it makes an initial investment. Otherwise, no amount appears on the balance sheet for the derivative.

3. At the end of each period, revalue the hedged asset or liability to fair value and include the resulting gain or loss in other comprehensive income.

4. At the end of each period, revalue the derivative instrument to fair value and include the resulting loss or gain in other comprehensive income.

5. Reclassify gains and losses from other comprehensive income to net income when the gain or loss on the hedged item affects net income. If the derivative is not highly effective in neutralizing the gain or loss on the hedged item, then the firm must reclassify the ineffective portion to net income immediately and not wait until the gain or loss on the hedged items affects net income.

6. Show the hedged asset and liability and its related derivative separately on the balance sheet. Also show the cumulative amount of net value changes for the hedged items and its related derivative in accumulated other comprehensive income.

7. Remove the hedged asset or liability and its related derivative from the accounts at the time of settlement (for example, at the time of interest payments).

SUMMARY OF EXAMPLES

Firms record changes in the market value of all derivatives each period. Changes in the value of derivatives and the related asset, liability, or commitment for fair value hedges flow through to net income immediately. Changes in the value of derivatives related to cash flow hedges initially increase or decrease other comprehensive income. They affect net income at the time the cash flows that they hedge affect net income. Although this section does not illustrate the accounting for derivatives held as speculative investments because of their infrequency, the accounting is the same as for fair value hedges.

DISCLOSURES RELATED TO DERIVATIVE INSTRUMENTS

Several FASB pronouncements address disclosures for derivatives. FASB *Statement No. 107*[15] requires firms to disclose the book value and the fair value of financial instruments. Financial instruments impose on one entity a right to receive

---

[15]Financial Accounting Standards Board, *Statement of Financial Accounting Standards Statement No. 107*, "Disclosures about Fair Value of Financial Instruments," 1991.

cash and an obligation on another entity to pay cash. Financial instruments include accounts receivable, notes receivable, notes payable, bonds payable, forward contracts, swap contracts, and most derivatives. Fair value is the current amount at which two willing parties would exchange the instrument for cash.

FASB *Statement No. 133* requires the following disclosures (among others) with respect to derivatives.

1. A description of the firm's risk management strategy and how particular derivatives help accomplish the firm's hedging objectives. The description should distinguish between derivative instruments designated as fair value hedges, cash flow hedges, and all other derivatives.
2. For fair value and cash flow hedges, firms must disclose the net gain or loss recognized in earnings resulting from the hedges' ineffectiveness (that is, not offsetting the risk hedged) and the line item on the income statement that includes this net gain or loss.
3. For cash flow hedges, firms must describe the transactions or events that will result in reclassifying gains and losses from other comprehensive income to net income and the estimated amount of such reclassifications during the next 12 months.
4. The net amount of gains and losses recognized in earnings because a hedged firm commitment no longer qualifies as a fair value hedge, or a hedged forecasted transaction no longer qualifies as a cash flow hedge.

Refer to the notes to PepsiCo's financial statements in Appendix A. PepsiCo discloses in Note 1 that it uses derivatives to hedge commodity prices, foreign exchange rates, interest rates, and PepsiCo's stock price. All hedges are either fair value or cash flow hedges (that is, PepsiCo does not use derivatives for speculative investment purposes). Note 1 also describes the types of derivatives PepsiCo uses (futures, options, swaps) for each type of risk and how each derivative serves to hedge the specified risk. Note 12 describes PepsiCo's use of interest rate and currency swaps to hedge risk. Note 13 indicates that the net gain or loss included in earnings from fair value and cash flow hedges is immaterial. PepsiCo therefore does not disclose the amount of the net gain or loss. It states that it expected to reclassify losses of approximately $1 million from accumulated other comprehensive income into earnings during the next 12 months. It also states that it did not discontinue any cash flow hedges and that it had no hedged firm commitments that no longer qualify as fair value hedges.

PepsiCo's Statement of Shareholders' Equity shows the change in accumulated other comprehensive income for Year 11. The firm discloses that it incurred net derivative losses of $21 million during Year 11 from cash flow hedges. This amount is less than one percent of net income for Year 11, support for PepsiCo's description that its net derivative gains and losses from cash flow hedges were immaterial.

Firms must report the impact on earnings of certain adverse changes in each of the major risk factors to which they are subject. Firms typically disclose this information in their management discussion and analysis of operations. PepsiCo discloses in Appendix B the effect on earnings of adverse changes in commodity prices, foreign exchange rates, interest rates, and its stock price (used in measuring deferred compensation expense). This information permits the analyst to assess the extent and effectiveness of hedging activities on each of these risks. The following summarizes PepsiCo's disclosures:

Adverse Change	Nature of Adverse Effect	Effect on Earnings
Commodity Prices	10% Increase	$12 million decrease
Foreign Exchange Rates	10% Unfavorable	$35 million decrease
Interest Rates	1 Percentage Point Increase	$3 million decrease
Stock Price	10% Unfavorable	$6 million decrease

Recall that PepsiCo reported earnings of $2,662 million for Year 11. Thus, none of these changes would have a material effect on net income, suggesting that PepsiCo's derivatives would be effective in hedging even larger adverse changes than actually occurred.

Many firms use a value-at-risk simulation model to estimate the impact of adverse price movements. The value-at-risk model develops a distribution of the changes in relevant interest rates, exchange rates, commodity prices, or other underlying for a particular period of prior years (for example, 10 years). Using the distribution of prior adverse changes and the average net position in various financial instruments for the current year, the model simulates with a 95 percent or other confidence level the minimum, maximum, or average amount of loss that a firm would incur.

ACCOUNTING QUALITY ISSUES AND DERIVATIVES

Firms must mark derivatives to market value each period. When active, established markets exist for derivatives, as is the case for most forward contracts and interest and currency swaps, market values are usually reliable and easy to obtain. When firms engage in derivative transactions for which active markets do not exist, questions arise about the reliability of the market valuations. Enron, for example, purchased and sold derivatives on the price and availability of broadband services. Broadband services were an emerging market at the time, with Enron one of only a few firms engaging in this type of derivative trading.

A second accounting quality concern involves the classification of derivatives as fair value hedges versus cash flow hedges. Recall that the firms in Examples 9 and 12 could have classified the exchange and commodity contracts as either fair value or cash flow hedges. Gains and losses on cash flow hedges affect earnings later than those on fair value hedges. When gains and losses on cash flow hedges, which GAAP includes in accumulated other comprehensive income, substantially exceed the gains and losses on fair value hedges included in earnings, then the analyst must at least question the firm's classification of its hedges.

When firms use derivatives effectively to manage risks, the net gain or loss each period should be relatively small. Large and varying amounts of gains or losses usually signal ineffective use of derivatives.

RETIREMENT BENEFITS

Employers typically provide two types of benefits to retired employees: (1) pension benefits and (2) health care and life insurance coverage.[16] Financial reporting, both in the United States and in most other countries, requires that the employer recognize the cost of these benefits as an expense while the employees work and generate revenues rather than when they receive the benefits during retirement. Estimating the expected cost of the benefits requires assumptions about employee turnover, future compensation and health care costs, interest rates, and other factors. Because the employer will not know the actual costs of these benefits until many years elapse, estimating their costs while the employees work requires estimation and judgments.

A further issue relates to the pattern for recognizing the costs as an expense. Should the employer recognize an equal amount each year over the employee's working years? Or should the amount increase over time as compensation levels increase? FASB pronouncements on pension and health care benefits further complicate the question of the timing of expense recognition. These pronouncements do not require immediate recognition of an expense and a liability for benefits already earned by employees at the time firms adopt these reporting standards. Instead, the costs of benefits already earned can become expenses in future periods. One consequence of this reporting procedure is that the amount that firms show as pension or health care liabilities on the balance sheet may understate the economic liability.

This section describes GAAP accounting and reporting for pensions, health care, and life insurance benefits, and discusses issues that the analyst should consider when interpreting disclosures related to retirement benefits.

PENSIONS

Pension plans work as follows:

1. Employers agree to provide certain pension benefits to employees. The arrangement may take the form of either a defined contribution plan or a defined benefit plan. Under a defined contribution plan, the employer agrees to contribute a certain amount to a pension fund each period (usually based on a percentage of employees' compensation), without specifying the benefits

---

[16]Some retired employees receive a third benefit from employers in the form of severance and similar benefits following active service but prior to retirement. The FASB addresses the reporting for these benefits in *Statement of Financial Accounting Standard No. 112*, "Employer's Accounting for Postemployment Benefits," 1992. The standard requires employers to accrue the cost of these benefits if they can be reasonably estimated and the employees have the unconditional right to the benefits. The statement only peripherally relates to the retiree benefits discussed in this section, however, because applying *Statement No. 112* is not conditional on retirement of the employee.

employees will receive during retirement. The amount employees eventually receive depends on the performance of the pension fund. Under a defined benefit plan, the employer agrees to make pension payments to employees during retirement using a benefits formula based on wages earned and number of years of employment. A typical plan might provide an annual pension benefit during retirement equal to two percent times the number of years worked times an average of the highest five years of compensation during working years. An employee who worked 30 years at an average highest five years of compensation of $50,000 would receive an annual pension of $30,000 (= .02 × 30 × $50,000). The plan does not specify the amount the employer will contribute to the pension fund. The employer must make contributions to the fund such that those amounts plus earnings from pension investments are sufficient to make the promised payments.

2. Employers periodically contribute cash to a pension fund. The trustee, or administrator, of the fund invests the cash received from the employer in stocks, bonds, and other investments. The assets in the pension fund accumulate each period from both employer contributions and income from investments. These assets appear on the balance sheet of the pension plan and not on the employer's balance sheet.

3. The employer satisfies its obligation to the employee under a defined contribution plan once it makes periodic contributions to the pension fund. The employer's obligation under a defined benefit plan increases each period from two factors. First, employees earn increased benefits each period as they work an additional period at a higher compensation level. Second, the employer's obligation increases each period because time passes and the remaining time until employees begin receiving their pensions decreases. Thus, the present value of the pension obligation increases. This obligation appears as a liability on the balance sheet of the pension plan and not on the employer's balance sheet.

4. The pension fund makes pension payments to retired employees under defined benefit plans. Both the assets and the liabilities of the pension plan decrease in the amount of the payments. The employer's obligation under a defined benefit plan, which does not appear on the employer's books, decreases by the amount paid.

Accounting Records of the Pension Plan

The balance sheet of the pension plan lists the assets in the pension fund and the liability for benefits earned but not yet paid to employees. Exhibit 8.8 indicates how the balance sheet changes each period. Assets increase from earnings on investments and from contributions received from the employer, and decrease from losses on investments and payments to retirees. Liabilities increase because (1) the remaining time until working employees will receive their pension decreases, and (2) employees work an additional year and earn rights to a larger pension. Liabilities decrease when the pension plan makes payments to retirees. Liabilities also increase or

EXHIBIT 8.8	
Activity Affecting a Defined Benefit Pension Plan	
Pension Fund Assets	**Pension Fund Liabilities**
Assets at Beginning of Period	Liabilities at Beginning of Period
± Actual Earnings on Investments	+ Increase in Liabilities Due to Passage of Time
+ Contributions Received from the Employer	+ Increase in Liabilities from Employee Services
	± Actuarial Gains and Losses Due to Changes in Assumptions
− Payments to Retirees	− Payments to Retirees
= Assets at End of Period	= Liabilities at End of Period

decrease if firms change the actuarial assumptions (discount rate, employee turnover rate, mortality rate) or the pension benefit formula underlying the pension plan.

Pension disclosures permit the analyst to assess the degree to which a firm has an overfunded or underfunded pension plan. These disclosures also permit an assessment of the performance of the pension fund during an accounting period.[17]

Obligations Under Defined Benefit Plans

GAAP requires firms to disclose the funded status of their pension plans at the end of each year. Refer to PepsiCo's Note 19, "Pension and Postretirement Benefits," in Appendix A. Exhibit 8.9 reports the status of PepsiCo's pension plan at the end of Year 10 and Year 11. The top portion of Exhibit 8.9 shows the assets and liabilities of the pension plan. The last line shows the amounts that PepsiCo records on its books related to the pension plan. The unrecognized items (middle three lines of the exhibit) represent amounts reflected in assets and liabilities of the pension plan but not yet recognized on the employer's books. We discuss the accounting entries on the employer's books later in this section.

Interpreting these disclosures requires several definitions:

Accumulated Benefit Obligation. The present value of amounts the employer expects to pay to retired employees (taking into consideration actuarial assumptions concerning employee turnover and mortality) based on employees' service to date

---

[17]The accounting and disclosures for pension plans follow two FASB pronouncements: Financial Accounting Standards Board, *Statement of Financial Accounting Standards Statement No. 87,* "Employer's Accounting for Pensions," 1985; Financial Accounting Standards Board, *Statement of Financial Accounting Standards Statement No. 132,* "Employer's Disclosures about Pensions and Other Retirement Benefits," 1998.

EXHIBIT 8.9		
Funded Status of PepsiCo's Pension Plan **(amounts in millions)**		
	December 31, Year 11	December 31, Year 10
Accounting Records of Pension Plan		
Actuarial present value of projected benefit obligation.....................	$(3,556)	$(3,170)
Plan assets at fair value....................	3,129	3,251
Projected benefit obligation (in excess of)/ less than plan assets....................	$ (427)	$ 81
Items that Reconcile the Two Sets of Records		
Unrecognized prior service	38	49
Unrecognized loss/(gain)	548	(349)
Unrecognized transition asset	(2)	(3)
Accounting Records of Employer		
Net amounts recognized (accrued pension asset (liability) on balance sheet)	$ 157	$ (222)

and current-year compensation levels. The accumulated benefit obligation indicates the present value of the benefits earned to date, excluding any future salary increases that will serve as the base for computing the pension payment and excluding future years of service prior to retirement.

Projected Benefit Obligation. The actuarial present value of amounts the employer expects to pay to retired employees based on employees' service to date but using the expected future salaries that will serve as the base for computing the pension payment. The difference between the accumulated and projected benefit obligation is the effect of future salary increases. Consequently, the projected benefit obligation exceeds the accumulated benefit obligation. The projected benefit obligation is also closer in amount to what one might view as an economic measure of the pension obligation: the present value of amounts the employer expects to pay to employees during retirement based on total expected years of service (past and future) and expected future salaries. *Statement No. 87* does not require disclosure of this economic obligation.

The required disclosures show the relationship between the market value of pension fund assets and the projected benefit obligation at each valuation date. The amounts on the books of the pension plan reflect current market values of both assets and liabilities at each valuation date. A pension plan can be overfunded or underfunded at any point in time.

At the end of Year 10, the assets in PepsiCo's pension plans of $3,251 million exceeded the benefit obligation of $3,170 million by $81 million. There are several implications of an *overfunded* pension plan:

1. In some circumstances, the sponsoring firm can reclaim the excess assets for corporate use. The amount reclaimed becomes immediately subject to income taxes, which discourages most firms from reclaiming excess amounts.
2. The sponsoring firm can discontinue contributions to the pension fund, subject to any minimum funding requirements of federal law, until such time as the assets in the pension fund equal the projected benefit obligation.
3. The sponsoring firm can continue its historical pattern of funding on the presumption that the overfunded status is due to temporary market appreciation of investments that could easily reverse in the future, as is the case for PepsiCo.

Although one might argue that an excess of pension fund assets over the projected benefit obligation represents an asset of the employer, *Statement No. 87* does not permit firms to recognize this resource on the balance sheet.

At the end of Year 11, the assets in PepsiCo's pension plan of $3,129 million were less than the benefit obligation of $3,556 million. Thus, the pension fund was underfunded by $427 million. Using arguments similar to that applied to overfunded situations, one might view an excess of the projected benefit obligation over pension fund assets as a liability that firms should report on the balance sheet. The FASB, responding to criticisms that the measurement of the projected benefit obligation requires subjective projections of future salary increases, stipulates instead that firms show an excess of the *accumulated* benefit obligation over pension fund assets on the balance sheet as a liability (included in what *Statement No. 87* labels the *minimum liability*). Because the accumulated benefit obligation is usually smaller than the projected benefit obligation, relatively few firms report a liability for underfunded benefits by this measure. We discuss this minimum liability in a later section.

GAAP also requires firms to show the reasons why their pension assets and pension liabilities changed during the year. Exhibit 8.10 summarizes PepsiCo's disclosures from Note 19. PepsiCo's pension plan moved from a slightly overfunded status at the end of Year 10 to a more significant underfunded status at the end of Year 11 as a result of the net effect of three factors:

1. An actuarial loss on the benefit obligation of $170 million, due primarily to a decrease in the discount rate used to compute the benefit obligations (increases the net underfunded status of the plan).
2. A net loss on investments for Year 11 of $382 million (increases the net underfunded status of the plan).
3. A substantial increase in PepsiCo's contribution to the pension fund from $103 million in Year 10 to $446 million in Year 11 (decreases the net underfunded status of the plan).

Next, we explore more fully each of these three contributing explanations for a change in the net funded status of a pension plan.

EXHIBIT 8.10		
Changes in the Funded Status of PepsiCo Pension Plan for Year 10 and Year 11 (amounts in millions)		
Accounting Records of Pension Plan	**Year 11**	**Year 10**
Assets at Beginning of Year.....................	$3,251	$3,053
Plus (minus) Earnings (Losses) from Investments ..	(382)	281
Plus Contribution from PepsiCo	446	103
Less Payments to Retirees (Plug)	(170)	(166)
Other Changes	(16)	(20)
Assets at End of Year..........................	$3,129	$3,251
Benefit Obligation at Beginning of Year...........	$3,170	$3,009
Plus Service Cost.............................	127	120
Plus Interest Cost	233	221
Less Payments to Retirees......................	(170)	(166)
Plus (Minus) Loss (Gain)	170	6
Other Changes	26	(20)
Benefit Obligation at End of Year................	$3,556	$3,170

Accounting Records of the Employer

The last line of Exhibit 8.9 shows the amounts on the books of PepsiCo. PepsiCo reports a net liability of $222 million at the end of Year 10 and a net asset of $157 million at the end of Year 11. PepsiCo indicates in Note 19 the particular accounts on the balance sheet that comprise these net amounts. The amounts that appear on the balance sheet of the employer generally result from three entries each period:

1. Recognition of pension expense.
2. Recognition of pension contribution.
3. Recognition of minimum underfunded pension liability.

We discuss each of these three entries next.

Employer's Entry 1: Recognition of Pension Expense

Firms must calculate net pension expense each year based on the projected benefit cost method, which means that actuarial calculations use accumulated service to date and projected future salaries. PepsiCo reports in Note 19 that its net pension cost (expense) for Year 11 is $56 million.[18] PepsiCo's recognition of net pension expense had the following effects on the financial statements (ignoring income taxes):

---

[18]PepsiCo also recognized separate charges to curtail or settle existing pension plans or provide special termination benefits. We do not consider these typically nonrecurring charges in the discussion of pensions in this section.

	C	+	N$A	=	L	+	CC	+	AOCI	+	RE
BS-BOP											
(1)					+56						−56
IBT											−56

PepsiCo's entry in its accounting records to recognize net pension expense (excluding curtailments and special termination benefits) is:

Pension Expense	56	
Pension Liability		56

Exhibit 8.11 summarizes the six elements comprising net pension expense and shows the amounts from PepsiCo's Note 19. We discuss each of these elements next.

Element 1: Service Cost. The present value of the projected benefit obligation on the books of the pension plan increases each year because employees work an additional year. GAAP refers to the increase as the *service cost.* The employer includes the service cost in pension expense each year (PepsiCo's service cost for Year 11 is $127 million).

Element 2: Interest Cost. The present value of the projected benefit obligation on the books of the pension plan also increases each year because pension payments are one year nearer to being made. GAAP refers to this increase as the *interest cost.* The employer includes this amount in pension expense on its books each year (PepsiCo's interest cost for Year 11 is $233 million). PepsiCo discloses in Note 19 that it used an interest rate of 7.7 percent at the end of Year 10 to value the pension fund obligation. Multiplying the pension obligation of $3,170 million on January 1, Year 11, by this interest rate approximately equals the $233 million amount recognized as interest cost for the year.

Element 3: Expected Return on Pension Investments. Pension plans must have sufficient assets to pay retirement benefits. Pension plans obtain the needed assets from employer contributions and from investment income. The higher is the return on pension investments, the less cash the employer needs to contribute to the pension plan. GAAP requires firms to reduce their pension expense for the return on pension fund investments. Recall from above that pension expense and the pension liability increase each year for service and interest costs. The sum of these two amounts is the additional assets needed in the pension fund to fund the increase in the pension obligation for the period. To the extent that earnings on pension fund investments fund this additional liability, the employer can contribute less to the pension fund. Thus, earnings on pension investment reduce the employer's pension expense.

GAAP requires firms to reduce pension expense each period by the *expected,* not the *actual,* return on investments. When deciding on its funding level for employer contributions, firms make an assumption as to the long-term expected return on pension fund investments. Note 19 indicates that PepsiCo assumed a long-term

EXHIBIT 8.11		
Components of Pension Expense for PepsiCo		
	Effect on Pension Expense	
	Debit (Increase)	**Credit (Decrease)**
1. Service Cost–the increase in the projected benefit obligation because employees worked an additional year...............	127	
2. Interest Cost–the increase in the projected benefit obligation because of the passage of time	233	
3. Expected Return on Plan Assets–the expected change in the market value of plan assets due to interest, dividends, and changes in the market value of investments.....................		301
4. Amortization of net pension asset (pension fund assets exceed projected benefit obligation) or net pension liability (pension fund assets are less than projected benefit obligation) as of the date of initial adoption of *Statement No. 87*, referred to as the transition asset or liability. The firm amortizes the net asset or net liability straight line over the average remaining service life of employees.		
Net Pension Liability......................................	N/A	
Net Pension Asset		2
5. Amortization of increases in the projected benefit obligation that arise because the firm sweetens the pension benefit formula and gives employees credit for their prior service under the sweetened benefit arrangement. The amortization period is generally the average remaining service life of employees, although a shorter period may be required if an employer regularly sweetens its pension plan.	8	
6. Amortization of gains and losses because actual experience differs from actuarial assumptions (e.g., salary interest rate, employee turnover, mortality, asset returns).		
Actuarial Loss	N/A	
Actuarial Gain...		9
7. Net pension expense	56	

return on pension assets of 9.9 percent as of the end of Year 10. Actual returns over time will vary around this amount but should average 9.9 percent over the long term. GAAP encourages firms to take a long-term view of its pension plan by reducing pension expense for the long-term expected return on investments. As we discuss later with respect to element 6 of pension expense, GAAP requires firms to amortize into pension expense over time any difference between expected and actual returns on investments. Note that PepsiCo's assets measured at fair value at the beginning of Year 11 totaled $3,251 million. The expected return on these assets for Year 11 at 9.9 percent approximately equals the $301 million reduction in pension expense that PepsiCo recognized for Year 11.

Recognizing the Effects of Unexpected Changes in Pension Plan Assets and Liabilities

If the assets in a pension fund equal the liabilities of the pension plan at the beginning of the year and the rate of return earned on pension assets exactly equals the discount rate used to compute the pension liability, then pension expense each year will equal the service cost. The return on pension investments will exactly offset the interest cost. This precise matching seldom occurs for the following reasons.

    a. Pension funds generate actual earnings on investments at a rate that differs from the long-term rate of return that actuaries assume in deciding on the appropriate level of employer contributions to the pension fund. GAAP does not permit firms to immediately increase pension expense for any investment returns shortfall or reduce pension expense for any excess investment returns.

    b. Firms change the pension benefit formula and give employees credit under the new formula for the years of service prior to the change (referred to as a *prior service cost*). The change immediately increases the projected benefit obligation of the pension fund. GAAP does not permit the employer, however, to immediately increase pension expense for the increase in the pension obligation.

    c. Actuarial experience with respect to employee turnover, mortality, compensation levels, and the discount rate may differ from that assumed or used at the beginning of the year. The employer may change its actuarial assumptions with respect to any of these factors, which immediately changes the amount of the projected benefit obligation of the pension fund (referred to as an *actuarial gain or loss*). GAAP again does not permit the employer to adjust pension expense immediately for the actuarial gain or loss.

Although these three items change either the assets or liabilities of the pension plan, GAAP does not require that firms recognize, or flow through, their full effect into the measurement of pension expense and earnings immediately when they occur. Instead, GAAP requires firms to defer their effects and amortize them over the remaining expected period of benefit, usually the remaining average working life of employees. The amortization smoothes the effect on pension expense and earnings. Items 4 through 6 in Exhibit 8.11 include the items subject to deferral and amortization.

***Element 4: Amortization of Excess Pension Asset or Pension Obligation Upon Adoption of FASB* Statement No. 87.** Most firms adopted FASB *Statement No. 87* between 1986 and 1988. At the time of adoption, firms typically had either more assets in the pension fund than the pension obligation or a larger pension obligation than pension fund assets. Instead of immediately reporting the difference as a gain or loss in measuring pension expense, GAAP requires employers to amortize the difference over the remaining working years of employees. This amortization is the fourth component of pension expense listed in Exhibit 8.11. PepsiCo had an overfunded pension plan at the time that it adopted *Statement No. 87*. It amortized $2 million as a reduction in pension expense during Year 11.

Element 5: Amortization of Prior Service Cost. Firms likewise defer and then amortize increases in the pension benefit obligation that arise from sweetening of the benefit formula. This amortization is the fifth component of pension expense in Exhibit 8.11. PepsiCo amortized $8 million as an addition to pension expense for Year 11.

Element 6: Amortization of Actuarial Gains and Losses. Actuarial gains and losses arise when actual returns on investments differ from expectations and when the actuarial assumptions underlying the pension plan change. GAAP likewise requires firms to defer and then amortize the gain or loss. PepsiCo amortized $9 million during Year 11 as a reduction in pension expense. Thus, PepsiCo had an accumulated but unamortized gain as of the beginning of Year 11. PepsiCo indicates in Note 19 that the amount of the unamortized gain at the end of Year 10 was $349 million. This unamortized gain at the end of Year 10 became an unamortized loss of $548 million at the end of Year 11. Most of the swing in this unamortized amount resulted from the net loss on pension investments. PepsiCo also lowered the discount rate used to compute the pension obligation from 7.7 percent at the end of Year 10 to 7.4 percent at the end of Year 11. This reduction in the discount rate increased the pension obligation and the amount of the unamortized loss. PepsiCo may also have changed other assumptions (for example, employee turnover, mortality) that affected the amount of the pension obligation and the amount of unamortized loss.

We noted earlier that if (1) pension assets equal pension liabilities, (2) the rate of return on pension assets equals the interest rate used to compute the present value of the pension liability, and (3) actuarial assumptions turn out as expected, then the employer's pension expense will equal the current employee service cost (item 1 in Exhibit 8.11). Items 2 and 3 will net to zero, and items 4, 5, and 6 will be zero. The lack of equality of pension assets and liabilities and the realization of a different rate of return on assets than the interest rate used to compute the pension liability result in unequal offsetting of items 2 and 3. This inequality plus changes in the pension benefit formula and an inability to realize actuarial assumptions create the need for larger or smaller employer contributions to the pension fund in the future. Because the employers' total expenses must ultimately equal the cash contributed to the pension fund, pension expense must increase or decrease as well. *Statement No. 87* requires firms to smooth the effect of these excess or deficient amounts (items 4 through 6), rather than including them in the calculation of pension expense immediately.

Pension expense each period is the net of these six elements. The six elements may result in a net pension expense or a net pension credit. If a pension plan is not significantly overfunded or underfunded, the six items typically net to a pension expense. This is the case for PepsiCo in Year 9, Year 10, and Year 11. During the late 1990s, stock market prices increased significantly and many firms found that the market value of pension investments far exceeded their pension obligations. The credit, or reduction, in pension expense for the expected return on pension assets exceeded the service and interest cost and resulted in a net pension credit instead of a net pension expense.

Employer's Entry 2: Recognition of Pension Contribution

The second entry that the employer will make on its books each year (the first entry is to recognize pension expense, as described above) is for its contribution of cash to the pension fund. Exhibit 8.10 and Note 19 indicate that PepsiCo contributed $446 million to its pension fund during Year 11. The effects of the (1) recognition of pension expense of $56 million and the pension contribution of $446 million on the financial statements is as follows:

BS-BOP	C	+	N$A	=	L	+	CC	+	AOCI	+	RE
(1)					+ 56						−56
(2)	−446				−446						
IBT											−56

PepsiCo's entry to record the pension contribution is:

Pension Liability............................	446	
Cash..................................		446

The amount that a firm recognizes as pension expense each period typically will not equal the amount the firm contributes to its pension fund. The firm measures the amount for pension expense in accordance with the provisions of *Statement No. 87.* The amount the firm contributes to its pension fund relies on actuaries' recommendations concerning the needed level of funding, minimum required funding dictated by government regulations, and decisions by the firm regarding investments of its financial resources. For example, a firm with a significantly overfunded pension plan might delay additional contributions for a few years and use the cash for other corporate purposes. In this case, the firm recognizes pension expense each year but does not contribute cash to the pension fund. Alternatively, a firm might contribute more than the amount of pension expense. Earnings on pension investments are not subject to income taxation, whereas earnings on cash left within a firm are subject to taxation. Within prescribed limits, firms can make excess pension contributions and delay or avoid taxes on investment earnings. PepsiCo contributed significantly more to its pension fund during Year 11, perhaps in part to make up for the net loss on pension investments during the year.

When a firm recognizes more pension expense than it contributes to the pension fund, a pension liability appears on the balance sheet. PepsiCo, for example, recognizes a net liability of $222 million on its balance sheet at the end of Year 10. Because of the large excess of PepsiCo's contribution over its pension expense for Year 11, it reports a net pension asset at the end of Year 11 of $157 million. Note that this pension asset (or pension liability) on the balance sheet bears no necessary relation to the more important measure of the status of a pension plan: the difference between the total assets in the pension fund and the projected benefit obligation. The latter is sometimes a much larger amount. Refer again to Exhibit 8.9, showing the status of PepsiCo's pension plan. The assets in PepsiCo's pension plans at the end of Year 10 exceed the projected benefit obligation by $81 million. Yet, PepsiCo reports a net liability on its balance sheet of $222 million at the end of Year 10 because its cumulative pension expense exceeds its cumulative pension contributions. At the end of Year 11, the pension obligation exceeds pension assets by $427 million. Yet, PepsiCo reports a net pension asset of $157 million on its balance sheet because cumulative pension contributions exceed cumulative pension expenses.

Employer's Entry 3: Recognition of Minimum Underfunded Pension Liability

If a firm has any pension plan (most firms maintain separate pension plans for each of the various groups of employees) for which the accumulated benefit obligation exceeds the assets in that pension plan, then the firm must report as a minimum a liability equal to this underfunded accumulated benefit obligation on its balance sheet. The entry to recognize the minimum liability adjusts any pension liability already on the employer's books resulting from a difference between pension expenses and pension contributions from the first two entries above. The entry to recognize the minimum liability is as follows:

Intangible Asset	X	
Accumulated Other Comprehensive Income	Y	
Pension Liability.		Z

The firm increases an intangible asset up to the amount of any unrecognized prior service cost on plans with underfunded accumulated benefit obligations. The increase in intangible assets reflects the expected benefits of future productivity of employees that should result from sweetening plan benefits and making those benefits retroactive. The remaining amount of any incremental liability recognized decreases Accumulated Other Comprehensive Income. The amounts debited to Accumulated Other Comprehensive Income primarily represent unamortized actuarial gains and losses. PepsiCo reports in Note 19 that plans with an accumulated benefit obligation in excess of plan assets have assets of $51 million and an accumulated benefit obligation of $252 million, for a net liability of $201 million. PepsiCo includes this $201 million underfunded accumulated benefit obligation for some of its pension plans in the accrued benefit liability account on its books, which at the end of Year 11 totals $261 million. PepsiCo must have already recognized a liability on its books for these underfunded accumulated benefit obligations equal to $179 million (= $201 − $0 in intangible assets and $22 million in Accumulated Other Comprehensive Income). Thus, its entry to recognize the additional underfunded accumulated benefit obligation was:

Accumulated Other Comprehensive ($22 − $8)...	14	
Intangible Assets ($1 − $0)..............		1
Accrued Benefit Liability (plug)		13

Thus, in addition to recognizing a minimum liability for the underfunded accumulated benefit obligation, PepsiCo also had pension plans for which cumulative pension expenses exceed cumulative pension contributions by $60 million (= $261 − $201).

ANALYSTS' TREATMENT OF PENSIONS

The analyst should consider several items when evaluating accounting quality with respect to pensions and analyzing profitability and risk.

Funded Status of Pension Plan

One question that the analyst might ask is: Should I adjust the balance sheet of the employer to recognize an overfunded pension plan as an asset and an underfunded pension plan as a liability? Possible responses include:

1. Make no adjustment to the employer's balance sheet for an underfunded or overfunded pension plan. The rationale for this approach is that the under- or overfunding is a temporary condition that will work itself out over a longer time period.
2. Recognize an underfunded projected benefit obligation as a liability. The employer may have to contribute an amount to the pension fund in the future equal to the underfunding. Including the obligation among liabilities provides a better measure for assessing financial structure risk. PepsiCo's underfunded projected benefit obligation is $427 million at the end of Year 11. The books of PepsiCo show a net pension asset of $157 million on this date. The analyst's adjustment to eliminate the net pension asset of $157 and to recognize a liability of $427 million, assuming an income tax rate of 35 percent, is as follows:

Year 11

Accumulated Other Comprehensive Income		
[(1 − .35) × ($157 + $427)]	380	
Deferred Tax Assets [.35 × ($157 + $427)]....	204	
Pension Asset (net)....................		157
Pension Liability......................		427

The debit to Accumulated Other Comprehensive Income represents unrecognized prior service costs and actuarial gains and losses (net of taxes), which the firm will amortize as an adjustment of pension expense in future periods. When the firm contributes cash to the pension fund to make up for the deficiency in pension assets, it will realize tax benefits. In the meantime, the analyst recognizes a deferred tax asset. The credit of $157 to net pension assets adjusts for the amount now appearing on the books of PepsiCo that gave rise to this net asset. The credit of $427 million to pension liability recognizes the underfunded status of the pension plan.

3. Recognize an overfunded projected benefit obligation as an asset and an underfunded projected benefit obligation as a liability. This approach shows the potential benefit of not having to contribute as much to the pension fund in the future because of its overfunding (pension asset) and the need to contribute more to the pension fund in the future because of its underfunding (pension liability). PepsiCo's pension plans at the end of Year 10 are overfunded by $81 million. The balance sheet of PepsiCo shows a net pension liability of $222 million for these plans. The analyst's adjustment to eliminate the net pension liability and reflect the $81 million asset of these plans, again assuming a 35 percent income tax rate, is:

Year 10

Pension Asset..........................	81	
Pensicn Liability (net)...................	222	
Deferred Tax Liability		
[.35 × ($81 + $222)]................		106
Other Comprehensive Income		
[(1 − .35) × ($81 + $222)]		197

The adjustment at the end of Year 11 is the same as in 2 above.

4. Include both the assets and liabilities of the pension fund on the employer's balance sheet. Include the return on pension assets as interest and dividend revenue, and the interest cost component of pension expense as interest expense on the employer's income statement. This approach consolidates the financial statements of the pension fund with those of the employer, much like those for a parent company and majority-owned subsidiaries (a topic discussed in Chapter 9). The case for consolidation rests on the employer's right to access pension assets and obligation to provide for pension liabilities. The counterargument for consolidation is that federal pension law significantly constrains the operational relation between the employer and its pension fund as compared to most parent/subsidiary relationships.

IMPACT OF ACTUARIAL ASSUMPTIONS

Firms must disclose in notes to the financial statements the assumptions made with respect to (1) the discount rate used to compute the pension benefit obligation, (2) the expected rate of return on pension investments, and (3) the rate of compensation increase, which affects the amount of the projected benefit obligation.

The amount of the pension benefit obligation is inversely related to the discount rate. *Statement No. 87* specifies that firms should use a long-term government bond rate as the discount rate. Thus, firms should not vary significantly with respect to the discount rate used. One must recognize, however, that even small differences in the discount rate can materially affect the size of the pension benefit obligation.

Firms use different expected rates of return on pension investments, in part because of different mixtures of investments in their pension portfolios. A firm with equal proportions of debt and equity should have a lower expected return than a firm that invests fully in equities. Firms may also use different expected rates of return in an effort to conserve cash or manage earnings. The assumed long-term rate of return on pension assets impacts the analysis of pensions in several ways. First, if the firm cannot generate returns on average equal to this rate, then the firm will need to contribute additional assets in the future. Second, the expected return on pension investments reduces pension expense each period and increases earnings. GAAP requires firms to amortize any difference between expected and actual returns, so a deficiency in returns because of assuming too high a level of expected returns shows up slowly in pension expense. Recent decreases in the market values of equity securities have led firms to decrease their expected rates of return on pension assets. Note, for example, that PepsiCo reduced its expected return rate from 10 percent to 9.8 percent between Year 9 and Year 11.

The amount of the pension benefit obligation is directly related to the assumed rate of compensation increases. Firms have incentives to use a lower rather than a higher assumed rate of compensation increases, both to lower their projected benefit obligation and to create lower expectations among employees about future compensation increases.

The analyst should compare a firm's assumptions over time and with other firms to evaluate the firm's level of aggressiveness in making assumptions.

SIGNALS ABOUT EARNINGS PERSISTENCE

Sharp swings in the market values of investments, as occurred in 1998 to early 2000 with the buildup of Internet technology businesses and in early 2000 to late 2002 with the technology meltdown, can impact pension expense and earnings significantly. Although firms use a long-term expected return on investments to compute the expected return on assets each period, they apply this rate to the market value of assets in the pension portfolio. When market values increase, as they did in 1998 and 1999, many firms found that their pension expenses became pension credits. For some firms during this period, a substantial portion of their increased earnings resulted from a swing from pension expense to pension credit. During the market meltdown that followed, the pension credits became pension expenses, exacerbating the downward pressure on earnings already experienced from weakened economic conditions. When using earnings of the current period to forecast earnings in the future, the analyst should recognize the impact of changing stock prices on the measurement of pension expense.

POSTRETIREMENT BENEFITS OTHER THAN PENSIONS

In addition to pensions, most employers provide health care and life insurance benefits to retired employees. This benefit may take the form of a fixed dollar amount to cover part or all of the cost of health and life insurance (analogous to the defined contribution type of pension plan) or the benefit may specify the level of health care or life insurance provided (analogous to the defined benefit type of pension plan).

The accounting issues related to these postretirement obligations are similar to those discussed previously for pensions. The employer must recognize the cost of the postretirement benefits during the employees' years of service. The employer may or may not set aside funds to cover the cost of these benefits. Health and life insurance expense each period includes an amount for current service plus interest on the health care or life insurance benefits obligation for the period. Expected earnings on investments in a postretirement benefits fund, if any, reduce these expenses. The employer defers and then amortizes actuarial gains and losses due to changes in employee turnover, health care costs, interest rates, and similar factors.

The major difference between the accounting for pensions and the accounting for other postretirement benefits is that firms need not report an excess of the accumulated benefits obligation over assets in a postretirement benefits fund as a liability on the balance sheet.[19] Firms must report this amount in the notes to the financial statements. During the deliberation process on the reporting standard for postretirement benefits, business firms exerted pressure on the FASB not to require recognition of the underfunded accumulated benefits obligation, particularly for health care benefits. These business firms argued that the amount of this obligation was both large, relative to other liabilities and shareholders' equity, and uncertain, because of uncertainties regarding future health care inflation rates. Some firms indicated that they would eliminate health care retirement benefits if the FASB required recognition of the liability. As a compromise, the FASB allows firms to recognize the obligation either in full upon adoption of *Statement No. 106* or piecemeal over employees' working years.[20] (Exhibit 6.4 in Chapter 6 shows the impact on Ford's income statement of recognizing its obligation in full when it adopted *Statement No. 106*.)

Refer to Note 19 to PepsiCo's financial statements in Appendix A. When PepsiCo adopted *Statement No. 106* in Year 3, it elected to recognize the full obligation for health care and life insurance benefits. By the end of Year 10, its balance sheet includes a liability of $810 million. This liability grew to $825 million by the end of Year 11. At the end of Year 10, the total benefit obligation exceeds plan assets by $834 million, and at the end of Year 11, the total benefit obligation exceeds plan assets by

---

[19]The accumulated benefits obligation for health care incorporates health care costs expected when employees receive benefits and is therefore more similar to the projected benefit pension obligation than the accumulated benefit pension obligation. See Financial Accounting Standards Board, *Statement of Financial Accounting Standards No. 106*, "Employer's Accounting for Postretirement Benefits Other than Pensions," 1990.

[20]The implications of the differences between the two methods allowed for adopting *Statement No. 106* are discussed in Eli Amir and Joshua Livnat, "Adoption Choices of SFAS No. 106: Implications for Financial Analysis," *The Journal of Financial Statement Analysis*, Winter 1997, pp. 51–60.

$911 million. Thus, the obligation for postretirement benefits at the end of both Year 10 and Year 11 exceed the liability that PepsiCo reports on its balance sheet. The difference between the two results from two factors:

1. PepsiCo apparently decreased the level of benefits for employees since adoption of *Statement No. 106* but has not yet fully recognized the reduction in cost for these benefits on its books. PepsiCo reports these unrecognized benefits as a prior service cost in Note 19.
2. PepsiCo has unrecognized losses of $41 million at the end of Year 10, and $91 million at the end of Year 11. PepsiCo does not set aside cash for these benefits, but contributes sufficient cash each year to fund required payments under its plans. Thus, the unrecognized loss must result from measuring the benefit obligation. The loss could result from providing increased benefits to employees or from increasing the assumed rate of health care cost increases.

Analysts' concerns with postretirement benefits other than pensions are similar to those for pensions. Should the analyst add the underfunded postretirement benefit obligation to liabilities in assessing risk? How reasonable are the firm's assumptions regarding health care cost increases, discount rates, and amortization periods? Is the postretirement benefit fund, if any, generating returns consistent with the expected rate of return?

INCOME TAXES

Income taxes affect the analysis of a firm's profitability (income tax expense is a subtraction when computing net income) and its cash flows (income tax payments payable require cash). Deferred tax assets and deferred tax liabilities on the balance sheet affect future cash flows. The note to the financial statements on income taxes contains useful information for assessing a firm's income tax position. This section reviews the required accounting for income taxes[21] and discusses how the analyst might use income tax disclosures when analyzing a firm's financial statements.

REVIEW OF INCOME TAX ACCOUNTING

Chapter 2 discussed the required accounting for income taxes. Review these important concepts:

1. Firms often use different methods of accounting for financial reporting and income tax reporting, which means that income before taxes will likely differ from taxable income.
2. Differences between income before taxes and taxable income are either permanent or temporary. Permanent differences arise from revenues and

---

[21]Financial Accounting Standards Board, *Statement of Financial Accounting Standards No. 109*, "Accounting for Income Taxes," 1992.

expenses that GAAP requires firms to include in income before taxes but that the income tax law excludes from taxable income. Interest earned on state and municipal bonds is an example of a permanent difference. Temporary differences result from including revenues and expenses in income before taxes in a different period than those items affect taxable income. Depreciation expense computed for financial reporting using the straight-line method and for tax reporting using an accelerated depreciation method is an example of a temporary difference.

3. GAAP requires firms to measure income tax expense each period based on income before taxes excluding permanent differences, not on taxable income. The objective is to match income tax expense against the pre-tax income recognized for financial reporting.

4. The amount of income tax expense for a period will often differ from the amount of income taxes currently payable because of temporary differences between income for financial reporting and tax reporting. Temporary differences give rise to either deferred tax assets or deferred tax liabilities. Deferred tax assets result in future tax savings when temporary differences reverse. Deferred tax liabilities require future tax payments when temporary differences reverse.

The description above sets forth the accounting for income taxes from an income statement perspective. Computing income tax expense and income taxes payable involves applying a tax rate to income before taxes excluding permanent differences and to taxable income, respectively. *Statement No. 109*, however, requires firms to follow a balance sheet approach when computing income tax expense. The results are similar in most instances. The following description summarizes the balance sheet approach:

1. Identify at each balance sheet date all differences between the *book basis* (that is, the book value for financial reporting) of assets, liabilities, and tax loss carryforwards, and the *tax basis* of assets, liabilities, and tax loss carryforwards.

2. Eliminate from Step 1 items that will not have a future tax consequence (that is, permanent differences).

3. Separate the remaining differences after the first two steps into those that give rise to future tax deductions and those that give rise to future taxable income. Financial reporting refers to these differences as *temporary differences*. Multiply differences between the book and tax basis of assets and liabilities that give rise to future tax deductions by the *enacted* marginal tax rate expected to apply in those future periods. The result is a *deferred tax asset*. Multiply differences between the book and tax basis of assets and liabilities that give rise to future taxable income by the *enacted* marginal tax rate expected to apply in those future periods. The result is a *deferred tax liability*.

Firms may have unused net operating loss and tax credit carryforwards as of a balance sheet date. These items have the potential to reduce future taxable income (operating loss carryforwards) or future taxes payable (tax credit carryforwards).

The firm includes the tax effect of these carryforwards in deferred tax assets at each balance sheet date.

4. Assess the likelihood that the firm will realize the benefits of deferred tax assets in the future. This assessment should consider the nature (for example, cyclical or noncyclical) and characteristics (for example, growing, mature, or declining) of the firm's business and its tax planning strategies for the future. If realization of the benefits of deferred tax assets is "more likely than not" (that is, exceeds 50 percent), then deferred tax assets equal the amounts computed in Step 3 above. However, if it is more likely than not that a firm will not realize some or all of the deferred tax assets, then the firm must reduce the deferred tax assets for a *valuation allowance* (similar in concept to the allowance for uncollectible accounts). The valuation allowance reduces the deferred tax assets to the amounts the firm expects to realize by way of reduced taxes in the future.

The result of following this four-step procedure is a deferred tax asset and a deferred tax liability at each balance sheet date. Income tax expense each period equals:

1. Income taxes currently payable on taxable income.
2. Plus a net credit change in the deferred tax asset or liability and minus a net debit change in the deferred tax asset or liability between the beginning and the end of the period.

Exhibit 8.12 provides a comparison between the components of income tax expense using the income statement approach and the balance sheet approach. The principal difference between these two approaches relates to item (2) versus item (5). Item (2) includes only temporary differences for the current year between financial and tax reporting incomes, whereas item (5) includes temporary differences, enacted changes during a period in future income tax rates, and changes in the valuation allowance as a result of new information regarding the realizability of deferred tax assets. When tax rates do not change and a firm recognizes no valuation allowance, the income statement and balance sheet approaches yield identical amounts for income tax expense.

EXHIBIT 8.12
Comparison of Income Statement and Balance Approaches for Measuring Income Tax Expense

Income Statement Approach	Balance Sheet Approach
(1) Taxes Currently Payable on Taxable Income	(4) Taxes Currently Payable on Taxable Income
(2) Taxes Potentially Saved or Payable in the Future from Temporary Differences between Current Period's Income for Financial and Tax Reporting	(5) Change in Deferred Tax Assets and Deferred Tax Liabilities during the Current Period
(3) Income Tax Expense = (1) + (2)	(6) Income Tax Expense = (4) + (5)

REQUIRED INCOME TAX DISCLOSURES

The note to the financial statements on income taxes is a rich source of information for not only understanding a firm's income tax position but for understanding much about its operations as well. This section describes four specific GAAP disclosures, using amounts for a hypothetical firm:

1. Components of income tax expense.
2. Components of income before taxes.
3. Reconciliation of income taxes at statutory rate with income tax expense.
4. Components of deferred tax assets and liabilities.

1. Components of Income Tax Expense

Firms must disclose the amount of income taxes currently payable and the amount deferred, broken down by governmental entity (federal, foreign, state and local).

Components of Income Tax Expense		Year 3	Year 2	Year 1
Current — Federal		$191	$105	$123
— Foreign		128	75	61
— State and Local		18	12	13
Total Current		$337	$192	$197
Deferred — Federal		$ 35	$ 40	$ 70
— Foreign		38	30	19
Total Deferred		$ 73	$ 70	$ 89
Total Income Tax Expense		$410	$262	$286

The journal entries made to record income taxes each year appear below:

	Year 3		Year 2		Year 1	
Income Tax Expense	410		262		286	
Income Tax Payable		337		192		197
Deferred Tax Asset or						
Deferred Tax Liability		73		70		89

2. Components of Income before Taxes

Assessing a firm's tax position over time or relative to other firms requires some base for scaling the amount of income tax expense. Income before taxes serves this purpose.

Components of Income before Taxes

	Year 3	Year 2	Year 1
United States	$ 700	$450	$600
Foreign......................................	350	250	200
Total......................................	$1,050	$700	$800

The average, or effective, tax rates for the three years on total income before taxes are:

Year 1: $286/$800 = 35.7%
Year 2: $262/$700 = 37.4%
Year 3: $410/$1,050 = 39.0%

Thus, the effective tax rate increased over the three-year period.

3. Reconciliation of Income Taxes at Statutory Rate with Income Tax Expense

The third required disclosure explains why the effective tax rates shown above differ from the statutory federal tax rate on income before taxes. Firms can express reconciling items in either dollar amounts or percentage terms.

Reconciliation of Income Taxes at Statutory Rate with Income Tax Expense

	Year 3	Year 2	Year 1
(1) Income Taxes on Income before Taxes at Statutory Rate........................	35.0%	35.0%	35.0%
(2) Foreign Tax Rates Greater (Less) than Statutory Federal Rate	4.1	2.5	1.3
(3) State and Local Taxes	1.1	1.1	1.1
(4) Dividend Deduction.....................	(0.6)	(0.5)	(0.7)
(5) Tax Exempt Income	(0.4)	(0.4)	(0.5)
(6) Goodwill Amortization	0.6	0.4	0.2
(7) Percentage Depletion in Excess of Cost	(0.8)	(0.7)	(0.7)
Income Tax Expense	39.0%	37.4%	35.7%

The statutory federal tax rate was 35 percent in each year. The effective tax rates were greater than the statutory rates. The reconciliation includes two types of reconciling items: (1) tax rate differences, and (2) permanent differences. The sections that follow discuss each of these reconciling items more fully.

Foreign Rates Greater (Less) than Statutory Rate. The denominator of the effective tax rate computation combines both U.S.-source and foreign-source income for financial reporting. The initial assumption on line (1) is that all of this income is subject to taxes at a rate equal to the U.S. federal statutory rate. Foreign tax rates are usually different from the U.S. federal rate, however. This line indicates how much the overall effective tax rate increased or decreased because of these foreign rate differences.

Refer to the first two types of income tax disclosures discussed earlier. Foreign tax expense for Year 3 totaled $166 (= $128 + $38). Pre-tax book income from foreign sources was $350. If this income were subject to tax at the federal rate of 35 percent, foreign income tax expense would have been $123 (= .35 × $350). Foreign tax expense of $166 exceeded the amount at the federal statutory rate by $43 (= $166 − $123). The excess tax as a percentage of *total* pre-tax book income, the denominator of the effective tax rate, is 4.1 percent (= $43/$1,050). Foreign-source income was taxed at a rate of 47.4 percent (= $166/$350).

It would be desirable to have a breakdown of total foreign income and foreign taxes by individual countries, but firms rarely disclose such information.

State and Local Taxes. The statutory tax rate on line (1) reflects federal taxes only. The reconciliation adds state and local taxes on income for financial reporting because such taxes are part of income tax expense. The amount of the reconciling item is state and local taxes net of their federal tax benefit. State and local taxes are deductible in determining taxable income for federal purposes, so the incremental effect of state and local taxes beyond the federal statutory rate appears on line (3).

Refer to the disclosure of the components of income tax expense discussed previously. State and local taxes for Year 3 were $18. Net of the federal tax benefit of 35 percent, state and local taxes are $12 [(1 − .35)($18)]. This $12 amount increases the effective tax rate by 1.1 percent (= $12/$1,050) for Year 3.

As with foreign taxes, the income tax note to the financial statements does not give any further detail on the income and taxes by jurisdictional unit within the United States.

Dividends Received Deduction. Depending on the investor's ownership percentage, only 20 percent or 30 percent of dividends received from unconsolidated domestic subsidiaries and affiliates is subject to federal taxation. The dividend deduction is intended to reduce the effect of triple taxation of the corporate organization form. The full dividend received is included in income for financial reporting. The calculation on line (1) presumes that the dividend is subject to tax at the statutory rate. The reduction on line (4) indicates the tax savings due to the 70 percent or 80 percent dividends received deduction.

Tax Exempt Income. Income for financial reporting includes interest revenue on state and municipal obligations. Such interest revenue, however, is never included in taxable income. The income tax savings from this permanent difference appears on line (5).

Goodwill Amortization. A firm that acquires another firm and pays a higher price than the market value of its identifiable assets and liabilities must allocate the excess to goodwill. (Chapter 9 addresses accounting for business acquisitions.) Prior to 2002, GAAP required firms to amortize goodwill over a period not exceeding 40 years for financial reporting purposes, but it often cannot amortize goodwill for tax purposes. By subtracting goodwill amortization in computing income before taxes, line (1) presumes a tax benefit equal to the amortization times the statutory tax rate. The addition on line (6) reflects the fact that no tax benefit accrues to this permanent difference. Since 2002, GAAP no longer requires firms to amortize goodwill for financial reporting. Thus, goodwill amortization should not appear as a reconciling item for 2003 and later years.

Percentage Depletion in Excess of Cost. The Internal Revenue Code permits firms involved in mineral extraction to claim a depletion deduction equal to a specified percentage times the gross income from the property each year. Over the life of a mineral property, total percentage depletion will likely exceed the acquisition cost of the property. For financial reporting purposes, total depletion cannot exceed acquisition cost under GAAP. The excess of percentage depletion over book depletion represents a permanent difference that reduces the effective tax rate.

The foregoing discussion illustrates the reconciling items most commonly encountered in corporate annual reports. Other items reported have characteristics similar to those discussed above.

4. Components of Deferred Tax Assets and Liabilities

The fourth disclosure item in the income tax note is a listing of the components of the deferred tax asset and the deferred tax liability at the beginning and the end of each year. Exhibit 8.13 presents the required disclosures. The change in deferred tax asset and deferred tax liability each year represents deferred income tax expense for that year. Note that Deferred Tax Assets experienced a net credit change of $34 (= $240 − $274) between Year 2 and Year 3, and Deferred Tax Liabilities experienced a net credit change of $39 (= $819 − $780). The total credit change in these accounts of $73 (= $34 + $39) equals the deferred component of income tax expense for Year 3 (see the first income tax disclosure item). The following sections discuss the components of deferred taxes.

Uncollectible Accounts Receivable. Firms provide for estimated uncollectible accounts in the year of sale for financial reporting but cannot recognize bad debt expense for tax purposes until an actual customer's account becomes uncollectible. Thus, the book value of accounts receivable will be less than its tax basis. The difference represents the future tax deductions for bad debt expense. These future tax benefits times the tax rate give rise to a deferred tax asset. The deferred tax asset relating to uncollectible accounts increased between Year 0 and Year 2, suggesting that bad debt expense for financial reporting continued to exceed bad debt expense for tax reporting. Such a relation characterizes a firm with increasing sales. The decrease in the deferred tax asset during Year 3 suggests that sales declined, causing bad debt expense for tax reporting to exceed the amount for financial reporting.

EXHIBIT 8.13					
Disclosures Related to Deferred Taxes— Components of Deferred Tax Assets and Liabilities					

		December 31			
		Year 3	Year 2	Year 1	Year 0
Deferred Tax Asset					
(8)	Uncollectible Accounts Receivable.	$ 16	$ 19	$ 17	$ 15
(9)	Warranties	91	105	89	76
(10)	Pensions	71	83	67	53
(11)	Leases	62	54	42	32
(12)	Net Operating Losses.	—	13	—	—
	Total Deferred Tax Asset	$240	$274	$215	$176
Deferred Tax Liability					
(13)	Depreciable Assets	$476	$421	$355	$275
(14)	Inventories	59	58	49	41
(15)	Installment Receivables	193	205	171	149
(16)	Intangible Drilling and Development Costs	91	96	76	58
	Total Deferred Tax Liability.	$819	$780	$651	$523

Warranties. Firms expense estimated warranty costs in the year of sale for financial reporting but cannot deduct warranty expense for tax reporting until the firm makes actual expenditures to provide warranty services. Thus, the book value of the warranty liability (a positive amount) will exceed the tax basis of the warranty liability (zero, because the income tax law does not permit recognition of a warranty liability). The difference represents the future tax deductions for warranty expense. The increase in the deferred tax asset relating to warranties between Year 0 and Year 2 is consistent with a growing firm, whereas the decrease in Year 3 indicates a firm whose sales of product under warranty plans probably declined.

Pensions. Firms recognize pension expense each year as employees render services for financial reporting and when the firm contributes cash to the pension fund for tax reporting. As discussed in the previous section on pensions in this chapter, the income tax law limits a firm's ability to claim tax deductions when a pension fund is overfunded. Thus, firms may curtail making pension fund contributions even though they must recognize pension expense each year. The book basis of the pension liability (a positive amount) will exceed the tax basis (not recognized). The future tax deductions for pension expense result in a deferred tax asset. For our illustrative firm, pension expense for financial reporting exceeded the amount for tax reporting during Year 1 and Year 2, and the deferred tax asset relating to pensions increased. The deferred tax asset decreased in Year 3, indicating a larger expense for tax reporting than for financial reporting (that is, the book basis of the pension liability decreased during the year). Several explanations might account for such a decrease. First, the firm resumed funding the pension obligation and made a multi-year contribution. Second, the firm curtailed employment during Year 3 in light of the decrease in sales, reducing pension expense, but made a pension contribution sufficient to reduce the pension liability. Third, the firm experienced a negative pension expense (that is, a pension credit) during Year 3 because of an overfunded pension plan. The negative pension expense reduces the pension liability and thereby the amount of future tax deductions previously considered available.

Leases. Our illustrative firm leases equipment from other entities (lessors). As discussed in the previous section on leases in this chapter, firms may treat leases as either operating leases or as capital leases for financial and tax reporting. If the leases qualify as operating leases, the lessor recognizes rent revenue and depreciation expense and the lessee recognizes rent expense. If leases qualify as capital leases, the lessor recognizes a gain on the "sale" of the leased property at the inception of the lease and recognizes interest revenue each year from financing the lessee's "purchase" of the property. The lessee depreciates the assets each period and recognizes interest expense on its borrowing from the lessor.

Leasing arose as an industry in part to shift tax deductions on property from firms that needed the use of property but did not have sufficient taxable income to take advantage of the tax deductions to other entities with higher tax rates that could take advantage of the deductions. If a lease qualifies as an operating lease for tax purposes, the lessor gets the tax deductions for depreciation and can possibly pass through some of these benefits to the lessee in the form of lower lease payments.

The earlier section of this chapter on leases indicates that the criteria for an operating lease and a capital lease for financial reporting are not identical to those for tax reporting. It is possible to structure leases that are operating leases for tax reporting, even though they qualify as capital leases for financial reporting. Our illustrative firm shows a deferred tax asset relating to leases. The likely scenario is that this firm treats leases as capital leases for financial reporting and as operating leases for tax reporting. Thus, the book basis of the leased asset and lease liability (a positive amount) exceeds the tax basis of the asset and liability (not recognized). Depreciation and interest expense recognized for financial reporting exceed rent expense recognized for tax reporting. In later years, rent expense for tax reporting will exceed depreciation and interest expense. These future tax deductions give rise to a deferred tax asset. The deferred tax asset increased each year, suggesting that this firm increased its involvement in leasing during the three-year period (that is, the firm has more leased assets in the early years of the lease period when the book expenses exceed the tax deduction than in the later years when the tax deduction exceeds the book expenses).

Net Operating Losses. A firm may operate for both financial and tax reporting at a net loss for the year. The firm can carry back this net loss to offset taxable income of the three preceding years and receive a refund for income taxes paid in those years. The firm recognizes the refund as an income tax credit in the year of the net loss.

If the firm either has no positive taxable income in the three preceding years against which to carry back the net loss or if the net loss exceeds the taxable income of those three preceding years, the firm must carry forward the net loss. This carryforward provides future tax benefits in that it can offset positive taxable incomes and thereby reduce income taxes otherwise payable. The benefits of the net operating loss carryforward give rise to a deferred tax asset.

Our illustrative firm recognized a deferred tax asset during Year 2 and realized the benefits of the net operating loss carryforward during Year 3. Referring back to the disclosure of the components of income tax expense, we see that this firm paid taxes to all three governmental units during Year 2. Thus, the firm must have been unable to offset the net operating loss incurred by some sub-unit during the year against the taxable income of the overall entity. One possibility is that the firm owns a majority interest in a subsidiary and therefore consolidates it for financial reporting. Its ownership percentage, however, is less than the 80 percent required to include the subsidiary in a consolidated tax return. Thus, the net loss of the subsidiary can only offset net income of that subsidiary in a later year. The firm recognizes this future benefit as a deferred tax asset. This firm shows no valuation allowance related to the deferred tax asset, indicating a greater than 50 percent probability of realizing the tax benefits in the future.

Depreciable Assets. Firms claim depreciation on their tax returns using accelerated methods over periods shorter than the expected useful lives of depreciable assets. Most firms depreciate assets for financial reporting using the straight-line method over the expected useful lives of such assets. Thus, the book value of depreciable assets will likely exceed their tax basis. Depreciation expense for tax reporting in future years will be less than the amounts for financial reporting, giving rise to a liability for future tax payments. The deferred tax liability relating to depreciable assets increased each year, suggesting that this firm has more assets in their early years when tax depreciation exceeds book depreciation. The deferred tax liability increased, however, at a decreasing rate, suggesting a slowdown in the growth rate of capital expenditures.

Inventories. The book value of inventories for our illustrative firm exceeds their tax basis, giving rise to future tax liabilities. Perhaps this firm includes certain elements of cost as part of manufacturing overhead for financial reporting but deducts them when incurred for tax reporting.

Installment Receivables. Firms that sell assets on account and permit customers to pay over two or more future years often recognize revenue at the time of sale for financial reporting and when they collect cash using the installment method for tax reporting. The book basis of these receivables exceeds their tax basis and gives rise to deferred tax liabilities. The deferred tax liability relating to installment sales increased between Year 0 and Year 2, characteristic of a growing firm (that is, revenues from sales during the current period exceed collections this period from sales made in prior periods). The deferred tax liability on installment sales decreased during Year 3, consistent with the decline in sales noted above in the discussion of deferred taxes related to uncollectible accounts and warranties.

Intangible Drilling and Development Costs. Firms can deduct in the year of the cash expenditure for tax purposes certain costs of acquiring rights to drill and for drilling a property to ascertain the existence of mineral resources. These firms must capitalize and amortize such costs for financial reporting. The book basis of the property will exceed the tax basis and give rise to a deferred tax liability. The deferred tax liability for this item increased between Year 0 and Year 2, indicating a growth in drilling and development activity. The decrease in the liability during Year 3 suggests a cutback in such expenditures.

ASSESSING A FIRM'S TAX POSITION

The note to the financial statements on income taxes defines the effective tax rate as:

$$\text{Effective Tax Rate} = \frac{\text{Income Tax Expense}}{\text{Book Income before Income Taxes}}$$

Exhibit 8.14 presents an analysis of effective tax rates. This analysis separates the amounts for each year into domestic and foreign components. The combined effective tax rate based on income tax expense increased each year. The effective tax rate on the domestic portion remained relatively steady at a rate close to the 35 percent federal statutory tax rate. Differences in the domestic tax position due to rate differences and permanent differences offset each other. On the other hand, the effective tax rate on the foreign portion exceeded 35 percent and that rate increased each year. The analyst should explore the reasons for this increase in the foreign effective tax rate more fully with management. Perhaps the portions of the firm's foreign operations in higher tax rate countries grew more rapidly than foreign operations in lower tax rate countries. The firm may need to search for more tax-effective ways of operating abroad. For example, the firm might:

1. Shift some operations (manufacturing, marketing) to the United States where the effective tax rate is lower.
2. Assess whether transfer prices or cost allocations can be adjusted to shift income from high to low tax rate jurisdictions.
3. Shift from domestic to foreign borrowing to increase deductions for interest against foreign-source income.
4. Shift from equity to debt financing of foreign operations to increase interest deductions against foreign-source income.

The increasing tax rates abroad and an increasing proportion of income derived from abroad suggest a continuing increase in the combined effective tax rate that could hurt future profitability unless the firm takes counteractions.

EXHIBIT 8.14

Analysis of Effective Tax Rates

	Year 3		Year 2		Year 1	
	Domestic	Foreign	Domestic	Foreign	Domestic	Foreign
(1) Net Income Before Income Taxes ..	$700	$350	$450	$250	$600	$200
Income Taxes at 35% Statutory						
Federal Rate	$245	$123	$157	$ 87	$210	$ 70
Foreign Tax Rates Greater						
than 35%.	—	43	—	18	—	10
State and Local Taxes.	11	—	8	—	9	—
Dividends Deduction	(6)	—	(3)	—	(4)	—
Tax Exempt Income.	(4)	—	(3)	—	(4)	—
Goodwill Amortization	6	—	3	—	1	—
Percentage Depletion.	(8)	—	(5)	—	(6)	—
(2) Income Tax Expense	$244	$166	$157	$105	$206	$ 80
Effective Tax Rates: (2)÷(1).	34.9%	47.4%	34.9%	42.0%	34.3%	40.0%
Combined Effective Tax Rates.	39.0%		37.4%		35.7%	

ANALYZING PEPSICO'S INCOME TAX DISCLOSURES

Refer to PepsiCo's income tax disclosures in Note 14 to its financial statements in Appendix A. PepsiCo's effective tax rate was 41.4 percent in Year 9, 32.4 percent in Year 10, and 33.9 percent in Year 11.

The larger effective tax rate in Year 9 is due to bottling transactions. Note 10 indicates that, during Year 9, PepsiCo recognized a pre-tax gain of $1 billion when it sold a large portion of its interest in previously wholly owned bottlers. PepsiCo recognized taxes at a rate of 52.4 percent on this gain. PepsiCo does not explain the reason for this high tax rate on the gain. It is possible that PepsiCo's tax basis for the stock was lower than the book basis, so that the gain was larger for tax reporting than for financial reporting. To appear as a reconciling item, the difference in tax basis must have been a permanent difference, not a temporary difference. Another possibility is that the stock involved bottlers located in high tax rate foreign countries. An analysis of the domestic versus foreign effective tax rates supports this explanation. The effective tax rates each year, computed by dividing domestic or foreign income tax expense by domestic or foreign income before taxes, respectively, were:

	Domestic	Foreign
Year 9	43.7%	33.0%
Year 10	41.2%	13.3%
Year 11	39.3%	19.6%

The most significant change in effective tax rates between Year 9 and Year 10 occurred for foreign operation. The higher effective tax rate in Year 9 appears to be due to a nonrecurring event and is not persistent.

PepsiCo's tax reconciliation also shows that merger-related costs, impairment charges, and restructuring charges affected the effective tax rate in Year 10 and Year 11. Most of the reconciling amount occurred in Year 11 and relates to merger-related costs incurred in connection with the merger with Quaker Oats. The increase in the effective tax rate in Year 11 for merger-related costs suggests that PepsiCo incurred some costs that are never deductible for tax purposes. The source of the increase in the effective tax rate, at least as to the amount, appears to be nonrecurring and is not likely to persist. PepsiCo indicates in Appendix B that its effective tax rate—if it eliminated the effects of the bottling transactions, merger costs, and other unusual items—would have been 32.9 percent in Year 9, 32.7 percent in Year 10, and 32.0 percent in Year 11. Thus, the analyst might project an effective tax rate between 32 percent and 33 percent for future years.

The disclosures of current and deferred taxes by PepsiCo indicate that most of the firm's tax expense each year is also currently payable. We can gain additional insights about the operations of PepsiCo by examining the components of its deferred tax assets and liabilities.

Investment in Unconsolidated Affiliates. PepsiCo owns less than a controlling interest in its bottlers and uses the equity method to account for its investments in these bottlers. As Chapter 9 explains more fully, PepsiCo recognizes its share of the earnings of these bottlers each year and includes it in "bottling equity income" on its income statement. Income before taxes for Year 11 includes $160 million of bottling equity income. The income tax law taxes this income only when PepsiCo receives a dividend from the bottlers. PepsiCo subtracts this $160 from net income when computing cash flow from operations for Year 11 but does not show an addition for dividends received. Deferred tax liabilities for these investments totaled $672 million at the end of Year 10 and $702 million at the end of Year 11, indicating that PepsiCo has deferred a significant amount of income tax payments because of this temporary difference.

Property, Plant, and Equipment. PepsiCo indicates in Note 1 to its financial statements that it principally uses the straight-line depreciation method for financial reporting. Income tax laws provide for accelerated depreciation. PepsiCo has deferred taxes of $804 million as of the end of Year 11 due to depreciating assets faster for tax than for financial reporting. The deferred tax liability increased during Year 11, indicating that PepsiCo has more depreciable assets in the early years of their lives when accelerated depreciation exceeds straight-line depreciation than they have depreciable assets in the later years when straight-line depreciation exceeds accelerated depreciation.

Safe Harbor Leases. PepsiCo does not disclose any additional information about these leases to understand why they give rise to deferred tax liabilities. One possibility is that PepsiCo is the lessee on leases that it accounts for as operating leases for financial reporting and capital leases for tax reporting. Expenses for interest and depreciation on capital leases usually exceed rent expense on operating leases during the early years of the life of a leased asset. The additional expenses for the capital leases permit the firm to delay paying income taxes, which results in a deferred tax liability. The decrease in the amount of deferred tax liabilities for safe harbor leases during Year 11 suggest that the leases are now in the later years of their lives and PepsiCo is beginning to pay the deferred taxes.

Zero Coupon Notes. PepsiCo indicates in Note 12 that it has issued zero coupon notes as a liability. The recognition of a deferred tax liability suggests that the firm has recognized more interest expense on these notes for tax reporting than for financial reporting and thereby deferred the payment of income taxes. PepsiCo likewise does not disclose sufficient information to understand why this item gives rise to a deferred tax liability. One possible explanation is that PepsiCo uses the effective interest method to amortize the discount on these notes for tax reporting and the straight-line method for financial reporting.

Intangible Asset Other than Nondeductible Goodwill. PepsiCo indicates in Note 1 to its financial statements that it amortizes intangibles other than goodwill over periods ranging from 5 to 20 years. The reporting of a deferred tax liability for these items suggests that PepsiCo writes off these intangibles more quickly for tax purposes.

Net Carryforwards. PepsiCo recognizes deferred tax assets for the future saving in taxes when it can offset net operating losses previously incurred against the positive income of future periods. PepsiCo indicates in Note 14 that it has $3.2 billion of net operating loss carryforwards and $90 million of tax credit carryforwards as of the end of Year 11. The deferred tax asset of $556 million related to carryforwards at the end of Year 11 includes $90 million of tax credit carryforwards and potential tax saving on net operating loss carryforwards of $466 (= $556 − $90). The average tax rate on the net operating loss carryforwards is 14.6 percent (= $466/$3,200). This low rate is consistent with the low average effective tax rate for PepsiCo's overall foreign operations. The deferred tax asset related to carryforwards decreased significantly during Year 11, indicating that the firm was able to realize some of the benefits of these loss carryforwards.

Postretirement Benefits. PepsiCo uses the term "postretirement benefits" in Note 18 to refer to medical benefits. PepsiCo recognized a liability for postretirement benefits when it adopted FASB *Statement No. 106*. PepsiCo cannot claim a tax deduction for medical benefits until it funds this obligation. Thus, PepsiCo reports a deferred tax asset for the future tax savings. At the end of Year 11, the deferred tax asset totals $320 million and the postretirement liability on the balance sheet (see Note 18) is

$825 million. Thus, PepsiCo recognized deferred taxes at a tax rate of 38.8 percent (= $320/$825). This tax rate is similar to its effective tax rate on domestic operations.

Deferred Tax Asset Valuation Allowances. Recall that firms must recognize a valuation allowance if it is more likely than not that they will not realize the tax benefits of deferred tax assets. PepsiCo's valuation allowance is approximately equal to the deferred tax asset for net carryforwards each year, suggesting that the valuation allowance likely relates to these items. The decrease in the valuation allowance for Year 11 matches closely the reduction in the deferred tax asset for carryforwards.

SUMMARY OF INCOME TAXES

Income taxes affect each of the principal financial statements.

1. The income statement reports the amount of income tax expense and its relation to income before taxes, a relation referred to as a firm's effective tax rate. The effective tax rate affects analysis of a firm's profitability. The income tax note explains the major reasons why the effective tax rate differs from the statutory federal tax rate.
2. The statement of cash flows usually shows an adjustment to net income for the change in deferred taxes ($162 million for PepsiCo for Year 11), which converts tax expense to tax payable when computing cash flow from operations. The income tax note indicates the mix of current and deferred taxes, and the extent to which a firm has delayed or accelerated the payment of income taxes. It also indicates the components of deferred tax assets and liabilities, which the analyst can tie to analysis of various other transactions of the firm (for example, intercorporate investments, retirement obligations).
3. The balance sheet shows the amount of deferred tax assets and deferred tax liabilities. The income tax note indicates the line items on the balance sheet that include deferred taxes. These amounts affect assessments of a firm's financial position (for example, current ratio, debt ratios).

UNDERSTANDING RESERVES IN THE FINANCIAL STATEMENTS

This chapter and the previous one emphasize two important concepts underlying the financial statements:

1. Income over sufficiently long time periods equals cash inflows minus cash outflows from operating, investing, and financing activities (except dividends and capital transactions with shareholders).
2. Because accountants prepare financial statements for discrete periods of time shorter than the life of a firm, the recognition of revenues does not necessarily coincide with the receipt of cash, and the recognition of expenses does not necessarily coincide with the disbursement of cash.

Assets such as inventories, investments, property, plant, equipment, and intangibles result from past cash outflows. The costs of these assets become expenses in future periods when the firm uses the services of these assets in operations or through sales. Liabilities, such as salaries payable, interest payable, taxes payable, and pensions payable reflect the cost of services already received by a firm. They generally require a future cash outflow. Thus, most asset and liability accounts result from efforts to match revenues with expenses for discrete periods of time.

Because revenues must ultimately equal the total cash inflows and expenses must ultimately equal the total cash outflows (except for dividends and capital transactions), firms in the long run cannot alter the total *amount* of revenues and expenses. In the short run, however, firms can only estimate ultimate cash flows. In addition, accounting allocates benefits received in the form of revenues, and services consumed in the form of expenses, to discrete accounting periods with some imprecision. As Chapter 6 discusses, management may have incentives to shift revenues or expenses between accounting periods to accomplish certain reporting objectives. Audits by the firm's independent accountants, taxing authorities, and government regulators serve as control mechanisms on management's behavior.

The analyst should develop a heightened sensitivity to financial reporting areas where firms enjoy flexibility in measuring revenues, expenses, assets, and liabilities. This chapter and the previous one discuss reporting areas that allow management to select from acceptable alternatives to influence reported earnings (for example, percentage-of-completion versus completed contract method for revenue recognition, FIFO versus LIFO cost-flow assumptions, or depreciation methods). These chapters also discuss reporting areas that require firms to make estimates in applying accounting principles (for example, useful lives for depreciable assets, assumed investment return on pension fund assets, or future salary increases for pensions). Management's latitude for influencing reported earnings correlates directly with the role or significance of estimates in applying accounting principles.

In the United States, all major revenues, gains, expenses, and losses flow through the income statement (exceptions apply to certain items that initially flow through Accumulated Other Comprehensive Income, such as unrealized gains and losses on marketable equity securities, and adjustments to recognize a minimum pension obligation). The analyst can study the time-series pattern of earnings to assess the extent to which firms attempt to shift income through time.

In some countries outside of the United States, certain income items do not flow through the income statement but instead increase or decrease a shareholders' equity account directly. In addition, common practice in certain countries permits liberal shifting of income between accounting periods either to minimize income taxes or to smooth earnings, especially in those countries where financial reporting and tax reporting follow similar rules. The accounting mechanism used to accomplish these reporting results is called a *reserve*. This section briefly discusses the nature and use of reserves.

NATURE OF A RESERVE ACCOUNT

As the sections below discuss, reserve accounts may appear on the balance sheet as a deduction from an asset, as a liability, or as a component of shareholders' equity. (Thus, reserve accounts always carry a credit balance.) They may appear for a limited period of time or represent a permanent account. Firms may use reserve accounts to shift earnings between periods or they may not affect earnings in any period. These multiple uses of reserve accounts and the implication that firms have set aside assets equal to the reserve result in considerable confusion among financial statement users, and even some professional analysts.

Using the term *reserve* in the title of an account in the United States is generally unacceptable. When firms use an account that functions similar to a reserve, U.S. firms generally use more descriptive terminology. Reserve accounts—and use of this terminology in an account title—commonly appear in the financial statements of non-U.S. firms. The next section illustrates some of the ways firms both inside and outside of the United States use reserve accounts and the issues they raise for analysts.

USE OF RESERVE ACCOUNTS

Matching Expenses with Associated Revenues

The recognition of an expense during the current period could result in an increase in a reserve account. The reserve account might appear on the balance sheet as a reduction in an asset. For example, firms provide for bad debt expense and increase the account, Reserve for Bad Debts (U.S. firms use the account, Allowance for Uncollectible Accounts). This reserve account appears as a subtraction from Accounts Receivable on the balance sheet. Likewise, firms recognize depreciation expense and increase the account, Reserve for Depreciation (U.S. firms use the account, Accumulated Depreciation). The reserve account appears as a reduction from fixed assets on the balance sheet. Alternatively, the reserve account might appear as a liability on the balance sheet. For example, a firm might provide for warranty expense or pension expense and increase the accounts, Reserve for Warranties (Estimated Warranty Liability in the United States) or Reserve for Retirement Benefits (Accrued Retirement Liability in the United States).

When used properly, reserve accounts serve the same functions as the corresponding accounts that U.S. firms use: to permit an appropriate matching of revenues and expenses, and appropriate valuation of assets and liabilities. Of course, firms in both the United States and abroad can misuse these accounts (that is, understating or overstating the provisions each year) to manage earnings, as discussed in Chapter 6. In addition to searching for situations where such management occurs, the analyst's main concern with these reserves is understanding the nature of the reserve account in each case. There is usually an analogous account used in the United States that helps the analyst in this interpretation.

Keeping Expenses Out of the Income Statement

A practice in some countries is to create a reserve account by reducing the Retained Earnings account. For example, a firm might decrease Retained Earnings and increase Reserve for Price Increases or Reserve for Contingencies. These accounts appear among the shareholders' equity accounts and may carry a title such as Retained Earnings Appropriated for Price Increases or Retained Earnings Appropriated for Contingencies. When firms later experience the price increase or contingency, they charge the cost against the reserve account rather than include it in expenses. These costs therefore bypass the income statement and usually result in an overstatement of earnings. Note that this use of reserves does not misstate total shareholders' equity because all of the affected accounts (Retained Earnings, reserve accounts, expense accounts) are components of shareholders' equity. Thus, the analyst's primary concern with these reserves is assessing whether the reported net income that excludes these items is an appropriate base for estimating future earnings. The analyst can study the shareholders' equity portion of the balance sheet to ascertain whether firms have used reserve accounts to avoid sending legitimate expenses through the income statement. Reserves of this type have been particularly common in the German reporting system.

Revaluing Assets but Delaying Income Recognition Effect

Firms might use reserves in situations where they revalue assets but do not desire the income effect of the revaluation to affect income of the current period. The next chapter points out that firms in the United States account for investments in marketable equity securities using the market value method. When market value differs from acquisition costs, U.S. firms write up or write down the investment account. Financial reporting in the United States does not generally permit the immediate recognition of this increase or decrease in market value in measuring income (except for securities held for "trading" purposes, as defined in the next chapter). Instead, these firms increase or decrease Accumulated Other Comprehensive Income, a shareholders' equity account. When the firm sells the securities, it eliminates the unrealized gain or loss account and recognizes a realized gain or loss in measuring net income.

Another example of this use of the reserve account relates to foreign currency translation (also discussed in the next chapter). U.S. firms with foreign operations usually translate the financial statements of their foreign entities into U.S. dollars each period using the exchange rate at the end of the period. Changes in the exchange rate cause an unrealized foreign currency gain or loss. Firms do not recognize this gain or loss in measuring income each period but instead increase or decrease Accumulated Other Comprehensive Income. When the firm disposes of the foreign unit, it eliminates the unrealized foreign currency adjustment from Accumulated Other Comprehensive Income and recognizes a gain or loss on disposal.

Financial reporting in the United Kingdom permits periodic revaluations of fixed assets and intangible assets to their current market value. The increased valuation of assets that usually occurs leads to an increase in a revaluation reserve account included in the shareholders' equity section of the balance sheet. Depreciation or amortization of the revalued assets may appear fully on the income statement each period as an expense, or split between the income statement (depreciation or amortization based on acquisition cost) and a reduction in the revaluation reserve (depreciation or amortization based on the excess of current market value over acquisition cost).

The analyst's concern with this type of reserve is the appropriateness of revaluing the asset and delaying recognition of its income effect. Note that total shareholders' equity is the same regardless of whether the unrealized gain or loss immediately affects net income or whether it affects another shareholders' equity account and later affects net income. This use of reserves does affect net income of the current period. The analyst may wish to restate reported net income of the current period to incorporate changes in these reserves.

Permanently Reclassifying Retained Earnings

Local laws or practices may dictate that firms transfer an amount from retained earnings, which is available for dividends, to a more permanent account that is not available for dividends. U.S. firms typically "capitalize" a portion of retained earnings when they issue a stock dividend. Several other countries require firms to report a certain amount of legal capital on the balance sheet. Such firms reduce retained earnings and increase an account titled Legal Capital or Legal Reserve. The implication of such disclosures is that assets equal to the amount of this legal capital are not available for dividends. This use of reserves has no effect on net income of the current or future periods.

SUMMARY OF RESERVES

The quality of disclosures regarding reserves varies considerably across countries. Analysts will often encounter difficulties attempting to understand, much less adjust for, the effect of changes in reserves. An awareness of the ways that firms might use reserve accounts should help the analyst in knowing the kinds of questions to raise when studying the financial statements. Until greater standardization occurs across countries in the use of reserves, the analyst must recognize the lack of comparability of net income and balance sheet amounts, and perhaps the increased importance of a statement of cash flows.

SUMMARY

This chapter explores various reporting areas where expense measurement and liability recognition interact. These reporting areas therefore affect both profitability analysis and risk analysis. The desire to keep debt off the balance sheet, with the hope of lowering the cost of financing, should put the analyst on guard for the existence of unreported liabilities and potential for lower quality of financial position reporting by firms. The lack of physical existence of liabilities (unlike most assets) increases the difficulty experienced by both the independent auditor and the analyst in identifying the existence of unreported liabilities. This chapter described some of the areas that the analyst should consider when engaging in this search.

PROBLEMS AND CASES

8.1 ACHIEVING OFF-BALANCE-SHEET FINANCING (ADAPTED FROM MATERIALS BY R. DIETER, D. LANDSITTEL, J. STEWART, AND A. WYATT). Brion Company wishes to raise $50 million cash but, for various reasons, does not wish to do so in a way that results in a newly recorded liability. It is sufficiently solvent and profitable that its bank is willing to lend up to $50 million at the prime interest rate. Brion Company's financial executives have devised six different plans, described in the following sections.

Transfer of Receivables with Recourse

Brion Company will transfer to Credit Company its long-term accounts receivable, which call for payments over the next 2 years. Credit Company will pay an amount equal to the present value of the receivables, less an allowance for uncollectibles, as well as a discount, because it is paying now but will collect cash later. Brion Company must repurchase from Credit Company at face value any receivables that become uncollectible in excess of the allowance. In addition, Brion Company may repurchase any of the receivables not yet due at face value less a discount specified by formula and based on the prime rate at the time of the initial transfer. (This option permits Brion Company to benefit if an unexpected drop in interest rates occurs after the transfer.) The accounting issue is whether the transfer is a sale (where Brion Company increases Cash, reduces Accounts Receivable, and recognizes expense or loss on transfer) or whether the transfer is merely a loan collateralized by the receivables (where Brion Company increases Cash and increases Notes Payable at the time of transfer).

Product Financing Arrangement

Brion Company will transfer inventory to Credit Company, who will store the inventory in a public warehouse. Credit Company may use the inventory as collateral for its own borrowings, whose proceeds will be used to pay Brion Company. Brion Company will pay storage costs and will repurchase all of the inventory within the next 4 years at contractually fixed prices plus interest accrued for the time elapsed between the transfer and later repurchase. The accounting issue is whether the inventory is sold to Credit Company, with later repurchases treated as new acquisitions for Brion's inventory, or whether the transaction is merely a loan, with the inventory remaining on Brion's balance sheet.

Throughput Contract

Brion Company wants a branch line of a railroad built from the main rail line to carry raw material directly to its own plant. It could, of course, borrow the funds and build the branch line itself. Instead, it will sign an agreement with the railroad to ship specified amounts of material each month for 10 years. Even if it does not ship the specified amounts of material, it will pay the agreed shipping costs. The railroad will take the contract to its bank and, using it as collateral, borrow the funds to build the branch line. The accounting issue is whether Brion Company would increase an asset for future rail services and increase a liability for payments to the railroad. The alternative is to make no accounting entry except when Brion makes payments to the railroad.

Construction Partnership

Brion Company and Mission Company will jointly build a plant to manufacture chemicals both need in their own production processes. Each will contribute $5 million to the project, called Chemical. Chemical will borrow another $40 million from a bank, with Brion the only guarantor of the debt. Brion and Mission are each to contribute equally to future operating expenses and debt service payments of Chemical, but, in return for its guaranteeing the debt, Brion will have an option to purchase Mission's interest for $20 million four years hence. The accounting issue is whether Brion Company should recognize a liability for the funds borrowed by Chemical. Because of the debt guarantee, debt service payments will ultimately be Brion Company's responsibility. Alternatively, the debt guarantee is a commitment merely to be disclosed in notes to Brion Company's financial statements.

Research and Development Partnership

Brion Company will contribute a laboratory and preliminary findings about a potentially profitable gene-splicing discovery to a partnership, called Venture. Venture will raise funds by selling the remaining interest in the partnership to outside investors for $2 million and borrowing $48 million from a bank with Brion Company guaranteeing the debt. Although Venture will operate under the management of Brion Company, it will be free to sell the results of its further discoveries and development efforts to anyone, including Brion Company. Brion Company is not obligated to purchase any of Venture's output. The accounting issue is whether Brion Company would recognize the liability.

Hotel Financing

Brion Company owns and operates a profitable hotel. It could use the hotel as collateral for a conventional mortgage loan. Instead, it considers selling the hotel to a partnership for $50 million cash. The partnership will sell ownership interests to outside investors for $5 million and borrow $45 million from a bank on a conventional mortgage loan, using the hotel as collateral. Brion Company guarantees the debt. The accounting issue is whether Brion Company would record the liability for the guaranteed debt of the partnership.

Required

Discuss the appropriate treatment of each of these proposed arrangements from the viewpoint of the auditor, who must apply GAAP in deciding whether the transaction will result in a liability to be recorded or whether footnote disclosure will suffice. Does the GAAP reporting result in accurately portraying the economics of the arrangement in each case?

8.2 ACCOUNTING FOR SECURITIZATION OF RECEIVABLES.

Sears, Roebuck, and Co. discloses the following information with respect to credit card receivables (amounts in millions).

December 31:	Year 11	Year 10
Credit Card Receivables............................	$27,639	$27,060
Securitized Balances Sold	—	(7,834)
Retained Interest in Securitized Balances Sold..........	—	(3,051)
Credit Card Receivables on Balance Sheet	$27,639	$16,175

NOTES TO FINANCIAL STATEMENTS

The company utilizes credit card securitizations as part of its overall funding strategy. The company transfers certain credit card receivables to master trusts. The trusts then securitize the receivables by issuing certificates representing undivided interests in the trusts' receivables to both outside investors and to the company (retained interest). These certificates entitle the holder to a series of scheduled cash flows under present terms and conditions, the receipt of which is dependent upon cash flows generated by the related trusts' assets. In each securitization transaction, the company has retained certain subordinated interests which serve as a credit enhancement to the certificates held by the outside investors. As a result, the credit quality of certificates held by outside investors is enhanced. However, the investors and the trusts have no recourse against the company beyond the trust assets. The addition of previously uncommitted assets to the securitization trusts in April, Year 11, required the company to consolidate the securitization structure for financial reporting purposes on a prospective basis. Accordingly, the company recognized approximately $8.1 billion of previously unconsolidated securitized credit card receivables and related securitization borrowings in the second quarter of Year 11. In addition, approximately $3.9 billion of assets were reclassified to credit card receivables from retained interest in transferred credit card receivables. The company now accounts for securitizations as secured borrowings. In connection with the consolidation of the securitization structure, the company recognized a non-cash, pretax charge of $522 million to establish an allowance for uncollectible accounts related to the receivables, which were previously considered as sold or accounted for as retained interests in transferred credit card receivables.

Required

a. Applying the criteria for the sale of receivables from FASB *Statement No. 140*, justify Sears' treatment of the securitization of receivables on December 31, Year 10, as a sale instead of as a collateralized loan.

b. Assume that the receivables disclosed as securitized on December 31, Year 10, had been initially securitized on that day. Give the journal entry that Sears would have made to securitize these receivables, assuming that it securitized the receivables at no gain or loss.

c. Give the journal entry that Sears made on April, Year 11, to consolidate the securitization structure.

d. Applying the criteria for the sale of receivables from FASB *Statement No. 140*, justify Sears' consolidation of the securitization structure beginning in April, Year 11.

e. Identify the likely events that required Sears to consolidate the securitization structure.

8.3 ACCOUNTING FOR ATTEMPTED OFF-BALANCE-SHEET FINANCING ARRANGEMENTS.

Part a.   International Paper Company (IP) is in need of $100 million of additional financing but, because of restrictions in existing debt covenants, cannot place any more debt on its balance sheet. To obtain the needed funds, it plans to transfer cutting rights to a mature timber tract to a newly created trust as of January 1, Year 8. The trust will use the cutting rights to obtain a $100 million, five-year, 10 percent interest rate bank loan due in five equal installments with interest on December 31 of each year.

The timber will be harvested each year and sold to obtain funds to service the loan and pay operating costs. Based on current prices, there is 10 percent more standing wood available for cutting than should be needed to service the loan and pay ongoing operating costs of the tract (including wind, fire, and erosion insurance). If the selling price of timber decreases in the future, the volume of timber harvested will be increased sufficiently to service the debt. If the selling price of timber increases in the future, the volume harvested will remain as originally anticipated, but any cash left over after debt service and coverage of operating costs will be invested by the trust to provide a cushion for possible future price decreases. The value of any cash or uncut timber at the end of five years will revert to IP.

IP will not guarantee the debt. The bank, however, has the right to inspect the tract at any time and to replace IP's forest management personnel with managers of its own choosing if it feels the tract is being mismanaged.

Required (Part a)

Discuss the appropriate accounting for this transaction by IP in light of other FASB pronouncements on off-balance-sheet financing.

Part b.   On June 24, Year 4, Delta Air Lines entered into a revolving accounts receivable facility (Facility) providing for the sale of $489 million of a defined pool of accounts receivable (Receivables) through a wholly owned subsidiary to a trust in exchange for a senior certificate in the principal amount of $300 million (Senior Certificate) and a subordinate certificate in the principal amount of $189 million (Subordinate Certificate). The subsidiary retained the Subordinate Certificate and the company received $300 million in cash from the sale of the Senior Certificate to a third party. The principal amount of the Subordinate Certificate fluctuates daily depending upon the volume of Receivables sold, and is payable to the subsidiary only to the extent the collections received on the Receivables exceed amounts due on the Senior Certificate. The full amount of the allowance for doubtful accounts related to the Receivables sold has been retained, as the company has substantially the same credit risk as if the Receivables had not been sold. Under the terms of the Facility, the company is obligated to pay fees, which approximate the purchaser's cost of issuing a like amount of commercial paper plus certain administrative costs.

Required (Part b)

Delta requests your advice on the appropriate accounting for this transaction. How would you respond?

Part c. In Year 2, a wholly owned subsidiary of Sun Company became a one-third partner in Belvieu Environmental Fuels (BEF), a joint venture formed for the purpose of constructing, owning, and operating a $220 million methyl tertiary butyl ether (MTBE) production facility in Mont Belvieu, Texas. As of December 31, Year 3, BEF had borrowed $128 million against a construction loan facility of which the company guarantees one-third, or $43 million. The plant, which has a designed daily capacity of 12,600 barrels of MTBE, is expected to begin production in mid-Year 4. When production commences, the construction loan will be converted into a five-year, nonrecourse term loan with a first priority lien on all project assets.

In order to obtain a secure supply of oxygenates for the manufacture of reformu-lated fuels, Sun has entered into a 10-year take-or-pay agreement with BEF which commences when the plant becomes operational. Pursuant to this agreement, Sun will purchase all of the MTBE production from the plant. The minimum per unit price to be paid for the MTBE production while the nonrecourse term loan is out-standing will be equal to BEF's annual raw material and operating costs and debt service payments divided by the plant's annual designed capacity. Notwithstanding this minimum price, Sun has agreed to pay BEF a price during the first three years of the off-take agreement, which approximates prices included in current MTBE long-term sales agreements in the marketplace. This price is expected to exceed the minimum price required by the loan agreement. Sun will negotiate a new pricing arrangement with BEF for the remaining years the take-or pay agreement is in effect, which will be based upon the expected market conditions existing at such time.

Required (Part c)

How should Sun account for this transaction?

8.4 ACCOUNTING FOR A LEASE BY THE LESSOR AND THE LESSEE. Ford Motor Company (Ford) needs to acquire computer equipment from IBM as of January 1, Year 4. Ford can borrow the necessary funds to purchase the computer for $10,000,000. Ford, however, desires to keep debt off of its balance sheet and to struc-ture an operating lease with IBM. The computer has an estimated life to IBM of five years. Ford will lease the computer for three years, at which time the computer reverts back to IBM. The cost to IBM to manufacture the computer is $8,000,000. Ford's borrowing rate for three-year, secured financing is 8 percent.

Required

a. Assume that Ford must make rental payments on December 31 of Year 4 through December 31 of Year 6. What is the maximum annual rental (to the nearest dollar) that Ford can make and still permit this lease to qualify as an operating lease?

b. Assume that Ford must make rental payments on January 1, Year 4, through January 1, Year 6. What is the maximum annual rental (to the nearest dollar) that Ford can make and still permit this lease to qualify as an operating lease?

c. Assume for the remaining parts of this problem that Ford will make annual payments of $3,880,335 on December 31, Year 4, through December 31, Year 6. Indicate the nature and amount of revenues and expenses (excluding income taxes) each company would report for each of the Years 4 through 6, assuming that they accounted for the lease as an operating lease.

d. Repeat part c assuming each company accounted for the lease as a capital lease.

e. Assume that these firms treat the lease as a capital lease for financial reporting and an operating lease for tax reporting. Compute the amount of deferred tax asset or deferred tax liability each firm would report related to the lease on December 31, Year 4, through December 31, Year 6. The income tax rate is 35 percent.

8.5 ACCOUNTING FOR CAPITAL LEASES. Wal-Mart Stores leases most of its office, warehouse, and retail space under a combination of capital and operating leases. The disclosures related to *capital leases* for its fiscal year ending January 31, Year 11, appear below (amounts in millions):

	January 31	
	Year 11	Year 10
Property, Plant, and Equipment under		
Capital Leases	$4,626	$4,620
Less Accumulated Depreciation	(1,432)	(1,303)
Net Property, Plant, and Equipment under		
Capital Leases	$3,194	$3,317
Capitalized Lease Obligation.	$3,193	$3,295

The weighted average discount rate used to compute the present value of the capitalized lease obligation was 7 percent. Assume that new leases capitalized and lease payments occur evenly throughout the year.

Required

a. Prepare an analysis that explains the change in the following accounts during the Year 11 fiscal year.

(1) Property, Plant, and Equipment under Capital Leases

(2) Accumulated Depreciation

(3) Capitalized Lease Obligation

b. Assume that Wal-Mart treats these capitalized leases as operating leases for income tax purposes. The income tax rate is 35 percent. Compute the total amount of pre-tax expenses related to these leased assets for financial and tax reporting for the Year 11 fiscal year.

c. Compute the amount of deferred tax asset and/or deferred tax liability that Wal-Mart would report on its January 31, Year 11, balance sheet related to these leases.

8.6 EFFECT OF CAPITALIZING OPERATING LEASES ON BALANCE SHEET RATIOS.

Some retailing companies own their own stores or acquire their premises under capital leases. Other retailing companies acquire the use of store facilities under operating leases, contracting to make future payments. An analyst comparing the capital structure risks of retailing companies may wish to make adjustments to reported financial statement data to put all firms on a comparable basis.

Certain data from the financial statements of The Gap and Limited Brands appear below (amounts in millions):

	The Gap	Limited Brands
Balance Sheet as of End of Year 12		
Current Liabilities	$2,056	$1,319
Long-term Debt...........................	2,027	272
Other Noncurrent Liabilities...............	564	229
Shareholders' Equity......................	3,008	2,921
Total..................................	$7,655	$4,741
Minimum Payments Under Operating Leases		
Year 13	$ 816	$ 587
Year 14	771	544
Year 15	718	490
Year 16	612	423
Year 17	477	347
After Year 17............................	1,844	863
Total..................................	$5,238	$3,254

Required

a. Compute the present value of operating lease obligations using an 8 percent discount rate for The Gap and Limited Brands at the end of Year 12. Assume that all cash flows occur at the end of each year. Also assume that the minimum lease payment each year after Year 17 equals the amount for Year 17 and continues until the aggregate payments after Year 17 have been made (that is, $1,844 million for The Gap and $863 million for Limited Brands).

b. Compute each of the following ratios for The Gap and Limited Brands as of the end of Year 12 using the amounts as originally reported in their balance sheets for the year.

(1) Liabilities to Assets Ratio = Total Liabilities/Total Assets

(2) Long-term Debt Ratio = Long-term Debt /(Long-term Debt + Shareholders' Equity)

c. Repeat part b but assume that these firms capitalize operating leases.

d. Comment on the results from parts b and c.

8.7 FINANCIAL STATEMENT EFFECTS OF CAPITAL AND OPERATING LEASES. Northwest Airlines leases aircraft used in its operations. Information taken from its financial statements and notes for Year 10 and Year 11 appear below (amounts in millions).

Balance Sheet	December 31, Year 11	December 31, Year 10
Property Rights under Capital Leases (net of accumulated depreciation)	$543	$565
Capitalized Lease Obligation	$586	$556

NOTES TO THE FINANCIAL STATEMENTS

Leases: The present value of minimum lease payments under *capital leases* as of December 31, Year 10 and Year 11, when discounted at 8 percent, are:

	December 31, Year 11	December 31, Year 10
Lease Payments on December 31 of:		
Year 11	$ —	$106
Year 12	287	280
Year 13	101	87
Year 14	75	62
Year 15	64	51
After Year 15		146
Total		$732
Year 16	50	
After Year 16	527	
Total	$1,104	
Less Discount	(518)	(176)
Present Value	$ 586	$556

Minimum lease payments under *operating leases* as of December 31, Year 10 and Year 11, appear below:

	December 31, Year 11	December 31, Year 10
Lease Payment on December 31 of:		
Year 11	—	$ 655
Year 12	$ 707	668
Year 13	699	650
Year 14	679	641
Year 15	654	622
After Year 15............................	—	5,924
Year 16	659	—
After Year 16............................	5,649	—
Total	$9,047	$9,160

Required

a. Complete the analyses below relating to capital leases for Year 11. Assume that all cash flows occur at the end of the year and new capital leases were signed at the end of the year.

Property Rights under Capital Leases, December 31, Year 10........
New Capital Leases Entered into During Year 11 ....
Amortization of Property Rights for Year 11..................... _____
Property Rights under Capital Leases, December 31, Year 11........ _____

Capitalized Lease Obligation, December 31, Year 10..............
Increase in Capitalized Lease Obligation for
   Interest During Year 11 ....
New Capitalized Lease Obligations Entered into During Year 11....
Cash Payments under Capital Leases During Year 11 .... _____
Capitalized Lease Obligation, December 31, Year 11.............. _____

b. Determine the amount that Northwest would have reported as rent expense for Year 11 if it had treated all capital leases as operating leases.

c. Determine the amount reported as rent expense for Year 11 for all operating leases.

d. Compute the present value of commitments under operating leases on December 31, Year 10 and Year 11, assuming that 8 percent is an appropriate discount rate and that all cash flows occur at the end of each period. Cash flows after the fifth year occur in the same amount as those in the fifth year

($622 million at the end of Year 10 and $659 million at the end of Year 11) until the aggregate payments ($5,924 million and $5,649 million, respectively) have been made.

e. Assume that Northwest had capitalized all operating leases using the amounts computed in part d. Complete the following analysis for Year 11:

Capitalized Value of Operating Leases, December 31, Year 10 ......

Increase in Capitalized Value for Interest During Year 11..........

New Operating Leases Capitalized During Year 11...............

Cash Payments under Capitalized Operating Leases
During Year 11. ....   _____

Capitalized Value of Operating Leases, December 31, Year 11 ......   _____

---

f. Northwest Airlines treats *all* of its leases as operating leases for tax purposes. The income tax rate is 35 percent and Northwest expects this rate to continue into the foreseeable future. Compute the amount of deferred tax asset or deferred tax liability that Northwest Airlines will recognize at the end of Year 10 and the end of Year 11. Indicate whether the change in the deferred tax asset or liability during Year 11 increased or decreased income tax expense for the year.

8.8 ACCOUNTING FOR FORWARD FOREIGN EXCHANGE CONTRACT AS A FAIR VALUE HEDGE.   Refer to Examples 5 and 9 in the chapter. Firm A places its firm order for the equipment on June 30, Year 1. It simultaneously signs a forward foreign exchange contract for 10,000 GBP. The forward rate on June 30, Year 1, for settlement on June 30, Year 2, is $1.64 per GBP. Firm A designates the forward foreign exchange contract as a fair value hedge of the firm commitment.

a. GAAP does not require Firm A to record either the purchase commitment or the forward foreign exchange contract on the balance sheet as a liability and an asset on June 30, Year 1. What is the GAAP logic for this accounting?

b. On December 31, Year 1, the forward foreign exchange rate for settlement on June 30, Year 2, is $1.73 per GBP. Give the journal entries to record the *change* in the value of the purchase commitment and the *change* in the value of the forward contract for Year 1. Assume an 8 percent per year interest rate for discounting cash flows to their present values on December 31, Year 1.

c. Give the journal entries on June 30, Year 2, to record the change in the present value of the purchase commitment and the forward foreign exchange contract for the passage of time.

d. On June 30, Year 2, the spot foreign exchange rate is $1.75 per GBP. Give the journal entries to record the *change* in the value of the purchase commitment and the *change* in the value of the forward contract due to changes in the exchange rate during the first six months of Year 2.

e. Give the journal entry on June 30, Year 2, to purchase 10,000 GBP with U.S. dollars and acquire the equipment.

f. Give the journal entry on June 30, Year 2, to settle the forward foreign exchange contract.

g. How would the entries in parts b through f differ if Firm A had chosen to designate the forward foreign exchange contract as a cash flow hedge instead of a fair value hedge?

h. Suggest a scenario that would justify Firm A treating the forward foreign exchange contract as a fair value hedge, and a scenario that would justify the firm treating the contract as a cash flow hedge.

8.9 ACCOUNTING FOR FORWARD COMMODITY PRICE CONTRACT AS A CASH FLOW HEDGE.   Refer to Examples 8 and 12 in the chapter. Firm D holds 10,000 gallons of whiskey in inventory on October 31, Year 1, that costs $225 per gallon. Firm D contemplates selling the whiskey on March 31, Year 2, when it completes the aging process. Uncertainty about the selling price of whiskey on March 31, Year 2, leads Firm D to acquire a forward contract on whiskey. The forward contract does not require an initial investment of funds. Firm D designates the forward commodity contract as a cash flow hedge of an anticipated transaction. The forward price on October 31, Year 1, for delivery on March 31, Year 2, is $320 per gallon.

a. Give the journal entry, if any, that Firm D would make on October 31, Year 1, when it acquires the forward commodity price contract.

b. On December 31, Year 1, the end of the accounting period for Firm D, the forward price of whiskey for March 31, Year 2, delivery is $310 per gallon. Give the journal entry to record the *change* in the value of the forward commodity price contract. Ignore the discounting of cash flows in this part and for the remainder of the problem.

c. Give the journal entry that Firm D must make on December 31, Year 1, for the decline in value of the whiskey inventory.

d. On March 31, Year 2, the price of whiskey declines to $270 per gallon. Give the journal entry that Firm D must make to revalue the forward contract.

e. Give the entry that Firm D must make on March 31, Year 2, to reflect the decline in value of the inventory.

f. Give the journal entry that Firm D would make on March 31, Year 2, to settle the forward contract.

g. Assume that Firm D sells the whiskey on March 31, Year 2, for $270 a gallon. Give the journal entries to record the sale and recognize the cost of goods sold.

h. How would the entries in parts b through g differ if Firm D had chosen to designate the forward commodity price contract as a fair value hedge instead of a cash flow hedge?

i   Suggest a scenario that would justify the firm treating the forward commodity price contract as a fair value hedge, and a scenario that would justify treating it as a cash flow hedge.

8.10 INTERPRETING DERIVATIVES DISCLOSURES.   Excerpts from the disclosures on derivatives by The Coca-Cola Company (Coke) appear below.

> Our Company uses derivative financial instruments primarily to reduce our exposure to adverse fluctuations in interest rates and foreign exchange rates. When entered into, the Company formally specifies the

risk management objectives and strategies for undertaking the hedge transactions and designates the financial instruments as a hedge of a specific underlying exposure. The Company formally assesses, both at the inception and at least quarterly thereafter, whether the financial instruments that are used in hedging transactions are effective at offsetting changes in either the fair value or cash flows of the related underlying exposures. The Company does not enter into derivative financial instruments for trading purposes.

Our Company maintains a percentage of fixed and variable rate debt within defined parameters. We enter into interest rate swap agreements to maintain the fixed-to-variable mix within these parameters. These contracts have maturities ranging from one to two years. After giving effect to interest rate management instruments, the principal amount of our long-term debt that had fixed and variable interest rates, respectively, was $1,262 million and $113 million on December 31, Year 11. The fair value of our Company's interest rate swap agreements was approximately $5 million at December 31, Year 11. Interest rate swap agreements are accounted for as fair value hedges. There was no ineffective portion of gains and losses on interest rate swaps during Year 11.

We enter into forward exchange contracts to hedge certain portions of forecasted cash flows denominated in foreign currencies. These contracts have maturities ranging from one to two years. The purpose of our foreign currency hedging activities is to reduce the risk that our eventual U.S. dollar net cash inflows resulting from sales outside the U.S. will be adversely affected by changes in exchange rates. We designate these derivatives as cash flow hedges. During Year 11, we increased accumulated other comprehensive income net by $311 million ($189 million after tax) for changes in the fair value of cash flow hedges. The amount recorded in earnings for the ineffective portion of cash flow hedges during Year 11 was not significant. We also reclassified net gains for $160 million ($97 million after tax) from accumulated other comprehensive income to earnings. The accumulated net gain on cash flow derivatives on December 31, Year 11, is $234 million ($142 million after tax). The carrying and fair value of foreign exchange contracts on December 31, Year 11 is $266 million.

Our Company monitors our exposure to financial market risks using value-at-risk models. Our value-at-risk calculations use a historical simulation model to estimate potential future losses in the fair value of our derivatives and other financial instruments that could occur as a result of adverse movements in interest rates and foreign exchange rates. We examined historical weekly returns over the previous 10 years to calculate our value at risk. The average value at risk represents the simple average of quarterly amounts over the past year. As a result of our calculations, we estimate with a 95 percent confidence that the impact of adverse movements in interest rates over a one-week period would not have a material impact on our earnings for Year 11 or on our financial position on December 31, Year 11. Similar calculations for adverse movements in foreign exchange rates indicate a maximum impact on earnings over a one-week period is $43 million. Net income for Year 11 was $3,969 million.

Required

a. Coke indicates that it "formally specifies the risk management objectives and strategies for undertaking the hedge transactions." Identify the risk management objective and describe how the particular derivative accomplishes this objective with respect to interest rate swap agreements.

b. Repeat part a for forward exchange contracts.

c. What is the rationale for Coke's designation of the interest rate swaps as fair value hedges and the forward exchange contracts as cash flow hedges?

d. Why does Coke assess both initially and at least quarterly the effectiveness of these hedging instruments?

e. Compute the amount that Coke initially recorded on its books for foreign exchange contracts outstanding on December 31, Year 11. What events will cause the carrying value of these contracts at any later date to differ from the amounts initially recorded?

f. Coke reports a net gain from changes in the value of cash flow hedges of $311 million for Year 11. What does the disclosure that Coke recognized a net gain instead of a net loss suggest about the direction of changes in exchange rates between the U.S. dollar and the foreign currencies underlying the foreign exchange contracts? Will the forward exchange contracts likely appear on Coke's balance sheet as assets or as liabilities? Explain.

g. Justify Coke's treatment of the $311 million net gain from changes in the value of cash flow hedges during Year 11 as an increase in accumulated other comprehensive income instead of as an ineffective cash flow hedge that should be included in earnings.

h. The income tax law taxes gains and losses from changes in the fair value of foreign exchange contracts at the time of settlement. Will the tax effects of the $311 million pre-tax gain for Year 11 affect current taxes payable or deferred taxes? If deferred taxes, then will it affect deferred tax assets or deferred tax liabilities? Explain.

i. Describe the likely event that will cause Coke to reclassify amounts from accumulated other comprehensive income to earnings.

j. Assess the effectiveness of Coke management of risk changes from interest and foreign exchange rates for Year 11.

8.11 INTERPRETING RETIREMENT BENEFIT PLAN DISCLOSURES.

Ford Motor Company (Ford) provides pension, health care, and life insurance benefits for retired employees. Exhibit 8.15 presents the components of pension expense and health care and life insurance expense for Year 10 and Year 11. Exhibit 8.16 presents the funded status and changes in the funded status of pension plans and health care and life insurance plans for Year 10 and Year 11. Exhibit 8.16 also indicates the

EXHIBIT 8.15

Elements of Pension, Health Care, and Life Insurance Expenses for Ford Motor Company
(amounts in millions)
(Problem 8.11)

	Pensions				Health Care and Life Insurance	
	U.S. Plans		Non-U.S. Plans			
	Year 11	Year 10	Year 11	Year 10	Year 11	Year 10
Service Cost	$ 531	$ 495	$ 396	$ 405	$ 374	$ 320
Interest Cost.	2,410	2,345	974	918	1,697	1,483
Expected Return on Assets	(3,697)	(3,281)	(1,184)	(1,162)	(161)	(135)
Amortization of Prior Service Cost.	532	620	138	133	(114)	(38)
Amortization of (Gains)/Losses	(367)	(418)	(101)	17	161	28
Other	245	51	8	184	(35)	(105)
Total Expense/(Income)	$ (346)	$ (188)	$ 231	$ 495	$1,922	$1,553

EXHIBIT 8.16

Funded Status of Retirement Plans for Ford Motor Company
(amounts in millions)
(Problem 8.11)

	Pensions				Health Care and Life Insurance	
	U.S. Plans		Non-U.S. Plans			
	Year 11	Year 10	Year 11	Year 10	Year 11	Year 10
Benefit Obligation, January 1. . . .	$33,282	$31,846	$16,918	$16,484	$23,374	$15,744
Service Cost	531	495	396	405	374	320
Interest Cost	2,410	2,345	974	918	1,697	1,483
Amendments.	6	—	133	232	(923)	(226)
Actuarial (Gains) Losses.	1,120	689	(962)	229	1,968	3,338
Benefits Paid	(2,496)	(2,273)	(768)	(744)	(1,145)	(1,055)
Other.	370	180	(700)	(606)	88	3,770
Benefit Obligation, December 31	$35,223	$33,282	$15,991	$16,918	$25,433	$23,374

	Pensions				Health Care and Life	
	U.S. Plans		Non-U.S. Plans		Insurance	
Exhibit 8.16—(continued)	Year 11	Year 10	Year 11	Year 10	Year 11	Year 10
Fair Value of Plan						
Assets, January 1	$39,830	$40,845	$14,714	$15,432	$ 3,135	$ 1,258
Actual Return on Assets	(1,558)	979	(931)	233	200	168
Contributions	—	8	277	185	142	1,935
Benefits Paid	(2,496)	(2,273)	(768)	(744)	(758)	(651)
Other.	43	271	(357)	(392)	(27)	425
Fair Value of Plan Assets,						
December 31	$35,819	$39,830	$12,935	$14,714	$ 2,692	$ 3,135
Net Funded Asset (Liability)	$ 596	$ 6,548	$(3,056)	$(2,204)	$(22,741)	$(20,239)
Unamortized Prior						
Service Costs	3,358	3,912	768	814	(1,043)	(231)
Unamortized Actuarial (Gains)						
Losses	(1,939)	(8,557)	1,642	430	6,655	4,850
Net Asset (Liability)						
Recognized	$ 2,015	$ 1,903	$ (646)	$ (960)	$(17,129)	$(15,620)
Recognized in:						
Prepaid Assets	$ 3,099	$ 2,856	$ 1,259	$ 1,040	$ —	$ —
Accrued Liabilities	(1,356)	(1,244)	(2,779)	(2,900)	(17,129)	(15,620)
Other Accounts.	272	291	874	900	—	—
Net Asset (Liability)						
Recognized.	$ 2,015	$ 1,903	$ (646)	$ (960)	$(17,129)	$(15,620)
Pension Plans with Underfunded						
Accumulated Benefit						
Obligations.	$ 1,118	$ 1,023	$ 2,388	$ 2,423	$ —	$ —
Weighted Average Assumptions:						
Discount Rate	7.25%	7.50%	6.10%	6.10%	7.25%	7.50%
Expected Return on Assets	9.50%	9.50%	8.70%	8.80%	6.00%	6.00%
Rate of Compensation Increase . .	5.20%	5.20%	3.80%	4.10%	—	—
Initial Health Care Cost						
Trend Rate	—	—	—	—	9.45%	8.97%
Ultimate Health Care Cost						
Trend Rate	—	—	—	—	5.00%	5.00%
Number of Years to Ultimate						
Trend Rate	—	—	—	—	6	7

assumptions that Ford used for these various plans each year. Ford discloses that the average rate of return on pension fund investments has exceeded 9.5 percent for the last 10-, 20-, and 30-year periods. A one-half point decrease/increase in the assumed U.S. rate of return on pension investments would increase/decrease U.S. pension expense by $190 million and would have no effect on the funded status of the pension plan. A one percentage point increase in the assumed health care cost trend rate would increase the service and interest component of health care and life insurance expense by $310 million, and the health care and insurance obligation by $3.1 billion. A one percentage point decrease in the assumed health care cost trend rate would decrease the service and interest component of health care and life insurance expense by $241 million, and the health care and insurance obligation by $2.6 billion.

Required

a. Why do the U.S. pension plans report pension *income* for Year 10 and Year 11, whereas the non-U.S. plans report pension *expense*?

b. Why is the net expense for the health care and life insurance plans so much larger than the income or expense for pension plans?

c. Why does the net funded asset or liability of these retirement plans differ from the net asset or net liability recognized in Ford's balance sheet?

d. Why does Ford recognize both assets and liabilities on its books for pension plans?

e. Why is the recognized liability for health care and life insurance plans so much larger than the asset or liability recognized for pension plans?

f. Prepare the entry to recognize the underfunded benefit obligation for non-U.S. plans at the end of Year 10 and Year 11. Assume that the amounts that Ford now recognizes on its books for non-U.S. pension plans appears in a single net liability account instead of the separate asset and liability accounts indicated in Exhibit 8.16. Also assume an income tax rate of 35 percent. The income tax law does not permit a deduction for pensions until a firm funds its obligation.

g. Give the entry to recognize the underfunded health care and life insurance obligation at the end of Year 10 and Year 11. Assume an income tax rate of 35 percent. The income tax law does not permit a deduction for health care and life insurance benefits until a firm funds its obligation.

h. What is the likely reason for the decrease in the service cost of non-U.S. pensions between Year 10 and Year 11?

i. What is the likely reason for the increase in the interest cost of health care and life insurance plans between Year 10 and Year 11?

j. Why might have the prior service cost for U.S. pension plans increased between Year 10 and Year 11 whereas the prior service cost decreased for the health care and life insurance plans between these two years?

k. Evaluate the investment performance of the pension fund and the health care and life insurance fund during Year 10 and Year 11.

l. What is the likely reason for the large decrease in the unamortized actuarial gain for U.S. pension plans between Year 10 and Year 11?

m. Ford indicates that a one-half point change in the expected rate of return on assets in U.S. pension plans would change pension expense by $190 million. How might an analyst check the reasonableness of this $190 million amount from the disclosures given?

n. Ford indicates that a change in the expected rate of return on assets would not affect the funded status on the pension plans at the end of Year 11. Why should there be no effect on the funded status of the pension plans?

o. Ford indicates that a one percentage point change in the health care trend rate would have a significant effect on the health care and life insurance obligation at the end of each year. Why is the health care obligation so much more sensitive to this change in assumption than the pension obligation is sensitive to changes in the expected rate of return on assets?

8.12 INTERPRETING RETIREMENT BENEFIT PLAN DISCLOSURES. The General Electric Company (GE) provides pension, health care, and life insurance benefits to its retired employees. Exhibit 8.17 presents the components of pension expense and health care and life insurance expense for Year 9 to Year 11. Exhibit 8.18 presents the funded status of the plan on December 31, Year 10 and Year 11.

Required

a. Why do GE's pension plans give rise to a net *income* for Year 11, whereas its health care and life insurance plans give rise to a net *expense*?

b. Why does the net funded asset or liability of GE's retirement plans at the end of Year 10 and Year 11 differ from the net asset or liability recognized on GE's balance sheet?

EXHIBIT 8.17

Elements of Pension, Health Care, and Life Insurance Expense for General Electric
(amounts in millions)
(Problem 8.12)

	Pensions			Health Care and Life Insurance		
	Year 11	Year 10	Year 9	Year 11	Year 10	Year 9
Service Cost	$ 884	$ 780	$ 693	$191	$165	$107
Interest Cost.	2,065	1,966	1,804	459	402	323
Expected Return on Assets.	(4,327)	(3,754)	(3,407)	(185)	(178)	(165)
Amortization of:						
Transition Gain	—	(154)	(154)	—	—	—
Prior Service Cost	244	237	151	90	49	8
Actuarial (Gain) Loss.	(961)	(819)	(467)	60	40	45
Net Expense (Income)	$(2,095)	$(1,744)	$(1,380)	$615	$478	$318

EXHIBIT 8.18

Funded Status of Pension, Health Care, and Life Insurance Plans for General Electric
(amounts in millions)
(Problem 8.12)

	Pensions		Health Care and Life Insurance	
	Year 11	Year 10	Year 11	Year 10
Benefit Obligation, January 1	$28,535	$25,522	$ 6,422	$ 4,926
Service Cost	884	780	191	165
Interest Cost	2,065	1,966	459	402
Plan Amendments	—	1,155	—	948
Actuarial (Gains) Losses	889	970	287	534
Participant Contributions	141	140	30	25
Benefits Paid	(2,091)	(1,998)	(593)	(578)
Benefit Obligation, December 31	$30,423	$28,535	$ 6,796	$ 6,422
Fair Value of Plan Assets, January 1	$49,757	$50,243	$ 2,031	$ 2,369
Actual Return on Assets	(2,876)	1,287	(163)	(85)
Employer Contributions	75	85	466	300
Participant Contributions	141	140	30	25
Benefits Paid	(2,091)	(1,998)	(593)	(578)
Fair Value of Plan Assets, December 31	$45,006	$49,757	$ 1,771	$ 2,031
Net Funded Asset (Liability)	$14,583	$21,222	$(5,025)	$(4,391)
Unrecognized Prior Service Cost	1,373	1,617	909	999
Unrecognized Net Actuarial (Gain) Loss	(3,541)	(12,594)	1,393	818
Net Asset (Liability) Recognized	$12,415	$10,245	$(2,723)	$(2,574)
Recognized in:				
Prepaid Assets	$13,740	$11,377	$ 66	$ 8
Accrued Liabilities	(1,325)	(1,132)	(2,789)	(2,582)
Net Asset (Liability) Recognized	$12,415	$10,245	$(2,723)	$(2,574)
Actuarial Assumptions:				
Discount Rate	7.25%	7.5%	7.25%	7.5%
Expected Return on Assets	9.5%	9.5%	9.5%	9.5%
Rate of Compensation Increase	5.0%	5.0%	—	—
Initial Health Care Cost Trend Rate	—	—	11.6%	10.0%
Ultimate Health Care Cost Trend Rate	—	—	5.0%	5.0%
Number of Years to Ultimate Trend Rate	—	—	9	9

c. Why does GE recognize both assets and liabilities on its balance sheet for retirement plans?

d. Give the entry that the analyst would make to recognize GE's underfunded health care and life insurance benefits obligation at the end of Year 10 and Year 11. Assume that the amounts now recognized on GE's books appear in a single net liability account instead of the separate net asset and net liability accounts shown in Exhibit 8.17. Also assume an income tax rate of 35 percent. The income tax law does not permit a firm to take a tax deduction for health care and life insurance benefits until it funds the obligation.

e. What is the most likely reason that GE reports an actuarial loss for Year 11 in measuring its pension obligation and its health care and life insurance obligation?

f. Evaluate the investment performance of the pension, health care, and life insurance funds during Year 10 and Year 11.

g. What is the likely reason that the unrecognized net actuarial gain related to pensions decreased so significantly between Year 10 and Year 11?

8.13 INTERPRETING RETIREMENT BENEFIT PLAN DISCLOSURES. The Goodyear Tire and Rubber Company (Goodyear) provides pension, health care, and life insurance benefits to its retired employees. Exhibit 8.19 presents the components of pension expense and health care and life insurance expense for Year 9 to Year 11. Exhibit 8.20 presents the funded status of the plans on December 31, Year 10 and Year 11.

EXHIBIT 8.19

Elements of Pension, Health Care, and Life Insurance Expense for Goodyear Tire and Rubber Company
(amounts in millions)
(Problem 8.13)

	Pensions			Health Care and Life Insurance		
	Year 11	Year 10	Year 9	Year 11	Year 10	Year 9
Service Cost............................	$110.3	$119.6	$118.0	$ 17.8	$ 19.5	$ 21.5
Interest Cost	377.4	353.0	314.6	183.2	164.2	145.6
Expected Return on Assets	(441.0)	(470.7)	(389.2)	—	—	—
Amortization of:						
Transition Gain......................	.6	.4	.3	—	—	—
Prior Service Cost...................	84.1	69.1	65.9	10.4	(2.2)	(2.3)
Actuarial (Gain) Loss................	6.8	(7.1)	14.2	13.6	14.7	9.0
Net Expense (Income)...............	$138.2	$ 64.3	$123.8	$225.0	$196.2	$173.8

EXHIBIT 8.20

Funded Status of Pension, Health Care, and Life Insurance Plans for Goodyear Tire and Rubber Company
(amounts in millions)
(Problem 8.13)

	Pensions		Health Care and Life Insurance	
	Year 11	Year 10	Year 11	Year 10
Benefit Obligation, January 1..................	$ 5,051.4	$4,878.1	$ 2,153.7	$ 2,124.3
Service Cost	110.3	119.6	17.8	19.5
Interest Cost.............................	377.4	353.0	183.2	164.2
Plan Amendments	11.1	248.6	150.1	3.0
Actuarial (Gains) Losses.....................	157.6	(153.8)	138.0	75.4
Participant Contributions	20.2	23.6	4.2	2.2
Benefits Paid.............................	(448.4)	(332.3)	(258.1)	(230.5)
Other Items	(64.6)	(85.4)	(5.2)	(4.4)
Benefit Obligation, December 31...............	$ 5,215.0	$5,051.4	$ 2,383.7	$ 2,153.7
Fair Value of Plan Assets, January 1............	$ 4,749.6	$5,178.9	—	—
Actual Return on Assets.....................	(230.6)	(117.2)	—	—
Employer Contributions	186.5	81.0	253.9	228.3
Participant Contributions	20.2	23.6	4.2	2.2
Benefits Paid.............................	(448.4)	(332.3)	(258.1)	(230.5)
Other Items	(101.1)	(84.4)	—	—
Fair Value of Plan Assets, December 31.........	$ 4,176.2	$4,749.6	$ —	$ —
Net Funded Asset (Liability)	$(1,038.8)	$ (301.8)	$(2,383.7)	$(2,153.7)
Unrecognized Prior Service Cost.	573.4	645.7	119.0	(23.1)
Unrecognized Net Actuarial (Gain) Loss........	798.3	(10.2)	440.8	313.5
Unrecognized Transition Obligations	4.7	6.7	—	—
Net Asset (Liability) Recognized...............	$ 337.6	$ 340.4	$(1,823.9)	$(1,863.3)
Recognized in:				
Prepaid Assets	$ 633.6	$ 641.5	$ —	$ —
Accrued Liabilities.......................	(1,215.1)	(594.2)	(1,823.9)	(1,863.3)
Other Accounts	919.1	293.1	—	—
Net Asset (Liability) Recognized...............	$ 337.6	$ 340.4	$(1,823.9)	$(1,863.3)
Actuarial Assumptions:				
Discount Rate	7.25%	7.5%	7.75%	8.0%
Expected Return on Assets	10.0%	9.5%	—	—
Rate of Compensation Increase	4.0%	4.0%	—	—
Initial Health Care Cost Trend Rate	—	—	7.5%	7.5%
Ultimate Health Care Cost Trend Rate........	—	—	5.0%	5.0%
Number of Years to Ultimate Trend Rate	—	—	11	11

Required

a. Why does Goodyear's health care and life insurance expense exceed pension expense each year, despite the fact that the pension benefit obligation exceeds the health care and life insurance obligation?

b. Why does the net liability of Goodyear's pension plans and of its health care and life insurance plans differ from the amounts reported for these plans on Goodyear's balance sheet?

c. Give the entry that the analyst would make to recognize Goodyear's underfunded pension obligation at the end of Year 10 and Year 11. Assume that the amounts now recognized on Goodyear's books appear in a single net pension asset or net pension liability account instead of the multiple accounts shown in Exhibit 8.20. Also assume an income tax rate of 35 percent. The income tax law does not permit a firm to take a tax deduction for pension benefits until it funds the obligation.

d. Repeat part c for Goodyear's underfunded health care and life insurance obligation.

e. Compute the amount by which the actual return on pension investments exceeded or fell short of expectations for Year 11.

f. What are the likely reasons that the unrecognized net actuarial gain or loss related to Goodyear's pension plans changed from a net gain to a net loss during Year 11?

g. What is the likely explanation for the change in the unrecognized prior service cost of the health care and life insurance plan between the end of Year 10 and the end of Year 11?

8.14 INTERPRETING RETIREMENT BENEFIT PLAN DISCLOSURES. The Boeing Company (Boeing) provides pension, health care, and life insurance benefits to retired employees. Exhibit 8.21 presents the components of pension expense and health care and life insurance expense for Year 9 to Year 11. Exhibit 8.22 presents the funded status of the plans on December 31, Year 10 and Year 11.

a. Why does Boeing report net benefit income for its pension plans but net benefit expense for its health care and life insurance plans?

b. Why does the net funded asset for Boeing's pension plans differ from the asset recognized on Boeing's balance sheet?

c. Why does the net funded liability for Boeing's health care and life insurance plans differ from the liability recognized on Boeing's balance sheet?

d. Why does Boeing show a net asset on its balance sheet with respect to its pension plans but a net liability with respect to its health care and life insurance plans?

e. When assessing the financial position and risk of Boeing, would you restate Boeing's assets from the reported net asset for its pension plans to the net funded asset for these plans? Explain your reasoning.

f. Give the adjustment that the analyst would make to restate Boeing's balance sheet for the difference between its reported net asset for pension plans and the funded net asset. Assume that the amounts now appearing on Boeing's

	EXHIBIT 8.21					

Elements of Pension, Health Care, and Life Insurance Expense for The Boeing Company
(amounts in millions)
(Problem 8.14)

	Pensions			Health Care and Life Insurance		
	Year 11	Year 10	Year 9	Year 11	Year 10	Year 9
Service Cost	$ 591	$ 636	$ 651	$132	$138	$111
Interest Cost	2,187	2,079	1,879	478	419	302
Expected Return on Assets...........	(3,452)	(3,117)	(2,689)	(3)	(2)	(2)
Amortization of:						
Transition Asset	(26)	(103)	(106)	—	—	—
Prior Service Cost	150	149	139	(69)	(66)	(47)
Actuarial (Gain) Loss.	(370)	(72)	1	60	44	10
Net Expense (Income)	$ (920)	$ (428)	$ (125)	$598	$533	$374

balance sheet are in a single net pension asset account. Also assume an income tax rate of 35 percent. The income tax law does not permit a firm to claim an income tax deduction for pension plans until it contributes cash to its pension plans.

g. When assessing the financial position and risk of Boeing, would you restate Boeing's liabilities from the reported net liability for health care and life insurance benefits to the net funded liability for these plans? Explain your reasoning.

h. Give the adjustment that the analyst would make to restate Boeing's balance sheet for the difference between its reported net liability for health care and life insurance benefits and the funded net liability. Assume an income tax rate of 35 percent. The income tax law does not permit a firm to claim an income tax deduction for health care and life insurance benefits until it contributes cash to its health care and life insurance benefits plans.

i. What is the likely reason for the actuarial loss related to the pension obligation and the health care and life insurance benefit obligation for Year 11?

j. What are the likely reasons that the unrecognized net actuarial gain at the end of Year 10 related to Boeing's pension plans became an unrecognized net actuarial loss at the end of Year 11?

k. Prepare an analysis that explains the change in the unrecognized prior service cost for Boeing's pension plans from $1,427 million at the end of Year 10 to $1,465 million at the end of Year 11.

EXHIBIT 8.22

Funded Status of Pension, Health Care, and Life Insurance Plans for The Boeing Company
(amounts in millions)
(Problem 8.14)

	Pensions		Health Care and Life Insurance	
	Year 11	Year 10	Year 11	Year 10
Benefit Obligation, January 1..............	$29,102	$27,621	$ 6,268	$ 5,569
Service Cost	591	636	132	138
Interest Cost...........................	2,187	2,079	478	419
Plan Amendments	188	196	73	(178)
Actuarial (Gains) Losses.................	2,562	(666)	258	539
Participant Contributions	12	1	—	—
Benefits Paid...........................	(1,949)	(1,925)	(375)	(347)
Acquisitions/dispositions.................	—	1,160	(34)	128
Benefit Obligation, December 31..........	$32,693	$29,102	$ 6,800	$ 6,268
Fair Value of Plan Assets, January 1........	$42,856	$37,026	$ 30	$ 22
Actual Return on Assets..................	(7,150)	6,022	—	2
Employer Contributions	19	30	14	10
Participant Contributions	12	1	—	—
Benefits Paid...........................	(1,949)	(1,925)	(5)	(4)
Acquisitions/dispositions.................	6	1,684	—	—
Other Items	16	18	—	—
Fair Value of Plan Assets, December 31........	$33,810	$42,856	$ 39	$ 30
Net Funded Asset (Liability)	$ 1,117	$13,754	$(6,761)	$(6,238)
Unrecognized Prior Service Cost (Benefit)	1,465	1,427	(360)	(502)
Unrecognized Net Actuarial (Gain) Loss........	2,897	(10,652)	1,652	1,484
Unrecognized Transition Asset	(5)	(30)	—	—
Other	7	8	102	93
Net Asset (Liability) Recognized	$ 5,481	$ 4,507	$(5,367)	$(5,163)
Recognized in:				
Prepaid Assets	$ 5,838	$ 4,845	$ —	$ —
Accrued Liabilities.....................	(1,300)	(415)	(5,367)	(5,163)
Other Accounts	943	77	—	—
Net Asset (Liability) Recognized.............	$ 5,481	$ 4,507	$(5,367)	$(5,163)
Actuarial Assumptions:				
Discount Rate	7.00%	7.75%	7.00%	7.75%
Expected Return on Assets	9.25%	9.25%	9.25%	9.25%
Rate of Compensation Increase	5.5%	5.5%	—	—
Initial Health Care Cost Trend Rate	—	—	9.0%	9.0%
Ultimate Health Care Cost Trend Rate.......	—	—	5.0%	5.0%
Number of Years to Ultimate Trend Rate	—	—	9	9

8.15 INTERPRETING INCOME TAX DISCLOSURES.   Disclosures related to income taxes for Sun Microsystems for its fiscal years ending June 30, Year 9 to Year 11, appear in Exhibits 8.23 and 8.24 (amounts in millions).

Required

a. Compute the pre-tax profit margin percentage (that is, income before taxes divided by revenues) for each year for domestic operations, foreign operations, and combined domestic and foreign operations.

b. Compute the after-tax profit margin percentage (that is, net income after taxes divided by revenues) for each year for domestic operations, foreign operations, and combined domestic and foreign operations.

EXHIBIT 8.23

Components of Income Tax Expense for Sun Microsystems
(amounts in millions)
(Problem 8.15)

	Year 11	Year 10	Year 9
Revenues			
Domestic	$ 8,647	$ 8,134	$ 6,106
Foreign...........................	9,603	7,587	5,700
Total	$18,250	$15,721	$11,806
Income Before Income Taxes			
Domestic	$ 388	$ 1,647	$ 975
Foreign...........................	1,196	1,124	630
Total	$ 1,584	$ 2,771	$ 1,605
Income Tax Expense			
Current			
U.S. Federal	$ 438	$ 684	$ 381
State	56	85	45
Foreign..........................	295	234	130
Total Current.	$ 789	$ 1,003	$ 556
Deferred			
U.S. Federal	$ (204)	$ (20)	$ (2)
State	7	12	7
Foreign..........................	11	(78)	14
Total Deferred...................	$ (186)	$ (86)	$ 19
Total Income Tax Expense	$ 603	$ 917	$ 575

**Income Tax Reconciliation and Components of Deferred Taxes for Sun Microsystems
(amounts in millions)
(Problem 8.15)**

	Year 11	Year 10	Year 9
Income Tax Reconciliation			
Expected Taxes at 35%.	$ 554	$ 970	$ 562
State Taxes, net of Federal Tax Benefit	41	63	32
Foreign Earnings Permanently Reinvested	(80)	(118)	(82)
Goodwill Amortization	96	26	8
Acquired In-Process R&D	27	3	44
R&D Credit	(42)	(23)	(18)
Other	7	(4)	29
Total Income Tax Expense	$ 603	$ 917	$ 575
Components of Deferred Taxes on June 30:			
Deferred Tax Assets			
Inventory Valuation	$ 69	$ 91	$ 80
Reserves and Accrued Expenses.	321	235	215
Fixed Assets	—	44	75
Compensation Not Currently Deductible.	77	93	40
Deferred Revenue.	33	59	—
Tax Credit Carryforward	230	—	—
Other	136	99	96
Total Deferred Tax Assets	$ 866	$ 621	$ 506
Deferred Tax Liabilities			
Undistributed Profits of Subsidiaries	$ (62)	$(214)	$(172)
Unrealized Gains on Investments	(22)	(85)	—
Acquisition-related Intangibles	(99)	(13)	—
Other	(30)	—	(20)
Total Deferred Tax Liabilities	$(213)	$(312)	$(192)
Net Deferred Tax Asset	$ 653	$ 309	$ 314
Tax Benefit of Employee Stock Options for the Year.	$ 816	$ 708	$ 222

c. Compute the effective tax rate (that is, income tax expense divided by income before income taxes) for each year for domestic operations, foreign operations, and combined domestic and foreign operations. Assume that the reconciling items for goodwill amortization, acquired in-process R&D, and the R&D credit relate to domestic operations.

d. Prepare an income tax reconciliation for Sun Microsystems in a form similar to that in Exhibit 8.24, but separate the amounts for the firm as a whole into the portions attributable to domestic operations and to foreign operations. The reconciliation should explain the reasons for the differences in the effective tax rates computed in part c. The line for "Other" will be the plug required to reconcile to income tax expense in each case, but the net of the domestic and foreign plug must equal $29 for Year 9, ($4) for Year 10, and $7 for Year 11, as shown in the income tax reconciliation.

e. What role do income taxes appear to play in understanding differences in the profit margins of domestic versus foreign operations?

f. Suggest reasons why the amounts for deferred income tax expense for Year 10 of ($86) and for Year 11 of ($186) do not equal the changes in the net deferred tax asset each year.

g. Approximate the amount of income taxes payable in cash each year, assuming only an immaterial change in the Income Taxes Payable account on the balance sheet.

h. Indicate the adjustments to net income required to compute cash flow from operations each year to the extent permitted by the given information.

8.16 INTERPRETING INCOME TAX DISCLOSURES. Disclosures related to income taxes for The Coca-Cola Company (Coke) for Year 9 to Year 11 appear in Exhibits 8.25 and 8.26.

Required

a. Compute the pre-tax profit margin percentage (that is, income before taxes divided by revenues) for each year for domestic operations, foreign operations, and combined domestic and foreign operations.

b. Compute the after-tax profit margin percentage (that is, net income after taxes divided by revenues) for each year for domestic operations, foreign operations, and combined domestic and foreign operations.

c. Compute the effective tax rate (that is, income tax expense divided by income before income taxes) for each year for domestic operations, foreign operations, and combined domestic and foreign operations.

d. What role do income taxes play in understanding changes in the profit margin of Coke over this three-year period?

e. Is it likely that Coke has recognized a net asset or a net liability on its balance sheet for pension and other postretirement benefit plans? Explain your reasoning.

f. Interpret Coke's recognition of deferred tax assets, instead of deferred tax liabilities, for asset impairment charges.

	EXHIBIT 8.25		

Components of Income Tax Expense for The Coca-Cola Company
(amounts in millions)
(Problem 8.16)

	Year 11	Year 10	Year 9
Revenues			
Domestic	$ 7,526	$ 7,372	$ 7,086
Foreign.........................	12,566	12,517	12,198
Total	$20,092	$19,889	$19,284
Income Before Income Taxes			
Domestic	$ 2,430	$ 1,497	$ 1,504
Foreign.........................	3,240	1,902	2,315
Total	$ 5,670	$ 3,399	$ 3,819
Income Tax Expense			
Current			
U.S. Federal	$ 552	$ 48	$ 395
State	102	16	67
Foreign..........................	981	1,155	829
Total Current....................	$ 1,635	$ 1,219	$ 1,291
Deferred			
U.S. Federal	$ 70	$ (9)	$ 182
State	(15)	46	11
Foreign..........................	1	(34)	(96)
Total Deferred...................	$ 56	$ 3	$ 97
Total Income Tax Expense	$ 1,691	$ 1,222	$ 1,388

g. Coke discloses that the valuation allowance on deferred tax assets relates primarily to asset impairment charges and net operating loss carryforwards. Assume for purposes of this question that Coke had recognized a valuation allowance each year exactly equal to the deferred tax assets recognized for asset impairment charges and net operating loss carryforwards. Indicate the effect on income tax expense and income tax payable in the year Coke initially recognizes the asset impairment charges and the net operating loss carryforwards.

h. Refer to part g. Indicate the effect on income tax expense and income tax payable in the year that Coke claims an income tax deduction for the asset impairment charges and benefits from the net operating loss carryforwards.

EXHIBIT 8.26		

Income Tax Reconciliation and Components of Deferred Taxes for The Coca-Cola Company
(amounts in millions)
(Problem 8.16)

	Year 11	Year 10	Year 9
Income Tax Reconciliation			
Expected Taxes at 35%....................................	$35.0%	$35.0%	$35.0%
State Taxes, net of Federal Tax Benefit.	1.0	.8	1.0
Foreign Earnings Taxed at Lower Rates.	(4.9)	(4.0)	(6.0)
Equity Income or Loss..................................	(.9)	2.9	1.6
Other Operating Charges.	—	1.9	5.3
Other	(.4)	(.6)	(.6)
Effective Tax Rate	$29.8%	$36.0%	$36.3%
Components of Deferred Taxes on December 31:			
Deferred Tax Assets			
Benefit Plans...	$ 377	$ 261	$ 311
Asset Impairment Charges...............................	489	456	169
Net Operating Loss Carryforwards	286	375	196
Other Operating Charge.	169	321	254
Other..	232	126	272
Total Deferred Tax Assets (Gross)......................	$ 1,553	$ 1,539	$ 1,202
Valuation Allowance....................................	(563)	(641)	(443)
Total Deferred Tax Asset (Net)	$ 990	$ 898	$ 759
Deferred Tax Liabilities			
Property, Plant, and Equipment..........................	$ (391)	$ (425)	$ (320)
Equity Investments....................................	(196)	(228)	(397)
Intangible Assets.....................................	(248)	(224)	(197)
Other..	(185)	(129)	(99)
Total Deferred Tax Liabilities........................	$(1,020)	$(1,006)	$(1,013)
Net Deferred Tax Asset (Liability)	$ (30)	$ (108)	$ (254)

i. Interpret Coke's recognition of deferred tax liabilities, instead of deferred tax assets, for equity investments.

j. Why does Coke report tax effects of equity income and investments in both the income tax reconciliation and in deferred tax liabilities?

k. Interpret Coke's recognition of deferred tax liabilities, instead of deferred tax assets, for intangible assets.

8.17 ANALYZING INCOME TAX DISCLOSURES. Exhibit 8.27 presents information from the income tax notes of TRW, Inc. for Year 6.

   a. Give the journal entry to record income tax expense for Year 5.

   b. Was taxable income greater or less than book income before income taxes for Year 5? Explain.

EXHIBIT 8.27

Income Tax Disclosures for TRW, Inc.
(amounts in millions)
(Problem 8.17)

	Year 6	Year 5	Year 4
Earnings Before Income Taxes			
U.S.	$213	$(156)	$178
Non-U.S.	135	27	165
	$348	$(129)	$343
Provision for Income Taxes			
Current:: U.S.	$ 81	$ 25	$ 97
Non-U.S.	59	39	75
Deferred: U.S.	11	(39)	(44)
Non-U.S.	3	(14)	7
	$154	$ 11	$135
Effective Tax Rate Reconciliation			
U.S. Statutory Tax Rate	35.0%	(35.0%)	35.0%
U.S. State and Local Taxes	3.6	.3	4.2
Non-U.S. Tax Rate Variances	4.2	14.9	3.0
Losses on Restructuring Without Income Tax Benefit	3.6	23.1	—
Other	(2.1)	4.9	(2.8)
Effective Income Tax Rate	44.3%	8.2%	39.4%
Components of Deferred Taxes			
Deferred Tax Assets			
Post Retirement Benefits Other than Pensions	$244	$ 232	$ —
Restructuring Charges	124	121	50
Pensions	—	—	115
Non-U.S. Net Operating Loss Carryforwards	36	30	—
Valuation Allowance	(36)	(30)	—
Total	$368	$ 353	$165
Deferred Tax Liabilities			
Depreciation	$470	$ 431	$351
Pensions	45	55	—
Total	$515	$ 486	$351

c. Why is there a positive amount for income tax expense for Year 5 if earnings before income taxes is negative for the year?
d. Give the journal entry to record income tax expense for Year 6.
e. Was taxable income greater or less than book income before income taxes for Year 6? Explain.
f. Why do restructuring charges appear in both the income tax reconciliation and in deferred tax assets?
g. What is the likely reason for the change in the deferred tax asset for postretirement benefits other than pensions?
h. What is the likely reason for the change in deferred taxes related to pensions from a deferred tax asset at the end of Year 4 to a deferred tax liability at the end of Year 5?
i. What is the likely reason for the valuation allowance related to deferred tax assets?
j. What is the likely explanation for the behavior of the deferred tax liability related to depreciation?

Note: See Problems 2.5, 2.6, and 2.7 in Chapter 2 for additional problems on income taxes.

CASE 8.1

AMERICAN AIRLINES AND UNITED AIRLINES: A PENSION FOR DEBT

American Airlines and United Airlines maintain dominant market positions in the airline market in the United States. Airlines carry heavy investments in fixed assets. Their high proportions of fixed operating costs provide potential benefits and risks of economies and diseconomies of scale.

Airlines rely heavily on debt financing for their fixed asset investments. The financing may take the form of borrowing to purchase fixed assets or leasing under a capital lease arrangement. Airlines have increasingly turned, in recent years, to operating leases as a means to keep debt off of their balance sheets. The fixed costs of servicing on-balance-sheet debt and off-balance-sheet leasing commitments add to the potential scale economies and diseconomies.

Most airlines are unionized and provide pension, health care, and other postretirement benefits to employees. The obligations under various benefit plans are not fully reflected in liabilities on the balance sheet.

An effective analysis of the risk of airlines requires consideration of the effects of commitments under operating leases and underfunded retirement benefit obligations. This case analyzes the disclosures of American and United with respect to leases, pensions, and health care benefits. Data for American and United appear in the following exhibits:

Exhibit 8.28: Balance sheet data.

Exhibit 8.29: Income and cash flow data.
Exhibit 8.30: Capital and operating lease data.
Exhibit 8.31: Pension, health care, and other retirement data for American Airlines.
Exhibit 8.32: Pension, health care, and other retirement data for United Airlines.

EXHIBIT 8.28

Balance Sheet Data for American Airlines and United Airlines
(amounts in millions)
(Case 8.1)

| | American | | United | |
| | December 31 | | December 31 | |
	Year 11	Year 10	Year 11	Year 10
Assets				
Current Assets..................................	$ 6,540	$ 5,179	$ 5,086	$ 4,779
Property, Plant, and Equipment:				
Cost	$26,838	$25,380	$19,230	$19,412
Accumulated Depreciation	(8,850)	(8,288)	(4,716)	(5,583)
Net	$17,988	$17,092	$14,514	$13,829
Property, Plant, and Equipment under Capital Leases:				
Cost	$ 2,821	$ 2,777	$ 2,766	$ 3,154
Accumulated Depreciation	(1,154)	(1,233)	(472)	(640)
Net	$ 1,667	$ 1,544	$ 2,294	$ 2,514
Other Assets	$ 6,646	$ 2,398	$ 3,303	$ 3,233
Total Assets	$32,841	$26,213	$25,197	$24,355
Liabilities and Shareholders' Equity				
Current Operating Liabilities......................	$ 6,740	$ 6,194	$ 6,612	$ 6,070
Current Maturities of Long-term Debt	556	569	1,217	170
Current Maturities of Capital Leases	216	227	237	269
Total Current Liabilities......................	$ 7,512	$ 6,990	$ 8,066	$ 6,509
Long-term Debt	8,310	4,151	6,622	4,688
Capital Leases	1,524	1,323	1,943	2,261
Pension, Health Care and Other Retirement Obligations ..	3,201	1,952	3,051	1,908
Other Noncurrent Liabilities	6,921	4,621	2,307	3,129
Total Liabilities.............................	$27,468	$19,037	$21,989	$18,495
Preferred Stock	$ —	$ —	$ 175	$ 403
Common Stock.................................	3,047	3,093	4,992	4,791
Retained Earnings..............................	4,188	5,950	(199)	1,998
Accumulated Other Comprehensive Income...........	(146)	(2)	(275)	152
Treasury Stock................................	(1,716)	(1,865)	(1,485)	(1,484)
Total Shareholders' Equity.....................	$ 5,373	$ 7,176	$ 3,208	$ 5,860
Total Liabilities and Shareholders' Equity...........	$32,841	$26,213	$25,197	$24,355

EXHIBIT 8.29

Income and Cash Flow Data for American Airlines and United Airlines
(amounts in millions)
(Case 8.1)

	American		United	
	Year 11	Year 10	Year 11	Year 10
Operating Revenues	$18,963	$19,703	$16,138	$19,352
Operating Expenses	(21,433)	(18,322)	(19,257)	(18,698)
Operating Income	$(2,470)	$ 1,381	$(3,119)	$ 654
Interest Expense	(538)	(467)	(525)	(402)
Other Income (Expense)	252	373	287	179
Income Before Taxes	$(2,756)	$ 1,287	$(3,357)	$ 431
Income Taxes	994	(508)	1,226	(160)
Net Income	$(1,762)	$ 779	$(2,131)	$ 271
Cash Flow from:				
Operations	$ 511	$ 3,142	$ (160)	$ 2,472
Investing	(4,691)	(3,275)	(1,969)	(2,521)
Financing	4,211	137	2,138	1,418
Change in Cash	$ 31	$ 4	$ 9	$ 1,369
Capital Lease Obligations Incurred	$ 429	$ —	$ —	$ 339
Rent Expense	$ 1,700	$ 1,300	$ 1,400	$ 1,500

EXHIBIT 8.30

Capital and Operating Lease Data for American Airlines and United Airlines
(amounts in millions)
(Case 8.1)

	American		United	
	Year 11	Year 10	Year 11	Year 10
Commitments Under Capital Leases				
Payable In:				
Year 11	$ —	$ 320	$ —	$ 472
Year 12	326	276	413	415
Year 13	243	195	315	316
Year 14	295	246	323	325
Year 15	229	178	292	293
After Year 15....................................	—	867	—	1,867
Year 16	231	—	317	—
After Year 16....................................	1,233	—	1,501	—
Total...	$ 2,557	$ 2,082	$ 3,161	$ 3,688
Less Imputed Interest	(817)	(532)	(981)	(1,158)
Total Present Value	$ 1,740	$ 1,550	$ 2,180	$ 2,530
Current Portion	(216)	(227)	(237)	(269)
Long-term Portion	$ 1,524	$ 1,323	$ 1,943	$ 2,261
Commitments Under Operating Leases				
Payable In:				
Year 11	$ —	$ 984	$ —	$ 1,553
Year 12	1,336	921	1,580	1,496
Year 13	1,276	931	1,572	1,513
Year 14	1,199	913	1,591	1,522
Year 15	1,138	900	1,593	1,526
After Year 15....................................	—	11,306	—	18,724
Year 16	1,073	—	1,578	—
After Year 16....................................	11,639	—	16,624	—
Total...	$17,661	$15,955	$24,538	$26,334

EXHIBIT 8.31

Pension, Health Care and Other Retirement Data for American Airlines
(amounts in millions)
(Case 8.1)

Elements of Pension, Health Care, and Other Retirement Benefits Expense

	Pensions			Health Care and Other Benefits		
	Year 11	Year 10	Year 9	Year 11	Year 10	Year 9
Service Cost.........................	$260	$213	$236	$ 66	$ 43	$ 56
Interest Cost	515	467	433	175	108	108
Expected Return on Assets	(539)	(490)	(514)	(9)	(7)	(6)
Amortization of:						
Transition Asset	(1)	(1)	(4)	—	—	—
Prior Service Cost..................	11	10	5	(5)	(5)	(5)
Actuarial (Gain) Loss..............	22	17	21	—	(14)	—
Net Expense (Income).................	$268	$216	$177	$227	$125	$153

Funded Status of Pension, Health Care, and Other Retirement Benefit Plans

	Pensions		Health Care and Other Benefits	
	Year 11	Year 10	Year 11	Year 10
Benefit Obligation, January 1.................	$6,434	$5,628	$1,708	$1,306
Service Cost	260	213	66	43
Interest Cost.............................	515	467	175	108
Plan Amendments	168	—	(12)	—
Actuarial (Gains) Losses....................	416	499	205	328
Benefits Paid.............................	(371)	(373)	(117)	(77)
Acquisitions/dispositions....................	—	—	734	—
Benefit Obligation, December 31..............	$7,422	$6,434	$2,759	$1,708
Fair Value of Plan Assets, January 1............	$5,731	$5,282	$ 88	$ 72
Actual Return on Assets.....................	1	735	(5)	5
Employer Contributions	121	85	129	88
Participant Contributions	—	—	—	—
Benefits Paid.............................	(371)	(373)	(117)	(77)
Acquisitions/dispositions.....................	—	—	—	—
Other Items	—	2	—	—
Fair Value of Plan Assets, December 31.........	$5,482	$5,731	$ 95	$ 88

Funded Status of Pension, Health Care, and Other Retirement Benefit Plans

Exhibit 8.31—continued	Pensions		Health Care and Other Benefits	
	Year 11	Year 10	Year 11	Year 10
Net Funded Asset (Liability)	$(1,940)	$(703)	$(2,664)	$(1,620)
Unrecognized Prior Service Cost (Benefit)	286	129	(42)	(35)
Unrecognized Net Actuarial (Gain) Loss........	1,454	523	168	(51)
Unrecognized Transition Asset	(5)	(6)	—	—
Other	—	—	—	—
Net Asset (Liability) Recognized	$ (205)	$ (57)	$(2,538)	$(1,706)
Recognized in:				
Prepaid Assets	$ 123	$ 107	$ —	$ —
Accrued Liabilities......................	(663)	(246)	(2,538)	(1,706)
Intangible Asset........................	163	72	—	—
Accumulated Other Comprehensive Income ..	172	10	—	—
Net Asset (Liability) Recognized	$ (205)	$ (57)	$(2,538)	$(1,706)
Actuarial Assumptions:				
Discount Rate	7.50%	7.75%	7.50%	7.75%
Expected Return on Assets	9.50%	9.50%	9.50%	9.50%
Rate of Compensation Increase	4.3%	4.3%	—	—
Initial Health Care Cost Trend Rate	—	—	6.0%	6.0%
Ultimate Health Care Cost Trend Rate.......	—	—	4.5%	4.5%
Number of Years to Ultimate Trend Rate	—	—	3	3

EXHIBIT 8.32

Pension, Health Care, and Other Retirement Data for United Airlines
(amounts in millions)
(Case 8.1)

Elements of Pension, Health Care, and Other Retirement Benefits Expense

	Pensions			Health Care and Other Benefits		
	Year 11	Year 10	Year 9	Year 11	Year 10	Year 9
Service Cost..........................	$352	$269	$295	$ 68	$ 47	$ 53
Interest Cost	722	629	583	149	120	116
Expected Return on Assets	(805)	(740)	(665)	(9)	(9)	(9)
Amortization of:						
Prior Service Cost..................	73	58	57	—	—	—
Actuarial (Gain) Loss	16	(7)	1	2	(9)	(5)
Other	74	—	—	4	—	—
Net Expense (Income)................	$432	$209	$271	$214	$149	$155

Funded Status of Pension, Health Care, and Other Retirement Benefit Plans

	Pensions		Health Care and Other Benefits	
	Year 11	Year 10	Year 11	Year 10
Benefit Obligation, January 1................	$ 9,252	$7,381	$1,706	$1,465
Service Cost	352	269	68	47
Interest Cost...........................	722	629	149	120
Participant Contributions	1	1	11	8
Plan Amendments	4	260	—	3
Actuarial (Gains) Losses..................	284	1,162	473	164
Benefits Paid...........................	(518)	(435)	(117)	(101)
Other	(2)	(15)	69	—
Benefit Obligation, December 31.............	$10,095	$9,252	$2,359	$1,706
Fair Value of Plan Assets, January 1...........	$ 8,511	$8,701	$ 116	$ 113
Actual Return on Assets....................	(457)	21	7	8
Employer Contributions	43	230	101	88
Participant Contributions	1	1	11	8
Benefits Paid...........................	(518)	(435)	(117)	(101)
Other Items	(5)	(7)	—	—
Fair Value of Plan Assets, December 31.........	$ 7,575	$8,511	$ 118	$ 116

Funded Status of Pension, Health Care, and Other Retirement Benefit Plans

Exhibit 8.32—continued	Pensions		Health Care and Other Benefits	
	Year 11	Year 10	Year 11	Year 10
Net Funded Asset (Liability)	$(2,520)	$(741)	$(2,241)	$(1,590)
Unrecognized Prior Service Cost (Benefit)	692	806	2	2
Unrecognized Net Actuarial (Gain) Loss........	1,508	14	484	(54)
Unrecognized Transition Obligation...........	15	—	—	—
Net Asset (Liability) Recognized	$ (305)	$ 79	$(1,755)	$(1,642)
Recognized in:				
Prepaid Assets	$ —	$ 79	$ —	$ —
Accrued Liabilities......................	(1,296)	(266)	(1,755)	(1,642)
Intangible Asset.......................	562	255		
Accumulated Other Comprehensive Income	429	11	—	
Net Asset (Liability) Recognized	$ (305)	$ 79	$(1,755)	$(1,642)
Actuarial Assumptions:				
Discount Rate	7.50%	7.75%	7.50%	7.75%
Expected Return on Assets	9.75%	9.75%	8.00%	8.00%
Rate of Compensation Increase	4.2%	4.4%	—	—
Initial Health Care Cost Trend Rate	—	—	8.0%	8.0%
Ultimate Health Care Cost Trend Rate.......	—	—	4.5%	4.5%
Number of Years to Ultimate Trend Rate.....	—	—	5	5

CAPITAL LEASES

a. Complete the following analysis of changes in the capitalized lease assets and capitalized lease obligation of American for Year 11.

Capitalized Lease Assets (gross), December 31, Year 10 ....
Plus New Leases Signed During Year 11 ....
Less Capitalized Cost of Leases Terminated (plug) ....
Capitalized Lease Asset (gross), December 31, Year 11 ....

Accumulated Deprecation on Capitalized Lease Assets,
    December 31, Year 10 ....
Less Accumulated Depreciation on Leases Terminated.........
Plus Depreciation Recognized for Year 11 (Plug) ....
Accumulated Depreciation on Capitalized Lease Assets,
    December 31, Year 11 ....

Capitalized Lease Liability, December 31, Year 10[a] . . . .
Plus Interest on Lease Liability for Year 11 (Plug) . . . .
Plus New Leases Capitalized During Year 11 . . . .
Less Cash Payments on Capital Leases During Year 11 . . . .   _____
Capitalized Lease Liability, December 31, Year 11[a] . . . .   _____

[a]Be sure to include current and noncurrent portions.

b.   Repeat part a for United for Year 11.

OPERATING LEASES

c.   Assume for this part that 6 percent is the appropriate interest rate to capitalize the operating lease commitments of American and United, and that all lease payments occur at the end of each year. Also assume that each firm pays the aggregate amount of payments after the fifth year in an amount each year beginning in the sixth year equal to the minimum lease payment in the fifth year until the aggregate amount is fully paid. Compute the present value of the operating lease commitments of each airline as of December 31, Year 10 and Year 11.

d.   Compare the total expenses for operating leases for Year 11 assuming that American and United accounted for these leases as operating leases (that is, as reported) versus as capital leases.

e.   Compute the long-term debt ratio [long-term debt ÷ (long-term debt + shareholders' equity)] as of December 31, Year 11, based on the reported amounts for American and United. Include in long-term debt the amounts reported on the balance sheet as long-term debt, capital leases, and pension, health care, and other retirement obligations.

f.   Repeat question e above but now include the present value of operating lease commitments as computed in question c above. Assume no change in retained earnings as a result of capitalizing operating leases.

PENSION, HEALTH CARE, AND OTHER RETIREMENT OBLIGATIONS

g.   Why does the amount that each firm reports on its balance sheet as the net asset or net liability recognized for pension, health care, and other retirement benefits differ from the net funded asset or liability of the benefit plans?

h.   Give the entry that the analyst would make on the balance sheet on December 31, Year 11, to recognize any difference between the net liability now recognized on the balance sheet of each firm and the net funded liability for pension benefits. Assume an income tax rate of 35 percent. The income tax law does not permit a deduction for pension and other retirement benefits until the firm contributes amounts to retirement plans.

i.   Repeat part h for health care and other retirement benefits.

j. Refer to questions e and f under Operating Leases. Compute the long-term debt ratio at the end of Year 11 for each firm by including in the numerator long-term debt, capital leases, pension, health care, and other retirement benefit obligations reported on the balance sheet, the present value of operating lease commitments from question c, and the incremental amounts of pension, health care, and other retirement benefits from questions h and i.

k. Evaluate the investment performance of each firm's pension plan during Year 10 and Year 11.

l. Did either firm sweeten its pension benefit formula during Year 11 and make the benefits retroactive for employees? How can you tell?

m. What is the likely reason for the actuarial loss in the pension benefit obligation and the health care and other retirement benefit obligations for each firm during Year 11?

n. What is the likely reason for the significant increase in the *unrecognized* net actuarial loss for each firm in both their pension plans and health care and other retirement benefit plans?

CASE 8.2

CIFRA: REMODELING THE FINANCIAL STATEMENTS

CIFRA, S.A. de C.V. and Subsidiaries (CIFRA) is a leading retailer in Mexico. At the end of Year 8, Year 9, and Year 10, it operated the following retailing establishments:

	Year 10		Year 9		Year 8	
	No. of Stores	Square Feet	No. of Stores	Square Feet	No. of Stores	Square Feet
Self-Service Stores.........	33	2,285,800	33	2,253,788	38	2,775,508
Discount Warehouse						
Stores.................	45	2,216,577	39	1,821,193	29	1,308,127
Supermarkets.............	37	568,371	35	505,176	34	479,030
Department Stores	31	1,698,075	28	1,501,578	29	1,545,771
Restaurants	106	21,818[a]	89	18,274[a]	78	16,616[a]
Hypermarkets	5	871,819	2	361,832	—	—
Membership Clubs	7	688,788	3	291,704	—	—

[a]Seating capacity.

CIFRA follows an "everyday-low-price" strategy in its stores. CIFRA commenced a major remodeling effort in all of its retailing establishments in Year 8. It expects to complete these renovations by the end of Year 11. CIFRA created an account, Fund for Remodeling, which it uses to cover the cost of remodeling. Financial statements for CIFRA for Year 8, Year 9, and Year 10 appear in Exhibit 8.33 (balance sheet), Exhibit 8.34 (statement of earnings), and Exhibit 8.35 (statement of changes in financial position). Selected notes follow these financial statements.

Required

a. Prepare an analysis of the changes in the Funds for Remodeling account during Year 8, Year 9, and Year 10.

b. Which of the amounts from part a did CIFRA charge against earnings for each year?

c. Which amounts (if any) related to remodeling do you think CIFRA should have charged against earnings each year? Explain your reasoning.

d. What adjustments must be made to the financial statements for Year 8, Year 9, and Year 10 to conform to the accounting suggested in your response to part c?

e. Suggest reasons why CIFRA chose to account for remodeling costs as it did.

f. Using your restated financial statements from part d, assess the profitability and risk of CIFRA for Year 8 through Year 10.

EXHIBIT 8.33

CIFRA, S.A. de C.V. and Subsidiaries
Consolidated Balance Sheet
(in millions of constant December 31, Year 10 Mexican Pesos)
(Case 8.2)

	December 31			
	Year 10	Year 9	Year 8	Year 7
ASSETS				
Current Assets				
Cash and Short-term Investments	P 1,940	P2,180	P1,382	P 942
Accounts Receivable	234	152	231	144
Inventories......................................	1,319	1,080	804	814
Prepayments	38	47	15	8
Total Current Assets	P 3,531	P3,459	P2,432	P1,908
Property, Plant, and Equipment..................	P 7,378	P5,389	P4,188	P3,668
Accumulated Depreciation	(1,298)	(1,079)	(1,013)	(930)
Net Property, Plant, and Equipment	P 6,080	P4,310	P3,175	P2,738
Investments in Securities.......................	P —	P —	P 69	P —
Surplus Pension Funds	593	—	—	—
Total Assets..............................	P10,204	P7,769	P5,676	P4,646
Current Liabilities				
Accounts Payable—Trade	P 2,279	P1,882	P1,494	P1,336
Other Accounts Payable	571	627	570	496
Fund for Remodeling (Note 1)...................	51	261	111	—
Total Current Liabilities......................	P 2,901	P2,770	P2,175	P1,832
Reserve for Seniority Premiums (Note 2).............	P 22	P 21	P —	P —

Exhibit 8.33—continued	December 31			
	Year 10	**Year 9**	**Year 8**	**Year 7**
Shareholders' Equity				
Capital Stock	P 900	P 900	P 900	P 900
Legal Reserve	264	264	229	201
Retained Earnings	3,726	2,678	1,995	1,469
Surplus on Restatement of Fixed Assets and				
Capital Stock.	1,447	782	501	410
Treasury Stock	(124)	(38)	(124)	(166)
Majority Shareholders' Equity	P 6,213	P4,586	P3,501	P2,814
Minority Shareholders' Equity	1,068	392	—	—
Total Shareholders' Equity	P 7,281	P4,978	P3,501	P2,814
Total Liabilities and Shareholders' Equity.	P10,204	P7,769	P5,676	P4,646

EXHIBIT 8.34

CIFRA, S.A. de C.V. and Subsidiaries
Consolidated Statement of Earnings
(in millions of constant December 31, Year 10 Mexican Pesos)
(Case 8.2)

	Year 10	**Year 9**	**Year 8**
Net Sales	P14,231	P12,417	P10,287
Cost of Goods Sold	(11,135)	(9,525)	(7,870)
Operating Expenses	(2,306)	(2,154)	(1,859)
Operating Income	P 790	P 738	P 558
Comprehensive Financing Income:			
Financial Income.	324	338	239
Gain on Monetary Position.	9	42	91
Other Income (Expenses)—Net	(17)	(39)	16
Earnings Before Taxes	P 1,106	P 1,079	P 904
Income Taxes and Employees' Statutory Profit Sharing	(308)	(309)	(250)
Earnings Before Special Items	P 798	P 770	P 654
Special Items Net of Applicable Income Taxes			
Net Effect of Bulletin D-3 on Labour Obligations (Note 2).	233	—	—
Reversion of Surplus in Pension Funds (Note 2)	—	549	309
Fund for Remodeling (Note 1)	—	(270)	(179)
Reserve for Seniority Premiums (Note 2)	—	(21)	—
Net Earnings.	P 1,031	P 1,028	P 784
Minority Interest in Earnings	3	(15)	—
Majority Share	P 1,034	P 1,013	P 784

EXHIBIT 8.35
CIFRA, S.A. de C.V. and Subsidiaries Consolidated Statement of Changes in Financial Position (in millions of constant December 31, Year 10 Mexican Pesos) (Case 8.2)

	Year 10	Year 9	Year 8
Net Earnings Before Special Items.........................	P 798	P 770	P 654
Depreciation and Amortization...........................	237	199	174
Other Addbacks	3	—	—
Change in:			
Accounts Receivable	(83)	77	(87)
Inventories...	(245)	(285)	19
Prepayments	11	(32)	(8)
Accounts Payable—Trade	397	388	158
Other Accounts Payable	(41)	15	(17)
Resources Provided by Operations	P 1,077	P 1,132	P 893
Reimbursement of Pension Surplus (Note 2)	P —	P 549	P 309
Investment of Minority Shareholders	P 676	P 446	P —
Other Investments	—	—	(69)
Payment of Dividends	(323)	(289)	(210)
Premium on Sale of Shares	279	71	5
Resources Provided by Financing	P 632	P 228	P (274)
Acquisition of Property and Equipment	P(1,739)	P (991)	P (420)
Application of Fund for Remodeling (Note 1)	(210)	(120)	(68)
Resources Used for Investing............................	P(1,949)	P(1,111)	P (488)
(Decrease) Increase in Cash and Short-term Investments	P (240)	P 798	P 440
Cash and Short-term Investments—Beginning of Year	2,180	1,382	942
Cash and Short-term Investments—End of Year	P 1,940	P 2,180	P1,382

NOTES TO EXHIBITS 8.33–8.35

Note 1: CIFRA commenced a major remodeling effort of its retailing establishments in Year 8. It created a Fund for Remodeling account on its balance sheet, which CIFRA increased by provisions of P179 million (net of taxes) in Year 8 and P270 million (net of taxes) in Year 9. CIFRA charges a portion of remodeling expenditures (net of taxes) each year against the Fund for Remodeling account and capitalizes a portion in fixed assets.

Note 2: The Mexican government instituted a mandatory pension program on May 1, Year 9. All CIFRA employees participate in this program from the effective date forward. Retirement benefits earned in CIFRA's retirement plans prior to the effective date remain the responsibility of CIFRA. CIFRA's pension plan for non-senior employees had pension assets in excess of pension liabilities. CIFRA reverted part of the excess back to the Company during Year 8 and Year 9. Its pension plan for senior employees had pension liabilities in excess of pension assets on May 1, Year 9. CIFRA recognized a liability for the excess. On December 31, Year 10, the pension plan for non-senior employees had pension assets in excess of pension liabilities of P593 million. CIFRA recognized this excess as an asset on this date. It credited retained earnings for P360 million (relating to returns on pension fund investments for years prior to Year 10) and earnings for Year 10 for P233 million (relating to returns on pension fund investments during Year 10).

Note 3: CIFRA recognizes deferred taxes for *nonrecurring* timing differences between income before taxes for financial reporting and taxable income. There were no *recurring* timing differences qualifying for the recognition of deferred taxes under Mexican accounting principles in Year 8, Year 9, or Year 10.

Chapter 9

INTERCORPORATE ENTITIES

Learning Objectives
1. **Understand the effect on the financial statements of the purchase method of accounting for a corporate acquisition, both at the time of the acquisition and in subsequent years.**
2. **Understand the financial statement effects of the market value, equity, proportionate consolidation, and full consolidation methods.**
3. **Understand the accounting for variable interest entities, commonly referred to as special purpose entities, including the requirement to consolidate them with the firm identified as the primary beneficiary.**
4. **Prepare a set of translated financial statements using the all-current method and the monetary/nonmonetary method and understand the conditions when each method best portrays the operating relationship between a U.S. parent firm and its foreign subsidiary.**
5. **Understand the accounting for the options given to employees to acquire shares of common stock at a price that is less than the market price of the shares.**

This chapter concludes the four-chapter unit (Chapters 6 through 9) that focuses on how a firm's selection of accounting methods and the way it implements them affect its *accounting information quality*, its *earnings quality*, and its *balance sheet quality*. Similar to the previous three chapters, this chapter emphasizes those transactions and reporting techniques that have the greatest interpretative impact on financial statements issued by a firm. Recall that the overall objective of this unit of the text is to understand both the *reported* corporate financial data released by a firm and the relevant *adjusted* financial data for analyzing the profitability and risk of the firm, with valuation of the firm often the culminating goal. Chapters 10 through 13 address firm valuation, drawing on many of the issues discussed in this unit.

This chapter addresses three reporting topics related to intercorporate investments:

1. Corporate acquisitions.
2. Investments in securities, including investments in variable interest entities.
3. Foreign currency translation.

The chapter concludes with a discussion of accounting for stock-based compensation, a topic that straddles themes of this chapter and Chapter 8. When a firm grants stock options to employees that are "out of the money," the firm currently has the choice to report or not report the stock-based compensation as an expense on the income statement. When employees subsequently exercise the stock options, the firm often issues shares to the employees out of treasury shares, which represent past repurchases the firm has made in its own securities.[1]

CORPORATE ACQUISITIONS

Corporate acquisitions occur when one corporation acquires all, or substantially all, of another corporation's common shares. Prior to the issuance of *Statement No. 141*[2], GAAP required firms to use one of two methods to account for corporate acquisitions: the purchase method or the pooling-of-interests method. After the acquisition, the results reported for the combined company differed substantially as a result of the accounting for the acquisition, so acquiring companies were concerned about the methods they used. *Statement No. 141* prohibits the use of the pooling-of-interests method, requiring firms to account for all acquisitions using the purchase method.

Recall from the discussion in Chapter 1 that PepsiCo was able to account for its acquisition of Quaker Oats using the pooling-of-interests method because the merger was initiated prior to the effective date of *Statement No. 141*. In Appendix A (Note 2), PepsiCo states: "The provisions of *Statement No. 141* are effective for transactions accounted for using the purchase method that are completed after June 30, Year 11. Since our merger with Quaker was initiated in December, Year 10, adoption of this statement does not have an impact on the accompanying consolidated financial statements." Given this, we provide background on the pooling-of-interests method both to understand the PepsiCo/Quaker Oats merger and to understand the issues faced by the FASB in disallowing the pooling-of-interests method and requiring the purchase method for all corporate acquisitions.

---

[1] Treasury stock is reported as a reduction in a firm's shareholders' equity. In Appendix A, note that PepsiCo reports that it holds 26 million shares of its common stock on December 29, Year 11, with a historical cost of $1,268 million. PepsiCo uses the term "repurchased common stock" for its shares held in treasury.
[2] Financial Accounting Standards Board, *Statement of Financial Accounting Standards No. 141*, "Business Combinations," 2001.

OVERVIEW OF THE PURCHASE AND POOLING-OF-INTERESTS METHODS

The following summarizes the most important differences between the purchase method and the pooling-of-interests method.

Purchase Method

The purchase method views a corporate acquisition as conceptually identical to the purchase of any single asset (for example, inventory or a machine). The purchaser records the intercorporate investment in the common stock of the acquired company at the *market value of the consideration given.* If the purchase price exceeds the book value of the net assets acquired, the purchaser allocates the excess to identifiable assets and liabilities to revalue them to market values. The purchaser allocates any remaining excess to goodwill. This allocation occurs as part of the work sheet entry to eliminate the investment account when preparing consolidated financial statements for the two entities, a topic discussed later in this chapter. The purchaser must also write off the excess purchase price allocated to individual assets and liabilities over the expected service lives of the assets and liabilities. Prior to the issuance of *Statement No. 142*[3], firms also amortized any amount allocated to goodwill and other intangibles with indefinite lives, but as Chapter 7 discussed in detail, firms need no longer amortize goodwill and other intangibles with indefinite lives. However, as Chapters 6 and 7 discuss, firms must test goodwill and other intangibles not requiring amortization at least annually for impairment.

Pooling-of-Interests Method

The pooling-of-interests method views a corporate acquisition as a uniting of the ownership interests of two entities that, while legally combined, continue operating as they did as separate entities prior to the acquisition. To qualify for the pooling-of-interests method under the rules when it was an allowable reporting technique, the "acquiring" firm had to exchange shares of its common stock for the common stock of the "acquired" company. Thus, the shareholders of the two previously separate companies became shareholders in the new combined entity. The pooling criteria also precluded the entities from disposing of significant operations shortly before or after the acquisition. These criteria helped insure the continuity of ownership interests and operations envisioned by the pooling-of-interests concept. The purchaser recorded the intercorporate investment in the common stock of the acquired company at the *book value of the contributed capital (common stock, additional paid-in capital)* of the acquired company. Because the investment account equals the book value of the contributed capital, no excess purchase price arose that the acquiring company had to allocate to individual assets and liabilities. The book values of the

---

[3]Financial Accounting Standards Board, *Statement of Financial Accounting Standards No. 142*, "Goodwill and Other Intangible Assets," 2001.

acquired company's net assets carried over to the consolidated financial statements of the new, combined entity. The retained earnings of the acquired company also carried over. Because the pooling-of-interests method did not give rise to an excess purchase price related to either identifiable assets and liabilities or goodwill, it did not require subsequent charges to earnings.

Most firms preferred to account for corporate acquisitions as poolings of interests rather than as purchases because of the positive effect on earnings subsequent to the acquisition.[4] Firms also argued that the required amortization of goodwill under the purchase method neglected to consider that many of the intangible qualities that comprise goodwill (brand names, reputation, distribution networks, customer loyalty, quality management, for example) do not necessarily lose their future benefits with time, as amortization implies.

Opponents of the pooling-of-interests method argued that few acquisitions result in a mutual sharing of ownership. One firm, usually the acquiring firm, is much larger than the acquired firm, as is the case with PepsiCo and Quaker Oats. The shareholders of the acquiring firm therefore own a majority of the common stock of the new combined entity. The managers of the acquiring firm often maintain their positions after the acquisition. Thus, most acquisitions result in one firm being "acquired" instead of merely "combined." Critics of the pooling-of-interests method also argue that the accounting ignores the market valuation of the acquired company indicated by the number of shares exchanged. Finally, the pooling-of-interests method allows the new combined entity to manage earnings by selling assets carried over at lower book values but subsequently sold at their currently higher market values.

ILLUSTRATION OF THE PURCHASE METHOD

Exhibit 9.1 shows financial information for Company P and Company S. Columns (1) and (2) show the book values of P's and S's assets, liabilities, and shareholders' equity on the date of the acquisition. Column (3) shows the corresponding market values on this date for S. Assume that Company P pays $1,848,000 for 100 percent of the outstanding shares of Company S on the first day of the fiscal year. Company P makes the following entry on its books at the time of the acquisition:

Investment in Stock of Company S	1,848,000	
Cash		1,848,000

The market value of S's shareholders' equity of $1,848,000 exceeds its book value of $450,000 by $1,398,000. There are three reasons for this difference:

---

[4]Compared to the purchase method, earnings are positively affected three ways: no deduction for excess depreciation on stepped-up values in individual assets, no amortization of goodwill and other intangibles with indefinite lives, and a full year's earnings combined with the acquiring firm's earnings regardless of when during the year the merger took place.

	EXHIBIT 9.1			
Consolidated Financial Statements for P and S Using the Purchase Method				

	Historical Cost P (1)	Historical Cost S (2)	S Shown at Current Market Values (3)	Consolidated at Date of Acquisition Purchase Method (4)
Balance Sheets				
Assets:				
Current Assets................	$1,500,000	$450,000	$ 450,000	$1,950,000
Depreciable Assets less				
Accumulated Depreciation.....	1,700,000	450,000	850,000	2,550,000
Goodwill	—	—	1,138,000	1,138,000
Total Assets....................	$3,200,000	$900,000	$2,438,000	$5,638,000
Equities:				
Liabilities.....................	$1,300,000	$450,000	$ 450,000	$1,750,000
Deferred Income Tax Liability	—	—	140,000	140,000
Shareholders' Equity...........	1,900,000	450,000	1,848,000	3,748,000
Total Equities	$3,200,000	$900,000	$2,438,000	$5,638,000
Income Statements				
Precombination Income Before				
Income Taxes.................	$ 300,000	$160,000		$ 460,000
From Combination:				
Extra Depreciation Expense	—	—		(80,000)
Net Income Before Taxes	$ 300,000	$160,000		$ 380,000
Income Tax Expense	(105,000)	(56,000)		(133,000)
Net Income....................	$ 195,000	$104,000		$ 247,000

1. Long-term depreciable assets have a market value of $850,000 but a book value of only $450,000. The lower book value of depreciable assets results from accounting's use of historical cost valuations for assets. Company S initially recorded its depreciable assets at acquisition cost. Over time, Company S recognized a portion of this acquisition cost as depreciation expense. GAAP does not permit the firm to recognize increases in the market values of these assets. The market value of Company S, as measured by the market value of its common stock, reflects the economic values, not book values, of assets.

2. Deferred income taxes of $140,000 arise because the acquiring firm cannot deduct the $400,000 excess of the market value over the book value of depreciable assets as depreciation expense for income tax purposes in future years. Although this $400,000 appears to be a permanent difference between book

and taxable income, GAAP requires the firm to recognize deferred taxes of $140,000 (=.35 × $400,000) for it. The $140,000 amount represents the extra income taxes that the firm will pay in future years because taxable income will exceed book income before income taxes. Stated another way, the $140,000 represents the loss in future tax benefits because the company cannot base depreciation on the $850,000 market value of depreciable assets. We might show the $140,000 as a reduction in the market value of depreciable assets ($850,000 − $140,000 = $710,000) on the premise that the market value of these assets to P is only $710,000, not $850,000. As discussed later, GAAP includes the $140,000 in the Deferred Income Tax Liability account.

3. Goodwill of $1,138,000 exists. The $1,138,000 amount for goodwill equals the difference between the acquisition cost ($1,848,000) and the market value of identifiable assets and liabilities ($450,000 + $850,000 − $450,000 − $140,000 = $710,000). As discussed earlier, goodwill includes intangible attributes that a firm cannot separately identify, as well as any merger premium that the acquirer had to pay to consummate the corporate acquisition. Goodwill generates no Deferred Income Tax Liability account because the firms structured the merger in such a way that the firm does not amortize goodwill for either book or tax purposes.

Consolidation on the Date of Acquisition

Column (4) of Exhibit 9.1 shows the consolidated balance sheet on the date of the acquisition. The following worksheet entry eliminates the investment account on Company P's books and the shareholders' equity accounts of Company S, revalues the depreciable assets of Company S, and recognizes the goodwill.

Shareholders' Equity (S)	450,000	
Depreciable Assets (individual assets would be debited)	400,000	
Goodwill	1,138,000	
Deferred Tax Liability.		140,000
Investment in Stock of Company S (P)		1,848,000

Note that the revaluation of depreciable assets and the recognition of goodwill do not appear on the separate books of either company. These accounts and amounts emerge on the consolidation worksheet as part of the entry to eliminate the investment account.

Net Income Subsequent to the Acquisition

The lower portion of Exhibit 9.1 shows the effect of the purchase method on net income for the first year after the acquisition. The two firms anticipated pretax net income of $300,000 and $160,000, respectively, for the year assuming the acquisition had not occurred. The consolidated financial statements must recognize depreciation on the excess purchase price allocated to depreciable assets. The extra depreciation, assuming a five-year remaining life using the straight-line method, is $80,000 (= $400,000/5). The extra depreciation reduces the Deferred Tax Liability and income tax expense by $28,000 (= .35 × $80,000). Consolidated net income is less than the combined income of the two companies because of the need to amortize the excess purchase price allocated to assets with finite lives.

A quality of accounting issue related to corporate acquisitions is the allocation of any excess purchase price. To enhance future earnings, firms have an incentive to allocate as much of the excess purchase price to goodwill and other intangibles with indefinite lives. In this way, they avoid future amortization charges. To counter this tendency, *Statement No. 141* relaxes the usual criterion for asset recognition (resource with reliably measured future benefits) in favor of a new scheme. Firms must allocate a portion of the purchase price to intangibles with finite lives if:

1. They arise from contractual or other legal rights (regardless of whether those rights are transferable or separable from the firm), or
2. They are separable (capable of being sold, transferred, licensed, rented, or exchanged), regardless of whether the firm intends to do so.

Examples of contractual or other legal rights are airport landing slots, management contracts, patents, and order backlog. Customer lists and unpatented technology are examples of separable intangibles. However, such items as a well-trained labor force or an efficient product distribution network would not qualify as an intangible with either a finite or infinite life. And recall from Chapter 7 that firms amortize intangibles with a finite useful life over their expected useful lives, taking into consideration the legal, regulatory, economic, competitive, or contractual provisions that may limit the useful life.

To counter firms' efforts to allocate as much of the purchase price to goodwill and other intangibles with indefinite lives, again as discussed in Chapter 7, firms must test such assets at least annually for impairment and recognize an impairment loss if the book values exceed fair values.

Consolidation Subsequent to the Acquisition

Each year, subsequent to the acquisition, Company P applies the equity method to account for its investment in Company S, a technique that the next section discusses. During the first year after the acquisition, S generates net income of $104,000. P recognizes this income on its books with the following entry:

Investment in Stock of Company S	104,000	
Equity in Earnings of Company S		104,000

The investment account shows a balance of $1,952,000 (=$1,848,000 + $104,000) at the end of the first year on P's books. The entry on the consolidation worksheet to eliminate the shareholders' equity of S and the investment account on P's books, and recognize the excess purchase price is as follows:

Shareholders' Equity (S)	450,000	
Depreciable Assets ($400,000 – $80,000)	320,000	
Depreciation Expense	80,000	
Equity in Earnings of Company S	104,000	
Goodwill	1,138,000	
Deferred Tax Liability ($140,000 – $28,000)		112,000
Income Tax Expense.		28,000
Investment in Stock of Company S		1,952,000

These entries adjust the separate income amounts of P and S to produce the amounts in the lower panel of Exhibit 9.1 labeled Net Income.

Acquisition Reserves

Oftentimes the purchase method entails establishing "acquisition reserves" at the time one company acquires another company because the acquiring company may not know the potential losses inherent in the acquired assets or the potential liabilities of the acquired company. Acquisition reserve accounts always have credit balances. The acquiring company will allocate a portion of the purchase price to various types of acquisition reserves (for example, estimated losses on long-term contracts, estimated liabilities for unsettled lawsuits). An acquiring company has up to one year after the date of acquisition to revalue these acquisition reserves as new information becomes available. After that, the acquisition reserve amounts remain in the accounts and absorb losses as they occur. That is, the acquiring firm charges actual losses against the acquisition reserves instead of against income for the period of the loss.

To illustrate, assume in the example above that S Company has an unsettled lawsuit in which P Company anticipates a $10 million pre-tax loss will ultimately result. It allocates $10 million to an acquisition reserve (liability account) and debits Deferred Tax Assets for the $3.5 million (= .35 × $10 million) tax effect. The acquiring firm would presumably pay less for this company because of this potential liability. Assume that settlement of the lawsuit occurs three years after the date of the acquisition for $8 million (pre-tax). The accountant charges the $8 million loss against the $10 million reserve instead of against net income for the year and reduces Deferred Tax Assets by $2.8 million (= .35 × $8 million). Furthermore, the accountant eliminates the $2 million remaining in the acquisition reserve and the $.7 million remaining in Deferred Tax Assets, increasing net income by $1.3 million (= $2 million – .7 million) in the year of the settlement. The benefit of this scenario to the acquiring firm is twofold: (1) no *charges* for the settlement reduce net income; but (2) the "cleaning up" *credit* increases net income in the year of the settlement.

Acquisition reserves can affect assessments of the quality of accounting information, and regulators carefully monitor their use (and abuse). When used properly, acquisition reserves are an accounting mechanism that helps insure that the assets and liabilities of an acquired company reflect market values. However, given the estimates required in establishing such reserves, management has some latitude in managing earnings under the purchase method.

CORPORATE ACQUISITIONS AND INCOME TAXES

Most corporate acquisitions involve a transaction between the acquiring corporation and the *shareholders* of the acquired corporation. Although the Board of Directors and management of the acquired company may closely monitor the discussions and negotiations, the acquisition usually takes place with the acquiring corporation giving some type of consideration to the shareholders of the acquired corporation in exchange for their stock. From a legal viewpoint, the acquired corporation remains a legally separate entity that has simply had a change in the make-up of its shareholder group.

The income tax treatment of corporate acquisitions follows these legal entity notions. In most acquisitions, the acquired company does not restate its assets and liabilities for tax purposes to reflect the amount that the acquired corporation paid for the shares of common stock. Instead, the tax basis of assets and liabilities of the acquired company before the acquisition carries over after the acquisition.[5] In this sense, the tax treatment of a corporate acquisition is analogous in concept to a pooling of interests. Thus, even if the combining entities use the purchase method for financial reporting, they treat the transaction like a pooling of interests for tax purposes (termed a *nontaxable reorganization* by the Internal Revenue Code).

Example 1

Refer to Appendix A, Note 2 of PepsiCo's annual report. The firm states:

> Under the Quaker merger agreement dated December 2, Year 10, Quaker shareholders received 2.3 shares of PepsiCo common stock in exchange for each share of Quaker common stock, including a cash payment for fractional shares. We issued approximately 306 million shares of our common stock in exchange for all the outstanding common stock of Quaker.
>
> The merger was accounted for as a tax-free transaction and as a pooling of interests. As a result, all prior period consolidated financial statements presented have been restated to include the results of operations,

---

[5]An acquiring company can elect Section 338 of the Internal Revenue Code and thereby record assets and liabilities at their market values for tax purposes. However, the acquired company must pay taxes immediately on differences between these market values and the tax basis of assets and liabilities.

Any goodwill resulting from the restatement of assets and liabilities that qualifies as a Section 197 intangible is amortized over a 15-year period as specified in the Revenue Recognition Act of 1993. To qualify for the amortization deduction, the goodwill had to be acquired after August 10, 1993. Goodwill amortization usually is not deducted for tax purposes, however, because few acquired firms restate their assets and liabilities.

financial position, and cash flows of both companies as if they had always been combined. Certain reclassifications were made to conform the presentation of the financial statements, and the fiscal calendar and certain interim reporting policies were also conformed.

Note that PepsiCo uses the term, "tax-free transaction" instead of the more technical term, "nontaxable reorganization," found in the tax code to describe the accounting for the transaction for tax purposes. The meanings of the two terms are the same. Also note, as discussed earlier in this section, that for financial reporting purposes, PepsiCo accounts for the merger using the pooling-of-interests method because it took place prior to the effective date of *Statement No. 141*.

CORPORATE DISCLOSURES ON ACQUISITIONS

Although PepsiCo accounted for the Quaker Oats merger using the pooling-of-interests method, the transaction could have been structured in such a way that the purchase method would have been used for financial reporting but still qualify for a tax-free transaction for tax reporting. In fact, this is often the case, given *Statement No. 141*'s elimination of the pooling-of-interests method. Consider the following example.

Example 2

AT&T Wireless is one of the largest wireless communications service providers in the United States, and it operates one of the largest digital wireless networks. In Year 10, AT&T Wireless acquired TeleCorp Wireless. At the time of the acquisition, TeleCorp Wireless provided digital wireless personal communications services to a large portion of the customer base of AT&T Wireless.

AT&T Wireless provides several key disclosures related to the transaction in its quarterly and annual filings with the SEC:

Accounting Treatment. In accordance with recently issued *Statement of Financial Accounting Standards No. 141*, "Business Combinations," and *Statement of Financial Accounting Standards No. 142*, "Goodwill and Other Intangible Assets," AT&T Wireless will use the purchase method of accounting for a business combination to account for the merger, as well as new accounting and reporting regulations for goodwill and other intangibles.

Tax Consequences. We have structured the merger to be a tax-free reorganization for U.S. federal income tax purposes. Holders of TeleCorp class A voting common stock will not recognize gain or loss for U.S. federal income tax purposes in the merger, except for gain or loss recognized because of cash received instead of fractional shares of AT&T Wireless common stock.

Goodwill Consequences for Financial and Tax Reporting. In accordance with SFAS No. 142, goodwill and licensing costs related to TeleCorp Wireless will not be amortized. Instead, AT&T Wireless Services will test these items for impairment as part of its periodic impairment test of total consolidated goodwill and total consolidated licensing costs. None of the goodwill recorded is deductible for tax purposes.

In addition to these disclosures, AT&T Wireless provides selected pro forma information assuming the two firms had been combined in Year 10. The firm does *not* restate prior periods' financial statements (as is the case with PepsiCo in Example 1).

INVESTMENTS IN SECURITIES

Firms invest in the securities (debt, preferred stock, common stock) of other entities (corporations, special purpose entities, variable interest entities, joint ventures, partnerships) for a variety of reasons, such as:

1. Short-term investments of temporarily excess cash.
2. Long-term investments to:
   a. Lock in high yields on debt securities.
   b. Exert significant influence on an important raw materials supplier, customer, technological innovator, or other valued entity.
   c. Gain voting control of another entity whose operations mesh well strategically with the investing firm.
3. Short- or long-term investments designed to meet specific operational goals, such as commercial real estate leasing, research and development programs, or reinsurance.

Accounting for investments in other entities has been under heightened scrutiny in recent years both because of what Robert Swieringa, former FASB board member, refers to as the "flexible and fluid organizations" formed to meet the needs of firms[6] (see the discussion on intangibles in Chapter 7), and the spate of reporting scandals in the early part of this decade, with the most notable case being Enron's abuse of special purpose entities as investment vehicles.

ACCOUNTING FOR INVESTMENTS

Exhibit 9.2 lists the rulings that address accounting for investments in one entity by another. In general, firms must consider two paths for deciding the appropriate accounting for its investments:

1. Percentage of ownership that one firm has in another entity.
2. Whether the reporting firm is deemed the primary beneficiary of the investment it has made in a variable interest entity (VIE), as defined in FASB *Interpretation No. 46.*[7]

---

[6]Robert J. Swieringa, "Should Accounting be 'Green and Smooth and Inviting'?" *The Journal of Financial Statement Analysis*, Winter 1997, pp. 75–87.

[7]Financial Accounting Standards Board, *Interpretation No. 46*, "Consolidation of Variable Interest Entities: An Interpretation of ARB No. 51," 2003. *Statement No. 140*, discussed in Chapter 8, addresses the accounting for the sale of receivables. Entities formed by the transferor for the sale of receivables, often referred to as qualifying special-purpose entities, are excluded from the scope of *Interpretation No. 46* and, thus, are never classified as variable interest entities.

EXHIBIT 9.2

Rulings on Accounting for Investments

Accounting Research Bulletin No. 51, "Consolidated Financial Statements," as amended by *Statement of Financial Accounting Standards No. 94*, "Consolidation of Majority-Owned Subsidiaries," 1987 (referred to as *ARB No. 51* and *Statement No. 94*).

Statement of Financial Accounting Standards No. 115, "Accounting for Certain Investments in Debt and Equity Securities," 1993 (referred to *Statement No. 115*).

FASB Interpretation No. 46, "Consolidation of Variable Interest Entities: An Interpretation of ARB No. 51," 2003 (referred to as *Interpretation No. 46*).

The goal of each path is to assess the level of "controlling financial interest" by the firm making the investment, with the first path the more common situation for determining the appropriate accounting for investments.[8] However, it is important to note that the appropriate reporting is determined *only after considering both paths*. Each path, in turn, will be discussed next.

PERCENTAGE OF VOTING STOCK

Exhibit 9.3 identifies three types of investments.

1. Minority, Passive Investments

Firms view debt securities or shares of capital stock of another corporation as a good investment and acquire them for their anticipated interest or dividends and capital gains (increases in the market prices of the securities). The percentage owned of another corporation's voting shares is not so large that the acquiring company can control or exert significant influence over the other company, and the investing firm is not deemed the VIE primary beneficiary as defined by *Interpretation No. 46* (discussed in a later section). Financial reporting views investments in debt securities, preferred stock, or common stock where the firm holds less than 20 percent of the voting stock as a minority, passive investment.

2. Minority, Active Investments

Firms acquire shares of another corporation so that the acquiring corporation can exert significant influence over the other company's activities. This significant influence is usually at a broad policy-making level through representation on the other

---

[8]ARB No. 51, which addresses when consolidation accounting is appropriate, states that the most common condition for determining "controlling financial interest" is percent of voting interest by the investing firm of another firm.

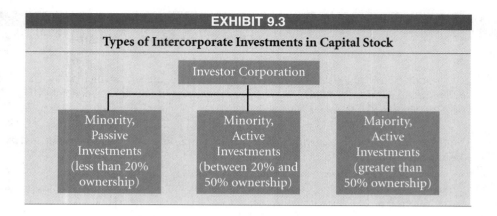

corporation's Board of Directors. Because of the wide dispersion of ownership of most publicly held corporations, many of whose shareholders do not vote their shares, firms can exert significant influence over another corporation with ownership of less than a majority of the voting stock. Financial reporting views investments of between 20 percent and 50 percent of the voting stock of another company as a minority, active investment *unless* evidence indicates that the acquiring firm cannot exert significant influence or the investing firm is deemed the VIE primary beneficiary as defined by *Interpretation No. 46* (discussed in a later section).

3. Majority, Active Investments

Firms acquire shares of another corporation so that the acquiring corporation can control the other company. This control is typically at both the broad policy-making level and at the day-to-day operational level. Ownership of more than 50 percent of the voting stock of another company implies an ability to control, unless available evidence indicates to the contrary.

The accounting for these three types of investments attempts to reflect the different purpose of each. Exhibit 9.4 summarizes the accounting for each type of investment in the financial statements.

MINORITY, PASSIVE INVESTMENTS

If a firm does not own a sufficient percentage of the voting stock of another corporation to control or significantly influence it, the management of the investment involves two activities: awaiting the receipt of interest or dividends and deciding when to sell the investment for a capital gain or loss. Financial reporting requires firms to account for minority, passive investments using either amortized acquisition cost or the market value method.[9]

---

[9]Financial Accounting Standards Board, *Statement of Financial Accounting Standards No. 115*, "Accounting for Certain Investments in Debt and Equity Securities," 1993.

	EXHIBIT 9.4		
	Reporting Investments in Securities in the Financial Statements		
Financial Statement	**Minority, Passive Investments***	**Minority, Active Investments***	**Majority, Active Investments**
Income Statement	Interest and dividend revenue Unrealized increases and decreases in the market value of securities classified as trading securities Realized gains and losses on sales of securities	Investor's share of investee's net income	Individual revenues and expenses of investee minus the minority interest's share of investee's net income included in consolidated net income
Balance Sheet	Marketable securities and investments in securities reported at market value (except that debt securities held to maturity reported at amortized acquisition cost) Unrealized increases and decreases in the market value of securities classified as available for sale included in Accumulated Other Comprehensive Income in the shareholders' equity section of the balance sheet	Investments reported at acquisition cost plus investor's cumulative share of investee's net income minus dividends received from investee since acquisition	Investment in securities account eliminated and replaced by investee's individual assets and liabilities in preparing consolidated balance sheet Minority interest's claim on investee's net assets shown in the shareholders' equity section of consolidated balance sheet
Statement of Cash Flows	Cash received from interest and dividends included in cash flow from operations; cash flows associated with purchases and sales included in cash flows from investing	Cash received from interest and dividends included in cash flow from operations. Cash flows associated with purchases and sales included in cash flows from investing	Individual cash flows from operating, investing, and financing activities of investee included in consolidated statement of cash flows

*The accounting for minority, passive and minority, active investments illustrated in the exhibit assumes that the investing firm is not a VIE primary beneficiary as defined by FASB *Interpretation No. 46*. If the investing firm is a VIE primary beneficiary, the firm must follow the reporting for investments in securities categorized as majority, active investments.

Example 15 in Chapter 2 details the accounting for an available-for-sale investment (category 3c below) by Microsoft, labeled investments in "Marketable Securities" in that chapter. Exhibit 2.1 in that chapter summarizes the various valuation techniques employed for all assets and liabilities, including investments in marketable debt and equity securities. A review of the example and exhibit at this point is helpful. A summary of the accounting for minority, passive investments follows:

1. Firms initially record investments at acquisition cost.
2. Revenues each period equal interest and dividends received or receivable.
3. The accounting at the end of each period depends on the type of security and the firm's reason for holding it. *Statement No. 115* requires firms to classify securities into three categories:
   a. Debt securities for which a firm has a positive intent and ability to hold to maturity.
   b. Debt and equity securities held as *trading securities.*
   c. Debt and equity securities held as *available for sale.*
4. Firms must account for debt securities expected to be held until maturity at amortized acquisition cost. That is, the firm must amortize any difference between the acquisition cost and maturity value of these debt securities as an adjustment to interest revenue over the life of the debt. Firms report all other debt and equity securities at market value at the end of each period. The reporting of any unrealized holding gain or loss depends on the purpose of holding the securities. If firms actively buy and sell securities to take advantage of short-term differences or changes in market values, then these firms classify the securities as *trading securities,* a current asset on the balance sheet. Commercial banks, for example, often trade securities in different capital markets worldwide to take advantage of temporary differences in market prices. Manufacturers, retailers, and other nonfinancial firms occasionally invest funds for trading purposes, but such situations are unusual. Firms include unrealized holding gains and losses on trading securities in the calculation of net income each period.[10] Firms classify debt and equity securities that do not fit one of these first two categories (debt securities held to maturity or trading securities) as securities *available for sale,* including them as either current assets or noncurrent assets depending on the expected holding period. Unrealized holding "gains" or "losses" on securities available for sale are not included in net income each period but instead appear as a component of comprehensive income, labeled Unrealized Holding Gain or Loss on Securities Available for Sale. The cumulative unrealized holding gain or loss

---

[10]As Chapter 8 discusses, if a firm chooses not to designate a particular derivative as either a fair value hedge or a cash flow hedge, GAAP requires that the firm account for the derivative as a speculative investment. The accounting for trading securities and derivatives classified as a speculative investment is similar in that firms must revalue the derivatives to market value each period and recognize the resulting unrealized gain or loss in earnings.

on securities available for sale appears in the shareholders' equity section of the balance sheet as part of Accumulated Other Comprehensive Income.

5. When a firm sells a trading security, it recognizes the difference between the selling price and the book value (that is, the market value at the end of the most recent accounting period prior to sale) as a gain or loss in measuring net income. When a firm sells a security classified as available for sale, it recognizes the difference between the selling price and the *acquisition cost* of the security as a realized gain or loss. The firm must eliminate at the time of sale any amount in the shareholders' equity account, Accumulated Other Comprehensive Income, for the unrealized holding gain or loss related to that security.

Example 3

Refer to Note 1 of PepsiCo's annual report in Appendix A, "Summary of Significant Accounting Policies—Cash Equivalents and Short-Term Investments." PepsiCo provides minimal disclosures related to its minority, passive investments, only indicating in the note that the investments are "short-term" in nature. The immaterial nature of PepsiCo's investments, less than one-half of one percent of total assets at the end of Year 11, justifies the minimal disclosures.

Example 4

Qualcomm, Inc. develops, manufactures and markets digital wireless telecommunications products and services. The company generates revenues by licensing its proprietary digital technology and through ongoing royalty payments received on the sale of equipment by domestic and international wireless telecommunications equipment suppliers.

Qualcomm provides the following disclosures in a note to a recent annual report, labeled "Marketable Securities":

> Management determines the appropriate classification of marketable securities at the time of purchase and re-evaluates such designation as of each balance sheet date. Held-to-maturity securities are carried at amortized cost, which approximates fair value. Available-for-sale securities are stated at fair value as determined by the most recently traded price of each security at the balance sheet date. The net unrealized gains or losses on available-for-sale securities are reported as a component of Comprehensive Income (Loss), Net of Tax, unless the company provides a valuation allowance against the tax benefit or liability resulting from the loss or gain. The specific identification method is used to compute the realized gains and losses on debt and equity securities.
>
> Available-for-sale securities were comprised as follows at September 30, Year 11 (in thousands):

	Cost	Unrealized Gains	Unrealized Losses	Fair Value
Year 11				
Equity Securities	$ 210,769	$18,520	$ (74,067)	$ 155,222
Debt Securities......	1,343,703	21,535	(17,175)	1,348,063
Total	$1,554,472	$40,055	$ (91,242)	$1,503,285
Year 10				
Equity Securities	$ 227,537	$ 3,388	$(108,494)	$ 122,431
Debt Securities	790,793	16,070	(70,594)	736,269
Total	$1,018,330	$19,458	$(179,088)	$ 858,700

Components of Accumulated Other Comprehensive Loss consisted of the following (in thousands):

	September 30,	
	Year 11	**Year 10**
Foreign Currency Translation	$ (79,762)	$ (64,537)
Unrealized Loss on Marketable Securities,		
net of income taxes	(51,187)	(159,630)
	$(130,949)	$(224,167)

Note that the Unrealized Loss on Marketable Securities, net of income taxes, at the end of fiscal Year 11 of $51,187 (= $40,055 − $91,242) and at the end of Year 10 of $159,630 (= $19,458 − $179,088) appear as part of Accumulated Other Comprehensive Loss for the respective years. These amounts result from netting the unrealized gains and unrealized losses reported for securities classified as available-for-sale for each year.

In assessing the quality of accounting information, analysts must decide whether or not to include any change in the holding gain or loss on securities classified as available for sale in earnings for the period. The principal argument for excluding it is that the unrealized "gain" or "loss" may well reverse and perhaps will not be realized for many years, if ever. The principal argument for including it relates to the fact that firms have some latitude in deciding how to classify securities; as such, firms can manage earnings by classifying securities as available for sale versus trading. If the analyst adjusts reported income statement amounts to include *all* changes in holding gains or losses on securities, then any earnings management practiced by firms is eliminated.

Because firms invest in marketable securities with temporarily excess cash, the analyst can generally presume that firms could sell these securities for an amount at least equal to the amount shown on the balance sheet. This is a reasonable presumption for firms located in countries that require the market method, such as France and Great Britain. Certain countries, such as Canada, Japan, and Germany, require the valuation of marketable securities at acquisition cost unless firms consider a price decline to be permanent. Firms in the latter countries seldom disclose the market value of their marketable securities. If interest rates have increased or stock prices have declined materially in one of these countries during the last several months of the accounting period, the analyst should interpret the reported amounts for these securities cautiously.

MINORITY, ACTIVE INVESTMENTS

When a firm owns less than a majority of the voting stock of another corporation, the accountant must exercise judgment in ascertaining whether the firm can exert significant influence. For the sake of uniformity, GAAP presumes that one company can significantly influence another company when it owns 20 percent or more of the voting stock of the other company. Ownership of less than 20 percent may permit a firm to exert significant influence, but in these cases management must demonstrate to the independent accountant that it is possible (for example, by placing individuals on the investee's Board of Directors).

GAAP requires firms to account for minority, active investments, generally those where ownership is between 20 and 50 percent, using the *equity method*.[11] Under the equity method, the firm owning shares in another firm recognizes as revenue (expense) each period its share of the net income (loss) of the other firm. See, for example, the income statement of PepsiCo in Appendix A. The line, "Bottling Equity Income and Transaction Gains/(Losses)" includes PepsiCo's share of the earnings from 20 percent- to 50 percent-owned affiliates. The investor treats dividends received from the investee as a return of investment and not as income. In the discussion that follows, we designate the firm owning shares as P and the firm whose shares P owns as S.

The rationale for using the equity method when significant influence is present is best understood by considering the financial statement effects of using the market value method for securities classified as available-for-sale in these circumstances. Under the market value method, P recognizes income or loss on the income statement only when it receives a dividend or sells all or part of the investment. Suppose, as often happens, that S follows a policy of financing its own growing operations through retention of earnings and consistently declares dividends significantly less than its net income. The market price of S's shares will probably increase to reflect the retention of assets generated by earnings. Under the market value method, P's only reported income from the investment will be the modest dividends received.

P, because of its ownership percentage, can influence the dividend policy of S and thereby the amount of income recognized under the market value method. Under these conditions, the market value method may not reasonably reflect the earnings of S generated under P's influence. The equity method provides a better measure of a

---

[11]Accounting Principles Board, *Accounting Principles Board Opinion No. 18*, "The Equity Method of Accounting for Investments in Common Stock," 1971.

firm's earnings and of its investment when, because of its ownership interest, it can significantly influence the operations and dividend policy of another firm.

Under the equity method, firms report investments on the balance sheet at acquisition cost plus (minus) the investor's share of the investee's net income (loss) each period. The statement of cash flows reports cash flows and not equity method earnings. Thus, in deriving cash flow from operations, the statement of cash flows subtracts the investor's share of the investee's earnings from net income and adds the cash dividends received. Many firms report this adjustment as a subtraction for the investor's share of the *undistributed* earnings (equity income minus dividends) of the investee. The analyst should address two questions in particular when examining the financial statements of firms with significant equity method intercorporate investments:

1. What is the relation between equity method income and cash flows received from the investees?
2. Are assets and liabilities essential to a firm's operations submerged in the intercorporate investment account?

The analyst answers the first question by comparing equity method income on the income statement with the adjustment to net income for undistributed earnings of investees in the statement of cash flows. PepsiCo reports "Bottling equity income and transaction gain/(losses), net" of $160 million on its income statement for Year 11. Its statement of cash flows shows a subtraction from net income to compute cash flow from operations of $160 million for "Bottling equity income and transactions (gains)/losses, net," suggesting that PepsiCo did not receive any dividends from these intercorporate investments during Year 11. PepsiCo derived less than 5 percent of its pre-tax earnings during Years 11 and 10 from equity method investees. (As discussed in Example 17 in Chapter 6, the amount for Year 9 includes a non-recurring bottling transaction gain of $1.0 billion.)

The analyst answers the second question by studying the notes on intercorporate investments. Firms must disclose partial balance sheet and income statement information for significant intercorporate investments. PepsiCo maintains less than a controlling interest in its major bottling operations for the strategic reasons discussed in Chapter 1 and Appendix B. The assets and liabilities of these bottlers do not appear on PepsiCo's balance sheet. A later section demonstrates the procedure an analyst might follow to incorporate amounts for such investments on the balance sheet.

The analyst should also exert caution when examining the financial statements of firms in other countries. Firms commonly use the equity method for minority, active investments in Canada, France, Great Britain and in certain filings with the Ministry of Finance in Japan. Countries that follow a strict legal definition of the entity, such as Germany, tend to report these intercorporate investments at acquisition cost, even when significant influence is present.

MAJORITY, ACTIVE INVESTMENTS

When one firm, P, owns more than 50 percent of the voting stock of another company, S, P can control the activities of S. This control may occur at both a broad policy-making level and a day-to-day operational level. The majority investor in this case is the *parent* and the majority-owned company is the *subsidiary*. Financial reporting requires the combining or *consolidating* of the financial statements of majority-owned companies with those of the parent (unless the parent cannot for legal or other reasons exercise control).[12]

Reasons for Legally Separate Corporations

There are many reasons why a business firm prefers to operate as a group of legally separate corporations rather than as a single legal entity. From the viewpoint of the parent company, the more important reasons for maintaining legally separate subsidiary companies include the following:

1. To reduce financial risk. Separate corporations may mine raw materials, transport them to a manufacturing plant, produce the product, and sell the finished product to the public. If any one part of the total process proves to be unprofitable or inefficient, losses from insolvency fall only on the owners and creditors of the one subsidiary corporation. Furthermore, creditors have a claim on the assets of the subsidiary corporation only, not on the assets of the parent company. For corporations with potential environmental and product liabilities, legal separation through the use of subsidiaries can be especially advantageous.

2. To meet more effectively the requirements of state corporation laws and tax legislation. If a firm does business in many states, it must often contend with overlapping and inconsistent taxation, regulations, and requirements. Organizing separate corporations to conduct the operations in the various states may reduce administrative costs.

3. To expand or diversify with a minimum of capital investment. A firm may absorb another company by acquiring a controlling interest in its voting stock. It may accomplish this result with a substantially smaller capital investment, as well as with less difficulty, inconvenience, and risk, than if it had constructed a new plant or geared up for a new line of business.

Purpose of Consolidated Statements

For a variety of reasons, then, a parent and several legally separate subsidiaries may exist as a single economic entity. A consolidation of the financial statements of the parent and each of its subsidiaries presents the results of operations, financial position, and changes in cash flows of an affiliated group of companies under the

---

[12]Committee on Accounting Procedure, *Accounting Research Bulletin No, 51*, "Consolidated Financial Statements," as amended by Financial Accounting Standards Board, *Statement No. 94*, "Consolidation of Majority-Owned Subsidiaries," 1987.

control of a parent, essentially as if the group of companies were a single entity. The parent and each subsidiary are legally separate entities, but they operate as one centrally controlled *economic entity*. Consolidated financial statements generally provide more useful information to the shareholders of the parent corporation than would separate financial statements of the parent and each subsidiary.

Consolidated financial statements also generally provide more useful information than the equity method used to account for minority, active investments. The parent, because of its voting interest, can effectively control the use of the subsidiary's individual assets. Consolidation of the individual assets, liabilities, revenues, and expenses of both the parent and the subsidiary provides a more realistic picture of the operations and financial position of the single economic entity.

In a legal sense, consolidated statements merely supplement, and do not replace, the separate statements of the individual corporations, although it is common practice in the United States to present only the consolidated statements in published annual reports.

Disclosure of Consolidation Policy

The note to the financial statements that describes significant accounting policies includes a statement about the consolidation policy of the parent. If a parent does not consolidate a significant majority-owned subsidiary, the notes will disclose that fact.

Example 5

Note 1 to PepsiCo's annual report in Appendix A states:

> The financial statements include the consolidated accounts of PepsiCo, Inc. and its controlled affiliates. Intercompany balances and transactions have been eliminated. Investments in unconsolidated affiliates over which we exercise significant influence, but not control, are accounted for by the equity method. Our definition of control for majority-owned affiliates considers the exercisability of the minority interest rights, and consolidation would be precluded to the extent that the minority interest holds substantive participating rights. Our share of the net income or loss of unconsolidated affiliates accounted for by the equity method is included in consolidated net income.

Note that PepsiCo summarizes its accounting and reporting for both minority, passive (equity method) and majority, active (consolidation method) investments in this first footnote.

Understanding Consolidated Statements

This section discusses three concepts essential for understanding consolidated financial statements:

1. The need to eliminate intercompany balances and transactions, as PepsiCo details in Example 5 above.

2. The meaning of consolidated net income.
3. The nature of the external minority interest.

The Need to Eliminate Intercompany Activity. State corporation laws typically require each legally separate corporation to maintain its own set of books. Thus, during the accounting period, the accounting system of each corporation records transactions of that entity with all other entities (both affiliated and nonaffiliated). At the end of the period, each corporation prepares its own set of financial statements. The consolidation of these financial statements involves summing the amounts for various financial statement items across the separate company statements. The amounts resulting from the summation require adjustments, however, to eliminate double counting resulting from *intercompany transactions.* Consolidated financial statements reflect the results of an affiliated group of companies operating as a single company. Thus, consolidated financial statements include only the transactions between the consolidated entity and others outside the group.

The eliminations to remove intercompany transactions typically appear on a *consolidation worksheet* and not on the books of any of the legal entities comprising the consolidated group. The accountant prepares the consolidated financial statements directly from the worksheet. The consolidated entity generally maintains no separate set of books.

To illustrate the need for, and the nature of, *elimination entries,* refer to the data for Company P and Company S in Exhibit 9.5. Column (1) shows the balance sheet and income statement data for Company P taken from its separate company books. Column (2) shows similar data for Company S. Column (3) sums the amounts from columns (1) and (2). The amounts in column (3) include the effects of several intercompany items and, therefore, do not represent the correct amounts for *consolidated* assets, equities, revenues, or expenses.

Eliminating Double Counting of Intercompany Payables. Separate company records indicate that $12,000 of Company S's accounts receivable represent amounts payable by Company P. The amounts in column (3) count the current assets underlying this transaction twice: once as part of Accounts Receivable on Company S's books and a second time as Cash (or Other Assets) on Company P's books. Also, Accounts Payable in column (3) includes the liability shown on Company P's books, even though the amount is not payable to an entity external to the consolidated group. To eliminate double counting on the asset side and to report Accounts Payable at the amount payable to external entities, the elimination entry reduces the amounts for Accounts Receivable and Accounts Payable in column (3) by $12,000.

Eliminating Double Counting of Investment. Company P's balance sheet shows an asset, Investment in Stock of Company S. The subsidiary's balance sheet shows its individual assets and liabilities. The combined balance sheets in column (3) include both Company P's investment in Company S's net assets and the assets and liabilities themselves. We must eliminate Company P's account, Investment in Stock of Company S, from the sum of the balance sheets. Because the consolidated balance sheet must maintain the accounting equation, we must make corresponding

	EXHIBIT 9.5		
Illustrative Data for Preparation of Consolidated Financial Statements			

	Single-Company Statements		
	Company P (1)	Company S (2)	Combined (3)=(1)+(2)
Condensed Balance Sheets on December 31			
Assets:			
Accounts Receivable	$ 200,000	$ 25,000	$ 225,000
Investment in Stock of Company S (at equity)	705,000	—	705,000
Other Assets.....................................	2,150,000	975,000	3,125,000
Total Assets	$3,055,000	$1,000,000	$4,055,000
Equities:			
Accounts Payable................................	$ 75,000	$ 15,000	$ 90,000
Other Liabilities.................................	70,000	280,000	350,000
Common Stock	2,500,000	500,000	3,000,000
Retained Earnings	410,000	205,000	615,000
Total Equities	$3,055,000	$1,000,000	$4,055,000
Condensed Income Statement for Current Year			
Revenues:			
Sales	$ 900,000	$ 250,000	$1,150,000
Equity in Earnings of Company S....................	48,000	—	48,000
Total Revenues	$ 948,000	$ 250,000	$1,198,000
Expenses:			
Cost of Goods Sold (excluding depreciation)..........	$ 440,000	$ 80,000	$ 520,000
Depreciation Expense	120,000	50,000	170,000
Administrative Expenses	80,000	40,000	120,000
Income Tax Expense	104,000	32,000	136,000
Total Expenses.............................	$ 744,000	$ 202,000	$ 946,000
Net Income	$ 204,000	$ 48,000	$ 252,000
Dividend Declarations.............................	50,000	13,000	63,000
Increase in Retained Earnings for the Year	$ 154,000	$ 35,000	$ 189,000

eliminations on the right-hand, or equities, side as well. To understand the eliminations from the right-hand side of the balance sheet, recall that the right-hand side shows the sources of the firm's financing. Creditors (liabilities) and owners (shareholders' equity) finance Company S. Company P owns 100 percent of Company S's voting shares. Thus, the creditors of both companies and Company P's shareholders finance the assets on the consolidated balance sheet of the single economic entity. In other words, the equities of the consolidated entity are the liabilities of both companies but the shareholders' equity of Company P alone. If we added the shareholders' equity accounts of Company S to those of Company P, we would count twice the financing from Company P's shareholders (once on the parent's books and once on the subsidiary's books). Hence, when we eliminate Company P's investment account from the sum of the two companies' assets, we maintain the accounting equation by eliminating the shareholders' equity accounts of Company S.

Eliminating Double Counting of Income. Similarly, we must eliminate certain intercompany items from the sum of income statement accounts to present meaningfully the operating performance of the consolidated entity. Company P's accounts show Equity in Earnings of Company S of $48,000. Company S's records show individual revenues and expenses that net to $48,000. If we merely summed the revenues and expenses of the two companies, as column (3) of Exhibit 9.5 illustrates, we would double count the earnings of Company S. We must eliminate the account, Equity in Earnings of Company S, in preparing consolidated statements.

Eliminating Intercompany Sales. Another example of an intercompany item involves intercompany sales of inventory. Separate company records indicate that Company S sold merchandise to Company P for $40,000 during the year. None of this inventory remains in Company P's inventory on December 31. The sale of the merchandise inventory increases Sales Revenue on both Company S's books (sale to Company P for $40,000) and on Company P's books (sale to an external entity for probably a higher price). Thus, the combined amounts for Sales Revenue overstate sales from the standpoint of the consolidated entity by $40,000. Likewise, Cost of Goods Sold of both companies includes the separate company costs of the goods sold. To eliminate double counting, we must eliminate $40,000 from consolidated Cost of Goods Sold.

The Meaning of Consolidated Income. The amount of consolidated net income for a period exactly equals the amount that the parent shows on its separate company books from applying the equity method; that is, consolidated net income equals

Parent Company's Net Income from Its Own Activities	+	Parent Company's Share of Subsidiary's Net Income	−	Profit (or + Loss) on Intercompany Transactions

A consolidated income statement differs from an equity method income statement in the *components* presented. When using the equity method for an unconsolidated subsidiary, the parent's share of the subsidiary's net income minus gain (or plus loss) on intercompany transactions appears on a single line, Equity in Earnings of Unconsolidated Subsidiary. In a consolidated income statement, we combine the individual revenues and expenses of the subsidiary (less intercompany adjustments) with those of the parent, and eliminate the account, Equity in Earnings of Unconsolidated Subsidiary, shown on the parent's books. Some accountants refer to the equity method as a *one-line consolidation* because it nets the individual revenues and expenses of the subsidiary into the one account, Equity in Earnings of Unconsolidated Subsidiary.

The Nature of External Minority Interest in Consolidated Subsidiary. The parent does not always own 100 percent of the voting stock of a consolidated subsidiary. Accountants refer to the owners of the remaining shares of voting stock as the *minority interest.* These shareholders have a proportionate interest in the net assets (= total assets – total liabilities) of the subsidiary as shown on the subsidiary's separate corporate records. They also have a proportionate interest in the earnings of the subsidiary.

One issue that the accountant must confront in preparing consolidated statements is whether the statements should show only the parent's share of the assets and liabilities of the subsidiary or whether they should show all of the subsidiary's assets and liabilities along with the minority interests' claim on them. GAAP requires firms to show all of the assets and liabilities of the subsidiary, because the parent, with its controlling voting interest, effectively directs the use of all the assets and liabilities, not merely an amount equal to the parent's percentage of ownership. The consolidated balance sheet and income statement in these instances, however, must disclose the interest of the minority shareholders in the consolidated subsidiary.

The amount of the minority interest appearing on the balance sheet results from multiplying the common shareholders' equity of the subsidiary by the minority's percentage of ownership. For example, if the common shareholders' equity (or assets minus liabilities) of a consolidated subsidiary totals $500,000 and the minority owns 20 percent of the common stock, the minority interest appears on the consolidated balance sheet at $100,000 (=.20 × $500,000). The consolidated balance sheet shows the minority interest as part of shareholders' equity. The financial statements of PepsiCo give no indication that a minority interest exists in any of its consolidated subsidiaries.

The amount of the minority interest in the subsidiary's income results from multiplying the subsidiary's net income by the minority's percentage of ownership. The consolidated income statement shows the proportion of consolidated income applicable to the parent company and the proportion of the subsidiary's income applicable to the minority interest. Typically, the minority interest in the subsidiary's income appears as a subtraction in calculating consolidated net income.

Limitations of Consolidated Statements

The consolidated statements do not replace those of individual corporations; rather, they supplement those statements and aid in their interpretation. Creditors must rely on the resources of one corporation and may be misled if forced to rely entirely on consolidated statements that combine the data of a company in good financial condition with one verging on insolvency. Firms can legally declare dividends only from their own retained earnings. When the parent company does not own all of the shares of the subsidiary, the outside or minority shareholders can judge the dividend constraints, both legal and financial, only by inspecting the subsidiary's statements.

Consolidation of Unconsolidated Subsidiaries and Affiliates

The analyst may wish to assess the financial position of a firm with all important majority-owned subsidiaries and minority-owned affiliates consolidated. For example, firms frequently join together in joint ventures to carry out their business activities. Chiron Corporation (Case 7.2 in Chapter 7) uses joint ventures and collaborative research agreements to develop new biotechnology-related products. Chiron does not consolidate the financial statements of the joint ventures with its financial statements, but, rather, uses the equity method to account for the joint ventures because they are not majority-owned by the firm.

As discussed in this chapter and Chapter 1, PepsiCo has significant investments in bottlers that are integral to its operations. As with Chiron, PepsiCo does not consolidate the bottlers because they are less than majority-owned. However, consolidation of the financial statements of these affiliates with those of PepsiCo presents a more realistic picture of the assets and liabilities of PepsiCo as an *operating* enterprise.

Exhibit 9.6 presents a consolidation worksheet for PepsiCo and its bottlers. PepsiCo's balance sheet (from Appendix A) provides the amounts in column (1). Note 9 to PepsiCo's financial statements provides the amounts for columns (2), (3), and (4). The amounts in column (5) eliminate amounts in the intercorporate investment accounts on PepsiCo's books against the shareholders' equity accounts of the affiliates. The column also shows the reclassification of a portion of the shareholders' equity accounts of the affiliates to recognize the minority or external interest claims. The amount that Exhibit 9.6 shows for the external interest equals the total shareholders' equity of the affiliates times the external interests' ownership percentages. This percentage is 58 percent for PBG and 63 percent for PepsiAmericas. Unfortunately, PepsiCo does not disclose its ownership percentage in Other Equity Investments (see Note 9). In addition, PepsiCo doesn't disclose the amount of equity income related to the specific category of bottlers, and furthermore, the line on PepsiCo's income statement, "Bottling Equity Income and Transaction Gains/(Losses) Net," captures several different types of transactions. We estimate the external interests in Other Equity Investments at 60.5 percent by averaging the external interests in PBG and PepsiAmericas that are disclosed to the analyst.

Consider now the effect of consolidating PepsiCo's bottlers on its rate of return on assets. For Year 11, Chapter 4 calculates an ROA (adjusted for two nonrecurring items totaling $341 million) of

$$14.8\% = \frac{\$2,662 + \$341 + (1 - .35)(\$219) + \$0}{.5(\$20,757 + \$21,695)} = \frac{\$3,145}{\$21,226}$$

Operating income in the numerator of ROA does not change as a result of consolidation. To exclude the effect of financing from the numerator of ROA, we must add back the interest expense (net of taxes) recognized by PepsiCo's bottlers. Note 9 does not provide the amount of interest expense for those entities. We estimate the

EXHIBIT 9.6

PepsiCo and Equity Method Affiliates
Consolidation Worksheet
December 31, Year 11
(in millions)

	PepsiCo (1)	PBG (2)	Pepsi-Americas (3)	Other Equity Investments (4)	Eliminations (5)	Consolidated (6)
Current Assets	$ 5,853	$1,548	$ 481	$ 953		$ 8,835
Investments in Securities	2,871	—	—		(A) −962[a] (B) −746[a] (C) −906[a]	257
Noncurrent Assets	12,971	6,309	2,938	1,970	(A) +156[c] (B) +217[e] (C) +266[g]	24,827
Total Assets	$21,695	$7,857	$3,419	$2,923		$33,919
Current Liabilities	$ 4,998	$1,081	$ 653	$1,053		$ 7,785
Noncurrent Liabilities	8,023	4,856	1,336	249		14,464
Preferred Stock	26	—	—			26
External Interests (Minority Interest)	—	—	—		(A) +1,114[b] (B) +901[d] (C) +981[f]	2,996
Common Shareholders' Equity	$ 8,648	$1,920	$1,430	$1,621	(A) −1,920[a] (B) −1,430[a] (C) −1,621[a]	8,648
	$21,695	$7,857	$3,419	$2,923		$33,919

[a]Information provided in PepsiCo's Note 9.
[b]$1,114 = .58 × $1,920
[c]$156 = [$962 − (.42 × $1,920)]
[d]$901 = .63 × $1,430
[e]$217 = $746 − (.37 × $1,430)
[f]$981 = (1 − .395) × ($1,621)
[g]$266 = $906 − (.395 × $1,621)

amount by assuming that the noncurrent liabilities of the bottlers represent interest-bearing debt. Using the disclosures in PepsiCo's Note 12, assume an average interest rate of 7.0 percent on long-term debt. The debt of PepsiCo's investees and amounts for noncurrent liabilities from Note 9 yield interest expense of $449 million [= .07 × .5($4,856 + $4,817 + $1,336 + $999 + $249 + $578)] for Year 11. Obviously we inject some error into the calculation of ROA to the extent that some of the current liabilities of these entities bear interest, that some of the noncurrent liabilities do not bear interest, and that 7.0 percent is not a reasonable interest rate.

The final adjustment to the numerator of ROA to consolidate these bottlers is to add the external interest in earnings. This adjustment permits the numerator to include 100 percent of the operating income of PepsiCo and its bottlers and the denominator to include 100 percent of the assets of these entities. PepsiCo's Note 9 shows the total income of these bottlers for Year 11 of $433 ($305 + $19 + $109), as well as PepsiCo's bottling equity income and transaction gains/losses of $160. The share of the external interest is therefore approximately $273 million (= $433 − $160). Consolidating PepsiCo's bottlers results in the following recomputed ROA for Year 11 of

$$11.1\% = \frac{\$2,662 + \$341 + (1 - .35)(\$219 + \$449) + 273}{.5[\$33,919 + 33,054]} = \frac{\$3,710}{\$33,487}$$

Thus, PepsiCo's ROA for Year 11 drops from 14.8 percent to 11.1 percent, a twenty-five percent decline. The capital intensive nature of bottling reveals itself in this pro forma ratio analysis in that the asset base for PepsiCo increases dramatically when the bottling companies are consolidated. The analysis clearly points out the benefit to PepsiCo of not bottling its own product, and captures one of the key reasons PepsiCo divested itself of its bottlers in Year 9.

The consolidation of majority-owned subsidiaries is a relatively recent phenomenon in some countries (for example, Germany and Japan). These countries tended to follow strict legal definitions of the reporting entity. Financial reporting in these countries now generally requires the preparation of consolidated financial statements, although the requirement in Japan applies only to filings with the Ministry of Finance.

Proportionate Consolidation of Unconsolidated Subsidiaries and Affiliates

An alternative to full consolidation of PepsiCo's bottlers is proportionate consolidation. Under proportionate consolidation, the investor's share of the assets and liabilities of the affiliate appear in separate sections on the asset and liabilities sides of the balance sheet, with the equity investment account eliminated (recall that PepsiCo currently accounts for its investments using the equity method).

This alternative is especially appealing for firms that enter into joint ventures where ownership of the venture is equally split between two firms. Chapter 7 provides several examples of these types of arrangements. Currently, firms account for investments in joint ventures using the equity method (unless FASB *Interpretation*

No. 46 applies) because these investments fall between minority, active investments and majority, active investments. Some accountants argue that proportionate consolidation better captures the economics of transactions where joint control is present. The FASB has been reviewing joint venture accounting for some time, but is having difficulty identifying a standard that is operational.

PRIMARY BENEFICIARY OF A VARIABLE INTEREST ENTITY

As discussed at the beginning of this section, firms must consider two paths for deciding the appropriate accounting for its investments. Both paths are necessary because a determination of "controlling financial interest" through levels of voting interest may not be appropriate (first path). For example, applying the majority voting interest rule to assess controlling financial interest will not work for investments in which control is achieved through arrangements that do *not* include voting rights, such as partnerships or trusts without governing boards. For these investments, controlling financial interest is assessed through application of *Interpretation No. 46* and a determination of the whether the investing firm is the primary beneficiary in a variable interest entity (VIE).

As detailed below, if a firm's investment in another entity is classified as a VIE investment, accounting for the investment must follow the rules established in *Interpretation No. 46*. That is, the accounting based on the percentage of voting stock discussed above is superseded by the reporting and disclosure requirements of *Interpretation No. 46*.

The FASB does not provide a precise definition of a VIE in *Interpretation No. 46*, only stating that the term refers "to an entity subject to consolidation according to the provisions of this Interpretation." VIEs can take the form of a corporation, partnership, trust, or any other legal structure used for business purposes. Examples include entities that administer real estate leases, research and development agreements, or energy-related foreign exchange contracts. Oftentimes VIEs hold financial assets, real estate, or other property. The VIE may be passive and simply carry out a function on behalf of one or more firms (administer a commercial real estate lease, for example), or it may actively engage in some activity on behalf of one or more firms (conduct research and development research). *Interpretation No. 46* uses the term "variable interest" to capture the fact that investors in VIEs have levels of interest that will vary with the success or failure of the VIE.

Although many individuals in business commonly use the term *special-purpose entities* (SPEs) instead of VIEs, the FASB purposely does not use the term because *Interpretation No. 46* applies to a larger set of entities than just SPEs. However, the fact is that *Interpretation No. 46* is the direct result of the Enron debacle and the firm's abusive use of SPEs. Congress directed the FASB to swiftly address the reporting sins of Enron. The deliberative process for *Interpretation No. 46* followed a record-breaking pace, with some of its requirements taking effect almost immediately after its release by the FASB.

Application of *Interpretation No 46*

The primary objectives of *Interpretation No. 46* are to (1) provide guidance on identifying entities for which control is achieved through means other than voting rights, and (2) determine which firm should consolidate the VIE, labeled the primary beneficiary. The FASB concluded that consolidation by the primary beneficiary of the assets, liabilities and results of activities of the VIE will provide the most complete information about the resources, obligations, risks, and opportunities of the consolidated company. In addition, *Interpretation No. 46* stipulates disclosures required by both the primary beneficiary and all other enterprises with a significant variable interest in a VIE.

When Is an Entity Classified as a VIE? A firm's investment in another entity is classified as a VIE investment and thus, subject to *Interpretation No. 46*, if any one of the following four conditions is met:

1. The total equity investment at risk is not sufficient to permit the VIE to finance its activities without additional subordinated financial support from other parties, which would absorb some of the expected losses of the entity. *Interpretation No. 46* interprets this condition to be when "the equity investment at risk is not greater than the expected losses of the VIE." Also, the presumption is that an equity investment of less than 10 percent of the entity's *total assets* is not sufficient to permit the VIE to finance its activities without additional support.
2. The equity investing firms do not have the direct or indirect ability to make decisions about the VIE's activities through voting rights or similar rights. Contractual arrangements with the subordinated providers of funds usually restrict the ability of the equity investing firms to make decisions about the VIE's activities.
3. The equity investing firms do not have the obligation to absorb the expected losses of the VIE if they occur. The subordinated providers of funds absorb some of the expected losses.
4. The investing firms do not have the right to receive the expected residual returns of the VIE if they occur. The subordinated providers of funds have a claim on some of the expected residual returns.

Which Entity Should Consolidate the VIE? Determining whether an investing firm should consolidate the VIE is at the heart of *Interpretation No. 46*. An investing firm consolidates the VIE if it absorbs the *majority* of the entity's expected losses if they occur, receive a *majority* of the entity's expected residual returns if they occur, or both. The consolidating firm is labeled the primary beneficiary. The firm considers the rights and obligations conveyed by its variable interests and the relationship of its variable interests to variable interests held by other firms to determine whether it will absorb a majority of expected losses, receive a majority of expected residual returns, or both. If one firm absorbs a majority of the expected losses and another firm receives a majority of the expected residual returns, the firm absorbing a majority of the losses consolidates the variable interest entity.

Disclosure Requirements of **Interpretation No. 46.** Both the primary beneficiary firm and the firms holding a significant variable interest in a VIE are subject to *Interpretation No. 46* disclosure rules. The primary beneficiary must disclose the (1) nature, purpose, size, and activities of the VIE, (2) carrying amount and classification of the consolidated assets that represent collateral for the VIE's obligations, and (3) status of VIE creditor recourse to the assets of the primary beneficiary. Firms holding significant variable interest in a VIE must disclose the (1) nature of its involvement with the VIE and when that involvement began, (2) nature, purpose, size, and activities of the VIE, and (3) the investing firm's maximum exposure to loss given its involvement with the VIE.

Identifying VIEs, determining the level of involvement (variable interests), and quantifying VIE activity is a difficult and subjective task. *Interpretation No. 46* provides only limited guidance, especially related to quantifying expected losses (condition 1 above), which is a crucial dimension to the interpretation. Furthermore, *Interpretation No. 46* provides no guidance on how to proportion the expected losses when more than one firm has made an investment in the VIE.

To date, there is limited experience with implementing the interpretation. Analysts should view the quality of accounting information for VIEs with skepticism, especially when the investing firm determines that consolidation of the VIE is not appropriate.

INCOME TAX CONSEQUENCES OF INVESTMENTS IN SECURITIES

For income tax purposes, investments fall into two categories:

1. Investments in debt securities, in preferred stock, and in less than 80 percent of the common stock of another entity. Firms recognize interest or dividends received or receivable each period as taxable income (subject to a partial dividend exclusion), as well as gains or losses when they sell the securities.
2. Investments in 80 percent or more of the common stock of another entity. Firms can prepare consolidated tax returns for these investments.

As is evident, the methods of accounting for investments for financial and tax reporting do not overlap precisely. Thus, temporary differences will likely arise for which firms must recognize deferred taxes. PepsiCo, for example, cannot file consolidated tax returns with PBG, PepsiAmericas, or other equity investments because its ownership percentage is less than 80 percent. PepsiCo reports in Note 14 of Appendix A deferred tax liabilities of $702 million at December 29, Year 11, relating to these equity investments because it includes its share of the investees' earnings each year for financial reporting but recognizes dividends received as income on its tax return.

FOREIGN CURRENCY TRANSLATION

Firms headquartered in the United States often have substantial operations outside of the country. For example, PepsiCo indicates in Appendix B that it generates approximately 20 percent of its operating profits internationally (defined as outside of the United States and Canada).[13] For Coke, its largest beverage competitor, the percent is much larger, representing over 70 percent of its operating profits.

U.S. parent companies must translate the financial statements of foreign branches and subsidiaries into U.S. dollars before preparing consolidated financial statements for shareholders and creditors. This section describes and illustrates the translation methodology and discusses the implications of the methodology both for managing international operations and for interpreting financial statement disclosures regarding such operations.

Two general issues arise in translating the financial statements of a foreign branch or subsidiary.

1. Should the firm translate individual financial statement items using the exchange rate at the time of the transaction (referred to as the *historical exchange rate*) or the exchange rate during or at the end of the current period (referred to as the *current exchange rate*)? Financial statement items that firms translate using the historical exchange rates appear in the financial statements at the same U.S. dollar equivalent amount each period regardless of changes in the exchange rate. For example, land acquired in France for 10,000 euros when the exchange rate was $1.05 per euro appears on the balance sheet at $10,500 each period. Financial statement items that firms translate using the current exchange rate appear in the financial statements at a different U.S. dollar amount each period when exchange rates change. Thus, a change in the exchange rate to $1.10 per euro results in reporting the land at $11,000 in the balance sheet. Financial statement items for which firms use the current exchange rate give rise to a *foreign exchange adjustment* each period.
2. Should the firm recognize the foreign exchange adjustment as a gain or loss in measuring net income each period as it arises or should the firm defer its recognition until a future period? The foreign exchange adjustment represents an unrealized gain or loss, much the same as changes in the market value of derivatives, marketable securities, inventories, or other assets. Should financial reporting require realization of the gain or loss through sale of the foreign operation before recognizing it or should the unrealized gain or loss flow directly to the income statement as the exchange rate changes?

The sections that follow address these two questions.

---

[13]Financial reporting requires firms to disclose segment data by geographic location (foreign versus domestic), as well as by reportable operating segments and major customers (Financial Accounting Standards Board, *Statement of Financial Accounting Standards No. 131*, "Disclosures about Segments of an Enterprise and Related Information," 1997). PepsiCo reports extensive geographic segment information in Note 21 in Appendix A. Chapter 4 provides profitability analysis of PepsiCo's geographic segment information.

FUNCTIONAL CURRENCY CONCEPT

Central to the translation of foreign currency items is the *functional currency concept*.[14] Determination of the functional currency drives the accounting for translating the financial statements of foreign entities of U.S. firms into U.S. dollars.

Foreign entities (whether branches or subsidiaries) are of two general types:

1. A foreign entity operates as a relatively self-contained and integrated unit within a particular foreign country. The functional currency for these operations is the currency of that foreign country.
2. The operations of a foreign entity are a direct and integral component or extension of the parent company's operations. The functional currency for these operations is the U.S. dollar.

Statement No. 52 sets out characteristics for determining whether the currency of the foreign unit or the U.S. dollar is the functional currency. Exhibit 9.7 summarizes these characteristics. The operating characteristics of a particular foreign operation may provide mixed signals regarding which currency is the functional currency. Management must exercise judgment in determining which functional currency best captures the economic effects of a foreign entity's operations and financial position. As a later section discusses, management may wish to structure certain financing or other transactions to swing the balance to favor selecting either the foreign currency or the U.S. dollar as the functional currency. Once a firm determines the functional currency of a foreign entity, it must use it consistently over time unless changes in economic circumstances clearly indicate a change in the functional currency.

Statement No. 52 provides for one exception to the guidelines in Exhibit 9.7 for determining the functional currency. If the foreign entity operates in a highly inflationary country, GAAP considers its currency to be too unstable to serve as the functional currency and the firm must use the U.S. dollar instead. A highly inflationary country is one that has experienced cumulative inflation of at least 100 percent over a three-year period. Some developing nations fall within this exception and pose particular problems for the U.S. parent company, as a later section discusses.

TRANSLATION METHODOLOGY—FOREIGN CURRENCY IS FUNCTIONAL CURRENCY

When the functional currency is the currency of the foreign unit, GAAP requires firms to use the *all-current translation method*. The left-hand column of Exhibit 9.8 summarizes the translation procedure under the all-current method.

Firms translate revenues and expenses at the average exchange rate during the period and balance sheet items at the end-of-the-period exchange rate. Net income

---

[14]Financial Accounting Standards Board, *Statement of Financial Accounting Standards No. 52* (as amended by *Statement No. 130*, "Reporting Comprehensive Income"), "Foreign Currency Translation," 1981.

EXHIBIT 9.7

Factors for Determining Functional Currency of a Foreign Unit

	Foreign Currency Is Functional Currency	U.S. Dollar Is Functional Currency
Cash Flows of Foreign Entity	Receivables and payables denominated in foreign currency and not usually remitted to parent currently	Receivables and payables denominated in U.S. dollars and readily available for remittance to parent
Sales Prices	Influenced primarily by local competitive conditions and not responsive on a short-term basis to exchange rate changes	Influenced by worldwide competitive conditions and responsive on a short-term basis to exchange rate changes
Cost Factors	Foreign unit obtains labor, materials, and other inputs primarily from its own country	Foreign unit obtains labor, materials, and other inputs primarily from the United States
Financing	Financing denominated in currency of foreign unit or generated internally by the foreign unit	Financing denominated in U.S. dollars or ongoing fund transfers by the parent
Relations between Parent and Foreign Unit	Low volume of intercompany transactions and little operational interrelations between parent and foreign unit	High volume of intercompany transactions and extensive operational interrelations between parent and foreign unit

includes only *transaction* exchange gains and losses of the foreign unit. That is, a foreign unit that has receivables and payables denominated in a currency other than its own must make a currency conversion on settlement of the account. The gain or loss from changes in the exchange rate between the time the account originated and the time of settlement is a transaction gain or loss. Firms recognize this gain or loss during the period the account is outstanding, even though it is not yet realized or settled. As Chapter 8 discusses, firms often acquire derivatives to hedge the risk of foreign currency gains and losses. Firms include the offsetting loss or gain on the derivative to the gain or loss on the item hedged in net income each period. Thus, net income increases or decreases net only to the extent that the derivative did not perfectly hedge the change in exchange rates.

When a foreign unit operates more or less independently of the U.S. parent, financial reporting assumes that only the parent's equity investment in the foreign unit is subject to exchange rate risk. The firm measures the effect of exchange rate changes on this investment each period, but includes the resulting "translation adjustment"

EXHIBIT 9.8		
Summary of Translation Methodology		
	Foreign Currency Is the Functional Currency (all-current method)	U.S. Dollar Is the Functional Currency (monetary/non-monetary method)
Income Statement	Firms translate revenues and expenses as measured in foreign currency into U.S. dollars using the average exchange rate during the period. Income includes (1) realized and unrealized transaction gains and losses, and (2) realized translation gains and losses when the firm sells the foreign unit.	Firms translate revenues and expenses using the exchange rate in effect when the firm made the original measurements underlying the valuations. Firms translate revenues and most operating expenses using the average exchange rate during the period. However, they translate cost of goods sold and depreciation using the historical exchange rate appropriate to the related asset (inventory, fixed assets). Net income includes (1) realized and unrealized transaction gains and losses, and (2) unrealized translation gains and losses on the net monetary position of the foreign unit each period.
Balance Sheet	Firms translate assets and liabilities as measured in foreign currency into U.S. dollars using the end-of-the-period exchange rate. Use of the end-of-the-period exchange rate gives rise to unrealized transaction gains and losses on receivables and payables requiring currency conversions in the future. Firms include an unrealized translation adjustment on the net asset position of the foreign unit in a separate shareholders' equity account, not in net income, until the firm sells the foreign unit.	Firms translate monetary assets and liabilities using the end-of-the-period exchange rate. They translate nonmonetary assets and equities using the historical exchange rate.

as a component of Other Comprehensive Income, rather than net income. GAAP's rationale for this treatment is that the firm's investment in the foreign unit is for the long term; short-term changes in exchange rates should not, therefore, affect periodic net income. Firms recognize the cumulative amount in the translation adjustment account when measuring any gain or loss from disposing of the foreign unit.

The "translation adjustment" reported by a firm can include a second component in addition to the effect of exchange rate changes on the parent's equity investment in foreign subsidiaries or branches. Firms can hedge their investment in foreign operations using forward contracts, currency swaps, or other derivative instruments. GAAP requires firms to report the change in fair value of a derivative that qualifies as a hedge of the net investment in a foreign entity as part of the translation adjustment.[15] In this sense, the foreign currency hedge is treated similar to a cash-flow hedge (discussed and illustrated in Chapter 8) in that the change in the fair value of the hedge appears in Other Comprehensive Income. The difference is that firms do not separately disclose the change in the fair value of the hedge, but rather, embed it in the translation adjustment, which also captures the effect of exchange rate changes on the parent's equity investment in the foreign entity.

Example 6

The functional currency for PepsiCo's foreign subsidiaries is the currency of the foreign unit. As a result, PepsiCo reports the currency translation adjustment in comprehensive income. PepsiCo's comprehensive income for Year 11 is $2,390 million. As detailed in Chapter 1, PepsiCo reports Currency Translation Adjustment of −$218 million for the year as a component of comprehensive income. The statement of changes in common shareholders' equity for PepsiCo includes the $218 million currency translation adjustment in reconciling the change in Accumulated Other Comprehensive Income for Year 11. In addition, Note 16 in Appendix A, labeled "Other Comprehensive Loss," reports the ending accumulated balance in Currency Translation Adjustment of −$1,587 million for Year 11 and −$1,369 million for Year 10. The difference between the two ending balances is −$218 million, the amount reported as part of comprehensive income for Year 11.

Illustration—Foreign Currency Is Functional Currency

Exhibit 9.9 illustrates the all-current method for a foreign unit *during its first year of operations*. The exchange rate was $1:1FC on January 1, $2:1FC on December 31, and $1.5:1FC on average during the year. Thus, the foreign currency increased in value relative to the U.S. dollar during the year (that is, it takes fewer foreign currency units to acquire $1 at the end of the year than at the beginning of the year). The firm

---

[15]Financial Accounting Standards Board, *Statement of Financial Accounting Standards No. 133*, "Accounting for Derivative Instruments and Hedging Activities," 1998. However, if the foreign currency hedge does not qualify as a hedge of the net investment, then the criteria established in this standard for fair value and cash flow hedges are applied to determine the appropriate accounting. See Chapter 8 for a discussion of the accounting for derivatives used in fair value and cash flow hedging activities.

EXHIBIT 9.9			
Illustration of Translation Methodology when the Foreign Currency Is the Functional Currency			
	Foreign Currency	**U.S. Dollars**	
Balance Sheet			
Assets			
Cash	FC 10	$2.0:1FC	$ 20.0
Receivables.......................	20	$2.0:1FC	40.0
Inventories.......................	30	$2.0:1FC	60.0
Fixed Assets (net).................	40	$2.0:1FC	80.0
Total	FC 100		$200.0
Liabilities and Shareholders' Equity			
Accounts Payable..................	FC 40	$2.0:1FC	$ 80.0
Bonds Payable	20	$2.0:1FC	40.0
Total	FC 60		$120.0
Common Stock	FC 30	$1.0:1FC	$ 30.0
Retained Earnings	10		12.5[a]
Accumulated Other Comprehensive Income			
Unrealized Translation Adjustment	—		37.5[b]
Total	FC 40		$ 80.0
Total	FC 100		$200.0
Income Statement			
Sales Revenue.....................	FC 200	$1.5:1FC	$300.0
Realized Transaction Gain.	2[c]	$1.5:1FC	3.0[c]
Unrealized Transaction Gain.........	1[d]	$1.5:1FC	1.5[d]
Cost of Goods Sold	(120)	$1.5:1FC	(180.0)
Selling & Administrative Expense......	(40)	$1.5:1FC	(60.0)
Depreciation Expense	(10)	$1.5:1FC	(15.0)
Interest Expense...................	(2)	$1.5:1FC	(3.0)
Income Tax Expense	(16)	$1.5:1FC	(24.0)
Net Income	FC 15		$ 22.5

	Foreign Currency		**U.S. Dollars**
[a]Retained Earnings, Jan. 1	FC 0.0		$ 0.0
Plus Net Income.................................	15.0		22.5
Less Dividends	(5.0)	$2.0:1FC	$(10.0)
Retained Earnings, Dec. 31........................	FC 10.0		$ 12.5

Exhibit 9.9—continued	Foreign Currency		U.S. Dollars
[b] Net Asset Position, Jan. 1	FC 30.0	$1.0:1FC	$ 30.0
Plus Net Income...............................	15.0		22.5
Less Dividends	(5.0)	$2.0:1FC	$(10.0)
Net Asset Position, Dec. 31.......................	FC 40.0		$ 42.5
		$2.0:1FC	80.0
Unrealized Translation "Gain"			$ 37.5

[c] The foreign unit had receivables and payables denominated in a currency other than its own. When it settled these accounts during the period, the foreign unit made a currency conversion and realized a transaction gain of FC2.
[d] The foreign unit has receivables and payables outstanding that will require a currency conversion in a future period when the foreign unit settles the accounts. Because the exchange rate changed while the receivables/payables were outstanding, the foreign unit reports an unrealized transaction gain for financial reporting.

translates all assets and liabilities on the balance sheet at the exchange rate on December 31. It translates common stock at the exchange rate on the date of issuance; the translation adjustment account includes the effects of changes in exchange rates on this investment. The translated amount of retained earnings results from translating the income statement and dividends. Note that the firm translates all revenues and expenses of the foreign unit at the average exchange rate. The foreign unit realized a transaction gain during the year and recorded it on its books. In addition, the translated amounts for the foreign unit include an unrealized transaction gain arising from exposed accounts that are not yet settled. Note a to Exhibit 9.9 shows the computation of translated retained earnings. The foreign unit paid the dividend on December 31.

Note b shows the calculation of the translation adjustment. By investing $30 in the foreign unit on January 1 and allowing the $22.5 of earnings to remain in the foreign unit throughout the year while the foreign currency was increasing in value relative to the U.S. dollar, the parent has a potential exchange "gain" of $37.5. It reports this amount as a component of comprehensive income.

TRANSLATION METHODOLOGY—U.S. DOLLAR IS FUNCTIONAL CURRENCY

When the functional currency is the U.S. dollar, financial reporting requires firms to use the *monetary/nonmonetary translation method*. The right-hand column of Exhibit 9.8 summarizes the translation procedure under the monetary/nonmonetary method.

The underlying premise of the monetary/nonmonetary method is that the translated amounts reflect amounts that the firm would have reported if it had originally made all measurements in U.S. dollars. To implement this underlying premise, financial reporting makes a distinction between monetary items and nonmonetary items.

A monetary item is an account whose nominal maturity amount does not change as the exchange rate changes. From a U.S. dollar perspective, these accounts give rise to exchange gains and losses because the number of U.S. dollars required to settle the fixed foreign currency amounts fluctuates over time with exchange rate changes. Monetary items include cash, receivables, accounts payable, and other accrued liabilities and long-term debt. Firms translate these items using the end-of-the-period exchange rate and recognize translation gains and losses. These translation gains and losses increase or decrease net income each period, whether or not the foreign unit must make an actual currency conversion to settle the monetary item.

A nonmonetary item is any account that is not monetary and includes inventories, fixed assets, common stock, revenues, and expenses. Firms translate these accounts using the historical exchange rate in effect when the foreign unit initially made the measurements underlying these accounts. Inventories and cost of goods sold translate at the exchange rate when the foreign unit acquired the inventory items. Fixed assets and depreciation expense translate at the exchange rate when the foreign unit acquired the fixed assets. Most revenues and operating expenses other than cost of goods sold and depreciation translate at the average exchange rate during the period. The objective is to state these accounts at their U.S. dollar-equivalent historical cost amounts. In this way, the translated amounts will reflect the U.S. dollar perspective that is appropriate when the U.S. dollar is the functional currency.

Illustration—U.S. Dollar Is Functional Currency

Exhibit 9.10 shows the application of the monetary/nonmonetary method to the data considered in Exhibit 9.9. Net income again includes both realized and unrealized transaction gains and losses. Net income under the monetary/nonmonetary translation method also includes a $22.5 translation loss.

As Exhibit 9.10 (note b) shows, the firm was in a net monetary liability position during a period when the U.S. dollar decreased in value relative to the foreign currency. The translation loss arises because the U.S. dollars required to settle these foreign-denominated net liabilities at the end of the year exceed the U.S. dollar amount required to settle the net liability position before the exchange rate changed.

IMPLICATIONS OF FUNCTIONAL CURRENCY DETERMINATION FOR ANALYSIS

As Exhibit 9.9 and Exhibit 9.10 demonstrate, the functional currency and related translation method can significantly affect translated financial statement amounts for a foreign unit. Some summary comparisons follow:

Functional Currency Is:	Foreign Currency	U.S. Dollar
Net Income............................	$ 22.5	$ 5.0
Total Assets............................	200.0	145.0
Shareholders' Equity.....................	80.0	25.0
Return on Assets........................	11.3%	3.4%
Return on Equity	28.1%	20.0%

	EXHIBIT 9.10		

Illustration of Translation Methodology when the U.S. Dollar Is the Functional Currency

	Foreign Currency		U.S. Dollars
Balance Sheet			
Assets			
Cash	FC	10	$2.0:1FC	$ 20.0
Receivables......................		20	$2.0:1FC	40.0
Inventories......................		30	$1.5:1FC	45.0
Fixed Assets (net).................		40	$1.0:1FC	40.0
Total	FC	100		$145.0
Liabilities and Shareholders' Equity			
Accounts Payable.................	FC	40	$2.0:1FC	$ 80.0
Bonds Payable		20	$2.0:1FC	40.0
Total	FC	60		$120.0
Common Stock	FC	30	$1.0:1FC	$ 30.0
Retained Earnings		10		(5.0)[a]
Total	FC	40		$ 25.0
Total	FC	100		$145.0
Income Statement			
Sales Revenue....................	FC	200	$1.5:1FC	$300.0
Realized Transaction Gain...........		2	$1.5:1FC	3.0
Unrealized Transaction Gain.........		1	$1.5:1FC	1.5
Unrealized Translation Loss		—		(22.5)[b]
Cost of Goods Sold		(120)	$1.5:1FC	(180.0)
Selling & Administrative Expense......		(40)	$1.5:1FC	(60.0)
Depreciation Expense		(10)	$1.0:1FC	(10.0)
Interest Expense..................		(2)	$1.5:1FC	(3.0)
Income Tax Expense		(16)	$1.5:1FC	(24.0)
Net Income	FC	15		$ 5.0

	Foreign Currency		U.S. Dollars
[a]Retained Earnings, Jan. 1	FC	0	—	$ 0.0
Plus Net Income...............................		15		5.0
Less Dividends		(5)	$2.0:1FC	(10.0)
Retained Earnings, Dec. 31........................	FC	10		$(5.0)

Exhibit 9.10—continued

[b]Income for financial reporting includes any unrealized translation gain or loss for the period. The net monetary position of a foreign unit during the period serves as the basis for computing the translation gain or loss. The foreign unit was in a net monetary liability position during a period when the U.S. dollar decreased in value relative to the foreign currency. The translation loss arises because the U.S. dollars required to settle the net monetary liability position at the end of the year exceed the U.S. dollars required to settle the obligation at the time the firm initially recorded the transactions, that give rise to change in net monetary liabilities during the period. The calculations appear below:

	Foreign Currency		U.S. Dollars
Net Monetary Position, Jan. 1	FC 0.0	—	$ 0.0
Plus:			
Issue of Common Stock	30.0	$1.0:1FC	$ 30.0
Sales for Cash and on Account	200.0	$1.5:1FC	300.0
Settlement of Exposed Receivable/Payable			
at a Gain	2.0	$1.5:1FC	3.0
Unrealized Gain on Exposed Receivable/Payable	1.0	$1.5:1FC	1.5
Less:			
Acquisition of Fixed Assets	(50.0)	$1.0:1FC	(50.0)
Acquisition of Inventory	(150.0)	$1.5:1FC	(225.0)
Selling & Admin. Costs Incurred	(40.0)	$1.5:1FC	(60.0)
Interest Cost Incurred	(2.0)	$1.5:1FC	(3.0)
Income Taxes Paid	(16.0)	$1.5:1FC	(24.0)
Dividend Paid	(5.0)	$2.0.1FC	(10.0)
Net Monetary Liability Position, Dec. 31	(30.0)		$(37.5)
	└──────→ $2.0.1FC		–(60.0)
Unrealized Translation Loss			$ 22.5

These differences arise for two principal reasons:

1. The all-current translation method (foreign currency is the functional currency) uses current exchange rates, whereas the monetary/nonmonetary translation method (U.S. dollar is the functional currency) uses a mixture of current and historical rates. Not only are net income and total asset amounts different, but the relative proportions of receivables, inventories, and fixed assets to total assets, debt/equity ratios, and gross and net profit margins differ. When firms use the all-current translation method, the translated amounts reflect the same financial statement relationships (for example, debt/equity ratios) as when measured in the foreign currency. When the U.S. dollar is the functional currency, financial statement relationships get measured in U.S. dollar-equivalent amounts and financial ratios differ from their foreign currency amounts.

2. The other major reason for differences between the two translation methods is the inclusion of unrealized translation gains and losses in net income under the monetary/nonmonetary method. Much of the debate with respect to the predecessor to *Statement No. 52*, which was *Statement No. 8*, involved the inclusion of this unrealized translation gain or loss in net income. Many

companies argued that the gain or loss was a bookkeeping adjustment only and lacked economic significance, particularly when the transaction required no currency conversion to settle a monetary item. Also, its inclusion in net income often caused wide, unexpected swings in earnings, particularly in quarterly reports.

As discussed earlier, the organizational structure and operating policies of a particular foreign unit determine its functional currency. The two acceptable choices and the corresponding translation methods were designed to capture the different economic and operational relationships between a parent and its foreign affiliates. However, firms have some latitude in deciding the functional currency, and, therefore, the translation method, for each foreign unit. In many cases, the signals about the appropriate functional currency will be mixed and firms will have latitude to select between them. Some actions that management might consider to swing the balance of factors toward use of the foreign currency as the functional currency include:

1. *Decentralize decision making to the foreign unit.* The greater the degree of autonomy of the foreign unit, the more likely its currency will be the functional currency. The U.S. parent company can design effective control systems to monitor the activities of the foreign unit while at the same time permitting the foreign unit to operate with considerable freedom.
2. *Minimize remittances/dividends.* The greater the degree of earnings retention by the foreign unit, the more likely its currency will be the functional currency. The parent may obtain cash from a foreign unit indirectly rather than directly through remittances or dividends. For example, a foreign unit with mixed signals about its functional currency might, through loans or transfer prices for goods or services, send cash to another foreign unit whose functional currency is clearly its own currency. This second foreign unit can then remit it to the parent. Other possibilities for interunit transactions are possible to insure that *some* foreign currency rather than the U.S. dollar is the functional currency.

Research suggests that approximately 80 percent of U.S. firms with foreign operations use the foreign currency as the functional currency and the remainder use the U.S. dollar.[16] Few firms select the foreign currency for some operations and the U.S. dollar for other operations (except for operations in highly inflationary countries, when firms must use the U.S. dollar as the functional currency). Thus, it appears that firms have a preference for the all-current translation method, in large part because they can exclude unrealized foreign currency "gains and losses" from earnings each period, and experience fewer earnings surprises. Inclusion of the change in the foreign currency translation adjustment account each period in earnings can cause large, unexpected variations in reporting earnings, a result that most managers prefer to avoid.

---

[16]Eli Bartov and Gordon M. Bodnar, "Alternative Accounting Methods, Information Asymmetry and Liquidity: Theory and Evidence," *The Accounting Review*, July 1996, pp. 397–418.

The question for the analyst assessing earnings quality is whether to include the change in the foreign currency translation account in earnings, or to leave it as a component of comprehensive income. The principal argument for excluding it is that the unrealized "gains or losses" may well reverse in the long term, and, in any case, will not be realized perhaps for many years. The principal arguments for including it in earnings are (1) management has purposely chosen the foreign currency as the functional currency in order to avoid including such "gains or losses" in earnings, not because the firm allows its foreign units to operate as independent units, and (2) the change in the foreign currency translation adjustment represents the current period's portion of the eventual net gain or loss that *will* be realized. When using earnings to value a firm, Chapter 12 suggests that earnings should include all recognized value changes regardless of whether GAAP includes them in net income or other comprehensive income.

A study[17] examining the valuation relevance of the translation adjustment regressed excess, or unexpected, returns on (1) earnings excluding exchange gains and losses, (2) transaction exchange gains and losses included in earnings, and (3) changes in the translation adjustment reported as a component of comprehensive income. The study found that the coefficient on the translation adjustment was statistically significant but smaller than that on earnings excluding all exchange gains and losses, suggesting that the market considers the translation adjustment relevant for security valuation but less persistent (as discussed in Chapter 6) than earnings excluding gains and losses. Given this finding, the FASB's decision to require firms to report the translation adjustment change as a *separate and distinct* component of comprehensive income appears on target in that it mandates the highlighting of the change.

FOREIGN CURRENCY TRANSLATION AND INCOME TAXES

Income tax laws make a distinction between a foreign branch of a U.S. parent and a subsidiary of a U.S. parent. A subsidiary is a legally separate entity from the parent, while a branch is not. The translation procedure of foreign branches is essentially the same as for financial reporting (except that taxable income does not include translation gains and losses until realized). That is, a firm selects a functional currency for each foreign branch and uses the all-current or monetary/nonmonetary translation method as appropriate.

For foreign subsidiaries, taxable income includes only dividends received each period (translated at the exchange rate on the date of remittance). Because parent companies typically consolidate foreign subsidiaries for financial reporting but cannot consolidate them for tax reporting, temporary differences that require the provision of deferred taxes likely arise.

---

[17]Billy S. Soo and Lisa Gilbert Soo, "Accounting for the Multinational Firm: Is the Translation Process Valued by the Stock Market?" *The Accounting Review*, October 1995, pp. 617–637.

ACCOUNTING FOR STOCK-BASED COMPENSATION

Firms often give employees the right, or option, to acquire shares of common stock at a price that is less than the market price of the shares at the time they exercise the option. Use of stock options, especially as a form of employee compensation, skyrocketed in the last twenty years. The technology sector, especially since the Internet boom of the 1990s, has used options as the dominant component of their employee compensation packages.

It is especially common for firms to grant stock options to senior management each year as an element of their compensation. The stock options permit the employees to purchase shares of common stock at a price usually set equal to the market price of the stock at the time the firm grants the stock option. Employees exercise these stock options at a later time, assuming that the stock price has increased. Firms adopt stock option plans to motivate employees to take actions that will increase the market value of a firm's common shares. Unlike compensation in the form of salaries, stock options do not require firms to use cash during the period when they grant stock options to employees.

Example 7

Note 17 in Appendix A describes the stock options PepsiCo granted to employees under four different plans. The PepsiCo long-term incentive plan (LTIP) is typical of plans offered by many firms. Note that PepsiCo identifies the participants as "senior management and certain middle management," and bases the awards on a multiple of base salaries. Also note that there is a vesting period (defined below) for the options. At the end of Year 11, 57 million shares were available for grants under the LTIP.

An understanding of the accounting for stock options requires several definitions. Refer to Exhibit 9.11. The *grant date* is the date a firm gives a stock option to employees. The *vesting date* is the first date employees can exercise their stock options. The *exercise date* is the date employees exchange the option and cash for shares of common stock. The *exercise price* is the price specified in the stock option contract for purchasing the common stock. The *market price* is the price of the stock as it trades in the market. Firms usually structure stock option plans so that a period of time elapses between the grant date and the vesting date. Firms may either preclude employees from exercising the option for one or more years or set an exercise price sufficiently high that the employee would not desire to exercise the option until the stock price increases.

The value of a stock option has two elements: (1) the benefit realized on the exercise date because the market price of the stock exceeds the exercise price (the *benefit element*), and (2) the length of the period during which the holder can exercise the option (the *time value element*).

The amount of the benefit element is not known until the exercise date. In general, stock options with exercise prices less than the current market price of the stock (described as *in the money*) have a higher value than stock options with exercise prices exceeding the current market price of the stock (described as *out of the money*). The time value element of an option's value results from the benefit it provides its holder

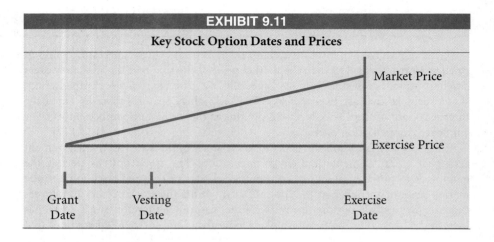

EXHIBIT 9.11

Key Stock Option Dates and Prices

for increases in the market price of the stock during the exercise period. An option provides the holder the right to enjoy the benefits of market price increases for the stock. This second element of an option will have more value the longer the exercise period, the more volatile the market price of the stock, the lower the dividend yield, and the lower the discount rate. Note that a stock option may have an exercise price that exceeds the current market price (zero value for the first element) but still have a value because of the possibility that the market price will exceed the exercise price on the exercise date (positive value for the second element). As the expiration date of the option approaches, the value of the second element approaches zero.[18]

Three FASB rulings address accounting for stock options.[19] The history of these three rulings is intriguing. APB *Opinion No. 25* recommended, but did not require, firms to recognize the cost of stock options as an expense on the date of the grant. In the 1990s, the FASB issued an exposure draft of a new reporting standard that would require firms to recognize the cost of stock options as compensation expense. This proposal would have superceded *Opinion No. 25*, which recommended but did not require expensing of stock options grants. This proposal was never adopted, however, because the business community lobbied various congressional interests so vigorously that some senators brought pressure on FASB to withdraw its proposal. The FASB eventually passed *Statement No. 123*, which reaffirmed the conclusions of *Opinion No. 25* but required new pro forma stock option disclosures in the notes to the financial statements about the impact of stock option grants on earnings.

Subsequent to issuance of *Statement No. 123*, and importantly, after the reporting and accounting scandals of the early 2000s, firms began to *voluntarily* treat the cost

---

[18]For an elaboration on the theory of option pricing, see Fischer Black and Myron Scholes, "The Pricing of Options and Corporate Liabilities," *Journal of Political Economy* (May–June 1973), pp. 637–654.

[19]Accounting Principles Board, *Opinion No. 25*, "Accounting for Stock Issued to Employees," 1972; Financial Accounting Standards Board, *Statement No. 123*, "Accounting for Stock-Based Compensation," 1995; and Financial Accounting Standards Board, *Statement No 148*, "Accounting for Stock-Based Compensation—Transition and Disclosure," 2002.

of stock options given to employees as an expense. These firms decided either that expensing the cost of stock options is theoretically more sound reporting, a position that we subscribe to as well, or that investors would view these firms more favorably for taking this voluntary move.

One issue that firms face in the first year that they expense stock options is whether to measure the expense just for stock options granted in that year (the so-called *prospective method* prescribed by *Statement No. 123*) or to also include the expense for stock options granted during previous years for which the vesting period had not yet lapsed and the firm would still be amortizing the cost (the so-called *retroactive method*). Given the movement to begin voluntarily recognizing the cost of stock options, the FASB felt obliged to issue *Statement No. 148* in response to concerns that the prospective application of the fair value recognition provisions for expensing stock options prescribed by *Statement No. 123* were no longer appropriate. The point was made that the basis for requiring prospective application—lack of historical data—was no longer applicable since seven years had passed since issuance of *Statement No. 123* and, in fact, historical data was available now.

The end result of this tumultuous time is that GAAP now allows firms to choose between two methods of accounting for employee stock options, and two methods for reporting a *voluntary* adoption of *Statement No. 123*'s expense recognition provisions.

Acceptable Methods of Accounting

Firms can choose between two acceptable methods of accounting for employee stock options: (1) fair value method; and (2) intrinsic (*Opinion No. 25*) method. However, the FASB makes it clear that the fair value method is preferable. With the fair value method, firms measure the value of stock options on the date of grant. The preferred valuation method for valuing stock options is the Black-Scholes options pricing model referenced in footnote 18. Firms then amortize this cost over the accounting periods between the date of the grant and the date when the stock options vest with employees, typically a period of three to five years.

With the intrinsic (*Opinion No. 25*) method, firms never recognize an expense for the options unless the market price of the stock is greater than the exercise price on the grant date. Most firms set the exercise price equal to or greater than the market price on the grant date, so no compensation expense arises.

Acceptable Methods of Transition

Firms that voluntarily elect to adopt the fair value method for stock options may report the change in accounting using any one of several transition methods. They are the (1) prospective (original *Statement No. 123*) method[20], in which compensation expense is recognized only for awards granted, modified, or settled after the beginning of the fiscal year in which the change is made; (2) modified prospective

---

[20]The Prospective transition option is acceptable only when firms commence the expensing of options prior to December 15, 2003. Firm commencing the expensing of options after that date must use either the modified prospective method or the retroactive restatement method.

method, in which compensation expense for the year of change is equal to that which would have been recognized had the recognition provisions of *Statement No. 123* been applied from the original effective date of the *Statement*; or (3) retroactive restatement method, in which compensation expense for the year of change is recognized in that year and financial statements for all prior periods are presented as though the fair value recognition provisions of *Statement No. 123* had been applied as of the original effective date of the *Statement*.

Disclosure Requirements

In addition to addressing issues of transition, *Statement No. 148* also modified the disclosures required under *Statement No. 123*. FASB particularly had comparability concerns in mind as a result of a greater number of companies deciding to adopt the fair value method of accounting.

All firms with significant stock options must disclose the following information:

1. The method of accounting for stock options used in each period presented.
2. Until such time as a firm recognizes compensation expense in measuring earnings for all periods reported, they must provide a tabular presentation showing (a) any stock-based employee compensation expense included in net income each period, (b) stock-based employee compensation cost that would have been included in net income had the fair value recognition provisions been applied from the original effective date of *Statement No. 123*, and (c) pro forma net income and earnings per share as if the fair value recognition provisions had been applied from the original effective date of *Statement No. 123*.

PepsiCo uses the intrinsic (*Opinion No. 25*) method for accounting for stock-based compensation, reported in Note 1 of Appendix A, "Summary of Significant Accounting Policies—Stock-Based Compensation." As is common with this method, PepsiCo records no stock-based compensation, which it confirms in Note 1. PepsiCo provides stock options disclosures in Note 17. Note that PepsiCo reports pro forma earnings per share (basic) of $1.33 for Year 11 when taking stock-based compensation into consideration using the Black-Scholes option pricing model to value the options. This compares to reported earnings per share (basic) of $1.51 for the year. The disclosures provided by PepsiCo are slightly different than those detailed above because *Statement No. 148* was not effective for Year 11.

Accounting for stock-based compensation is not uniform across firms. In addition, the reporting for stock-based compensation is in transition worldwide as the IASB has tentatively concluded that the fair value of shares given as remuneration should be expensed on the income statement. These issues make the quality of the accounting information suspect because of lack of comparability.

Fortunately, analysts have sufficient information for U.S. firms to convert a firm's income statement from the intrinsic (*Opinion No. 25*) method to the fair value method, in our opinion the preferred method. Using the information provided by a firm, such as that provided by PepsiCo in Note 17, analysts can use earnings and earnings per share adjusted for stock-based compensation in profitability and risk analyses, and in valuation models based on earnings. Pro forma adjustments are appropriate, especially when the magnitude of the difference between the two methods is large. This is especially true for firms in the technology sector such as Cisco Systems, Sun Microsystems, and Microsoft.

Chapter 12 discusses the valuation implications of employee stock options.

SUMMARY

Unlike reporting topics such as revenue recognition, inventories, derivatives, leases, and deferred taxes (covered in Chapters 7 and 8), which affect one or only a few line items in the financial statements, the topics discussed in this chapter tend to affect many line items in the financial statements. The accounting for corporate acquisitions, intercorporate investments, and foreign currency translation are therefore more pervasive in their financial statement effects. This situation both increases their potential significance to the financial analyst and provides a source for concern. Full disclosure of the effects of using the purchase method or translating the financial statements of a foreign unit using the all-current method instead of the monetary/nonmonetary method is cumbersome and possibly confusing. The final topic discussed in the chapter, accounting for stock options, also suffers from inconsistent reporting across firms. As always, the analyst must learn to work with comparability limitations and less than sufficient disclosures when interpreting financial statements affected by the topics considered in this chapter.

We now move on to the valuation of firms in Chapters 10 through 13.

PROBLEMS AND CASES

9.1 EFFECT OF THE PURCHASE METHOD ON THE BALANCE SHEET.   Sun Company acquired all of the outstanding common stock of Snow Company on January 1, Year 5. Sun gave shares of its common stock with a market value of $504 million in exchange for the Snow common stock. Snow will remain a legally separate entity after the exchange, but Sun will prepare consolidated financial statements each period with Snow. The transaction qualifies as a nontaxable exchange for income tax purposes. Exhibit 9.12 presents the balance sheets of Sun and Snow on January 1, Year 5, just prior to the acquisition. The income tax rate in 40 percent. The following information applies to Snow.

1. The market value of Snow's fixed assets exceeds their book value by $80 million.
2. Snow owns a copyright with a market value of $50 million.
3. Snow is a defendant in a lawsuit that it expects to settle during Year 5 at a pretax cost of $30 million. The firm carries no insurance against such lawsuits. Sun desires to establish an acquisition reserve for this lawsuit.
4. Snow has an unrecognized and unfunded pension benefits obligation totaling $40 million on January 1, Year 5.

EXHIBIT 9.12

Sun Company and Snow Company
Balance Sheets
January 1, Year 5
(amounts in millions)
(Problem 9.1)

	Sun Company	Snow Company
Cash	$ 100	$ 30
Accounts Receivable..........................	240	90
Fixed Assets (net)............................	1,000	360
Copyright..................................	—	—
Deferred Tax Asset...........................	40	—
Goodwill...................................	—	—
Total Assets	$1,380	$480
Accounts Payable and Accruals	$ 240	$ 80
Long-term Debt..............................	480	100
Deferred Tax Liability	160	—
Other Noncurrent Liabilities...................	120	—
Common Stock	320	100
Retained Earnings	60	200
Total Equities............................	$1,380	$480

Required

a. Prepare an analysis that determines the excess purchase price and shows the allocation of the excess to individual assets and liabilities under the purchase method.

b. Prepare a consolidated balance sheet for Sun and Snow on January 1, Year 5, under the purchase method. Show your supporting calculations for any amount that is not simply the sum of the amounts for Sun and Snow from their separate financial records.

9.2 EFFECT OF THE PURCHASE METHOD ON THE BALANCE SHEET AND THE INCOME STATEMENT. Condensed balance sheet data for Moran Corporation and Napolitano Corporation as of January 1, Year 8, follows (amounts in millions):

	Book Values		Market Values
	Moran (1)	Napolitano (2)	Napolitano (3)
Current Assets.	$1,200	$ 800	$ 900
Fixed Assets.	1,800	1,200	1,500
Goodwill.	—	—	
	$3,000	$2,000	$
Current Liabilities.	$1,000	$ 600	$ 600
Noncurrent Liabilities	1,400	1,000	1,000
Shareholders' Equity.	600	400	
	$3,000	$2,000	$

The shares of Moran Corporation currently sell on the market for $40 per share. Moran Corporation wishes to acquire all of the common stock of Napolitano Corporation as of January 1, Year 8. Moran Corporation will issue at par 10-percent, 20-year bonds for $1,200. It will use the proceeds to acquire all of the common stock of Napolitano Corporation. The firms will account for the transaction using the purchase method for financial reporting. This transaction is a taxable exchange to the shareholders of Napolitano Corporation but a nontaxable exchange for Napolitano Corporation.

Required

a. Prepare a pro forma balance sheet as of January 1, Year 8, accounting for the transaction using the purchase method of accounting. The income tax rate is 40 percent.

b. Before considering the effects of the acquisition, Moran Corporation projects net income of $300 and Napolitano Corporation projects net income of $200 for Year 8. Compute the amount of pro forma net income for Year 8 for the merged firm. Both firms use a LIFO cost-flow assumption for inventories and do not expect to liquidate a LIFO layer during Year 8. Depreciable assets have a 10-year remaining life as of January 1, Year 8. Both firms use the straight-line depreciation method. Assume that the test for goodwill impairment indicates that no impairment charge is necessary for Year 8.

9.3 EFFECT OF THE PURCHASE METHOD ON THE CONSOLIDATED BALANCE SHEET AND INCOME STATEMENT. AT&T launched a hostile takeover bid for NCR in Year 5, which was consummated in early Year 6. AT&T was successful in acquiring all of the common stock of NCR for $7,800 million of AT&T common stock. Financial statement data for these companies for Year 5, taken from their most recent annual reports prior to the transaction, reveal the following (amounts in millions):

	AT&T	NCR
December 31, Year 5 (Before Takeover)		
Total Assets	$43,775	$4,547
Total Liabilities	29,682	2,757
Total Shareholders' Equity	14,093	1,790
	$43,775	$4,547

Required

a. Assume that AT&T used the purchase method to account for its acquisition of NCR. Also assume that $2 billion of any excess purchase price relates to depreciable assets with a market value in excess of their book value. These depreciable assets have an average remaining life of 10 years at the date of acquisition. AT&T uses the straight-line depreciation method. The income tax rate is 34 percent. Prepare a consolidated balance sheet as of January 2, Year 6, the date in the first quarter in which the merger became effective.

b. Repeat part a, but assume that all of any excess purchase price relates to goodwill.

c. Compute the amount of consolidated net income for Year 6 following the assumptions in part a. Assume combined net income of the two companies for Year 6 is $2,880 million before taking into consideration any additional expenses that must be recorded as a result of using the purchase method to account for the merger.

d. Compute the amount of consolidated net income for Year 6 following the assumptions in part b. Assume combined net income of the two companies for Year 6 is $2,880 million before taking into consideration any additional expenses that must be recorded as a result of using the purchase method to account for the merger. Assume that the test for goodwill impairment indicates that an impairment charge of $1,050 million needs to be recognized in the fourth quarter of Year 6.

9.4 EFFECT OF THE PURCHASE METHOD ON THE BALANCE SHEET AND INCOME STATEMENT.   Ormond Co. acquired all of the outstanding common stock of Daytona Co. on January 1, Year 5. Ormond Co. gave shares of its common stock with a market value of $312 million in exchange for 100 percent of the Daytona Co. common stock. Daytona Co. will remain a legally separate entity after the exchange but Ormond Co. will prepare consolidated financial statements each period with Daytona Co. The transaction qualifies as a nontaxable exchange for income tax purposes. Exhibit 9.13 presents the balance sheets of Ormond Co. and Daytona Co. on January 1, Year 5, just prior to the acquisition. The income tax rate is 40 percent. The following information applies to Daytona Co.

EXHIBIT 9.13

Ormond Co. and Daytona Co.
Balance Sheets on January 1, Year 5
(amounts in millions)
(Problem 9.4)

	Ormond Co.	Daytona Co.
Cash	$ 25	$ 15
Accounts Receivable.	60	40
Fixed Assets (net).	250	170
Patent.	—	—
Deferred Tax Asset.	10	—
Goodwill	—	—
Total Assets	$345	$225
Accounts Payable & Accruals.	$ 60	$ 40
Long-term Debt.	120	60
Deferred Tax Liability	40	—
Other Noncurrent		
Liabilities.	30	—
Common Stock	80	50
Retained Earnings	15	75
Total Equities	$345	$225

1. The market value of Daytona Co.'s fixed assets exceeds their book value by $50 million.
2. Daytona Co. owns a patent with a market value of $40 million.
3. Daytona Co. is a defendant in a lawsuit that it expects to settle during Year 5 at a pre-tax cost of $25 million. The firm carries no insurance against such lawsuits. If permitted, Ormond Co. desires to establish an "acquisition reserve" for this lawsuit.
4. Daytona Co. has an unrecognized and unfunded retirement health care benefits obligation totaling $20 million on January 1, Year 5.

Required

a. Prepare a consolidated balance sheet for Ormond Co. and Daytona Co. on January 1, Year 5, assuming that Ormond Co. accounts for the acquisition using the purchase method.

b. Exhibit 9.14 presents income statements and balance sheets taken from the separate-company books at the end of Year 5 assuming that Ormond Co. had accounted for its acquisition of Daytona Co. using the *purchase* method. The following information applies to these companies.

EXHIBIT 9.14

Ormond Co. and Daytona Co.
Consolidation Worksheet for Year 5
(in millions)
(Problem 9.4)

	Ormond Co.	Daytona Co.
Income Statement for Year 5		
Sales	$600	$450
Equity in Earnings of Daytona Co.	18	—
Operating Expenses.	(550)	(395)
Interest Expense.	(10)	(5)
Loss on Lawsuit	—	(20)
Income Tax Expense	(23)	(12)
Net Income	$ 35	$ 18
Balance Sheet on December 31, Year 5		
Cash	$ 45	$ 25
Accounts Receivable.	80	50
Investment in Daytona Co.	327[a]	—
Fixed Assets	280	195
Patent	—	—
Deferred Tax Asset.	15	—
Goodwill	—	—
Total Assets	$747	$270
Accounts Payable and Accruals	$ 85	$ 55
Long-term Debt.	140	75
Deferred Tax Liability	50	—
Other Noncurrent Liabilities.	40	—
Common Stock	392	50
Retained Earnings	40	90
Total Equities	$747	$270

[a]$312 initial investment + $18 equity in earnings – $3 dividend received = $327

1. The fixed assets of Daytona Co. had an average remaining life of 5 years on January 1, Year 5. The firms use the straight-line depreciation method.
2. The patent of Daytona Co. had a remaining life of 10 years on January 1, Year 5.
3. Daytona Co. settled the lawsuit during Year 5 and expects no further liability.

4. Daytona Co. will amortize and fund its retirement health care benefits obligation over 20 years. It included $1 million in operating expenses during Year 5 related to amounts unrecognized and unfunded as of January 1, Year 5.

5. Assume that the test for goodwill impairment indicates that no impairment charge is necessary for Year 5.

Prepare a consolidated income statement for Year 5 and a consolidated balance sheet on December 31, Year 5, following the purchase method of accounting.

9.5 HISTORICAL PERSPECTIVE OF POOLING-OF-INTERESTS VERSUS PURCHASE METHOD. Bristol-Myers Company and Squibb Company, both pharmaceutical firms, agreed to merge as of October 1, Year 9. Bristol-Myers exchanged 234 million shares of its common stock for the outstanding shares of Squibb. The shares of Bristol-Myers sold for $55 per share on the merger date, resulting in a transaction with a market value of $12.87 billion. The firms were able to account for the merger using the pooling-of-interests method because it took place prior to the effective date of *Statement Nos. 141 and 142.*

Required

a. The most recent balance sheets of Bristol-Myers and Squibb prior to the merger reveal the following (amounts in millions):

	Bristol-Myers	Squibb
Assets	$5,190	$3,083
Liabilities	$1,643	$1,682
Shareholders' Equity	3,547	1,401
	$5,190	$3,083

Prepare a summary consolidated balance sheet such as those above for Bristol-Myers and Squibb assuming that the firms accounted for the merger using the (1) pooling-of-interests method, and (2) the purchase method. Assume that any excess of market value over book value relates to goodwill.

b. Net Income of Bristol-Myers and Squibb prior to and subsequent to the merger appear below (amounts in millions). The amounts for Year 9 exclude a special charge for merger-related expenses. Compute the amount of net income that Bristol-Myers Squibb would report for Year 9 using the pooling-of-interests method.

c. Compute the amount of net income that Bristol-Myers Squibb would report for Year 9 using the purchase method. For this part, assume that *Statement Nos. 141 and 142* were not effective for Year 9, and that the firm amortizes

	Pre-Merger			Post-Merger	
	Year 7	Year 8	First Nine Months of Year 9	Last Three Months of Year 9	Year 10
Bristol-Myers	$710	$829	$716	—	—
Squibb	$358	$425	$384	—	—
Combined	—	—	—	$340	$1,748

goodwill over 40 years. Note that net income under the purchase method excludes earnings of Squibb prior to the merger.

d. Repeat part c, but assume that *Statement Nos. 141 and 142* were effective for Year 9. Assume that the test for goodwill impairment indicates that no impairment charge is necessary for Year 9.

e. Repeat part d for Year 10 (that is, assume that *Statement Nos. 141 and 142* are effective for Year 9 *and* Year 10). But, in this part, assume that Bristol-Myers Squibb's test of goodwill impairment concludes that the goodwill is totally impaired and is written off in Year 10.

f. Complete the following schedule of net income, and comment on the reasons for the differences between the earnings reported using the two methods:

	Bristol-Myers Company		Bristol-Myers Squibb Company	
	Year 7	Year 8	Year 9 (part d)	Year 10 (part e)
Pooling of Interests Method . . .				
Purchase Method.				

g. Comment on the goodwill impairment write-down in Year 10 and how an analyst might view this charge when assessing the profitability of Bristol-Myers Squibb for the year.

9.6 APPLICATION OF *STATEMENT NO. 115* FOR INVESTMENTS IN MARKETABLE EQUITY SECURITIES. Suntrust Bank owns a large block of Coca-Cola Company (Coke) common stock that it has held for many years. Suntrust indicates in a note to its financial statements that all equity securities held by the bank, including its investment in Coke stock, are classified as *available for sale*. A recent annual report of Suntrust reports the following information for its Coke investment (in thousands):

Coke common stock investment, market value at December 31, Year 8	$1,791,894
Coke common stock investment, market value at December 31, Year 9	$1,242,862
Net income for Year 9	$ 565,476

Required

a. Calculate the effect of the change in the market value of Suntrust's investment in Coke common stock on Year 9's (1) net income, and (2) shareholders' equity for the bank. The income tax rate is 35 percent.

b. How does your answer to part a differ if Suntrust classified its investment in Coke's common stock as a *trading* security?

c. Does the value reported on Suntrust's balance sheet for the investment in Coke's stock differ depending on the firm's reason for holding the stock (that is, whether it is classified as *available-for-sale* versus *trading* by management)? Explain your answer.

9.7 EFFECT OF MARKET VALUE AND EQUITY METHODS ON BALANCE SHEET AND INCOME STATEMENT. Seagram acquired 11.7 percent of Time Warner on January 2, Year 3. Financial statement data for these firms at the end of Year 3 reveal the following (amounts in millions):

Seagram

Assets—December 31, Year 3

Investment in Time Warner at Market Value (11.7% ownership)	$ 1,769
All Other Assets	9,949
Total Assets.	$11,718
Liabilities.	$ 6,717

Shareholders' Equity

Unrealized Appreciation in Market Value of Time Warner (pre-tax).	13
All Other Shareholders' Equity	4,988
Total Liabilities and Shareholders' Equity	$11,718

Income Statement for Year 3

Dividend Revenue from Time Warner (net of taxes)	$ 8
All Other Revenue and Expenses (net of taxes).	371
Net Income.	$ 379

Time Warner—December 31, Year 3

Assets	$16,892
Liabilities	$15,522
Shareholders' Equity.	1,370
	$16,892
Net Loss for Year 3	$ (339)

Required

a. The total common shareholders' equity of Time Warner on January 1, Year 3, was $1,810. Assume that any excess purchase price relates to goodwill. Compute the amount of goodwill related to Seagram's investment in Time Warner on the date of acquisition.

b. Assume for this part that Seagram had used the equity method instead of the market value method to account for its investment in Time Warner during Year 3. Compute the maximum amount of net income that Seagram would report for Year 3. Assume that the test for goodwill impairment indicates that no impairment charge is necessary for Year 3. The income tax rate is 35 percent.

c. Compute the total assets for Seagram on December 31, Year 3, if it had used the equity method instead of the market value method throughout Year 3.

9.8 APPLYING THE EQUITY, PROPORTIONATE CONSOLIDATION, AND FULL CONSOLIDATION METHODS.   Mylan Laboratories (Mylan) is a leading firm in the generic pharmaceutical industry. Generic drugs have chemical compositions similar to ethical drugs but sell for a significantly lower price. Once the patent period ends on an ethical drug, generic drug companies break down the drug into its basic chemical elements. They then submit an application to the Food and Drug Administration to sell a generic equivalent of the ethical drug. The ability to sell generic drugs at a lower price results from lower research and development, marketing, and other costs.

Mylan owns 50 percent of the common stock of Somerset Pharmaceuticals (Somerset). Somerset sells an ethical drug for Parkinson's Disease. Exhibit 9.15 presents financial statement data for Mylan. Mylan accounts for its investment in Somerset using the equity method. Equity in earnings of Somerset includes Mylan's 50 percent share of Somerset's earnings minus amortization of intangible assets resulting from the acquisition of Somerset. Such intangible assets are amortized over 15 years. Amortization expense for intangibles totaled $924,000 in each of the Years 6 through 8. Additionally, Mylan charges Somerset a management services fee each year and includes it in the Equity in Earnings of Somerset account. Somerset records this fee as an expense in measuring earnings. Exhibit 9.16 presents financial statement data for Somerset.

EXHIBIT 9.15

Mylan Laboratories
Financial Statement Data
(amounts in thousands)
(Problem 9.8)

	Year 5	Year 6	Year 7	Year 8
Balance Sheet				
Current Assets.................................	$ 94,502	$120,014	$180,482	$209,572
Investment in and Advances to Somerset	18,045	13,674	14,844	17,964
Noncurrent Assets.............................	74,408	93,032	155,779	175,789
Total Assets....................................	$186,955	$226,720	$351,105	$403,325
Current Liabilities..............................	$ 12,931	$ 17,909	$ 26,482	$ 17,926
Noncurrent Liabilities...........................	6,493	5,359	7,348	5,430
Shareholders' Equity............................	167,531	203,452	317,275	379,969
Total Liabilities and Shareholders' Equity.........	$186,955	$226,720	$351,105	$403,325

	Year 6	Year 7	Year 8
Income Statement			
Sales..	$131,936	$211,964	$251,773
Costs and Expenses............................	(100,458)	(135,759)	(188,304)
Operating Income	$ 31,478	$ 76,205	$ 63,469
Equity in Earnings of Somerset	18,664	21,136	23,596
Income Before Taxes...........................	$ 50,142	$ 97,341	$ 87,065
Income Tax Expense...........................	(10,028)	(26,720)	(13,998)
Net Income...................................	$ 40,114	$ 70,621	$ 73,067

	Year 6	Year 7	Year 8
Cash Flow Statement			
Net Income....................................	$40,114	$70,621	$73,067
Equity in Earnings of Somerset	(18,664)	(21,136)	(23,596)
Cash Received from Somerset	23,035	19,966	20,676
Other Addbacks and Subtractions................	5,962	7,959	14,690
Changes in Working Capital Accounts..............	(4,519)	(9,073)	(49,204)
Cash Flow from Operations	$45,928	$68,337	$35,633

EXHIBIT 9.16

Somerset Pharmaceuticals
Financial Statement Data
(amounts in thousands)
(Problem 9.8)

	Year 5	Year 6	Year 7	Year 8
Balance Sheet				
Current Assets..............................	$22,801	$24,597	$30,409	$27,931
Noncurrent Assets...........................	2,802	2,791	2,670	6,043
Total Assets...........................	$25,603	$27,388	$33,079	$33,974
Current Liabilities...........................	$ 7,952	$15,413	$20,675	$14,918
Payable to Owners	7,274	1,490	1,796	1,002
Other Noncurrent Liabilities	3,302	975	808	642
Shareholders' Equity..........................	7,075	9,510	9,800	17,412
Total Liabilities and Shareholders' Equity.........	$25,603	$27,388	$33,079	$33,974

		Year 6	Year 7	Year 8
Income Statement				
Sales......................................		$93,513	$108,518	$111,970
Costs and Expenses...........................		(42,041)	(49,872)	(50,465)
Income Before Taxes		$51,472	$ 58,646	$ 61,505
Income Tax Expense		(18,806)	(21,789)	(19,547)
Net Income		$32,666	$ 36,857	$ 41,958

Required

a. Prepare an analysis of the changes in the shareholders' equity of Somerset for each of the Years 6 through 8.

b. Prepare an analysis of the changes in the Investment in and Advances to Somerset account on Mylan's books for each of the Years 6 through 8. Be sure to indicate the amounts for equity in earnings of Somerset, management fee, dividend received, and other cash payments received.

c. Does the equity method, proportionate consolidation method, or full consolidation method best reflect the operating relationships between Mylan and Somerset? Explain.

d. Prepare an income statement for Mylan and Somerset for Year 6, Year 7, and Year 8 using the proportionate consolidation method.

e. Repeat part d using the full consolidation method.

f. Compute the ratio of operating income before income taxes to sales for Year 6, Year 7, and Year 8 using the equity method, proportionate consolidation method, and full consolidation method.

g. Why do the ratios computed in part f differ across the three methods of accounting for the investment in Somerset?

h. Compute the effective tax rate (that is, income tax expense divided by income before income taxes) for Year 6, Year 7, and Year 8 using the equity method, proportionate consolidation method, and full consolidation method.

i. Why do the measures of the effective tax rate computed in part h differ across the three methods of accounting for the investment in Somerset?

9.9 CALCULATING THE TRANSLATION ADJUSTMENT UNDER THE ALL-CURRENT METHOD AND THE MONETARY/NONMONETARY METHOD. Foreign Sub is a wholly owned subsidiary of U.S. Domestic Corporation. U.S. Domestic Corporation acquired the subsidiary several years ago. The financial statements for Foreign Sub for Year 4 in its own currency appear in Exhibit 9.17.

The exchange rates between the U.S. dollar and the foreign currency of the subsidiary were:

December 31, Year 3:	$10:1FC
Average–Year 4:	$8:1FC
December 31, Year 4:	$6:1FC

On January 1, Year 4, Foreign Sub issued FC100 of long-term debt and FC100 of common stock in the acquisition of land costing FC200. Operating activities occurred evenly over the year.

Required

a. Assume that the currency of Foreign Sub is the functional currency. Compute the change in the cumulative translation adjustment for Year 4. Indicate whether the change increases or decreases shareholders' equity.

b. Assume that the U.S. dollar is the functional currency. Compute the amount of the translation gain or loss for Year 4. Indicate whether the amount is a gain or loss.

EXHIBIT 9.17

Foreign Sub
Financial Statement Data
(Problem 9.9)

	December 31			
	Year 3		Year 4	
Cash	FC	100	FC	150
Accounts Receivable....................		300		350
Inventories		350		400
Land		500		700
	FC	1,250	FC	1,600
Accounts Payable	FC	150	FC	250
Long-term Debt........................		200		300
Common Stock		500		600
Retained Earnings		400		450
	FC	1,250	FC	1,600

	For Year 4	
Sales..	FC	4,000
Cost of Goods Sold....................................		(3,200)
Selling and Administrative		(400)
Income Taxes.......................................		(160)
Net Income	FC	240
Dividend Declared and Paid on December 31		(190)
Increase in Retained Earnings...........................	FC	50

9.10 TRANSLATING THE FINANCIAL STATEMENTS OF A FOREIGN SUBSIDIARY; COMPARISON OF TRANSLATION METHODS. Stebbins Corporation established a wholly owned Canadian subsidiary on January 1, Year 6, by contributing US$500,000 for all of the subsidiary's common stock. The exchange rate on that date was C$1:US$.90 (that is, one Canadian dollar equaled 90 U.S. cents). The Canadian subsidiary invested C$500,000 in a building with an expected life of 20 years and rented it to various tenants for the year. The average exchange rate during Year 6 was C$1:US$.85 and the exchange rate on December 31, Year 6, was C$1:US$.80. Exhibit 9.18 shows the amounts taken from the books of the Canadian subsidiary at the end of Year 6 measured in Canadian dollars.

EXHIBIT 9.18

Canadian Subsidiary
Financial Statements
Year 6
(Problem 9.10)

Balance Sheet: December 31, Year 6

Assets

Cash	C$ 77,555
Rent Receivable...............................	25,000
Building (net)................................	475,000
	C$577,555

Liabilities and Equity

Accounts Payable	6,000
Salaries Payable..............................	4,000
Common Stock..................................	555,555
Retained Earnings.............................	12,000
	C$577,555

Income Statement for Year 6

Rent Revenue	C$125,000
Operating Expenses	(28,000)
Depreciation Expense..........................	(25,000)
Translation Exchange Loss	—
Net Income...................................	C$ 72,000

Retained Earnings Statement for Year 6

Balance, January 1, Year 6....................	C$ —
Net Income...................................	72,000
Dividends	(60,000)
Balance, December 31, Year 6.................	C$ 12,000

Required

a. Prepare a balance sheet, income statement, and retained earnings statement for the Canadian subsidiary for Year 6 in U.S. dollars assuming that the Canadian dollar is the functional currency. Include a separate schedule showing the computation of the translation adjustment account.

b. Repeat question a but assume that the U.S. dollar is the functional currency. Include a separate schedule showing the computation of the translation gain or loss.

c. Why is the sign of the translation adjustment for Year 6 under the all-current translation method and the translation gain or loss for Year 6 under the monetary/nonmonetary translation method the same? Why do their amounts differ?

d. Assuming that the firm could justify either translation method, which method would the management of Stebbins Corporation likely prefer for Year 6? Why?

9.11 TRANSLATING THE FINANCIAL STATEMENTS OF A FOREIGN SUBSIDIARY; SECOND YEAR OF OPERATIONS. Refer to Problem 9.10 for Stebbins Corporation for Year 6, its first year of operations. Exhibit 9.19 shows the amounts for the Canadian subsidiary for Year 7. The average exchange rate during

---

EXHIBIT 9.19

Canadian Subsidiary
Financial Statements
Year 7
(Problem 9.11)

Balance Sheet:
Assets

Cash	C$116,555
Rent Receivable	30,000
Building (net)	450,000
	C$596,555

Liabilities and Equity

Accounts Payable.	7,500
Salaries Payable	5,500
Common Stock	555,555
Retained Earnings	28,000
	C$596,555

Income Statement

Rent Revenue.	C$150,000
Operating Expenses.	(34,000)
Depreciation Expense	(25,000)
Translation Exchange Gain	—
Net Income	C$ 91,000

Retained Earnings Statement

Balance, January 1, Year 7	C$ 12,000
Net Income	91,000
Dividends.	(75,000)
Balance, December 31, Year 7	C$ 28,000

Year 7 was C$1:US$.82 and the exchange rate on December 31, Year 7, was C$1:US$.84. The Canadian subsidiary declared and paid dividends on December 31, Year 7.

Required

a. Prepare a balance sheet, income statement, and retained earnings statement for the Canadian subsidiary for Year 7 in U.S. dollars assuming that the Canadian dollar is the functional currency. Include a separate schedule showing the computation of the translation adjustment for Year 7 and the change in the translation adjustment account.

b. Repeat part a but assume that the U.S. dollar is the functional currency. Include a separate schedule showing the computation of the translation gain or loss.

c. Why is the sign of the translation adjustment for Year 7 under the all current translation method and the translation gain or loss under the monetary/nonmonetary translation method the same? Why do their amounts differ?

d. Assuming that the firm could justify either translation method, which method would the management of Stebbins Corporation likely prefer for Year 7? Why?

9.12 INTERPRETING FOREIGN CURRENCY TRANSLATION DISCLOSURES. Hewlett-Packard (HP) and Sun Microsystems (Sun) derive similar proportions of their sales from the United States, Europe, Japan and other countries. Recent annual reports of the two companies indicate that HP uses the U.S. dollar as its functional currency, whereas Sun uses the currency of each foreign operation as its functional currency.

Required

a. The shareholders' equity section of the balance sheet of Sun reveals the following (amounts in thousands):

	June 30	
	Year 8	Year 9
Common Stock..........................	$1,089,550	$1,164,421
Retained Earnings.......................	1,205,483	1,662,355
Cumulative Translation Adjustment.........	33,629	21,620
Treasury Stock..........................	(206,067)	(596,910)
Total	$2,122,595	$2,251,486

Did the U.S. dollar likely increase or decrease in value on average during the year ended June 30, Year 9, against the foreign currencies of the countries in which Sun conducts its operations? Explain.

b. Sun uses a FIFO cost-flow assumption for inventories and cost of goods sold. Would the gross margin in U.S. dollars (that is, sales minus cost of goods sold) of Sun likely have increased or decreased for the year ended June 30, Year 9, if it had used the U.S. dollar as its functional currency instead of the currency of its foreign operations? Explain.

c. HP also uses a FIFO cost-flow assumption for inventories and cost of goods sold. Both companies maintain net monetary asset positions in their foreign operations. HP generated a pre-tax return from foreign operations of 12.3 percent for the year ended June 30, Year 9, whereas Sun generated a pre-tax return of 5.1 percent. Would the profit margin of HP likely increase or decrease if it had used the currency of its foreign units as the functional currency? Explain.

9.13 IDENTIFYING THE FUNCTIONAL CURRENCY.   Electronic Computer Systems (ECS) designs, manufactures, sells, and services networked computer systems, associated peripheral equipment, and related network, communications, and software products.

Exhibit 9.20 presents segment geographical data. ECS conducts sales and marketing operations outside the United States principally through sales subsidiaries in Canada, Europe, Central and South America, and the Far East, by direct sales from the parent corporation, and through various representative and distributorship arrangements. The Company's international manufacturing operations include plants in Canada, the Far East, and Europe. These manufacturing plants sell their output to the Company's sales subsidiaries, the parent corporation, or other manufacturing plants for further processing.

ECS accounts for intercompany transfers between geographic areas at prices representative of unaffiliated party transactions.

Sales to unaffiliated customers outside the United States, including U.S. export sales, were $5,729,879,000 for Year 5, $4,412,527,000 for Year 4, and $3,179,143,000 for Year 3; which represented 50 percent, 47 percent, and 42 percent, respectively, of total operating revenues. The international subsidiaries have reinvested substantially all of their earnings to support operations. These accumulated retained earnings, before elimination of intercompany transactions, aggregated $2,793,239,000 at the end of Year 5, $2,070,337,000 at the end of Year 4, and $1,473,081,000 at the end of Year 3.

The company enters into forward exchange contracts to reduce the impact of foreign currency fluctuations on operations and the asset and liability positions of foreign subsidiaries. The gains and losses on these contracts increase or decrease net income in the same period as the related revenues and expenses, and for assets and liabilities, in the period in which the exchange rate changes.

Required

Discuss whether ECS should use the U.S. dollar or the currencies of its foreign subsidiaries as its functional currency.

EXHIBIT 9.20

**Electronic Computer Systems
Geographical Segment Data
(amounts in thousands)
(Problem 9.13)**

	Year 3	Year 4	Year 5
Revenues			
United States customers	$4,472,195	$5,016,606	$ 5,810,598
Intercompany.....................................	1,354,339	1,921,043	2,017,928
Total	$5,826,534	$6,937,649	$ 7,828,526
Europe customers	2,259,743	3,252,482	4,221,631
Intercompany.....................................	82,649	114,582	137,669
Total	$2,342,392	$3,367,064	$ 4,359,300
Canada, Far East, Americas customers	858,419	1,120,356	1,443,217
Intercompany.....................................	577,934	659,204	912,786
Total	$1,436,353	$1,779,560	$ 2,356,003
Eliminations.....................................	(2,014,922)	(2,694,829)	(3,068,383)
Net revenue	$7,590,357	$9,389,444	$11,475,446
Income			
United States	$ 342,657	$ 758,795	$ 512,754
Europe	405,636	634,543	770,135
Canada, Far East, Americas.....................	207,187	278,359	390,787
Eliminations.....................................	(126,771)	(59,690)	(38,676)
Operating income	828,709	1,612,007	1,635,000
Interest income	116,899	122,149	143,665
Interest expense.................................	(88,079)	(45,203)	(37,820)
Income before income taxes	$ 857,529	$1,688,953	$ 1,740,845
Assets			
United States	$3,911,491	$4,627,838	$ 5,245,439
Europe	1,817,584	2,246,333	3,093,818
Canada, Far East, Americas.....................	815,067	843,067	1,293,906
Corporate assets (temporary cash investments).........	2,035,557	1,979,470	2,057,528
Eliminations.....................................	(1,406,373)	(1,289,322)	(1,579,135)
Total assets.....................................	$7,173,326	$8,407,386	$10,111,556

9.14 STOCK-BASED COMPENSATION. Exhibit 9.21 includes a footnote excerpt from the annual report of John Deere & Company for Year 11. Deere manufactures tractors and other equipment, primarily for use by farmers. The note describes the

---

EXHIBIT 9.21

John Deere & Company
Stock Option Disclosures
(amounts in millions)
(Problem 9.14)

Note —Stock Options (partial footnote from Year 11 annual report)

Deere issues stock options and restricted stock to key employees under plans approved by stockholders. Restricted stock is also issued to nonemployee directors under a plan approved by stockholders. Options are generally awarded with the exercise price equal to the market price and become exercisable in one to three years after grant. Certain other options have been awarded with the exercise prices greater than the market price and become exercisable in one year or longer after grant, depending on the achievement of company performance goals. Options generally expire 10 years after the date of grant. According to these plans at October 31, Year 11, the company is authorized to grant an additional 10.0 million shares related to stock options or restricted stock.

The company has retained the intrinsic value method of accounting for its plans in accordance with APB Opinion No. 25, and no compensation expense for stock options was recognized under this method. For disclosure purposes only under FASB *Statement No. 123*, Accounting for Stock Based Compensation, the Black-Scholes option pricing model was used to calculate the "fair values" of stock options on the date the options were awarded. Based on this model, the weighted-average fair values of stock options awarded during Year 11, Year 10, and Year 9, with the exercise price equal to the market price, were $12.06, $12.06, and $7.96 per option, respectively. Those awarded during Year 9 with the exercise price greater than the market price had a fair value of $4.26 per option.

Pro forma net income and earnings per share, as if the fair value method in FASB *Statement No. 123* had been used to account for stock-based compensation, and the assumptions used, are as follows:

	Year 11	Year 10	Year 9
Net income (loss) (in millions):			
As reported	$(64)	$ 486	$ 239
Pro forma	$(96)	$ 446	$ 216
Net income (loss) per share:			
As reported—basic	$(.27)	$2.07	$1.03
Pro forma—basic	$(.41)	$1.91	$ .93
As reported—diluted	$(.27)	$2.06	$1.02
Pro forma—diluted	$(.41)	$1.89	$ .92
Black-Scholes assumptions*			
Risk-free interest rate	5.4%	6.2%	4.6%
Dividend yield	2.1%	2.1%	2.7%
Stock volatility	33.2%	30.4%	27.9%
Expected option life (years)	4.1	4.5	5.0

---

*Weighted-averages

stock options and restricted stock Deere offers to key employees under plans approved by stockholders. Note that the disclosure requirements of *Statement No. 148* were not in effect in Year 11.

Required

Review Exhibit 9.21 and answer the following questions:
a. Deere uses the intrinsic (*Opinion No. 25*) method of accounting for its stock option plans related to stock-based compensation. Speculate why Deere chooses to use the intrinsic method instead of the fair value method for accounting for its stock-based compensation.
b. Deere states in the footnote excerpt that it recognized no compensation expense for stock options in any of the years reported by the firm. Why is that the case; that is, what characteristics of the options offered to employees must be present (which, in fact, Deere discloses in the footnote excerpt) so that it recognized no compensation expense using the intrinsic method?
c. Under what circumstances does a firm recognize stock-based compensation using the intrinsic method? Is this a very likely set of circumstances?

9.15 STOCK-BASED COMPENSATION. Exhibit 9.22 includes a footnote excerpt from the annual report of Nike, Inc. for Year 11. Nike is the world's largest seller of athletic footwear and athletic apparel. The period covered in the note is the same as that covered in Exhibit 9.21 for John Deere & Company (Problem 9.14). Note that the disclosure requirements of *Statement No. 148* were not in effect in Year 11.

EXHIBIT 9.22

Nike, Inc.
Common Stock and Stock Option Disclosures
(amounts in millions)
(Problem 9.15)

Note —Common Stock and Stock Options (partial footnote from Year 11 annual report)

Statement of Financial Accounting Standards No.123, "Accounting for Stock-Based Compensation," (FAS 123) defines a fair value method of accounting for employee stock compensation and encourages, but does not require, all entities to adopt that method of accounting. Entities electing not to adopt the fair value method of accounting must make pro forma disclosures of net income and earnings per share, as if the fair value based method of accounting defined in this statement had been applied.

The company has elected not to adopt the fair value method; however, as required by *FAS 123*, the company has computed for pro forma disclosure purposes, the fair value of options granted during the years ended May 31, Year 11, Year 10, and Year 9, using the Black-Scholes option pricing model. The weighted average assumptions used for stock option grants for each of these years were a dividend yield of 1%; expected volatility of the market price of the company's common stock of 39%, 37%, and 34%, for the years ended May 31, Year 11, Year 10, and Year 9, respectively; a weighted-average expected life of the options of approximately five years; and interest rates of 5.4% for the year ended May 31, Year 11, 5.8%, 6.2%, and 6.6%, for the year ended May 31, Year 10, and 5.5% and 4.9% for the year ended May 31,Year 9. These interest rates are reflective of option grant dates throughout the year.

Exhibit 9.22—continued

Options were assumed to be exercised over the five-year expected life for purposes of this valuation. Adjustments for forfeitures are made as they occur. For the years ended May 31, Year 11, Year 10, and Year 9, the total value of the options granted, for which no previous expense has been recognized, was computed as approximately $5.0 million, $129.8 million, and $61.6 million, respectively, which would be amortized on a straight-line basis over the vesting period of the options. The weighted average fair value per share of the options granted in the years ended May 31, Year 11, Year 10, and Year 9 are $17.27, $15.81, and $17.33, respectively.

If the company had accounted for these stock options issued to employees in accordance with *FAS 123*, the company's pro forma net income and pro forma earnings per share (EPS) would have been reported as follows:

	Year 11			Year 10			Year 9		
	Net Income	Diluted EPS	Basic EPS	Net Income	Diluted EPS	Basic EPS	Net Income	Diluted EPS	Basic EPS
(in millions, except per share data)									
As Reported.........	$589.7	$2.16	$2.18	$579.1	$2.07	$2.10	$451.4	$1.57	$1.59
Pro Forma	$559.0	$2.05	$2.07	$551.2	$1.97	$2.00	$434.3	$1.51	$1.53

The pro forma effects of applying *FAS 123* may not be representative of the effects on reported net income and earnings per share for future years since options vest over several years and additional awards are made each year.

Required

Review Exhibit 9.21 (Deere) and Exhibit 9.22 (Nike) and answer the following questions:

a. What method does Nike use for accounting for its stock option plans related to stock-based compensation? Speculate on why Nike chose this method of accounting. Is this the preferred method of accounting for stock options?

b. Both Deere and Nike provide pro forma earnings per share information using the Black-Scholes options pricing model for calculating stock-based compensation expense, as required by *Statement No. 123*. Both firms also disclose the key assumptions made in applying the Black-Scholes options pricing model.

(1) Prepare a chart that compares the firms' reported earnings per share (diluted) with pro forma earnings per share (diluted) for both Year 10 and 11. Also include in the chart the percentage decrease in reported earnings per share (diluted) when stock-based compensation is taken into consideration.

(2) Speculate on the directional effects of the key assumptions made in applying the Black-Scholes options pricing model. That is, which assumptions will result in a higher fair value for stock options and which will result in a lower fair value, and why?

c. Which ratio do you believe is more relevant to the analyst: (1) reported earnings per share or (2) pro forma earnings per share taking into consideration stock-based compensation? Why?

9.16 STOCK-BASED COMPENSATION PLANS AND VESTING.   Exhibit 9.21
and Exhibit 9.22 provide footnote excerpts to the annual reports of John Deere and
Nike that discuss the firm's stock option plans. Each firm uses options extensively to
reward employees for their performance.

Required

Review Exhibit 9.21 and Exhibit 9.22 and answer the following questions:

a. Explain the concept of vesting and discuss why firms typically include a vesting feature in the stock-based compensation plans that they offer to their
   employees.

b. What are the vesting characteristics of the two plans discussed in the exhibits
   and what effect do they have on stock-based compensation expense using the
   fair value method?

c. Discuss how the vesting characteristic in a stock-based compensation plan is
   treated in the year of a switch in each of the transition options available to firms
   that switch from the intrinsic (*Opinion No. 25*) method to the fair value method.

9.17 INTERPRETING STOCK OPTION DISCLOSURES.   Exhibit 9.23 summa-
rizes the information disclosed by the General Electric Company regarding its stock
option plans for Year 9 to Year 11. Assume an income tax rate of 35 percent.

EXHIBIT 9.23

General Electric Company
Stock Option Disclosures
(Problem 9.17)

	Year 11	Year 10	Year 9
Number of Options Granted*	60.946	46.278	51.281
Average Option Price per Share	$ 41.15	$ 47.84	$ 37.93
Average Market Price at Time of Grant	$ 41.15	$ 47.84	$ 37.93
Fair Value of Option Granted per Share	$ 12.15	$ 15.76	$ 11.23
Option Valuation Assumptions:			
Discount Rate	4.9%	6.4%	5.8%
Volatility	30.5%	27.1%	23.7%
Dividend Yield	1.6%	1.2%	1.3%
Time to Exercise in Years	6.0	6.4	6.5
Net Income Reported*	$13,684	$12,735	$10,717
Pro Forma Net Income Reflecting			
Stock Option Expense (net of tax)*	$13,388	$12,502	$10,572
Number of Options Exercised*	31.801	44.758	61.679
Average Option Exercise Price	$ 10.04	$ 8.82	$ 7.82
Average Market Price at Time of Exercise	$ 43.95	$ 53.00	$ 39.72

* Amounts in millions.

Required

a. Compute the total fair value of options granted for Year 9, Year 10, and Year 11.

b. Compute the difference between reported net income and pro forma net income each year.

c. Why do the amounts in part a differ from the amounts in part b?

d. What are the likely reasons that the fair value of options granted per share increased between Year 9 and Year 10?

e. What are the likely reasons that the fair value of options granted per share decreased between Year 10 and Year 11?

f. Compute the amount that GE received from the exercise of stock options each year versus the amount it would have received if it had issued the same number of shares on the market.

g. Compute a pro forma net income for each year assuming that stock option expense equaled the difference between the market price and the exercise price of options exercised.

h. Discuss the strengths and weaknesses of each of the following approaches to recognizing the cost of stock options: (1) no expense as long as the option price equals the market price on the date stock options are granted, (2) expense in the year of the grant equal to value of options granted, and (3) expense in the year of exercise equal to the benefit realized by employees from purchasing shares for less than market value.

CASE 9.1

FISHER CORPORATION*

Effective January 1, Year 12, Weston Corporation (Weston) and Fisher Corporation (Fisher) will merge their respective companies. Under the terms of the merger agreement, Weston will acquire all of the outstanding common shares of Fisher. Fisher will remain a legally separate entity. However, Weston will consolidate its financial statements with those of Fisher at the end of each accounting period. According to the merger agreement, Weston can structure the transaction under either of the following two alternatives:

ALTERNATIVE A

Weston would acquire all of the outstanding common shares of Fisher for $58,500,000 in cash. To obtain the necessary cash, Weston would issue $59 million of 10 percent, 20-year bonds on the open market. For financial reporting purposes, Weston would account for the merger using the purchase method. For tax purposes, the merger transaction is a taxable event to Fisher's shareholders. They would pay

*The authors gratefully acknowledge the assistance of Gary M. Cypres in the preparation of this case.

income taxes at capital gains rates on any difference between the amount received and the tax basis of their shares. The transaction would not directly involve Fisher Corporation. The tax basis of Fisher's net assets, therefore, remains the same after the acquisition as before the acquisition. The firms would choose not to do a Section 338 election to obtain a step-up in tax basis of the net assets in this case.

ALTERNATIVE B

Weston would acquire all of the outstanding common shares of Fisher for the issuance of 1,800,000 shares of a new Weston preferred stock. The preferred stock would carry an annual dividend of $2 per share and would be convertible into .75 shares of Weston common stock at any time. The exchange ratio would be one share of the new preferred stock for each outstanding common share of Fisher. An independent investment banking firm has valued the preferred shares at $50 million. For financial reporting purposes, Weston would account for the merger using the purchase method. For tax purposes, the merger transaction is a nontaxable event to Fisher's shareholders. The tax basis of Fisher's net assets carry over after the acquisition. Summarizing the alternatives:

	Alternative A	Alternative B
Type of Consideration Given	Cash	Convertible Preferred Stock
Value of Consideration Given	$58,500,000	$50,000,000
Financial Reporting Method	Purchase	Purchase
Tax Reporting Method—Shareholders	Taxable	Nontaxable
Tax Reporting Method—Fisher	Nontaxable	Nontaxable

FINANCIAL STATEMENTS FOR WESTON

For the five years ended December 31, Year 11 (See Exhibit 9.24), the Weston Company's revenues, net income, and earnings per share had each grown at an average compounded annual rate of 23 percent. Growth in Year 11 exceeded the average in all categories. These five-year growth rates include the recession year of Year 7 when the company's net income increased by 14 percent despite a sales decline of 5 percent. Weston accomplished this growth rate both from operations and from aggressive corporate acquisitions. The company intends to continue making acquisitions in the future.

Although the company has exhibited strong financial growth, it has consistently maintained a conservative balance sheet (see Exhibit 9.25). The company's debt has steadily declined from 29 percent of long-term capital in Year 8, to 24 percent in Year 11 (see Exhibit 9.26). Dividends per share have ranged between 27 percent and 32 percent of earnings per share in each of the last five years.

The company currently projects 25 percent growth in net income and earnings per share in Year 12, with revenues increasing by 16 percent.

EXHIBIT 9.24

Weston Corporation
Income Statements
For the Years Ended December 31,
(amounts in thousands, except per share amounts)
(Case 9.1)

	Year 7	Year 8	Year 9	Year 10	Year 11	Estimated Year 12*
Sales	$233,000	$321,300	$306,500	$361,500	$482,100	$560,000
Cost & Expenses						
Cost of Sales	(180,700)	(251,100)	(232,800)	(273,900)	(360,600)	(415,700)
Selling & Admin...........	(36,500)	(51,600)	(51,900)	(58,300)	(86,921)	(105,632)
Operating Income	$ 15,800	$ 18,600	$ 21,800	$ 29,300	$ 34,579	$ 38,668
Equity in net income of						
nonconsolidated entities.....	2,300	3,800	3,600	2,600	3,200	4,000
Other income (expense)	(1,300)	(2,100)	(900)	(400)	(1,600)	(1,000)
Income before taxes	$ 16,800	$ 20,300	$ 24,500	$ 31,500	$ 36,179	$ 41,668
Provision for income taxes	(6,800)	(7,500)	(9,900)	(14,000)	(14,179)	(14,584)
Net income	$ 10,000	$ 12,800	$ 14,600	$ 17,500	$ 22,000	$ 27,084
Earnings per share	$ 1.25	$ 1.60	$ 1.83	$ 2.22	$ 2.82	$ 3.47
Dividends per share of						
common stock	$ .40	$ .40	$ .45	$ .63	$ .88	$ 1.20
Average number of shares of						
common stock outstanding ..	8,000	8,000	8,000	7,900	7,800	7,800

*Before consideration of the merger with Fisher.

EXHIBIT 9.25

Weston Corporation
Consolidated Balance Sheets
December 31,
(amounts in thousands)
(Case 9.1)

	Year 10	Year 11	Estimated Year 12*
Assets			
Cash	$ 28,000	$ 28,000	$ 32,000
Accounts Receivable...........................	84,000	90,000	100,000
Inventory	58,000	71,000	82,000
Other	4,000	13,000	13,000
Total Current Assets	$174,000	$202,000	$227,000
Property, Plant, and Equipment	$ 96,000	$116,000	$131,000
Less Accumulated Depreciation......................	(29,000)	(38,000)	(48,000)
Net..	$ 67,000	$ 78,000	$ 83,000
Investment in Nonconsolidated Entities................	42,000	45,000	47,000
Goodwill...	8,400	8,000	7,800
Other Assets	6,000	7,000	7,200
Total Assets	$297,400	$340,000	$372,000
Liabilities			
Current Portion Long-term Debt	$ 400	$ 2,000	$ —
Accounts Payable	23,000	30,000	40,000
Accrued Liabilities and Advances	67,000	78,000	91,000
Income Taxes	12,000	21,000	14,000
Total Current Liabilities	$102,400	$131,000	$145,000
Long-term Debt...................................	48,000	48,000	48,000
Deferred Taxes	9,000	10,000	10,000
Total Liabilities	$159,400	$189,000	$203,000
Shareholders' Equity			
Common Stock	$ 11,000	$ 11,000	$ 11,000
Capital Surplus...................................	55,000	55,000	55,000
Retained Earnings	72,000	85,000	103,000
Total Shareholders' Equity	$138,000	$151,000	$169,000
Total Liabilities and Shareholders' Equity	$297,400	$340,000	$372,000

*Before consideration of the merger with Fisher.

	EXHIBIT 9.26				

Weston Corporation
Key Financial Highlights
Year 8–Year 12
(Case 9.1)

	Year 8	Year 9	Year 10	Year 11	Estimated Year 12*
Earnings per Share	$ 1.60	$ 1.83	$ 2.22	$ 2.82	$ 3.53
Dividends per Share	$ .40	$ .45	$ .63	$ .88	$ 1.20
Current Ratio	1.8	2.0	1.7	1.5	1.6
Long-term Debt as a Percentage of Long-term Capital	28.9%	26.5%	25.8%	24.1%	22.1%
Return on Average Common Shareholders' Equity	12.4%	12.9%	13.6%	15.2%	16.9%
Book Value per Share	$ 13.50	$ 14.88	$ 17.69	$ 19.36	$ 21.68
Tangible Net Worth ($000).	$99,300	$111,600	$129,600	$143,000	$161,200
Times Interest Earned.	5.7	7.8	9.8	10.9	10.0

*Before consideration of the merger with Fisher.

FINANCIAL STATEMENTS FOR FISHER CORPORATION

Exhibit 9.27 presents comparative income statements and Exhibit 9.28 presents comparative balance sheets for Fisher. Fisher's management estimates that revenues will remain approximately flat between Year 11 and Year 12, but that Fisher's net income for Year 12 will decline to $2,500,000, compared with $6,602,000 in Year 11. This decrease in net income results from a $1,000,000 increase in labor costs in Year 12, a $3,000,000 loss in the construction of a crystallization system, a $1,000,000 expenditure to meet expected OSHA requirements, and a $1,000,000 expenditure to relocate one of its product lines to a new plant facility. Fisher has 1,800,000 shares outstanding on January 1, Year 12. It currently pays a dividend of $1.22 per share.

EXHIBIT 9.27

Fisher Corporation
Income Statement
(amounts in thousands)
(Case 9.1)

	Year 7	Year 8	Year 9	Year 10	Year 11	Estimated Year 12
Sales	$41,428	$53,541	$76,328	$109,373	$102,699	$100,000
Other Revenue and Gains	0	41	0	0	211	200
Cost of Goods Sold	(33,269)	(43,142)	(60,000)	(85,364)	(80,260)	(85,600)
Sell. & Admin. Expense	(6,175)	(7,215)	(9,325)	(13,416)	(12,090)	(10,820)
Other Expenses and Losses	(2)	0	(11)	(31)	(1)	—
Earnings before Interest and Taxes	$ 1,982	$ 3,225	$ 6,992	$ 10,562	$ 10,559	$ 3,780
Interest Expense.	(43)	(21)	(284)	(276)	(13)	—
Income Tax Expense	(894)	(1,471)	(2,992)	(3,703)	(3,944)	(1,323)
Net Income.	$ 1,045	$ 1,733	$ 3,716	$ 6,583	$ 6,602	$ 2,457

EXHIBIT 9.28

Fisher Corporation
Balance Sheet
(amounts in thousands)
(Case 9.1)

	Year 6	Year 7	Year 8	Year 9	Year 10	Year 11
Assets						
Cash	$ 955	$ 961	$ 865	$ 1,247	$ 1,540	$ 3,100
Marketable Securities.	0	0	0	0	0	2,900
Accounts/Notes Receivable	6,545	7,295	9,718	13,307	18,759	15,000
Inventories	7,298	8,686	12,797	20,426	18,559	18,000
Total Current Assets	$14,798	$16,942	$23,380	$34,980	$38,858	$39,000
Property, Plant, and Equipment.	12,216	12,445	13,126	13,792	14,903	15,000
Less: Accum. Depreciation.	(7,846)	(8,236)	(8,558)	(8,988)	(9,258)	(9,000)
Other Assets.	470	420	400	299	343	1,000
Total Assets	$19,638	$21,571	$28,348	$40,083	$44,846	$46,000
Liabilities						
Accounts Payable—Trade	$ 2,894	$ 4,122	$ 6,496	$ 7,889	$ 6,779	$ 7,000
Notes Payable—Non-trade	0	0	700	3,500	0	0
Current Part Long-term Debt	170	170	170	170	170	0
Other Current Liabilities.	550	1,022	3,888	8,624	12,879	8,000
Total Current Liabilities	$ 3,614	$ 5,314	$11,254	$20,183	$19,828	$15,000
Long-term Debt.	680	510	340	170	0	0
Deferred Taxes	0	0	5	228	357	1,000
Total Liabilities	$ 4,294	$ 5,824	$11,599	$20,581	$20,185	$16,000

Exhibit 9.28—continued	Year 6	Year 7	Year 8	Year 9	Year 10	Year 11
Shareholders' Equity						
Preferred Stock.....................	$ 0	$ 0	$ 0	$ 0	$ 0	$ 0
Common Stock	2,927	2,927	2,927	5,855	7,303	9,000
Additional Paid-in Capital...........	5,075	5,075	5,075	5,075	5,061	5,000
Retained Earnings	7,342	7,772	8,774	8,599	12,297	16,000
Treasury Stock	0	−27	−27	−27	0	0
Total Shareholders' Equity	$15,344	$15,747	$16,749	$19,502	$24,661	$30,000
Total Liabilities and Shareholders' Equity...........	$19,638	$21,571	$28,348	$40,083	$44,846	$46,000

ALLOCATION OF PURCHASE PRICE

Exhibit 9.29 shows the calculation of the purchase price and the allocation of any excess cost under each of the two alternatives for structuring the acquisition of Fisher. Notes to the calculations are as follows (amounts in thousands):

Note 1: Acquisition costs consist of printing, legal, auditing, and finder's fees, and increase the cost of the shares of Fisher acquired.

Note 2: The book value of certain long-term contracts of Fisher (relating to a crystallization system) exceeds their market value by $3,000. Fisher expects to complete these contracts during Year 12. Weston establishes a "reserve" for this loss as of the date of acquisition and includes it among current liabilities. When Fisher completes the contracts in Year 12, the consolidated entity will charge the actual loss against the "reserve" for financial reporting. It will then claim a deduction for the loss in calculating taxable income.

Note 3: The market value of Fisher's property, plant, and equipment on January 1, Year 12, is $23,000. Their book value and tax basis is $6,000. Thus, Weston allocates $17,000 (= 23,000 − $6,000) of the excess cost to property, plant, and equipment. The consolidated entity will depreciate the excess using the straight-line method over 10 years for financial reporting. It cannot depreciate the excess for tax purposes.

Note 4: Fisher has an unfunded pension obligation of $5,000 on January 1, Year 12. Fisher had planned to straight-line amortize this obligation over 20 years from January 1, Year 12. Weston allocates a portion of the purchase price to this obligation on the date of the acquisition.

Note 5: Fisher expects to incur $1,000 of costs during Year 12 on its facilities to comply with various health and safety provisions of OSHA. Weston allocates a portion of the purchase price to recognize this expected cost.

Note 6: Weston intends to relocate the manufacture of certain product lines of Fisher to a new plant facility during Year 12. The estimated costs of relocation are $1,000. Weston allocates a portion of the purchase price to recognize this expected cost.

Note 7: *Statement No. 109* requires firms to provide deferred taxes for differences between the book basis and tax basis of assets and liabilities. Weston allocates the

EXHIBIT 9.29

**Calculation of Purchase Price and Allocation of
Excess Cost
(amounts in thousands)
(Case 9.1)**

	Alternative A	Alternative B
Purchase Price:		
Base Price.	$58,500	$50,000
Acquisition Costs (Note 1)	500	500
Total.	$59,000	$50,500
Book Value of Contributed Capital of Fisher.	(30,000)	(30,000)
Excess of Cost over Book Value to be Allocated to Assets and Liabilities	$29,000	$20,500
Allocation of Excess Cost:		
Recognition of "Reserve" for Losses on Long-term Contracts (Note 2).	3,000 Cr.	3,000 Cr.
Write-up of Building and Equipment (Note 3).	17,000 Dr.	17,000 Dr.
Recognition of Unfunded Pension Liability (Note 4)	5,000 Cr.	5,000 Cr.
Recognition of Estimated Liability to meet OSHA Requirements (Note 5).	1,000 Cr.	1,000 Cr.
Recognition of Estimated Costs to Relocate Facilities in Connection with Product Move (Note 6).	1,000 Cr.	1,000 Cr.
Total Allocated to Identifiable Assets and Liabilities	7,000 Dr.	7,000 Dr.
Deferred Tax Effect (Note 7)	2,450 Cr.	2,450 Cr.
Residual to Goodwill (Note 8)	24,450 Dr.	15,950 Dr.
Total Allocated	$29,000 Dr.	$20,500 Dr.

$7,000 amount of excess cost shown in Exhibit 9.29 above to individual assets and liabilities for financial reporting. For tax reporting, the basis of these assets and liabilities remain the same as the amounts shown on Fisher's books before the acquisition. Thus, Weston provides deferred taxes of $2,450 (= .35 × $7,000). It reports $1,750 [=.35 × ($3,000 Cr. + $1,000 Cr. + $1,000 Cr.)] as a current deferred tax asset, $1,750 (= .35 × $5,000) as a noncurrent deferred tax asset, and $5,950 (= .35 × $17,000) as a noncurrent deferred tax liability. The consolidated entity eliminates these deferred taxes as it amortizes the related asset or liability.

Note 8: Weston allocates the remaining excess cost to goodwill. *Statement No. 142* does not require the firm to amortize goodwill.

Exhibits 9.30 to 9.34 present pro forma consolidated financial statements for Weston and Fisher under each of the two alternatives.

EXHIBIT 9.30

Weston Corporation and Fisher Corporation
Pro Forma Consolidated Balance Sheet as of January 1, Year 12
Alternative A (Cash Exchange)
(amounts in thousands)
(Case 9.1)

	Weston (Before Acquisition)	To Record Acquisition of Fisher's Shares		Weston (After Acquisition)	Fisher (After Acquisition)	Worksheet Consolidation Entries		Pro Forma Consolidated
	(1)	(2)	(3)	(4)	(5)	(6)	(7)	(8)
Assets								
Cash	$ 28,000	(A) 59,000	(B) 59,000	$ 28,000	$ 6,000			$ 34,000
Accounts Receivable	90,000			90,000	15,000			105,000
Inventory	71,000			71,000	18,000			89,000
Other	13,000			13,000	—	(C) 1,750		14,750
Total Current Assets	$202,000			$202,000	$39,000			$242,750
Property, Plant, and Equipment	$116,000			$116,000	$15,000	(C) 8,000		$139,000
Less: Accumulated Depreciation	(38,000)			(38,000)	(9,000)	(C) 9,000		(38,000)
Net Property, Plant, and Equip.	$ 78,000			$ 78,000	$ 6,000			$101,000
Investment in Nonconsolidated Entities	45,000			$ 45,000	—			$ 45,000
Investment in Fisher	—	(B) 59,000		59,000	—		(C) 59,000	—
Goodwill	8,000			8,000	—	(C) 24,450		32,450
Other Assets	7,000			7,000	1,000	(C) 1,750		9,750
Total Assets	$340,000			$399,000	$46,000			$430,950

Liabilities

Current Portion Long-term Debt	$ 2,000	$ —			$ 2,000
Accounts Payable	30,000	7,000	(C) 3,000		37,000
Accrued Liabilities & Advances	78,000	7,000	(C) 1,000		90,000
Income Taxes	21,000	1,000	(C) 1,000		22,000
Total Current Liabilities	$131,000	$15,000			$151,000
Long-term Debt	48,000	—	(A) 59,000		107,000
Other Liabilities	—	1,000		(C) 5,000	6,000
Deferred Taxes	10,000			(C) 5,950	15,950
Total Liabilities	$189,000	$16,000			$279,950

Shareholders' Equity

Preferred Stock	$ —	$ —			$ —
Common Stock	11,000	9,000	(C) 9,000		11,000
Additional Paid-In Capital	55,000	5,000	(C) 5,000		55,000
Retained Earnings	85,000	16,000	(C) 16,000		85,000
Total Shareholders' Equity	$151,000	$30,000			$151,000
Total Liabilities and Shareholders' Equity	$340,000	$46,000			$430,950

(A) Issue of bonds for cash and payment of acquisition costs.

(B) Purchase of Fisher's outstanding common stock.

(C) Elimination of investment in Fisher and Fisher's shareholders' equity accounts and allocation of excess purchase price (see Exhibit 9.29 for amounts).

EXHIBIT 9.31

Weston Corporation and Fisher Corporation
Pro Forma Consolidated Income Statement
for the Year Ending December 31, Year 12
Alternative A (Cash Exchange)
(amounts in thousands)
(Case 9.1)

	Weston	Fisher	Consolidation Work-Sheet Entries Dr.	Consolidation Work-Sheet Entries Cr.	Consolidated Pro Forma
Sales	$560,000	$100,000			$660,000
Cost of Sales	(415,700)	(85,600)	(B) 1,700	(D) 5,000	(498,000)
Selling & Administrative	(105,632)	(10,820)		(C) 250	(116,202)
Operating Income	38,668	3,580			$ 45,798
Equity in Net Income of					
Nonconsolidated Entities	4,000	—			4,000
Other Income (expense)	(1,000)	200	(A) 5,900		(6,700)
Income before Taxes.	41,668	3,780			$ 43,098
Provision for Income Taxes	(14,584)	(1,323)	(C) 88	(A) 2,065	
			(D) 1,750	(B) 595	15,085
Net Income.	$ 27,084	$ 2,457			$ 28,013
Basic Earnings per Share	$ 3.47	$ 1.37			$ 3.59
Average Number Shares of Common					
Stock Outstanding.	7,800	1,800			7,800

(A) Interest on Debt: .10 × $59,000 = $5,900, Tax Effect: .35 × $5,900 = $2,065
(B) Depreciation Expense: $17,000 ÷ 10 = $1,700; Deferred Tax Effects = .35 × $1,700 = $595
(C) Elimination of Pension Expense: $5,000 ÷ 20 = $250, Deferred Tax Effect = .35 × $250 = $88
(D) Elimination of Contract Loss, OSHA cost, and relocation costs = $5,000; Deferred Tax Effect: .35 × $5,000 = $1,750

EXHIBIT 9.32

Weston Corporation and Fisher Corporation
Pro Forma Consolidated Balance Sheet as of January 1, Year 12
Alternative B (Preferred Stock Exchange)
(amounts in thousands)
(Case 9.1)

	Weston (Before Acquisition)	To Record Acquisition of Fisher's Shares		Weston (After Acquisition)	Fisher (After Acquisition)	Consolidation Worksheet Entries		Pro Forma Consolidated
	(1)	(2)	(3)	(4)	(5)	(6)	(7)	(8)
Assets								
Cash	$ 28,000		(A) 500	$ 27,500	$ 6,000			$ 33,500
Accounts Receivable	90,000			90,000	15,000			105,000
Inventory	71,000			71,000	18,000			89,000
Other	13,000			13,000	—	(B) 1,750		14,750
Total Current Assets	$202,000			$201,500	$39,000			$242,250
Property, Plant, and Equipment	$116,000			$116,000	$15,000	(B) 8,000		$139,000
Less: Accum. Depreciation	(38,000)			(38,000)	(9,000)	(B) 9,000		(38,000)
Net Property, Plant, and Equip.	$ 78,000			$ 78,000	$ 6,000			$101,000
Investment in Nonconsolidated Entities	45,000			$ 45,000	—			$ 45,000
Investment in Fisher	—	(A) 50,500		50,500	—		50,500 (B)	—
Goodwill	8,000			8,000	—	(B)15,950		23,950
Other Assets	7,000			7,000	1,000	(B) 1,750		9,750
Total Assets	$340,000			$390,000	$46,000			$421,950
Liabilities								
Current Portion Long-term Debt	$ 2,000			$ 2,000	$ —			$ 2,000
Accounts Payable	30,000			30,000	7,000		3,000 (B)	37,000
Accrued Liabilities & Advances	78,000			78,000	7,000		1,000 (B)	90,000
Income Taxes	21,000			21,000	1,000		1,000 (B)	22,000
Total Current Liabilities	$131,000			$131,000	$15,000			$151,000

continued

Exhibit 9.32—continued

	Weston (Before Acquisition) (1)	To Record Acquisition of Fisher's Shares (2)	(3)	Weston (After Acquisition) (4)	Fisher (After Acquisition) (5)	Consolidation Worksheet Entries (6)	(7)	Pro Forma Consolidated (8)
Long-term Debt..............	48,000			48,000	—			48,000
Other Liabilities............	—			—	1,000		5,000 (B)	6,000
Deferred Taxes.............	10,000			10,000			5,950 (B)	15,950
Total Liabilities...........	$189,000			$189,000	$16,000			$220,950
Shareholders' Equity								
Preferred Stock.............	$ —		(A) 50,000	$ 50,000	$ —			$ 50,000
Common Stock	11,000			11,000	9,000	(B) 9,000		11,000
Additional Paid-In Capital....	55,000			55,000	5,000	(B) 5,000		55,000
Retained Earnings	85,000			85,000	16,000	(B)16,000		85,000
Total Shareholders' Equity	$151,000			$201,000	$30,000			$201,000
Total Liabilities and Shareholders' Equity.........	$340,000			$390,000	$46,000			$421,950

(A) Issue of preferred stock for the outstanding common shares of Fisher and payment of acquisition costs.
(B) Elimination of investment in Fisher and Fisher's shareholders' equity accounts and allocation of excess purchase price (see Exhibit 9.29 for amounts).

<table>
<tr><th colspan="8" align="center">EXHIBIT 9.33</th></tr>
</table>

Weston Corporation and Fisher Corporation
Pro Forma Consolidated Income Statement
for the Year Ending December 31, Year 12
Alternative B (Preferred Stock Exchange)
(amounts in thousands)
(Case 9.1)

	Weston	Fisher	Consolidation Work-Sheet Entries Dr.	Cr.	Consolidated Pro Forma
Sales	$560,000	$100,000			$660,000
Cost of Sales	(415,700)	(85,600)	(A) 1,700	(C) 5,000	(498,000)
Selling & Administrative	(105,632)	(10,820)		(B) 250	(116,202)
Operating Income	38,668	3,580			$ 45,798
Equity in Net Income of					
Nonconsolidated Entities	4,000	—			4,000
Other Income (expense)	(1,000)	200			(800)
Income before Taxes.	$ 41,668	$ 3,780			$ 48,998
Provision for Income Taxes	(14,584)	(1,323)	(B) 88	(A) 595	
			(C) 1,750		17,150
Net Income.	$ 27,084	$ 2,457			$ 31,848
Basic Earnings per Share	$ 3.47	$ 1.37			*
Average Number Shares of Common					
Stock Outstanding.	7,800	1,800			7,800

(A) Depreciation expense = $17,000 ÷ 10 = $1,700;
    Deferred tax effect = .35 × 1,700=595
(B) Pension expense: $5,000 ÷ 20=$250; Deferred tax effect = .35 × $250 = $88
(C) Loss on contract, OSHA and relocation costs = $5,000;
    Deferred tax effect = .35 × $5,000 = $1,750

*Basic EPS: $\dfrac{\$(31,848 - \$3,600)}{7,800} = 3.62$

Diluted EPS: $\dfrac{\$31,848}{7,800+1,350} = 3.48$

EXHIBIT 9.34

Weston Corporation and Fisher Corporation
Key Financial Highlights
(Case 9.1)

	Actual for Weston Corporation				Weston Corporation and Fisher Corporation Pro Forma for Year 12	
	Year 8	Year 9	Year 10	Year 11	Alternative A	Alternative B
Earnings per Common Share						
Basic	$ 1.60	$ 1.83	$ 2.22	$ 2.82	$ 3.51	$ 3.62
Diluted	—	—	—	—	—	$ 3.48
Dividends per Common Share...	$ .40	$ .45	$ .63	$ .88	$ 1.20	$ 1.20
Current Ratio*	1.8	2.0	1.7	1.5	1.6	1.6
Long-term Debt as Percentage of Long-term Capital*	28.9%	26.5%	25.8%	24.1%	41.5%	19.3%
Return on Average Common Shareholders' Equity........	12.4%	12.9%	13.6%	15.2%	17.5%	17.6%
Book Value per Common Share	$13.50	$ 14.88	$ 17.69	$ 19.36	$ 19.36	$ 19.36
Tangible Net Worth ($000)*.....	$99,300	$111,600	$129,600	$143,000	$118,550	$127,050
Times Interest Earned	5.7	7.8	9.8	10.9	5.1	11.3
(with preferred dividend)....	—	—	—	—	—	6.4

*Pro forma amounts for these ratios are at date of acquisition of Fisher.

Calculation of Key Financial Ratios – Alternative A

Basic Earnings per Share: $28,013 ÷ 7,800 = $3.59

Current Ratio: $242,750 ÷ $151,000 = 1.6

Long-term Debt to Long-term Capital: $107,000 ÷ ($107,000 + $151,000) = 41.5%

Return on Common Equity: $28,013 ÷ .5[$151,000 + ($151,000 + $28,013 – $9,360)] = 17.5%

Common Dividend = 7,800 × $1.20 = $9,360

Book Value per Share: $151,000 ÷ 7,800 = $19.36

Tangible Net Worth: $430,950 – $32,450 – $279,950 = $118,550

Times Interest Earned: ($28,013 + $15,085 + $4,741 + $5,900) ÷ ($4,741 + $5,900) = 5.1
  Interest Expense with No Merger: ($27,084 + $15,584 + X) ÷ X = 10.0; X = $4,741

Calculation of Key Financial Ratios – Alternative B

Basic Earnings Per Share: ($31,848 – $3,600) ÷ 7,800 = $3.62
  Preferred Dividend = 1,800 × $2.00 = $3,600

Diluted Earnings Per Share: $31,848 ÷ (7,800 + 1,350) = 3.48
  Common Shares Issued Upon Conversion of Preferred: 1,800 × .75 = 1,350

Current Ratio: $242,250 ÷ $151,000 = 1.6

Long-term Debt to Long-term Capital: $48,000 ÷ ($48,000+$201,000) = 19.3%

Return on Common Equity: ($31,848 – $3,600) ÷ .5[$151,000 + ($151,000 + $31,848 – $3,600 – $9,360)] = 17.6%

Book Value per Common Share: $151,000 ÷ 7,800 = $19.36

Tangible Net Worth: $421,950 – $23,950 – $220,950 – $50,000 = $127,050

Times Interest Earned: ($31,848 + $17,150 + $4,741) ÷ $4,741 = 11.3
  With Preferred Dividend: ($31,848 + $17,150 + $4,741) ÷ ($4,741 + $3,600) = 6.4

Required

a. As a shareholder of Fisher, which alternative would you choose and why? The income tax rate on capital gains is 20 percent. Would your answer differ if you were an individual investor versus a pension fund?

b. As the chief financial officer of Weston, which alternative would you choose and why?

CASE 9.2

CLARK EQUIPMENT COMPANY: ANALYZING A JOINT PROBLEM

Clark Equipment Company, through its wholly owned subsidiaries, operates in three principal product markets:

1. Small "lift and carry" products, including excavators for digging and loaders for hauling various materials. Its Bobcat® skid steer loader maintains a 50 percent worldwide market share.

2. Axles and transmissions for use by manufacturers of cranes and large material handling machinery used in construction, mining, logging, and other industrial applications.

3. Axles and transmissions for use by manufacturers of automobiles, trucks, and tractors in the Brazilian market.

Sales for these product groups for Year 10 to Year 12 appear below:

	Year 10		Year 11		Year 12	
Off-highway:						
Lift-and-carry products....	$385	44%	$347	48%	$410	51%
Axles and Transmissions ...	274	32	240	33	241	30
On-highway:						
Axles and Transmissions ...	205	24	140	19	152	19
	$864	100%	$727	100%	$803	100%

The geographical source of its product sales (that is, the location of its manufacturing facilities) for Year 10 to Year 12 are as follows:

	Year 10		Year 11		Year 12	
North America.............	$504	58%	$439	60%	$501	62%
Europe	165	19	153	21	157	20
South America.............	195	23	135	19	145	18
	$864	100%	$727	100%	$803	100%

Since Year 5, Clark Equipment Company has engaged in a 50 percent-owned joint venture with Volvo of Sweden. The joint venture, called VME Group, manufactures heavy earthmoving construction and mining equipment worldwide. Its principal competitors are Caterpillar, Komatsu, and, to a lesser extent, Deere & Company. Clark Equipment Company accounts for its investment in this joint venture using the equity method.

Key economic characteristics of the equipment manufacturing industry, which includes industrial, construction, and agricultural equipment, are as follows:

1. **Product Lines.** Products include tractors, excavators, loaders, haulers, cranes, compactors, and similar products. Manufacturers range from worldwide, full-line producers to regional niche players. There are currently over 700 producers in the United States, yet six companies command over 70 percent of the domestic market. Manufacturers compete on the basis of machine performance, price, aftermarket support, and parts availability. Approximately 20–30 percent of a manufacturer's sales typically come from the aftermarket. A large tractor, for example, will usually consume parts and service equal to the cost of the equipment within approximately two years of initial purchase.

2. **Production.** Equipment manufacturing is capital intensive. Manufacturers tend to centralize production around key machine components, such as engines, axles, transmissions, and hydraulics. Customizing products to particular customers' needs typically occurs at the assembly stage.

3. **Technology.** Electronic and computer-based technologies have played an increasingly important role in recent years, both in the design of the final product and its manufacturing. Robotics in particular has been applied successfully in the manufacturing process.

4. **Demand.** The relatively high cost of equipment and the cyclicality of many of the industries to which equipment manufacturers sell their products (for example, construction, mining, automotive) result in highly cyclical sales patterns. The level of interest rates, general conditions in the economy, and income tax considerations (for example, depreciation rates) significantly impact sales.

5. **Marketing.** Manufacturers use a distributor network to sell their products (original equipment and parts). The distributors usually sell a single manufacturer's products, but complement the product offering with products of other manufacturers unique to the market.

6. **Financing.** The capital-intensive nature of the manufacturing process leads these firms to rely on extensive long-term debt financing. Responsibility for arranging customer financing for equipment purchases may fall on the manufacturer, the distributor, or both.

Exhibit 9.35 presents condensed balance sheets for Clark Equipment Company as of December 31, Year 9, through December 31, Year 12, and condensed income statements for Year 10 through Year 12. These financial statements report Clark Equipment Company's investment in VME Group using the equity method. Exhibit 9.36 presents similar condensed financial statement data for VME Group.

EXHIBIT 9.35

Clark Equipment Company
Condensed Financial Statement Data with VME Group Accounted for Using the Equity Method
(amounts in millions)
(Case 9.2)

	December 31			
	Year 9	Year 10	Year 11	Year 12
Balance Sheet				
Current Assets..................................	$ 551	$ 468	$ 520	$396
Investment in VME Group......................	142	168	139	125
Noncurrent Assets.............................	319	466	465	444
Total Assets...........................	$1,012	$1,102	$1,124	$965
Current Liabilities............................	$ 265	$ 282	$ 328	$187
Noncurrent Liabilities........................	255	238	554	519
Shareholders' Equity.........................	492	582	242	259
Total Equities......................	$1,012	$1,102	$1,124	$965

	For the Year:		
	Year 10	Year 11	Year 12
Income Statement			
Sales..	$864	$727	$803
Equity in Earnings of VME.....................	26	(29)	(47)
Cost of Goods Sold...........................	(717)	(638)[a]	(664)
Interest Expense	(22)	(26)	(26)
Other Expenses, including Taxes	(109)	(85)	(92)
Net Income (Loss)...........................	$ 42	$(51)	$(26)

[a]Includes $20 million of charges for restructuring operations and environmental cleanup.

EXHIBIT 9.36

VME Group
Condensed Financial Statement Data
(amounts in millions)
(Case 9.2)

	December 31			
	Year 9	**Year 10**	**Year 11**	**Year 12**
Balance Sheet				
Current Assets..........................	$594	$665	$ 801	$649
Noncurrent Assets.....................	177	231	392	321
Total Assets........................	$771	$896	$1,193	$970
Current Liabilities.....................	$326	$354	$ 642	$516
Noncurrent Liabilities.................	187	232	299	230
Shareholders' Equity..................	258	310	252	224
Total Equities	$771	$896	$1,193	$970

	For the Year:		
	Year 10	**Year 11**	**Year 12**
Income Statement			
Sales......................................	$1,325	$1,368	$1,357
Cost of Goods Sold........................	(1,037)	(1,110)	(1,159)
Interest Expense	(20)	(33)	(29)
Other Expenses, including Taxes	(216)	(283)	(263)
Net Income (Loss)........................	$ 52	$ (58)	$ (94)

Required

a. Prepare an analysis of the changes in the Investment in VME Group account on the books of Clark for Year 9 through Year 12.

b. Exhibit 9.37 presents partial condensed balance sheets and income statements for Clark Equipment Company assuming that it accounted for its investment in VME Group using the proportionate consolidation method (that is, Clark Equipment Company recognizes its 50 percent share of the assets, liabilities, revenues, and expenses of VME Group). Complete Exhibit 9.37 by preparing a balance sheet as of December 31, Year 12, and an income statement for Year 12 following the proportionate consolidation method.

c. Exhibit 9.38 presents partial condensed balance sheets and income statements for Clark Equipment Company assuming that it accounted for its investment

 EXHIBIT 9.37

Clark Equipment Company
Condensed Financial Statement Data
with VME Group Accounted for Using the Proportionate Consolidation Method
(amounts in millions)
(Case 9.2)

	December 31			
	Year 9	Year 10	Year 11	Year 12
Balance Sheet				
Current Assets......................................	$ 848.0	$ 800.5	$ 920.5	
Noncurrent Assets...............................	407.5	581.5	661.0	
Goodwill	13.0	13.0	13.0	
Total Assets.....................................	$1,268.5	$1,395.0	$1,594.5	
Current Liabilities...............................	$428.0	$459.0	$649.0	
Noncurrent Liabilities............................	348.5	354.0	703.5	
Shareholders' Equity	492.0	582.0	242.0	
Total Equities	$1,268.5	$1,395.0	$1,594.5	

	For the Year:		
	Year 10	Year 11	Year 12
Income Statement			
Sales..	$1,526.5	$1,411.0	
Cost of Goods Sold.............................	(1,235.5)	(1,193.0)	
Interest Expense	(32.0)	(42.5)	
Other Expenses, including Taxes	(217.0)	(226.5)	
Net Income (Loss).............................	$ 42.0	$ (51.0)	

in VME Group using the full consolidation method (that is, Clark Equipment Company consolidated 100 percent of the assets, liabilities, revenues, and expenses of VME Group, and reports Volvo's share of these items as a joint-owner's interest. Complete Exhibit 9.38 by preparing a balance sheet as of December 31, Year 12, and an income statement for Year 12 following the full consolidation method.

d. Which of three methods of accounting for Clark's investment in VME Group (equity, proportionate consolidation, full consolidation) portrays better the economics of the relationship between the entities? Explain.

	EXHIBIT 9.38

Clark Equipment Company
Condensed Financial Statement Data
with VME Group Accounted for Using the Full Consolidation Method
(amounts in millions)
(Case 9.2)

	December 31			
	Year 9	Year 10	Year 11	Year 12
Balance Sheet				
Current Assets.....................................	$1,145	$1,133	$1,321	
Noncurrent Assets...............................	496	697	857	
Goodwill	13	13	13	
Total Assets..................................	$1,654	$1,843	$2,191	
Current Liabilities...............................	$ 591	$ 636	$ 970	
Noncurrent Liabilities...........................	442	470	853	
Joint-Owners Interest	129	155	126	
Shareholders' Equity.............................	492	582	242	
Total Equities	$1,654	$1,843	$2,191	

	For the Year:		
	Year 10	Year 11	Year 12
Income Statement			
Sales..	$2,189	$2,095	
Cost of Goods Sold.............................	(1,754)	(1,748)	
Interest Expense	(42)	(59)	
Other Expenses, including Taxes	(325)	(368)	
Joint-Owners Interest	(26)	29	
Net Income (Loss).............................	$ 42	$ (51)	

e. Exhibit 9.39 presents selected financial statement ratios for Clark Equipment Company and VME Group under each of the three methods of accounting. Calculate these ratios for Year 12. The income tax rate is 34 percent.

f. Identify the likely reasons for changes in the profitability and risk of Clark Equipment Company during the period Year 10 to Year 12.

EXHIBIT 9.39

Clark Equipment Company
Profitability and Risk Ratios
(Case 9.2)

	Equity Method			Proportionate Consolidation			Full Consolidation		
	Year 10	Year 11	Year 12	Year 10	Year 11	Year 12	Year 10	Year 11	Year 12
Profit Margin for ROA	6.31%	(4.93%)		4.00%	(1.77%)		4.28%	(2.06%)	
Assets Turnover	.82	.65		1.15	.95		1.25	1.04	
Return on Assets	5.16%	(3.23%)		4.59%	(1.67%)		5.36%	(2.14%)	
Profit Margin for ROCE	4.86%	(7.02%)		2.75%	(3.61%)		1.92%	(2.43%)	
Capital Structure Leverage	1.97	2.71		2.48	3.65		3.26	4.92	
Return on Common Equity	7.46%	(12.96%)		7.46%	(12.96%)		7.46%	(12.96%)	
Current Ratios (December 31)	1.66	1.59		1.74	1.42		1.78	1.36	
Fixed Asset Turnover[a]	2.20	1.56		3.09	2.27		3.67	2.70	
Long-term Debt Ratio (Dec. 31)[b]	29.10%	69.95%		37.90%	74.72%		39.00%	70.09%	
Cost of Goods Sold/Sales	82.99%	87.76%		80.94%	84.55%		80.13%	83.44%	

	Clark–Separate Co.			VME–Separate Co.		
	Year 10	Year 11	Year 12	Year 10	Year 11	Year 12
Profit Margin for ROA	3.30%	.88%		4.92%	(2.65%)	
Assets Turnover	.96	.76		1.59	1.31	
Return on Assets	3.16%	.66%		7.82%	(3.47%)	
Profit Margin for ROCE	1.85%	(3.03%)		3.92%	(4.24%)	
Capital Structure Leverage	1.68	2.35		2.94	3.72	
Return on Common Equity	2.61%	(2.64%)		18.3%	(20.64%)	
Current Ratios (December 31)	1.66	1.59		1.88	1.25	
Fixed Asset Turnover[a]	2.20	1.56		6.50	4.39	
Long-term Debt Ratio (Dec. 31)[b]	29.10%	69.95%		42.80%	54.27%	
Cost of Goods Sold/Sales	82.99%	87.76%		78.26%	81.14%	

[a]Assuming that noncurrent assets represent property, plant, and equipment.
[b]Assuming that noncurrent liabilities represent long-term debt.

CASE 9.3

LOUCKS CORPORATION: OBTAINING SECURITY IN TRANSLATION

Loucks Corporation (Loucks), a U.S. company, manufactures and markets security alarm systems. Based on predictions of rapid economic growth in South America during the next decade, Loucks plans to establish a wholly owned subsidiary in Colombia as of January 1, Year 8, to manufacture and market security alarm systems in that country. The Colombian subsidiary will use technology developed by Loucks for the alarm systems. It will import from Loucks a portion of the electronic software needed for the systems. Assembly will take place in Colombia.

Loucks plans to contribute $100,000 to establish the subsidiary on January 1, Year 8. The exchange rate between the Colombian peso and the U.S. dollar is expected to be $.02:P1 on this date. Exhibit 9.40 presents pro forma financial statements for Year 8 for the Colombian subsidiary during its first year of operations. Exhibit 9.41 presents a partial pro forma consolidation worksheet for Loucks and its Colombian subsidiary for Year 8. The following additional information pertains to these companies during Year 8.

1. Loucks expects to sell electronic software to its Colombian subsidiary during Year 8 at a transfer (selling) price of P3,000,000. The Colombian subsidiary expects to sell all alarm systems in which this software is a component by the end of Year 8. The firms will denominate the transfers in Colombian pesos. Loucks plans to hedge its exchange exposure, including any transaction gain or loss and related loss or gain on the hedging instrument in other expenses.
2. The subsidiary expects to declare and pay a dividend to Loucks on December 31, Year 8.

Required

a. Discuss whether Loucks should use the U.S. dollar or the Colombian peso as the functional currency for its Colombian subsidiary.
b. Loucks expects the exchange rate between the U.S. dollar and the Colombian peso to change as follows during Year 8:

January 1, Year 8	$.020:P1
Average, Year 8.	$.018:P1
December 31, Year 8	$.015:P1

Complete Exhibit 9.40 showing the translation of the subsidiary's accounts into U.S. dollars assuming that the Colombian peso is the functional currency. Include a separate calculation of the translation adjustment. Using the

EXHIBIT 9.40

Columbian Subsidiary
Translation of Financial Statements—Year 8
(Case 9.3)

	Colombian Pesos	Exchange Rate	U.S. Dollars
Balance Sheet:			
Assets			
Cash	P 700,000		
Accounts Receivable	2,000,000		
Inventories	3,500,000		
Fixed Assets (net)	5,700,000		
	P 11,900,000		
Liabilities and Equity			
Accounts Payable	P 2,400,000		
Bonds Payable.	4,000,000		
Common Stock	5,000,000		
Translation Adjustment	—		
Retained Earnings	500,000		
	P 11,900,000		
Income Statement:			
Revenues.	P 15,000,000		
Cost of Goods Sold	(10,000,000)		
Depreciation Expense.	(300,000)		
Other Expenses.	(2,500,000)		
Net Income	P 2,200,000		
Retained Earnings Statement:			
Balance, January 1, Year 1	P —		
Plus Net Income.	2,200,000		
Less Dividends	(1,700,000)		
Balance, December 31, Year 1	P 500,000		

EXHIBIT 9.41

Loucks Corporation and Colombian Subsidiary
Consolidation Worksheet
(Case 9.3)

	Loucks Corp.	Colombian Subsidiary	Adjustments and Eliminations	Consolidated
Balance Sheet				
Cash	$ 48,000			
Accounts Receivable	125,000			
Inventories	260,000			
Investment in Colombian Subsidiary	?			
Fixed Assets (net).	120,000			
Total Assets	$?			
Accounts Payable	$280,000			
Bonds Payable	50,000			
Common Stock	100,000			
Translation Adjustment.	—			
Retained Earnings	?			
Total Equities	$?			
Income Statement				
Sales Revenue.	$500,000			
Equity in Earnings of Colombian Subs..	?			
Cost of Goods Sold	(400,000)			
Depreciation Expense	(20,000)			
Other Expenses	(30,000)			
Net Income	$ 89,600			
Dividends.	(20,000)			
Increase in Retained Earnings	$?			
Retained Earnings, Jan. 1	167,500			
Retained Earnings, Dec. 31	$?			

translated amounts from part b, complete the consolidation worksheet in Exhibit 9.41.

c. Repeat part b, assuming that the U.S. dollar is the functional currency. Include a separate calculation of the translation gain or loss. The Colombian subsidiary expects to issue bonds denominated in Colombian pesos and acquire fixed assets on January 1, Year 8.

d. Why does the sign of the translation adjustment in part b differ from the sign of the translation gain or loss in part c?

e. Assume that actual financial statement amounts for Year 8 turn out to be exactly as projected in Exhibit 9.40 and 9.41 but that the exchange rate changes as follows:

January 1, Year 8	$.020:P1
Average, Year 8.....................................	$.022:P1
December 31, Year 8	$.025:P1

Calculate the amount of the translation adjustment under the all-current method and the translation adjustment under the monetary/nonmonetary method for Year 8. Why do the signs of the translation adjustments in part e differ from those in parts b and c?

f. Compute the net income to revenues ratio based on (1) amounts originally measured in Colombian pesos, (2) amounts measured in U.S. dollars from part b, and (3) amounts measured in U.S. dollars from part c. Why is the net income to revenues percentage the same under (1) and (2) but different under (3)?

Chapter 10

FORECASTING PRO FORMA FINANCIAL STATEMENTS

Learning Objectives
1. Develop the skills to build complete forecasts of pro forma balance sheets, income statements, and statements of cash flows. These pro forma financial statements should provide reliable forecasts of expected future earnings, cash flows, and dividends that the analyst can use in valuation models to estimate share value. The analyst can also use these forecasts in a wide array of decision contexts, such as strategic planning, credit analysis, corporate management, and mergers and acquisitions.
2. Understand and apply the six-step framework for building pro forma financial statements: (a) revenue growth, (b) expense control, (c) net operating assets turnover and efficiency, (d) leverage and capital structure, (e) interest and taxes, and (f) cash flows.
3. Identify and incorporate important business and strategic factors into forecasts of accounting numbers.
4. Understand when and how to use shortcut forecasting techniques.
5. Develop forecast models that are flexible and complete, allowing the analyst to respond quickly and appropriately to important announcements by firms.

OVERVIEW

Thus far, this text has discussed the first four steps of the five-step analysis framework. Drawing on the disciplines of accounting, finance, economics, and strategy, the text has demonstrated how to apply the framework to analyze: (a) the economics of a firm's industry, (b) the competitive advantages and risks of the firm's strategy, (c) the quality of the firm's accounting, and (d) the firm's performance and risk.

In the next four chapters, we take the final, culminating step of the framework: firm valuation. Valuation is in itself a two-part process. The first part of the process involves forecasting future value-relevant payoffs to the firm. The second part applies valuation models to the forecasts of future payoffs to determine the economic value of an investment.

In this chapter, the focus shifts to the future. The economic value of any resource is a function of the expected future returns from the resource, and the risks inherent in those expected returns. Therefore, this chapter demonstrates how to capture expectations of the firm's future operating, investing, and financing activities in forecasts of pro forma financial statements—income statements, balance sheets, and statements of cash flows—in order to determine expectations of future value-relevant payoffs to the firm, including future earnings, free cash flows, and dividends. Chapters 11 to 13 introduce and apply valuation models that use forecasts of expected future earnings, cash flows, and dividends to determine firm value. Chapter 11 describes and implements valuation models that presume the value-relevant payoffs are expected future "free" cash flows that the firm that can eventually pay to shareholders as dividends. Chapter 12 illustrates and implements valuation models that presume earnings reflect shareholder value-creation, and, therefore, are value-relevant. Chapter 13 illustrates and applies valuation approaches that rely on comparable companies and valuation multiples, such as price-earnings ratios and market-to-book ratios.

INTRODUCTION TO FORECASTING

The objective of forecasting is to develop a set of realistic expectations for future value-relevant payoffs—earnings, cash flows, and dividends—which are the fundamental bases for firm value. The analytical tool used to capture these expectations is a set of *forecasts of pro forma financial statements*.[1] Financial statement forecasts represent an integrated, articulated portrayal of all of the firm's future operating, investing, and financing activities that will determine the firm's future profitability, financial position, and risk. Using a forecasted set of financial statements, the analyst aims to capture expectations for *all* of the factors that will determine the firm's future value-relevant payoffs to stakeholders.

---

[1]Throughout this chapter, we use the term *pro forma financial statements* to denote the expected future income statements, balance sheets, and statements of cash flows that capture the analyst's forecasts of the firm's future operating, investing, and financing activities.

Pro forma financial statements are important analysis tools because forecasts of future payoffs play a central role in valuation and many other financial decision contexts. A firm's share value is a function of its expected future payoffs to equity stakeholders, discounted for time and risk. Credit decisions require forecasts of future cash flows available to make required future interest and principal payments. Managers' decisions about firm strategy, potential customer or supplier relationships, potential mergers or acquisitions, potential carve-outs of divisions or subsidiaries, and even whether a firm presents a good employment opportunity, depend on their expected future payoffs and the risks of those payoffs.

Developing forecasts of future payoffs is in many ways the most difficult step of the five-step framework because it requires estimating the effects of what might occur in the future, and therefore involves the highest degree of uncertainty. Forecast errors can be very costly. Excessively optimistic forecasts of future earnings and cash flows can lead to overestimating a firm's value, and therefore paying more for a share than it is worth. On the other hand, overly conservative forecasts can lead to understating a firm's future earnings and cash flows, and consequently missing valuable investment opportunities or selling shares for less than they are worth. The goal is to develop *realistic* (unbiased and objective—not optimistic or conservative) expectations of future earnings and cash flows and to make intelligent investment decisions.

Superior forecasting has the potential to earn superior returns. As Chapter 1 discussed, empirical research results from the Ball and Brown (1968) study demonstrate the potential to earn abnormal returns by forecasting simply the *sign* of the change in annual earnings numbers.[2] Their findings indicate that if one could have predicted accurately the sign of the change in earnings one year ahead for each firm in their sample during their 9-year study period, one could have earned on average above-market-returns of 7 percent per year by investing in those firms experiencing earnings increases, and one could have earned above-market-returns of 9 percent per year by selling short those firms experiencing earnings decreases. In a subsequent study, empirical results in Beaver, Clarke, and Wright (1979) demonstrate that the potential to earn abnormal returns increases substantially if one can correctly forecast the future *sign* and *magnitude* of the change in one-year-ahead earnings.[3] Their findings imply that stock returns for the firms experiencing significant increases in earnings tend to beat the market as a whole by 10 to 20 percent per year, whereas stock returns for firms experiencing significant decreases in earnings tend to be 10 to 20 percent less than the market as a whole. To be sure, analysts do not have perfect foresight and cannot perfectly predict the amount of earnings increases and decreases one year ahead. Nonetheless, these results are encouraging because they imply that analysts that are better than average at forecasting future earnings changes may be able to generate superior returns.

---

[2]Ray Ball and Philip Brown, "An Evaluation of Accounting Income Numbers," *Journal of Accounting Research*, Autumn 1968, pp. 159–178.

[3]See William Beaver, Roger Clarke, and William Wright, "The Association Between Unsystematic Security Returns and the Magnitude of Earnings Forecast Errors," *Journal of Accounting Research*, Autumn 1979, Vol. 17 Issue 2, pp. 316–341.

More recently, accounting researchers have investigated whether financial statement ratios like those described throughout this text can be used to build forecast models for future earnings. For example, Ou and Penman (1989) built earnings prediction models by regressing earnings changes on a set of financial statement ratios. The earnings prediction models provide probability estimates of the likelihood of an earnings increase.[4] They find that their probability estimates correctly predict earnings increases and decreases one year ahead roughly 67 percent of the time. Taking long positions in firms with a high probability of an earnings increase next year, and short positions in firms with a high probability of an earnings decrease next year, results in average market-adjusted returns of roughly 8 percent per year. This study and subsequent related studies provide encouraging results to suggest that a fundamental analysis of financial statement ratios can produce more informed forecasts of future earnings, which in turn analysts can use to make better investment decisions.

To maximize the potential to develop reliable pro forma financial statements and to minimize the potential for costly forecast errors, this chapter first outlines a set of six steps for forecasting pro forma financial statements. The chapter then illustrates each of the steps by applying them to PepsiCo, developing detailed pro forma financial statements for each of the three primary financial statements. The chapter also describes a set of techniques to enhance the reliability of forecasts, including sensitivity analysis, iteration, and validity checks. The chapter also describes some simplifying steps for "shortcut" forecasts based on time-series projections of sales, future earnings, and cash flows, and the conditions under which such shortcuts are less likely to create forecast errors.

The analyst should base pro forma financial statements on expectations that reflect the economics of the industry, the competitive advantages and risks of the firm's strategy, the quality of the firm's accounting, and the drivers of the firm's profitability and risk. The first four steps of the framework of this text provide the necessary foundation for forecasting. These four steps should inform the analyst about the critical risk and success factors of the firm and the key drivers of the firm's profitability and risk. The same critical factors that are the focal points for the analysis of the firm's strategy, accounting, profitability, and risk are the focal points for forecasting pro forma financial statements.

PREPARING PRO FORMA FINANCIAL STATEMENTS

Preparing a set of pro forma financial statements can be an overwhelming task because of the numerous assumptions and relations an analyst must consider. It is helpful to establish at the outset a flow, or a sequence of steps, to project the three principal financial statements. It is also helpful to implement these steps while

---

[4]See Jane Ou and Stephen Penman, "Financial Statement Analysis and the Prediction of Stock Returns," *Journal of Accounting and Economics* (November 1989), pp. 295–330. For examples of recent studies in this area, see Baruch Lev and Ramu Thiagarajan, "Fundamental Information Analysis," *Journal of Accounting Research* (Autumn 1993), pp. 190–215; and Jeffery Abarbanell and Brian Bushee, "Abnormal Stock Returns to a Fundamental Analysis Strategy," *The Accounting Review 73* (January 1998), pp. 19–46.

following several general but important principles. This section offers a set of principles to guide the preparation and development of a set of pro forma financial statements, describes a six-step forecasting game plan, and then concludes with several practical coaching tips on implementing the six-step sequence.

GENERAL FORECASTING PRINCIPLES

Several key principles of forecasting deserve mention (or are worth repeating) right at the outset. **First, as noted earlier, the objective of forecasting is to produce objective and realistic expectations of the future value-relevant payoffs to investment.** To maximize forecast reliability and minimize costly forecast errors, pro forma financial statements should provide unbiased predictions of the firm's future operating, investing, and financing activities, and should not be conservative or optimistic.

Second, pro forma financial statements should be comprehensive. The pro forma financial statements should include *all* expected future operating, investing, and financing activities for the forecasts to be complete. For example, suppose one forecasts expected future sales growth and then simply projects expected future earnings assuming a constant profit margin on sales. This approach is incomplete because it fails to consider all of the elements that determine profitability from sales, which can cause the earnings forecasts to be incomplete. By assuming a constant profit margin on sales, one would ignore whether costs of good sold and selling, general, and administrative expenses will increase or decrease disproportionately relative to sales growth based on potential economies of scale or scope, or operating synergies.

Third, pro forma financial statements should be based on internally consistent assumptions and relations. Pro forma financial statements should rely on the *additivity* within financial statements and the *articulation* across financial statements to avoid internal inconsistencies in forecasts. The analyst can rely on the internal discipline of accounting across the three primary financial statements to reduce the possibility of errors from internally inconsistent assumptions. For example, sales growth forecasts will likely drive forecasts of growth in related elements of the financial statements, including future costs of sales, inventory, accounts receivable, and property, plant, and equipment. In turn, forecasts of future growth in inventory, receivables and property, plant, and equipment will likely affect growth in related elements, including accounts payable, depreciation, short-term and long-term borrowing, interest expense, and equity capital issues. Each of these elements will, in turn, have implications for the cash flows of the firm. To capture the many complex relations among operating, investing, and financing activities, pro forma financial statements should add up and should articulate with each other—the balance sheet should reflect all of the elements of financial position and should balance; the income statement should reflect all of the revenues, expenses, gains, and losses each period; the statement of cash flows should reflect all of the cash flow implications of the income statement and the changes in the firm's balance sheet.

Fourth, pro forma financial statements should be based on externally valid assumptions. Forecast assumptions should pass the test of common sense. The analyst should impose reality checks on the forecast assumptions. For example, are the sales growth forecast assumptions consistent with the competitive conditions in the industry, including market demand and price elasticity for the firm's products? The analyst should be sure that the assumptions in the pro forma financial statements are consistent with the past or reflect changes that management intends to make and can make in the future. In addition, the analyst should avoid building forecasts based on wishful thinking. That is, forecasts should not be based on what the analyst hopes the firm will do, or on what the analyst thinks the firm should do, but instead the forecasts should capture what the analyst believes the firm actually will do in the future.

SIX-STEP FORECASTING GAME PLAN

To prepare a set of pro forma financial statements, it is helpful to organize the numerous assumptions and relations an analyst must consider into related operating, investing, and financing activities. This activity-based forecasting perspective enables the analyst to identify the necessary sequence of steps to project the three principal financial statements. The particular sequence of steps may vary, depending on the reason for preparing the pro forma financial statements. For most forecasts of pro forma financial statements, this six-step sequence works well:

1. Project revenues from sales and other activities.
2. Project operating expenses (for example, costs of goods sold, selling, general, and administrative expenses) and derive projected operating income (income before interest expense, interest income, and income taxes).
3. Project the operating assets and liabilities (for example, cash, inventory, receivables, property, plant, and equipment, accounts payable, accrued expenses) necessary to support the level of operations projected in steps 1 and 2.
4. Project the financial capital structure (for example, short-term and long-term borrowing, short-term and long-term investments in financial assets, and shareholders' equity except for retained earnings) necessary to support the level of operations projected in step 3.
5. Determine the cost of financing the capital structure projected in step 4. From projected operating income from step 2, subtract interest expense on short-term and long-term borrowing and add interest income on short-term and long-term financial asset investments to derive projected income before tax. Next, subtract projected income tax to derive projected net income. Subtract expected dividends from net income to obtain the projected change in retained earnings. At this point, check to be sure the projected balance sheets are in balance. If they are not in balance, it may indicate that the financial structure may need to be adjusted (for example, additional financing may be needed), and steps 4 and 5 will have to be repeated until the balance sheet is in balance.
6. Derive the statement of cash flows from the projected income statements and balance sheets.

Exhibit 10.1 summarizes this procedure.

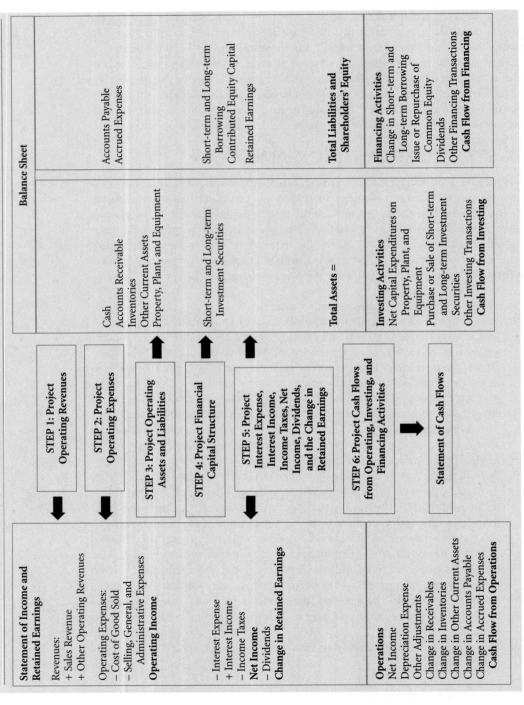

EXHIBIT 10.1

Preparing Pro Forma Financial Statements

PRACTICAL TIPS FOR IMPLEMENTING THE SIX-STEP GAME PLAN

Several practical coaching tips on implementing the six-step sequence are in order. **These six steps are integrated and interdependent. They are not strictly sequential and linear for all firms.** The order in which the analyst implements these six steps and the amount of emphasis placed on each step will depend on the integration of the firm's operating, investing, and financing activities. For example, forecasts of revenues for a retail chain or restaurant chain may first require forecasts of the number of new stores to be opened. The sales forecasts for a manufacturer may depend on whether new productive plants can be built, which may depend on whether long-term debt financing can be obtained.

Be sure that the amounts on the three pro forma financial statements articulate with each other. For example, be sure that net income minus dividends agrees with the change in retained earnings. Be sure that the change in accumulated depreciation on the balance sheet reflects depreciation expense on the income statement. Also be sure that the change in the property, plant, and equipment amounts on the balance sheet incorporates the effects of any capital expenditures, and that the statement of cash flows reflects the amounts of depreciation expense and capital expenditures. Be sure that the net cash flow on the statement of cash flows agrees with the change in the cash balance on the balance sheet.

Preparing pro forma financial statements requires at least one financial "flexible" account, and an iterative and circular process. Firms rely on flexible accounts—usually financial assets and liabilities—to expand and contract with the firm's need for capital. For example, a firm that needs capital to finance growth in assets may need to increase short-term or long-term borrowing, or reduce investments in short-term or long-term financial assets, or issue equity shares. A firm generating excess cash may deploy that cash by paying down debt, investing it in financial assets, paying dividends, or repurchasing its own shares. Therefore, the analyst must be prepared to adjust flexible financial accounts as necessary to appropriately match the firm's future financial capital structure with the firm's future operations. This means that the process of producing a set of pro forma financial statements will likely require several iterations and a degree of circularity. For example, after the first pass through a set of pro forma financial statements, the analyst may discover that the firm will need to increase borrowing to finance future capital expenditures. However, by forecasting increased borrowing the analyst will also have to forecast increased interest expense to reflect the cost of the additional debt capital, which in turn means that income taxes will fall and net income will fall. As a consequence, retained earnings will fall, which means the analyst may have to increase borrowing a bit more, and the process will have to be repeated until the balance sheet is in balance and it articulates with the income statement and the statement of cash flows.

The quality of the pro forma financial statements, and therefore the quality of the decisions on which they will be based, is no better than the quality of the forecast assumptions. The analyst should spend time thinking through and justifying each assumption, especially the most important assumptions that reflect the critical risk and success factors of the firm's strategy. In addition, the analyst can impose reality checks on the assumptions by analyzing ratios and common-size financial statements using the pro forma financial statements. These analytical tools may reveal that certain assumptions are unrealistic or are inconsistent with one another.

The analyst should also conduct sensitivity analysis on the pro forma financial statements. The analyst should assess, for example, the extent to which earnings will vary across different sales growth scenarios (for example, comparing across the most likely, optimistic, and pessimistic growth rate assumptions). Some of the assumptions will be more critical than others, and sensitivity analyses will help the analyst assess the extent to which pro forma forecast results are dependent on key assumptions.

The subsequent sections of this chapter illustrate the six-step procedure described above by using the analysis of PepsiCo's financial statements through Year 11. Appendix A presents the financial statements and notes for PepsiCo for Year 11. Appendix C presents printouts for PepsiCo from FSAP, the financial statement analysis package discussed in Chapter 1. In the chapter, we use PepsiCo's financial statement data and our analysis of those data to carefully develop forecast assumptions and to compute pro forma financial statements for PepsiCo for Year 12 to Year 16, which we label Year +1 to Year +5 to denote that they are forecasts.

USING FSAP TO PREPARE PRO FORMA FINANCIAL STATEMENTS

FSAP contains a Forecast spreadsheet that permits the analyst to prepare pro forma financial statements.[5] If you have not previously designed an Excel spreadsheet to prepare pro forma financial statements, you should do so *before* using the Forecast spreadsheet within FSAP. The proper design of a spreadsheet and the preparation of pro forma financial statements provide an excellent learning device to enhance and solidify understanding of the relationships between various financial statement items. Once you become comfortable with pro forma financial statements and spreadsheets, then using the Forecast spreadsheet will save time.

Note that the Forecast spreadsheet in FSAP is a general and adaptable template to use to construct pro forma financial statements. To illustrate the use of the Forecast spreadsheet template, we incorporate in FSAP the specific pro forma assumptions we make for PepsiCo. Appendix D presents printouts of the Forecast spreadsheet within FSAP for PepsiCo, with explicit financial statement forecast assumptions through Year +11. To use the Forecast spreadsheet template within FSAP for other companies, the analyst will need to program the template with the specific forecast assumptions the analyst makes for other companies.

All financial statement amounts throughout this chapter appear in millions. The spreadsheets take all computations to multiple decimal places. Because we express all

---

[5]The web site for this text (http://stickney.swlearning.com) contains both FSAP and a user manual for easy downloading and use.

amounts in this chapter in millions, some minor rounding differences will occasionally arise and make it appear that various subtotals and totals disagree with the sum of the individual items that make up the subtotal or total.

STEP 1: PROJECT SALES AND OTHER REVENUES

PROJECTING SALES

The key starting point is to project revenues from the principal business activities of the firm, which often involve sales of products or services. The expected level of revenues can serve as a basis for deriving many of the other amounts in the pro forma financial statements.

Sales numbers are determined by both a volume component and a price component. In the case of sales *volume*, some firms (for example, automobile manufacturing, beverages) report sales volume figures, enabling the analyst to assess separately volume and price as drivers of historical sales growth, and to use them as a framework for predicting future sales. Other firms report volume-related measures of operating activities that the analyst can use to forecast sales, such as new stores for retailers and restaurant chains, and passengers and passenger-seat-miles for airlines. A firm in a mature industry (for example, consumer foods) with little expected change in its market share might anticipate volume increases equal to the growth rate in the population within its geographic markets. A firm that has increased its operating capacity consistent with the high growth rate anticipated in a particular industry (for example, biotechnology or computer software) might use this growth rate when projecting volume increases.

Projecting *price* increases involves consideration of the expected rate of general price inflation in the economy, and the effects of changes in foreign currency exchange rates on sales denominated in foreign currencies. Projecting prices also depends on factors specific to the firm and its industry that might affect demand and price elasticity, such as excess capacity, shortages of raw materials, substitute products, technological changes in products or production methods, and similar factors. A firm in a capital-intensive industry, such as paper manufacturing, may require several years to add new capacity. If a firm competes in a capital-intensive industry that is expected to operate near capacity for the next few years, then price increases are likely to occur. On the other hand, if a firm competes in an industry in which excess capacity already exists or new capacity is expected to become available soon, then price increases are less likely. A firm operating in an industry that is expected to transition from the high growth to the maturity phase of its life cycle, or to experience technological improvements in its production processes (for example, some portions of the computer industry), might expect increases in sales volume but decreases in sales prices per unit. If a firm has established a competitive position for its brand name in its markets, or has successfully differentiated unique characteristics for its products, then that firm may have a greater potential to increase prices, or to avoid price declines, than another firm with generic products.

If sales have grown at a reasonably steady rate in prior periods and there is no indication that economic, industry, or firm-specific factors will change significantly, then the analyst can project this growth rate into the future. If a major acquisition or sale affected the historical growth rate, then the analyst should filter out the effect of this event when making projections (unless the firm's strategy is to make additional acquisitions). It can be difficult to project sales for firms with cyclical sales patterns (for example, heavy machinery, property-casualty insurance, investment banking). Their historical growth rates for sales might reflect wide variations in both direction and amount from year to year. The analyst should project a varying growth rate that maintains this cyclical sales pattern in these cases.

Earlier chapters indicated that the consumer foods industry in the United States is in its maturity phase. Industry sales have grown recently at the growth rate for the general population, approximately 2 percent per year. The primary vehicles for growth by consumer foods companies are international sales and corporate acquisitions. PepsiCo has defied these industry averages, generating an average sales growth rate of 7.3 percent between Year 9 and Year 11. PepsiCo discloses (see PepsiCo's management's discussion and analysis of operations in Appendix B) information about comparable net sales over these years, which it has adjusted for items affecting comparability with Year 11 sales, including removing the sales of previously consolidated bottlers from reported results for Year 9, removing the effect on sales from a fifty-third week in Year 10, and incorporating the effects of the merger with Quaker as if it had been in effect throughout this time period. Comparable net sales amounts and growth rates for PepsiCo appear below:

	Year 9	Year 10	Year 11
Amounts in millions.................	$23,385	$25,185	$26,935
Growth rates		+7.7%	+6.9%
Compound growth rate			+7.3%

PepsiCo also discloses information about sales and operating profits for each of its three major operating segments, which it grouped by product market: Snack Foods (including Frito-Lay North America and Frito-Lay International); Worldwide Beverages (including Pepsi-Cola North America, Gatorade/Tropicana North America, and PepsiCo Beverages International); and Quaker Foods North America. PepsiCo also discloses sales volume growth for each segment, which the analyst can use to infer price growth for each segment. These segment and sales volume data reveal significant differences in volume and price growth rates across segments. Comparable net sales amounts, sales growth rates, volume growth rates, and price growth rates by segment for PepsiCo appear in Exhibit 10.2.

By analyzing these volume and price growth data across different segments, an analyst can develop more detailed and accurate sales forecasts for each segment.

Snack Foods Sales Growth

The Snack Foods segment, PepsiCo's largest segment in terms of sales, generated a compound annual sales growth rate of 7.7 percent between Years 9 and 11, driven

EXHIBIT 10.2			
PepsiCo Sales Growth Analysis by Segment			
	Year 9	**Year 10**	**Year 11**
Snack Food Segment			
Sales.....................................	$12,506	$13,621	$14,504
Percent of total sales	53.5%	54.1%	53.8%
Growth rates		+8.9%	+6.5%
Compound annual growth rate			+7.7%
Compound annual growth in sales volume ...			+5.4%
Compound annual growth rate in prices.....			+2.2%
Worldwide Beverages Segment			
Sales.....................................	$ 8,886	$ 9,592	$10,440
Percent of total sales	38.0%	38.1%	38.8%
Growth rates		+7.9%	+8.8%
Compound annual growth rate			+8.4%
Compound annual growth in sales volume ...			+5.0%
Compound annual growth rate in prices.....			+3.2%
Quaker Segment			
Sales.....................................	$ 1,993	$ 1,972	1,991
Percent of total sales	8.5%	7.8%	7.4%
Growth rates		−1.1%	+1.0%
Compound annual growth rate			0.1%
Compound annual growth in sales volume ...			−1.0%
Compound annual growth rate in prices.....			+1.0%

largely by increases in sales volume (5.4 percent) coupled with modest increases in prices (2.2 percent). Sales volume growth has been led by strength in their core brands, as well as new product introductions. The modest increase in prices likely reflects the relatively price-competitive snack foods markets. An analyst might expect that sales volume growth will continue at 5 percent per year into the future, and that price increases will be limited to 2 percent per year, which will produce an overall sales growth rate of 7.1 percent (that is, $1.071 = 1.05 \times 1.02$.) Snack Foods segment sales over the first five years of the forecast horizon would then be:

Year 11 (actual)...........................	$14,504	
Year +1 (forecast)	$15,534	+7.1%
Year +2 (forecast)	$16,637	+7.1%
Year +3 (forecast)	$17,818	+7.1%
Year +4 (forecast)	$19,083	+7.1%
Year +5 (forecast)	$20,438	+7.1%

Worldwide Beverages Sales Growth

PepsiCo's Worldwide Beverages segment experienced a compound annual sales growth rate of 8.4 percent between Years 9 and 11, which includes sales volume growth of 5.0 percent and sales price growth of 3.2 percent. PepsiCo discloses that Pepsi-Cola North America and Gatorade/Tropicana North America have generated the strongest sales growth rates in the beverages segment, with slower growth occurring in the PepsiCo Beverages International division. New products and acquisitions have driven the strong growth, with weaker growth in trademark brands. The beverage segment experienced greater price growth (3.2 percent) than the snack foods segment (2.2 percent), which likely reflects a more concentrated, less price-competitive product market for beverages. An analyst might expect PepsiCo's beverage segment to sustain 5.0 percent growth in sales volume, and 3.0 percent growth in prices into the future, creating a compound sales growth rate of 8.2 percent. Sales for the Worldwide Beverage segment over the first five years of the forecast horizon would then be:

Year 11 (actual)	$10,440	
Year +1 (forecast)	$11,296	+8.2%
Year +2 (forecast)	$12,222	+8.2%
Year +3 (forecast)	$13,225	+8.2%
Year +4 (forecast)	$14,309	+8.2%
Year +5 (forecast)	$15,482	+8.2%

Quaker Foods Sales Growth

The Quaker Foods North America segment has experienced virtually flat sales growth, with a 1.0 percent decline in sales volume offset by a 1.0 percent increase in prices. Looking ahead, an analyst might expect this segment to stem the tide of falling sales volume and maintain 1.0 percent price increases, leading to a steady 1.0 percent growth in net sales. If so, then sales for the Quaker Foods North America segment over the first five years of the forecast horizon would be:

Year 11 (actual)	$1,991	
Year +1 (forecast)	$2,011	+1.0%
Year +2 (forecast)	$2,031	+1.0%
Year +3 (forecast)	$2,051	+1.0%
Year +4 (forecast)	$2,072	+1.0%
Year +5 (forecast)	$2,093	+1.0%

Combined Segment Sales Growth

Combining all three sets of sales forecasts for these three segments, PepsiCo's total net sales and sales growth rates over the first five years of the forecast horizon would be:[6]

Year 11 (actual)...............................	$26,935	
Year +1 (forecast)	$28,841	+7.1%
Year +2 (forecast)	$30,890	+7.1%
Year +3 (forecast)	$33,094	+7.1%
Year +4 (forecast)	$35,464	+7.2%
Year +5 (forecast)	$38,013	+7.2%

The Forecast spreadsheet of FSAP gives the analyst the opportunity to specify forecast parameters (such as sales growth rates) for Year +1 through Year +11. The forecast parameters for Year +11 represent forecast assumptions for the long-run horizon. We assume that PepsiCo will maintain sales growth of 7.2 percent until Year +10. We then assume a 5.0 percent sales growth rate in Year +11 and beyond, consistent with long-run growth in the economy of 2.0 percent and long-run expected inflation of 3.0 percent.

PROJECTING OTHER REVENUES

Other revenues for PepsiCo primarily include earnings from bottling operations and other equity-method affiliates. Apart from an unusually large $1.0 billion gain recognized in Year 9 as a result of sales of certain bottling operation investments, other revenues as a percentage of sales have been steady at roughly 0.5 percent of sales in Years 10 and 11. For projection purposes, one can assume that gains of the magnitude experienced in Year 9 will not recur and that other revenues will remain steady at 0.5 percent of sales.

As an alternative, one can assume PepsiCo will earn a normal rate of return on its investment in these bottling affiliates, in which case the rate of expected return and the level of investment will drive other revenues in unconsolidated affiliates. In Year 11, for example, PepsiCo recognized $160 million in equity income on an average investment of $2,925 million [= .5($2,871 + $2,979)], for a return of 5.5 percent. This rate of return is probably reasonable because bottling companies are relatively low risk, low margin businesses, and the income recognized by PepsiCo on these investments has already been adjusted for the income taxes paid by the affiliates

---

[6]Note 1 in PepsiCo's Year 11 annual report describes adoption of a new accounting standard (EITF 01-9). Beginning in forecast Year +1, this new standard will reduce reported amounts for sales and selling and administrative expenses by equivalent amounts, which reflect payments received from customers for cooperative marketing, advertising, and promotion programs. For Year 11, this new accounting standard would have reduced reported sales, and selling and administrative expenses, by $3.4 billion each. Because these amounts offset, net income and cash flows are not changed. To maintain consistency with prior reported amounts of sales and selling and administrative expenses, we develop our forecasts based on the old reporting standard.

(PepsiCo does not have to pay taxes on these investments until it receives dividends or sells a portion of the investment). Therefore, we will project Other Revenues in future years to be 5.5 percent of the annual average Investment in Unconsolidated Affiliates. We will describe our projections of amounts of Investment in Unconsolidated Affiliates when we project the assets on the balance sheet, so for now, accept the projected investment amounts below as given. The projected amounts for Other Revenues appear below:

Year	Investments in Unconsolidated Affiliates			Rate of Return	Other Revenues
	Beginning	Ending	Average		
+1	$2,871	$3,287	$3,079	5.5%	$169
+2	$3,287	$3,524	$3,405	5.5%	$187
+3	$3,524	$3,779	$3,651	5.5%	$201
+4	$3,779	$4,052	$3,915	5.5%	$215
+5	$4,052	$4,346	$4,199	5.5%	$231

STEP 2: PROJECT OPERATING EXPENSES

The procedure for projecting operating expenses depends on the degree to which the various operating expense items have fixed or variable components. If all operating expenses behave as variable costs and the analyst anticipates no changes in their behavior relative to sales, then the common-size income statement percentages can serve as the basis for projecting future operating expenses. We would multiply projected sales by the cost of goods sold percentage, by the selling and administrative expense percentage, and so on, to derive the amounts for operating expenses. Equivalently, we can project each operating expense to grow at the same rate as sales.

Alternatively, if the cost structure reflects a proportion of fixed cost that will not change (or will change relatively slowly) as sales increase (that is, the firm experiences economies of scale), then using the common size income statement approach described above can result in expense projections that are too high. In this case, the analyst should attempt to estimate the variable and fixed cost structure of the firm. Capital-intensive manufacturing firms often have high proportions of fixed costs in their cost structures. One clue suggesting the presence of fixed costs is that the percentage change in cost of goods sold or selling and administrative expenses in prior years is significantly less than the percentage change in sales. Using the historical growth rates for individual cost items is one way of reflecting the effects of different mixes of variable and fixed costs.

When projecting operating expenses as a percent of sales, the analyst should be careful to keep in mind that an expense as a percent of sales can change over time as: (a) expenses change, holding sales constant, or (b) sales change holding expenses constant, or (c) both types of change occur simultaneously. As an example of case (a), the analyst may expect an expense to become a smaller fraction of sales over time if the firm is expected to reduce the expense relative to each dollar of sales through economies of scale or increased operating efficiencies. As an example of case (b), the analyst may expect the firm will hold expenses constant, but will face increased competition for sales and therefore may be forced to lower sales prices, causing the expected expense-to-sales ratio to increase. In scenario (c), if the analyst expects both effects will occur simultaneously, the net result on the projected expense-to-sales percentage will depend on which of the two effects is expected to be proportionally greater.

Cost of Goods Sold

PepsiCo's cost of goods sold percentage declined from 43.0 percent of sales in Year 8 to 41.2 percent in Year 9, and declined further to 40.1 percent in Year 10, and 39.9 percent in Year 11. This pattern suggests that PepsiCo has some proportion of cost of goods sold that behaves like a fixed cost. Based on their recent performance and the apparent presence of a proportion of fixed costs, we assume that PepsiCo will be able to achieve additional reductions in the cost of goods sold percentage over time, gradually reducing this cost to roughly 39.0 percent of sales by Year +5, and that PepsiCo's cost of goods sold will remain at 39.0 percent through Year +10 and beyond. As an alternative, one could also reasonably assume that PepsiCo will gain further efficiencies in cost of goods sold in the future. For example, Coca-Cola's cost of good sold percentage has varied between 36 percent and 38 percent of sales over Years 8 to 11, and it may be possible for PepsiCo to further reduce its cost of sales to approach Coca-Cola's cost levels. We do not make this assumption, however, because PepsiCo's sales include a high proportion of snack foods and breakfast foods, which likely have higher costs as a percent of sales than beverages. Our cost of goods sold forecasts through Year +5 appear below:

	Sales	Percentage of Sales	Cost of Goods Sold
Year +1 Projected	$28,841	39.7%	$11,450
Year +2 Projected	$30,890	39.5%	$12,202
Year +3 Projected	$33,094	39.3%	$13,006
Year +4 Projected	$35,464	39.1%	$13,866
Year +5 Projected	$38,013	39.0%	$14,825

Selling and Administrative Expenses

The selling and administrative expense varied between 43.1 percent and 43.9 percent of sales during Years 8 through 11. We project selling and administrative expenses to equal roughly 43.1 percent of sales in the future. Again, an analyst might also reasonably assume that PepsiCo will achieve further selling and administrative expense efficiencies in the future as a result of the merger with Quaker, and reduce this percentage over time. Coca-Cola maintained selling and administrative expenses at roughly 40 percent of sales over those same years.

	Sales	Percentage of Sales	Selling and Administrative Expenses
Year +1 Projected	$28,841	43.1%	$12,429
Year +2 Projected	$30,890	43.1%	$13,312
Year +3 Projected	$33,094	43.1%	$14,262
Year +4 Projected	$35,464	43.1%	$15,284
Year +5 Projected	$38,013	43.1%	$16,382

Other Operating Expenses

PepsiCo recognized other recurring operating expenses that represent between 0.6 percent and 0.8 percent of sales during Years 8 through 11. These expenses largely represent amortization of intangibles, such as goodwill, trademarks, and brands. Beginning in forecast Year +1, U.S. GAAP will no longer require amortization of goodwill, which represents roughly 70 percent of PepsiCo's intangible assets. We therefore forecast that other operating expenses will decrease as a percent of sales in Year +1 by roughly 70 percent. We project other operating expenses will equal 0.2 percent of sales in Year +1 and beyond.

Exhibit 10.3 presents pro forma statements of income and retained earnings for Years +1 through +5. We discuss the projections of interest income, interest expense, income tax expense, net income, and the change in retained earnings after projecting PepsiCo's balance sheet.

STEP 3: PROJECT THE ASSETS ON THE BALANCE SHEET

We prepare the asset side of the pro forma balance sheet next. We project individual assets and then sum individual asset amounts to obtain total assets. We take this approach first to illustrate how to develop forecasts that capture different drivers of growth in different types of assets, allowing the mix of the firm's assets to change over time. Later in the chapter, we also briefly describe shortcut approaches for projecting total assets, such as using sales and total asset turnover rates to forecast total assets and then using the common-size balance sheet percentages to allocate this total among individual asset items.

To develop forecasts of individual assets, the analyst must first link historical growth rates for individual assets to historical growth rates in sales (or other activity-based drivers). The analyst can then use those links to develop forecasts of individual assets based on sales growth forecasts, particularly for assets integrally related to operations (accounts receivable, inventories, and fixed assets). By using turnover rates to develop

	EXHIBIT 10.3				
	Pro Forma Statements of Income and Retained Earnings for PepsiCo **(amounts in millions; allow for rounding errors)**				
	Year +1 Projected	Year +2 Projected	Year +3 Projected	Year +4 Projected	Year +5 Projected
Sales[a]........................	$28,841	$30,890	$33,094	$35,464	$38,013
Cost of Goods Sold[b]..............	(11,450)	(12,202)	(13,006)	(13,866)	(14,825)
Gross Margin	$17,391	$18,688	$20,088	$21,598	$23,188
Selling and Administrative Expense[c] ...	(12,429)	(13,312)	(14,262)	(15,284)	(16,382)
Other Revenues[d].................	169	187	201	215	231
Other Expenses[e]	(58)	(62)	(66)	(71)	(76)
Operating Income	$ 5,073	$ 5,501	$ 5,960	$ 6,458	$ 6,961
Interest Income[f]	73	80	86	92	99
Interest Expense[g]	(189)	(199)	(194)	(203)	(216)
Income before Income Taxes	$ 4,957	$ 5,382	$ 5,852	$ 6,347	$ 6,844
Income Tax Expense[h]	(1,586)	(1,722)	(1,873)	(2,031)	(2,190)
Net Income.....................	$ 3,371	$ 3,660	$ 3,980	$ 4,316	$ 4,654
Preferred Dividends[i]..............	(4)	(4)	(4)	(4)	(4)
Common Dividends[j]	(1,600)	(1,692)	(1,572)	(2,395)	(1,920)
Change in Retained Earnings........	$ 1,767	$ 1,964	$ 2,404	$ 1,917	$ 2,730

[a]Projected using expected growth rates for the three primary product market segments.
[b]Projected assuming a steady decline from 39.7 percent to 39.0 percent of sales.
[c]Projected assuming 43.1 percent of sales.
[d]Projected assuming 5.5 percent return on investments.
[e]Projected assuming 0.2 percent of sales.
[f]Projected assuming an interest rate of 4.2 percent earned on average cash and short-term investments.
[g]Projected assuming an interest rate of 6 percent on average short-term borrowing, current maturities of long-term debt, and long-term debt.
[h]Projected assuming an effective tax rate of 32.0 percent of income before taxes.
[i]Projected assuming a constant preferred stock dividend.
[j]Projected assuming a dividend payout rate of 38.0 percent of net income, plus any necessary adjustment to balance the balance sheet.

forecasts for individual assets, the analyst can capture the projected levels of operating activity and permit changes in the expected relations between individual assets and operating activities, such as sales. Our projections of individual assets for PepsiCo illustrate the use of a combination of drivers, including common-size percentages, growth rates, and asset turnovers. Exhibit 10.4 presents the projected balance sheets through Year +5. The sections below discuss the projection of individual assets.

Cash and Marketable Securities

PepsiCo has reduced its cash holdings between Years 9 to 11, while at the same time it has increased its holdings of marketable securities. At the end of Year 11, PepsiCo had a cash balance roughly equivalent to 9.3 days of sales (computed as 365

EXHIBIT 10.4

Pro Forma Balance Sheets for PepsiCo
(amounts in millions; allow for rounding errors)

	Year +1 Projected	Year +2 Projected	Year +3 Projected	Year +4 Projected	Year +5 Projected
Assets					
Cash	$ 790	$ 846	$ 907	$ 972	$ 1,041
Short-term Investments	1,057	1,133	1,215	1,302	1,397
Accounts Receivable	2,291	2,454	2,629	2,818	3,020
Inventories	1,316	1,402	1,495	1,594	1,704
Other Current Assets	822	881	945	1,013	1,086
Total Current Assets.............	$ 6,276	$ 6,716	$ 7,191	$ 7,699	$ 8,248
Investments......................	3,287	3,524	3,779	4,052	4,346
Property, Plant, and					
Equipment (cost)................	13,598	15,117	16,744	18,488	20,357
Accumulated Depreciation...........	(6,207)	(7,174)	(8,210)	(9,320)	(10,510)
Other Assets	6,526	6,990	7,489	8,025	8,602
Total Assets	$23,481	$25,173	$26,993	$28,944	$31,043
Liabilities and Shareholders' Equity					
Accounts Payable	$ 1,287	$ 1,380	$ 1,471	$ 1,569	$ 1,678
Short-term Borrowings..	117	126	135	145	155
Current Maturities of					
Long-term Debt.................	485	441	167	602	310
Other Current Liabilities	3,647	3,906	4,185	4,484	4,807
Total Current Liabilities...........	$ 5,536	$ 5,853	$ 5,958	$ 6,800	$ 6,950
Long-term Debt	2,700	2,769	2,834	2,894	3,104
Deferred Income Taxes.	1,602	1,716	1,838	1,970	2,111
Other Noncurrent Liabilities	4,150	4,445	4,762	5,103	5,470
Total Liabilities	$13,989	$14,782	$15,394	$16,768	$17,636
Preferred Stock....................	$ 26	$ 26	$ 26	$ 26	$ 26
Common Stock....................	43	43	43	43	43
Retained Earnings..................	13,286	15,251	17,655	19,572	22,302
Other Equity Adjustments	(1,646)	(1,646)	(1,646)	(1,646)	(1,646)
Treasury Stock	(2,217)	(3,283)	(4,479)	(5,819)	(7,318)
Total Shareholders' Equity.........	$ 9,492	$10,391	$11,599	$12,176	$13,407
Total Liabilities and					
Shareholders' Equity	$23,481	$25,173	$26,993	$28,944	$31,043

days divided by the ratio of sales to ending cash, or 365 / [$26,935 /$683]). PepsiCo needs a certain amount of cash on hand to maintain sufficient liquidity for day-to-day operations. We assume PepsiCo will maintain year-end cash balances equivalent to roughly 10 days of sales.

	Annual Sales	Average Sales per Day	Days Sales in Cash	Year-end Cash Balance
Year +1 Projected............	$28,841	$ 79.0	10 days	$ 790
Year +2 Projected............	$30,890	$ 84.6	10 days	$ 846
Year +3 Projected............	$33,094	$ 90.7	10 days	$ 907
Year +4 Projected............	$35,464	$ 97.2	10 days	$ 972
Year +5 Projected............	$38,013	$104.1	10 days	$1,041

Marketable securities (also commonly referred to as Short-term Investments, as is the case on PepsiCo's Year 11 balance sheet) have grown to represent 4.5 percent of total assets by the end of Year 11. We will assume that the marketable securities balance will continue to grow but remain in the same proportion to total assets, at 4.5 percent of total assets. We will therefore project the dollar amount of marketable securities each year as a function of all of the other asset amounts.

As discussed in more detail later, projecting future balance sheet amounts by projecting individual assets, liabilities, and shareholders' equity items requires the analyst to plug a flexible financial asset or liability account on the balance sheet to bring about an equality of assets with liabilities and shareholders' equity. For some firms, the plug may be cash. For such firms, the cash account represents the financial liquidity "safety valve," where cash is kept in a liquid account that the firm can use to meet periodic cash needs. For these firms, analysts typically forecast the cash balance as the plug needed to balance the balance sheet after all the other balance sheet amounts have been determined. If the analyst considers the projected level of cash to be too large, the analyst can then assume that the firm will invest the excess in marketable securities (if the excess is considered temporary), or pay down borrowing. If the analyst projects the balance in cash will be too low or negative, the analyst might then assume that the firm will need to engage in short-term borrowing to bring about a desired level of cash. PepsiCo, like many other firms, manages cash to provide sufficient liquidity while minimizing amounts tied up in assets that do not earn high rates of return. For such firms, analysts use other flexible financial accounts, such as investment securities, short-term or long-term debt, or dividends, as the balance sheet plug.

To make the three primary pro forma financial statements articulate with each other, the change in cash balance on the balance sheet each year should agree with the net change in cash on the projected statement of cash flows. We will demonstrate how to compute the implied statement of cash flows later in this chapter. We will also include on the pro forma income statements any interest income that the cash and marketable securities can be expected to earn.

Accounts Receivable

PepsiCo's accounts receivable collection period has declined steadily from an average of 37 days in Year 7 to an average of 29 days in Years 10 and 11. We project accounts receivable by assuming PepsiCo will maintain an average 29-day collection period in the future, turning over accounts receivable approximately 12.6 times a year (365/29). The projected amounts appear below:

	Sales	Accounts Receivable Collection	Average Accounts Receivable
Year +1 Projected	$28,841	29 days	$2,291
Year +2 Projected	$30,890	29 days	$2,454
Year +3 Projected	$33,094	29 days	$2,629
Year +4 Projected	$35,464	29 days	$2,818
Year +5 Projected	$38,013	29 days	$3,020

Because we rely on average accounts receivable balances to compute turnover rates and collection periods, the above approach produces estimates of the *average* accounts receivable balance for the year (and the same will be true whenever we use average turnover rates to forecast any asset or liability amounts, including inventory, fixed assets, and payables). This approach will produce accurate forecasts of year-end account balances *if* the firm generates sales evenly throughout the year. However, if the firm is likely to experience significant growth in sales and receivables over the year, or experience substantial seasonality in sales and receivables, then this approach may introduce a degree of estimation error.

In the case of PepsiCo, for example, we expect 7.1 percent sales growth, so estimating average accounts receivable balances will tend to underestimate year-end balances. For the analyst interested in greater forecast precision, a number of alternatives exist. One alternative is to base the forecasts on asset turnover rates using year-end account balances, which assumes a degree of stationarity in the relation between sales and ending balances. Another possibility is to forecast average balances and then increase them proportionately to year-end amounts using the expected growth rate in sales from the average (or midpoint) of the year to the end of the year. A third possibility is to compute the ending balance implied by the beginning balance and the average (that is, the implied ending balance should equal two times the average balance minus the beginning balance). To illustrate, we compute below the ending accounts receivable balances implied by the annual averages, and the differences between the average and ending balances.

		Accounts Receivable			Difference:
	Sales	Average	Beginning of Year	End of Year	Average Minus End of Year
Year +1 Projected ...	$28,841	$2,291	$2,142	$2,440	$–149
Year +2 Projected ...	$30,890	$2,454	$2,440	$2,468	$ –14
Year +3 Projected ...	$33,094	$2,629	$2,468	$2,790	$–161
Year +4 Projected ...	$35,464	$2,818	$2,790	$2,846	$ –28
Year +5 Projected ...	$38,013	$3,020	$2,846	$3,194	$ –74

A desirable feature of computing implied ending balances is that it reduces the potential understatement inherent in average balances. In the case of PepsiCo, using the forecast for the average balance in accounts receivable would understate the Year +1 ending balance by $149 million (roughly 6.5 percent, which is just under 2 days of sales), whereas in Year +2 it would only understate by $14 million (roughly 0.5 percent). A less desirable feature of this approach is that it can introduce artificial volatility in ending balances. For example, the Year +1 projected increase in receivables is quite large, partially to compensate for an unusually small increase in receivables relative to sales in Year 11, just prior to our forecast period. The large increase in Year +1 then triggers an unusually small increase in Year +2 to compensate, and so on. Exhibit 10.5 depicts this type of "sawtooth" pattern. The analyst can mitigate the variability in this pattern by estimating the average rate of growth in receivables expected over a long horizon, and then smooth each year-end balance using this growth rate. For example, the compound growth rate in receivables over the 5-year forecast horizon shown above is 8.3 percent. One could forecast receivables to grow at this rate, creating a smooth growth rate in receivables.

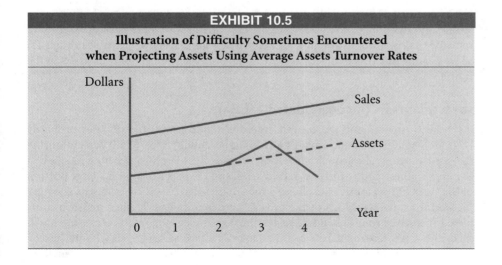

EXHIBIT 10.5

Illustration of Difficulty Sometimes Encountered when Projecting Assets Using Average Assets Turnover Rates

For our purposes, we will rely on average turnover rates because the degree of measurement error introduced by using average balances as estimates of year-end balances is relatively slight.

Inventories

PepsiCo has experienced slowing inventory turnover rates during the last four years. The average number of days in inventory increased from 38 days in Year 7 to 42 days in Years 10 and 11. We project inventories using an average inventory turnover period of 42 days, or equivalently, an average turnover rate of 8.7 times per year. The projected amounts appear below:

	Cost of Goods Sold	Inventory Turnover	Average Inventories
Year +1 Projected	$11,450	8.7	$1,316
Year +2 Projected	$12,202	8.7	$1,402
Year +3 Projected	$13,006	8.7	$1,495
Year +4 Projected	$13,866	8.7	$1,594
Year +5 Projected	$14,825	8.7	$1,704

Remember that this approach uses forecasts of average inventory balances as estimates of year-end inventory balances, which may slightly understate ending inventory. If greater forecast precision is desirable, then the analyst can apply one of the more precise but more cumbersome methods described above in the discussion of accounts receivable.

Other Current Assets

Other current assets usually vary in relation to the level of operating activity, such as sales, production, or total assets. In the case of PepsiCo, other current assets have remained fairly steady at roughly 3.5 percent of total assets over Years 9 through 11, so we assume that other current assets will remain at 3.5 percent of total assets in the future.

Investments in Unconsolidated Affiliates

PepsiCo's investments represent its interests in unconsolidated affiliates, primarily bottlers. These investments grew at a compound annual rate of 15.9 percent during the last five years. The growth reflects the effects of (1) PepsiCo accruing its share of earnings in these equity method subsidiaries, and (2) PepsiCo selling a large portion of the stock of previously consolidated subsidiaries that PepsiCo now treats as equity method investments. Much of the growth occurred in Year 9, when PepsiCo completed this sale. From the end of Year 9 through the end of Year 11, investments in securities have remained between 13.2 percent and 14.4 percent of total assets. Assuming that the increase in Year 9 was unusual, we assume that equity method investments will grow in proportion with total assets and remain at 14.0 percent of total assets in the future.

Property, Plant, and Equipment

PepsiCo's fixed assets turnover ratio increased steadily from 2.8 to 4.0 between Year 7 and Year 11. The increase likely results from the sale of interests in previously consolidated bottlers, as well as the consolidation of fixed assets acquired in the Quaker merger. We assume that PepsiCo's fixed asset efficiency will remain at a turnover rate of 4.0 in the future. Thus, we expect that PepsiCo's net fixed assets will grow at approximately the same rate as sales. To be more specific, we assume that sales growth will drive capital expenditures on gross property, plant, and equipment at cost, which in turn will drive growth in depreciation expense. Growth in net property, plant, and equipment will therefore reflect the capital expenditures minus depreciation expenses. PepsiCo's statement of cash flows and Note 20 reveal that capital expenditures amounted to $1,324 million in Year 11. Note 8 reveals that depreciation expense related to property, plant, and equipment in Year 11 amounted to $843 million. The projected amounts appear below.

Year	Sales Growth	Property, Plant, and Equipment				
		Capital Expenditures	Ending Balance at Cost	Depreciation Expense	Accumulated Depreciation	Ending Balance Net
11 actual		$1,324	$12,180	$ −843	($5,304)	$6,876
+1	+ 7.1%	$1,418	$13,598	$ −903	($6,207)	$7,391
+2	+ 7.1%	$1,519	$15,117	$ −967	($7,174)	$7,943
+3	+ 7.1%	$1,627	$16,744	$−1,036	($8,210)	$8,534
+4	+ 7.2%	$1,744	$18,488	$−1,110	($9,320)	$9,168
+5	+ 7.2%	$1,869	$20,357	$−1,190	($10,510)	$9,847

When forecasting fixed assets for capital-intensive firms or firms for which fixed asset growth is a critical driver of future sales growth and earnings (for example, new stores for retail chains or restaurant chains), the analyst should invest considerable time and effort in developing detailed forecasts of capital expenditures and depreciation expense schedules. For such firms, capital expenditures are typically an economically large part of the balance sheet and have a material impact on the analysts' forecasts of earnings, cash flows, and firm value.

Other Assets

Other assets for PepsiCo primarily include goodwill, trademarks, brands, and other identifiable intangibles from acquisitions. In the normal course of business, these assets usually decline ratably over time as they are amortized over their estimated useful lives. Beginning in the first forecast year, U.S. GAAP will no longer require amortization of goodwill, which constitutes the majority of PepsiCo's other assets. However, these assets will be subject to periodic impairment tests, which could trigger significant write-downs of goodwill if they are deemed impaired. These intangible assets can also increase or decrease dramatically in a given year as a result of an acquisition of another firm with significant intangible assets, or the sale of consolidated subsidiaries with significant recognized intangible assets.

In the case of PepsiCo, other assets decreased by 32.9 percent in Year 7, increased by 46.0 percent in Year 8, and then decreased again by 43.9 percent in Year 9. It is difficult to project with confidence substantial increases or decreases in other intangible assets from corporate events such as acquisitions, sales of subsidiaries, or impairment test write-downs. We can project, however, that PepsiCo will likely continue to invest in other intangible assets as it acquires companies with new products and brands in order to drive future sales growth. Therefore, we forecast that other intangible assets will grow at the same rate as sales. The projected amounts for other assets are:

	Year-end Other Assets	Percentage Increase
Year 11 Actual	$6,095	
Year +1 Projected......................	$6,526	7.1%
Year +2 Projected......................	$6,990	7.1%
Year +3 Projected......................	$7,489	7.1%
Year +4 Projected......................	$8,025	7.2%
Year +5 Projected......................	$8,602	7.2%

Assets that Vary as a Percent of Total Assets

We can now project asset amounts that we expect will vary as a percentage of total assets, including marketable securities (4.5 percent), other current assets (3.5 percent), and investment securities (14.0 percent), for a total of 22.0 percent. Projected amounts for Year +1 for all of the individual assets other than these three assets are as follows:

Cash..	$ 790
Accounts Receivable	2,291
Inventories..	1,316
Property, Plant, and Equipment (net)	7,391
Other Assets..	6,526
Subtotal of assets..	$18,314

The $18,314 subtotal represents 78.0 percent (= 1.0 − .045 − .035 − .140) of total assets. Projected total assets therefore equal $23,481 (= $18,314/0.78). Marketable securities equal $1,057 (= 0.045 × $23,481); other current assets equal $822 (= 0.035

× \$23,481); and investments equal \$3,287 (= 0.140 × \$23,481). The projected amounts for total assets, marketable securities, other current assets, and investments in Years +1 to +5 are as follows:

Year:	Total Assets	Marketable Securities (4.5%)	Other Current Assets (3.5%)	Investments (14.0%)
+1	\$23,481	\$1,057	\$ 822	\$3,287
+2	\$25,173	\$1,133	\$ 881	\$3,524
+3	\$26,993	\$1,215	\$ 945	\$3,779
+4	\$28,944	\$1,302	\$1,013	\$4,052
+5	\$31,043	\$1,397	\$1,086	\$4,346

STEP 4: PROJECT LIABILITIES AND SHAREHOLDERS' EQUITY

Once the analyst completes forecasting the asset side of the pro forma balance sheet, projections of liabilities and shareholders' equity come next. For firms that target and maintain a particular capital structure over time, the analyst can use the common-size balance sheet percentages to project amounts of individual liabilities and shareholders' equities. The common-size balance sheet for PepsiCo in Appendix C shows that the balance sheet percentages for total liabilities fluctuated from 68.5 percent of total assets in Year 7, up to 73.9 percent in Year 8, followed by steady declines each year down to 60.0 percent in Year 11. Complementarily, shareholders' equity fluctuated from 31.5 percent of total assets in Year 7, down to 26.1 percent in Year 8, followed by increases each year up to 40.0 percent in Year 11. If the analyst believes that PepsiCo's capital structure will consist of 60.0 percent liabilities and 40.0 percent equities in the future, then these common-size percentages could be used to project individual liabilities and equities. Alternatively, the analyst can project individual liabilities and shareholders' equity accounts using historical growth rates or turnover ratios. In this chapter, we illustrate forecasting individual liabilities and equities using a combination of common-size percentages, growth rates, and turnover ratios for PepsiCo, in order to develop forecasts that incorporate the projected levels of operating activities and permit changes in the expected behavior of individual liability and equity amounts over time. We consider each account next.

Accounts Payable

PepsiCo includes accounts payable and other current liabilities, which primarily represent accrued expenses, on a single line on its balance sheet amounting to \$4,461 million at the end of Year 11. Note 11 identifies that \$1,238 million of that total is attributable to accounts payable, and the remainder ($3,223 million) is attributable to accruals for selling, advertising, marketing, compensation, and other expenses. Different factors may drive the future amounts of accounts payable and accrued expenses. Future credit purchases of inventory and PepsiCo's payment policy to its suppliers will likely drive accounts payable, whereas accrued expenses will likely grow with future selling and administrative expenses. Therefore, we forecast accounts payable and accrued expenses separately.

PepsiCo's days payable varied between 39 and 51 days during the last five years. During the last three years, the average payables period has declined from 48 days in Year 9, to 45 days in Year 10, to 41 days in Year 11. We assume PepsiCo will maintain an accounts payable period of 41 days in the future. To forecast future accounts payable balances, we begin by calculating forecasts of inventory purchases on account.

	Year +1	Year +2	Year +3	Year +4	Year +5
Cost of Goods Sold.......	$11,450	$12,202	$13,006	$13,866	$14,825
Plus Ending Inventory	1,316	1,402	1,495	1,594	1,704
Less Beginning Inventory..	(1,310)	(1,316)	(1,402)	(1,495)	(1,594)
Inventory Purchases	$11,456	$12,288	$13,099	$13,965	$14,935

The projection of accounts payable using an average of 41 days payable is as follows. For illustration purposes, we also compute the implied beginning and ending balances of accounts payable to assess the extent to which using average days in payables understates the likely ending balances in payables:

	Accounts Payable					Difference: Average Minus End of Year
	Inventory Purchases	Days	Average	Beginning of Year	End of Year	
Year +1 Projected	$11,456	41	$1,287	$1,238	$1,336	$–49
Year +2 Projected	$12,288	41	$1,380	$1,336	$1,424	$–44
Year +3 Projected	$13,099	41	$1,471	$1,424	$1,518	$–47
Year +4 Projected	$13,965	41	$1,569	$1,518	$1,620	$–51
Year +5 Projected	$14,935	41	$1,678	$1,620	$1,736	$–58

In this case, because we forecast PepsiCo's purchases of inventory to grow over time smoothly with costs of sales and because we assume the payables period will be a constant 41 days, using the average balance in accounts payable introduces only minor understatements as compared to the implied ending balances. Again, for the analyst who needs a higher degree of forecast precision, it may be worthwhile to use implied end-of-year balances.

Other Current Liabilities

Note 11 states that, at the end of Year 11, PepsiCo has current accruals of $3,223 million, which are largely attributable to selling, advertising, marketing, compensation, and other expenses. On the Year 11 balance sheet, PepsiCo also recognizes a relatively small current accrued liability for income taxes payable of $183 million. Because these accrued liability amounts relate to operating expenses and taxes, which vary with sales and income, we combine them for forecasting purposes. Our forecasts of income for PepsiCo assumed that selling and administrative expenses would remain a steady percentage of sales, and therefore grow proportionately with sales. We therefore forecast that the combined total of other current liabilities and income taxes payable will grow with selling and administrative expenses.

	Year-end Other Current Liabilities	Percentage Increase
Year 11 Actual ($3,223 + $183)	$3,406	
Year +1 Projected	$3,647	7.1%
Year +2 Projected	$3,906	7.1%
Year +3 Projected	$4,185	7.1%
Year +4 Projected	$4,484	7.2%
Year +5 Projected	$4,807	7.2%

Short-term Borrowings

Note 12 discloses that PepsiCo's short-term borrowings represent current maturities of long-term debt, short-term notes payable, and amounts borrowed under a $750 million revolving line of credit for temporary cash needs. Note 12 reveals that, at the end of Year 11, for example, total short-term borrowings were $354 million, which included $319 million of current maturities of long-term debt. Short-term borrowings also includes $410 million in other borrowings; however, that includes $375 million borrowed under the revolving line of credit, which PepsiCo reclassified as long-term debt because of its intent and ability to refinance on a long-term basis. Therefore, net short-term borrowings amount to only $35 million at the end of Year 11. We forecast the amounts relating to current maturities of long-term debt and the revolving line of credit as components of PepsiCo's long-term financing strategy and we forecast separately the amounts relating to other short-term borrowings.

Note 12 implies that PepsiCo does not rely heavily on short-term borrowings through notes payable to meet temporary cash flow needs (the revolving line of credit is used for those needs). PepsiCo generates substantial amounts of cash from its operations and investments. The statement of cash flows for PepsiCo in Appendix A indicates that the firm generates approximately $2 billion of net cash flow after operating and investing activities, and uses this cash flow primarily to pay dividends and repurchase common stock. Therefore, it is not surprising that short-term borrowings are a minor element of PepsiCo's financial capital structure. We project that short-term borrowings will be 0.5 percent of total assets in the future.

Long-term Debt and Current Maturities of Long-term Debt

Long-term debt as a percentage of total assets declined steadily from 25.6 percent in Year 7, to 12.2 percent in Year 11. A portion of this decline is attributable to reduced long-term debt to finance previously consolidated bottlers. Note 12 reveals that, at the end of Year 11, PepsiCo has $2,970 million in long-term debt, including $319 million in current maturities of long-term debt and $375 million under the revolving line of credit, which is classified as long-term debt. The outstanding long-term debt is due at varying maturity dates, extending to Year +25. Note 12 reveals the amounts due to be repaid in Years +1 ($319 million) through +5 ($602 million). The amount maturing in Year +2 ($485 million) will become the current maturity of long-term debt at the end of Year +1, the amount maturing in Year +3 ($441 million) will become the current maturity of long-term debt at the end of Year +2, and so on. We use these amounts and maturities to project the current portion of long-term debt through the end of Year +4; thereafter, we assume the current portion represents 10 percent of the long-term debt. We assume that PepsiCo will continue to slowly reduce its long-term debt to total assets ratio to approximately 10 percent by Year +4 and beyond. The projected amounts are as follows:

	Current Maturity of Long-term Debt	Year-end Long-term Debt	Percentage of Total Assets
Year +1 Projected	$485	$2,700	11.5%
Year +2 Projected	$441	$2,769	11.0%
Year +3 Projected	$167	$2,834	10.5%
Year +4 Projected	$602	$2,894	10.0%
Year +5 Projected	$310	$3,104	10.0%

Deferred Income Taxes

The income tax note for PepsiCo indicates that deferred taxes relate to a variety of operating items (investments in unconsolidated affiliates, property, plant, and equipment, employee benefits plans). Thus, we assume that deferred tax liabilities will increase at the growth rate in sales, which is the primary driver of operating activities. The amounts are as follows:

	Year-end Deferred Income Taxes	Percentage Increase
Year 11 Actual	$1,496	
Year +1 Projected.........................	$1,602	7.1%
Year +2 Projected.........................	$1,716	7.1%
Year +3 Projected.........................	$1,838	7.1%
Year +4 Projected.........................	$1,970	7.2%
Year +5 Projected.........................	$2,111	7.2%

Other Noncurrent Liabilities

Other noncurrent liabilities relate to pension obligations, health care obligations, and other operating and administrative expenses. We therefore project other noncurrent liabilities to grow with selling and administrative expenses, which are expected to grow with sales.

	Year-end Other Non-current Liabilities	Percentage Increase
Year 11 Actual........................	$3,876	
Year +1 Projected	$4,150	7.1%
Year +2 Projected	$4,445	7.1%
Year +3 Projected	$4,762	7.1%
Year +4 Projected	$5,103	7.2%
Year +5 Projected	$5,470	7.2%

Preferred Stock and Minority Interest

PepsiCo has $26 million in outstanding preferred stock at the end of Year 11 and no common equity capital from minority interest shareholders. We assume that these amounts will remain constant in the future.

Common Stock and Capital in Excess of Par Value

These paid-in capital accounts increase as the firm raises capital by selling shares to investors, and they decrease as the firm retires shares. Common stock and capital in excess of par value have steadily decreased for PepsiCo from $2,212 million at the end of Year 7, down to only $43 million at the end of Year 11. These accounts are not likely to decrease any further. In the past several years, PepsiCo has conducted its stock issue transactions for the Quaker merger and to meet stock option exercises through previously acquired treasury shares. We expect PepsiCo to continue to issue stock through the Treasury Stock account. Therefore, we project Common Stock and Capital in Excess of Par Value to remain constant, and we project the effects of stock issue and buyback transactions using the Treasury Stock accounts (discussed below).

Accumulated Other Comprehensive Loss

According the PepsiCo's Statement of Common Shareholders' Equity at the end of Year 11, Accumulated Other Comprehensive Loss primarily includes the cumulative effects of losses from foreign currency translation adjustments. The foreign currency translation adjustments have been consistently negative during the last five years. PepsiCo appears to have international operations in countries whose currencies have decreased in value relative to the U.S. dollar. We assume PepsiCo will continue to hold and possibly expand these international operations. It is difficult to forecast, however, whether the U.S. dollar will continue to increase in value relative to the foreign currencies of PepsiCo's international operations. One might also expect that PepsiCo will either hedge or limit their exposure to these adverse foreign currency movements. Thus, we project that PepsiCo will not experience continuing negative foreign currency translation adjustments, and that Accumulated Other Comprehensive Loss will remain at its current level. This assumption is equivalent to assuming that PepsiCo's future foreign currency translation adjustments are equally likely to be positive or negative in any given year and that, on average, they will be zero over time.

Other Equity Adjustments

PepsiCo's other equity adjustments relate primarily to accrued deferred compensation. Over the five years leading up to Year 11, this account steadily declined and in Year 11 it was reduced to a zero balance. We project that the balance will remain zero in the future.

Treasury Stock

The treasury stock account decreases (that is, becomes more negative) when the firm repurchases some of its shares. The treasury stock account increases (becomes less negative) when the firm's treasury shares are reissued on the open market, are used to meet stock option exercises, are exchanged in merger or acquisition transactions, or are retired. Over Years 9, 10, and 11, PepsiCo has repurchased significant amounts of its common stock and used treasury shares to meet stock options exercises. In addition, in Year 11, PepsiCo reduced the treasury stock account $7,243 million to reflect the issue of treasury shares to execute the merger with Quaker.

The stock market often interprets share repurchases as "good news," inferring that management, with its in-depth knowledge of the firm, thinks that the market is underpricing the firm's stock. The stock market typically reacts to this positive signal by bidding up the price of the firm's shares. Stock repurchases also represent a form of implicit dividend to shareholders which may be taxed at capital gains rates (depending on the shareholders' holding period and tax status), which may be lower than the ordinary income tax rates on dividends.

During Years 9 to 11, PepsiCo repurchased increasing amounts of treasury stock each year, from $1,285 million in Year 9 to $1,430 million in Year 10 (see PepsiCo's Statement of Changes in Common Shareholders' Equity in Appendix A). In Year 11, PepsiCo acquired $1,716 million in treasury stock in the aftermath of the September 11 tragedy. Repurchase transactions alone would have increased the treasury stock account in excess of 20 percent per year over this period. It is likely that PepsiCo will continue to make significant stock repurchases. We assume that PepsiCo will repurchase $1,700 million in treasury stock in Year +1, and that amount will increase by 10 percent per year. We may need to revisit this assumption at the end of our analysis, if we determine that PepsiCo will not have sufficient cash flow for these repurchases, or if our equity valuation estimates indicate that PepsiCo stock is overpriced in the market.

PepsiCo reissued treasury shares amounting to $514 million in Year 9, $816 million in Year 10, and $751 million in Year 11, to meet stock option exercises by employees (see PepsiCo's Statement of Changes in Common Shareholders' Equity in Appendix A). We assume that employees will continue to exercise stock options in future years (but we may need to reevaluate that assumption if it turns out we expect PepsiCo stock to fall in the future and the options are likely to become "out-of-the-money"). We project that treasury stock reissues for stock options grants will again be $751 million in Year +1 and will grow in the future at the same rate as sales.

We also project that PepsiCo's issue of treasury stock in the Quaker merger was unusual and that such large treasury stock issues for purposes of mergers and acquisitions will not continue in future years. Therefore, the projected amounts for treasury stock are as follows:

			Treasury Stock				
Year	Beginning Balance	Share Repurchases	Repurchase Growth Rate	Share Reissues	Reissue Growth Rate	Ending Balance	Implied Rate of Growth
+1	$–1,268	$–1,700	na	$751	na	$–2,217	74.8%
+2	$–2,217	$–1,870	10%	$804	7.1%	$–3,283	48.1%
+3	$–3,283	$–2,057	10%	$861	7.1%	$–4,479	36.4%
+4	$–4,479	$–2,263	10%	$923	7.2%	$–5,819	29.9%
+5	$–5,819	$–2,489	10%	$990	7.2%	$–7,318	25.8%

Beyond Year +5, we project treasury stock to continue to experience significant growth but at declining rates over time, and that growth in treasury stock will be 10 percent per year until Year +10, and 5.0 percent per year in Year +11, and thereafter.

STEP 5: PROJECT INTEREST EXPENSE, INTEREST INCOME, INCOME TAX EXPENSE, AND THE CHANGE IN RETAINED EARNINGS

Interest Expense

We can now project our first-iteration estimate of interest expense, based on our projected balances in interest-bearing capital, including short-term borrowing, current maturities of long-term debt, and long-term debt. Note 12 to PepsiCo's Year 11 financial statements indicates that the interest rate on short-term borrowing was 6.4 percent at the end of Year 11. Note 12 also indicates that the interest rate on roughly two-thirds of the long-term debt (including current maturities of long-term debt) was 4.1 percent and the weighted average interest rate on long-term debt was between 5.5 and 6.0 percent at the end of Year 11. We assume that interest expense will equal 6 percent on average short-term borrowing and 6 percent on average long-term debt (including current maturities of long-term debt) during Year +1 through Year +5. Projected interest expense appears below:

	Year +1	Year +2	Year +3	Year +4	Year +5
Average Short-term Borrowing	$ 235.5	$ 121.5	$ 130.5	$ 140.0	$ 150.0
Interest Rate	× .06	× .06	× .06	× .06	× .06
Interest Expense on Short-term Borrowing	$ 14.1	$ 7.3	$ 7.8	$ 8.4	$ 9.0
Average Long-term Debt	$2,918.0	$3,197.5	$3,105.5	$3,248.5	$3,455.0
Interest Rate	× .06	× .06	× .06	× .06	× .06
Interest Expense on Long-term Debt	$ 175.1	$ 191.8	$ 186.3	$ 194.9	$ 207.3
Total Interest Expense	$ 189.2	$ 199.1	$ 194.1	$ 203.3	$ 216.3

We can now enter these "first-pass" interest expense amounts in the projected income statements. If our projected balance sheets imply that PepsiCo will need larger amounts of long-term debt to finance future asset growth, then we will need to recompute the interest expense projections to reflect additional debt.

Interest Income

We can also project our first-iteration estimates of PepsiCo's interest income on financial assets, such as cash and cash equivalents and short-term investments in marketable securities. Recall that we accounted for returns earned on investments in unconsolidated affiliates (that is, bottling affiliates) as part of other revenues, and so we do not include them here. In Year 11, PepsiCo recognized $67 million in income on an average investment in cash and short-term investments of $1,577 million (=[$1,649 + $1,505]/2), for an average return of 4.2 percent. This rate of return is probably reasonable because it approximates the risk-free rate of return during Year 11, and it is likely that cash and short-term investments are held in very low risk but highly liquid instruments. The projected amounts for interest income appear below:

| | Cash and Short-term Investments | | | | |
Year	Beginning	Ending	Average	Rate of Return	Interest Income
+1	$1,649	$1,847	$1,748	4.2%	$73
+2	$1,847	$1,979	$1,913	4.2%	$80
+3	$1,979	$2,121	$2,050	4.2%	$86
+4	$2,121	$2,274	$2,198	4.2%	$92
+5	$2,274	$2,438	$2,356	4.2%	$99

If our projected balance sheets imply that PepsiCo will generate larger amounts of cash flow in future years and if we expect they will retain larger amounts of cash and short-term investments, then we will need to recompute the interest income projections to reflect additional interest-earning assets.

Income Taxes

As Chapter 8 discusses, PepsiCo's income tax note (Note 14 in Appendix A) shows the reconciliation between the statutory tax rate and the average, or effective, tax rate. The statutory U.S. Federal income tax rate was 35 percent during Year 9 to Year 11. PepsiCo experienced increases in its effective tax rate of 1.0 percent from state income taxes and decreases in its effective tax rate of approximately 4.0 percent from lower tax rates in other tax jurisdictions, yielding an effective tax rate of approximately 32 percent. PepsiCo realized one-time increases in the effective tax rate in Year 11 from the effects of the merger with Quaker and in Year 9 from the sale of the bottling operations. We assume that the effective tax rate for Year +1 and beyond will be 32 percent.

Net Income

We have now projected all of the elements of the income statement, including first-iteration assumptions about interest expense, interest income, and income taxes. Exhibit 10.3 presents these income statement projections. As it stands, our projected net income amounts and the implied growth rates in net income are as follows:

	Net Income	Percentage Increase
Year 11 Actual	$3,003	
Year +1 Projected	$3,371	12.3%
Year +2 Projected	$3,660	8.6%
Year +3 Projected	$3,980	8.7%
Year +4 Projected	$4,316	8.5%
Year +5 Projected	$4,654	7.8%

Retained Earnings

The retained earnings account typically increases by the amount of net income (or decreases for net loss) and decreases for dividends. In Year 11, PepsiCo's retained earnings also decreased because of the issue of treasury shares in the merger with Quaker, which was accounted for as a pooling of interests (see the discussion in Chapter 9). PepsiCo's dividend payout policy for common shareholders has been relatively constant during Years 9 to 11, averaging 38 percent of net income each year. We project that PepsiCo's dividend payout policy will remain at 38 percent in the future. Therefore, our forecasts of dividends to common shareholders will vary over time with net income. PepsiCo also pays a small dividend to preferred stockholders, which we expect will remain constant at $4 million. Thus, the implied changes in retained earnings are as follows:

	Year +1	Year +2	Year +3	Year +4	Year +5
Beginning of Year	$11,519	$13,605	$15,870	$18,334	$21,006
Plus Net Income	3,371	3,660	3,980	4,316	4,654
Less Dividends to Common Shareholders	(1,281)	(1,391)	(1,512)	(1,640)	(1,768)
Less Dividends to Preferred Shareholders	(4)	(4)	(4)	(4)	(4)
End of Year	$13,605	$15,870	$18,334	$21,006	$23,888

Balancing the Balance Sheet

Even though we have completed first-iteration forecasts of all of the amounts on the income statement and balance sheet, our balance sheet will not balance, because we have forecast individual asset and liability accounts to capture their individual operating activities, which do not vary together perfectly. Currently, our projections of total assets minus our projections of liabilities, shareholders' equity other than retained earnings (which is a negative amount because of PepsiCo's extensive treasury stock), and retained earnings indicate the amounts by which our balance sheets do not balance:

Projections:	Year +1	Year +2	Year +3	Year +4	Year +5
Total Assets	$23,481	$25,173	$26,993	$28,944	$31,043
Liabilities.	$13,989	$14,782	$15,394	$16,768	$17,636
Shareholders' Equity (other than Retained Earnings).	(3,794)	(4,860)	(6,056)	(7,396)	(8,895)
Retained Earnings.	13,605	15,870	18,334	21,006	23,888
Total Liabilities and Shareholders' Equity	$23,800	$25,792	$27,672	$30,378	$32,629
Difference	$ −319	$ −619	$ −679	$−1,435	$−1,586
Change in the difference	$ −319	$ −300	$ −60	$ −756	$ −151

The difference between the projected totals of assets and the projected total liabilities and shareholders' equity each year represents the total amount by which we must adjust a flexible financial account to balance the balance sheet. The change in the difference represents the increment by which we must adjust the flexible financial account each year. Thus, in Year +1, our first-iteration forecasts project that liabilities and equities will exceed assets by $319 million (or about 1.4 percent of total assets). We need to adjust a flexible financial account by $319 million (either increase a financial asset account or decrease a financial liability or shareholders' equity account) to balance the balance sheet. In Year +2, our first-iteration projections indicate liabilities and equities will exceed assets by $619 million, so we will need an additional adjustment of $300 million in Year +2, and so on.

We could use a number of PepsiCo's flexible financial accounts for this adjustment, depending on PepsiCo's strategy for investments and capital structure. We could consider the following options:

1. Increase cash or marketable securities if we expect PepsiCo will reinvest this capital in liquid securities;
2. Increase investment securities if we expect PepsiCo will reinvest this capital in long-term investments;
3. Decrease long-term debt if we expect PepsiCo will use this capital to reduce interest-bearing debt;
4. Increase dividends or treasury stock repurchases if we expect PepsiCo will distribute this capital to shareholders.

Our forecasts imply that PepsiCo will continue to generate substantial amounts of excess capital, so we assume that dividends will increase in the future. We therefore adjust upwards our dividends forecasts each year by the amount of the necessary adjustment to balance the balance sheet. We refer to this amount as an *implied dividend*. Note that we could have assumed that PepsiCo will distribute the excess capital to shareholders through treasury stock repurchases rather than implied dividends. In either case, the assumption that PepsiCo will return the excess capital to shareholders through increased dividends or treasury stock repurchases will have equivalent effects on total assets, total liabilities, total shareholders' equity, and net income. After adjusting our dividends projections to include the implied dividends necessary to balance the balance sheet, the implied changes in retained earnings are as follows:

	Year +1	Year +2	Year +3	Year +4	Year +5
Beginning of Year	$11,519	$13,286	$15,251	$17,655	$19,572
Plus Net Income	3,371	3,660	3,980	4,316	4,654
Less Dividends to Common Shareholders	(1,600)	(1,691)	(1,572)	(2,395)	(1,920)
Less Dividends to Preferred Shareholders	(4)	(4)	(4)	(4)	(4)
End of Year	$13,286	$15,251	$17,655	$19,572	$22,302

The final pro forma balance sheet total amounts are as follows:

Projections:	Year +1	Year +2	Year +3	Year +4	Year +5
Total Assets..............................	$23,481	$25,173	$26,993	$28,944	$31,043
Liabilities...............................	$13,989	$14,782	$15,394	$16,768	$17,636
Shareholders' Equity					
(other than Retained Earnings).............	(3,794)	(4,860)	(6,056)	(7,396)	(8,895)
Retained Earnings........................	13,286	15,251	17,655	19,572	22,302
Total Liabilities and Shareholders' Equity	$23,481	$25,173	$26,993	$28,944	$31,043
Difference................................	$ 0	$ 0	$ 0	$ 0	$ 0

CLOSING THE LOOP: SOLVING FOR CO-DETERMINED VARIABLES

If we had plugged the excess capital to interest-earning accounts (for example, cash, marketable securities, or investment securities) or to interest-bearing accounts (for example, short-term or long-term debt), then we would need to adjust accordingly the projected amounts for interest income or interest expense on the income statement. This would create an additional set of co-determined variables within our pro forma financial statements forecasts. For example, assume we use long-term debt as our flexible financial account and adjust long-term financing by the amount PepsiCo will require to balance assets with liabilities and shareholders' equity. To determine the necessary plug to long-term debt, we need to know all of the other asset, liability, and shareholders' equity amounts, including retained earnings. To forecast retained earnings, we must know net income, which depends on interest expense on long-term debt. To determine retained earnings, we also need to know dividends, which depend on net income. Thus, we need to solve for at least five unknown variables simultaneously.

This problem is not as intractable as it might seem, thanks to computational capabilities of computer spreadsheet programs such as Excel. To solve for variables simultaneously in Excel, for example, first click on the Tools menu, and then click on the Calculations menu, and then click on the Iterations box, so that Excel will solve and resolve circular references 100 times until all the calculations fall within the specified tolerance for precision. Then, we can program each cell to calculate the variables we need, even if they are simultaneously determined. FSAP users should follow these steps to check that the Excel-based Forecast spreadsheet in FSAP is programmed to compute co-determined variables simultaneously.

STEP 6: PROJECTING THE STATEMENT OF CASH FLOWS

The final step involves preparing a projected statement of cash flows. We prepare the statement of cash flows directly from the projected income statement and projected balance sheets. We follow the usual procedure for preparing this statement described in Chapter 3. We capture all of the changes in the pro forma balance sheets each year and express these changes in terms of their implied effects on cash. Increases in assets imply uses of cash; decreases in assets imply sources of cash. Increases in liabilities and shareholders' equity imply sources of cash; decreases in liabilities and shareholders' equity imply uses of cash. Exhibit 10.6 presents the pro forma statement of cash flows for PepsiCo for Years +1 through +5. The derivation of each of the line items appears below.

(1) Net Income: We use the amounts in the pro forma income statement (Exhibit 10.3).
(2) Depreciation and Amortization Expense: We assume that the addback for depreciation expense equals the projection of depreciation expense used to compute the net change in property, plant, and equipment. If the analyst has explicitly projected the accumulated depreciation account, then depreciation expense should reconcile with the change in accumulated depreciation on the pro forma balance sheet (plus any change in accumulated depreciation from assets that were sold or retired, which we have assumed to be zero). The addback for amortization expense is zero because we forecast that under U.S. GAAP beginning in Year +1, PepsiCo will no longer amortize goodwill. Other Assets on the pro forma balance sheet, which includes goodwill, also includes other intangible assets that will be amortized, but it is a relatively small amount. Thus, adding back zero amortization expense is an error but the error is not material. This error primarily understates the amount of cash flow from operations (by the amount of the omitted intangible asset amortization addback) and overstates cash flow from investing (where the change in Other Assets appears), but does not affect net cash flows.
(3), (4), (5), (6), (7): Changes in operating current asset and current liability accounts other than cash appearing on the pro forma balance sheet.
(8), (9): Changes in noncurrent accrued expenses: Changes in long-term accruals for expenses that are part of operations, including deferred taxes and other noncurrent liabilities, that appear on the pro forma balance sheet.
(10): Property, Plant, and Equipment: The amount on this line equals the projected capital expenditures included in the change in property, plant, and equipment on the pro forma balance sheet in Exhibit 10.4. We assume that PepsiCo did not sell or retire depreciable assets each year. As a check, the analyst should be sure that the statement of cash flows captures the net cash flow implications of property, plant, and equipment (for example, the addback for depreciation expense minus capital expenditures, net of any

EXHIBIT 10.6

Pro Forma Statements of Cash Flows for PepsiCo
(amounts in millions; allow for rounding errors)

	Year +1 Projected	Year +2 Projected	Year +3 Projected	Year +4 Projected	Year +5 Projected
Operations					
(1) Net Income..........................	$ 3,371	$ 3,660	$ 3,980	$ 4,316	$ 4,654
(2) Depreciation.........................	903	967	1,036	1,110	1,190
(3) (Increase) Decrease in Accounts Receivable..................	(149)	(163)	(175)	(188)	(203)
(4) (Increase) Decrease in Inventories........	(6)	(86)	(92)	(99)	(110)
(5) (Increase) Decrease in Other Current Assets	(70)	(59)	(64)	(68)	(74)
(6) Increase (Decrease) in Accounts Payable...	49	93	91	97	109
(7) Increase (Decrease) in Other Current Liabilities..................	241	259	279	300	322
(8) Increase (Decrease) in Deferred Tax	106	114	122	132	142
(9) Increase (Decrease) in Other Noncurrent Liabilities	274	295	317	341	367
Cash Flow from Operations..............	$ 4,719	$ 5,080	$ 5,494	$ 5,941	$ 6,397
Investing					
(10) Acquisition of Property, Plant, and Equipment (at cost)	$(1,418)	$(1,519)	$(1,627)	$(1,744)	$(1,869)
(11) Acquisition of Marketable Securities (net)......................	(91)	(76)	(82)	(88)	(95)
(12) Acquisition of Investment Securities (net)......................	(416)	(237)	(254)	(273)	(294)
(13) Other Assets	(431)	(464)	(499)	(536)	(577)
Cash Flow from Investing	$(2,356)	$(2,295)	$(2,461)	$(2,641)	$(2,834)
Financing					
(14) Increase (Decrease) in Short-term Borrowing	$ (237)	$ 8	$ 9	$ 10	$ 10
(15) Increase (Decrease) in Long-term Debt	534	25	(209)	495	(82)
(16) Increase (Decrease) in Preferred Stock......................	0	0	0	0	0
(17) Increase (Decrease) in Common Stock	0	0	0	0	0
(18) Increase (Decrease) in Other Equity Adjustments..........	0	0	0	0	0
(19) Acquisition of Treasury Stock	(949)	(1,066)	(1,196)	(1,340)	(1,499)
(20) Dividends	(1,604)	(1,696)	(1,576)	(2,400)	(1,923)
Cash Flow from Financing..............	$(2,256)	$(2,729)	$(2,972)	$(3,235)	$(3,494)
(21) Net Change in Cash	$ 107	$ 56	$ 61	$ 65	$ 69
Cash—Beginning of Year	683	790	846	907	972
Cash—End of Year	$ 790	$ 846	$ 907	$ 972	$ 1,041

asset sales or retirements) is equal to the change in net property, plant, and equipment on the pro forma balance sheet.

(11), (12): Marketable Securities and Investment Securities (net): The statement of cash flows classifies purchases and sales of marketable securities (current asset) and investment securities (noncurrent asset) as investing transactions. We use the changes in these accounts on the pro forma balance sheet to derive the amounts for these items on the statement of cash flows. There is likely to be some error in the implied cash flow amount from investment securities. This change should be increased (become less negative) for the excess (if any) of equity earnings over dividends received from unconsolidated affiliates (which is a non-cash increase in this asset amount). Similarly, the excess of equity earnings over dividends received should also be subtracted from net income in the operating section of the statement of cash flows. Rather than making assumptions about this relatively immaterial item (the effects of which completely offset each other), we chose to simply treat the change in investments fully as an investing transaction. This choice means that cash flows from operating activities may be slightly overstated, and cash flows from investing activities may be slightly understated by an equivalent amount, but the net change in cash each year is not affected.

(13): Other Assets: We enter the change in other assets (intangibles and goodwill) on this line. The change in other assets on the pro forma balance sheet is the net of acquisitions and amortization. As discussed in item (2), we assume that the amount of amortization of goodwill is zero, and the amortization of other intangible assets is sufficiently immaterial that we treat the change in other assets fully as an investing transaction.

(14), (15): Debt Capital: Changes in debt capital (short-term notes payable, current maturities of long-term debt, and long-term debt) on the pro forma balance sheet are financing activities.

(16): Minority Interest and Preferred Stock: The amounts entered on line (16) represent the changes in minority interest and preferred stock on the pro forma balance sheet, which are financing activities.

(17): Changes in Common Stock: The amounts entered on line (17) represent the changes in the common stock and paid-in capital accounts on the pro forma balance sheet.

(18): Changes in Accumulated Other Comprehensive Income and Other Equity Adjustments: The amounts entered on line (18) represent the changes in the adjustment accounts that are components of shareholders' equity on the pro forma balance sheet.

(19): Treasury Stock: The amounts entered on line (19) represent the cash flow implications of treasury stock transactions, captured in the net change in the treasury stock account on the pro forma balance sheet.

(20) Dividends: The amount for common and preferred dividends equals the projected amount each year (discussed earlier in the section on Retained Earnings in the pro forma balance sheet).

(21) Net Change in Cash: The aggregate of the amounts on lines (1) to (20), which should equal the change in cash on the pro forma balance sheet.

The analyst should note that the statement of cash flows will not reconcile with the pro forma income statement and balance sheets if the balance sheets do not balance and if the income statement does not articulate with the balance sheets (that is, net income should be included in the change in retained earnings).

It is important to be aware that, unlike historical balance sheets and income statements, historical statements of cash flows commonly do not provide good bases for projecting the future because many of the line items on the statement of cash flows are difficult to reconcile with historical changes in balance sheets. This is because, in preparing the statement of cash flows, the accountant can aggregate numerous cash flows on each line item of this statement and the analyst may not be able to determine what amounts have been aggregated. For example, the accountant could choose to report separately the aggregate cost of a business acquisition on one line of the statement, but the business acquisition could cause changes in many asset and liability accounts, recognizing the acquisition of various assets and liabilities. In addition, the accountant may choose to disclose details of cash flows that the analyst cannot verify. For example, the accountant might choose to disclose separately in the statement of cash flows the amount of marketable securities purchased and sold, and there is no way for the analyst to verify those amounts because the analyst can only observe the net change in the marketable securities balance from the beginning to the end of the year. Thus, we recommend simply computing the implied statement of cash flows from the pro forma income statements and balance sheets, which the analyst can observe and verify.

SHORTCUT APPROACHES TO FORECASTING

Throughout the chapter thus far we have emphasized a methodical, detailed approach to forecasting individual accounts on the pro forma income statement and balance sheet, allowing the analyst to incorporate expected changes in operating activities related to each account. In some circumstances, however, it may be necessary to forecast income statement and balance sheet totals directly without carefully considering each account. This shortcut approach has the potential to introduce forecasting error if the shortcut assumptions do not fit each account very well. On the other hand, if the firm is stable and mature in an industry in steady-state equilibrium, then it may be efficient and reliable to use shortcut forecasting techniques that project current steady-state conditions to the future. We next illustrate shortcut approaches for forecasting PepsiCo's income statements and balance sheets.

Projected Sales and Income Approach

We can develop shortcut projections for total sales and net income using PepsiCo's recent sales growth rates and profit margins. PepsiCo's compound growth rate in sales over Years 9 to 11 was 7.3 percent. During that period, PepsiCo generated an average profit margin of 10.2 percent. If we simply use these ratios to forecast sales and net income over Years +1 to +5, the projected amounts would be as follows:

Year	Sales Growth Rate	Projected Sales	Net Profit Margin	Projected Net Income
11 actual		$26,935		
+1	7.3%	$28,901	10.2%	$2,948
+2	7.3%	$31,011	10.2%	$3,163
+3	7.3%	$33,275	10.2%	$3,394
+4	7.3%	$35,704	10.2%	$3,642
+5	7.3%	$38,310	10.2%	$3,908

These shortcut projections for sales are slightly higher than the more detailed sales projections we developed earlier, and the net income projections are significantly lower. By forecasting individual expense amounts, the more detailed projections capture expected changes in expenses relative to sales, whereas the shortcut approach assumes existing relations between sales and expenses will persist indefinitely into the future. In this case, we projected a steady decline in the cost of goods sold as a percent of sales relative to the past, which is one reason why our detailed projections of net income are higher than these shortcut projections.

Projected Total Assets Approach

We can project total assets using the recent historical growth rate in total assets. Between the end of Year 9 and the end of Year 11, PepsiCo's total assets grew at a 4.3 percent compound annual growth rate. If this growth rate continues, total assets will increase as follows:

Year	Asset Growth Rate	Projected Total Assets
11 actual		$21,695
+1	4.3%	$22,628
+2	4.3%	$23,601
+3	4.3%	$24,616
+4	4.3%	$25,674
+5	4.3%	$26,778

Using historical growth rates to project total assets can result in erroneous projections if the analyst fails to consider the link between sales growth and asset growth. We assumed a sales growth rate for PepsiCo of 7.3 percent in the shortcut approach to sales projections, but only a 4.3 percent growth in assets, which implies a steady increase in total asset turnover from 1.3 in Years 10 and 11, to 1.46 in Year +5. An alternative shortcut approach to projecting total assets uses the total asset turnover ratio, explicitly linking sales growth and asset growth. Assume that PepsiCo's total asset turnover will remain at 1.3 over the next five years. Also assume that we use the shortcut approach to estimate sales growth at 7.3 percent per year as above. The calculation of projected total assets using the asset turnover ratio shortcut appears below:

Year	Projected Sales	Average Asset Turnover Rate	Projected Average Total Assets	Projected Beginning Total Assets	Projected Ending Total Assets	Implied Percent Change in Total Assets
+1	$28,901	1.3	$22,232	$21,695	$22,769	5.0%
+2	$31,011	1.3	$23,855	$22,769	$24,941	9.5%
+3	$33,275	1.3	$25,596	$24,941	$26,251	5.3%
+4	$35,704	1.3	$27,467	$26,251	$28,683	9.3%
+5	$38,310	1.3	$29,469	$28,683	$30,255	5.5%

This approach ties the projection of total assets to the level of projected sales. One difficulty sometimes encountered with using total assets turnover to project total assets is that it can result in unusual patterns for projected total assets. The total assets turnover uses *average* total assets in the denominator. If total assets changed by an unusually large (small) percentage in the most recent year preceding the projections, then the next year's assets must change by an unusually small (large) proportion to compensate. This "sawtooth" pattern, which is described earlier in the chapter and is illustrated in Exhibit 10.5, makes little intuitive sense, given a smooth growth in sales.

We encounter this problem projecting total assets for PepsiCo using its total assets turnover. Note that PepsiCo's total assets increased 5.0 percent during Year +1, and 9.5 percent in Year +2, and then 5.3 percent in Year +3, and so on, whereas PepsiCo's sales are expected to grow smoothly at 7.3 percent per year. The analyst can deal with that sawtooth problem by basing the asset turnover ratio on the ending balance, instead of the average balance, in total assets. An alternative approach to dealing with the sawtooth problem is to arbitrarily smooth the rate of increase in assets over a period of time. An increase in assets from $21,695 million in Year 11, to $30,255 million in Year +5 reflects a compound average annual growth rate of 6.88 percent. The table below shows the revised projected assets following this smoothed approach. Note that total assets equal $30,255 million at the end of Year +5 in both cases. We could use these smoothed total assets amounts in preparing the pro forma balance sheets for PepsiCo.

Year	Asset Growth Rate	Projected Total Assets
11 actual		$21,695
+1	6.88%	$23,188
+2	6.88%	$24,783
+3	6.88%	$26,488
+4	6.88%	$28,310
+5	6.88%	$30,255

Once the analyst projects total assets, common-size balance sheet percentages provide the basis for allocating this total to individual assets, as well as to liabilities and shareholders' equity. In using these common-size percentages, the analyst assumes that the firm maintains a constant mix of assets, liabilities, and equities, regardless of the level of total assets. Equivalently, the analyst assumes that each asset, liability, and equity account grows at the same growth rate as total assets. For example, the common-size balance sheet for Year 11 for PepsiCo in Appendix C indicates that total liabilities represent 60.0 percent of total assets, and equities represent 40.0 percent of total assets. If we use these proportions and the smoothed projections of total assets, we can project total liabilities and shareholders' equity for Years +1 through +5, as follows:

Year	Projected Total Assets	Projected Total Liabilities (60%)	Projected Shareholders' Equity (40%)
+1	$23,188	$13,913	$ 9,275
+2	$24,783	$14,870	$ 9,913
+3	$26,488	$15,893	$10,595
+4	$28,310	$16,986	$11,324
+5	$30,255	$18,153	$12,102

Using common-size balance sheet percentages to project individual assets, liabilities, and shareholders' equity encounters (at least) two potential shortcomings. First, the common-size percentages for individual assets, liabilities, and shareholders' equity are not independent of each other. For example, a firm such as PepsiCo that acquires and disposes of its bottlers on an ongoing basis may experience a changing proportion for investments in securities among its assets. Other asset categories may show decreasing percentages in some years even though their dollar amounts are increasing. The analyst must interpret these decreasing percentages carefully.

Second, using the common-size percentages does not permit the analyst to easily change the assumptions about the future behavior of an individual asset. For example, assume that PepsiCo intended to implement inventory control systems that should increase its inventory turnover in the future. Inventory will likely comprise a smaller percentage of total assets in the future than it has in the past. The analyst encounters difficulties adjusting the common-size balance sheet percentages to reflect the changes in inventory policies.

The following diagram summarizes the approaches to projecting assets:

	Project Individual Assets	**Project Total Assets**
Use Historical Growth Rates for Projections		
Use Asset Turnovers for Projections		

These four possible combinations yield similar projections for assets when a firm has experienced relatively stable historical growth rates for total assets and individual asset items, and relatively stable asset turnovers. If historical growth rates have varied significantly from year to year, then using *average* historical growth rates provides more reasonable projections than asset turnovers. One desirable feature of using asset turnovers, however, is that projected asset amounts incorporate projections of the level of sales. Also, management's actions to improve profitability often focus on improving asset turnovers. The analyst can incorporate the effects of these actions into the projections more easily by using the asset turnover approach than by adjusting the compound annual growth rates or common-size balance sheet percentages.

ANALYZING PRO FORMA FINANCIAL STATEMENTS

As a reality check on the reasonableness of our forecast assumptions and their internal consistency with one another, we can analyze the pro forma financial statements using the same ratios and other analytical tools discussed in previous chapters. Exhibit 10.7 presents a ratio analysis for PepsiCo based on the pro forma financial statement forecasts for Year +1 to Year +5. The FSAP Forecasts spreadsheet provides these ratio computations based on the pro forma financial statements.

Sales growth rates are consistent with our assumptions for sales growth. Net income growth rates are greater than the sales growth rates, in part because we project PepsiCo will enjoy an increasing profit margin, which is driven largely by the projected decrease in PepsiCo's cost of goods sold percentage. The projected rate of return on assets (ROA) increases slightly from 15.5 percent in Year +1 to 16.0 percent in Year +5, and then remains steady thereafter. The main driver of the increase in projected ROA is the expected increase in profit margin for ROA from 12.1 percent in Year +1 to 12.6 percent in Year +5. On the other hand, the projected rate of return on common equity (ROCE) declines between Year +1 and Year +5, from 37.2 percent to 36.4 percent. This occurs because the projected increase in net profit margin for

		EXHIBIT 10.7			
Financial Ratio Analysis based on Pro Forma Financial Statements for PepsiCo (allow for rounding errors)					
	Year +1	Year +2	Year +3	Year +4	Year +5
Growth Rates:					
Sales............................	7.1%	7.1%	7.1%	7.2%	7.2%
Net Income	12.3%	8.6%	8.7%	8.5%	7.8%
Total Assets	8.2%	7.2%	7.2%	7.2%	7.3%
Return on Assets:					
Profit Margin for ROA	12.1%	12.3%	12.4%	12.6%	12.6%
× Asset Turnover	1.3	1.3	1.3	1.3	1.3
= Return on Assets	15.5%	15.6%	15.8%	15.9%	16.0%
Return on Common Equity:					
Profit Margin for ROCE	11.7%	11.8%	12.0%	12.2%	12.2%
× Asset Turnover	1.3	1.3	1.3	1.3	1.3
× Capital Structure Leverage.......	2.5	2.5	2.4	2.4	2.3
= Return on Common Equity	37.2%	36.9%	36.2%	36.4%	36.4%
Operating Performance:					
Gross Margin / Sales	60.3%	60.5%	60.7%	60.9%	61.0%
Operating Profit / Sales...........	11.7%	11.8%	12.0%	12.2%	12.2%
Asset Turnover:					
Sales / Average Accounts Receivable	13.0	13.0	13.0	13.0	13.0
COGS / Average Inventory	8.7	9.0	9.0	9.0	9.0
Sales/ Average Fixed Assets	4.0	4.0	4.0	4.0	4.0
Liquidity:					
Current Ratio	1.1	1.1	1.2	1.1	1.2
Quick Ratio......................	0.7	0.8	0.8	0.7	0.8
Solvency:					
Total Liabilities / Total Assets	0.6	0.6	0.6	0.6	0.6
Interest Coverage..................	27.2	28.0	31.1	32.2	32.6

ROCE (from 11.7 percent in Year +1 to 12.2 percent by Year +5, a relative increase of 4.3 percent) is more than offset by the decrease in capital structure leverage (from 2.5 to 2.3 by Year +5, a relative decrease of −8.0 percent).

The projected decrease in capital structure leverage is the net result of several forecast assumptions, two of which have opposite effects on financial leverage. We assumed that PepsiCo would reduce long-term debt to 10 percent of total assets by Year +5, which should reduce financial leverage. In contrast, we also assumed that PepsiCo would continue to make significant repurchases of its common stock and to increase its dividend payout policy. PepsiCo is expected to finance the treasury stock repurchases and dividends with cash flow from operations, which will reduce shareholders' equity relative to debt, thereby increasing the capital structure leverage ratio. The net effect of decreasing long-term debt as a percent of assets, while at the same time repurchasing shares and paying dividends, suggests PepsiCo is expected to generate very healthy cash flows after operating and investing activities.

The asset turnover ratios, liquidity ratios, and solvency ratios remain fairly steady over time. Consistent with the decline in long-term debt as a percent of total assets, PepsiCo's interest coverage ratio increases over time.

These ratios confirm that our forecast assumptions are reasonable and that they appear to be implemented correctly (that is, the computations appear to be working). Unfortunately, these ratios cannot confirm whether our assumptions are correct. These ratios do not tell us whether we have accurately and realistically captured PepsiCo's sales growth and profitability in the future. For this confirmation, only time will tell.

SENSITIVITY ANALYSIS AND REACTIONS TO ANNOUNCEMENTS

These pro forma financial statement forecasts can serve as the base case from which the analyst assesses the impact of various critical forecast assumptions for the firm, and from which the analyst reacts to new announcements from the firm. For example, with these pro forma financial statements, the analyst can assess the sensitivity of projected net income and cash flows to key assumptions about the firm's sales growth rates, gross profit margins, control over selling, general and administrative expenses, and other assumptions. For example, using the pro forma financial statements in Appendix D as the base case, the analyst can assess the impact on PepsiCo's profitability from a one-point increase or decrease in sales growth, or from a one-point increase or decrease in the gross profit margin.

The analyst can also use the pro forma financial statements to assess the sensitivity of the firm's liquidity and leverage to changes in key balance sheet assumptions. For example, the analyst can assess the impact on PepsiCo's liquidity and solvency ratios by varying the long-term debt to assets assumptions and the interest expense assumptions. Lenders and credit analysts can use the pro forma financial statements to assess the conditions under which the firm's debt covenants may become binding. For example, suppose PepsiCo's long-term debt and revolving line of credit agreements require that PepsiCo maintain certain minimum liquidity and interest coverage ratios. The pro forma financial statements provide the analyst a structured approach to assess how far net income and cash flows would need to decrease, and how much long-term debt and interest expense would need to increase, before the minimum interest coverage ratio becomes binding.

The pro forma financial statements also enable the analyst to react quickly and efficiently to new announcements by the firm. Suppose PepsiCo announces at the beginning of Year +1 that it has signed a new contract with a key distribution channel that should enable PepsiCo to increase beverage sales by an additional $1 billion by Year +3, and that this new level of sales should be sustainable into the future. The projected pro forma financial statements enable the analyst to incorporate the effects of this announcement relatively efficiently into expectations for PepsiCo's future earnings, balance sheets, and cash flows.

As an alternative example, suppose PepsiCo announces that it plans to discontinue purchases of treasury stock in Year +1 (other than to acquire shares needed to meet stock options exercises), and that it intends to use this cash to reduce long-term debt. Our original projections included $1,700 million in treasury stock repurchases in Year +1, which will now be zero, and that PepsiCo will instead use this capital to reduce long-term debt. The analyst can efficiently incorporate the effects of this announcement into the pro forma financial statements. PepsiCo's original and revised projected ratios for Year +1 appear below:

	Year +1 Originally Projected	Year +1 Revised Projected
Net Profit Margin for ROA	11.5%	11.7%
Rate of Return on Assets	14.7%	14.9%
Rate of Return on Common Equity	37.2%	34.3%
Capital Structure Leverage...............	2.5	2.3
Total Liabilities / Total Assets.............	59.6%	52.3%
Interest Coverage Ratio	27.2	37.2

Thus, the assumptions about the growth in treasury stock and long-term debt have significant effects on pro forma amounts for PepsiCo. Various other changes in assumptions are possible. By designing a flexible computer spreadsheet for projecting pro forma financial statements, the analyst can change any one or a combination of assumptions and observe the effect on the financial statements and ratios. FSAP provides a flexible spreadsheet for forecasting.

SUMMARY

The preparation of pro forma financial statements requires numerous assumptions about the growth rate in sales, cost behavior of various expenses, levels of investment in working capital and fixed assets, mix of financing, and others. The analyst should carefully develop realistic expectations for these activities, and capture those expectations in pro forma financial statements that provide an objective and realistic portrait of the firm in the future. The analyst should study the sensitivity of the pro forma financial statements to the assumptions made and to the impact of different assumptions. Spreadsheet computer programs can assist in this sensitivity analysis.

After developing careful and realistic expectations for future earnings, cash flows, and dividends using pro forma financial statement projections, the analyst can then begin to make decisions with these data, including decisions about the firm as a potential equity investment or a potential credit risk. In the next three chapters, we demonstrate how to incorporate expectations for future dividends, cash flows, and earnings into estimates of firm value.

PROBLEMS AND CASES

10.1 PROJECTING GROSS MARGINS FOR CAPITAL-INTENSIVE, CYCLICAL BUSINESSES. AK Steel is an integrated manufacturer of high quality steel and steel products in capital-intensive steel mills. Sales for Year 11 totaled $3,994 million and cost of goods sold totaled $3,373 million. Its manufacturing cost structure is $785 million fixed cost plus $.648 variable cost as a percentage of sales. Nucor manufactures more commodity-level steel at the lower end of the market in less capital-intensive mini-mills. Sales for Year 11 totaled $4,139 million and cost of goods sold totaled $3,820 million. Its manufacturing cost structure is $389 million fixed cost and $.829 variable cost as a percentage of sales.

Industry analysts anticipate the following annual changes in sales for the next five years: Year 12, 2 percent increase; Year 13, 6 percent increase; Year 14, 10 percent increase; Year 15, 4 percent decrease; Year 16, 12 percent decrease.

Required

a. Discuss the structure of manufacturing cost (that is, fixed versus variable) for each firm in light of the manufacturing process and type of steel produced.
b. Using the analysts' forecasts of sales changes, compute the projected sales, cost of goods sold, and gross margin of each firm for Year 12 through Year 16.
c. Compute the gross margin percentage for each firm for Year 12 through Year 16.
d. Why do the levels and variability of the gross margin percentages differ for these two firms?

10.2 IDENTIFYING THE COST STRUCTURE. Sony Corporation manufactures and markets consumer electronics products. Selected income statement data for Year 7 and Year 8 appear below (in billions of yen):

	Year 7	Year 8
Sales.....................................	¥ 4,571	¥ 5,636
Cost of Goods Sold...........................	(3,439)	(4,161)
Selling and Administrative Expenses	(918)	(1,132)
Operating Income Before Income Taxes	¥ 214	¥ 343

Required

a. The analyst can sometimes estimate the variable cost as a percentage of sales for a particular cost (for example, cost of goods sold) by dividing the yen amount of the change in the cost item between two years by the yen amount of the change in sales for those two years. The analyst can then multiply the variable cost percentage times sales to determine the total variable cost. Subtracting the variable cost from the total cost yields the fixed cost for that particular cost item. Follow this procedure to determine the cost structure (fixed cost plus variable cost as a percentage of sales) for cost of goods sold for Sony.

b. Repeat part a for selling and administrative expenses.

c. Sony Corporation projects sales to grow at the following percentages in future years: Year 9, 12 percent; Year 10, 10 percent; Year 11, 8 percent; Year 12, 6 percent. Project sales, cost of goods sold, selling and administrative expenses, and operating income before income taxes for Sony for Year 9 to Year 12, using the cost structure amounts derived in parts a and b.

d. Compute the ratio of operating income before income taxes to sales for Year 9 through Year 12.

e. Interpret the changes in the ratio computed in part d in light of the expected changes in sales.

10.3 SMOOTHING CHANGES IN ACCOUNTS RECEIVABLE. Hasbro manufactures and markets toys and games for children and adults. Sales during Year 5 totaled $3,002 million. Accounts receivable totaled $791 million at the beginning of Year 5 and $807 million at the end of Year 5.

Required

a. Compute the accounts receivable turnover ratio for Hasbro for Year 5.

b. Hasbro anticipates that sales will grow at a compound annual rate of 6 percent each year between Year 5 and Year 10 and that the accounts receivable turnover ratio each year will equal the ratio computed in part a for Year 5. Compute the projected *implied* amount of accounts receivable at the end of Year 6 through Year 10 based on the accounts receivable turnover computed in part a. Also compute the percentage change in accounts receivable between each of the year-ends between Year 5 and Year 10.

c. The changes in accounts receivable computed in part b display the "sawtooth" pattern depicted in Exhibit 10.5 in the chapter. Smooth the changes in accounts receivable between the end of Year 5 and the end of Year 10 from part b using the compound annual growth rate in accounts receivable between Year 5 and Year 10.

d. Smooth the changes in accounts receivable from part b using the compound annual growth rate in accounts receivable between the end of Year 5 and the end of Year 9. Apply this growth rate to compute accounts receivable at the end of Year 6 through Year 10. Why do the amounts for ending accounts receivable using the growth rate from part c differ from those using the growth rate from this part?

e. Compute the accounts receivable turnover for Year 5 by dividing sales by the balance in accounts receivable at the end of Year 5 (instead of using average accounts receivable as in part a).

f. Using the measure and amount of the accounts receivable turnover determined in part e, compute the projected balance in accounts receivable at the end of Year 6 through Year 10. Also compute the percentage change in accounts receivable between the year-ends for Year 5 through Year 10.

10.4 SMOOTHING CHANGES IN INVENTORIES.   Land's End sells men's, women's, and children's clothing through catalogs. Sales totaled $1,118,743 thousand and cost of goods sold totaled $609,913 thousand during Year 7. Inventories totaled $164,816 thousand at the end of Year 6 and $142,445 thousand at the end of Year 7.

Required

a. Compute the inventory turnover ratio for Land's End for Year 7.

b. Lands' End projects that sales will grow at a compound annual rate of 4 percent between Year 7 and Year 12, and that the cost of goods sold to sales percentage will equal that realized in Year 7. Compute the projected *implied* amount of inventory at the end of Year 8 through Year 12 using the inventory turnover ratio computed in part a. Also compute the percentage change in inventories between each of the year-ends between Year 7 and Year 12.

c. The changes in inventories in part b display the "sawtooth" pattern depicted in Exhibit 10.5 in the chapter. Smooth the changes in inventories between the end of Year 7 and the end of Year 12, using the compound annual growth rate in inventories between Year 7 and Year 12.

d. Smooth the changes in inventories using the compound annual growth rate between Year 7 and Year 11. Apply this growth rate to determine the amount of inventories at the end of Year 8 through the end of Year 12. Why do the amounts for ending inventories using the growth rate in part c differ from those using the growth rate in this part?

e. Compute the inventory turnover for Year 7 using the balance in inventories at the end of Year 7 (instead of using average inventories as in part a).

f. Using the measure and the amount of inventory turnover determined in part e, compute the amount of inventories at the end of Year 8 through Year 12. Also compute the percentage change in inventories between the year-ends of Year 8 through Year 12.

10.5 IDENTIFYING PRO FORMA FINANCIAL STATEMENT RELATIONS. Partial pro forma financial statements for Watson Corporation appear in Exhibit 10.8 (income statement), Exhibit 10.9 (balance sheet), and Exhibit 10.10 (statement of cash flows). Selected items have been omitted, as well as all totals (indicated by XXXX).

EXHIBIT 10.8
Partial Pro Forma Income Statement for Watson Corporation
(Problem 10.5)

	Year 10 Actual	Year 11 Projected	Year 12 Projected	Year 13 Projected	Year 14 Projected
Sales	$46,000	$50,600	$56,672	$64,606	$74,943
Cost of Goods Sold	(29,900)	(32,890)	XXXX	(40,702)	(46,465)
Selling and Administrative	(10,580)	(11,638)	(12,468)	(13,567)	(14,989)
Interest.....	(3,907)	(4,298)	d	(3,866)	(5,227)
Income Taxes.....	(565)	(621)	(1,372)	(2,265)	(2,892)
Net Income	$XXXX	$XXXX	$XXXX	$XXXX	$XXXX

EXHIBIT 10.9
Partial Pro Forma Balance Sheet for Watson Corporation
(Problem 10.5)

	Year 10 Actual	Year 11 Projected	Year 12 Projected	Year 13 Projected	Year 14 Projected
Assets					
Cash.....	$ 1,200	$ 664	$ 206	$ 416	$ 1,262
Accounts Receivable	8,000	8,433	8,855	10,420	12,286
Inventories.....	7,500	8,223	c	10,711	11,333
Fixed Assets:					
Cost.....	110,400	120,445	126,467	f	169,895
Accumulated Depreciation.....	(33,100)	(36,112)	(37,917)	(45,352)	(50,938)
Total Assets	$XXXX	$XXXX	$XXXX	$XXXX	$XXXX
Liabilities and Shareholders' Equity					
Accounts Payable.....	$ 2,500	$ 2,801	$ 3,107	$ 3,376	$ 3,828
Notes Payable.....	6,500	6,852	7,195	8,467	9,982
Other Current Liabilities.....	3,300	3,630	e	4,635	5,376
Long-term Debt.....	45,000	49,094	51,549	h	69,251
Total Liabilities.....	$XXXX	$XXXX	$XXXX	$XXXX	$XXXX
Common Stock	$15,000	$17,233	$17,539	$22,434	$24,319
Retained Earnings	21,700	22,043	23,700	g	31,082
Total Shareholders' Equity	$XXXX	$XXXX	$XXXX	$XXXX	$XXXX
Total Liabilities and Shareholders' Equity ...	$XXXX	$XXXX	$XXXX	$XXXX	$XXXX

EXHIBIT 10.10

Pro Forma Statement of Cash Flows for Watson Corporation
(Problem 10.5)

	Year 10 Actual	Year 11 Projected	Year 12 Projected	Year 13 Projected	Year 14 Projected
Operations					
Net Income	$ 1,048	$ 1,153	$XXXX	$ 4,206	$ 5,370
Depreciation	2,378	b	1,805	7,435	5,586
Change in Accounts Receivable.	(394)	(433)	(422)	(1,565)	(1,866)
Change in Inventories.	(657)	(723)	(1,322)	(1,166)	(622)
Change in Accounts Payable	274	301	306	269	452
Change in Other Current Liabilities.	300	330	436	569	741
Cash Flow from Operations.	$XXXX	$ XXXX	$XXXX	$ XXXX	$ XXXX
Investing					
Acquisition of Fixed Assets	$(9,130)	$(10,045)	$(6,022)	$(24,796)	$(18,632)
Financing					
Change in Notes Payable.	$ 320	$ 352	$ 343	$ 1,272	$ 1,515
Change in Long-term Debt.	3,721	4,094	2,455	10,107	7,595
Change in Common Stock	2,029	2,233	306	4,895	1,885
Dividends.	(750)	a	(891)	(1,016)	(1,178)
Cash Flow from Financing.	$XXXX	$ XXXX	$XXXX	$ XXXX	$ XXXX
Change in Cash	$XXXX	$ XXXX	$XXXX	$ XXXX	$ XXXX

Required

Determine the amount of each of the following items:
a. Dividends declared and paid during Year 11.
b. Depreciation expense for Year 11, assuming Watson Corporation neither sold nor retired depreciable assets during Year 11.
c. Inventories at the end of Year 12.
d. Interest expense on borrowing during Year 12. The interest rate is 7 percent.
e. Other current liabilities at the end of Year 12.
f. Property, plant, and equipment at the end of Year 13, assuming Watson Corporation neither sold nor retired depreciable assets during Year 13.
g. Retained earnings at the end of Year 13.
h. Long-term debt at the end of Year 13.
i. The income tax rate for Year 14.
j. Purchases of inventories during Year 14.

10.6 PREPARING AND INTERPRETING PRO FORMA FINANCIAL STATEMENTS. Wal-Mart Stores (Wal-Mart) is the largest retailing firm in the world. Building on a base of discount stores, Wal-Mart has expanded into warehouse clubs and supercenters, which sell traditional discount store items and grocery products.

Exhibits 4.48 to 4.50 in Chapter 4 (Case 4.1) present the financial statements of Wal-Mart for Year 10, Year 11, and Year 12. Exhibit 4.51 presents selected financial statement ratios.

Required (Additional requirements follow on pages 794 and 795.)

a. Design a spreadsheet and prepare a set of pro forma financial statements for Wal-Mart for Year 13 to Year 17, following the assumptions set forth below. Project the amounts in the order presented (unless indicated otherwise), beginning with the income statement, then the balance sheet, and then the statement of cash flows.

INCOME STATEMENT

Sales

Sales grew 19.9 percent in Year 10, 15.9 percent in Year 11, and 13.8 percent in Year 12, primarily as a result of significant increases in same store sales, opening new stores, and corporate acquisitions. The compound annual growth rate during the last five years was 16.2 percent. Although Wal-Mart will continue to grow internationally by acquiring other firms and domestically by converting discount stores to super-centers, competition will likely constrain increases in same store sales to the level of 5 percent to 6 percent experienced in Year 12. Also, market saturation of stores will limit sales increases. Thus, assume that sales will grow 12 percent each year between Year 12 and Year 17.

Other Revenues

Other revenues have been approximately one percent of sales during the last three years. Assume that other revenues will continue at this historical pattern.

Cost of Goods Sold

The cost of goods sold to sales percentage steadily increased between Year 10 and Year 12. Wal-Mart's everyday low-price strategy, its movement into grocery products, and competition will likely result in additional increases in this expense percentage. Assume that the cost of goods sold to sales percentage will be 79 percent for Year 13 to Year 17.

Selling and Administrative Expenses

The selling and administrative expense percentage has steadily increased from 16.5 percent of sales in Year 10, to 16.7 percent of sales in Year 12. Identifying and transacting international corporate acquisitions and opening additional supercenters will put upward pressure on this expense percentage, but the slowdown in sales growth will moderate this upper pressure. Assume that the selling and administrative expense to sales percentage will be 16.8 percent for Year 13 to Year 17.

Interest Expense

Wal-Mart has engaged in long-term borrowing to construct new stores domestically, and in both short- and long-term borrowing to finance corporate acquisitions. The average interest rate on all interest-bearing debt was approximately 7.5 percent during Year 12. Assume this interest rate for all outstanding borrowing (notes payable, long-term debt, and current portion of long-term debt) for Wal-Mart for Year 13 through Year 17. Compute interest expense on the average amount of interest-bearing debt outstanding each year (that is, the sum of the beginning and end of the year divided by 2). Note: Projecting the amount of interest expense must await projection of interest-bearing debt on the balance sheet.

Income Tax Expense

Wal-Mart's average income tax rate as a percentage of income before income taxes has varied between 36.9 percent and 37.5 percent during the last three years. Assume an income tax rate of 37.1 percent of income before income taxes for Year 13 through Year 17. Note: Projecting the amount of income tax expense must await computation of net income before taxes.

BALANCE SHEET

Cash

Cash will be the amount necessary to equate total assets with total liabilities plus shareholders' equity. Projecting the amount of cash must await projections of all other balance sheet amounts.

Accounts Receivable

Accounts receivable will increase at the growth rate in sales.

Inventories

Wal-Mart increased its inventory turnover ratio during the last three years. The increasing role of grocery products should result in even faster inventory turnover in the future. However, the stocking of new stores and the distribution of merchandise to stores worldwide should slow the inventory turnover. Assume that inventory will grow at the growth rate in sales.

Prepayments

Prepayments relate to ongoing operating costs, such as rent and insurance. Assume that prepayments will grow at the growth rate in sales.

Property, Plant, and Equipment

Property, plant, and equipment grew 17.1 percent annually during the most recent five years. The construction of new supercenters and the acquisition of established retail chains abroad will require additional investments in property, plant, and equipment. However, increasing market saturation of stores will slow the growth rate. Assume that property, plant, and equipment will grow 13 percent each year between Year 13 and Year 17.

Other Assets

Other assets primarily include goodwill arising from corporate acquisitions abroad. Assume that other assets will grow at the growth rate in property, plant, and equipment.

Accounts Payable

Accounts payable will grow at the growth rate in sales.

Notes Payable

Wal-Mart used short-term borrowing (Notes Payable) to help finance corporate acquisitions in recent years. These funds were used to finance the inventories of the acquired companies. Assume that notes payable will grow at the growth rate in property, plant, and equipment.

Current Maturities of Long-term Debt

The notes to Wal-Mart's financial statements indicate that current maturities of long-term debt on January 31 of each year are as follows: Year 12 (already appears on the January 31, Year 12 balance sheet), $2,405; Year 13, $3,667; Year 14, $2,004; Year 15, $798; Year 16, $2,327; Year 17, $1,350.

Other Current Liabilities

Other current liabilities relate to ongoing operating activities and are expected to grow at the growth rate in sales.

Long-term Debt

Wal-Mart uses long-term debt to finance acquisitions of property, plant, and equipment, and acquisition of existing retail chains abroad. Assume that long-term debt will decrease by the amount of long-term debt reclassified as a current liability each year and then the remaining amount will increase at the growth rate in property, plant, and equipment, and other assets. For example, the January 31, Year 12, balance sheet of Wal-Mart shows the current portion of long-term debt to be $2,405. Wal-Mart will repay this amount during the fiscal Year 13. During fiscal Year 13, Wal-Mart will reclassify $3,667 from long-term debt to the current portion of long-term debt. This will leave a preliminary balance in long-term debt of $19,844 (= $23,511 − $3,667). Wal-Mart will increase this amount of long-term debt by the 13 percent growth rate in property, plant and equipment, and other assets. The projected amount for long-term debt on the January 31, Year 13, balance sheet is $22,424 (= $19,844 × 1.13).

Other Noncurrent Liabilities

Other noncurrent liabilities include amounts related to health care benefits and deferred taxes. Assume that other noncurrent liabilities will increase at the growth rate in sales.

Common Stock

Assume that common stock and additional paid-in capital will not change.

Retained Earnings

The increase in retained earnings equals net income minus dividends. Wal-Mart's dividends increased at an average annual rate of 20.5 percent between Year 9 and Year 12. Assume that dividends will grow 20.5 percent each year between Year 13 and Year 17.

Note: Project the amount of cash at this point.

STATEMENT OF CASH FLOWS

Depreciation Addback

Assume that depreciation expense will increase at the growth rate in property, plant, and equipment.

Other Addbacks

Assume that changes in other noncurrent liabilities on the balance sheet are an operating activity.

Other Investing Transactions

Assume that changes in other noncurrent assets on the balance sheet are an other investing activity.

Other Financing Transactions

The Other Financing line amount of $84 for Year 12 represents foreign exchange gains and losses. Ignore such gains and losses for Year 13 to Year 17. (That is, set the amounts at zero.)

Required (continued from page 791)

b. If you have programmed your spreadsheet correctly, the projected amount of cash is negative at the end of each year between Year 13 and Year 17, and the projected cash balance at the end of Year 17 is a negative $11,501 million. Given the profitability and growth projected for Wal-Mart, a negative balance in cash seems unlikely. Identify the likely reason for the negative projected amount of cash.

c. Assume now that long-term debt is projected to grow in Year 13 and Year 14 at twice the growth rate in property, plant, and equipment, and other assets (that is, 26 percent), and in Year 15 to Year 17 at 1.5 times the growth rate in property, plant, and equipment, and other assets (that is, 19.5 percent). Assess whether these growth rates in long-term debt provide more reasonable forecast amounts for cash.

d. Calculate the financial statement ratios listed in Exhibit 4.51 for Wal-Mart using the forecast amounts for Year 13 to Year 17. Assess the projected changes in the profitability and risk of Wal-Mart for Year 13 to Year 17.

10.7 PREPARING PRO FORMA FINANCIAL STATEMENTS. The Gap and Limited Brands operate specialty retail chains featuring clothing and personal care items. Case 4.2 in Chapter 4 presents financial statements and financial statement ratios for these two firms for Year 10, Year 11, and Year 12.

Required

a. Design spreadsheets and prepare pro forma financial statements for The Gap and Limited Brands for Year 13 through Year 17. Exhibit 10.11 presents the assumptions to be made. Also calculate the values of the profitability and risk ratios presented in Case 4.2 for each firm for Year 13 through Year 17. Note that the pro forma amounts for accounts receivable, inventories, fixed assets, and accounts payable use turnovers based on year-end values for these balance sheet items to avoid the "sawtooth" problem. Adjust the amount in the treasury stock to maintain the desired long-term debt to shareholders' equity ratios. The balance in accumulated depreciation at the end of Year 12 is $4,002 million for The Gap and $2,559 million for Limited Brands.

b. Discuss the principal assumptions that give rise to the differences in the pro forma profitability and risk ratios of The Gap versus Limited Brands.

c. The managers of Limited Brands are disturbed that the pro forma amounts indicate that The Gap will have a higher ROCE than Limited Brands. These managers are contemplating several strategic changes to enhance the return to the common shareholders of Limited Brands and desire to examine the impact on the following financial ratios for Year 14: (1) profit margin for rate of return on common shareholders' equity, (2) capital structure leverage ratio, (3) rate of return on common shareholders' equity, (4) cash flow from operations to average total liabilities ratio, and (5) interest coverage ratio. Indicate the pro forma amounts of these five ratios for The Gap and Limited Brands from part a and the revised amounts for Limited Brands for each of the following three independent strategic actions:

Scenario 1: Decrease the accounts payable turnover ratio from the 23.5 level assumed in part a to the 8.3 level of The Gap. The stretching out of payments to suppliers will result in Limited Brands losing some purchase discounts, leading to an increase in the cost of goods sold to sales percentage from 63.0 percent assumed in part a to 63.5 percent.

Scenario 2: Increase the amount of treasury stock repurchased to achieve the same 1.9 debt-equity ratio forecasted for The Gap.

Scenario 3: Long-term debt will increase at 2.0 times the growth rate in property, plant, and equipment instead of the 1.0 times assumed in part a.

d. Evaluate the three alternative scenarios in light of the analysis in part b.

EXHIBIT 10.11		

Pro Forma Assumptions for The Gap and Limited Brands
(Problem 10.7)

	The Gap	Limited Brands
Sales Growth	6%	3%
Other Revenues/Sales	.000%	.002%
Cost of Goods Sold/Sales	60%	63%
Selling and Administrative/Sales.	27%	25%
Interest Rate on Notes Payable		
Term Debt	4%	4%
Interest Rate on Long-term Debt	8%	8%
Effective Tax Rate	36.5%	40.0%
Minority Interest in Earnings	Not Applicable	15% of Net Income
		Before Minority Int.
Growth in Dividends.	Growth Rate in Sales	Growth Rate in Sales
Cash.	Plug	Plug
Marketable Securities	0	0
Sales/Ending Accounts Receivable	Not applicable	120.0
Cost of Goods Sold/Ending Inventory . . .	5.6	5.8
Sales/Ending Net Fixed Assets.	1.7	2.4
Growth in Fixed Assets at Cost.	Growth in Fixed Assets–Net	Growth in Fixed Assets–Net
Growth in Accumulated		
Depreciation	Growth in Fixed Assets–Net	Growth in Fixed Assets–Net
Growth in Other Assets.	Growth Rate in Sales	Growth Rate in Sales
Purchases/Ending Accounts Payable.	8.3	23.5
Notes Payable.	0	0
Growth Rate in Other Current		
Liabilities	Growth Rate in Sales	Growth Rate in Sales
Growth in Long-term Debt.	Growth Rate in	Growth Rate in
	Fixed Assets at Cost	Fixed Assets at Cost
Growth Rate in Other Noncurrent		
Liabilities	Growth Rate in Sales	Growth Rate in Sales
Increase in Minority Interest		
in Net Assets	Not Applicable	60% of Minority
		Interest in Earnings
Long-term Debt/Shareholders' Equity . . .	1.9	.9
Growth in Accumulated Other		
Comprehensive Income	0.00%	0.00%

CASE 10.1

MASSACHUSETTS STOVE COMPANY: ANALYZING STRATEGIC OPTIONS*

THE WOOD STOVE MARKET

Since the early 1990s, wood stove sales have declined from 1,200,000 units per year to approximately 100,000 units per year. The decline has occurred because of (1) stringent new federal EPA regulations, which set maximum limits on stove emissions beginning in 1992, (2) stable energy prices, which reduced the incentive to switch to wood stoves to save heating costs, and (3) changes in consumers' lifestyles, particularly the growth of two-income families.

During this period of decline in industry sales, the market was flooded with wood stoves at distressed prices as companies closed their doors or liquidated inventories made obsolete by the new EPA regulations. Downward pricing pressure forced surviving companies to cut prices, output, or both. Years of contraction and pricing pressure left many of the surviving manufacturers in a precarious position financially, with excessive inventory, high debt, little cash, uncollectible receivables, and low margins.

The shakeout and consolidation among wood stove manufacturers and, to a lesser extent, among wood stove specialty retailers, have been dramatic. The number of manufacturers selling over 2,000 units a year (characterized within the industry as "large manufacturers") has declined from approximately 90 to 35 in the last 10 years. The number of manufacturers selling less than 2,000 units per year (characterized as "small manufacturers") has declined from approximately 130 to 6. Because the current wood stove market is not large enough to support all of the surviving producers, manufacturers have attempted to diversify in order to stay in business. Seeking relief, virtually all of the survivors have turned to the manufacture of gas appliances.

THE GAS APPLIANCE MARKET

The gas appliance market includes three segments: (1) gas log sets, (2) gas fireplaces, and (3) gas stoves. Gas log sets are "faux fires," which can be installed in an existing fireplace. They are primarily decorative, and have little heating value. Gas fireplaces are fully assembled fireboxes, which can be installed in new construction or in renovated buildings and houses by a builder or contractor. They are mainly decorative, and are less expensive and easier to maintain than a masonry/brick fireplace. Gas stoves are freestanding appliances with a decorative appearance and efficient heating characteristics.

---

*The authors acknowledge the assistance of Tom P. Morrissey in the preparation of this case.

The first two segments of the gas appliance market (log sets and fireplaces) are large, established, and stable markets. Established manufacturers control these markets, and distribution is primarily through mass merchandisers. The third segment (gas stoves) is less than five years old. Although it is growing steadily, it has an annual volume of only about 100,000 units (almost identical to the annual volume of the wood stove market). This is the market to which wood stove manufacturers have turned for relief.

The gas stove market is not as heavily regulated as the wood stove market, and there are currently no EPA regulations governing the emissions of gas heating appliances. Gas stoves are perceived as more appropriate to an aging population because they provide heat and ambiance but require no effort. They can be operated with a wall switch, thermostat, or by remote control. Actual fuel cost (or cost savings) is not an issue for many buyers, so a big advantage of heating with wood is no longer a consideration for many consumers. Gas stoves are sold and distributed through mass merchandisers, or natural gas or propane dealers. The gas industry has the financial, promotional, organizational, and lobbying clout to support the development of the gas stove market, attributes that the tiny wood stove industry lacks.

Unfortunately, life has not been rosy for all of the wood stove companies entering this new market. Development costs and selling costs for new products using a different fuel and different distribution system have been substantial. Improvements in gas logs and gas burners have required rapid changes in product design. In contrast, wood stove designs are fairly stable and slow to change. Competition for market share has renewed pricing pressure on gas stove producers. Companies trying to maintain their wood stove sales while introducing gas products must carry large inventories to service both product lines. Failure to accurately forecast demand has left many companies with inventory shortages during the selling season, or large inventories of unsold product at the end of the season.

Many surviving manufacturers who looked to gas stoves for salvation are now quietly looking for suitors to acquire them. A combination of excessive debt and inventory levels, together with high development and distribution costs, has made financial success highly uncertain. There will be continued consolidation in this difficult market during the next five years.

MASSACHUSETTS STOVE COMPANY

Massachusetts Stove Company (MSC) is one of the six "small manufacturers" to survive the EPA regulation and industry meltdown. It has just completed its sixth consecutive year of slow but steady growth in revenue and profit since complying with the EPA regulations. Exhibits 10.12 to 10.14 present the financial statements of MSC for Year 3 to Year 7. Exhibit 10.15 presents selected financial statement ratios.

The success of MSC in recent years is a classic case of a company staying small, marketing in a specific niche, and vigorously applying a "stick to your knitting" policy. MSC is the only wood stove producer that has not developed gas products; 100 percent of its sales currently come from wood stove sales. MSC is the only wood stove producer that sells by mail order directly to consumers. The mail order market has sheltered MSC from some of the pricing pressure that other manufacturers have had

	EXHIBIT 10.12				
	Income Statements for Massachusetts Stove Company				
	(Case 10.1)				

	Year Ended December 31:				
	Year 3	Year 4	Year 5	Year 6	Year 7
Sales	$1,480,499	$1,637,128	$2,225,745	$2,376,673	$2,734,986
Cost of Goods Sold	(727,259)	(759,156)	(1,063,135)	(1,159,466)	(1,380,820)
Depreciation.	(56,557)	(73,416)	(64,320)	(66,829)	(72,321)
Facilities Costs	(59,329)	(47,122)	(66,226)	(48,090)	(45,309)
Facilities Rental Income.	25,856	37,727	38,702	42,142	41,004
Selling Expenses.	(452,032)	(563,661)	(776,940)	(874,000)	(926,175)
Administrative Expenses	(36,967)	(39,057)	(46,444)	(48,046)	(111,199)
Operating Income	$ 174,211	$ 192,443	$ 247,382	$ 222,384	$ 240,166
Interest Income	712	2,242	9,541	9,209	16,665
Interest Expense.	(48,437)	(44,551)	(47,535)	(52,633)	(42,108)
Net Income Before					
Income Taxes.	$ 126,486	$ 150,134	$ 209,388	$ 178,960	$ 214,723
Income Taxes Expense	(35,416)	(42,259)	(64,142)	(45,794)	(60,122)
Net Income	$ 91,070	$ 107,875	$ 145,246	$ 133,166	$ 154,601

to bear. The combination of high entry costs and high risks make it unlikely that another competitor will enter the mail order niche.

MSC's other competitive advantages are the high efficiency and unique features of its wood stoves. MSC equips its wood stoves with a catalytic combuster, which reburns gases emitted from burning wood. This reburning not only increases the heat generated by the stoves but reduces pollutants in the air. MSC offers a wood stove with inlaid soapstone. This soapstone heats up and provides warmth even after the fire has dwindled in the stove. The soapstone also adds to the attractiveness of the stove as a piece of furniture. MSC's customer base includes many middle- and upper-income individuals.

MSC feels that profitable growth of wood stove sales beyond gross revenues of three million dollars a year in the mail order niche is unlikely. However, no one is selling gas appliances by mail order. Many of MSC's customers and prospects have asked if MSC plans to produce a gas stove.

The management of MSC is contemplating the development of several gas appliances to sell by mail order. There are compelling reasons for MSC to do this, as well as some good reasons to be cautious.

Availability of Space

MSC owns a 25,000 square foot building, but occupies only 15,000 square feet. MSC leases the remaining 10,000 square feet to two tenants. The tenants pay rent

EXHIBIT 10.13

Balance Sheets for Massachusetts Stove Company
(Case 10.1)

	December 31:					
	Year 2	Year 3	Year 4	Year 5	Year 6	Year 7
Assets						
Cash	$ 50,794	$ 19,687	$ 145,930	$ 104,383	$ 258,148	$ 351,588
Accounts Receivable	12,571	56,706	30,934	41,748	30,989	5,997
Inventories	251,112	327,627	347,883	375,258	409,673	452,709
Other Current Assets	1,368	—	—	—	—	—
Total Current Assets	$ 315,845	$ 404,020	$ 524,747	$ 521,389	$ 698,810	$ 810,294
Property, Plant, and Equipment:						
At Cost	1,056,157	1,148,806	1,164,884	1,184,132	1,234,752	1,257,673
Accumulated Depreciation	(296,683)	(353,240)	(426,656)	(490,975)	(557,804)	(630,125)
Other Assets	121,483	94,000	61,500	12,200	—	—
Total Assets	$1,196,802	$1,293,586	$1,324,475	$1,226,746	$1,375,758	$1,437,842
Liabilities and Shareholders' Equity						
Accounts Payable	$ 137,104	$ 112,815	$ 43,229	$ 60,036	$ 39,170	$ 47,809
Notes Payable	25,000	12,000	—	—	—	—
Current Portion of Long-term Debt	27,600	29,000	21,570	113,257	115,076	27,036
Other Current Liabilities	39,530	100,088	184,194	189,732	244,241	257,252
Total Current Liabilities	$ 229,234	$ 253,903	$ 248,993	$ 363,025	$ 398,487	$ 332,097
Long-term Debt	972,446	953,491	881,415	599,408	574,332	547,296
Deferred Income Taxes	—	—	—	—	5,460	6,369
Total Liabilities	$1,201,680	$1,207,394	$1,130,408	$ 962,433	$ 978,279	$ 885,762
Common Stock	2,000	2,000	2,000	2,000	2,000	2,000
Additional Paid-in Capital	435,630	435,630	435,630	435,630	435,630	435,630
Retained Earnings (Deficit)	(442,508)	(351,438)	(243,563)	(98,317)	34,849	189,450
Treasury Stock	—	—	—	(75,000)	(75,000)	(75,000)
Total Shareholders' Equity	$ (4,878)	$ 86,192	$ 194,067	$ 264,313	$ 397,479	$ 552,080
Total Liabilities and Shareholders' Equity	$1,196,802	$1,293,586	$1,324,475	$1,226,746	$1,375,758	$1,437,842

| | EXHIBIT 10.14 | | | | |

Statements of Cash Flows for Massachusetts Stove Company
(Case 10.1)

	Year Ended December 31:				
	Year 3	Year 4	Year 5	Year 6	Year 7
Operations					
Net Income	$ 91,070	$107,875	$ 145,246	$133,166	$ 154,601
Depreciation and Amortization	56,557	73,416	64,320	66,829	72,321
Other Addbacks.	27,483	32,500	49,300	17,660	909
(Increase) Decrease in Receivables	(44,135)	25,772	(10,814)	10,759	24,992
(Increase) Decrease in Inventories	(76,515)	(20,256)	(27,375)	(34,415)	(43,036)
Decrease in Other Current Assets.	1,368	—	—	—	—
Increase (Decrease) in Payables	(24,289)	(69,586)	16,807	(20,866)	8,639
Increase in Other Current Liabilities.	60,558	84,106	5,538	54,509	13,011
Cash Flow from Operations	$ 92,097	$233,827	$ 243,022	$227,642	$ 231,437
Investing					
Capital Expenditures.	$(92,649)	$(16,078)	$ (19,249)	$(50,620)	$ (22,921)
Cash Flow from Investing	$(92,649)	$(16,078)	$ (19,249)	$(50,620)	$ (22,921)
Financing					
Increase in Long-term Debt	$ 10,000	$ —	$ —	$ —	$ —
Decrease in Short-term Debt	(13,000)	(12,000)	—	—	—
Decrease in Long-term Debt	(27,555)	(79,506)	(190,320)	(23,257)	(115,076)
Acquisition of Common Stock.	—	—	(75,000)	—	—
Cash Flow from Financing	$(30,555)	$(91,506)	$(265,320)	$(23,257)	$(115,076)
Change in Cash	$(31,107)	$126,243	$ (41,547)	$153,765	$ 93,440
Cash—Beginning of Year	50,794	19,687	145,930	104,383	258,148
Cash—End of Year	$ 19,687	$145,930	$ 104,383	$258,148	$ 351,588

EXHIBIT 10.15					
Financial Statement Ratios for Massachusetts Stove Company **(Case 10.1)**					
	Year 3	Year 4	Year 5	Year 6	Year 7
Profit Margin for ROA..................	8.5%	8.5%	8.1%	7.2%	6.8%
Total Assets Turnover....................	1.2	1.3	1.7	1.8	1.9
Rate of Return on Assets	10.1%	10.7%	14.1%	13.1%	13.1%
Profit Margin for ROCE	6.2%	6.6%	6.5%	5.6%	5.7%
Capital Structure Leverage Ratio...........	30.6	9.3	5.6	3.9	3.0
Rate of Return on Common Equity	224.0%	77.0%	63.4%	40.2%	32.6%
Cost of Goods Sold/Sales.................	49.1%	46.4%	47.8%	48.8%	50.5%
Depreciation Expense/Sales...............	3.8%	4.5%	2.9%	2.8%	2.6%
Facilities Costs Net of Rental Income/Sales....	2.3%	.6%	1.2%	.3%	.2%
Selling Expense/Sales....................	30.5%	34.4%	34.9%	36.8%	33.9%
Administrative Expenses/Sales.............	2.5%	2.4%	2.1%	2.0%	4.0%
Interest Income/Sales....................	—	.1%	.4%	.4%	.6%
Interest Expense/Sales	3.3%	2.7%	2.1%	2.2%	1.5%
Income Tax Expense/Income Before Taxes	28.0%	28.1%	30.6%	25.6%	28.0%
Accounts Receivable Turnover.............	42.7	37.4	61.2	65.3	147.9
Inventory Turnover	2.5	2.2	2.9	3.0	3.2
Fixed Asset Turnover	1.9	2.1	3.1	3.5	4.2
Current Ratio...........................	1.59	2.11	1.44	1.75	2.44
Quick Ratio	.30	.71	.40	.73	1.08
Days Accounts Receivable	9	10	6	6	3
Days Inventory Held	146	166	126	122	114
Days Accounts Payable...................	51	33	16	14	11
Cash Flow from Operations/Average Current Liabilities	38.1%	93.0%	79.4%	59.8%	63.4%
Debt-Equity Ratio	1,106.2%	454.2%	226.8%	144.5%	99.1%
Cash Flow from Operations/Average Total Liabilities.............................	7.6%	20.0%	23.2%	23.5%	24.8%
Interest Coverage Ratio	3.6	4.4	5.4	4.4	6.1

plus their share of insurance, property taxes, and maintenance costs. The addition of gas appliances to its product line would require MSC to use 5,000 square feet of the space currently rented to tenants. MSC would have to give the tenant six months' notice to cancel its lease.

Availability of Capital

MSC has its own internal funds for product development and inventory, as well as an unused line of credit. But it will lose interest income (or incur interest expense) as it invests these funds in development and increased inventory.

Existing Demand

MSC receives approximately 50,000 requests for catalogues each year, and has a mailing list of approximately 220,000 active prospects and 15,000 recent owners of wood stoves. There is anecdotal evidence of sufficient demand that MSC could introduce its gas stoves with little or no additional marketing expense, other than the cost of printing some catalogue pages each year. MSCs management worries about the risk of the gas stove sales cannibalizing its existing wood stove sales. Also, if the current base of wood stove sales is eroded through mismanagement, inattention, or cannibalization, then attempts to grow the business through expansion into gas appliances will be self-defeating.

Vacant Market Niche

No other manufacturer is selling gas stoves by mail order. The entry costs are high and the unit volume is small, so it is unlikely that another producer will enter the niche. MSC has had the mail order market for wood stoves to itself for approximately seven years. MSC feels that this lack of existing competition will give it additional time to develop new products. However, management also feels that a timely entry will help to solidify its position in this niche.

Suppliers

MSC has existing relationships with many of the suppliers necessary to manufacture new gas products. The foundry that produces MSC's wood stove castings is one of the largest suppliers of gas heating appliances in central Europe. On the other hand, MSC will be a small, new customer for the vendors that provide the ceramic logs and gas burners. This could lead to problems with price, delivery, or service for these parts.

Synergies in Marketing and Manufacturing

MSC would sell gas appliances through its existing direct mail marketing efforts. It will incur additional marketing expenses for photography, printing, and customer service. MSC's existing plant is capable of manufacturing the shell of the gas units. It will require additional expertise to assemble fireboxes for the gas units (valves, burners, and log sets). MSC will have to increase both its space and number of employees to process and paint the metal parts of the new gas stoves. The gross margin for the gas products should be similar to that of the wood stoves.

Lack of Management Experience

Managing new product development, larger production levels and inventories, and a more complex business will require MSC to hire more management expertise. MSC will also have to institute a new organization structure for its more complex business and define responsibilities and accountability more carefully. Up to now, MSC has operated with a fairly loose organizational philosophy.

Required (Requirements continue on page 806.)

a. Identify clues from the financial statements and financial statement ratios for Year 3 to Year 7 that might suggest that Massachusetts Stove Company is in a mature business.

b. Design a spreadsheet for the preparation of pro forma income statements, balance sheets, and statements of cash flows for MSC for Year 8 to Year 12 and prepare pro forma financial statements for each of these years under three scenarios: (1) best case, (2) most likely, and (3) worst case. The sections below describe the assumptions to be made.

Development Costs

MSC plans to develop two gas stove models, but not concurrently. It will develop the first gas model during Year 8 and begin selling it during Year 9. It will develop the second gas model during Year 9 and begin selling it during Year 10. MSC will capitalize the development costs in the year incurred (Year 8 and Year 9) and amortize them straight line over five years, beginning with the year the particular stove is initially sold (Year 9 and Year 10). Estimated development cost for each stove are:

Best Case: $100,000.
Most Likely Case: $120,000.
Worst Case: $160,000.

Capital Expenditures

Capital expenditures, other than development costs, will be: Year 8, $20,000; Year 9, $30,000; Year 10, $30,000; Year 11, $25,000; Year 12, $25,000. Assume a six-year depreciable life, straight-line depreciation, and a full year of depreciation in the year of acquisition.

Sales Growth

Changes in total sales relative to total sales of the preceding year are as follows:

	Best Case			Most Likely Case			Worst Case		
Year	Wood Stoves	Gas Stoves	Total	Wood Stoves	Gas Stoves	Total	Wood Stoves	Gas Stoves	Total
8	+2%	—	+2%	−2%	—	−2%	−4%	—	−4%
9	+2%	+6%	+8%	−2%	+4%	+2%	−4%	+2%	−2%
10	+2%	+12%	+14%	−2%	+8%	+6%	−4%	+4%	+0%
11	+2%	+12%	+14%	−2%	+8%	+6%	−4%	+4%	+0%
12	+2%	+12%	+14%	−2%	+8%	+6%	−4%	+4%	+0%

Because sales of gas stoves will start at zero, the projections of sales should *use the growth rates in total sales above.* The growth rates shown for wood stove sales and gas stove sales simply indicate the components of the total sales increase.

Cost of Goods Sold

Manufacturing costs of the gas stoves will equal 50 percent of sales, the same as for wood stoves.

Depreciation

Depreciation will increase for the amortization of the product development costs on the gas stoves and depreciation of additional capital expenditures.

Facilities Rental Income and Facilities Costs

Facilities rental income will decrease by 50 percent beginning in Year 9 when MSC takes over 5,000 square feet of its building now rented to others and remain at that reduced level for Year 10 to Year 12. Facilities costs will increase by $30,000 beginning in Year 9 for facilities costs now paid by the tenants and for additional facilities costs required by gas stove manufacturing. These costs will remain at that increased level for Year 10 to Year 12.

Selling Expenses

Selling expenses as a percentage of sales are as follows:

Year	Best Case	Most Likely Case	Worst Case
8	34%	34.0%	34%
9	33%	33.5%	35%
10	32%	33.0%	36%
11	31%	32.5%	37%
12	30%	32.0%	38%

Administrative Expenses

Administrative expenses will increase by $30,000 in Year 8, $30,000 in Year 9, $20,000 in Year 10, and then remain at the Year 10 level in Year 11 and Year 12.

Interest Income

MSC will earn 5 percent interest on the average balance in cash each year.

Interest Expense

The interest rate on interest-bearing debt will be 6.8 percent on the average amount of debt outstanding each year.

Income Tax Expense

MSC is subject to an income tax rate of 28 percent.

Accounts Receivable and Inventories

Accounts receivable and inventories will increase at the growth rate in sales.

Property, Plant, and Equipment

Property, plant, and equipment at cost will increase each year by the amounts of capital expenditures and expenditures on development costs. Accumulated depreciation will increase each year by the amount of depreciation and amortization expense.

Accounts Payable and Other Current Liabilities

Accounts payable will increase with the growth rate in inventories. Other current liabilities primarily include advances by customers for stoves manufactured soon after the year end. Other current liabilities will increase with the growth rate in sales.

Current Portion of Long-term Debt

Scheduled repayments of long-term debt are as follows: Year 8, $27,036; Year 9, $29,200; Year 10, $31,400; Year 11, $33,900; Year 12, $36,600; Year 13, $39,500.

Deferred Income Taxes

Deferred income taxes relate to the use of accelerated depreciation for tax purposes and the straight-line method for financial reporting. Assume that deferred income taxes will not change.

Shareholders' Equity

Assume that there will be no changes in the contributed capital of MSC. Retained earnings will change each year in the amount of net income.

Required (continued from page 804)

c. Calculate the financial statements ratios listed in Exhibit 10.15 for MSC under each of the three scenarios for Year 8 to Year 12.
Note: You should create a fourth spreadsheet as part of your preparation of the pro forma financial statements that will compute the financial ratios.

d. What advice would you give to the management of MSC regarding its decision to enter the gas stove market? Your recommendation should consider the profitability and risks of this action as well as other factors you deem relevant.

Chapter 11

VALUATION: CASH-FLOW-BASED APPROACHES

Learning Objectives

1. Understand how cash-flow-based valuation models work, and their conceptual and practical strengths and weaknesses.

2. Develop practical valuation techniques to deal with many of the difficult issues involved in estimating firm value using the present value of expected future cash flows:
   - (a) cash flows versus earnings versus dividends,
   - (b) cash flows to the investor versus cash flows to the firm,
   - (c) nominal versus real cash flows,
   - (d) pre-tax versus after-tax cash flows,
   - (e) free cash flows for all debt and equity capital stakeholders versus free cash flows for common equity shareholders,
   - (f) the forecast horizon,
   - (g) continuing value, and
   - (h) risk, discount rates, and the cost of capital.

3. Apply all of these techniques to estimate firm value using the present value of future cash flows valuation methods.

4. Develop techniques to assess the sensitivity of firm value estimates to key valuation parameters, such as discount rates and expected long-term growth rates.

INTRODUCTION AND OVERVIEW

Economic theory teaches that the value of any resource equals the present value of the expected future returns from the resource discounted at a rate that reflects the risk inherent in those expected returns. A general model for the present value of a security (denoted as V_0 with present value denoted at time $t = 0$) with an expected life of n future periods is as follows:[1]

$$V_0 = \sum_{t=1}^{n} \frac{\text{Expected Future Returns}_t}{(1 + \text{Discount Rate})^t}$$

Even in relatively efficient securities markets, *price* does not necessarily equal *value* for every security at all times. When an investor buys a security, the investor pays the security's price and receives the security's value. When the investor sells a security, the investor receives the selling price and gives up the security's value. Price is observable, value is not; value has to be estimated. Estimating the value of a security in order to make intelligent investment decisions is therefore a common objective of financial statement analysis. Investors, analysts, investment bankers, and managers design the financial statement analysis process to culminate in a reliable appraisal of the value of shares of common equity. The questions they typically address include: What do I think a share of common stock in a particular company is worth? Considering the current price, should I make a buy, sell, or hold recommendation on a particular firm's common shares? What price should I assign to the initial public offering of a firm's common shares? What is a reasonable price to accept (seller) or pay (buyer) for a firm involved in a corporate acquisition?

We designed the five-step analysis framework that forms the structure of this book (Exhibit 1.1) as a logical set of steps to determine intelligent estimates of value. We first analyze the economics of the industry and the particular firm's strategy. We then assess the quality of the firm's accounting, making adjustments if necessary. Next, we evaluate the firm's risk and performance with a set of financial ratios. We then use all of this information to project the firm's pro forma financial statements to develop realistic forecasts of expected future earnings, cash flows, and dividends. Finally, we apply valuation models to these forecasts to estimate the value of the firm. Forecasts of expected future returns (the numerator in the valuation model) depend on forecasts of future earnings, cash flows, or dividends. Assessing an appropriate risk-adjusted discount rate (the denominator in the valuation model) requires an objective assessment of the inherent riskiness in the set of expected future returns. Therefore, objective estimates of firm value depend on objective estimates of expected future returns and an appropriate risk-adjusted discount rate, all of which depend on all five steps of the framework.

---

[1]Throughout this chapter, t refers to accounting periods. The valuation process determines an estimate of firm value, denoted V_0, in present value as of today, when $t = 0$. The period $t = 1$ refers to the first accounting period being discounted to present value. Period $t = n$ is the period of the expected final, or liquidating, return.

When the analyst derives internally consistent forecasts of future earnings, cash flows, and dividends from a set of internally consistent pro forma financial statements, and uses the same discount rate to compute the present values of those expected earnings, cash flows, and dividends, then the valuation models yield a consistent estimate of value for a firm. That is, the valuation models are complementary and equivalent approaches to valuation. In Chapters 11 and 12, we illustrate this equivalence both in the theoretical development of the models and in their application to the pro forma financial statements for PepsiCo developed in Chapter 10. In Chapter 13, we describe practical shortcuts (such as market multiples like price-earnings ratios or market-to-book ratios) that analysts take in some instances in applying these valuation models. The analyst will not necessarily derive the identical valuations across the various valuation models when using these shortcuts, so we describe some of the biases that these shortcuts may trigger in valuation.

Cash-flow-based and earnings-based equity valuation models have been the subject of considerable theoretical and empirical research in recent years. The results indicate that these models generally provide significant explanatory power for share prices.[2] In the same vein, empirical research has shown that cash flows and earnings for most firms display high positive correlations with stock returns. It is therefore no surprise that analysts and investors commonly use cash flows and earnings as the value-relevant attributes on which they base valuation models. This chapter describes and applies cash-flow-based valuation models. Chapter 12 describes and applies earnings-based and dividends-based valuation models. Both chapters discuss and illustrate the important issues that determine the conceptual and practical strengths and weaknesses of each approach.

Our experience indicates that applying several valuation approaches yields better insights about the value of a firm than relying on one approach in all cases. In addition, all three valuation chapters—Chapters 11 through 13— emphasize that the objective of the valuation process is not a single point estimate of value per se, but instead the objective is to determine the distribution of value estimates across the relevant ranges of critical valuation parameters. By estimating share value using cash flows, earnings, and dividends, and by assessing the sensitivity of these value estimates across a distribution of relevant valuation parameters, we seek to determine the most likely range of values for a share, which can then be compared to the share's price for an intelligent investment decision.

RATIONALE FOR CASH-FLOW-BASED VALUATION

In theory, the value of a share of common equity is the present value of the expected future dividends.[3] Dividends are the most fundamental value-relevant

---

[2]For examples, see Stephen Penman and Theodore Sougiannis, "A Comparison of Dividend, Cash Flow, and Earnings Approaches to Equity Valuation," *Contemporary Accounting Research* Vol. 15 No. 3 (Fall 1998), pp. 343–383, and Jennifer Francis, Per Olsson, and Dennis Oswald, "Comparing the Accuracy and Explainability of Dividend, Free Cash Flow, and Abnormal Earnings Equity Value Estimates," *Journal of Accounting Research* Vol. 38 No. 1 (Spring 2000), pp. 45–70.

[3]John Burr Williams, *The Theory of Investment and Value*, Cambridge, Mass.: Harvard University Press, 1938.

attributes of expected future returns to use to value shares because they represent the distribution of wealth to shareholders. The equity shareholder invests cash when the share is purchased, and then receives dividends as the payoffs from holding the share, including the final "liquidating" dividend when the share is sold. In dividends-based valuation, dividends are therefore defined to be all-inclusive measures of cash flows between the firm and the common equity shareholders. Therefore, in valuation, "all-inclusive dividends" encompass cash flows from the firm to shareholders through periodic dividend payments, stock buybacks, and the firm's liquidating dividend, as well as cash flows from the shareholders to the firm when shares are issued (in a sense, *negative* dividends).

As a practical matter, however, periodic dividend payment amounts are arbitrary (except for the final liquidating dividend), established by a dividend policy. Periodic dividend payments do not vary closely with firm performance from one period to the next. Some firms do not pay a regular periodic dividend, particularly young, high growth firms. For most firms, the final liquidating dividend plays a very important role, usually representing a very large proportion of the value of the firm in a dividends-based valuation. Therefore, to value a firm's shares using dividends, one must forecast dividends over the life of the firm (or the expected length of time the share will be held), including the final liquidating dividend (that is, the future price at which the share will be sold). Thus, the analyst faces the challenge of needing to forecast the value of a share in the future at the time of the liquidating dividend in order to value the share today.

Cash-flow-based valuation is an alternative approach that is equivalent to dividends-based valuation. The analyst can forecast and value the cash flows the firm will generate and use to pay dividends, instead of forecasting the dividends per se. Instead of focusing on wealth distribution, the cash-flow-based approach focuses on dividend-paying capacity. The cash-flow-based valuation approach measures and values the cash flows that are "free" to be distributed to shareholders. That is, *"free" cash flows* are the cash flows each period that are available to be distributed to shareholders, unencumbered by necessary reinvestments in operating assets or required payments to debt holders. Free cash flows can be used instead of dividends in the numerator of the general value model as the value-relevant measures of expected future returns to the investor. Both approaches, if implemented with consistent assumptions, will lead to identical estimates of value.

The rationale for using expected free cash flows in valuation is twofold:

1. **Cash is the ultimate source of value.** When individuals and firms invest in any resource, they delay current consumption in favor of future consumption. Cash is the medium of exchange that will permit them to consume various goods and services in the future. A resource has value because of its ability to provide future cash flows.
2. **Cash serves as a measurable common denominator for comparing the future benefits of alternative investment opportunities.** One might compare investment opportunities involving the holding of a bond, a stock, or an office building, but comparing these alternatives requires a common measuring unit of their future benefits. The future cash flows derived from their future services serve such a function.

Economists sometimes argue that free cash flows are superior to earnings as the value-relevant attribute in valuation models. When addressing the free cash flows versus earnings issue, economists sometimes argue that: (1) firms pay dividends in cash, not earnings; investors can spend cash but cannot spend earnings for future consumption; (2) earnings are subject to accounting methods that may no longer reflect underlying economic values (for example, acquisition cost valuations of assets, past expenses for research and development that have turned out to be successful); and (3) earnings can be subject to purposeful management by a firm. Thus, they assert that earnings are not as reliable or as meaningful as cash as the common measurement attribute for comparing investment alternatives. They assert that a dollar of cash is a dollar of cash, but a dollar of earnings by one firm is not necessarily equal to a dollar of earnings by another firm. Chapter 12 addresses these concerns and presents an earnings-based valuation model that is as practical and as reliable as the cash-flow-based model.

OVERVIEW OF CASH-FLOW-BASED VALUATION

The valuation of any resource using cash flows involves measuring three elements:

1. The expected future free cash flows over the forecast horizon.
2. The expected free cash flow at the final period of the forecast horizon, referred to as the *continuing free cash flow,* and a forecast of the long-run growth rate in the continuing free cash flow beyond the forecast horizon.
3. The discount rate used to compute the present value of the future free cash flows.

The sections below discuss measuring each of these elements.

MEASURING PERIODIC FREE CASH FLOWS

In this section, we describe and illustrate measuring value-relevant cash flows. We first confront conceptual measurement issues regarding cash flows to the investor versus cash flows to the firm, nominal versus real cash flows, and before- versus after-tax cash flows. We then present a conceptual framework for measuring free cash flows, and describe specific practical steps to take to measure free cash flows from two different perspectives—free cash flows to all debt and equity stakeholders and free cash flows to common equity shareholders—and when to use each free cash flow measure. We conclude this section by discussing free cash flow forecasting horizons.

Cash Flows to the Investor versus Cash Flows to the Firm

This chapter primarily considers valuation settings that involve valuing the common stock equity of a firm. In the previous section, we asserted that the analyst can use the free cash flows expected to be generated by the firm as the value-relevant measure of expected future returns instead of the dividends expected to be paid to the investor. Will using free cash flows in valuation result in the same estimate of value as using dividends? Cash flows paid to the investor via dividends and free cash flows available for common equity shareholders will differ each period to the extent that the firm reinvests a portion (or all) of the cash flows generated. However, if the firm generates a rate of return on reinvested free cash flow equal to the discount rate used by the investor (that is, the cost of equity capital), then either set of cash flows will yield the same valuation of a firm's shares at a point in time. Consider the following scenarios.

Example 1. A firm expects to generate free cash flows of 15 percent annually on invested equity capital for the rest of its life, which is likely to continue for an indefinitely long period of time into the future (until say $t=n$). Equity investors in this firm require a 15 percent return each year, considering the riskiness of the firm. Assume that the firm pays out 100 percent of the free cash flows each year as a dividend. Thus, the free cash flows generated by the firm equal the cash dividends received by the investor. Each dollar of capital committed by the investor has a present value of future cash flows equal to one dollar. That is,

$$\$1 = \sum_{t=1}^{n} \frac{\$.15}{(1.15)^t}$$

Example 2. Assume the same facts as Example 1, except that the firm pays out none of the free cash flows as a dividend. The firm retains the $0.15 free cash flow on each dollar of capital and reinvests it in projects expected to earn 15 percent return per year. In this case, the investor receives no periodic dividends and receives cash only when the investor sells the shares or the firm liquidates at date $t = n$. By the terminal date, n periods in the future, each dollar of capital invested in the firm today will have earned a compound rate of return of 15 percent, equal to the required rate of return. In this case also, each dollar of invested capital has a present value of future cash flows equal to one dollar. That is,

$$\$1 = \frac{(\$1.15)^n}{(1.15)^n}$$

Example 3. Assume the same facts as Example 1, except that the firm pays out 25 percent of the free cash flow each period as a dividend and reinvests the other 75 percent in projects expected to generate a return of 15 percent. In this case also, each dollar of invested capital has a present value of future cash flows equal to one dollar. That is,

$$\$1 = \sum_{t=1}^{n} \frac{(\$.25)(.15)}{(1.15)^t} + \frac{(\$.75)(1.15)^n}{(1.15)^n}$$

These three examples illustrate the irrelevance of dividend policy in firm valuation.[4] The same valuation should arise whether the analyst discounts (1) the expected

---

[4]Merton Miller and Franco Modigliani, "Dividend Policy, Growth and the Valuation of Shares," *Journal of Business* (October 1961), pp. 411–433. Penman and Sougiannis test empirically the replacement property of dividends for future earnings and find support for the irrelevance of dividend policy in valuation. See Stephen H. Penman and Theodore Sougiannis, "The Dividend Displacement Property and the

periodic dividends plus the liquidating dividend to the investor, or (2) the expected free cash flows to the firm that are available to pay dividends to equity shareholders some time in the future. Because liquidating dividends are seldom observable, as a practical matter analysts and investors commonly use the present value of the firm's expected future free cash flows to assess the value of a firm's common equity shares.

Nominal Versus Real Cash Flows

Changes in general price levels (that is, inflation or deflation) cause the purchasing power of the monetary unit to change over time. Should the valuation use projected *nominal* free cash flows, which include the effects of inflation or deflation, or *real* free cash flows, which filter out the effects of changes in general purchasing power?[5] The valuation of a resource should be the same whether one uses nominal or real free cash flow amounts as long as the discount rate used is the nominal or real rate of return, consistent with the cash flows. That is, if projected free cash flows are nominal and include the effects of changes in general purchasing power of the monetary unit, then the discount rate should be nominal and include an inflation component. If projected free cash flows are real amounts that filter out the effects of general price changes, then the discount rate should be a real rate of return, excluding the inflation component.

Example 4. A firm owns an asset that it expects to sell one year from today for $115.5 million. The firm expects the general price level to increase 10 percent during this period. The real interest rate is 5 percent. The nominal discount rate should be 15.5 percent to measure the effects of the real rate of interest and inflation ($1.155 = 1.10 \times 1.05$). Discounting either nominal or real cash flows, the value of the asset today to the firm is $100 million, as shown below:

Nominal Cash Flow	×	Discount Rate Including Expected Inflation	=	Value
$115.5 million	×	$1/[(1.05)(1.10)]$	=	$100 million

Real Cash Flow	×	Discount Rate Excluding Expected Inflation	=	Value
$115.5 million/(1.10)$	×	$1/(1.05)$	=	$100 million

Substitution of Anticipated Earnings for Dividends in Equity Valuation," *The Accounting Review* (January 1997), pp. 1–21.

[5]Note that the issue here is not with specific price changes of a firm's particular assets, liabilities, revenues, and expenses. These specific price changes affect cash flows and should enter into the valuation of the firm. The issue is whether some portion, all, or more than all of the specific price changes represent simply a change in the purchasing power of the monetary unit, which should not affect the value of a firm.

As a practical matter, analysts usually find it more straightforward to discount nominal cash flows using nominal discount rates than to first adjust nominal cash flows to real cash flows and then discount real cash flows using real interest rates.

Pre-tax Versus After-tax Free Cash Flows

Will the same valuation arise if the analyst discounts pre-tax free cash flows at a pre-tax cost of capital and after-tax free cash flows at an after-tax cost of capital? The answer is no if costs of debt and equity capital receive different tax treatments. For tax purposes, firms can typically deduct the costs of debt capital but cannot deduct the costs of equity capital.

Example 5. Suppose the firm faces the following costs of capital:

	Proportion in Capital Structure	Pre-tax Cost	Tax Effect	After-tax Cost	Weighted Average Cost of Capital Pre-tax	Weighted Average Cost of Capital After-tax
Debt	.33	10%	.4	6%	3.33%	2.00%
Equity.	.67	18%	—	18%	12.00%	12.00%
	1.00				15.33%	14.00%

Assume that this firm expects to generate $90 million of pre-tax free cash flows and $54 million of after-tax free cash flows [= (1 − 0.4) × $90 million] one year from today. This firm would be valued using pre-tax and after-tax amounts (assuming a one-year horizon) as follows:

Pre-tax:	$90 million × 1/1.1533 = $78.04 million
After-tax:	$54 million × 1/1.14 = $47.37 million

These values are not equivalent because cash inflows from assets are taxed at 40 percent and cash outflows to service debt give rise to a tax savings of 40 percent. The cost of equity capital, however, does not provide a tax benefit. The appropriate valuation in this case is $47.37 million. Thus, the analyst should use after-tax free cash flows and the after-tax cost of capital.

A Framework for Free Cash Flows

A conceptual framework for free cash flows to the firm emanates from the familiar balance sheet equation, in which assets equal liabilities plus shareholders' equity:

$$A = L + SE$$

Separate all of the assets and liabilities into two categories, operating or financing:

$$OA + FA = OL + FL + SE$$

Operating assets and liabilities relate to the firm's day-to-day operations in the normal course of business. For most firms, operating assets (denoted OA) include cash and short-term investment securities necessary for liquidity purposes, accounts receivable, inventory, property, plant, and equipment, intangible assets (licenses, patents, trademarks, goodwill, etc.), and investments in affiliated companies. Operating liabilities (denoted OL) typically include accounts payable, accrued expenses, accrued taxes, deferred taxes, pension obligations, and other retirement benefits obligations. Assets and liabilities related to financing activities typically include interest-earning assets and interest-bearing liabilities that are part of the financial capital structure of the firm. Financial liabilities (denoted FL) include such interest-bearing items as notes payable, current maturities of long-term debt, and long-term debt in the forms of mortgages, bonds, notes, and capital lease obligations. Insofar as outstanding preferred stock contains features that indicate it is economically similar to debt (that is, features such as limited life, mandatory redemption, guaranteed dividends), then the analyst should include preferred stock with financial liabilities. In some circumstances, firms may hold financial assets (denoted FA), which reflect capital savings as opposed to borrowings in the financial capital structure. Financial assets include amounts of capital that are not necessary to support the liquidity needs of the firm's operating activities and are held in interest-earning accounts such as cash and cash equivalents, short-term investment securities, and long-term investment securities.[6] Note that capital held in these types of accounts for purposes of liquidity for operating activities, or investments in affiliated companies with related operating activities, should be considered operating assets and not financial assets.

Rearrange the balance sheet to put operating activities on one side and financing activities on the other:

$$OA - OL = FL - FA + SE,$$

which is equivalent to

$$NetOA = NetFL + SE$$

where NetOA = OA − OL and NetFL = FL − FA. For most firms, operating assets are likely to exceed operating liabilities, and financial liabilities are likely to exceed financial assets (financial borrowing usually exceeds financial savings).

This rearrangement of the balance sheet provides a useful basis from which to conceptualize free cash flows to the firm. If we substitute for each term the present

---

[6]The calculation of the rate of return on assets, or ROA, in Chapter 4 assumed that all assets were operating assets and that operating income is equal to net income excluding the after-tax cost of financial liabilities. Thus, we made no adjustment to eliminate interest income on financial assets from net income in the numerator of ROA and no adjustment to eliminate financial assets in the denominator. Most manufacturing, retailing, and service firms hold only minor amounts of financial assets, so ignoring adjustments for financial assets does not usually introduce a material amount of bias to the calculation of ROA. A more precise calculation of ROA for firms with a material amount of financial assets in the capital structure adjusts the numerator to eliminate interest income and adjusts the denominator of ROA for the portions of financial assets (cash, marketable securities, and investment securities) that are part of the financial capital structure and are not directly related to operating activities.

values of the expected future net cash flows associated with operating activities, financing activities, and shareholders' equity, we can express the balance sheet in the following cash flow terms:

$$\text{PVNetCFs from Operations} = \text{PVNetCFs to Debt Financing}$$
$$+ \text{PVNetCFs to Shareholders' Equity}$$

This expression indicates the sum of the values of the debt and equity claims on the firm is determined by the present value of the net cash flows the operations of the firm will produce. Therefore, one can estimate the value of the debt and equity capital of the firm by projecting the net cash flows from operations that are "free" to service debt and equity claims, and discounting those free cash flows to present value. We refer to this measure of free cash flows as the *free cash flows for all debt and equity capital stakeholders*, because they reflect the cash flows that are available to the capital stakeholders in the firm as a whole.

We can rearrange the balance sheet equation slightly further:

$$\text{NetOA} - \text{NetFL} = \text{SE}$$

Using the same present value cash flow terms as before, we can express this form of the balance sheet in terms of present values of expected future cash flows as follows:

$$\text{PVNetCFs from Operations} - \text{PVNetCFs to Debt Financing}$$
$$= \text{PVNetCFs to Shareholders' Equity}$$

With this expression, we can conceptualize free cash flows specifically attributable to the equity shareholders of the firm. The present value of free cash flows produced by the operations of the firm minus the present value of cash flows necessary to service claims of the net debt holders yields the free cash flows available for equity shareholders. We refer to this measure of free cash flows as the *free cash flows for common equity shareholders* because they capture the net free cash flows available to equity shareholders after satisfying debt claims.

Free Cash Flows Measurement

Under U.S. GAAP, firms report the statement of cash flows by decomposing the net change in cash into operating, investing, and financing activity components. These three categories do not match exactly the operating and financing classifications we need for computing free cash flows. Thus, the analyst needs to reclassify some of the components of the statement of cash flows in order to compute free cash flows for valuation purposes. In the following sections, we describe how to use the statement of cash flows to measure free cash flows from two different perspectives: *free cash flows for all debt and equity capital stakeholders* and *free cash flows for common equity shareholders*, and when to use each free cash flow measure. Exhibit 11.1 describes the computation of each of these two measures of free cash flows.

Measuring Free Cash Flows: The Starting Point. In practice, analysts use a number of different starting points. We use cash flow from operations from the projected statement of cash flows as the starting point to compute both measures of free cash

---

EXHIBIT 11.1

Measurement of Free Cash Flows for All Debt and Equity Capital Stakeholders and Free Cash Flows for Common Equity Shareholders

---

Operating Activities:

Cash Flow from Operations

Begin with cash flow from operations on the projected statement of cash flows.

Net Interest After Tax

Add back cash outflows for interest expense and subtract cash inflows for interest income, net of tax effects. Net interest cash flows are considered financing cash flows and are included below.

Cash Requirements for Liquidity

Subtract an increase or add a decrease in cash required for purposes of liquidity for operations.

Equals Free Cash Flow from Operations

Capital Expenditures

Subtract cash outflows for capital expenditures and add cash inflows from sales of assets that comprise the productive capacity of the operations of the firm, including property, plant, and equipment, affiliated companies, and intangible assets. Note that cash outflows for purchases or cash inflows from sales of financial assets that are part of the financial capital structure of the firm and are not part of the operations of the firm (that is, savings of cash in short-term or long-term securities of non-affiliated companies that are not necessary for the liquidity of the firm) should be considered cash flows related to financing activities of the firm. Therefore, such cash inflows or outflows for such financial assets should not be included in investing activity cash flows but instead should be included below in financing activity cash flows.

Equals Free Cash Flows for All Debt and Equity Capital Stakeholders

Financing Activities:

Debt Cash Flows

Add cash inflows from new borrowings or subtract cash outflows from repayments of short-term and long-term interest-bearing debt capital.

Financial Asset Cash Flows

Subtract cash outflows invested in cash, short-term or long-term investment securities (or add cash inflows from these accounts) if these financial assets are deemed to be part of the financial capital structure of the firm and are not part of the operating activities of the firm.

Adjust for Net Interest After Tax

Subtract net cash outflows for interest expense and add cash inflows for interest income, net of tax effects.

Adjust for Preferred Stock Cash Flows

Add cash inflows from new issues of preferred stock or subtract cash outflows from preferred stock retirements and dividend payments.

Equals Free Cash Flows to Common Equity Shareholders

flows because it is the most direct starting point, requiring the fewest adjustments. Recall from Chapter 3 that the statement of cash flows measures cash flow from operations by beginning with net income, adding back any non-cash elements of income (such as depreciation and amortization expenses), and then adjusting for net cash flows for operating activities (such as changes in receivables, inventory, accounts payable). Thus, some analysts will compute free cash flows by beginning with projected net income, then adding back non-cash income items, and then including adjustments for operating activities. Other analysts will begin the computation of free cash flows with EBITDA (earnings before interest, taxes, depreciation, and amortization), which already includes the addback for non-cash income items for depreciation and amortization, as well as an addback for interest expense (but usually not interest income) and an addback of *all* the income taxes. Still others will begin the computation using NOPAT (net operating profit after tax), which includes net income with net interest (adjusted for tax savings) added back. The starting point of the computation of free cash flows is less important than the ending point. The analyst can begin the computation of free cash flows with net income, EBITDA, NOPAT, or some other number, so long as the analyst makes all of the necessary adjustments to compute a complete measure of free cash flows as described in Exhibit 11.1.

Free Cash Flows for All Debt and Equity Capital Stakeholders. Free cash flows for all debt and equity capital stakeholders are the cash flows available to make interest and principal payments to debt holders, redeem preferred shares or pay dividends to preferred shareholders, and to pay dividends and buy back shares from common equity shareholders. To measure these free cash flows, we begin with cash flow from operations from the projected statement of cash flows. To remove the effects of the cash flows related to the firm's financial capital structure from cash flows from operations, we must add back the cash flows for interest on the financial capital structure, net of tax effects. Procedurally, the analyst adds back to reported cash flow from operations the cash outflow for interest expense on financial liabilities minus the cash inflow from interest income on financial assets, net of their combined effect on income taxes. Firms typically report the cash outflow for interest expense as additional information at the bottom of the statement of cash flows; however, the cash inflow from interest income is usually not reported separately, so the analyst may instead have to use interest income recognized on the income statement. To adjust net interest for tax effects, the analyst typically multiplies net interest by one minus the firm's marginal tax rate.

The analyst should also add or subtract any change in the cash balance that the firm will require for operating liquidity. Cash that the firm must maintain for liquidity purposes is not available to be distributed to debt or equity stakeholders, and is therefore not part of free cash flow. For example, suppose an analyst is valuing a retail store chain, and that it is necessary for the chain to maintain the equivalent of two days of sales in checking accounts and as cash on hand at each store for purposes of conducting retail sales transactions. In this case, as the chain opens new stores it is required to hold additional cash as part of operations (just like it would need to invest in additional inventory). These additional cash requirements are not available for debt and equity capital providers if the firm intends to maintain its operations. If the firm improves its cash management efficiency and reduces the amount of cash required for liquidity, then the firm has additional free cash flow that can be distributed to debt or equity stakeholders. Procedurally, the analyst should project the required change each period in cash for working capital purposes, and add or subtract that amount to determine free cash flow from operations.

After computing free cash flow from operations, the analyst adjusts for cash flows for capital expenditures on long-lived assets that are a part of the firm's productive capacity, such as property, plant, and equipment, affiliated companies, intangible assets, and other investing activities. The analyst should subtract cash outflows for purchases and add cash inflows from sales of assets related to the firm's long-term productive activities.

The analyst must make a judgment call to estimate the extent to which the cash the firm retains in financial asset accounts, such as in cash and cash equivalents, short-term securities, or long-term investment securities, is (a) necessary for the liquidity and operating capacity of the firm, or (b) a financial asset that is part of the financial capital structure of the firm and therefore distributable to debt or equity stakeholders. For example, if the analyst projects that the firm will retain financial assets by saving some portion of its cash flows each period in a securities account, and that this cash can ultimately be used to repay debt, make dividends payments, or buy back shares, then the analyst should deem these cash flows as free cash flows for debt and equity capital. In this case, the analyst should not subtract the amount of cash used to purchase the securities (or add the amount of cash received from selling such securities) each period to measure free cash flows for debt and equity capital.[7]

This adjustment requires a judgment call by the analyst because, in some circumstances, firms will retain seemingly excess cash in the cash, marketable securities, or investment securities accounts, when this cash is not in fact free for potential distribution to capital stakeholders. For example, in some cases, firms with seasonal business need to maintain large balances in cash or securities accounts in order to provide needed liquidity during particular seasons. In other cases, firms may build up large balances in investment securities accounts that represent investments in key affiliates, such as PepsiCo's and Coca-Cola's investments in bottling companies. In scenarios like these, the analyst should not assess these cash flows as "free" for potential distribution to capital stakeholders, but instead should consider these cash flows necessary investments in the productive capacity of the firm.

Together, these computations result in free cash flows for all debt and equity capital stakeholders, which are available to service debt, pay dividends to preferred and common shareholders, buy back shares, and finance future assets. To estimate the present value of the sum of the debts and equity claims on the firm, the analyst can discount free cash flows for debt and equity capital using the weighted average cost

---

[7]If the analyst measures cash flows for capital expenditures using the amount reported as net cash flow for investing activities on the firm's statement of cash flows, this amount usually includes a subtraction for cash outflows for securities purchases or an addition for cash inflows from securities sales. Therefore, if it is necessary to reverse these effects, the analyst should add back the amount of cash outflows for purchases of securities or subtract the cash inflows from sales of securities to the net cash flow from investing activities in order to measure cash flows for capital expenditures.

of capital of the firm. From this sum, the analyst can subtract the present value of debt and preferred claims to isolate an estimate of the value of common equity.

Free Cash Flows for Common Equity Shareholders. Free cash flows for common equity shareholders are the cash flows specifically available to the common shareholders after making all debt service payments to lenders and paying dividends to preferred shareholders. Therefore, we can measure the free cash flows for common equity by narrowing the measure of free cash flows to all debt and equity capital. To begin, the analyst should incorporate cash flows to debt claims by adding cash inflows from new borrowing or subtracting cash outflows for repayments related to the change in short- and long-term borrowing. In calculating free cash flows to debt and equity capital, if the analyst made the judgment call that the firm saves financial capital beyond its immediate liquidity needs in a cash or investment securities account, then these cash flows reflect financing activities. Therefore, the analyst must now subtract the amount of cash outflow used to purchase the securities or add the amount of cash inflow received from selling such securities. Likewise, the analyst also must adjust free cash flows for net interest. To measure free cash for equity shareholders, the analyst should subtract cash outflow for interest expense on financial liabilities and add cash inflow for interest income on financial assets, net of related tax effects (this adjustment simply reverses the adjustment made for net interest to determine free cash flow from operations). Finally, the analyst should also add cash inflows from new issues of preferred stock and subtract cash outflows from preferred stock retirements and dividend payments.[8] The result of these computations is free cash flows for common equity shareholders. These are the cash flows available to common shareholders for common share dividends, stock buybacks, or reinvestment in future assets. Free cash flows for common equity can be discounted at the cost of equity capital to determine the present value of the common equity of the firm.

Which free cash flow measure should be used? The appropriate free cash flow measure depends on the resource to be valued.

(1) If the objective is to value *operating assets net of operating liabilities*, or equivalently, the *sum of the debt and equity capital* of a firm, then the *free cash flow for all debt and equity capital* is the appropriate cash flow measure. A later section of this chapter indicates that the appropriate discount rate is the weighted average cost of capital.

(2) If the objective is to value the *common shareholders' equity* of a firm, then the *free cash flow for common equity shareholders* is the appropriate cash flow measure. A later section indicates that the appropriate discount rate is the cost of equity capital.

---

[8]It might seem inappropriate to include changes in debt and preferred stock financing, which appear in the financing section of the statement of cash flows, in the valuation of a firm. Economic theory suggests that the capital structure (that is, the proportion of debt versus equity) should not affect the value. Changes in debt and preferred stock, however, affect the amount of cash available to the common shareholders. The analyst includes cash flows related to debt and preferred stock financing in free cash flows for common equity shareholders but adjusts the cost of equity capital to reflect the amounts of such senior financing in the capital structure.

The difference between these two valuations is, of course, the value of total interest-bearing liabilities and preferred stock. To reconcile the two valuations, one could always value interest-bearing liabilities by discounting all the future debt service cash flows (including repayments of principal) at the after-tax cost of debt capital and all the preferred stock dividends at the cost of preferred equity. Subtracting the present value of interest-bearing liabilities and preferred stock from the present value of the sum of debt and equity capital will yield the present value of common equity. The approach followed depends on the valuation setting.

Example 6. One firm desires to acquire the net operating assets of a division of another firm. The acquiring firm will replace the financing structure of the division with a financing structure that matches its own. The relevant cash flows for valuing the division's net operating assets are the free operating cash flows those assets will generate minus the expected capital expenditures in operating assets, or equivalently, the free cash flows for all debt and equity capital. The acquiring firm would then discount these projected free cash flows for all debt and equity capital at the expected future weighted average cost of capital of the division to be acquired, which will match the weighted average cost of capital of the acquiring firm because the acquiring firm will use a similar capital structure for the division.

Example 7. An investor desires to value a potential investment in the common stock equity in a firm. The relevant cash flows are the free cash flows available to be distributed to common equity shareholders. These free cash flows measure the cash flows generated from using debt capital, minus the cash required to service the debt. Thus, free cash flows for common equity shareholders should capture any beneficial effects of financial leverage on the value of the common equity, less the cash flows required to service debt capital. The investor should discount these projected free cash flows at the required return on equity capital.

Example 8. The managers of a firm intend to acquire a firm through a leveraged buyout (LBO). The managers will offer to purchase the outstanding shares of the target firm by investing their own equity (usually 20 to 25 percent of the total) and borrowing the remainder from various lenders. The tendered shares serve as collateral for the loan (often called a *bridge loan*) during the transaction. After gaining voting control of the firm, the managers will have the firm engage in sufficient new borrowing to repay the bridge loan. Following an LBO, the firm will likely have a significantly higher debt level in the capital structure from the use of leverage to execute the takeover.

Determining the value of the common shares acquired follows the usual procedure for an equity investment (see Example 7 above). This value should equal the present value of free cash flows for common equity discounted at the cost of common equity capital. The valuation of the equity must reflect the new capital structure and the related increase in debt service costs. Also, the cost of equity capital will likely increase as a result of the higher level of debt in the capital structure; the common shareholders bear more risk as residual claimants on the assets of the firm. The valuation must therefore be based on the expected new cost of equity capital.

As an alternate approach that will produce the same value for the common equity, the analyst can treat an LBO as a purchase of assets (similar to Example 6 above). That is, compute the present value of the free cash flows for all debt and equity capital stakeholders using the expected future weighted average cost of debt and equity capital, using weights that reflect the newly leveraged capital structure of the acquired firm. This amount represents the value of net operating assets. Subtract from the present value of net operating assets the present value of debt raised to execute the LBO.[9] The result is the present value of the common equity.

Selecting a Forecast Horizon

For how many future years should the analyst project periodic free cash flows? The correct answer is the expected life of the resource to be valued. This life is a finite number of years for a resource such as a machine, building, or similar resource with limits to its physical existence, or a financial instrument with a finite stated maturity (such as a bond, a mortgage, or a lease). In many valuation contexts, however, the resource to be valued is an equity claim on the firm, a resource that has a potentially infinite life. In the case of an equity security, the analyst must therefore project future periodic free cash flows that, in theory, extend to infinity.

Of course, as a practical matter, the analyst cannot precisely predict a firm's free cash flows very many years into the future. Therefore, analysts commonly develop specific projections of all of the elements of the income statements and balance sheets for the firm and use those elements to derive forecasts of free cash flows over an explicit forecast horizon, say five or ten years, depending on the industry, the maturity of the firm, and the expected growth and predictability of the firm's cash flows. After the explicit forecast horizon, analysts then commonly use general growth assumptions to project the future income statements and balance sheets, and use them to derive the free cash flows that will persist each period to infinity. The analyst will therefore find it desirable to develop specific forecasts of income statements, balance sheets, and free cash flows over an explicit forecast horizon that extends until the point at which a firm's growth pattern is expected to settle into steady-state equilibrium, during which free cash flows might be expected to grow at a steady, predictable rate.

Selecting a forecast horizon involves tradeoffs. One can develop reasonably reliable projections over longer forecast horizons for stable and mature firms. Projections for such firms, like the case of PepsiCo demonstrated in Chapter 10, capture relatively steady-state operations. On the other hand, it is much more difficult to develop reliable projections over long forecast horizons for young, high-growth firms because their future operating performance is uncertain. In addition, a much higher proportion of the value of young growth firms will be achieved in distant future years, after their potential has been reached. Thus, the analyst faces the dilemma of depending most heavily on long-run forecasts for young growth firms

---

[9]It is irrelevant whether any debt on the books of the target firm remains outstanding after the LBO or whether the firm engages in additional borrowing to repay existing debt, as long as the weighted average cost of capital properly includes the costs of each financing arrangement.

for which long-run projections are likely to be most uncertain. The forecasting and valuation process is particularly difficult for growth firms when the near-term free cash flows are projected to be negative, as is common for rapidly growing firms financing growth by issuing common stock. In this case, most of the firm's value depends on free cash flows to be generated in the long-term years.

Unfortunately, there is no way to avoid this dilemma. The predictive accuracy of cash flow forecasts many years into the future is likely to be questionable for even the most stable and predictable firms. The analyst must recognize that forecasts and value estimates for all firms, but especially growth firms, have a high degree of uncertainty and estimation risk. To mitigate this uncertainty and estimation risk, we emphasize the following points:

1. Diligently and comprehensively follow all five steps of the analysis framework. By thoroughly analyzing the firm's industry and strategy, the firm's accounting quality, and the firm's financial performance and risk ratios, the analyst will have more information to use to develop long-term forecasts that are as reliable as possible.

2. To the extent possible, confront directly the problem of long-term uncertainty by developing specific projections of free cash flows derived from projected income statements and balance sheets that extend five or ten years into the future, at which point the firm is projected to reach steady-state growth.

3. Assess the sensitivity of the forecast projections and value estimates across the reasonable range of long-term growth parameter assumptions. Suppose an analyst is valuing a young, high-growth company, and can reliably forecast free cash flows five years into the future. After that horizon, the analyst expects the firm to grow at 6 percent per year, but this is highly uncertain, and long-run growth could range from –3 percent per year to as much as 9 percent per year. The analyst should conduct sensitivity analysis on the projections and valuation, varying long-run growth across the range from –3 to 9 percent per year.

CONTINUING VALUE OF FUTURE FREE CASH FLOWS

In the previous section, we described measuring periodic free cash flows over an explicit forecast horizon. In this section, we describe techniques to project free cash flows using a steady-state growth rate continuing beyond the explicit forecast horizon, and to measure the present value of continuing free cash flows beyond the explicit forecast horizon. In a subsequent section, we describe specific techniques to measure appropriate risk-adjusted rates to discount free cash flows to present value.

As described earlier, the analyst will find it desirable to forecast free cash flows over an explicit forecast horizon, until the point at which the analyst expects a firm's growth pattern to settle into steady-state growth, during which free cash flows might be expected to grow at a steady, predictable rate. We refer to these free cash flows as *continuing* free cash flows, because they reflect the free cash flows continuing into the long-run future of the firm. The long-run steady-state growth rate in future continuing free cash flows could be positive, negative, or zero. Steady-state growth in free cash flows could be driven by long-run expectations for inflation, the industry's sales, the economy in general, or the population. The analyst should select a growth rate that captures realistic expectations for the long run.

If a firm's growth pattern can be projected to settle into steady-state growth rate (denoted g) continuing after the end of the explicit forecast horizon, say after Year T, then the analyst can derive the continuing free cash flows from the projected income statements and balance sheets. To do so correctly, the analyst should use the expected long-run growth rate (g) to project all of the items of the Year T+1 income statement and balance sheet. That is, each item on the Year T+1 income statement should be projected by multiplying each item on the Year T income statement times (1 + g). Each item on the Year T+1 balance sheet should be projected by multiplying each item on the Year T balance sheet times (1 + g). The Year T+1 statement of cash flows, and thus Year T+1 free cash flows, can then be derived from the Year T+1 income statement and balance sheet projections. It is necessary to impose the long-run growth rate assumption (1 + g) uniformly on the Year T+1 income statement and balance sheet projections in order to derive correctly the free cash flows for Year T+1. In steady state, earnings, assets, liabilities, shareholders' equity, and cash flows are assumed to grow at equivalent rates. By applying a uniform growth rate, the analyst achieves internally consistent steady-state growth across all of the projections of the firm, keeping the balance sheet in balance throughout the continuing forecast horizon and keeping the cash flows, earnings, and dividends internally consistent with the assumed long-run growth rate.

A shortcut sometimes used to compute the continuing free cash flow for Year T+1 is to apply the multiple (1 + g) to the free cash flow for Year T, instead of deriving the Year T+1 free cash flow from changes in the income statement and balance sheet for Year T+1. If the analyst wishes to compute internally consistent and identical estimates of firm value using free cash flows, earnings, and dividends, then the analyst should *not* project free cash flows for Year T+1 by simply multiplying free cash flows for Year T by (1 + g). Doing so ignores the necessary growth in all of the elements of the balance sheet and the income statement, which can introduce inconsistent forecast assumptions for cash flows, earnings, and dividends. Even if the analyst simply projects Year T+1 free cash flows, earnings, and dividends to grow at an identical rate (1 + g), it may impound inconsistent assumptions and lead to inconsistent value estimates if Year T cash flows, earnings, and dividends are not consistent with their long-run continuing amounts.

Example 9. Suppose the analyst develops the following forecasts for the firm in Year T−1 and Year T:

	Assets	=	Liabilities	+	Shareholders' Equity
Year T−1 Balances	$100	=	$60	+	$40
+ Net Income	+20				+20
+ New Borrowing	+6		+6		
− Dividends Paid	−10				−10
Year T Balances	$116	=	$66	+	$50

The analyst would compute Year T free cash flows for common equity shareholders to equal $10 (= $20 net income – $16 increase in assets + $6 increase in liabilities). Now suppose the analyst projects that the firm will grow at a steady-state rate of 10 percent in Year T+1 and thereafter. The analyst should project Year T+1 net income, assets, liabilities, and shareholders' equity to each grow by 10 percent, and then compute Year T+1 free cash flows, as follows:

	Assets	**=**	**Liabilities**	**+**	**Shareholders' Equity**
Year T Balances	$116	=	$66	+	$50
Growth	× 1.10		× 1.10		× 1.10
Year T+1 Balances	$127.6	=	$72.6	+	$55

The projected net income would be $22 (= $20 × 1.10). The Year T+1 free cash flow projection would be $17 (= $22 net income – $11.6 increase in assets + $6.6 increase in liabilities). However, if the analyst would have simply projected Year T free cash flows to grow by 10 percent, the Year T+1 projections would only be $11 (= $10 Year T free cash flow × 1.10), which is not correct. This error would reduce the estimated value of the firm using free cash flows, relative to the value estimate using earnings, because of the inconsistent assumptions.

Once the analyst has computed free cash flows for Year T+1, then the analyst can compute continuing value (sometimes called residual value or terminal value) of future free cash flows continuing in Years T+1 and beyond using the following perpetuity-with-growth valuation model.[10]

$$\begin{matrix} \text{Continuing Value} \\ \text{At End of Forecast} \\ \text{Horizon (Year T)} \end{matrix} = \begin{matrix} \text{Continuing} \\ \text{Free Cash Flow} \\ \text{Projection for T+1} \end{matrix} \times 1/(R - g)$$

where g denotes the projected steady-state growth rate for Years T+1 and beyond, and is applied uniformly to project the income statement and balance sheet in Year T+1, which are then used to project the continuing free cash flows in Year T+1; and R denotes the appropriate risk-adjusted discount rate (which will be described in detail in the next section).

Example 10. An analyst forecasts that the free cash flow of a firm in Year +5 will be $30 million, and that Year +5 earnings and dividends will also be $30 million. The analyst expects that the firm's income statements and balance sheets will grow uniformly over the long run, and that therefore cash flows, earnings, and dividends will all grow uniformly over the long run, but the analyst is uncertain about the steady-state long-run growth rate in Year +6 and beyond. The analyst believes the growth rate will most likely be zero but could reasonably fall in the range between +6 to –6

---

[10]This formula is simply the algebraic simplification for the present value of a growing perpetuity.

percent per year. Assuming a 15 percent cost of capital, the table below shows the range of possible continuing values (in millions) for the firm in present value at the beginning of the continuing value period (that is, the beginning of Year +6), and in present value as of today (that is, the continuing value is discounted to today using a factor of $1/(1.15)^5$):

Free Cash Flow in Year T	Long-run Growth Assumption	Free Cash Flow in Year T+1	Perpetuity with Growth Valuation Factor	Continuing Value in Present Value as of:	
				Beginning of Year T+1	Today
$30	0%	$30	$\dfrac{1}{0.15-0.0}=6.67$	$200.0	$ 99.4
$30	+6%	$31.80	$\dfrac{1}{0.15-0.06}=11.11$	$353.3	$175.7
$30	−6%	$28.20	$\dfrac{1}{0.15+0.06}=4.76$	$134.3	$ 66.8

Analysts can also estimate a continuing value using a multiple of free cash flow in the first year of the continuing value period to value the common stock of a firm. The table below shows the cash flow multiples using $1/(R-g)$ for various costs of equity capital and growth rates. The multiples increase with growth for a given cost of capital, and they decrease as cost of capital increases for a given level of growth.

Continuing Value Multiples				
Cost of Equity Capital	Growth Rates			
	0%	2%	4%	6%
10%	10.00	12.50	16.67	25.00
12%	8.33	10.00	12.50	16.67
15%	6.67	7.69	9.09	11.11
18%	5.56	6.25	7.14	8.33
20%	5.00	5.56	6.25	7.14

The continuing value computation using the perpetuity-with-growth valuation model does not work when the growth rate equals or exceeds the discount rate (that is, when $g \geq R$) because the denominator in the computation is zero or negative and the resulting continuing value estimate is meaningless. In this case, the analyst cannot use the perpetuity computation illustrated above. Instead, the analyst must forecast free cash flow amounts for each year beyond the forecast horizon using the terminal period growth rate, and then discount each year's cash flows to present value using the discount rate. The analyst should probably also reconsider whether it is realistic to expect the firm's free cash flow growth rate to exceed the discount rate (the expected rate of return) in perpetuity. This scenario can exist for some years, but is not likely to be sustainable indefinitely. Competition, technological change, new entrants into an industry, and similar factors eventually reduce growth rates. Thus, in applying the model, the analyst must attempt to estimate the long-term sustainable growth rate in cash flows (refer to the discussion of sustainable earnings in Chapter 6).

An alternate approach for estimating the continuing value is to use the free cash flow multiples for comparable firms that currently trade in the market. The analyst identifies comparable companies by studying characteristics such as industry, firm size and age, past growth rates in free cash flows, profitability, risk, and similar factors. We discuss valuation multiples in more depth in Chapter 13.

Non-operating Assets and Liabilities

For completeness, the analyst should check the most recent balance sheet to insure all of the firm's assets and liabilities are captured in the free cash flow computations. In some circumstances, a firm may have an asset or liability that may have been omitted from the free cash flows computations because it is not part of normal business activities. For example, suppose a firm owns a piece of land for possible future expansion, but the land is not part of the operations of the firm and does not incur material cash flows. The analyst can simply add or subtract the book value (or fair value, if disclosed) of non-operating assets or liabilities (if any) to the present value of free cash flows for a more complete valuation of the firm.

DISCOUNT RATES

The prior two sections describe measurements of expected free cash flows during the explicit forecast horizon and continuing after that horizon. To determine the value of the firm, we need to measure the third parameter in the cash flows valuation model—the risk-adjusted discount rate—to compute the present value of all the projected free cash flows. The discount rate equals the expected rate of return that providers of capital require the firm to generate to induce them to commit capital, given the level of risk involved. If the analyst discounts free cash flows for common equity shareholders, then the analyst should use a discount rate that reflects the required rate of return on equity capital. If the analyst discounts free cash flows for all debt and equity capital stakeholders, then the analyst should use a discount rate that reflects the weighted average required rate of return that encompasses the debt, preferred, and common equity capital used to finance the net operating assets of the firm.

The discount rate should be a forecast of the required rate of return, conditional on the expected future riskiness of the firm and expected future interest rates, over the future period during which the free cash flows will be generated. The historical discount rate of the firm may be a good indicator of the appropriate discount rate to apply to the firm in the future, but only if the following three conditions hold:

a) the current risk of the firm is the same as the expected future risk of the firm;
b) prevailing interest rates are good indicators of expected future interest rates; and
c) the existing financial capital structure of the firm (that is, the current mix of debt and equity financing) is the same as the expected future capital structure of the firm.

On the other hand, if one or more of these conditions change in the future, then the analyst will need to project discount rates that appropriately capture the future risk and capital structure of the firm and future interest rates in the economy over the forecast horizon.

As a starting point to estimate expected rates of return on capital, analysts often compute the prevailing after-tax cost of each type of capital invested in the firm. Existing costs of capital reflect the required rates of return for the firm's existing capital structure, and they may be good indicators of appropriate discount rates for the firm in the future if the analyst expects the three conditions above will hold. Developing discount rates using costs of capital assumes that the capital markets price capital to reflect risk and, at a minimum, the firm's value is a function of its ability to generate returns that at least cover its cost of capital. We next describe techniques to estimate the firm's cost of debt, preferred, and equity capital. Following these descriptions, we illustrate how to compute a weighted average cost of capital for the firm.

Cost of Debt Capital

The analyst computes the after-tax cost of debt capital, including notes payable, mortgages, bonds, and capital lease obligations, as the yield to maturity of the debt times one minus the marginal tax rate appropriate to income tax deductions for interest. The yield to maturity is the rate that discounts the contractual cash flows on the debt to the debt's current fair value. If the fair value of the debt is equal to face value, then the yield to maturity equals the stated interest rate on the debt. If the fair value of the debt exceeds the face value of the debt, then yield to maturity is lower than the stated rate. This can occur after interest rates fall; previously issued fixed-rate debt will have a stated rate that exceeds current market yields for debt with comparable credit quality and terms. On the other hand, after interest rates rise, fixed-rate debt may have a stated rate that is lower than prevailing market rates for comparable debt, in which case the debt will have a fair value that is less than face value, and the yield to maturity will be greater than the stated rate.

Firms disclose in notes to their financial statements the stated interest rates on their existing interest-bearing debt capital. Firms also disclose in notes the estimated fair values of their interest-bearing debt, which should reflect the present value of the debt using prevailing market yields to maturity on the debt. Together, these disclosures allow the analyst to estimate prevailing market yields to maturity on the outstanding debt.

In computing costs of debt capital, analysts typically exclude accounts payable and other operating liability accounts (for example, accounts payable, deferred income tax liability, retirement benefit liabilities). Instead, analysts typically treat these items as part of the firm's operating activities, and include cash flows related to these liabilities in the computation of free cash flows from operations.

Capitalized lease obligations have an implicit after-tax cost of capital equal to the after-tax yield to maturity on collateralized borrowing with equivalent risk and maturity. Firms recognize capital lease obligations on the balance sheet as financial liabilities; however, as described in Chapter 8, firms may also have significant off-balance-sheet obligations in operating leases. If the firm has significant commitments under operating leases, then the analyst should consider including them as a component of debt capital in the computation of the weighted average cost of capital. Procedurally, the analyst should make three sets of adjustments. First, the analyst should include the present value of operating lease commitments in the calculation of the weights of capital in the capital structure. Second, the analyst should include the after-tax interest rate implicit in operating lease commitments in the computation of the weighted average cost of capital. The lessor bears more risk in an operating lease than in a capital lease so the cost of capital represented by operating leases is likely to be higher than for capital leases. Third, if the analyst treats operating leases as part of debt financing, then the cash outflow for rent payments under operating leases should be reclassified as interest and principal payments of debt when computing free cash flows. Chapter 8 discusses techniques for the required adjustments to convert operating leases to capital leases, as well as techniques to adjust for other, less-common forms of off-balance-sheet financing, including contingent liabilities for receivables sold with recourse and product financing arrangements.

The income tax rate used to compute the tax effects of interest should be the marginal tax rate for interest expense deductions. The statutory federal marginal tax rate applicable to interest expense deductions in the United States is 35 percent. However, state and foreign taxes may increase or decrease the combined marginal tax rate, depending on where the firm raises its debt capital. Firms do not separately disclose statutory state or foreign tax rates, but do show the effect of these taxes in the income tax reconciliation found in the income tax note. To achieve greater precision, the analyst could approximate the combined marginal tax rate applicable to interest expense deductions using information in the income tax footnote.

Cost of Preferred Equity Capital

The cost of preferred stock capital depends on the preference conditions. Preferred stock that has preference over common shares with respect to dividends and priority ordering in liquidation generally sells near its par value. Its cost is therefore the dividend rate on the preferred stock. Depending on the attributes of the preferred stock, dividends on preferred stock may give rise to a tax deduction, in which case the after-tax cost of capital will be lower than the pre-tax cost. Preferred stock that is convertible into common stock has both preferred and common equity attributes. Its cost is a blending of the cost of nonconvertible preferred stock and common equity.

Cost of Common Equity Capital

Analysts commonly estimate the cost of equity capital using the theory underlying the capital asset pricing model (CAPM). The CAPM hypothesizes that, in equilibrium, a firm's cost of common equity capital should equal the rate of return the market requires to hold the firm's stock within a diversified portfolio of stocks. In theory, the market's required rate of return is a function of prevailing risk-free rates of interest, the premium demanded for bearing systematic risk by a market comprised of risk-averse investors, and the level of systematic risk inherent in the firm's common stock.[11] Systematic risk refers to the degree of covariation between a firm's stock returns and an index of stock returns for all firms in the market. Systematic risk is often measured using the market beta for a firm's common stock, which is estimated as a regression coefficient from a regression of the firm's stock returns on a market index of returns over a relevant period of time (for example, over the last 60 months). The CAPM projects the expected return on common equity capital for firm j as follows:

$$E[R_{Ej}] = E[R_F] + \beta_j \times \left\{ E[R_M] - E[R_F] \right\}$$

where E denotes that the related variable is an expectation; R_{Ej} denotes return on common equity in firm j; R_F denotes the risk-free rate of return; β_j denotes the market beta for firm j; and R_M denotes the return on a diversified marketwide portfolio of stocks. According to the CAPM, a common equity security with no systematic risk (that is, a stock with $\beta_j = 0$) is expected to earn a return equal to the expected rate of return on risk-free securities. Of course, most equity securities are not risk-free. An equity security with systematic risk equal to the average amount of systematic risk of all equity securities in the market has a market beta of 1.0. The subtraction term in brackets above represents the average market risk premium, equal to the excess return that equity investors in the capital markets require for bearing systematic risk. Therefore, the cost of common equity capital for a firm with an average level of systematic risk should be equal to the average expected return on the market portfolio. A firm with a market beta greater than 1.0 has higher systematic risk than average and faces a higher cost of equity capital because the capital markets expect the firm to yield a commensurately higher return to investors for risk. A firm with a market beta less than 1.0 has lower than average systematic risk and faces a lower cost of equity capital because the capital markets expect the firm to yield a commensurately lower return to investors for risk. Exhibit 11.2 depicts the relations graphically.

Exhibit 11.3 reports industry median market betas for a sample of 36 industries over the years 1992–2001. These data depict wide variation in systematic risk across industries during this ten-year period, with industry median market betas ranging from a low of 0.24 (Forestry) to a high of 1.30 (Transportation by Air). Various financial reference sources and web sites regularly publish market betas for common equity in publicly traded firms, including Standard & Poor's *Stock Reports* and Yahoo! Finance (http://finance.yahoo.com/). It is not uncommon to find considerable variation in the published amounts for market beta among the various sources. This

---

[11]Note that this model views nonsystematic risk as diversifiable by the investor. The market, according to CAPM, does not provide a return for a firm's nonsystematic risk.

EXHIBIT 11.2

Relation Between Cost of Equity Capital and Systematic Risk

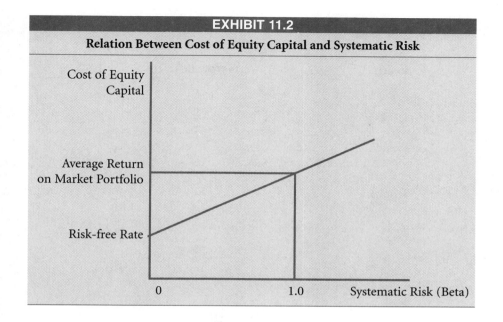

occurs in part because of differences in the period and methodology used to calculate the betas.[12]

The analyst should use the market return on securities with zero systematic risk as the risk-free interest rate in the CAPM. Returns on such securities exhibit no correlation with returns on a diversified marketwide portfolio of stocks. It might seem appropriate to use the yield on long-term U.S. government securities. However, yields on long-term U.S. government securities tend to exhibit greater sensitivity to changes in inflation and interest rates, and therefore have a greater degree of systematic risk (although the systematic risk is still quite low), than short-term U.S. government securities. Common practice uses the yield on either short- or intermediate-term U.S. government securities as the risk-free rate. This rate has historically averaged around six percent. The average return on the market portfolio depends on the period studied. Historically, the realized rate of return on the market portfolio has varied between nine and thirteen percent. Thus, the excess return over the risk-free rate has varied between three and seven percent.

---

[12]Eugene Fama and Kenneth French developed an empirical model that explains realized stock returns using three factors that they found to be correlated with returns during their study period. Their model and results indicate that, during their sample period (1963–1990), firms' stock returns were related to firms' market betas, market capitalizations (size), and market-to-book ratios (see Eugene F. Fama and Kenneth R. French, "The Cross Section of Expected Stock Returns," *The Journal of Finance* (June 1992), pp. 427–465.) Data to implement their model can be obtained from the following web site: http://mba.tuck.dartmouth.edu/pages/faculty/ken.french/data_library.html. Although the model deserves and has received a lot of attention in academics and practice, more research is necessary to determine the theoretical basis for the model, and the risk factors and risk premia that comprise the model. In addition, more research is needed to assess the empirical applicability of the model as a predictor of expected stock returns in periods following their sample period.

EXHIBIT 11.3	
Relation between Industry and Systematic Risk over 1992–2001	
Industry:	**Median Beta during 1992–2001**
Forestry	0.24
Metal Mining	0.37
Utilities	0.44
Real Estate	0.58
Oil and Gas Extraction	0.64
Depository Institutions	0.68
Petroleum and Coal	0.72
Grocery Stores	0.76
Insurance	0.77
Textiles	0.80
Food Processors	0.81
Amusements	0.84
Printing and Publishing	0.84
Wholesalers–Nondurables	0.87
Lumber	0.91
Metal Products	0.92
Paper	0.92
Tobacco	0.94
Transportation Equipment	0.94
Wholesalers–Durables	0.94
Restaurants	0.97
Motion Pictures	0.98
Retailers–General Merchandise	0.98
Instruments and Related Products	0.99
Metals	0.99
Personal Services	1.04
Hotels	1.08
Business Services	1.09
Chemicals	1.10
Industrial Machinery and Equipment	1.11
Communication	1.13
Electronic and Electric Equipment	1.15
Retailing–Apparel	1.20
Security Brokers	1.22
Health Services	1.24
Transportation by Air	1.30

Adjusting Market Equity Beta to Reflect a New Capital Structure

Recall from the discussion in Chapter 5 that market equity beta reflects operating leverage, financial leverage, variability of sales, and other firm characteristics. In some settings, such as a leveraged buyout, firms plan to make significant changes in the financial capital structure. The market beta computed using historical market price data reflects the firm's historical capital structure. The analyst can adjust this beta to project what it is likely to be after changing the capital structure. The analyst can unlever the current beta and then relever it to reflect the new capital structure. The formula below describes an approach to estimate an unlevered market beta (sometimes referred to as an *asset beta*):

$$\text{Current Levered Market Beta} = \text{Unlevered Market Beta} \times$$

$$\left[1 + \left(1 - \text{Income Tax Rate} \right) \times \left(\frac{\text{Current Market Value of Debt}}{\text{Current Market Value of Equity}} \right) \right]$$

To estimate the new levered beta, the analyst takes two steps. First, the analyst solves for the unlevered beta using the model above. Second, the analyst projects the new levered beta by multiplying the unlevered beta by the last term on the right-hand side of this model after substituting the projected new debt-to-equity ratio in place of the current debt-to-equity ratio.

Example 11. Suppose a firm has a market beta of 0.9, is subject to an income tax rate of 35 percent, and has a debt-to-equity ratio of 60 percent. If the risk-free rate is 6 percent and if the market risk premium is 7 percent, then according to the CAPM the market expects this firm to generate equity returns of 12.3 percent [$0.123 = 0.06 + (0.9 \times 0.07)$]. The firm intends to adopt a new capital structure that will have a debt-to-equity ratio of 140 percent. To project the firm's levered beta under the new capital structure, we first solve for the unlevered beta, denoted X:

$$0.9 = X \times [1 + (1 - 0.35) \times (0.60/1.00)]$$
$$X = 0.65$$

Because financial leverage is positively related to market beta, removing the effect of financial leverage reduces market beta. The unlevered beta should reflect the effects of the firm's operating risk, sales volatility, and other operating factors, but not risk related to financial leverage. We relever the unlevered beta to reflect the new debt to equity ratio as follows:

$$Y = 0.65 \times [1 + (1 - 0.35) \times (1.40/1.00)] = 1.24$$

According to the CAPM, this firm will face an equity cost of capital of 14.68 percent [$0.1468 = 0.06 + (1.24 \times 0.07)$] under the new capital structure.

Evaluating the Use of the CAPM to Measure the Cost of Equity Capital

The use of the CAPM to calculate the cost of equity capital has been subject to various criticisms:

1. Market betas should vary for a firm over time as the systematic risk of the firm changes; however, market beta estimates are quite sensitive to the time period and methodology used in their computation.
2. In theory, the CAPM measures expected returns based on the stock's risk relative to a diversified portfolio of assets across the economy, but a return index for a diversified portfolio of assets for the entire economy does not exist. Measuring a stock's systematic risk relative to a stock market return index such as the S&P 500 Index fails to consider covariation between the stock's returns and returns on assets outside of the stock market, including other financial investments (for example, U.S. Government and corporate debt securities and privately held equity), real estate, and human capital.
3. The excess market rate of return is not stable over time and is likewise sensitive to the time period used in its calculation. Considerable uncertainty surrounds the appropriate adjustment for the market risk premium. It is not clear whether the appropriate adjustment should be on the order of 3 percent, 7 percent, or somewhere in between.[13]

In light of these criticisms of the CAPM, and considering the crucial role of the risk-adjusted discount rate for common equity in valuation, our experience suggests it is important to conduct thorough sensitivity analyses to evaluate the sensitivity of share value estimates across different discount rates for common equity. For example, the analyst should estimate values for a share of common equity in a particular firm across a relevant range of discount rates for common equity by varying the market risk premium from 3 percent to 7 percent.

Chapter 13 describes techniques to estimate the implicit expected rate of return in common equity securities. Chapter 13 also describes an approach to estimating the implicit discount in share price for risk by using risk-free discount rates. These techniques do not require the assumption of an asset pricing model like the CAPM.

Computing the Weighted Average Cost of Capital

If the analyst discounts free cash flows for all debt and equity capital stakeholders, then the analyst should use a discount rate that reflects the weighted average required rate of return that encompasses the debt, preferred, and common equity capital used to finance the net operating assets of the firm. A formula for the weighted average cost of capital (denoted R_A) is given below:

$$R_A = w_D \times R_D \times (1 - \textit{tax rate}) + w_P \times R_P + w_E \times R_E$$

in which w denotes the weight on each type of capital, R denotes the cost of each type of capital, and *tax rate* denotes the tax rate applicable to debt capital costs. The

---

[13]See, for example, James Claus and Jacob Thomas, "Equity Premia as Low as Three Percent? Empirical Evidence from Analysts' Earnings Forecasts for Domestic and International Stock Markets," *Journal of Finance* 56, 5 (October 2001), pp. 1629–1666. Also see Peter Easton, Gary Taylor, Pervin Shroff, and Theodore Sougiannis, "Using Forecasts of Earnings to Simultaneously Estimate Growth and the Rate of Return on Equity Investment," *Journal of Accounting Research* 40 (June 2000), pp. 657–676.

weights used to compute the weighted average cost of capital should be the market values of each type of capital in proportion to the total market value of the financial capital structure of the firm (that is, $w_D + w_P + w_E = 1.0$).

Example 12. A firm has the following capital structure on its balance sheet:

Long-term Debt, 10 percent annual coupon, issued at par	$20,000,000
Preferred Stock, 4 percent dividend, issued at par	5,000,000
Common Equity	25,000,000
Total.	$50,000,000

The market values of the securities are as follows: bonds, $22,000,000; preferred equity, $5,000,000; common equity, $33,000,000. The market has priced the debt to yield 8 percent. The firm's income tax rate is 35 percent, so the after-tax cost of debt is 5.2 percent [$= (1 - 0.35) \times 8.0$ percent]. Note that this rate is less than the coupon rate of 10 percent, and the market value of the debt is greater than its par value. Use of coupon rates and book values in this case would result in a higher cost of debt capital (6.5 percent $= 0.65 \times 10.0$ percent) but a smaller weight in the weighted average. Assuming that the dividend on the preferred stock is not tax deductible, its cost is the dividend rate of 4 percent because it is selling for par value. The market equity beta is 0.9. Assuming a risk-free interest rate of 6 percent and a market premium of 7 percent, the cost of equity capital is 12.3 percent [$= 6.0$ percent $+ 0.9 \times 7$ percent]. The calculation of the weighted average cost of capital is as follows:

Security	Market Value	Weight	After-tax Cost	Weighted Average
Long-term Debt	$22,000,000	37%	5.2%	1.92%
Preferred Equity	5,000,000	8%	4.0%	.32%
Common Equity.	33,000,000	55%	12.3%	6.77%
Total.	$60,000,000	100%		9.01%

Over time, the weights for debt, preferred, and equity capital may change if the analyst expects the firm's capital structure to change over the forecast horizon. In addition, the analyst may expect yields to maturity on debt capital and required rates of return on equity capital to change as interest rates in the economy change, or the risk of the firm changes, or the firm's tax status changes. Thus, to capture these changes in the weighted average cost of capital, the analyst may need to compute a weighted average cost of capital for each period over the forecast horizon.

To determine the appropriate weights to use in the weighted average cost of capital, the analyst will need to determine the market values of the debt, preferred, and common equity capital. Market values for debt will only be observable for firms that have issued publicly traded debt; however, under U.S. GAAP, firms are required to disclose the fair value of their outstanding debt capital in notes to the financial statements each year. Fair value disclosures may not be available, however, if the firm is privately owned or is a foreign firm that is not required to follow U.S. GAAP, or if the firm is a division and does not publish its own financial statements. If market values are not observable and fair values for the firm's debt are not disclosed, then the analyst can either (a) estimate the fair value of the firm's debt if sufficient data are available about the firm's credit quality and the maturity and terms of the debt, or (b) rely on the book value of debt. The book value of debt can be a reliable estimate of fair value if the debt is recently issued, or if the debt bears a variable rate of interest, or if the debt bears a fixed rate of interest but interest rates and the firm's credit quality have been stable since the debt was issued. Because the yield to maturity of debt is inversely related to its market value, analysts sometimes approximate the cost of debt by simply using the coupon rate and the book value of debt when computing the weighted average cost of capital, particularly in circumstances in which interest rates are stable and the market value of debt is likely to be close to book value.

If available, market price quotations for equity securities provide the amounts for determining the market value of equity. Market prices for equity may not be available, however, if the firm is privately owned or if it is a division of another firm. The analyst can then use the book value of equity as a starting point to compute the weight of equity in the capital structure for purposes of estimating a weighted average cost of capital.

The above discussion reveals circular reasoning in computing weighted average costs of capital for valuation purposes. Analysts use the market values of debt and equity to compute the weighted average cost of capital, which is in turn used to compute the value of the debt and equity in the firm. This is circular reasoning because the analyst needs to know the market values to determine the weights but needs to know the weights to determine the weighted average cost of capital used in estimating firm value. In practice, analysts can use two approaches to avoid this circularity. One approach assumes that the firm will maintain a target debt-to-equity structure in the future, based on benchmarks such as the firm's past debt-to-equity ratios, the firm's stated strategy with respect to financial leverage, or industry averages. The other approach computes iteratively the weighted average cost of capital and the value of debt and equity capital, until the weights and the values converge. Example 13 below illustrates this iterative approach.

Example 13. Suppose that one wishes to compute the weighted average cost of capital and the market value of equity for a firm for which no market or fair value data are available. Also suppose that the firm has outstanding debt with a book value of $40 million. The debt is recently issued and carries a stated rate of 8 percent, so the analyst can assume this is a reliable measure of the cost of debt capital. The book value of equity is $60 million. Similar firms in the same industry with comparable risks have a market beta of 1.2. Using the same risk-free rate and market risk premium as in Example 11, the cost of equity capital is 14.4 percent [= 6.0 percent + 1.2 × 7.0 percent]. The firm faces a 35 percent tax rate. The first estimate of the weighted average cost of capital is:

Security	Amount	Weight	After-tax Cost	Weighted Average
Debt	$ 40,000,000	40%	5.2%	2.08%
Common Equity	60,000,000	60%	14.4%	8.64%
Total..................	$100,000,000	100%		10.72%

After using the 10.72 percent weighted average cost of capital to discount the free cash flows to present value, the analyst determines that the firm's equity value is roughly $120 million (calculations not shown). Therefore, the values and weights used to compute the weighted average cost of capital are inconsistent with value estimates for equity. The first iteration estimates placed too much weight on debt and too little weight on equity. The analyst should use the revised estimate of the value of equity to recompute the weighted average cost of capital, and recompute the value of the firm. Using the revised estimates produces a weighted average cost of capital estimate of:

Security	Amount	Weight	After-tax Cost	Weighted Average
Debt	$40,000,000	25%	5.2%	1.30%
Common Equity	120,000,000	75%	14.4%	10.80%
Total..................	$160,000,000	100%		12.10%

The analyst should now use the revised estimate of the weighted average cost of capital of 12.10 percent to recompute the value of equity once again, and iterate this process until the values of debt and equity converge with the weights of debt and equity.

CASH-FLOW-BASED VALUATION EQUATIONS

In this chapter thus far, we have discussed all of the elements of free cash-flow-based valuation. To bring all of the elements together, we present below equations to describe the free cash-flow-based valuation models. In each of these equations, all of the variables used to compute firm value are *expectations* of future free cash flows, future discount rates, and future growth rates. We present the equations with and without explicit terms for continuing values. Recall that Exhibit 11.1 describes the computations for free cash flows for all debt and equity capital stakeholders, and free cash flows for common equity shareholders.

Valuation Models for Free Cash Flows for All Debt and Equity Capital Stakeholders

The following equation summarizes the computation of the present value of future free cash flows for all debt and equity capital stakeholders to determine the value of the net operating assets of a firm as of time t = 0 (denoted $VNOA_0$):

$$VNOA_0 = \sum_{t=1}^{\infty} [FreeCashFlowAll_t / (1 + R_A)^t]$$

In this equation, *FreeCashFlowAll* denotes the analyst's forecasts (as of time t = 0) of future free cash flows for all debt and equity capital stakeholders, and R_A denotes the expected future weighted average cost of capital.[14]

The next equation summarizes the same computation but uses the analyst's forecasts of free cash flows for all debt and equity capital stakeholders over a finite forecast horizon through year T (where T is 5 or 10 years in the future), plus the present value of continuing value. The analyst computes continuing value based on the forecast assumption that the firm will grow indefinitely at rate g beginning in Year T+1 and continuing thereafter. The analyst derives free cash flows for all debt and equity capital stakeholders in Year T+1 from the projected income statement and balance sheet for Year T+1, in which all of the elements of the Year T income statement and balance sheet are projected to grow at rate g beginning in Year T+1. The equation is as follows:

$$VNOA_0 = \sum_{t=1}^{T} [FreeCashFlowAll_t / (1 + R_A)^t]$$

$$+ [FreeCashFlowAll_{T+1}] \times [1/(R_A - g)] \times [1/(1 + R_A)^T]$$

Both of the prior equations represent estimates of the value of the net operating assets of the firm, which is equivalent to the sum of the values of debt, preferred, and common equity capital. To isolate the value of common equity capital, the analyst must subtract the present value of all interest-bearing debt and preferred stock. The equation to compute the value of equity (denoted V_0) is:

$$V_0 = VNOA_0 - VDebt_0 - VPreferred_0$$

The Valuations spreadsheet within FSAP provides a template that will calculate $VNOA_0$ and V_0 using the present value of free cash flows for all debt and equity capital stakeholders, including the continuing value computation.

---

[14]The analyst should also remember to add any non-operating assets or subtract any non-operating liabilities that the firm may have on the balance sheet at time t = 0 that are not included in free cash flows.

Valuation Models for Free Cash Flows for Common Equity Shareholders

The following equation summarizes the computation of the value of the common equity of a firm as of time t = 0 (denoted V_0) using the present value of free cash flows for common equity shareholders:

$$V_0 = \sum_{t=1}^{\infty} [FreeCashFlowEquity_t / (1 + R_E)^t]$$

This equation differs from the prior models because it includes the analyst's forecasts of future free cash flows to common equity shareholders (denoted *FreeCashFlowEquity*) rather than free cash flows to all debt and equity, and R_E denotes the required rate of return to equity rather than the weighted average cost of capital (R_A).

The following equation summarizes the computation of the value of common equity as of time t = 0, but in this equation, the analyst bases the valuation on the forecasts of free cash flows for common equity shareholders over a finite forecast horizon through year T, plus the present value of continuing value. The analyst computes continuing value based on the forecast assumption that the firm will grow indefinitely at rate g beginning in Year T+1 and continuing thereafter. The analyst derives free cash flows for common equity shareholders in Year T+1 from the projected income statement and balance sheet for Year T+1, in which all of the elements of the Year T income statement and balance sheet are projected to grow at rate g beginning in Year T+1. The equation is as follows:

$$V_0 = \sum_{t=1}^{T} [FreeCashFlowEquity_t / (1 + R_E)^t]$$

$$+ [FreeCashFlowEquity_{T+1}] \times [1 / (R_E - g)] \times [1 / (1 + R_E)^T]$$

Both of these free cash-flow-based equations represent the value of the common equity of the firm. Therefore, it is not necessary to subtract the market value of all interest-bearing debt and preferred stock. The Valuations spreadsheet within FSAP provides a template that will calculate V_0 using the present value of free cash flows for common equity shareholders, including the continuing value computation.

Minor Refinements to Present Value Calculations

The analyst interested in a slightly higher degree of precision in the free cash-flow-based value estimates can consider implementing the following two refinements to the valuation calculations.

Mid-Year Discounting. Present value calculations like those illustrated above discount cash flows for full periods. Thus, the valuation discounts Year +1 cash flows for a full year, Year +2 cash flows for two years, and so on, which is appropriate if the cash flows being discounted occur at the end of the year. Free cash flows of businesses generally occur throughout the period. Thus, present value computations with full-year discounting will over-discount these flows. To avoid over-discounting, the analyst can compute the present value discount factors as of the mid-point of each year, thereby effectively discounting the cash flows as if they occur on average in the middle of each year. Suppose the analyst uses a discount rate of 10 percent ($R = 0.10$). The Year +1 cash flows would be discounted using a factor of $1/(1 + R)^{0.5} = 1/(1.10)^{0.5} = 0.9535$; the Year +2 cash flows would be discounted using a factor of $1/(1 + R)^{1.5} = 1/(1.10)^{1.5} = 0.8668$; and so on. The analyst can also use a shortcut approach to this correction by adjusting the total present value to a mid-year approximation by adding back one-half of a year of discounting. To make this mid-year adjustment, the analyst multiplies the total present value of the discounted cash flows by a factor of $1 + (R/2)$. For example, if $R = 0.10$, then the midyear adjustment is 1.05 [$= 1 + (0.10/2)$]. The Valuation spreadsheet computations in FSAP use this shortcut adjustment.

Partial Year Accumulation of Value. The valuation models described in this chapter estimate the present value of the firm as of the first day of the first year of the forecast horizon; for example, January 1 of Year +1 for a firm with an accounting period that matches the calendar year. However, analysts estimate valuations every day of the year. Suppose the analyst values a firm as of June 17, and compares the value estimate to a market price for the firm's shares on June 17. A present value calculation that determines the value of the firm as of January 1 will ignore the value accumulation between January 1 and June 17 of that year. To refine the calculation, the analyst can adjust the present value as of January 1 to a present value as of June 17 by multiplying V_0 by a future value factor that reflects value accumulation for the appropriate number of days (in this case, 168 days). If the valuation date is June 17, for example, then the analyst can update the January 1 value estimate by multiplying V_0 by $(1 + R)^{168/365} = (1 + 0.10)^{168/365} = 1.0448$, if $R = 0.10$.

ILLUSTRATIONS OF CASH-FLOW-BASED VALUATION

We next illustrate cash-flow-based valuation methods in this section, first with a simple example involving a single project and then a more complex example involving the valuation of PepsiCo using the projections developed in Chapter 10.

VALUATION OF A SINGLE PROJECT

Assume that a firm is considering an investment that is expected to cost $10,000,000 and is expected to generate free cash flows of $2,000,000 a year forever for all debt and equity capital stakeholders. The firm will finance the investment with $6,000,000 debt and $4,000,000 of common equity. The debt is issued at par and bears interest at 10 percent each year, payable at the end of each year. The income tax rate is 40 percent. The cost of equity capital is 25.625 percent.

Example 14–Value of Common Equity. We can determine the value of the common equity investment using the present value of free cash flows for common equity shareholders. The free cash flow to common equity each year is as follows:

Free Cash Flow for All Debt and Equity Capital.	$2,000,000
Interest Paid on Debt: 0.10 × $6,000,000	(600,000)
Income Tax Savings on Interest: 0.40 × $600,000.	240,000
Free Cash Flow for Common Equity Shareholders	$1,640,000

The value of the common equity in the project is $6,400,000 (= $1,640,000/0.25625). Dividing by the discount rate is appropriate because the $1,640,000 annual free cash flow for common equity is a perpetuity with no growth. The present value of the gain to the common equity shareholders in excess of their initial investment is $2,400,000 (= $6,400,000 – $4,000,000).

Example 15–Value of Debt Plus Equity. Alternatively, for the same project we can determine the value of the sum of the debt plus common equity invested in the project by discounting the free cash flow for all debt and equity capital at the weighted average cost of capital. The debt carries an after-tax cost of 6 percent [= 0.10 × (1 – 0.40)].

The weights to compute the weighted average cost of capital are the relative market values of the debt and the equity. Recall that the $6,000,000 of debt is issued at par, so that its market value is $6,000,000. We know from the previous example that the common equity has a market value of $6,400,000. The weighted average cost of capital is:

Type of Capital	Amount	Weight	After-tax Cost	Weighted Average
Debt.	$ 6,000,000	0.48387	0.06000	0.02903
Common Equity	6,400,000	0.51613	0.25625	0.13226
Total.	$12,400,000	1.00000		0.16129

The present value of debt plus equity is $12,400,000 (= $2,000,000/0.16129).[15] Subtracting the $6,000,000 value of the debt yields a $6,400,000 value for the common equity, the same as in the previous example.

Example 16–Adjusted Present Value Approach. An alternate approach to valuing the debt plus equity is the *adjusted present value* approach. This approach values the debt and equity (or net operating assets) in two steps:

---

[15]There is a small difference from $12,400,000 due to rounding various calculations.

1. Value the free cash flows to all debt and equity capital at the unlevered cost of equity.
2. Add the present value of the tax savings from deducting interest expense on debt using the cost of debt capital.

The first component requires the calculation of an unlevered cost of equity capital. Conceptually, this is the rate of return required by equity investors if the firm had no debt financing. Because leverage typically increases risk to equity holders, the unlevered cost of equity capital is usually lower than the levered cost of equity capital. We assumed above that the levered cost of equity capital is 25.625 percent. To unlever this cost of equity capital, we solve the following equation:

Unlevered Cost of Equity Capital = Levered Cost of Equity Capital −

$$\left[\left(\frac{\text{Debt}}{\text{Equity}}\right) \times (1 - \text{Income Tax Rate}) \times \left(\text{Unlevered Cost of Equity Capital} - \text{Cost of Debt Capital}\right)\right]$$

$$X = 0.25625 - \left[(\$6,000 / \$6,400) \times (1-0.40) \times (X-0.10)\right]$$

Solving for X yields an unlevered cost of equity capital of 20 percent.

The second component requires the cost of debt capital. We assumed above that the firm issued the debt at par, so its pre-tax cost is 10 percent. The valuation of the debt plus equity is as follows:

1. Value of Free Cash Flows to Debt and Equity at Unlevered Cost of Equity Capital: $2,000,000/0.20	$10,000,000
2. Value of Tax Savings on Interest at Cost of Debt: (0.40 × 0.10 × $6,000,000)/0.10	2,400,000
Total Value of Debt Plus Equity	$12,400,000

This total is the same as in Example 14. We can subtract the value of the debt of $6,000,000 to obtain the $6,400,000 value of the equity, the same as in Example 13. Note that, in order to use the adjusted present value approach, we need to know the amount of debt that will be outstanding that will give rise to interest deductions.

VALUATION OF PEPSICO

At the end of Year 11, PepsiCo shares closed trading at $49.05 per share on the New York Stock Exchange. We therefore know the *price* at which we can buy or sell PepsiCo shares. But what is the *value* of these shares? We illustrate the valuation of PepsiCo shares using the techniques described in this chapter and the forecasts developed in Chapter 10. The forecasts and valuation estimates are also developed using the FSAP Forecast and Valuation spreadsheets.

We will estimate the present value of a share of common equity in PepsiCo at the end of Year 11 (equivalently, the start of forecast Year +1) two ways: (1) by estimating the present value of free cash flows to all debt and equity capital stakeholders (discounted using PepsiCo's weighted average cost of capital) and then subtracting the present value of debt and preferred stock claims; and (2) by estimating the present value of free cash flows to common equity shareholders directly, discounted at the required rate of return to common equity. To proceed with each valuation, we will follow five steps: (a) determine the free cash flows from the pro forma financial statements for PepsiCo described in Chapter 10, and make assumptions about free cash flows growth in the continuing periods beyond the forecast horizon; (b) estimate the appropriate discount rate; (c) discount the free cash flows to present value, including continuing value; (d) make necessary adjustments to convert the present value computation to an estimate of share value for PepsiCo; and (e) conduct sensitivity analysis for our estimate of PepsiCo's share value to determine the reasonable range of values for PepsiCo shares. In the end, we compare this range of reasonable values to PepsiCo's share price in the market and suggest an appropriate investment decision indicated by our analysis.

VALUATION OF PEPSICO USING FREE CASH FLOWS TO ALL DEBT AND EQUITY CAPITAL STAKEHOLDERS

PepsiCo's Free Cash Flows to All Debt and Equity Capital Stakeholders

Chapter 10 described detailed projections of PepsiCo's future statements of cash flows by making specific assumptions regarding each item in the income statement and balance sheet and then deriving the related cash flow effects using a five-year forecast horizon. For projections beyond Year +5, Chapter 10 essentially assumed that PepsiCo would continue to grow, and that the assumptions in Year +5 would continue to hold until Year +10. We use these projections of PepsiCo's statements of cash flows to compute projected free cash flows to all debt and equity capital stakeholders, and we present these projections in Exhibit 11.4.

As described earlier in this chapter, we begin the computation of free cash flows with cash flows from operations from the projected statements of cash flows. In Year +1, for example, we project PepsiCo's cash flows from operations to be $4,718.6 million. We then adjust for net interest, adding back interest expense after tax. Specifically, we add back in Year +1 $128.7 million in interest expense after tax (= $189.2 million × (1 − 0.32)). We do not make an adjustment to subtract interest income after tax because we assume that all of PepsiCo's interest income relates to financial assets (cash and short-term investments) that are used for liquidity in operating activities and are not part of the capital structure. We also adjust cash flow from operations for required investments in operating cash. In Chapter 10, we projected PepsiCo would need to maintain roughly 10 days of sales in cash for liquidity purposes, therefore PepsiCo's required cash balance grows with sales. For example, in Year +1 PepsiCo's cash balance will grow by $107.2 million. The additional

EXHIBIT 11.4
Valuation of PepsiCo:
Present Value of Free Cash Flows to All Debt and Equity Capital Stakeholders
Year +1 through Year +10

	Year +1	Year +2	Year +3
NET CASH FLOW FROM OPERATIONS.	$ 4,718.6	$5,079.9	$5,493.7
Add back: Interest Expense after tax.	128.7	135.4	132.0
Subtract: Interest Income after tax	0.0	0.0	0.0
+/− Investment in operating cash.	−107.2	−56.1	−60.4
FREE CASH FLOWS FROM OPERATIONS.	4,740.1	5,159.2	5,565.3
NET CASH FLOW FROM INVESTING	−2,356.0	−2,295.3	−2,461.7
Net Cash Flow into Marketable Securities	0.0	0.0	0.0
FREE CASH FLOWS FOR ALL DEBT AND EQUITY	$ 2,384.1	$2,864.0	$3,103.6
Present Value Factors (R$_A$ = 7.90%)	0.927	0.859	0.796
PVs of Free Cash Flows.	$ 2,209.6	$2,460.1	$2,470.8
Sum of PV Free Cash Flows Year +1 through Year +10	$24,317.6		

increments of cash required for liquidity are therefore not free cash flows, so we subtract them. The result of these adjustments is the free cash flow from operations for PepsiCo, which we project will be $4,740.1 million in Year +1.

We next subtract cash flows for capital expenditures, using the amount of net cash flow for investing from PepsiCo's projected statements of cash flows. In the projected statement of cash flows for PepsiCo in Year +1, we projected net cash flows for investing activities will be $2,356.0 million. These investing cash flows include cash outflows for purchases of short-term investment securities, which is appropriate because we assumed above these securities are for purposes of operating liquidity and are not financial assets that are part of the financing structure of PepsiCo. Note also that PepsiCo's investing cash flows include cash outflows for long-term investments that primarily relate to affiliated bottling companies, which we deem to be part of PepsiCo's operations. Therefore, we subtract the full amount of net cash flow for investing activities from the free cash flow from operations. We therefore forecast PepsiCo's free cash flows for all debt and equity capital stakeholders will be $2,384.1 million (= $4,740.1 million − $2,356.0 million) in Year +1. We repeat these steps each year through Year +10.

To project PepsiCo's free cash flows continuing in Year +11 and beyond, we forecast that PepsiCo can sustain a long-run growth rate of 5.0 percent in sales, earnings, and free cash flows, consistent with long-term growth in the economy of 2 percent and long-term inflation of 3 percent. To compute continuing free cash flows in Year +11, we first project each line item on PepsiCo's Year +10 income statement and balance sheet to grow at 5.0 percent per year in Year +11. We use these Year +11 projected income statement and balance sheet amounts to derive the Year +11 free cash flows for all debt and equity capital, which we project will be $5,925.5 million. We assume

	EXHIBIT 11.4					

Exhibit 11.4—continued

Year+4	Year +5	Year +6	Year +7	Year +8	Year +9	Year +10
$5,940.4	$6,396.8	$6,863.2	$7,356.0	$7,884.8	$8,451.6	$9,061.5
138.3	147.1	151.0	161.9	173.7	186.3	199.8
0.0	0.0	0.0	0.0	0.0	0.0	0.0
−64.9	−69.8	−74.9	−80.2	−86.0	−92.2	−99.0
6,013.7	6,474.0	6,939.2	7,437.7	7,972.5	8,545.7	9,162.3
−2,640.3	−2,833.9	−3,038.7	−3,257.1	−3,491.2	−3,742.1	−4,013.3
0.0	0.0	0.0	0.0	0.0	0.0	0.0
$3,373.4	$3,640.1	$3,900.6	$4,180.6	$4,481.3	$4,803.6	$5,149.0
0.738	0.684	0.634	0.587	0.544	0.505	0.468
$2,489.0	$2,489.2	$2,472.1	$2,455.7	$2,439.6	$2,423.7	$2,407.8

this free cash flow amount is the beginning amount of a perpetuity of continuing free cash flows that PepsiCo will generate beginning in Year +11 and growing at 5 percent each year thereafter. The computations are shown in detail in the Forecast and Valuation spreadsheets in FSAP, which permits specific forecast assumptions to extend as far as Year +10 into the future, with continuing value assumptions after that.

PepsiCo Discount Rates

To discount free cash flows to all debt and equity capital, we need to compute PepsiCo's weighted average cost of capital. With respect to the cost of equity capital, at the end of Year 11 PepsiCo common stock had a market beta of roughly 0.76. At that time, U.S. Treasury Bills with one to five years to maturity traded with a yield of approximately 4.2 percent, which we use as the risk-free rate. Assuming a 5 percent market risk premium, the CAPM indicates that PepsiCo has a cost of common equity capital of 8.0 percent $[0.080 = 0.042 + (0.76 \times 0.05)]$. At the end of Year 11, PepsiCo had 1,756 million shares outstanding and a share price of $49.05 for a total market capital of common equity of $86,132 million.

With respect to debt capital, on the Year 11 balance sheet PepsiCo had interest-bearing debt from short-term borrowing and long-term debt totaling $3,005 million (= $354 + $2,651; see Appendix A). Recall that in Chapter 10 we used information disclosed in Note 12 to assess stated interest rates on PepsiCo's interest-bearing debt. We determined that in Year 11 PepsiCo's outstanding debt carries a weighted average interest rate of approximately 5.5 to 6.0 percent. In Note 13, PepsiCo discloses that the fair value of PepsiCo's outstanding debt at the end of Year 11 is $3,266 million. Thus, PepsiCo has experienced an unrealized (and unrecognized) loss on its debt capital. This unrealized loss implies that their outstanding debt carries stated rates of interest that exceed prevailing market yields, which at the end of Year 11 are at historically low levels in the U.S. economy. Expecting that prevailing yields to maturity are temporarily low, we forecast PepsiCo's cost of debt capital to approximate 6 percent in Year +1 and beyond. We therefore also use the current fair value (as a proxy for market value) of PepsiCo's debt for weighting purposes. Note 14 to PepsiCo's Year 11 financial statements suggests that the combined federal, state, and foreign marginal tax rate is approximately 32 percent in Year 10 and Year 11. Separately, we also forecast that PepsiCo will face an effective tax rate of roughly 32 percent in Year +1 and beyond. Therefore, our projections imply that PepsiCo faces an after-tax cost of debt capital of 4.1 percent $[0.041 = 0.06 \times (1 - 0.32)]$.

PepsiCo also has $26 million in preferred stock at book value on the Year 11 balance sheet. The preferred stock pays a dividend of $4 million, so the implied cost of preferred stock capital is 15.4 percent. This cost of capital seems high relative to the risk of this preferred stock, and relative to the cost of PepsiCo's debt and common equity capital. We therefore assume that PepsiCo's preferred stock is approximately as risky as PepsiCo's common stock, and has a similar 8.0 percent cost of capital. This implies that the preferred stock has a fair value of $50 million (=$4 million/0.080), which we use for weighting purposes. We assume this cost of preferred capital is not tax deductible. Because the preferred stock is an immaterial amount relative to the common equity and debt capital of PepsiCo, it will have little effect on PepsiCo's weighted average cost of capital or valuation, but we include it for completeness.

Bringing these three costs of capital together, we compute our initial estimate of PepsiCo's weighted average cost of capital to be 7.858 percent as follows:

Capital	Value Basis	Amount	Weight	After-tax Cost of Capital	Weighted-Average Component
Debt	Fair	$ 3,266	0.0365	0.041	0.00150
Preferred.......	Fair	50	0.0006	0.080	0.00005
Common	Market	86,132	0.9629	0.080	0.07703
Total		$89,448	1.0000		0.07858

As described earlier, the weighted average cost of capital must be computed iteratively until the weights used are consistent with the present values of debt, preferred, and equity capital. After iterating the computation, we determine that the internally consistent weighted average cost of capital is 7.90 percent. We use this rate to discount to present value the expected future free cash flows to all debt and equity capital.

Discounting PepsiCo's Free Cash Flows to All Debt and Equity Capital Stakeholders to Present Value

We discount free cash flows to all debt and equity capital stakeholders to present value using PepsiCo's 7.90 percent weighted average cost of capital. Exhibit 11.4

shows that PepsiCo's free cash flows for all debt and equity capital in Year +1 through Year +10 have a present value of $24,317.6 million.

To compute the present value of PepsiCo's continuing value, we compute the continuing value beyond Year +10 using the perpetuity-with-growth model. First, as described above, we project that PepsiCo will generate free cash flows of $5,925.5 million in Year +11, and that these free cash flows will grow at a rate of 5 percent indefinitely. We use the discount rate of 7.90 percent to compute present value, as follows:

$$ContinuingValue_0 = [FreeCashFlowAll_{11}] \times [1/(R_A - g)] \times [1/(1 + R_A)^{10}]$$

$$= [\$5{,}925.5 \ million] \times [1/(0.079 - 0.05)] \times [1/(1 + 0.079)^{10}]$$

$$= \$5925.5 \ million \times 34.4889 \times 0.468$$

$$= \$95{,}642.4 \ million$$

The total present value of PepsiCo's free cash flows to all debt and equity capital stakeholders is the sum of these two parts:

PV Free Cash Flows through Year +10..................	$ 24,317.6 million
PV of Continuing Value Year +11 and beyond	95,642.4 million
PV of Free Cash Flows for All Debt and Equity Capital	$119,960.0 million

Necessary Adjustments to Compute Common Equity Share Value

To narrow this computation to the present value of common equity, we need to subtract the present value of interest-bearing debt and preferred stock and add the present value of interest-earning financial assets that are part of the firm's financial capital structure. Relying on PepsiCo's fair values, we subtract $3,266 million for outstanding debt and $50 million for preferred stock. We assumed that PepsiCo's financial assets are not part of the financial capital structure, so we make no adjustment for them. After subtracting the value of debt and preferred stock, the present value of PepsiCo's common equity capital is $116,644.0 million (= $119,960.0 million − $3,266 million − $50 million.)

As described earlier, our present value calculations have over-discounted these cash flows because we have discounted each year's cash flows for a full period when, in fact, PepsiCo generates cash flows throughout each period and we should discount them from the midpoint of the year to the present. Therefore, to make the correction, we multiply the present value sum by the mid-year adjustment factor $[1 + (R_A/2) = 1 + (0.079/2) = 1.0395]$. Therefore, the total present value of free cash flows to common equity capital stakeholders is $121,249.8 million (= $116,644.0 million × 1.0395).[16]

---

[16]The last adjustment we need to make to compute the value is to add the present value of any non-operating assets and liabilities not captured in the free cash flows computations. After reviewing PepsiCo's Year 11 balance sheet, it appears that we have incorporated the free cash flows implications of all of PepsiCo's assets and liabilities into our free cash flows, so this adjustment is zero.

The total value of common equity of PepsiCo as of the beginning of Year +1 is $121,249.8 million. Dividing by 1,756 million shares outstanding indicates that PepsiCo's common equity shares have a value of $69.05 per share. Exhibit 11.5 summarizes the computations to arrive at PepsiCo's common equity share value.

Note that our calculation of the present value of PepsiCo's common equity ($121,249.8 million) is inconsistent with our use of the current market value of PepsiCo common equity ($86,132 million) in the initial weighted average cost of capital computation because it did not place enough weight on equity in the initial cost of capital computation. We iterated the valuation computations until the weights and values converged. The weighted average cost of capital of 7.90 percent and the equity value estimate of $121,249.8 million are the internally consistent values.

VALUATION OF PEPSICO USING FREE CASH FLOWS TO COMMON EQUITY SHAREHOLDERS

We also estimate the value of PepsiCo's common equity by using free cash flows to common equity shareholders. We describe each step next.

PepsiCo's Free Cash Flows to Common Equity

Exhibit 11.6 presents estimates of PepsiCo's free cash flows for common equity shareholders through Year +10. The computations begin with the free cash flows for all debt and equity capital, as described earlier. To refine these cash flows to free cash

EXHIBIT 11.5		
Valuation of PepsiCo using Free Cash Flows to All Debt and Equity Capital		
Valuation Steps	**Computations**	**Amounts**
PV Free Cash Flows Year +1 through Year +10	See Exhibit 11.4.	+ $ 24,317.6
PV Free Cash Flows Years +11 and Beyond	Long-run growth rate assumed to be 5.0%; discounted at 7.90%. Computations in FSAP.	+ $ 95,642.4
PV of All Debt and Equity Capital		= $119,960.0
Subtract Debt Capital	Fair Value of Debt	− $ 3,266.0
Subtract Preferred Stock	Fair Value of Preferred Stock	− $ 50.0
Add Financial Assets	Assumed to be zero	+ $ 0.0
PV of Common Equity		= $116,644.0
Adjust for Mid-year Discounting	Multiply by 1 + ($R_A/2$)	× 1.0395
Total PV of Common Equity		= $121,249.8
Divide by Number of Shares Outstanding	In millions of shares	÷ 1,756
Value per Share of Common Equity		= $ 69.05
Current Price per Share		$ 49.05
Percent Difference	(Positive number indicates under-pricing.)	41%

flows available to common equity, we need to adjust them for financing cash flows. We first add any cash inflows from new borrowing and subtract any cash outflows for debt repayments. For example, in Year +1, we begin with $2,384.1 million in free cash flow for all debt and equity capital, and add $297.7 million in cash flows from PepsiCo's projected new borrowing. Next, we add inflows and subtract outflows related to transactions with preferred stock and minority equity shareholders (if any). In Year +1, we subtract $4.0 million for preferred stock dividends. We also subtract any cash outflows and add any cash inflows related to financial asset accounts that are part of PepsiCo's capital structure (which we have deemed to be zero). Finally, we subtract interest expense after tax (projected to be $128.7 million in Year +1) and add interest income after tax (projected to be zero), as financing cash flows. The computations project $2,549.1 million in free cash flows for common equity shareholders for PepsiCo in Year +1. We repeat these steps each year through Year +10.

To project PepsiCo's free cash flows continuing in Year +11 and beyond, we again forecast that PepsiCo can sustain long-run growth of 5 percent. We project the income statement and balance sheet to grow at 5 percent in Year +11, and derive free cash flows to common equity from these statements. Our computations indicate that free cash flows to common equity in Year +11 will be $5,966.3 million (shown in detail in the Forecast and Valuation spreadsheets in FSAP). We assume these free cash flows will continue to grow at 5 percent per year thereafter.

Discount Rates for Free Cash Flows for Common Equity

To compute the appropriate discount rate, we use the CAPM to compute the market's required rate of return on PepsiCo's common stock. As described earlier, the CAPM implies that the required rate of return on PepsiCo stock is 8.0 percent.

Discounting to Present Value PepsiCo's Free Cash Flows to Common Equity Shareholders

We discount these free cash flows to present value using PepsiCo's 8.0 percent cost of equity capital. Exhibit 11.6 shows that PepsiCo's free cash flows for common equity through Year +10 have a present value of $24,426.2 million. The present value of PepsiCo's continuing value is computed as the present value of a growing perpetuity. We project continuing free cash flows for Year +11 will be $5,966.3. We project these free cash flows to grow at 5.0 percent and discount them to present value using the 8.0 percent discount rate. The present value of these cash flows is $92,118.0 million, computed as follows (allowing for rounding):

$$ContinuingValue_0 = [FreeCashFlowEquity_{11}] \times [1/(R_E - g)] \times [1/(1+R_E)^{10}]$$

$$= [\$5,966.3 \ million] \times [1/(0.080-0.05)] \times [1/(1+0.080)^{10}]$$

$$= \$5,966.3 \ million \times 33.333 \times 0.463$$

$$= \$92,118.0 \ million$$

EXHIBIT 11.6			
Valuation of PepsiCo:			
Present Value of Free Cash Flows to Common Equity Year +1 through Year +10			
	Year +1	Year +2	Year +3
FREE CASH FLOWS FOR ALL DEBT AND EQUITY	$ 2,384.1	$2,864.0	$3,103.6
Net Cash Flows from Debt Financing.....................	297.7	33.3	−199.9
Net Cash Flows from Preferred and Minority Interest........	−4.0	−4.0	−4.0
Net Cash Flows into Marketable Securities	0.0	0.0	0.0
Subtract: Interest Expense after tax......................	−128.7	−135.4	−132.0
Add back: Interest Income after tax	0.0	0.0	0.0
FREE CASH FLOWS FOR COMMON EQUITY	$ 2,549.1	$2,757.8	$2,767.6
Present Value Factors (R$_E$ = 8.0%)	0.926	0.857	0.794
PVs of Free Cash Flows..................................	$ 2,360.3	$2,364.4	$2,197.0
Sum of PV Free Cash Flows for Common Equity			
Year +1 through Year +10	$24,426.2		

The total present value of PepsiCo's free cash flows to common equity shareholders is the sum of these two parts:

PV Free Cash Flows through Year +10	$ 24,426.2 million
PV of Continuing Value in Year +11 and beyond.........	92,118.0 million
Present Value of Common Equity.....................	$116,544.2 million

As described above, we need to correct our present value calculations for over-discounting. To make the correction, we multiply the present value sum by the mid-year adjustment factor $[1 + (R_E/2) = 1 + (0.080/2) = 1.040]$. The total present value of free cash flows to common equity shareholders should be $121,205.9 million $[= $116,544.2 million × 1.040]$.

Necessary Adjustments to Compute Common Equity Share Value

Dividing the total value of common equity of PepsiCo by 1,756 million shares outstanding indicates that PepsiCo's common equity shares have a value of $69.02 per share. This share value estimate is within $0.03 of the share value estimate using free cash flows to all debt and equity capital, and subtracting the value of debt and preferred.[17] Exhibit 11.7 summarizes the computations to arrive at PepsiCo's common equity share value.

---

[17]The minor difference is attributable to our use of rough approximations of PepsiCo's costs of capital for debt and preferred stock, rather than using precise estimates of yields to maturity on debt and preferred as implied by their present values.

	EXHIBIT 11.6					

Exhibit 11.6—continued

Year+4	Year +5	Year +6	Year +7	Year +8	Year +9	Year +10
$3,373.4	$3,640.1	$3,900.6	$4,180.6	$4,481.3	$4,803.6	$5,149.0
504.9	−71.0	259.5	278.2	298.2	319.6	343.0
−4.0	−4.0	−4.0	−4.0	−4.0	−4.0	−4.0
0.0	0.0	0.0	0.0	0.0	0.0	0.0
−138.3	−147.1	−151.0	−161.9	−173.7	−186.3	−199.8
0.0	0.0	0.0	0.0	0.0	0.0	0.0
$3,736.0	$3,418.0	$4,005.2	$4,292.9	$4,601.8	$4,932.9	$5,288.1
0.735	0.681	0.630	0.583	0.540	0.500	0.463
$2,746.1	$2,326.2	$2,523.9	$2,504.9	$2,486.2	$2,467.7	$2,449.4

Sensitivity Analysis and Investment Decision-Making

One should not place too much confidence in the *precision* of firm value estimates using these (or any) forecasts of cash flows over the remaining life of any firm, even a mature firm like PepsiCo. Although we have constructed these forecasts and value estimates with care, the forecasting and valuation process has an inherently high degree of uncertainty and estimation error. Therefore, the analyst should not rely too

	EXHIBIT 11.7	
	Valuation of PepsiCo using Free Cash Flows to Common Equity	
Valuation Steps	**Computations**	**Amounts**
PV of Free Cash Flows Year +1 through Year +10	See Exhibit 11.6.	+ $ 24,426.2
PV of Free Cash Flows Years +11 and Beyond	Long-run growth rate assumed to be 5.0%; discounted at 8.0%. Computations in FSAP.	+ $ 92,118.0
Total Present Value Sum		= $116,544.2
Adjust for Mid-year Discounting	Multiply by $1+(R_E/2)$	× 1.040
Total PV of Common Equity		= $121,205.9
Divide by Number of Shares Outstanding	In millions of shares	÷ 1,756
Value per Share of Common Equity		= $ 69.02
Current Price per Share		$ 49.05
Percent Difference	(Positive number indicates underpricing.)	41%

heavily on any one point estimate of the value of a firm's shares, and instead should describe a reasonable range of values for a firm's shares.

Two critical forecasting and valuation parameters are the long-run growth assumption (5 percent) and the cost of equity capital (8.0 percent). Under these assumptions, our base case estimate is that PepsiCo common shares should be valued in the neighborhood of $69 per share. We can assess the sensitivity of our estimates of PepsiCo's share value by varying these two parameters (or any other key parameters in the valuation) across reasonable ranges. Exhibit 11.8 contains the results of sensitivity analysis varying the long-run growth assumption from 0 to 10 percent, and the cost of equity capital from 5 to 20 percent. The data in Exhibit 11.8 show that as the discount rate increases, holding growth constant, share value estimates of PepsiCo fall. Likewise, value estimates fall as growth rates decrease, holding discount rates constant. Note that we omit value estimates from this analysis when the assumed growth rate equals or exceeds the assumed discount rate, because then the continuing value computation is meaningless.

Under our base case assumptions, we estimate PepsiCo share value to be roughly $69, which is 41% greater than the market price of $49.05 a share for PepsiCo at the time of the valuation. Our base case assumptions indicate PepsiCo shares are underpriced, or our forecasts and valuation estimates are more optimistic than those of the

EXHIBIT 11.8
Valuation of PepsiCo:
Sensitivity Analysis of Value to Growth and Equity Cost of Capital

Discount Rates	Long-run Growth Assumptions				
	0%	1%	2%	3%	4%
5%	59.48	70.17	87.99	123.63	230.53
6%	48.49	55.00	64.77	81.05	113.62
7%	40.70	44.96	50.92	59.86	74.75
8%	34.93	37.85	41.75	47.20	55.38
9%	30.48	32.56	35.24	38.81	43.81
10%	26.96	28.49	30.40	32.86	36.13
11%	24.12	25.27	26.67	28.42	30.68
12%	21.78	22.66	23.71	25.00	26.61
13%	19.82	20.50	21.31	22.28	23.46
14%	18.16	18.70	19.33	20.07	20.96
15%	16.74	17.17	17.67	18.25	18.93
16%	15.51	15.86	16.26	16.71	17.25
17%	14.45	14.73	15.05	15.41	15.83
18%	13.51	13.74	14.00	14.29	14.63
19%	12.67	12.87	13.08	13.32	13.59
20%	11.94	12.09	12.27	12.47	12.69

market. The data in Exhibit 11.8 allow the analyst to build greater confidence in the prediction that PepsiCo shares are under-priced. For example, if we reduce the long-run growth assumption to as low as 3.0 percent, holding the discount rate constant at 8.0 percent, PepsiCo shares have a value of $47.20, slightly below current market price.

PepsiCo's share value is more sensitive to the discount rate assumption. Holding growth constant, if we increase the discount rate for common equity capital from 8.0 percent to 9.0 percent, then PepsiCo's share value estimate falls to $51.31, slightly above current market price. Increasing the discount rate to 10.0 percent drops the value further, to $40.72 per share. On the other hand, if we reduce the discount rate to 7 percent, holding growth constant, the value estimate jumps to $104.55 per share. The data in Exhibit 11.8 also allow the analyst to vary both valuation parameters jointly, for additional insights into the correlation between share value and the growth and discount rate assumptions implicit in our estimate of PepsiCo share value. These data suggest our value estimate is sensitive to PepsiCo's discount rate assumption. If our forecast and valuation assumptions are realistic, then PepsiCo shares were underpriced at the end of Year 11 and would have supported a buy recommendation at that time.

		EXHIBIT 11.8			

Exhibit 11.8—continued

5%	6%	7%	8%	9%	10%
#DIV/0!	na	na	na	na	na
211.33	#DIV/0!	na	na	na	na
104.55	193.93	#DIV/0!	na	na	na
69.02	96.30	178.14	#DIV/0!	na	na
51.31	63.81	88.81	163.79	#DIV/0!	na
40.72	47.60	59.06	81.98	150.75	#DIV/0!
33.68	37.89	44.20	54.72	75.76	138.88
28.68	31.44	35.31	41.10	50.77	70.09
24.94	26.85	29.39	32.94	38.27	47.15
22.05	23.42	25.17	27.50	30.77	35.67
19.75	20.75	22.01	23.62	25.77	28.78
17.88	18.63	19.56	20.71	22.20	24.18
16.32	16.91	17.60	18.46	19.52	20.89
15.02	15.47	16.01	16.65	17.44	18.42
13.90	14.26	14.68	15.18	15.77	16.50
12.94	13.23	13.56	13.95	14.41	14.95

EVALUATION OF PRESENT VALUE OF CASH FLOWS VALUATION METHOD

The principal advantages of the present value of future cash flows valuation method include the following:

1. This valuation method focuses on cash flows, a base that economists would argue has more economic meaning than earnings.
2. Projected amounts of cash flows result from projecting likely amounts of revenues, expenses, assets, liabilities, and shareholders' equities, therefore requiring the analyst to think through many future operating, investing, and financing decisions of a firm.

The principal disadvantages of the present value of future cash flows valuation method include the following:

1. The continuing value (terminal value) tends to dominate the total value in many cases. This continuing value is sensitive to assumptions made about growth rates after the forecast horizon and discount rates.
2. The projection of cash flows can be time-consuming for the analyst, making it costly when the analyst follows many companies and must regularly identify under- and over-valued firms.

SUMMARY

This chapter illustrates valuation using the present value of future cash flows. As with the preparation of pro forma financial statements in Chapter 10, the reasonableness of the valuations depends on the reasonableness of the assumptions. The analyst should assess the sensitivity of the valuation to alternative assumptions regarding growth and discount rates. To validate value estimates using the cash-based approach, the analyst should also compute the value of the firm using other approaches, such as the earnings-based approaches discussed in Chapter 12 and the valuation multiples approaches described in Chapter 13.

PROBLEMS AND CASES

11.1 CALCULATION OF FREE CASH FLOWS. Exhibit 11.9 presents information from the statement of cash flows and income statement for the 3M Company for Year 9 to Year 11. Marketable securities represent investments of excess cash that 3M does not need in its operations. Because of the slow growth of 3M, it does not require incremental investments in cash to sustain operations. The income tax rate is 35 percent.

EXHIBIT 11.9

3M Company
Selected Statement of Cash Flows Information
(amounts in millions)
(Problem 11.1)

	Year 11	Year 10	Year 9
Cash Flow from Operations	$ 3,080	$ 2,419	$ 3,061
Investing Activities:			
Fixed Assets Acquired.	$ (878)	$(1,011)	$ (942)
Acquisition of Businesses.	(207)	(471)	(125)
Acquisition (Sale) of Marketable Securities. .	35	109	(47)
Cash Flow from Investing Activities	$(1,050)	$(1,373)	$(1,114)
Financing Activities:			
Inc. (Dec). in Short-term Borrowing.	$ (20)	$ (236)	$ (164)
Inc. (Dec.) in Long-term Debt.	129	472	(177)
Inc. (Dec.) in Common Stock	(860)	(389)	(478)
Dividends Paid	(965)	(978)	(952)
Cash Flow from Financing Activities	$(1,716)	$(1,131)	$(1,771)
Inc. (Dec.) in Cash	$ 314	$ (85)	$ 176
Cash at Beginning of Year.	302	387	211
Cash at End of Year.	$ 616	$ 302	$ 387
Interest Revenue on Marketable Securities.	$ 37	$ 27	$ 33
Interest Expense on Short- and Long- term Borrowing	$ 124	$ 111	$ 109
Interest Paid in Cash on Short- and Long-term Borrowing	$ 137	$ 104	$ 114

Required

a. Calculate the amount of free cash flows to all debt and equity capital stakeholders for 3M for Year 9 to Year 11.

b. Calculate the amount of free cash flows for common equity shareholders for
   3M for Year 9 to Year 11.

11.2 EFFECT OF CONTINUING VALUE ON COMMON EQUITY VALUATION.
Problem 10.6 projected the following cash flows for Wal-Mart Stores for Year 13 to
Year 17 (in millions):

	Year 13	Year 14	Year 15	Year 16	Year 17
Cash Flow from					
Operations	$10,418	$11,739	$13,222	$14,833	$16,639
Cash Flow for Investing.	(11,516)	(13,013)	(14,704)	(16,616)	(18,776)
Cash Flow from Debt					
Financing	2,851	2,422	3,614	5,454	4,872
Free Cash Flow for					
Common Equity					
Shareholders.	$ 1,753	$ 1,148	$ 2,132	$ 3,671	$ 2,735

Wal-Mart does not report marketable securities on its balance sheet or interest revenue on its income statement. The market equity beta for Wal-Mart at the end of Year 7 is .83. Assume that the risk-free interest rate is 4.2 percent and the market risk premium is 5 percent.

Required

a. Valuing the common equity of Wal-Mart requires some assumption about the continuing free cash flows to common equity shareholders after Year 17. One approach grows the income statement and balance sheet amounts and the related free cash flows after Year 17 at a constant growth rate. Free cash flows to common equity shareholders are projected to grow 11.8 percent between Year 13 and Year 17. Assuming a continuation of this growth rate, the analyst increases each income statement and balance sheet amount of Year 17 by 11.8 percent to obtain forecasted income statement and balance sheet amounts for Year 18 and then derives the forecasted free cash flows. The analyst then applies a multiple to the projected free cash flows for Year 18 equal to $1/(R - g)$, where R is the cost of equity capital and g is the assumed growth rate in free cash flows after Year 17. Why doesn't this continuing value model work well in this case when the assumed growth rate in free cash flows to common equity shareholders is 11.8 percent in perpetuity?

b. Assume that the growth rate in free cash flows to common equity shareholders will decline one percentage point each year between Year 17 and Year 22 (that is, growth of 10.8 percent for Year 18, 9.8 percent for Year 19, 8.8 percent in Year 20, 7.8 percent in Year 21, and 6.8 percent in Year 22). The growth rate will stabilize at 6.8 percent after Year 22. Compute the value of the common equity of Wal-Mart as of the end of Year 12. Apply these growth rates each year directly to free cash flows to common equity shareholders of the preceding year, instead of first adjusting income statement and balance sheet amounts. Include the midyear adjustment related to the assumption that cash flows occur evenly throughout the year for this and the remaining parts of this problem.

c. Repeat part b but assume that the growth rate will equal 5.8 percent after Year 22.

d. What do the results of parts b and c suggest about the role of the growth rate in valuation?

e. The actual market value of Wal-Mart at the end of Year 12 was $244,915 million. One approach to dealing with a growth rate that approximately equals or exceeds the cost of equity capital is to solve for the growth rate implicit in the actual market price. Assume that the analyst is confident about the projected free cash flows to common equity shareholders for Year 13 to Year 17 and desires to solve for the growth in free cash flows after Year 17 implicit in the total market value of $244,915 million at the end of Year 12. Compute the value of this growth rate.

f. One criticism of using the present value of projected cash flows as a valuation method is that the continuing value tends to dominate the value. One suggestion for dealing with this criticism is to extend the number of years in the forecast horizon before computing the continuing value. Compare the effect of the continuing value on the total value when the analyst values Wal-Mart at the end of Year 17 in part e versus at the end of Year 22 in part b. How well does extending the forecast horizon deal with this continuing value concern?

11.3 CALCULATING THE COST OF CAPITAL. Crown Cork & Seal Co. manufactures aluminum, steel, and plastic containers. IBM develops and manufactures computer technologies and offers related services. Target Stores operates a chain of discount retail stores. Selected data for these companies appear below (in millions):

	Crown Cork & Seal Co.	IBM	Target Stores
Total Assets	$9,620	$ 88,313	$24,154
Interest-bearing Debt	$4,856	$ 15,963	$ 8,993
Average Pre-tax Borrowing Cost. . .	9.1%	2.6%	6.0%
Common Equity:			
Book Value	$ 804	$ 23,614	$ 7,860
Market Value	$1,407	$135,207	$28,133
Income Tax Rate	35.0%	35.0%	35.0%
Market Equity Beta	1.61	1.46	1.13

Required

a. One issue in computing the cost of equity capital is whether the analyst should use short-term, intermediate-term, or long-term riskless rates and market premia. Appropriate rates for each of these time horizons have recently been as follows:

Time Horizon	Riskless Rate	Market Premium
Short	3.4%	5.7%
Intermediate	4.2%	5.0%
Long	4.8%	4.4%

Compute the cost of equity capital for each of these three companies using (1) short-, (2) intermediate-, and (3) long-term riskless rates and market premia. Under what conditions will the cost of equity capital differ little versus much with respect to the time frame selected?

b. For the remaining parts of this problem, use the intermediate-term riskless rate and risk premium from part a. Compute the weighted average cost of capital for each of the three companies. Assume that the market value of the debt equals its book value.

c. Compute the unlevered market (asset) beta for each of the three companies. Assume that the market value of the debt equals its book value.

d. Assume for this part that each company is a potential leveraged buyout candidate. The buyers intend to put in place a capital structure that has 75 percent debt with a pre-tax borrowing cost of 10 percent and 25 percent common equity. Compute the weighted average cost of capital for each company based on the new capital structure. Why do these revised weighted average costs of capital differ so little from those computed in part b?

11.4 VALUATION OF EQUITY USING PRESENT VALUE OF FREE CASH FLOWS TO COMMON EQUITY SHAREHOLDERS. Problem 10.7 projects the financial statements for The Gap and Limited Brands for Year 13 to Year 17. Exhibit 11.10 presents the amounts from their pro forma statements of cash flows. The last column of Exhibit 11.10 provides the cash amounts for Year 18 assuming that income statement and balance sheet amounts for Year 17 increase by the long-term growth rate of 6 percent for The Gap and 3 percent for Limited Brands. (Note: If you prepared pro forma financial statements for Problem 10.7, you may wish to verify the amounts for Year 18.) The market equity beta of The Gap is 1.61 and of Limited Brands is 1.37 at the end of Year 12. Assume a risk-free interest rate of 4.2 percent and a market risk premium of 5 percent.

Required

a. Compute the present value of the projected free cash flows to common equity shareholders for each firm as of the end of Year 12. These firms need any increase in cash each year for operating purposes. Apply the midyear adjustment related to the assumption that cash flows occur evenly throughout the year.

b. Repeat part a, but apply the growth rates of 6 percent and 3 percent directly to the free cash flows for Year 17, instead of deriving them from income statement and balance sheet amounts, when computing the continuing value.

EXHIBIT 11.10

The Gap and Limited Brands
Pro Forma Cash Flows
(amounts in millions)
(Problem 11.4)

	Year 13	Year 14	Year 15	Year 16	Year 17	Year 18[a]
The Gap						
Operations.................	$1,337	$1,282	$1,334	$1,414	$1,499	$1,585
Investing.................	(969)	(802)	(849)	(900)	(954)	(1,012)
Financing:						
Borrowing.............	415	376	398	422	447	474
Dividends	(89)	(94)	(100)	(106)	(112)	(639)
Treasury Stock.........	(529)	(665)	(705)	(747)	(792)	(315)
Change in Cash	$ 165	$ 97	$ 78	$ 83	$ 88	$ 93
Limited Brands						
Operations.................	$ 565	$ 579	$ 599	$ 617	$ 635	$ 649
Investing.................	(319)	(222)	(228)	(236)	(242)	(250)
Financing:						
Borrowing.............	(22)	86	88	91	94	96
Minority Interests........	51	53	54	56	58	14
Dividends	(133)	(137)	(141)	(145)	(150)	(424)
Treasury Stock.........	(149)	(320)	(330)	(340)	(350)	(39)
Change in Cash	$ (7)	$ 39	$ 42	$ 43	$ 45	$ 46

[a]The amounts for Year 18 result from increasing each income statement and balance sheet amount of Year 17 of The Gap by 6 percent and of Limited Brands by 3 percent and then deriving the cash flow amounts. Dividends on common stock are the plug to reconcile net income minus dividends to the change in retained earnings on the balance sheet.

Assess the extent to which the shortcut for computing the continuing value amounts for Year 18 in this part affected the valuation as compared to the more theoretically sound method in part a.

c. The total market value of The Gap is $14,192 million and of Limited Brands is $8,889 million at the end of Year 12. Assuming that the analyst is confident of the projected free cash flows for common equity shareholders for Year 13 to Year 17, compute the growth rate in free cash flows after Year 17 implicitly assumed by the market in arriving at the market values above at the end of Year 12. Use the methodology from part a for determining the undiscounted cash flow for Year 18.

d. Evaluate the reasonableness of the implied growth rates computed in part c.

11.5 VALUING A LEVERAGED BUYOUT CANDIDATE.   May Department Stores (May) operates retail department store chains throughout the United States. At the end of Year 12, May reports debt of $4,658 million and common shareholders' equity

at book value of $3,923 million. The market value of its common stock is $6,705 and its market equity beta is .88.

An equity buyout group is considering a leveraged buyout of May as of the beginning of Year 13. The group intends to finance the buyout with 75 percent debt carrying an interest rate of 10 percent and 25 percent common equity. They project that the free cash flows to all debt and equity capital stakeholders of May will be as follows: Year 13, $798 million; Year 14, $861 million; Year 15, $904 million; Year 16, $850 million; Year 17, $834 million; Year 18, $884 million; Year 19, $919 million; Year 20, $947 million; Year 21, $985 million; and Year 22, $1,034 million. The group projects free cash flows to grow 3 percent annually after Year 22.

This problem sets forth the steps that the analyst might follow in deciding to acquire May and the value to place on the firm.

Required

a. Compute the unlevered market equity (asset) beta of May before consideration of the leveraged buyout. Assume that the book value of the debt equals its market value. The income tax rate is 35 percent.

b. Compute the cost of equity capital with the new capital structure that results from the leveraged buyout. Assume a risk-free rate of 4.2 percent and a market premium of 5 percent.

c. Compute the weighted average cost of capital of the new capital structure.

d. Compute the present value of the projected free cash flows to all debt and equity capital stakeholders at the weighted average cost of capital. Ignore the midyear adjustment related to the assumption that cash flows occur on average over the year. Apply the projected growth rate in free cash flows after Year 22 of 3 percent directly to the free cash flows of Year 22 in computing the continuing value.

e. Assume that the buyout group acquires May for the value determined in part d. Will May generate sufficient cash flow each year to service the interest on the debt, assuming that the realized free cash flows coincide with projections?

11.6 VALUING A LEVERAGED BUYOUT CANDIDATE.   Experian Information Systems (Experian) is a wholly owned subsidiary of TRW, a publicly traded company. The subsidiary has total assets of $555,443 thousand, long-term debt of $1,839 thousand, and common equity at book value of $402,759 thousand.

An equity buyout group is planning to acquire Experian from TRW in a leveraged buyout as of the beginning of Year 6. The group plans to finance the buyout with 60 percent debt that has an interest cost of 10 percent per year and 40 percent common equity. Analysts for the buyout group project free cash flows to all debt and equity capital stakeholders as follows (in thousands): Year 6, $52,300; Year 7, $54,915; Year 8, $57,112; Year 9, $59,396; Year 10, $62,366. Because Experian is not a publicly traded firm, it does not have a market equity beta. The company most comparable to Experian is Equifax. Equifax has an equity beta of .86. The market value of Equifax's debt is $366.5 thousand and its common equity is $4,436.8 thousand. Assume an income tax rate of 35 percent throughout this problem.

This problem sets forth the steps that the analyst might follow in valuing a leveraged buyout candidate.

Required

a. Compute the unlevered market equity (asset) beta of Equifax.

b. Assuming that the unlevered market equity beta of Equifax is appropriate for Experian, compute the equity beta of Experian after the buyout with its new capital structure.

c. Compute the weighted average cost of capital of Experian after the buyout. Assume a risk-free interest rate of 4.2 percent and a market premium of 5 percent.

d. The analysts at the buyout firm project that free cash flows for all debt and equity capital stakeholders of Experian will increase 5 percent each year after Year 10. Compute the present value of the free cash flows at the weighted average cost of capital. Ignore the midyear adjustment related to the assumption that cash flows occur on average over the year. Apply the projected growth rate in free cash flows after Year 10 of 5 percent directly to the free cash flows of Year 10 in computing the continuing value.

e. Assume that the buyout group acquires Experian for the value determined in part d. Will Experian generate sufficient cash flow each year to service the debt, assuming that actual free cash flows to all debt and equity capital stakeholders coincide with projections?

11.7 APPLYING VARIOUS PRESENT VALUE APPROACHES TO VALUATION.

An equity buyout group intends to acquire Wedgewood Products (Wedgewood) as of the beginning of Year 8. The buyout group intends to finance 40 percent of the acquisition price with 10 percent annual coupon debt, and 60 percent with common equity. The income tax rate is 40 percent. The cost of equity capital is 14 percent. Analysts at the buyout firm project the following free cash flows for all debt and equity capital stakeholders for Wedgewood (in millions): Year 8, $2,100; Year 9, $2,268; Year 10, $2,449; Year 11, $2,645; and Year 12, $2,857. The analysts project that free cash flows for all debt and equity capital stakeholders will increase 8 percent each year after Year 12.

Required

a. Compute the weighted average cost of capital for Wedgewood based on the proposed capital structure.

b. Compute the total purchase price of Wedgewood (debt plus common equity). To do this, discount the free cash flows for all debt and equity capital stakeholders at the weighted average cost of capital. Ignore the midyear adjustment related to the assumption that cash flows occur on average over the year. Apply the projected growth rate in free cash flows after Year 12 of 8 percent directly to the free cash flows of Year 12 in computing the continuing value.

c. Given the purchase price determined in part b, compute the total amount of debt, the annual interest cost, and the free cash flows to common equity shareholders for Year 8 to Year 12.

d. The present value of the free cash flows for common equity shareholders when discounted at the 14 percent cost of equity capital should equal the common equity portion of the total purchase price computed in part b. Determine the growth rate in free cash flows for common equity shareholders after Year 12 that will result in a present value of free cash flows for common equity shareholders equal to 60 percent of the purchase price computed in part b.

e. Why does the implied growth rate in free cash flows to common equity shareholders determined in part d differ from the 8 percent assumed growth rate in free cash flows for all debt and equity capital stakeholders?

f. The adjusted present value valuation approach separates the total value of the firm into the value of an all-equity firm and the value of the tax savings from interest deductions. Assume that the cost of unlevered equity is 11.33 percent. Compute the present value of the free cash flows to all debt and equity capital stakeholders at this unlevered equity cost. Compute the present value of the tax savings from interest expense deductions using the pre-tax cost of debt as the discount rate. Compare the total of these two present values to the purchase price determined in part b.

11.8 VALUING THE EQUITY OF A PRIVATELY HELD FIRM.   Refer to the pro forma financial statements for Massachusetts Stove Company (MSC) prepared for Case 10.1. The management of MSC desires to know the equity valuation implications of not adding gas stoves versus adding gas stoves under the best, most likely, and worst scenarios. Under the three scenarios from Case 10.1 and a fourth scenario involving not adding gas stoves, the projected free cash flows to common equity shareholders for Year 8 to Year 12, and assumed growth rates thereafter, are as follows:

Year	Best	Most Likely	Worst	No Gas
8	$ 73,967	$ 47,034	$ 3,027	$162,455
9	$ 52,143	$ −3,120	$−84,800	$132,708
10	$213,895	$135,939	$ 48,353	$106,021
11	$315,633	$178,510	$ 36,605	$ 81,840
12	$432,232	$220,010	$ 10,232	$ 60,007
13–17	20% Growth	10% Growth	Zero Growth	Zero Growth
After Year 17	10% Growth	5% Growth	Zero Growth	Zero Growth

MSC is not publicly traded and therefore does not have a market equity beta. Using the market equity beta of the one publicly traded wood and gas stove manufacturing firm and adjusting it for differences in the debt to equity ratio, income tax rate, and privately owned status of MSC yields a cost of equity capital for MSC of 13.55 percent.

Required

a. Calculate the value of the equity of MSC as of the end of Year 7 under each of the four scenarios. Ignore the midyear adjustment related to the assumption that cash flows occur on average over the year. Apply the growth rates in free cash flows to common equity shareholders after Year 12 directly to the free cash flow of the preceding year (that is, Year 13 free cash flow equals the free cash flow for Year 12 times the given growth rate; Year 18 free cash flow equals the free cash flow for Year 17 times the given growth rate).

b. How do these valuations affect your advice to the management of MSC regarding the addition of gas stoves to its wood stove line?

CASES

Note: To provide up-to-date integrated valuation cases, we include additional cases for Chapters 11 to 13 on the web site for this book (http://stickney. swlearning.com) instead of in the text.

CASE 11.1

HOLMES CORPORATION: LBO VALUATION

Holmes Corporation is a leading designer and manufacturer of material handling and process equipment for heavy industry in the United States and abroad. Its sales have more than doubled and its earnings increased more than sixfold in the past five years. In material handling, Holmes is a major producer of electric overhead and gantry cranes, ranging from 5 tons in capacity to 600-ton giants, the latter used primarily in nuclear and conventional power generating plants. It also builds underhung cranes and monorail systems for general industrial use carrying loads up to 40 tons, railcar movers, railroad and mass transit shop maintenance equipment, plus a broad line of advanced package conveyors. Holmes is a world leader in evaporation and crystallization systems, and also furnishes dryers, heat exchangers, and filters to complete its line of chemical processing equipment sold internationally to the chemical, fertilizer, food, drug, and paper industries. For the metallurgical industry, it designs and manufactures electric arc and induction furnaces, cupolas, ladles, and hot metal distribution equipment.

The information on the following pages appears in the Year 15 annual report of Holmes Corporation.

HIGHLIGHTS

	Year 15	Year 14
Net Sales	$102,698,836	$109,372,718
Net Earnings	6,601,908	6,583,360
Net Earnings per Share	3.62*	3.61*
Cash Dividends Paid	2,241,892	1,426,502
Cash Dividends per Share.................	1.22*	.78*
Shareholders' Equity	29,333,803	24,659,214
Shareholders' Equity per Share	16.07*	13.51*
Working Capital	23,100,863	19,029,626
Orders Received.........................	95,436,103	80,707,576
Unfilled Orders at End of Period	77,455,900	84,718,633
Average Number of Common Shares Outstanding During Period.............	1,824,853*	1,824,754*

*Adjusted for June, Year 15, and June, Year 14, 5-for-4 stock distributions.

Net Sales, Net Earnings, and Net Earnings per Share by Quarter
(adjusted for 5-for-4 stock distribution in June, Year 15, and June, Year 14)

	Year 15			Year 14		
	Net Sales	Net Earnings	Per Share	Net Sales	Net Earnings	Per Share
First Quarter...........	$ 25,931,457	$1,602,837	$ .88	$ 21,768,077	$1,126,470	$ .62
Second Quarter........	24,390,079	1,727,112	.95	28,514,298	1,716,910	.94
Third Quarter.........	25,327,226	1,505,118	.82	28,798,564	1,510,958	.82
Fourth Quarter........	27,050,074	1,766,841	.97	30,291,779	2,229,022	1.23
	$102,698,836	$6,601,908	$3.62	$109,372,718	$6,583,360	$3.61

Common Stock Prices and Cash Dividends Paid per Common Share by Quarter
(adjusted for 5-for-4 stock distribution in June, Year 15, and June, Year 14)

	Year 15			Year 14		
	Stock Prices		Cash Dividends Per Share	Stock Prices		Cash Dividends Per Share
	High	Low		High	Low	
First Quarter	22\frac{1}{2}$	18\frac{1}{2}$	$ .26	11\frac{1}{4}$	9\frac{1}{2}$	$.16
Second Quarter	25$\frac{1}{4}$	19$\frac{1}{2}$	.26	12$\frac{3}{8}$	8$\frac{7}{8}$	.16
Third Quarter	26$\frac{1}{4}$	19$\frac{3}{4}$	.325	15$\frac{7}{8}$	11$\frac{5}{8}$	.20
Fourth Quarter	28$\frac{1}{8}$	23$\frac{1}{4}$	.375	20$\frac{7}{8}$	15$\frac{7}{8}$	.26
			$1.22			$.78

MANAGEMENT'S REPORT TO SHAREHOLDERS

Year 15 was a pleasant surprise for all of us at Holmes Corporation. When the year started, it looked as though Year 15 would be a good year but not up to the record performance of Year 14. However, due to the excellent performance of our employees and the benefit of a favorable acquisition, Year 15 produced both record earnings and the largest cash dividend outlay in the company's 93-year history.

There is no doubt that some of the attractive orders received in late Year 12 and early Year 13 contributed to Year 15 profit. But of major significance was our organization's favorable response to several new management policies instituted to emphasize higher corporate profitability. Year 15 showed a net profit on net sales of 6.4 percent, which not only exceeded the 6.0 percent of last year but represents the highest net margin in several decades.

Net sales for the year were $102,698,836, down 6 percent from the $109,372,718 of a year ago but still the second largest volume in our history. Net earnings, however, set a new record at $6,601,908, or $3.62 per common share, which slightly exceeded the $6,583,360, or $3.61 per common share earned last year.

Cash dividends of $2,241,892 paid in Year 15 were 57 percent above the $1,426,502 paid a year ago. The record total resulted from your Board's approval of two increases during the year. When we implemented the 5-for-4 stock distribution in June, Year 15, we maintained the quarterly dividend rate of $.325 on the increased number of shares for the January payment. Then, in December, Year 15, we increased the quarterly rate to $.375 per share.

Year 15 certainly was not the most exuberant year in the capital equipment markets. Fortunately, our heavy involvement in ecology improvement, power generation, and international markets continued to serve us well, with the result that new orders of $95,436,103 were 18 percent over the $80,707,576 of Year 14.

Economists have predicted a substantial capital spending upturn for well over a year, but, so far, our customers have displayed stubborn reluctance to place new orders amid the uncertainty concerning the economy. Confidence is the answer. As soon as potential buyers can see clearly the future direction of the economy, we expect the unleashing of a large latent demand for capital goods, producing a much-expanded market for Holmes' products.

Fortunately, the accelerating pace of international markets continues to yield new business. Year 15 was an excellent year on the international front as our foreign customers continue to recognize our technological leadership in several product lines. Net sales of Holmes products shipped overseas and fees from foreign licensees amounted to $30,495,041, which represents a 31 percent increase over the $23,351,980 of a year ago.

Management fully recognizes and intends to take maximum advantage of our technological leadership in foreign lands. The latest manifestation of this policy was the acquisition of a controlling interest in Societé Francaise Holmes Fermont, our Swenson process equipment licensee located in Paris. Holmes and a partner started this firm 14 years ago as a sales and engineering organization to function in the Common Market. The company currently operates in the same mode. It owns no physical manufacturing assets, subcontracting all production. Its markets have expanded to include Spain and the East European countries.

Holmes Fermont is experiencing strong demand in Europe. For example, in early May, a $5.5 million order for a large potash crystallization system was received from a French engineering company representing a Russian client. Management estimates that Holmes Fermont will contribute approximately $6 to $8 million of net sales in Year 16.

Holmes' other wholly owned subsidiaries—Holmes Equipment Limited in Canada, Ermanco Incorporated in Michigan, and Holmes International, Inc., our FSC (Foreign Sales Corporation)—again contributed substantially to the success of Year 15. Holmes Equipment Limited registered its second best year. However, capital equipment markets in Canada have virtually come to a standstill in the past two quarters. Ermanco achieved the best year in its history, while Holmes International, Inc. had a truly exceptional year because of the very high level of activity in our international markets.

The financial condition of the company showed further improvement and is now unusually strong as a result of very stringent financial controls. Working capital increased to $23,100,863 from $19,029,626, a 21 percent improvement. Inventories decreased 6 percent from $18,559,231 to $17,491,741. The company currently has no long-term or short-term debt, and has considerable cash in short-term instruments. Much of our cash position, however, results from customers' advance payments which we will absorb as we make shipments on the contracts. Shareholders' equity increased 19 percent to $29,393,803 from $24,690,214 a year ago.

Plant equipment expenditures for the year were $1,172,057, down 18 percent from $1,426,347 of Year 14. Several appropriations approved during the year did not require expenditures because of delayed deliveries beyond Year 15. The major emphasis again was on our continuing program of improving capacity and efficiency through the purchase of numerically controlled machine tools. We expanded the Ermanco plant by 50 percent, but since this is a leasehold arrangement, we made only minor direct investment. We also improved the Canadian operation by adding more manufacturing space and installing energy-saving insulation.

Labor relations were excellent throughout the year. The Harvey plant continues to be nonunion. We negotiated a new labor contract at the Canadian plant, which extends to March 1, Year 17. The Pioneer Division in Alabama has a labor contract that does not expire until April, Year 16. While the union contract at Ermanco expired June 1, Year 15, work continues while negotiation proceeds on a new contract. We anticipate no difficulty in reaching a new agreement.

We exerted considerable effort during the year to improve Holmes' image in the investment community. Management held several informative meetings with security analyst groups to enhance the awareness of our activities and corporate performance.

The outlook for Year 16, while generally favorable, depends in part on the course of capital spending over the next several months. If the spending rate accelerates, the quickening pace of new orders, coupled with present backlogs, will provide the conditions for another fine year. On the other hand, if general industry continues the reluctant spending pattern of the last two years, Year 16 could be a year of maintaining market positions while awaiting better market conditions. Management takes an optimistic view and thus looks for a successful Year 16.

The achievement of record earnings and the highest profit margin in decades demonstrates the capability and the dedication of our employees. Management is most grateful for their efforts throughout the excellent year.

T.R. Varnum
President

T.L. Fuller
Chairman

March 15, Year 16

REVIEW OF OPERATIONS

Year 15 was a very active year although the pace was not at the hectic tempo of Year 14. It was a year that showed continued strong demand in some product areas but a dampened rate in others. The product areas that had some special economic circumstances enhancing demand fared well. For example, the continuing effort toward ecological improvement fostered excellent activity in Swenson process equipment. Likewise, the energy concern and the need for more electrical power generation capacity boded well for large overhead cranes. On the other hand, Holmes' products that relate to general industry and depend on the overall capital spending rate for new equipment experienced lesser demand, resulting in lower new orders and reduced backlogs. The affected products were small cranes, underhung cranes, railcar movers, and metallurgical equipment.

Year 15 was the first full year of operations under some major policy changes instituted to improve Holmes' profitability. The two primary revisions were the restructuring of our marketing effort along product division lines, and the conversion of the product division incentive plans to a profit-based formula. The corporate organization adapted extremely well to the new policies. The improved profit margin in Year 15, in substantial part, was a result of the changes.

International activity increased markedly during the year. Surging foreign business and the expressed objective to capitalize on Holmes' technological leadership overseas resulted in the elevation of Mr. R.E. Foster to officer status as Vice President-International. The year involved heavy commitments of the product division staffs, engineering groups, and manufacturing organization to such important contracts as the $14 million Swenson order for Poland, the $8 million Swenson project for Mexico, the $2 million crane order for Venezuela, and several millions of dollars of railcar movers for all areas of the world.

The acquisition of control and commencement of operating responsibility of Societé Francaise Holmes Fermont, the Swenson licensee in Paris, was a major milestone in our international strategy. This organization has the potential of becoming a very substantial contributor in the years immediately ahead. Its long-range market opportunities in Europe and Asia are excellent.

Material Handling Products

Material handling equipment activities portrayed conflicting trends. During the year, when total backlog decreased, the crane division backlog increased. This was a result of several multimillion dollar contracts for power plant cranes. The small crane market, on the other hand, experienced depressed conditions during most of the year as general industry withheld appropriations for new plant and equipment. The underhung crane market experienced similar conditions. However, as Congressional attitudes and policies on investment unfold, we expect capital spending to show a substantial upturn.

The Transportation Equipment Division secured the second order for orbital service bridges, a new product for the containment vessels of nuclear power plants. This design is unique and allows considerable cost savings in erecting and maintaining containment shells.

The Ermanco Conveyor Division completed its best year with the growing acceptance of the unique XenoROL design. We expanded the Grand Haven plant by 50 percent to effect further cost reduction and new concepts of marketing.

The railcar moving line continued to produce more business from international markets. We installed the new 11TM unit in six domestic locations, a product showing signs of exceptional performance. We shipped the first foreign 11TM machine to Sweden.

Process Equipment Products

Process equipment again accounted for slightly more than half of the year's business.

Swenson activity reached an all-time high level with much of the division's effort going into international projects. The large foreign orders required considerable additional work to cover the necessary documentation, metrification when required, and general liaison.

We engaged in considerably more subcontracting during the year to accommodate one-piece shipment of the huge vessels pioneered by Swenson to effect greater equipment economies. The division continued to expand the use of computerization for design work and contract administration. We developed more capability during the year to handle the many additional tasks associated with turnkey projects. Swenson research and development efforts accelerated in search of better technology and new products. We conducted pilot plant test work at our facilities and in the field to convert several sales prospects into new contracts.

The metallurgical business proceeded at a slower pace in Year 15. However, with construction activity showing early signs of improvement, and automotive and farm machinery manufacturers increasing their operating rates, we see intensified interest in metallurgical equipment.

FINANCIAL STATEMENTS

The financial statements of Holmes Corporation and related notes appear in Exhibits 11.11 through 11.13. Exhibit 11.14 presents five-year summary operating information for Holmes.

EXHIBIT 11.11

Holmes Corporation
Balance Sheet
(amounts in thousands)
(Case 11.1)

	Year 10	Year 11	Year 12	Year 13	Year 14	Year 15
Cash	$ 955	$ 962	$ 865	$ 1,247	$ 1,540	$ 3,857
Marketable Securities	0	0	0	0	0	2,990
Accounts/Notes Receivable	6,545	7,295	9,718	13,307	18,759	14,303
Inventories...................	7,298	8,685	12,797	20,426	18,559	17,492
Current Assets	$14,798	$16,942	$23,380	$34,980	$38,858	$38,642
Investments	0	0	0	0	0	422
Property, Plant, & Equipment......	12,216	12,445	13,126	13,792	14,903	15,876
Less: Accumulated Depreciation....	(7,846)	(8,236)	(8,558)	(8,988)	(9,258)	(9,703)
Other Assets...................	470	420	400	299	343	276
Total Assets.................	$19,638	$21,571	$28,348	$40,083	$44,846	$45,513
Accounts Payable–Trade	$ 2,894	$ 4,122	$ 6,496	$ 7,889	$ 6,779	$ 4,400
Notes Payable–Non-trade	0	0	700	3,500	0	0
Current Portion Long-term Debt...	170	170	170	170	170	0
Other Current Liabilities..........	550	1,022	3,888	8,624	12,879	11,142
Current Liabilities	$ 3,614	$ 5,314	$11,254	$20,183	$19,828	$15,542
Long-term Debt	680	510	340	170	0	0
Deferred Tax (NCL)	0	0	0	216	328	577
Other Noncurrent Liabilities.......	0	0	0	0	0	0
Total Liabilities...............	$ 4,294	$ 5,824	$11,594	$20,569	$20,156	$16,119
Common Stock.................	$ 2,927	$ 2,927	$ 2,927	$ 5,855	$ 7,303	$ 9,214
Additional Paid-in Capital	5,075	5,075	5,075	5,075	5,061	5,286
Retained Earnings...............	7,342	7,772	8,774	8,599	12,297	14,834
Accumulated Other Comprehensive Income	0	0	5	12	29	60
Treasury Stock..................	0	(27)	(27)	(27)	0	0
Total Shareholders' Equity	$15,344	$15,747	$16,754	$19,514	$24,690	$29,394
Total Liabilities and Shareholders' Equity	$19,638	$21,571	$28,348	$40,083	$44,846	$45,513

EXHIBIT 11.12				

Holmes Corporation
Income Statement
(amounts in thousands)
(Case 11.1)

	Year 11	Year 12	Year 13	Year 14	Year 15
Sales	$41,428	$53,541	$76,328	$109,373	$102,699
Other Revenues and Gains	0	41	0	0	211
Cost of Goods Sold	(33,269)	(43,142)	(60,000)	(85,364)	(80,260)
Selling and Administrative Expense	(6,175)	(7,215)	(9,325)	(13,416)	(12,090)
Other Expenses and Losses	(2)	0	(11)	(31)	(1)
Operating Income	$ 1,982	$ 3,225	$ 6,992	$ 10,562	$ 10,559
Interest Expense.	(43)	(21)	(284)	(276)	(13)
Income Tax Expense	(894)	(1,471)	(2,992)	(3,703)	(3,944)
Net Income	$ 1,045	$ 1,733	$ 3,716	$ 6,583	$ 6,602

NOTES TO CONSOLIDATED FINANCIAL STATEMENTS
YEAR 15 AND YEAR 14

Note A—Summary of Significant Accounting Policies

Significant accounting policies consistently applied appear below to assist the reader in reviewing the company's consolidated financial statements contained in this report.

Consolidation—The consolidated financial statements include the accounts of the company and its subsidiaries after eliminating all intercompany transactions and balances.

Inventories—Inventories generally appear at the lower of cost or market, with cost determined principally on a first-in, first-out method.

Property, plant, and equipment—Property, plant, and equipment appear at acquisition cost less accumulated depreciation. When the company retires or disposes of properties, it removes the related costs and accumulated depreciation from the respective accounts and credits, or charges any gain or loss to earnings. The company expenses maintenance and repairs as incurred. It capitalizes major betterments and renewals. Depreciation results from applying the straight-line method over the estimated useful lives of the assets as follows:

Buildings	30 to 45 years
Machinery and equipment	4 to 20 years
Furniture and fixtures	10 years

EXHIBIT 11.13

Holmes Corporation
Statement of Cash Flow
(amounts in thousands)
(Case 11.1)

	Year 11	Year 12	Year 13	Year 14	Year 15
Operations					
Net Income	$1,045	$1,733	$3,716	$ 6,583	$ 6,602
Depreciation and Amortization	491	490	513	586	643
Other Addbacks.......................	20	25	243	151	299
Other Subtractions	0	0	0	0	(97)
(Inc.) Dec. in Receivables	(750)	(2,424)	(3,589)	(5,452)	4,456
(Inc.) Dec. in Inventories	(1,387)	(4,111)	(7,629)	1,867	1,068
Inc. (Dec.) Accounts Payable–Trade	1,228	2,374	1,393	1,496	(2,608)
Inc. (Dec.) in Other Current Liabilities	473	2,865	4,737	1,649	(1,509)
Cash from Operations	$1,120	$ 952	$ (616)	$ 6,880	$ 8,854
Investing					
Fixed Assets Acquired (net)...............	$ (347)	$ (849)	$ (749)	$(1,426)	$(1,172)
Investments Acquired	0	0	0	0	(3,306)
Other Investing Transactions	45	0	81	(64)	39
Cash Flow from Investing	$ (302)	$ (849)	$ (668)	$(1,490)	$(4,439)
Financing					
Inc. in Short-term Borrowing..............	$ 0	$ 700	$2,800	$ $0	$ 0
Dec. in Short-term Borrowing	0	0	0	(3,500)	0
Inc. in Long-term Borrowing	0	0	0	0	0
Dec. in Long-term Borrowing..............	(170)	(170)	(170)	(170)	(170)
Issue of Capital Stock	0	0	0	0	315
Acquisition of Capital Stock	(27)	0	0	0	0
Dividends............................	(614)	(730)	(964)	(1,427)	(2,243)
Other Financing Transactions..............	0	0	0	0	0
Cash Flow from Financing.............	$ (811)	$ (200)	$1,666	$(5,097)	$(2,098)
Net Change in Cash.....................	$ 7	$ (97)	$ 382	$ 293	$ 2,317
Cash, Beginning of Year	955	962	865	1,247	1,540
Cash, End of Year	$ 962	$ 865	$1,247	$ 1,540	$ 3,857

	EXHIBIT 11.14				
Five-Year Summary of Operations for Holmes Corporation **(Case 11.1)**					
	Year 15	Year 14	Year 13	Year 12	Year 11
Orders Received................	$ 95,436,103	$ 80,707,576	$121,445,731	$89,466,793	$55,454,188
Net Sales.....................	102,698,836	109,372,718	76,327,664	53,540,699	41,427,702
Backlog of Unfilled Orders	77,455,900	84,718,633	113,383,775	68,265,708	32,339,614
Earnings before Taxes on					
Income	$ 10,546,213	$ 10,285,943	$ 6,708,072	$ 3,203,835	$ 1,939,414
Taxes on Income	3,944,305	3,702,583	2,991,947	1,470,489	894,257
Net Earnings	6,601,908	6,583,360	3,716,125	1,733,346	1,045,157
Net Property, Plant, and					
Equipment	$ 6,173,416	$ 5,644,590	$ 4,803,978	$ 4,568,372	$ 4,209,396
Net Additions to Property........	1,172,057	1,426,347	748,791	848,685	346,549
Depreciation and					
Amortization	643,231	585,735	513,402	490,133	491,217
Cash Dividends Paid	$ 2,242,892	$ 1,426,502	$ 963,935	$ 730,254	$ 614,378
Working Capital...............	23,100,463	19,029,626	14,796,931	12,126,491	11,627,875
Shareholders' Equity	29,393,803	24,690,214	19,514,358	15,754,166	15,747,116
Earnings per Common					
Share (1).................	$3.62	$3.61	$2.03	$.96	$.57
Dividends per Common					
Share (1).................	1.22	.78	.53	.40	.34
Book Value per Common					
Share (1).................	16.07	13.51	10.68	9.18	8.62
Number of Shareholders					
December 31...............	2,157	2,024	1,834	1,792	1,787
Number of Employees					
December 31...............	1,549	1,550	1,551	1,425	1,303
Shares of Common Outstanding					
December 31 (1)............	1,824,853	1,824,754	1,824,754	1,824,941	1,827,515
% Net Sales by Product Line					
Material Handling Equipment	46.1%	43.6%	51.3%	54.4%	63.0%
Processing Equipment..........	53.9%	56.4%	48.7%	45.6%	37.0%

Note: (1) Based on number of shares outstanding on December 31 adjusted for the 5-for-4 stock distributions in June, 1993, 1994, and 1995.

Intangible assets—The company has amortized the unallocated excess of cost of a subsidiary over net assets acquired (that is, goodwill) over a 17-year period. Beginning in Year 16, GAAP no longer requires amortization of goodwill.

Research and development costs—The company charges research and development costs to operations as incurred ($479,410 in Year 15, and $467,733 in Year 14).

Pension plans—The company and its subsidiaries have noncontributory pension plans covering substantially all of their employees. The company's policy is to fund accrued pension costs as determined by independent actuaries. Pension costs amounted to $471,826 in Year 15, and $366,802 in Year 14.

Revenue recognition—The company generally recognizes income on a percentage-of-completion basis. It records advance payments as received and reports them as a deduction from billings when earned. The company recognizes royalties, included in net sales, as income when received. Royalties total $656,043 in Year 15, and $723,930 in Year 14.

Income taxes—The company provides no income taxes on unremitted earnings of foreign subsidiaries since it anticipates no significant tax liabilities should foreign units remit such earnings. The company makes provision for deferred income taxes applicable to timing differences between financial statement and income tax accounting, principally on the earnings of a foreign sales subsidiary which existing statutes defer in part from current taxation.

Note B—Foreign Operations

The consolidated financial statements in Year 15 include net assets of $2,120,648 ($1,847,534 in Year 14), undistributed earnings of $2,061,441 ($1,808,752 in Year 14), sales of $7,287,566 ($8,603,225 in Year 14), and net income of $454,999 ($641,454 in Year 14) applicable to the Canadian subsidiary.

The company translates balance sheet accounts of the Canadian subsidiary into U.S. dollars at the exchange rates at the end of the year, and operating results at the average of exchange rates for the year.

Note C—Inventories

Inventories used in determining cost of sales appear below:

	Year 15	Year 14	Year 13
Raw materials and supplies.....	$ 8,889,147	$ 9,720,581	$ 8,900,911
Work in process	8,602,594	8,838,650	11,524,805
	$17,491,741	$18,559,231	$20,425,716

Note D—Short-term Borrowing

The company has short-term credit agreements which principally provide for loans of 90-day periods at varying interest rates. There were no borrowings in Year 15. In Year 14, the maximum borrowing at the end of any calendar month was $4,500,000 and the approximate average loan balance and weighted average interest rate, computed by using the days outstanding method, was $3,435,000 and 7.6 percent. There were no restrictions upon the company during the period of the loans and no compensating bank balance arrangements required by the lending institutions.

Note E—Income Taxes

Provision for income taxes consists of:

	Year 15	Year 14
Current		
Federal	$2,931,152	$2,633,663
State	466,113	483,240
Canadian	260,306	472,450
	$3,657,571	$3,589,353
Deferred		
Federal	$ 263,797	$ 91,524
Canadian	22,937	21,706
	286,734	113,230
	$3,944,305	$3,702,583

Reconciliation of the total provision for income taxes to the current federal statutory rate of 35 percent is as follows:

	Year 15		Year 14	
	Amount	%	Amount	%
Tax at statutory rate	$3,691,000	35.0%	$3,600,100	35.0%
State taxes, net of U.S.				
tax credit	302,973	2.9	314,106	3.1
All other items	(49,668)	(.5)	(211,623)	(2.1)
	$3,944,305	37.4%	$3,702,583	36.0%

Note F—Pensions

The components of pension expense appear below:

	Year 15	Year 14
Service Cost	$476,490	$429,700
Interest Cost.............................	567,159	446,605
Expected Return on Pension Investments.......	(558,373)	(494,083)
Amortization of Actuarial Gains and Losses.....	(13,450)	(15,420)
Pension Expense..........................	$471,826	$366,802

The funded status of the pension plan appears below.

	December 31,	
	Year 15	Year 14
Accumulated Benefit Obligation..............	$5,763,450	$5,325,291
Effect of Salary Increases....................	1,031,970	976,480
Projected Benefit Obligation..................	6,795,420	6,301,771
Pension Fund Assets	6,247,940	5,583,730
Excess Pension Obligation....................	$ 547,480	$ 718,041

Assumptions used in accounting for pensions appear below:

	Year 15	Year 14
Expected Return on Pension Assets............	10%	10%
Discount Rate for Projected Benefit Obligation ..	9%	8%
Salary Increases	5%	5%

Note G—Common Stock

As of March 20, Year 15, the company increased the authorized number of shares of common stock from 1,800,000 shares to 5,000,000 shares.

On December 29, Year 15, the company increased its equity interest (from 45 percent to 85 percent) in Societé Francaise Holmes Fermont, a French affiliate, in exchange for 18,040 of its common shares in a transaction accounted for as a purchase. The company credited the excess of the fair value ($224,373) of the company's shares issued over their par value ($90,200) to additional contributed capital. The excess of the purchase cost over the underlying value of the assets acquired was insignificant.

The company made a 25 percent common stock distribution on June 15, Year 14, and on June 19, Year 15, resulting in increases of 291,915 shares in 1994 and 364,433 shares in Year 15, respectively. We capitalized the par value of these additional shares by a transfer of $1,457,575 in Year 14 and $1,822,165 in Year 15 from retained earnings to the common stock account. In Year 14 and Year 15, we paid cash of $2,611 and $15,340, respectively, in lieu of fractional share interests.

In addition, the company retired 2,570 shares of treasury stock in June, Year 14. The earnings and dividends per share for Year 14 and Year 15 in the accompanying consolidated financial statements reflect the 25 percent stock distributions.

Note H—Contingent Liabilities

The company has certain contingent liabilities with respect to litigation and claims arising in the ordinary course of business. The company cannot determine the ultimate disposition of these contingent liabilities but, in the opinion of management, they will not result in any material effect upon the company's consolidated financial position or results of operations.

Note I—Quarterly Data (unaudited)

Quarterly sales, gross profit, net earnings, and earnings per share for Year 15 appear below:

	Net Sales	Gross Profit	Net Earnings	Earnings per Share
First	$ 25,931,457	$ 5,606,013	$1,602,837	$ .88
Second	24,390,079	6,148,725	1,727,112	.95
Third	25,327,226	5,706,407	1,505,118	.82
Fourth	27,050,074	4,977,774	1,766,841	.97
Year	$102,698,836	$22,438,919	$6,601,908	$3.62

The first quarterly results are restated for the 25 percent stock distribution on June 19, Year 15.

Auditors' Report

Board of Directors and Stockholders
Holmes Corporation

We have examined the consolidated balance sheets of Holmes Corporation and Subsidiaries as of December 31, Year 15 and Year 14, and the related consolidated statements of earnings and cash flows for the years then ended. Our examination was made in accordance with generally accepted auditing standards, and accordingly included such tests of the accounting records and such other auditing procedures as we considered necessary in the circumstances.

In our opinion, the financial statements referred to above present fairly the consolidated financial position of Holmes Corporation and Subsidiaries at December 31,

Year 15 and Year 14, and the consolidated results of their operations and changes in cash flows for the years then ended, in conformity with generally accepted accounting principles applied on a consistent basis.

SBW, LLP
Chicago, Illinois
March 15, Year 16

Required

A group of Holmes' top management is interested in acquiring Holmes in a leveraged buyout.

 a. Describe briefly the factors that make Holmes an attractive and, conversely, an unattractive leveraged buyout candidate.
 b. (This question requires coverage of Chapter 10.) Prepare pro forma financial statements for Holmes Corporation for Year 16 through Year 20 excluding all financing (that is, project the amount of operating income after taxes, assets, and cash flows from operating and investing activities). State the underlying assumptions made.
 c. (This question requires coverage of Chapter 11.) Ascertain the value of Holmes' common shareholders' equity using the present value of its future cash flows valuation approach. Assume a risk-free interest rate of 4.2 percent and a market premium of 5 percent. Ignore the midyear adjustment related to the assumption that cash flows occur on average over the year for this and the remaining parts of this case. Note that information in part e below may be helpful in this valuation. Assume the following financing structure for the leveraged buyout:

Type	Proportion	Interest Rate	Term
Term Debt	50%	8%	7-Year Amortization[a]
Subordinated Debt..........	25	12%	10-Year Amortization[a]
Shareholders' Equity.........	25		
	100%		

[a]Holmes must repay principal and interest in equal annual payments.

 d. (This question requires coverage of Chapter 12.) Ascertain the value of Holmes' common shareholders' equity using the residual income approach.
 e. (This question requires coverage of Chapter 13.) Ascertain the value of Holmes' common shareholders' equity using the residual ROCE model, and the price-to-earnings ratio and the market value to book value of comparable companies' approaches. Selected data for similar companies for Year 15 appear below (amounts in millions):

	Agee Robotics	GI Handling Systems	LJG Industries	Gelas Corp.
Industry:	Conveyor Systems	Conveyor Systems	Cranes	Industrial Furnaces
Sales	$4,214	$28,998	$123,034	$75,830
Net Income	$ 309	$ 2,020	$ 9,872	$ 5,117
Assets	$2,634	$15,197	$ 72,518	$41,665
Long-term Debt.	$ 736	$ 5,098	$ 23,745	$ 8,869
Common Shareholders' Equity	$1,551	$ 7,473	$ 38,939	$26,884
Market Value of Common Equity. . .	$6,915	$20,000	$102,667	$41,962
Market Beta	1.12	.88	.99	.93

f. Would you attempt to acquire Holmes Corporation after completing the analyses in parts a to e? If not, how would you change the analyses to make this an attractive leveraged buyout?

Chapter 12

VALUATION: EARNINGS-BASED APPROACHES

Learning Objectives

1. Understand earnings-based valuation, particularly the value-relevance of earnings versus dividends versus cash flows.

2. Understand the conceptual and practical strengths and weaknesses of the residual income valuation method.

3. Develop conceptual understanding and practical techniques to deal with the important issues involved in estimating firm value using the present value of expected future residual income:
   (a) the role of book values, earnings, dividends, and "clean surplus" accounting,
   (b) required (or "normal") income versus residual (or "abnormal") income,
   (c) the forecast horizon and continuing value, and
   (d) risk, discount rates, and the cost of capital.

4. Apply all of these techniques to estimate common shareholders' equity value using the residual income valuation method. For completeness, develop a conceptual and practical understanding of the dividends-based valuation method. Demonstrate the residual income and dividends valuation approaches by valuing the common shareholders' equity of PepsiCo.

5. Assess the sensitivity of firm value estimates to key valuation parameters, such as discount rates and expected long-term growth rates.

6. Identify potential causes of valuation errors if the residual income, free cash flows, and dividends valuations do not determine identical value estimates.

INTRODUCTION AND OVERVIEW

The earnings number is the single most widely followed measure of firm performance. The accounting profession and firms themselves have designed the accrual accounting process to measure earnings as the "bottom line" of the firm's profitability each period. As a result, firms' earnings numbers play central roles as the primary measures of performance used in the capital markets for capital allocation.

Because of the demand in the capital markets for earnings numbers, firms usually release quarterly and annual income numbers to the public as soon as the accountants have prepared and verified them, often weeks *before* the firms distribute their detailed quarterly and annual income statements, balance sheets, and statements of cash flows. Firms commonly release earnings numbers during conference calls and press conferences that investors, analysts, managers, board members, and the financial press attend. Analysts often spend enormous time and effort building (and monitoring and revising) forecasts of firms' upcoming quarterly and annual earnings numbers. Sell-side analysts sell their earnings forecasts to interested investors, brokers, and fund managers. Commercial firms such as I/B/E/S and First Call have built businesses on compiling and distributing daily data on analysts' earnings forecasts. The financial media provide daily coverage of firms' earnings announcements. For example, the *Wall Street Journal* provides a summary report of firms' earnings announcements each day in the "Earnings Digest" section. The *Wall Street Journal* also reports daily data on each firm's stock trading activity, including a daily price-earnings ratio. In fact, because of the demand for and attention to earnings among capital markets participants, earnings numbers are the *only* accounting numbers that U.S. GAAP requires firms to report scaled on a *per-share* basis (see related discussion in Chapter 4).[1]

When firms announce earnings, their share prices usually react quickly to the announcement, and the direction and magnitude of the market's reaction depends on the direction and magnitude of the earnings news relative to the market's expectations. Firms that announce earnings that exceed the market's expectations often experience significant jumps in share price in the days following the announcement. Likewise, firms that announce earnings that fall short of the market's expectations usually experience a decline in share price, and, in some circumstances, severe drops during the days following the announcement. As we have noted in several prior chapters, the seminal Ball and Brown (1968) study[2] and many other research studies have shown that firms' stock returns are highly positively correlated with earnings numbers.

Because of the importance of earnings to investors and other stakeholders, corporate governance processes often reward and punish managers based on whether firm performance meets certain earnings targets. Managers that meet or exceed specified earnings targets are usually rewarded with substantial bonuses. Managers that consistently fall short of earnings targets typically need to explain why they failed to

---

[1]Financial Accounting Standards Board, *Statement of Financial Accounting Standard No. 128*, "Earnings per Share," 1997.

[2]Ray Ball and Philip Brown, "An Evaluation of Accounting Income Numbers," *Journal of Accounting Research*, Autumn 1968, pp. 159–178.

meet the targets, and if the explanations are not satisfactory, they may find themselves fired and replaced.

It is natural that accounting earnings numbers provide a basis for valuation because earnings are the primary measures of firm performance in the accrual accounting system, and because earnings numbers play such a critical role in the capital markets and in corporate management. This chapter describes the conceptual and practical strengths and weaknesses of the earnings-based valuation model known as the residual income valuation model. The residual income valuation model uses expected future net income and the book value of common shareholders' equity as the basis for valuation.

To describe and explain the residual income valuation model, and to demonstrate the practical application of the model, this chapter takes four important steps. Exhibit 12.1 illustrates these steps, and some of the key questions we will address in this chapter. First, we describe the rationale behind earnings-based valuation. Second, we describe and explain the theoretical and conceptual foundation for residual income valuation, with a number of illustrations and examples. Third, we demonstrate the practical application of the residual income model by applying the model to value the common shareholders' equity of PepsiCo. As we apply the model to PepsiCo, we describe the key measurement and implementation issues. Fourth, we come full circle in valuation by describing and applying the dividends-based valuation model, demonstrating the equivalence (and internal consistency) in dividends, free cash flows, and residual income valuation. We demonstrate that these three valuation approaches yield identical valuations if applied properly. We also help the analyst understand where to look to identify valuation errors if the three valuation models do not agree.

The residual income valuation model in this chapter provides a powerful approach that is a complementary equivalent to the classical dividends-based valuation approach and to the free cash-flow-based valuation approach presented in Chapter 11. The residual income valuation model in this chapter forms the basis for the market-based multiples described in Chapter 13, including the market-to-book ratio and the price-earnings ratio.

RATIONALE FOR EARNINGS-BASED VALUATION

As Exhibit 12.1 illustrates, the first step we need to take to understand residual income valuation is to understand how accrual accounting earnings can be a valid foundation for value. As Chapter 11 discusses, economic theory teaches that the value of any resource equals the present value of the expected future returns from the resource discounted at a rate that reflects the risk inherent in those expected returns. We start with a general model for the present value of a security (denoted as V_0, with present value denoted as of time t = 0) with an expected life of n future periods, as follows:[3]

---

[3]Throughout this chapter, t refers to accounting periods. The valuation process determines an estimate of firm value, denoted V_0, in present value as of today, when t=0. The period t=1 refers to the first accounting period being discounted to present value. Period t=n is the period of the expected final, or liquidating, return.

EXHIBIT 12.1
Steps to Understanding Residual Income Valuation

---

1. Rationale
- What is the rationale for using earnings as a basis for valuation?
- What are the practical advantages and common concerns associated with using earnings to determine common shareholders' equity value?

2. Theoretical and Conceptual Foundations for Residual Income Valuation
- What theories and concepts support residual income valuation?
- How do we measure residual income? What does it represent?

3. Practical Applications
- What steps do we take to determine value using residual income valuation methods?
- What value estimate do we get from this approach for the common shareholders' equity of PepsiCo? How does that value estimate compare with the estimate from Chapter 11 using the free cash flows approach?
- What implementation issues do we need to understand in order to use the residual income model?

4. Linking Residual Income Valuation to Dividends Valuation and Free Cash Flow Valuation
- How do we measure value using dividends?
- What value estimate do we obtain by applying the dividends value model to PepsiCo? Does it agree with the free cash flow value estimate and the residual income value estimate?
- What if the value estimates do not agree across these three models? Where do we look for possible valuation errors?

$$V_0 = \sum_{t=1}^{n} \frac{Expected\ Future\ Returns_t}{(1 + Discount\ Rate)^t}$$

As Chapter 11 describes, in theory, the value of a share of common equity should equal the present value of the *expected future dividends* the shareholder will receive.[4] Dividends are the fundamental, value-relevant attribute of expected future returns because they represent the distribution of wealth from the firm to the shareholders. The equity shareholder receives dividends as the payoffs from holding a share, including the final "liquidating" dividend when the firm liquidates the share or the investor sells the share. Thus, to value a firm's shares using dividends, one must forecast dividends over the life of the firm (or the expected length of time the share will be held), including the final liquidating dividend.

---

[4]John Burr Williams, *The Theory of Investment and Value*, Cambridge, Mass.: Harvard University Press, 1938.

The residual income valuation approach presented in this chapter is parallel to the dividends-based valuation approach and to the cash-flow-based valuation approach, except that it uses a different measure of returns. The residual income valuation approach uses expected future earnings and book value of common shareholders equity to determine the value-relevant expected future returns to the investor (that is, the numerator of the general value model above), in place of future dividends or future free cash flows. The rationale for using expected earnings as a basis for valuation is straightforward: Earnings provide the ultimate measure of profitability. Earnings numbers measure the net profits of the firm for the shareholders, the ultimate residual claimants of the performance and risk of the firm. Over the life of the firm, earnings measure the total wealth created by the firm for the shareholders. Instead of focusing valuation on wealth distribution through dividends payments, and instead of focusing valuation on dividend-paying capacity in free cash flows, residual income valuation focuses on *earnings as a periodic measure of shareholder wealth creation.*

Accrual accounting produces periodic performance statements—income statements that measure and report net income—that are informative estimates of the net amount of economic resources earned and consumed by the firm each period. Accrual accounting also produces periodic statements of financial position—balance sheets that measure assets, liabilities, and shareholders' equity—that report the economic resources that the firm can control and use to produce expected future economic benefits and the claims on those resources. To produce informative measures of financial performance and position that are relevant and reliable, the accounting profession develops and implements accounting principles through which the accrual accounting process measures income, assets, liabilities, and shareholders' equity using estimates of economic resources earned and consumed each period, rather than just relying on simplistic measures of cash inflows and cash outflows, which often do not reflect economic value received and consumed each period. For some examples, consider that to measure a firm's economic performance and position in a given period, it makes sense to measure the:

- revenues *earned* from operating performance during that period, not just those activities that resulted in cash inflows that period;
- expenses incurred for resources that were *consumed* in that period, not just those activities that resulted in cash outflows that period;
- portion of the long-lived resources consumed during that period, such as periodic depreciation of a building each year of its useful life, rather than recognizing the full cost of the building in the year the firm pays for it and ignoring the consumption of the building in all the other years that the firm uses it;
- cost of commitments made during that period to pay retirement benefits to employees in future periods, rather than ignoring those commitments and only measuring their effects when the firm pays cash.

Accrual accounting earnings are far from perfect performance measures, but, by virtue of accounting principles, they are closer to the firm's underlying economic performance in a given period than are cash flows.

Over the life of a firm, the capital invested in the firm by the shareholders plus the income of the firm (the wealth created by the firm for the shareholders) will reflect the value of the firm to the shareholders. Cash is the ultimate medium of exchange; therefore, over the life of the firm, the cash flows that are distributable to shareholders will equal the shareholders' capital investments in the firm plus the lifetime earnings of the firm. Thus, valuation of shareholders' equity in a firm using the capital invested in the firm plus earnings over the life of the firm is equivalent to valuation using distributable cash flows over the life of the firm, and both are equivalent to valuation using dividends over the life of the firm.[5]

EARNINGS-BASED VALUATION: PRACTICAL ADVANTAGES AND COMMON CONCERNS

Although earnings, cash flows, and dividends are equally valid bases for valuation, the emphasis placed on earnings by firms and the capital markets makes it a natural starting point for valuation. Earnings numbers provide a measure of performance each period that can be used more directly and efficiently in valuation than cash flows or dividends. Earnings numbers are directly aligned with the focus of the capital markets and corporate managers and boards of directors on periodic performance measurement. Analysts, investors, the capital markets, managers, boards, and the financial press focus on earnings forecasts and earnings reports, rather than free cash flow forecasts and free cash flow amounts. Firms usually don't hold press conferences to announce free cash flows. Analysts rarely publish free cash flow forecasts. The *Wall Street Journal* does not publish a "free cash flow digest" every day. Boards of directors do not establish managers' bonus plans based on achieving free cash flow targets. As a practical matter, it is therefore more direct for the analyst to go straight from earnings into valuation, rather than taking a detour to free cash flows.[6]

As Exhibit 12.2 depicts, estimating firm value using free cash flows adds an intermediary step to the valuation process. As Chapter 11 discusses, valuing a firm using

---

[5]Over sufficiently long time periods, net income equals free cash flows to common equity. The effect of year-end accruals to convert cash flows to net income lessens as the measurement period lengthens. The correlation between firms' earnings and stock returns increases as the earnings measurement interval increases. The values of R^2 for various intervals are: one year, 5 percent; two years, 15 percent; five years, 33 percent, 10 years, 63 percent. See Peter D. Easton, Trevor S. Harris, and James A. Ohlson, "Aggregate Accounting Earnings Can Explain Most of Security Returns," *Journal of Accounting and Economics* (1992), pp. 119–142.

[6]Considerable research interest has been directed at the question as to whether cash flows or earnings are more closely associated with stock returns. This research indicates that both earnings and cash flows are similarly correlated with stock returns over long periods (for example, five-year periods), but that, for shorter periods, earnings show a higher association with stock returns than cash flows. See Patricia M. Dechow, "Accounting Earnings and Cash Flows as Measures of Firm Performance: The Role of Accounting Accruals," *Journal of Accounting and Economics* (1994), pp. 3–42; C.S. Cheng, Chao-Shin Liu, and Thomas F. Schaefer, "Earnings Permanence and the Incremental Information Content of Cash Flow from Operations," *Journal of Accounting Research* (Spring 1996), pp. 173–181; Richard G. Sloan, "Do Stock Prices Fully Reflect Information in Accruals and Cash Flows about Future Earnings," *The Accounting Review* (July 1996), pp. 289–315.

free cash flows requires the analyst to initially forecast future income statements and balance sheets. Then the analyst derives the implied forecasts of cash flows from these income statements and balance sheets by making adjustments for the accruals in earnings, for the cash flows invested in working capital, and for capital expenditures. Then the analyst uses these cash flows to determine free cash flows and to compute value. Under the residual income model, valuation can begin immediately after the analyst forecasts future income statements and balance sheets. The two valuations should ultimately be the same, but the free cash flows approach requires more computations, which increases the potential for an error.

Economists sometimes argue that earnings are not a value-relevant attribute on which to base valuation. They assert that earnings are not as reliable or as meaningful as cash or dividends for valuing investments. When considering earnings, economists sometimes point out that firms pay dividends in cash, not earnings; investors can spend cash but cannot spend earnings for future consumption. This concern is alleviated in valuation, however, by the fact that, over the life of the firm, the present values of future earnings, cash flows, and dividends will be equal.

Some economists worry that accrual accounting earnings numbers reflect accounting methods that no longer reflect underlying economic values; for example, depreciation or amortization expenses based on outdated acquisition cost valuations of assets; or expenses for research and development that have turned out to be successful; or advertising expenses that have created economically valuable brand equity. Value measurement based on expected earnings over the remaining life of the firm alleviates this concern. Over time, the accrual accounting process will ultimately self-correct measurement errors in accounting numbers. For example, if fixed asset book values are "too high" or "too low" for a company, over time (and it usually does not take long) accrual accounting will correct itself because the subsequent depreciation

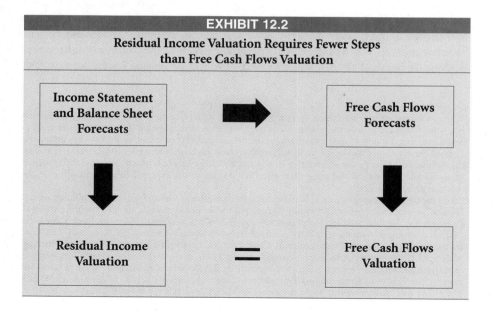

EXHIBIT 12.2

Residual Income Valuation Requires Fewer Steps than Free Cash Flows Valuation

| Income Statement and Balance Sheet Forecasts | → | Free Cash Flows Forecasts |

| Residual Income Valuation | = | Free Cash Flows Valuation |

expenses will be "too high" or "too low," accordingly. If the current balance sheet does not recognize intellectual capital value created by successful research and development, or brand value created by successful marketing, accrual accounting will correct itself over time as the firm earns returns on this intangible capital.[7]

Some economists voice concerns that earnings can be subject to purposeful management by a firm. To be sure, analysts should always be alert to the possibility that earnings management may occur in some periods by some firms, but this is more of a concern about earnings as a measure of current period performance than about a firm's lifetime expected earnings for valuation purposes. In addition, this concern is not really an issue for valuation because residual income valuation is based on the *analyst's forecasts* of expected future earnings, not on past earnings reports that the firm may have managed. Ironically, cash flows in a given period are explicitly managed. Cash flows each period depend on cash inflows and outflows, which the firm can control by accelerating or delaying certain cash payments or cash collections in that particular period. Over the remaining lifetime of the firm, which is the focus of the analyst's forecasting and valuation, the firm's earnings and cash flows are determined ultimately by the success of the firm's operating, investing, and financing activities, not by the manipulation of past earnings or cash flows.

THEORETICAL AND CONCEPTUAL FOUNDATIONS FOR RESIDUAL INCOME VALUATION[8]

As Exhibit 12.1 illustrates, the second step toward understanding residual income valuation is to establish the theoretical and conceptual foundation for the residual income valuation approach. The foundation for residual income valuation is the classical dividends-based valuation model in which the value of common shareholders' equity in the firm is the present value of all future dividends to shareholders over the life of the firm. In dividends-based valuation, we define dividends to be all-inclusive measures of the cash flows between the firm and the common equity shareholders. Therefore, "all-inclusive dividends" (which we denote D) encompass cash

---

[7]When an analyst asserts that a firm's current balance sheet accounting numbers do not reflect underlying economic values, how does the analyst know that? When an analyst asserts that a firm's balance sheet omits a valuable intangible asset in the form of intellectual property or brand equity, how has the analyst assessed the amount of the omission? Usually, analysts base assertions like these on their assessments that the firm will generate future profits from operations that utilize these economic assets. Earnings-based valuation captures *exactly* the same idea. Firm value depends on expected future earnings over the remaining life of the firm.

[8]Credit for the rigorous development of the residual income valuation model goes to James Ohlson in: J.A. Ohlson, "A Synthesis of Security Valuation Theory and the Role of Dividends, Cash Flows, and Earnings," *Contemporary Accounting Research* (Spring 1990), pp. 648–676; J.A. Ohlson, "Earnings, Book Values, and Dividends in Equity Valuation," *Contemporary Accounting Research* (Spring 1995), pp. 661–687; G.A. Feltham and J.A. Ohlson, "Valuation and Clean Surplus Accounting for Operating and Financial Activities," *Contemporary Accounting Research* (Spring 1995), pp. 216–230. The ideas underlying the earnings-based valuation approach trace to early work by G.A.D. Preinreich, "Annual Survey of Economic Theory: The Theory of Depreciation," *Econometrica* (1938), pp. 219–241, and E. Edwards and P.W. Bell, *The Theory and Measurement of Business Income* (Berkeley, CA: University of California Press), 1961.

flows from the firm to shareholders through periodic dividend payments, stock buy-backs, and the firm's liquidating dividend, as well as cash flows from the sharehold-ers to the firm when the firm issues shares (in a sense, *negative* dividends).

As Chapter 11 discusses, we assume that we can estimate (using the CAPM or some other asset-pricing model) an appropriate rate of return (denoted R_E) that the capital markets expect for the risk associated with common equity capital in the firm. The dividends-based valuation approach expresses the value of common sharehold-ers' equity (denoted V_0) as the present value of all expected future all-inclusive divi-dends with the following general model:

$$V_0 = \sum_{t=1}^{\infty} \frac{D_t}{(1+R_E)^t} = \frac{D_1}{(1+R_E)^1} + \frac{D_2}{(1+R_E)^2} + \frac{D_3}{(1+R_E)^3} + \cdots$$

Analysts and investors commonly find it desirable to identify and forecast economic variables that determine the firm's future dividends and that can therefore substitute for dividends to yield a valuation that is equivalent to the value estimate one would obtain using dividends. Accounting numbers provide a solution. Accounting for the book value of common shareholders' equity (denoted BV) in a firm can be expressed as follows:

$$BV_t = BV_{t-1} + NI_t - D_t$$

In this expression, book value of common shareholders' equity at the end of Year t (BV_t) is equal to book value at the end of Year t−1 (BV_{t-1}) plus net income for Year t (NI_t) minus the all-inclusive dividends during Year t (D_t). We assume that account-ing for net income and book value of shareholders' equity follows *clean surplus accounting*. Clean surplus accounting simply means net income includes all of the recognized elements of income of the firm for common equity shareholders (that is, all of the amounts in the income statement and all of the other comprehensive income items) and dividends include all direct capital transactions between the firm and the common equity shareholders. We can rearrange the accounting equation for the book value of common shareholders' equity to isolate dividends, as follows:

$$D_t = NI_t + BV_{t-1} - BV_t$$

In this expression, dividends equal net income plus the change in book value from transactions with common shareholders.

Example 1. Suppose the firm had shareholders' equity on the balance sheet at a book value of $100 at the end of Year t−1. Suppose during Year t, the firm earns net income of $50, pays dividends to shareholders of $25, issues new stock to raise $10 of capital, and uses $5 to repurchase common shares. The book value of sharehold-ers' equity the end of Year t is:

$$BV_t = BV_{t-1} + NI_t - D_t = \$100 + \$50 - \$25 + \$10 - \$5 = \$100 + \$50 - \$20 = \$130$$

In this example, all-inclusive dividends (D_t) in year t amount to $20. Using the expression for dividends shows that:

$$D_t = NI_t + BV_{t-1} - BV_t = \$50 + \$100 - \$130 = \$20$$

Because dividends equal net income plus the change in book value of common shareholders' equity, we can substitute net income plus the change in the book value of common shareholders' equity into the dividends valuation model, as follows:

$$V_0 = \sum_{t=1}^{\infty} \frac{D_t}{(1+R_E)^t} = \sum_{t=1}^{\infty} \frac{NI_t + BV_{t-1} - BV_t}{(1+R_E)^t}$$

$$= \frac{NI_1 + BV_0 - BV_1}{(1+R_E)^1} + \frac{NI_2 + BV_1 - BV_2}{(1+R_E)^2} + \frac{NI_3 + BV_2 - BV_3}{(1+R_E)^3} + \cdots$$

Algebraically,

$$\frac{BV_{t-1}}{(1+R_E)^t} = \frac{BV_{t-1}}{(1+R_E)^{t-1}} - \frac{R_E \times BV_{t-1}}{(1+R_E)^t}$$

We substitute the right-hand side expression for the present value of BV_{t-1} into the equation for V_0, rearrange terms, and simplify to obtain the following expression for the *residual income valuation model*—a valuation model for common shareholders' equity that is consistent with dividends-based valuation, yet relies on earnings and book values:

$$V_0 = BV_0 + \sum_{t=1}^{\infty} \frac{NI_t - (R_E \times BV_{t-1})}{(1+R_E)^t}$$

$$= BV_0 + \frac{NI_1 - (R_E \times BV_0)}{(1+R_E)^1} + \frac{NI_2 - (R_E \times BV_1)}{(1+R_E)^2} + \frac{NI_3 - (R_E \times BV_2)}{(1+R_E)^3} + \cdots$$

The intuition for the residual income valuation model is straightforward. The value of common shareholders' equity is equal to the book value of common equity, plus the present value of all expected future *residual income*, which is the amount by which expected future earnings exceed the required earnings, for the remaining life of the firm. The *required earnings* (also known as *normal earnings*) of the firm equals the product of the required rate of return on common equity capital times the book value of common equity capital at the beginning of the period. We compute required earnings for period t as $R_E \times BV_{t-1}$. Required earnings reflect the earnings the firm must earn in period t simply to provide a return to common equity that is equal to the cost of common equity capital.

We measure *residual income* (sometimes called *abnormal earnings*) by the subtraction term $NI_t - (R_E \times BV_{t-1})$. Residual income is the difference between the net income the analyst expects the firm to generate and the required earnings of the firm. Residual income in period t measures the amount of wealth that the analyst expects the firm to earn in period t for common equity shareholders above (or below) the earnings required to cover the cost of equity capital. If the analyst expects the firm will generate net income each period in the future that is exactly equal to required earnings (that is, $NI_t - (R_E \times BV_{t-1}) = 0$ for all future periods), then the analyst expects the firm to exactly cover the cost of equity capital, no more, no less. In that case, the value of the firm is exactly equal to the book value of common shareholders' equity. On the other hand, if the analyst expects the firm will earn positive amounts of residual income, then the value of the firm is equal to book value of common shareholders' equity plus the present value of all expected future residual income.[9]

Example 2. Suppose investors have invested $10,000 in common equity in a company. Given the risk of the company, the investors expect to earn a 12 percent return, and they expect the company to pay out 100 percent of income in dividends each year. The required earnings of the company each period are:

$$R_E \times BV_{t-1} = 0.12 \times \$10,000 = \$1,200$$

Suppose the investors forecast that the company will generate exactly $1,200 in net income each year. The investors should compute the residual income of the firm as follows:

$$NI_t - (R_E \times BV_{t-1}) = \$1,200 - (0.12 \times \$10,000) = \$0$$

Using the residual income approach, investors would value this firm based on book value plus expected future residual income as follows:

$$V_0 = BV_0 + \sum_{t=1}^{\infty} \frac{NI_t - (R_E \times BV_{t-1})}{(1 + R_E)^t}$$

$$= \$10,000 + \sum_{t=1}^{\infty} \frac{\$12,000_t - (0.12 \times \$10,000_{t-1})}{(1 + 0.12)^t}$$

$$= \$10,000 + \sum_{t=1}^{\infty} \frac{\$0_t}{(1 + 0.12)^t} = \$10,000$$

In this case, the firm's expected future income exactly equals the required level of earnings necessary to cover the cost of equity capital, so residual income is zero, and the value of the firm is equal to the book value of common equity invested in the firm. The value of the firm under the residual income model is identical to the value determined using the dividends valuation model, which would value the company as a stream of dividends in perpetuity with no growth:

$$V_0 = \frac{\$1,200}{.12} = \$10,000$$

---

[9]Recent applications of the concept of residual income in valuation and corporate governance practices can be found in G.B. Stewart, *The Quest for Value* (New York: Harper Collins), 1991, and in the expanding literature on EVA®. As noted earlier, the concept of residual income in the economics literature and the accounting literature predates the popularization of "Economic Value Added" by decades.

Example 3. Now assume the same facts as in Example 2, but suppose investors expect the firm will earn net income of $1,000 in Year +1, $2,000 in Year +2, $1,500 in Year +3, and $1,200 each year thereafter. Assume the firm maintains 100 percent dividend payout. Investors should compute the residual income valuation as follows:

$$V_0 = BV_0 + \sum_{t=1}^{\infty} \frac{NI_t - (R_E \times BV_{t-1})}{(1+R_E)^t}$$

$$= \$10,000 + \frac{\$1,000 - (0.12 \times \$10,000)}{(1.12)^1} + \frac{\$2,000 - (0.12 \times \$10,000)}{(1.12)^2}$$

$$+ \frac{\$1,500 - (0.12 \times \$10,000)}{(1.12)^3} + \sum_{t=4}^{\infty} \frac{\$1,200_t - (0.12 \times \$10,000_{t-1})}{(1+0.12)^t}$$

$$= \$10,000 + \frac{-\$200}{(1.12)^1} + \frac{\$800}{(1.12)^2} + \frac{\$300}{(1.12)^3} + \sum_{t=4}^{\infty} \frac{\$0_t}{(1+0.12)^t}$$

$$= \$10,000 - \$178 + \$638 + \$214 + \$0$$

$$= \$10,674$$

In this example, the firm will generate residual income amounts of −$200 in Year +1, $800 in Year +2, $300 in Year +3, and $0 each year thereafter. The firm destroys share-holder wealth in Year +1 by failing to earn sufficient income to cover the cost of equity capital, but the firm generates shareholder wealth in Years +2 and +3, and exactly covers the cost of equity capital each year thereafter. Given these assumptions, the present value of the firm under the residual income model is $10,674.

RESIDUAL INCOME MODEL WITH FINITE HORIZON EARNINGS FORECASTS AND CONTINUING VALUE COMPUTATION

As Chapter 11 discusses, analysts cannot precisely forecast income statements and balance sheets of firms for many years into the future. Therefore, analysts commonly forecast income statements and balance sheets over a foreseeable, finite horizon and then make simplifying growth rate assumptions for the years continuing after the fore-cast horizon. We can modify the residual income valuation model to include explicit forecasts of net income and book value of common equity through Year T (where T is a finite horizon, say 5 or 10 years in the future) and then apply a constant growth rate assumption (denoted g) to project residual income for Year T+1 and all years thereafter. As Chapter 11 describes, the analyst will find it desirable to forecast net income, book value of shareholders' equity, and residual income over an explicit forecast horizon, until the point at which the analyst expects the firm's growth pattern to settle into steady-state growth, during which earnings, dividends, and cash flows will grow at a steady, predictable rate. We refer to residual income in this long-run steady-state growth period as *continuing* residual income, because it reflects residual income earned by the firm continuing into the long-run future. The long-run steady-state growth rate in future continuing residual income could be positive, negative, or zero. Steady-state growth in residual income could be driven by long-run expectations for inflation, the industry's sales, the economy in general, or the population. In some industries, competitive dynamics eventually drive long-run projections of the future returns earned by the firm (for example, the future ROCE) to an equilibrium level equal to the long-run expected cost of equity capital in the firm. Once a firm reaches that point, the firm can be expected to earn zero residual income in the future. The analyst should select a continuing growth rate in residual income that captures realistic long-run expectations for the firm.

To compute residual income in Year T+1, the analyst should first project Year T+1 net income by multiplying Year T net income by the growth factor $(1 + g)$. Year T+1 residual income (denoted RI_{T+1}) can then be computed as follows:

$$RI_{T+1} = [NI_T \times (1 + g)] - [R_E \times BV_T]$$

By estimating RI_{T+1} this way, the analyst will also be able to apply the same uniform long-run growth factor $(1 + g)$ to estimate Year T+1 income statement and balance sheet amounts, and compute internally consistent projections for Year T+1 free cash flows and dividends, which the analyst can then use in free cash flow value models and dividends value models to determine internally consistent value estimates.

In addition, by computing RI_{T+1} this way, the analyst will avoid a potential mistake in forecasting RI_{T+1} by simply projecting $RI_{T+1} = RI_T \times (1 + g)$. This shortcut projection implicitly assumes:

$$RI_T \times (1 + g) = [NI_T - (R_E \times BV_{T-1})] \times (1+g) = NI_T \times (1 + g) - R_E \times BV_{T-1} \times (1 + g)$$

This assumption requires $BV_T = BV_{T-1} \times (1 + g)$, which is not necessarily true. In words, residual income in Year T+1 depends on book value at the end of Year T. We assume constant growth at rate $(1 + g)$ in residual income beginning in Year T+1. Thus, the only way residual income in Year T+1 will equal residual income in Year T times $(1 + g)$ is if book value in Year T happened to grow at the same rate $(1 + g)$. This will not necessarily be the case. The analyst can avoid this forecast error for RI_{T+1} by correctly computing $RI_{T+1} = [NI_T \times (1 + g)] - [R_E \times BV_T]$.

After computing RI_{T+1}, the analyst can treat RI_{T+1} as a growing perpetuity of residual income beginning in Year T+1. The analyst can discount the perpetuity of residual income to present value using the perpetuity-with-growth value model described in Chapter 11. We include the continuing value computation into the finite-horizon residual income model as follows:

$$V_0 = BV_0 + \sum_{t=1}^{\infty} \frac{NI_t - (R_E \times BV_{t-1})}{(1+R_E)^t}$$

$$= BV_0 + \sum_{t=1}^{T} \frac{NI_t - (R_E \times BV_{t-1})}{(1+R_E)^t} + \left[\left(\left(NI_T \times (1+g) \right) - \left(R_E \times BV_T \right) \right) \times \frac{1}{(R_E - g)} \times \frac{1}{(1+R_E)^T} \right]$$

    (1)   (2)   (3)

This model computes the value of common equity based on three parts: (1) book value of shareholders' equity at time t = 0 (the BV_0 term); (2) the present value of residual income over the explicit forecast horizon through Year T (the summation term); and (3) continuing value based on the present value of residual income as a perpetuity with growth beginning in Year T+1 (the term in brackets). To compute continuing value, we first compute residual income in Year T+1 (the term $NI_T \times (1 + g) - (R_E \times BV_T)$). We assume that residual income in Year T+1 will grow at constant rate g in perpetuity, beginning in Year T+1, so we compute continuing value as of the start of Year T+1 using the perpetuity-with-growth valuation factor (the term $1/(R_E - g)$). Finally, we discount continuing value to present value at time t = 0 using the present value factor (the term $1/(1 + R_E)^T$).

VALUATION OF PEPSICO USING THE RESIDUAL INCOME MODEL

Step three toward understanding residual income valuation, as Exhibit 12.1 illustrates, is the practical application step. In this step, we apply the residual income valuation approach to value the common shareholders' equity in PepsiCo. As Chapter 11 describes, PepsiCo shares closed trading at $49.05 on the New York Stock Exchange at the end of Year 11. In Chapter 11, we estimated the value of PepsiCo shares at the end of Year 11 to be roughly $69 using the pro forma financial statement forecasts developed in Chapter 10 and applying the free cash flow valuation techniques. We next illustrate the valuation of PepsiCo shares using the residual income valuation model techniques described in this chapter and the forecasts developed in Chapter 10. The Forecast and Valuation spreadsheets of FSAP (Appendix D) also demonstrate the forecasts and valuation estimates.

We value PepsiCo with the residual income approach, following these five steps:

(1) estimate the appropriate discount rate;
(2) determine the book value of common shareholders' equity on PepsiCo's Year 11 balance sheet, project expected future residual income from the pro forma financial statement forecasts for PepsiCo described in Chapter 10, and project long-run growth in residual income in the continuing periods beyond the forecast horizon;
(3) discount the expected future residual income to present value, including continuing value;
(4) add the book value of equity and the present value of expected future residual income to determine the total value of common shareholders' equity, and then divide by the number of shares outstanding to convert this total to an estimate of share value for PepsiCo; and
(5) examine sensitivity analysis for the estimate of PepsiCo's share value to determine the reasonable range of values for PepsiCo shares.

After illustrating this five-step valuation process, we will compare the range of reasonable values to PepsiCo's share price in the market, and suggest an appropriate investment decision indicated by our analysis.

DISCOUNT RATES FOR RESIDUAL INCOME

To compute the appropriate discount rate for residual income, we use the CAPM to estimate the market's required rate of return on PepsiCo's common stock. At the end of Year 11, PepsiCo's common stock had a market beta of roughly 0.76. At the same time, U.S. Treasury Bills with one to five years to maturity traded with a yield of approximately 4.2 percent, which we use as the risk-free rate. Assuming a 5 percent market risk premium, the CAPM indicates that PepsiCo had a cost of common equity capital of 8.0 percent $[R_E = 0.080 = 0.042 + (0.76 \times 0.05)]$ at the end of Year 11, the beginning of the valuation period. This is the same cost of common equity capital used in Chapter 11 to value PepsiCo using the present value of future free cash flows valuation model.

Using the residual income valuation model, we do not need to compute the weighted average cost of capital. This does not mean that we ignore debt capital or the costs related to debt capital. Instead, we rely on accounting to capture the effects of debt. We project book value of shareholders' equity after subtracting debt from total assets, and we project net income after subtracting interest expense net of tax effects.

PEPSICO'S BOOK VALUE OF EQUITY AND RESIDUAL INCOME

According to PepsiCo's balance sheet (in Appendix A), book value of common shareholders' equity is $8,648.0 million at the end of Year 11. This amount is the starting point for the residual income valuation model (the term denoted BV_0 in the valuation equations).

We project residual income each period in the finite forecast horizon in four steps. First, we compute forecasts of expected future net income for each period. Second, we compute forecasts of expected future book value of common shareholders' equity at the beginning of each period. Third, we compute expected future required income, which is the product of the cost of equity capital times the book value of common shareholders' equity at the beginning of each period (that is, required income is computed as $R_E \times BV_{t-1}$). Fourth, we determine expected future residual income by subtracting expected future required income from expected future net income $[= NI_t - (R_E \times BV_{t-1})]$.

Chapter 10 developed our projections of PepsiCo's future net income by making specific assumptions regarding each line item in the income statement. Chapter 10 also developed specific forecasts of common shareholders' equity on the balance sheet by making specific assumptions about PepsiCo's assets, liabilities, and common equity, including specific forecasts of dividends, stock issues, and stock buybacks. For projections of net income and book value of shareholders' equity beyond Year +5, Chapter 10 essentially assumed that PepsiCo would continue to grow in steady state and that the Year +5 assumptions would continue to hold until Year +10. Exhibit 12.3 presents projections of PepsiCo's net income, book value of shareholders' equity, required income, and residual income through Year +10 using the forecasts discussed in Chapter 10 and an 8.0 percent cost of equity capital.

	EXHIBIT 12.3		
	Valuation of PepsiCo:		
	Present Value of Residual Income Year +1 through Year +10		
	Year +1	Year +2	Year +3
COMPREHENSIVE INCOME AVAILABLE FOR COMMON SHAREHOLDERS........................	$ 3,367.3	$3,656.4	$ 3,975.8
Common Shareholders' Equity (at beginning of year).........	$ 8,648.0	$9,466.2	$10,364.7
Required Income $(R_E \times BV_{t-1})$	$ 691.8	$ 757.3	$ 829.2
Residual Income $[NI_t - (R_E \times BV_{t-1})]$........................	$ 2,675.5	$2,899.1	$ 3,146.6
Present Value Factors (at $R_E = 8.0$ percent)..................	0.926	0.857	0.794
PV Residual Income.....................................	$ 2,477.3	$2,485.5	$ 2,497.9
Sum of PV Residual Income Year +1 through Year +10	$24,613.0		

In Year +1, for example, we projected PepsiCo's net income to be $3,371.3 million. We forecasted other comprehensive income items to be zero, so projected comprehensive income and net income are equal. We projected preferred dividends of $4 million in Year +1 so the portion of net income available to common shareholders is $3,367.3 million. The book value of common shareholders' equity at the beginning of Year +1 is $8,648.0 million. We estimate PepsiCo's cost of equity capital to be 8.0 percent, so we project Year +1 required earnings to be $691.8 million (= 0.08 × $8,648.0) and residual income to be $2,675.5 million (= $3,367.3 – $691.8).

During Years +6 to +10, our forecasts of residual income grow at roughly 7.2 percent, consistent with growth rates in PepsiCo's sales and earnings. To project PepsiCo's residual income continuing in Year +11, we forecast that PepsiCo can sustain long-run growth of 5.0 percent per year, consistent with long-run growth in the economy of 2 percent and long-run inflation of 3 percent. It is the same assumption we made in forecasting long-run growth in free cash flows in Year +11 and beyond in Chapter 11. The Forecast spreadsheet in FSAP permits forecast assumptions to extend as far as 10 years into the future, with continuing value assumptions after that. We project Year +11 residual income will be $5,394.1 million, computed by projecting Year +10 net income to grow by 5.0 percent and subtracting required earnings, measured as the equity cost of capital times book value at the end of Year +10, as follows:

$$RI_{11} = [NI_{10} \times (1 + g)] - [R_E \times BV_{10}]$$

$$= (\$6,590.4 \text{ million} \times 1.05) - (0.080 \times \$19,073.7 \text{ million}) = \$5,394.1 \text{ million}$$

			EXHIBIT 12.3			

Exhibit 12.3—continued

Year +4	Year +5	Year +6	Year +7	Year +8	Year +9	Year +10
$ 4,312.3	$ 4,649.6	$ 4,991.0	$ 5,350.0	$ 5,734.9	$ 6,147.5	$ 6,590.4
$11,572.9	$12,149.2	$13,380.8	$14,366.6	$15,423.7	$16,556.8	$17,771.4
$ 925.8	$ 971.9	$ 1,070.5	$ 1,149.3	$ 1,233.9	$ 1,324.5	$ 1,421.7
$ 3,386.5	$ 3,677.6	$ 3,920.5	$ 4,200.7	$ 4,501.0	$ 4,822.9	$ 5,168.7
0.735	0.681	0.630	0.583	0.540	0.500	0.463
$ 2,489.1	$ 2,502.9	$ 2,470.6	$ 2,451.1	$ 2,431.8	$ 2,412.7	$ 2,394.1

DISCOUNTING PEPSICO'S RESIDUAL INCOME TO PRESENT VALUE

We discount residual income to present value using PepsiCo's 8.0 percent cost of equity capital. Exhibit 12.3 shows that the sum of the present value of PepsiCo's residual income from Year +1 through Year +10 is $24,613.0 million.

We compute the present value of PepsiCo's continuing value of residual income as a perpetuity beginning in Year +11 with growth at a 5.0 percent rate. To compute the continuing value estimate, we use the perpetuity-with-growth valuation model, which determines the present value of the growing perpetuity at the start of the perpetuity period. We then discount that value back to present value at time t = 0. We compute the present value of the continuing value of PepsiCo's residual income as follows (allowing for rounding):

$$Continuing Value_0 = [NI_{10} \times (1+g) - (R_E \times BV_{10})] \times [1/(R_E - g)] \times [1/(1+R_E)^{10}]$$

$$= [(\$6,590.4 \text{ million} \times 1.05) - (0.080 \times \$19,073.7 \text{ million})] \times [1/(0.080 - 0.05)] \times [1/(1+0.080)^{10}]$$

$$= \$5,394.1 \text{ million} \times 83.333 \times 0.4632$$

$$= \$83,283.2 \text{ million}$$

The total present value of PepsiCo's residual income is the sum of these two parts:

PV Residual Income Year +1 through Year +10 (Exhibit 12.3)	$ 24,613.0 million
PV of Continuing Value in Year +11 and beyond.........	$ 83,283.2 million
Present Value of Residual Income	$107,896.2 million

NECESSARY ADJUSTMENTS TO COMPUTE COMMON EQUITY SHARE VALUE

To compute the total value of common equity, we add PepsiCo's book value of common equity to the present value of residual income. The total value of common equity of PepsiCo as of the beginning of Year +1 is $116,544.2 million (= $8,648.0 million + $107,896.2 million).

As Chapter 11 describes, our present value calculations over-discount because they discount each year's residual income for full periods when, in fact, income is generated throughout each period and should be discounted from the midpoint of each year to the present. Therefore, to make the correction we multiply the total by the mid-year adjustment factor $[1 + (R_E/2) = 1 + (0.080/2) = 1.040]$. Therefore, the total present value of common shareholders' equity should be $121,205.9 million [= $116,544.2 million × 1.040].

Dividing by 1,756 million shares outstanding indicates that PepsiCo's common equity shares have a value of $69.02 per share. This value estimate is identical to the value estimate based on free cash flows to common equity shareholders in Chapter 11. Exhibit 12.4 summarizes the computations to arrive at PepsiCo's common equity share value.

SENSITIVITY ANALYSIS AND INVESTMENT DECISION-MAKING

We cautioned in Chapter 11 and we reiterate here that one should not place too much confidence in the *precision* of firm value estimates using these (or any) forecasts for residual income over the remaining life of any firm, even a mature firm like PepsiCo. Although we have constructed these forecasts and value estimates with care, the forecasting and valuation process has an inherently high degree of uncertainty and estimation error. Therefore, the analyst should not rely too heavily on any one point estimate of the value of a firm's shares, and instead should describe a reasonable range of values for a firm's shares.

Two critical forecasting and valuation parameters are the long-run growth assumption, which we forecast to be 5.0 percent, and the cost of equity capital, which we forecast to be 8.0 percent. With these assumptions, our base case estimate is that PepsiCo common shares should be valued at roughly $69 per share. As in Chapter 11, we assess the sensitivity of our estimate of PepsiCo's share value by varying these two parameters across reasonable ranges. Exhibit 12.5 contains the results of sensitivity

EXHIBIT 12.4		
Valuation of PepsiCo using the Residual Income Valuation Model		
Valuation Steps	**Computations**	**Amounts**
Sum of PV Residual Income Year +1 through Year +10	See Exhibit 12.3.	+$ 24,613.0
Add Continuing Value in Present Value	Year +11 residual income assumed to grow at 5.0%; discounted at 8.0%. Computations in FSAP.	+ 83,283.2
Total PV Residual Income		=$107,896.2
Add: Beginning Book Value of Equity	Beginning Book Value of Equity from Year 11 Balance Sheet.	+ 8,648.0
		=$116,544.2
Adjust to Midyear	Multiply by 1+(R_E/2)	× 1.040
Total PV of Common Equity		=$121,205.9
Shares Outstanding		÷ 1,756.0
Estimated Value per Share		=$ 69.02
Current Price per Share		$ 49.05
Percent Difference	(Positive number indicates underpricing.)	41%

analysis varying the long-run growth assumption from 0 to 10 percent and the cost of equity capital from 5 to 20 percent. The data in Exhibit 12.5 show that value estimates of PepsiCo are inversely related to discount rates, holding growth constant. In contrast, share value estimates are positively related to growth rates, holding discount rates constant. We omit value estimates from this analysis when the growth rate equals or exceeds the discount rate, because then the continuing value computation is meaningless.

Under our base case assumptions, we estimate PepsiCo's share value to be $69.02, which is roughly 41 percent greater than the market prices of $49.05 a share for PepsiCo at the time of the valuation. Our base case assumptions indicate that either PepsiCo shares are underpriced or our forecasts and valuation assumptions are more optimistic than those of the market. The data in Exhibit 12.5 allow the analyst to build greater confidence in the prediction that PepsiCo shares are underpriced. For example, if we reduce the long-run growth assumption to 3.0 percent, holding the discount rate constant, PepsiCo shares have a value of $49.29, roughly equal to the market price. These data also show the value of long-run growth to PepsiCo shareholders: if we increase our long-run growth projection from 5.0 percent to 6.0 percent, holding the discount rate constant, PepsiCo's share value jumps to $93.69.

PepsiCo's share value is sensitive to the discount rate assumption. Holding growth constant, increasing the discount rate for common equity from 8.0 percent to 9.0 percent decreases PepsiCo's share value estimate to $51.31. Increasing the discount

	EXHIBIT 12.5			
	Valuation of PepsiCo:			
	Sensitivity Analysis of Share Value Estimates to Growth and			
	Equity Cost of Capital			

Discount Rates	Long-Run Growth Assumptions				
	0%	1%	2%	3%	4%
5%	66.32	77.01	94.83	130.46	237.36
6%	53.69	60.00	69.46	85.22	116.75
7%	44.79	48.77	54.35	62.71	76.66
8%	38.20	40.84	44.36	49.29	56.69
9%	33.14	34.96	37.30	40.41	44.77
10%	29.16	30.45	32.05	34.11	36.87
11%	25.95	26.88	28.02	29.43	31.25
12%	23.32	24.00	24.82	25.82	27.07
13%	21.13	21.64	22.24	22.96	23.84
14%	19.28	19.67	20.11	20.64	21.28
15%	17.70	18.00	18.33	18.73	19.19
16%	16.35	16.57	16.83	17.12	17.47
17%	15.17	15.34	15.54	15.76	16.02
18%	14.13	14.27	14.42	14.59	14.79
19%	13.22	13.33	13.45	13.58	13.73
20%	12.42	12.50	12.59	12.70	12.81

rate to 10.0 percent drops the value to $40.72, well below current market price. On the other hand, reducing the discount rate to 7.0 percent and holding growth constant, the value estimate jumps to $104.55. The data in Exhibit 12.5 also allow the analyst to vary both valuation parameters jointly, for additional insights into the correlation between share value estimates and the growth and discount rate assumptions implicit in the valuation of PepsiCo. These data suggest our value estimate is sensitive to PepsiCo's discount rate assumption. If our forecast and valuation assumptions are realistic, then, at the end of Year 11, PepsiCo's shares were underpriced at the prevailing market price of $49.05, and would have supported a buy recommendation at that time.

RESIDUAL INCOME MODEL IMPLEMENTATION ISSUES

The residual income valuation model is a rigorous and straightforward valuation approach, but the analyst should be aware of three important implementation issues: (1) "dirty surplus" accounting items, (2) common stock transactions, and (3) portions of net income attributable to equity claimants other than common shareholders. The next three sections describe these three issues.

EXHIBIT 12.5					

Exhibit 12.5—continued

5%	6%	7%	8%	9%	10%
#DIV/0!	na	na	na	na	na
211.33	#DIV/0!	na	na	na	na
104.55	188.21	#DIV/0!	na	na	na
69.02	93.69	167.67	#DIV/0!	na	na
51.31	62.21	84.01	149.41	#DIV/0!	na
40.72	46.50	56.13	75.39	133.16	#DIV/0!
33.68	37.08	42.19	50.69	67.69	118.71
28.68	30.82	33.82	38.32	45.82	60.83
24.94	26.36	28.25	30.89	34.86	41.47
22.05	23.02	24.27	25.93	28.26	31.75
19.75	20.43	21.29	22.38	23.85	25.89
17.88	18.37	18.97	19.72	20.68	21.96
16.32	16.68	17.11	17.64	18.29	19.14
15.02	15.28	15.60	15.97	16.43	17.01
13.90	14.10	14.33	14.61	14.93	15.34
12.94	13.09	13.26	13.47	13.70	13.99

Dirty Surplus Accounting

The first implementation issue arises because the residual income model requires that the analyst follow clean surplus accounting in developing expectations for future earnings, dividends, and book values. This means that the expected future income amounts should include all of the income recognized by the firm for the common equity shareholders, and all-inclusive dividends should include all capital transactions with common equity shareholders. Currently, U.S. GAAP does not follow clean surplus accounting. U.S. GAAP admits several dirty surplus items—the other comprehensive income amounts that are recognized directly in shareholders' equity, and bypass the income statement. These items include adjustments for unrealized fair value gains and losses on available-for-sale investment securities, foreign currency translation gains and losses, minimum pension liability adjustments, and the effects of cash flow hedges. U.S. GAAP includes these items in *comprehensive income*. Firms usually report comprehensive income in the Statement of Common Shareholders' Equity or in a note to the financial statements.

In Year 11, for example, PepsiCo reported in Note 16 other comprehensive loss adjustments that totaled −$272 million. As a result of these adjustments in Year 11, PepsiCo's comprehensive income was $2,390 million, as compared to net income of

$2,662 million. In Year 11, total accumulated other comprehensive loss (which measures total accumulated comprehensive income adjustments over the life of PepsiCo and is included as a component of shareholders' equity) declined from –$1,374 million to –$1,646 million. As Chapters 9 and 10 describe, the main culprit driving other comprehensive losses for PepsiCo has been foreign currency translation adjustments, amounting to –$218 million in Year 11, and a cumulative total of –$1,587 million.

These dirty surplus items in U.S. GAAP typically arise because of unrealized gains and losses attributable to changes in market prices, such as changes in investment security fair values, foreign currency exchange rates, or interest rates. Thus, in expectation, the analyst may determine that such gains and losses are certain to occur, but that it is impossible to predict with precision either the sign or amount of the future unrealized gains and losses. In that case, the analyst would likely forecast the expected future dirty surplus items to be zero, on average, and therefore forecast net income and comprehensive income to be equal. We used this assumption in building forecasts for PepsiCo in Chapter 10.

On the other hand, if the analyst can project the amounts and timing of future unrealized gains and losses from available-for-sale investment securities, foreign currency translations, minimum pension liability adjustments, or cash flow hedges, then the analyst should incorporate these unrealized gains and losses in comprehensive income forecasts, and base the residual income valuation on comprehensive income rather than net income. To allow for either possibility (expectations of zero or non-zero comprehensive income adjustments in the future), the residual income model in the Valuation spreadsheet in FSAP begins with forecasts of future comprehensive income.

Common Stock Transactions

Common stock transactions that change the intrinsic value of existing common shareholders' equity can also cause violations of the clean surplus accounting relation and hinder the ability of the residual income model to measure firm value. To illustrate, consider that when the firm sells common shares or repurchases common shares at transaction prices that *exactly* reflect the intrinsic value of the shares (that is, share sales or repurchases that are zero net present value projects for existing shareholders), then these transactions leave the existing shareholders' value unchanged, and clean surplus accounting holds for these transactions. On the other hand, suppose the firm issues common shares at a price that is lower than their intrinsic value. This transaction has a dilutive effect on (that is, reduces the value of) all of the existing common shares. Net income and the all-inclusive dividend do not reflect this loss in value to existing shareholders, so it violates clean surplus accounting.

It is reasonable to assume that clean surplus accounting for most common stock transactions holds, in expectation, because most issues and repurchases of common shares are accounted for at market value. Most of these capital transactions will likely have zero net present value effects on existing shareholders and will conform to clean surplus accounting.

The most prominent exception, however, is the issuance of common equity shares for employee stock options exercises. As Chapter 9 discusses, the exercise of stock options by employees at strike prices below the prevailing market price dilutes the existing shareholders' equity value. If the firm estimates the fair value of the employee stock options at the time they are granted, and recognizes the estimated value of the grants as an expense in measuring net income, then it mitigates the violation of clean surplus accounting. In this case, the analyst should forecast the fair value of expected future options grants and subtract these estimated expenses in forecasting expected future net income. Beginning in 2002 and 2003, following the lead of firms like Boeing, Winn-Dixie, and Coca-Cola, more firms are beginning to recognize stock option compensation expense in income at the time they grant stock options. Under SFAS 123, firms that elect not to recognize this expense in income must disclose an estimate of the expense in the notes to the annual financial statements. The analyst can use these disclosures to estimate future expenses for stock options grants.

PepsiCo does not recognize stock option compensation expense in income but instead discloses this expense in Note 17 to the Year 11 financial statements. After recognizing pro forma compensation expense based on fair values for stock-based awards, pro forma net income in Year 11 was $2,356 million, which is $306 million lower than reported net income.

It is not uncommon for firms to repurchase common equity shares in the market and then use these shares to fulfill stock option exercises. In that case, the accounting for the stock repurchase at market value and the issue of the treasury share at the option strike price captures the dilutive effect of the option exercise on shareholders' equity. For example, if the firm repurchases a share in the market for $60 and issues it to an employee exercising an option with a strike price of $40, then the net effect of the accounting will capture the $20 decrease in shareholders' equity. On the other hand, if the firm fulfills stock option exercises by issuing new shares (or treasury shares repurchased in prior periods at prices that do not reflect the current period market value), then the accounting will reflect the issue of the shares at the option's strike price, and the dilutive effect on existing shareholders will violate clean surplus accounting.

In Year 11, PepsiCo reports in the Statement of Common Shareholders' Equity that it repurchased a total of 35 million shares for $1,716 million, implying an average cost of just over $49 per share. PepsiCo also discloses in that statement that it issued 20 million treasury shares for options exercises, thereby increasing equity capital by $833 million (the sum of $82 million in the Capital in Excess of Par Value account and $751 million in Repurchased Common Stock account), for an average book value of $41.65 per share issued. The difference between the average cost of $49 per share and average book value of $41.65 per share indicates an average dilution of $7.35 per share issued. Given that PepsiCo issued 20 million shares, the total dilution is $147 million. With 1,756 shares outstanding, that amounts to $0.084 dilution per outstanding share, which is roughly 0.2 percent of the year-end share price of $49.05.

If the analyst is valuing a firm with substantial amounts of options outstanding that the analyst expects will be exercised (options that the analyst expects will ultimately expire or be forfeited pose no problems for valuation), or a firm that is likely to grant large numbers of options in the future that are likely to be exercised, then the analyst should explicitly forecast future stock-based compensation expenses that include the fair values of future options grants, and forecast the future dilutive effects of options exercises on the book value of common equity, and include these effects in valuation.[10]

Portions of Net Income Attributable to Equity Claimants Other than Common Shareholders

In some circumstances, a portion of net income is attributable to equity claimants other than common shareholders. For example, preferred stockholders may be entitled to preference in dividends over common shareholders. Also, minority shareholders have a claim on the portion of net income that is attributable to their share of the equity in the subsidiary they own. For purposes of residual income measurement and valuation, these portions of net income do not represent net income to the common equity shareholders and should be excluded from residual income. Residual income valuation should be based on the net income available for common equity shareholders. In the case of PepsiCo in Year 11, for example, PepsiCo paid a $4 million preferred stock dividend, so we measure residual income after subtracting this dividend. PepsiCo did not have any minority equity shareholders at the end of Year 11.

DIVIDENDS VALUATION MODEL

As Exhibit 12.1 illustrates, the fourth and final step toward understanding residual income valuation, and valuation in general, is to understand and apply the classical dividends-based valuation approach. Throughout Chapters 11 and 12, we have anchored the discussions of free cash flows valuation and residual income valuation on dividends valuation as the most fundamental valuation approach. Therefore, to complete our analysis and valuation of PepsiCo, and to demonstrate the equivalence of value estimates based on residual income, free cash flows, and dividends, we also apply the classical dividends valuation model.

We described earlier that the dividends valuation model determines the value of common shareholders' equity in the firm as the present value of all future dividends to shareholders over the life of the firm. Recall that the dividends-based approach values "all-inclusive dividends" (which we denote D) that encompass cash flows from the firm to shareholders through periodic dividend payments, stock buybacks, and the firm's liquidating dividend, as well as cash flows from the shareholders to the firm (*negative* dividends) when the firm issues shares. Assuming the required return on common equity capital in the firm is R_E, we expressed the dividends valuation approach with the following general model:

$$V_0 = \sum_{t=1}^{\infty} \frac{D_t}{(1+R_E)^t} = \frac{D_1}{(1+R_E)^1} + \frac{D_2}{(1+R_E)^2} + \frac{D_3}{(1+R_E)^3} + \cdots$$

---

[10]For an illustration of stock options and valuation, see Leonard Soffer, "SFAS No. 123 Disclosures and Discounted Cash Flow Valuation," *Accounting Horizons* Vol. 14, No. 2 (June 2000), pp. 169–189.

At some future date T, the firm will be liquidated (acquired, taken private, bankrupted) or the investors will sell their shares. At that time, the value of the firm will equal the present value of all expected future all-inclusive dividends beyond Year T, which can be expressed as:

$$V_T = \sum_{t=1}^{\infty} \frac{D_{T+1}}{(1+R_E)^t}$$

Thus, the value of the firm today can be expressed using dividends over a finite horizon to Year T plus continuing value based on dividends in Year T+1 and beyond as follows:

$$V_0 = \sum_{t=1}^{\infty} \frac{D_t}{(1+R_E)^t} = \frac{D_1}{(1+R_E)^1} + \frac{D_2}{(1+R_E)^2} + \frac{D_3}{(1+R_E)^3} + \cdots \frac{D_T}{(1+R_E)^T} + \frac{V_T}{(1+R_E)^T}$$

This equation reveals that the estimate of value today (V_0) depends on the estimate of value in the future (V_T), where V_T represents the continuing value of dividends beyond Year T.

The dividends in the continuing value period beyond Year T can be projected using the expected, long-run growth of the firm, which we specified as $(1 + g)$ in the free cash flows and residual income valuation models. To be consistent with those models, we must specify the same long-run growth in dividends. Thus, we project the Year T+1 dividend in the same manner as we projected the Year T+1 free cash flows and residual income, by forecasting each line item on the Year T income statement and balance sheet to grow at rate $(1 + g)$ and then deriving the Year T+1 dividend. Relying on clean surplus accounting and the projected net income and book value of shareholders' equity in Year T+1, we can derive the Year T+1 dividend, as follows:

$$D_{T+1} = NI_{T+1} + BV_T - BV_{T+1}$$

We rely on the assumption that growth in net income and book value in Year T+1 equals $(1 + g)$. We rewrite the D_{T+1} equation as follows:

$$D_{T+1} = [NI_T \times (1 + g)] + BV_T - [BV_T \times (1 + g)]$$

We assume that D_{T+1} will grow in perpetuity at rate g, so we can value the firm at Year T using the now familiar perpetuity-with-growth model:

$$V_T = \sum_{t=1}^{\infty} \frac{D_{T+1}}{(1+R_E)^t} = \frac{D_{T+1}}{(R_E - g)} = \frac{[NI_T \times (1+g)] + BV_T - [BV_T \times (1+g)]}{(R_E - g)}$$

Thus, the present value of common equity today can be expressed using dividends as follows:

$$V_0 = \sum_{t=1}^{\infty} \frac{D_t}{(1+R_E)^t}$$

$$= \frac{D_1}{(1+R_E)^1} + \frac{D_2}{(1+R_E)^2} + \frac{D_3}{(1+R_E)^3} + \cdots + \frac{D_T}{(1+R_E)^T} + \frac{V_T}{(1+R_E)^T}$$

$$= \frac{D_1}{(1+R_E)^1} + \frac{D_2}{(1+R_E)^2} + \frac{D_3}{(1+R_E)^3} + \cdots + \frac{D_T}{(1+R_E)^T} + \frac{[NI_T \times (1+g)] + BV_T - [BV_T \times (1+g)]}{(R_E - g) \times (1+R_E)^T}$$

APPLICATION OF THE DIVIDENDS VALUATION MODEL TO PEPSICO

The all-inclusive dividends to common equity shareholders of PepsiCo include three sets of capital transactions between PepsiCo and common shareholders, all based on the forecasts of common equity developed in detail in Chapter 10. First, we include cash flows to shareholders through the periodic dividend payments of PepsiCo. Second, we include negative dividends in the form of stock issues. Third, we include cash flows to shareholders through stock repurchases.

As described in detail in Chapter 10, we project Year +1 dividend payments to common shareholders to be $1,600.3 million. We project common stock issues to be zero in Year +1 (and each year through Year +10). We project cash flows to common shareholders through stock repurchases will amount to $948.8 million in Year +1. Thus, our projections forecast all-inclusive dividends in Year +1 will be $2,549.1 million. Exhibit 12.6 summarizes the computations of PepsiCo's all-inclusive dividends in Years +1 to +10. Discounting these future dividends using PepsiCo's equity cost of capital (8.0 percent) yields a present value estimate of $24,426.2 million.

To compute the continuing value of PepsiCo's dividends in Year +11 and beyond, we again project that dividends, like residual income and free cash flows, will grow in perpetuity at a 5 percent growth rate. We forecast Year +11 dividends as follows:

EXHIBIT 12.6			
Valuation of PepsiCo:			
Present Value of Dividends Year +1 through Year +10			
	Year +1	Year +2	Year +3
Dividends Paid to Common Shareholders.	$ 1,600.3	$1,691.5	$1,571.6
Less: Common Stock Issues	0.0	0.0	0.0
Plus: Common Stock Repurchases.	948.8	1,066.3	1,196.1
All-inclusive Dividends to Common Equity Shareholders	$ 2,549.1	$2,757.8	$2,767.6
Present Value Factors (at R_E = 8.0 percent)	0.926	0.857	0.794
Present Value of Periodic Dividends	$ 2,360.3	$2,364.4	$2,197.0
Sum of Present Value Net Dividends Year +1 through Year +10 . . .	$24,426.2		

$$D_{11} = [NI_{10} \times (1+g)] + BV_{10} - [BV_{10} \times (1+g)]$$

$$= [\$6,590.4 \text{ million} \times 1.05] + \$19,073.7 \text{ million} - [\$19,073.7 \text{ million} \times 1.05]$$

$$= \$6,920.0 \text{ million} + \$19,073.7 \text{ million} - \$20,027.4 \text{ million}$$

$$= \$5,966.3 \text{ million.}$$

We use the perpetuity-with-growth model to discount dividends in the continuing value period to present value at PepsiCo's 8.0 percent cost of equity capital, as follows (allowing for rounding):

$$ContinuingValue_0 = D_{11} \times [1/(R_E - g)] \times [1/(1+R_E)^{10}]$$

$$= \$5,966.3 \text{ million} \times [1/(0.080 - 0.050)] \times [1/(1+0.080)^{10}]$$

$$= \$5,966.3 \text{ million} \times 33.33 \times 0.4632$$

$$= \$92,118.0 \text{ million}$$

The sum of the present value of dividends through Year +10 plus the present value of the continuing value of dividends in Year +11 and beyond is $116,544.2 million (= $24,426.2 million + $92,118.0 million). We correct this present value for overdiscounting by multiplying this sum by the mid-year adjustment factor $[1+(R_E/2) = 1 + (0.080/2) = 1.040]$. Therefore, the total present value of dividends is $121,205.9 million [= $116,544.2 million × 1.040]. Exhibit 12.7 summarizes the dividends valuation computations.

Dividing by 1,756 million shares outstanding indicates that PepsiCo's common equity shares have a value of $69.02 per share, a value estimate that is identical to the value estimate based on residual income presented earlier in this chapter and the value estimate based on free cash flows to common equity shareholders in Chapter 11. All three value estimates indicate that PepsiCo shares at the end of Year 11 are

EXHIBIT 12.6						
Exhibit 12.6—continued						
Year +4	Year +5	Year +6	Year +7	Year +8	Year +9	Year +10
$2,395.8	$1,918.9	$2,175.6	$2,463.3	$2,955.2	$3,670.5	$3,899.5
0.0	0.0	0.0	0.0	0.0	0.0	0.0
1,340.2	1,499.1	1,829.6	1,829.6	1,646.6	1,262.4	1,388.7
$3,736.0	$3,418.0	$4,005.2	$4,292.9	$4,601.8	$4,932.9	$5,288.1
0.735	0.681	0.630	0.583	0.540	0.500	0.463
$2,746.1	$2,326.2	$2,523.9	$2,504.9	$2,486.2	$2,467.7	$2,449.4

EXHIBIT 12.7		
Valuation of PepsiCo using Dividends		
Valuation Steps	**Computations**	**Amounts**
Sum of PV Dividends Year +1 through Year +10	See Exhibit 12.6.	+$ 24,426.2
Add continuing value in present value	Year +11 dividends assumed to grow at 5.0%; discounted at 8.0%. Computations in FSAP.	+ 92,118.0
Total		=$116,544.2
Adjust to midyear	Multiply by 1+(R$_E$/2)	× 1.040
Total PV Dividends		=$121,205.9
Shares Outstanding		÷ 1,756.0
Estimated Value per Share		=$ 69.02
Current Price per Share		$ 49.05
Percent Difference	(Positive number indicates underpricing.)	41%

underpriced by roughly 41 percent. Not surprisingly, sensitivity analysis of the share value estimate using the dividends valuation model reveals the same sensitivity of PepsiCo's share value to growth and equity cost of capital as we observed with the residual income value estimates and the free cash flows estimates.

CAUSES OF DIFFERENCES IN RESIDUAL INCOME, DIVIDENDS, AND FREE CASH FLOW VALUE ESTIMATES

The former baseball player and coach Yogi Berra is reported to have said, "In theory, practice and theory are the same. In practice, they're not." In theory, all three valuation models, when correctly implemented with internally consistent assumptions, will produce the same estimates of value. In practice, the analyst may discover that the three models yield different value estimates. If so, the analyst should check the analysis for one or more of the following three common errors (errors that we have experienced ourselves).[11]

1. *Incomplete or inconsistent earnings and cash flow forecasts.* The analyst should be sure that projected earnings, cash flows, and dividends are complete and based on assumptions that are consistent with one another. The analyst can

---

[11]For a more complete description of diagnosing errors that can cause differences in the three value model estimates, see Russell Lundholm and Terry O'Keefe, "Reconciling Value Estimates from the Discounted Cash Flow Model and the Residual Income Model," *Contemporary Accounting Research* 2001 (Summer), pp. 1–26.

reduce the chance of incomplete or inconsistent forecasts by forecasting complete pro forma financial statements in which the balance sheets balance, the income statements add up, and the statements of cash flows articulate with the income statements and the changes in the balance sheets. The analyst should also insure that projected shareholders' equity reflects clean surplus accounting. As suggested in Chapter 10, relying on the additivity and articulation of financial statements will help the analyst avoid inconsistent forecasts.

2. *Inconsistent estimates of weighted average costs of capital.* Suppose the analyst computes the present value of free cash flows to all debt and equity capital using the weighted average cost of capital as a discount rate, and then subtracts the present value of debt and preferred stock to determine the present value of common equity value (as shown in Chapter 11). The only way the value estimates from this approach will be identical with value estimates from the residual income approach or the dividends approach is if the weighted average cost of capital uses weights that are perfectly internally consistent with the present values of debt, preferred stock, and common equity. Thus, the analyst may have to iterate the computation of the weighted average cost of capital a number of times until the weights and present values are all internally consistent.

3. *Incorrect continuing value computations.* In Chapters 11 and 12, we have emphasized that the analyst must take care to estimate the continuing value estimate, particularly the Year T+1 amount for residual income, free cash flow, and dividends. If the analyst uses inconsistent assumptions to project the beginning amounts used to compute continuing value, then the value estimates will not agree. To avoid this problem, the analyst should first project the Year T+1 income statement and balance sheet amounts assuming a uniform rate of growth $(1 + g)$, and then use these projections to derive the Year T+1 amounts for residual income, free cash flow, and dividends. The derived amounts for Year T+1 can then be used as the starting values of the perpetuity to calculate continuing value. A common error analysts make is to simply assume that residual income, free cash flows, and dividends in Year T will all grow at the same rate g. This shortcut will *not* insure consistent assumptions and valuation. As described in the past two chapters, that shortcut may impound inconsistent assumptions in the Year T+1 amounts, and therefore inconsistent value estimates.

SUMMARY COMMENTS ON VALUATION

Chapters 11 and 12 have described and applied multiple approaches to valuation, using the present value of projected free cash flows, the present value of projected residual income, and the present value of projected dividends. Together, these approaches provide theoretically sound and practically applicable approaches to convert forecasts of future cash flows, earnings, and dividends into estimates of firm value. In Chapter 13, we examine a variety of additional valuation techniques, including the use of valuation multiples. Our experience with valuation suggests that using multiple valuation approaches yields more useful insights than using just one method in all circumstances.

PROBLEMS AND CASES

12.1 VALUATION OF EQUITY USING RESIDUAL INCOME AND DIVIDENDS DISCOUNT VALUATION MODELS. Problem 10.7 presents assumptions for the preparation of pro forma financial statements for The Gap and Limited Brands for Year 13 to Year 17. Problem 11.4 presents the cash flows from these pro forma financial statements for Year 13 to Year 17, and the amounts for Year 18 to compute the continuing value of each firm assuming that The Gap grows at 6 percent and Limited Brands grows at 3 percent in perpetuity. The market equity beta of The Gap is 1.61 and of Limited Brands is 1.37 at the end of Year 12. Assume a risk-free interest rate of 4.2 percent and a market premium of 5 percent. Exhibit 12.8 presents the changes in common shareholders' equity for each firm for Year 13 through Year 17, as well as projected amounts for Year 18, assuming that each item on the income statement and balance sheet of The Gap grows 6 percent and those for Limited Brands grow 3 percent.

EXHIBIT 12.8

The Gap and Limited Brands
Changes in Pro Forma Common Shareholders' Equity
(amounts in millions)
(Problem 12.1)

	Year 13	Year 14	Year 15	Year 16	Year 17	Year 18
The Gap						
Start of Year....................	$3,008	$3,295	$3,493	$3,702	$3,924	$4,160
Net Income.....................	905	957	1,014	1,075	1,140	1,208
Accumulated Other Comprehensive						
Income.......................	—	—	—	—	—	(4)
Dividends	(89)	(94)	(100)	(106)	(112)	(639)
Treasury Stock Purchases	(529)	(665)	(705)	(747)	(792)	(315)
End of Year	$3,295	$3,493	$3,702	$3,924	$4,160	$4,409[a]
Limited Brands						
Start of Year....................	$2,744	$2,947	$2,989	$3,032	$3,077	$3,123
Net Income.....................	485	500	515	530	546	562
Accumulated Other Comprehensive						
Income.......................	—	—	—	—	—	(5)
Dividends	(133)	(137)	(141)	(145)	(150)	(424)
Treasury Stock Purchases	(149)	(320)	(330)	(340)	(350)	(39)
End of Year	$2,947	$2,989[a]	$3,032[a]	$3,077	$3,123	$3,218[a]

[a]Amounts do not sum due to rounding.

Required

a. Compute the value of each firm at the end of Year 12 using the residual income model. Include the midyear adjustment, assuming discounting from the midpoint each year to present value.

b. Compute the value of each firm at the end of Year 12 using the dividends discount model. Include the midyear adjustment, assuming discounting from the midpoint each year to present value.

c. Compare the valuations in part a and b (as well as with those in part a of Problem 11.4, if assigned). What are the likely reasons for any differences?

12.2 VALUATION OF EQUITY USING RESIDUAL INCOME MODEL.
Morrissey Tool Company manufactures machine tools for various other manufacturing firms. The firm is wholly owned by Kelsey Morrissey. The firm's accountant developed the following long-term forecasts of net income:

Year 12: $213,948
Year 13: $192,008
Year 14: $187,444
Year 15: $196,442
Year 16: $206,667

The accountant expects net income to grow 5 percent annually after Year 16. Kelsey withdraws 30 percent of net income each year as a dividend. Total common shareholder's equity on January 1, Year 12, is $1,111,141. Kelsey expects to earn a rate of return on her invested equity capital of 12 percent each year.

Required

a. Using the residual income valuation model, compute the value of Morrissey Tool Company as of January 1, Year 12.

b. What advice would you give Kelsey regarding her ownership of the firm?

12.3 VALUATION OF EQUITY USING RESIDUAL INCOME AND DIVIDEND
DISCOUNT MODELS. Priority Contractors provides maintenance and cleaning services to various corporate clients in New York City. The firm has provided you with the following forecasts of net income for Year 12 to Year 16:

Year 12: $478,246
Year 13: $491,882
Year 14: $485,568
Year 15: $515,533
Year 16: $554,198

Total common shareholders' equity was $2,224,401 on January 1, Year 12. The firm does not expect to pay a dividend during the period of Year 12 to Year 16. The cost of equity capital is 12 percent.

EXHIBIT 12.9				
Steak N Shake				
Selected Financial Information				
(amounts in millions)				
(Problem 12.4)				
	Year 12	Year 13	Year 14	Year 15
Common Equity, Beginning of Year	$165.8	$177.6	$192.0	$206.0
Net Income.....................................	24.5	25.8	27.6	29.6
Dividends......................................	(12.7)	(11.4)	(13.6)	(19.0)
Common Equity, End of Year[b]......................	$177.6	$192.0	$206.0	$216.6
Cash Flow from Operations........................	$ 45.4	$ 51.2	$ 56.3	$ 61.5
Cash Flow for Investing...........................	(35.2)	(41.1)	(41.9)	(42.7)
Cash Flow for Long-term Debt	(.5)	2.0	—	1.0
Cash Flow for Dividends	(12.7)	(11.4)	(13.6)	(19.0)
Net Change in Cash..............................	$ (3.0)	$ .7	$ .8	$ .8

[a]The amounts for Year 22 result from increasing each income statement and balance sheet amount by the expected long-term growth rate of 3 percent and then deriving the amounts for the statement of cash flows.
[b]Amounts on this line may differ from the amounts above due to rounding of intermediate computations.

Required

a. Compute the value of Priority Contractors on January 1, Year 12, using the residual income valuation model. The firm expects net income to grow 5 percent annually after Year 16.

b. Compute the value of Priority Contractors on January 1, Year 12, using the dividend discount model.

12.4 VALUATION OF EQUITY USING PRESENT VALUES OF FREE CASH FLOWS, RESIDUAL INCOME, AND DIVIDEND DISCOUNT MODELS. Exhibit 12.9 presents selected pro forma financial information for Steak N Shake for Year 12 to Year 22. The amounts for Year 22 reflect a long-term growth assumption of 3 percent. The cost of equity capital is 9.34 percent.

Required

a. Compute the value of Steak N Shake as of January 1, Year 12, using the present value of expected free cash flows to the common equity shareholders.

b. Repeat part a using the residual income model.

c. Repeat part a using the dividend discount model.

d. Identify the reasons for any differences in the valuations in parts a, b, and c.

e. The market value of Steak N Shake on January 1, Year 12, is $309.98 million. Based on your valuations in parts a, b, and c, what is your assessment of the market value of this firm?

	EXHIBIT 12.9	

Exhibit 12.9—continued

Year 16	Year 17	Year 18	Year 19	Year 20	Year 21	Year 22[a]
$216.6	$227.7	$234.2	$238.1	$239.4	$255.8	$269.5
31.8	34.2	36.8	39.5	53.9	57.0	58.7
(20.8)	(27.7)	(32.9)	(38.2)	(37.4)	(43.3)	(50.6)
$227.7	$234.2	$238.1	$239.4	$255.8	$269.5	$277.6
$ 67.1	$ 72.9	$ 78.9	$ 85.2	$ 85.6	$ 92.4	$ 73.2
(43.5)	(44.4)	(45.2)	(46.0)	(47.3)	(48.1)	(22.1)
(2.0)	—	—	—	—	—	—
(20.8)	(27.7)	(32.9)	(38.2)	(37.4)	(43.3)	(50.6)
$ .8	$ .8	$ .8	$ 1.0	$ .9	$ 1.0	$ .5

CASES

Note: To provide up-to-date integrated valuation cases, we include cases for Chapters 11 to 13 on the web site for this book (http://stickney.swlearning.com) instead of in the text.

Chapter 13

VALUATION: MARKET-BASED APPROACHES

Learning Objectives

1. Understand the practical advantages and disadvantages of using market multiples in valuation.

2. Apply a version of the residual income valuation model to estimate the value-to-book ratio (VB) as a theoretically correct valuation multiple. Understand how to compare the value-to-book ratio to the market-to-book ratio (MB). Also understand how to compare VB ratios and MB ratios to analyze values of firms over time and to compare values across firms.

3. Understand and estimate the firm's value-earnings ratio (VE) as a theoretically correct earnings-valuation multiple. Understand how to incorporate growth into the VE ratio to determine the value-earnings-growth ratio (VEG). Compare the VE and VEG ratios to the price-earnings ratio (PE) and the price-earnings-growth ratio (PEG). Use VE and VEG ratios and PE and PEG ratios to evaluate firms over time and compare valuations across firms.

4. Understand the role of the following factors on market multiples: (a) risk and the cost of equity capital, (b) growth rates, (c) differences between current and expected future earnings, and (d) alternative accounting methods and principles. Use these factors to explain how VB, VE, and VEG ratios should differ across firms, and why MB, PE, and PEG ratios actually do differ across firms.

5. Estimate the price differential—the difference between market price and "risk-free value," which is computed using the residual income model and the risk-free discount rate.

> **6. Reverse engineer the firm's stock price by using the residual income model to determine either the implicit expected return or the implicit expected long-run growth rate.**
>
> **7. Understand the role of market efficiency in valuation, and the academic evidence on the degree to which the market efficiently impounds earnings information into share prices.**

INTRODUCTION AND OVERVIEW

Chapters 1 to 12 have all focused on using the information in a firm's accounting numbers, financial statements, and related notes to analyze the firm's fundamental characteristics of profitability, risk, growth, and value. These prior chapters have established a coherent framework to attack a very difficult problem—how to analyze and value a business. Using this framework to analyze and value a business, we must first understand the firm's industry and business strategy, and then we use that understanding to assess the quality of the firm's accounting, making adjustments as necessary. We then evaluate the firm's profitability, risk, growth, efficiency, liquidity, and leverage, using a set of financial ratios. On the foundation of these steps, we construct forecasts of future financial statements, from which we derive the expected future earnings, cash flows, and dividends that form the bases for valuation. We apply the free cash flows model, the residual income model, and the dividends model to value the firm, and we use these models to assess the sensitivity of firm value to key valuation parameters, such as costs of capital and expected growth rates. To culminate this process, we describe the realistic range of firm value estimates and compare this range of values to the firm's market share price for an intelligent investment decision.

Exhibit 13.1 provides a summary representation of the fundamentals-driven valuation process. The bottom of the exhibit depicts the firm's value drivers, such as expected future earnings, cash flows, growth, and risk, which comprise the economic foundations of valuation. We capture these value drivers in forecasts of future pro forma financial statements, and then convert these forecasts into value estimates using valuation models, such as the residual income model, the free cash flows model, and the dividends model.

In this chapter, we continue our focus on the firm's fundamental characteristics of profitability, risk, growth, and value, but now we augment that analytical approach with techniques that allow us to exploit the information in the firm's *market value*. We describe and apply a variety of techniques that compare the firm's market value (or share price) to firm fundamentals. The techniques we describe in this chapter include commonly used market multiples—market-to-book ratios, price-earnings ratios, and price-earnings-growth ratios. Market multiples provide efficient shortcuts to the valuation process. As Exhibit 13.2 depicts, market multiples rest on the same foundation of value drivers in the valuation process as the valuation models discussed in Chapters 11 and 12—expected future earnings, cash flows, growth, and risk—but market multiples collapse the valuation process in two important ways.

EXHIBIT 13.1
Fundamentals of Valuation

Firm Value

Estimate:
Book Value of Common Equity plus Present Value of Expected Future Residual Income
= Present Value of Expected Future Free Cash Flows to Common Equity Shareholders
= Present Value of Expected Future Dividends

Pro Forma Financial Statement Forecasts

Fundamental Value Drivers over the Remaining Life of the Firm:
Expected Future Earnings, Cash Flows, Growth, Risk

---

(1) Instead of developing complete pro forma financial statement forecasts, multiples use just one or two summary accounting numbers to represent the value drivers.

(2) Instead of using extensive present value model computations, market multiples summarize value using relatively simple ratios of market value of common equity to summary accounting numbers.

EXHIBIT 13.2
Market Multiples

Firm Value

Market Multiples:
Market-to-Book Ratios, Price-Earnings Ratios, Price-Earnings-Growth Ratios

Summary Accounting Numbers:
Earnings; Book Value of Common Shareholders' Equity; Long-run Growth

Fundamental Value Drivers over the Remaining Life of the Firm:
Expected Future Earnings, Cash Flows, Growth, Risk

In this chapter, we also introduce techniques to infer and exploit the information in share prices, including computing price differentials and reverse engineering share prices. In the last section of the chapter, we briefly summarize a few key insights from the last 40 years of accounting, finance, and economics research on how efficiently the market uses accounting earnings to price stocks. The research findings are very encouraging for those interested in using accounting numbers for fundamental analysis and valuation of stocks.

MARKET MULTIPLES OF ACCOUNTING NUMBERS

The market price for a share of common equity is a very special and important number: it reflects the aggregated expectations of all of the market participants following that particular stock. The market price reflects the result of the market's trading activity in that stock. It summarizes the aggregate information the market participants have about the firm, and the aggregate expectation for the firm's future profitability, growth, and risk. The market price of a share does not mean that all market participants agree that the price is the correct *value* for the share; indeed, the market price simply indicates the equilibrium point at which the forces of supply (participants potentially willing to sell the stock—the "ask" side of trading) and the forces of demand (participants potentially willing to buy the stock—the "bid" side of trading) are momentarily in balance. Stock prices are dynamic, constantly changing with the arrival of new information that changes investors' expectations about share value and triggers trading in the firm's shares in the market. We can analyze share price for value-relevant information.

Market participants commonly calibrate firm valuation using market value or share price expressed as a multiple of a fundamental summary accounting number, such as the market-to-book ratio or the price-earnings ratio. Thus, market multiples capture *relative* valuation per dollar of book value or per dollar of earnings. In this way, market multiples measure value relative to a key accounting number as a common denominator, thereby enabling analysts to draw inferences about a particular firm's relative market capitalization, to assess changes in relative valuation over time, to make comparisons of valuation across firms, and to make projections about comparable firms' values. For example, price-earnings ratios allow an analyst to quickly gauge and compare the multiples at which the market is capitalizing different firms' annual earnings.

Market multiples can provide useful and efficient fundamental valuation ratios but they must be applied and interpreted carefully, after considering the firm's expected future profitability, growth, and risk. Multiples like market-to-book ratios and price-earnings ratios are relative value metrics and therefore are not meaningful by themselves. For example, whether a particular firm's price-earnings ratio should be 10, 20, 30, or some other number cannot be determined unless the analyst knows the firm's fundamental characteristics—expected future profitability, growth, and risk.

Analysts sometimes apply market multiples to estimate value in *ad hoc* ways. Valuation using market multiples may be efficient (the so-called "quick and dirty" approach) but may also be misleading. An analyst might be tempted to value a firm using that firm's historical average or the industry average market multiple. The firm's historical average market-to-book ratio, for example, may be an appropriate fit for the firm today, but only if the firm's fundamental characteristics today match those of the firm's past. In the same vein, an industry average price-earnings multiple may be an appropriate yardstick for valuing a particular firm, but only if that firm matches the industry average fundamental characteristics. If the firm is different today than it was in the past, or if the firm does not match the industry average, then market multiples must be adjusted to reflect the firm's fundamental characteristics.

This chapter continues to emphasize the distinction between *value* and *price*. The chapter focuses attention on how to compute *value*-based multiples that reflect the firm's fundamentals and that can be compared to market *price*-based multiples. This focus also directs our attention to the factors that drive multiples, so that the analyst can avoid being ad hoc and can correctly adjust historical or industry average multiples to reflect appropriately the firm's expected profitability, growth, and risk.

MARKET-TO-BOOK AND VALUE-TO-BOOK RATIOS[1]

The market-to-book ratio (MB) can be computed by dividing the firm's market value of common equity at a point in time by the book value of common shareholders' equity from the firm's most recent balance sheet. For example, at the end of Year 11, PepsiCo's market value was $86,131.8 million (= $49.05 per share × 1,756 million shares), and PepsiCo's Year 11 book value of common shareholders' equity was $8,648.0 million (Appendix A). Thus, PepsiCo was trading at an MB ratio equal to 9.96 (=$86,131.8 million/$8,648.0 million). The MB ratio measures market value as a multiple of accounting book value at a point in time. The MB ratio reflects market value but it does not tell us what the ratio *should be*, given our estimate of value.

A THEORETICAL MODEL OF THE VALUE-TO-BOOK RATIO

To compute a ratio that reflects our expectation of the firm's intrinsic value to book value, we need to compute the value-to-book ratio (VB)—the value of common shareholders' equity divided by the book value of common shareholders' equity. The VB ratio can be derived directly from the residual income model developed in Chapter 12. In fact, the VB ratio model is simply a version of the residual income model that is scaled by book value of common shareholders' equity. The numerator of the VB ratio is the estimated value of common equity, which takes into account the book value of common shareholders' equity, expected future profitability, growth, risk, and the time

---

[1]As we noted in Chapter 12, credit for the rigorous development of the residual income model, and its extension to the value-to-book ratio model, goes to James Ohlson in: J. A. Ohlson, "A Synthesis of Security Valuation Theory and the Role of Dividends, Cash Flows, and Earnings," *Contemporary Accounting Research* (Spring 1990), pp. 648–676; J. A. Ohlson, "Earnings, Book Values, and Dividends in Equity Valuation," *Contemporary Accounting Research* (Spring 1995), pp. 661–687; G. A. Feltham and J. A. Ohlson, "Valuation and Clean Surplus Accounting for Operating and Financial Activities," *Contemporary Accounting Research* (Spring 1995), pp. 216–230. The ideas underlying the value-to-book ratio also trace to early work by G.A.D. Preinreich, "Annual Survey of Economic Theory: The Theory of Depreciation," *Econometrica* (1938), pp. 219–241 and E. Edwards and P. W. Bell, *The Theory and Measurement of Business Income* (Berkeley, CA: University of California Press), 1961.

value of money. The VB ratio can be compared to the market-to-book ratio to identify whether the stock is correctly priced in the market. The VB ratio of one firm can also be used to estimate the value of a different but comparable firm, provided the analyst makes the appropriate and necessary adjustments to the VB ratio so that it matches the comparable firm's fundamental characteristics. This section explores the theoretical and empirical relation between estimated value, book value, and market value.

Using the same notation from prior chapters, we can compute the VB ratio with the following model:

$$\frac{V_0}{BV_0} = 1 + \sum_{t=1}^{\infty} \frac{[ROCE_t - R_E] \times \dfrac{BV_{t-1}}{BV_0}}{(1+R_E)^t}$$

In short, the VB ratio should be equal to one, plus the present value of expected future abnormal return on common equity (the $[ROCE_t - R_E]$ term above) times cumulative growth in book value (the BV_{t-1}/BV_0 term above). The growth in book value indicates the increase in net assets on which firms can earn abnormal earnings. The growth in book value depends on ROCE, dividend policy, and changes in common stock.

To show how we derive this model, recall from Chapter 12 the following expression for the residual income valuation model:

$$V_0 = BV_0 + \sum_{t=1}^{\infty} \frac{NI_t - (R_E \times BV_{t-1})}{(1+R_E)^t}$$

Under the residual income valuation model, the value of common shareholders' equity is equal to the book value of common equity plus the present value of all expected future *residual income*, which is the amount by which expected future earnings exceed required earnings, for the remaining life of the firm.[2] We compute the required earnings (or "normal" earnings) of the firm in year t as the product of the required rate of return on common equity capital times the book value of common equity at the beginning of year t $(R_E \times BV_{t-1})$. Required earnings captures the amount of net income the firm must generate in order to provide a return to common equity capital that is equal to the cost of common equity capital. We measure *residual income* (or "abnormal" earnings) by the subtraction term, $NI_t - (R_E \times BV_{t-1})$. Residual income is the difference between expected net income and required earnings of the firm in year t. Residual income measures the amount of wealth that the analyst expects the firm to create (or destroy) in year t for common equity shareholders above (or below) the cost of equity capital.

---

[2]Chapter 12 describes that the residual income valuation model depends on clean surplus accounting for book value of common shareholders' equity, which requires that expected future earnings forecasts are comprehensive measures of income for the firm's common equity shareholders, and that expected future dividends reflect all capital transactions between the firm and common equity shareholders. Throughout this chapter, when we refer to expected future "earnings" or "net income" in the context of residual income valuation, we mean expected future comprehensive income available for common shareholders.

To convert the residual income model into a model for the VB ratio, we scale both sides of the equation by BV_0, which produces the following equation:

$$\frac{V_0}{BV_0} = \frac{BV_0}{BV_0} + \sum_{t=1}^{\infty} \frac{\dfrac{NI_t}{BV_0} - \left(R_E \times \dfrac{BV_{t-1}}{BV_0}\right)}{(1+R_E)^t}$$

We rewrite BV_0 divided by BV_0 as equal to one. We rewrite the NI_t/BV_0 term as follows:

$$\frac{NI_t}{BV_0} = \frac{NI_t}{BV_{t-1}} \times \frac{BV_{t-1}}{BV_0} = ROCE_t \times \frac{BV_{t-1}}{BV_0}$$

To rewrite NI_t/BV_0 this way, we state $ROCE_t = NI_t/BV_{t-1}$. Note that this computation of $ROCE_t$ divides net income in period t by book value of common equity at the beginning of period t. This ROCE computation differs slightly from the approach in Chapter 4 in which we compute ROCE as net income divided by the average book value of equity during period t.[3] Also, note that BV_{t-1}/BV_0 is the cumulative growth factor in book value of common equity between year 0 (the date of the valuation) and period t − 1. As indicated above, growth in book value is a function of the earnings generated each period plus additional capital contributions by shareholders, less equity capital paid out to shareholders through dividends and stock buybacks. The growth in book value indicates growth in net assets invested, on which a firm can earn abnormal returns.

By decomposing the term NI_t/BV_0 into these two parts, we can restate NI_t/BV_0 as the product of ROCE in year t times the cumulative growth in book value from year 0 to the start of year t. Return on common equity is a function of profitability on beginning of year common equity; beginning of year common equity is a function of cumulative growth. We can substitute these two components of NI_t/BV_0 into the VB equation, as follows:

$$\frac{V_0}{BV_0} = 1 + \sum_{t=1}^{\infty} \frac{\left(ROCE_t \times \dfrac{BV_{t-1}}{BV_0}\right) - \left(R_E \times \dfrac{BV_{t-1}}{BV_0}\right)}{(1+R_E)^t}$$

Now both terms in the numerator of the summation term are multiplied by the same cumulative book value growth factor. We rearrange that equation as follows:

---

[3]Theoretical and empirical research on the VB ratio typically defines ROCE as net income to common shareholders for a year divided by common shareholders' equity at the *beginning* of the year. In contrast, we have used *average* common shareholders' equity in the denominator of ROCE throughout this book. The theoretical development and application of the VB model in this section uses shareholders' equity at the beginning of the year, although the bias in using average shareholders' equity should not be particularly significant.

$$\frac{V_0}{BV_0} = 1 + \sum_{t=1}^{\infty} \frac{[ROCE_t - R_E] \times \dfrac{BV_{t-1}}{BV_0}}{(1 + R_E)^t}$$

We now have a useful model for the value-to-book ratio. Next we consider each term.

First, as a starting point, the VB ratio will equal one, to reflect the book value of common equity invested in the firm. The summation term indicates how the VB ratio should differ from one as a function of the firm's expected future abnormal profitability (the $ROCE_t - R_E$ term) times the firm's cumulative growth in book value (the BV_{t-1}/BV_0 term), all of which is discounted to present value, reflecting the firm's cost of equity capital (R_E) and the time value of money. Thus, the residual income model specifies the firm's VB ratio as a function of the firm's value drivers: capital in place, profitability, cost of equity capital, growth, and time value of money. The VB model provides a valuation approach in which all of the inputs to valuation can be expressed as forecasts of *rates*—expected future ROCE, R_E, and growth. The only dollar amount the analyst needs in order to use the VB ratio to compute the dollar value of common shareholders' equity is the book value of common shareholders' equity, which is observable from the shareholders' equity section of the balance sheet.

The expression for the VB ratio provides some insights into valuation:

- Economics teaches that, in equilibrium, firms will earn a return equal to the cost of capital (that is, ROCE = R_E). The VB model indicates that a firm in steady-state equilibrium earning ROCE = R_E will maintain (not create or destroy) shareholder wealth and will be valued at book value (that is, VB = 1).

- A firm's value should be greater than its book value of common equity insofar as the firm will generate wealth for common equity shareholders by earning a return (ROCE) that exceeds the cost of capital (R_E). That is, VB > 1 if ROCE > R_E. Firms that earn a return that is less than the cost of equity capital (that is, ROCE < R_E) will destroy shareholder wealth and will be valued below book value (that is, VB < 1).

- Growth is not value-adding in itself. Growth adds value to shareholders *only* if the growth is abnormally profitable. If expected ROCE equals R_E on new projects (that is, zero NPV projects), then these new projects will not create (or destroy) common shareholders' equity value. New projects will be "abnormally profitable" only when their expected ROCE exceeds R_E.

- The risk of the firm increases the equity cost of capital. Increasing the equity cost of capital reduces firm value in two ways: (1) by increasing the required ROCE the firm must earn to cover the increased cost of capital R_E (that is, the "hurdle rate" goes up); and (2) by increasing the discount rate used to compute the present value of residual income.

- If a firm's VB ratio differs from the industry average VB ratio, it should be because the firm's expected future ROCE, R_E, or book value growth differ from the industry averages. If a firm's VB ratio changes over time, it should be because current expectations for the firm's future ROCE, R_E, or book value growth differ from the past expectations for the firm's future ROCE, R_E, or book value growth.

Example 1. Suppose an analyst is evaluating a firm with $1,000 of book value of common equity and a cost of equity capital equal to 10 percent. Assume that the analyst forecasts that the firm will earn ROCE of 15 percent until Year +3, but then after Year +3 the firm will earn ROCE equal to 10 percent. The analyst also expects the firm will reinvest all net income (that is, pay zero dividends), and it will not issue or buy back stock. Using the VB ratio approach, the analyst should assign the firm a VB ratio equal to one plus the present value of future residual ROCE times growth. The present value of future residual ROCE times growth is determined as follows:

Year	Expected ROCE	Residual ROCE $= ROCE - R_E$	Cumulative Book Value Growth Factor to Year t–1	Residual ROCE times Cumulative Growth	PV Factor	PV of Residual ROCE times Cumulative Growth
+1	0.15	0.05	$1.00 = (1.15)^0$	0.05000	0.9091	0.04545
+2	0.15	0.05	$1.15 = (1.15)^1$	0.05750	0.8264	0.04752
+3	0.15	0.05	$1.3225 = (1.15)^2$	0.06613	0.7513	0.04968
+4	0.10	0.00	$1.52088 = (1.15)^3$	0.00000	0.6830	0.00000

The sum of the present values of residual ROCE times cumulative growth through Year +3 equals 0.14265, and the sum in all years after Year +3 is zero. The VB ratio of this firm is therefore 1.14265. We can multiply the VB ratio by book value of equity to determine that firm value is $1,142.65 (= 1.14265 VB ratio × $1,000 book value equity). Note that we have determined this VB ratio with all of the inputs expressed in rates. We can confirm this value using dollar amounts and the residual income model approach from Chapter 12, as follows:

Year	Expected ROCE	Expected Earnings	Cumulative Book Value at the end of Year t – 1 (BV_{t-1})	Required Income $= BV_{t-1} \times R_E$	Residual Income	PV Factor	PV of Residual Income
+1	0.15	$150.00 $= 0.15 \times 1,000$	$1,000	$100 $= 1,000 \times 0.10$	$50.00 $= 150 - 100$	0.9091	$45.45
+2	0.15	$172.50 $= 0.15 \times 1,150$	$1,150 $= 1,000 + 150$	$115 $= 1,150 \times 0.10$	$57.50 $= 172.50 - 115$	0.8264	$47.52
+3	0.15	$198.38 $= 0.15 \times 1,322.5$	$1,322.5 $= 1,150 + 172.50$	$132.25 $= 1,322.5 \times 0.10$	$66.13 $= 198.38 - 132.25$	0.7513	$49.68
+4	0.10	$152.09 $= 0.10 \times 1,520.88$	$1,520.88 $= 1,322.50 + 198.38$	$152.09 $= 1,520.88 \times 0.10$	$0.00 $= 152.09 - 152.09$	0.6830	$ 0.00

The sum of the present values of residual income through Year +3 equals $142.65, the sum in all years after Year +3 is zero, and book value of equity is $1,000, so the residual income model confirms that firm value is $1,142.65.

REASONS WHY VB RATIOS AND MB RATIOS MAY DIFFER FROM ONE

We described above a number of *economic* reasons why VB and MB ratios may differ from one. For example, the firm may have competitive advantages that enable it to earn an ROCE that is greater than R_E. To the extent that the firm can create and sustain these competitive advantages, the firm will increase the magnitude and persistence over time of the degree to which ROCE exceeds R_E, thereby increasing the VB and MB ratios. In addition, to the extent the firm will generate future growth by investing in abnormally profitable projects, the VB and MB ratios will differ from one.

A firm's VB and MB ratio may differ from one for *accounting* reasons in addition to economic reasons.[4] The firm may have investments in projects for which accounting methods and principles cause ROCE to differ from R_E. For example, firms may make substantial investments in successful research and development projects, brand equity, or human capital. If these investments were internally generated through research and development activities, marketing and advertising activities, or human capital recruiting and training activities, and if the investments in these activities were expensed according to conservative accounting principles (as is common under GAAP in the United States and most countries), then the firm will have substantial off-balance sheet assets and off-balance sheet common shareholders' equity. These off-balance sheet assets generate net income, but common shareholders' equity is understated, so ROCE will be relatively high. These effects can be observed among certain firms in many different industries, such as pharmaceuticals, biotechnology, software, and consumer goods.

In the case of PepsiCo and Coca-Cola, for example, these firms have created substantial off-balance sheet brand equity over many years of successful product development, advertising, and brand-building activities, and the investments in these activities have been expensed. Thus, for these firms, the book value of common shareholders' equity does not recognize the off-balance sheet value of brand equity. Relative to R_E, ROCE for PepsiCo and Coca-Cola is very high and likely will continue to be very high for many years in the future.

Over a sufficiently long period of time, however, the impact of accounting principles on the VB and MB ratio will diminish because economics teaches us to expect that competitive equilibrium forces will drive ROCE to converge to R_E in the long run. Also, the self-correcting nature of accounting will eventually eliminate biases in ROCE and book value of equity. For example, consider a biotechnology company that invests for several years in research and development to develop a particular drug. During the initial years of research, the firm incurs research costs that GAAP

---

[4]Stephen Ryan found that book value changes lag market value changes in part because of GAAP's use of historical cost valuations for assets. The lag varies in part based on the degree of capital intensity of firms. See Stephen Ryan, "A Model of Accrual Measurement and Implications for the Evolution of the Book-to-Market Ratio," *Journal of Accounting Research* (Spring 1995), pp. 95–112.

requires the firm to expense. Its ROCE and book value of equity will be "low" during these years. After developing and then marketing the final drug, ROCE will be "high" because the firm generates revenues without offsetting research costs. The "high" ROCE will increase retained earnings, and, over time, the initial conservative biases in ROCE and book value will be corrected.

EMPIRICAL DATA ON MB RATIOS

Exhibit 13.3 presents descriptive statistics for MB ratios across 36 industries during the decade from 1991 to 2000.[5] The descriptive statistics include the 25th percentile, median, and 75th percentile MB ratios for the sample as a whole and for each industry, listed in ascending order of the median MB ratio. The median MB ratio for the 64,297 firm-years in this sample is 1.85. These data reveal substantial variation in MB ratios across industries and within industries during this period.

The differences in industry median MB ratios in Exhibit 13.3 likely relate in part to differences in competitive conditions driving differences in growth and ROCE relative to R_E, as well as differences in alternative accounting principles. Economically, in an industry that can be characterized as mature and competitive, the median firm will likely generate ROCE that is close to R_E and will not likely generate unusually high rates of growth. Such firms tend to have median MB ratios closer to one. For example, firms in mature competitive industries such as textiles, real estate, insurance, banking, metals, and metal products tend to have MB ratios that are lower than the sample average.

With respect to accounting, the assets of firms in some of these industries—particularly banks and insurers—are primarily investments in financial assets, some of which appear on the balance sheet at fair value, and thus MB ratios are closer to one. In contrast, some of the industries with relatively high MB ratios are more likely to have off-balance sheet assets and shareholders' equity. For example, the chemical industry includes pharmaceutical firms, which expense research and development expenditures in the year incurred. The health services, personal services, and business services industries expense compensation costs in the year incurred and do not capitalize the value of their employees on the balance sheet. The balance sheet understates the economic value of key resources in each of these industries. These industries have MB ratios considerably in excess of one.

EMPIRICAL RESEARCH RESULTS ON THE PREDICTIVE POWER OF MB RATIOS

Several empirical studies have found that MB ratios are fairly stable, mean reverting slowly over time, and that MB ratios are reliable predictors of future growth in book value and expected future ROCE (implying that ROCE also mean reverts

---

[5]To compute these descriptive statistics on market-to-book value ratios, we deleted firm-years with negative book value of equity. We also deleted firm-year observations in the top 1 percent of the distribution as potential outliers with undue influence on the descriptive statistics.

EXHIBIT 13.3			
Descriptive Statistics on Market-to-Book Ratios, 1991–2000			
	25th Percentile	Median	75th Percentile
Full Sample* on Compustat (N = 64,297 firm-years)	1.13	1.85	3.34
Industry:			
Textiles	0.78	1.28	2.00
Real Estate...................................	0.73	1.31	2.50
Insurance	0.94	1.33	1.93
Depository Institutions	0.98	1.34	1.82
Metals	0.89	1.45	2.31
Metal Products	0.96	1.47	2.27
Hotels	0.80	1.48	2.44
Retailers—General Merchandise	0.83	1.49	3.01
Wholesale—Durables..........................	0.90	1.55	2.77
Lumber.....................................	1.06	1.61	2.43
Utilities	1.32	1.62	2.00
Paper......................................	1.17	1.64	2.58
Motion Pictures	1.02	1.68	3.11
Security Brokers	1.09	1.69	3.28
Metal Mining	0.97	1.70	3.05
Oil and Gas Extraction........................	1.09	1.74	2.84
Grocery Stores...............................	1.05	1.76	3.02
Restaurants	1.04	1.81	3.02
Transportation by Air.........................	1.15	1.82	3.10
Petroleum and Coal	1.28	1.83	2.55
Wholesale—Nondurables......................	1.14	1.84	3.16
Transportation Equipment.....................	1.21	1.90	2.93
Amusements	1.11	1.91	3.42
Retailing—Apparel...........................	1.14	1.95	3.50
Forestry....................................	0.90	2.02	2.85
Industrial Machinery and Equipment	1.25	2.08	3.67
Food Processors	1.23	2.15	3.75
Electronic and Electric Equipment	1.25	2.21	3.85
Health Services	1.30	2.21	3.83
Personal Services.............................	1.45	2.34	3.69
Instruments and Related Products..............	1.37	2.39	4.46
Printing and Publishing	1.40	2.41	3.74
Communication	1.84	2.93	5.51
Business Services.............................	1.61	3.06	5.82
Chemicals	1.96	3.34	5.96
Tobacco.....................................	2.87	4.20	11.63

*To compute these descriptive statistics on market-to-book value ratios, we deleted firm-years with negative book value of equity. We also deleted firm-year observations in the top 1 percent of the distribution as potential outliers with undue influence on the descriptive statistics.

slowly).[6] For example, Victor Bernard grouped roughly 1,900 firms into 10 portfolios each year between 1972 and 1981 based on their MB ratios. He then computed the mean ROCE for each portfolio in the formation year and for each of the ten subsequent years. Exhibit 13.4 summarizes a portion of Bernard's results, grouping firms in the lowest 3 MB portfolios, middle 4 MB portfolios, and highest 3 MB portfolios.[7]

The data in Exhibit 13.4 indicate that firms with the highest MB ratios tend to have the highest ROCEs through Year +10, and firms with the lowest MB ratios tend to have the lowest ROCEs through Year +10. The results from the Bernard study also indicate that firms with the highest MB ratios have the highest growth rates in book value of equity through Year +10, and firms with the lowest MB ratios have the lowest growth rates through Year +10. The results in the Bernard study also indicate (although it is not apparent from the summary of results in Exhibit 13.4) that the predictive power of MB ratios for future ROCEs does tend to diminish as the horizon lengthens. In Year +10, for example, there is relatively little difference in ROCEs across firms in the 3rd through 9th MB portfolios, as these firms experience ROCEs that tend to converge to 14 percent. These results are consistent with the steady mean

EXHIBIT 13.4					
The Relation between MB Ratios and Future ROCE and Future Book Value Growth					
		Median ROCE for Year:			
MB Portfolio	**Mean MB Ratio**	**0**	**+1**	**+5**	**+10**
Low	0.67	0.11	0.09	0.12	0.12
Medium	1.15	0.11	0.13	0.14	0.14
High	2.65	0.10	0.17	0.16	0.20
		Cumulative Percent Increase in Book Value through Year:			
		0	**+1**	**+5**	**+10**
Low	0.67	0%	15%	54%	190%
Medium	1.15	0%	15%	69%	204%
High	2.65	0%	21%	139%	394%

---

[6]Victor L. Bernard, "Accounting-Based Valuation Methods, Determinants of Market-to-Book Ratios and Implications for Financial Statement Analysis," *Working Paper*, University of Michigan, 1993; Jane A. Ou and Stephen H. Penman, "Financial Statement Analysis and the Evaluation of Market-to-Book Ratios," *Working Paper*, Columbia University, 1995; Stephen H. Penman, "The Articulation of Price-Earnings Ratios and Market-to-Book Ratios and the Evaluation of Growth," *Journal of Accounting Research*, Vol. 34, No. 2 Autumn 1996, pp. 235–259; William H. Beaver and Stephen G. Ryan, "Biases and Lags in Book Value and Their Effects on the Ability of the Book-to-Market Ratio to Predict Book Return on Equity," *Journal of Accounting Research*, Vol. 38, No. 1 (Spring 2000), pp. 127–149.

[7]To reduce the effects of survivorship bias, Bernard included firms that did not survive the entire 10-year future horizon, and included any gain or loss on the cessation of the firm (from bankruptcy, takeover, or liquidation) in the final year ROCE.

reversion in ROCEs over time, consistent with movement toward competitive equilibrium.

APPLICATION OF THE VALUE-TO-BOOK MODEL TO PEPSICO

In Chapter 12, we estimated PepsiCo's share value at the end of Year 11 to be roughly $69, based on the pro forma financial statement forecasts developed in Chapter 10 and the residual income model valuation. We next illustrate the valuation of PepsiCo shares using the value-to-book model, implementing the same forecasts developed in Chapter 10, the same equity cost of capital (8.0 percent), and the same long-run growth rate (5.0 percent). We also demonstrate the forecasts and valuation estimates in the FSAP Forecasts and Valuation spreadsheets in Appendix D.

To proceed with the VB model, we will follow seven steps:

(1) estimate the expected ROCE each period, computed as NI_t/BV_{t-1};
(2) compute expected residual ROCE each period by subtracting the equity cost of capital from expected ROCE;
(3) determine the cumulative growth factor in book value of common shareholders' equity to the beginning of each period (computed as BV_{t-1}/BV_0);
(4) multiply the expected residual ROCE by the cumulative growth factor;
(5) discount the expected residual ROCE with growth to present value, including continuing value;
(6) compute the implied VB ratio by adding one (the ratio of book value over book value) to the sum of the present value of the expected residual ROCE with growth;
(7) compare the implied VB ratio to the MB ratio to determine whether market price is greater than, equal to, or less than our estimate of value. Equivalently, we can multiply the implied VB ratio by book value of equity to determine the value of common shareholders' equity, and then divide by the number of shares outstanding to convert this total to a per-share estimate of value for PepsiCo, which we then compare to market price.

We next illustrate each of these seven steps with PepsiCo. The Year +1 projected ROCE is 38.9 percent, computed as net income available for common shareholders in Year +1 divided by book value of common equity at the start of Year +1 (= $3,367.3 million/$8,648.0 million). The residual ROCE is 30.9 percent after subtracting 8.0 percent for the cost of equity capital. The cumulative growth in book value (BV_{t-1}/BV_0) in Year +1 is 1.0, because Year +1 is the first year of the valuation horizon.[8] The product of Year +1 residual ROCE and cumulative growth is 30.9 percent, which we discount to present value using an 8.0 percent cost of equity capital. Exhibit 13.5 presents these

---

[8]We project PepsiCo's book value of common equity will grow to $9,466.2 million during Year +1. Therefore the cumulative growth factor in book value of common equity as of the start of Year +2 will be 1.095 (= $9,466.2 million/$8,648.0 million).

	EXHIBIT 13.5		
	Valuation of PepsiCo:		
	Present Value of Residual ROCE in Year +1 through Year +10		
	Year +1	**Year +2**	**Year +3**
COMPREHENSIVE INCOME AVAILABLE FOR			
COMMON SHAREHOLDERS	$3,367.3	$3,656.4	$ 3,975.8
Common Shareholders' Equity (at beginning of year)	$8,648.0	$9,466.2	$10,364.7
Implied ROCE (Comp Inc./Begin. Common Equity)	0.389	0.386	0.384
Residual ROCE (assuming $R_E = 0.08$)	0.309	0.306	0.304
Cumulative Book Value Growth Factor as of the			
Beginning of Year.	1	1.095	1.199
Residual ROCE times Cumulative Book Value Growth Factor . . .	0.309	0.335	0.364
Present Value Factors	0.926	0.857	0.794
PV Residual ROCE times Growth	0.286	0.287	0.289
Sum of PV Residual ROCE in Year +1 through Year +10	2.846		

computations for PepsiCo for Year +1 through Year +10. The sum of the present value of residual ROCE times growth in Year +1 through Year +10 is 2.846.[9]

We use the same steps to compute the Year +11 residual ROCE for purposes of computing continuing value. As described in the previous chapter, we project net income in Year +11 to grow by the 5.0 percent long-run growth rate. We compute book value as of the start of Year +11 (the end of Year +10), compute implied residual ROCE, and multiply by the cumulative growth factor in book value up to the beginning of Year +11. The projected $ROCE_{11}$ is 36.3 percent (= NI_{11}/BV_{10} = $6,920.0 million/$19,073.7 million). The projected residual $ROCE_{11}$ is therefore 28.3 percent. Cumulative growth in book value from Year 0 to the beginning of Year +11 (the end of Year +10) is 2.206 (= BV_{10}/BV_0 = $19,073.7 million/$8,648.0 million). We therefore project in Year +11 the product of residual ROCE times cumulative growth is 62.4 percent (= 28.3 percent × 2.206).

We use the Year +11 residual ROCE with growth (62.4 percent) in the continuing value computation, as follows (allowing for rounding):

$$ContinuingValue_0 = [(NI_{10} \times (1+g)/BV_{10}) - R_E] \times [BV_{10}/BV_0] \times [1/(R_E - g)] \times [1/(1+R_E)^{10}]$$

$$= [(\$6,590.4 \times 1.05/\$19,073.7) - 0.08] \times [\$19,073.7/\$8,648.0] \times [1/(0.08 - 0.05)] \times [1/(1+0.08)^{10}]$$

$$= 0.283 \times 2.206 \times 33.33 \times 0.463$$

$$= 9.630$$

---

[9]This value should be interpreted as a component of the VB ratio, because all of the computations in the model are scaled by BV_0. Thus, the amount 2.846 can be interpreted as an estimate that PepsiCo will create residual income in Years +1 through +10 that, in present value, is equal to 2.846 times the current book value of common equity. To reconcile this computation with the residual income model computations in Chapter 12, recognize that 2.846 times book value of $8,648.0 million equals $24,613.0 (allow for rounding), which is the present value of residual income through Year +10 computed in Exhibit 12.2.

	EXHIBIT 13.5					
Exhibit 13.5—continued						

Year +4	Year +5	Year +6	Year +7	Year +8	Year +9	Year +10
$ 4,312.3	$ 4,649.6	$ 4,991.0	$ 5,350.0	$ 5,734.9	$ 6,147.5	$ 6,590.4
$11,572.9	$12,149.2	$13,380.8	$14,366.6	$15,423.7	$16,556.8	$17,771.4
0.373	0.383	0.373	0.372	0.372	0.371	0.371
0.293	0.303	0.293	0.292	0.292	0.291	0.291
1.338	1.405	1.547	1.661	1.783	1.915	2.055
0.392	0.425	0.453	0.486	0.520	0.558	0.598
0.735	0.681	0.630	0.583	0.540	0.500	0.463
0.288	0.289	0.286	0.283	0.281	0.279	0.277

The total present value of PepsiCo's expected residual ROCE with growth, expressed as components of the VB ratio, is the sum of these two parts:

Present Value of Residual ROCE in Year +1 through Year +10	2.846
Present Value of Continuing Value of ROCE in Year +11 and beyond	9.630
Present Value of Residual ROCE.	12.476

Necessary Adjustments to Compute the Value-to-Book Ratio

To compute the VB ratio for common equity, we need to add PepsiCo's beginning book value of common equity expressed as a ratio of beginning book value of equity, which is, of course, equal to one. As described in Chapters 11 and 12, our present value calculations overdiscount because they discount each year's residual ROCE for full periods when, in fact, the firm generates residual ROCE throughout each period and we should discount from the midpoint of each year to the present. Therefore, to make the correction, we multiply the present value sum by the mid-year adjustment factor $[1 + (R_E/2) = 1 + (0.080/2) = 1.040]$. Making these two adjustments produces the implied VB ratio as follows:

Present Value of Residual ROCE	12.476
Add: Beginning Book Value	+ 1.000
Total.	13.476
Multiply by the Mid-Year Correction Factor	× 1.040
Implied VB Ratio	14.015

These computations suggest that PepsiCo common equity should be valued at 14.015 times the book value of equity at the start of the valuation horizon, which is the end of Year 11. At that time, PepsiCo's market value was $86,131.8 million (= $49.05 per share × 1,756 million shares). Thus, PepsiCo was trading at an MB ratio equal to 9.96 (= $86,131.8 million/$8,648.0 million). The VB ratio is 41 percent greater than the MB ratio, implying PepsiCo shares were underpriced by 41 percent at that time.

Equivalently, we can convert the VB ratio into a share value estimate for purposes of comparing to price. If we multiply book value equity by the VB ratio, we obtain the value estimate of PepsiCo common equity of $121,205.9 million (= $8,648.0 million × 14.015 VB ratio; allow for rounding). Dividing by 1,756 million shares outstanding indicates that PepsiCo's common equity shares have a value of $69.02 per share, a value estimate that is identical to the value estimates we obtained from the residual income and dividend models in Chapter 12 and the free cash flows to common equity shareholders model in Chapter 11. The computations to arrive at PepsiCo's common equity share value are summarized in Exhibit 13.6.

We can conduct a sensitivity analysis for the estimate of PepsiCo's VB ratio to assess a reasonable range of VB ratios for PepsiCo. We will find that the sensitivity of the VB ratio estimate is identical to the sensitivity of the residual income model value estimates demonstrated in Chapter 12. This is to be expected because both models use the same forecasts and valuation assumptions. The VB model is simply a scaled version of the residual income model.

EXHIBIT 13.6		
Valuation of PepsiCo using the Residual ROCE Valuation Model		
Valuation Steps	**Computations**	**Amounts**
Sum of PV Residual ROCE in Year +1 through Year +10	See Exhibit 13.5.	+ 2.846
Add Continuing Value in Present Value	Year +11 residual ROCE assumed to grow at 5.0%; discounted at 8.0%. Computations in FSAP.	+ 9.630
Total PV Residual ROCE		= 12.476
Add: Beginning Book Value of Equity Ratio	Beginning Book Value of Equity from Year 11 Balance Sheet.	+ 1.000
		= 13.476
Adjust to Midyear	Multiply by 1 + (R$_E$/2)	× 1.040
Value-to-Book Ratio of Common Equity		= 14.015
Book Value of Common Equity		×$ 8,648.0
Value of Common Equity		=$121,205.9
Shares Outstanding		÷ 1,756.0
Estimated Value per Share		=$ 69.02
Current Price per Share		$ 49.05
Percent Difference	(Positive number indicates underpricing.)	41%

PRICE-EARNINGS AND VALUE-EARNINGS RATIOS

As we noted in Chapter 12, the capital markets devote enormous amounts of time and energy to forecasting and analyzing firms' earnings numbers. It is, therefore, no surprise that the market multiple that receives most frequent use and attention is the price-earnings (PE) ratio. Analysts' reports and the financial press make frequent references to PE ratios. The *Wall Street Journal* reports PE ratios as part of the daily coverage of stock prices and trading. The capital markets increasingly evaluate ratios that integrate the PE ratio with expected future earnings growth, to capture explicitly the links between price, earnings, and growth.

This section first describes the theoretical model for computing value-earnings ratios. The section then describes computing and using PE ratios from a practical perspective because of the widespread use of PE ratios in practice. We then discuss the strict assumptions implied by PE ratios, and describe the conditions in which PE ratios may not capture appropriately the theoretical relation between value and earnings for most firms and the difficulties one encounters in reconciling actual PE ratios with those indicated by the theoretical value-earnings model. In this section, we also incorporate the role of earnings growth and examine price-earnings-growth (PEG) ratios. We conclude the section by describing empirical data on PE ratios, the predictive power of PE ratios, and the empirical evidence on the articulation between PE ratios and MB ratios.

A THEORETICAL MODEL FOR THE VALUE-EARNINGS RATIO

The VE ratio is the ratio of the value of common shareholders' equity divided by earnings for a single period. The previous chapter described how to determine common equity value as a function of present value of expected *future* earnings and the residual income model. In the residual income model, we use clean surplus accounting and measure future earnings as expected future comprehensive income (that is, income that includes all of the income to common shareholders). Thus, in theory, the analyst should measure the VE ratio as the value of common equity divided by *next* period's expected comprehensive income. This way, the VE ratio achieves consistent alignment of *perspective* (numerator and denominator both forward-looking) and *measurement* (numerator and denominator both based on income measurement that is comprehensive).

If one has already computed firm value using the forecasting and valuation models developed in the last three chapters, then computing the VE ratio is a simple matter of division. For example, in prior chapters we estimated PepsiCo's common shareholders' equity value to be $121,205.9 million at the end of Year 11. We also projected Year +1 comprehensive income will equal net income available for common shareholders, which will equal $3,367.3 million. Thus, we can compute the VE ratio for PepsiCo at the end of Year 11 as:

$$V_0/E_1 = \$121,205.9 \text{ million}/\$3,367.3 \text{ million} = 36.0$$

Or equivalently, on a per-share basis as:

$$\text{Vps}_0/\text{Eps}_1 = (\$121{,}205.9 \text{ million}/1{,}756 \text{ million shares})/(\$3{,}367.3 \text{ million}/1{,}756 \text{ million shares}) = \$69.02/\$1.92 = 36.0$$

We can also derive the VE ratio from the VB ratio determined using the residual income model in the previous section. We can employ an algebraic step to derive the firm's VE ratio from the firm's VB ratio, as follows:

$$V_0/E_1 = V_0/BV_0 \times BV_0/E_1 = V_0/BV_0 \times (1/\text{ROCE}_1)$$

Using this approach, we can derive PepsiCo's VE ratio from the VB ratio we computed in the previous section, as follows:

$$V_0/E_1 = V_0/BV_0 \times BV_0/E_1 = V_0/BV_0 \times (1/\text{ROCE}_1)$$
$$= (\$121{,}205.9 \text{ million}/\$8{,}648.0 \text{ million}) \times (\$8{,}648.0 \text{ million}/\$3{,}367.3 \text{ million})$$
$$= 14.015 \times 2.5682$$
$$= 14.015 \times (1/0.389)$$
$$= 36.0$$

Thus, we compute that PepsiCo's VE ratio should equal 36.0. We convert PepsiCo's VB ratio of 14.015 into the VE ratio by multiplying by $1/\text{ROCE}_1$, which we project will be the inverse of 38.9 percent.

Notice that we simply derived the VE ratio from the computation that PepsiCo's value is equal to $121,205.9 million, which is based on specific forecasts of PepsiCo's future earnings. Obviously, using value to compute a VE ratio will not provide any new information about PepsiCo's value. So what is the point of computing a VE ratio?

The VE ratio provides the theoretically correct benchmark to evaluate the firm's PE ratio. We can compare PepsiCo's VE ratio of 36.0 to PepsiCo's PE ratio to assess the market value of PepsiCo shares. This comparison is equivalent to comparing V to P (that is, value to price). With the theoretically correct VE ratio, we can also project VE ratios for other firms, including making adjustments as necessary to capture the other firms' fundamental characteristics of profitability, growth, and risk. In addition, with the theoretically correct VE ratio, we have a benchmark to gauge other firms' PE ratios in order to assess whether the market is under- or overpricing their shares. In the next section, we discuss the practical advantages and disadvantages in using PE ratios as shortcut valuation metrics.

PRICE-EARNINGS RATIOS

As a practical matter, analysts, the financial press, and financial databases commonly measure PE ratios as current period share price divided by reported earnings per share for either the most recent prior fiscal year or the most recent four quarters (sometimes referred to as the trailing-twelve-months earnings).[10] The *Wall Street Journal* and financial data web sites such as Yahoo! Finance commonly compute PE ratios this way. With this approach, we compute the PE ratio for PepsiCo as of the end of Year 11 as follows: Price per share$_{11}$/Earnings per share$_{11}$ = \$49.05/\$1.51 = 32.5. Thus, at the end of Year 11, PepsiCo shares traded at a multiple of 32.5 times Year 11 earnings per share.[11]

The common approach to compute the PE ratio by dividing market price by earnings per share for the most recent year is practical because analysts can readily observe price per share and historical earnings per share for most firms. However, this common approach creates a logical misalignment for valuation purposes because it divides share price—which reflects the present value of *future* earnings—by *historical* earnings. If historical earnings contain unusual or nonrecurring gains or losses that are not expected to persist in future earnings, then the analyst should cleanse the reported historical earnings of these effects in order to compute a PE ratio that reflects earnings that are likely to persist in the future. Chapter 6 describes techniques to identify elements of income that are unusual and nonrecurring, adjust reported earnings to eliminate their effects, and thereby measure recurring, persistent earnings.

As an alternative approach to create a more logical alignment of price and earnings, the analyst can compute the PE ratio by dividing share price by the analyst's forecast of future earnings per share—for example, expected earnings per share one year ahead. A PE ratio based on expected future earnings, however, requires the analyst to forecast future earnings (or have access to another analyst's forecast). The reliability of a forward-looking PE ratio then depends on the reliability of the earnings forecast. Earnings forecast errors will distort forward-looking PE ratios.

We compute the forward-looking PE ratio for PepsiCo as of the end of Year 11 using our forecast that Year +1 earnings will be \$3,367.3 million as follows: Price per share$_0$/Earnings per share$_{+1}$ = \$49.05 per share/(\$3,367.3 million/1,756 million shares) = 25.6. Thus, at the end of Year 11, PepsiCo shares traded at a multiple of 25.6 times the Year +1 earnings forecast. PepsiCo's VE ratio of 36.0 is 41 percent greater than PepsiCo's PE ratio of 25.6 at the end of Year 11, consistent with our prior estimates of PepsiCo's value.[12]

---

[10]In theory, to be consistent with clean surplus accounting and residual income valuation, the denominator should be based on comprehensive income per share. However, analysts, the financial press, and financial databases rarely, if ever, compute PE ratios based on comprehensive income per share, in part because (a) U.S. GAAP does not yet require reporting comprehensive income on a per-share basis, and (b) the other comprehensive income items are usually unrealized gains and losses that are not likely to be a permanent component of income each period. We follow traditional practice in this chapter and compute PE ratios using reported earnings figures.

[11]If we compute PepsiCo's PE ratio using amounts in millions rather than per-share amounts, we obtain a PE ratio of 32.4 (= \$86,131.8 million/(Net Income of \$2,662 million − \$4 million preferred dividends)). This PE ratio is slightly lower than the PE ratio of 32.5 based on per-share amounts because PepsiCo reports earnings per share based on the weighted average number of common shares outstanding during the year (which is consistent with U.S. GAAP) rather than the number of shares outstanding at year-end.

[12]In this case, our forecasts of net income and comprehensive income for PepsiCo in Year +1 are the same, so the PE ratio using earnings per share is equal to that using comprehensive income per share.

Notice that we simply derived the PE ratio by dividing PepsiCo's market share price by either earnings per share of the past year or by our forecasts of PepsiCo's future earnings per share. Obviously, using price to compute a PE ratio will not provide any new information about PepsiCo's share *value*. So what is the point of computing a PE ratio?

PE ratios are practical tools used by analysts interested in valuation shortcuts. In some circumstances, analysts need to react with timely ballpark-estimates of valuation, and PE ratios provide a quick and efficient way to estimate firm value as a multiple of earnings. Analysts commonly assess benchmark PE ratios that they expect a firm to have based on past PE ratios for that firm, or industry-average PE ratios, or comparable firms' PE ratios. Analysts use benchmarks like these to project a firm's PE ratio quickly, using one-period earnings as a common denominator for relative valuations, rather than engaging in the extensive computations necessary to determine the correct value-earnings ratio to assess whether the market has priced the firm's shares appropriately.

Analysts also use PE ratios as potentially informative benchmarks to project earnings-based valuation multiples that they use to compare valuations across companies or to project the valuations of other companies. For example, we could compare PepsiCo's PE ratio to the PE ratios of Coca-Cola, Cadbury-Schweppes, or other beverage companies. We might also use PepsiCo's PE ratio to project valuations for these beverage companies, or to project valuations for privately held firms or divisions of companies. Investment bankers use comparable companies' PE ratios, for example, to benchmark reasonable ranges of share prices for IPOs.

PE ratios have the advantage of speed and efficiency, but they are not necessarily precise valuation estimates. When using PE ratios, therefore, the analyst must be careful to adjust them to match the fundamental characteristics of different companies. For example, PepsiCo's PE ratio should differ from Coca-Cola's insofar as the fundamental characteristics of profitability, growth, and risk differ across these two firms. Such differences might arise, for example, because PepsiCo derives a major portion of earnings from the snack food business, which Coca-Cola does not have. Similarly, Coca-Cola derives more of its earnings from international sales than PepsiCo. These and other factors cause the profitability, growth, and risk of PepsiCo and Coca-Cola to differ, and therefore cause their PE ratios to differ. We will describe PE ratio differences in more detail after we first describe the conceptual basis for PE ratios.

PE Ratios Project Firm Value from Permanent Earnings

What should a firm's PE ratio be? What is an appropriate valuation multiple for a firm's earnings? We have seen that, in theory, the firm's PE ratio should equal the firm's VE ratio. However, if the analyst has not computed value in order to determine the VE ratio and wishes to use a shortcut PE ratio instead, what is the correct PE ratio to use?

In projecting firm value using a simple PE ratio (that is, one that ignores earnings-growth), the analyst imposes a strong assumption on the earnings number for a single period: the analyst treats this earnings number (whether it is a trailing earnings number or a one-period-ahead forecast) as the beginning amount of a permanent stream of earnings, valued as a perpetuity. Conceptually, suppose that the firm's common shareholders' equity value equals its market value, that the firm's earnings will be constant in the future, and that the firm's investors expect a rate of return R_E. Under these conditions, we can value the firm's common equity using the perpetuity model based on one-year-ahead earnings (denoted E_1), as follows:

$$V_0 = P_0 = E_1/R_E$$

Rearranging slightly, the firm's VE and PE ratios are:

$$V_0/E_1 = P_0/E_1 = 1/R_E$$

Thus, strictly speaking, the PE multiple assumes that firm value is the present value of a constant stream of expected future earnings, discounted at a constant expected future discount rate. Under these conditions, the analyst can value the firm simply using a multiple of one-period-ahead earnings, and the PE ratio of the firm is simply the inverse of the discount rate.

To illustrate this model with an example, assume that the market expects the firm to generate earnings of $700 next period and requires a 14 percent return on equity capital. The market value of the firm at the beginning of the next period should be $5,000 (= $700/0.14). Note that the inverse of the 14 percent discount rate translates into a PE ratio of 7.14 (= 1/0.14). Thus, $700 times 7.14 equals $5,000.

The simple PE ratio assumes future earnings will be permanent, which is not realistic for most firms. Most firms' earnings are not expected to remain constant; most firms' earnings grow. Not surprisingly, such strict assumptions match the fundamental characteristics of very few firms. We have already seen that such strict assumptions do not fit PepsiCo. Under the assumptions that PepsiCo's earnings will be constant in the future, and that PepsiCo's constant future ROCE will equal the 8.0 percent cost of equity capital, then PepsiCo's PE ratio should be 12.5 (= 1/0.080). This PE ratio is far below the theoretically derived VE ratio of 36.0 for PepsiCo.

Descriptive Data on PE Ratios

The table below includes descriptive statistics of price-earnings ratios (share price to one-year-ahead earnings: P_t/E_{t+1}, as well as share price to trailing earnings: P_t/E_t) during the years 1991–2000. These data represent a broad cross-sectional sample of 38,219 firm-years drawn from the Compustat database, excluding all firm-years with negative earnings.[13]

Price-Earnings Ratio	25th percentile	Median	75th percentile
P_t/E_{t+1}	9.60	13.91	21.39
P_t/E_t	11.09	15.72	24.12

---

[13]It does not make sense to compute PE ratios on the basis of negative earnings. PE ratios assume earnings are permanent; negative earnings are not likely to be permanent.

Exhibit 13.7 includes descriptive statistics on forward-looking PE ratios (share price to one-year-ahead earnings: P_t/E_{t+1}) for the same 36 industries described in Exhibit 13.3 (MB ratios) and Exhibit 11.3 (market betas) during the years 1991 to 2000. Exhibit 13.7 lists the industries in ascending order of the median PE ratios. To describe the industry-wide variation in PE ratios, Exhibit 13.7 also includes the 25th percentile PE ratio and the 75th percentile PE ratio for each industry.

These descriptive data indicate substantial differences in median PE ratios across industries during 1991 to 2000. The firms in the forestry, security brokers, and insurance industries experienced the lowest median PE ratios during that period, whereas firms in the metal mining, business services, communications, and personal services industries experienced the highest median PE ratios. These data also depict wide variation in PE ratios across firms within each industry. For example, most of these 36 industries experienced wide differences between the 25th percentile and the 75th percentile PE ratio during 1991 to 2000. With only a few exceptions, the 75th percentile PE ratio was more than double the 25th percentile PE ratio.[14]

What Factors Cause the PE Ratio to Differ Across Firms?

The same set of *economic* factors that may cause firms' MB ratios to differ will also cause PE ratios to differ. The primary drivers of differences in PE ratios across firms are the fundamental drivers of value: risk, profitability, and growth. In addition to economic factors, differences across firms in accounting methods and accounting principles, and differences across time in accounting earnings, can also drive differences in PE ratios. We describe the effects of each of these determinants of PE ratios in the sections that follow, saving growth for last because we will expand on the role of growth in determining PE ratios.

Risk and the Cost of Capital. As the previous discussion points out, firms with equivalent amounts of earnings but different levels of risk and therefore different costs of equity capital will experience different PE ratios (and different VE ratios). All else equal, more risky firms will experience a lower market value and PE ratio. However, only firms facing rare circumstances experience PE ratios that equal the inverse of the equity cost of capital, so a variety of other forces also cause PE ratios to differ.

Profitability. A firm with competitive advantages will be able to earn ROCE that exceeds R_E. To the extent that the firm can sustain these competitive advantages, the persistence over time of the degree to which ROCE exceeds R_E will increase, thereby increasing the PE ratio relative to similar firms that do not have sustainable competitive advantages. Thus, both the magnitude and the persistence of the difference between ROCE and R_E will increase PE ratios across firms.

---

[14]The analyst must be careful with PE ratios because they are sensitive to earnings numbers that are near zero. Firms with earnings that are positive but temporarily very low will experience PE ratios that are temporarily very high.

EXHIBIT 13.7		
Descriptive Statistics on Share Price to One-Year-Ahead Earnings Ratios (P_t/E_{t+1}), 1991–2000		

Industry	Price-Earnings Ratios (P_t/E_{t+1})		
	25th Percentile	**Median**	**75th Percentile**
Forestry	4.5	5.8	11.3
Security Brokers	6.3	9.9	16.2
Insurance	7.8	10.9	16.5
Depository Institutions	8.8	11.5	15.6
Lumber	8.1	11.6	17.4
Transportation by Air	8.1	11.7	17.3
Metal Products	8.4	11.8	17.2
Transportation Equipment	8.8	12.1	18.6
Tobacco	11.0	12.8	17.2
Wholesale—Durables	8.4	12.8	20.5
Metals	8.7	12.9	20.2
Wholesale—Nondurables	9.2	13.0	21.0
Utilities	10.8	13.0	16.1
Textiles	10.0	13.3	19.6
Real Estate	8.0	13.4	24.7
Industrial Machinery and Equipment	9.7	14.4	23.9
Retailers—General Merchandise	11.5	14.8	22.5
Retailing—Apparel	10.2	14.8	21.9
Petroleum and Coal	11.4	14.9	19.7
Hotels	8.1	15.0	21.4
Motion Pictures	9.7	15.3	25.5
Electronic and Electric Equipment	9.7	15.6	25.4
Printing and Publishing	11.2	15.6	22.0
Oil and Gas Extraction	8.9	15.7	27.2
Restaurants	10.7	15.7	24.8
Paper	10.8	16.0	23.2
Grocery Stores	12.2	16.1	23.3
Health Services	11.3	16.6	26.6
Instruments and Related Products	11.2	16.8	26.5
Amusements	10.0	17.4	26.6
Chemicals	12.5	17.6	26.5
Food Processors	11.9	17.6	26.1
Personal Services	14.3	18.8	24.2
Communication	13.4	18.8	35.0
Business Services	12.4	19.4	31.7
Metal Mining	12.0	21.0	37.6

To compute these descriptive statistics on price-earnings ratios, we divided firm value (computed as year-end closing price times number of shares outstanding) by one-year-ahead net income. We deleted firm-years with negative one-year-ahead net income.

Accounting Differences. In addition to economic factors, firms' PE ratios may differ for *accounting* reasons—especially differences in accounting methods, principles, and the periodic nature of earnings measurement. Some firms select accounting methods that are conservative with respect to income recognition and asset measurement (for example, LIFO for inventories during periods of rising input prices and accelerated depreciation of fixed assets). Some firms invest in projects for which accounting principles are conservative. For example, firms may make substantial investments in intangible activities that must be expensed under conservative accounting principles, leading to economic assets that are off-balance sheet, such as successful research and development, brand equity, or human capital. The effects of accounting methods and principles on reported earnings and PE ratios will likely change over the firm's lifetime. All else held equal, conservative accounting will reduce reported earnings early in the life of the firm (for example, when accelerated depreciation charges are high or research and development is being expensed), thereby increasing the PE ratio. Ironically, later in the life of the firm, after the investments have been completely expensed, reported earnings will be higher, and PE ratios will be lower.

Accounting measures earnings in annual periods. Firms' PE ratios will be significantly different when one-period earnings are unusually high or low and therefore not representative of earnings in perpetuity. For example, if the analyst expects Year +1 earnings will include an unusual loss that will not persist, then the firm's PE ratio will be unusually high. The transitory nature of a single period of accounting earnings can cause PE ratios to be more volatile than the long-run expectations of earnings warrant. In particular, if the analyst uses PE ratios based on trailing twelve months earnings that include non-recurring gains or losses that are not expected to persist, the PE ratios will be artificially volatile.

Continuing the example, assume that the analyst expects the firm to generate earnings next period of $650 instead of $700 because the firm will recognize a $50 restructuring charge. If the market views this charge as nonrecurring (that is, not a permanent change in earnings), then the market price should fall to roughly $4,950 (= $5,000 − $50) in the no-growth scenario, and the PE ratio for the period will be 7.62 (= $4,950/$650), instead of 7.14 (= $5,000/$700). Conversely, if the current period's earnings exceed their expected permanent level, then the PE ratio will be less than normal.

The analyst must assess whether the lower or higher level of earnings for the period (and therefore higher or lower PE ratio) represents a transitory phenomenon or a change to a new lower or higher level of permanent earnings. If the analyst expects the decrease in earnings from $700 to $650 will be permanent, then the market price (assuming no change in risk or growth) should decrease to $4,643 (= $650/.14). Thus, the PE ratio remains the same at 7.14 (= 1/.14).

To illustrate the effects of accounting differences on PE ratios across firms, consider the table below, which includes PE ratios (computed as year-end share price over trailing earnings per share) for PepsiCo and Coca-Cola for the Years 10 and 11.

		PE Ratio	Price per Share	Earnings per Share
Year 10:	PepsiCo	34.2	$49.56	$1.45
	Coca-Cola	69.3	$60.94	$0.88
Year 11:	PepsiCo	32.5	$49.05	$1.51
	Coca-Cola	29.5	$47.15	$1.60

Considered at face value, the PE ratios for PepsiCo and Coca-Cola in Year 10 indicate that the market valued Coca-Cola's earnings at a multiple of 69.3, more than twice PepsiCo's earnings multiple of 34.2, implying Coca-Cola had lower cost of capital, higher growth, and/or greater profitability than PepsiCo. To the contrary, however, Coca-Cola recognized a restructuring charge in income in Year 10, driving EPS down to only $0.88, thereby inflating Coca-Cola's PE ratio. Thus, the big jump in Coca-Cola's PE ratio occurred largely because earnings temporarily declined that year, and did not reflect the market's expectations for Coca-Cola's long-term earnings. In Year 11, both firms reported earnings closer to normal levels and their PE ratios were quite similar.

Growth. Holding all else equal, PE ratios will be greater for firms that the market expects will generate greater earnings growth with future investments in abnormally profitable projects. In the next section, we discuss techniques analysts use to incorporate earnings growth into PE ratios.

Incorporating Earnings Growth into Price-Earnings Ratios

Analysts commonly modify the PE ratio to incorporate earnings growth. In this section, we describe and apply two related approaches to include expected future earnings growth in the computation of the PE ratio: (1) the perpetuity-with-growth approach; and (2) the price-earnings-growth approach.[15]

The Perpetuity-with-Growth Approach. The perpetuity-with-growth approach assumes that the firm can be valued as the present value of a permanent stream of future earnings that will grow at constant rate g. In this case, we can express VE and PE ratios as perpetuity-with-growth models, as follows:

$$V_0 = P_0 = E_1 \times 1/(R_E - g), \text{ so } V_0/E_1 = P_0/E_1 = 1/(R_E - g)$$

To continue the illustration, assume that the market expects the firms' earnings will be $700 next year and will grow 5 percent each year thereafter. The model suggests

---

[15]In recent research, James Ohlson and Beate Juettner-Narouth develop a theoretical model for the price-earnings ratio that incorporates short-term and long-term earnings per share growth. The model appears to be a promising addition to the earnings-based valuation literature, providing new insights into the relation between value, earnings, and growth. However, the model has not yet been subject to extensive empirical testing or practical application. See James Ohlson and Beate Juettner-Nauroth, "Expected EPS and EPS Growth as Determinants of Value," *Working Paper*, New York University, 2000.

the PE ratio should be 11.11 [= 1.0/(0.14 − 0.05)] and market value should be $7,778 (= $700 × 11.11). The present value of the growth in earnings adds $2,778 (= $7,778 − $5,000) to the value of the firm.

PE ratios are particularly sensitive to the growth rate. If the growth rate is 6 percent instead of 5 percent, the ratio becomes 12.50 [= 1.0/(0.14 − 0.06)] and the market value becomes $8,750 (= $700 × 12.50). The sensitivity occurs because the model assumes that the firm will grow at the specified growth rate forever. Competition, new discoveries or technologies, or other factors eventually erode rapid growth rates in an industry. In using the constant growth version of the PE ratio, the analyst should select a long-run equilibrium growth rate in earnings.

This expression for the VE and PE ratio underscores the joint importance of risk and growth in valuation. Given the relation between expected return (R_E) and risk, the VE and PE ratio should be inversely related to risk. Holding earnings and growth constant, higher risk levels should translate into lower PE and VE ratios, and vice versa. Investors will not pay as much for a higher risk security as for a lower risk security with identical expected earnings and growth. In contrast, VE and PE should relate positively to growth. Holding earnings and R_E constant, firms with high expected long-run growth rates in earnings should experience higher VE and PE ratios.

With respect to PepsiCo at the end of Year 11, we assumed that PepsiCo would experience a long-run growth rate of 5.0 percent. Thus, using the perpetuity-with-growth approach, we calculate the PE ratio as:

$$P_0/E_1 = 1/(R_E − g) = 1/(0.080 − 0.050) = 33.33$$

Clearly, incorporating growth makes a big difference in PepsiCo's PE ratio (as compared to the PE ratio of 12.5 that ignores growth). Assuming PepsiCo's earnings grow at 5.0 percent per year beginning in Year +1, this PE with growth ratio would value PepsiCo shares at a multiple of 33.33 times the Year +1 earnings forecast. This PE ratio is still less than the theoretically correct VE ratio of 36.0, however, because it does not take into account our forecast that PepsiCo earnings would grow at roughly 7.2 percent from Year +1 to Year +10. Thus, this PE ratio understates the value of PepsiCo's expected earnings growth during those years.

The Price-Earnings-Growth Approach. An alternative *ad hoc* approach to incorporate growth into PE ratios has emerged from practice in recent years, in which analysts' divide the price-earnings ratio by the expected short-term earnings growth rate (expressed as a percent; some analysts will use the expected earnings growth rate for the medium-term horizon of 3 to 5 years). This approach produces the so-called PEG ratio seen with increasing frequency in practice. Analysts compute the PEG ratio as follows:

$$PEG_0 = (Price\ per\ share_0/Earnings\ per\ share_0)/(g × 100)$$

Analysts and the financial press use the PEG ratio as a rule-of-thumb to assess share price relative to earnings and expected future earnings growth. Although there is little theoretical foundation for this rule-of-thumb (which tends to vary across analysts), proponents of PEG ratios generally assert that firms normally have PEG ratios near 1.0, indicating market price fairly reflects expected earnings growth. Using this rule-of-thumb, proponents assert that market prices for firms with low PEG ratios (0.5 and below) are low relative to growth, and market prices for firms with high PEG ratios (1.5 and above) are high relative to growth. Proponents of PEG ratios argue that this heuristic provides a convenient means to rank stocks, taking into account one-year-ahead earnings and expected earnings growth.[16]

In Chapter 10, we assumed that PepsiCo would experience earnings growth of roughly 7.2 percent per year through Year +5. Using this growth rate assumption and our Year 11 reported earnings per share, we compute PepsiCo's PEG ratio at the end of Year 11 as follows:

$$PEG_{11} = (\text{Price per share}_{11}/\text{Earnings per share}_{11})/(g \times 100)$$
$$= (\$49.05/\$1.51)/(0.072 \times 100)$$
$$= 32.5/7.2 = 4.51$$

Thus, PepsiCo shares traded at the end of Year 11 at a PEG ratio of 4.51. Based on the PEG heuristic, PepsiCo's PEG ratio of 4.51 suggests the market price for PepsiCo shares reflect substantial overpricing of PepsiCo's growth. This heuristic does not take into account, however, the fact that PepsiCo's expected future ROCE is significantly greater than PepsiCo's R_E because of PepsiCo's substantial off-balance sheet brand equity. The PEG ratio deserves considerable attention from researchers and practitioners so that its uses and limitations can be tested and understood.

PE Ratio Measurement Issues

Thus far, we have discussed a variety of different measurement issues for PE ratios. Forward-looking PE ratios divide share price by one-year-ahead earnings forecasts, which is theoretically more correct; however, such forecasts are not readily available for all firms, and they depend on analysts' forecast assumptions, which can differ widely. Therefore, as noted earlier, in practice the analyst is most likely to encounter PE ratios in the *Wall Street Journal* or on financial data web sites that are most commonly measured as share price divided by earnings per share for either the most recent prior fiscal year or the most recent four quarters. This is a sensible approach because historical earnings are observable and unique; however, computation of PE ratios using historic earnings introduces the potential for bias. To recap, the analyst should be aware of (at least) the following two types of measurement error:

(1) *Growth.* Simple ratios of price over earnings do not explicitly consider firm-specific differences in long-term earnings growth. The price-earnings ratios described in the prior sections provide mechanisms that incorporate growth into price-earnings multiples.

(2) *Transitory earnings.* Past earnings are historical and may not be indicative of expected future "permanent" earnings levels. Insofar as historic earnings

---

[16]Mark Bradshaw demonstrates an empirical link between PEG ratios and sell-side analysts' target price recommendations in "The Use of Target Prices to Justify Sell-Side Analysts' Stock Recommendations," *Accounting Horizons*, Vol. 16, No. 1 (March 2002), pp. 27–41.

contain transitory gains or losses, or other elements that are not expected to recur, it can cause the PE ratio to vary wildly.

In addition, the analyst must also be aware of the potential bias in PE ratios because of differences in firms' dividend payouts. *Dividends displace future earnings.* A dividend paid in year t reduces market price by the amount of the dividend, but the dividend is not subtracted from earnings. The dividend paid will cause future earnings to decline because the firm has paid out a portion of its resources to shareholders. Price should therefore decline by the present value of the firm's foregone amount of expected future return on assets distributed as dividends. Thus, for dividend-paying firms, dividends cause a mismatch between current period price and lagged earnings. To eliminate this mismatch, the analyst should compute a PE ratio with growth for a dividend-paying firm as follows: $(P_t + D_t)/E_t = 1/(R_E - g)$.

Empirical Properties of PE Ratios

The theoretical models indicate that the PE ratio is related to R_E, the cost of equity capital, and g, the growth rate in future earnings. Several empirical studies have examined the relation between PE ratios, risk (measured using market beta), and growth (measured using realized prior growth rates or analysts forecasts of future growth). These studies have found that approximately 50 percent to 70 percent of the variability in PE ratios across firms relates to risk and growth.[17]

PE Ratios as Predictors of Future Earnings Growth. Stephen Penman, a leading scholar in the relation between earnings, book values, and market values, studied the relation between PE ratios and changes in earnings per share for all firms on the Compustat database for the years 1968 to 1985.[18] For each year, Penman grouped firms into 20 portfolios based on the level of their PE ratios. He then computed the percentage change in earnings per share for the formation year, and for each of the nine subsequent years. Penman then aggregated the results across years. The table below presents a subset of the aggregate results.

PE Portfolio:	Median Percentage Change in Earnings per Share in:				
	Year 0	Year +1	Year +2	Year +3	Year +4
High	3.9%	52.2%	17.5%	17.8%	15.0%
Medium............	14.0%	11.8%	11.6%	13.7%	15.8%
Low	18.4%	4.8%	10.2%	12.3%	13.1%

[17]See William Beaver and Dale Morse, "What Determines Price-Earnings Ratios?," *Financial Analysts Journal* (July–August 1978), pp. 65–76, and Paul Zarowin, "What Determines Earnings-Price Ratios: Revisited," *Journal of Accounting, Auditing and Finance* (Summer 1990), pp. 439–454.

[18]Stephen H. Penman, "The Articulation of Price-Earnings Ratios and Market-to-Book Ratios and the Evaluation of Growth," *Journal of Accounting Research* (Autumn 1996), pp. 235–259.

The results for the formation year are consistent with transitory components in earnings. Firms with high PE ratios experienced low percentage changes in earnings during the formation year relative to the preceding year. Firms with low PE ratios experienced high percentage changes in earnings during the formation year. The results for Year 1 after the formation year suggest a counter-balancing effect of the earnings change in the formation year. A low percentage increase in earnings is followed by a high percentage earnings increase for the high PE portfolios, and vice-versa for the low PE portfolios.

The results for subsequent years reflect the tendency toward mean reversion in percentage earnings changes to a level in the mid-teens. This result is consistent with the data presented in Exhibit 13.4 for ROCE, where Bernard observed a mean reversion in ROCE toward the mid-teens. The mean reversion suggests systematic directional changes in earnings growth over time (that is, serial autocorrelation), but the reversion takes several years to occur.

Articulation of MB and PE Ratios. In the same research study, Stephen Penman also utilized the residual income valuation model and empirical data to examine the articulation between firms' PE and MB ratios.[19] Penman predicts that MB should be "normal" (that is, equal to one) when the market expects the firm to earn zero residual income in the future. The MB ratio will be high (above one) or low (below one) if the market expects the firm to earn positive or negative future residual income. At the same time, Penman predicts that PE ratios will be normal (that is, equal to the inverse of R_E) when the firm earns current period residual income that is equal to expected future residual income (that is, a firm with current ROCE equal to long-run expected ROCE, which should equal long-run expected R_E). In contrast, PE ratios should be high when the firm earns current residual income below long-run expected residual income (that is, current ROCE is unusually low, causing PE to be high). PE ratios should be low when the firm earns current residual income that is greater than long-run expected residual income (that is, current ROCE is temporarily high, causing PE to be low.) Thus, MB ratios will be determined primarily by expected future residual income, whereas PE ratios will be a function of the difference between current and expected future residual income.

To study the articulation of PE and MB ratios, Penman collected data from the CRSP and Compustat databases on roughly 2,574 firms during the years 1968–1985. Each sample year, Penman ranked and grouped these firms into 20 portfolios based on PE ratios. He also ranked and grouped the same firms each year into 3 MB ratio portfolios, classifying MB ratios below 0.90 as low, MB ratios above 1.10 as high, and MB ratios in between as normal.

Exhibit 13.8 presents a matrix summarizing a portion of the results from Penman's study. Exhibit 13.8 presents residual income figures after assuming a 10.0 percent cost of capital for all firm-years, and after scaling by beginning of period book value of common equity (so they are essentially residual ROCE figures). We denote current period residual income as CRI, and future residual income one-year-ahead and six-years-ahead as FRI_1 and FRI_6, respectively.

---

[19]Stephen H. Penman, *op cit.*

EXHIBIT 13.8

The Articulation of Market-to-Book (MB) and Price-Earnings (PE) Ratios

PE Ratio Portfolios:	MB Ratio Portfolios:		
	High	Normal	Low
High (Portfolios 15–20)	CRI < FRI > 0 CRI: −0.50 to 0.07 FRI$_1$: −0.07 to 0.08 FRI$_6$: 0.01 to 0.11	CRI < FRI = 0 CRI: −0.36 to −0.04 FRI$_1$: −0.13 to −0.03 FRI$_6$: −0.06 to 0.07	CRI < FRI < 0 CRI: −0.24 to −0.06 FRI$_1$: −0.13 to −0.06 FRI$_6$: −0.01 to 0.02
Normal (Portfolios 7–14)	CRI = FRI > 0 CRI: 0.07 to 0.10 FRI$_1$: 0.08 to 0.10 FRI$_6$: 0.11 to 0.14	CRI = FRI = 0 CRI: −0.02 to 0.04 FRI$_1$: −0.02 to 0.04 FRI$_6$: 0.01 to 0.06	CRI = FRI < 0 CRI: −0.05 to 0.00 FRI$_1$: −0.04 to 0.00 FRI$_6$: −0.02 to 0.03
Low (Portfolios 1–6)	CRI > FRI > 0 CRI: 0.12 to 0.41 FRI$_1$: 0.12 to 0.25 FRI$_6$: 0.11 to 0.24	CRI > FRI = 0 CRI: 0.05 to 0.22 FRI$_1$: 0.05 to 0.15 FRI$_6$: 0.07 to 0.12	CRI > FRI < 0 CRI: 0.00 to 0.06 FRI$_1$: −0.01 to 0.04 FRI$_6$: 0.03 to 0.05

Source: We obtained these data from Table 4 in Stephen H. Penman, "The Articulation of Price-Earnings Ratios and Market-to-Book Ratios and the Evaluation of Growth," *Journal of Accounting Research* Vol. 34, No. 2, Autumn 1996, pp. 235–259.

Penman's research results generally support his predictions and shed light on the residual income conditions that cause MB ratios and PE ratios to covary. Examining future residual income across columns of the matrix, Penman's results suggest that MB ratios correlate positively with future residual income, consistent with the results from Bernard in Exhibit 13.4. Future residual income is substantially higher for high MB firms than for low MB firms. Examining the results across rows, high PE ratio firms tend to have current period residual income that is much lower than future residual income, suggesting PE ratios for these firms are temporarily high because residual income is temporarily low. In contrast, firms with low PE ratios tend to have current residual income amounts that are greater than the future residual income amounts, suggesting these firms are experiencing low PE ratios because residual income is temporarily high. Penman's results provide intuition about when MB ratios should be high, low, or normal, and concurrently, when PE ratios should be high, low, or normal.

SUMMARY OF VE AND PE RATIOS

Summarizing, the VE and PE ratios are determined by:

1. Risk
2. Growth
3. Differences between current and expected future (permanent) earnings
4. Alternative accounting methods and principles.

The analyst must assess each of these elements when estimating VE and PE ratios, particularly when evaluating PE ratios based on reported earnings and when projecting PE ratios to value non-traded firms. The theoretical model indicates the factors affecting the PE ratio but does not provide an unambiguous signal of the "correct" PE ratio for a particular firm. The analyst should be aware of the following considerations when using PE ratios:

1. The PE ratio is particularly sensitive to the cost of equity capital and to the earnings growth rate because it assumes a firm can grow earnings at that rate forever. The analyst should select a sustainable long-term growth rate when applying the PE model.

2. The theoretical PE model does not work when the growth rate in earnings exceeds the cost of equity capital. Firms are unlikely to grow earnings at rates exceeding the cost of equity capital forever. Competition will eventually force growth rates to decrease.

3. The theoretical PE model does not work when the cost of equity capital and the growth rate in earnings are similar in amount. The denominator of the theoretical model approaches zero and the theoretical PE ratio becomes exceeding large.

4. The PE model does not work when earnings are negative.

5. Before concluding that the market is undervaluing or overvaluing a firm because the actual PE ratio differs from the theoretically correct VE ratio, the analyst should assess whether earnings of the period include transitory elements. The analyst should adjust the current period's earnings for unusual, nonrecurring income items before measuring the PE ratio for the period.

6. When comparing actual PE ratios of firms, the analyst should consider the impact of their use of different accounting methods and principles.

USING MARKET MULTIPLES OF COMPARABLE FIRMS

The analyst can use the PE and MB ratios of comparable firms to assess the corresponding ratios of publicly traded firms. The analyst can also value firms whose common shares are not publicly traded by using PE ratios and MB ratios of comparable firms that are publicly traded. The theoretical models assist in this valuation task by identifying the variables that the analyst should use in selecting comparable firms. Bhojraj and Lee demonstrate a technique for selecting comparable firms in multiples-based valuation by computing "warranted multiples" based on factors that drive cross-sectional differences in multiples, such as expected profitability, growth, and cost of capital.[20] Alford examined the accuracy of the PE valuation models using industry, risk, ROCE, and earnings growth as the bases for selecting comparable

---

[20]Sanjeev Bhojraj and Charles M.C. Lee, "Who is My Peer? A Valuation-Based Approach to the Selection of Comparable Firms," *Journal of Accounting Research* Vol. 40, No. 2 (May 2002), pp. 407–439.

firms.[21] The results indicate that industry membership, particularly at a three-digit SIC code level, provides a useful basis for comparisons if firms in the same industry experience similar profitability, face similar risks, and grow at similar rates. Thus, in some circumstances, industry membership serves as an effective proxy for the variables in the PE valuation model. However, as the data in Exhibit 13.7 reveal, substantial differences commonly exist in PE ratios of firms within the same industry. The warranted-multiples approach of Bhojraj and Lee provides a mechanism to determine comparable companies within industries and across different industries.

PRICE DIFFERENTIALS[22]

To what extent has the market discounted the value of a firm's common equity for risk? On a per-share level, what is the per-share price impact of risk? Is the market's discount for risk implicit in a firm's share price sufficient to compensate for risk? Or is the discount too large or too small relative to risk? We rely on an adaptation of the residual income model to address these questions. We use the residual income model and risk-free rates of return to estimate *risk-free value*. We then subtract market price from risk-free value to assess the *price differential*—the amount the market has discounted share price for risk.

As we described in detail in the previous chapter, the residual income model determines the present value of common shareholders' equity as follows:

$$V_0 = BV_0 + \sum_{t=1}^{\infty} \frac{NI_t - (R_E \times BV_{t-1})}{(1 + R_E)^t}$$

To implement this model, the analyst must estimate the cost of equity capital (R_E) for purposes of computing residual income $[NI_t - (R_E \times BV_{t-1})]$ and for discounting residual income to present value at $1/(1 + R_E)^t$. But the state-of-the-art in financial economics does not provide a clear picture of how R_E should be determined. Substantial controversy surrounds expected returns models like the CAPM. What is the appropriate measure for market beta? In addition to market betas, do other risk factors belong in the expected returns model, such as firm size or some other set of risk factors? Assuming one can identify the appropriate risk factors that are priced in the market, what are the appropriate risk premia to use to determine expected returns? At an even more fundamental level, questions arise about whether risk and expected returns should be measured based on covariation between a firm's returns and a market index of returns. These questions arise in part because market-based models like the CAPM are essentially circular—should stock prices and realized returns be used to estimate risk to determine expected returns to evaluate stock prices? Or should risk

---

[21]Andrew W. Alford, "The Effect of the Set of Comparable Firms on the Accuracy of the Price-Earnings Valuation Method," *Journal of Accounting Research* (Spring 1992), pp. 94–108.

[22]This section relies heavily on Stephen Baginski and James Wahlen, "Residual Income Risk, Intrinsic Values, and Share Prices," *The Accounting Review* Vol. 78, No. 1 (January 2003), pp. 327–351.

and expected returns be based on covariation between a firm's returns and an economy-wide measure of consumption, on the theory that investors' risk aversion is driven by the need to diversify volatility in expected future consumption?

In light of the critical role of risk and expected returns in valuation, and in light of the uncertainty surrounding how to measure risk and expected returns, the analyst needs a variety of tools to assess the impact of risk on share prices and firm values. One such tool involves computing price differentials. If the analyst substitutes the prevailing risk-free rate of interest (denoted R_F; for example, the yield on one- to five-year U.S. Treasury securities) for the cost of equity capital, the residual income model can be used to determine risk-free value (denoted RFV_0), which is an estimate of the value of the firm in a risk-neutral market:

$$RFV_0 = BV_0 + \sum_{t=1}^{\infty} \frac{NI_t - (R_F \times BV_{t-1})}{(1 + R_F)^t}$$

Risk-free value represents the value of the firm, based on book value of equity and forecasts of expected future earnings, in the absence of discounting for risk. On a per-share basis, risk-free value per share represents the hypothetical value at which shares would trade in a risk-neutral market. Market price of a share of common equity reflects the risk-discounted value. Therefore, market price can be subtracted from risk-free value per share to determine the total discount in share price for risk. We refer to this difference as the *price differential* (denoted *PDIFF*), computed as follows:

$$PDIFF_0 = RFV_0 - MV_0$$

The analyst can evaluate the price differential to assess whether the market discount for risk is sufficient to compensate the investor to hold the firm's shares and bear risk. If the analyst assesses that $PDIFF_0$ is large relative to the risk of the firm, then perhaps the firm's shares may be over-discounted for risk (undervalued). On the other hand, if the analyst assesses that $PDIFF_0$ is small relative to firm risk, then perhaps the firm's shares are under-discounted for risk (overvalued). In the next section, we illustrate how to compute the PDIFF for PepsiCo. In the following section that discusses reverse engineering, we describe and apply more formal methods to gauge the magnitude of PDIFF.

COMPUTING PDIFF FOR PEPSICO

To compute the price differential of PepsiCo as of the end of Year 11, we rely on the forecast assumptions developed in Chapter 10 and the residual income model developed in the previous chapter. However, instead of using an 8.0 percent cost of equity capital for PepsiCo for purposes of computing residual income and discounting it to present value, we instead use the risk-free interest rate at the time of the valuation. At the end of Year 11, U.S. Treasury bills with one to five years to maturity yielded roughly 4.2 percent. Exhibit 13.9 reports the present value of PepsiCo's expected future residual income in Year +1 through Year +10, computed using the 4.2 percent risk-free discount rate.

	EXHIBIT 13.9		
	Price Differential of PepsiCo: **Present Value of Residual Income in Year +1 through Year +10 after** **Discounting at the Risk-Free Rate of Interest**		
	Year +1	**Year +2**	**Year +3**
COMPREHENSIVE INCOME AVAILABLE FOR COMMON SHAREHOLDERS	$ 3,367.3	$3,656.4	$ 3,975.8
Common Shareholders' Equity (at beginning of year)	$ 8,648.0	$9,466.2	$10,364.7
Required Income $(R_F \times BV_{t-1})$	$ 363.2	$ 397.6	$ 435.3
Residual Income $[NI_t - (R_F \times BV_{t-1})]$	$ 3,004.1	$3,258.8	$ 3,540.4
Present Value Factors (at R_F = 4.2 percent)	0.960	0.921	0.884
PV Residual Income	$ 2,883.0	$3,001.4	$ 3,129.4
Sum of PV Residual Income in Year +1 through Year +10	$33,946.3		

To compute continuing value, we cannot use the perpetuity-with-growth model [= $1/(r - g)$], because our long-term growth assumption for PepsiCo is 5.0 percent, which is greater than the risk-free discount rate of only 4.2 percent. Therefore, we derive PepsiCo's Year +11 residual income, project it to grow uniformly at the long-term growth rate for an arbitrarily long time (until Year +50), and then discount each year of residual income to present value.[23] The present value of continuing value under this approach is $181,404.5 million. After adding book value of common equity at the end of Year 11, adjusting for mid-year discounting, and dividing by the number of shares outstanding, we estimate the PepsiCo shares have a risk-free value of $130.24. Subtracting the market price at Year 11 of $49.05 per share, we estimate the PDIFF to be $81.19. These computations suggest that PepsiCo shares have been discounted by the risk-averse market by roughly $81.19 per share below the value at which they would trade in a hypothetical risk-neutral market, conditional on the forecast assumptions in Chapter 10. These computations indicate PepsiCo shares traded at the end of Year 11 at a price equal to roughly 38 percent of risk-free value (= $49.05/$130.24). Exhibit 13.10 presents these computations.

In Chapters 11 and 12, we estimated that PepsiCo shares may have been under-priced at the end of Year 11. The price differential computation indicates that the market imposed a substantial discount to PepsiCo's expected future residual income, relative to the risk of PepsiCo. To more formally evaluate the relative magnitude of the price differential, we next turn to the method of reverse engineering market values.

---

[23]Although we compute present value of continuing value over an arbitrarily long horizon, it will nonetheless understate continuing value (and therefore the risk-free value) because the present value computation does not extend to infinity. By using a long horizon, we seek to reduce the understatement.

EXHIBIT 13.9

Exhibit 13.9—continued

Year +4	Year +5	Year +6	Year +7	Year +8	Year +9	Year +10
$ 4,312.3	$ 4,649.6	$ 4,991.0	$ 5,350.0	$ 5,734.9	$ 6,147.5	$ 6,590.4
$11,572.9	$12,149.2	$13,380.8	$14,366.6	$15,423.7	$16,556.8	$17,771.4
$ 486.1	$ 510.3	$ 562.0	$ 603.4	$ 647.8	$ 695.4	$ 746.4
$ 3,826.2	$ 4,139.3	$ 4,429.0	$ 4,746.6	$ 5,087.1	$ 5,452.1	$ 5,844.0
0.848	0.814	0.781	0.750	0.720	0.691	0.663
$ 3,245.6	$ 3,369.7	$ 3,460.2	$ 3,558.9	$ 3,660.4	$ 3,764.9	$ 3,872.9

EXHIBIT 13.10

Price Differential of PepsiCo

Valuation Steps	Computations	Amounts
Sum of PV Residual Income in Year +1 through Year +10	Discounted at the risk-free rate of interest. See Exhibit 13.9.	+$ 33,946.3
Add Continuing Value in Present Value	Year +11 residual income assumed to grow at 5.0%; projected to Year +50, discounted at 4.2%. Computations not shown.	+$181,404.5
Total PV Residual Income		=$215,350.8
Add: Beginning Book Value of Equity	Beginning Book Value of Equity from Year 11 Balance Sheet.	+$ 8,648.0
		=$223,998.8
Adjust to Midyear	Multiply by $1+(R_E/2)$	× 1.021
PV of Common Equity		=$228,702.8
Shares Outstanding		÷$ 1,756.0
Estimated Value per Share		$ 130.24
Current Price per Share		$ 49.05
Price Differential		$ 81.19

REVERSE ENGINEERING

Throughout this text we have emphasized the process of using a firm's fundamental characteristics to estimate firm value. This process can be characterized essentially as a puzzle with four missing pieces, or as an equation with four unknown variables: value, expected future profitability, expected long-run future growth, and expected risk-adjusted discount rates. Thus far, we have developed forecasts and expectations about three of the variables—expected future profitability, long-run growth, and risk-adjusted discount rates—and we have used them to solve for the fourth, firm value. In fact, we can make assumptions about any three of the four variables and then solve for the fourth variable.

We can, for example, treat the market value of common equity as one of the "known" variables. We can assume that V_0 equals market value. We can then build forecasts for any two other variables, and solve for the missing fourth variable. We refer to this process as *reverse engineering* stock prices because it takes the valuation process and reverses it. It is a process in which the analyst takes market value as given, and then solves for the assumptions the market appears to be making in order to value the firm's stock at market price. For example, if we take a firm's market price as given, and if we use an analyst's forecasts for future earnings and growth as reasonable proxies for the market's expectations, then we can solve for the implied expected risk-adjusted rate of return on common equity that is consistent with the observed market value, expected future earnings, and growth. This is essentially equivalent to solving for the internal rate of return on the stock.

As another example, suppose we take market value as given, we assume that the risk-adjusted expected return on a stock can be determined by an asset pricing model such as the CAPM, and we assume analysts' consensus earnings forecasts through Year +5 are reasonable proxies for the market's earnings expectations. We can then solve for the long-run growth rate implicit in the firm's stock price, conditional on the other assumptions.

The process of reverse engineering stock prices allows the analyst to infer a set of assumptions that appear to be impounded into the firm's share price. The analyst can then assess whether the assumptions the market appears to be making are realistic, optimistic, or pessimistic. If the analyst determines that the market's assumptions seem optimistic, then it suggests the market has overpriced the stock (or perhaps the analyst is just too pessimistic). Alternatively, if the analyst determines that the market's assumptions are pessimistic, then it suggests the market has underpriced the stock (or again, the analyst may be wrong). Reverse engineering is a mechanism by which the analyst can infer and judge the assumptions implicit in a stock price.

REVERSE ENGINEERING PEPSICO'S STOCK PRICE

To illustrate the process of reverse engineering, we will apply the approach to PepsiCo, using the end of Year 11 market price of $49.05 per share. To reverse engineer PepsiCo's $49.05 share price, we will again rely on the residual income model in the previous chapter and the forecasts developed in Chapter 10.

Assume we want to solve for the expected return (that is, the risk-adjusted discount rate) on PepsiCo's stock implied by the Year 11 share price of $49.05. Assume also that we believe our forecasts of earnings and book value of common equity for PepsiCo through Year +10 and our forecast of 5.0 percent long-run growth are realistic proxies for the market's expectations. Armed with share price, specific profitability and growth forecasts through Year +10, and a constant long-run growth assumption beyond Year +10, we can use the residual income value model to solve for the discount rate that reduces future earnings and book value to a present value equal to $49.05 per share.

Procedurally, one way to solve for the implied expected return on PepsiCo stock, conditional on the price, earnings, and growth assumptions, is to begin by estimating the value of common equity using the risk-free discount rate, as in the price differential illustration above. The initial value will likely far exceed the market price because the future residual income has not been discounted for risk. In applying the price differential model to PepsiCo in the previous section, we determined that PepsiCo's risk-free value was $130.24 per share. We then steadily increase the discount rate as necessary until the residual income model value exactly agrees with the market price of $49.05 per share. Following this approach, the implied expected rate of return on PepsiCo stock is 9.178 percent. At this discount rate, conditional on the residual income and growth assumptions, the present value of PepsiCo shares is $49.05 per share, exactly equal to market price. Recall we assumed PepsiCo common equity had a required rate of return of 8.0 percent based on the CAPM. However, this reverse engineering approach indicates that if we buy a share of PepsiCo stock at the market price of $49.05, it will yield a 9.178 percent rate of return, conditional on our other assumptions. The Valuation spreadsheet in FSAP allows the analyst to make these iterative computations easily by simply varying the discount rate for equity capital.

We can also reverse engineer PepsiCo's Year 11 stock price to solve for the implicit long-run growth assumption. To illustrate, we again take the market price of $49.05 per share as given, and our earnings and book value forecasts through Year +10 as reasonable proxies for the market's expectations. We now return to our original assumption that the risk-adjusted discount rate for PepsiCo stock is 8.0 percent, based on the CAPM. With this, we have established three assumptions—value, earnings through Year +10, and the risk-adjusted discount rate—and we can solve for the missing piece of the puzzle: long-run implied growth. We begin with the long-run growth assumption set at zero growth. We compute our first estimate of firm value using the zero growth assumption, and we compare that estimate to market price. The first estimate will likely be substantially lower than market price because market price probably includes the present value of the market's expectations for long-run growth. For PepsiCo, the initial value estimate assuming zero growth is $38.20 per share. We steadily increase the long-run growth parameter assumption as necessary until the present value from the residual income model equals market price. In the case of PepsiCo at the end of Year 11, market price of $49.05 only reflects long-run growth of 2.96 percent (significantly lower than our expectation of 5.0 percent long-run growth). That is, conditional on our assumptions for residual income through

Year +10 and on our assumption that PepsiCo's cost of equity capital is 8.0 percent, if the market expects long-run growth will be 2.96 percent, then the present value of PepsiCo shares exactly agrees with the market price of $49.05. Again, note that the Valuation spreadsheet in FSAP is a useful tool that allows the analyst to establish assumptions for earnings and cost of capital, and then vary the long-run growth assumption for reverse engineering.

THE RELEVANCE OF ACADEMIC RESEARCH FOR THE WORK OF THE SECURITY ANALYST[24]

Academic accounting researchers develop and test models to explain the observed relation between accounting information and stock prices. The research usually proposes theories and models for this relation analytically and then tests the models empirically on large data sets involving many firms for many years. The results of this research have provided many insights into multi-faceted dimensions of the relations between accounting numbers and a wide variety of capital market variables such as stock prices, stock returns reactions around announcements, stock returns cumulated over long periods of time, trading volume, analysts' and managements' earnings forecasts, equity costs of capital, implied market risk premia, market betas, other risk factors, bankruptcy, earnings management, and many others. Throughout this text, we have referred to relevant examples of empirical accounting research, including the classic study by Ball and Brown that helped set the stage for future research by being the first to show that changes in earnings correlate with unexpected changes in stock prices.[25] As we described in Chapter 1, the Ball and Brown results indicate that, in their sample, merely the difference in the sign of the change in annual earnings (whether positive or negative) was associated with nearly a 16 percent difference in annual market-adjusted stock returns. Firms that reported increases in earnings experienced returns that on average "beat" the market average by 7 percent, while firms that reported decreases in earnings experienced returns that on average fell 9 percent short of the market average.

Accounting academics and the research process itself provide important elements that should lead to reliable insights into the relation between accounting numbers and stock market variables. For example, as researchers, academics are trained to base their predictions and hypotheses as much as possible on formal theory integrating economics, finance, and accounting (rather than ad hoc or ex post reasoning). Academics commonly test these predictions with rigorous quasi-scientific methods on large empirical samples of real data. Academics usually have no commercial interest in the results, so the findings should not be biased by the need to obtain a particular conclusion, or the need to sell. Furthermore, academic research is not published

---

[24]This section draws heavily from Clyde P. Stickney, "The Academic's Approach to Securities Research: Is It Relevant to the Analyst?" *Journal of Financial Statement Analysis* (Summer 1997), pp. 52–60.

[25]Ray Ball and Philip Brown, "An Empirical Evaluation of Accounting Income Numbers," *Journal of Accounting Research* (Autumn 1968), pp. 159–178.

in a leading scholarly research journal until after it passes the stringent peer review process. Few research studies pass the "publish" test; most "perish."

Despite these strong advantages leading the academic accounting research process toward reliable conclusions and insights about the relation between accounting numbers and market variables, the natural question for the security analyst is: Of what relevance are the academic research models and empirical findings to my task of making buy, sell, or hold recommendations on individual firms? This concluding section offers some thoughts on this important question. This section also summarizes the role of market efficiency, and describes some of the empirical evidence to date on the relative degree of market efficiency with respect to earnings numbers. We consider the results to date to be very encouraging for analysts.

LEVEL OF AGGREGATION ISSUE

Both the academic and professional analyst communities must recognize that their interests involve different levels of aggregation. The academic is interested primarily in "big picture" explanations; conclusions and results that predict and explain the relation between accounting information and stock market variables in general. The analyst is concerned with specific assessments of the value of individual firms. The academic might seek to answer the question, what is the sign and significance of the relation between investments in research and development and stock market returns? Does this relation differ across industries? The analyst is more concerned with whether the specific investments in research and development by a particular firm, such as Eli Lilly or Intel, are likely to enhance profitability and stock returns. Academic research describes general tendencies that provide a basis for the analyst to assess the link between accounting numbers and a firm's value, and to identify deviations from the average for individual firms. Professional analysts create value by acting on the deviations (that is, taking positions in under- or overpriced stocks). Academics should not expect immediate application of their research findings to the work of the professional analyst. Professional analysts should not expect to apply the results of academic research immediately and specifically to their day-to-day responsibilities.

THEORY DEVELOPMENT AND PRACTICE FEED EACH OTHER

The previous section suggests the common meeting place between the academic and professional analyst communities. Both communities share the desire to understand better how accounting information relates to stock prices. The activities of each community do influence the other. Academics are keenly interested in predicting and explaining analysts' earnings forecasts and price targets, and, more generally, in explaining the actions of market participants on the whole. Analysts, directly or indirectly, rely on theories and results from academic research to inform their analysis. Much of what analysts learn in their academic training (such as in undergraduate and MBA programs) and in professional development training, is developed and validated by academic work (including textbooks like this one, that seek to link practice, theory, and research). Consider, for example, the impact that academic research relating to earnings forecasts, market reactions to earnings, risk and expected returns, and bankruptcy prediction have had on the work of the securities analyst during the last several decades. Consider the success of the academic community to identify and explain market pricing "anomalies," such as why the market does not fully incorporate information about past earnings changes when making earnings predictions, and the numerous portfolios and trading strategies that have emerged to exploit these anomalies.

HAS THE THEORY OF CAPITAL MARKET EFFICIENCY GOTTEN IN THE WAY?

For most of the last several decades, academic research has presumed that the capital markets exhibit a relatively high degree of efficiency with respect to accounting information. In contrast, many analysts view their task as the constant pursuit of market inefficiencies—mispriced securities. Academics generally perceive market efficiency from the perspective of the big picture, with a view of large samples and market movements in general, whereas analysts see market efficiency from the front lines, experiencing daily swings in market prices which are sometimes hard to explain in the context of an efficient market. Thus, it is not surprising that at times the differences in perspective on the degree of market efficiency may create more of a wall, rather than a bridge, between academics and professional analysts. This section seeks to reach a common understanding, and the next section provides some striking evidence on the degree of market efficiency with respect to earnings.

Capital markets may be described as "efficient" with regard to accounting information if market prices react *completely* and *quickly* to available accounting information. Notice that efficiency should be described as a matter of degree, not as an absolute. The issue is not whether the capital markets are or are not efficient. Rather, the issue is the degree to which the capital markets impound in prices all the available value-relevant information.

The term "completely" in this description implies the degree to which market participants identify the value-relevant implications of all available accounting information so that market prices reflect economic values without systematic bias. For example, a market that reflects a relatively high degree of information efficiency would impound in prices the value-relevant information in the persistence of earnings over time, and accounting information disclosed in footnotes as well as in the financial statements. A market that is relatively efficient will impound in stock prices the economic implications of all value-relevant accounting information, even including items such as comprehensive income or pro forma stock options expense, which may be disclosed in the notes.

The term "quickly" in this description suggests that market participants cannot consistently earn abnormal returns using accounting information for a long period of time after the information has been made publicly available. If capital markets exhibit a high degree of efficiency, market prices should react quickly (within a matter of hours or days) to capture any value-relevant signals in the accounting information.

The degree of efficiency with respect to complete and quick reactions in an information-efficient capital market depends on analysts and financial statement analysis. Analysts study accounting information to assess appropriate values for stocks and to take positions in under- or overvalued securities, thereby driving stock market prices to efficient levels. The speed with which analysts can forecast, anticipate, and react to accounting information causes prices to move before accounting information is released, and to react quickly to surprises in the information when it is released.

Also consider what a high degree of market efficiency *does not* imply. A capital market with a high degree of information efficiency does not necessarily price all stocks correctly every day. As a practical matter, relatively efficient markets experience valuation errors at the level of the individual firm; but these random inefficiencies cancel out at an aggregated market level and do not tend to persist for long periods of time.[26] Analysts are driving forces involved in identifying and correcting security mispricings. A capital market with a high degree of information efficiency does not necessarily have perfect foresight—surprises happen. Firms frequently surprise the market by announcing earnings numbers that are higher or lower than the market's expectations. Again, analysts drive market prices to react quickly and completely to new information.

STRIKING EVIDENCE ON THE DEGREE OF MARKET EFFICIENCY AND INEFFICIENCY WITH RESPECT TO EARNINGS

Two studies by Victor Bernard and Jacob Thomas provide the most striking evidence to date on the degree of market efficiency and inefficiency with respect to accounting earnings.[27] Bernard and Thomas collected a sample of 84,792 quarterly earnings announcements for firms on the CRSP and Compustat databases over the years 1974 to 1986. They ranked each firm each quarter into 10 portfolios on the basis of each firm's standardized unexpected earnings (denoted SUE—the seasonal quarterly change in earnings standardized by the firm's standard deviation in earnings changes over the prior 16 quarters). They studied the average abnormal (market-adjusted) stock returns to each portfolio over the 60 trading days leading up to the quarterly earnings announcement, and over the 60 trading days following the announcement. Exhibit 13.11 depicts a portion of their results.

The results in Exhibit 13.11 during the pre-announcement period indicate that the market is highly efficient in anticipating and reacting to quarterly earnings surprises. Firms with quarterly earnings surprises in the "good news" portfolios—portfolios 7 through 10—experience positive cumulative abnormal returns during the 60 days prior to and including the release of earnings. Firms with quarterly earnings surprises in the "bad news" portfolios—portfolios 1 through 4—experience negative cumulative abnormal returns during the 60 days prior to and including the release of earnings. The average difference in cumulative abnormal returns between portfolio

---

[26]For a discussion of these issues, see Ray Ball, "The Earnings-Price Anomaly," *Journal of Accounting and Economics* (1992), pp. 319–345.

[27]Victor Bernard and Jacob Thomas, "Post-Earnings Announcement Drift: Delayed Price Response or Risk Premium?" *Journal of Accounting Research* Vol. 27, (Supplement, 1989), pp. 1–36; and "Evidence that Stock Prices Do Not Fully Reflect the Implications of Current Earnings for Future Earnings," *Journal of Accounting and Economics* Vol. 13, No. 4 (1990), pp. 305–340.

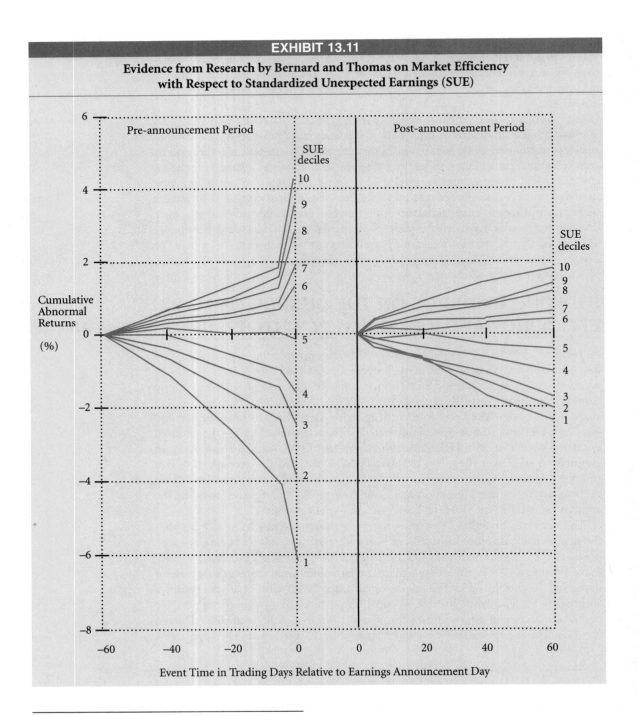

EXHIBIT 13.11

Evidence from Research by Bernard and Thomas on Market Efficiency with Respect to Standardized Unexpected Earnings (SUE)

Source: Victor Bernard and Jacob Thomas, "Post-Earnings Announcement Drift: Delayed Price Response or Risk Premium?" *Journal of Accounting Research* Vol. 27, (Supplement, 1989), pp.1–36.

10 (roughly +4 percent) and portfolio 1 (roughly –6 percent) was more than 10 percent *per quarter!* These results suggest the market anticipates and reacts quickly to quarterly earnings information.

The results in Exhibit 13.11 during the post-announcement period suggest that the market's reaction to quarterly earnings news is highly, but not completely, efficient. In the post-announcement period, Bernard and Thomas measured the cumulative abnormal returns to the exact same portfolios over the 60 trading days after the earnings announcements. If the market's reactions to quarterly earnings were on average quick and complete, these portfolios should exhibit no systematic abnormal returns in the post-announcement period. Upon the announcement of earnings, market prices should adjust efficiently. Post-announcement abnormal returns should only arise from new information that arrives during those 60 days, and the post-announcement abnormal returns should not be associated with the prior quarter's earnings news.

The results for the post-announcement period clearly indicate significant cumulative abnormal returns for the firms in portfolio 10 (best news) and portfolio 1 (worst news). Mean cumulative abnormal returns amount to roughly +2 percent and –2 percent for the best and worst news portfolios, respectively. In their second study, Bernard and Thomas show that, in part, the market seems to underreact to the persistence in current period earnings for future period earnings, failing to fully anticipate the momentum in quarterly earnings changes.

Taken together, the Bernard and Thomas studies reveal that the market is highly but not completely efficient with respect to quarterly earnings. We consider these results to be very encouraging for analysts. We interpret the results to suggest that analysts who can sharpen their ability to forecast future changes in earnings, and take long positions in (buy) shares of firms experiencing earnings increases and short positions in (sell) shares of firms experiencing earnings decreases during the 60-day pre-announcement period have the potential to earn some portion of the pre-announcement abnormal returns. Similarly, analysts who can sharpen their ability to react appropriately once earnings are announced have some potential to earn a portion of the post-announcement abnormal returns. These findings suggest that there are returns to be earned by being good at forecasting and reacting to earnings.

We believe the state-of-the-art of market efficiency is *exactly* where analysts would like it to be. The market is very efficient with respect to accounting information, but not perfectly efficient. Some stocks are temporarily mispriced, but the market tends to correct mispricings in a relatively short period of time. Financial statements analysis, particularly focusing on earnings, can help the analyst identify stocks whose prices may be temporarily out of equilibrium. Insightful financial statement analysis can lead to intelligent investment decisions and better-than-average returns.

SUMMARY

This chapter relies on the residual income model to develop the theoretical rationale relating market prices to economic drivers of value and to accounting fundamentals. This chapter describes the conceptual basis and practical application of market multiples—the market-to-book value (MB) ratio and the price-earnings (PE) ratio. The chapter focuses on four variables, or factors, that affect the market-to-book ratio and the price-earnings ratio: (1) risk and the cost of equity capital, (2) the expected future growth rate in earnings, (3) the presence of permanent and transitory components in the earnings of a particular year, and (4) the effects of accounting methods and principles on reported earnings and the book value of common shareholders' equity. For decades, analysts have relied heavily on PE ratios to relate market prices to earnings. However, in recent years, analysts and academics alike increasingly recognize that transitory elements in earnings and earnings growth can cloud the interpretation of the PE ratio as an indicator of value. Analysts and academics are shifting emphasis to the price-earnings-growth ratio and to the MB ratio. Transitory earnings elements of a particular period have less effect on the MB ratio. This chapter also demonstrates techniques to exploit the information in market value by calculating price differentials and by reverse engineering stock prices to infer the assumptions the market must be making. The chapter concludes by describing the relevance of academic research for the professional analyst, including highlighting key research results that appear to be very encouraging for the analyst interested in using earnings and financial statement data to analyze and value firms.

PROBLEMS

13.1 USING MARKET MULTIPLES TO ASSESS VALUES AND MARKET PRICES.
This problem continues Case 5.2 and Problems 10.7, 11.4, and 12.1 for The Gap and Limited Brands.

Required
  a. Compute the value-to-book ratio of each firm as of January 1, Year 13, using the residual ROCE valuation method.
  b. Using analyses developed in the case and problems listed above and in part a, prepare an exhibit summarizing the following ratios for each firm as of January 1, Year 13:
   1. Value-to-book ratio (use the values derived from the value-to-book ratio in part a).
   2. Market-to-book ratio (Problem 11.4 gives market value information).
   3. Value-to-earnings ratio, where earnings are reported earnings for Year 12 (Case 5.2 provides reported earnings information).
   4. Price-to-earnings ratio, where earnings are reported earnings for Year 12.
   5. Value-to-earnings ratio, where earnings are projected earnings for Year 13 (use the amounts of projected earnings in Problem 12.1).
   6. Price-to-earnings ratio, where earnings are projected earnings for Year 13.
  c. Compute the risk-free value of each firm as of January 1, Year 13, using a risk-free rate of 4.2 percent. Use the projected earnings for Year 13 to Year 17 developed in Problem 10.7, and the projected comprehensive income for Year 18 developed in Problem 12.1. Maintain the continuing value growth assumptions of 6 percent for The Gap and 3 percent for Limited Brands. Forecast

amounts out 50 years in total (that is, the initial five years plus 45 additional years). Compute the ratio of market value to risk-free value for each firm as of January 1, Year 13.

d. Solve for the growth rate in continuing residual income implicitly impounded in the market value of each firm on January 1, Year 13. Use the residual income amounts in Problem 12.1 for Year 13 to Year 17 before solving for the growth rate in continuing residual income.

e. Using the analyses in parts a to d, evaluate the extent of mispricing of each firm by the market.

13.2 USING MARKET MULTIPLES TO ASSESS VALUES AND MARKET PRICES.
Problem 12.4 presents selected pro forma financial information for Steak N Shake for Year 12 to Year 22.

Required

a. Compute the value-to-book ratio as of January 1, Year 12, using the residual ROCE valuation method.

b. Using analyses developed in part a and in Problem 12.4, prepare an exhibit summarizing the following ratios for Steak N Shake as of January 1, Year 12:
   1. Value-to-book ratio (use the amounts from part a).
   2. Market-to-book ratio.
   3. Value-to-earnings ratio, where earnings are reported earnings for Year 11 of $21.8 million.
   4. Price-to-earnings ratio, where earnings are reported earnings for Year 11.
   5. Value-to-earnings ratio, where earnings are projected earnings for Year 12.
   6. Price-to-earnings ratio, where earnings are projected earnings for Year 12.

c. Compute the risk-free value of Steak N Shake as of January 1, Year 12, using a risk-free rate of 4.2 percent. Use the projected earnings for Year 12 to Year 21, and the projected net income for Year 22 given in Problem 12.4. Maintain the continuing value growth assumption of 3 percent. Forecast amounts out 50 years in total (that is, the initial ten years plus 40 additional years). Compute the ratio of market value to risk-free value for Steak N Shake as of January 1, Year 12.

d. Solve for the growth rate in continuing residual income implicitly impounded in the market value of Steak N Shake on January 1, Year 12. Use the residual income amounts in Problem 12.4 for Year 12 to Year 21 before solving for the growth rate in continuing residual income.

e. Using the analyses in parts a to c, evaluate the extent of mispricing of Steak N Shake by the market.

13.3 APPLYING VARIOUS VALUATION METHODS FOR COMMON EQUITY.
The Coca-Cola Company (Coke) is a principal competitor of PepsiCo. This problem asks you to compute the value of Coke using various valuation methods discussed in Chapters 11 to 13 and to compare the results to those illustrated in the chapters for PepsiCo. Exhibit 13.12 presents selected information from the actual financial state-

EXHIBIT 13.12

The Coca-Cola Company
Selected Financial Information
(amounts in millions)
(Problem 13.3)

	Actual	Forecast					
	Year 11	Year 12	Year 13	Year 14	Year 15	Year 16	Year 17[a]
Common Equity,							
Beginning of Year.......	$ 9,694	$11,366	$13,563	$15,947	$18,536	$21,345	$24,395
Net Income	3,733	3,930	4,171	4,426	4,691	4,973	5,122
Other Comprehensive							
Income	(157)	(167)	(178)	(189)	(199)	(212)	(112)
Change in Common Stock ..	(113)	341	422	515	621	743	(199)
Dividends...............	(1,791)	(1,907)	(2,031)	(2,163)	(2,304)	(2,454)	(4,079)
Common Equity, End							
of Year...............	$11,366	$13,563	$15,947	$18,536	$21,345	$24,395	$25,127
Cash Flow from							
Operations	$ 4,065	$ 3,828	$ 3,958	$ 4,209	$ 4,469	$ 4,746	$ 4,863
Cash Flow for Investing.....	(1,188)	(513)	(616)	(653)	(692)	(734)	(389)
Cash Flow for Long-term							
Debt	(926)	297	163	333	354	376	199
Cash Flow from							
Common Stock	(113)	341	422	515	621	743	(199)
Cash Flow for Dividends....	(1,791)	(1,907)	(2,031)	(2,163)	(2,304)	(2,454)	(4,079)
Net Change in Cash........	$ 47	$ 2,046	$ 1,896	$ 2,241	$ 2,448	$ 2,677	$ 395

[a]The amounts for Year 17 result from increasing each income statement and balance sheet amount by the expected long-term growth rate of 6 percent and then deriving the amounts for the statement of cash flows.

ments of Coke for Year 11 and the forecasted amounts for Year 12 to Year 16. Exhibit 13.12 also shows the forecasted amounts for Year 17 assuming that all amounts on the income statement and balance sheet for Year 16 grow 6 percent. The market equity beta for Coke is 0.419. Assume a risk-free interest rate of 4.2 percent and a market risk premium of 5 percent. The market value of Coke on January 1, Year 12, is $117,214.9 million (2,486 million shares outstanding at a market price per share of $47.15).

Required

a. Compute the value of Coke on January 1, Year 12, using the present value of projected free cash flows to common equity capital.
b. Repeat part a using the dividends discount model.
c. Repeat part a using the residual income model.
d. Repeat part a using the residual ROCE model.

	EXHIBIT 13.13

PepsiCo and Coke
Value and Market Multiples and Financial Ratios
(dollar amounts in millions)
(Problem 13.3)

	PepsiCo	Coke
Value-to-Book Ratio:		
$121,205.9/$8,648	14.02	
Market-to-Book Ratio:		
$86,131.8/$8,648	9.96	
Value-Earnings Ratio (Year 11 Actual Net		
Income): $121,205.9/$2,658	45.60	
Price-Earnings Ratio (Year 11 Actual Net		
Income): $86,131.8/$2,658	32.40	
Value-Earnings Ratio (Year 12 Projected Net		
Income): $121,205.9/$3,367.3...................	35.99	
Price-Earnings Ratio (Year 12 Projected Net		
Income): $86,131.8/$3,367.3...................	25.58	
Year 16 Forecasted Financial Ratios:		
Profit Margin for ROA	12.1%	19.3%
Total Assets Turnover	1.26	.72
Rate of Return on Assets.......................	15.3%	14.0%
Profit Margin for ROCE	12.2%	18.5%
Capital Structure Leverage Ratio	2.37	1.62
Rate of Return on Common Shareholders' Equity....	36.4%	21.7%

e. Exhibit 13.13 shows the amounts for various multiples for PepsiCo as of January 1, Year 12. This exhibit also shows financial ratios from the forecast financial statements for each firm for Year 16. Enter the missing amounts in Exhibit 13.13 for Coke.

f. Using the analyses in parts a to e, evaluate the extent of mispricing of PepsiCo and Coke by the market.

13.4 INTERPRETING MARKET-TO-BOOK RATIOS. Exhibit 13.14 presents selected data for seven pharmaceutical companies for a recent year. The growth rate in earnings and the dividend payout ratios are five-year averages. The excess earnings years represent the number of years that each firm would need to earn a rate of return on common shareholders' equity (ROCE) equal to that in Exhibit 13.14 in order to produce the market-to-book ratios shown. For example, Bristol-Myers Squibb would need to earn an ROCE of 48.9 percent for 58.3 years in order for the present value of the excess earnings over the cost of equity capital to produce a market-to-book ratio of 13.9 when applying the theoretical model. For several years just prior to the most recent year, Bristol-Myers Squibb recognized significant estimated losses related to breast implant claims.

EXHIBIT 13.14
Selected Data for Pharmaceutical Companies
(Problem 13.4)

Company	MB	ROCE	Cost of Equity	Dividend Payout Percentage	PE	Growth in Earnings	Excess Earnings Years
Bristol-Myers Squibb..........	13.9	.489	.134	.77	32.4	.068	58.3
Warner Lambert..............	13.0	.350	.133	.48	42.7	.051	32.2
Eli Lilly....................	12.4	.281	.155	.42	49.3	.110	89.8
Pfizer	11.2	.350	.143	.43	40.4	.152	27.8
Abbott Laboratories..........	10.4	.428	.113	.39	26.9	.116	13.5
Merck......................	10.3	.331	.154	.46	31.8	.130	41.9
Wyeth......................	6.9	.340	.138	.51	25.0	.065	24.6

Required

Considering the variables in the theoretical market-to-book ratio, discuss the likely reasons for the ordering of these seven companies on their market-to-book ratios.

13.5 SENSITIVITY OF THE THEORETICAL MODELS OF PRICE-EARNINGS AND MARKET-TO-BOOK TO CHANGES IN ASSUMPTIONS. This problem explores the sensitivity of the price-earnings and market-to-book models to changes in underlying assumptions. We recommend that you design a computer spreadsheet to perform the calculations, particularly for the market-to-book ratio.

Required

a. Compute the price-earnings ratio under each of the following sets of assumptions:

Scenario	Cost of Equity Capital	Growth Rate in Earnings
A	.15	.06
B	.15	.08
C	.15	.10
D	.13	.06
E	.13	.08
F	.13	.10
G	.11	.06
H	.11	.08
I	.11	.10

b. Assess the sensitivity of the price-earnings ratio to changes in the cost of equity capital and changes in the growth rate.

c. Compute the market-to-book ratio under each of the following sets of assumptions:

Scenario	ROCE	Cost of Equity Capital	Dividend Payout Percentage	Years of Excess Earnings
A	.20	.13	.30	10
B	.18	.13	.30	10
C	.14	.13	.30	10
D	.18	.15	.30	10
E	.18	.11	.30	10
F	.18	.13	.40	10
G	.18	.13	.20	10
H	.18	.13	.30	15
I	.18	.13	.30	20

d. Assess the sensitivity of the market-to-book ratio to changes in the assumptions made about the various underlying variables.

CASES

Note: To provide up-to-date integrated valuation cases, we include cases for Chapters 11 to 13 on the web site for this book (http://stickney.swlearning.com) instead of the text.

Appendix A

FINANCIAL STATEMENTS AND NOTES FOR PEPSICO, INC. AND SUBSIDIARIES

Consolidated Statements of Income
PepsiCo, Inc. and Subsidiaries
Fiscal years ended December 29, Year 11, December 30, Year 10, and December 25, Year 9

(in millions except per share amounts)	Year 11	Year 10	Year 9
New PepsiCo	$26,935	$25,479	$22,970
Bottling Operations.............................	—	—	2,123
Total Net Sales	26,935	25,479	25,093
Costs and Expenses			
Costs of sales	10,754	10,226	10,326
Selling, general, and administrative expenses	11,608	11,104	11,018
Amortization of intangible assets	165	147	193
Merger-related costs	356	—	—
Other impairment and restructuring charges...........	31	184	73
Total Costs and Expenses	22,914	21,661	21,610
Operating Profit			
New PepsiCo	4,021	3,818	3,430
Bottling operations and equity investments............	—	—	53
Total Operating Profit..........................	4,021	3,818	3,483
Bottling equity income and transaction gains/(losses), net	160	130	1,083
Interest expense................................	(219)	(272)	(421)
Interest income	67	85	130
Income Before Income Taxes	4,029	3,761	4,275
Provision for Income Taxes	1,367	1,218	1,770
Net Income	$ 2,662	$ 2,543	$ 2,505
Basic	$ 1.51	$ 1.45	$ 1.41
Diluted	$ 1.47	$ 1.42	$ 1.38

See accompanying notes to consolidated financial statements.

Consolidated Statements of Cash Flows
PepsiCo, Inc. and Subsidiaries
Fiscal years ended December 29, Year 11,
December 30, Year 10, and December 25, Year 9

(in millions)	Year 11	Year 10	Year 9
Operating Activities			
Net income........................	$2,662	$2,543	$2,505
Adjustments to reconcile net income to net cash provided by operating activities			
Bottling equity income and transaction (gains)/losses, net	(160)	(130)	(1,083)
Depreciation and amortization	1,082	1,093	1,156
Merger-related costs..................	356	—	—
Other impairment and restructuring charges...........................	31	184	73
Cash payments for merger-related costs and other restructuring charges........	(273)	(38)	(98)
Deferred income taxes	162	33	573
Deferred compensation – ESOP	48	36	32
Other noncash charges and credits, net....	209	303	368
Changes in operating working capital, excluding effects of acquisitions and dispositions			
Accounts and notes receivable	7	(52)	(141)
Inventories......................	(75)	(51)	(202)
Prepaid expenses and other current assets...................	(6)	(35)	(209)
Accounts payable and other current liabilities.....................	(236)	219	357
Income taxes payable	394	335	274
Net change in operating working capital...	84	416	79
Net Cash Provided by Operating Activities ...	4,201	4,440	3,605
Investing Activities			
Capital spending	(1,324)	(1,352)	(1,341)
Acquisitions and investments in unconsolidated affiliates..................	(432)	(98)	(430)
Sales of businesses	—	33	513
Sales of property, plant, and equipment	—	57	130
Short-term investments, by original maturity			
More than three months—purchases	(2,537)	(4,950)	(2,209)
More than three months—maturities.......	2,078	4,585	2,220
Three months or less, net................	(41)	(9)	12
Other, net	(381)	(262)	(67)
Net Cash Used for Investing Activities	(2,637)	(1,996)	(1,172)

(in millions)	Year 11	Year 10	Year 9
Financing Activities			
Proceeds from issuances of long-term debt	324	130	3,480
Payments of long-term debt	(573)	(879)	(1,216)
Short-term borrowings, by original maturity			
More than three months—proceeds	788	198	3,699
More than three months—payments	(483)	(155)	(2,758)
Three months or less, net.	(397)	1	(2,814)
Cash dividends paid.	(994)	(949)	(935)
Share repurchases—common	(1,716)	(1,430)	(1,285)
Share repurchases—preferred	(10)	—	—
Quaker share repurchases	(5)	(254)	(382)
Proceeds from reissuance of shares.	524	—	—
Proceeds from exercises of stock options	623	690	383
Net Cash Used for Financing Activities.	(1,919)	(2,648)	(1,828)
Effect of exchange rate changes on cash and			
cash equivalents	—	(4)	3
Net (decrease)/Increase in Cash and			
Cash Equivalents.	(355)	(208)	608
Cash and Cash Equivalents,			
Beginning of Year	1,038	1,246	638
Cash and Cash Equivalents,			
End of Year.	$ 683	$1,038	$1,246
Supplemental Cash Flow Information			
Interest paid.	$ 159	$ 226	$ 384
Income taxes paid	$ 857	$ 876	$ 689
Acquisitions:			
Fair value of assets acquired	$ 604	$ 80	$ 717
Cash paid and debt issued.	(432)	(98)	(438)
Liabilities assumed.	$ 172	$ (18)	$ 279

See accompanying notes to consolidated financial statements.

Consolidated Balance Sheets
PepsiCo, Inc. and Subsidiaries
December 29, Year 11, and December 30, Year 10

(in millions except per share amounts)	Year 11	Year 10
ASSETS		
Current Assets		
Cash and cash equivalents.....................	$ 683	$ 1,038
Short-term investments, at cost.................	966	467
	1,649	1,505
Accounts and notes receivable, net	2,142	2,129
Inventories...................................	1,310	1,192
Prepaid expenses and other assets..............	752	791
Total Current Assets	5,853	5,617
Property, Plant, and Equipment, net............	6,876	6,558
Intangible Assets, net	4,841	4,714
Investments in Unconsolidated Affiliates........	2,871	2,979
Other Assets	1,254	889
Total Assets	$21,695	$20,757
LIABILITIES AND SHAREHOLDERS' EQUITY		
Current Liabilities		
Short-term borrowings	$ 354	$ 202
Accounts payable and other current liabilities	4,461	4,529
Income taxes payable........................	183	64
Total Current Liabilities	4,998	4,795
Long-term Debt	2,651	3,009
Other Liabilities	3,876	3,960
Deferred Income Taxes......................	1,496	1,367
Preferred Stock, no par value..................	26	49
Deferred Compensation—preferred............	—	(27)
Common Shareholders' Equity		
Common stock, par value 1 2/3¢ per share		
(issued 1,782 and 2,029 shares, respectively)	30	34
Capital in excess of par value...................	13	375
Deferred compensation.......................	—	(21)
Retained earnings............................	11,519	16,510
Accumulated other comprehensive loss	(1,646)	(1,374)
	9,916	15,524
Less: repurchased common stock, at cost		
(26 and 280 shares, respectively)	(1,268)	(7,920)
Total Common Shareholders' Equity	8,648	7,604
Total Liabilities and Shareholders' Equity	$21,695	$20,757

See accompanying notes to consolidated financial statements.

Consolidated Statements of Common Shareholders' Equity
PepsiCo, Inc. and Subsidiaries
Fiscal years ended December 29, Year 11, December 30, Year 10, and December 25, Year 9

(in millions)	Year 11 Shares	Year 11 Amount	Year 10 Shares	Year 10 Amount	Year 9 Shares	Year 9 Amount
Common Stock						
Balance, beginning of year	2,029	$ 34	2,030	$ 34	2,037	$ 34
Share repurchases	—	—	(9)	—	(13)	—
Stock option exercises	6	—	—	—	—	—
Quaker stock option exercises	3	—	8	—	6	—
Shares issued to effect merger	(256)	(4)	—	—	—	—
Balance, end of year	1,782	30	2,029	34	2,030	34
Capital in Excess of Par Value						
Balance, beginning of year		375		559		904
Share repurchases		—		(236)		(370)
Stock option exercises[a]		82		52		(21)
Reissued shares		150		—		—
Shares issued to effect merger		(595)		—		—
Other		1		—		46
Balance, end of year		13		375		559
Deferred Compensation						
Balance, beginning of year		(21)		(45)		(68)
Net activity		21		24		23
Balance, end of year		—		(21)		(45)
Retained Earnings						
Balance, beginning of year		16,510		14,921		13,356
Net income		2,662		2,543		2,505
Shares issued to effect merger		(6,644)		—		—
Cash dividends declared—common . . .		(1,005)		(950)		(936)
Cash dividends declared—preferred . . .		(4)		(4)		(4)
Balance, end of year		11,519		16,510		14,921
Accumulated Other Comprehensive Loss						
Balance, beginning of year		(1,374)		(1,085)		(1,139)
Currency translation adjustment (CTA)		(218)		(289)		(136)
CTA reclassification adjustment		—		—		175
Cash flow hedges, net of tax:						
Cumulative effect of accounting change		3		—		—
Derivative (losses)/gains, net		(21)		—		—

(in millions)	Year 11		Year 10		Year 9	
	Shares	Amount	Shares	Amount	Shares	Amount
Minimum pension liability						
adjustment, net of tax		(38)		(2)		17
Other		2		2		(2)
Balance, end of year		(1,646)		(1,374)		(1,085)
Repurchased Common Stock						
Balance, beginning of year	(280)	(7,920)	(271)	(7,306)	(255)	(6,535)
Shares repurchased	(35)	(1,716)	(38)	(1,430)	(36)	(1,285)
Stock option exercises	20	751	29	816	20	514
Reissued shares	13	374	—	—	—	—
Shares issued to effect merger	256	7,243	—	—	—	—
Balance, end of year	(26)	(1,268)	(280)	(7,920)	(271)	(7,306)
Total Common Shareholders' Equity		$ 8,648		$ 7,604		$ 7,078

(a)Includes total tax benefit of $212 in Year 11, $177 in Year 10, and $105 in Year 9.
See accompanying notes to consolidated financial statements.

NOTES TO CONSOLIDATED FINANCIAL STATEMENTS

NOTE 1—SUMMARY OF SIGNIFICANT ACCOUNTING POLICIES

On August 2, Year 11, we completed our merger transaction, which resulted in The Quaker Oats Company (Quaker) becoming a wholly owned subsidiary of PepsiCo. As a result, we restated all prior period consolidated financial statements presented to reflect the combined results of operations, financial position, and cash flows of both companies as if they had always been merged. See Note 2.

The preparation of the consolidated financial statements in conformity with generally accepted accounting principles requires us to make estimates and assumptions that affect reported amounts of assets, liabilities, revenues, expenses, and disclosure of contingent assets and liabilities. Actual results could differ from these estimates.

Tabular dollars are in millions, except per-share amounts. All per-share amounts reflect common per-share amounts, assume dilution unless noted, and are based on unrounded amounts. Certain reclassifications were made to the Year 10 and Year 9 amounts to conform to the Year 11 presentation.

Items Affecting Comparability

Our fiscal year ends on the last Saturday in December and, as a result, a fifty-third week is added every five or six years. The fiscal year ended December 30, Year 10, consisted of fifty-three weeks. The fifty-third week increased Year 10 net sales by an estimated $294 million, operating profit by an estimated $62 million, and net income by an estimated $44 million or $0.02 per share. See Note 21 for the impact on our business segments.

The consolidated financial statements subsequent to the dates of the bottling transactions described in Note 10 are not comparable to the consolidated financial statements presented for prior periods as certain bottling operations that were previously consolidated are now accounted for under the equity method. In addition, the merger costs described in Note 2, other impairment and restructuring charges described in Note 3, and the income tax adjustment described in Note 14 affect comparability.

Principles of Consolidation

The financial statements include the consolidated accounts of PepsiCo, Inc. and its controlled affiliates. Intercompany balances and transactions have been eliminated. Investments in unconsolidated affiliates over which we exercise significant influence, but not control, are accounted for by the equity method. Our definition of control for majority owned affiliates considers the exercisability of the minority interest rights, and consolidation would be precluded to the extent that the minority interest holds substantive participating rights. Our share of the net income or loss of unconsolidated affiliates accounted for by the equity method is included in consolidated net income.

Issuances of Subsidiary Stock

The issuance of stock by one of our subsidiaries to third parties reduces our proportionate ownership interest in the subsidiary. Unless the issuance of such stock is part of a broader corporate reorganization, we recognize a gain or loss equal to the difference between the issuance price per share and our carrying amount per share. Such gain or loss, net of the related tax, is recognized in consolidated net income when the transaction occurs.

Revenue Recognition

We recognize revenue when products are delivered to customers consistent with sales terms. Sales terms generally do not allow a right of return.

Marketing Costs

Marketing costs are reported in selling, general, and administrative expenses, and include costs of advertising, promotional programs and other marketing activities. Advertising expenses were $1.7 billion in Year 11 and Year 10, and $1.6 billion in Year 9. Deferred advertising expense classified as prepaid expenses in the Consolidated Balance Sheet was $111 million in Year 11, and $127 million in Year 10. Deferred advertising costs are expensed in the year first used and consist of:

- media and personal service prepayments,
- promotional materials in inventory, and
- production costs of future media advertising.

We classify promotional payments to customers, including cooperative advertising, as either a reduction of net sales or as marketing costs. During Years 10 and 11, the Financial Accounting Standards Board's (FASB) Emerging Issues Task Force (EITF) addressed various issues related to the income statement classification of certain promotional payments, including consideration from a vendor to a reseller or another party that purchases the vendor's products. EITF 01-9, *Accounting for Consideration Given by a Vendor to a Customer or a Reseller of the Vendor's Products,* was issued in November Year 11, and codified earlier pronouncements. Primarily effective for Year 12, adoption of EITF 01-9 will reduce our net sales by $3.4 billion in Year 11, $3.1 billion in Year 10, and $2.9 billion in Year 9, with selling, general, and administrative expenses reduced by the same amounts.

Distribution Costs

Distribution costs are reported in either cost of sales or selling, general, and administrative expenses depending on the distribution method, and include the costs of shipping and handling activities. Shipping and handling expenses classified as selling, general, and administrative expenses were $2.6 billion in Year 11, $2.5 billion in Year 10, and $2.4 billion in Year 9.

Research and Development Costs

Research and development costs are expensed in the year incurred. Research and development costs were $206 million in Year 11, $207 million in Year 10, and $187 million in Year 9.

Stock-based Compensation

We measure stock-based compensation cost as the excess of the quoted market price of PepsiCo common stock at the grant date over the amount the employee must pay for the stock (exercise price). Our policy is to generally grant stock options with an exercise price equal to the stock price at the date of grant, and accordingly, no compensation cost is recognized. Under certain prior incentive programs, compensation cost for cash payments expected to be paid to employees in lieu of stock options was based on the grant date value and recognized over the vesting period of the award.

Pension and Postretirement Benefits

Our pension plans cover substantially all full-time U.S. employees and certain international employees. Benefits depend on years of service and earnings and are based on stated amounts for each year of service. Our postretirement plans provide medical and life insurance benefits principally to U.S. retirees and their dependents. Employees are eligible for benefits if they meet age and service requirements and qualify for retirement benefits. Plans generally use a measurement date of September 30. The pre-merger Quaker plans used a measurement date of December 31. Prior service costs are amortized on a straight-line basis over the average remaining service period of employees expected to receive benefits.

Derivative Instruments and Hedging

We manage risks associated with commodity prices, foreign exchange rates, interest rates, and our stock price, and may use derivatives to hedge these risks. Hedging transactions are executed in accordance with our policies. As a matter of policy, we do not use derivative instruments unless there is an underlying exposure and, therefore, we do not use derivative instruments for trading or speculative purposes. Any change in the value of our derivative instruments would be substantially offset by an opposite change in the value of the underlying hedged items. All derivative instruments are recognized in our Consolidated Balance Sheet at fair value. The fair value of our derivative instruments is generally based on quoted market prices. There is no significant concentration of credit risk or activity with any of the counterparts.

Using qualifying criteria defined in Statement of Financial Accounting Standards No. (SFAS) 133, *Accounting for Derivative Instruments and Hedging Activities*, derivative instruments are designated and accounted for as either fair value or cash flow hedges. Our evaluations of hedge effectiveness are subject to assumptions based on the terms and timing of the underlying exposures. For a fair value hedge, both the effective and ineffective portions of the change in fair value of the derivative instrument, along with an adjustment to the carrying amount of the hedged item for fair value changes attributable to the hedged risk, are recognized in earnings. For a cash flow hedge, changes in the fair value of a derivative instrument that is highly effective are deferred in accumulated other comprehensive income or loss until the underlying hedged item is recognized in earnings. The ineffective portion is recognized in earnings immediately. If a fair value or cash flow hedge was to cease to qualify for hedge accounting or be terminated, it would continue to be carried on the balance sheet at fair value until settled, but hedge accounting would be discontinued prospectively. If a forecasted transaction were no longer probable of occurring, amounts previously deferred in accumulated other comprehensive income would be recognized immediately in earnings.

We are subject to market risk with respect to the cost of commodities because our ability to recover increased costs through higher pricing may be limited by the competitive environment in which we operate. We manage this risk primarily through the use of fixed-price purchase orders, pricing agreements, geographic diversity, and derivative instruments. Derivative instruments, including futures, options, and swaps, are used to hedge fluctuations in prices of a portion of anticipated commodity purchases, primarily corn, oats, natural gas, heating oil, vegetable oil, and packaging materials. Our use of derivative instruments is not significant to our commodity purchases. Derivative instruments designated as hedges of anticipated commodity purchases are accounted for generally as cash flow hedges. The earnings impact from commodity hedges is classified as either cost of sales or selling, general, and administrative expenses consistent with the expense classification of the underlying hedged items.

International operations constitute about one-fifth of our annual business segment operating profit. Operating in international markets involves exposure to movements in foreign exchange rates, primarily the Mexican peso, British pound, Canadian dollar, euro, and Brazilian real, which principally impacts the translation of our international operating profit into U.S. dollars. On occasion, we may enter into derivative financial instruments, as necessary, to reduce the effect of foreign exchange rate changes. We manage the use of foreign exchange derivatives centrally. Derivative instruments designated as foreign exchange hedges are generally accounted for as fair value hedges. The earnings impact from these hedges is classified as either cost of sales or selling, general, and administrative expenses consistent with the expense classification of the underlying hedged items.

We centrally manage our debt and investment portfolios considering investment opportunities and risks, tax consequences, and overall financial strategies. We use interest rate and currency swaps to effectively change the interest rate and currency of specific debt issuances, with the objective of reducing our overall borrowing costs. These swaps are entered into concurrently with the issuance of the debt that they are intended to modify. The notional amount, interest payment, and maturity date of the swaps match the principal, interest payment, and maturity date of the related debt. Our credit risk related to interest rate and currency swaps is considered low because such swaps are entered into only with strong creditworthy counterparties, are generally settled on a net basis, and are of relatively short duration. Interest rate and currency swaps are designated as hedges of underlying fixed rate obligations and accounted for as fair value hedges. The earnings impact from these hedges is classified as interest expense.

The portion of our deferred compensation liability, which is based on our stock price, is subject to market risk. Prepaid forward contracts with financial institutions are used to hedge this risk and are accounted for as natural hedges. The earnings impact from these hedges is classified as selling, general, and administrative expenses consistent with the expense classification of the deferred compensation liability. Prior to the adoption of SFAS 133, the earnings impact from these equity derivative contracts was classified as interest income.

The cash flows related to the above derivative instruments are classified in the Consolidated Statement of Cash Flows in a manner consistent with those of the transactions being hedged.

Cash Equivalents and Short-term Investments

Cash equivalents represent funds temporarily invested with original maturities of three months or less. All other investment portfolios are primarily classified as short-term investments.

Inventories

Inventories are valued at the lower of cost (computed on the average, first-in, first-out (FIFO) or last-in, first-out (LIFO) method) or at net realizable value.

Property, Plant, and Equipment

Property, plant, and equipment are stated at cost. Depreciation is calculated primarily on a straight-line basis. Buildings and improvements are depreciated over their estimated useful lives, generally ranging from 15 to 40 years. Machinery and equipment (including fleet) are depreciated over their estimated useful lives, generally ranging from 5 to 15 years.

Intangible Assets

Goodwill, the excess of our investments in unconsolidated affiliates over our equity in the underlying net assets of these investments, and trademarks and brands are amortized on a straight-line basis over their estimated useful lives, generally ranging from 20 to 40 years. Other identifiable intangibles are amortized on a straight-line basis over their estimated useful lives, generally ranging from 5 to 20 years.

Asset Impairment

All long-lived assets, including goodwill, investments in unconsolidated affiliates and other identifiable intangibles, are evaluated for impairment on the basis of undiscounted cash flows whenever events or changes in circumstances indicate that the carrying amount of an asset may not be recoverable. An impaired asset is written down to its estimated fair market value based on the best information available. Estimated fair market value is generally measured by discounting estimated future cash flows. Considerable management judgment is necessary to estimate discounted future cash flows.

The depreciation or amortization periods for long-lived assets to be held and used are periodically evaluated to determine whether events or circumstances have occurred that warrant revision to the useful lives.

Income Taxes

Deferred taxes are recorded to give recognition to temporary differences between the tax bases of assets or liabilities and their reported amounts in the financial statements. Deferred tax assets generally represent items that can be used as a tax deduction or credit in future years. Deferred tax liabilities generally represent items for which we have taken a tax deduction, but have not yet recorded in the Consolidated Statement of Income. Valuation allowances are established for deferred tax assets where the amount of expected future taxable income from operations does not support the realization of these deferred tax assets.

Deferred tax liabilities are not recognized for temporary differences related to investments in foreign subsidiaries and in unconsolidated foreign affiliates that are essentially permanent in duration. It would not be practicable to determine the amount of any such deferred tax liabilities.

Commitments and Contingencies

We are subject to various claims and contingencies related to lawsuits, taxes, and environmental matters, as well as commitments under contractual and other commercial obligations. We recognize liabilities for contingencies and commitments when a loss is probable and estimable.

Accounting Changes

In July, Year 11, the FASB issued SFAS 141, *Business Combinations*. SFAS 141 eliminates the pooling-of-interests method of accounting for business combinations and modifies the application of the purchase accounting method. The elimination of the pooling-of-interests method is effective for transactions initiated after June 30, Year 11. The remaining provisions of SFAS 141 are effective for transactions accounted for using the purchase method that are completed after June 30, Year 11. Since our merger with Quaker (see Note 2) was initiated in December, Year 10, and our acquisition of South Beach Beverage Company, LLC (see Note 4) was completed in January, Year 11, adoption of this statement does not have an impact on the accompanying consolidated financial statements.

In July, Year 11, the FASB also issued SFAS 142, *Goodwill and Intangible Assets*. SFAS 142 eliminates the current requirement to amortize goodwill and indefinite-lived intangible assets, addresses the amortization of intangible assets with finite lives, and addresses impairment testing and recognition for goodwill and intangible assets. SFAS 142 applies to existing goodwill and intangible assets, as well as to transactions completed after the statement's effective date. SFAS 142 is effective for Year 12. Adoption of SFAS 142 will increase income before taxes by approximately $87 million in Year 12, reflecting the cessation of goodwill amortization and changes in the lives of other intangibles. The required transition impairment evaluations are not expected to result in impairment charges.

In June, Year 11, the FASB issued SFAS 143, *Accounting for Asset Retirement Obligations*. SFAS 143 addresses the financial accounting and reporting for obligations associated with the retirement of tangible long-lived assets and the associated asset retirement costs. It requires that we recognize the fair value of a liability for an asset retirement obligation in the period in which it is incurred if a reasonable estimate of fair value can be made. We are currently assessing SFAS 143 and the impact that adoption, in Year 13, will have on our consolidated financial statements.

In August, Year 11, the FASB issued SFAS 144, *Accounting for the Impairment or Disposal of Long-Lived Assets*. SFAS 144 establishes a single model for the impairment of long-lived assets and broadens the presentation of discontinued operations to include more disposal transactions. SFAS 144 is effective for Year 12. Adoption will not have a material impact on our consolidated financial statements.

NOTE 2—MERGER OF PEPSICO AND THE QUAKER OATS COMPANY

Under the Quaker merger agreement dated December 2, Year 10, Quaker shareholders received 2.3 shares of PepsiCo common stock in exchange for each share of Quaker common stock, including a cash payment for fractional shares. We issued approximately 306 million shares of our common stock in exchange for all the outstanding common stock of Quaker.

In connection with the merger transaction, we sold the global rights in our All Sport beverage brand to The Monarch Company, Inc. of Atlanta. As part of the terms of the sale, we agreed that, for 10 years after the Quaker transaction closing date, we would not distribute Gatorade sports drink through our bottling system in the United States and would not include Gatorade with Pepsi-Cola products in certain marketing or promotional arrangements covering specific distribution channels.

The merger was accounted for as a tax-free transaction and as a pooling-of-interests. As a result, all prior period consolidated financial statements presented have been restated to include the results of operations, financial position, and cash flows of both companies as if they had always been combined. Certain reclassifications were made to conform the presentation of the financial statements, and the fiscal calendar and certain interim reporting policies were also conformed. There were no material transactions between pre-merger PepsiCo and Quaker.

The results of operations of the separate companies and the combined company for the most recent interim period prior to the merger, and for the years presented in the consolidated financial statements, are as follows:

	24 Weeks Ended 6/16/Year 11 (unaudited)	Year 10	Year 9
Net Sales:			
PepsiCo.....................	$ 9,820	$20,438	$20,367
Quaker	2,741	5,041	4,726
Adjustments[a].................	(518)	—	—
Combined....................	$12,043	$25,479	$25,093
Net Income:			
PepsiCo.....................	$ 1,150	$ 2,183	$ 2,050
Quaker	279	360	455
Adjustments[a].................	(61)	—	—
Combined....................	$ 1,368	$ 2,543	$ 2,505

[a]Adjustments reflect the impact of changing Quaker's fiscal calendar to conform to PepsiCo's and conforming the accounting policies of the two companies applicable to interim reporting. These changes have no impact on full year net sales or net income.

During Year 11, we recognized costs of $356 million associated with our merger with Quaker. The components of these merger-related costs were as follows:

Transaction costs	$ 117
Integration and restructuring costs.........	$ 239
Total merger-related costs	$ 356
After-tax	$ 322
Per Share.............................	$0.18

Transaction costs were incurred to complete the merger and consist primarily of fees and expenses for investment bankers, attorneys, and accountants, SEC filing fees, stock exchange listing fees, and financial printing and other related charges.

Integration costs represent incremental one-time merger-related costs. Such costs include consulting fees and expenses, expenses for accelerated vesting under change-in-control provisions, information system integration costs, and employee-related costs.

The restructuring charges primarily reflect termination costs for approximately 580 corporate, sales, distribution, manufacturing, research, and marketing employees. Employee termination costs include retirement benefit costs, severance costs, and expenses associated with change-in-control provisions of pre-merger employment contracts. As of December 29, Year 11, approximately 380 of the terminations have occurred. The terminations are expected to be completed during Year 12.

We expect to incur additional costs to integrate the two companies.

Analysis of merger-related integration and restructuring reserves:

	Integration	Employee-related	Facility and Other Exit	Total
Year 11 costs.	$124	$106	$9	$239
Cash payments.	(80)	(33)	(2)	(115)
Reclassification of postretirement/ postemployment liabilities.	—	(22)	—	(22)
Other noncash utilization	(22)	—	(3)	(25)
Reserves, December 29, Year 11.	$ 22	$ 51	$4	$ 77

These reserves are included in accounts payable and other current liabilities in the Consolidated Balance Sheet.

NOTE 3—OTHER IMPAIRMENT AND RESTRUCTURING CHARGES

	Year 11	Year 10	Year 9
Asset impairment charges			
Held and used in the business: property, plant, and equipment.	$ 19	$ 125	$ 8
Held for disposal/abandonment: property, plant, and equipment	—	—	34
Total asset impairment.	19	125	42
Restructuring charges			
Employee-related costs.	—	41	20
Other charges	12	18	11
Total restructuring.	12	59	31
Total.	$ 31	$ 184	$ 73
After-tax.	$ 19	$ 111	$ 45
Per share.	$0.01	$0.06	$0.02

Year 11 and Year 10

The Year 11 and Year 10 other impairment and restructuring charges relate to a three-year supply chain reconfiguration project announced in Year 9 to upgrade and optimize Quaker's manufacturing and distribution capabilities across all of its North American businesses.

The asset impairment charges primarily reflect the reduction in the carrying value of the land, buildings, and production machinery and equipment to their estimated fair market value based on analyses of the liquidation values of similar assets. The restructuring charges primarily included severance and termination benefits for approximately 1,000 employees and other shutdown costs. No future charges are expected on this project.

Year 9

The Year 9 other impairment and restructuring charges of $73 million were comprised of the following:

- A charge of $65 million, for asset impairment of $37 million and restructuring charges of $28 million, related to the closure of three plants and impairment of equipment at Frito-Lay North America. The asset impairment charges primarily reflected the reduction in the carrying value of the land and buildings to their estimated fair market value based on selling prices for comparable real estate, less costs to sell, and the write-off of the net book value of equipment which could not be redeployed. The plant closures were completed during Year 9. The majority of these assets were either disposed of or abandoned in Year 9. The restructuring charges of $28 million primarily included severance costs and plant closing costs.
- A charge of $8 million, for asset impairment of $5 million and restructuring charges of $3 million, related to the previously discussed Quaker supply chain reconfiguration project. The charge included costs to consolidate several cereal manufacturing liens and employee-related costs.

The employee-related costs for Year 9 of $20 million primarily included severance and early retirement benefits for approximately 930 employees. Substantially all of the terminations occurred during Year 9.

Analysis of other restructuring reserves:

	Employee-related	Facility Closure	Third-Party Termination	Other	Total
Reserve, December 26, Year 8.	$70	$28	$62	$1	$161
Year 9 restructuring charges.	20	8	—	3	31
Cash payments.	(44)	(5)	(47)	(2)	(98)
Noncash utilization	(3)	(4)	—	—	(7)
Separation of PBG (see Note 10).	(25)	(5)	(5)	—	(35)

	Employee-related	Facility Closure	Third-Party Termination	Other	Total
Reserve, December 25, Year 9	18	22	10	2	52
Year 10 restructuring charges	41	18	—	—	59
Cash payments	(13)	(24)	(1)	—	(38)
Noncash utilization	(3)	(3)	—	—	(6)
Changes in estimate	—	(4)	—	—	(4)
Reserve, December 30, Year 10	43	9	9	2	63
Year 11 restructuring charges	—	12	—	—	12
Cash payments	(28)	(17)	—	—	(45)
Changes in estimate	1	(1)	—	—	—
Reclassification to postretirement liabilities . . .	(7)	—	—	—	(7)
Reserve, December 29, Year 11	$ 9	$ 3	$ 9	$2	$23

The restructuring reserves are included in accounts payable and other current liabilities in the Consolidated Balance Sheet. Third-party termination costs involve indemnifications by PepsiCo for ongoing litigation.

NOTE 4—ACQUISITION OF SOUTH BEACH BEVERAGE COMPANY, LLC

On January 5, Year 11, we completed the acquisition of South Beach Beverage Company, LLC, for approximately $337 million in cash. As of December 29, Year 11, we own a 93% interest in the newly formed South Beach Beverage Company, Inc. (SoBe). SoBe manufactures and markets an innovative line of alternative non-carbonated beverages including fruit blends, energy drinks, dairy-based drinks, exotic teas and other beverages with herbal ingredients, which prior to our acquisition were distributed under license by a network of independent distributors, primarily in the United States.

NOTE 5—NET INCOME PER COMMON SHARE

Basic net income per common share is calculated by dividing net income available to common shareholders by the weighted average of common shares outstanding during the period. Diluted net income per common share is calculated using the weighted average of common shares outstanding adjusted to include the potentially dilutive effect of convertible stock or stock options.

The computation of basic and diluted net income per common share is as follows:

| | Year 11 | | Year 10 | | Year 9 | |
	Income	Average Shares Outstanding	Income	Average Shares Outstanding	Income	Average Shares Outstanding
Net Income...............	$2,662		$2,543		$2,505	
Preferred shares:						
Dividends	(4)		(4)		(4)	
Redemption.............	(1)		—		—	
Net income available for common shareholders.......	$2,657	1,763	$2,539	1,748	$2,502	1,774
Basic net income per common share............	$ 1.51		$ 1.45		$ 1.41	
Net income available for common shareholders.......	$2,657	1,763	$2,539	1,748	$2,501	1,774
Dilutive Securities:						
Stock options.............	—	39	—	38	—	37
ESOP convertible preferred stock..........	3	4	2	4	2	5
Unvested stock awards.........	—	1	—	1	—	1
Diluted	$2,660	1,807	$2,541	1,791	$2,503	1,817
Diluted net income per common share	$ 1.47		$ 1.42		$ 1.38	

Diluted net income per common share excludes incremental shares of 0.4 million in Year 11, 0.1 million in Year 10, and 49.0 million in Year 9 related to employee stock options due to their antidilutive effect at each respective year end.

NOTE 6—ACCOUNTS AND NOTES RECEIVABLES, NET

	Year 11	Year 10	Year 9
Trade receivables	$1,663	$1,613	
Receivables from affiliates	171	190	
Other receivables	429	452	
	2,263	2,255	
Allowance, beginning of year	126	109	$148
Charged to expense	41	42	32
Other additions	2	8	5
Deductions............................	(48)	(33)	(76)
Allowance, end of year	121	126	$109
Net receivables	$2,142	$2,129	

Other additions include acquisitions, currency translation effects, and reclassifications. Deductions include the impact of the bottling transactions, accounts written off, and currency translation effects.

NOTE 7—INVENTORIES

	Year 11	Year 10
Raw materials	$ 535	$ 503
Work-in-process	205	160
Finished goods	570	529
	$1,310	$1,192

The cost of approximately 20% of Year 11 and Year 10 inventories was computed using the LIFO method. The differences between LIFO and FIFO methods of valuing these inventories for Year 11 and Year 10 are not material.

NOTE 8—PROPERTY, PLANT, AND EQUIPMENT, NET

	Year 11	Year 10
Land and improvements	$ 464	$ 435
Buildings and improvements	2,846	2,722
Machinery and equipment, including fleet.	8,135	7,522
Construction in progress.	735	787
	12,180	11,466
Accumulated Depreciation	(5,304)	(4,908)
	$ 6,876	$ 6,558

Depreciation expense was $843 million in Year 11, $840 million in Year 10, and $873 million in Year 9.

NOTE 9—INTANGIBLE ASSETS, NET

	Year 11	Year 10
Goodwill	$3,374	$3,522
Trademarks and brands.	1,320	994
Other identifiable intangibles	147	198
	$4,841	$4,714

Identifiable intangible assets possess economic value but lack physical substance. These assets primarily arise from the allocation of purchase prices of businesses acquired. Amounts assigned to such identifiable intangibles are based on independent appraisals or internal estimates. Goodwill represents the excess purchase price after allocation to all identifiable net assets.

The above amounts are presented net of accumulated amortization of $1 billion at year-end Year 11, and $0.9 billion at year-end Year 10.

NOTE 10—INVESTMENTS IN UNCONSOLIDATED AFFILIATES

During Year 9, we completed a series of transactions creating our anchor bottlers that manufacture, sell, and distribute carbonated and non-carbonated Pepsi-Cola beverages under master bottling agreements with us.

In April, Year 9, certain wholly owned bottling businesses, referred to as The Pepsi Bottling Group (PBG), completed an initial public offering with PepsiCo retaining a direct noncontrolling ownership interest of 35.5%. We received $5.5 billion of debt proceeds as settlement of pre-existing intercompany amounts due to us and recognized a pre-tax gain of $1.0 billion ($476 million after-tax or $0.26 per share) as a result of the transaction. In May, we combined certain other bottling operations with Whitman Corporation to create new Whitman, retaining a noncontrolling ownership interest of approximately 38%. The transaction resulted in an after-tax loss to PepsiCo of $206 million or $0.11 per share. In July, we combined certain other bottling operations with PepCom Industries, Inc., retaining a noncontrolling interest of 35% in the combined entity renamed Pepsi Bottling Ventures, LLC. This transaction was accounted for as a nonmonetary exchange for book purposes. However, a portion of the transaction was taxable and resulted in income tax expense of $25 million or $0.01 per share. In October, we formed a business venture with Pohlad Companies, a Pepsi-Cola franchisee, retaining a noncontrolling ownership interest of approximately 24% in the venture's principal operating subsidiary, PepsiAmericas, Inc. The transaction was structured as a fair value exchange with no resulting gain or loss.

In December, Year 10, Whitman merged with PepsiAmericas. At year-end Year 11, we owned approximately 37% of the combined company. As part of the merger, we participate in an earn-out option whereby we may receive additional shares when certain performance targets are met. Effective January, Year 11, the name of the combined company was changed to PepsiAmericas.

PBG

In addition to approximately 38% of PBG's outstanding common stock that we own at year-end Year 11, we own 100% of PBG's class B common stock and approximately 7% of the equity of Bottling Group, LLC, PBG's principal operating subsidiary. This gives us economic ownership of approximately 42% of PBG's combined operations.

PBG's summarized financial information is as follows:

	Year 11	Year 10
Current assets	$1,548	$1,584
Noncurrent assets	6,309	6,152
Total assets	$7,857	$7,736
Current liabilities.	$1,081	$ 967
Noncurrent liabilities	4,856	4,817
Minority interest	319	306
Total liabilities	$6,256	$6,090
Our equity investment	$ 962	$ 934

	Year 11	Year 10	Year 9
Net sales.	$8,443	$7,982	$7,505
Gross profit	$3,863	$3,577	$3,209
Operating profit	$ 676	$ 509	$ 412
Net income	$ 305	$ 229	$ 118

The excess of our investment in PBG over our equity in the underlying net assets, net of amortization, was approximately $24 million at year-end Year 11. Based upon the quoted closing value of our direct investment in PBG, excluding our investment in Bottling Group, LLC, exceeded our carrying value by approximately $1.9 billion.

PepsiAmericas (formerly Whitman)

PepsiAmericas' summarized financial information is as follows:

	Year 11	Year 10
Current assets	$ 481	$ 477
Noncurrent assets	2,938	2,859
Total assets	$3,419	$3,336
Current liabilities.	$ 653	$ 887
Noncurrent liabilities	1,336	999
Total liabilities	$1,989	$1,886
Our equity investment	$ 746	$ 741

	Year 11	Year 10	Year 9
Net sales.	$3,171	$2,528	$2,138
Gross profit	$1,259	$1,033	$ 890
Operating profit	$ 268	$ 223	$ 182
Income from continuing operations.	$ 90	$ 72	$ 43
Net income/(loss)	$ 19	$ 80	$ (9)

The above financial information for Year 10 includes the results of the former PepsiAmericas after the date of the merger with Whitman.

The excess of our investments in PepsiAmericas over our equity in the underlying net assets, net of amortization, was approximately $212 million at year-end Year 11. Based upon the quoted closing price at year-end Year 11, the calculated market value of our investment in PepsiAmericas exceeded our carrying value by approximately $68 million.

Other Equity Investments

Summarized financial information regarding our principal equity investments, other than PBG and PepsiAmericas, follows. These investments are noncontrolling interests in bottling and snack food businesses. Information is presented in the aggregate and generally from the acquisition date.

	Year 11	Year 10
Current assets	$ 953	$1,033
Noncurrent assets	1,970	2,200
Total assets	$2,923	$3,233
Current liabilities	$1,053	$ 972
Noncurrent liabilities	249	578
Minority interest	3	35
Total liabilities	$1,305	$1,585
Our related equity investments	$ 906	$1,030

	Year 11	Year 10	Year 9
Net sales	$4,314	$4,714	$3,754
Gross profit	$2,132	$2,066	$1,691
Net Income/(loss)	$ 109	$ 79	$ (10)

Related Party Transactions

Our significant related party transactions involve our investments in unconsolidated bottling affiliates. We sell concentrate to these affiliates that is used in the production of carbonated soft drinks and non-carbonated beverages. We also sell certain finished goods and we receive royalties for the use of our trademark for certain products. The affiliates purchase sweeteners and certain other raw materials through us. The raw material purchases on behalf of these bottling affiliates, related payments to suppliers, and collections from the bottlers are not reflected in our consolidated financial statements. We also provide certain administrative and other services to these bottling affiliates under negotiated fee arrangement.

Further, because we share a common business objective with these bottling affiliates of increasing the availability and consumption of Pepsi-Cola beverages, we provide various forms of marketing support, market programs, capital equipment investment, and shared media expense. Based on the objective of the programs and initiatives, we record marketing support as an adjustment to net sales or as selling, general, and administrative expenses.

These transactions with our unconsolidated bottling affiliates are reflected in the Consolidated Statement of Income as follows:

	Year 11	Year 10	Year 9
Net sales..................................	$2,976	$2,706	$1,924
Selling, general, and administrative expenses....	$ 925	$ 733	$ 627

As of December 29, Year 11, the receivables from these bottling affiliates are $119 million and payables to these affiliates are $108 million. As of December 30, Year 10, the receivables from these bottling affiliates were $187 million and payables to these affiliates were $125 million. Such amounts are selected on terms consistent with other trade receivables and payables. See Notes 13 and 20 regarding our guarantee of PBG related debt.

NOTE 11—ACCOUNTS PAYABLE AND OTHER CURRENT LIABILITIES

	Year 11	Year 10
Accounts payable..................................	$1,238	$1,212
Accrued selling, advertising, and marketing............	861	986
Accrued compensation and benefits..................	789	809
Dividends payable..................................	255	240
Insurance accruals..................................	158	227
Other current liabilities............................	1,160	1,055
	$4,461	$4,529

NOTE 12—SHORT-TERM BORROWINGS AND LONG-TERM DEBT

	Year 11	Year 10
Short-term borrowings		
Current maturities of long-term debt.................	$319	$453
Other borrowings (6.4% and 7.1%)..................	410	499
Amounts reclassified to long-term debt..............	(375)	(750)
	$354	$202

	Year 11	Year 10
Long-term debt		
Short-term borrowings, reclassified	$ 375	$ 750
Notes due Year 12–Year 36 (4.1% and 6.7%)	1,986	1,924
Various foreign currency debt, due Year 11 (6.5%)	—	219
Zero coupon notes, $735 million		
due Year 21–Year 22 (13.4%)	356	339
Other, due Year 12–Year 15 (6.9% and 7.6%).	253	230
	2,970	3,462
Less current maturities of long-term debt	(319)	(453)
	$2,651	$3,009

The weighted average interest rates in the above table include the effects of associated interest rate and currency swaps at year-end Year 11 and Year 10. Also, see Notes 1 and 13 for a discussion of our use of interest rate and currency swaps, our management of the inherent credit risk and fair value information related to debt and interest rate and currency swaps.

Interest Rate Swaps

The following table indicates the notional amount and weighted average interest rates of interest rate swaps outstanding at year-end Year 11 and Year 10. The weighted average variable interest rates that we pay, which are primarily linked to either commercial paper or LIBOR rates, are based on rates as of the respective balance sheet date and are subject to change.

	Year 11	Year 10
Received fixed-pay variable		
Notional amount	$1,077	$1,335
Weighted average receive rate.	5.6%	4.4%
Weighted average pay rate	1.7%	4.9%

The terms of the interest rate swaps match the terms of the debt they modify. The swaps terminate at various dates, through Year 21. At year-end Year 11, approximately 52% of total debt, including the effects of the associated interest rate swaps, was exposed to variable interest rates, compared to 55% in Year 10. In addition to variable rate long-term debt, all short-term borrowings are categorized as variable for purposes of this measure.

Currency Swaps

We entered into current swaps to hedge our currency exposure on certain non-US. dollar-dominated debt upon issuance of such debt. The terms of the currency swaps matched the terms of the debt they modify. We have no currency swaps at December 29, Year 11.

At year-end Year 10, the foreign currency risk that related to debt denominated in Swiss francs and Luxembourg francs with an aggregate carrying amount of $122 million was hedged by currency swaps. The payables under related currency swaps were $43 million, resulting in an effective U.S. dollar liability of $165 million with a weighted average interest rate of 6.6%.

Revolving Credit Facilities

At year-end Year 11, we maintained $750 million of revolving credit facilities. Of the $750 million, approximately $375 million expires in June, Year 12, with the remaining $375 million expiring in June, Year 16. The credit facilities exist largely to support issuances of short-term debt and remain unused at year-end Year 11. Annually, these facilities are extendable an additional year upon the mutual consent of PepsiCo and the lending institutions. These facilities are subject to normal banking terms and conditions.

The reclassification of short-term borrowings to long-term debt reflects our intent and ability, through the existence of the unused credit facilities, to refinance these borrowings on a long-term basis.

Long-term debt outstanding at December 29, Year 11, matures as follows:

	Year 12	Year 13	Year 14	Year 15	Year 16	Thereafter
Maturities	$319	$485	$441	$167	$602	$956

NOTE 13—DERIVATIVE AND FINANCIAL INSTRUMENTS

On December 31, Year 10, we adopted SFAS 133. SFAS 133 established accounting and reporting standards for derivative instruments and hedging activities. It requires that we recognize all derivative instruments as either assets or liabilities in the Consolidated Balance Sheet and measure those instruments at fair value. The adoption of SFAS 133 on December 31, Year 10, increased assets by approximately $12 million and liabilities by approximately $10 million, with approximately $3 million recognized in accumulated other comprehensive income and a loss of less than $1 million recognized in the Consolidated Statement of Income. Accumulated other comprehensive loss included net accumulated derivative losses of $18 million as of December 29, Year 11.

Cash Flow Hedges

During the next twelve months, we expect to reclassify losses of approximately $1 million from accumulated other comprehensive income into earnings. All cash flow hedges at December 29, Year 11, are for periods of less than two years. Ineffectiveness resulting from cash flow hedging activities was not material to our results of operations. No cash flow hedges were discontinued during the year ended December 29, Year 11, as a result of anticipated transactions that are no longer probable of occurring.

Fair Value Hedges

Ineffectiveness resulting from fair value hedging activities was not material to our results of operations. All components of each derivative's gain or loss are included in the assessment of hedge effectiveness. In Year 11, there were no hedged firm commitments that no longer qualified as fair value hedges. See Note 12 for the notional amounts, related interest rates, and maturities of the interest rate and currency swaps.

Prepaid Forward Contracts

The change in the fair value of these equity derivative contracts resulted in $1 million of expense during Year 11, $19 million of income during Year 10, and $6 million of expense during Year 9. These changes in fair value were substantially offset by opposite changes in the amount of the underlying deferred compensation liability.

Fair Value

Carrying amounts and fair values of our derivative and financial instruments:

	Year 11		Year 10	
	Carrying Amount	Fair Value	Carrying Amount	Fair Value
Assets				
Cash and cash equivalents	$ 683	$ 683	$1,038	$1,038
Short-term investments	$ 966	$ 966	$ 467	$ 467
Forward exchange contracts[a]	$ 6	$ 6	$ —	$ —
Commodity contracts[a]	$ 1	$ 1		
Equity derivative contracts[a]	$ 65	$ 65	$ 66	$ 66
Interest rate swaps	$ 32	$ 32	$ —	$ 12
Liabilities				
Forward exchange contracts[b]	$ 2	$ 2	$ 9	$ 9
Commodity contracts[b]	$ 17	$ 17	—	—
Short-term borrowings and long-term debt,				
excluding capital leases	$3,001	$3,266	$3,205	$3,392
Interest rate swaps[b]	$ —	$ —	$ —	$ 5
Combined currency and interest rate swaps[c]	$ —	$ —	$ 43	$ 46

Included in the Consolidated Balance Sheet under the captions noted above or as indicated below.
[a]Included in Prepaid Expenses and Other Current Assets.
[b]Included in Accounts Payable and Other Current Liabilities.
[c]Included in Long-term Debt.

Because of the short maturity of cash equivalents and short-term investments, the carrying amounts approximate fair values. Short-term investments consist primarily of debt securities and have been classified as held-to-maturity. The fair values of commodity contracts, debt, debt-related derivatives, and foreign exchange derivatives were estimated using market quotes and calculations based on market rates. We have unconditionally guaranteed $2.3 billion of Bottling Group, LLC's long-term debt. The guarantee had a fair value of $59 million at December 29, Year 11, and $66 million at December 30, Year 10, based on market rates.

NOTE 14—INCOME TAXES

	Year 11	Year 10	Year 9
Income before income taxes:			
U.S..	**$2,922**	$2,574	$3,350
Foreign.............................	**1,107**	1,187	925
	$4,029	$3,761	$4,275
Provision for income taxes:			
Current: U.S. Federal	**$ 926**	$ 958	$ 819
Foreign....................	**226**	165	322
State	**53**	62	56
	$1,205	$1,185	$1,197
Deferred: U.S. Federal	**159**	31	559
Foreign....................	**(8)**	(7)	(17)
State	**11**	9	31
	162	33	573
	$1,367	$1,218	$1,770
Tax rate reconciliation:			
U.S. Federal statutory tax rate............	**35.0%**	35.0%	35.0%
State income tax, net of U.S. Federal tax benefit........................	**1.0**	1.2	1.3
Lower taxes on foreign results............	**(4.3)**	(2.9)	(2.5)
Bottling transactions	**—**	—	9.0
Merger-related costs and other impairment and restructuring charges.............	**2.3**	(0.2)	—
Other, net...........................	**(0.1)**	(0.7)	(1.4)
Effective tax rate	**33.9%**	32.4%	41.4%

In Year 9, Quaker adjusted its tax accruals and tax assets to reflect developments and information received during the year. The net effect of these adjustments, which are included above in Other, net, reduced our Year 9 provision for income taxes by $59 million or $0.03 per share.

Deferred tax liabilities (assets):

	Year 11	Year 10
Investments in unconsolidated affiliates	$ 702	$ 672
Property, plant, and equipment	804	742
Safe harbor leases	82	94
Zero coupon notes	68	73
Intangible assets other than nondeductible goodwill	121	105
Other..	480	448
Gross deferred tax liabilities	$2,257	$2,134
Net carryforwards................................	(556)	(816)
Postretirement benefits............................	(320)	(311)
Various current and noncurrent liabilities.............	(805)	(869)
Gross deferred tax assets...........................	(1,681)	(1,996)
Deferred tax asset valuation allowances...............	529	822
Deferred tax assets, net...........................	(1,152)	(1,174)
Net deferred tax liabilities.........................	$1,105	$ 960
Included in:		
Prepaid expenses and other current assets	$ (391)	$ (407)
Deferred income taxes	$1,496	$1,367
	$1,105	$ 960

Net operating loss carryforwards totaling $3.2 billion at year-end Year 11 are being carried forward and are available to reduce future taxable income of certain subsidiaries in a number of foreign and state jurisdictions. These net operating losses will expire as follows: $0.1 billion in Year 12, $2.8 billion between Year 12 and Year 27, and $0.3 billion may be carried forward indefinitely. In addition, tax credit carryforwards of approximately $90 million are available to reduce certain foreign tax liabilities through Year 21.

Analysis of valuation allowances:

	Year 11	Year 10	Year 9
Balance, beginning of year..................	$822	$810	$926
(Benefit)/provision	(291)	10	73
Other (deductions)/additions.............	(2)	2	(189)
Balance, end of year......................	$529	$822	$810

Other deductions/additions include the effects of currency translation and, in Year 9, the impact of the bottling transactions.

NOTE 15—PREFERRED AND COMMON STOCK

As of December 29, Year 11, there were 3.6 billion shares of common stock and 3 million shares of convertible preferred stock authorized, which are designated as $5.46 cumulative preferred convertible stock. Of the authorized convertible preferred shares, 803,953 shares were issued and 736,152 shares were outstanding. Each share is convertible at the option of the holder into 4.9625 shares of common stock. The convertible preferred shares may be called for redemption at $78 per share plus accrued and unpaid dividends upon written notice. The convertible preferred stock was issued only for the ESOP and will not be traded on the open market.

Preferred stock activity:

(in millions)	Year 11 Shares	Year 11 Amount	Year 10 Shares	Year 10 Amount	Year 9 Shares	Year 9 Amount
Balance, beginning of year	0.8	$49	0.9	$61	1.0	$70
Redemption.	(0.1)	(23)	(0.1)	(12)	(0.1)	(9)
Balance, end of year	0.7	$26	0.8	$49	0.9	$61

NOTE 16—OTHER COMPREHENSIVE LOSS

The accumulated balances related to each component of other comprehensive loss were as follows:

	Year 11	Year 10	Year 9
Currency translation adjustment	$(1,587)	$(1,369)	$(1,080)
Cash flow hedges, net of tax:[a]			
Cumulative effect of accounting change	3	—	—
Derivative (losses)/gains, net	(21)	—	—
Minimum pension liability adjustment[a][b]	(43)	(5)	(3)
Other	2	—	(2)
Accumulated other comprehensive loss	$(1,646)	$(1,374)	$(1,085)

[a]Includes $7 for our share of our equity investees' accumulated derivative losses and $29 for our share of our equity investees' minimum pension liability adjustments.
[b]Net of taxes of $22 in Year 11, $3 in Year 10, and $2 in Year 9.

NOTE 17—EMPLOYEE STOCK OPTIONS

Stock options have been granted to employees under four different incentive plans:
- the PepsiCo SharePower Stock Option Plan (SharePower);
- the PepsiCo Long-Term Incentive Plan (LTIP);
- the PepsiCo Stock Option Incentive Plan (SOIP); and
- the Quaker Long-Term Incentive Plan (Quaker LTIP).

SharePower

SharePower stock options are granted to essentially all full-time employees. SharePower options generally have a 10-year term. Beginning in Year 8, the number of SharePower options granted is based on each employee's annual earnings and tenure. These options generally become exercisable after three years. Prior to Year 8, the number of options granted was based on each employee's annual earnings and generally became exercisable ratably over five years.

LTIP

All senior management and certain middle management awards are made under LTIP. Under the LTIP, awards are generally based on a multiple base salary. The options generally become exercisable at the end of three years and have a 10-year term. In Year 11, the entire award was made in stock options with an exercise price equal to the average stock price on the day of the award. From Year 8 through Year 10, two-thirds of the award consisted of stock options with the balance paid in stock options or cash. At the date of these awards, the employee selected whether the remaining one-third of the award will be granted in stock options or paid in cash at the end of three years. The number of options granted or the cash payment, if any, depended on the attainment of prescribed performance goals over the three-year measurement period. If stock options were selected, they will be granted with an exercise price equal to the average stock price on the date of the grant, will vest immediately, and will have a 10-year term. If a cash payment is selected, one dollar of cash will be received for every four dollars of the award. Amounts expensed for expected cash payments were $64.0 million in Year 11, $36.7 million in Year 10, and $17.9 million in Year 9. At year-end Year 11, 57 million shares were available for grants under the LTIP.

SOIP

Grants under the SOIP are available to middle management employees. Under the SOIP, an employee generally receives an award based on a multiple of base salary. The options generally become exercisable at the end of three years and have a 10-year term. The entire award is made in stock options with an exercise price equal to the average stock price on the date of the award. At year-end Year 11, 39 million shares were available for grants under the SOIP.

Quaker LTIP

Grants under the Quaker LTIP were made to officers and other key employees. This program provided for benefits to be awarded in a variety of ways, with stock options being used most frequently. Approximately 12 million shares of Quaker common stock were authorized for grant under the Quaker LTIP. Stock options were granted for the purchase of common stock at a price not less than the fair market value on the date of grant. Options were generally exercisable after one or more years and expire no later than 10 years from the date of grant. This plan provided that, in the event of a change in control of Quaker, stock options become exercisable. Accordingly, upon approval by the Quaker shareholders of the merger, unvested options under this plan were vested. Upon consummation of the merger, these options were converted to PepsiCo stock options.

Stock option activity: (Options in thousands)	Year 11 Options	Year 11 Weighted Average Exercise Price	Year 10 Options	Year 10 Weighted Average Exercise Price	Year 9 Options	Year 9 Weighted Average Exercise Price
Outstanding at beginning of year.....	170,640	$28.08	188,661	$25.82	173,691	$22.43
Granted........................	40,432	43.53	28,660	31.92	48,711	33.90
Exercised.......................	(29,064)	21.59	(37,039)	18.40	(24,846)	15.84
Forfeited/expired.................	(5,086)	34.83	(9,642)	33.93	(8,895)	32.06
Outstanding at end of year..........	176,922	32.35	170,640	28.08	188,661	25.82
Exercisable at end of year[a]	83,521	$26.32	75,129	$21.27	90,826	$18.65
Weighted average fair value of options granted		$13.53		$12.04		$10.65

[a]In connection with the Year 9 bottling transactions, substantially all unvested PepsiCo stock options held by bottling employees vested. The acceleration resulted in a $46 pre-tax charge included in the determination of the related net gain.

Stock options outstanding and exercisable (in thousands) at December 29, Year 11:

Range of Exercise Price	Options Outstanding			Options Exercisable	
	Options	Weighted Average Remaining Contractual Life	Weighted Average Exercise Price	Options	Weighted Average Exercise Price
$4.25 to $14.20	2,975	1.49 yrs.	$ 8.56	2,975	$ 8.56
$14.28 to $33.04	77,165	4.85	24.99	56,023	22.37
$34.00 to $49.00	96,782	8.02	39.13	24,523	37.43
	176,922	6.44	32.35	83,521	26.32

Pro forma income and pro forma income per common share, as if we had recorded compensation expense based on fair value for stock-based awards:

	Year 11	Year 10	Year 9
Reported			
Net income	$2,662	$2,543	$2,505
Net income per common share—basic	$ 1.51	$ 1.45	$ 1.41
Net income per common share—diluted	$ 1.47	$ 1.42	$ 1.38
Pro forma			
Net income	$2,356	$2,343	$2,343
Net income per common share—basic	$ 1.33	$ 1.34	$ 1.32
Net income per common share—diluted	$ 1.30	$ 1.31	$ 1.29

We estimate the fair value of stock-based awards using the Black-Scholes options pricing model based on the following weighted average assumptions for options granted during the year:

	Year 11	Year 10	Year 9
Risk-free interest rate	4.8%	6.7%	5.2%
Expected life	5 yrs.	5 yrs.	5 yrs.
Expected volatility	29%	29%	27%
Expected dividend yield	0.98%	1.08%	1.34%

NOTE 18—DEFERRED COMPENSATION—ESOP

Quaker established an ESOP for the benefit of its employees to issue debt and to use the proceeds of such debt to acquire shares of stock for future allocation to ESOP participants. The final ESOP award was made in June, Year 11. The ESOP borrowings are included in long-term debt in the Consolidated Balance Sheet. As annual contributions were made to the ESOP, these contributions, along with the dividends accumulated on the common and preferred stock held by the ESOP, were used to repay the outstanding loans. As the loans were repaid, common and preferred stock were allocated to ESOP participants and deferred compensation was reduced by the amount of the principal payments on the loans.

The following table presents the ESOP loan payments:

	Year 11	Year 10
Principal payments	**$40**	$37
Interest payments	**3**	6
Total ESOP payments	**$43**	$43

As of December 29, Year 11, 11 million shares of common stock and 0.7 million shares of preferred stock were held in the accounts of ESOP participants.

NOTE 19—PENSION AND POSTRETIREMENT BENEFITS

	Year 11	Year 10	Year 9
Components of net periodic pension cost:			
Service cost	**$127**	$120	$133
Interest cost.	**233**	221	209
Expected return on plan assets.	**(301)**	(277)	(269)
Amortization of transition asset	**(2)**	(3)	(3)
Amortization of prior service amendments . . .	**8**	13	11
Amortization of (gain)/loss	**(9)**	(18)	15
Net periodic benefit cost	**56**	56	96
Curtailment/settlement loss	**1**	6	54
Special termination benefits.	**26**	—	10
Net pension cost	**$ 83**	$ 62	$160
Components of periodic postretirement cost:			
Service cost	**$ 20**	$ 22	$ 23
Interest cost.	**63**	58	54
Amortization of prior service amendments . . .	**(12)**	(12)	(14)
Amortization of gain	**—**	(1)	(1)
Net periodic benefit cost	**71**	67	62
Curtailment loss	**—**	2	—
Special termination benefits.	**1**	—	3
Net postretirement cost	**$ 72**	$ 69	$ 65

	Year 11	Year 10	Year 11	Year 10
	Pension		Postretirement	
Change in benefit obligation:				
Obligation at beginning of year	$3,170	$3,009	$ 834	$ 740
Service cost	127	120	20	22
Interest cost.	233	221	63	58
Plan amendments	10	3	1	—
Participant contributions	5	6	—	1
Actuarial loss.	170	6	50	48
Acquisitions.	—	3	—	
Benefit payments	(170)	(166)	(58)	(43)
Curtailment/settlement loss	2	6		8
Special termination benefits.	26	—	1	—
Foreign currency adjustment	(17)	(38)	—	—
Obligation at end of year	$3,556	$3,170	$ 911	$ 834
Change in fair value of plan assets:				
Fair value at beginning of year	$3,251	$3,053	$ —	$ —
Actual (loss)/gain on plan assets	(382)	281	—	—
Acquisitions.	—	14	—	—
Employer contributions	446	103	58	42
Participant contributions	5	6	—	1
Benefit payments	(170)	(166)	(58)	(43)
Foreign currency adjustment	(21)	(40)	—	—
Fair value at end of year	$3,129	$3,251	$ —	$ —
Funded status as recognized in the **Consolidated Balance Sheet:**				
Funded status at end of year.	$ (427)	$ 81	$(911)	$(834)
Unrecognized prior service cost	38	49	(5)	(17)
Unrecognized loss/(gain)	548	(349)	91	41
Unrecognized transition asset	(2)	(3)	—	—
Net amounts recognized.	$ 157	$ (222)	$(825)	$(810)
Net amounts as recognized in the **Consolidated Balance Sheet:**				
Prepaid benefit cost	$ 396	$ 141	$ —	$ —
Intangible assets	—	1	—	—
Accrued benefit liability	(261)	(372)	(825)	(810)
Accumulated other comprehensive income	22	8	—	
Net amounts recognized.	$ 157	$ (222)	$(825)	$(810)
Selected information for plans with **accumulated benefit obligation in excess** **of plan assets:**				
Projected benefit obligation	$ (419)	$ (307)	$(911)	$(834)
Accumulated benefit obligation	$ (252)	$ (193)	$(911)	$(834)
Fair value of plan assets	$ 51	$ 36	$ —	$ —

In Year 9, as a result of the bottling transactions, $717 million of pension benefit obligation and $205 million of postretirement benefit obligations were assumed by bottling affiliates. In addition, bottling affiliate plans assumed ownership of $659 million of pension assets. The net gain on the bottling transactions includes a curtailment/settlement net loss of $52 million.

Weighted-average pension assumptions at end of year:

	Year 11	Year 10	Year 9
Discount rate for benefit obligation.......	7.4%	7.7%	7.7%
Expected return on plan assets...........	9.8%	9.9%	10.0%
Rate of compensation increase...........	4.6%	4.5%	4.5%

The discount rate assumption used to compute the postretirement benefit obligation at year-end was 7.5% in Year 11, and 7.8% in Year 10.

Pension Assets

The pension plan assets are principally invested in stocks and bonds. These assets include approximately 4.7 million shares of PepsiCo common stock with a fair value of $227 million in Year 11, and $214 million in Year 10. Subsequent to the measurement date of September 30, Year 11, 0.8 million shares of PepsiCo common stock were purchased and, during Year 10, 1.8 million shares were sold. A one-percentage point decrease in our expected return on assets would have increased our net pension cost by approximately $31 million in Year 11.

Health Care Cost Trend Rates

An average increase of 7.5% in the cost of covered postretirement medical benefits is assumed for Year 12. This average increase is then projected to decline gradually to 4.5% in Year 18 and thereafter. Generally, our costs are capped at a specified dollar amount.

Assumed health care cost trend rates have a significant effect on the amount reported for postretirement medical plans. A one-percentage point change in assumed health care costs would have the following effects:

	1% Increase	1% Decrease
Year 11 service and interest cost components....	$ 7	$ (6)
Year 11 accumulated benefit obligation.........	$61	$(52)

NOTE 20—COMMITMENTS, CONTINGENCIES, AND LEASES

Contingent liabilities primarily reflect guarantees to support financial arrangements of certain unconsolidated affiliates, including the unconditional guarantee for $2.3 billion of Bottling Group, LLC's long-term debt. We believe that the ultimate liability, if any, in excess of amounts already recognized arising from such claims or contingencies is not likely to have a material adverse effect on our results of operations, financial condition, or liquidity.

In March, Year 10, we entered into a 10-year lease for office space to be constructed in Chicago, Illinois. The new Chicago office is currently in development and is expected to be completed in Year 12. Our obligations under the lease are contingent upon completion of the building and satisfaction of certain other obligations by the lessor.

Certain equipment and operating properties are rented under non-cancelable and cancelable operating leases and may provide for renewal options or escalation clauses. Total rent expense under operating leases was $165 million in Year 11, $171 million in Year 10, and $137 million in Year 9. The following is a schedule of future minimum annual rentals on non-cancelable operating leases, in effect as of December 29, Year 11:

	Year 12	Year 13	Year 14	Year 15	Year 16	Thereafter	Total
Total payments....	$138	$111	$95	$57	$42	$162	$605

NOTE 21—BUSINESS SEGMENTS

In early Year 9, in contemplation of the separation from PepsiCo of our bottling operations, we completed a reorganization of our beverage businesses and presented our operating results for Year 9, consistent with the new beverage organization. Therefore, the results of previously consolidated bottling operations in which we now own an equity interest through the applicable transaction closing dates in Year 9 are presented separately with the first quarter Year 9 equity income or loss of other unconsolidated bottling affiliates. From the applicable transaction closing dates in Year 9, the equity income of those previously consolidated bottling operations, and the equity income or loss of other unconsolidated bottling affiliates from the second quarter of Year 9 are presented separately below operating profit in the Consolidated Statement of Income. The combined results of our six ongoing reportable segments are referred to as New PepsiCo. The North American segments include the United States and Canada.

The accounting policies of the segments are the same as those described in Note 1. Merger-related costs and other impairment and restructuring charges are not included in segment results. All intersegment net sales and expenses are immaterial and have been eliminated in computing net sales and operating profit.

Frito-Lay North America

Frito-Lay North America (FLNA) manufactures, markets, sells, and distributes salty, sweet, and grain-based snacks. Products manufactured and sold include Lay's potato chips, Doritos and Tostitos tortilla chips, Cheetos cheese-flavored snacks, Ruffles potato chips, Fritos corn chips, a variety of dips and salsas, Quaker Chewy granola bars, Rold Gold pretzels, Sunchips multigrain snacks, and Funyuns onion-flavored rings.

Frito-Lay International

Frito-Lay International (FLI) manufactures, markets, sells, and distributes primarily salty and sweet snacks. Products include Sabritas snack foods and Alegro and Gamesa sweet snacks in Mexico, Walkers snack foods in the United Kingdom, and Smith's snack foods in Australia. Frito-Lay International also includes non-snack products, such as cereals, that are not material.

Pepsi-Cola North America

Pepsi-Cola North America (PCNA) markets, promotes, and manufactures concentrates for Pepsi, Mountain Dew, MUG, Sierra Mist, Slice and other brands for sale to franchised bottlers. It also sells syrups for these brands to national fountain accounts. Pepsi-Cola North America receives a royalty fee for licensing the processing, distribution, and sale of Aquafina bottled water; manufactures, markets and distributes ready-to-drink tea and coffee products through joint ventures with Lipton and Starbucks; and manufactures and sells SoBe and Dole beverages for distribution and sale through our franchise bottling system.

Gatorade/Tropicana North America

Gatorade/Tropicana North America (GTNA) produces, markets, sells, and distributes Gatorade sports drinks, Tropicana Pure Premium, Tropicana Season's Best, Tropicana Twister, and Dole juices.

PepsiCo Beverages International

PepsiCo Beverages International (PBI) manufactures concentrates of Pepsi, 7UP, Mirinda, KAS, Mountain Dew, and other brands internationally for sale to franchised and company-owned bottlers. PBI also produces, markets, sells, and distributes Gatorade sports drinks as well as Tropicana and other juices. In addition, PBI operates bottling plants and distribution facilities in certain international markets for the production, distribution, and sale of company-owned and licensed brands.

Quaker Foods North America

Quaker Foods North America (QFNA) manufactures, markets, and sells ready-to-eat cereals, hot cereals, flavored rice and pasta products, mixes and syrups, hominy grits, and cornmeal in North America. Products manufactured and sold include Quaker oatmeal, Cap'n Crunch and Life ready-to-eat cereals, Rice-A-Roni products, Aunt Jemima mixes and syrups, and Quaker grits.

Fiscal Year

Comparisons of Year 10 to Year 11 and Year 9 are affected by an additional week of results in the Year 10 reporting period. The estimated impact of the fifty-third week on Year 10 segment results is as follows:

	Net Sales	Operating Profit
Frito-Lay North America....................	$164	$40
Frito-Lay International	61	10
Pepsi-Cola North America....................	36	13
Gatorade/Tropicana North America.............	33	5
	$294	68
Corporate unallocated.......................		(6)
		$62

Business Segments

	Year 11	Year 10	Year 9
Net Sales			
Worldwide Snacks			
–Frito-Lay North America................	$ 9,374	$ 8,971	$ 8,232
–Frito-Lay International	5,130	4,875	4,274
Worldwide Beverages			
–Pepsi-Cola North America..............	3,842	3,289	2,605
–Gatorade/Tropicana North America	4,016	3,841	3,452
–PepsiCo Beverages International	2,582	2,531	2,407
Quaker Foods North America	1,991	1,972	1,993
Combined Segments	26,935	25,479	22,963
Quaker Divested Business	—	—	7
Bottling Operations/Investments...........	—	—	2,123
	$26,935	$25,479	$25,093
Operating Profit			
Worldwide Snacks			
–Frito-Lay North America................	$ 2,056	$ 1,915	$ 1,679
–Frito-Lay International	627	546	455
Worldwide Beverages			
–Pepsi-Cola North America..............	927	833	751
–Gatorade/Tropicana North America	530	500	433
–PepsiCo Beverages International	221	169	108
Quaker Foods North America	415	392	363

	Year 11	Year 10	Year 9
Combined Segments	**4,776**	4,355	3,789
Merger-related costs....................	**(356)**	—	—
Other impairment and restructuring charges.	**(31)**	(184)	(73)
Corporate[a]	**(368)**	(353)	(286)
Bottling Operations/Investments...........	—	—	53
	$ 4,021	$ 3,818	$ 3,483

Total Assets
Worldwide Snacks

–Frito-Lay North America................	**$ 4,623**	$ 4,282	$ 4,146
–Frito-Lay International	**4,381**	4,352	4,425
Worldwide Beverages			
–Pepsi-Cola North America...............	**1,325**	836	729
–Gatorade/Tropicana North America	**4,328**	4,143	3,927
–PepsiCo Beverages International	**1,747**	1,923	1,988
Quaker Foods North America	**917**	952	1,036
Combined Segments	**17,321**	16,488	16,251
Quaker Divested Business	—	—	2
Corporate[b]	**1,927**	1,737	1,226
Bottling Operations/Investments...........	**2,447**	2,532	2,469
	$21,695	$20,757	$19,948

Amortization of Intangible Assets
Worldwide Snacks

–Frito-Lay North America................	**$ 7**	$ 7	$ 8
–Frito-Lay International	**46**	46	46
Worldwide Beverages			
–Pepsi-Cola North America...............	**19**	2	2
–Gatorade/Tropicana North America	**69**	68	69
–PepsiCo Beverages International	**16**	16	16
Quaker Foods North America	**8**	8	8
Combined Segments	**165**	147	149
Bottling Operations/Investments...........	—	—	44
	$ 165	$ 147	$ 193

	Year 11	Year 10	Year 9
Depreciation and Other Amortization Expense			
Worldwide Snacks			
–Frito-Lay North America................	$ 377	$ 374	$ 345
–Frito-Lay International	187	182	158
Worldwide Beverages			
–Pepsi-Cola North America..............	64	94	72
–Gatorade/Tropicana North America	129	118	107
–PepsiCo Beverages International..........	99	111	104
Quaker Foods North America.............	43	51	53
Combined Segments	899	930	839
Corporate............................	18	16	10
Bottling Operations/Investments...........	—	—	114
	$ 917	$ 946	$ 963
Capital Spending			
Worldwide Snacks			
–Frito-Lay North America................	$ 514	$ 524	$ 485
–Frito-Lay International	291	278	295
Worldwide Beverages			
–Pepsi-Cola North America..............	70	59	22
–Gatorade/Tropicana North America	289	261	216
–PepsiCo Beverages International..........	95	98	128
Quaker Foods North America.............	57	96	58
Combined Segments	1,316	1,316	1,204
Corporate............................	8	36	42
Bottling Operations/Investments...........	—	—	95
	$ 1,324	$1,352	$1,341
Investments in Unconsolidated Affiliates			
Frito-Lay International	$ 361	$ 373	$ 284
Pepsi-Cola North America..............	25	32	50
Gatorade/Tropicana North America	10	13	17
PepsiCo Beverages International...........	6	6	4
Quaker Foods North America.............	—	1	1
Combined Segments	402	425	356
Corporate............................	22	22	22
Bottling Operations/Investments...........	2,447	2,532	2,469
	$ 2,871	$2,979	$2,847

	Year 11	Year 10	Year 9
Equity Income/(Loss) and Transaction Gains/(Losses)			
Frito-Lay International	$ 32	$ 26	$ 3
Pepsi-Cola North America................	40	33	31
Gatorade/Tropicana North America	(3)	—	1
PepsiCo Beverages International	3	2	1
Quaker Foods North America	(8)	(4)	—
Combined Segments	64	57	36
Bottling Operations/Investments[c]	160	130	1,076
	$ 224	$ 187	$ 1,112
Net Sales			
United States	$18,215	$17,051	$15,406
International.........................	8,720	8,428	7,564
Combined Segments	26,935	25,479	22,970
Bottling Operations/Investments...........	—	—	2,123
	$26,935	$25,479	$25,093
Long-Lived Assets[d]			
United States	$ 9,689	$ 9,285	$ 9,093
International.........................	4,899	4,966	5,099
Combined Segments	$14,588	$14,251	$14,192

[a]Corporate expenses include unallocated corporate headquarters expenses and costs of centrally managed initiatives and insurance programs, foreign exchange transaction gains and losses, and certain one-time charges.

[b]Corporate assets consist principally of cash and cash equivalents, short-term investments primarily held outside the United States, property, plant, and equipment, and other investments in unconsolidated affiliates.

[c]Includes our share of the net earnings or losses from our bottling equity investments and any gains or losses from disposals, as well as other transactions related to our bottling investments. Includes in Year 9, a gain of $1 billion ($270 million after-tax or $0.15 per share) related to our PBG and PepsiAmericas bottling transactions.

[d]Long-lived assets represent net property, plant, and equipment, net intangible assets, and investments in unconsolidated affiliates.

NOTE 22—SELECTED QUARTERLY FINANCIAL DATA (UNAUDITED)

	First Quarter		Second Quarter		Third Quarter		Fourth Quarter	
	Yr 11	Yr 10[g]	Yr 11	Yr 10[g]	Yr 11	Yr 10[g]	Yr 11	Yr 10[g]
PepsiCo............	$4,539	4,191	5,281	4,928		4,909		6,410
Quaker	1,227	1,172	1,514	1,398		1,475		996
Adjustments[a]	(436)	(422)	(82)	(76)	37	461		
Net Sales.........	$5,330	4,941	6,713	6,250	6,906	6,421	7,986	7,867
PepsiCo...........	$2,748	2,514	3,250	3,037		3,044		3,900
Quaker	677	649	846	761		831		512
Adjustments[a]	(240)	(229)	(52)	(45)	7	272		
Gross profit	$3,185	2,934	4,044	3,753	4,178	3,882	4,774	4,684
Merger-related costs[b]	$ —	—	—	—	235	—	12	—
Quaker	$ 4	173	5	4		—		6
Adjustments........	—	(172)	(1)	167		6		—
Other impairment and restructuring charges[c]	$ 4	1	4	171	13	6	10	6
PepsiCo...........	$ 498	422	652	563		587		611
Quaker	109	2	170	151		159		48
Adjustments[a]	(37)	72		(120)		9		39
Net income.........	$ 570	496	798	594	627	755	667	698
Net income per common share– basic[d]	$ 0.33	0.28	0.45	0.34	0.35	0.43	0.38	0.40
Net income per common share– diluted[d]	$ 0.32	0.28	0.44	0.33	0.34	0.42	0.37	0.39
Cash dividends declared per common share[e] ..	$ 0.14	0.135	0.145	0.14	0.145	0.14	0.145	0.14
Stock price share [f]								
High	$49.50	38.63	46.61	42.50	47.99	47.06	50.46	49.94
Low	$40.25	29.69	40.90	31.56	43.12	39.69	45.76	41.31
Close	$43.85	33.00	43.26	41.25	47.40	42.31	49.05	49.56

[a]Adjustments reflect the impact of changing Quaker's fiscal calendar to conform to PepsiCo's, conforming the accounting policies of the two companies applicable to interim periods, and certain reclassifications for gross profit and other impairment and restructuring charges.

[b]Merger-related costs in Year 11 (Note 2):

	Third Quarter	Fourth Quarter
Pre-tax.................	$ 235	$ 121
After-tax	$ 231	$ 91
Per share	$0.13	$0.05

(c)Other impairment and restructuring charges (Note 3):

	First Quarter		Second Quarter		Third Quarter		Fourth Quarter	
	Year 11	Year 10	Year 11	Year 10	Year 11	Year 10	Year 11	Year 10
Pre-tax	$ 4	$ 1	$ 4	$171	$13	$ 6	$10	$ 6
After-tax	$ 2	$ –	$ 3	$103	$ 8	$ 4	$ 6	$ 4
Per share	$ –	$ –	$ –	$ 0.06	$ 0.01	$ –	$ –	$ –

(d)The net income per common share amounts prior to the effective date of the merger are calculated by (1) combining the weighted average of pre-merger PepsiCo and Quaker common stock after adjusting the number of shares of Quaker common stock to reflect the exchange ratio of 2.3 shares of PepsiCo common stock for each share of Quaker common; and (2) dividing the combined net income by the result in (1) above.

(e)Cash dividends declared per common share are those of pre-merger PepsiCo prior to the effective date of the merger.

(f)Represents the composite high and low sales price and quarterly closing prices for one share of PepsiCo's common stock. Pre-merger amounts are those of PepsiCo prior to the effective date of the merger.

(g)Fiscal Year 10 consisted of fifty-three weeks and Year 9 consisted of fifty-two weeks. The impact for the fourth quarter and full year to net sales was an estimated $294, to operating profit was an estimated $62, and to net income was an estimated $44 or $0.02 per share.

Management's Responsibility for Financial Statements

To Our Shareholders:

Management is responsible for the reliability of the consolidated financial statements and related notes. The financial statements were prepared in conformity with generally accepted accounting principles and include amounts based upon our estimates and assumptions, as required. The financial statements have been audited by our independent auditors, KPMG LLP, who were given free access to all financial records and related data, including minutes of the meetings of the Board of Directors and Committees of the Board. We believe that our representations to the independent auditors are valid and appropriate.

Management maintains a system of internal controls designed to provide reasonable assurance as to the reliability of the financial statements, as well as to safeguard assets from unauthorized use or disposition. The system is supported by formal policies and procedures, including an active Code of Conduct program intended to ensure employees adhere to the highest standards of personal and professional integrity. Our internal audit function monitors and reports on the adequacy of and compliance with the internal control system and appropriate actions are taken to address significant control deficiencies and other opportunities for improving the system as they are identified. The Audit Committee of the Board of Directors consists solely of directors who are not salaried employees and who are, in the opinion of the Board of Directors, free from any relationship that would interfere with the exercise of independent judgment as a committee member. The Committee meets during the year with representatives of management, including internal auditors and the independent accountants to review our financial reporting process and our controls to safeguard assets. Both our independent auditors and internal auditors have free access to the Audit Committee.

Although no cost-effective internal control system will preclude all errors and irregularities, we believe our controls as of December 29, Year 11 provide reasonable assurance that the financial statements are reliable and that our assets are reasonably safeguarded.

Peter A. Bridgman
Senior Vice President and Controller

Indro K. Nooyi
President and Chief Financial Officer

Independent Auditor's Report

Board of Directors and Shareholders
PepsiCo, Inc.:

We have audited the accompanying Consolidated Balance Sheet of PepsiCo, Inc. and Subsidiaries as of December 29, Year 11 and December 30, Year 10 and the related Consolidated Statements of Income, Cash Flows and Common Shareholders' Equity for each of the years in the three-year period ended December 29, Year 11. These consolidated financial statements are the responsibility of PepsiCo, Inc.'s management. Our responsibility is to express an opinion on these consolidated financial statements based on our audits.

We conducted our audits in accordance with auditing standards generally accepted in the United States of America. Those standards require that we plan and perform the audit to obtain reasonable assurance about whether the financial statements are free of material misstatement. An audit includes examining, on a test basis, evidence supporting the amounts and disclosures in the financial statements. An audit also includes assessing the accounting principles used and significant estimates made by management, as well as evaluating the overall financial statement presentation. We believe that our audits provide a reasonable basis for our opinion.

In our opinion, the consolidated financial statements referred to above present fairly, in all material respects, the financial position of PepsiCo, Inc. and Subsidiaries as of December 29, Year 11 and Decembers 30, Year 10, and the results of their operations and their cash flows for each of the years in the three-year period ended December 29, Year 11, in conformity with accounting principles generally accepted in the United States of America.

KPMG LLP
New York, New York
February 6, Year 12

Appendix B

MANAGEMENT'S DISCUSSION AND ANALYSIS OF RESULTS OF OPERATIONS AND FINANCIAL CONDITION FOR PEPSICO, INC. AND SUBSIDIARIES

On August 2, Year 11, we completed a merger transaction, which resulted in The Quaker Oats Company (Quaker) becoming a wholly owned subsidiary of PepsiCo. As a result, we restated all prior periods presented to reflect the combined results of operations, financial position and cash flows of both companies as if they had always been merged. For further detail, see Merger of PepsiCo and The Quaker Oats Company.

Tabular dollars are in millions, except per share amounts. All per share amounts reflect common per share amounts, assume dilution unless noted, and are based on unrounded amounts. Percentage changes are based on unrounded amounts.

Management's Discussion and Analysis is presented in four sections. The first section discusses critical accounting policies, transactions with related and other parties, items affecting comparability, new accounting standards and market and other risk factors. The second section analyzes the results of operations, first on a consolidated basis and then for each of our business segments. The final two sections address consolidated cash flows and liquidity and capital resources.

Cautionary Statements

From time to time, in written reports and in oral statements, we discuss expectations regarding our future performance including synergies from the merger, the impact of the euro conversion and the impact of global macroeconomic issues. These "forward-looking statements" are based on currently available competitive, financial, and economic data and our operating plans. They are inherently uncertain, and investors must recognize that events could turn out to be significantly different from our expectations.

INTRODUCTION TO OUR BUSINESS

Critical Accounting Policies

An understanding of our accounting policies is necessary for a complete analysis of our results, financial positions, liquidity, and trends. We focus your attention on the following:

Principles of consolidation – The financial statements include the consolidated accounts of PepsiCo, Inc. and its controlled affiliates. Investments in unconsolidated affiliates over which we exercise significant influence, but not control, are accounted for by the equity method. Our definition of control for majority owned affiliates considers the exercisability of the minority interest rights, and consolidation would be precluded to the extent that the minority interest holds substantive participating rights. Our share of the net income or loss of unconsolidated affiliates accounted for by the equity method is included in our consolidated net income. As a result of changes in the operations of our European snack joint venture, we have determined that, effective in Year 12, consolidation is required.

Revenue recognition – We recognize revenue when products are delivered to customers consistent with sales terms. Sales terms generally do not allow a right of return.

Derivative instruments and hedging – We manage risks associated with commodity prices, foreign exchange rates, interest rates, and our stock price, and may use derivative instruments to hedge these risks. As a matter of policy, we do not use derivative instruments unless there is an underlying exposure, and therefore, we do not use derivative instruments for trading or speculative purposes. The evaluation of hedge effectiveness is subject to assumptions based on the terms and timing of the underlying exposures. All derivative instruments are recognized in our Consolidated Balance Sheet at fair value. The fair value of our derivative instruments is generally based on quoted market prices.

Asset impairment – All long-lived assets, including goodwill, investments in unconsolidated affiliates and other identifiable intangibles, are evaluated for impairment on the basis of undiscounted cash flows whenever events or changes in circumstances indicate that the carrying amount of an asset may not be recoverable. An impaired asset is written down to its estimated fair market value based on the best information available. Estimated fair market value is generally measured by discounting estimated future cash flows. Considerable management judgment is necessary to estimate discounted future cash flows. Assumptions used in these cash flows are consistent with internal forecasts.

Income taxes – Our effective tax rate and the tax bases of our assets and liabilities reflect our best estimate of the ultimate outcome of tax audits. Valuation allowances are established where expected future taxable income does not support the realization of the deferred tax assets.

Commitments and contingencies – We are subject to various claims and contingencies related to lawsuits, taxes, and environmental matters, as well as commitments under contractual and other commercial obligations. We recognize liabilities for contingencies and commitments when a loss is probable and estimable. Our contractual and other commercial obligations primarily relate to the procurement of goods and services in the normal course of business and to guarantees related to our equity investees.

Refer to **Note 1** to the consolidated financial statements for additional information on our accounting policies.

Transactions with Related and Other Parties

Significant related parties include our bottling franchisees in which we own an equity interest. We have entered into agreements with these bottlers and expect these arrangements to continue. These agreements cover the prices and terms for the sale of concentrate and full goods bearing our trademarks, as well as the manufacturing and distribution of our fountain products. In addition, we provide various forms of marketing support to or on behalf of our bottlers covering a variety of initiatives including marketplace support, marketing programs, capital equipment, and shared media expense. The level of this support is negotiated annually and can be increased or decreased at our discretion. We provide this support because we share a common business objective with our bottlers of increasing the availability and consumption of Pepsi-Cola beverages and the level of support has a direct impact on these objectives. See Liquidity and Capital Resources for related party commitments and guarantees and **Note 10** to our consolidated financial statements for additional information on related parties.

Certain members of our Board of Directors also serve on the boards of certain vendors and customers. Our transactions with these vendors and customers are in the normal course of business and consistent with terms negotiated with other vendors and customers. Those Board members do not participate in vendor selection and negotiations or in customer negotiations. In addition, certain officers serve on the boards of our anchor bottlers and other equity investees and may receive compensation from such entities consistent with that of other members serving on those boards.

ITEMS AFFECTING COMPARABILITY

Fifty-third Week in Year 10

Comparisons of Year 10 to Year 11 and Year 9 are affected by an additional week of results in the Year 10 reporting year. Because our fiscal year ends on the last Saturday in December, a fifty-third week is added every five or six years. The fifty-third week increased Year 10 net sales by an estimated $294 million, operating profit by an estimated $62 million, and net income by an estimated $44 million or $0.02 per share.

Merger of PepsiCo and The Quaker Oats Company

Under the Quaker merger agreement dated December 2, Year 10, Quaker shareholders received 2.3 shares of PepsiCo common stock in exchange for each share of Quaker common stock, including a cash payment for fractional shares. We issued approximately 306 million shares of our common stock in exchange for all the outstanding common stock of Quaker.

In connection with the merger transaction, we sold the global rights in our All Sport beverage brand to The Monarch Company, Inc. of Atlanta. As part of the terms of the sale, we agreed that, for 10 years after the Quaker transaction closing date, we would not distribute Gatorade sports drink through our bottling system in the United States and would not include Gatorade with Pepsi-Cola products in certain marketing or promotional arrangements covering specific distribution channels.

The merger was accounted for as a tax-free transaction and as a pooling-of-interests. As a result, all prior period consolidated financial statements presented have been restated to include the results of the operations, financial position, and cash flows of both companies as if they had always been combined. Certain reclassifications were made to conform the presentation of the financial statements, and the fiscal calendar and certain interim reporting policies were also conformed. There were no material transactions between pre-merger PepsiCo and Quaker.

The results of operations of the separate companies and the combined company for the most recent interim period prior to the merger and for the years presented in the consolidated financial statements are as follows:

	24 Weeks Ended June 16, Year 11	Year 10	Year 9
Reported Net Sales:			
PepsiCo.	$ 9,820	$20,438	$20,367
Quaker	2,741	5,041	4,726
Adjustments[a]	(518)	—	—
Combined	$12,043	$25,479	$25,093
Reported Net Income:			
PepsiCo.	$ 1,150	$ 2,183	$ 2,050
Quaker	279	360	455
Adjustments[a]	(61)	—	—
Combined	$ 1,368	$ 2,543	$ 2,505

[a]Adjustments reflect the impact of changing Quaker's fiscal calendar to conform to PepsiCo's and conforming the accounting policies of the two companies applicable to interim reporting. These changes have no impact on full year net sales or net income.

During Year 11, we recognized costs of $356 million associated with our merger with Quaker. The components of these merger-related costs were as follows:

Transaction costs	**$ 117**
Integration and restructuring cost	**239**
Total merger-related cost.	**$ 356**
After-tax.	**$ 322**
Per share.	**$0.18**

Transaction costs were incurred to complete the merger and consist primarily of fees and expenses for investment bankers, attorneys, and accountants, SEC filing fees, stock exchange listing fees, and financial printing and other related charges.

Integration costs represent incremental one-time merger-related costs. Such costs include consulting fees and expenses, expenses for accelerated vesting under change-in-control provisions, information system integration costs, and employee-related costs.

The restructuring charges primarily reflect termination costs for approximately 580 corporate, sales, distribution, manufacturing, research, and marketing employees. Employee termination costs include retirement benefit costs, severance costs, and expenses associated with change-in-control provisions of pre-merger employment contracts. As of December 29, Year 11, approximately 380 of the terminations have occurred. The terminations are expected to be completed during Year 12.

Additional merger-related actions are expected to bring the total integration costs and restructuring charges to between $450 million and $550 million. Ongoing merger-related cost savings and revenue enhancement opportunities are expected to reach $400 million a year by Year 15. We expect to achieve up to $175 million of the synergies by the end of Year 12.

Other Impairment and Restructuring Charges

	Year 11	Year 10	Year 9
Asset impairment charges			
Held and used in the business:			
Property, plant, and equipment.	$ 19	$ 125	$ 8
Held for disposal/abandonment:			
Property, plant, and equipment.	—	—	34
Total asset impairment	$ 19	$ 125	$ 42
Restructuring charges			
Employee-related costs.	—	41	20
Other charges	12	18	11
Total restructuring	12	59	31
Total	$ 31	$ 184	$ 73
After-tax	$ 19	$ 111	$ 45
Per share	$0.01	$0.06	$0.02

Year 11 and Year 10

The Year 11 and Year 10 other impairment and restructuring charges relate to a three-year supply chain reconfiguration project announced in Year 9 to upgrade and optimize Quaker's manufacturing and distribution capabilities across all of its North American businesses.

The asset impairment charges primarily reflect the reduction in the carrying value of the land, buildings, and production machinery and equipment to their estimated fair market value based on analyses of the liquidation values of similar assets. The restructuring charges primarily included severance and termination benefits for approximately 1,000 employees and other shutdown costs. No future charges are expected on this project.

Year 9

The Year 9 other impairment and restructuring charges of $73 million were comprised of the following:

- A charge of $65 million for asset impairment of $37 million and restructuring charges of $28 million, related to the closure of three plants and impairment of equipment at Frito-Lay North America. The asset impairment charges primarily reflected the reduction in the carrying value of the land and buildings to their estimated fair market value based on selling prices for comparable real estate, less costs to sell, and the write-off of the net book value of equipment which could not be redeployed. The plant closures were completed during Year 9. The majority of these assets were either disposed of or abandoned in Year 9. The restructuring charges of $28 million primarily included severance costs and plant closing costs.
- A charge of $8 million, for asset impairment of $5 million and restructuring charges of $3 million, related to the previously discussed Quaker supply chain reconfiguration project. The charge included costs to consolidate several cereal manufacturing lines and employee-related costs.

The employee-related costs for Year 9 of $20 million primarily included severance and early retirement benefits for approximately 930 employees. Substantially all of the terminations occurred during Year 9.

Total restructuring reserves of $100 million, including merger-related reserves, at December 29, Year 11, are included in accounts payable and other current liabilities in the Consolidated Balance Sheet.

Bottling Transactions

During Year 9, we completed a series of transactions creating our anchor bottlers. In April Year 9, certain wholly owned bottling businesses, referred to as The Pepsi Bottling Group (PBG), completed an initial public offering with PepsiCo retaining a direct noncontrolling ownership interest of 35.5%. In May, we combined certain other bottling operations with Whitman Corporation retaining a noncontrolling ownership interest of approximately 38%. In July, we combined certain other bottling operations with PepCom Industries, Inc., retaining a noncontrolling interest of 35% in the combined entity renamed Pepsi Bottling Ventures, LLC. In October, we formed a business venture with Pohlad Companies, a Pepsi-Cola franchisee, retaining a noncontrolling ownership interest of approximately 24% in the venture's principal operating subsidiary, PepsiAmericas, Inc.

Our financial statements include the results of our bottling operations on a consolidated basis through the transaction dates above, and our proportionate share of income under the equity method subsequent to those dates.

In December, Year 10, Whitman merged with PepsiAmericas. We now own approximately 37% of the combined company, which has since changed its name to PepsiAmericas. As part of the merger, we participate in an earn-out option whereby we may receive additional shares when certain performance targets are met.

Our three anchor bottlers distribute approximately three-fourths of our beverage products in North America.

Tax Item

In Year 9, Quaker adjusted its tax accruals and tax assets to reflect developments and information received during the year. The net effect of these adjustments reduced the income tax provision by $59 million or $0.03 per share.

New Accounting Standards

On December 31, Year 10, we adopted Statement of Financial Accounting Standard No. (SFAS) 133, *Accounting for Derivative Instruments and Hedging Activities.* SFAS 133 establishes accounting and reporting standards for derivative instruments and hedging activities. It requires that we recognize all derivative instruments as either assets or liabilities in the Consolidated Balance Sheet and measure those instruments at fair value. The adoption of SFAS 133 on December 31, Year 10 increased assets by approximately $12 million and liabilities by approximately $10 million, with approximately $3 million recognized in accumulated other comprehensive income and a loss of less than $1 million recognized in the Consolidated Statement of Income.

During Year 10 and Year 11, the Financial Accounting Standards Board's (FASB) Emerging Issues Task Force (EITF) addressed various issues related to the income statement classification of certain promotional payments, including consideration from a vendor to a reseller or another party that purchases the vendor's products. EITF 01-9, *Accounting for Consideration Given by a Vendor to a Customer or a Reseller of the Vendor's Products,* was issued in November, Year 11 and codified earlier pronouncements. Primarily effective for Year 12, adoption of EITF 01-9 will reduce our net sales by $3.4 billion in Year 11, $3.1 billion in Year 10, and $2.9 billion in Year 9, with selling, general, and administrative expenses reduced by the same amounts.

In July, Year 11, the FASB issued SFAS 141, *Business Combination.* SAFS 141 eliminated the pooling-of-interests method of accounting for business combinations and modified the application of the purchase accounting method. The elimination of the pooling-of-interests method is effective for transactions initiated after June 30, Year 11. The remaining provisions of SFAS 141 are effective for transactions accounted for using the purchase method that are completed after June 30, Year 11. Since our merger with Quaker (see Note 2 to the consolidated financial statements) was initiated in December, Year 10, and our acquisition of South Beach Beverage Company, LLC (see Note 4 to the consolidated financial statements) was completed in January, Year 11, adoption of this statement does not have an impact on our consolidated financial statements.

In July, Year 11, the FASB also issued SFAS 142, *Goodwill and Intangibles.* SFAS 142 eliminates the current requirement to amortize goodwill and indefinite-lived intangible assets, addresses the amortization of intangible assets with finite lives, and addresses impairment testing and recognition for goodwill and intangible assets. SFAS 142 applies to existing goodwill and intangible assets, as well as to transactions completed after the statement's effective date. SAFS 142 is effective for Year 12. Adoption of SFAS 142 will increase income before taxes by approximately $87 million in Year 12, reflecting the cessation of goodwill amortization and changes in the lives of other intangibles. The required transition evaluations are not expected to result in impairment charges.

In June, Year 11, the FASB issued SFAS 143, *Accounting for Asset Retirement Obligations*. SFAS 143 addresses financial accounting and reporting for obligations associated with the retirement of tangible long-lived assets and the associated asset retirement costs. It requires that we recognize the fair value of a liability for an asset retirement obligation in the period in which it is incurred if a reasonable estimate of fair value can be made. We are currently assessing SFAS 143 and the impact that adoption, in Year 13, will have on our consolidated financial statements.

In August, Year 11, the FASB issued SFAS 144, *Accounting for the Impairment of Disposal of Long-lived Assets*. SFAS 144 establishes a single model for the impairment of long-lived assets and broadens the presentation of discontinued operations to include more disposal transactions. SFAS 144 is effective for Year 12. Adoption will not have a material impact on our consolidated financial statements.

MARKET AND OTHER RISK FACTORS

Market Risks

The principal market risks (i.e., the risk of loss arising from adverse changes in market ranges and prices) to which we are exposed are:
- commodity prices, affecting the cost of our raw materials and fuel;
- foreign exchange risk;
- interest rates on our debt and short-term investment portfolios; and
- our stock price.

In the normal course of business, we manage these risks through a variety of strategies, including the use of hedging transactions, executed in accordance with our policies.

Our hedging transactions include, but are not limited to, the use of various derivative instruments. As a matter of policy, we do not use derivative instruments unless there is an underlying exposure and, therefore, we do not use derivative instruments for trading or speculative purposes. Any change in the value of our derivative instruments would be substantially offset by an opposite change in the value of the underlying hedged items.

Commodity Prices

We are subject to market risk with respect to the cost of commodities because our ability to recover increased costs through higher pricing may be limited by the competitive environment in which we operate. We manage this risk primarily through the use of fixed-price purchase orders, pricing agreements, geographic diversity, and derivative instruments. Derivative instruments, including futures, options, and swaps, are used to hedge fluctuations in prices of a portion of anticipated commodity purchases, primarily corn, oats, natural gas, heating oil, vegetable oil, and packaging materials. Our use of derivative instruments is not significant to our commodity purchases.

Our commodity derivative positions were $252 million at December 29, Year 11 and $52 million at December 30, Year 10. Our commodity derivative positions resulted in a net unrealized loss of $16 million at December 29, Year 11 and a net unrealized gain of $3 million at December 30, Year 10. We estimate that a 10% decline in commodity prices would have increased the loss by $18 million in Year 11 and reduced the gain by $6 million, resulting in a loss in Year 10.

Foreign Exchange

International operations constitute about one-fifth of our annual business segment operating profit. Operating in international markets involves exposure to movements in foreign exchange rates, primarily the Mexican peso, British pound, Canadian dollar, euro, and Brazilian real, which principally impacts the translation of our international operating profit into U.S. dollars. On occasion, we may enter into derivative instruments, as necessary, to reduce the effect of foreign exchange rate changes. We manage the use of foreign exchange derivatives centrally.

Our foreign currency derivative positions had an aggregate notional value of $355 million, with $223 million relating to contracts to exchange British pounds for U.S. dollars, at December 29, Year 11, with $336 million relating to contracts to exchange British pounds to U.S. dollars, at December 30, Year 10. These forward contracts had a net gain of $4 million at December 29, Year 11 and losses of $9 million at December 30, Year 10. We estimate that an unfavorable 10% change in the exchange rates would have decreased the Year 11 gain by $35 million, resulting in a loss, and increased the Year 10 losses by $35 million.

Interest Rates

We centrally manage our debt and investment portfolios considering investment opportunities and risks, tax consequences, and overall financing strategies. We use interest rate and currency swaps to effectively change the interest rate and currency of specific debt issuances, with the objective of reducing our overall borrowing costs. These swaps are entered into concurrently with the issuance of the debt that they are intended to modify. The notional amount, interest payment, and maturity date of the swaps match the principal, interest payment, and maturity date of the related debt. Our credit risk related to interest rate and currency swaps is considered low because such swaps are entered into only with strong creditworthy counterparties, are generally settled on a net basis, and are of relatively short duration.

Assuming year-end Year 11 and Year 10 variable rate debt and investment levels, a one-point increase in interest rates would have increased net interest expense by $3 million in Year 11 and $7 million in Year 10. The change in this impact from Year 10 resulted from decreased variable debt levels and increased investment levels at year-end Year 11. This sensitivity analysis includes the impact of existing interest rate and currency swaps.

Stock Price

The portion of our deferred compensation liability, which is based on our stock price, is subject to market risk. Prepaid forward contracts with financial institutions with an aggregate notional amount of $52 million at year-end Year 11 were used to hedge this risk and are accounted for as natural hedges. The change in fair value of these equity derivative contracts results in $1 million of expense in Year 11, $19 million of income in Year 10, and $6 million of expense in Year 9. We estimate that a 10% unfavorable change in the year-end stock price would have increased the Year 11 loss by $6 million and reduced the Year 10 gain by $7 million.

Euro Conversion

Our operating subsidiaries affected by the euro conversion successfully addressed the issues raised by the euro currency conversion including, among others, adapting computer and financial systems, business processes and equipment, such as vending machines, to accommodate euro-denominated transactions, and taking actions to reduce the impact of one common currency on cross-border pricing. We have experienced no business interruption as a result of the issuance and circulation of euro-denominated bills and coins and the withdrawal of legacy currencies. The system and equipment conversion costs were not material. Due to numerous uncertainties, we cannot reasonably estimate the long-term effects one common currency may have on pricing and the resulting impact, if any, on financial condition or results of operations.

RESULTS OF OPERATIONS

General

In the discussions below, the year-over-year dollar change in unit sales is referred to as volume. Price changes over the prior year and the impact of product, package, and country sales mix changes are referred to as effective net pricing.

Comparable results in all periods presented below exclude:
- the costs associated with our merger with Quaker,
- the impact of the fifty-third week in Year 10,
- other impairment and restructuring charges and various Quaker one-time items,
- the gain on the bottling transactions in Year 9, and also
- the impact of certain reclassifications and tax items.

In addition, comparable net sales and operating profit present the deconsolidation of our bottling operations as if it had occurred at the beginning of Year 8.

CONSOLIDATED REVIEW

Net Sales

	Year 11	Year 10	Year 9	% Change Year 11	% Change Year 10
Reported..................	**$26,935**	$25,479	$25,093	**6**	2
Comparable	**$26,935**	$25,185	$23,385	**7**	8

In Year 11, comparable net sales increased 7%. This increase is primarily due to volume gains and higher effective net pricing of worldwide snacks and worldwide beverages, as well as the acquisition of South Beach Beverage Company, LLC (SoBe). These gains were partially offset by a net unfavorable foreign currency impact. The SoBe acquisition enhanced comparable net sales growth by nearly 1 percentage point and the unfavorable foreign currency impact, primarily in Brazil and Europe, reduced comparable net sales growth by more than 1 percentage point.

In Year 10, comparable net sales increased 8%. This increase is primarily due to volume gains and higher effective net pricing of worldwide snacks, Pepsi-Cola North America and PepsiCo Beverages International. These increases were partially offset by a net unfavorable foreign currency impact, primarily in Europe, which reduced comparable net sales growth by 1 percentage point. The fifty-third week enhanced reported net sales growth by 1 percentage point.

Volume

Servings are based on U.S. Food and Drug Administration guidelines for single-serving sizes of our products.

Total servings increased 4% in Year 11 compared to Year 10 primarily due to contributions from our international divisions and Pepsi-Cola North America.

Total servings increased 5% in Year 10 compared to Year 9 driven by our international divisions, as well as contributions from Frito-Lay North America and Gatorade/Tropicana North America.

Operating and Profit Margin

	Year 11	Year 10	Year 9	% Change Year 11	% Change Year 10
Reported					
Operating profit	**$4,021**	$3,818	$3,483	**5%**	10%
Operating profit margin. . . .	**14.9%**	15.0%	13.9%	**(0.1)**	1.1
Comparable					
Operating profit	**$4,406**	$3,957	$3,487	**11%**	13%
Operating profit margin. . . .	**16.4%**	15.7%	14.9%	**0.7**	0.8

In Year 11, comparable operating profit margin increased 0.7 percentage points primarily reflecting the favorable margin impact of higher effective net pricing and increased volume. These improvements were partially offset by the margin impact of increased advertising and marketing and general and administrative expenses.

In Year 10, comparable operating profit margin increased 0.8 percentage points primarily reflecting the favorable margin impact of higher effective net pricing and increased volume. These improvements were partially offset by the margin impact of increases in selling and distribution expenses, primarily in Frito-Lay International, advertising and marketing, and general and administrative expenses.

Bottling Equity Income and Transaction Gains and Losses

Bottling equity income and transaction gains and losses includes our share of the net earnings or losses from our bottling equity investments. From time to time, we may increase or dispose of particular bottling investments. Any gains or losses from disposals, as well as other transactions related to our bottling investments, are also reflected on a pre-tax basis in equity income and transaction gains and losses.

In Year 11, comparable net bottling equity income and transaction gains and losses increased 28% to $160 million, primarily reflecting the strong performance of PBG. Results for Year 11 also include a gain of $59 million from the sale of approximately 2 million shares of PBG stock and a net credit of $23 million related to the resolution of issues for which a prior year accrual was established in connection with the creation of our anchor bottler system. These increases were offset by impairment charges of $62 million related to certain international bottling investments, primarily our equity investment in Turkey, reflecting a major currency devaluation and adverse macroeconomic conditions. Additionally, $27 million for our share of a charge recorded by PepsiAmericas for environmental liabilities relating to discontinued operations is included in our share of the net earnings from our bottling equity investments in Year 11.

In Year 10, comparable net bottling equity income and transaction gains and losses increased 51% to $125 million. Our share of net earnings from our bottling equity investments includes $18 million from the favorable impact of an accounting change by PBG. In addition, results for Year 10 include our share of charges related to restructuring actions in certain other bottling affiliates and the net loss from changes in our equity ownership interests. The fifty-third week in Year 10 enhanced reported net bottling equity income and transaction gains and losses by $5 million.

In Year 9, reported bottling equity income and transaction gains and losses includes a gain on bottling transactions of $1.0 billion ($270 million after-tax or $0.15 per share) relating to the second quarter PBG and Whitman bottling transactions. The PBG transaction resulted in a pre-tax gain of $1.0 billion ($476 million after-tax or $0.26 per share). The majority of the taxes are expected to be deferred indefinitely. The Whitman transaction resulted in an after-tax loss to us of $206 million or $0.11 per share. The Year 9 PepCom transaction was accounted for as a nonmonetary exchange for book purposes. However, a portion of the transaction was taxable which resulted in income tax expense of $25 million or $0.01 per share. The Year 9 Pohlad transaction was structured as a fair value exchange with no resulting gain or loss. Further, Year 9 bottling equity income and transaction gains and losses reflects $83 million for the equity income of our previously consolidated bottling operations from the applicable transaction closing dates and the equity income or loss of other unconsolidated bottling affiliates for the second, third, and fourth quarters.

Interest Expense, net

	Year 11	Year 10	Year 9	% Change Year 11	% Change Year 10
Reported					
Interest expense	$(219)	$(272)	$(421)	20	35
Interest income...........	67	85	130	(22)	(34)
Interest expense, net.......	$(152)	$(187)	$(291)	19	36
Comparable					
Interest expense	$(219)	$(268)	$(421)	19	36
Interest income...........	67	66	136	—	(51)
Interest expense, net.......	$(152)	$(202)	$(285)	25	29

Reported and comparable interest income in Year 11 includes a loss on investments used to economically hedge a portion of our deferred compensation liability. Reported interest income in Year 10 and Year 9 includes gains or losses from the equity derivative contracts used to hedge a portion of our deferred compensation liability. These equity derivative gains or losses are now classified in selling, general, and administrative expenses in connection with the Year 11 adoption of the accounting standard on derivative instruments. Comparable interest income for Year 10 and Year 9 reflects this reclassification. The fifty-third week increased reported net interest expense in Year 10 by $3 million.

In Year 11, comparable net interest expense declined 25%. Interest expense declined primarily as a result of significantly lower average debt levels. Interest income remained nearly flat as the increase from higher average investment balances was offset by lower average interest rates and a loss on the investments hedging a portion of our deferred compensation liability.

In Year 10, comparable net interest expense declined 29%. Interest expense declined reflecting significantly lower average debt levels, partially offset by higher average interest rates. Lower average debt levels reflect the third quarter Year 9 repayment of borrowings used to finance the Tropicana acquisition and the absence of the financing related to PBG. Interest income declined primarily due to lower average investment balances.

Provision for Income Taxes

	Year 11	Year 10	Year 9
Reported			
Provision for income taxes...........	**$1,367**	$1,218	$1,770
Effective tax rate..................	**33.9%**	32.4%	41.4%
Comparable			
Provision for income taxes...........	**$1,412**	$1,270	$1,099
Effective tax rate..................	**32.0%**	32.7%	32.9%

In Year 11, the comparable effective tax rate decreased 0.7 percentage points primarily due to lower taxes on foreign results. The reported effective tax rate increased 1.5 percentage points primarily due to limited tax benefits associated with merger-related costs recognized during the year.

In Year 10, the comparable effective tax rate remained nearly flat. The reported effective tax rate decreased 9 percentage points primarily as a result of the Year 9 bottling transactions.

Net Income and Net Income Per Common Share – Assuming Dilution

				% Change	
	Year 11	Year 10	Year 9	Year 11	Year 10
Reported					
Net income..............	**$2,662**	$2,543	$2,505	**5**	2
Net income per					
common share.........	**$ 1.47**	$ 1.42	$ 1.38	**4**	3
Comparable					
Net income..............	**$3,002**	$2,610	$2,239	**15**	17
Net income per					
common share.........	**$ 1.66**	$ 1.46	$ 1.23	**14**	18

In Year 11, comparable net income increased 15% and the related net income per common share increased 14%. These increases primarily reflect increased operating profit, lower net interest expense, and a lower effective tax rate.

In Year 10, comparable net income increased 17% and the related net income per common share increased 18% reflecting higher operating profit and lower net interest expense. The increase in net income per common share also reflects the benefit from a 1.4% reduction in average shares outstanding.

Business Segments

Additional information concerning our operating segments is presented in Note 21 to our consolidated financial statements.

Worldwide Snacks

Worldwide Snacks primarily include our salty, sweet, and grain-based snack businesses. Products manufactured and sold by Frito-Lay North America include Lay's potato chips, Doritos and Tostitos tortilla chips, Cheetos cheese-flavored snacks, Ruffles potato chips, Fritos corn chips, a variety of dips and salsas, Quaker Chewy granola bars, Rold Gold pretzels, Sunchips multigrain snacks, and Funyuns onion-flavored rings. Frito-Lay International includes Sabritas snack food and Alegro and Gamesa sweet snacks in Mexico, Walker snack foods in the United Kingdom, and Smith's snack food in Australia. Frito-Lay International also includes non-snack products, such as cereals that are not material.

Volume growth is reported on a system-wide basis, which includes joint ventures.

Frito-Lay North America

	Year 11	Year 10	Year 9	% Change Year 11	% Change Year 10
Net sales					
Reported	**$9,374**	$8,971	$8,232	4	9
Comparable	**$9,374**	$8,807	$8,232	6	7
Operating profit					
Reported	**$2,056**	$1,915	$1,679	7	14
Comparable	**$2,056**	$1,875	$1,679	10	12

Year 11 vs. Year 10

Pound volume advanced 3% excluding the impact of the fifty-third week in Year 10. This growth was led by single-digit growth in Lay's potato chips, Cheetos cheese-flavored snacks, Doritos tortilla chips, Fritos cornchips, and the introduction of our new Lay's Bistro Gourmet potato chips. These gains were partially offset by a double-digit decline in Ruffles potato chips. Pound volume growth including the fifty-third week in Year 10 was 1%.

Comparable net sales grew 6% due to higher effective net pricing and the increased volume. Lay's Bistro Gourmet potato chips contributed 1 percentage point to this growth.

Comparable operating profit increased 10% primarily reflecting the higher effective net pricing and increased volume, partially offset by increased advertising and marketing expenses. Advertising and marketing expenses grew at a faster rate than sales primarily due to increased promotional allowances.

Year 10 vs. Year 9

Pound volume advanced 5% excluding the impact of the fifty-third week. This growth was primarily driven by most of our core brands, excluding the low-fat and no-fat versions, and by our new Snack Kit products. The growth in core brands was led by solid single-digit growth in Lay's potato chips, Cheetos cheese-flavored snacks and Ruffles potato chips, as well as double-digit growth in Tostitos tortilla chips. These gains were partially offset by continued decline in WOW! Products. Pound volume growth including the fifty-third week was 7%.

Comparable net sales increased 7% primarily due to the volume gains and higher effective net pricing. Sales of our new Snack Kit and Snack Mix products and Oberto natural beef jerky snacks accounted for almost 30% of this growth. The fifty-third week enhanced reported net sales growth by 2 percentage points.

Comparable operating profit increased 12% primarily reflecting the higher volume, the higher effective net pricing, and reduced vegetable oil costs, partially offset by higher energy and fuel costs. Advertising and marketing expenses grew at a slightly slower rate than sales. The margin impact of these favorable factors contributed to the comparable operating profit margin improvement of 0.9 percentage points. The fifty-third week enhanced reported operating profit growth by 2 percentage points.

Frito-Lay International

	Year 11	Year 10	Year 9	% Change Year 11	% Change Year 10
Net sales					
Reported	$5,130	$4,875	$4,274	5	14
Comparable	$5,130	$4,814	$4,274	7	13
Operating profit					
Reported	$ 627	$ 546	$ 455	15	20
Comparable	$ 627	$ 536	$ 455	17	17

Year 11 vs. Year 10

Kilo volume increased 6%, excluding the impact of the fifty-third week in Year 10. This growth was primarily driven by a 9% increase in salty snack kilos and a 5% increase in sweet snack kilos. The salty snack growth was led by double-digit growth at our European joint venture in Brazil and in Poland, and single-digit growth at Walkers. Acquisitions contributed 2 percentage points of salty growth. The sweet snack increase was primarily attributable to growth at Gamesa. Kilo volume growth including the fifty-third week in Year 10 was 5%.

Comparable net sales increased 7%, primarily driven by the volume growth in Walkers, Gamesa, and Poland, and effective net pricing at Sabritas and Gamesa. Acquisitions contributed 1 percentage point to sales growth. Weaker foreign currencies in Brazil and the United Kingdom decreased net sales growth by 4 percentage points.

Operating profit increased 17%, led by solid results from Sabritas, Walkers, Poland, and Gamesa, partially offset by a decrease in Argentina as a result of macroeconomic conditions. The weaker foreign currencies, primarily in Brazil and the United Kingdom, decreased operating profit growth by 2 percentage points.

Year 10 vs. Year 9

Kilo volume increased 10%, excluding the impact of the fifty-third week. This growth was primarily driven by a 13% increase in salty snack kilos and a 9% increase in other non-snack food kilos. The salty snack growth was led by double-digit increases at Sabritas, our European and Latin American joint ventures, and Walkers. The other non-snack food growth was led by our business in Brazil. Acquisitions did not significantly impact the kilo growth. Kilo volume growth including the fifty-third week was 11%.

Comparable net sales increased 13% primarily driven by the volume growth at Sabritas, Walkers, and in Turkey, largely due to promotional programs, and effective net pricing at Gamesa and Sabritas. The net impact from acquisitions/divestitures contributed 2 percentage points to sales growth. Weaker foreign currencies, primarily in the United Kingdom and Australia, decreased net sales growth by 3 percentage points.

Comparable operating profit grew 17%, reflecting strong operating performances at Sabritas, Gamesa and in Turkey. The net impact from acquisitions/divestitures decreased operating profit growth by 3 percentage points. Weaker foreign currencies, primarily in the United Kingdom, decreased operating profit growth by 2 percentage points.

Worldwide Beverages

Our worldwide beverage operations include Pepsi-Cola North America, Gatorade/Tropicana North America, and PepsiCo Beverages International.

Pepsi-Cola North America markets, promotes, and manufactures concentrates for Pepsi, Mountain Dew, MUG, Sierra Mist, Slice and other brands for sale to franchised bottlers. It also sells syrups for these brands to national fountain accounts. Pepsi-Cola North America receives a royalty fee for licensing the processing, distribution, and sale of Aquafina bottled water; manufactures, markets, and distributes ready-to-drink tea and coffee products through joint ventures with Lipton and Starbucks; and manufactures and sells SoBe and Dole beverages for distribution and sale through our franchise bottling system.

Gatorade/Tropicana North America produces, markets, sells, and distributes Gatorade sports drinks, Tropicana Pure Premium, Tropicana Season's Best, Tropicana Twister and Dole juices.

PepsiCo Beverages International (PBI) manufactures concentrates of Pepsi, 7UP, Miranda, KAS, Mountain Dew and other brands internationally for sale to franchised and company-owned bottlers. PBI also produces, markets, sells and distributes Gatorade sports drinks as well as Tropicana and other juices. In addition, PBI operates bottling plants and distribution facilities in certain international markets for the production, distribution, and sale of company-owned and licensed brands.

Pepsi-Cola North America

	Year 11	Year 10	Year 9	% Change Year 11	% Change Year 10
Net sales					
Reported	**$3,842**	$3,289	$2,605	**17**	26
Comparable.............	**$3,842**	$3,253	$3,005	**18**	8
Operating profit					
Reported	**$ 927**	$ 833	$ 751	**11**	11
Comparable.............	**$ 927**	$ 820	$ 751	**13**	9

Year 11 vs. Year 10

Concentrate shipments and equivalents increased 4%, excluding the impact of the fifty-third week in Year 10. This increase was primarily driven by high single-digit growth in Mountain Dew reflecting the introduction of Code Red, strong growth in Sierra Mist and Aquafina, the acquisition of SoBe and the launch of Dole. These gains were partially offset by a low single-digit decline in trademark Pepsi, which was mitigated, in part, by the successful launch of Pepsi Twist, and a double-digit decline in Slice reflecting the strong growth of Sierra Mist. Bottler case sales volume increased 4%. The carbonated soft drink portfolio and the acquisition of SoBe each contributed 1 percentage point to both concentrate shipments and equivalents and bottler case sales growth.

Comparable net sales growth increased 18% primarily due to the increased volume and higher effective net pricing. The acquisition of SoBe and our new products Dole, Mountain Dew Code Red, Sierra Mist, and Pepsi Twist, accounted for the majority of the volume growth. These gains were partially offset by increased customer support. SoBe and Dole are sold as finished products to our bottling system. Accordingly, net sales growth was accelerated due to their significantly higher price per unit. The SoBe acquisition contributed 7 percentage points to net sales growth.

DON'T THROW THIS CARD AWAY!

THIS MAY BE REQUIRED FOR YOUR COURSE!

Bring Wall Street to the Classroom with Thomson Analytics!

Thomson Analytics–*Business School Edition* is a web-based portal product that provides integrated access to Thomson Financial content for the purpose of financial analysis. This is an educational version of the same financial resources used by Wall Street analysts on a daily basis!

For 500 companies, this online resource provides seamless access to:

- **Current and Past Company Data:** Worldscope which includes company profiles, financials and accounting results, market per-share data, annual information, and monthly prices going back to 1980.

- **Financial Analyst Data and Forecasts:** I/B/E/S Consensus Estimates which provides consensus estimates, analyst-by-analyst earnings coverage, and analysts' forecasts.

- **SEC Disclosure Statements:** Disclosure SEC Database which includes company profiles, annual and quarterly company financials, pricing information and earnings.

- *And More!*

Thomson Analytics *Business School Edition*

HOW DO I GET STARTED?

Follow these easy steps to gain access to Thomson Analytics–
Business School Edition!

STEP 1:
Visit the Thomson Analytics for Accounting website (http://tabseacct.swlearning.com).

STEP 2:
Click on "register" to enter your serial number.

STEP 3:
Enter your serial number exactly as it appears on this card and select a User ID.

STEP 4:
When prompted, select a password and submit the necessary information. Record your User ID and password in a secure location.

STEP 5:
You are now registered. Return to the above URL and click on "enter" to access Thomson Analytics–*Business School Edition*.

SERIAL #: SC-0008H9MN-ACTA

If you need technical assistance in registering, contact our Technical Support Team at support@thomsonlearning.com.

Thomson Analytics *Business School Edition*

ISBN: 0-324-20156-7

THOMSON
SOUTH-WESTERN

Comparable operating profit increased 13% primarily due to the increased volume and higher effective net pricing. These gains were partially offset by the increased advertising and marketing expenses related to bottler funding and other programs, increased general and administrative expenses, and the increased customer support. General and administrative expenses grew at a significantly faster rate than sales, while advertising and marketing expenses grew at a significantly slower rate. The SoBe acquisition reduced operating profit growth by 4 percentage points.

Year 10 vs. Year 9

Bottler case sales volume increased 1%, driven by double-digit growth in Aquafina and distribution gains from Fruitworks. In addition, the introduction of Sierra Mist and low single-digit decline in Diet Pepsi contributed to the increase. These gains were partially offset by a low single-digit decline in Pepsi and double-digit declines in Pepsi One and Lemon Lime Slice. Concentrate shipments were in line with bottler case sales. On a fifty-three week basis, concentrate shipments increased 1.3%.

Comparable net sales increased 8%. Higher concentrate and fountain pricing and higher Aquafina royalties contributed 8 percentage points of growth, and the increased volume, including the launch of Sierra Mist and our new Dole juice product, contributed 2 percentage points. These increases were partially offset by increased customer support. The fifty-third week enhanced reported net sales growth by 1 percentage point.

Comparable operating profit increased 9% primarily due to the higher concentrate pricing, increased volume, and the higher Aquafina royalties. These increases were partially offset by higher advertising and marketing expenses, increased customer support, and increased general and administrative expenses.

Other Beverages

	Year 11	Year 10	Year 9	% Change Year 11	% Change Year 10
Net sales					
Reported	**$4,016**	$3,841	$3,452	5	11
Comparable	**$4,016**	$3,808	$3,452	5	10
Operating profit					
Reported	**$ 530**	$ 500	$ 433	6	16
Comparable	**$ 530**	$ 495	$ 433	7	15

Year 11 vs. Year 10

Volume grew 4% excluding the impact of the fifty-third week in Year 10. This growth was led by three new Gatorade flavors and double-digit growth in Tropicana Pure Premium nutritionals, offset by low double-digit declines in Tropicana Season's Best.

Comparable net sales increased 5% due to the volume gains and higher effective net pricing for Gatorade.

Comparable operating profit increased 7% due to the volume gains, the higher effective net pricing, and lower general and administrative expenses. These increases were partially offset by higher promotional allowances and higher manufacturing costs primarily resulting from lower fruit yields, higher energy costs, and lower production leverage.

Year 10 vs. Year 9

Volume grew 10% due to the introduction of two new Gatorade flavors, multiple packs, and expanded distribution. Continued double-digit growth in Tropicana Pure Premium, including strong double-digit growth in Tropicana Pure Premium nutritionals and blends, also contributed to this growth. On a fifty-three week basis, volume increased 11%.

Comparable net sales increased 10% primarily due to the volume gains. Lower effective net pricing at Tropicana was substantially offset by increased pricing of selected Gatorade products.

Comparable operating profit increased 15% primarily due to the volume gains. These gains were partially offset by increased advertising and marketing expenses, including costs to support the launch of Propel fitness water, and increased packaging and transportation costs.

PepsiCo Beverages International

	Year 11	Year 10	Year 9	% Change Year 11	% Change Year 10
Net sales					
Reported	**$2,582**	$2,531	$2,407	**2**	5
Comparable	**$2,582**	$2,531	$2,429	**2**	4
Operating profit	**$ 221**	$ 169	$ 108	**31**	56

Year 11 vs. Year 10

Volume increased 4.5% due to broad-based increases led by Russia, China, and Brazil. These increases were partially offset by pricing-related declines in Mexico and Saudi Arabia, coupled with a macroeconomic decline in Turkey. Total carbonated soft drink concentrate shipments to franchisees, including those bottlers in which we own an equity interest, grew 3%, while their bottler case sales grew at about the same rate.

Net sales increased 2%. This increase was primarily due to the volume gains and higher effective net pricing, partially offset by a net unfavorable foreign currency impact. The net unfavorable foreign currency impact, primarily in Europe, reduced operating profit growth by 12 percentage points. Overall margin improvements contributed to operating profit growth.

Operating profit increased 31% primarily reflecting the volume gains and higher effective net pricing, partially offset by a net unfavorable foreign currency impact. The net unfavorable foreign currency impact, primarily in Europe, reduced operating profit growth by 12 percentage points. Overall margin improvements contributed to operating profit growth.

Year 10 vs. Year 9

Volume increased 6%. This reflects broad-based increases led by a doubling of volume in Russia, where volumes recovered from the effects of the Year 8 ruble devaluation. Volume growth was also driven by double-digit growth in China, India, and Thailand, and by growth in Mexico. Total carbonated soft drink concentrate shipments to franchisees, including those bottlers in which we own an equity interest, grew 2%, while their bottler case sales grew at a higher rate.

Comparable net sales increased 4% due to the volume gains and higher effective net pricing, partially offset by a broad-based net unfavorable foreign currency impact led by Europe. The net unfavorable foreign currency impact reduced net sales growth by 5 percentage points.

Operating profit increased 56% primarily reflecting the volume gains and higher effective net pricing, partially offset by a net unfavorable foreign currency impact led by Europe. The net unfavorable foreign currency impact reduced net sales growth by 5 percentage points.

Operating profit increased 56% primarily reflecting the volume gains and higher effective net pricing, partially offset by a net unfavorable foreign currency impact, primarily in Europe, higher advertising and marketing, and higher general and administrative expenses to support top-line growth.

Quaker Foods North America

Quaker Foods North America manufactures, markets, and sells ready-to-eat cereals, hot cereals, flavored rice and pasta products, mixes and syrups, hominy grits and cornmeal in North America. Products manufactured and sold include Quaker oatmeal, Cap'n Crunch and Life ready-to-eat cereals, Rice-A-Roni products, Aunt Jemima mixes and syrups, and Quaker grits.

	Year 11	Year 10	Year 9	% Change Year 11	% Change Year 10
Net sales....................	**$1,991**	$1,972	$1,993	1	(1)
Operating profit.............	**$ 415**	$ 392	$ 363	6	8

Year 11 vs. Year 10

Volume decreased 1%, driven by declines in ready-to-eat cereals and bulk corn-meal and oats products, largely offset by growth in hot cereals. The hot cereals growth resulted primarily from new products and flavor varieties.

Net sales increased 1%, primarily due to higher effective net pricing reflecting a mix shift to higher priced products, as well as price increases for cereals. This increase was offset by the lower overall volume.

Operating profit increased 6%, reflecting the higher effective net price from growth in higher priced products and the price increases in cereals.

Year 10 vs. Year 9

Volume declined 1%, driven by price competition in the ready-to-eat cereal category, partially offset by gains from the introduction of new varieties of hot cereals.

Net sales declined 1% primarily due to the lower overall volume.

Operating profit increased 8%, reflecting the higher-margin hot cereals volume growth, productivity gains, and lower marketing spending. Advertising and marketing expenses declined at a faster rate than sales.

Consolidated Cash Flows

Operating cash flow for Year 11 was $2.9 billion compared with $3.1 billion for Year 10. Operating cash flow primarily reflects externally reported net cash provided by operating activities of $4.2 billion, excluding after-tax net interest payments and the cash payments for merger-related costs and other impairment and restructuring charges, less capital spending, sales of property, plant, and equipment, and other net investing activity. Our Year 11 operating cash flow reflects a $421 million contribution to our U.S. pension plans compared to a $70 million contribution in Year 10. The Year 11 payment was made following a review of our anticipated future sources and uses of cash. We do not expect to make a cash contribution to our U.S. pension plans in Year 12. Additionally, in Year 11, we received tax refunds to $62 million versus $145 million in Year 10.

As shown in our Consolidated Statement of Cash Flows, our Year 11 cash and cash equivalents decreased $355 million to $683 million, reflecting cash used for investing and financing activities primarily funded from net cash provided by operations. The cash used in investing activities reflects capital spending, net purchases of short-term investments, the acquisition of SoBe, and the contribution to our pension plans. The cash used in financing activities reflects share repurchases and dividend payments, partially offset by proceeds from the exercise of stock options and the net proceeds of $524 million from the issuance of shares in connection with the merger with Quaker. We issued 13.2 million shares of our repurchased common stock to qualify for pooling-of-interests accounting treatment.

Our Year 10 cash and cash equivalents decreased $208 million to $1 billion, reflecting cash used for financing and investment activities primarily funded from net cash provided by operations. The cash used in financing activities reflects share repurchases, dividend payments, and net long-term debt payments, partially offset by proceeds from the exercise of stock options. The cash used in investing activities reflects capital spending and net purchases of short-term investments.

Common Share Repurchases

Common share repurchase activity was as follows:

	Year 11	Year 10	Year 9
Cost	**$1,716**	$1,430	$1,285
Shares repurchased:			
Number of shares (in millions)	**35**	38	36
% of shares outstanding at beginning of year	**2.4%**	2.6%	2.4%

Quaker repurchased common shares totaling $242 million in Year 10 and $373 million in Year 9.

Subsequent to our merger with Quaker, we repurchased 35 million shares of our common stock at a cost of $1.7 billion under the emergency and exemptive orders from the Securities and Exchange Commission aimed at facilitating the reopening of the U.S. equities market on September 17, Year 11, following the September 11th terrorist attacks. Our Board of Directors authorized the repurchase of up to $2 billion worth of our common stock during the terms of the orders. Repurchases under the orders did not compromise our ability to account for the merger with Quaker as a pooling-of-interests. All authorizations for share repurchases have been rescinded as a result of the PepsiCo and Quaker merger.

Liquidity and Capital Resources

Our strong cash-generating capability and financial condition give us ready access to capital markets throughout the world. Our principal source of liquidity is operating cash flows, which are derived from net sales. Macroeconomic conditions may impact the demand for and pricing of our products. Our debt rating of A1 from Moody's and A from Standard & Poor's contributes to our accessibility to global capital markets. These ratings reflect our strong operating cash flows and include the impact of the cash flows and debt of our anchor bottlers. We have maintained these healthy ratings for many years, demonstrating the stability of our operating cash flows.

At year-end Year 11, we maintained $750 million of revolving credit facilities. Of the $750 million, approximately $375 million expires in June, Year 12, with the remaining $375 million expiring in June, Year 16. Annually, these facilities are extendable for an additional year upon the mutual consent of PepsiCo and the lending institutions. The credit facilities exist largely to support issuances of short-term debt and remain unused at year-end Year 11. At year-end Year 11, $375 million of short-term borrowings were reclassified as long-term, reflecting our intent and ability, through the existence of the unused credit facilities, to refinance these borrowings on a long-term basis.

Quaker integration costs will require cash, of which $228 million was paid in Year 11. We expect the balance will be paid in Year 12 and Year 13.

Long-term financial obligations and other commercial commitments

Long-term financial obligations:

		Payments Due by Period			
	Total	Less than 1 year	1–3 years	4–5 years	After 5 years
Long-term debt, including current maturities[a]	$2,970	$319	$ 926	$769	$ 956
Operating leases	605	138	206	99	162
Total	$3,575	$457	$1,132	$868	$1,118

[a]As recognized in our Consolidated Balance Sheet.

Our other commercial commitments at December 29, Year 11 include:
- the unconditional guarantee of $2.3 billion of Bottling Group, LLC's long-term debt (see **Notes 13** and **20** to our consolidated financial statements);
- guarantees of approximately $45 million of debt and other obligations of unconsolidated affiliates;
- commitments for the purchase of goods and services used in the production of our products approximating $425 million that, if triggered, will result in increasing our ownership;
- guarantees of approximately $90 million with terms that extend over 5 years related primarily to leases of Tricon Global Restaurants, Inc. (which we spun-off in Year 7), and
- other commitments in the normal course of business, including obligations for customer promotional incentives, approximating $60 million with terms primarily extending up to 5 years.

Our commitments for goods and services purchases do not exceed our projected requirements over the related terms and are in the normal course of business.

Appendix C

OUTPUT OF ANALYSIS SPREADSHEET IN FINANCIAL STATEMENT ANALYSIS PACKAGE (FSAP) FOR PEPSICO, INC. AND SUBSIDIARIES

PROFITABILITY ANALYSIS FOR: Pepsico
A #DIV/0! message indicates that a ratio denominator is zero.

	RETURN ON ASSETS		
Level 1	Year 9	Year 10	Year 11
	12.3%	13.4%	13.2%

Level 2	PROFIT MARGIN FOR ROA			ASSETS TURNOVER		
	Year 9	Year 10	Year 11	Year 9	Year 10	Year 11
	11.1%	10.7%	10.4%	1.1	1.3	1.3

Level 3	Year 9	Year 10	Year 11	Year 9	Year 10	Year 11	
Sales	100.0%	100.0%	100.0%	10.7	12.5	12.6	Receivable
Interest Revenues	.5%	.3%	.2%				Turnover
Other Revenues	4.3%	.5%	.6%	8.5	8.7	8.6	Inventory
Cost of Goods Sold	41.2%	40.1%	39.9%				Turnover
Selling & Administrative				3.4	3.9	4.0	Fixed Asset
Expense	43.9%	43.6%	43.1%				Turnover
Other Expenses—I	0.8%	0.6%	0.6%				
Other Expenses—II	0.3%	0.7%	1.4%				
Income Tax Expense	7.6%	5.2%	5.4%				
Operating Margin	11.1%	10.7%	10.4%				

ROCE PROFITABILITY ANALYSIS FOR: Pepsico

RETURN ON COMMON SHAREHOLDERS' EQUITY

Year 9	Year 10	Year 11
36.7%	34.6%	32.7%

PROFIT MARGIN FOR ROCE

Year 9	Year 10	Year 11
10.0%	10.0%	9.9%

ASSET TURNOVER

Year 9	Year 10	Year 11
1.1	1.3	1.3

CAPITAL STRUCTURE LEVERAGE

Year 9	Year 10	Year 11
3.3	2.8	2.6

PROFITABILITY FACTORS:

A #DIV/0! message indicates that a ratio denominator is zero.

	Year 7	Year 8	Year 9	Year 10	Year 11
RETURN ON ASSETS:					
Profit Margin for ROA	3.6%	9.5%	11.1%	10.7%	10.4%
× Asset Turnover	1.0	1.1	1.1	1.3	1.3
= Return on Assets	3.6%	10.8%	12.3%	13.4%	13.2%
RETURN ON COMMON EQUITY:					
Profit Margin for ROCE	2.2%	8.4%	10.0%	10.0%	9.9%
× Asset Turnover	1.0	1.1	1.1	1.3	1.3
× Capital Structure Leverage	3.4	3.5	3.3	2.8	2.6
= Return on Common Equity	7.5%	33.2%	36.7%	34.6%	32.7%
OPERATING PERFORMANCE:					
Gross Margin / Sales	57.2%	57.0%	58.8%	59.9%	60.1%
Operating Profit Before Taxes / Revenues	6.9%	11.5%	17.9%	15.7%	15.1%
Net Income—Continuous Ops / Revenues	2.2%	8.4%	9.5%	9.9%	9.9%
Comprehensive Income / Revenues	1.3%	8.1%	9.4%	8.8%	8.9%
ASSET TURNOVER:					
Sales / Avg. Accounts Receivable	9.8	10.5	10.7	12.5	12.6
COGS / Average Inventory	9.6	10.3	8.5	8.7	8.6
Sales / Average Fixed Assets	2.8	3.4	3.4	3.9	4.0

RISK FACTORS:

A #DIV/0! message indicates that a ratio denominator is zero.

LIQUIDITY:	Year 7	Year 8	Year 9	Year 10	Year 11
Current Ratio	1.42	0.61	1.09	1.17	1.17
Quick Ratio	1.04	0.39	0.70	0.76	0.76
Days Receivables Held	37	35	34	29	29
Days Inventory Held	38	35	43	42	42
Days Payables Held	51	39	48	45	41
Net Wk. Capital Days	24	31	29	26	30
Operating Cash Flow to Current Liabilities	66.8%	52.7%	52.8%	93.3%	85.8%

SOLVENCY:					
Total Liabilities / Total Assets	68.5%	73.9%	64.4%	63.3%	60.0%
LT Debt / (LT Debt + Share Equity)	44.8%	42.3%	33.2%	28.3%	23.4%
LT Debt / Share Equity	81.2%	73.4%	49.7%	39.5%	30.6%
Operating Cash Flow to Total Liabilities	21.3%	21.8%	22.9%	34.2%	32.1%
Interest Coverage Ratio	3.21	6.72	11.15	14.83	19.40
Price-Earnings Ratio	80.55	28.36	28.20	34.09	32.36
Market-to-Book-Value Ratio	6.3	9.9	10.2	11.4	10.0

INCOME STATEMENT ITEMS AS % OF SALES:
A #DIV/0! message indicates that a ratio denominator is zero.

	Year 7	Year 8	Year 9	Year 10	Year 11
Sales	100.0%	100.0%	100.0%	100.0%	100.0%
Cost of Goods Sold	42.8%	43.0%	41.2%	40.1%	39.9%
GROSS MARGIN	57.2%	57.0%	58.8%	59.9%	60.1%
Interest Revenues	.5%	.3%	.5%	.3%	.2%
Other Revenues & Gains	0%	0%	4.3%	.5%	.6%
Selling & Admin. Expense	43.1%	43.4%	43.9%	43.6%	43.1%
Other Expenses & Losses—I	.8%	.8%	.8%	.6%	.6%
Other Expenses & Losses—II	6.9%	1.5%	.3%	.7%	1.4%
Income Tax Expense	3.4%	2.0%	7.6%	5.2%	5.4%
OPERATING MARGIN	3.6%	9.5%	11.1%	10.7%	10.4%
Interest Expense	2.2%	1.7%	1.7%	1.1%	.8%
Income Tax Savings on Interest	.8%	.6%	.6%	.4%	.3%
Minority Interest in Earnings	0%	0%	0%	0%	0%
Income from Continuing Ops	2.2%	8.4%	10.0%	10.0%	9.9%
Income from Discontinued Ops	2.5%	0%	0%	0%	0%
Extraordinary Gains (Losses)	0%	0%	0%	0%	0%
Changes in Actg. Principles	0%	0%	0%	0%	0%
NET INCOME	4.7%	8.4%	10.0%	10.0%	9.9%
Change in Accum. Other Comprehensive Income	-.8%	-.3%	-.1%	-1.1%	-1.0%
COMPREHENSIVE INCOME	1.3%	8.1%	9.9%	8.8%	8.9%

INCOME STATEMENT ITEMS—INTERPERIOD % CHANGES:

A #DIV/0! message indicates that a ratio denominator is zero.

INTERPERIOD % CHANGES	Year 7	Year 8	Year 9	Year 10	Year 11	COMPOUND GROWTH RATE
Sales	#DIV/0!	4.9%	-7.7%	1.5%	5.7%	1.0%
Cost of Goods Sold	#DIV/0!	5.5%	-11.8%	-1.0%	5.2%	-.8%
GROSS MARGIN	#DIV/0!	4.3%	-4.6%	3.3%	6.1%	2.2%
Selling & Admin. Expense	#DIV/0!	5.5%	-6.6%	.8%	4.5%	.9%
Income Tax Expense	#DIV/0!	-38.2%	252.0%	-31.5%	9.9%	18.9%
OPERATING MARGIN	#DIV/0!	178.2%	7.7%	-2.1%	3.1%	31.9%
Interest Expense	#DIV/0!	-17.6%	-9.5%	-35.4%	-19.5%	-21.1%
Income Tax Savings on Interest	#DIV/0!	-17.6%	-9.5%	-35.4%	-19.5%	-21.1%
Minority Interest in Earnings	#DIV/0!	#DIV/0!	#DIV/0!	#DIV/0!	#DIV/0!	#DIV/0!
Income from Continuing Ops	#DIV/0!	306.1%	10.0%	1.5%	4.7%	47.6%
Income from Discontinued Ops	#DIV/0!	-100.0%	#DIV/0!	#DIV/0!	#DIV/0!	#NUM!
Extraordinary Gains (Losses)	#DIV/0!	#DIV/0!	#DIV/0!	#DIV/0!	#DIV/0!	#DIV/0!
Changes in Actg. Principles	#DIV/0!	#DIV/0!	#DIV/0!	#DIV/0!	#DIV/0!	#DIV/0!
NET INCOME	#DIV/0!	88.0%	10.0%	1.5%	4.7%	21.7%
Change in Accum. Other Comprehensive Income	#DIV/0!	-67.7%	-63.4%	1011.5%	-5.9%	5.4%
COMPREHENSIVE INCOME	#DIV/0!	547.2%	12.3%	-9.1%	6.0%	62.7%

BALANCE SHEET COMMON SIZE STATEMENT:
A #DIV/0! message indicates that a ratio denominator is zero.

ASSETS:	Year 7	Year 8	Year 9	Year 10	Year 11
Cash and Marketable Securities	13.0%	3.0%	6.7%	7.3%	7.6%
Accounts Receivable—Trade	10.8%	10.9%	9.8%	10.3%	9.9%
Inventories	4.3%	5.1%	5.8%	5.7%	6.0%
Other Current Assets	4.3%	2.8%	3.5%	3.8%	3.5%
CURRENT ASSETS	32.4%	21.8%	25.9%	27.1%	27.0%
Investments in Securities	5.3%	5.5%	14.3%	14.4%	13.2%
Property, Plant, & Equipment—at cost	32.6%	33.3%	31.9%	31.6%	31.7%
Less: Accumulated Depreciation	0%	0%	0%	0%	0%
Other Assets	29.8%	39.4%	27.9%	27.0%	28.1%
TOTAL ASSETS	100.0%	100.0%	100.0%	100.0%	100.0%
LIABILITIES:					
Accounts Payable—Trade	5.4%	5.4%	6.7%	5.8%	5.7%
Notes Payable—Non Trade	.7%	16.1%	1.9%	1.0%	1.6%
Current Portion of Long-term Debt	0%	0%	0%	0%	0%
Other Current Liabilities	16.7%	14.0%	15.1%	16.3%	15.7%
CURRENT LIABILITIES	22.8%	35.5%	23.7%	23.1%	23.0%
Long-term Debt	25.6%	19.2%	17.7%	14.5%	12.2%
Deferred Tax	7.6%	8.0%	6.1%	6.6%	6.9%
Other Noncurrent Liabilities	12.5%	11.3%	17.0%	19.1%	17.9%
NONCURRENT LIABILITIES	45.7%	38.4%	40.7%	40.2%	37.0%
TOTAL LIABILITIES	68.5%	73.9%	64.4%	63.3%	60.0%
STOCKHOLDERS' EQUITY					
Minority Interest in Subsidiaries	0%	0%	0%	0%	0%
Preferred Stock	.1%	.1%	.1%	.1%	.1%
Common Stock	.1%	.1%	.2%	.2%	.1%
Additional Paid-in Capital	9.6%	3.6%	2.8%	1.8%	.1%
Retained Earnings	52.6%	53.1%	74.8%	79.5%	53.1%
Treasury Stock	25.8%	26.0%	36.6%	38.2%	5.8%
Accumulated Other Comprehensive Income	−2.7%	−4.3%	−4.2%	−5.4%	−6.6%
Other Equity Adjustments	−.8%	−.6%	−.2%	−.1%	0%
SHAREHOLDERS' EQUITY	31.5%	26.1%	35.6%	36.7%	40.0%
TOTAL EQUITIES	100.0%	100.0%	100.0%	100.0%	100.0%

Appendix C *Output of Financial Statement Analysis Package (FSAP) for PepsiCo*

BALANCE SHEET—INTERPERIOD % CHANGES:
A #DIV/0! message indicates that a ratio denominator is zero.

INTERPERIOD % CHANGES	Year 7	Year 8	Year 9	Year 10	Year 11	COMPOUND GROWTH RATE
ASSETS:						
Cash and Mkt. Securities	231.1%	−74.8%	78.9%	12.3%	9.6%	13.0%
Accounts Receivable—Trade	−12.6%	11.4%	−28.4%	8.7%	.6%	−5.3%
Inventories	−24.8%	29.3%	−8.8%	2.3%	9.9%	0%
Other Current Assets	−3.6%	−26.5%	−1.1%	11.9%	−4.9%	−5.7%
CURRENT ASSETS	22.5%	−25.8%	−5.6%	8.6%	4.2%	−.6%
Investments in Securities	−12.7%	16.2%	103.9%	4.7%	−3.6%	15.9%
Property, Plant, & Equipment—at cost	−34.8%	13.0%	−24.0%	2.9%	4.8%	−9.6%
Less: Accumulated Depreciation	#DIV/0!	#DIV/0!	#DIV/0!	#DIV/0!	#DIV/0!	#DIV/0!
Other Noncurrent Assets	−32.9%	46.0%	−43.9%	.8%	8.8%	−9.6%
TOTAL ASSETS	−21.1%	10.4%	−20.7%	4.1%	4.5%	−5.6%
LIABILITIES:						
Accounts Payable—Trade	−30.3%	8.9%	−1.0%	−9.2%	2.1%	−7.0%
Notes Payable—Non-Trade	−71.5%	2300.6%	−90.4%	−47.9%	75.2%	−9.8%
Current Portion of Long-term Debt	#DIV/0!	#DIV/0!	#DIV/0!	#DIV/0!	.7%	#DIV/0!
Other Current Liabilities	−8.0%	−7.3%	−14.6%	12.5%	4.2%	−3.8%
CURRENT LIABILITIES	−19.9%	71.5%	−47.0%	1.4%	4.2%	−5.1%
Long-term Debt	−38.2%	−17.3%	−26.9%	−14.7%	−11.9%	−22.4%
Deferred Tax	−14.0%	15.6%	−39.6%	13.1%	9.4%	−5.8%
Other Noncurrent Liabilities	−8.1%	.1%	18.9%	17.0%	−2.1%	4.6%
NONCURRENT LIABILITIES	−28.4%	−7.1%	−16.1%	2.7%	−3.8%	−11.2%
TOTAL LIABILITIES	−25.8%	19.1%	−30.9%	2.2%	−0.8%	−9.1%
STOCKHOLDERS' EQUITY						
Minority Interest in Subsidiaries	#DIV/0!	#DIV/0!	#DIV/0!	#DIV/0!	#DIV/0!	#DIV/0!
Preferred Stock	10.5%	4.8%	4.5%	−4.3%	18.2%	6.5%
Common Stock	0%	0%	0%	0%	−11.8%	−2.5%
Additional Paid-in Capital	7.0%	−58.5%	−38.2%	−32.9%	−96.5%	−63.6%
Retained Earnings	12.1%	11.3%	11.7%	10.6%	−30.2%	1.5%
Treasury Stock	47.8%	11.0%	11.8%	8.4%	−84.0%	−20.5%
Accumulated Other Comprehensive Income	28.6%	7.2%	2.5%	26.6%	19.8%	−100.0%
Other Equity Adjustments	.6%	−14.5%	−69.6%	−53.3%	−100.0%	#DIV/0!
SHAREHOLDERS' EQUITY	−8.7%	−8.5%	8.0%	7.4%	13.7%	2.0%
TOTAL EQUITIES	−21.1%	10.4%	−20.7%	4.1%	4.5%	−5.6%

Appendix D

OUTPUT OF FORECASTS AND VALUATIONS SPREADSHEETS IN FINANCIAL STATEMENT ANALYSIS PACKAGE (FSAP) FOR PEPSICO

FSAP OUTPUT: **PRO FORMA FINANCIAL STATEMENT FORECASTS**
FIRM NAME: **PEPSICO**
ANALYST NAME: **Stickney, Brown, & Wahlen**

Format
Actual Amounts
Common Size Percent
Rate of Change Percent

	Actuals		
	Year 9	Year 10	Year 11
INCOME STATEMENT			
Sales..	**25093**	**25479**	**26935**
common size	100.0%	100.0%	100.0%
rate of change................................		1.5%	5.7%
Cost of Goods Sold...........................	**10326**	**10226**	**10754**
common size	41.2%	40.1%	39.9%
rate of change................................		−1.0%	5.2%
GROSS MARGIN	**14767**	**15253**	**16181**
common size	58.8%	59.9%	60.1%
rate of change................................		3.3%	6.1%
Selling & Admin. Expense	**11018**	**11104**	**11608**
common size	43.9%	43.6%	43.1%
rate of change................................		0.8%	4.5%
Other Revenues & Gains	**83**	**130**	**160**
common size	0.3%	0.5%	0.6%
rate of change................................		56.6%	23.1%
Other Expenses & Losses—I	**193**	**147**	**165**
common size	0.8%	0.6%	0.6%
rate of change................................		−23.8%	12.2%
Other Expenses & Losses—II	**0**	**0**	**0**
common size	0.0%	0.0%	0.0%
rate of change................................		#DIV/0!	#DIV/0!
OPERATING MARGIN	**3639**	**4132**	**4568**
common size	14.5%	16.2%	17.0%
rate of change................................		13.5%	10.6%
Interest Income..............................	**130**	**85**	**67**
common size	0.5%	0.3%	0.2%
rate of change................................		−34.6%	−21.2%
Interest Expense	**421**	**272**	**219**
common size	1.7%	1.1%	0.8%
rate of change................................		−35.4%	−19.5%

Format:
Forecast Amounts
Forecast Assumptions
Forecast Assumption Explanation

Forecasts for Year +11 and Beyond:
Long-run Growth Rate Assumption: 5.0%
Long-run Growth Factor: 105%

Forecasts

	Year +1	Year +2	Year +3	Year +4	Year +5	Year +6	Year +7	Year +8	Year +9	Year +10	Year +11
	28841	30890	33094	35464	38013	40745	43674	46813	50178	53791	56480
	7.1%	7.1%	7.1%	7.2%	7.2%	7.2%	7.2%	7.2%	7.2%	7.2%	
Sales growth rate											
	11450	12202	13006	13866	14825	15891	17033	18257	19569	20978	22027
	39.7%	39.5%	39.3%	39.1%	39.0%	39.0%	39.0%	39.0%	39.0%	39.0%	
Cost of goods sold as % of sales											
	17391	18688	20088	21597	23188	24855	26641	28556	30609	32812	34453
	60.3%	60.5%	60.7%	60.9%	61.0%	61.0%	61.0%	61.0%	61.0%	61.0%	
	7.5%	7.5%	7.5%	7.5%	7.4%	7.2%	7.2%	7.2%	7.2%	7.2%	
	12429	13312	14262	15284	16382	17560	18822	20175	21625	23182	24341
	43.1%	43.1%	43.1%	43.1%	43.1%	43.1%	43.1%	43.1%	43.1%	43.1%	
Selling & Admin. Expenses as % of sales											
	169	187	201	215	231	248	266	285	306	328	344
	5.5%	5.5%	5.5%	5.5%	5.5%	5.5%	5.5%	5.5%	5.5%	5.5%	
Assume 5.5% return on unconsolidated affiliates											
	58	62	66	71	76	81	87	94	100	108	113
	0.2%	0.2%	0.2%	0.2%	0.2%	0.2%	0.2%	0.2%	0.2%	0.2%	
As % of sales											
	0	0	0	0	0	0	0	0	0	0	0
	0.0%	0.0%	0.0%	0.0%	0.0%	0.0%	0.0%	0.0%	0.0%	0.0%	
As % of sales											
	5073	5502	5960	6458	6961	7461	7998	8573	9189	9851	10343
	17.6%	17.8%	18.0%	18.2%	18.3%	18.3%	18.3%	18.3%	18.3%	18.3%	
	11.1%	8.4%	8.3%	8.4%	7.8%	7.2%	7.2%	7.2%	7.2%	7.2%	
	73	80	86	92	99	106	114	122	131	140	147
	4.2%	4.2%	4.2%	4.2%	4.2%	4.2%	4.2%	4.2%	4.2%	4.2%	
Interest rate earned on avg. financial assets											
	189	199	194	203	216	222	238	255	274	294	309
	6.0%	6.0%	6.0%	6.0%	6.0%	6.0%	6.0%	6.0%	6.0%	6.0%	
Interest rate paid on avg. financial liabilities											

	Actuals		
	Year 9	Year 10	Year 11
Income before Tax	**3348**	**3945**	**4416**
common size	13.3%	15.5%	16.4%
rate of change..............................		17.8%	11.9%
Income Tax Expense.........................	**1068**	**1291**	**1413**
common size	4.3%	5.1%	5.2%
rate of change..............................		20.9%	9.5%
Income from Continuing Ops	**2280**	**2654**	**3003**
common size	9.1%	10.4%	11.1%
rate of change..............................		16.4%	13.1%
Income (Loss) from Discontinued Operations	**0.0%**	**0.0%**	**0.0%**
common size	0.0%	0.0%	0.0%
rate of change..............................		#DIV/0!	#DIV/0!
Extraordinary Gains (Losses)	**0**	**0**	**0**
common size	0.0%	0.0%	0.0%
rate of change..............................		#DIV/0!	#DIV/0!
Changes in Actg. Principles.....................	**0**	**0**	**0**
common size	0.0%	0.0%	0.0%
rate of change..............................		#DIV/0!	#DIV/0!
Minority Interest in Earnings...................	**0**	**0**	**0**
common size	0.0%	0.0%	0.0%
rate of change..............................		#DIV/0!	#DIV/0!
NET INCOME................................	**2280**	**2654**	**3003**
common size	9.1%	10.4%	11.1%
rate of change..............................		16.4%	13.1%
Change in Accum. Other Comp. Income..........	**−26**	**−289**	**−272**
common size	−0.1%	−1.1%	−1.0%
rate of change..............................		1011.5%	−5.9%
COMPREHENSIVE INCOME	**2254**	**2365**	**2731**
common size	9.0%	9.3%	10.1%
rate of change..............................		4.9%	15.5%
Preferred Stock Dividends	**4**	**4**	**4**
common size	0.0%	0.0%	0.0%
rate of change..............................		0.0%	0.0%
COMPREHENSIVE INCOME AVAILABLE FOR COMMON SHAREHOLDERS	**2250**	**2361**	**2727**
common size	9.0%	9.4%	10.9%
rate of change..............................		4.9%	15.5%

Forecasts

	Year +1	Year +2	Year +3	Year +4	Year +5	Year +6	Year +7	Year +8	Year +9	Year +10	Year +11
	4958	**5383**	**5852**	**6347**	**6843**	**7345**	**7873**	**8439**	**9046**	**9697**	**10182**
	17.2%	17.4%	17.7%	17.9%	18.0%	18.0%	18.0%	18.0%	18.0%	18.0%	
	12.3%	8.6%	8.7%	8.5%	7.8%	7.3%	7.2%	7.2%	7.2%	7.2%	
	1586	**1722**	**1873**	**2031**	**2190**	**2350**	**2519**	**2700**	**2894**	**3103**	**3258**
	32.0%	32.0%	32.0%	32.0%	32.0%	32.0%	32.0%	32.0%	32.0%	32.0%	
Effective income tax rate											
	3371	**3660**	**3980**	**4316**	**4654**	**4995**	**5354**	**5739**	**6151**	**6594**	**6924**
	11.7%	11.8%	12.0%	12.2%	12.2%	12.3%	12.3%	12.3%	12.3%	12.3%	
	12.3%	8.6%	8.7%	8.5%	7.8%	7.3%	7.2%	7.2%	7.2%	7.2%	
	0.0%	**0.0%**	**0.0%**	**0.0%**	**0.0%**	**0.0%**	**0.0%**	**0.0%**	**0.0%**	**0.0%**	
	0.0%	0.0%	0.0%	0.0%	0.0%	0.0%	0.0%	0.0%	0.0%	0.0%	
Random walk											
	0	**0**	**0**	**0**	**0**	**0**	**0**	**0**	**0**	**0**	**0**
	0.0%	0.0%	0.0%	0.0%	0.0%	0.0%	0.0%	0.0%	0.0%	0.0%	
Random walk											
	0	**0**	**0**	**0**	**0**	**0**	**0**	**0**	**0**	**0**	**0**
	0.0%	0.0%	0.0%	0.0%	0.0%	0.0%	0.0%	0.0%	0.0%	0.0%	
Random walk											
	0	**0**	**0**	**0**	**0**	**0**	**0**	**0**	**0**	**0**	**0**
	0.0%	0.0%	0.0%	0.0%	0.0%	0.0%	0.0%	0.0%	0.0%	0.0%	
Random walk											
	3371	**3660**	**3980**	**4316**	**4654**	**4995**	**5354**	**5739**	**6151**	**6594**	**6924**
	11.7%	11.8%	12.0%	12.2%	12.2%	12.3%	12.3%	12.3%	12.3%	12.3%	
	12.3%	8.6%	8.7%	8.5%	7.8%	7.3%	7.2%	7.2%	7.2%	7.2%	
	0	**0**	**0**	**0**	**0**	**0**	**0**	**0**	**0**	**0**	**0**
	0.0%	0.0%	0.0%	0.0%	0.0%	0.0%	0.0%	0.0%	0.0%	0.0%	
Changes follow a random walk											
	3371	**3660**	**3980**	**4316**	**4654**	**4995**	**5354**	**5739**	**6151**	**6594**	**6924**
	11.7%	11.8%	12.0%	12.2%	12.2%	12.3%	12.3%	12.3%	12.3%	12.3%	
	23.4%	8.6%	8.7%	8.5%	7.8%	7.3%	7.2%	7.2%	7.2%	7.2%	
	4	**4**	**4**	**4**	**4**	**4**	**4**	**4**	**4**	**4**	**4**
	4	4	4	4	4	4	4	4	4	4	
Constant											
	3367	**3656**	**3976**	**4312**	**4650**	**4991**	**5350**	**5735**	**6147**	**6590**	**6920**
	11.7%	11.8%	12.0%	12.2%	12.2%	12.2%	12.2%	12.3%	12.3%	12.3%	
	23.5	8.6%	8.7%	8.5%	7.8%	7.3%	7.2%	7.2%	7.2%	7.2%	

FSAP OUTPUT: PRO FORMA FINANCIAL STATEMENT FORECASTS
FIRM NAME: PEPSICO
ANALYST NAME: Stickney, Brown, & Wahlen

Format
Actual Amounts
Common Size Percent
Rate of Change Percent

	Actuals		
	Year 9	Year 10	Year 11
BALANCE SHEET			
ASSETS:			
Cash	**1247**	**1038**	**683**
common size	6.3%	5.0%	3.1%
rate of change		−16.8%	−34.2%
Marketable Securities	**93**	**467**	**966**
common size	0.5%	2.2%	4.5%
rate of change		402.2%	106.9%
Accounts Receivable—Trade	**1958**	**2129**	**2142**
common size	9.8%	10.3%	9.9%
rate of change		8.7%	0.6%
Inventories	**1165**	**1192**	**1310**
common size	5.8%	5.7%	6.0%
rate of change		2.3%	9.9%
Other Current Assets	**707**	**791**	**752**
common size	3.5%	3.8%	3.5%
rate of change		11.9%	−4.9%
CURRENT ASSETS	**5170**	**5617**	**5853**
common size	25.9%	27.1%	27.0%
rate of change		8.6%	4.2%
Investments in Securities	**2846**	**2979**	**2871**
common size	14.3%	14.4%	13.2%
rate of change		4.7%	−3.6%
Property, Plant, & Equipment—at cost	**6373**	**6558**	**6876**
common size	31.9%	31.6%	31.7%
rate of change		2.9%	4.8%
Less: Accumulated Depreciation			
common size	0.0%	0.0%	0.0%
rate of change		#DIV/0!	#DIV/0!
Other Assets	**5559**	**5603**	**6095**
common size	27.9%	27.0%	28.1%
rate of change		0.8%	8.8%
TOTAL ASSETS	**19948**	**20757**	**21695**
common size	100.0%	100.0%	100.0%
rate of change		4.1%	4.5%

Format:
Forecast Amounts
Forecast Assumptions
Forecast Assumption Explanation

Forecasts for Year +11 and Beyond:
Long-run Growth Rate Assumption: 5.0%
Long-run Growth Factor: 105%

Forecasts

Year +1	Year +2	Year +3	Year +4	Year +5	Year +6	Year +7	Year +8	Year +9	Year +10	Year +11
790	846	907	972	1041	1116	1197	1283	1375	1474	1547
10	10	10	10	10	10	10	10	10	10	
Number of days sales in cash										
1057	1133	1215	1302	1397	1498	1607	1724	1849	1983	2082
4.5%	4.5%	4.5%	4.5%	4.5%	4.5%	4.5%	4.5%	4.5%	4.5%	
As a percent of assets										
2291	2454	2629	2818	3020	3237	3470	3719	3987	4274	4487
29	29	29	29	29	29	29	29	29	29	
Average number of days sales in receivables										
1316	1402	1495	1594	1704	1827	1958	2099	2249	2411	2532
8.7	8.7	8.7	8.7	8.7	8.7	8.7	8.7	8.7	8.7	
Average inventory turnover rate										
822	881	945	1013	1086	1165	1250	1341	1438	1543	1620
3.5%	3.5%	3.5%	3.5%	3.5%	3.5%	3.5%	3.5%	3.5%	3.5%	
As a percent of assets										
6276	6717	7190	7698	8249	8844	9482	10165	10898	11685	12269
26.7%	26.7%	26.6%	26.6%	26.6%	26.6%	26.5%	26.5%	26.5%	26.5%	
7.2%	7.0%	7.0%	7.1%	7.2%	7.2%	7.2%	7.2%	7.2%	7.2%	
3287	3524	3779	4052	4346	4662	5001	5364	5753	6170	6479
14.0%	14.0%	14.0%	14.0%	14.0%	14.0%	14.0%	14.0%	14.0%	14.0%	
As a percent of assets										
7391	7943	8534	9167	9846	10573	11353	12189	13085	14046	14748
515	552	591	633	679	728	780	836	896	7.2%	
Net PP&E growth with sales = CAPEX – deprec exp										
										0
6526	6990	7489	8025	8602	9220	9883	10593	11355	12172	12781
7.1%	7.1%	7.1%	7.2%	7.2%	7.2%	7.2%	7.2%	7.2%	7.2%	
Grow with sales										
23481	25174	26992	28942	31043	33299	35718	38311	41091	44073	46277
100.0%	100.0%	100.0%	100.0%	100.0%	100.0%	100.0%	100.0%	100.0%	100.0%	
8.2%	7.2%	7.2%	7.2%	7.3%	7.3%	7.3%	7.3%	7.3%	7.3%	

	Actuals		
	Year 9	Year 10	Year 11
LIABILITIES:			
Accounts Payable—Trade	**1335**	**1212**	**1238**
common size	6.7%	5.8%	5.7%
rate of change.................................		−9.2%	2.1%
Notes Payable—Non-trade	**388**	**202**	**354**
common size	1.9%	1.0%	1.6%
rate of change.................................		−47.9%	75.2%
Current Portion of Long-term Debt			
common size	0.0%	0.0%	0.0%
rate of change.................................		#DIV/0!	#DIV/0!
Other Current Liabilities.......................	**3004**	**3381**	**3406**
common size	15.1%	16.3%	15.7%
rate of change.................................		12.5%	0.7%
CURRENT LIABILITIES	**4727**	**4795**	**4998**
common size	23.7%	23.1%	23.0%
rate of change.................................		1.4%	4.2%
Long-term Debt	**3527**	**3009**	**2651**
common size	17.7%	14.5%	12.2%
rate of change.................................		−14.7%	−11.9%
Deferred Tax	**1209**	**1367**	**1496**
common size	6.1%	6.6%	6.9%
rate of change.................................		13.1%	9.4%
Other Noncurrent Liabilities	**3384**	**3960**	**3876**
common size	17.0%	19.1%	17.9%
rate of change.................................		17.0%	−2.1%
TOTAL LIABILITIES	**12847**	**13131**	**13021**
common size	64.4%	63.3%	60.0%
rate of change.................................		2.2%	−0.8%

Forecasts

Year +1	Year +2	Year +3	Year +4	Year +5	Year +6	Year +7	Year +8	Year +9	Year +10	Year +11
1287	1380	1471	1569	1678	1799	1928	2067	2215	2375	2493
41	41	41	41	41	41	41	41	41	41	
Number of days payables held										
117	126	135	145	155	166	179	192	205	220	231
0.5%	0.5%	0.5%	0.5%	0.5%	0.5%	0.5%	0.5%	0.5%	0.5%	
One-half of one percent of total assets										
485	441	167	602	310	333	357	383	411	441	463
$485	$441	$167	$602	10.0%	10.0%	10.0%	10.0%	10.0%	10.0%	
Maturities in Note 12; 10% of long-term debt after Year +5										
3647	3906	4185	4484	4807	5152	5523	5920	6345	6802	7142
7.1%	7.1%	7.1%	7.2%	7.2%	7.2%	7.2%	7.2%	7.2%	7.2%	
Grow with sales										
5536	5853	5958	6800	6950	7451	7986	8561	9177	9838	10330
23.6%	23.3%	22.1%	23.5%	22.4%	22.4%	22.4%	22.3%	22.3%	22.3%	
10.8%	5.7%	1.8%	14.1%	2.2%	7.2%	7.2%	7.2%	7.2%	7.2%	
2700	2769	2834	2894	3104	3330	3572	3831	4109	4407	4628
11.5%	11.0%	10.5%	10.0%	10.0%	10.0%	10.0%	10.0%	10.0%	10.0%	
Decline to 10 percent of assets										
1602	1716	1838	1970	2111	2263	2426	2600	2787	2988	3137
7.1%	7.1%	7.1%	7.2%	7.2%	7.2%	7.2%	7.2%	7.2%	7.2%	
Grow with sales										
4150	4445	4762	5103	5470	5863	6285	6737	7221	7741	8128
7.1%	7.1%	7.1%	7.2%	7.2%	7.2%	7.2%	7.2%	7.2%	7.2%	
Grow with sales										
13989	14783	15393	16767	17636	18907	20269	21729	23293	24973	26222
59.6%	58.7%	57.0%	57.9%	56.8%	56.8%	56.7%	56.7%	56.7%	56.7%	
7.4%	5.7%	4.1%	8.9%	5.2%	7.2%	7.2%	7.2%	7.2%	7.2%	

	Actuals		
	Year 9	Year 10	Year 11
STOCKHOLDERS' EQUITY			
Minority Interest in Subsidiaries			
common size	0.0%	0.0%	0.0%
rate of change...............................		#DIV/0!	#DIV/0!
Preferred Stock	23	22	26
common size	0.1%	0.1%	0.1%
rate of change...............................		−4.3%	18.2%
Common Stock and Paid-in Capital	593	409	43
common size	3.0%	2.0%	0.2%
rate of change...............................		−31.0%	−89.5%
Retained Earnings.............................	14921	16510	11519
common size	74.8%	79.5%	53.1%
rate of change...............................		10.6%	−30.2%
Accumulated Other Comprehensive Income	−1085	−1374	−1646
common size	−5.4%	−6.6%	−7.6%
rate of change...............................		26.6%	19.8%
Other Equity Adjustments	−45	−21	0
common size	−0.2%	−0.1%	0.0%
rate of change...............................		−53.3%	−100.0%
Treasury Stock................................	−7306	−7920	−1268
common size	−36.6%	−38.2%	−5.8%
rate of change...............................		8.4%	−84.0%
SHAREHOLDERS' EQUITY	7101	7626	8674
common size	35.6%	36.7%	40.0%
rate of change...............................		7.4%	13.7%
TOTAL LIABILITIES AND EQUITIES	19948	20757	21695
common size	100.0%	100.0%	100.0%
rate of change...............................		4.1%	4.5%
Check figures: Balance Sheet A = L + OE?	0	0	0

Forecasts

	Year +1	Year +2	Year +3	Year +4	Year +5	Year +6	Year +7	Year +8	Year +9	Year +10	Year +11
	0	**0**	**0**	**0**	**0**	**0**	**0**	**0**	**0**	**0**	**0**
	0	0	0	0	0	0	0	0	0	0	
No changes in minority interest											
	26	**26**	**26**	**26**	**26**	**26**	**26**	**26**	**26**	**26**	**27**
	0	0	0	0	0	0	0	0	0	0	
No changes in preferred stock											
	43	**43**	**43**	**43**	**43**	**43**	**43**	**43**	**43**	**43**	**45**
	0	0	0	0	0	0	0	0	0	0	
Add capital from new equity issues											
	13286	**15251**	**17655**	**19572**	**22302**	**25118**	**28004**	**30784**	**33261**	**35952**	**37750**
	38%	38%	38%	38%	38%	38%	38%	38%	38%	38%	
Add net income and subtract implied dividends—see dividends forecast below											
	−1646	**−1646**	**−1646**	**−1646**	**−1646**	**−1646**	**−1646**	**−1646**	**−1646**	**−1646**	**−1728**
	0.0%	0.0%	0.0%	0.0%	0.0%	0.0%	0.0%	0.0%	0.0%	0.0%	
Changes follow a random walk											
	0	**0**	**0**	**0**	**0**	**0**	**0**	**0**	**0**	**0**	**0**
	0	0	0	0	0	0	0	0	0	0	
Changes follow a random walk											
	−2217	**−3283**	**−4479**	**−5819**	**−7318**	**−9148**	**−10978**	**−12624**	**−13887**	**−15275**	**−16039**
	74.8%	48.1%	36.4%	29.9%	25.8%	25%	20%	15%	10%	10%	
Stock buybacks net of stock repurchases											
	9492	**10391**	**11599**	**12175**	**13407**	**14393**	**15450**	**16583**	**17797**	**19100**	**20055**
	40.4%	41.3%	43.0%	42.1%	43.2%	43.2%	43.3%	43.3%	43.3%	43.3%	
	9.4%	9.5%	11.6%	5.0%	10.1%	7.4%	7.3%	7.3%	7.3%	7.3%	
	23481	**25174**	**26992**	**28942**	**31043**	**33299**	**35718**	**38311**	**41091**	**44073**	**46277**
	100.0%	100.0%	100.0%	100.0%	100.0%	100.0%	100.0%	100.0%	100.0%	100.0%	
	8.2%	7.2%	7.2%	7.2%	7.3%	7.3%	7.3%	7.3%	7.3%	7.3%	
	0	**0**	**0**	**0**	**0**	**0**	**0**	**0**	**0**	**0**	**0**
Adjustment needed to balance the balance sheet:											
	−319	−301	−59	−756	−151	−277	−429	−774	−1333	−1394	0
Account adjusted: Dividends											
Dividends forecast:											
	1281	1391	1512	1640	1768	1898	2035	2181	2338	2506	5122
	319	301	59	756	151	277	429	774	1333	1394	0
	1600	1692	1572	2396	1919	2176	2463	2955	3671	3899	5122

FSAP OUTPUT: PRO FORMA FINANCIAL STATEMENT FORECASTS
FIRM NAME: PEPSICO
ANALYST NAME: Stickney, Brown, & Wahlen

	Actuals		
	Year 9	Year 10	Year 11

IMPLIED STATEMENT OF CASH FLOWS

The following statements of cash flows are derived from the above income statements and balance sheets, and are not the reported statements of cash flows.

		Year 10	Year 11
NET INCOME		2654	3003
Depreciation and Amortization		0	0
WORKING CAPITAL FROM OPS		2654	3003
(Incr.) Decrease in Receivables—Trade		−171	−13
(Incr.) Decrease in Inventories		−27	−118
(Incr.) Decr. in Other Curr. Assets		−84	39
Incr. (Decr.) in Acct. Payable—Trade		−123	26
Incr. (Decr.) in Other Current Liabilities		377	25
Incr. (Decr.) in Deferred Tax		158	129
Incr. (Decr.) in Other Noncurrent Liabilities		576	−84
NET CF FROM OPERATIONS		3360	3007
(Incr.) Decrease in Prop., Plant, Equip.		−185	−318
(Incr.) Decrease in Marketable Securities		−374	−499
(Incr.) Decrease in Investment Securities		−133	108
(Incr.) Decrease in Other Assets		−44	−492
NET CF FROM INVESTING		−736	−1201
Incr. (Decr.) in ST Debt		−186	152
Incr. (Decr.) in LT Debt		−518	−358
Incr. (Decr.) in Minority Int. and Prefd. Stock		−1	4
Incr. (Decr.) in Com. Stock and Paid-in Capital		−184	−366
Incr. (Decr.) in Accum. OCI and Oth. Eq. Adjs.		−265	−251
Incr. (Decr.) in Treasury Stock		−614	6652
Dividends (Preferred)		−4.0	−4.0
Dividends (Common)		−1061	−7990
NET CF FROM FINANCING		−2833	−2161
NET CHANGE IN CASH		−209	−355
Check Figure: Net change in cash − Change in cash balance		0	0

Forecasts

Year +1	Year +2	Year +3	Year +4	Year +5	Year +6	Year +7	Year +8	Year +9	Year +10	Year +11
3371	3660	3980	4316	4654	4995	5354	5739	6151	6594	6924
903	967	1036	1110	1190	1275	1367	1465	1570	1684	1768
4274	4627	5016	5426	5843	6270	6721	7204	7722	8278	8692
−149	−163	−175	−188	−203	−217	−233	−249	−267	−287	−214
−6	−86	−92	−99	−110	−122	−131	−141	−151	−162	−121
−70	−59	−64	−68	−74	−79	−85	−91	−97	−104	−77
49	93	91	97	109	121	129	139	149	160	119
241	259	279	300	322	346	370	397	426	457	340
106	114	122	132	142	152	163	174	187	201	149
274	295	317	341	367	393	421	452	484	520	387
4719	5080	5494	5940	6397	6863	7356	7885	8452	9062	9276
−1418	−1518	−1627	−1743	−1869	−2003	−2147	−2301	−2467	−2644	−2470
−91	−76	−82	−88	−95	−102	−109	−117	−125	−134	−99
−416	−237	−254	−273	−294	−316	−339	−363	−389	−418	−309
−431	−464	−499	−536	−577	−618	−663	−710	−761	−818	−609
−2356	−2295	−2462	−2640	−2834	−3039	−3257	−3491	−3742	−4013	−3486
−237	8	9	10	11	11	12	13	14	15	11
534	25	−209	495	−82	248	266	285	306	328	242
0	0	0	0	0	0	0	0	0	0	1
0	0	0	0	0	0	0	0	0	0	2
0	0	0	0	0	0	0	0	0	0	−82
−949	−1066	−1196	−1340	−1499	−1830	−1830	−1647	−1262	−1389	−764
−4	−4	−4	−4	−4	−4	−4	−4	−4	−4	−4
−1600	−1692	−1572	−2396	−1919	−2176	−2463	−2955	−3671	−3899	−5122
−2255	−2729	−2972	−3235	−3493	−3750	−4019	−4308	−4617	−4949	−5716
107	56	60	65	70	75	80	86	92	99	74
0	0	0	0	0	0	0	0	0	0	0

FSAP OUTPUT: **PRO FORMA FINANCIAL STATEMENT FORECASTS**
FIRM NAME: **PEPSICO**
ANALYST NAME: **Stickney, Brown, & Wahlen**

	Actuals		
	Year 9	**Year 10**	**Year 11**
FORECAST VALIDITY CHECK DATA:			
GROWTH			
Sales Growth Rates:	−7.7%	1.5%	5.7%
Net Income Growth Rates:.	−10.6%	16.4%	13.1%
Total Asset Growth Rates	−20.7%	4.1%	4.5%
RETURN ON ASSETS:			
Profit Margin for ROA.	10.2%	11.1%	11.7%
× Asset Turnover.	1.1	1.3	1.3
= Return on Assets	11.3%	13.9%	14.8%
RETURN ON COMMON EQUITY:			
Profit Margin for ROCE.	9.1%	10.4%	11.1%
× Asset Turnover.	1.1	1.3	1.3
× Capital Structure Leverage	3.3	2.8	2.6
= Return on Common Equity	33.4%	36.1%	36.9%
OPERATING PERFORMANCE:			
Gross Margin / Sales.	58.8%	59.9%	60.1%
Operating Profit Before Taxes / Revenues	14.6%	16.0%	16.6%
ASSET TURNOVER:			
Sales / Avg. Accounts Receivable	10.7	12.5	12.6
COGS / Average Inventory.	8.5	8.7	8.6
Sales / Average Fixed Assets	3.4	3.9	4.0
LIQUIDITY:			
Current Ratio	1.1	1.2	1.2
Quick Ratio	0.7	0.8	0.8
SOLVENCY:			
Total Liabilities / Total Assets.	0.6	0.6	0.6
Total Liabilities / Total Equity	1.8	1.7	1.5
Interest Coverage Ratio	9.0	15.5	21.2

Forecasts for Year +11 and Beyond:

Long-run Growth Rate Assumption: 5.0%

Long-run Growth Factor: 105%

Forecasts

Year +1	Year +2	Year +3	Year +4	Year +5	Year +6	Year +7	Year +8	Year +9	Year +10	Year +11
7.1%	7.1%	7.1%	7.2%	7.2%	7.2%	7.2%	7.2%	7.2%	7.2%	5.0%
12.3%	8.6%	8.7%	8.5%	7.8%	7.3%	7.2%	7.2%	7.2%	7.2%	5.0%
8.2%	7.2%	7.2%	7.2%	7.3%	7.3%	7.3%	7.3%	7.3%	7.3%	5.0%
12.1%	12.3%	12.4%	12.6%	12.6%	12.6%	12.6%	12.6%	12.6%	12.6%	12.6%
1.3	1.3	1.3	1.3	1.3	1.3	1.3	1.3	1.3	1.3	1.3
15.5%	15.6%	15.8%	15.9%	16.0%	16.0%	16.0%	16.0%	16.0%	16.0%	15.8%
11.7%	11.8%	12.0%	12.2%	12.2%	12.2%	12.2%	12.3%	12.3%	12.3%	12.3%
1.3	1.3	1.3	1.3	1.3	1.3	1.3	1.3	1.3	1.3	1.3
2.5	2.5	2.4	2.4	2.3	2.3	2.3	2.3	2.3	2.3	2.3
37.2%	36.9%	36.2%	36.4%	36.4%	36.0%	35.9%	35.9%	35.8%	35.8%	35.4%
60.3%	60.5%	60.7%	60.9%	61.0%	61.0%	61.0%	61.0%	61.0%	61.0%	61.0%
11.7%	11.8%	12.0%	12.2%	12.2%	12.3%	12.3%	12.3%	12.3%	12.3%	12.3%
13.0	13.0	13.0	13.0	13.0	13.0	13.0	13.0	13.0	13.0	12.9
8.7	9.0	9.0	9.0	9.0	9.0	9.0	9.0	9.0	9.0	8.9
4.0	4.0	4.0	4.0	4.0	4.0	4.0	4.0	4.0	4.0	3.9
1.1	1.1	1.2	1.1	1.2	1.2	1.2	1.2	1.2	1.2	1.2
0.7	0.8	0.8	0.7	0.8	0.8	0.8	0.8	0.8	0.8	0.8
0.6	0.6	0.6	0.6	0.6	0.6	0.6	0.6	0.6	0.6	0.6
1.5	1.4	1.3	1.4	1.3	1.3	1.3	1.3	1.3	1.3	1.3
27.2	28.0	31.1	32.2	32.6	34.1	34.1	34.0	34.0	34.0	34.0

FSAP OUTPUT: **VALUATIONS**
FIRM NAME: **PEPSICO**
ANALYST NAME: **Stickney, Brown, & Wahlen**

VALUATION PARAMETER ASSUMPTIONS

COST OF EQUITY CAPITAL:		COST OF DEBT CAPITAL	
Equity risk (i.e. beta)	0.76	Debt capital	$3,266
Risk-free rates	4.2%	Average cost of debt capital, before tax	6.0%
Market risk premium	5.0%	Effective tax rate	32%
Required rate of return on common equity:	8.00%		
		COST OF PREFERRED STOCK	
		Preferred Stock Capital	$ 50
		Dividends	$ 4
		Implied Yield	8.0%
Current share price	$ 49.05	WEIGHTED AVERAGE COST OF CAPITAL	
Number of shares outstanding (millions)	1,756.0	Weight of equity in capital structure	0.97
Current market value (millions)	$ 86,132	Weight of debt in capital structure	0.03
Implied value of equity (millions)	$121,206	Weight of preferred in capital structure	0.00
Long-run growth assumption	5.0%	Weighted average cost of capital	7.90%

FSAP OUTPUT: **VALUATIONS**
FIRM NAME: **PEPSICO**
ANALYST NAME: Stickney, Brown, & Wahlen

Free Cash Flows for All Debt and Equity Stakeholders

	1 Year +1	2 Year +2	3 Year +3	4 Year +4
Net Cash Flow from Operations	4,718.6	5,079.9	5,493.7	5,940.4
Add back: Interest Expense after tax	128.7	135.4	132.0	138.3
Subtract: Interest Income after tax	0.0	0.0	0.0	0.0
+/– Change in Operating Cash	–107.2	–56.1	–60.4	–64.9
Free Cash Flow from Operations	4,740.1	5,159.2	5,565.3	6,013.7
Net Cash Flow from Investing.	–2,356.0	–2,295.3	–2,461.7	–2,640.3
Add back: CFs into Financial Assets	0.0	0.0	0.0	0.0
Free Cash Flow—All Debt and Equity	2,384.1	2,864.0	3,103.6	3,373.4
Present Value Factors.	0.927	0.859	0.796	0.738
PV Free Cash Flows	2,209.6	2,460.1	2,470.8	2,489.0
Sum of PV Free Cash Flows	24,317.6			
PV of Continuing Value	95,642.4			
Total PV Free Cash Flows	119,960.0			
Less: Outstanding Debt (FV or BV)	–3,266.0			
Less: Preferred Stock (FV or BV)	–50.0			
Plus: Financial Assets (FV or BV)	0.0			
PV of Equity	116,644.0			
Adjust to midyear discounting	1.0395			
Total PV of Equity.	121,249.8			
Shares Outstanding	1,756.0			
Estimated Value per Share.	$69.05			
Current share price	$49.05			
Percent difference	41%			
(Value/price)–1: positive number indicates underpricing.				

5 Year +5	6 Year +6	7 Year +7	8 Year +8	9 Year +9	10 Year +10	Continuing Value Year +11
6,396.8	6,863.2	7,356.0	7,884.8	8,451.6	9,061.5	9,275.7
147.1	151.0	161.9	173.7	186.3	199.8	209.8
0.0	0.0	0.0	0.0	0.0	0.0	0.0
−69.8	−74.9	−80.2	−86.0	−92.2	−99.0	−73.7
6,474.0	6,939.2	7,437.7	7,972.5	8,545.7	9,162.3	9,411.8
−2,833.9	−3,038.7	−3,257.1	−3,491.2	−3,742.1	−4,013.3	−3,486.3
0.0	0.0	0.0	0.0	0.0	0.0	0.0
3,640.1	3,900.6	4,180.6	4,481.3	4,803.6	5,149.0	5,925.5
0.684	0.634	0.587	0.544	0.505	0.468	
2,489.2	2,472.1	2,455.7	2,439.6	2,423.7	2,407.8	

FSAP OUTPUT: **VALUATIONS**
FIRM NAME: **PEPSICO**
ANALYST NAME: Stickney, Brown, & Wahlen

Free Cash Flows for Common Equity Shareholders

	1 Year +1	2 Year +2	3 Year +3	4 Year +4
Free Cash Flow—All Debt and Equity	2,384.1	2,864.0	3,103.6	3,373.4
Net CFs from Debt Financing.	297.7	33.3	−199.9	504.9
Net CFs—Pref. Stock and Minority Int.	−4.0	−4.0	−4.0	−4.0
Net CFs into Financial Assets	0.0	0.0	0.0	0.0
Subtract: Interest Expense after tax.	−128.7	−135.4	−132.0	−138.3
Add back: Interest Income after tax	0.0	0.0	0.0	0.0
Free Cash Flow for Common Equity	2,549.1	2,757.8	2,767.6	3,736.0
Present Value Factors.	0.926	0.857	0.794	0.735
PV Free Cash Flows	2,360.3	2,364.4	2,197.0	2,746.1
Sum of PV Free Cash Flows	24,426.2			
PV of Continuing Value	92,118.0			
Total	116,544.2			
Adjust to midyear discounting	1.040			
Total PV Free Cash Flows to Equity	121,205.9			
Shares Outstanding	1,756.0			
Estimated Value per Share.	$69.02			
Current share price	$49.05			
Percent difference	41%			
(Value/price)−1: positive number indicates underpricing.				

5 Year +5	6 Year +6	7 Year +7	8 Year +8	9 Year +9	10 Year +10	Continuing Value Year +11
3,640.1	3,900.6	4,180.6	4,481.3	4,803.6	5,149.0	5925.5
−71.0	259.5	278.2	298.2	319.6	343.0	253.4
−4.0	−4.0	−4.0	−4.0	−4.0	−4.0	−2.9
0.0	0.0	0.0	0.0	0.0	0.0	0.0
−147.1	−151.0	−161.9	−173.7	−186.3	−199.8	−209.8
0.0	0.0	0.0	0.0	0.0	0.0	0.0
3,418.0	4,005.2	4,292.9	4,601.8	4,932.9	5,288.1	5,966.3
0.681	0.630	0.583	0.540	0.500	0.463	
2,326.2	2,523.9	2,504.9	2,486.2	2,467.7	2,449.4	

FSAP OUTPUT: **VALUATIONS**
FIRM NAME: **PEPSICO**
ANALYST NAME: **Stickney, Brown, & Wahlen**

Free Cash Flow Valuation Sensitivity Analysis:

Long-run Growth Assumptions:

	69.02	0%	1%	2%	3%	4%
Discount	5%	59.48	70.17	87.99	123.63	230.53
Rates:	6%	48.49	55.00	64.77	81.05	113.62
	7%	40.70	44.96	50.92	59.86	74.75
	8%	34.93	37.85	41.75	47.20	55.38
	9%	30.48	32.56	35.24	38.81	43.81
	10%	26.96	28.49	30.40	32.86	36.13
	11%	24.12	25.27	26.67	28.42	30.68
	12%	21.78	22.66	23.71	25.00	26.61
	13%	19.82	20.50	21.31	22.28	23.46
	14%	18.16	18.70	19.33	20.07	20.96
	15%	16.74	17.17	17.67	18.25	18.93
	16%	15.51	15.86	16.26	16.71	17.25
	17%	14.45	14.73	15.05	15.41	15.83
	18%	13.51	13.74	14.00	14.29	14.63
	19%	12.67	12.87	13.08	13.32	13.59
	20%	11.94	12.09	12.27	12.47	12.69

5%	6%	7%	8%	9%	10%
#DIV/0!	na	na	na	na	na
211.33	#DIV/0!	na	na	na	na
104.55	193.93	#DIV/0!	na	na	na
69.02	96.30	178.14	#DIV/0!	na	na
51.31	63.81	88.81	163.79	#DIV/0!	na
40.72	47.60	59.06	81.98	150.75	#DIV/0!
33.68	37.89	44.20	54.72	75.76	138.88
28.68	31.44	35.31	41.10	50.77	70.09
24.94	26.85	29.39	32.94	38.27	47.15
22.05	23.42	25.17	27.50	30.77	35.67
19.75	20.75	22.01	23.62	25.77	28.78
17.88	18.63	19.56	20.71	22.20	24.18
16.32	16.91	17.60	18.46	19.52	20.89
15.02	15.47	16.01	16.65	17.44	18.42
13.90	14.26	14.68	15.18	15.77	16.50
12.94	13.23	13.56	13.95	14.41	14.95

FSAP OUTPUT: **VALUATIONS**
FIRM NAME: **PEPSICO**
ANALYST NAME: **Stickney, Brown, & Wahlen**

Residual Income Valuation

	1 Year +1	2 Year +2	3 Year +3	4 Year +4
Comprehensive Income Available for Common Shareholders	3,367.3	3,656.4	3,975.8	4,312.3
Book Value of Common Shareholders' Equity (at t–1)	8,648.0	9,466.2	10,364.7	11,572.9
Required Earnings	691.8	757.3	829.2	925.8
Residual Income	2,675.5	2,899.1	3,146.6	3,386.5
Present Value Factors	0.926	0.857	0.794	0.735
PV Residual Income	2,477.3	2,485.5	2,497.9	2,489.1
Sum of PV Residual Income	24,613.0			
PV of Continuing Value	83,283.2			
Total	107,896.2			
Add: Beginning Book Value of Equity	8,648.0			
PV of Equity	116,544.2			
Adjust to midyear discounting	1.040			
Total PV of Equity	121,205.9			
Shares Outstanding	1,756.0			
Estimated Value per Share	$69.02			
Current share price	$49.05			
Percent difference	41%			
(Value/price)–1: positive number indicates underpricing.				

5 Year +5	6 Year +6	7 Year +7	8 Year +8	9 Year +9	10 Year +10	Continuing Value Year +11
4,649.6	4,991.0	5,350.0	5,734.9	6,147.5	6,590.4	6,920.0
12,149.2	13,380.8	14,366.6	15,423.7	16,556.8	17,771.4	19,073.7
971.9	1,070.5	1,149.3	1,233.9	1,324.5	1,421.7	1,525.9
3,677.6	3,920.5	4,200.7	4,501.0	4,822.9	5,168.7	5,394.1
0.681	0.630	0.583	0.540	0.500	0.463	
2,502.9	2,470.6	2,451.1	2,431.8	2,412.7	2,394.1	

FSAP OUTPUT: **VALUATIONS**
FIRM NAME: **PEPSICO**
ANALYST NAME: **Stickney, Brown, & Wahlen**

Residual Income Valuation Sensitivity Analysis:

	Long-run Growth Assumptions:					
	69.02	0%	1%	2%	3%	4%
Discount	5%	66.32	77.01	94.83	130.46	237.36
Rates:	6%	53.69	60.00	69.46	85.22	116.75
	7%	44.79	48.77	54.35	62.71	76.66
	8%	38.20	40.84	44.36	49.29	56.69
	9%	33.14	34.96	37.30	40.41	44.77
	10%	29.16	30.45	32.05	34.11	36.87
	11%	25.95	26.88	28.02	29.43	31.25
	12%	23.32	24.00	24.82	25.82	27.07
	13%	21.13	21.64	22.24	22.96	23.84
	14%	19.28	19.67	20.11	20.64	21.28
	15%	17.70	18.00	18.33	18.73	19.19
	16%	16.35	16.57	16.83	17.12	17.47
	17%	15.17	15.34	15.54	15.76	16.02
	18%	14.13	14.27	14.42	14.59	14.79
	19%	13.22	13.33	13.45	13.58	13.73
	20%	12.42	12.50	12.59	12.70	12.81

5%	6%	7%	8%	9%	10%
#DIV/0!	na	na	na	na	na
211.33	#DIV/0!	na	na	na	na
104.55	188.21	#DIV/0!	na	na	na
69.02	93.69	167.67	#DIV/0!	na	na
51.31	62.21	84.01	149.41	#DIV/0!	na
40.72	46.50	56.13	75.39	133.16	#DIV/0!
33.68	37.08	42.19	50.69	67.69	118.71
28.68	30.82	33.82	38.32	45.82	60.83
24.94	26.36	28.25	30.89	34.86	41.47
22.05	23.02	24.27	25.93	28.26	31.75
19.75	20.43	21.29	22.38	23.85	25.89
17.88	18.37	18.97	19.72	20.68	21.96
16.32	16.68	17.11	17.64	18.29	19.14
15.02	15.28	15.60	15.97	16.43	17.01
13.90	14.10	14.33	14.61	14.93	15.34
12.94	13.09	13.26	13.47	13.70	13.99

FSAP OUTPUT: VALUATIONS
FIRM NAME: PEPSICO
ANALYST NAME: Stickney, Brown, & Wahlen

Residual Income Valuation
Market-to-Book Approach

	1 Year +1	2 Year +2	3 Year +3	4 Year +4
Comprehensive Income Available for Common Shareholders	3,367.3	3,656.4	3,975.8	4,312.3
Book Value of Common Shareholders' Equity (at t–1)	8,648.0	9,466.2	10,364.7	11,572.9
Implied ROCE	38.9%	38.6%	38.4%	37.3%
Residual ROCE	30.9%	30.6%	30.4%	29.3%
Cumulative growth factor as of t–1.	100.0%	109.5%	119.9%	133.8%
Residual ROCE times growth	30.9%	33.5%	36.4%	39.2%
Present Value Factors.	0.926	0.857	0.794	0.735
PV Residual ROCE times growth	0.286	0.287	0.289	0.288
Sum of PV Residual ROCE times growth. . .	2.85			
PV of Continuing Value	9.63			
Total PV Residual ROCE.	12.48			
Add one for book value of equity at t–1	1.0			
Sum	13.48			
Adjust to mid-year discounting.	1.040			
Implied Market-to-Book Ratio	14.015			
Times Beginning Book Value of Equity	8,648.0			
Total PV of Equity.	121,205.9			
Shares Outstanding	1,756.0			
Estimated Value per Share.	69.02			
Current share price	$49.05			
Percent difference	41%			

(Value/price)–1: positive number indicates underpricing.

Sensitivity analysis for the market-to-book approach should be identical to that of the residual income approach.

5 Year +5	6 Year +6	7 Year +7	8 Year +8	9 Year +9	10 Year +10	Continuing Value Year +11
4,649.6	4,991.0	5,350.0	5,734.9	6,147.5	6,590.4	6,920.0
12,149.2	13,380.8	14,366.6	15,423.7	16,556.8	17,771.4	19,073.7
38.3%	37.3%	37.2%	37.2%	37.1%	37.1%	36.3%
30.3%	29.3%	29.2%	29.2%	29.1%	29.1%	28.3%
140.5%	154.7%	166.1%	178.3%	191.5%	205.5%	220.6%
42.5%	45.3%	48.6%	52.0%	55.8%	59.8%	62.4%
0.681	0.630	0.583	0.540	0.500	0.463	
0.289	0.286	0.283	0.281	0.279	0.277	

FSAP OUTPUT: **VALUATIONS**
FIRM NAME: **PEPSICO**
ANALYST NAME: Stickney, Brown, & Wahlen

Dividends Based Valuation

	1 Year +1	2 Year +2	3 Year +3	4 Year +4
Dividends Paid to Common Shareholders.	1,600.3	1,691.5	1,571.6	2,395.8
Less: Common Stock Issues.	0.0	0.0	0.0	0.0
Plus: Common Stock Repurchases	948.8	1,066.3	1,196.1	1,340.2
All-Inclusive Dividends to Common Equity.	2,549.1	2,757.8	2,767.6	3,736.0
Present Value Factors.	0.926	0.857	0.794	0.735
PV Net Dividends	2,360.3	2,364.4	2,197.0	2,746.1
Sum of PV Net Dividends.	24,426.2			
PV of Continuing Value	92,118.0			
Total.	116,544.2			
Adjust to midyear discounting	1.040			
Total PV Dividends	121,205.9			
Shares Outstanding	1,756.0			
Estimated Value per Share.	$69.02			
Current share price	$49.05			
Percent difference	41%			

(Value/price)−1: positive number indicates underpricing.

5 Year +5	6 Year +6	7 Year +7	8 Year +8	9 Year +9	10 Year +10	Continuing Value Year +11
1,918.9	2,175.6	2,463.3	2,955.2	3,670.5	3,899.5	
0.0	0.0	0.0	0.0	0.0	0.0	
1,499.1	1,829.6	1,829.6	1,646.6	1,262.4	1,388.7	
3,418.0	4,005.2	4,292.9	4,601.8	4,932.9	5,288.1	5,966.3
0.681	0.630	0.583	0.540	0.500	0.463	
2,326.2	2,523.9	2,504.9	2,486.2	2,467.7	2,449.4	

INDEX

SUMMARY OF KEY FINANCIAL STATEMENT RATIOS

PROFITABILITY RATIOS

$$\text{Profit Margin for ROA} = \frac{[\text{Net Income} + (1 - \text{Tax Rate})(\text{Interest Expense}) + \text{Minority Interest in Earnings}]}{\text{Sales}}$$

$$\text{Total Assets Turnover} = \frac{\text{Sales}}{\text{Average Total Assets}}$$

$$\text{Return on Assets (ROA)} = \frac{[\text{Net Income} + (1 - \text{Tax Rate})(\text{Interest Expense}) + \text{Minority Interest in Earnings}]}{\text{Average Total Assets}}$$

$$\text{Profit Margin for ROCE} = \frac{(\text{Net Income} - \text{Preferred Dividends})}{\text{Sales}}$$

$$\text{Capital Structure Leverage Ratio} = \frac{\text{Average Total Assets}}{\text{Average Common Shareholders' Equity}}$$

$$\text{Return on Common Equity (ROCE)} = \frac{(\text{Net Income} - \text{Preferred Dividends})}{\text{Average Common Shareholders' Equity}}$$

$$\text{Cost of Goods Sold Percentage} = \frac{\text{Cost of Goods Sold}}{\text{Sales}}$$

$$\text{Selling and Administrative Expense Percentage} = \frac{\text{Selling and Administrative Expense}}{\text{Sales}}$$

$$\text{Income Tax Expense Percentage (on operating income)} = \frac{[\text{Income Tax Expense} + (\text{Tax Rate})(\text{Interest Expense})]}{\text{Sales}}$$

$$\text{Accounts Receivable Turnover} = \frac{\text{Sales}}{\text{Average Accounts Receivable}}$$

$$\text{Inventory Turnover} = \frac{\text{Cost of Goods Sold}}{\text{Average Inventories}}$$

$$\text{Fixed Asset Turnover} = \frac{\text{Sales}}{\text{Average Fixed Assets}}$$